KU-023-455

The HUTCHINSON
DICTIONARY OF
WORLD
HISTORY

Helicon

Copyright © Helicon Publishing Ltd 1993, 1998

All rights reserved

Helicon Publishing Ltd
42 Hythe Bridge Street
Oxford OX1 2EP
e-mail: admin@helicon.co.uk
Web site:http://www.helicon.co.uk

First published 1993
Paperback edition first published 1994
Reprinted 1995, 1997
Reissued and updated paperback edition published 1998
Reprinted 1999

Printed and bound in Great Britain by
The Bath Press Ltd, Bath, Somerset

ISBN 1-85986-246-2

British Cataloguing in Publication Data

A catalogue record for this book is available
from the British Library

The HUTCHINSON

DICTIONARY OF

WORLD
HISTORY

Contents

Introduction

The Dictionary of World History has been compiled with the intention of providing as great a coverage as possible of global events from earliest times to the present day within a single volume.

Inevitably constraints imposed by the format of this dictionary have made it necessary to be highly selective in the inclusion of material. However, it is hoped that the reasoning behind the selection procedure has produced a balanced coverage of the main features of human development while maintaining the excitement of history as a living discipline.

Consequently a policy was established to form a basis for editorial decisions of a detailed nature of coverage.

The earliest part of our history, that which is, strictly speaking, prehistory since it was before the invention of written records, has largely been omitted from the A to Z section. However, in order to give as broad a perspective as possible, chronologies have been added to the end of the dictionary covering the earliest historic, and prehistoric, periods, thus providing a balanced view of historical development around the world.

The emphasis of the dictionary is on what is generally recognized as the historical era: that is, the period more properly the province of the historian working from surviving records, than that of the archeologist working from surviving artefacts. The coverage is based on the three main divisions of history – period, nation and topic. Major civilizations, events, and leaders, as well as the world's nations, have all been included.

Within the chosen areas, entries have been selected by their historical significance. Cities, places, popes, saints, archeologists, historians, and biblical figures, are included only if they were of historical significance or they gave their names to an empire or civilization.

Maps and chronologies are listed within the A to Z sequence where appropriate, and further information displayed in chronological form at the end of the book.

Arrangement of entries

Entries are ordered alphabetically, as if there were no spaces between words.

Cross-references

These are shown by a ◊ symbol immediately preceding the reference. Cross-referencing is selective; a cross-reference is shown when another entry contains material which is relevant to the subject matter of an entry, in cases where the reader may not otherwise think of looking.

CONTRIBUTORS

Consultant Editor
Ian D Derbyshire PhD, GBIM

Subject Consultants
Kent Fedorowich BA, MA,
   PhD
Peter Fleming PhD
Joseph Harrison BA, PhD
Gerald M D Howat MA,
   MLitt, PhD, FRHistS
Graham Ley MPhil
Isabel Miller BA, PhD
Bob Moore PhD
Michael Pudlo MSc, PhD

EDITORS

Content Editor
Jennifer Speake

Project Editors
Emma Callery
Sheila Dallas

Text Editors
Jane Anson
Ruth Barratt
Sean Callery
Ingrid von Essen
Frances Lass
Helen Maxey
Lorna Williams

Production
Tony Ballsdon

Illustrations

Abbadid dynasty 11th century Muslim dynasty based in Seville, Spain, which lasted from 1023 until 1091. The dynasty was founded by Abu-el-Kasim Muhammad Ibn Abbad, who led the townspeople against the Berbers when the Spanish caliphate fell. The dynasty continued under Motadid (ruled 1042–69) and Motamid (ruled 1069–91) when the city was taken by the ◊Almoravids.

Abbas I *the Great c.* 1557–1629. Shah of Persia from 1588. He expanded Persian territory by conquest, defeating the Uzbeks near Herat in 1597 and also the Turks. The port of Bandar-Abbas is named after him. At his death his empire reached from the river Tigris to the Indus. He was a patron of the arts.

Abbas II Hilmi 1874–1944. Last ◊khedive (viceroy) of Egypt, 1892–1914. On the outbreak of war between Britain and Turkey in 1914, he sided with Turkey and was deposed following the establishment of a British protectorate over Egypt.

Abbasid dynasty family of rulers of the Islamic empire, whose ◊caliphs reigned in Baghdad 750–1258. They were descended from Abbas, the prophet Muhammad's uncle, and some of them, such as Harun al-Rashid and Mamun (reigned 813–33), were outstanding patrons of cultural development. Later their power dwindled, and in 1258 Baghdad was burned by the Tatars. From then until 1517 the Abbasids retained limited power as caliphs of Egypt.

Abd Allah Sudanese dervish leader *Abdullah el Taaisha* 1846–1899. Successor to the Mahdi as Sudanese ruler from 1885, he was defeated by British forces under General ◊Kitchener at Omdurman 1898 and later killed in Kordofan.

Abd al-Malik Ibn Marwan 647–705. Caliph who reigned 685–705. Based in Damascus, he waged military campaigns to unite Muslim groups and battled against the Greeks. He instituted a purely Arab coinage and replaced Syriac, Coptic, and Greek with Arabic as the language for his lands. His reign was turbulent but succeeded in extending and strengthening the power of the ◊Omayyad dynasty. He was also a patron of the arts.

Abd el-Kader *c.* 1807–1873. Algerian nationalist. Emir (Islamic chieftain) of Mascara from 1832, he led a struggle against the French until his surrender in 1847.

Abd el-Krim el-Khettabi 1881–1963. Moroccan chief known as the 'Wolf of the Riff'. With his brother Muhammad, he led the *Riff revolt* against the French and Spanish invaders, inflicting disastrous defeat on the Spanish at Anual in 1921, but surrendered to a large French army under Pétain in 1926. Banished to the island of Réunion, he was released in 1947 and died in voluntary exile in Cairo.

abdication crisis in British history, the constitutional upheaval of the period 16 Nov 1936 to 10 Dec 1936, brought about by the English king Edward VIII's decision to marry Wallis Simpson, an American divorcee. The marriage of the 'Supreme Governor' of the Church of England to a divorced person was considered unsuitable and the king was finally forced to abdicate on 10 Dec and left for voluntary exile in France. He was created Duke of Windsor and married Mrs Simpson on 3 June 1937.

Abdul-Hamid II 1842–1918. Last sultan of Turkey 1876–1909. In 1908 the ◊Young Turks under Enver Pasha forced Abdul-Hamid to restore the constitution of 1876 and in 1909 insisted on his deposition. He died in confinement. For his part in the ◊Armenian massacres suppressing the revolt of 1894–96 he was known as 'the Great Assassin'; his actions still motivate Armenian violence against the Turks.

Abdullah el Taaisha alternative name for ◊Abd Allah, Sudanese dervish leader.

Abdullah ibn Hussein 1882–1951. King of Jordan from 1946. He worked with the British guerrilla leader T E ◊Lawrence in the Arab revolt of World War I. Abdullah became king of Trans-Jordan 1946; on the incorporation of Arab Palestine (after the 1948–49 Arab–Israeli War) he renamed the country the Hashemite Kingdom of Jordan. He was assassinated.

Abdullah Sheik Muhammad 1905–1982. Indian politician, known as the 'Lion of Kashmir'. He headed the struggle for constitutional government against the Maharajah of Kashmir, and in 1948, following a coup, became prime minister. He agreed to the accession of the state to India, but was dismissed and imprisoned from 1953 (with brief intervals) until 1966, when he called for Kashmiri self-determination. He became chief minister of Jammu and Kashmir 1975, accepting the sovereignty of India.

Abdul Mejid I 1823–1861. Sultan of Turkey from 1839. During his reign the Ottoman Empire was increasingly weakened by internal nationalist movements and the incursions of the great European powers.

Aberdeen George Hamilton Gordon, 4th Earl of Aberdeen 1784–1860. British Tory politician, prime minister 1852–55 when he resigned because of the criticism aroused by the miseries and mismanagement of the ◊Crimean War.

Aberdeen began his career as a diplomat. In 1828 and again in 1841 he was foreign secretary under Wellington. In 1852 he became prime minister in a government of Peelites and Whigs (Liberals), but resigned 1855 because of the Crimean War losses. Although a Tory, he supported Catholic emancipation and followed Robert Peel in his conversion to free trade.

Abkhazia autonomous republic in Georgia, situated on the Black Sea.

history Abkhazia, a Georgian kingdom from the 4th century, was inhabited traditionally by Abkhazis, an ethnic group converted from Christianity to Islam in the 17th century. By the 1980s some 17% of the population were Muslims and two-thirds were of Georgian origin. In 1989, Abkhazis demanded secession from Georgia and reinstatement as a full Union republic. The dispute triggered civil unrest in Abkhazia and nationalist demonstrations throughout Georgia. In July 1992 the local parliament unilaterally declared Abkhazia's independence. After the kidnapping of senior Georgian officials in Aug, Georgian troops invaded and took control. By early Sept Russia's president Boris Yeltsin had successfully brokered a cease-fire, but in a surprise Oct offensive, secessionist guerillas reclaimed half of Abkhazia, gaining control of all of the region N of the capital, Sukhumi. By Oct 1993, all but a small area of the republic was in rebel hands, and the capital had fallen. A cease-fire was signed April 1994, providing for the deployment of 2,500 Russian peacekeepers. The parliament adopted a new constitution Nov 1994 proclaiming Abkhazian sovereignty, and Vladislav Ardzinba was elected president. In Nov 1996 elections were held to a separatist Abkhaz parliament, but were condemned as illegal by the Georgian government, which organized a counter-referendum of Abkhaz refugees in Georgia.

abolitionism in UK and US history, a movement culminating in the late 18th and early 19th centuries that aimed first to end the slave trade, and then to abolish the institution of ◊slavery and emancipate slaves.

In the USA, slavery was officially abolished by the ◊Emancipation Proclamation 1863 of President Abraham Lincoln, but it could not be enforced until 1865 after the Union victory in the Civil War. The question of whether newly admitted states would allow slavery had been a major issue in the break-up of the Union.

Aborigine, Australian see ◊Australian Aborigine.

Aboukir Bay, Battle of also known as the *Battle of the Nile*; naval battle between Great Britain and France, in which Admiral Nelson defeated Napoleon's fleet at Aboukir, E of Alexandria, on 1 Aug 1798.

Abraham *c.* 2300 BC. In the Old Testament, founder of the Jewish nation. In his early life he was called Abram. God promised him heirs and land for his people in Canaan (Israel), renamed him Abraham ('father of many nations'), and tested his faith by a command (later retracted) to sacrifice his son Isaac.

Abraham was born in Ur, in Mesopotamia, the son of Terah. With his father, wife Sarah, and nephew Lot, he migrated to Haran, N Mesopotamia, then to Canaan where he received God's promise of land. After visiting Egypt, he separated from Lot at Bethel and settled in Hebron (now in Israel). He was still childless at the age of 76, subsequently had a son (Ishmael) with his wife's maidservant Hagar, and then, at the age of 100, a son Isaac with his wife Sarah. God's promise to Abraham that his descendants would be a nation and Canaan their land was fulfilled when the descendants of Abraham's grandson, Jacob, were led out of Egypt by Moses. Abraham was buried in Machpelah Cave, Hebron.

Abraham, Plains of plateau near Québec City, Canada, where the British commander ◊Wolfe defeated the French under ◊Montcalm, 13 Sept 1759, during the French and Indian War (1754–63). The outcome of the battle established British supremacy in Canada.

absolutism or *absolute monarchy* system of government in which the ruler or rulers have unlimited power. The principle of an absolute monarch, given a right to rule by God (see ◊divine right of kings), was extensively used in Europe during the 17th and 18th centuries.

Absolute monarchy is contrasted with limited or constitutional monarchy, in which the sovereign's powers are defined or limited.

Abu Bakr or *Abu-Bekr* 573–634. 'Father of the virgin', name used by Abd-el-Ka'aba from about 618 when the prophet Muhammad married his daughter Ayesha. He was a close adviser to Muhammad in the period 622–32. On the prophet's death, he became the first ◊caliph, adding Mesopotamia to the Muslim world and instigating expansion into Iraq and Syria.

Traditionally he is supposed to have encouraged some of those who had known Muhammad to memorize his teachings; these words were later written down to form the ◊Koran.

Achaea in ancient Greece, an area of the N Peloponnese. The *Achaeans* were the predominant society during the Mycenaean period and are said by Homer to have taken part in the siege of Troy.

Achaean League union in 275 BC of most of the cities of the N Peloponnese, which managed to defeat ◊Sparta, but was itself defeated by the Romans 146 BC.

Achaemenid dynasty family ruling the Persian Empire 550–330 BC, and named after Achaemenes, ancestor of Cyrus the Great, founder of the empire. His successors included Cambyses, Darius I, Xerxes, and Darius III, who, as the last Achaemenid ruler, was killed after defeat in battle against Alexander the Great 330 BC.

Acheson Dean (Gooderham) 1893–1971. US politician. As undersecretary of state 1945–47 in Truman's Democratic administration, he was associated with George C Marshall in preparing the ◊Marshall Plan, and succeeded him as secretary of state 1949–53.

Acre or *'Akko* seaport taken by the Crusaders 1104, it was captured by Saladin 1187 and retaken by Richard I (the Lionheart) 1191. Napoleon failed in a siege 1799. British field marshal Allenby captured the port 1918. From being part of British mandated Palestine, it became part of Israel 1948.

acropolis (Greek 'high city') citadel of an ancient Greek town. The Acropolis of Athens contains the ruins of the Parthenon and surrounding complexes, built there during the days of the Athenian empire.

Action Française French extreme nationalist political movement founded 1899, first led by Charles Maurras (1868–1952). It stressed the essential unity of all French people in contrast to the socialist doctrines of class warfare. Its influence peaked in the 1920s.

Initially nationalist and republican, it was opposed to capitalism and parliamentarianism, but from 1914 it became predominantly nationalist. In the 1920s the movement obtained a degree of respectability through an alliance with the former prime minister Clemenceau, and seats in the chamber of deputies. By the 1930s, Action Française had been superseded by more radical right-wing movements such as the Jeunesses Patriotes and the Croix de Feu.

Actium, Battle of naval battle in which Octavian defeated the combined fleets of ◊Mark Antony and ◊Cleopatra 31 BC to become the undisputed ruler of the Roman world (as the emperor ◊Augustus). The site is at Akri, a promontory in W Greece.

act of Parliament in Britain, a change in the law originating in Parliament and called a statute. Before an act receives the royal assent and becomes law it is a *bill*. The US equivalent is an *act of Congress*.

An act of Parliament may be either public (of general effect), local, or private. The body of English statute law comprises all the acts passed by Parliament: the existing list opens with the Statute of Merton, passed in 1235. An act (unless it is stated to be for a definite period and then to come to an end) remains on the statute book until it is repealed.

AD in the Christian chronological system, abbreviation for ◊*anno domini.*

Adams John 1735–1826. 2nd president of the USA 1797–1801, and vice president 1789–97. He was a member of the Continental Congress 1774–78 and signed the Declaration of Independence. In 1779 he went to France and negotiated the treaty of 1783 that ended the American Revolution. In 1785 he became the first US ambassador in London.

Adams John Quincy 1767–1848. 6th president of the USA 1825–29. Eldest son of President John Adams, he was born in Quincy, Massachusetts, and became US minister in The Hague, Berlin, St Petersburg, and London. He negotiated the Treaty of Ghent to end the ◊War of 1812 (fought between Britain and the USA) on generous terms for the USA. In 1817 he became ◊Monroe's secretary of state, formulated the ◊Monroe Doctrine 1823, and was elected president by the House of Representatives, despite receiving fewer votes than his main rival, Andrew ◊Jackson. As president, Adams was an advocate of strong federal government.

Addams Jane 1860–1935. US social reformer, feminist, and pacifist. In 1889 she founded and led the social settlement of Hull House, Chicago, one of the earliest community welfare centres. She was vice president of the National American Women Suffrage Alliance 1911–14, and in 1915 led the Women's Peace Party and the first Women's Peace Congress. She shared the Nobel Peace Prize 1931.

Addington Henry 1757–1844. British Tory politician and prime minister 1801–04, he was created Viscount Sidmouth 1805. As home secretary 1812–22, he was responsible for much reprieve legislation, including the notorious ◊Six Acts.

Addled Parliament the English Parliament that met for two months in 1614 but failed to pass a single bill before being dissolved by James I.

Aden main port and commercial centre of ◊Yemen, on a rocky peninsula at the southwest corner of Arabia, commanding the entrance to the Red Sea. A British territory from 1839, Aden became part of independent South Yemen 1967; it was the capital of South Yemen until 1990.

history After annexation by Britain, Aden and its immediately surrounding area (121 sq km/47 sq mi) were developed as a ship-refuelling station following the opening of the Suez Canal 1869. It was a colony 1937–63 and then, after a period of transitional violence among rival nationalist groups and British forces, was combined with the former Aden protectorate (290,000 sq km/112,000 sq mi) to create the Southern Yemen People's Republic 1967, which was renamed the People's Democratic Republic of Yemen 1970–90.

History is the sum total of the things that could have been avoided.

Konrad Adenauer

Adenauer Konrad 1876–1967. German Christian Democrat politician, chancellor of West Germany 1949–63. With the French president de Gaulle he achieved the postwar reconciliation of France and Germany and strongly supported all measures designed to strengthen the Western bloc in Europe.

Adrian IV (Nicholas Breakspear) *c.* 1100–1159. Pope 1154–59, the only British pope. He secured the execution of Arnold of Brescia; crowned Frederick I Barbarossa as German emperor; refused Henry II's request that Ireland should be granted to the English crown in absolute ownership; and was at the height of a quarrel with the emperor when he died.

Adullam biblical city with nearby caves in which David and those who had some grievance took refuge (1 Samuel 22). An Adullamite is a person who is disaffected or who secedes from a political party; the term was used to describe about 40 British Liberal MPs who voted against their leaders to defeat the 1866 Reform Bill.

Aduwa, Battle of defeat of the Italians by the Ethiopians at Aduwa in 1896 under Emperor ◊Menelik II. It marked the end of Italian ambitions in this part of Africa until Mussolini's reconquest in 1935.

Aegean civilization the cultures of Bronze Age Greece, including the ◊*Minoan civilization* of Crete and the ◊*Mycenaean civilization* of the Peloponnese and mainland Greece.

aerial bombardment another name for ◊Blitzkrieg.

Aetolia district of ancient Greece on the NW of the gulf of Corinth. The *Aetolian League* was a confederation of the cities of Aetolia which, following the death of Alexander the Great, became the chief rival of Macedonian power and the Achaean League. In 189 BC the Aetolians were forced to accept a treaty as subject allies of Rome.

Afghanistan mountainous, landlocked country in S central Asia, bounded N by Tajikistan, Turkmenistan, and Uzbekistan, W by Iran, and S and E by Pakistan and China.

history Part of the ancient Persian Empire, the region was used by Darius I and Alexander the Great as a path to India; Islamic conquerors arrived in the 7th century, then the Mongol leaders Genghis Khan and Tamerlane in the 13th and 14th centuries respectively. Afghanistan first became an independent emirate 1747 under Ahmed Shah Durrani. During the 19th century two ◊Afghan Wars were fought in which imperial Britain checked Russian influence extending towards India. The Anglo-Russian treaty 1907 gave autonomy to Afghanistan, with independence achieved by the Treaty of Rawalpindi 1919 following the third Afghan War. The kingdom was founded 1926 by Emir Amanullah.

During the 1950s, Lt-Gen Sardar Mohammad Daud Khan, cousin of King Mohammad Zahir Shah (ruled 1933–73), governed as prime minister and introduced a programme of social and economic modernization with Soviet aid. Opposition to his authoritarian rule forced Daud's resignation 1963; the king was made a constitutional monarch, but political parties were outlawed.

republic After a famine 1972, General Daud Khan overthrew the monarchy in a Soviet-backed military coup 1973. The king fled to exile, and a republic was declared. President Daud, after steering a centrist course, was assassinated 1978 in a military coup, and Nur Mohammad Taraki, the imprisoned leader of the radical Khalq (masses) faction of the banned communist People's Democratic Party of Afghanistan (PDPA), took charge as president of a revolutionary council. A one-party constitution was adopted, a treaty of friendship signed with the USSR, and major land and social reforms introduced. Conservative Muslims opposed these initiatives, and 5 million refugees fled to Iran and Pakistan. Taraki was replaced 1979 by prime minister Hafizullah Amin.

Soviet invasion Internal unrest continued, and the USSR organized a further coup Dec 1979. Amin was executed and Babrak Karmal (1929–), the exiled leader of the gradualist Parcham (banner) faction of the PDPA, was installed as leader. The numbers of Soviet forces in Afghanistan grew to over 120,000 by 1985 as Muslim guerrilla resistance by the mujaheddin ('holy warriors') continued. A war of attrition developed.

Soviet withdrawal Faced with high troop casualties and a drain on economic resources, the new Soviet administration of Mikhail Gorbachev moved towards a compromise settlement 1986. Karmal was replaced as PDPA leader May 1986 by Najibullah Ahmadzai (1947–), and several noncommunist politicians joined the new government. In 1987 the Afghan government announced a unilateral cease-fire and a new multiparty Islamic constitution was ratified. Concurrently, the USSR carried out a phased withdrawal of its troops. On its completion Feb 1989, a state of emergency was imposed by the Najibullah government. It was faced with a mounting military onslaught by the mujaheddin, who resisted the regime's power-sharing proposals. In March 1991, the garrison of Khost, near the Pakistan border, fell to the mujaheddin.

A UN peace plan was accepted by the government May 1991, but rejected by the mujaheddin. Pakistan, the USA, and the USSR halted all weapons supplies Jan 1992.

Mujaheddin seize power The Najibullah regime collapsed April 1992 when Kabul was captured by Mujaheddin forces. A moderate interim government failed to resore order and power was transferred to guerilla leader Burhanuddin Rabbani, with Hezb-i-Islami representative Abdul Sabur Farid as prime minister. Rabbani, a member of the Tajik minority,

pledged to seek unity between the warring guerillas and abolished all laws contrary to *Sharia* (Islamic law). Tensions between the government and Hezb-iIslami fundamentalists culminated Aug 1992 in heavy bombardment of Kabul by rebels. Farid was removed and Hezb-i-Islami banned from government activity. Elected president 1992, Rabbani signed a peace agreement March 1993 with Hezb-i-Islami leader Gulbiddin Hekmatyar, who became prime minister. Kabul came under renewed attack Jan 1994 after Hekmatyar formed an alliance with Mujaheddin leader, Rashid Doestam against the Rabbani government. By June, the rebel forces were driven out, and in Nov Hekmatyar was replaced. In March 1995 government forces repelled forces of the Talibaan (Islamic theology students).

The Talibaan In May 1996 the government concluded a peace agreement with Hekmatyar, who returned as prime minister. But Talibaan rocket attacks on Kabul were renewed, and the city fell Aug 1996. The Talibaan seized power and strict Islamic law was imposed.

Afghan Wars three wars waged between Britain and Afghanistan to counter the threat to British India from expanding Russian influence in Afghanistan.

First Afghan War 1838–42, when the British garrison at Kabul was wiped out.

Second Afghan War 1878–80, when General ◊Roberts captured Kabul and relieved Kandahar.

Third Afghan War 1919, when peace followed the dispatch by the UK of the first aeroplane ever seen in Kabul.

Afonso six kings of Portugal, including:

Afonso I 1094–1185. King of Portugal from 1112. He made Portugal independent from León.

Africa *see map illustrations* (Africa in the early modern era; Africa in 1880) *and see chronology* (Occupation of Africa 16th century to 1919).

African National Congress (ANC) multiracial nationalist organization formed in South Africa 1912 to extend the franchise to the whole population and end all racial discrimination there. Its president is Nelson ◊Mandela. Although originally nonviolent, the ANC was banned by the government from 1960 to Jan 1990, and in exile in Mozambique developed a military wing, *Umkhonto we Sizwe*, which engaged in sabotage and guerrilla training. The armed struggle was suspended Aug 1990 after the organization's headquarters were moved from Zambia

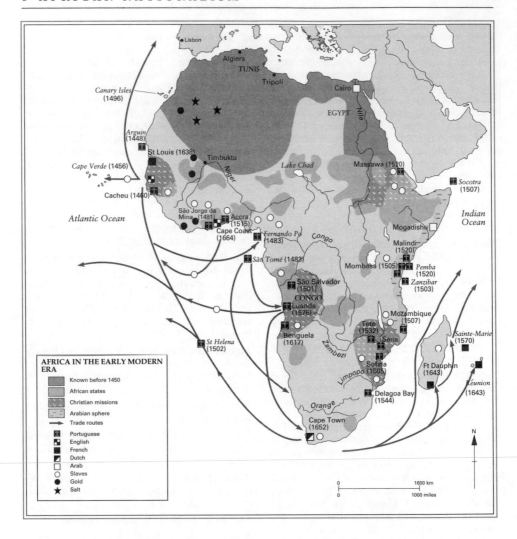

Africa in the early modern era *By the mid-15th century European exploration, led by the Portuguese, began to encounter new and sophisticated African societies south of the Sahara. Eager to exploit the flourishing trade, especially in gold and slaves, by the mid-17th century many European nations had established important economic and strategic toeholds for future expansion into the interior.*

to Johannesburg. Talks between the ANC and the South African government began Dec 1991 and culminated in the adoption of a nonracial constitution 1993 and the ANC's agreement to participate in a power-sharing administration, as a prelude to full majority rule.

In the country's first universal suffrage elections April 1994, the ANC won a sweeping victory, capturing 62% of the vote, and Mandela was elected president. The ANC also won a majority in South Africa's first democratic local government elections Nov 1995, when it won 66.3% of the vote. The ANC's vice president from 1991 is Walter ▷Sisulu.

African nationalism political movement for the unification of Africa. African nationalism has its roots among the educated elite (mainly 'returned' Americans of African descent and freed slaves or their descendants) in W Africa in the 19th century. Christian mission-educated, many challenged overseas mission control and founded independent churches. These were often involved in anticolonial rebellions, for example in Natal 1906 and Nyasaland 1915. The Kitwala (Watchtower Movement) and Kimbanguist churches provided strong support for the nationalist cause in the 1950s. Early African political organizations included

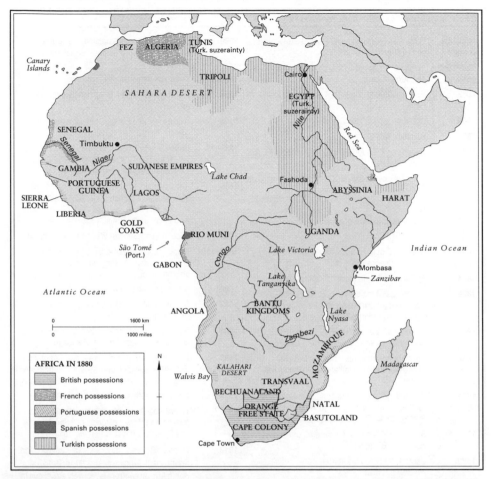

Africa in 1880 *European settlement in Africa was largely confined to the coasts and the navigable waterways provided by the Nile, Congo, and Niger rivers. Although European commerce made inroads, African resistance to European encroachment remained strong. However, increased commercial competition among the European powers, combined with growing military and diplomatic rivalry, was set to alter the map of Africa after 1880.*

the Aborigines Rights Protection Society in the Gold Coast 1897, the African National Congress in South Africa 1912, and the National Congress of West Africa 1920.

After World War I, nationalists fostered moves for self-determination. The ◊Fourteen Points encouraged such demands in Tunisia, and delegates to London 1919 from the Native National Congress in South Africa stressed the contribution to the war effort by the South African Native Labour Corps. Most nationalist groups functioned within the territorial boundaries of single colonies, for example the Tanganyika African Association and the Rhodesian Bantu Voters Association. One or two groups, including the National Congress of British West Africa, had wider pan-African visions.

The first pan-African Congress was held in London 1900 and others followed after 1919.

Pan-African sentiment in Africa and the Americas was intensified with the Italian invasion of ◊Ethiopia in 1935. By 1939 African nationalist groups existed in nearly every territory of the continent. Africa's direct involvement in World War II, the weakening of the principal colonial powers, increasing anticolonialism from America (the ◊Atlantic Charter 1941 encouraged self-government), and Soviet criticism of imperialism inspired African nationalists.

Since 1958 pan-Africanism has become partially absorbed into wider Third World movements. In May 1963 it was decided to establish the ◊Organization of African Unity (OAU).

Occupation of Africa: 16th century to 1919	
Mid–15th century	Portuguese began exploration and exploitation of W African coast.
Mid–16th century	Portuguese in control of Arab trading towns on E African coast.
1652	Dutch made first settlement at Cape of Good Hope.
1806	British occupied Cape Colony.
1822	Foundation of Liberia.
1830	French occupied Algiers and began occupation of Algeria.
1836	Great Trek by Afrikaner (Boer) settlers north to escape British rule at Cape.
1843	British annexed Natal.
1851	British attacked and occupied Lagos.
1857	French occupied Dakar.
1869	Suez Canal opened. Increasing British and French influence in Egypt.
1871	British annexed diamond fields of Kimberley.
1880	Beginnings of major Anglo-French colonial rivalry and annexations of territory introducing a period of formal imperialism.
1881	French established control in Tunisia. First South African War between Boers and British.
1882	British bombarded Alexandria in Egypt to quell Arabi Pasha revolt and establish formal control.
1884	Germans occupied Togo and Cameroon, W Africa, and acquired South West Arica. First South African goldfields opened.
1884–85	Berlin Conference on the partition of Africa chaired by Bismarck.
1885	General Gordon killed at Khartoum. British evacuated Sudan.
1886	(British) Royal Niger Company given charter. French occupied Ivory Coast.
1890	British protectorate established over East Africa. German protectorate declared over Tanganyika.
1893	French declared Guinea a colony.
1895–96	French established a protectorate over Madagascar.
1896	Italians invaded Ethiopia but were repulsed at Adowa (Adwa).
1896–97	British South Africa Company (formed 1889) penetrated N of Zambezi river. Northern Rhodesian Protectorate created.
1898	British army destroyed Sudanese resistance at Omdurman. French under Marchand forced to withdraw from Fashoda. Sudan combined with Egypt under British rule.
1899	Second South African War (Boer War) began.
1899–1901	Anglo-French agreement on colonial frontiers. Frontiers between other European colonies also finalized.
1900	British occupied Nigeria.
1902	Second South African War ended with Peace of Vereeniging.
1904	Entente Cordiale between Britain and France settled their remaining colonial disputes.
1908	Belgian state took over running of Congo Free State after scandals of private maladministration.
1910	Union of South Africa constituted.
1912	French declared protectorate over Morocco. Italians established colonies of Tripolitania and Cyrenaica (Libya) after war 1911–12.
1919	Former German colonies Tanganyika and South West Africa transferred to British and South African control respectively as League of Nations mandates after World War I.

Afrika Korps German army in the western desert of North Africa 1941–43 during World War II, commanded by Field Marshal Erwin Rommel. They were driven out of N Africa by May 1943.

Afrikaner (formerly known as *Boer*) inhabitant of South Africa descended from the original Dutch, Flemish, and ◊Huguenot settlers of the 17th century. Comprising approximately 60% of the white population in South Africa, they were originally farmers but have now become mainly urbanized. Their language is Afrikaans.

Afro-Caribbean West Indian person of African descent. Afro-Caribbeans are the descendants of W Africans captured or obtained in trade from African procurers. European slave traders then shipped them to the West Indies to Eng-lish, French, Dutch, Spanish, and Portuguese colonies founded from the 16th century. Since World War II many Afro-Caribbeans have migrated to North America and to Europe, especially to the USA, the UK, and the Netherlands.

aga (Turkish 'lord') title of nobility, applied by the Turks to military commanders and, in general, to men of high station in some Muslim countries.

Agadir Incident or the *Second Moroccan Crisis* international crisis provoked by Kaiser Wilhelm II of Germany, July–Nov 1911. By sending the gunboat *Panther* to demand territorial concessions from the French, he hoped to drive a wedge into the Anglo-French entente. In fact, German aggression during the second

Moroccan crisis merely served to reinforce Anglo-French fears of Germany's intentions. The crisis gave rise to the term *gunboat diplomacy*.

Agincourt, Battle of battle of the Hundred Years' War in which Henry V of England defeated the French on 25 Oct 1415, mainly through the overwhelming superiority of the English longbow. The French lost more than 6,000 men to about 1,600 English casualties. As a result of the battle, Henry gained France and the French princess, Catherine of Valois, as his wife. The village of Agincourt (modern *Azincourt*) is south of Calais, in N France.

agitprop (Russian 'agitation propaganda') Soviet government bureau established Sept 1920 in charge of Communist agitation and propaganda. The idea was developed by later left-wing groups in the West for the use of theatre and other entertainment to convey political messages.

agora in an ancient Greek town, the public meeting place and market, equivalent to the Roman ◊forum. The limits were marked with boundary stones, and trade was regulated. The Agora at Athens contained an altar to the twelve Olympian gods, sanctuaries of Zeus, Apollo, and Hephaestus, the mint, administrative offices of state, fountain houses, shops, and covered arcades (stoas).

Agra city of Uttar Pradesh, India, on the river Jumna, 160 km/100 mi SE of Delhi. It was the capital of the Mogul empire 1526–1628, from which period the Taj Mahal dates.

history ◊Zahir ud-din Muhammad (known as 'Babur'), the first great Mogul ruler, made Agra his capital 1526. His grandson Akbar rebuilt the Red Fort of Salim Shah 1566, and is buried outside the city in the tomb at Sikandra. In the 17th century the buildings of ◊Shah Jahan made Agra one of the most beautiful cities in the world. The *Taj Mahal*, erected as a tomb for the emperor's wife Mumtaz Mahal, was completed 1650. Agra's political importance dwindled from 1648, when Shah Jahan moved the capital back to Delhi. It was taken from the ◊Marathas by Lord Lake 1803.

Agricola Gnaeus Julius AD 37–93. Roman general and politician. Born in Provence, he became consul AD 77, and then governor of Britain AD 78–85. He extended Roman rule to the Firth of Forth in Scotland and won the battle of Mons Graupius. His fleet sailed round the north of Scotland and proved Britain an island.

agricultural revolution sweeping changes that took place in British agriculture over the period 1750–1850 in response to the increased demand for food from a rapidly expanding population. Recent research has shown these changes to be only part of a much larger, ongoing process of development.

Changes of the latter half of the 18th century included the enclosure of open fields, the introduction of four-course rotation together with new fodder crops such as turnips, and the development of improved breeds of livestock. Pioneers of the new farming were Viscount ◊Townshend (known as 'Turnip' Townshend), Jethro Tull, Robert Bakewell, and enlightened landowners such as Thomas Coke of Norfolk (1752–1842).

Many of the changes were in fact underway before 1750 and other breakthroughs, such as farm mechanization, did not occur until after 1859. Scientific and technological advances in farming during the second half of the 20th century have further revolutionized ◊agriculture.

agriculture the practice of farming, including the cultivation of the soil (for raising crops) and the raising of domesticated animals.

history Agriculture developed in the Middle East and Egypt at least 10,000 years ago. Farming communities soon became the base for society in China, India, Europe, Mexico, and Peru, then spread throughout the world. Reorganization along more scientific and productive lines took place in Europe in the 18th century in response to dramatic population growth (see ◊agricultural revolution).

Mechanization made considerable progress in the USA and Europe during the 19th century. After World War II, there was an explosive growth in the use of agricultural chemicals. In the 1960s there was development of high-yielding species, and the industrialized countries began intensive farming of cattle, poultry, and pigs. In the 1980s, there was also a reaction against some forms of intensive agriculture because of the pollution and habitat destruction caused. One result of this was a growth of alternative methods, including organic agriculture.

overproduction The greater efficiency in agriculture achieved since the 19th century, coupled with post–World War II government subsidies for domestic production in the USA and the European Community (EC), have led to the development of high stocks, nicknamed 'lakes' (wine, milk) and 'mountains' (butter, beef, grain). Increasing concern about the starving and the cost of storage has led the USA and the EC to develop measures for limiting production, such as letting arable land lie fallow to reduce grain crops. The USA had some success at selling surplus wheat to the USSR when

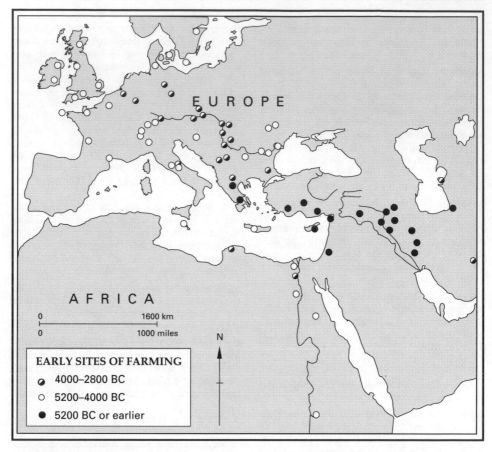

Agriculture: early sites of farming *The earliest evidence for farming techniques comes from Anatolia (modern Turkey) and the Middle East. The harvesting of wild grasses dates from about 9500 BC, sheep-herding in N Iraq from about 9000, and Jericho was settled by 8000. Çatal Hüyük (near Konya, Turkey) demonstrated a developed urban life dependent on farming by 6000 and from then, farming techniques spread from the Middle East into the Balkans and the Danube Valley (Lepenski Vir), and into N Europe. There were flourishing farming communities in Egypt and China by 5000.*

History of agriculture

10,000–8000 BC	Holocene (post-glacial) period of hunters and gatherers. Harvesting and storage of wild grains in SW Asia. Herding of reindeer in N Eurasia. Domestic sheep in N Iraq.	**3200**	Records of ploughing, raking, and manuring, by Egyptians.
		***c.* 3100**	River Nile dammed during the rule of King Menes.
8000	Neolithic revolution with cultivation of domesticated wheats and barleys, sheep, and goats in SW Asia. Domestication of pigs in New Guinea.	**3000**	First record of asses used as beasts of burden in Egypt. Sumerian civilization used barley as main crop with wheat, dates, flax, apples, plums, and grapes.
7000–6000	Domestic goats, sheep, and cattle in Anatolia, Greece, Persia, and the Caspian basin. Planting and harvesting techniques transferred from Asia Minor to Europe.	**2900**	Domestication of pigs in E Asia.
		2640	Reputed start of Chinese silk industry.
5000	Beginning of Nile valley civilization. Millet cultivated in China.	**2500**	Domestic elephants in the Indus valley. Potatoes a staple crop in Peru.
3400	Flax used for textiles in Egypt. Widespread corn production in the Americas.	**2350 BC**	Wine-making in Egypt.
		2250	First known irrigation dam.

History of agriculture *continued*

1600	Important advances in the cultivation of vines and olives in Crete.
1500	*Shadoof* (mechanism for raising water) used for irrigation in Egypt.
1400	Iron ploughshares in use in India.
1300	Aqueducts and reservoirs used for irrigation in Egypt.
1200	Domestic camels in Arabia.
1000–500	Evidence of crop rotation, manuring and irrigation in India.
600	First windmills used for corn grinding in Persia.
350	Rice cultivation well established in parts of W Africa. Hunting and gathering in the E, central, and S parts of the continent.
c. 200	Use of gears to create ox-driven water wheel for irrigation. Archimedes screw used for irrigation.
100	Cattle-drawn iron ploughs in use in China.
AD 65	*De Re Rustica/On Rural Things*, Latin treatise on agriculture and irrigation.
500	'Three fields in two years' rotation used in China.
630	Cotton introduced into Arabia.
800	Origins of the 'open field' system in N Europe.
900	Wheeled ploughs in use in W Europe. Horse collar, originating in China, allowed horses to be used for ploughing as well as carrying.
1000	Frisians (NW Netherlanders) began to build dykes and reclaim land. Chinese began to introduce Champa rice which cropped much more quickly than other varieties.
11th century	Three-field system replaced the two-field system in W Europe. Concentration on crop growing.
1126	First artesian wells, at Artois, France.
12th century	Increasing use of water mills and windmills. Horses replaced oxen for pulling work in many areas.
12th–14th centuries	Expansion of European population brought more land into cultivation. Crop rotations, manuring, and new crops such as beans and peas helped increase productivity. Feudal system at its height.
13th–14th centuries	Agricultural recession in W Europe with a series of bad harvests, famines, and pestilence.
1347	Black Death killed about a third of the European population.
16th century	Decline of the feudal system in W Europe.
	More specialist forms of production were now possible with urban markets. Manorial estates and serfdom remained in E Europe. Chinese began cultivation of non-indigenous crops such as corn, sweet potatoes, potatoes, and peanuts.
17th century	Potato introduced into Europe. Norfolk crop rotation became widespread in England, involving wheat, turnips, barley and then ryegrass/clover.
1700–1845	Agricultural revolution began in Britain. Two million hectares of farmland in England enclosed. Removal of open fields in other parts of Europe followed.
c. 1701	Jethro Tull developed the seed drill and the horse-drawn hoe.
1747	First sugar extracted from sugar beet in Prussia.
1762	Veterinary school founded in Lyon, France.
1783	First plough factory in England.
1785	Cast-iron ploughshare patented.
1793	Invention of the cotton gin.
1800	Early threshing machines developed in England.
1820s	First nitrates for fertilizer imported from S America.
1830	Reaping machines developed in Scotland and the US. Steel plough made by John Deere in Illinois, US.
1840s	Extensive potato blight in Europe.
1850s	Use of clay pipes for drainage well established throughout Europe.
1862	First steam plough used in the Netherlands.
1850–1890s	Major developments in transport and refrigeration technology altered the nature of agricultural markets with crops, dairy products, and wheat being shipped internationally.
1890s	Development of stationary engines for ploughing.
1892	First petrol-driven tractor in the USA.
1921	First attempt at crop dusting with pesticides from an aeroplane near Dayton, Ohio, US.
1938	First self-propelled grain combine harvester used in the USA.
1942–62	Huge increase in the uses of pesticides, later curbed by disquiet about their effects and increasing resistance of pests to standard controls such as DDT.
1945 onwards	Increasing use of scientific techniques, crop specialization and larger scale of farm enterprises throughout N America and W Europe.

the Soviet crop was poor, but the overall cost of bulk transport and the potential destabilization of other economies have acted against high producers exporting their excess on a regular basis to needy countries.

Agrippa Marcus Vipsanius 63–12 BC. Roman general and admiral, instrumental in the successful campaigns and rise to power of ◊Augustus. He commanded the victorious fleet at the battle of ◊Actium and married Augustus's daughter Julia.

AH with reference to the Muslim calendar, abbreviation for *anno hegirae* (Latin 'year of the flight' -of ◊Muhammad, from Mecca to Medina).

Ahab c. 875–854 BC. King of Israel. His empire included the suzerainty of Moab, and Judah was his subordinate ally, but his kingdom was weakened by constant wars with Syria. By his marriage with Jezebel, princess of Sidon, Ahab introduced into Israel the worship of the Phoenician god Baal, thus provoking the hostility of Elijah and other prophets. Ahab died in battle against the Syrians at Ramoth Gilead.

Ahasuerus (Latinized Hebrew form of the Persian *Khshayarsha*, Greek *Xerxes*) name of several Persian kings in the Bible, notably the husband of Esther. Traditionally it was also the name of the Wandering Jew.

Ahmadiyya Islamic religious movement founded by Mirza Ghulam Ahmad (1839–1908). His followers reject the doctrine that Muhammad was the last of the prophets and accept Ahmad's claim to be the Mahdi and Promised Messiah. In 1974 the Ahmadis were denounced as non-Muslims by other Muslims.

Ahmad Shah Durrani 1724–1773. Founder and first ruler of Afghanistan. Elected shah in 1745, he had conquered the Punjab by 1751 and defeated the ◊Maratha people's confederacy at Panipat, Punjab, in 1761.

Aigun, Treaty of treaty between Russia and China signed 1858 at the port of Aigun in China on the Amur River. The left bank was ceded to Russia, but this has since been repudiated by China.

Ainu aboriginal people of Japan, driven north in the 4th century AD by ancestors of the Japanese. They now number about 25,000, inhabiting Japanese and Russian territory on Sakhalin, Hokkaido, and the Kuril Islands.

air raid aerial attack, usually on a civilian target such as a factory, railway line, or communications centre. In World War II (1939–45), raids were usually made by bomber aircraft, but many thousands were killed in London 1944 by German V1 and V2 rockets. The air raids on Britain 1940–41 became known as *the Blitz*. The Allies made retaliatory raids over European cities 1942–45.

During the ◊Gulf War 1991 the UN coalition forces made thousands of air raids on Baghdad, Iraq, to destroy the Iraqi infrastructure and communications network (some 250,000 civilians were killed).

Akbar Jalal ud-Din Muhammad 1542–1605. Mogul emperor of N India from 1556, when he succeeded his father. He gradually established his rule throughout N India. He is considered the greatest of the Mogul emperors, and the firmness and wisdom of his rule won him the title 'Guardian of Mankind'; he was a patron of the arts.

Akbar was tolerant towards the majority Hindu population, suspending discriminatory taxes. He created his own eclectic royal religion (Din Illahi), reformed the land tax system and created a more centralized system of political control. He moved the Mogul court-capital temporarily from ◊Agra to the nearby new city of Fatehpur Sikri 1569–85.

A monarch should be ever intent on conquest, otherwise his neighbours rise in arms against him.

Jalal ud-Din Muhammad Akbar
Abu-l-Fazl Allami *Ain-e Akbari*
c. 1590, tr. Jarrett.

Akhenaton another name for ◊Ikhnaton, pharaoh of Egypt.

Akhetaton capital of ancient Egypt established by the monotheistic pharaoh ◊Ikhnaton as the centre for his cult of the Aton, the sun's disc; it is the modern Tell el Amarna 300 km/190 mi S of Cairo. Ikhnaton's palace had formal enclosed gardens. After his death it was abandoned, and the clay *Amarna tablets*, found in the ruins, were probably discarded by his officials.

Akkad northern Semitic people who conquered the Sumerians in 2350 BC and ruled Mesopotamia. The ancient city of Akkad or Agade in central Mesopotamia, founded by ◊Sargon I, was an imperial centre in the late 3rd millennium BC; the site is unidentified, but it was on the river Euphrates somewhere near Babylon.

Akko Israeli seaport formerly called ◊Acre.

Aksum or *Axum* ancient Greek-influenced Semitic kingdom that flourished in the 1st–6th centuries AD and covered a large part of modern Ethiopia as well as the Sudan. The ruins of its capital, also called Aksum, lie NW of Aduwa, but the site has been developed as a modern city.

Alamanni alternative spelling of ◊Alemanni.

Alamein, El, Battles of in World War II, two decisive battles in the western desert, N Egypt. In the *First Battle of El Alamein* 1–27 July 1942 the British 8th Army under Auchinleck held the German and Italian forces under Rommel. In the *Second Battle of El Alamein* 23 Oct–4 Nov 1942 ◊Montgomery defeated Rommel.

Before Alamein we never had a victory. After Alamein we never had a defeat.

On the Battles *of El Alamein*
Winston Churchill *The Hinge of Fate* 1951

Alamo, the mission fortress in San Antonio, Texas, USA. It was besieged 23 Feb–6 March 1836 by ◊Santa Anna and 4,000 Mexicans; they killed the garrison of about 180, including Davy ◊Crockett and Jim ◊Bowie.

Alanbrooke Alan Francis Brooke, 1st Viscount Alanbrooke 1883–1963. British army officer, Chief of Staff in World War II and largely responsible for the strategy that led to the German defeat.

He was commander in chief of the Home Forces 1940–41 and chief of the Imperial General Staff 1941–46. He became a field marshal in 1944, was created a baron 1945 and viscount 1946.

Alaric c. 370–410. King of the Visigoths. In 396 he invaded Greece and retired with much booty to Illyria. In 400 and 408 he invaded Italy, and in 410 captured and sacked Rome, but died the same year on his way to invade Sicily.

Alaska largest state of the USA, on the northwest extremity of North America, separated from the lower 48 states by British Columbia. Various groups of Indians crossed the Bering land bridge 60,000–15,000 years ago; the Eskimo began to settle the Arctic coast from Siberia about 2000 BC; the Aleuts settled the Aleutian archipelago about 1000 BC. The first European to visit Alaska was Vitus Bering 1741. Alaska was a Russian colony from 1744 until purchased by the USA 1867 for $7,200,000; gold was discovered five years later. It became a state 1959.

Alba alternative spelling of ◊Alva.

Albania country in SE Europe, bounded N and E by Yugoslavia, SE by Greece, and W and SW by the Adriatic Sea.

history In the ancient world the area was occupied by the Illyrians, later becoming a Roman province until the end of the 4th century AD. Albania then came under Byzantine rule, which lasted until 1347. There followed about 100 years of invasions by Bulgarians, Serbs, Venetians, and finally Turks, who arrived 1385 and, after the death of the nationalist leader Skanderbeg (George Castriota) (1403–1468), eventually made Albania part of the ◊Ottoman Empire after the siege of Scutari 1478.

independence Albania became independent 1912, after the First Balkan War, and a republic 1925. In 1928 President Ahmed Beg Zogu was proclaimed King Zog. Overrun by Italy and Germany 1939–44, Albania became a republic with a communist government 1946 after a guerrilla struggle led by Enver ◊Hoxha.

the 'Hoxha experiment' At first closely allied with Yugoslavia, Albania backed the Soviet dictator Stalin in his 1948 dispute with the Yugoslav ruler Tito and developed close links with the USSR 1949–55, entering the trade organization ◊Comecon 1949. Hoxha imposed a Stalinist system with rural collectivization, industrial nationalization, central planning, and one-party control. Mosques and churches were closed in an effort to create the 'first atheist state'. Hoxha remained a committed Stalinist and broke off diplomatic relations with the USSR 1961. Choosing isolation and neutrality, Albania also severed diplomatic relations with China 1978. The 'Hoxha experiment' left Albania with the lowest income per head of population in Europe. After Hoxha's death 1985, there was a widening of external economic contacts.

open dissent Opposition to the regime began to mount during 1990. In early July unprecedented antigovernment street demonstrations erupted in Tiranë. Faced with a government crackdown, 5,000 demonstrators sought refuge in foreign embassies and were later allowed to leave the country. Later the same month diplomatic relations with the USSR were restored and embassies re-established.

end of one-party system In Dec 1990, amid continuing protests in Tiranë and economic collapse, the Communist Party leadership announced that the existence of opposition parties had finally been authorized and the ban on religion lifted. An opposition party was immediately formed: the Democratic Party (DP), led by Sali Berisha.

civil unrest A huge bronze statue of Hoxha in Tiranë was toppled by demonstrators Feb 1991, and there were riots in several other towns. President Alia replaced the unpopular premier Adil Çarçani with Fatos Nano (1951–), a reform economist. Alia also declared the imposition of presidential rule and tanks were moved into the streets of Tiranë. Fears of a right-wing coup prompted a flight of thousands of Albanians to neighbouring countries. 'Nonpolitical' refugees were sent back.

first multiparty elections Diplomatic relations with the USA and the UK, suspended since 1946, were restored March and May 1991 respectively. In Albania's first free multiparty elections, held March–April 1991, the ruling Party of Labour of Albania (PLA) secured sufficient seats for the necessary two-thirds majority to make constitutional changes.

economic problems An interim constitution was adopted April 1991, with the country renamed the Republic of Albania and the PLA's leading role being abandoned. The new People's Assembly elected Ramiz Alia as both the new executive president of the republic, replacing the presidium, and commander in chief of the armed forces. In May 1991 Fatos Nano was reappointed prime minister, but resigned in June. The economy deteriorated rapidly. Nano was replaced by Ylli Bufi, the former food minister, heading a new, interim 'government of national stability' with members from the opposition parties. In June 1991 the PLA renamed itself the Socialist Party of Albania (PSS), with Fatos Nano elected as its chair. In July 1991 a land-privatization bill was passed to restore land to peasants dispossessed under communist rule. From late summer 1991 Albania began to receive emergency aid from the European Community.

first noncommunist leaders The DP withdrew from the coalition government, claiming that it was being manipulated by former communists, and on 6 Dec 1991 prime minister Bufi resigned. On 18 Dec 1991 President Alia appointed Vilson Ahmeti, a former nutrition minister, as Albania's first noncommunist premier. In Jan 1992, 20 former Albanian communist officials were arrested on corruption charges. The DP won 62% of the national vote in March 1992 elections against 25% for the PSS. The newly formed parliament elected Dr Sali Berisha, founder and leader of the DP, as the country's president and granted him increased executive powers. Alexander Meksi succeeded Ahmeti as prime minister. In July 1992 a ban was imposed on all 'fascist, antinational, chauvinistic, racist, totalitarian, communist, Marxist-Leninist, Stalinist, or Enverist (following Enver Hoxha)' political organizations. The DP was renamed the Democratic

Party of Albania (PDS) in 1993. A national referendum in 1994 rejected proposals for a new presidential-style constitution. In May-June 1996, the ruling PDS claimed an overwhelming victory in the parliamentary elections amidst opposition allegations of rigging and intimidation. In July 1996 Berisha asked Meksi to form a new coalition government.

chaos In Jan 1997 nine high-risk 'pyramid' investment schemes collapsed. Almost half the population had participated. Widespread protest followed, resulting in violence and demands for political change. Berisha reached agreement with northern opposition parties and appointed as prime minister Bakshim Fino. In elections of summer 1997, the socialists and their allies won a two-thirds majority.

Alberdi Juan Bautista 1810–1884. Argentine diplomat and political theorist. Forced into exile 1838 because of his opposition to Juan Manuel de ◊Rosas, he wrote his great work *Bases y punto de partida para la organización política de la república argentina/Bases and Starting Points for the Organization of the Argentine Republic* in Chile 1852. It formed the basis for Argentina's constitution the following year.

Alberoni Giulio 1664–1752. Spanish-Italian priest and politician, born in Piacenza, Italy. Philip V made him prime minister of Spain in 1715. He became a cardinal 1717. Despite many domestic reforms, his foreign policies failed. He was forced to flee to Italy in 1719.

Albert Prince Consort 1819–1861. Husband of British Queen ◊Victoria from 1840; a patron of the arts, science, and industry. Albert was the second son of the Duke of Saxe Coburg-Gotha and first cousin to Queen Victoria, whose chief adviser he became. He planned the ◊Great Exhibition of 1851; the profit was used to buy the sites in London of all the South Kensington museums and colleges and the Royal Albert Hall, built 1871. He died of typhoid.

Albert I 1875–1934. King of the Belgians from 1909, the younger son of Philip, Count of Flanders, and the nephew of Leopold II. In 1900 he married Duchess Elisabeth of Bavaria. In World War I he commanded the Allied army that retook the Belgian coast in 1918.

Albigenses heretical sect of Christians (associated with the ◊Cathars) who flourished in S France near Albi and Toulouse during the 11th–13th centuries. They adopted the manichean belief in the duality of good and evil and pictured Jesus as being a rebel against the cruelty of an omnipotent God.

An inquisition was initiated against the Albigensians in 1184 by pope Lucius III (although the ◊Inquisition as we know it was not established until 1233); it was, however, ineffective, and in 1208 a crusade (1208–29) was launched against them under the elder Simon de Montfort. Thousands were killed before the movement was crushed in 1244.

Alboin 6th century. King of the ◊Lombards about 561–573. At that time the Lombards were settled north of the Alps. Early in his reign he attacked the Gepidae, a Germanic tribe occupying present-day Romania, killing their king and taking his daughter Rosamund to be his wife. About 568 he crossed the Alps to invade Italy, conquering the country as far S as Rome. He was murdered at the instigation of his wife, after he forced her to drink wine from a cup made from her father's skull.

Albuquerque Afonso de 1453–1515. Viceroy and founder of the Portuguese East Indies with strongholds in Ceylon, Goa, and Malacca 1508–15, when the king of Portugal replaced him by his worst enemy. He died at sea on the way home when his ship *Flor del Mar* was lost between Malaysia and India.

Alcazarquivir, Battle of battle on 4 Aug 1578 between the forces of Sebastian, king of Portugal (1554–1578), and those of the Berber kingdom of Fez. Sebastian's death on the field of battle paved the way for the incorporation of Portugal into the Spanish kingdom of Philip II.

Alcibiades 450–404 BC. Athenian politician and general. He organized a confederation of Peloponnesian states against Sparta that collapsed after the battle of Mantinea 418 BC. Although accused of profaning the Eleusinian Mysteries (ceremonies in honour of Greek deities), he was eventually accepted as the commander of the Athenian fleet. He achieved several victories such as Cyzicus 410 BC, before his forces were defeated at Notium 406. He was murdered in Phrygia by the Persians.

Alcmaeonidae noble family of ancient Athens; its members included ◊Pericles and ◊Alcibiades.

Alemanni or *Alamanni* Germanic people who from the 4th century AD occupied an area bounded by the Rhine, Danube, and Main rivers. They were part of the medieval western German grouping of peoples which also included Franks, Saxons, Frisians, and Thuringians. During the 5th century they crossed the Rhine and Danube and settled in what is now Alsace and N Switzerland, where they introduced the German language. They were fully absorbed into the East Frankish kingdom in the 9th century.

Alençon François, duke of, later duke of Anjou 1554–1584. Fourth son of Henry II of France and Catherine de' Medici. At one time he was considered as a suitor to Elizabeth I of England.

Alessandri Palma Arturo 1868–1950. Chilean president 1920–25, 1932–37. Reforms proposed in his first presidential term were blocked by an opposition-controlled Congress. Forced into exile, he returned to achieve a measure of economic recovery at the expense of the repression of opponents, a policy which made him a controversial figure in Chilean history.

Alexander eight popes, including:

Alexander III (Orlando Barninelli) Pope 1159–81. His authority was opposed by Frederick I Barbarossa, but Alexander eventually compelled him to render homage 1178. He supported Henry II of England in his invasion of Ireland, but imposed penance on him after the murder of Thomas à ◊Becket.

Alexander VI (Rodrigo Borgia) 1431–1503. Pope 1492–1503. Of Spanish origin, he bribed his way to the papacy, where he furthered the advancement of his illegitimate children, who included Cesare and Lucrezia ◊Borgia. When ◊Savonarola preached against his corrupt practices, Alexander had him executed.

Alexander three tsars of Russia:

Alexander I 1777–1825. Tsar from 1801. Defeated by Napoleon at Austerlitz 1805, he made peace at Tilsit 1807, but economic crisis led to a break with Napoleon's ◊Continental System and the opening of Russian ports to British trade; this led to Napoleon's ill-fated invasion of Russia 1812. After the Congress of Vienna 1815, Alexander hoped through the Holy Alliance with Austria and Prussia to establish a new Christian order in Europe.

It is better to abolish serfdom from above than to wait for it to abolish itself from below

Alexander II speech to the Moscow nobility
March 1856

Alexander II 1818–1881. Tsar from 1855. He embarked on reforms of the army, the government, and education, and is remembered as 'the Liberator' for his emancipation of the serfs 1861, but he lacked the personnel to implement his reforms. However, the revolutionary element remained unsatisfied, and Alexander became increasingly autocratic and reactionary. He was assassinated by an anarchistic terrorist group, the ◊Nihilists.

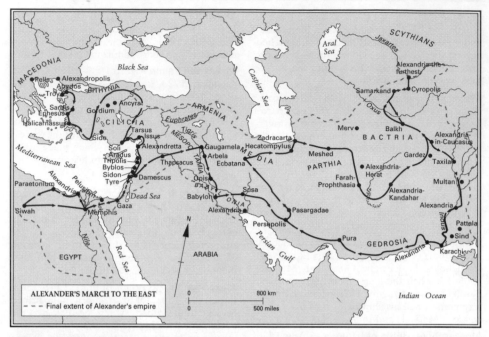

Alexander's march to the east *Alexander's conquests reached the furthest extent of the Persian Empire. He crossed into Asia 334 BC with an army of 40,000. His first victory at Granicus (near Troy) was followed by a second at Issus 333. He occupied Egypt and the Phoenician port of Tyre, and decisively defeated Darius III at Gaugamela 331, occupying the Persian capitals. In Bactria he faced strong resistance and pressed on as far as the Indus valley (327–325), before a gruelling return journey downriver and then overland to Babylon.*

Alexander III 1845–1894. Tsar from 1881, when he succeeded his father, Alexander II. He pursued a reactionary policy, promoting Russification and persecuting the Jews. He married Dagmar (1847–1928), daughter of Christian IX of Denmark and sister of Queen Alexandra of Britain, 1866.

Alexander three kings of Scotland including:

Alexander III 1241–1285. King of Scotland from 1249, son of Alexander II. In 1263, by military defeat of Norwegian forces, he extended his authority over the Western Isles, which had been dependent on Norway. He strengthened the power of the central Scottish government.

Alexander I Karageorgevich 1888–1934. Regent of Serbia 1912–21 and king of Yugoslavia 1921–34, as dictator from 1929. Second son of ◊Peter I, King of Serbia, he was declared regent for his father 1912, and on his father's death became king of the state of South Slavs – Yugoslavia – that had come into being 1918.

Rivalries with neighbouring powers and among the Croats, Serbs, and Slovenes within the country led Alexander to establish a personal dictatorship. He was assassinated on a state visit to France, and Mussolini's government was later declared to have instigated the crime.

Alexander Nevski, St 1220–1263. Russian military leader, son of the grand duke of Novgorod. In 1240 he defeated the Swedes on the banks of the Neva (hence Nevski), and 1242 defeated the Teutonic Knights on the frozen Lake Peipus.

Alexander Obrenovich 1876–1903. King of Serbia from 1889 while still a minor, on the abdication of his father, King Milan. He took power into his own hands 1893 and in 1900 married a widow, Draga Mashin. In 1903 Alexander and his queen were murdered, and ◊Peter I was placed on the throne.

Alexander the Great 356–323 BC. King of Macedonia. The son of King Philip of Macedonia and Queen Olympias, Alexander was educated by the philosopher Aristotle. At the age of 20, when his father was murdered, he assumed command of the throne and the army. He secured his northern frontier, suppressed an attempted rising in Greece by his capture of Thebes, and in 334 crossed the Dardanelles for the campaign against the vast Persian empire. In 333 he routed Darius at Issus, and then set out for Egypt, where he was greeted as

Pharaoh. Meanwhile, Darius assembled half a million men for a final battle at Gaugamela, near Arbela on the Tigris 331 but Alexander, with 47,000 men, drove the Persians into retreat. After the victory he stayed a month in Babylon, then marched to Susa and Persepolis and in 330 to Ecbatana (now Hamadán, Iran). Soon after, he learned that Darius was dead. In Afghanistan he founded colonies at Herat and Kandahar, and in 328 reached the plains of Sogdiana, where he married Roxana, daughter of King Oxyartes. India was his next objective, and he pressed on to the Indus. Near the river Hydaspes (now Jhelum) he fought one of his fiercest battles against the rajah Porus. At the river Hyphasis (now Beas) his depleted troops refused to go farther, and reluctantly he turned back down the Indus and along the coast. They reached Susa 324, where Alexander made Darius' daughter his second wife. He died in Babylon of a malarial fever.

I will not steal a victory.

Alexander the Great
refusing to fall on the army of King Darius before the Battle of Gaugamela 331 BC, quoted in Plutarch *Lives*

Alexandra 1872–1918. Last tsarina of Russia 1894–1917. She was the former Princess Alix of Hessen and granddaughter of Britain's Queen Victoria. She married ◊Nicholas II and, from 1907, fell under the spell of ◊Rasputin, a 'holy man' brought to the palace to try to cure her son of haemophilia. She was shot with the rest of her family by the Bolsheviks in the Russian Revolution.

Alexandria or *El Iskandariya* city, chief port, and second largest city of Egypt. The principal centre of Hellenistic culture, Alexandria has since the 4th century AD been the seat of a Christian patriarch. In 641 it was captured by the Muslim Arabs, and after the opening of the Cape route its trade rapidly declined. Early in the 19th century it began to recover its prosperity, and its growth was encouraged by its use as the main British naval base in the Mediterranean during both world wars. Of the large European community, most were expelled after the Suez Crisis 1956 and their property confiscated.

Few relics of antiquity remain. The Pharos, the first lighthouse and one of the seven wonders of the ancient world, has long since disappeared. The library, said to have contained 700,000 volumes, was destroyed by the caliph ◊Omar 640. Pompey's Pillar is a column erected by the emperor Diocletian, as a landmark visible from the sea. Two obelisks that once stood before the Caesareum temple are now in London (Cleopatra's Needle) and New York respectively.

Alexius five emperors of Byzantium, including:

Alexius I (Comnenus) 1048–1118. Byzantine emperor 1081–1118. The Latin (W European) Crusaders helped him repel Norman and Turkish invasions, and he devoted great skill to buttressing the threatened empire. His daughter ◊Anna Comnena chronicled his reign.

Alexius III (Angelos) died c. 1210. Byzantine emperor 1195–1203. He gained power by deposing and blinding his brother Isaac II, but Isaac's Venetian allies enabled him and his son Alexius IV to regain power as coemperors.

Alexius IV (Angelos) 1182–1204. Byzantine emperor from 1203, when, with the aid of the army of the Fourth Crusade, he deposed his uncle Alexius III. He soon lost the support of the Crusaders (by that time occupying Constantinople), and was overthrown and murdered by Alexius Mourtzouphlus (son-in-law of Alexius III) 1204, an act which the Crusaders used as a pretext to sack the city the same year.

Alfaro Eloy 1842–1912. Ecuadorian general and politician, president 1895–1901, 1906–11. He was involved in various revolts before overthrowing President Luis Cordero 1895, backed by the military. Despite his liberal support, he was unable to avoid political conflict or run an orderly government.

At 22, Alfaro kidnapped the governor of Manabí and was a revolutionary leader for the next 25 years. During his first term in office he promoted religious freedom, instituted civil marriage, and encouraged state education. After his second period as president he was forced into exile and later lynched by opponents in Quito.

Alfonso thirteen kings of León, Castile, and Spain, including:

Alfonso VII c. 1107–1157. King of León and Castile from 1126 who attempted to unite Spain. Although he protected the Moors, he was killed trying to check a Moorish rising.

Alfonso X *el Sabio* ('the Wise') 1221–1284. King of Castile from 1252. His reign was politically unsuccessful but he contributed to learning: he made Castilian the official language of the country and commissioned a history of Spain and an encyclopedia, as well as several translations from Arabic concerning, among other subjects, astronomy and games.

Alfonso XI *the Avenger* 1311–1350. King of Castile and León from 1312. He ruled cruelly, repressed a rebellion by his nobles, and defeated the last Moorish invasion 1340.

Alfonso XIII 1886–1941. King of Spain 1886–1931. He assumed power 1906 and married Princess Ena, granddaughter of Queen Victoria of the United Kingdom, in the same year. He abdicated 1931 soon after the fall of the Primo de Rivera dictatorship 1923–30 (which he supported), and Spain became a republic. His assassination was attempted several times.

Assassination – an accident of my trade.

Alfonso XIII of Spain
after an attempt on his life May 1906

Alfred *the Great* c. 848–c. 900. King of Wessex from 871. He defended England against Danish invasion, founded the first English navy, and put into operation a legal code. He encouraged the translation of works from Latin (some he translated himself), and promoted the development of the ◊Anglo-Saxon Chronicle.

Alfred was born at Wantage, Berkshire, the youngest son of Ethelwulf (died 858), king of the West Saxons. In 870 Alfred and his brother Ethelred fought many battles against the Danes. He gained a victory over the Danes at Ashdown 871, and succeeded Ethelred as king April 871 after a series of defeats. Five years of uneasy peace followed while the Danes were occupied in other parts of England. In 876 the Danes attacked again, and in 878 Alfred was forced to retire to the stronghold of Athelney, from where he finally emerged to win the victory of Edington, Wiltshire. By the Peace of Wedmore 878 the Danish leader Guthrum (died 890) agreed to withdraw from Wessex and from Mercia west of Watling Street. A new landing in Kent encouraged a revolt of the East Anglian Danes, which was suppressed 884–86, and after the final foreign invasion was defeated 892–96, Alfred strengthened the navy to prevent fresh incursions.

Algeciras Conference international conference held Jan–April 1906 when France, Germany, Britain, Russia, Austria–Hungary, USA, Spain, the Low Countries, Portugal, and Sweden met to settle the question of Morocco. The conference was prompted by increased German demands in what had traditionally been seen as a French area of influence, but it resulted in a reassertion of Anglo-French friendship and the increased isolation of Germany. France and Spain gained control of Morocco.

Algeria country in N Africa, bounded E by Tunisia and Libya, SE by Niger, SW by Mali and Mauritania, NW by Morocco, and N by the Mediterranean Sea.

history From the 9th century BC the area now known as Algeria was ruled by ◊Carthage, and subsequently by Rome 2nd century BC–5th century AD. In the early Christian era, St Augustine was bishop of Hippo (now called Annaba) 396–430. The area was invaded by the ◊Vandals after the decline of Roman rule and was ruled by ◊Byzantium from the 6th–8th centuries, after which the Arabs invaded the region, introducing Islam and Arabic. Islamic influence continued to dominate, despite Spain's attempts to take control in the 15th–16th centuries. From the 16th century Algeria was under Ottoman rule and flourished as a centre for the slave trade. The sultan's rule was often nominal, and in the 18th century Algeria became a pirate state, preying on Mediterranean shipping. European intervention became inevitable, and an Anglo-Dutch force bombarded Algiers 1816.

French colonization A French army landed 1830 and seized Algiers. By 1847 the north had been brought under French control, and was formed 1848 into the *départements* of Algiers, Oran, and Constantine. Many French colonists settled in these *départements*, which were made part of metropolitan France 1881. The mountainous region inland, inhabited by the Kabyles, was occupied 1850–70, and the Sahara region, subdued 1900–09, remained under military rule.

Struggle for independence After the defeat of France by Germany 1940 in World War II, Algeria came under the control of the Vichy government, which collaborated with the Nazis, until the Allies landed in N Africa 1942. Postwar hopes of integrating Algeria more closely with France were frustrated by opposition in Algeria from both those of non-French and French origin. An embittered struggle for independence from France continued 1954–62, when referenda in Algeria and France resulted 1962 in the recognition of Algeria as an independent one-party republic with ◊Ben Bella as prime minister 1962 and the country's first president from 1963. Colonel Houari ◊Boumédienne deposed Ben Bella in a military coup 1965, suspended the constitution, and ruled through a revolutionary council.

Chadli's presidency A new constitution confirmed Algeria as an Islamic, socialist, one-party state 1976. Boumédienne died 1978, and power was transferred to Benjedid ◊Chadli, secretary general of the National Liberation Front (FLN). During Chadli's presidency, relations with France and the USA improved, and there was some progress in achieving greater cooperation with neighbouring states, such as Tunisia. Algeria acted as an intermediary in securing the release of the US hostages in Iran 1981. A proposal by Colonel ◊Khaddhafi for political union with Libya received a cool response 1987. Riots and protests at economic austerity measures Oct 1988 prompted reforms and a revised constitution, deleting references to socialism and opening the way to a multiparty system. Reforms were partly designed to stem the growing fundamentalist movement.

military rule In first-round assembly elections Dec 1991 the Islamic Front for Salvation (FIS) won an overwhelming majority and Chadli resigned. The army cancelled the second round, forming a junta under Muhammad Boudiaf. Religious political activity was restricted. Disquiet persisted; Boudiaf was assassinated June 1992 and replaced by Ali Kafi.

From 1993 Islamic fundamentalists launched a retaliatory campaign of violence against the government, which responded with brutal tactics. Under new president General Lamine Zeroual, talks were conducted unsuccessfully with the fundamentalists 1994. Opposition peace proposals 1995 were rejected by the military regime. The imposition of a new constitution 1996, banning the political exploitation of Islam, fuelled the civil war.

Algiers, Battle of bitter conflict in Algiers 1954–62 between the Algerian nationalist population and the French colonial army and French settlers. The conflict ended with Algerian independence 1962.

Ali *c.* 598–660. 4th caliph of Islam. He was born in Mecca, the son of Abu Talib, uncle to the prophet Muhammad, who gave him his daughter Fatima in marriage. On Muhammad's death 632, Ali had a claim to succeed him, but this was not conceded until 656. After a stormy reign, he was assassinated. Around Ali's name the controversy has raged between the Sunni and the Shi'ites (see ◊Islam), the former denying his right to the caliphate and the latter supporting it.

Ali (Ali Pasha) 1741–1822. Turkish politician, known as *Arslan* ('the Lion'). An Albanian, he was appointed pasha (governor) of the Janina region 1788 (now Ioánnina, Greece). His court

was visited by the British poet Byron. He was assassinated.

Ali Mustafa 1541–1600. Historian and writer of the Ottoman Empire. Ali was responsible for much of the myth of the preceding reign of Suleiman (1520–66) as a golden age.

Alia Ramiz 1925– . Albanian communist politician, head of state 1982–92. He gradually relaxed the isolationist policies of his predecessor Hoxha, and following public unrest introduced political and economic reforms, including free elections 1991, when he was elected executive president.

Alien and Sedition Acts four laws passed by the US Congress 1798, when war with France seemed likely. The acts lengthened the period of residency required for US citizenship, gave the president the power to expel 'dangerous' aliens, and severely restricted criticism of the government. They were controversial because of the degree of power exercised by central government; they are now also seen as an early manifestation of US xenophobia (fear of foreigners).

Aliens Act in the UK, an act of Parliament passed by the Conservative government 1905 to restrict the immigration of 'undesirable persons' into Britain; it was aimed at restricting Jewish immigration.

Ali Pasha Mehmed Emin 1815–1871. Grand vizier (chief minister) of the Ottoman Empire 1855–56, 1858–59, 1861, and 1867–71, noted for his attempts to westernize the Ottoman Empire.

After a career as ambassador to the UK, minister of foreign affairs 1846, delegate to the Congress of ◊Vienna 1855 and of Paris 1856, he was grand vizier a total of five times. While promoting friendship with Britain and France, he defended the vizier's powers against those of the sultan.

Allen Ethan 1738–1789. US military leader who founded the ◊Green Mountain Boys 1770. At the outbreak of the American Revolution 1775 they joined with Benedict ◊Arnold and captured Fort Ticonderoga, the first victory for the American side. Captured by the British in the subsequent invasion of Canada, Allen continued his campaign for Vermont's independence after his release in 1778. He died before it achieved statehood in 1791.

Allenby Edmund Henry Hynman, 1st Viscount Allenby 1861–1936. English field marshal. In World War I he served in France before taking command 1917–19 of the British forces in the Middle East. His defeat of the Turkish forces at Megiddo in Palestine in Sept 1918 was followed almost at once by the capitulation of Turkey. He was high commissioner in Egypt 1919–35.

Allende (Gossens) Salvador 1908–1973. Chilean left-wing politician. Elected president 1970 as the candidate of the Popular Front alliance, Allende never succeeded in keeping the electoral alliance together in government. His failure to solve the country's economic problems or to deal with political subversion allowed the army, backed by the CIA, to stage the 1973 coup which brought about the death of Allende and many of his supporters.

Allende became a Marxist activist in the 1930s and rose to prominence as a presidential candidate in 1952, 1958, and 1964. In each election he had the support of the socialist and communist movements but was defeated by the Christian Democrats and Nationalists. As president, his socialism and nationalization of US-owned copper mines led the CIA to regard him as a communist and to their involvement in the coup that replaced him by General Pinochet.

Allies, the in World War I, the 23 countries allied against the Central Powers (Germany, Austria–Hungary, Turkey, and Bulgaria), including France, Italy, Russia, the UK, Australia and other Commonwealth nations, and, in the latter part of the war, the USA; and in World War II, the 49 countries allied against the ◊Axis powers (Germany, Italy, and Japan), including France, the UK, Australia and other Commonwealth nations, the USA, and the USSR.

In the 1991 Gulf War, there were 28 countries in the Allied coalition.

Alma, Battle of the in the Crimean War, a battle 20 Sept 1854 in which British, French, and Turkish forces defeated Russian troops, with a loss of about 9,000 men, of whom 6,000 were Russian.

Almagro Diego de 1475–1538. Spanish soldier who partnered Francisco ◊Pizarro in the conquest of Peru. Almagro arrived in Panama 1514 with the expedition of Pedro Arias de Ávila. Almagro recruited followers and arranged shipments for the expeditions led by Pizarro 1524–28. He led an expedition of conquest to Chile 1535–36, and returned to break the siege of Cuzco, taking its governorship.

He was assassinated by Pizarro's brother Hernando 1538, and his supporters killed Francisco Pizarro three years later.

Almansa, Battle of in the War of the Spanish Succession, battle 25 April 1707 in which British, Portuguese and Spanish forces were defeated by the French under the Duke of Berwick at a Spanish town in Albacete, about 80 km/50 mi NW of Alicante.

Almohad Berber dynasty 1130–1269 founded by the Berber prophet Muhammad ibn Tumart (c. 1080–1130). The Almohads ruled much of Morocco and Spain, which they took by defeating the ◊Almoravids; they later took the area that today forms Algeria and Tunis. Their policy of religious 'purity' involved the forced conversion and massacre of the Jewish population of Spain. The Almohads were themselves defeated by the Christian kings of Spain 1212, and in Morocco 1269.

Almoravid Berber dynasty 1056–1147 founded by the prophet Abdullah ibn Tashfin, ruling much of Morocco and Spain in the 11th–12th centuries. The Almoravids came from the Sahara, and in the 11th century began laying the foundations of an empire covering the whole of Morocco and parts of Algeria; their capital was the newly founded Marrakesh. In 1086 they defeated Alfonso VI of Castile to gain much of Spain. They were later overthrown by the ◊Almohads.

Alsace-Lorraine area of NE France, lying west of the river Rhine. Alsace-Lorraine formed part of Celtic Gaul in Caesar's time, was invaded by the Alemanni and other Germanic tribes in the 4th century, and remained part of the German Empire until the 17th century. In 1648 part of the territory was ceded to France; in 1681 Louis XIV seized Strasbourg. The few remaining districts were seized by France after the French Revolution. Conquered by Germany 1870–71 (chiefly for its iron ores), it was regained by France 1919, then again annexed by Germany 1940–44, when it was liberated by the Allies.

Altamira caves decorated with Palaeolithic wall paintings, the first such to be discovered, 1879. The paintings are realistic depictions of bison, deer, and horses in polychrome (several colours). The caves are near the village of Santillana del Mar in Santander province, N Spain; other well-known Palaeolithic cave paintings are in ◊Lascaux, SW France.

Alva or *Alba* Ferdinand Alvarez de Toledo, duke of 1508–1582. Spanish politician and general. He successfully commanded the Spanish armies of the Holy Roman emperor Charles V and his son Philip II of Spain. In 1567 he was appointed governor of the Netherlands, where he set up a reign of terror to suppress Protestantism and the revolt of the Netherlands. In 1573 he was recalled at his own request. He later led a successful expedition against Portugal 1580–81.

I have tamed men of iron and why then shall I not be able to tame these men of butter?

Duke of Alva
reply to King Philip II of Spain on being appointed governor general of the Netherlands 1567

Alvarado Pedro de 1485–1541. Spanish conquistador, ruler of Guatemala 1524–41. Alvarado joined Hernán ◊Cortés' army 1519 and became his principal captain during the conquest of New Spain. Left in command at Tenochtitlán, Mexico, he provoked the Aztec rebellion which resulted in the death of ◊Montezuma II 1520. He conquered Guatemala 1523–24 and was its governor and captain general until his death. He also attacked Ecuador 1534 in a bid for a share of the former Inca empire, but was paid off.

Amal radical Lebanese ◊Shi'ite military force, established by Musa Sadr in the 1970s; its headquarters are in Borj al-Barajneh. The movement split into extremist and moderate groups 1982, but both sides agreed on the aim of increasing Shi'ite political representation in Lebanon.

Amal guerrillas were responsible for many of the attacks and kidnappings in Lebanon during the 1980s, although subsequently the group came to be considered one of the more mainstream elements on the Lebanese political scene. The Amal militia under Nabih ◊Berri fought several bloody battles against the Hezbollah (Party of God) in 1988.

Amalekite in the Old Testament, a member of an ancient Semitic people of SW Palestine and the Sinai peninsula. According to Exodus 17 they harried the rear of the Israelites after their crossing of the Red Sea, were defeated by Saul and David, and were destroyed in the reign of Hezekiah.

Amanullah Khan 1892–1960. Emir (ruler) of Afghanistan 1919–29. Third son of Habibullah Khan, he seized the throne on his father's assassination and concluded a treaty with the British, but his policy of westernization led to rebellion 1928. Amanullah had to flee, abdicated 1929, and settled in Rome, Italy.

Amarna tablets collection of Egyptian clay tablets with cuneiform inscriptions, found in the ruins of the ancient city of ◊Akhetaton on the east bank of the Nile.

Amenhotep four Egyptian pharaohs, including:

Amenhotep III King of Egypt (*c.* 1400 BC) who built great monuments at Thebes, including the temples at Luxor. Two portrait statues at his tomb were known to the Greeks as the colossi of Memnon. His son *Amenhotep IV* changed his name to ◊Ikhnaton.

American Civil War 1861–65; see ◊Civil War, American.

American Federation of Labor and Congress of Industrial Organizations (AFL–CIO) federation of North American trade unions, representing (1996) about 14% of the workforce in North America.

The AFL was founded 1886 by Samuel ◊Gompers and was initially a union of skilled craftworkers. The CIO, representing unskilled workers, broke away from the AFL in the mid-1930s. A merger reunited them 1955, bringing most unions into the national federation.

American Independence, War of alternative name of the ◊American Revolution, the revolt 1775–83 of the British North American colonies that resulted in the establishment of the United States of America.

American Indian one of the aboriginal peoples of the Americas. Columbus named them Indians 1492 because he believed he had found not the New World, but a new route to India. The Asian ancestors of the Indians are thought to have entered North America on the land bridge, Beringia, exposed by the lowered sea level between Siberia and Alaska during the last ice age, 60,000–35,000 BC.

Hunting, fishing, and moving camp throughout the Americas, the migrants inhabited both continents and their nearby islands, and settled all the ecological zones, from the most tropical to the most frozen, including the woodlands, deserts, plains, mountains, and river valleys. As they specialized, many kinds of societies evolved, speaking many languages. Some became farmers, the first cultivators of maize, potatoes, sweet potatoes, manioc, peanuts, peppers, tomatoes, pumpkins, cacao, and chicle. They also grew tobacco, coca, peyote, and cinchona (the last three are sources of cocaine, mescalin, and quinine respectively.)

distribution: Canada 300,000, including the Inuit; the largest group is the Six Nations (Iroquois), with a reserve near Brantford, Ontario, for 7,000. They are organized in the National Indian Brotherhood of Canada. *United States* 1.6 million, almost 900,000 (including Inuit and Aleuts) living on or near reservations, mainly in Arizona, New Mexico, Utah (where the Navajo have the largest of all reservations),

The American Revolution

1773	A government tax on tea led Massachusetts citizens disguised as North American Indians to board British ships carrying tea and throw it into Boston harbour, the Boston Tea Party.	26 Dec	Washington recrossed the Delaware River and defeated the British at Trenton, New Jersey.
1774–75	The First Continental Congress was held in Philadelphia to call for civil disobedience in reply to British measures such as the Intolerable Acts, which closed the port of Boston and quartered British troops in private homes.	1777 3 Jan	Washington defeated the British at Princeton, New Jersey.
		11 Sept–4 Oct	British general William Howe defeated Washington at Brandywine and Germantown and occupied Philadelphia.
1775 19 April	Hostilities began at Lexington and Concord, Massachusetts. The first shots were fired when British troops, sent to seize illegal military stores and arrest rebel leaders John Hancock and Samuel Adams, were attacked by the local militia (minutemen).	17 Oct	British general John Burgoyne surrendered at Saratoga, New York, and was therefore unable to link up with Howe.
		1777–78	Washington wintered at Valley Forge, Pennsylvania, enduring harsh conditions and seeing many of his troops leave to return to their families.
10 May	Fort Ticonderoga, New York, was captured from the British.	1778	France, with the support of its ally Spain, entered the war on the US side (John Paul Jones led a French-sponsored naval unit).
17 June	The colonialists were defeated in the first battle of the Revolution, the Battle of Bunker Hill (which actually took place on Breed's Hill, nearby); George Washington was appointed colonial commander in chief soon afterwards.	1780 12 May	The British captured Charleston, South Carolina, one of a series of British victories in the South, but alienated support by enforcing conscription.
1776 4 July	The Second Continental Congress issued the Declaration of Independence, which specified some of the colonists' grievances and proclaimed an independent government.	1781 19 Oct	British general Charles Cornwallis, besieged in Yorktown, Virginia, by Washington and the French fleet, surrendered.
27 Aug	Washington was defeated at Long Island and was forced to evacuate New York and retire to Pennsylvania.	1782 1783 3 Sept	Peace negotiations opened. The Treaty of Paris recognized American independence.

Oklahoma, Texas, Montana, Washington, and North and South Dakota. The population level is thought to be about the same as at the time of Columbus, but now includes many people who are of mixed ancestry. Indians were made citizens of the USA 1924. There is an organized American Indian Movement (AIM). *Latin America* has many mestizo (mixed Indian-Spanish descent), of whom some six million (half the population) are in Bolivia and Peru. Since the 1960s they have increasingly stressed their Indian inheritance in terms of language and culture. The few Indians formerly beyond white contact are having their environment destroyed by the clearing and industrialization of the Amazon Basin.

American Revolution revolt 1775–83 of the British North American colonies that resulted in the establishment of the United States of America. It was caused by colonial opposition to British economic exploitation and by the unwillingness of the colonists to pay for a standing army. It was also fuelled by the colonists' antimonarchist sentiment and a desire to participate in the policies affecting them.

American System, the in US history, a federal legislative programme following the ◊War of 1812 designed to promote an integrated national economy. It introduced tariffs to protect US industry from foreign competition, internal improvements to the transport network, and a national bank to facilitate economic growth.

American West see ◊West, American.

Amethyst Incident UK–China episode arising when on 20 April 1949 a British frigate, HMS *Amethyst*, sailing on the Chang Jiang (Yangtze) River, was fired at by communist Chinese forces. The ship was trapped for 14 weeks before breaking free and completing the journey to the sea. The temporary detention of this British vessel has been interpreted as an attempt by the Chinese to assert their sovereignty over what had been considered an international waterway.

Amiens ancient city of NE France. It gave its name to the battles of Aug 1918, when British field marshal Douglas Haig launched his victorious offensive in World War I.

Amin (Dada) Idi 1926– . Ugandan politician, president 1971–79. He led the coup that deposed Milton Obote 1971, expelled the Asian community 1972, and exercised a reign of terror over his people. He fled to Libya when insurgent Ugandan and Tanzanian troops invaded the country 1979.

I captured some of the people who tried to assassinate me. I ate them before they ate me.

Idi Amin (Dada)

Ammonite member of an ancient Semitic people, mentioned in the Old Testament or Jewish Bible, who lived NW of the Dead Sea. Their capital was Amman, in present day Jordan. They worshipped the god Moloch, to whom they offered human sacrifices. They were frequently at war with the Israelites.

Amorites ancient people of Semitic or Indo-European origin who were among the inhabitants of ◊Canaan at the time of the Israelite invasion. They provided a number of Babylonian kings.

Amritsar industrial city in the Punjab, India. It is the holy city of ◊Sikhism, with the Golden Temple, from which armed demonstrators were evicted by the Indian army under General Dayal 1984, 325 being killed. Subsequently, Indian prime minister Indira Gandhi was assassinated in reprisal. In 1919 the city was the scene of the ◊Amritsar Massacre.

Amritsar Massacre also called *Jallianwallah Bagh massacre* the killing of 379 Indians (and wounding of 1,200) in ◊Amritsar, at the site of a Sikh religious shrine 1919. British troops under General Edward Dyer (1864–1927) opened fire without warning on a crowd of some 10,000, assembled to protest against the arrest of two Indian National Congress leaders (see ◊Congress Party).

Dyer was subsequently censured and resigned his commission, but gained popular support in the UK for his action, spurring Mahatma ◊Gandhi to a policy of active noncooperation with the British.

Anabaptist (Greek 'baptize again') member of any of various 16th-century radical Protestant sects. They believed in adult rather than child baptism, and sought to establish utopian communities. Anabaptist groups spread rapidly in N Europe, particularly in Germany, and were widely persecuted.

Notable Anabaptists included those in Moravia (the Hutterites) and also Thomas Müntzer (1489–1525), a peasant leader who was executed for fomenting an uprising in Mühlhausen (now Mulhouse in E France). In Münster, Germany, Anabaptists controlled the city 1534–35. A number of Anabaptist groups, such as the Mennonites, Amish, and Hutterites, emigrated to North America, where they became known for their simple way of life and pacifism.

anarchism (Greek *anarkhos* 'without ruler') political belief that society should have no government, laws, police, or other authority, but should be a free association of all its members. It does not mean 'without order'; most theories of anarchism imply an order of a very strict and symmetrical kind, but they maintain that such order can be achieved by cooperation. Anarchism should be distinguished from nihilism (a purely negative and destructive activity directed against society); anarchism is essentially a pacifist movement.

Anastasia 1901–1918. Russian Grand Duchess, youngest daughter of ◊Nicholas II. During the Russian Revolution she was presumed shot with her parents by the Bolsheviks after the Revolution of 1917, but it has been alleged that Anastasia escaped.

Those who claimed her identity included Anna Anderson (1902–1984). Alleged by some detractors to be a Pole, Franziska Schanzkowska, she was rescued from a Berlin canal 1920. The German Federal Supreme Court found no proof of her claim 1970.

ANC abbreviation for ◊African National Congress

ancien régime the old order; the feudal, absolute monarchy in France before the French Revolution 1789.

Andean Group (Spanish *Grupo Andino*) South American organization aimed at economic and social cooperation between member states. It was established under the Treaty of Cartagena 1969 by Bolivia, Chile, Colombia, Ecuador, and Peru. Venezuela joined 1973, but Chile withdrew 1976 and Peru suspended membership and became an observer 1992.

Andean Indian any indigenous inhabitant of the Andes range in South America, stretching from Ecuador to Peru to Chile, and including both the coast and the highlands. Many Andean civilizations developed in this region from local fishing-hunting-farming societies, all of which predated the ◊Inca, who consolidated the entire region and ruled from about 1200.

The earliest pan-Andean civilization was the Chavin, about 1200–800 BC, which was followed by large and important coastal city-states, such as the Mochica, the Chimú, the Nazca, and the Paracas. The region was dominated by the Tiahuanaco when the Inca started to expand, and took them and outlying peoples into their empire, imposing the Quechua language on all.

Andorra landlocked country in the E Pyrenees. Co-princes have ruled Andorra since 1278 (now the bishop of Urgel, Spain, and the French president). In the 1980s there were growing signs of fragile democracy. A constitution was adopted 1993, giving the country virtual independence, while external security is the responsibility of France and Spain.

Andrássy Gyula, Count Andrássy 1823–1890. Hungarian revolutionary and statesman who supported the Dual Monarchy of Austro-Hungary 1867 and was Hungary's first constitutional prime minister 1867–71. He became foreign minister of the Austro-Hungarian Empire 1871–79 and tried to halt Russian expansion into the Balkans.

Andreotti Giulio 1919– . Italian Christian Democrat politician. He headed six post-war governments: 1972–73, 1976–79 (four successive terms), and 1989–92. In addition he was defence minister eight times, and foreign minister five times.

Andropov Yuri 1914–1984. Soviet communist politician, president of the USSR 1983–84. As chief of the KGB 1967–82, he established a reputation for efficiently suppressing dissent.

Angevin relating to the reigns of the English kings Henry II and Richard I (also known, with the later English kings up to Richard III, as the ◊*Plantagenets*). Angevin derives from Anjou, the region in France controlled by English kings at this time. The *Angevin Empire* comprised the territories (including England) that belonged to the Anjou dynasty.

Anglican Communion family of Christian churches including the Church of England, the US Episcopal Church, and those holding the same essential doctrines, that is the Lambeth Quadrilateral 1888 Holy Scripture as the basis of all doctrine, the Nicene and Apostles' Creeds, Holy Baptism and Holy Communion, and the historic episcopate.

Anglo-Irish Agreement or *Hillsborough Agreement* concord reached 1985 between the UK premier Margaret Thatcher and Irish premier Garret FitzGerald. One sign of the improved relations between the two countries was increased cooperation between police and security forces across the border with Northern

Ireland. The pact also gave the Irish Republic a greater voice in the conduct of Northern Ireland's affairs. However, the agreement was rejected by Northern Ireland Unionists as a step towards renunciation of British sovereignty. In March 1988 talks led to further strengthening of the agreement.

Anglo-Saxon one of the several Germanic invaders (Angles, Saxons, and ◊Jutes) who conquered much of Britain between the 5th and 7th centuries. After the conquest kingdoms were set up, which are commonly referred to as the ◊*heptarchy*; these were united in the early 9th century under the overlordship of Wessex. The Norman invasion 1066 brought Anglo-Saxon rule to an end.

The Jutes probably came from the Rhineland and not, as was formerly believed, from Jutland. The Angles and Saxons came from Schleswig-Holstein, and may have united before invading. The Angles settled largely in East Anglia, Mercia, and Northumbria; the Saxons in Essex, Sussex, and Wessex; and the Jutes in Kent and S Hampshire.

Anglo-Saxon Chronicle history of England from the Roman invasion to the 11th century, in the form of a series of chronicles written in Old English by monks, begun in the 9th century (during the reign of King Alfred), and continuing to the 12th century.

The Chronicle, comprising seven different manuscripts, forms a unique record of early English history and of the development of Old English prose up to its final stages in the year 1154, by which date it had been superseded by Middle English.

Angola country in SW Africa, bounded W by the Atlantic Ocean, N and NE by Zaire, E by Zambia, and S by Namibia.

history Angola became a Portuguese colony 1491 and an Overseas Territory of Portugal 1951. A movement for complete independence, the People's Movement for the Liberation of Angola (MPLA), was established 1956, based originally in the Congo. This was followed by the formation of two other nationalist movements, the National Front for the Liberation of Angola (FNLA) and the National Union for the Total Independence of Angola (UNITA). War for independence from Portugal broke out 1961, with MPLA supported by socialist and communist states, UNITA helped by the Western powers and FNLA backed by the 'nonleft' power groups of southern Africa.

republic Three months of civil war followed the granting of full independence 1975, with MPLA and UNITA the main contestants, and foreign mercenaries and South African forces helping FNLA. By 1975 MPLA, with the help of mainly Cuban forces, controlled most of the country and had established the People's Republic of Angola in Luanda. Agostinho Neto, the MPLA leader, became its first president. FNLA and UNITA had, in the meantime, proclaimed their own People's Democratic Republic of Angola, based in Huambo. President Neto died 1979 and was succeeded by José Eduardo dos Santos, who maintained Neto's links with the Soviet bloc.

Lusaka Agreement UNITA guerrillas, supported by South Africa, continued to operate, and combined forces raided Angola 1980–81 to attack bases of the South-West Africa People's Organization (◊SWAPO), who were fighting for Namibia's independence. South Africa proposed a complete withdrawal of its forces 1983 if Angola could guarantee that the areas vacated would not be filled by Cuban or SWAPO units.

Angola accepted South Africa's proposals 1984, and a settlement was made (the *Lusaka Agreement*), whereby a Joint Monitoring Commission was set up to oversee South Africa's withdrawal, which was completed 1985. Relations between the two countries deteriorated 1986 when further South African raids into Angola took place. UNITA also continued to receive South African support. Despite the securing of a peace treaty with South Africa and Cuba 1988, guerrilla activity by the UNITA rebels began again 1989.

cease-fire and peace A cease-fire negotiated June 1989 between the Luanda government and UNITA's Jonas ◊Savimbi collapsed two months later. After an official peace treaty May 1991, President dos Santos promised a return to multiparty politics and freed all political prisoners. A general election victory Sept 1992 by MPLA was disputed by UNITA, which recommenced the civil war. UNITA accepted an offer of seats in government, but fighting between government and rebels resumed. Hostilties intensified 1993. A formal peace treaty, preceded by heavy fighting, was signed 1994, in Savimbis absence. A national unity government was formed April 1997, but Savimbi, who had refused the vice presidency, boycotted it.

Anguilla island in the E Caribbean. A British colony from 1650, Anguilla was long associated with St Christopher-Nevis but revolted against alleged domination by the larger island and in 1969 declared itself a republic. A small British force restored order, and Anguilla retained a special position at its own request; since 1980 it has been a separate dependency of the UK.

Anjou old countship and former province in N France. In 1154 the count of Anjou became king of England as Henry II, but the territory was lost by King John 1204. In 1480 the countship was annexed to the French crown.

Anna Comnena 1083–after 1148. Byzantine historian, daughter of the emperor ◊Alexius I, who was the historian of her father's reign. After a number of abortive attempts to alter the imperial succession in favour of her husband, Nicephorus Bryennius (*c.* 1062–1137), she retired to a convent to write her major work, the *Alexiad*. It describes the Byzantine view of public office, as well as the religious and intellectual life of the period.

Annales school or *total history* group of historians formed in France in 1929, and centred around the journal *Annales d'histoire économique et sociale* which pioneered new methods of historical enquiry. Its leading members included Fernand Braudel (1902–1985), who coined the term total history, and Marc Bloch (1886–1944). Their view was that to arrive at worthwhile conclusions on broad historical debates, all aspects of a society had to be considered. Thus they widened the scope of research away from political history to include social and economic factors as well.

The main criticism of this historical tradition comes from Marxists who complain that it has no overall theory of societal development.

Annam former country of SE Asia, incorporated in ◊Vietnam 1946 as Central Vietnam. A Bronze Age civilization was flourishing in the area when China conquered it about 214 BC. The Chinese named their conquest An-Nam, 'peaceful south'. Independent from 1428, Annam signed a treaty with France 1787 and became a French protectorate, part of Indochina 1884. During World War II, Annam was occupied by Japan.

Anne 1665–1714. Queen of Great Britain and Ireland 1702–14. She was the second daughter of James, Duke of York, who became James II, and Anne Hyde. She succeeded William III 1702. Events of her reign include the War of the Spanish Succession, Marlborough's victories at Blenheim, Ramillies, Oudenarde, and Malplaquet, and the union of the English and Scottish parliaments 1707. Anne was succeeded by George I.

She received a Protestant upbringing, and in 1683 married Prince George of Denmark (1653–1708). Of their many children only one survived infancy, William, Duke of Gloucester (1689–1700). For the greater part of her life

Anne was a close friend of Sarah Churchill (1650–1744), wife of John Churchill (1650–1722), afterwards Duke of Marlborough; the Churchills' influence helped lead her to desert her father for her brother-in-law, William of Orange, during the Revolution of 1688, and later to engage in Jacobite intrigues. Her replacement of the Tories by a Whig government 1703–04 was her own act, not due to Churchillian influence. Anne finally broke with the Marlboroughs 1710, when Mrs Masham succeeded the duchess as her favourite, and supported the Tory government of the same year.

Anne of Austria 1601–1666. Queen of France from 1615 and regent 1643–61. Daughter of Philip III of Spain, she married Louis XIII of France (whose chief minister, Cardinal Richelieu, worked against her). On her husband's death she became regent for their son, Louis XIV, until his majority.

Anne of Cleves 1515–1557. Fourth wife of ◊Henry VIII of England 1540. She was the daughter of the Duke of Cleves, and was recommended to Henry as a wife by Thomas ◊Cromwell, who wanted an alliance with German Protestantism against the Holy Roman Empire. Henry did not like her looks, had the marriage declared void after six months, pensioned her, and had Cromwell beheaded.

anno Domini (Latin 'in the year of our Lord') in the Christian chronological system, refers to dates since the birth of Jesus, denoted by the letters AD. There is no year 0, so AD 1 follows immediately after the year 1 BC (before Christ). The system became the standard reckoning in the Western world after being adopted by the English historian Bede in the 8th century. The abbreviations CE (Common Era) and BCE (before Common Era) are often used instead by scholars and writers as objective, rather than religious, terms.

The system is based on the calculations made 525 by Dionysius Exiguus, a Scythian monk, but the birth of Jesus should more correctly be placed about 4 BC.

anno hegirae year of the flight of Muhammad from Mecca to medina; see ◊AH.

Anschluss (German 'union') the annexation of Austria with Germany, accomplished by the German chancellor Adolf Hitler 12 March 1938.

Anson George, 1st Baron Anson 1697–1762. English admiral who sailed around the world 1740–44. In 1740 he commanded the squadron attacking the Spanish colonies and shipping in South America; he returned home by circum-navigating the world, with £500,000 of Spanish treasure. He carried out reforms at the Admiralty, which increased the efficiency of the British fleet and contributed to its success in the Seven Years' War (1756–63) against France.

antebellum (Latin *ante bellum*, 'before the war') in US usage, an adjective referring to the period just before the Civil War (1861–65).

Anthony Susan B(rownell) 1820–1906. US pioneering campaigner for women's rights who also worked for the antislavery and temperance movements. Her causes included equality of pay for women teachers, married women's property rights, and women's suffrage. In 1869, with Elizabeth Cady ◊Stanton, she founded the National Woman Suffrage Association.

anticlericalism hostility to the influence of the clergy in affairs outside the sphere of the church. Identifiable from the 12th century onwards, it became increasingly common in France in the 16th century and especially after the French Revolution of 1789. More recently apparent in most western European states, anticlericalism takes many forms, for example, opposition to the clergy as reactionary and against the principles of liberalism and the enlightenment, also opposition to clerics as representatives of religion or as landowners, tax-gatherers, or state servants.

Anti-Comintern Pact (Anti-Communist Pact) agreement signed between Germany and Japan 25 Nov 1936, opposing communism as a menace to peace and order. The pact was signed by Italy 1937 and by Hungary, Spain, and the Japanese puppet state of Manchukuo in 1939. While directed against the USSR, the agreement also had the effect of giving international recognition to Japanese rule in Manchuria.

Anti-Corn Law League in UK history, an extra-parliamentary pressure group formed 1838, led by the Liberals ◊Cobden and ◊Bright, which argued for free trade and campaigned successfully against duties on the import of foreign corn to Britain imposed by the ◊Corn Laws, which were repealed 1846.

Antietam, Battle of bloody but indecisive battle of the American Civil War 17 Sept 1862 at Antietam Creek, off the Potomac River. General McClellan of the Union blocked the advance of the Confederates under Robert E Lee on Maryland and Washington DC. This battle paved the way for Abraham Lincoln's proclamation of emancipation, and also persuaded the British not to recognize the Confederacy.

Antigua and Barbuda country comprising three islands in the E Caribbean (Antigua, Barbuda, and uninhabited Redonda).

history The original inhabitants of Antigua and Barbuda were Carib Indians. The first Europeans to visit Antigua were with Christopher Columbus 1493, although they did not go ashore. He named the island after the church of Santa María de la Antigua at Seville. Antigua was first colonized by Britain 1632. Charles II leased Barbuda 1685 to the Codrington family, who ran a sugar plantation on Antigua. Barbuda was a source of stock and provisions for the plantation and was inhabited almost entirely by black slaves, who used the relatively barren land cooperatively. The Codringtons finally surrendered the lease 1870. Barbuda reverted to the crown in the later 19th century. The Antiguan slaves were freed 1834 but remained poor, totally dependent on the sugar crop market. Between 1860 and 1959 the islands were administered by Britain within a federal system known as the ◊Leeward Islands. Antigua and Barbuda was made an associated state of the UK and given full internal independence 1967, with Britain retaining responsibility for defence and foreign affairs. Barbuda, with a population of about 1,200 people, started a separatist movement 1969, fearing that Antigua would sell Barbudan land to foreign developers.

independence from Britain In the 1971 general election, the Progressive Labour Movement (PLM) won a decisive victory, and its leader, George Walter, replaced Vere Bird, leader of the Antigua Labour Party (ALP), as prime minister. The PLM fought the 1976 election on a call for early independence while the ALP urged caution until a firm economic foundation had been laid. The ALP won and declared 1978 that the country was ready for independence. Opposition from the inhabitants of Barbuda delayed the start of constitutional talks, and the territory eventually became independent as Antigua and Barbuda 1981. Despite its policy of nonalignment, the government actively assisted the US invasion of Grenada 1983. The ALP won sweeping victories in elections of 1984 and 1989. Bird's government was tarnished 1990 by allegations that his son, a cabinet minister, was involved in illegal arms deals. Calls for Birds resignation 1991 were unsuccessful, but he stepped down 1993 and, after a close election, was succeeded by his younger son, Lester. The ALP won the 1994 general election.

Antiochus thirteen kings of Syria of the Seleucid dynasty, including:

Antiochus I *c.* 324–*c.* 261 BC. King of Syria from 281 BC, son of Seleucus I, one of the generals of Alexander the Great. He earned the title of Antiochus Soter, or Saviour, by his defeat of the Gauls in Galatia 276.

Antiochus II *c.* 286–*c.* 246 BC. King of Syria 261–246 BC, son of Antiochus I. He was known as Antiochus Theos, the Divine. During his reign the eastern provinces broke away from the Graeco-Macedonian rule and set up native princes. He made peace with Egypt by marrying the daughter of Ptolemy Philadelphus, but was a tyrant among his own people.

Antiochus III the Great *c.* 241–187 BC. King of Syria from 223 BC, nephew of Antiochus II. He secured a loose control over Armenia and Parthia 209, overcame Bactria, received the homage of the Indian king of the Kabul valley, and returned by way of the Persian Gulf 204. He took possession of Palestine, entering Jerusalem 198. He crossed into NW Greece, but was decisively defeated by the Romans at Thermopylae 191 and at Magnesia 190. The Peace of Apamea 188 BC confined Seleucid rule to Asia.

Antiochus IV *c.* 215–164 BC. King of Syria from 175 BC, known as Antiochus Epiphanes, the Illustrious, son of Antiochus III. He occupied Jerusalem about 170, seizing much of the Temple treasure, and instituted worship of the Greek type in the Temple in an attempt to eradicate Judaism. This produced the revolt of the Hebrews under the Maccabees; Antiochus died before he could suppress it.

Antiochus VII *c.* 159–129 BC. King of Syria from 138 BC. The last strong ruler of the Seleucid dynasty, he took Jerusalem 134, reducing the Maccabees to subjection. He was defeated and killed in battle against the Parthians.

Antiochus XIII 1st century BC. King of Syria 69–65 BC, the last of the Seleucid dynasty. During his reign Syria was made a Roman province by Pompey the Great.

anti-Semitism literally, prejudice against Semitic people but in practice it has meant prejudice or discrimination against, and persecution of, the Jews as an ethnic group. Historically this was practised for almost 2,000 years by European Christians. Anti-Semitism was a tenet of Hitler's Germany, and in the Holocaust 1933–45 about 6 million Jews died in concentration camps and in local extermination ◊pogroms, such as the siege of the Warsaw ghetto.

The destruction of Jerusalem AD 70 led many Jews to settle in Europe and throughout the Roman Empire. In the 4th century Christianity was adopted as the official religion of the Empire, which reinforced existing prejudice (dating back to pre-Christian times and referred to in the works of Seneca and Tacitus) against Jews who refused to convert. Anti-Semitism increased in the Middle Ages because of the Crusades and the Inquisition, and legislation forbade Jews to own land or be members of a craft guild; to earn a living they had to become moneylenders and traders (and were then resented when they prospered). Britain expelled many Jews 1290, but they were formally readmitted 1655 by Cromwell. From the 16th century Jews were forced by law in many cities to live in a separate area, or *ghetto*.

Late 18th- and early 19th-century liberal thought improved the position of Jews in European society. In the Austro-Hungarian Empire, for example, they were allowed to own land, and after the French Revolution the 'rights of man' were extended to French Jews 1790. The rise of 19th-century nationalism and unscientific theories of race instigated new resentments. Anti-Semitism became strong in Austria, France (see ◊Dreyfus), and Germany, and from 1881 pogroms in Poland and Russia caused refugees to flee to the USA (where freedom of religion was enshrined in the constitution), to the UK, and to other European countries as well as Palestine (see ◊Zionism).

In the 20th century, fascism and the Nazi Party's application of racial theories led to organized persecution and genocide. After World War II, the creation of Israel 1948 provoked Palestinian anti-Zionism, backed by the Arab world. Anti-Semitism is still fostered by extreme right-wing groups, such as the National Front in the UK and France and the Neo-Nazis in the USA and Germany.

Antonescu Ion 1882–1946. Romanian general and politician who headed a pro-German government during World War II and was executed for war crimes 1946.

Antonine Wall Roman line of fortification built AD 142. It was the Roman Empire's northwest frontier, between the Clyde and Forth rivers, Scotland. It was defended until *c*. 200.

Antoninus Pius AD 86–161. Roman emperor who had been adopted 138 as Hadrian's heir, and succeeded him later that year. He enjoyed a prosperous reign, during which the Antonine Wall was built. His daughter married his successor ◊Marcus Aurelius.

Antwerp (Flemish *Antwerpen*, French *Anvers*) port in Belgium on the river Scheldt. Antwerp rose to prominence in the 15th century and from 1500 to 1560 it was the richest

port in N Europe. Later Antwerp was beset by religious troubles and the Netherlands' revolt against Spain. In 1648 the Treaty of Westphalia gave both shores of the Scheldt estuary to the United Provinces, which closed it to Antwerp trade. The Treaty of Paris 1814 opened the estuary to all nations on payment of a small toll to the Dutch, abandoned 1863. During World War I Antwerp was occupied by ◊Germany Oct 1914–Nov 1918; during World War II, May 1940–Sept 1944.

ANZAC (acronym for *A*ustralian and *N*ew *Z*ealand *A*rmy *C*orps) general term for all troops of both countries serving in World War I and to some extent those in World War II.

The date of their World War I landing in ◊Gallipoli, Turkey, 25 April 1915, is marked by a public holiday, *Anzac Day*, in both Australia and New Zealand.

Anzam Treaty (*A*ustralia, *N*ew *Z*ealand, *a*nd *M*alaya) arrangement to coordinate service planning in defending air and sea communications in the region 1948. Cover was extended to the defence of Malaya 1954–55, but this was incorporated into the Anglo-Malayan Defence Agreement shortly after Malayan independence 1957.

Anzio, Battle of in World War II, the beachhead invasion of Italy 22 Jan–23 May 1944 by Allied troops; failure to use information gained by deciphering German codes led to Allied troops being stranded temporarily after German attacks.

ANZUS acronym for *A*ustralia, *N*ew *Z*ealand, and the *U*nited *S*tates (Pacific Security Treaty), a military alliance established 1951. It was replaced 1954 by the ◊Southeast Asia Treaty Organization (SEATO).

It appears that violence does not lead to a solution.

Michel Aoun *Observer* Dec 1990

Aoun Michel 1935– . Lebanese soldier and Maronite Christian politician, president 1988–90. As commander of the Lebanese army, he was made president without Muslim support, his appointment precipitating a civil war between Christians and Muslims. His unwillingness to accept a 1989 Arab League-sponsored peace agreement increased his isolation until the following year when he surrendered to military pressure. He left the country 1991 and was pardoned by the new government the same year.

Apache member of a group of North ◊American Indian peoples who lived as hunters in the Southwest. They are related to the Navajo, and now number about 10,000, living in reservations in Arizona, SW Oklahoma, and New Mexico. They were known as fierce raiders and horse warriors in the 18th and 19th centuries.

apartheid (Afrikaans 'apartness') racial-segregation policy of the government of South Africa, which was legislated 1948, when the Afrikaner National Party gained power. Non-whites (Bantu, coloured or mixed, or Indian) do not share full rights of citizenship with the 4.5 million whites (for example, the 23 million black people cannot vote in parliamentary elections), and many public facilities and institutions were until 1990 (and in some cases remain) restricted to the use of one race only; the establishment of ◊Black National States is another manifestation of apartheid. In 1991 President de Klerk repealed the key elements of apartheid legislation.

The term 'apartheid' was coined in the late 1930s by the South African Bureau for Racial Affairs (SABRA), which called for a policy of 'separate development' of the races.

Internally, organizations opposed to apartheid were banned, for example the African National Congress and the United Democratic Front, and leading campaigners for its abolition have been, like Steve Biko, killed, or, like Archbishop Tutu, harassed. Anger at the policy has sparked off many uprisings, from ◊Sharpeville 1960 and Soweto 1976 to the Crossroads squatter camps 1986.

Abroad, there are anti-apartheid movements in many countries. In 1961 South Africa was forced to withdraw from the Commonwealth because of apartheid; during the 1960s and 1970s there were calls for international ◊sanctions, especially boycotts of sporting and cultural links; and in the 1980s advocates of sanctions extended them into trade and finance.

The South African government's reaction to internal and international pressure was twofold: it abolished some of the more hated apartheid laws (the ban on interracial marriages was lifted 1985 and the pass laws, which restricted the movement of nonwhites, were repealed 1986); and it sought to replace the term 'apartheid' with 'plural democracy'. Under states of emergency 1985 and 1986 it used force to quell internal opposition, and from 1986 there was an official ban on the reporting of it in the media. In Oct 1989 President F W de Klerk permitted anti-apartheid demonstrations; the Separate Amenities Act was abolished 1990

and a new constitution promised. In 1990 Nelson Mandela, a leading figure in the African National Congress, was finally released. In 1991 the remaining major discriminating laws embodied in apartheid were repealed, including the Population Registration Act, which had made it obligatory for every citizen to be classified into one of nine racial groups.

appeasement historically, the conciliatory policy adopted by the British government, in particular under Neville Chamberlain, towards the Nazi and Fascist dictators in Europe in the 1930s in an effort to maintain peace. It was strongly opposed by Winston Churchill, but the ◊Munich Agreement 1938 was almost universally hailed as its justification. Appeasement ended when Germany occupied Bohemia–Moravia March 1939.

Appomattox village in Virginia, USA, scene of the surrender 9 April 1865 of the Confederate army under Robert E Lee to the Union army under Ulysses S Grant, which ended the American Civil War.

Aquino (Maria) Corazon (born Cojuangco) 1933– . President of the Philippines 1986–92. She was instrumental in the nonviolent overthrow of President Ferdinand Marcos 1986. As president, she sought to rule in a conciliatory manner, but encountered opposition from left (communist guerrillas) and right (army coup attempts), and her land reforms were seen as inadequate.

The daughter of a sugar baron, she studied in the USA and in 1956 married the politician Benigno Aquino (1933–1983). The chief political opponent of the right-wing president Marcos, he was assassinated by a military guard at Manila airport on his return from exile. Corazon Aquino was drafted by the opposition to contest the Feb 1986 presidential election and claimed victory over Marcos, accusing the government of ballot-rigging. She led a nonviolent 'people's power' campaign, which overthrew Marcos 25 Feb.

Aquitaine region of SW France, coinciding roughly with the Roman province of Aquitania and the ancient French province of Aquitaine. Eleanor of Aquitaine married the future Henry II of England 1152 and brought it to him as her dowry; it remained in English hands until 1452.

Arab any of a Semitic people native to the Arabian peninsula, but now settled throughout North Africa and the nations of the Middle East.

The homeland of the Arabs comprises Saudi Arabia, Qatar, Kuwait, Bahrain, United Arab Emirates, Oman, and Yemen. Predominantly

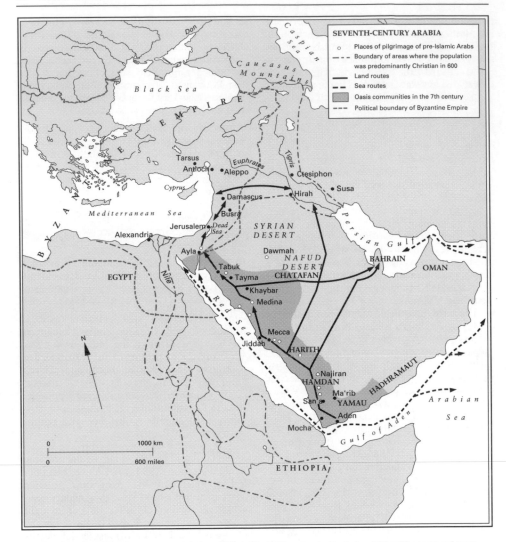

SEVENTH-CENTURY ARABIA

- ○ Places of pilgrimage of pre-Islamic Arabs
- --- Boundary of areas where the population was predominantly Christian in 600
- ▬ Land routes
- ▬▬ Sea routes
- Oasis communities in the 7th century
- ---- Political boundary of Byzantine Empire

Arabia In the 7th century Arabia was the birthplace of Islam. Most of the area was harsh desert fringed by oases and mountains; many of its inhabitants were nomads. In oasis cities such as Mecca, a merchant class developed, trading across the peninsula and as far as Damascus. Muhammad, the Prophet of Islam, was a member of this class in Mecca. Mecca also attracted pilgrims who came to the shrine known as the Kaaba.

Arab nations also include Iraq, Syria, Lebanon, and Jordan, and the N African Arab nations comprise Morocco, Algeria, Tunisia, Libya, Egypt, and Sudan, though the last-named has substantial non-Arab minorities. Although Mauritania and Somalia are not predominantly Arab, they support the ◊Arab League.

The term Arab was first recorded 853 BC but was not widely used until the end of the 6th century AD. The 7th century saw the rise of Islam and by the 8th century non-Arab converts were being assimilated by the Arabs. Arabic became the principal language of the

Arab Empire. In 1258 the empire was broken up by the Mongols and it was not until the decline of the Ottoman Empire at the end of World War I that the Arab nations emerged again as separate, if not independent, states.

Arabia peninsula between the Persian Gulf and the Red Sea, in SW Asia. The Arabian civilization was revived by Muhammad during the 7th century, but in the new empire created by militant Islam, Arabia became a subordinate state, and its cities were eclipsed by Damascus, Baghdad, and Cairo. Colonialism only touched the fringe of Arabia in the 19th century, and until the 20th century the interior was unknown to Europeans. Nationalism began actively to emerge at the period of World War I (1914–18), and the oil discoveries from 1953 gave the peninsula significant economic power.

Arab-Israeli Wars series of wars between Israel and various Arab states in the Middle East since the founding of the state of Israel 1948.

First Arab-Israeli War 14 Oct 1948–13 Jan/24 March 1949. As soon as the independent state of Israel had been proclaimed by the Jews, it was invaded by combined Arab forces. The Israelis defeated them and went on to annex territory until they controlled 75% of what had been Palestine under British mandate.

Second Arab-Israeli War 29 Oct–4 Nov 1956. After Egypt had taken control of the Suez Canal and blockaded the Straits of Tiran, Israel, with British and French support, invaded and captured Sinai and the Gaza Strip, from which it withdrew under heavy US pressure after the entry of a United Nations force.

Third Arab-Israeli War 5–10 June 1967, the *Six-Day War*. It resulted in the Israeli capture of the Golan Heights from Syria; the eastern half of Jerusalem and the West Bank from Jordan; and, in the south, the Gaza Strip and Sinai peninsula as far as the Suez Canal.

Fourth Arab-Israeli War 2–22/24 Oct 1973, the 'October War' or *Yom Kippur War*, so called because the Israeli forces were taken by surprise on the Day of Atonement (Yom Kippur), a Jewish holy day. It started with the recrossing of the Suez Canal by Egyptian forces who made initial gains, though there was some later loss of ground by the Syrians in the north.

Fifth Arab-Israeli War From 1978 the presence of Palestinian guerrillas in Lebanon led to Arab raids on Israel and Israeli retaliatory incursions, but on 6 June 1982 Israel launched a full-scale invasion. By 14 June Beirut was encircled, and ◊Palestine Liberation Organization (PLO) and Syrian forces were evacuated (mainly to Syria) 21–31 Aug, but in Feb 1985 there was a unilateral Israeli withdrawal from the country without any gain or losses incurred. Israel maintains a 'security zone' in S Lebanon and supports the South Lebanese Army militia as a buffer against Palestinian guerrilla incursions.

background Arab opposition to an Israeli state began after the Balfour Declaration 1917, which supported the idea of a Jewish national homeland. In the 1920s there were anti-Zionist riots in Palestine, then governed by the UK under a League of Nations mandate. In 1936 an Arab revolt led to a British royal commission that recommended partition (approved by the UN 1947, but rejected by the Arabs).

Tension in the Middle East remained high, and the conflict was sharpened and given East–West overtones by Soviet adoption of the Arab cause and US support for Israel. Several wars only increased the confusion over who had a claim to what territory. Particularly in view of the area's strategic sensitivity as an oil producer, pressure grew for a settlement, and in 1978 the ◊Camp David Agreements brought peace between Egypt and Israel, but this was denounced by other Arab countries. Israel withdrew from Sinai 1979–82, but no final agreement on Jerusalem and the establishment of a Palestinian state on the West Bank was reached. Israeli occupation of the Gaza strip and the West Bank continued into the 1990s in the face of a determined uprising (◊Intifada), but hope of a settlement emerged Sept 1993 when an Israeli-PLO preliminary peace accord was signed.

Arabistan former name of the Iranian province of Khuzestan, revived in the 1980s by the 2 million Sunni Arab inhabitants who demand autonomy. Unrest and sabotage 1979–80 led to a pledge of a degree of autonomy by Ayatollah Khomeini.

Arab League organization of Arab states established in Cairo 1945 to promote Arab unity, primarily in opposition to Israel. The original members were Egypt, Syria, Iraq, Lebanon, Transjordan (Jordan 1949), Saudi Arabia, and Yemen. In 1979 Egypt was suspended and the league's headquarters transferred to Tunis in protest against the Egypt-Israeli peace, but Egypt was readmitted as a full member May 1989, and in March 1990 its headquarters returned to Cairo.

Arafat Yassir 1929– . Palestinian nationalist politician, cofounder of al-◊Fatah 1957, and president of the ◊Palestinian Liberation Organization (PLO) from 1969. His support for Saddam Hussein after Iraq's invasion of Kuwait weakened his international standing, but he was subsequently in Middle East peace talks. In 1993 reached a peace accord of mutual recognition with Israel, under which the Gaza Strip and Jericho were transferred to PLO control. He returned to the former occupied territories 1994 as head of an embryonic Palestinian state, and in 1995 reached agreement on further Israeli troop withdrawals from areas in the West Bank. The assassination of Israeli prime minister Yitzhak Rabin 1995 threatened the peace process, but Rabin continued efforts for a lasting peace.

Aragón autonomous region of NE Spain. A Roman province until taken in the 5th century by the Visigoths, who lost it to the Moors in the 8th century; it became a kingdom 1035. It was united with Castile 1479 under Ferdinand and Isabella.

Araucanian Indian (Araucanian *Mapuche*) member of a group of South American Indian peoples native to central Chile and the Argentine pampas. They were agriculturalists and hunters, as well as renowned warriors, defeating the Incas and resisting the Spanish for 200 years.

Arawak member of an indigenous American people of the Caribbean and NE Amazon Basin. Arawaks lived mainly by shifting cultivation in tropical forests. They were driven out of many West Indian islands by another American Indian people, the Caribs, shortly before the arrival of the Spanish in the 16th century. Subsequently, their numbers on Hispaniola declined from some 4 million in 1492 to a few thousand after their exploitation by the Spanish in their search for gold; the remaining few were eradicated by disease (smallpox was introduced 1518). Arawakan languages belong to the Andean-Equatorial group.

Arbenz Guzmán Jácobo 1913–1971. Guatemalan social democratic politician and president from 1951 until his overthrow 1954 by rebels operating with the help of the US Central Intelligence Agency.

Guzmán brought in policies to redistribute land, much of which was owned by overseas companies, to landless peasants; he also encouraged labour organization. His last years were spent in exile in Mexico, Uruguay, and Cuba.

Arch Joseph 1826–1919. English Radical member of Parliament and trade unionist, founder of the National Agricultural Union (the first of its kind) 1872. He was born in Warwickshire, the son of an agricultural labourer. Entirely self-taught, he became a Methodist preacher, and was Liberal-Labour MP for NW Norfolk.

archaeology study of prehistory and history, based on the examination of physical remains. Principal activities include preliminary field (or site) surveys, excavation (where necessary), and the classification, dating, and interpretation of finds. Since 1958 radiocarbon dating has been used to establish the age of archaeological strata and associated materials.

history Interest in the physical remains of the past began in the Renaissance among dealers in and collectors of ancient art. It was further stimulated by discoveries made in Africa, the Americas, and Asia by Europeans during the period of imperialist colonization in the 16th–19th centuries, such as the antiquities discovered during Napoleon's Egyptian campaign in the 1790s. Towards the end of the 19th century archaeology became an academic study, making increasing use of scientific techniques and systematic methodologies.

related disciplines Useful in archaeological studies are stratigraphy (derived from the study of geological strata), dendrochronology (the establishment of chronological sequences through the study of tree rings), palaeobotany (the study of ancient pollens, seeds, and grains), epigraphy (the study of inscriptions), and numismatics (the study of coins).

Ardennes offensive alternative name for the World War II Battle of the ◊Bulge.

Areopagus, Council of in ancient Athens, the aristocratic council, composed of former magistrates, which took its name from the rocky outcrop where it met, immediately west of the ◊Acropolis. A sanctuary to the avenging Furies was located beneath the meeting place, in reference to the council's guardianship of the laws.

The council's power gradually diminished from the 5th century BC, though it remained a homicide court, a function sanctified by the mythical traditions that Orestes and the god Ares had been tried for murder on the hill.

Arevalo Bermejo Juan José 1904–1990. Guatemalan president 1945–51, elected to head a civilian government after a popular revolt ended a 14-year period of military rule. However, many of his liberal reforms were later undone by subsequent military rulers.

Argentina country in South America, bounded W and S by Chile, N by Bolivia, and E by Paraguay, Brazil, Uruguay, and the Atlantic Ocean.

history Originally inhabited by South American Indian peoples, Argentina was first visited by Europeans in the early 16th century. Buenos Aires was founded first 1536 and again 1580 after being abandoned because of Indian attacks. Argentina was made a Spanish viceroyalty 1776, and the population rose against Spanish rule 1810. Full independence was achieved 1816.

After the struggle with Spain, Argentina was in a state of chaos. From 1827 to 1852, the dictator Juan Manuel Rosas controlled Buenos Aires and established his authority over the interior. Later regimes committed themselves to laissez-faire economic policies which tied in Argentina to the international economy.

Archaeology

14th–16th centuries	The Renaissance revived interest in Classical Greek and Roman art and architecture, including ruins and buried art and artefacts.
1748	The buried Roman city of Pompeii was discovered under ash from Vesuvius.
1784	Thomas Jefferson excavated an Indian burial mound on the Rivanna River in Virginia and wrote a report on his finds.
1790	John Frere identified Old Stone Age (Palaeolithic) tools together with large extinct animals.
1822	Jean François Champollion deciphered Egyptian hieroglyphics.
1836	Christian Thomsen devised the Stone, Bronze, and Iron Age classification ('Three Age' system).
1840s	Austen Layard excavated the Assyrian capital of Nineveh.
1868	The Great Zimbabwe ruins in E Africa were first seen by Europeans.
1871	Heinrich Schliemann began excavations at Troy.
1879	Stone Age paintings were first discovered at Altamira, Spain.
1880s	Augustus Pitt-Rivers developed the concept of stratigraphy (identification of successive layers of soil within a site with successive archaeological stages; the most recent at the top).
1891	Flinders Petrie began excavating Akhetaton in Egypt.
1899–1935	Arthur Evans excavated Minoan Knossos in Crete.
1900–44	Max Uhle began the systematic study of the civilizations of Peru.
1911	The Inca city of Machu Picchu was discovered by Hiram Bingham in the Andes.
1911–12	The Piltdown skull was 'discovered'; it was proved to be a fake 1949.
1914–18	Osbert Crawford developed the technique of aerial survey of sites.
1917–27	John Eric Thompson (1898-1975) discovered the great Mayan sites in Yucatán, Mexico.
1922	Tutankhamen's tomb in Egypt was opened by Howard Carter.
1926	A kill site in Folsom, New Mexico, was found with human-made spearpoints in association with ancient bison.
1935	Dendrochronology (dating events in the distant past by counting tree rings) was developed by A E Douglas.
1939	An Anglo-Saxon ship-burial treasure was found at Sutton Hoo, England.
1947	The first of the Dead Sea Scrolls was discovered.
1948	The *Proconsul* prehistoric ape was discovered by Mary Leakey in Kenya.
1950s–1970s	Several early hominid fossils were found by Louis Leakey in Olduvai Gorge.
1953	Michael Ventris deciphered Minoan Linear B.
1960s	Radiocarbon and thermoluminescence measurement techniques were developed as aids for dating remains.
1961	The Swedish warship *Wasa* was raised at Stockholm.
1963	Walter Emery pioneered rescue archaeology at Abu Simbel before the site was flooded by the Aswan Dam.
1969	Human remains found at Lake Mungo, Australia, were dated at 26,000 years; earliest evidence of ritual cremation.
1974	The Tomb of Shi Huangdi was discovered in China. The footprints of a hominid called 'Lucy', 3 to 3.7 million years old, were found at Laetoli in Ethiopia.
1978	The tomb of Philip II of Macedon (Alexander the Great's father) was discovered in Greece.
1979	The Aztec capital Tenochtitlán was excavated beneath a zone of Mexico City.
1982	The English king Henry VIII's warship *Mary Rose* of 1545 was raised and studied with new techniques in underwater archaeology.
1985	The tomb of Maya, Tutankhamen's treasurer, was discovered at Saqqara, Egypt.
1988	The Turin Shroud was established as being of medieval origin by radiocarbon dating.
1989	The remains of the Globe and Rose Theatres, where many of Shakespeare's plays were originally performed, were discovered in London.
1991	Body of man from 5300 years ago, with clothing, bow, arrows, a copper axe, and other implements, found preserved in Italian Alps.
1992	The world's oldest surviving wooden structure, a well 15 m/49 ft deep made of huge oak timbers at Kückhoven, Germany, was dated by tree-rings to 5090 BC. The world's oldest sea-going vessel, dating from about 1400 BC, discovered Dover, southern England.

rise of Perón Since 1930 Argentina has been subject to alternate civilian and military rule. A military coup 1943 paved the way for the rise of Lt-Gen Juan Domingo ◊Perón. Strengthened by the popularity of his wife, María Eva Duarte de ◊Perón (the legendary 'Evita'), Perón created the Peronista party, based on extreme nationalism and social improvement. Evita Perón died 1952, and her husband was overthrown and civilian rule restored 1955. A coup 1966 restored military rule, and the success of a later Peronist party, Frente Justicialista de Liberación, brought Héctor Cámpora to the presidency 1973. After three months he resigned to make way for Juan Perón, with his third wife, María Estela Martínez de Perón ('Isabel'), as vice president. Perón died 1974 and was succeeded by his widow.

Videla and the 'dirty war' Two years later, a military coup ousted Isabel, and a three-person junta, led by Lt-Gen Jorge Videla, was installed. The constitution was amended, and political and trade-union activity banned. The years 1976–83 witnessed a ferocious campaign by the junta against left-wing elements, the 'dirty war', during which it is believed that between 6,000 and 15,000 people 'disappeared'. Videla retired 1978, to be succeeded by General Roberto Viola, who promised a return to democracy. Viola died 1981 and was replaced by General Leopoldo ◊Galtieri.

Falklands conflict Galtieri, seeking popular support and wishing to distract attention from the deteriorating economy, ordered 1982 the invasion of the *Islas Malvinas*, the ◊Falkland Islands, over which the UK's claim to sovereignty had long been disputed. After a short war, during which 750 Argentinians were killed, the islands were reoccupied by the UK. With the failure of the Falklands invasion, Galtieri was replaced in a bloodless coup by General Reynaldo Bignone. A military inquiry reported 1983 that Galtieri's junta was to blame for the defeat. Several officers were tried, and some, including Galtieri, given prison sentences, while an amnesty was granted to all those convicted of political crimes during the previous ten years. The ban on political and trade-union activity was lifted and general elections were held Oct 1983.

Alfonsín's reforms and investigations Having won the election, Alfonsín announced radical reforms in the armed forces (leading to the retirement of more than half the senior officers) and the trial of the first three military juntas that had ruled Argentina since 1976. He set up the National Commission on the Disappearance of Persons (CONADEP) to investi-

gate the 'dirty war'. A report by CONADEP 1984 listed over 8,000 people who had disappeared and 1,300 army officers who had been involved in the campaign of repression. Alfonsín's government was soon faced with enormous economic problems, resulting in recourse to help from the ◊International Monetary Fund and an austerity programme.

Menem tackles high inflation The presidential election of May 1989 was won by the Justicialist candidate, Carlos Menem. Alfonsín handed over power July 1989, five months before his term of office formally ended, to allow Menem to come to grips with the high inflation (more than 1,000% a year) that threatened to bring about increasing social unrest.

A financial scandal involving Menem's relatives and aides threatened the Justicialist Party's success in midterm elections, but support for Menem's economic policies secured a victory. In 1991 inflation was, at 84%, the lowest it had been since 1986. In Jan 1992 the government introduced a new currency, the peso, to replace the austral, which had been rendered almost worthless by inflation.

Argos city in ancient Greece, at the head of the Gulf of Nauplia, which was once a cult centre of the goddess Hera. In the Homeric age the name 'Argives' was sometimes used instead of 'Greeks'. In the classical period Argos repeatedly, but unsuccessfully, contested supremacy in S Greece with ◊Sparta.

Argyll Archibald Campbell, 5th Earl of Argyll 1530–1573. Adherent of the Scottish presbyterian John ◊Knox. A supporter of Mary Queen of Scots from 1561, he commanded her forces after her escape from Lochleven Castle 1568. He revised his position and became Lord High Chancellor of Scotland 1572.

Arianism system of Christian theology that denied the complete divinity of Jesus. It was founded about 310 by ◊Arius, and condemned as heretical at the Council of Nicaea 325.

Some 17th- and 18th-century theologians held Arian views akin to those of ◊Unitarianism (that God is a single being, and that there is no such thing as the Trinity). In 1979 the heresy again caused concern to the Vatican in the writings of such theologians as Edouard Schillebeeckx of the Netherlands.

arielism set of ideas rejecting North American materialism, inspired by Uruguayan writer José Enrique Rodó (1871–1917) in his short essay *Ariel* 1900.

Written after Spain's humiliating defeat in the ◊Spanish-American War 1898, the work was dedicated to 'the youth of America', and evoked the spirit of Latin America. It was highly influential throughout Latin America over the next two decades.

Aristides *c.* 530–468 BC. Athenian politician. He was one of the ten Athenian generals at the battle of ◊Marathon 490 BC and was elected chief archon, or magistrate. Later he came into conflict with the democratic leader Themistocles, and was exiled about 483 BC. He returned to fight against the Persians at Salamis 480 BC and in the following year commanded the Athenians at Plataea. As commander of the Athenian fleet he established the alliance of Ionian states known as the Delian League.

aristocracy (Greek *aristos* 'best', *kratos* 'power') social elite or system of political power associated with landed wealth, as in western Europe; monetary wealth, as in Carthage and Venice; or religious superiority, as with the Brahmins in India. The Prussian aristocracy based its legitimacy not only on landed wealth but also on service to the state. Aristocracies are also usually associated with monarchy but have frequently been in conflict with the sovereign over their respective rights and privileges. In Europe, their economic base was undermined during the 19th century by inflation and falling agricultural prices, leading to their demise as a political force after 1914.

Arius *c.* 256–336. Egyptian priest whose ideas gave rise to ◊Arianism, a Christian belief which denied the complete divinity of Jesus.

He was born in Libya, and became a priest in Alexandria 311. In 318 he was excommunicated and fled to Palestine, but his theology spread to such an extent that the emperor Constantine called a council at Nicaea 325 to resolve the question. Arius and his adherents were condemned and banished.

Armada fleet sent by Philip II of Spain against England 1588. See ◊Spanish Armada.

Armenia country in W Asia, bounded E by Azerbaijan, N by Georgia, W by Turkey, and S by Iran.

history Armenia was in ancient times a kingdom occupying what is now the Van region of Turkey, part of NW Iran, and what is now Armenia. Under King Tigranes II (95–55 BC) the kingdom reached the height of its power, controlling an empire that stretched from the Mediterranean to the Caucasus. Thereafter, it fell under the sway of the ◊Byzantine Empire, then the Muslim Turks from the late 11th century, the Mongols in the 13th century, and the Ottomans from the 16th century. This domination by foreign powers bred an intense

national consciousness and encouraged northward migration of the community.

under Soviet control With the advance of Russia into the Caucasus during the early 19th century, there was a struggle for independence which provoked an Ottoman backlash and growing international concern at Armenian maltreatment. In 1915 an estimated 1,750,000 Armenians were massacred or deported by the Turks. Conquered by Russia 1916, Armenia was briefly independent 1918 until occupied by the Red Army 1920. Along with Azerbaijan and Georgia, it formed part of the Transcaucasian Soviet Socialist Republic, but became a constituent republic of the USSR 1936.

growth of nationalism As a result of ◊glasnost, Armenian national identity was reawakened and in 1988 demands for reunion with ◊Nagorno-Karabakh led to a civil war 1989–91, resulting in the intervention of Soviet troops. The Armenian National Movement, which was formed Nov 1989 by Levon Ter-Petrossian and Vazguen Manukyan, and the militant Karabakh Committee were at the fore of this growing nationalist campaign. The campaign included attempts to secure full control over the Azeri enclave of Nakhichevan, leading to the flight of almost 200,000 Azeris from the republic. In the 1990 elections to the republic's supreme soviet (parliament) nationalists polled strongly and Ter-Petrossian and Manukyan were chosen as president and prime minister respectively.

struggle for independence On 23 Aug 1990 a declaration of independence was made but ignored by Moscow. The republic boycotted the March 1991 USSR referendum on the preservation of the Soviet Union and in April 1991 the property belonging to the Communist Party of Armenia (CPA) was nationalized. Four months later the CPA dissolved itself. In a referendum held Sept 1991, shortly after the failed anti-Gorbachev coup in Moscow, 94% voted for secession from the USSR. Two days later independence was formally proclaimed by President Ter-Petrossian, but this failed to secure Western recognition. A cease-fire agreement, brokered by the presidents of the Russian Federation and Kazakhstan, was signed by Armenia and Azerbaijan on 24 Sept 1991. It provided the basis for a negotiated settlement to the Nagorno-Karabakh dispute, including the disarming of local militias, the return of refugees, and the holding of free elections in the enclave.

However, the agreement collapsed Nov 1991 when the Azerbaijan parliament, nominated by communists-turned-nationalist, voted to annul

Nagorno-Karabakh's autonomous status. Soviet troops were gradually withdrawn from the enclave, leaving it vulnerable to Azeri attacks. In response, after a referendum and elections Dec 1991, Nagorno-Karabakh's parliament declared its 'independence', precipitating an intensification of the conflict.

Armenian independence achieved On 16 Oct 1991 Ter-Petrossian was overwhelmingly re-elected president, capturing 83% of the vote, in the republic's first direct election. In Dec 1991 Armenia agreed to join the new confederal ◊Commonwealth of Independent States (CIS), which was formed to supersede the Soviet Union. Also in Dec Armenia was accorded diplomatic recognition by the USA and in Jan 1992 was admitted into the ◊Conference on Security and Cooperation in Europe (CSCE); in March 1992 it became a member of the United Nations (UN).

Armenian member of the largest ethnic group inhabiting Armenia. There are Armenian minorities in Azerbaijan, as well as in Turkey and Iran. Christianity was introduced to the ancient Armenian kingdom in the 3rd century. There are 4–5 million speakers of Armenian, which belongs to the Indo-European family of languages.

Armenian massacres series of massacres of Armenians by Turkish soldiers between 1895 and 1915. Reforms promised to Armenian Christians by Turkish rulers never materialized; unrest broke out and there were massacres by Turkish troops 1895. Again in 1909 and 1915, the Turks massacred altogether more than a million Armenians and deported others into the N Syrian desert, where they died of starvation; those who could fled to Russia or Persia. Only some 100,000 were left.

Arminius 17 BC–AD 19. German chieftain. An ex-soldier of the Roman army, he annihilated a Roman force led by Varus in the Teutoburger Forest area AD 9, and saved Germany from becoming a Roman province. He was later treacherously killed by some of his kinsmen.

armistice cessation of hostilities while awaiting a peace settlement. 'The Armistice' refers specifically to the end of World War I between Germany and the Allies 11 Nov 1918. On 22 June 1940 French representatives signed an armistice with Germany in the same railway carriage at Compiègne as in 1918.

armour body protection worn in battle. Body armour is depicted in Greek and Roman art. Chain mail was developed in the Middle Ages but the craft of the armourer in Europe reached its height in design in the 15th century, when knights were completely encased in plate armour that still allowed freedom of movement.

The invention of gunpowder led, by degrees, to the virtual abandonment of armour until World War I, when the helmet reappeared as a defence against shrapnel.

arms control attempts to limit the arms race between the superpowers by reaching agreements to restrict the production of certain weapons; see ◊disarmament.

army organized military force for fighting on the ground. A national army is used to further a political policy by force either within the state or on the territory of another state. Most countries have a national army, maintained by taxation, and raised either by conscription (compulsory military service) or voluntarily (paid professionals). Private armies may be employed by individuals and groups.

ancient armies (to 1066) Armies were common to all ancient civilizations. The Spartans trained from childhood for compulsory military service from age 21 to 26 in a full-time regular force as a heavily armed infantryman, or *hoplite*. Roman armies were composed of *legions, cohorts*, and *centuries*. The concept of duty to military service continued following the collapse of the Roman Empire. For example, the Anglo-Saxon *fyrd* (local militia) obliged all able-bodied men to serve in defence of Britain against Danish and then Norman invasion.

armies of knights and mercenaries (1066–1648) Medieval monarchs relied on mounted men-at-arms, or *chevaliers*, who in turn called on serfs from the land. Feudal armies were thus inherently limited in size and could only fight for limited periods. Free *yeomen* armed with longbows were required by law to practise at the *butts* and provided an early form of indirect fire as *artillery*. In Europe paid troops, or *soldi*, and mounted troops, or *serviertes* (sergeants), made themselves available as *freelances*. By the end of the 15th century, *battles* or *battalions* of pikemen provided defence against the mounted knight. The hard gun, or *arquebus*, heralded the coming of infantrymen as known today. Those who wished to avoid military service could do so by paying *scutage*. For the majority, the *conpane*, or *company*, was their home; they were placed under royal command by *ordonnances* and led by crown office holders, or *officiers*. Increased costs led to the formation of the first mercenary armies. For example, the *Great Company* of 10,000 men acted as an international force, employing contractors, or *condottieri*, to serve the highest bidder. By the 16th century the long musket, pikemen, and the use of fortifications combined against the knight. *Sappers* became increasingly important in the creation and breaking of obstacles such as at Metz, a forerunner of the Maginot Line.

professional armies (1648–1792) The emergence of the European nation-state saw the growth of more professional standing armies which trained in drills, used formations to maximize firepower, and introduced service discipline. The invention of the ring bayonet and the flintlock saw the demise of pikemen and the increased capability to fire from three ranks (today still the standard drill formation in the British Army). Artillery was now mobile and fully integrated into the army structure. The defects of raw levies, noble amateurs, and mercenaries led Oliver Cromwell to create the New Model Army for the larger campaigns of the English Civil War. After the Restoration, Charles II established a small standing army, which was expanded under James II and William III. In France, a model regiment was set up under de Martinet which set standards of uniformity for all to follow. State taxation provided for a formal system of army administration (uniforms, pay, ammunition). Nevertheless, recruits remained mainly society's misfits and delinquents. Collectively termed *other ranks*, they were divided from commissioned officers by a rigid hierarchical structure. The sheer cost of such armies forced wars to be fought by manoeuvre rather than by pitched battle, aiming to starve one's opponent into defeat while protecting one's own logistic chain.

armies of the revolution (1792–1819) Napoleon's organization of his army into autonomous *corps* of two to three *divisions*, in turn comprising two *brigades* of two *regiments* of two *battalions*, was a major step forward in allowing a rapid and flexible deployment of forces. Small-scale skirmishing by *light infantry*, coupled with the increasing devastation created by artillery or densely packed formations, saw the beginnings of the *dispersed battlefield*. Victory in war was now synonymous with the complete destruction of the enemy in battle. Reservists were conscripted to allow the mass army to fight wars through to the bitter end. (Only Britain, by virtue of the English Channel and the Royal Navy, was able to avoid the need to provide such large land forces.) Officers were now required to be professionally trained; the Royal Military College was set up in Britain 1802, St Cyr in France 1808, the Kriegsakademie in

Berlin 1810, and the Russian Imperial Military Academy 1832. *Semaphore telegraph* and *observation balloons* were first steps to increasing the commander's ability to observe enemy movements. The British army, under Wellington, was very strong, but afterwards decreased in numbers and efficiency.

national armies (1792–1819) The defeat of Revolutionary France saw a return to the traditions of the 18th century and a reduction in conscription. Meanwhile the railway revolutionized the deployment of forces, permitting quick mobilization, continuous resupply to the front, and rapid evacuation of casualties to the rear. The US Civil War has been called the Railway War. By 1870, the limitation of supply inherent to the Napoleonic army had been overcome and once again armies of over 1 million could be deployed. By 1914, continental armies numbered as many as 3 million and were based on conscription. A general staff was now required to manage these. *Breechloading rifles* and *machine guns* ensured a higher casualty rate.

19th-century armies The 19th century saw the great development of rapidly produced missile weapons and the use of railways to move troops and materials.

technological armies (1918–45) The advent of the internal combustion engine allowed new advances in mobility to overcome the supremacy of the defensive over the offensive. The *tank* and the *radio* were vital to the evolution of armoured warfare or *Blitzkrieg*. Armies were able to reorganize into highly mobile formations, such as the German *Panzer Divisions*, which utilized speed, firepower, and surprise to overwhelm static defences and thereby dislocate the army's rear.

The armies of World War II were very mobile, and were closely coordinated with the navy and air force. The requirement to fuel and maintain such huge fleets of vehicles again increased the need to maintain supplies. The complexity of the mechanized army demanded a wide range of skills not easily found through conscription.

armies of the nuclear age (1945–   ) The advent of tactical nuclear weapons severely compounded the problems of mass concentration and thus mobility assumed greater importance to allow rapid concentration and dispersal of forces in what could be a high chemical threat zone. From the 1960s there were sophisticated developments in tanks and antitank weapons, mortar-locating radar, and heat-seeking missiles.

Arnhem, Battle of in World War II, airborne operation by the Allies, 17–26 Sept 1944, to secure a bridgehead over the Rhine, thereby opening the way for a thrust towards the Ruhr and a possible early end to the war.

Arnold Benedict 1741–1801. US soldier and military strategist who, during the American Revolution, won the turning-point battle at Saratoga 1777 for the Americans. He is chiefly remembered as a traitor to the American side, having plotted to betray the strategic post at West Point to the British.

Arras, Battle of battle of World War I, April–May 1917. It was an effective but costly British attack on German forces in support of a French offensive, which was only partially successful, on the ◊Siegfried Line. British casualties totalled 84,000 as compared to 75,000 German casualties.

Arras, Congress and Treaty of meeting in N France 1435 between representatives of Henry VI of England, Charles VII of France, and Philip the Good of Burgundy to settle the Hundred Years' War. The outcome was a diplomatic victory for France. Although England refused to compromise on Henry VI's claim to the French crown, France signed a peace treaty with Burgundy, England's former ally.

Arsacid dynasty rulers of ancient ◊Parthia *c.* 250 BC–*c.* AD 230 who took their titles from their founder Arsaces (*c.* 247–210 BC). At its peak the dynasty controlled a territory from eastern India to western Mesopotamia, with a summer capital at Ecbatana and a winter palace at Ctesiphon. Claiming descent from the Persian ◊Achaemenids, but adopting Hellenistic Greek methods of administration, they successfully challenged Roman expansion, defeating the Roman general Crassus at the battle of ◊Carrhae 53 BC. They were succeeded by the ◊Sassanian Empire.

Arthur 6th century AD. Legendary British king and hero in stories of ◊Camelot and the quest for the Holy Grail. Arthur is said to have been born in Tintagel, Cornwall, and buried in Glastonbury, Somerset. He may have been a Romano-Celtic leader against pagan Saxon invaders.

Arthur Chester Alan 1830–1886. 21st president of the USA 1881–85, a Republican. In 1880 he was chosen as James ◊Garfield's vice president, and was his successor when Garfield was assassinated the following year.

He was born in Vermont, the son of a Baptist minister, and became a lawyer and Republican political appointee in New York.

Artigas José Gervasio 1764–1850. Uruguayan independence campaigner. Artigas became governor of Montevideo 1815 but soon fell out with the Buenos Aires regime because it lacked commitment to his province's liberation. Although he was forced into exile, his federalist plans laid the foundations of an independent Uruguay 1828.

artillery collective term for military firearms too heavy to be carried. Artillery can be mounted on ships or aeroplanes and includes cannons and missile launchers.

14th century Cannons came into general use, and were most effective in siege warfare. The term had previously been applied to catapults used for hurling heavy objects.

16th century The howitzer, halfway between a gun and a mortar (muzzle-loading cannon), was first used in sieges.

early 19th century In the Napoleonic period, field artillery became smaller and more mobile.

1914–18 In World War I, howitzers were used to demolish trench systems. Giant cannons were used in the entrenched conditions of the Western Front and at sea against the lumbering, heavily armoured battleships, but their accuracy against small or moving targets was poor.

1939–45 In World War II artillery became more mobile, particularly in the form of self-propelled guns.

1980s The introduction of so-called smart munitions meant that artillery rounds could be guided to their target by means of a laser designator.

Artois former province of N France, bounded by Flanders and Picardie and almost corresponding with the modern *département* of Pas-de-Calais. Its capital was Arras. Its Latin name *Artesium* lent its name to the artesian well first sunk at Lillers 1126.

Aryan Indo-European family of languages; also the hypothetical parent language of an ancient people who are believed to have lived between central Asia and E Europe and to have reached Persia and India in one direction and Europe in another, sometime in the 2nd century BC, diversifying into the various Indo-European language speakers of later times. In Nazi Germany Hitler and other theorists erroneously propagated the idea of the Aryans as a white-skinned, blue-eyed, fair-haired master race.

Arya Samaj Hindu religious sect founded by Dayanand Saraswati (1825–1888) about 1875. He renounced idol worship and urged a return to the purer principles of the Vedas (Hindu scriptures). For its time the movement was quite revolutionary in its social teachings, which included forbidding ◊caste practices, prohibiting child-marriage, and allowing widows to remarry.

ASEAN acronym for ◊Association of South East Asian Nations.

Ashanti or *Asante* region of Ghana, W Africa; area 25,100 sq km/9,700 sq mi. For more than 200 years Ashanti was an independent kingdom. During the 19th century the Ashanti and the British fought for control of trade in West Africa. The British sent four expeditions against the Ashanti and formally annexed their country 1901. Otomfuo Sir Osei Agyeman, nephew of the deposed king, Prempeh I, was made head of the re-established Ashanti confederation 1935 as Prempeh II. The Golden Stool (actually a chair), symbol of the Ashanti peoples since the 17th century, was returned to Kumasi 1935 (the rest of the Ashanti treasure is in the British Museum). The Asantahene (King of the Ashanti) still holds ceremonies in which this stool is ceremonially paraded.

Ashikaga in Japanese history, the family who held the office of ◊shogun 1338–1573, a period of civil wars. Nō drama evolved under the patronage of Ashikaga shoguns. Relations with China improved intermittently and there was trade with Korea. The last (15th) Ashikaga shogun was ousted by Oda Nobunaga at the start of the ◊Momoyama period. The Ashikaga belonged to the ◊Minamoto clan.

Ashkenazi (plural *Ashkenazim*) a Jew of German or E European descent, as opposed to a Sephardi, of Spanish, Portuguese, or N African descent.

Asiento, Treaty of agreement between the UK and Spain 1713, whereby British traders were permitted to introduce 144,000 black slaves into the Spanish-American colonies in the course of the following 30 years. In 1750 the right was bought out by the Spanish government for $100,000.

Asoka c. 273–232 BC. ◊Mauryan emperor of India c. 268–232 BC, the greatest of the Mauryan rulers. He inherited an empire covering most of north and south-central India which, at its height, had a population of at least 30 million, with its capital at ◊Pataliputra. A devout Buddhist, he renounced militarism and concentrated on establishing an efficient administration with a large standing army and a secret police.

He had edicts encouraging the adoption of his faith carved on pillars and rocks throughout his kingdom.

Asquith Herbert Henry, 1st Earl of Oxford and Asquith 1852–1928. British Liberal politician, prime minister 1908–16. As chancellor of the Exchequer he introduced old-age pensions 1908. He limited the powers of the House of Lords and attempted to give Ireland Home Rule.

Asquith was born in Yorkshire. Elected a member of Parliament 1886, he was home secretary in Gladstone's 1892–95 government. He was chancellor of the Exchequer 1905–08 and succeeded Campbell-Bannerman as prime minister. Forcing through the radical budget of his chancellor ◊Lloyd George led him into two elections 1910, which resulted in the Parliament Act 1911, limiting the right of the Lords to veto legislation. His endeavours to pass the Home Rule for Ireland Bill led to the ◊Curragh 'Mutiny' and incipient civil war. Unity was reestablished by the outbreak of World War I 1914, and a coalition government was formed May 1915. However, his attitude of 'wait and see' was not adapted to all-out war, and in Dec 1916 he was replaced by Lloyd George. In 1918 the Liberal election defeat led to the eclipse of the party.

One to mislead the public, another to mislead the Cabinet, and the third to mislead itself.

Herbert Henry Asquith
(on the reason for the War Office keeping three sets of figures)

Assad Hafez al- 1930–   . Syrian Ba'athist politician, president from 1971. He became prime minister after a bloodless military coup 1970, and the following year was the first president to be elected by popular vote. Having suppressed dissent, he was re-elected 1978 and 1985. He is a Shia (Alawite) Muslim.

He has ruthlessly suppressed domestic opposition, and was Iran's only major Arab ally in its war against Iraq. He steadfastly pursued military parity with Israel, and has made himself a key player in any settlement of the Lebanese civil war or Middle East conflict generally. His support for UN action against Iraq following its invasion of Kuwait 1990 raised his international standing.

Assam state of NE India. A thriving region from 1000 BC, Assam migrants came from China and Burma. After Burmese invasion 1826, Britain took control and made Assam a separate province 1874; it was included in the Dominion of India, except for most of the

Muslim district of Silhet, which went to Pakistan 1947. Ethnic unrest started in the 1960s when Assamese was declared the official language. After protests, the Gara, Khasi, and Jainitia tribal hill districts became the state of Meghalaya 1971; the Mizo hill district became the Union Territory of Mizoram 1972. There were massacres of Muslim Bengalis by Hindus 1983. In 1987 members of the Bodo ethnic group began fighting for a separate homeland. In the early 1990s the Marxist-militant United Liberation Front of Assam (ULFA), which had extorted payments from tea-exporting companies, spearheaded a campaign of separatist terrorist violence.

assassination murder, usually of a political, royal, or public person. The term derives from the order of the ◊Assassins, a Muslim sect that, in the 11th and 12th centuries, murdered officials to further its political ends.

Assassins, order of the (Arabic *Assassiyun* 'fundamentalists' from *assass* 'foundation') militant offshoot of the Islamic Isma'ili sect 1089–1256, founded by Hassan Sabah (c. 1045–1124). They assassinated high officials in every Muslim town to further their political ends. Their headquarters from 1090 was the Alamut clifftop fortress in the Elburz Mountains, NW Iran.

Having converted to the persecuted, mystic Isma'ili sect, Hassan Sabah became a missionary and rebel against the Seljuk Empire. As grand master of the Assassins, he ran the order with strict asceticism. The assassins were members of a suicide squad: they remained at the scene of the crime to be martyred for their beliefs. Their enemies called them *hashishiyun* 'smokers of hashish'. Princes, viziers, and also Crusaders were among their victims. Hassan was a scholar and Alamut, built on a peak of 1,800 m/6,000 ft, held one of the largest libraries of the time.

assize in medieval Europe, the passing of laws, either by the king with the consent of nobles, as in the Constitutions of ◊Clarendon 1164 by Henry II of England, or as a complete system, such as the *Assizes of Jerusalem*, a compilation of the law of the feudal kingdom of Jerusalem in the 13th century.

The term remained in use in the UK for the courts held by judges of the High Court in each county; they were abolished under the Courts Act 1971.

Association of South East Asian Nations (ASEAN) regional alliance formed in Bangkok 1967; it took over the nonmilitary role of the Southeast Asia Treaty Organization 1975. Its members are Indonesia, Malaysia, the Philippines, Singapore, Thailand, and (from 1984) Brunei; its headquarters are in Jakarta, Indonesia.

The six member states signed an agreement 1992 to establish an ASEAN free trade area (AFTA) by the beginning of 2008.

Assyria empire in the Middle East c. 2500–612 BC, in N Mesopotamia (now Iraq); early capital Ashur, later Nineveh. It was initially subject to Sumer and intermittently to Babylon. The Assyrians adopted in the main the Sumerian religion and structure of society. At its greatest extent the empire included Egypt and stretched from the E Mediterranean coast to the head of the Persian Gulf.

The land of Assyria originally consisted of a narrow strip of alluvial soil on each side of the river Tigris. The area was settled about 3500 BC and was dominated by Sumer until about 2350 BC.

The first Assyrian kings are mentioned during the wars following the decline of the 3rd dynasty of Ur (in Sumer), but Assyria continued under Babylonian and subsequently Egyptian supremacy until about 1450 BC. Under King Ashur-uballit (reigned about 1380–1340 BC) Assyria became a military power. His work was continued by Adad-nirari I, Shalmaneser I, and Tukulti-enurta I, who conquered Babylonia and assumed the title of king of Sumer and Akkad.

During the reign of Nebuchadnezzar I (1150–1110 BC), Assyria was again subject to Babylonia, but was liberated by Tiglath-pileser I. In the Aramaean invasions, most of the ground gained was lost. From the accession of Adad-nirari II 911 BC Assyria pursued a course of expansion and conquest, culminating in the mastery over Elam, Mesopotamia, Syria, Palestine, the Arabian marches, and Egypt. Of this period the Old Testament records, and many 'documents' – such as the Black Obelisk celebrating the conquest of Shalmaneser III in the 9th century BC – survive.

The reign of Ashur-nazir-pal II (885–860 BC) was spent in unceasing warfare, evidenced by many bas-reliefs. Shalmaneser III warred against the Syrian states. At the battle of Qarqar 854 BC the Assyrian advance received a setback, and there followed a period of decline. The final period of Assyrian ascendancy began with the accession of Tiglath-pileser III (746–728 BC) and continued during the reigns of Sargon II, Sennacherib, Esarhaddon, and Ashurbanipal, culminating in the conquest of Egypt by Esarhaddon 671 BC. From this time the empire seems to have fallen into decay.

Nabopolassar of Babylonia and Cyaxares of Media (see ◊Mede) united against it; Nineveh was destroyed 612 BC; and Assyria became a Median province and subsequently a principality of the Persian Empire.

Much of Assyrian religion, law, social structure, and artistic achievement was derived from neighbouring sources. The Assyrians adopted the cuneiform script (invented by the Sumerians in 3500 BC) and took over the Sumerian pantheon, although the Assyrian god, Ashur (Assur), assumed the chief place in the cult. The library of Ashurbanipal excavated at Nineveh is evidence of the thoroughness with which Babylonian culture had been assimilated.

Astor prominent US and British family. *John Jacob Astor* (1763–1848) was a US millionaire. His great-grandson *Waldorf Astor*, 2nd Viscount Astor (1879–1952), was Conservative member of Parliament for Plymouth 1910–19, when he succeeded to the peerage. He was chief proprietor of the British *Observer* newspaper. His US-born wife Nancy Witcher Langhorne (1879–1964), *Lady Astor*, was the first woman member of Parliament to take a seat in the House of Commons 1919, when she succeeded her husband for the constituency of Plymouth. Government policy was said to be decided at Cliveden, their country home.

Grass is growing on the Front Bench.

> **Lady Astor** on Parliament
> *Observer* March 1940

Atahualpa *c.* 1502–1533. Last emperor of the Incas of Peru. He was taken prisoner 1532 when the Spaniards arrived, and agreed to pay a substantial ransom, but was accused of plotting against the conquistador Pizarro and sentenced to be burned. On his consenting to Christian baptism, the sentence was commuted to strangulation.

Atatürk Kemal. Name assumed 1934 by Mustafa Kemal Pasha 1881–1938. (Atatürk 'Father of the Turks') Turkish politician and general, first president of Turkey from 1923. After World War I he established a provisional rebel government and in 1921–22 the Turkish armies under his leadership expelled the Greeks who were occupying Turkey. He was the founder of the modern republic, which he ruled as virtual dictator, with a policy of consistent and radical westernization.

Kemal, born in Thessaloníki, was banished 1904 for joining a revolutionary society. Later he was pardoned and promoted in the army,

and was largely responsible for the successful defence of the Dardanelles against the British 1915. In 1918, after Turkey had been defeated, he was sent into Anatolia to implement the demobilization of the Turkish forces in accordance with the armistice terms, but instead he established a provisional government opposed to that of Constantinople (under Allied control), and in 1921 led the Turkish armies against the Greeks, who had occupied a large part of Anatolia. He checked them at the Battle of the Sakaria, 23 Aug–13 Sept 1921, for which he was granted the title of Ghazi (the Victorious), and within a year had expelled the Greeks from Turkish soil. War with the British was averted by his diplomacy, and Turkey in Europe passed under Kemal's control. On 29 Oct 1923, Turkey was proclaimed a republic with Kemal as first president.

I don't act for public opinion. I act for the nation and for my own satisfaction.

> **Kemal Atatürk**
> quoted in Lord Kinross *Atatürk*

Athelstan *c.* 895–939. King of the Mercians and West Saxons. Son of Edward the Elder and grandson of Alfred the Great, he was crowned king 925 at Kingston upon Thames. He subdued parts of Cornwall and Wales, and defeated the Welsh, Scots, and Danes at Brunanburh 937.

Atlantic, Battle of the continuous battle fought in the Atlantic Ocean during World War II by the sea and air forces of the Allies and Germany, to control the supply routes to the UK. The number of U-boats destroyed by the Allies during the war was nearly 800. At least 2,200 convoys of 75,000 merchant ships crossed the Atlantic, protected by US naval forces. Before the US entry into the war 1941, destroyers were supplied to the British under the Lend-Lease Act 1941.

Atlantic, Battle of the German naval campaign during World War I to prevent merchant shipping from delivering food supplies from the USA to the Allies, chiefly the UK. By 1917, some 875,000 tons of shipping had been lost. The odds were only turned by the belated use of naval *convoys* and *depth charges* to deter submarine attack.

Atlantic Charter declaration issued during World War II by the British prime minister Churchill and the US president Roosevelt after meetings Aug 1941. It stressed their countries' broad strategy and war aims and was largely a propaganda exercise to demonstrate public solidarity between the Allies.

The Atlantic Charter stated that the UK and the USA sought no territorial gains; desired no territorial changes not acceptable to the peoples concerned; respected the rights of all peoples to choose their own form of government; wished to see self-government restored to the occupied countries; would promote access by all states to trade and raw materials; desired international collaboration for the raising of economic standards; hoped to see a peace affording security to all nations, enabling them to cross the seas without hindrance; and proposed the disarmament of the aggressor states as a preliminary step to general disarmament.

atom bomb bomb deriving its explosive force from nuclear fission as a result of a neutron chain reaction, developed in the 1940s in the USA into a usable weapon.

Research began in the UK 1940 and was transferred to the USA after its entry into World War II the following year. Known as the *Manhattan Project*, the work was carried out under the direction of the US physicist Oppenheimer at Los Alamos, New Mexico.

After one test explosion, two atom bombs were dropped on the Japanese cities of Hiroshima (6 Aug 1945) and Nagasaki (9 Aug 1945), each nominally equal to 200,000 tonnes of TNT. The USSR first detonated an atom bomb 1949 and the UK 1952.

No country without an atom bomb could properly consider itself independent.

On the *atom bomb*
General Charles de Gaulle
New York Times 1968

---

attainder, bill of legislative device that allowed the English Parliament to declare guilt and impose a punishment on an individual without bringing the matter before the courts. Such bills were used intermittently from the Wars of the Roses until 1798. Some acts of attainder were also passed by US colonial legislators during the American Revolution to deal with 'loyalists' who continued to support the English crown.

Attila c. 406–453. King of the Huns in an area from the Alps to the Caspian Sea from 434, known to later Christian history as the 'Scourge of God'. He twice attacked the Eastern Roman Empire to increase the quantity of tribute paid to him, 441–43 and 447–49, and then attacked the Western Roman Empire 450–52.

Attila first ruled jointly with his brother Bleda, whom he murdered in 444. In 450 Honoria, the sister of the western emperor Valentinian III, appealed to him to rescue her from an arranged marriage, and Attila used her appeal to attack the West. He was forced back from Orléans by Aetius and Theodoric, king of the Visigoths, and defeated by them on the ◊Catalaunian Fields in 451. In 452 he led the Huns into Italy, and was induced to withdraw by Pope ◊Leo I.

He died on the night of his marriage to the German Ildico, either by poison, or, as Chaucer represents it in his *Pardoner's Tale*, from a nasal haemorrhage induced by drunkenness.

Attila lived in relative simplicity in his camp close to the Danube, which was described by the Greek historian Priscus after a diplomatic mission. But his advisers included a Greek Orestes, and his control over a large territory required administrative abilities. His conscious aims were to prevent the Huns from serving in the imperial armies, and to use force to exact as much tribute or land from both parts of the empire as he could. His burial place was kept secret.

Attlee Clement (Richard), 1st Earl 1883–1967. British Labour politician. In the coalition government during World War II he was Lord Privy Seal 1940–42, dominions secretary 1942–43, and Lord President of the Council 1943–45, as well as deputy prime minister from 1942. As prime minister 1945–51 he introduced a sweeping programme of nationalization and a whole new system of social services.

Attlee was educated at Oxford and practised as a barrister 1906–09. Social work in London's East End and cooperation in poor-law reform led him to become a socialist; he joined the Fabian Society and the Independent Labour Party 1908. He became lecturer in social science at the London School of Economics 1913. After service in World War I he was mayor of Stepney, E London, 1919–20; Labour member of Parliament for Limehouse 1922–50 and for W Walthamstow 1950–55. In the first and second Labour governments he was undersecretary for war 1924 and chancellor of the Duchy of Lancaster and postmaster general 1929–31. In 1935 he became leader of the opposition. In July 1945 he became prime minister after a Labour landslide in the general election. The government was returned to power with a much reduced majority 1950 and was defeated 1951. Created 1st Earl 1955 on his retirement as leader of the opposition.

Auchinleck Sir Claude John Eyre 1884–1981. British commander in World War II. He won the First Battle of El ◊Alamein 1942 in N Egypt. In 1943 he became commander in chief in India and founded the modern Indian and Pakistani armies. In 1946 he was promoted to field marshal; he retired 1947.

audiencia institution of colonial Spanish America. Audiencias were originally high courts of appeal, nominally subject to a viceroy, but they widened their powers and became in effect general administrative boards. They went into decline in the 17th century and virtually disappeared in the 18th century with the introduction of the ◊intendencia system.

Viceroys and audencias could work together as governments, but sometimes conflicts arose. The captaincy general of Venezuela and the presidency of Quito both had audencia status within the viceroyalty, or province, of ◊New Granada. Within ◊New Spain, the captaincy general of Guatemala had its own separate high courts.

Augsburg, Confession of statement of the Protestant faith as held by the German Reformers, composed by Philip Melanchthon (1497–1560). Presented to the holy Roman emperor Charles V, at the conference known as the Diet of Augsburg 1530, it is the creed of the modern Lutheran church.

Augsburg, Peace of religious settlement following the Diet of Augsburg 1555, which established the right of princes in the Holy Roman Empire (rather than the emperor himself, Ferdinand I) to impose a religion on their subjects – later summarized by the maxim *cuius regio, eius religio* ('those who live in a country shall adopt the religion of its leader'). It initially applied only to Lutherans and Catholics.

Augustus 63 BC–AD 14. Title of Octavian (Gaius Julius Caesar Octavianus), first of the Roman emperors. He joined forces with Mark Antony and Lepidus in the Second Triumvirate. Following Mark Antony's liaison with the Egyptian queen Cleopatra, Augustus defeated her troops at Actium 31 BC. As emperor (from 27 BC) he reformed the government of the empire, the army, and Rome's public services.

The son of a senator who married a niece of Julius Caesar, he became Caesar's adopted son and principal heir. Following Caesar's murder, Octavian formed with Mark Antony and Lepidus the Triumvirate that divided the Roman world between them and proceeded to eliminate the opposition. Antony's victory 42 BC over Brutus and Cassius had brought the republic to an end. Antony then became enamoured of Cleopatra and spent most of his time at Alexandria, while Octavian consolidated his hold on the western part of the Roman dominion. War was declared against Cleopatra, and the naval victory at Actium left Octavian in unchallenged supremacy, since Lepidus had been forced to retire.

After his return to Rome 29 BC, Octavian was created *princeps senatus*, and in 27 BC he was given the title of Augustus ('venerable'). He then resigned his extraordinary powers and received from the Senate, in return, the proconsular command, which gave him control of the army, and the tribunician power, whereby he could initiate or veto legislation. In his programme of reforms Augustus received the support of three loyal and capable helpers, Agrippa, Maecenas, and his wife, Livia, while Virgil and Horace acted as the poets laureate of the new regime.

A firm frontier for the empire was established: to the north, the friendly Batavians held the Rhine delta, and then the line followed the course of the Rhine and Danube; to the east, the Parthians were friendly, and the Euphrates gave the next line; to the south, the African colonies were protected by the desert; to the west were Spain and Gaul. The provinces were governed either by imperial legates responsible to the *princeps* or by proconsuls appointed by the Senate. The army was made a profession, with fixed pay and length of service, and a permanent fleet was established. Finally, Rome itself received an adequate water supply, a fire brigade, a police force, and a large number of public buildings.

The years after 12 BC were marked by private and public calamities: the marriage of Augustus' daughter Julia to his stepson ◊Tiberius proved disastrous; a serious revolt occurred in Pannonia AD 6; and in Germany three legions under Varus were annihilated in the Teutoburg Forest AD 9. He ensured the stability of the empire by handing his powers intact to his successor Tiberius.

I found Rome brick and I left it marble.

Emperor Augustus
quoted in Suetonius *Divus Augustus*

Aung San 1916–1947. Burmese (Myanmar) politician. He was a founder and leader of the Anti-Fascist People's Freedom League, which led Burma's fight for independence from Great Britain. During World War II he collaborated first with Japan and then with the UK. In 1947 he became head of Burma's provisional government but was assassinated the same year by political opponents. His daughter Suu Kyi

(1961–) spearheaded a nonviolent pro-democracy movement in Myanmar from 1988.

Aurangzeb or *Aurungzebe* 1618–1707. Mogul emperor of N India from 1658. Third son of ◊Shah Jahan, he made himself master of the court by a palace revolution. His reign was the most brilliant period of the Mogul dynasty, but his despotic tendencies and Muslim fanaticism aroused much opposition. His latter years were spent in war with the princes of Rajputana and the Marathas and Sikhs. His drive south into the Deccan overextended Mogul resources.

Aurelian (Lucius Domitius Aurelianus) *c.* AD 214–275. Roman emperor from 270. A successful soldier, he was chosen emperor by his troops on the death of Claudius II. He defeated the Goths and Vandals, and was planning a campaign against Parthia when he was murdered. The *Aurelian Wall*, a fortification surrounding Rome, was built by Aurelian in 271. It was made of concrete, and substantial ruins exist.

Aurignacian in archaeology, an Old Stone Age culture that came between the Mousterian and the Solutrian in the Upper Palaeolithic. The name is derived from a cave at Aurignac in the Pyrenees of France. The earliest cave paintings are attributed to the Aurignacian peoples of W Europe about 16,000 BC.

Auriol Vincent 1884–1966. French Socialist politician. He was president of the two Constituent Assemblies of 1946 and first president of the Fourth Republic 1947–54.

Auschwitz (Polish *Oswiecim*) town near Kraków in Poland, the site of a notorious ◊concentration camp used by the Nazis in World War II to exterminate Jews and other political and social minorities, as part of the 'final solution'. Each of the four gas chambers could hold 6,000 people.

Ausgleich compromise between Austria and Hungary 8 Feb 1867 that established the Austro-Hungarian Dual Monarchy under Habsburg rule. It endured until the collapse of Austria-Hungary 1918.

Austerlitz, Battle of battle on 2 Dec 1805 in which the French forces of Emperor Napoleon defeated those of Alexander I of Russia and Francis II of Austria at a small town in the Czech Republic (formerly in Austria), 19 km/12 mi E of Brno.

Austin Stephen Fuller 1793–1836. American pioneer and political leader. A settler in Texas 1821, he was a supporter of the colony's autonomy and was imprisoned 1833–35 for his

opposition to Mexican rule. Released during the Texas revolution, he campaigned for US support. After the end of the war 1836, he was appointed secretary of state of the independent Republic of Texas but died shortly afterwards.

Australia country occupying all of the Earth's smallest continent, situated S of Indonesia, between the Pacific and Indian oceans.

history Australia's first inhabitants, the Aborigines, arrived in Australia at least 40,000 years ago, according to present evidence. The first recorded sighting of Australia by Europeans was 1606, when the Dutch ship *Duyfken*, under the command of Willem Jansz, sighted the W coast of Cape York and the Spanish ship of Luis Vaez de Torres sailed N of Cape York and through Torres Strait, thus proving that New Guinea was separate from any southern continent. Later voyagers include Dirk Hartog 1616 – who left an inscribed pewter plate (Australia's most famous early European relic, now in Amsterdam) in W Australia – Abel ◊Tasman, and William Dampier. A second wave of immigration began 1788, after Capt James ◊Cook had claimed New South Wales as a British colony 1770.

colonies established The gold rushes of the 1850s and 1880s contributed to the exploration as well as to the economic and constitutional growth of Australia, as did the pioneer work of the ◊overlanders. The creation of other separate colonies followed the first settlement in New South Wales at Sydney 1788: Tasmania 1825, Western Australia 1829, South Australia 1836, Victoria 1851, and Queensland 1859. The system of transportation of convicts from Britain was never introduced in South Australia and Victoria, and ended in New South Wales 1840, Queensland 1849, Tasmania 1852, and Western Australia 1868. The convicts' contribution to the economic foundation of the country was considerable, and many would not have been convicted under a less harsh and capricious penal system than the one operating in Britain at that time.

inland exploration by Europeans Exploration of the interior began with the crossing of the barrier of the Blue Mountains 1813. Explorers include Hamilton Hume (1797–1873) and William Hovell (1786–1875) who reached Port Phillip Bay 1824 and were the first Europeans to see the Murray River; Charles Sturt; Thomas Mitchell (1792–1855), surveyor general for New South Wales 1828–55, who opened up the fertile western area of Victoria; Edward ◊Eyre, Ludwig Leichhardt, Robert O'Hara ◊Burke, William

Australia: history

30,000 –10,000 BC	Aboriginal immigration from S India, Sri Lanka, and SE Asia.	1911	Site for capital at Canberra acquired.
AD 1606	First European sightings of Australia include Dutch ship *Duyfken* off Cape York.	1914–18	World War I – Anzac troops in Europe including Gallipoli.
1770	Captain Cook claimed New South Wales for Britain.	1939–45	World War II – Anzac troops in Greece, Crete, and N Africa (El Alamein) and the Pacific (Battle of the Coral Sea).
1788	Sydney founded.	1941	Curtin's appeal to USA for help in World War II marks the end of the special relationship with Britain.
19th century	The great age of exploration: coastal surveys (Bass, Flinders), interior (Sturt, Eyre, Leichhardt, Burke and Wills, McDouall Stuart, Forrest). Also the era of the bushrangers, overlanders, and squatters, and individuals such as William Buckley and Ned Kelly.	1944	Liberal Party founded by Menzies.
		1948–75	Two million new immigrants, the majority from continental Europe.
1804	Castle Hill Rising by Irish convicts in New South Wales.	1950–53	Korean War – Australian troops formed part of the United Nations forces.
1813	Barrier of the Blue Mountains crossed.	1964–72	Vietnam War – Commonwealth troops in alliance with US forces.
1825	Tasmania seceded from New South Wales.	1966–74	Mineral boom typified by the Poseidon nickel mine.
1829	Western Australia formed.		
1836	South Australia formed.	1967	Australia becomes a member of ASEAN.
1840–68	Convict transportation ended.	1973	Britain entered the Common Market, and in the 1970s Japan became Australia's chief trading partner.
1851–61	Gold rushes (Ballarat, Bendigo).		
1851	Victoria seceded from New South Wales.	1974	Whitlam abolished 'white Australia' policy.
1855	Victoria achieved government.	1975	Constitutional crisis; Prime Minister Whitlam dismissed by the governor general.
1856	New South Wales, South Australia, Tasmania achieved government.	1975	United Nations trust territory of Papua New Guinea became independent.
1859	Queensland formed from New South Wales and achieved government.	1978	Northern Territory achieved self-government.
1860	(National) Country Party founded.	1979	Opening of uranium mines in Northern Territory.
1860s	Australian football developed.		
1890	Western Australia achieved government.	1983	Hawke convened first national economic summit.
1891	Depression gave rise to the Australian Labor Party.	1991	Paul Keating successfully challenged Hawke for the Labor Party leadership. He consequently replaced Hawke as prime minister.
1899–1900	South African War – forces offered by the individual colonies.		
1901	Creation of the Commonwealth of Australia.		

Wills (1834–1861), and John ◊Stuart. In the 1870s the last gaps were filled in by the crossings of W Australia by John Forrest, (William) Ernest Giles (1835–1897) 1875–76, and Peter Warburton (1813–1889) 1873.

economic depression and growth In the 1890s there was a halt in the rapid expansion that Australia had enjoyed, and the resulting depression led to the formation of the Australian Labor Party and an increase in trade-union activity, which has characterized Australian politics ever since. State powers waned following the creation of the Commonwealth of Australia 1901. Australia played an important role in both world wars, and after World War II it embarked on a fresh period of expansion, with new mineral finds playing a large part in economic growth. Since 1945 Australia has strengthened its ties with India and other SE Asian countries.

growth of nationalism After heading a Liberal–Country Party coalition government for 17 years, Robert Menzies resigned 1966 and was succeeded by Harold Holt, who died 1967. John Gorton became prime minister 1968 but lost a vote of confidence in the house of representatives and was succeeded by a Liberal– Country Party coalition under William McMahon 1971. At the end of 1972 the Australian Labor Party took office, led by Gough Whitlam. Under the Whitlam government, especially after Britain's entry into the European Community 1973, there was a growth of nationalism. The 1974 general election gave the

Labor Party a fresh mandate to govern despite having a reduced majority in the house of representatives.

1975 constitutional crisis The senate blocked the government's financial legislation 1975 and, with Whitlam unwilling to resign, the governor general took the unprecedented step of dismissing him and his cabinet and inviting Malcolm ◊Fraser to form a Liberal–Country Party coalition caretaker administration. The wisdom of this action was widely questioned, and eventually governor general John Kerr resigned 1977. In the 1977 general election the coalition was returned with a reduced majority that was further reduced 1980.

Hawke era In the 1983 general election the coalition was eventually defeated and the Australian Labor Party under Bob ◊Hawke again took office. Hawke called together employers and unions to a National Economic Summit to agree to a wage and price policy and to deal with unemployment. In 1984 he called a general election 15 months early and was returned with a reduced majority. Hawke placed even greater emphasis than his predecessors on links with SE Asia and imposed trading sanctions against South Africa as a means of influencing the dismantling of apartheid. In the 1987 general election, Labor marginally increased its majority in the House but did not have an overall majority in the Senate, where the balance was held by the Australian Democrats. The 1990 election was won by Labor, led by Bob Hawke, with a reduced majority in the house of representatives, for a record fourth term in office. The Australian Democrats maintained the balance of power in the senate. In Aug 1991 Hawke announced that agreement had been reached on greater cohesion of the states' economies.

Earth is here so kind that just tickle her with a hoe and she laughs with a harvest.

On *Australia*
Douglas William Jerrold (1803–1857)
A Man Made of Money 1849

Keating as prime minister In Dec 1991 Hawke's leadership of the Labor Party was successfully challenged by Paul Keating, who became the new party leader and prime minister. Keatings kickstart plan to boost a stagnant economy did not result in success, but after an expansionary budget the Labor Party won a surprising general election victory in 1993. But in elections in March 1996, the Labor Party was defeated by a Liberal-National coalition, under John Howard. Howard opposed Keating's public agenda for a referendum before 2000 on a republican future for Australia, but pledged to set up a convention to examine constitutional reforms.

Australian Aborigine any of the 500 groups of indigenous inhabitants of the continent of Australia, who migrated to this region from S Asia about 40,000 years ago. They were hunters and gatherers, living throughout the continent in small kin-based groups before European settlement. Several hundred different languages developed, the most important being Aranda (Arunta), spoken in central Australia, and Murngin, spoken in Arnhem Land. In recent years there has been a movement for the recognition of Aborigine rights and campaigning against racial discrimination in housing, education, wages, and medical facilities.

There are about 227,645 Aborigines in Australia, making up about 1.5% of Australia's population of 16 million. 12% of Australia is owned by Aborigines and many live in reserves as well as among the general population (65% of Aborigines live in cities or towns). They have an infant mortality rate four times the national average and an adult life expectancy 20 years below the average 76 years of Australians generally. Aboriginal culture has been protected by federal law since the passing of the Aboriginal and Torres Islander Heritage Protection Act in 1984.

Austria landlocked country in central Europe, bounded E by Hungary, S by Slovenia and Italy, W by Switzerland and Liechtenstein, NW by Germany, and N by the Czech and Slovak republics.

history Austria was inhabited in prehistoric times by Celtic tribes; the country south of the Danube was conquered by the Romans 14 BC and became part of the Roman Empire. After the fall of the empire in the 5th century AD, the region was occupied by Vandals, Goths, Huns, Lombards, and Avars. Having conquered the Avars 791, ◊Charlemagne established the East Mark, nucleus of the future Austrian empire. In 983 Otto II granted the Mark to the House of Babenburg, which ruled until 1246. Rudolf of Habsburg, who became king of the Romans and Holy Roman emperor 1273, seized Austria and invested his son as duke 1282. Until the empire ceased to exist 1806, most of the dukes (from 1453, archdukes) of Austria were elected Holy Roman emperor.

Turks kept at bay Austria, which acquired control of ◊Bohemia 1526, was throughout the

16th century a bulwark of resistance against the Turks, who besieged Vienna 1529 without success. The ◊Thirty Years' War (1618–48) did not touch Austria, but it weakened its rulers. A second Turkish siege of Vienna 1683 failed, and by 1697 Hungary was liberated from the ◊Ottoman Empire and incorporated in the Austrian dominion. As a result of their struggle with Louis XIV, the Habsburgs secured the Spanish Netherlands and Milan 1713. When Charles VI, last male Habsburg in the direct line, died 1740, his daughter Maria Theresa became archduchess of Austria and queen of Hungary, but the elector of Bavaria was elected emperor as Charles VII. Frederick II of Prussia seized Silesia, and the War of the ◊Austrian Succession (1740–48) followed. Charles VII died 1745, and Maria Theresa secured the election of her husband as Francis I, but she did not recover Silesia from Frederick. The archduke Francis who succeeded 1792 was also elected emperor as Francis II; sometimes opposing, sometimes allied with Napoleon, he proclaimed himself emperor of Austria 1804 as Francis I, and the name Holy Roman Empire fell out of use 1806. Under the Treaty of Vienna 1815, Francis failed to recover the Austrian Netherlands (annexed by France 1797) but received Lombardy and Venetia.

Austria-Hungary During the ◊revolutions of 1848 the grievances of mixed nationalities within the Austrian empire flared into a rebellion; revolutionaries in Vienna called for the resignation of ◊Metternich, who fled to the UK. By 1851 Austria had crushed all the revolts. As a result of the ◊Seven Weeks' War 1866 with Prussia, Austria lost Venetia to Italy. In the following year Emperor ◊Franz Joseph established the dual monarchy of Austria-Hungary. The treaty of Berlin 1878 gave Austria the administration of Bosnia-Herzegovina in the Balkans, though they remained nominally Turkish until Austria annexed them 1908. World War I was precipitated 1914 by an Austrian attack on Serbia, following the assassination of Archduke Franz Ferdinand (Franz Joseph's nephew) and his wife by a Serbian nationalist. Austria-Hungary was defeated 1918, the last Habsburg emperor overthrown, and Austria became a republic, comprising only Vienna and its immediately surrounding provinces. The Treaty of St Germain, signed 1919 by Austria and the Allies, established Austria's present boundaries. Austria was invaded by Hitler's troops 1938 and incor-porated into the German Reich (the ◊*Anschluss*).

partition and independence With the conclusion of World War II Austria returned to its 1920 constitution, with a provisional government led by Dr Karl Renner. The Allies divided both the country and Vienna into four zones, occupied by the USSR, the USA, Britain, and France. The country was occupied until independence was formally recognized 1955.

Waldheim controversy When Kurt Waldheim, former UN secretary general, became president 1986, he was diplomatically isolated by many countries because of controversy over his service in the German army during the Second World War.

Austrian Succession, War of the war 1740–48 between Austria (supported by England and Holland) and Prussia (supported by France and Spain).

1740 The Holy Roman emperor Charles VI died and the succession of his daughter Maria Theresa was disputed by a number of European powers. Frederick the Great of Prussia seized *Silesia* from Austria.

1743 At the battle of ◊*Dettingen* an army of British, Austrians, and Hanoverians under the command of George II was victorious over the French.

1745 An Austro-English army was defeated at *Fontenoy* but British naval superiority was confirmed, and there were gains in the Americas and India.

1748 The war was ended by the Treaty of Aix-la-Chapelle.

Austro-Hungarian Empire the Dual Monarchy established by the Habsburg Franz Joseph 1867 between his empire of Austria and his kingdom of Hungary (including territory that became Czechoslovakia as well as parts of Poland, the Ukraine, Romania, Yugoslavia, and Italy). It collapsed autumn 1918 with the end of World War I. Only two king-emperors ruled: Franz Joseph 1867–1916 and Charles 1916–18.

The Austro-Hungarian Empire came into being with an agreement known as the ◊Ausgleich. The two countries retained their own legal and administrative systems but shared foreign policy. In 1910 the empire had an area of 261,239 sq km/100,838 sq mi with a population of 51 million.

authoritarianism rule of a country by a dominant elite who repress opponents and the press to maintain their own wealth and power. They are frequently indifferent to activities not affecting their security, and rival power centres, such as trade unions and political parties, are often allowed to exist, although under tight control. An extreme form is ◊totalitarianism.

autocracy form of government in which one person holds absolute power. The autocrat has uncontrolled and undisputed authority. Russian government under the tsars was an autocracy extending from the mid-16th century to the early 20th century. The title *Autocratix* (a female autocrat) was assumed by Catherine II of Russia in the 18th century.

Autonomisti semiclandestine amalgam of Marxist student organizations in W Europe, linked with guerrilla groups and such acts as the kidnapping and murder of Italian former premier Aldo Moro by the Red Brigades 1978.

Avar member of a Central Asian nomadic people who in the 6th century invaded the area of Russia north of the Black Sea previously held by the Huns. They extended their dominion over the Bulgarians and Slavs in the 7th century and were finally defeated by Charlemagne 796.

Axis alliance of Nazi Germany and Fascist Italy before and during World War II. The *Rome–Berlin Axis* was formed 1936, when Italy was being threatened with sanctions because of its invasion of Ethiopia (Abyssinia). It became a full military and political alliance May 1939. A ten-year alliance between Germany, Italy, and Japan (*Rome–Berlin–Tokyo Axis*) was signed Sept 1940 and was subsequently joined by Hungary, Bulgaria, Romania, and the puppet states of Slovakia and Croatia. The Axis collapsed with the fall of Mussolini and the surrender of Italy 1943 and Germany and Japan 1945.

Axum kingdom which flourished 1st-6th centuries AD; see ◊Aksum.

ayatollah (Arabic 'sign of God') honorific title awarded to Shi'ite Muslims in Iran by popular consent, as, for example, to Ayatollah Ruhollah ◊Khomeini.

Ayesha 611–678. Third and favourite wife of the prophet Muhammad, who married her when she was nine. Her father, Abu Bakr, became ◊caliph on Muhammad's death 632. She bitterly opposed the later succession to the caliphate of Ali, who had once accused her of infidelity.

Ayub Khan Muhammad 1907–1974. Pakistani soldier and president from 1958 to 1969. He served in the Burma Campaign 1942–45, and was commander in chief of the Pakistan army 1951. In 1958 Ayub Khan assumed power after a bloodless army coup. He won the presidential elections 1960 and 1965, and established a stable economy and achieved limited land reforms. His militaristic form of government was unpopular, particularly with the Bengalis.

He resigned 1969 after widespread opposition and civil disorder, notably in Kashmir.

Azaña Manuel 1880–1940. Spanish politician and first prime minister 1931–33 of the second Spanish republic. He was last president of the republic during the Civil War 1936–39, before the establishment of a dictatorship under Franco.

Azerbaijan country in W Asia, bounded S by Iran, E by the Caspian Sea, W by Armenia and Georgia, and N by Russia.

history Azerbaijan shares a common language and culture with Turkey; however, before its conquest by tsarist Russia in the early 19th century, it was a province of Persia, and today 20 million Shi'ite Azeris live across the border in Iran. In the late 19th century, Baku became the centre of a growing oil industry. A member of the Transcaucasian Federation in 1917, Azerbaijan became an independent republic 1918, but was occupied by the Red Army two years later. The republic was secularized under Soviet rule.

growth of nationalism There was a growth in Azeri nationalism from the later 1980s, spearheaded by the Azeri Popular Front, founded in 1989, and fanned by the dispute with neighbouring Armenia over ◊Nagorno-Karabakh and Nakhichevan. This dispute, which reawakened centuries-old enmities, flared up into full civil war from Dec 1989, prompting Azeri calls for secession from the USSR. In Jan 1990 Soviet troops were sent to Baku to restore order, and a state of emergency was imposed. The Azerbaijan Communist Party (ACP), led by Ayaz Mutalibov, allied itself with the nationalist cause and rejected compromise in the Nagorno-Karabakh dispute.

backlash In the Sept 1990 supreme soviet elections the Popular Front, having been on the verge of power before the Jan 1990 crackdown, was convincingly defeated by the ACP. A new state flag was adopted in Dec 1990 and the words 'Soviet Socialist' were dropped from the republic's name. In the March 1991 USSR constitutional referendum, the Azerbaijan population voted overwhelmingly in favour of preserving the Union and the Aug 1991 anti-Gorbachev coup in Moscow was warmly welcomed by President Mutalibov, who ordered the military suppression of demonstrations organized by the Popular Front.

independence declared After the failure of the Moscow coup, Mutalibov resigned from the ACP, which was soon disbanded, and on 30 Aug 1991 independence was declared. The state of emergency, still in force in Baku, was

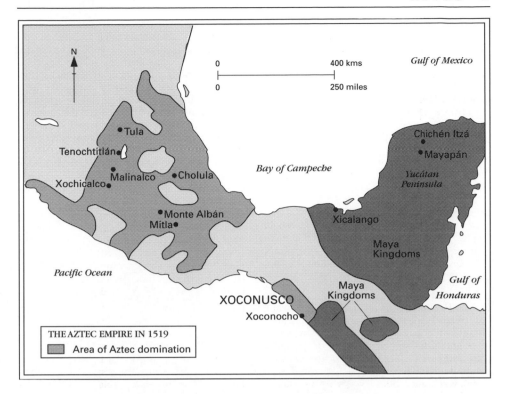

The Aztec empire in 1519 *The Aztec Empire in Central America (present-day Mexico) on the eve of the Spanish invasion 1519. The Aztecs reached Central America from the north during the 13th century, but the Aztec Empire only began growing during the hundred years or so before the Spanish invasion. At its peak it contained some five or six million people ruled either directly or as tribute-paying states. This populous empire was nonetheless conquered by a force of fewer than 600 men under Cortès.*

lifted. On 8 Sept 1991 Mutalibov was directly elected state president as the sole candidate in a contest boycotted by the opposition. In Dec 1991 Azerbaijan joined the new ◊Commonwealth of Independent States, which superseded the Soviet Union. In Jan 1992 Azerbaijan was admitted into the ◊Conference on Security and Cooperation in Europe (CSCE) and in March into the United Nations (UN). Azeri diplomatic and commercial links with Turkey improved and in Feb 1992 the republic joined the Economic Cooperation Organization (ECO), founded by Iran, Pakistan, and Turkey 1975, which aimed to reduce customs tariffs and eventually form a customs union. After independence, the state began to form its own armed forces. In Feb 1992 Azerbaijan switched from the Cyrillic alphabet, imposed by Moscow in 1937, to the Latin alphabet.

unstable leadership The Mutalibov administration and the supreme soviet remained under the domination of former members of the ACP, which was superseded by a new Republican Democratic Party, and much of the old system remained in place. Following Azeri defeats in Nagorno-Karabakh in March 1992, Mutalibov was forced to resign and various factions competed for power. In June 1992, Albufaz Elchibey, leader of the Popular Front, was elected president, pledging withdrawal from the CIS and a renewed campaign against Armenia over Nagorno-Karabakh. By Aug 1992 Azerbaijan had reclaimed much of its lost territory in the disputed enclave.

Azilian archaeological period following the close of the Old Stone (Palaeolithic) Age and regarded as one of the cultures of the Mesolithic Age. It was first recognized at Le Mas d'Azil, a village in Ariège, France.

Azincourt see ◊Agincourt, Battle of.

Aztec member of an ancient Mexican civilization that migrated south into the valley of

Mexico in the 12th century, and in 1325 began reclaiming lake marshland to build their capital, Tenochtitlán, on the site of present-day Mexico City. Under Montezuma I (reigned from 1440), the Aztecs created a tribute empire in central Mexico. After the conquistador Cortès landed 1519, Montezuma II (reigned from 1502) was killed and Tenochtitlán subsequently destroyed. Nahuatl is the Aztec language; it belongs to the Uto-Aztecan family of languages.

The Aztecs are known for their architecture, jewellery (gold, jade, and turquoise), sculpture, and textiles. Their form of writing combined hieroglyphs and pictographs, and they used a complex calendar that combined a sacred period of 260 days with the solar year of 365 days. Religious ritual included human sacrifice on a large scale, the priests tearing the heart from the living victim or flaying people alive. War captives were obtained for this purpose, but their own people were also used. The Aztec state was a theocracy with farmers, artisans, and merchants taxed to support the priestly aristocracy. Tribute was collected from a federation of conquered nearby states.

B

Baader-Meinhof gang popular name for the West German left-wing guerrilla group the *Rote Armee Fraktion*/Red Army Faction, active from 1968 against what it perceived as US imperialism. The three main founding members were Andreas Baader (1943–1977), Gudrun Ensslin, and Ulrike Meinhof (1934–1976).

Ba'ath Party ruling political party in Iraq and Syria. Despite public support of pan-Arab unity and its foundations 1943 as a party of Arab nationalism, its ideology has been so vague that it has fostered widely differing (and often opposing) parties in Syria and Iraq.

The Ba'ath party was founded in Damascus, Syria 1943 by three French-educated Syrian intellectuals, in opposition to both French rule and the older generation of Syrian Arab nationalists. Its constitution is an uncertain blend of neo-Marxist socialism and nationalism. The movement split into several factions after 1958 and again in 1966. In Iraq, the Ba'ath party took control briefly in 1963 and again from 1968 although its support here has always been limited. The rise of Saddam Hussein was not so much due to the popularity of the Ba'ath party itself as the exploitation and manipulation of an existing ideology by Saddam Hussein for his own purposes.

Babangida Ibrahim 1941– . Nigerian politician and soldier, president 1985-93. He became head of the Nigerian army 1983 and in 1985 led a coup against President Buhari, becoming president himself. In 1992 he promised a return to civilian rule but resigned 1993. His commitment to democracy was increasingly doubtful.

Babangida was an instructor in the Nigerian Defence Academy and by 1983 had reached the rank of major general. In 1983, after taking part in the overthrow of President Shehu Shagari, he was made army commander in chief.

Because of public pressure 1989, he allowed the formation of competing political parties, promising a return to a democratic civilian government 1992. Attempting to end corruption, he banned anyone who had ever held elective office from being a candidate in the new civilian government. Applications for recognition from former political parties were also rejected. Having twice blocked release of presidential election results (once in 1992 and once in 1993) after allegations of fraud, Babangida stepped down in 1993, nominating Ernest Shonekan as his successor.

Babel Hebrew name for the city of ◊Babylon.

Babeuf François-Noël 1760–1797. French revolutionary journalist, a pioneer of practical socialism. In 1794 he founded a newspaper in Paris, later known as the *Tribune of the People*, in which he demanded the equality of all people. He was guillotined for conspiring against the ruling Directory during the French Revolution.

Babington Anthony 1561–1586. English traitor who hatched a plot to assassinate Elizabeth I and replace her with ◊Mary *Queen of Scots*; its discovery led to Mary's execution and his own.

Babism religious movement founded during the 1840s by Mirza Ali Mohammad ('the Bab'). An offshoot of Islam, its main difference lies in the belief that Muhammad was not the last of the prophets. The movement split into two groups after the death of the Bab; Baha'ullah, the leader of one of these groups, founded the ◊Baha'i faith.

Babi Yar ravine near Kiev, Ukraine, where more than 100,000 people (80,000 Jews; the others were Poles, Russians, and Ukrainians) were killed by the Nazis 1941. The site was ignored until the Soviet poet Yevtushenko wrote a poem called 'Babi Yar' 1961 in protest at plans for a sports centre on the site.

Babur (Arabic 'lion') title given to ◊Zahir ud-Din Muhammad, founder of the Mogul Empire in N India.

Baby Doc nickname of Jean-Claude ◊Duvalier, right-wing president of Haiti 1971–86.

Babylon capital of ancient Babylonia, on the bank of the lower Euphrates River. The site is now in Iraq, 88 km/55 mi S of Baghdad and 8 km/5 mi N of Hilla, which is built chiefly of bricks from the ruins of Babylon. The *Hanging Gardens of Babylon*, one of the ◊Seven Wonders of the World, were probably erected on a vaulted stone base, the only stone construction in the mud-brick city. They formed a series of terraces, irrigated by a hydraulic system.

Babylonian captivity exile of Jewish deportees to Babylon after Nebuchadnezzar II's capture of Jerusalem in 586 BC. According to tradition, the captivity lasted 70 years, but Cyrus of Persia, who conquered Babylon, actually allowed them to go home in 536 BC. By analogy, the name has also been applied to the papal exile to Avignon, France, 1309–77.

By the waters of Babylon we sat down and wept: when we remembered thee, O Sion.

On the *Babylonian captivity* Psalms 147:2,
The Book of Common Prayer

Bacon Nathaniel 1647–1676. American colonial leader and wealthy plantation owner. An advocate of social reform in Virginia and an opponent of Governor William ◊Berkeley, he gained wide public support and was proclaimed 'General of Virginia'. In 1676 he organized Bacon's Rebellion, forcing Berkeley to flee from the capital at Jamestown. Bacon's sudden death ended the uprising but Berkeley was removed from power for his brutal treatment of the rebels.

Baden former state of SW Germany, which had Karlsruhe as its capital. Baden was captured from the Romans in 282 by the Alemanni; later it became a margravate and in 1806, a grand duchy. A state of the German empire 1871–1918, then a republic, and under Hitler a *Gau* (province), it was divided between the *Länder* of Württemberg-Baden and Baden in 1945 and in 1952 made part of Baden-Württemberg.

Baden-Powell Robert Stephenson Smyth, 1st Baron Baden-Powell 1857–1941. British general, founder of the Scout Association. He fought in defence of Mafeking (now Mafikeng) during the Second South African War. After 1907 he devoted his time to developing the Scout movement, which rapidly spread throughout the world.

Badoglio Pietro 1871–1956. Italian soldier and Fascist politician. A veteran of campaigns against the peoples of Tripoli and Cyrenaica, in 1935 he became commander in chief in Ethiopia, adopting ruthless measures to break patriot resistance. He was created viceroy of Ethiopia and duke of Addis Ababa in 1936. He resigned during the disastrous campaign into Greece 1940 and succeeded Mussolini as prime minister of Italy from July 1943 to June 1944, negotiating the armistice with the Allies.

Baghdad Pact military treaty of 1955 concluded by the UK, Iran, Iraq, Pakistan, and Turkey, with the USA cooperating; it was replaced by the ◊Central Treaty Organization (CENTO) when Iraq withdrew in 1958.

Bahadur Shah II 1775–1862. Last of the Mogul emperors of India. He reigned, though in name only, as king of Delhi 1837–57, when he was hailed by the mutineers of the ◊Indian Mutiny as an independent emperor at Delhi. After the rebellion he was exiled to Burma (now Myanmar) with his family.

Bahamas country comprising a group of about 700 islands and about 2,400 uninhabited islets and cays in the Caribbean, 80 km/50 mi from the SE coast of Florida. They extend for about 1,223 km/760 mi from NW to SE, but only 22 of the islands are inhabited.

history The Bahamas were reached 1492 by Christopher Columbus, who first landed at San Salvador. The British established a permanent settlement 1656, and in 1670 the Bahamas were given to the duke of Albemarle as a proprietary colony. The islands were a pirate area in the early 18th century and reverted to the British crown 1717 (although they were disputed by the Carolina colony until 1787). During the American War of Independence, Spanish forces captured the Bahamas 1782, but the islands were given back to Britain the following year.

independence The Bahamas achieved internal self-government in 1964, and the first elections for the national assembly on a full voting register were held 1967. The Progressive Liberal Party (PLP), drawing its support mainly from voters of African origin, won the same number of seats as the European-dominated United Bahamian Party (UBP). Lynden Pindling (1930–   ) became prime minister with support from outside his party. In the 1968 elections the PLP scored a resounding victory, repeated 1972, enabling Pindling to lead his country to full independence within the Commonwealth 1973.

Prime Minister Pindling The 1977 elections resulted in an increased majority for the PLP. The main contestants in the 1982 elections were the Free National Movement (FNM, consisting of a number of factions that had split and reunited) and the PLP. Despite allegations of government complicity in drug trafficking, the PLP was again successful, and Pindling was unanimously endorsed as leader at a party convention in 1984. The 1987 general election was won by the PLP, led by Pindling, but with a reduced majority. His time in office came to an end in Aug 1992, when the FNM wom 33 of the assembly's 49 seats and its leader Hubert Ingraham became prime minister.

Baha'ullah title of Mirza Hosein Ali 1817–1892. Persian founder of the Baha'i religion. Baha'ullah, 'God's Glory', proclaimed himself as the prophet the Bab had foretold.

Bahrain country comprising a group of islands in the Persian Gulf, between Saudi Arabia and Iran.

history Traditionally an Arab monarchy, Bahrain was under Portuguese rule during the 16th century and from 1602 was dominated by Persia (now Iran). Bahrain became a sheikdom 1783 under the control of the Khalifa dynasty. British assistance was sought to preserve the country's independence against claims of sovereignty made by Persia and the Ottoman Empire. It became a British protectorate 1861, with government shared between the ruling sheik and a British adviser. Iran (Persia) claimed sovereignty 1928 but accepted a United Nations report 1970 showing that the inhabitants of Bahrain preferred independence.

independence achieved Britain announced the withdrawal of its forces 1968, and Bahrain joined two other territories under British protection, Qatar and the Trucial States (now the ◊United Arab Emirates), to form the Federation of Arab Emirates. Qatar and the Trucial States left the federation 1971, and Bahrain became an independent state. A new constitution 1973 provided for an elected national assembly, but two years later the prime minister, Sheik al-Khalifa (1933-), complained of obstruction by the assembly, which was then dissolved.

absolute emirate Since 1975 the emir and his family have ruled with virtually absolute power. Bahrain has become a focal point on the Gulf, being the site of the Gulf University (1986) and an international airport, the centre of Gulf aviation. A causeway linking Bahrain with mainland Saudi Arabia was constructed 1986 (at 25 km/15.5 mi it is the longest in the world).

Since the Iranian revolution of 1979, relations between the two countries have been uncertain, with fears of Iranian attempts to disturb Bahrain's stability. During the 1991 Gulf War, Bahrain opposed Iraq's invasion of Kuwait.

bailiff officer of the court whose job, usually in the county courts, is to serve notices and enforce the court's orders involving seizure of the goods of a debtor.

Term originating in Normandy for a steward of an estate. It retained this meaning in England throughout the Middle Ages, and could also denote a sheriff's assistant. In France, the royal *bailli* or *bayle* was appointed to administer a large area of territory, the *baillage*, and was a leading local official.

Baker James (Addison), III 1930– . US Republican politician. Under President Reagan, he was White House chief of staff 1981–85 and Treasury secretary 1985-88. After managing George Bush's successful presidential campaign 1988, Baker was appointed secretary of state 1989 and played a prominent role in the 1990-91 Gulf crisis, and the subsequent search for a lasting Middle East peace settlement. In 1992 he left the State Department to become White House chief of staff and to oversee President Bush's unsuccessful re-election campaign.

bakufu (Japanese 'tent government') in Japanese history, the government of the ◊shogun. Originally meaning the headquarters of an army in the field, the term was adopted by Minamoto Yoritomo for his administration in Kamakura from 1185, and became a synonym for shogunate.

Bakunin Mikhail 1814–1876. Russian anarchist, active in Europe. In 1848 he was expelled from France as a revolutionary agitator. In Switzerland in the 1860s he became recognized as the leader of the anarchist movement. In 1869 he joined the First International (a coordinating socialist body) but, after stormy conflicts with Karl Marx, was expelled 1872.

To exploit and to govern mean the same thing... Exploitation and government are two inseparable expressions of what is called politics.

Mikhail Bakunin, *The Knouto-Germanic Empire and the Soviet Revolution*

Balaclava, Battle of in the Crimean War, an engagement on 25 Oct 1854 near a town in Ukraine, 10 km/6 mi SE of Sevastopol. It was the scene of the ill-timed ◊*Charge of the Light Brigade* of British cavalry against the Russian entrenched artillery. Of the 673 soldiers who took part, there were 272 casualties. *Balaclava helmets* were knitted hoods worn here by soldiers in the bitter weather.

balance of power in politics, the theory that the best way of ensuring international order is to have power so distributed among states that no single state is able to achieve a dominant position. The term, which may also refer more simply to the actual distribution of power, is one of the most enduring concepts in international relations. Since the development of nuclear weapons, it has been asserted that the balance of power has been replaced by a *balance of terror*.

Balboa Vasco Núñez de 1475–1519. Spanish ◊conquistador. He founded a settlement at Darien (now Panama) 1511 and crossed the Isthmus in search of gold, reaching the Pacific Ocean (which he called the South Sea) on 25 Sept 1513, after a 25-day expedition. He was made admiral of the Pacific and governor of Panama but was removed by Spanish court intrigue, imprisoned, and executed.

Baldwin Stanley, 1st Earl Baldwin of Bewdley 1867–1947. British Conservative politician, prime minister 1923–24, 1924–29, and 1935–37; he weathered the general strike 1926, secured complete adult suffrage 1928, and handled the ◊abdication crisis of Edward VIII 1936, but failed to prepare Britain for World War II.

Born in Bewdley, Worcestershire, the son of an iron and steel magnate, in 1908 he was elected Unionist member of Parliament for Bewdley, and in 1916 he became parliamentary private secretary to Bonar Law. He was financial secretary to the Treasury 1917–21, and then appointed to the presidency of the Board of Trade. In 1919 he gave the Treasury £50,000 of War Loan for cancellation, representing about 20% of his fortune. He was a leader in the disruption of the Lloyd George coalition 1922, and, as chancellor under Bonar Law, achieved a settlement of war debts with the USA.

As prime minister 1923–24 and again 1924–29, Baldwin passed the Trades Disputes Act of 1927 after the general strike, granted widows' and orphans' pensions, and complete adult suffrage 1928. He joined the national government of Ramsay MacDonald 1931 as Lord President of the Council. He handled the abdication crisis during his third premiership 1935–37, but was later much criticized for his failures to resist popular desire for an accommodation with the dictators Hitler and Mussolini, and to rearm more effectively.

Baldwin five kings of the Latin kingdom of Jerusalem, including:

Baldwin I 1058–1118. King of Jerusalem from 1100. A French nobleman, he joined his brother ◊Godfrey de Bouillon on the First Crusade in 1096 and established the kingdom of Jerusalem in 1100. It was destroyed by Islamic conquest in 1187.

Baldwin II Baldwin du Bourg died 1131. King of the Latin kingdom of Jerusalem from 1118.

During his reign Tyre became the seat of a Latin archbishop.

Balewa alternative title of Nigerian politician ◊Tafawa Balewa.

Balfour Arthur James, 1st Earl of Balfour 1848–1930. British Conservative politician, prime minister 1902–05 and foreign secretary 1916-19, when he issued the Balfour Declaration 1917 and was involved in peace negotiations after World War I, signing the Treaty of Versailles.

Son of a Scottish landowner, Balfour was elected a Conservative member of Parliament in 1874. In Lord Salisbury's ministry he was secretary for Ireland 1887, and for his ruthless vigour was called 'Bloody Balfour' by Irish nationalists. In 1891 and again in 1895 he became First Lord of the Treasury and leader of the Commons, and in 1902 he succeeded Salisbury as prime minister. His cabinet was divided over Joseph Chamberlain's tariff-reform proposals, and in the 1905 elections suffered a crushing defeat.

Balfour retired from the party leadership in 1911. In 1915 he joined the Asquith coalition as First Lord of the Admiralty. As foreign secretary 1916–19 he issued the Balfour Declaration in favour of a national home in Palestine for the Jews. He was Lord President of the Council 1919–22 and 1925–29. Created 1st Earl of Balfour 1922. He also wrote books on philosophy.

It is unfortunate, considering that enthusiasm moves the world, that so few enthusiasts can be trusted to speak the truth.

Arthur James Balfour
letter to Mrs Drew, May 1891

Balfour Declaration letter, dated 2 Nov 1917, from the British foreign secretary A J Balfour to Lord Rothschild (chair, British Zionist Federation) stating: 'HM government view with favour the establishment in Palestine of a national home for the Jewish people.' It helped form the basis for the foundation of Israel 1948.

Baliol John de *c.* 1249–1314. King of Scotland 1292–96. As an heir to the Scottish throne on the death of Margaret, the Maid of Norway, his cause was supported by the English king, Edward I, against 12 other claimants. Having paid homage to Edward, Baliol was proclaimed king but soon rebelled and gave up the kingdom when English forces attacked Scotland.

Balkans (Turkish 'mountains') peninsula of SE Europe, stretching into the Mediterranean Sea between the Adriatic and Aegean seas, comprising Albania, Bosnia-Herzegovina, Bulgaria, Croatia, Greece, Romania, Slovenia, Turkey-in-Europe, and Yugoslavia.

The great ethnic diversity resulting from successive waves of invasion has made the Balkans a byword for political dissension. The Balkans' economy developed comparatively slowly until after World War II, largely because of the predominantly mountainous terrain, apart from the plains of the Save-Danube basin in the N. Political differences have remained strong, for example, the confrontation of Greece and Turkey over Cyprus, and the civil war in Yugoslavia in the early 1990s. More recently, ethnic interfighting has dominated the peninsula as first Slovenia and Croatia, and then Bosnia-Herzegovina, have battled to win independence from the Serb-dominated Yugoslav federation. Despite international recognition being awarded to all three republics early 1992, fierce fighting between Serb, Croat, and Muslim factions in Bosnia-Herzegovina continued. To '*Balkanize*' is to divide into small warring states.

Balkan Wars two wars 1912–13 and 1913 (preceding World War I) which resulted in the expulsion by the Balkan states of Ottoman Turkey from Europe, except for a small area around Istanbul.

The *First Balkan War*, 1912, of Bulgaria, ◊Serbia, Greece, and Montenegro against Turkey, forced the Turks to ask for an armistice, but the London-held peace negotiations broke down when the Turks, while agreeing to surrender all Turkey-in-Europe W of the city of Edirne (formerly Adrianople), refused to give up the city itself. In Feb 1913 hostilities were resumed. Edirne fell on 26 March and on 30 May, by the Treaty of London, Turkey retained in Europe only a small piece of E Thrace and the Gallipoli peninsula.

The Balkans about 1400 During the 14th and 15th centuries the Balkan states fell under Ottoman control. Wallachia became part of the Ottoman Empire 1394; in 1396 Bulgaria was absorbed and Serbia became an Ottoman vassal – subsequently it too was incorporated into the empire 1459; Bosnia was conquered by the Ottomans 1463, and Herzegovina fell 1483. Constantinople, encircled by Ottoman territory, fell 1453.

The *Second Balkan War*, June–July 1913, took place when the victors fought over acquisitions in Macedonia, from most of which Bulgaria was excluded. Bulgaria attacked Greece and Serbia, which were joined by Romania. Bulgaria was defeated, and Turkey retained Thrace.

Ball John died 1381. English priest, one of the leaders of the ◊Peasants' Revolt 1381, known as 'the mad priest of Kent'. A follower of John Wycliffe and a believer in social equality, he was imprisoned for disagreeing with the archbishop of Canterbury. During the revolt he was released from prison, and when in Blackheath, London, incited people against the ruling clases by preaching from the text 'When Adam delved and Eve span, who was then the gentleman?' When the revolt collapsed he escaped but was captured near Coventry and executed.

Balmaceda José Manuel 1840–1891. Chilean president 1886–91. He inaugurated a vast reform programme including education, railways, communications, and public utilities, and invested revenue from Chile's nitrate fields in public works. The volatility of this key market led him to denounce foreign interests in Chile.

Balmaceda entered public life 1864 as secretary to former president Manuel ◊Montt. As minister of the interior after 1882 he sponsored a number of liberal reforms, including civil marriage. From 1888 he faced battles with congress over its demands for the removal of ministers, which eventually led to civil war. Forced out of the presidency by political opponents, he committed suicide in the Argentine embassy.

Baltic States collective name for the states of ◊Estonia, ◊Latvia, and ◊Lithuania, former constituent republics of the USSR (from 1940). They regained independence Sept 1991.

Banda Hastings Kamuzu 1902–1997. Malawi politician, president 1966-94. He led his country's independence movement and was prime minister of Nyasaland (the former name of Malawi) from 1964. Named president of Malawi for life in 1971, his rule was authoritarian. Bowing to opposition pressures for a pluralist system, he stood in free presidential elections 1994, but was defeated by Bakili Muluzi.

Bandaranaike Sirimavo (born Ratwatte) 1916 – . Sri Lankan politician who succeeded her husband Solomon Bandaranaike to become the world's first female prime minister, 1960–65 and 1970–77, but was expelled from parliament 1980 for abuse of her powers while in office.

Bandaranaike Solomon West Ridgeway Dias 1899–1959. Sri Lankan nationalist politician.

In 1952 he founded the Sri Lanka Freedom party and in 1956 became prime minister, pledged to a socialist programme and a neutral foreign policy. He failed to satisfy extremists and was assassinated by a Buddhist monk.

Bandung Conference first conference 1955 of the Afro-Asian nations, proclaiming anticolonialism and neutrality between East and West.

Bangladesh country in southern Asia, bounded N, W, and E by India, SE by Myanmar, and S by the Bay of Bengal.

history For history before 1947 see ◊India; for history 1947–71 see ◊Pakistan. Present-day Bangladesh formerly comprised East Bengal province and the Sylhet district of Assam in British India. Predominantly Muslim, it was formed into the eastern province of Pakistan when India was partitioned 1947. Substantially different in culture, language, and geography from the western provinces of Pakistan 1,600 km/1,000 mi away, and with a larger population, it resented the political and military dominance exerted by West Pakistan during the 1950s and 1960s. A movement for political autonomy grew after 1954, under the Awami League headed by Sheik Mujibur ◊Rahman. This gained strength as a result of West Pakistan's indifference 1970, when flooding killed 500,000 in East Pakistan.

republic proclaimed In Pakistan's first general elections, in 1970, the Awami League gained an overwhelming victory in East Pakistan and an overall majority in the all-Pakistan National Assembly. Talks on redrawing the constitution broke down, leading to East Pakistan's secession and the establishment of a Bangladesh ('Bengal nation') government in exile in Calcutta, India, 1971. Civil war resulted in the flight of 10 million East Pakistani refugees to India, administrative breakdown, famine, and cholera. The West Pakistani forces in East Pakistan surrendered 1971 after India intervened on the secessionists' side. A republic of Bangladesh was proclaimed and rapidly gained international recognition 1972.

first leader assassinated Sheik Mujibur Rahman became prime minister 1972 under a secular, parliamentary constitution. He introduced a socialist economic programme of nationalization but became intolerant of opposition, establishing a one-party presidential system Jan 1975. Rahman, his wife, and close relatives were assassinated in a military coup Aug 1975.

martial law under Zia Maj-Gen Zia ur-Rahman (1936–1981) became chief martial-law administrator 1976. President from 1977, he adopted an Islamic constitution and, after his Bangladesh Nationalist Party (BNP) won a parliamentary majority, martial law and the state of emergency were lifted 1979. The administration was undermined, however, by charges of corruption and by a guerrilla movement in the Chittagong Hill Tracts 1980, and on 30 May 1981 Zia was assassinated.

coup led by Ershad With disorder increasing, the civilian administration was overthrown March 1982 by by Lt-Gen Mohammad Hussain Ershad. Martial law was reimposed and political activity banned. Under Ershad the economy improved but a broad opposition coalition, the Movement for the Restoration of Democracy, developed.

contentious elections In parliamentary elections held in May 1986, Ershad's Jatiya Dal party gained a two-thirds majority after a substantial opposition boycott. Ershad was re-elected president in a direct election Oct 1986, and martial law was lifted Nov 1986.

opposition to government During 1987 the Awami League, led by Sheika Hasina Wazed (the daughter of Sheik Mujibur Rahman), and the BNP, led by Begum Khaleda Zia (the widow of Maj-Gen Zia ur-Rahman), stepped up their campaign against the Ershad government, demanding the president's resignation and free elections. In the wake of a wave of violent strikes and demonstrations, Ershad proclaimed a state of emergency Nov 1987. In fresh elections March 1988, as a result of further ballot-rigging and an opposition boycott, the ruling Jatiya Dal gained a sweeping victory. The state of emergency was lifted April 1988, and a bill was passed by parliament June 1988 making Islam the state religion.

Ershad resigns On 4 Dec 1990, after a protracted campaign for the government's removal, Ershad resigned and the state of emergency was lifted, parliament dissolved, and Shahabuddin Ahmad, the country's chief justice, became interim executive president. Police raids on Ershad's residence revealed large-scale corruption.

free elections When multiparty elections were held Feb 1991, the BNP emerged as the dominant force, capturing 140 of the 300 seats. Begum Khaleda Zia leader of the BNP, formed a coalition government, becoming the first woman prime minister of Bangladesh.

parliamentary government restored In late July 1991, the new government, rocked by a cyclone disaster, introduced a deregulationary New Industrial Policy to boost private enterprise and encourage foreign investment. A nationwide referendum Sept 1991 restored a parliamentary system of government, and in the same month by-elections secured an absolute majority in parliament for the BNP. In Oct 1991 parliament elected its speaker Abdur Rahman Biswas to succeed Shahabuddin Ahmad as state president.

foreign relations Bangladesh has remained a member of the Commonwealth since 1972. It has been heavily dependent on foreign economic aid but has pursued a broader policy of the ◊nonaligned movement. Relations with India have deteriorated since 1975 as a result of disputes over the sharing of Ganges water and the annual influx of 200,000 Bangladeshi refugees in Assam and West Bengal, which has prompted India to threaten to construct a frontier fence. In Jan 1992 Bangladesh became a refuge for around 60,000 Muslims fleeing military crackdowns in Myanmar.

Bannockburn, Battle of battle on 24 June 1314 in which ◊Robert I of Scotland (known as Robert the Bruce) defeated the English under Edward II, who had come to relieve the besieged Stirling Castle. Named after the town of Bannockburn, S of Stirling.

Bantustan or *homeland* name until 1978 for a ◊Black National State in the Republic of South Africa.

Baptist member of any of several Protestant and evangelical Christian sects that practise baptism by immersion only upon profession of faith. Baptists seek their authority in the Bible. They originated among English Dissenters who took refuge in the Netherlands in the early 17th century, and spread by emigration and, later, missionary activity. Of the world total of approximately 31 million, some 26.5 million are in the USA and 265,000 in the UK.

Formed 1792 in Britain, the Baptist Missionary Society pioneered the 19th-century missionary movement that spread the Baptist creed through Europe and to British colonies. The first Baptist church in America was organized in Rhode Island 1639. Baptism grew rapidly during the Great Awakening religious revival of the 18th century. After the American Revolution, Baptism spread into the South and among blacks, both slave and free.

Barbados island country in the Caribbean, one of the Lesser Antilles. It is about 483 km/300 mi N of Venezuela.

history Originally inhabited by Arawak Indians, who were wiped out soon after the arrival of the first Europeans, Barbados became a British colony 1627 and remained so until independence 1966. Universal adult suffrage was introduced 1951, and the Barbados Labour Party (BLP) won the first general election. Ministerial government was established 1954, and BLP leader Grantley Adams became the first prime minister. A group broke away from the BLP 1955 and formed the Democratic Labour Party (DLP). Six years later full internal self-government was achieved, and in the 1961 general election the DLP was victorious under its leader Errol Barrow.

independence When Barbados attained full independence 1966, Barrow became its first prime minister. The DLP was re-elected 1971, but in the 1976 general election the BLP – led now by Grantley Adams's son Tom – ended Barrow's 15-year rule.

foreign relations Both parties were committed to maintaining free enterprise and alignment with the USA, although the DLP government established diplomatic relations with Cuba 1972 and the BLP administration supported the US invasion of Grenada 1983.

end of two-party system The BLP was reelected 1981. After Adam's sudden death 1985, he was succeeded by his deputy Benard St John. The DLP was returned to power 1986 under Barrow, who was succeeded by Erskine Lloyd Sandiford 1987. The DLP was re-elected 1991, but the BLP returned to office 1994. Its leader, Owen Arthur, became prime minister.

Barbarossa nickname 'red beard' given to the Holy Roman emperor ◊Frederick I, and also to two brothers, Horuk and Khair-ed-Din, who were Barbary pirates. Horuk was killed by the Spaniards 1518; Khair-ed-Din took Tunis 1534 and died in Constantinople 1546.

Barbarossa, operation German code name for the plans to invade the USSR in 1941 during World War II.

Barbary Coast North African coast of the Mediterranean Sea (named after the ◊Berbers) from which pirates operated against US and European shipping (taking hostages for ransom) from the 16th up to the 19th century.

Barbary wars wars between the Barbary states of N Africa (Tripoli, Morocco, Algiers, and Tunis) and the USA after a dispute over protection money 1801–15. President Thomas Jefferson refused to pay more 'tribute money' in return for protection of merchant shipping from pirates in the Mediterranean. US warships blockaded Tripoli and intermittent warfare continued until the Sultan of Tripoli agreed to abandon the 'tribute' in exchange for a ransom for US prisoners 1805. A further

campaign in 1815 persuaded the other Barbary states to give up the tribute.

Barbie Klaus 1913–1991. German Nazi, a member of the ◊SS from 1936. During World War II he was involved in the deportation of Jews from the occupied Netherlands 1940–42 and in tracking down Jews and Resistance workers in France 1942–45.

His work as SS commander, based in Lyon, included the rounding-up of Jewish children from an orphanage at Izieu and the torture of the Resistance leader Jean Moulin. His ruthlessness during this time earned him the epithet 'Butcher of Lyon'. Having escaped capture 1945, Barbie was employed by the US intelligence services in Germany before moving to Bolivia 1951. Expelled from there in 1983, he was returned to France, where he was tried by a court in Lyon and convicted of crimes against humanity 1987. He died in prison.

Barcelona capital and port of Catalonia, NE Spain. As the chief centre of anarchism and Catalonian nationalism, it was prominent in the overthrow of the monarchy 1931 and was the last city of the republic to surrender to Franco 1939.

Founded in the 3rd century BC, Barcelona was ruled independently by the Counts of Barcelona from the 9th century, becoming a commercial centre for Aragon and Catalonia in the 13th–14th centuries and one of the leading ports of the Mediterranean. The city was devastated in the Catalonian Revolt 1652 and again during the War of the Spanish Succession 1714. At the forefront of the fight for regional autonomy during the Spanish Civil War, it suffered as a result of insurrections 1835, 1856, and 1909. It was held by the Republicans 1936–39.

Barebones Parliament English assembly called by Oliver ◊Cromwell to replace the 'Rump Parliament' July 1653. It consisted of 140 members nominated by the army and derived its name from one of its members, Praise-God Barbon (*c.* 1596–1679). Although they attempted to pass sensible legislation (civil marriage; registration of births, deaths, and marriages; custody of lunatics), its members' attempts to abolish tithes, patronage, and the court of chancery, and to codify the law, led to the resignation of the moderates and its dissolution Dec 1653.

Barikot garrison town in Konar province, E Afghanistan, near the Pakistan frontier. Besieged by Mujaheddin rebels 1985, the relief of Barikot by Soviet and Afghan troops was one of the largest military engagements of the Afghan war during Soviet occupation.

Barnet, Battle of in the English Wars of the ◊Roses, the defeat of Lancaster by York on 14 April 1471 in Barnet (now in NW London).

baron (Old High German *baro* 'freeman') any member of the higher nobility, a direct vassal (feudal servant) of the king, not bearing other titles such as duke or count. The term originally meant the vassal of a lord, but acquired its present meaning in the 12th century.

baronage collective title for all the landed nobility of medieval England, including earls and other important tenants-in-chief as well as the barons.

Barons' Wars civil wars in England:

1215–17 between King John and his barons, over his failure to honour Magna Carta.

1264–67 between Henry III (and the future Edward I) and his barons (led by Simon de Montfort).

1264 14 May *Battle of Lewes* at which Henry III was defeated and captured.

1265 4 Aug Simon de Montfort was defeated by Edward I at Evesham and killed.

Barotseland former kingdom in Western Province of ◊Zambia.

Barras Paul François Jean Nicolas, Count 1755 –1829. French revolutionary. He was elected to the National Convention 1792 and helped to overthrow Robespierre 1794. In 1795 he became a member of the ruling Directory (see ◊French Revolution). In 1796 he brought about the marriage of his former mistress, Joséphine de Beauharnais, with Napoleon and assumed dictatorial powers. After Napoleon's coup d'état 19 Nov 1799, Barras fell into disgrace.

Barrow Clyde 1900–1934. US criminal; see ◊Bonnie and Clyde.

Bartholomew, Massacre of St see ◊St Bartholomew, Massacre of.

Barton Clara 1821–1912. US health worker, founder of the American Red Cross 1881 and its president until 1904. A volunteer nurse, she tended the casualties of the American Civil War 1861–65 and in 1864 General Benjamin Butler named her superintendent of nurses for his forces.

Barton Edmund 1849–1920. Australian politician. He was leader of the federation movement from 1896 and first prime minister of Australia 1901–03.

Basil II *c.* 958–1025. Byzantine emperor from 976. His achievement as emperor was to contain, and later decisively defeat, the Bulgarians,

earning for himself the title 'Bulgar-Slayer' after a victory 1014. After the battle he blinded almost all 15,000 of the defeated, leaving only a few men with one eye to lead their fellows home. The Byzantine empire had reached its largest extent at the time of his death.

Basque member of a people inhabiting the Basque Country of central N Spain and the extreme SW of France. The Basques are a pre-Indo-European people who largely maintained their independence until the 19th century. During the Spanish Civil War 1936–39, they were on the republican side defeated by Franco. Their language (*Euskara*) is unrelated to any other language. The Basque separatist movement ETA (*Euskadi ta Askatasuna*, 'Basque Nation and Liberty') and the French organization Iparretarrak ('ETA fighters from the North Side') have engaged in guerrilla activity from 1968 in an attempt to secure a united Basque state.

bastard feudalism late medieval development of ◊feudalism in which grants of land were replaced by money as rewards for service. Conditions of service were specified in a contract, or indenture, between lord and retainer. The system allowed large numbers of men to be raised quickly for wars or private feuds.

Bastille castle of St Antoine, built about 1370 as part of the fortifications of Paris. It was made a state prison by Cardinal ◊Richelieu and was stormed by the mob that set the French Revolution in motion 14 July 1789. Only seven prisoners were found in the castle when it was stormed; the governor and most of the garrison were killed, and the Bastille was razed.

Bataan peninsula in Luzon, the Philippines, which was defended against the Japanese in World War II by US and Filipino troops under General MacArthur 1 Jan–9 April 1942. MacArthur was evacuated, but some 67,000 Allied prisoners died on the *Bataan Death March* to camps in the interior.

Batavian Republic name given to the Netherlands by the French 1795; it lasted until the establishment of the kingdom of the Netherlands 1814 at the end of the Napoleonic Wars.

Báthory Stephen 1533–1586. King of Poland, elected by a diet convened 1575 and crowned 1576. Báthory succeeded in driving the Russian troops of Ivan the Terrible out of his country. His military successes brought potential conflicts with Sweden, but he died before these developed.

Batista Fulgencio 1901–1973. Cuban dictator 1933–44, when he stood down, and again

1952–59, after siezing power in a coup. His authoritarian methods enabled him to jail his opponents and amass a large personal fortune. He was overthrown by rebel forces led by Fidel ◊Castro 1959.

Battenberg title (conferred 1851) of German noble family; its members included Louis Alexander, Prince of Battenberg, who anglicized his name to Mountbatten 1917 and was father of Louis ◊Mountbatten.

Baudouin 1930–1993. King of the Belgians from 1951. In 1950 his father, ◊Leopold III, abdicated and Baudouin was known until his succession July 1951 as *Le Prince Royal*. In 1960 he married Fabiola de Mora y Aragón (1928–   ), member of a Spanish noble family.

Bavaria (German *Bayern*) administrative region (German *Land*) of Germany. The last king, Ludwig III, abdicated 1918, and Bavaria declared itself a republic.

The original Bavarians were Teutonic invaders from Bohemia who occupied the country at the end of the 5th century. From about 555 to 788 Bavaria was ruled by Frankish dukes of the Agilolfing family. In the 7th and 8th centuries the region was christianized by Irish and Scottish monks. In 788 Charlemagne deposed the last of the Agilolfing dukes and incorporated Bavaria into the Carolingian Empire, and in the 10th century it became part of the Holy Roman Empire. The house of Wittelsbach ruled parts or all of Bavaria 1181–1918; Napoleon made the ruler a king 1806. In 1871 Bavaria became a state of the German Empire.

Bay of Pigs inlet on the S coast of Cuba about 145 km/90 mi SW of Havana. It was the site of an unsuccessful invasion attempt by 1,500 US-sponsored Cuban exiles 17–20 April 1961; 1,173 were taken prisoner.

Bazaine Achille François 1811–1888. Marshal of France. From being a private soldier 1831 he rose to command the French troops in Mexico 1862–67 and was made a marshal 1864. In the Franco-Prussian War Bazaine allowed himself to be taken in the fortress of Metz, surrendering 27 Oct 1870 with nearly 180,000 men. For this he was court-martialled 1873 and imprisoned; he escaped to Spain 1874.

Beaconsfield title taken by Benjamin ◊Disraeli, prime minister of Britain 1868 and 1874–80.

Beaker people people thought to be of Iberian origin who spread out over Europe from the 3rd millennium BC. They were skilled in metal-working, and are identified by their use of distinctive earthenware beakers with various designs, of which the bell-beaker type was widely distributed throughout Europe. They favoured inhumation (burial of the intact body), often under round barrows, or secondary burials in some form of chamber tomb. A beaker accompanied each burial, possibly to hold a drink for the deceased on their final journey. In Britain, the Beaker people have been associated with later stages of the construction of Stonehenge.

Beatty David, 1st Earl 1871–1936. British admiral in World War I. He commanded the cruiser squadron 1912–16 and bore the brunt of the Battle of Jutland.

In 1916 he became commander of the fleet, and in 1918 received the surrender of the German fleet.

Beaufort Henry 1375–1447. English priest, bishop of Lincoln from 1398, of Winchester from 1405. As chancellor of England, he supported his half-brother Henry IV, and made enormous personal loans to Henry V to finance war against France. As a guardian of Henry VI from 1421, he was in effective control of the country until 1426. In the same year he was created a cardinal. In 1431 he crowned Henry VI as king of France in Paris.

Beauharnais Alexandre, Vicomte de 1760–1794. French liberal aristocrat and general who served in the American Revolution and became a member of the National Convention in the early days of the French Revolution. He was the first husband of Josephine (consort of Napoleon I). Their daughter Hortense (1783–1837) married Louis, a younger brother of Napoleon, and their son became ◊Napoleon III. Beauharnais was guillotined during the Terror for his alleged lack of zeal for the revolutionary cause and his lack of success as Commander of the Republican Army of the North.

Beauregard Pierre Gustave Toutant 1818–1893. US military leader and Confederate general whose opening fire on ◊Fort Sumter, South Carolina, started the American Civil War 1861. His military successes were clouded by his conflicts with Confederate President Jefferson Davis.

Bebel August 1840–1913. German socialist. In 1869, with Wilhelm Liebknecht, he was a founding member of the Verband Deutsche Arbeitervereine (League of German Workers' Clubs), and became its leading speaker in the Reichstag. Also known as the Eisenach Party, it was based in Saxony and SW Germany before being incorporated into the SPD (Sozialdemokratische Partei Deutschlands/ German Social Democratic Party) 1875.

Bechuanaland former name of ◊Botswana.

Becket St Thomas à 1118–1170. English priest and politician. He was chancellor to ◊Henry II 1155–62, when he was appointed archbishop of Canterbury. The interests of the church soon conflicted with those of the crown and Becket was assassinated; he was canonized 1172.

A friend of Henry II, Becket was a loyal chancellor, but on becoming archbishop of Canterbury transferred his allegiance to the church. In 1164 he opposed Henry's attempt to regulate the relations between church and state, and had to flee the country; he returned 1170, but the reconciliation soon broke down. Encouraged by a hasty outburst from the king, four knights murdered Becket before the altar of Canterbury cathedral. He was declared a saint, and his shrine became the busiest centre of pilgrimage in England until the Reformation.

Bede c. 673–735. English theologian and historian, known as *the Venerable Bede*, active in Durham and Northumbria. He wrote many scientific, theological, and historical works. His *Historia Ecclesiastica Gentis Anglorum/Ecclesiastical History of the English People* 731 is a seminal source for early English history.

Beer-hall Putsch (Munich beer-hall putsch) unsuccessful uprising at Munich led by Adolf Hitler, attempting to overthrow the government of Bavaria on 8 Nov 1923. More than 2,000 Nazi demonstrators were met by armed police, who opened fire, killing 16 of Hitler's supporters. At the subsequent trial for treason, General Ludendorff, who had supported Hitler, was acquitted. Hitler was sentenced to prison, where he wrote ◊*Mein Kampf.*

BEF abbreviation for ◊British Expeditionary Force.

Begin Menachem 1913–1992. Israeli politician. He was leader of the extremist Irgun Zvai Leumi organization in Palestine from 1942, and prime minister of Israel 1977–83, as head of the right-wing Likud party. In 1978 Begin shared a Nobel Peace Prize with President Sadat of Egypt for work on the ◊Camp David Agreements for a Middle East peace settlement.

Begin was born in Brest-Litovsk, Poland, studied law in Warsaw, and fled to the USSR 1939. As leader of the Irgun group, he was responsible in 1946 for a bomb attack at the King David Hotel, Jerusalem, which killed over 100 people.

Beijing or *Peking* capital of China; part of its northeast border is formed by the Great Wall of China. Beijing, founded 2,000 years ago, was the 13th-century capital of the Mongol emperor Kublai Khan. Later replaced by Nanjing, it was again capital from 1421, except from 1928 to 1949, when it was renamed Peiping. Beijing was held by Japan 1937–45. In 1989 it was the site of the Tiananmen Square massacre of pro-democracy demonstrators.

Beirut or *Beyrouth* capital and port of ◊Lebanon, devastated by civil war in the 1970s and 1980s, when it was occupied by armies of neighbouring countries.

Beirut dates back to at least 1400 BC. Before the civil war 1975–76, Beirut was an international financial and educational centre, with four universities (Lebanese, Arab, French, and US); it was also a centre of espionage. Subsequent struggles for power among Christian and Muslim factions caused widespread destruction. From July to Sept 1982 the city was besieged and sections virtually destroyed by the Israeli army to enforce the withdrawal of the forces of the Palestinian Liberation Organization (PLO). After the cease-fire, 500 Palestinians were massacred in the Sabra–Shatila camps 16–18 Sept 1982, by dissident ◊Phalangist and ◊Maronite troops, with alleged Israeli complicity. Civil disturbances continued, characterized by sporadic street fighting and hostage taking. In 1987 Syrian troops entered the city and remained. Intensive fighting broke out between Christian and Syrian troops in Beirut, and by 1990 the strength of Syrian military force in greater Beirut and E Lebanon was estimated at 42,000. In Oct 1990 President Elias Hwari formally invited Syrian troops to remove the Maronite Christian leader General Michel ◊Aoun from his E Beirut stronghold; the troops then went on to dismantle the 'Green Line' separating Muslim western and Christian eastern Beirut. The Syrian-backed 'Greater Beirut Security Plan' was subsequently implemented by the Lebanese government, enforcing the withdrawal of all militias from greater Beirut.

Bekka, the or *El Beqa'a* governorate of E Lebanon separated from Syria by the Anti-Lebanon Mountains. Zahlé and the ancient city of Baalbek are the chief towns. The Bekka Valley was of strategic importance in the Syrian struggle for control of N Lebanon. In the early 1980s the valley was penetrated by Shia Muslims who established an extremist Hezbollah stronghold with the support of Iranian Revolutionary Guards.

Belarus or *Byelorussia* or *Belorussia* country in E central Europe, bounded S by Ukraine, E by Russia, W by Poland, and N by Latvia and Lithuania.

history A Byelorussian state developed in the Middle Ages around the city of Polotsk on the river Dvina. From the 13th century it became incorporated within the Slavonic Grand Duchy of Lithunia and from 1569 there was union with Poland.

brief independence Byelorussia was brought into the Russian Empire in the late 18th century and from the later 19th century there was an upsurge in national consciousness. Amid the chaos of the Bolshevik Revolution in Russia, an independent Byelorussian National Republic was declared in 1918, but failed to receive international recognition. Instead, a Byelorussian Soviet Republic was established in 1919, with some loss of territory to Poland.

nationalist revival National culture and language were encouraged until the Soviet dictator Stalin launched a Russification drive, with more than 100,000 people, predominantly writers and intellectuals, being executed between 1937 and 1941. Under the terms of the 1939 Nazi-Soviet pact, Byelorussia was reunified, but then suffered severely under German invasion and occupation 1941–44. Russification resumed in the 1960s and continued into the mid-1980s, when ◊glasnost brought a revival of national culture. A Popular Front, demanding greater autonomy, was established in Feb 1989. In the wake of the April 1986 Chernobyl nuclear disaster, which forced the resettlement of several hundred thousand people, the Byelorussian Ecological Union (BEU) had been formed. Both the Popular Front and BEU contested the March-April 1990 Byelorussian supreme soviet elections under the Democratic Bloc banner, capturing more than a quarter of the seats. In response, Byelorussian was re-established as the republic's official state language from Sept 1990.

independence achieved Byelorussia's communist president, Nikolai Dementei, expressed support for the Aug 1991 coup attempt against President Gorbachev in Moscow. When it failed, Dementei resigned and the republic's supreme soviet declared Byelorussia's independence on 25 Aug 1991, suspending the activities of the Communist Party. In Sept 1991 the supreme soviet voted to adopt the name of Republic of Belarus and elected Stanislav Shushkevich, an advocate of democratic reform, as its chair, which also made him state president. Shushkevich played an important role in the creation in Dec 1991 of a new ◊Commonwealth of Independent States (CIS), the confederal successor to USSR, with Mensk (Minsk) chosen as the CIS's early centre. In the same month Belarus was formally acknowledged as independent by the USA and granted diplomatic recognition. In Jan 1992 it was admitted into the ◊Conference on Security and Cooperation in Europe (CSCE). It has been a member of the United Nations since its foundation in 1945.

economy and armed forces Belarus was cautious in its implementation of market-centred economic reform, with privatization and price liberalization introduced very gradually. It remained heavily dependent upon Russia for industrial raw materials. Belarus inherited substantial nuclear arms from the USSR. The Shushkevich administration pledged to gradually remove these to become nuclear-free, but Belarus also planned to establish its own independent armed forces. In May 1992, Belarus and Russia (as a single signatory), along with the the Ukraine and Kazakhstan, signed protocols with the USA agreeing to comply with START. It was also agreed to return all tactical nuclear weapons to Russia for destruction.

Belaúnde Terry Fernando 1913– . President of Peru from 1963 to 1968 and from 1980 to 1985. He championed land reform and the construction of roads to open up the Amazon valley. He fled to the USA 1968 after being deposed by a military junta. After his return, his second term in office was marked by rampant inflation, enormous foreign debts, terrorism, mass killings, and human-rights violations by the armed forces.

Belau, Republic of (formerly *Palau*) self-governing island group in Micronesia. Spain held the islands from about 1600, and sold them to Germany 1899. Japan seized them in World War I, administered them by League of Nations mandate, and used them as a naval base during World War II. They were captured by the USA 1944, and became part of the US Trust Territory of the Pacific Islands three years later. Belau became internally self-governing 1980. It is the only remaining member of the Trust Territory.

Belgae the name given by Roman authors to the people who lived in Gaul, north of the Seine and Marne rivers. They were defeated by Caesar 57 BC. Many of the Belgae settled in SE England during the 2nd century BC. Belgic remains in Britain include coins, pottery made on a wheel, and much of the finest Iron Age Celtic art.

Belgium country in W Europe, bounded N by the Netherlands, NW by the North Sea, S and W by France, E by Luxembourg and Germany.

history The first recorded inhabitants were the Belgae, an ancient Celtic people. Conquered by the Romans, the area was known from 15 BC as the Roman province of Belgica; from the 3rd century AD onwards it was overrun by the Franks. Under ◊Charlemagne, Belgium became the centre of the Carolingian dynasty, and the peace and order during this period fostered the growth of such towns as Ghent, Bruges, and Brussels. Following the division of Charlemagne's empire 843 the area became part of Lotharingia.

late Middle Ages By the 11th century seven feudal states had emerged: the counties of Flanders, Hainaut, and Namur, the duchies of Brabant, Limburg, and Luxembourg, and the bishopric of Liège, all nominally subject to the French kings or the German emperor, but in practice independent. From the 12th century the economy flourished; Bruges, Ghent, and Ypres became centres of the textile industry, while the artisans of Dinant and Liège exploited the copper and tin of the Meuse valley. During the 15th century the states came one by one under the rule of the dukes of Burgundy, and in 1477, by the marriage of Mary (heir of Charles the Bold, duke of Burgundy) to Maximilian (archduke of Austria), passed into the ◊Habsburg dominions.

under Spanish rule Other dynastic marriages brought all the Low Countries under Spain, and in the 16th century the religious and secular tyranny of Philip II led to revolt in the Netherlands. The independence of the Netherlands as the Dutch Republic was recognized 1648; the south, reconquered by Spain, remained Spanish until the Treaty of ◊Utrecht 1713 transferred it to Austria. The Austrian Netherlands were annexed 1792 by revolutionary France. The Congress of Vienna 1815 reunited the North and South Netherlands as one kingdom under William, King of Orange-Nassau; but historical differences, and the fact that the language of the wealthy and powerful in the south was French, made the union uneasy.

recognition as an independent kingdom An uprising 1830 of the largely French-speaking people in the south, and continuing disturbances, led to the Great Powers' recognition 1839 of the South Netherlands as the independent and permanently neutral kingdom of Belgium, with Leopold of Saxe-Coburg (widower of Charlotte, daughter of George IV of England) as king, and a parliamentary constitution.

foreign relations Although Prussia had been a party to the treaty 1839 recognizing Belgium's permanent neutrality, Germany invaded Belgium 1914 and occupied a large part of it until 1918. In 1940 Belgium was again overrun by Germany, to whom Leopold III surrendered. His government escaped to London, and

Belgium had a strong resistance movement. After Belgium's liberation by the Allies 1944–45, the king's decision to remain in the country during the occupation caused acute controversy, ended only by his abdication 1951 in favour of his son Baudouin. Since 1945 Belgium has been a major force for international cooperation in Europe, being a founding member of the Benelux Economic Union 1948, the Council of Europe, and the European Economic Community. Between 1983 and 1985 there was much debate about the siting of US cruise missiles in Belgium before a majority vote in parliament allowed their installation.

language divisions Belgium's main problems stem from the division between French- and Flemish-speaking members of the population, aggravated by the polarization between the predominantly conservative Flanders in the north, and the mainly socialist French-speaking Wallonia in the south. About 55% of the population speak Flemish, 44% French, and the remainder German. During 1971–73 attempts to close the linguistic and social divisions included the transfer of greater power to the regions, the inclusion of German-speaking members in the cabinet, and linguistic parity in the government. Separate regional councils and ministerial committees were established 1974. The language conflict developed into open violence 1980, and it was eventually agreed that Flanders and Wallonia should be administered by separate regional assemblies, with powers to spend up to 10% of the national budget on cultural facilities, health, roads, and urban projects. Brussels was to be governed by a three-member executive. Linguistic divisions again threatened the government 1983. In Sept 1992 the government agreed, in principle, to introducing a federal system of government, based on Dutch-speaking Flanders and French-speaking Wallonia.

political instability Leo Tindemans (Flemish Christian Social Party (CVP)) resigned as prime minister 1978 and was succeeded by Wilfried Martens. By 1980 Martens had formed no fewer than four coalition governments. A new coalition 1981, led by Mark Eyskens (CVP), lasted less than a year, and Martens again returned to power. Economic difficulties 1981–82 resulted in a series of public-sector strikes, but Martens remained at the head of various coalitions until Jan 1992. With the government on the point of collapse, the king asked Jean-Luc Dehaene (CVP), a deputy prime minister, to form a new coalition government. The coalition, comprising the main centre-left parties, was formed March 1992.

Belgrano Manuel 1770–1820. Argentine revolutionary. He was a member of the military group that led the 1810 revolt against Spain. Later, he commanded the revolutionary army until he was replaced by José de ◊San Martín 1814.

Belisarius c. 505–565. Roman general under Emperor ◊Justinian I. He won major victories over the Persians in 530 and the Vandals in 533 when he sacked Carthage. Later he invaded Sicily and fought a series of campaigns against the Goths in Italy.

As a young man he was a member of Justinian's bodyguard before becoming commander of the eastern army. Although not always favoured by the Emperor, it was largely his military skill which preserved the Byzantine Empire from being overthrown.

Belize country in Central America, bounded N by Mexico, W and S by Guatemala, and E by the Caribbean Sea.

history Once part of the ◊Maya civilization, and colonized in the 17th century, British Honduras (as it was called until 1973) became a recognized British colony 1862. A 1954 constitution provided for internal self-government, with the UK responsible for defence, external affairs, and internal security.

The first general election under the the the new constitution, and all subsequent elections until 1984, were won by the People's United Party (PUP), led by George Price. Full internal self-government was achieved 1964, and Price became prime minister. The capital was moved 1970 from Belize City to the new town of Belmopan. British troops were sent 1975 to defend the long-disputed frontier with Guatemala. Negotiations begun 1977 were inconclusive.

full independence achieved The United Nations called 1980 for full independence for Belize. A constitutional conference broke up 1981 over Guatemala's demand for territory rather than just access to the Caribbean. Full independence was achieved 1981 with George Price as the first prime minister. The UK agreed to protect the frontier and to assist in the training of Belizean forces. The PUP's uninterrupted 30-year rule ended 1984 when the United Democratic Party (UDP) leader, Manuel Esquivel, became prime minister. The UK reaffirmed its undertaking to protect Belize's disputed frontier. Still led by George Price, the PUP unexpectedly won the Sept 1989 general election by a margin of 15 to 13 seats in the house of representatives.

agreement with Guatemala Diplomatic relations were established with Guatemala Sept 1991 after the latter announced its recognition of Belize's independence and withdrew threats of invasion.

Belorussia see ◊Belarus.

Belsen site of a Nazi ◊concentration camp in Lower Saxony, Germany.

Ben Ali Zine el Abidine 1936– . Tunisian politician, president from 1987. After training in France and the USA, he returned to Tunisia and became director-general of national security. He was made minister of the interior and then prime minister under the ageing president for life, Habib ◊Bourguiba, whom he deposed 1987 by a bloodless coup with the aid of ministerial colleagues. Ending Bourguiba's personality cult, he moved toward a political pluralism. Re-elected 1994, he won 99% of the vote.

Ben Barka Mehdi 1920–1965. Moroccan politician. He became president of the National Consultative Assembly 1956 on the country's independence from France. He was assassinated by Moroccan agents with the aid of the French secret service.

Ben Bella Ahmed 1916– . Algerian politician. He was leader of the National Liberation Front (FLN) from 1952, the first prime minister of independent Algeria 1962–63, and its first president 1963–65. In 1965 Ben Bella was overthrown by Col Houari ◊Boumédienne and detained until 1979. In 1985 he founded a new party, Mouvement pour la Démocratie en Algérie, and returned to Algeria 1990 after nine years in exile.

Benbow John 1653–1702. English admiral, hero of several battles with France. He ran away to sea as a boy, and from 1689 served in the navy. He fought at the battles of Beachy Head 1690 and La Hogue 1692, and died of wounds received in a fight with the French off Jamaica.

Benedictine order religious order of monks and nuns in the Roman Catholic church, founded by St Benedict at Subiaco, Italy, in the 6th century. It had a strong influence on medieval learning and reached the height of its prosperity early in the 14th century. St Augustine brought the order to England. At the Reformation there were nearly 300 Benedictine monasteries and nunneries in England, all of which were suppressed.

benefice in the early Middle Ages, a donation of land or money to the Christian church as an act of devotion; from the 12th century, the term came to mean the income enjoyed by clergy.

Under the ◊Carolingian dynasty, 'benefice' was used to mean a gift of land from a lord to a ◊vassal, in which sense it is often indistinguishable from a ◊fief.

Benelux (acronym from *Be*lgium, the *Nether*-lands, and *Lux*embourg) customs union agreed by Belgium, the Netherlands, and Luxembourg 1948, fully effective 1960. It was the precursor of the European Community.

Beneš Eduard 1884–1948. Czechoslovak politician. He worked with Tomáš ◊Masaryk towards Czechoslovak nationalism from 1918 and was foreign minister and representative at the League of Nations. He was president of the republic from 1935 until forced to resign by the Germans; he headed a government in exile in London during World War II. He returned home as president 1945 but resigned again after the Communist coup 1948.

Bengal former province of British India, divided 1947 into West Bengal, a state of India, and East Bengal, from 1972 ◊Bangladesh. A famine in 1943, caused by a slump in demand for jute and a bad harvest, resulted in over 3 million deaths.

Ben-Gurion David. Adopted name of David Gruen 1886–1973. Israeli statesman and socialist politician, one of the founders of the state of Israel, the country's first prime minister 1948–53, and again 1955–63.

He was born in Poland, and went to Palestine 1906 to farm. He was a leader of the Zionist movement, and as defence minister he presided over the development of Israel's armed forces into one of the strongest armies in the Middle East.

Benin country in W Africa, bounded E by Nigeria, N by Niger and Burkina Faso, W by Togo, and S by the Gulf of Guinea.

history In the 12th–13th centuries the country was settled by the Aja, whose kingdom reached its peak in the 16th century. In the 17th–19th centuries the succeeding Dahomey kingdom (which gave the country its name of Dahomey until 1975) captured and sold its neighbours as slaves to Europeans.

French colonial rule Under French influence from the 1850s, Dahomey formed part of French West Africa from 1899, and became a self-governing dominion within the French Community 1958.

independence Dahomey became fully independent 1960. The country went through a period of political instability 1960–72, with swings from civilian to military rule and disputes between regions.

people's republic The deputy chief of the army, Mathieu Kerekou, established 1972 a military regime pledged to give fair representation to each region. His initial instrument of

government was the National Council of the Revolution (CNR). Kerekou announced 1974 that as the People's Republic of Benin the country would follow 'scientific socialism', based on Marxist-Leninist principles. From 1975 to 1989 Benin was a one-party state, under the Party of the People's Revolution of Benin. CNR was dissolved 1977 and a 'national revolutionary assembly' established, which elected Kerekou 1980 as president and head of state. He was re-elected 1984 and, after initial economic and social difficulties, his government grew more stable.

foreign relations Relations with France (Benin's biggest trading partner) improved in the 1980s. President Mitterrand became the first French head of state to visit Benin 1983.

pluralism President Kerekou was re-elected Aug 1989 by the assembly for another five-year term. It was announced Dec 1989 that Marxist-Leninism was no longer the official ideology of Benin and that further constitutional reforms – allowing for more private enterprise – would be agreed upon. A preliminary referendum Dec 1990 showed overwhelming support for a multiparty political system, and multiparty elections were held Feb 1991. Kerekou was defeated and Nicéphore Soglo became president.

Benin former African kingdom 1200–1897, now a province of Nigeria. It reached the height of its power in the 14th–17th centuries when it ruled the area between the Niger Delta and Lagos.

Benin traded in spices, ivory, palm oil, and slaves until its decline and eventual incorporation into Nigeria. The oba (ruler) of Benin continues to rule his people as a divine monarch. The present oba is considered an enlightened leader and one who is helping his people to become part of modern Nigeria.

Benn Tony (Anthony Wedgwood) 1925– . British Labour politician, formerly the leading figure on the party's left wing. He was minister of technology 1966–70 and of industry 1974–75, but his campaign against entry to the European Community led to his transfer to the Department of Energy 1975–79. A skilled parliamentary orator, he unsuccessfully contested the Labour Party leadership 1988.

Bentinck Lord William Cavendish 1774–1839. British colonial administrator, first governor general of India 1828–35. He acted against the ancient Indian rituals of thuggee and suttee, and established English as the medium of instruction.

Ben Zvi Izhak 1884–1963. Israeli politician, president 1952–63. He was born in Atpoltava,

Russia, and became active in the Zionist movement in Ukraine. In 1907 he went to Palestine but was deported 1915 with ◊Ben-Gurion. They served in the Jewish Legion under Field Marshal Allenby, who commanded the British forces in the Middle East.

Berber member of a non-Semitic Caucasoid people of North Africa who since prehistoric times inhabited Barbary, the Mediterranean coastlands from Egypt to the Atlantic. Their language, present-day Berber (a member of the Afro-Asiatic language family), is spoken by about one-third of Algerians and nearly two-thirds of Moroccans, 10 million people. Berbers are mainly agricultural, but some are still nomadic.

Berchtold Count Leopold von 1863–1942. Prime minister and foreign minister of Austria–Hungary 1912–15 and a crucial figure in the events that led to World War I, because his indecisive stance caused tension with Serbia.

Beria Lavrenti 1899–1953. Soviet politician who in 1938 became minister of the interior and head of the Soviet police force that imprisoned, liquidated, and transported millions of Soviet citizens. On Stalin's death 1953, he attempted to seize power but was foiled and shot after a secret trial. Apologists for Stalin have blamed Beria for the atrocities committed by Soviet police during Stalin's dictatorship.

Berkeley Sir William 1606–1677. British colonial administrator in North America, governor of the colony of Virginia 1641–77. Siding with the Royalists during the English Civil War, he was removed from the governorship by Oliver Cromwell 1652. He was reappointed 1660 by Charles II after the Restoration of the monarchy. However, growing opposition to him in the colony culminated in Bacon's Rebellion 1676 and in 1677 Berkeley was removed from office for his brutal repression of that uprising.

Berlin capital of the Federal Republic of Germany. The Berlin Wall divided the city from 1961 to 1989, but in Oct 1990 Berlin became the capital of a unified Germany, once more with East and West Berlin reunited as the 16th *Land* (state) of the Federal Republic.

First mentioned about 1230, the city grew out of a fishing village, joined the Hanseatic League in the 15th century, became the permanent seat of the Hohenzollerns, and was capital of the Brandenburg electorate 1486–1701, of the kingdom of Prussia 1701–1871, and of united Germany 1871–1945. From the middle of the 18th century it developed into a commercial and cultural centre. In World War II air raids and conquest by the Soviet army 23 April–2 May 1945, destroyed much of the city. After the war, Berlin was divided into four sectors – British, US, French, and Soviet – and until 1948 was under quadripartite government by the Allies. Following the ◊Berlin blockade the city was divided, with the USSR creating a separate municipal government in its sector. The other three sectors (West Berlin) were made a *Land* of the Federal Republic May 1949, and in Oct 1949 East Berlin was proclaimed capital of East Germany.

Berlin blockade in June 1948, the closing of entry to Berlin from the west by Soviet forces. It was an attempt to prevent the other Allies (the USA, France, and the UK) unifying the western part of Germany. The British and US forces responded by sending supplies to the city by air for over a year (the *Berlin airlift*). In May 1949 the blockade was lifted; the airlift continued until Sept. The blockade marked the formal division of the city into Eastern and Western sectors.

Berlin, Conference of conference 1884–85 of the major European powers (France, Germany, the UK, Belgium and Portugal) called by Chancellor Otto von Bismarck to decide on the colonial partition of Africa.

Berlin, Congress of congress of the European powers (Russia, Turkey, Austria-Hungary, the UK, France, Italy, and Germany) held in Berlin 1878 to determine the boundaries of the Balkan states after the Russo-Turkish war 1877–78.

Berlinguer Enrico 1922–1984. Italian Communist who freed the party from Soviet influence. Secretary general of the Italian Communist Party, by 1976 he was near to the premiership, but the murder of Aldo Moro, the prime minister, by Red Brigade guerrillas, prompted a move toward support for the socialists.

Berlin Wall dividing barrier between East and West Berlin 1961–89, erected by East Germany to prevent East Germans from leaving for West Germany. Escapers were shot on sight.

From 13 Aug 1961, the East German security forces sealed off all but 12 of the 80 crossing points to West Berlin with a barbed wire barrier. It was reinforced with concrete by the Russians to prevent the escape of unwilling inhabitants of East Berlin to the rival political and economic system of West Berlin. The interconnecting link between East and West Berlin was *Checkpoint Charlie*, where both sides exchanged captured spies. On 9 Nov 1989 the East German government opened its borders to try to halt the mass exodus of its citizens to the West via other Eastern bloc countries, and the wall was gradually dismantled, with portions of it sold off as souvenirs.

Bermuda British colony in the NW Atlantic Ocean. The islands were named after Juan de Bermudez, who visited them 1515, and were settled by British colonists 1609. Indian and African slaves were transported from 1616, and soon outnumbered the white settlers. Racial violence 1977 led to intervention, at the request of the government, by British troops.

Bernadotte Count Folke 1895–1948. Swedish diplomat and president of the Swedish Red Cross. In 1945 he conveyed Nazi commander Himmler's offer of capitulation to the British and US governments, and in 1948 was United Nations mediator in Palestine, where he was assassinated by Israeli Stern Gang guerrillas. He was a nephew of Gustaf VI of Sweden.

Bernadotte Jean-Baptiste Jules 1764–1844. Marshal in Napoleon's army who in 1818 became ◊Charles XIV of Sweden. Hence, Bernadotte is the family name of the present royal house of Sweden.

Bernhard Prince of the Netherlands 1911– . Formerly Prince Bernhard of Lippe-Biesterfeld, he married Princess Juliana in 1937. When Germany invaded the Netherlands in 1940, he escaped to England and became liaison officer for the Dutch and British forces, playing a part in the organization of the Dutch Resistance.

Bernstein Edouard 1850–1932. German socialist thinker, journalist, and politician. He was elected to the Reichstag 1902. He was a proponent of reformist rather than revolutionary socialism, whereby a socialist society could be achieved within an existing parliamentary structure merely by workers' parties obtaining a majority.

Berri Nabih 1939– . Lebanese politician and soldier, leader of Amal ('Hope'), the Syrian-backed Shi'ite nationalist movement. He became minister of justice in the government of President ◊Gemayel 1984. In 1988 Amal was disbanded after defeat by the Iranian-backed Hezbollah ('Children of God') during the Lebanese civil wars, and Berri joined the cabinet of Selim Hoss 1989. In Dec 1990 Berri was made minister of state in the newly formed Karami cabinet, and in 1992 retained the same post in the cabinet of Rashid al-Sohl.

Betancourt Rómulo 1908–1981. Venezuelan president 1959–64 whose rule was plagued by guerrilla violence and economic and political division. He expanded welfare programmes, increased expenditure on education, encour-

aged foreign investment, and tried to diversify the Venezuelan economy to decrease its dependence on oil exports.

When he was a law student, Betancourt opposed the dictatorship (1908–35) of Juan Vicente ◊Gómez. He helped found the social democratic party Acción Democrática 1941, and was president of the junta which ruled 1945–47. Betancourt was exiled for a decade after the military rebellion led by Marcos ◊Pérez Jiménez 1948. Returning Dec 1958, he was elected president Feb 1959.

Bethmann Hollweg Theobald von 1856–1921. German politician, imperial chancellor 1909–17, largely responsible for engineering popular support for World War I in Germany, but his power was overthrown by a military dictatorship under ◊Ludendorff and ◊Hindenburg.

Bevan Aneurin (Nye) 1897–1960. British Labour politician. Son of a Welsh miner, and himself a miner at 13, he became member of Parliament for Ebbw Vale 1929–60. As minister of health 1945–51, he inaugurated the National Health Service (NHS); he was minister of labour Jan– April 1951, when he resigned (with Harold Wilson) on the introduction of NHS charges and led a Bevanite faction against the government. In 1956 he became chief Labour spokesperson on foreign affairs, and deputy leader of the Labour party 1959. He was an outstanding speaker.

Beveridge William Henry, 1st Baron Beveridge 1879–1963. British economist. A civil servant, he acted as Lloyd George's lieutenant in the social legislation of the Liberal government before World War I. The *Beveridge Report* 1942 formed the basis of the welfare state in Britain.

Bevin Ernest 1881–1951. British Labour politician. Chief creator of the Transport and General Workers' Union, he was its general secretary from 1921 to 1940, when he entered the war cabinet as minister of labour and national service. He organized the 'Bevin boys', chosen by ballot to work in the coal mines as war service, and was foreign secretary in the Labour government 1945–51.

My [foreign] policy is to be able to take a ticket at Victoria Station and go anywhere I damn well please.

Ernest Bevin *The Spectator* April 1951

Bhindranwale Sant Jarnail Singh 1947–1984. Indian Sikh fundamentalist leader who campaigned for the creation of a separate state of

Khalistan during the early 1980s, precipitating a bloody Hindu–Sikh conflict in the Punjab. Having taken refuge in the Golden Temple complex in Amritsar and built up an arms cache for guerrilla activities, Bhindranwale, along with around 500 followers, died at the hands of Indian security forces who stormed the temple in 'Operation Blue Star' June 1984.

Bhutan mountainous, landlocked country in the eastern Himalayas (SE Asia), bounded N and W by Tibet (China) and to the S and E by India.

history Bhutan was ruled by Tibet from the 16th century and by China from 1720. In 1774 the British ◊East India Company concluded a treaty with the ruler of Bhutan, and British influence grew during the 19th century. A short border war in 1863 ended with a treaty in 1865, under which an annual subsidy was paid by Britain to Bhutan. In 1907 the first hereditary monarch was installed, and under the Anglo-Bhutanese Treaty, signed three years later, Bhutan was granted internal autonomy while foreign relations were placed under the control of the British government in India.

foreign relations After India's independence 1947, an Indo-Bhutan Treaty of Friendship was signed 1949, under which Bhutan agreed to seek Indian advice on foreign relations but not necessarily to accept it. There is no formal defence treaty, but India would regard an attack on Bhutan as an act of aggression against itself. In 1959, after the Chinese annexation of Tibet, Bhutan gave asylum to some 4,000 Tibetan refugees, who in 1979 were given the choice of taking Bhutanese citizenship or returning to Tibet. Most became citizens, and the rest went to India. In 1983 Bhutan became a founding member of the South Asian Association for Regional Cooperation.

towards democracy In 1952 King Jigme Dorji Wangchuk came to power, and in 1953 a national assembly was established. In 1968 the king appointed his first cabinet. He died 1972 and was succeeded by his Western-educated son Jigme Singye Wangchuk.

ethnic tensions In 1988 the Buddhist Dzongkha ethnic minority, headed by King Jigme Singye Wangchuk, imposed its own language, religious practices, and national dress on the divided (although principally Hindu-Nepali) majority community and suppressed the Nepalese language and customs. Hundreds of thousands of non-Bhutanese were deported, beginning 1989. As a result, tension between the Dzongkha and Hindu Nepalese communities increased and the Nepalese illegally formed

a number of political parties to protest against Dzongkha policies. Several hundred people were reported to have been killed during security crackdowns on prodemocracy demonstrations in 1990.

Bhutto Zulfikar Ali 1928–1979. Pakistani politician, president 1971–73; prime minister from 1973 until the 1977 military coup led by General ◊Zia ul-Haq. In 1978 Bhutto was sentenced to death for conspiring to murder a political opponent and was hanged the following year. He was the father of *Benazir Bhutto* (1953–   ), Pakistan's prime minister 1988–90 and 1993-96.

Biafra, Republic of African state proclaimed in 1967 when fears that Nigerian central government was increasingly in the hands of the rival Hausa tribe led the predominantly Ibo Eastern Region of Nigeria to secede under Lt Col Odumegwu Ojukwu. On the proclamation of Biafra, civil war ensued with the rest of the federation. In a bitterly fought campaign federal forces confined the Biafrans to a shrinking area of the interior by 1968, and by 1970 Biafra ceased to exist.

Bidault Georges 1899–1983. French politician, prime minister 1946, 1949–50. He was a leader of the French resistance during World War II and foreign minister and president in de Gaulle's provisional government. He left the Gaullists over Algerian independence and in 1962 he became head of the ◊Organisation de l'Armée Secrète (OAS), formed 1961 by French settlers devoted to perpetuating their own rule in Algeria. He was charged with treason in 1963 and left the country, but was allowed to return in 1968.

The weak have one weapon: the errors of those who think they are strong.

Georges Bidault *Observer* July 1962

Bienville Jean Baptiste Le Moyne, Sieur de 1680–1768. French colonial administrator, governor of the North American colony of Louisiana 1706–13, 1717–23, and 1733–43. During his first term he founded the settlement at Mobile in Alabama and in his second term, established the Louisiana colonial capital at New Orleans. During his final term Bienville was drawn into a costly and ultimately unsuccessful war with the Indians of the lower Mississippi Valley.

Bikini atoll in the ◊Marshall Islands, W Pacific, where the USA carried out 23 atomic- and hydrogen-bomb tests (some underwater) 1946–58.

The islanders were relocated by the USA before 1946. Some returned after Bikini was declared safe for habitation 1969, but they were again removed in the late 1970s because of continuing harmful levels of radiation. In 1990 a US plan was announced to remove radioactive topsoil, allowing 800 islanders to return home.

Biko Steve (Stephen) 1946–1977. South African civil-rights leader. An active opponent of ◊apartheid, he was arrested in Sept 1977; he died in detention six days later. Since his death in the custody of South African police, he has been a symbol of the anti-apartheid movement.

He founded the South African Students Organization (SASO) in 1968 and was cofounder in 1972 of the Black People's Convention, also called the Black Consciousness movement, a radical association of South African students that aimed to develop black pride. His death in the hands of the police caused much controversy.

Bill of Rights in the USA, the first ten amendments to the US Constitution, incorporated 1791:

1 guarantees freedom of worship, of speech, of the press, of assembly, and to petition the government;

2 grants the right to keep and bear arms;

3 prohibits billeting of soldiers in private homes in peacetime;

4 forbids unreasonable search and seizure;

5 guarantees none be 'deprived of life, liberty or property without due process of law' or compelled in any criminal case to be a witness against him- or herself;

6 grants the right to speedy trial, to call witnesses, and to have defence counsel;

7 grants the right to trial by jury of one's peers;

8 prevents the infliction of excessive bail or fines, or 'cruel and unusual punishment';

9, 10 provide a safeguard to the states and people for all rights not specifically delegated to the central government.

Not originally part of the draft of the Constitution, the Bill of Rights was mooted during the period of ratification. Twelve amendments were proposed by Congress in 1789; the ten now called the Bill of Rights were ratified 1791.

Bill of Rights in Britain, an act of Parliament 1689 which established it as the primary governing body of the country. The Bill of Rights embodied the Declarations of Rights which contained the conditions on which William and Mary were offered the throne. It made provisions limiting royal prerogative with respect to legislation, executive power, money levies, courts, and the army and stipulated Parliament's consent to many government functions.

Billy the Kid nickname of William H Bonney 1859–1881. US outlaw, a leader in the 1878 Lincoln County cattle war in New Mexico, who allegedly killed his first victim at 12 and was reputed to have killed 21 men by age 22, when he died.

Birch John M 1918–1945. American Baptist missionary, commissioned by the US Air Force to carry out intelligence work behind the Chinese lines where he was killed by the communists; the US extreme right-wing *John Birch Society* 1958 is named after him.

Birkenhead Frederick Edwin Smith, 1st Earl of Birkenhead 1872–1930. British Conservative politician. A flamboyant character, known as 'FE', he joined with Edward Carson in organizing armed resistance in Ulster to Irish Home Rule. He was Lord Chancellor 1919–22 and a much criticized secretary for India 1924–28.

The world continues to offer glittering prizes to those who have stout hearts and sharp swords.

*Frederick Edwin Smith,
1st Earl of Birkenhead*
Rectorial Address, Glasgow University,
7 November 1923

Bismarck Otto Eduard Leopold, Prince von 1815–1898. German politician, prime minister of Prussia 1862–90 and chancellor of the German Empire 1871–90. He pursued an aggressively expansionist policy, waging wars against Denmark 1863–64, Austria 1866, and France 1870–71, which brought about the unification of Germany.

Bismarck was ambitious to establish Prussia's leadership within Germany and eliminate the influence of Austria. He secured Austria's support for his successful war against Denmark then, in 1866, went to war against Austria and its allies (the ◊Seven Weeks' War), his victory forcing Austria out of the German Bund and unifying the N German states into the North German Confederation under his own chancellorship 1867. He then defeated France, under Napoleon III, in the Franco-Prussian War 1870–71, proclaimed the German Empire 1871, and annexed Alsace-Lorraine. He tried to secure his work by the ◊Triple Alliance 1881 with Austria and Italy but ran into difficulties at home with the Roman Catholic church and the

socialist movement and was forced to resign by
Wilhelm II 18 March 1890.

---

*Not by speech-making and the decisions of
majorities will the questions of the day be
settled . . . but by iron and blood.*
Prince Otto von Bismarck Sept 1862

Bjelke-Petersen Joh(annes) 1911– . Australian right-wing politician, leader of the
Queensland National Party (QNP) and premier of Queensland 1968–87.

Bjelke-Petersen was born in New Zealand.
His Queensland state chauvinism and
extremely conservative policies, such as lack of
support for Aboriginal land rights or for conservation issues and attacks on the trade-union
movement, made him a controversial figure
outside as well as within Queensland, and he
was accused more than once of electoral gerry-
mandering. In 1987 he broke the coalition of
the QNP with the Australian Liberal Party to
run for prime minister, but his action, by splitting the opposition, merely strengthened the
hand of the Labor prime minister Bob Hawke.
Amid reports of corruption in his government,
Bjelke-Petersen was forced to resign the premiership 1987.

black English term first used 1625 to describe
West Africans, now used to refer to Africans
south of the Sahara and to people of African
descent living outside Africa.

Black Africans were first taken to the West
Indies in large numbers as slaves by the Spanish in the early 16th century and to the North
American mainland in the early 17th century.
They were transported to South America by
both the Spanish and Portuguese from the 16th
century. African blacks were also taken to
Europe to work as slaves and servants. Some of
the indigenous coastal societies in W Africa
were heavily involved in the slave trade and
became wealthy on its proceeds. Sometimes,
black sailors settled in European ports on the
Atlantic seaboard, such as Liverpool and Bristol, England. Although blacks fought beside
whites in the American Revolution, the US
Constitution (ratified 1788) did not redress the
slave trade, and slaves were given no ◊civil
rights.

Slavery was gradually abolished in the northern US states during the early 19th century,
but as the South's economy had been based
upon slavery, it was one of the issues concerning states' rights that led to the secession of
the South, which provoked the American Civil
War 1861–65. During the Civil War about
200,000 blacks fought in the Union (Northern)
army, but in segregated units led by white
officers.

The Emancipation Proclamation 1863 of
President Abraham Lincoln officially freed the
slaves (about 4 million), but it could not be
enforced until the Union victory 1865 and the
period after the war known as the ◊Recon-
struction. Freed slaves were often resented by
poor whites as economic competitors, and vigilante groups in the South, such as the ◊Ku
Klux Klan were formed to intimidate them. In
addition, although freed slaves had full US citizenship under the 14th Amendment to the
Constitution, and were thus entitled to vote,
they were often disenfranchised in practice by
state and local literacy tests and poll taxes.

A 'separate but equal' policy was established
when the US Supreme Court ruled 1896
(*Plessy* v. *Ferguson*) that segregation was legal if
equal facilities were provided for blacks and
whites. The ruling was overturned 1954
(*Brown* v. *Board of Education*) with the
Supreme Court decision outlawing segregation
in state schools. This led to a historic confrontation in Little Rock, Arkansas, 1957 when
Governor Orval Faubus attempted to prevent
black students from entering Central High
School, and President Eisenhower sent federal
troops to enforce their right to attend.

Another landmark in the blacks' struggle for
civil rights was the Montgomery bus boycott in
Alabama 1955, which first brought Martin
Luther ◊King Jr to national attention. In the
early 1960s the civil-rights movement had
gained impetus, largely under the leadership of
King, who in 1957 had founded the ◊Southern
Christian Leadership Conference (SCLC), a
coalition group advocating nonviolence. Moderate groups such as the National Association
for the Advancement of Colored People
(NAACP) had been active since early in the
century; for the first time they were joined in
large numbers by whites, in particular students,
as in the historic march converging on Washington DC 1963 from all over the USA. At
about this time, impatient with the lack of
results gained through moderation, the militant
◊Black Power movements began to emerge,
such as the Black Panther Party founded 1966,
and black separatist groups such as the ◊Black
Muslims gained support.

Increasing pressure led to the passage of federal legislation, the Civil Rights acts of 1964
and 1968, and the Voting Rights Act of 1965,
under President Johnson; they guaranteed
equal rights under the law and prohibited discrimination in public facilities, schools,

employment and voting. However, in the 1980s, despite some advances, legislation, and affirmative action (positive discrimination), blacks, who comprise some 12% of the US population, continued to suffer discrimination and inequality of opportunities in practice in such areas as education, employment, and housing. Despite these obstacles, many blacks have made substanital contributions in the arts, the sciences, and politics.

Blacks in Britain Unlike the USA, Britain does not have a recent history of slavery at home. The UK outlawed the slave trade 1807 and abolished slavery in the British Empire 1833. In the UK only a tiny proportion of the population was black until after World War II, when immigration from Commonwealth countries increased. Legislation such as the Race Relations Act 1976 specifically outlawed discrimination on grounds of race and emphasized the official policy of equality of opportunity in all areas, and the Commission for Racial Equality was established 1977 to work towards eliminating discrimination.

Black and Tans nickname of a special auxiliary force of the Royal Irish Constabulary employed by the British 1920–21 to combat the Sinn Féiners (Irish nationalists) in Ireland; the name derives from the colours of the uniforms, khaki with black hats and belts.

blackbirding formerly, the kidnapping of South Pacific islanders (kanakas) to provide virtual slave labour in Australia, Fiji, and Samoa. From 1847 to 1904 this practice was carried on extensively to provide workers for the sugar-cane plantations of Queensland. The Pacific Islanders Protection Act passed by the British Parliament 1872 brought the labour trade under control to some extent.

Black Death great epidemic of bubonic ◊plague that ravaged Europe in the 14th century, killing between one-third and half of the population. The cause of the plague was the bacterium *Pasteurella pestis*, transmitted by fleas borne by migrating Asian black rats. The name Black Death was first used in England in the early 19th century.

Blackfoot member of a Plains ◊American Indian people, some 10,000 in number and consisting of three subtribes: the Blackfoot proper, the Blood, and the Piegan, who live in Montana, USA, and Saskatchewan and Alberta, Canada. They were skilled, horse-riding buffalo hunters until their territories were settled by Europeans. Their name derives from their black moccasins. Their language belongs to the Algonquian family.

Black Friday 24 Sept 1869, a day on which Jay Gould (1836–1892) and James Fisk (1834–1872) stock manipulators, attempted to corner the gold market by trying to prevent the government from selling gold. President Grant refused to agree, but they spread the rumour that the president was opposed to the sales. George S Boutwell (1818–1905) with Grant's approval ordered the sale of $4 million in gold. The gold price plunged and many speculators were ruined. The two men made about $11 million.

Black Hawk or *Black Sparrow Hawk* (Sauk name *Makataimeshekiakiak*) 1767–1838. North American Sauk Indian leader. A principal opponent of the cession of Indian lands to the US government, he sided with the British during the Anglo-American War 1812–14 and joined his people in their removal to Iowa at the end of the war. In 1832 he led a large contingent back to Illinois to resettle the Sauk homeland. Defeated by Illinois militia in the bloody 'Black Hawk War', he was captured and permanently exiled to Iowa.

Black Hole of Calcutta incident in Anglo-Indian history: according to tradition, the nawab (ruler) of Bengal confined 146 British prisoners on the night of 20 June 1756 in one small room, of whom only 23 allegedly survived. Later research reduced the death count to 43, assigning negligence rather than intention.

Black Muslim member of a religious group founded 1929 in the USA and led, from 1934, by Elijah Muhammad (then Elijah Poole) (1897–1975) after he had a vision of Allah. Its growth from 1946 as a black separatist organization was due to Malcolm X (1926–1965), the son of a Baptist minister who, in 1964, broke away and founded his own Organization for Afro-American Unity, preaching 'active self-defence'. Under the leadership of Louis Farrakhan, the movement underwent a recent revival.

Black National State area on the Republic of South Africa set aside, 1971-94, for development towards self-government by black Africans, in accordance with ◊apartheid. Before 1980 these areas were known as *black homelands* or *bantustans*. Making up less than 14% of the country, they tended to be situated in arid areas (though some had mineral wealth), often in scattered blocks. Those that achieved nominal independence were Transkei 1976, Bophuthatswana 1977, Venda 1979, and Ciskei 1981. They were not recognised outside South Africa because of their racial basis.

The repeal of the Land Acts and Group Areas Acts 1991 promises progressively to change the status of Black National States. Since the accession of President de Klerk, outbreaks of violence have resulted in the overthrow of the governments in Ciskei and Venda, and calls for reintegration within South Africa in all four states. Some 11 million blacks live permanently in the country's white-designated areas.

Black Power movement towards black separatism in the USA during the 1960s, embodied in the *Black Panther Party* founded 1966 by Huey Newton and Bobby Seale. Its declared aim was the establishment of a separate black state in the USA.

The Black Power campaign arose when existing ◊civil rights organizations such as the National Association for Advancement of Colored People and the Southern Christian Leadership Conference were perceived to be ineffective in producing major change in the status of black people.

Black Prince nickname of ◊Edward, Prince of Wales, eldest son of Edward III of England.

Black September guerrilla splinter group of the ◊Palestine Liberation Organization formed 1970. Operating from bases in Syria and Lebanon, it was responsible for the kidnappings at the Munich Olympics 1972 that led to the deaths of 11 Israelis, and other hijack and bomb attempts. The group is named after the month in which Palestinian guerrillas were expelled from Jordan by King Hussein.

Blackshirts term widely used to describe fascist paramilitary organizations. Originating with Mussolini's fascist Squadristi in the 1920s, it was also applied to the Nazi SS (*Schutzstaffel*) and to the followers of Oswald Mosley's British Union of Fascists.

Blair Tony (Anthony Charles Lynton) 1953– . British politician, leader of the Labour Party from 1994, prime minister from 1997. A centrist like his predecessor John ◊Smith, he became Labour's youngest leader 1994. He won approval of a new party charter 1995, intended to distance Labour from its traditional socialist base and promote 'social market' values. His party won a 179-seat majority 1997.

Blake Robert 1599–1657. British admiral of the Parliamentary forces during the English ◊Civil War. Appointed 'general-at-sea' 1649, he destroyed Prince Rupert's privateering fleet off Cartagena, Spain, in the following year. In 1652 he won several engagements against the Dutch navy. In 1654 he bombarded Tunis, the stronghold of the Barbary corsairs, and in 1657 captured the Spanish treasure fleet in Santa Cruz.

Blamey Thomas Albert 1884–1951. Australian field marshal. Born in New South Wales, he served at Gallipoli, Turkey, and on the Western Front in World War I. After his recall to Australia 1942 and appointment as commander in chief, Allied Land Forces, he commanded operations on the Kokoda Trail and the recapture of Papua.

The rabbit that runs away is the rabbit that gets shot.

Field Marshal Blamey
addressing his troops

Blanc Louis 1811–1882. French socialist and journalist. In 1839 he founded the *Revue du progrès*, in which he published his *Organisation du travail*, advocating the establishment of cooperative workshops and other socialist schemes. He was a member of the provisional government of 1848 (see ◊revolutions of 1848) and from its fall lived in the UK until 1871.

Blanche of Castile 1188–1252. Queen of France, wife of ◊Louis VIII of France, and regent for her son Louis IX (St Louis of France) from the death of her husband 1226 until Louis IX's majority 1234, and again from 1247 while he was on a Crusade.

She quelled a series of revolts by the barons and in 1229 negotiated the Treaty of Paris, by which Toulouse came under control of the monarchy.

Blanqui Louis Auguste 1805–1881. French revolutionary politician. He formulated the theory of the 'dictatorship of the proletariat', used by Karl Marx, and spent a total of 33 years in prison for insurrection. Although in prison, he was elected president of the Commune of Paris 1871. His followers, the Blanquists, joined with the Marxists 1881. He became a martyr figure for the French workers' movement.

Blenheim, Battle of battle on 13 Aug 1704 in which English troops under ◊Marlborough defeated the French and Bavarian armies near the Bavarian village of Blenheim (now in Germany) on the left bank of the Danube.

Blitzkrieg (German 'lightning war') swift military campaign, as used by Germany at the beginning of World War II 1939–41. The abbreviated term *the Blitz* was applied to the attempted saturation bombing of London by the German air force between Sept 1940 and May 1941.

Blomberg Werner von 1878–1946. German general and Nazi politician, minister of defence

1933–35, minister of war, and head of the *Wehrmacht* (army) 1935–38 under Hitler's chancellorship. He was discredited by his marriage to a prostitute and dismissed in Jan 1938, enabling Hitler to exercise more direct control over the armed forces. In spite of his removal from office, Blomberg was interrogated about war crimes by the Nuremberg tribunal. He died during the trial and was never in the dock.

Blood and Iron (German *Blut und Eisen*) description of the methods used by German chancellor ◊Bismarck to unify Germany 1862–1871. The phrase came from Bismarck's speech in which he declared that 'the great questions of the day will be decided, not by speeches and majority votes ... but by iron and blood.'

Bloomer Amelia Jenks 1818–1894. US campaigner for women's rights. In 1849, when unwieldy crinolines were the fashion, she introduced a knee-length skirt combined with loose trousers gathered at the ankles, which became known as *bloomers* (also called 'rational dress'). She published the magazine *The Lily* 1849–54, which campaigned for women's rights and dress reform, and lectured with Susan B ◊Anthony in New York, USA.

The costume of woman ... should conduce at once to her health, comfort, and usefulness ... while it should not fail also to conduce to her personal adornment, it should make that end of secondary importance.
Amelia Jenks Bloomer letter June 1857

Blücher Gebhard Leberecht von 1742–1819. Prussian general and field marshal, popularly known as 'Marshal Forward'. He took an active part in the patriotic movement, and in the War of German Liberation defeated the French as commander in chief at Leipzig 1813, crossed the Rhine to Paris 1814, and was made prince of Wahlstadt (Silesia).

In 1815 he was defeated by Napoleon at Ligny but came to the aid of British commander Wellington at ◊Waterloo.

Blue Division Spanish volunteers who fought with the German army against the USSR during World War II.

Blum Léon 1872–1950. French politician. He was converted to socialism by the ◊Dreyfus affair 1899 and in 1936 became the first socialist prime minister of France. He was again premier for a few weeks 1938. Imprisoned under

the ◊Vichy government 1942 as a danger to French security, he was released by the Allies 1945. He again became premier for a few weeks 1946.

A revolution is legality on holiday.
Léon Blum

Boadicea alternative spelling of British queen ◊Boudicca.

Bodhidharma 6th century AD. Indian Buddhist and teacher. He entered China from S India about 520, and was the founder of the Ch'an school. Ch'an focuses on contemplation leading to intuitive meditation, a direct pointing to and stilling of the human mind. In the 20th century, the Japanese variation, Zen, has attracted many followers in the west.

Boeotia ancient district of central Greece, of which ◊Thebes was the chief city. The *Boeotian League* (formed by 10 city states in the 6th century BC) superseded ◊Sparta in the leadership of Greece in the 4th century BC.

Boer Dutch settler or descendant of Dutch and Huguenot settlers in South Africa; see also ◊Afrikaner.

Boer War the second of the ◊South African Wars 1899–1902, waged between Dutch settlers in South Africa and the British.

Bogomil member of a sect of Christian heretics who originated in 10th-century Bulgaria and spread throughout the Byzantine empire. Their derives from Bogomilus, or Theophilus, probably a Greek Orthodox priest who taught in Bulgaria 927–950. Despite persecution, they were expunged by the Ottomans only after the fall of Constantinople 1453.

Bohemia area of the Czech Republic, a kingdom of central Europe from the 9th century. It was under Habsburg rule 1526–1918, when it was included in Czechoslovakia. The name Bohemia derives from the Celtic Boii, its earliest known inhabitants.

It became part of the Holy Roman Empire as the result of Charlemagne's establishment of a protectorate over the Celtic, Germanic, and Slav tribes settled in this area. Christianity was introduced in the 9th century, the See of Prague being established 975, and feudalism was introduced by King Ottaker I of Bohemia (1197–1230). From the 12th century onward, mining attracted large numbers of German settlers, leading to a strong Germanic influence in culture and society. In 1310, John of Luxemburg (died 1346) founded a German-Czech royal dynasty that lasted until 1437. His son, Charles IV, became Holy Roman Emperor 1355, and during his reign the See of Prague was elevated to an archbishopric and a university was founded here. During the 15th century, divisions within the nobility and religious conflicts culminating in the Hussite Wars (1420–36) led to its decline.

Bokassa Jean-Bédel 1921– . President of the Central African Republic 1966–79 and later self-proclaimed emperor 1977–79. Commander in chief from 1963, in Dec 1965 he led the military coup that gave him the presidency. On 4 Dec 1976 he proclaimed the Central African Empire and one year later crowned himself as emperor for life.

His regime was characterized by arbitrary state violence and cruelty. Overthrown in 1979, Bokassa was in exile until 1986. Upon his return he was sentenced to death, but this was commuted to life imprisonment 1988.

Bokhara see ◊Bukhara.

Boleyn Anne 1507–1536. Queen of England 1533–36. Henry VIII broke with the pope (see ◊Reformation) in order to divorce his first wife and marry Anne. She was married to him 1533 and gave birth to the future Queen Elizabeth I in the same year. Accused of adultery and incest with her half-brother (a charge invented by Thomas ◊Cromwell), she was beheaded.

Bolingbroke title of Henry of Bolingbroke, ◊Henry IV of England.

Bolingbroke Henry John, Viscount Bolingbroke 1678–1751. British Tory politician and political philosopher. He was foreign secretary 1710–14 and a Jacobite conspirator. His books, such as *Idea of a Patriot King* 1738 and *The Dissertation upon Parties* 1735, laid the foundations for 19th-century Toryism.

Secretary of war 1704–08, he became foreign secretary in Robert ◊Harley's ministry 1710, and in 1713 negotiated the Treaty of Utrecht. His plans to restore the 'Old Pretender' James Francis Edward Stuart were ruined by Queen Anne's death only five days after he had secured the dismissal of Harley 1714. He fled abroad, returning 1723, when he worked to overthrow Robert Walpole.

Nations, like men, have their infancy.

Viscount Bolingbroke
On the Study of History

Bolívar Simón 1783–1830. South American nationalist, leader of revolutionary armies, known as *the Liberator*. He fought the Spanish colonial forces in several uprisings and eventually liberated his native Venezuela 1821, Colombia and Ecuador 1822, Peru 1824, and Bolivia (a new state named after him, formerly Upper Peru) 1825.

Born in Venezuela, he joined that country's revolution against Spain in 1810, and in the following year he declared Venezuela independent. His army was soon defeated by the Spanish, however, and he was forced to flee. Many battles and defeats followed, and it was not until 1819 that Bolívar won his first major victory, defeating the Spanish in Colombia and winning independence for that country. He went on to liberate Venezuela 1821 and (along with Antonio ◊Sucre) Ecuador 1822. These three countries were united into the republic of Gran Colombia with Bolívar as its president. In 1824 Bolívar helped bring about the defeat of Spanish forces in Peru, and the area known as Upper Peru was renamed 'Bolivia' in Bolívar's honour. Within the next few years, Venezuela and Ecuador seceded from the union, and in 1830 Bolívar resigned as president. He died the same year, despised by many for his dictatorial ways but since revered as South America's greatest liberator.

A people that loves freedom will in the end be free.

Simón Bolívar Letter from Jamaica

Bolivia landlocked country in central Andes mountains in South America, bounded N and E by Brazil, SE by Paraguay, S by Argentina, and W by Chile and Peru.

history Once part of the ◊Inca civilization, Bolivia was conquered by Spain 1538 and remained under Spanish rule until liberated by Simón ◊Bolívar 1825 (after whom the country took its name). Throughout most of the 19th century Bolivia was governed by a series of caudillos (military or political leaders). The first of these, Andrés Santa Cruz, seized power 1829 and created a Peru-Bolivia confederation 1836. The confederation lasted only three years: it was put down by Chilean troops 1839.

After the early 1870s, white and mixed-blood (*cholo*) landlords took virtually all the land remaining to the Indians.

loss of territory During the War of the Pacific 1881, Bolivia lost its coastal province and outlet to the sea. Two decades later, further territory was lost to Brazil. Between 1932 and 1935 the Bolivian army waged a disastrous war (the

Chaco War) with Paraguay over the border region between the two countries in the hot lowlands.

army vs reformers In the 1951 election, Dr Víctor Paz Estenssoro, the National Revolutionary Movement (MNR) candidate exiled in Argentina since 1946, failed to win an absolute majority, and an army junta took over. A popular uprising, supported by MNR and a section of the army, demanded the return of Paz, who became president and began a programme of social reform. He lost the 1956 election but returned to power 1960. In 1964 a coup, led by Vice President General René Barrientos, overthrew Paz and installed a military junta. Two years later Barrientos won the presidency. He was opposed by left-wing groups and in 1967 a guerrilla uprising led by Dr Ernesto 'Che' ◊Guevara was put down with US help.

frequent coups In 1969 President Barrientos died in an air crash and was replaced by the vice president. He was later replaced by General Alfredo Ovando, who was ousted by General Juan Torres, who in turn was ousted by Col Hugo Banzer Suárez 1971. Banzer announced a return to constitutional government, but another attempted coup 1974 prompted him to postpone elections, ban all trade union and political activity, and proclaim that military government would last until at least 1980. Banzer agreed to elections 1978, but they were declared invalid after allegations of fraud, and, in that year, two more military coups.

In the 1979 elections Dr Siles and Dr Paz received virtually equal votes, and an interim administration was installed. An election 1980 proved equally inconclusive and was followed by the 189th military coup in Bolivia's 154 years of independence. General Luis García became president but resigned the following year after allegations of drug trafficking. He was replaced by General Celso Torrelio, who promised to fight corruption and return the country to democracy within three years. In 1982 a mainly civilian cabinet was appointed, but rumours of an impending coup resulted in Torrelio's resignation. A military junta led by the hardline General Guido Vildoso was installed.

economy deteriorates With the economy deteriorating, the junta asked congress to elect a president, and Dr Siles Zuazo was chosen to head a coalition cabinet. Economic aid from Europe and the USA, cut off in 1980, was resumed, but the economy continued to deteriorate. The government's austerity measures proved unpopular, and in June the president was temporarily abducted by a group of rightwing army officers.

Siles resigned 1985 and an election was held. No candidate won an absolute majority and Dr Víctor Paz Estenssoro, aged 77, was chosen by congress. Austerity measures imposed by Estenssoro's administration reduced inflation from 24,000% in 1985 to 3% in the first half of 1989.

power-sharing In the 1989 congressional elections the MNR won marginally more votes in the chamber of deputies than the Nationalist Democratic Action Party (ADN), but did not obtain a clear majority. After an indecisive presidential contest, Jaime Paz Zamora of the Movement of the Revolutionary Left (MIR) was elected president by the congress after he negotiated a power-sharing arrangement with former military dictator Hugo Banzer Suárez. The 1993 presidential election was again inconclusive but, after Hugo Banzer withdrew his candidacy, the presidency went to the MNR leader, Gonzalo Sanchez do Lozada.

Christian theology is the grandmother of Bolshevism.

On the **Bolsheviks** Oswald Spengler
The Hour of Decision 1934

Bolshevik (from Russian *bolshinstvo* 'a majority') member of the majority of the Russian Social Democratic Party who split from the ◊Mensheviks 1903. The Bolsheviks, under ◊Lenin, advocated the destruction of capitalist political and economic institutions, and the setting-up of a socialist state with power in the hands of the workers. The Bolsheviks set the ◊Russian Revolution 1917 in motion. They changed their name to the Russian Communist Party 1918.

bomb container filled with explosive or chemical material and generally used in warfare. There are also incendiary bombs and nuclear bombs and missiles. Any object designed to cause damage by explosion can be called a bomb (car bombs, letter bombs). Initially dropped from aeroplanes (from World War I), bombs were in World War II also launched by rocket. The 1960s saw the development of missiles that could be launched from aircraft, land sites, or submarines. In the 1970s laser guidance systems were developed to hit small targets with accuracy.

Aerial bombing started in World War I (1914–18) when the German air force carried out 103 raids on Britain, dropping 269 tonnes of bombs. In World War II (1939–45) nearly twice this tonnage was dropped on London in a single night, and at the peak of the Allied air offensive against Germany, more than ten times this tonnage was regularly dropped in successive nights on one target. Raids in which nearly 1,000 heavy bombers participated were frequent. They were delivered either in 'precision' or 'area' attacks and advances were made in *blind bombing*, in which the target is located solely by instruments and is not visible through a bombsight. In 1939 bombs were commonly about 115 kg/250 lb and 230 kg/500 lb, but by the end of the war the ten-tonner was being produced.

Bonaparte Corsican family of Italian origin that gave rise to the Napoleonic dynasty: see ◊Napoleon I, ◊Napoleon II, and ◊Napoleon III. Others were the brothers and sister of Napoleon I.

Joseph (1768–1844) whom Napoleon made king of Naples 1806 and Spain 1808;

Lucien (1775–1840) whose handling of the Council of Five Hundred on 10 Nov 1799 ensured Napoleon's future;

Louis (1778–1846) the father of Napoleon III, who was made king of Holland 1806–10;

Caroline (1782–1839) who married Joachim ◊Murat 1800;

Jerome (1784–1860) made king of Westphalia 1807.

Bonapartism political system of military dictatorship by an individual, ostensibly based on popular appeal, with frequent use of the plebiscite. Derived from Napoleon's system of rule (1799–1815), the term has been applied to other regimes, for example that of Juan Perón in Argentina. In France, supporters of the Bonaparte family's claims to the French throne during the 19th century were known as Bonapartists.

Bonar Law British Conservative politician; see ◊Law, Andrew Bonar.

Bondfield Margaret Grace 1873–1953. British socialist who became a trade-union organizer to improve working conditions for women. She was a Labour member of Parliament 1923–24 and 1926–31, and was the first woman to enter the cabinet – as minister of labour 1929–31.

bondservant another term for a slave or serf used in the Caribbean in the 18th and 19th centuries; a person who was offered a few acres of land in return for some years of compulsory service. The system was a means of obtaining labour from Europe.

Bonney William H 1859–1881. US outlaw known by the nickname of ◊Billy the Kid.

Bonnie and Clyde Bonnie Parker (1911–1934) and Clyde Barrow (1900–1934). Infamous US criminals who carried out a series of small-scale robberies in Texas, Oklahoma, New Mexico, and Missouri between Aug 1932 and May 1934. They were eventually betrayed and then killed in a police ambush.

Bonnie Prince Charlie Scottish name for ◊Charles Edward Stuart, pretender to the throne.

Bonus Army or *Bonus Expeditionary Force* in US history, a march on Washington DC by unemployed ex-servicemen during the great ◊Depression to lobby Congress for immediate cash payment of a promised war veterans' bonus.

During the spring of 1932, some 15,000 veterans camped by the river Potomac or squatted in disused government buildings. They were eventually dispersed by troops.

Boone Daniel 1734–1820. US pioneer who explored the Wilderness Road (East Virginia–Kentucky) 1775 and paved the way for the first westward migration of settlers.

Booth John Wilkes 1839–1865. US actor and fanatical Confederate sympathizer who assassinated President Abraham ◊Lincoln 14 April 1865; he escaped with a broken leg and was later shot in a barn in Virginia when he refused to surrender.

Tell mother – tell mother – I died for my country.

John Wilkes Booth
having assassinated President Lincoln 1865

---

bootlegging illegal manufacture, distribution, or sale of a product. The term originated in the USA, when the sale of alcohol to American Indians was illegal and bottles were hidden for sale in the legs of the jackboots of unscrupulous traders. The term was later used for all illegal liquor sales during the period of ◊Prohibition in the USA 1920–33.

Bordeaux port on the river Garonne, capital of Aquitaine, SW France. Bordeaux was under the English crown for three centuries until 1453. In 1870, 1914, and 1940 the French government was moved here because of German invasion.

Borgia Cesare 1476–1507. Italian general, illegitimate son of Pope ◊Alexander VI. Made a cardinal at 17 by his father, he resigned to become captain-general of the papacy, campaigning successfully against the city republics of Italy. Ruthless and treacherous in war, he was an able ruler (the model for Machiavelli's *The Prince*), but his power crumbled on the death of his father. He was a patron of artists, including Leonardo da Vinci.

Borgia Lucrezia 1480–1519. Duchess of Ferrara from 1501. She was the illegitimate daughter of Pope ◊Alexander VI and sister of Cesare Borgia. She was married at 12 and again at 13 to further her father's ambitions, both marriages being annulled by him. At 18 she was married again, but her husband was murdered in 1500 on the order of her brother, with whom (as well as with her father) she was said to have committed incest. Her final marriage was to the duke of Este, the son and heir of the duke of Ferrara. She made the court a centre of culture and was a patron of authors and artists such as Ariosto and Titian.

Boris III 1894–1943. Tsar of Bulgaria from 1918, when he succeeded his father, Ferdinand I. From 1934 he was virtual dictator until his sudden and mysterious death following a visit to Hitler. His son Simeon II was tsar until deposed 1946.

Boris Godunov 1552–1605. See Boris ◊Godunov, tsar of Russia from 1598.

Bormann Martin 1900–1945. German Nazi leader. He took part in the abortive Munich ◊Beer-hall putsch (uprising) 1923 and rose to high positions in the Nazi (National Socialist) Party, becoming deputy party leader May 1941.

Bormann was believed to have escaped the fall of Berlin May 1945 and was tried in his absence and sentenced to death at the ◊Nuremberg trials 1945–46, but a skeleton uncovered by a mechanical excavator in Berlin 1972 was officially recognized as his by forensic experts 1973.

Borneo third-largest island in the world, one of the Sunda Islands in the W Pacific. It comprises the Malaysian territories of ◊*Sabah* and ◊*Sarawak*; ◊*Brunei* ; and, occupying by far the largest part, the Indonesian territory of *Kalimantan*. It was formerly under both Dutch and British colonial influence until Sarawak was formed 1841.

Bornu kingdom of the 9th–19th centuries to the west and south of Lake Chad, W central Africa. Converted to Islam in the 11th century, Bornu reached its greatest strength in the 15th–18th centuries. From 1901 it was absorbed in the British, French, and German colonies in this area, which became the states of Niger, Cameroon, and Nigeria. The largest section of ancient Bornu is now the *state of Bornu* in Nigeria.

Borodino, Battle of battle 7 Sept 1812 where French troops under Napoleon defeated the Russians under Kutusov. Named after the village of Borodino, 110km/70 mi NW of Moscow.

Boscawen Edward 1711–1761. English admiral who served against the French in the mid-18th-century wars, including the War of Austrian Succession and the Seven Years' War. He led expeditions to the East Indies 1748–50 and served as lord of the Admiralty from 1751, vice admiral from 1755, and admiral from 1758. To his men he was known as 'Old Dreadnought'.

Bosch Juan 1909– . President of the Dominican Republic 1963. His left-wing Partido Revolucionario Dominicano won a landslide victory in the 1962 elections. In office, he attempted agrarian reform and labour legislation. He was opposed by the USA, and overthrown by the army. His achievement was to establish a democratic political party after three decades of dictatorship.

Bosnia-Herzegovina Serbo-Croatian *Bosna-Hercegovina* country in central Europe, bounded N and W by Croatia, E by the Yugoslavian republic of Serbia, and E and S by the Yugoslavian republic of Montenegro.

history Once the Roman province of ◊Illyria, the area enjoyed brief periods of independence in medieval times, then was ruled by the Ottoman Empire 1463–1878 and Austria 1878–1918, when it was incorporated in the future Yugoslavia. It came under Nazi German rule 1941, and Marshal ◊Tito established his provisional government at liberated Jajce in Nov 1943. Bosnia-Herzegovina, kept undivided because of its ethnic and religious compound of Serbs (Orthodox Christians), Croats (Catholic Christians) and Serbo-Croatian-speaking Slavs (Muslims), became a republic within the Yugoslav Socialist Federal Republic in Nov 1945, after the expulsion of remaining German forces.

communist rule The republic's communist leadership became notorious for its corruption, racketeering, and authoritarianism, and from 1980 there was an upsurge in Islamic nationalism. Ethnic violence between Muslims and Serbs worsened 1989–90. In the Nov–Dec 1990 elections nationalist parties routed the ruling communists; subsequent divisions within the Bosnian ruling coalition, formed by the three leading Serb, Muslim, and Croatian parties, complicated the republic's dealings with Serbia.

civil unrest From spring 1991 the conflict between Serbia and Croatia and civil war in the latter spread disorder into Bosnia-Herzegovina. Croats set up barricades attempting to stop the mainly Serb Yugoslav National Army (JNA) moving through Croatia. In Aug 1991 president Alija Izetbegović expressed concern that Serbia wanted to divide Bosnia-Herzegovina between Serbia and Croatia, with a reduced Muslim buffer state between. From Sept border areas began to fall into Serb hands.

independence In Oct 1991 the republic's 'sovereignty' was declared by its parliament, but rejected by the Serbs, who established an alternative assembly. A referendum Feb 1992, requested by the EC, voted overwhelmingly in favour of independence, but was boycotted by Serbs. Violent clashes ensued. Its independence was recognised by the EC and the USA April, and it became a full UN member May.

In spring 1992 Bosnian Serb militia units, led by Radovan Karadic and effectively backed by Serbia, took control of E Bosnian border towns and launched attacks on the capital, Sarajevo. Croats and Muslims also struggled to gain disputed territory. In June the first UN troops were drafted in to Sarajevo. Bosnian Serb forces established control over two-thirds of the country and declared it independent. Croats declared an independent Croat state. There was increasing evidence of ethnic cleansing and reports of death camps.

peace plans UN negotiator Cyrus Vance and EC negotiator Lord Owen urged adoption of a peace plan 1993, but the warring factions disagreed over details and fighting continued. The UN created safe areas for Muslims fleeing Serbian aggression. In Oct Haris Siladzic became prime minister. A UN ultimatum Feb 1994 demanded withdrawal from Sarajevo; the Serbs agreed to withdraw when Russia intervened. A Muslim-Croat cease-fire in the N followed and a Bosnian Muslim-Croat federation was created. In April Bosnian Serb forces took control of Gorazde, but withdrew after a UN ultimatum. In July the Bosnian Serbs rejected a further pleace plan, leading Serbia, seeking a reduction in UN sanctions, to impose an economic blockade against its ex-allies.

Dayton Further fighting and intervention by the UN preceded a four-month cease-fire, taking effect Jan 1995, negotiated by former US president Jimmy Carter. But hostilities were renewed at the cease-fires end. In June the Serbs took UN peacekeepers hostage; a Rapid Reaction Force was deployed to protect the peacekeepers. Bosnian Serbs continued attacks on safe areas, while NATO started air attacks on their posts and depots around Sarajevo. Their military machine in disarray, the Bosnian Serbs agreed to recognize the Muslim-Croat federation. In Sept, the contending parties agreed to peace negotiations that led to the Dayton Peace Accord 21 Nov 1995, dividing land between the Bosnian Serbs and Muslim-Croats. A NATO-led force, IFOR, was drafted to police the agreement, replacing the UN.

Bosnian Crisis period of international tension 1908 when Austria attempted to capitalize on Turkish weakness after the ◊Young Turk revolt by annexing the provinces of Bosnia and Herzegovina. Austria obtained Russian approval in exchange for conceding Russian access to the Bosporus straits.

The speed of Austrian action took Russia by surprise, and domestic opposition led to the resignation of Russian foreign minister Izvolsky. Russia also failed to obtain necessary French and British agreements on the straits.

Boston Tea Party protest 1773 by colonists in Massachusetts, America, against the tea tax imposed on them by the British government before the ◊American Revolution.

When a valuable consignment of tea (belonging to the East India Company and intended for sale in the American colonies) arrived in Boston Harbor, it was thrown overboard by a group of Bostonians disguised as Indians during the night of 16 Dec 1773. The British government, angered by this and other colonial protests against British policy, took retaliatory measures 1774, including the closing of the port of Boston. The consignment, brought on three ships from England, was valued at £15,000.

Bosworth, Battle of last battle of the Wars of the ◊Roses, fought on 22 Aug 1485. Richard III, the Yorkist king, was defeated and slain by Henry of Richmond, who became Henry VII. The battlefield is near the village of Market Bosworth, 19 km/12 mi W of Leicester, England.

Botany Bay inlet on the east coast of Australia, 8 km/5 mi S of Sydney, New South Wales. Chosen 1787 as the site for a penal colony, it proved unsuitable. Sydney now stands there. The name Botany Bay was popularly used for any convict settlement in Australia.

Botha Louis 1862–1919. South African soldier and politician, a commande in the Second South African War (Boer War). In 1907 Botha became premier of the Transvaal and in 1910 of the first Union South African government. On the outbreak of World War I 1914 he rallied South Africa to the Commonwealth, suppressed a Boer revolt, and conquered German South West Africa.

Botha P(ieter) W(illem) 1916– . South African politician, prime minister from 1978. Botha initiated a modification of ◊apartheid, which later slowed in the face of Afrikaner (Boer) opposition. In 1984 he became the first executive state president. In 1989 he unwillingly resigned both party leadership and presidency after suffering a stroke, and was succeeded by F W de Klerk.

Bothwell James Hepburn, 4th Earl of Bothwell c. 1536–1578. Scottish nobleman, third husband of ◊Mary Queen of Scots, 1567–70, alleged to have arranged the explosion that killed Darnley, her previous husband, 1567.

Tried and acquitted a few weeks after the assassination, he abducted Mary and married her on 15 May. A revolt ensured, and Bothwell fled. In 1570 Mary obtained a divorce, and Bothwell was confined in a castle in the Netherlands where he died insane.

Botswana landlocked country in central southern Africa, bounded S and SE by South Africa, W and N by Namibia, and NE by Zimbabwe.

history The first inhabitants were the ◊Kung, the hunter-gatherer groups living chiefly in the Kalahari Desert; from the 17th century the Tswana people became the principal inhabitants of the area, followed by the arrival of Bantu peoples in the early 19th century. Fearing an invasion by Boer farmers (descendants of Dutch settlers), the local rulers appealed to Britain, and Bechuanaland (as it was originally called) became a British protectorate 1885.

On passing the Union of South Africa Act 1910, making South Africa independent, the British Parliament provided for the possibility of Bechuanaland becoming part of South Africa, but stipulated that this would not happen without popular consent. Successive South African governments requested the transfer, but Botswana preferred full independence.

The 1960 constitution provided for a legislative council, although remaining under British High Commission control. In 1963 High Commission rule ended, and in the legislative assembly elections the newly formed Bechuanaland Democratic Party (BDP) won a majority. Its leader, Seretse ◊Khama, had been deposed as chief of the Bamangwato tribe 1950 and had since lived in exile.

achieved independence In 1966 the country, renamed Botswana, became an independent state within the ◊Commonwealth with Sir Seretse Khama, as he had now become, as pres-

ident. He continued to be re-elected until his death 1980, when he was succeeded by the vice president, Dr Ketumile Masire, who was re-elected 1984. In the 1989 elections the BDP won overwhelmingly under Masire, and in 1994 the party was again returned to power.

relations with South Africa Since independence Botswana has earned a reputation for stability. It is a member of the ◊nonaligned movement. South Africa accused it of providing bases for the African National Congress (ANC) and Botswana was the target of several cross-border raids by South African forces. The presence of ANC bases was always denied by both Botswana and the ANC. Tension in this respect was dissipated by the legalization of the ANC by South Africa 1990.

I am not fighting for my kingdom and wealth now. I am fighting as an ordinary person for my lost freedom, my bruised body, and my outraged daughters.

Boudicca address to her army before the Icenian revolt, AD 61, quoted by *Tacitus*

Boudicca Queen of the Iceni (native Britons), often referred to by the Latin form *Boadicea*. Her husband, King Prasutagus, had been a tributary of the Romans, but on his death AD 60 the territory of the Iceni was violently annexed. Boudicca was scourged and her daughters raped. Boudicca raised the whole of SE England in revolt, and before the main Roman armies could return from campaigning in Wales she burned Londinium (London), Verulamium (St Albans), and Camulodunum (Colchester). Later the Romans under governor Suetonius Paulinus defeated the British between London and Chester; they were virtually annihilated and Boudicca poisoned herself.

Boulanger George Ernest Jean Marie 1837–1891. French general. He became minister of war 1886, and his anti-German speeches nearly provoked war with Germany 1887. In 1889 he was suspected of aspiring to dictatorship by a coup d'état. Accused of treason, he fled into exile and committed suicide on the grave of his mistress.

boulangist supporter of General George ◊Boulanger (1837–1891) who led the revanchist ('revenge') movement in France in the late 1880s. It focused on restoring French territory in Europe as an alternative to colonial expansion.

Boumédienne Houari. Adopted name of Mohammed Boukharouba 1925–1978. Algerian politician who brought the nationalist leader Ben Bella to power by a revolt 1962, and superseded him as president in 1965 by a further coup.

Bounty, Mutiny on the naval mutiny in the Pacific 1789 against British captain William ◊Bligh.

Bourbon Charles, Duke of 1490–1527. Constable of France, honoured for his courage at the Battle of Marignano 1515. Later he served the Holy Roman Emperor Charles V, and helped to drive the French from Italy. In 1526 he was made duke of Milan, and in 1527 allowed his troops to sack Rome. He was killed by a shot the artist Cellini claimed to have fired.

Bourbon, duchy of originally a seigneury (feudal domain) created in the 10th century in the county of Bourges, central France, held by the Bourbon family. It became a duchy 1327.

The lands passed to the Capetian dynasty (see ◊Capet) as a result of the marriage of the Bourbon heiress Beatrix to Robert of Clermont, son of Louis IX. Their son Pierre became the first duke of Bourbon 1327. The direct line ended with the death of Charles, Duke of Bourbon, in 1527.

Bourbon dynasty French royal house (succeeding that of ◊Valois) beginning with Henry IV, and ending with Louis XVI, with a brief revival under Louis XVIII, Charles X, and Louis Philippe. The Bourbons also ruled Spain almost uninterruptedly from Philip V to Alfonso XIII and were restored in 1975; at one point they also ruled Naples and several Italian duchies. The Grand Duke of Luxembourg is also a Bourbon by male descent.

Bourgeois Léon Victor Auguste 1851–1925. French politician. Entering politics as a Radical, he was prime minister in 1895, and later served in many cabinets. He was one of the pioneer advocates of the League of Nations. He was awarded the Nobel Peace Prize 1920.

bourgeoisie (French) the middle classes. The French word originally meant 'the freemen of a borough'. It came to mean the whole class above the workers and peasants, and below the nobility. Bourgeoisie (and *bourgeois*) has also acquired a contemptuous sense, implying commonplace, philistine respectability. By socialists it is applied to the whole propertied class, as distinct from the proletariat.

Bourguiba Habib ben Ali 1903–   . Tunisian politician, first president of Tunisia 1957–87. Educated at the University of Paris, he became a journalist and was frequently imprisoned by the French for his nationalist aims as leader of the Néo-Destour party. He became prime minister 1956, president (for life from 1974) and prime minister of the Tunisian republic 1957; he was overthrown in a bloodless coup 1987.

Bouvines, Battle of victory for Philip II (Philip Augustus) of France in 1214, near the village of Bouvines in Flanders, over the Holy Roman Emperor Otto IV and his allies. The battle, one of the most decisive in medieval Europe, ensured the succession of Frederick II as emperor and confirmed Philip as ruler of the whole of N France and Flanders; it led to the renunciation of all English claims to the region.

Bowie James 'Jim' 1796–1836. US frontiersman and folk hero. A colonel in the Texan forces during the Mexican War, he is said to have invented the single-edge, guarded hunting and throwing knife known as a *Bowie knife*. He was killed in the battle of the ◊Alamo.

Boxer member of the *I ho ch'üan* ('Righteous Harmonious Fists'), a society of Chinese nationalists dedicated to fighting European influence. The *Boxer Rebellion* or *Uprising* 1900 was instigated by the empress ◊Zi Xi. European and US legations in Beijing were besieged and thousands of Chinese Christian converts and missionaries murdered. An international punitive force was dispatched, Beijing was captured 14 Aug 1900, and China agreed to pay a large indemnity.

boyar landowner in the Russian aristocracy. During the 16th century boyars formed a powerful interest group threatening the tsar's power, until their influence was decisively broken in 1565 when Ivan the Terrible confiscated much of their land.

Boycott Charles Cunningham 1832–1897. English land agent in County Mayo, Ireland, who strongly opposed the demands for agrarian reform by the Irish Land League 1879–81, with the result that the peasants refused to work for him; hence the word *boycott*.

Boyer Jean-Pierre 1776–1850. Haitian president 1818–43 whose term saw the consolidation of a mulatto elite. A mulatto (one parent black, one white), Boyer joined the French army at 16 and went into exile after France was defeated by ◊Toussaint L'Ouverture. President for life, he annexed the Spanish-speaking E part of the island 1822. He was overthrown in a military revolt led by General Charles Hérard 1843.

Boyne, Battle of the battle fought 1 July 1690 in E Ireland, in which James II was defeated by

William III and fled to France. It was the decisive battle of the War of English Succession, confirming a Protestant monarch. It took its name from the river Boyne.

Brabant (Flemish *Braband*) former duchy of W Europe, comprising the Dutch province of North Brabant and the Belgian provinces of Brabant and Antwerp. They were divided when Belgium became independent 1830.

During the Middle Ages Brabant was an independent duchy, and after passing to Burgundy, and thence to the Spanish crown, was divided during the Dutch War of Independence. The southern portion was Spanish until 1713, then Austrian until 1815, when the whole area was included in the Netherlands. In 1830 the French-speaking part of the population in the S Netherlands rebelled, and when Belgium was recognized 1839, S Brabant was included in it.

Bradford William 1590–1657. British colonial administrator in America, the first governor of Plymouth colony, Massachusetts, 1621–57. As one of the Pilgrim Fathers, he sailed for America aboard the *Mayflower* 1620 and was among the signatories of the Mayflower Compact, the first written constitution in the New World. His memoirs, *History of Plimoth Plantation*, are an important source for the colony's early history.

Bradley Omar Nelson 1893–1981. US general in World War II. In 1943 he commanded the 2nd US Corps in their victories in Tunisia and Sicily, leading to the surrender of 250,000 Axis troops, and in 1944 led the US troops in the invasion of France. His command, as the 12th Army Group, grew to 1.3 million troops, the largest US force ever assembled.

Braganza the royal house of Portugal whose members reigned 1640–1910; another branch were emperors of Brazil 1822–89.

Brahma Samaj Indian monotheistic religious movement, founded in 1830 in Calcutta by Ram Mohun Roy who attempted to recover the simple worship of the Vedas and purify Hinduism. The movement had split into a number of sects by the end of the 19th century and is now almost defunct.

Brain Trust nickname of an informal group of experts who advised US president Franklin D Roosevelt on his ◊New Deal policy.

Brandt Willy. Adopted name of Karl Herbert Frahm 1913–92. German socialist politician, federal chancellor (premier) of West Germany 1969–74. He played a key role in the remoulding of the Social Democratic Party (SPD) as a moderate socialist force (leader 1964–87). As mayor of West Berlin 1957–66, Brandt became internationally known during the Berlin Wall crisis 1961. He won the Nobel Peace Prize 1971.

Brandt Commission officially the Independent Commission on International Development Issues, established 1977 and chaired by the former West German chancellor Willy ◊Brandt. Consisting of 18 eminent persons acting independently of governments, the commission examined the problems of developing countries and sought to identify corrective measures that would command international support. It was disbanded 1983.

Its main report, published 1980 under the title *North–South: A Programme for Survival,* made detailed recommendations for accelerating the development of poorer countries (involving the transfer of resources to the latter from the rich countries).

Brauchitsch Walther von 1881–1948. German field marshal. A staff officer in World War I, he became in 1938 commander in chief of the army and a member of Hitler's secret cabinet council. He was dismissed after his failure to invade Moscow 1941. Captured in 1945, he died before being tried in the ◊Nuremburg trials.

Braun Eva 1910–1945. German mistress of Adolf Hitler. Secretary to Hitler's photographer and personal friend, Heinrich Hoffmann, she became Hitler's mistress in the 1930s and married him in the air-raid shelter of the Chancellery in Berlin on 29 April 1945. The next day they committed suicide together.

Brazil largest country in South America (almost half the continent), bounded SW by Uruguay, Argentina, Paraguay and Bolivia; W by Peru and Colombia; N by Venezuela, Guyana, Surinam, and French Guiana; and NE and SE by the Atlantic Ocean.

history Inhabited by various South ◊American Indians, Brazil was colonized by the Portuguese from 1500, when the explorer Pedro Alvares Cobral landed there. The colony was named after a legendary island in the Atlantic and also a red dye wood which became the region's main export.

Later, the introduction of sugar cane from Madeira and São Tomé gave rise to a plantation economy in the coastal zone, based on slavery. Black slaves from Africa made up one-third of Brazil's population of 2 million around 1800. Of the rest, about two-thirds were black and mulatto and one-third of European origin.

empire In 1808, after the French emperor Napoleon invaded Portugal, King John VI moved his capital from Lisbon to Rio de Janeiro. In 1821 he returned to Lisbon, leaving his son, Crown Prince Pedro, as regent. In 1822 Pedro declared Brazil independent and took the title Emperor Pedro I. His son Pedro II persuaded large numbers of Portuguese to emigrate, and the centre of Brazil developed quickly, largely on the basis of slavery. In 1888 slavery was abolished and in 1889 a republic was founded by Marshal Manuel Deodoro de Fonseca, followed by the adoption of a constitution for a federated nation 1891.

First Republic The so-called First or Old Republic was a loose federation of states, dominated by São Paulo and Minas Gerais. At this time 3 million European immigrants came to Brazil, mainly settling on the coast. After social unrest in the 1920s and a series of revolts led by younger army officers, the First Republic was brought down by a revolution in 1930, prompted by the world economic crisis.

dictatorship and growth Dr Getúlio Vargas held presidential office, as a benevolent dictator, for the next 15 years. He expanded Brazilian industry and increased expenditure on state education, health, and social services. The army forced him to resign 1945 and General Eurico Gaspar Dutra became president. In 1951 Vargas returned to power as an elected president after the uninspiring regime of Dutra, but was brought down by military pressure and committed suicide 1954.

Vargas was succeeded by Dr Juscelino Kubitschek, who followed a policy of economic development combined with nationalism. This led to unprecedented growth and culminated in the construction of the country's new capital, Brasília.

military pressures The 1960s and 1970s brought a series of military dictatorships, which nevertheless achieved high levels of economic growth. In 1961 Dr Janio Quadros became president but resigned after seven months, to be succeeded by Vice President João Goulart. Suspecting him of left-wing leanings, the army forced a restriction of presidential powers and created the office of prime minister. A referendum brought back the presidential system 1963, with Goulart choosing his own cabinet.

free political parties banned In a bloodless coup 1964, General Castelo Branco assumed dictatorial powers and banned all political groupings except for two artificially created parties, the pro-government National Renewal Alliance (ARENA) and the opposition Brazilian Democratic Movement Party (PMBD). In

1967 Branco named Marshal da Costa e Silva as his successor, and a new constitution was adopted. In 1969 da Costa e Silva resigned because of ill health, and a military junta took over. In 1974 General Ernesto Geisel became president. He announced in 1967 the start of a gradual liberalization programme which led to amnesty for political prisoners. He was succeeded by General Baptista de Figueiredo 1978, and the ban on opposition parties was lifted 1979.

civilian presidency restored President Figueiredo held office until 1985, his last few years as president witnessing economic decline, strikes, and calls for the return of democracy. In 1985 Tancredo Neves became the first civilian president in 21 years, but died within months of taking office. He was succeeded by Vice President José Sarney, who continued to work with Neves's cabinet and policies. The constitution was again amended to allow direct presidential elections.

Collor accused of corruption. Fernando Collor of the National Reconstruction Party (PRN) narrowly won the 1989 presidential election, advocating free-market policies and a crackdown on corruption. Despite wins for the PRN in 1990 elections, widespread abstentions showed dissatisfaction with Collor. In Feb 1992 Collor was stripped of his power by congress, accused of corruption, and replaced by vice president Itamar Franco. Collor was later cleared of corruption charges. The 1994 presidential election was won by Fernando Henrique Cardoso of the Social Democratic Party.

Brest-Litovsk, Treaty of bilateral treaty signed 3 March 1918 between Russia and Germany, Austria-Hungary, and their allies. Under its terms, Russia agreed to recognize the independence of Georgia, Ukraine, Poland and the Baltic States, and pay heavy compensation. Under the Nov 1918 Armistice that ended World War I, it was annulled, since Russia was one of the winning allies.

Brétigny, Treaty of treaty made between Edward III of England and John II of France in 1360 at the end of the first phase of the Hundred Years' War, under which Edward received Aquitaine and its dependencies in exchange for renunciation of his claim to the French throne.

Bretton Woods township in New Hampshire, USA, where the United Nations Monetary and Financial Conference was held in 1944 to discuss postwar international payments problems. The agreements reached on financial assistance and measures to stabilize exchange rates led to the creation of the International Bank for Reconstruction and Development in 1945 and the International Monetary Fund (IMF).

Brezhnev Leonid Ilyich 1906–1982. Soviet leader. A protégé of Stalin and Khrushchev, he came to power (after he and ◊Kosygin forced Khrushchev to resign) as general secretary of the Soviet Communist Party (CPSU) 1964–82 and was president 1977–82. Domestically he was conservative; abroad the USSR was established as a military and political superpower during the Brezhnev era, extending its influence in Africa and Asia.

Brezhnev Doctrine Soviet doctrine 1968 designed to justify the invasion of Czechoslovakia. It laid down for the USSR as a duty the direct maintenance of 'correct' socialism in countries within the Soviet sphere of influence. In 1979 it was extended, by the invasion of Afghanistan, to the direct establishment of 'correct' socialism in countries not already within its sphere. The doctrine was renounced by Mikhail ◊Gorbachev in 1989. Soviet troops were withdrawn from Afghanistan and the satellite states of E Europe were allowed to decide their own forms of government.

Brian known as *Brian Boru* ('Brian of the Tribute') 926–1014. High king of Ireland from 976, who took Munster, Leinster, and Connacht to become ruler of all Ireland. He defeated the Norse at Clontarf, thus ending Norse control of Dublin, although he was himself killed. He was the last high king with jurisdiction over most of Scotland. His exploits were celebrated in several chronicles.

Briand Aristide 1862–1932. French radical socialist politician. He was prime minister 1909–11, 1913, 1915–17, 1921–22, 1925–26 and 1929, and foreign minister 1925–32. In 1925 he concluded the Pact ◊Locarno (settling Germany's western frontier) and in 1928 the ◊Kellogg–Briand Pact renouncing war; in 1930 he outlined a scheme for a United States of Europe.

Bridges Harry 1901–1990. Australian-born US labour leader. In 1931 he formed a trade union of clockworkers and in 1934, after police opened fire on a picket line and killed two strikers, he organized a successful general strike. He was head of the International Longshoremen's and Warehousemen's Union for many years.

Bright John 1811–1889. British Liberal politician, a campaigner for free trade, peace, and social reform. A Quaker millowner, he was among the founders of the Anti-Corn Law League in 1839, and was largely instrumental in securing the passage of the Reform Bill of 1867.

England is the mother of Parliaments.

John Bright

Brisbane Thomas Makdougall 1773–1860. Scottish soldier, colonial administrator, and astronomer. After serving in the Napoleonic Wars under Wellington, he was governor of New South Wales 1821–25. Brisbane in Queensland is named after him.

Brissot Jacques Pierre 1754–1793. French revolutionary leader, born in Chartres. He became a member of the legislative assembly and the National Convention, but his party of moderate republicans, the ◊Girondins, or Brissotins, fell foul of Robespierre, and Brissot was guillotined.

Britain or *Great Britain* island off the NW coast of Europe, one of the British Isles. It consists of England, Scotland, and Wales, and is part of the ◊United Kingdom. The name is derived from the Roman name Britannia, which in turn is derived from ancient Celtic name of the inhabitants, *Bryttas*.

Britain, ancient period in the British Isles (excluding Ireland) extending through prehistory to the Roman occupation (1st century AD). Settled agricultural life evolved in Britain during the 3rd millennium BC. Neolithic society reached its peak in southern England, where it was capable of producing the great stone circles of Avebury and Stonehenge early in the 2nd millennium BC. It was succeeded in central southern Britain by the Early Bronze Age Wessex culture, with strong trade links across Europe. The Iron Age culture of the Celts was predominant in the last few centuries BC, and the ◊Belgae (of mixed Germanic and Celtic stock) were partially Romanized in the century between the first Roman invasion of Britain under Julius Caesar (54 BC) and the Roman conquest (AD 43). For later history, see ◊England, history; ◊Roman Britain; ◊Scotland, history; ◊Wales, history; and ◊United Kingdom.

At the end of the last Ice Age, Britain had a cave-dwelling population of Palaeolithic hunter-gatherers, whose culture was called Creswellian, after Creswell Crags, Derbyshire, where remains of flint tools were found. Throughout prehistory successive waves of migrants from continental Europe accelerated or introduced cultural innovations. Important Neolithic remains include: the stone houses of Skara Brae, Orkney; so-called causewayed camps in which hilltops such as Windmill Hill, Wiltshire, were enclosed by concentric fortifications of ditches and banks; the first stages of the construction of the ritual monuments known as henges (for example, Stonehenge, Woodhenge); and the flint mines at Grimes Graves, Norfolk. Burial of the dead was in elongated earth mounds (long barrows).

The ◊Beaker people probably introduced copper working to the British Isles. The aristocratic society of the Bronze Age Wessex culture of southern England is characterized by its circular burial mounds (round barrows); the dead were either buried or cremated, and cremated remains were placed in pottery urns. Later invaders were the ◊Celts, a warrior aristocracy with an Iron Age technology; they introduced horse-drawn chariots, had their own distinctive art forms, and occupied fortified hilltops. The Belgae, who buried the ashes of their dead in richly furnished flat graves, were responsible for the earliest British sites large and complex enough to be called towns; settled in southern Britain, the Belgae resisted the Romans from centres such as Maiden Castle, Dorset.

Britain, Battle of World War II air battle between German and British air forces over Britain lasting 10 July–31 Oct 1940. The battle has been divided into five phases: 10 July–7 Aug, the preliminary phase; 8–23 Aug, attack on coastal targets; 24 Aug–6 Sept, attack on Fighter Command airfields; 7–30 Sept, daylight attack on London, chiefly by heavy bombers; and 1–31 Oct, daylight attack on London, chiefly by fighter-bombers. The main battle was between some 600 Hurricanes and Spitfires and the Luftwaffe's 800 Messerschmidt 109s and 1,000 bombers (Dornier 17s, Heinkel 111s, and Junkers 88s). Losses Aug–Sept were, for the RAF: 832 fighters totally destroyed; for the Luftwaffe: 668 fighters and some 700 bombers and other aircraft.

British Empire various territories all over the world conquered or colonized by Britain from about 1600, most now independent or ruled by other powers; the British Empire was at its largest at the end of World War I, with over 25% of the world's population and area. The ◊Commonwealth is composed of former and remaining territories of the British Empire.

The first successful British colony was Jamestown, Virginia, founded 1607. British settlement spread up and down the east coast of North America and by 1664, when the British secured New Amsterdam (New York) from the Dutch, there was a continuous fringe of colonies from the present South Carolina in the south to what is now New Hampshire. These colonies, and others formed later, had their own democratic institutions. The attempt of George III and his minister Lord North to coerce the colonists into paying special taxes to Britain roused them to resistance, which came to a head in the ◊American Revolution 1775–81 and led to the creation of the United States of America from the 13 English colonies then lost.

Colonies and trading posts were set up in many parts of the world by the British, who also captured them from other European empire builders. Settlements were made in Gambia and on the Gold Coast of Africa 1618; in Bermuda 1609 and other islands of the West Indies; Jamaica was taken from Spain 1655; in Canada, Acadia (Nova Scotia) was secured from France by the Treaty of Utrecht 1713, which recognized Newfoundland and Hudson Bay (as well as Gibraltar in Europe) as British. New France (Québec), Cape Breton Island, and Prince Edward Island became British as a result of the Seven Years' War 1756–63.

In the Far East, the ◊East India Company, chartered 1600, set up a number of factories, as their trading posts were called, and steadily increased its possessions and the territories over which it held treaty rights up to the eve of the ◊Indian Mutiny 1857.

Although this revolt was put down, it resulted in the taking over of the government of British India by the crown 1858; Queen Victoria was proclaimed empress of India 1 Jan 1877. Ceylon (now Sri Lanka) had also been annexed to the East India Company 1796, and Burma (now Myanmar), after a series of Anglo-Burmese Wars from 1824, became a province of British India 1886. Burma and Ceylon became independent 1948 and the republic of Sri Lanka dates from 1972. British India, as the two dominions of India and Pakistan, was given independence in 1947. In 1950 India became a republic but remained a member of the Commonwealth.

Constitutional development in Canada started with an act of 1791 which set up Lower Canada (Québec), mainly French-speaking, and Upper Canada (Ontario), mainly English-speaking. In the War of 1812, the USA wrongly assumed hat Canada would join the union. But there was sufficient discontent there to lead to rebellion 1837 in both Canadas. After the suppression of these risings, Lord Durham was sent out to advise on the affairs of British North America; his report, published 1839, became the basis for the future structure of the Empire. In accordance with his recommendations, the two Canadas were united 1840 and given a representative legislative council: the beginning of colonial self-government. With the British North America Act 1867, the self-governing dominion of Canada came into existence; to the original union of Ontario, Québec, New Brunswick, and Nova Scotia were later added further territories until the federal government of Canada controlled all the northern part of the continent except Alaska.

In Australia and New Zealand, colonization began with the desire to find a place for penal settlement after the loss of the original American colonies. The first shipload of British convicts landed in Australia 1788 on the site of the future city of Sydney. New South Wales was opened to free settlers 1819, and in 1853 transportation of convicts was abolished. Before the end of the century five Australian colonies – New South Wales, Western Australia, South Australia, Victoria, Queensland – and the island colony of Tasmania had each achieved self-government; an act of the Imperial Parliament at Westminster created the federal commonwealth of Australia, an independent dominion, 1901. New Zealand, annexed 1840, was at first a dependency of New South Wales. It became a separate colony 1853 and a dominion 1907.

The Cape of Good Hope in South Africa was occupied by two English captains 1620,

but neither the home government nor the East India Company was interested. The Dutch occupied it 1650, and Cape Town remained a port of call for their East India Company until 1795 when, French revolutionary armies having occupied the Dutch Republic, the British seized it to keep it from the French. Under the Treaty of Paris 1814, the UK bought Cape Town from the new kingdom of the Netherlands for $6 million. British settlement began 1824 on the coast of Natal, proclaimed a British colony 1843.

The need to find new farmland and establish independence from British rule led a body of Boers (Dutch 'farmers') from the Cape to make the Great Trek northeast 1836, to found Transvaal and Orange Free State. Conflict between the British government, which claimed sovereignty over those areas (since the settlers were legally British subjects), and the Boers culminated, after the discovery of gold in the Boer territories, in the South African War 1899–1902, which brought Transvaal and Orange Free State definitely under British sovereignty. Given self-government 1907, they were formed, with Cape Colony (self-governing 1872) and Natal (self-governing 1893), into the Union of South Africa 1910.

The British Empire 1815–1914 Britain's overseas empire consisted of a variety of possessions ranging from self-governing dominions and colonies to protectorates and crown colonies administered directly from London. There was great expansion in the 19th century, largely in Africa and Asia. The British Empire covered 25% of the world's surface by 1914.

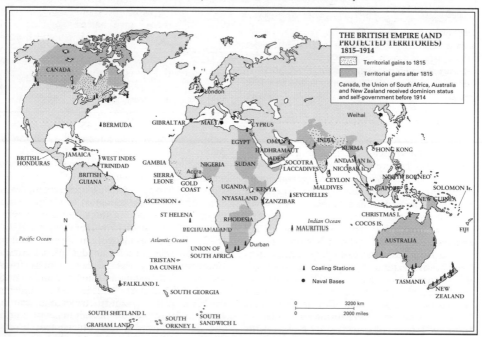

The British Empire

current name	colonial names and history	colonized	independent
India	East India Company 18th century–1858	18th century	1947
Pakistan	East India Company 18th century–1858	18th century	1947
Myanmar	Burma	1886	1948
Sri Lanka	Portuguese, Dutch 1602–1796; Ceylon 1802–1972	16th century	1948
Ghana	Gold Coast ; British Togoland integrated 1956	1618	1957
Nigeria		1861	1960
Cyprus	Turkish to 1878, then British rule 1878		1960
Sierra Leone	British protectorate	1788	1961
Tanzania	German East Africa to 1921; British mandate from League of Nations/UN as Tanganyika	19th century	1961
Jamaica	Spanish to 1655	16th century	1962
Trinidad & Tobago	Spanish 1532–1797; British 1797–1962	1532	1962
Uganda	British protectorate	1894	1962
Kenya	British colony from 1920	1895	1963
Malaysia	British interests from 1786; Federation of Malaya 1957–63	1874	1963
Malawi	British protectorate of Nyasaland 1907-53; Federation of Rhodesia & Nyasaland 1953-64	1891	1964
Malta	French 1798–1814	1798	1964
Zambia	N Rhodesia – British protectorate; Federation of Rhodesia & Nyasaland 1953–64	1924	1964
The Gambia		1888	1965
Singapore	Federation of Malaya 1963–65	1858	1965
Guyana	Dutch to 1796; British Guiana 1796-1966	1620	1966
Botswana	Bechuanaland – British protectorate	1885	1966
Lesotho	Basutoland	1868	1966
Bangladesh	East India Company 18th cent–1858; British India 1858–1947; E Pakistan 1947–71	18th century	1971
Zimbabwe	S Rhodesia from 1923; UDI under Ian Smith 1965–79	1895	1980
Belize	British Honduras	17th century	1981

In the early years of the century, a series of Colonial Conferences (renamed Imperial Conferences 1907) were held by the representatives of Australia, New Zealand, Canada, and South Africa, together with the United Kingdom. These four self-governing countries came to be known as Dominions within the British Empire. Their meetings were the basis for the idea of the Commonwealth of Nations.

The British South Africa Company, chartered 1889, extended British influence over Southern Rhodesia (a colony 1923) and Northern Rhodesia (a protectorate 1924); with Nyasaland, taken under British protection 1891, the Rhodesias were formed into a federation 1953–63 with representative government. Uganda was made a British protectorate 1894.

Kenya, formerly a protectorate, became a colony 1920, certain districts on the coast forming part of the sultan of Zanzibar's dominions remained a protectorate.

In W Africa, Sierra Leone colony was founded 1788 with the cession of a strip of land to provide a home for liberated slaves; a protectorate was established over the hinterland 1896. British influence in Nigeria began through the activities of the National Africa Company (the Royal Niger Company from 1886), which bought Lagos from an African chief 1861 and steadily extended its hold over the Niger Valley until it surrendered its charter 1899; in 1900 the two protectorates of North and South Nigeria were proclaimed. World War I ousted Germany from the African continent, and in 1921–22, under League of Nations mandate, Tanganyika was transferred to British administration, SW Africa to South Africa; Cameroons and Togoland, in West Africa, were divided between Britain and France. The establishment of the greater part of Ireland as the Irish Free State, with dominion status, occurred 1922. A new constitution adopted by the Free State 1937 dropped the name and declared Ireland (Eire) to be a 'sovereign independent state'; in 1949 Southern Ireland became a republic outside the Commonwealth. Hong Kong was a British crown colony before reverting to Chinese control July 1997.

British Expeditionary Force (BEF) British army serving in France in World War I 1914–18. Also the 1939–40 army in Europe in World War II, which was evacuated from Dunkirk, France.

British Honduras former name (until 1973) of ◊Belize.

British Somaliland British protectorate comprising over 176,000 sq km/67,980 sq mi of territory on the Somali coast of E Africa from 1884 until the independence of Somalia 1960. British authorities were harassed by Somali nationalists under the leadership of Muhammad bin Abdullah Hassan.

Broederbond (Afrikaans 'band of brothers') white South African secret society formed after the Boer War to protect Afrikaner interests. Its exact membership and power remains uncertain, but it was rumoured to have been highly influential during the governments of Hendrik Verwoerd and B J Vorster.

Bronze Age stage of prehistory and early history when copper and bronze became the first metals worked extensively and used for tools and weapons. It developed out of the Stone Age, preceded the Iron Age, and may be dated 5000–1200 BC in the Middle East and about 2000–500 BC in Europe. Recent discoveries in Thailand suggest that the Far East, rather than the Middle East, was the cradle of the Bronze Age.

Brooke James 1803–1868. British administrator who became rajah of Sarawak, on Borneo, 1841. In 1838 he headed a private expedition to Borneo, where he helped to suppress a revolt, for which the sultan gave him the title. Brooke became known as the 'the white rajah'.

Brookeborough Basil Brooke, Viscount Brookeborough 1888–1973. Unionist politician of Northern Ireland. He entered Parliament in 1929, held ministerial posts 1933–45,

and was prime minister of Northern Ireland 1943–63. He was a staunch advocate of strong links with Britain.

Brown John 1800–1859. US slavery abolitionist. With 18 men, on the night of 16 Oct 1859, he seized the government arsenal at Harper's Ferry in W Virginia, apparently intending to distribute weapons to runaway slaves who would then defend a mountain stronghold, which Brown hoped would become a republic of former slaves. On 18 Oct the arsenal was stormed by US Marines under Col Robert E ◊Lee. Brown was tried and hanged on 2 Dec, becoming a martyr and the hero of the popular song 'John Brown's Body' *c.* 1860.

Brownshirts the SA (*Sturmabteilung*), or Storm Troops, the private army of the German Nazi party, who derived their name from the colour of their uniform.

Bruce one of the chief Scottish noble houses. ◊Robert I (the Bruce) and his son, David II, were both kings of Scotland descended from Robert de Bruis (died 1094), a Norman knight who arrived in England with William the Conqueror 1066.

Bruce Robert de, 5th Lord of Annandale 1210–1295. Scottish noble, one of the unsuccessful claimants to the throne at the death of Alexander II 1290. His grandson was ◊Robert I (the Bruce).

Bruce Robert. King of Scotland; see ◊Robert I.

Brundtland Gro Harlem 1939–   . Norwegian Labour politician. Environment minister 1974–76, she briefly took over as prime minister, as post to which she was elected 1986, 1990, and again held 1993-96. She chaired the World Commission on Environment and Development, which produced the Brundtland Report, published as *Our Common Future* 1987.

Brunei country comprising two enclaves on the NW coast of the island of Borneo, bounded to the landward side by Sarawak and to the NW by the South China Sea.

history An independent Islamic sultanate from the 15th century, Brunei was a powerful state by the early 16th century, with dominion over all of Borneo, its neighbouring islands, and parts of the Philippines. With the growing presence of the Portuguese and Dutch in the region, its influence declined in the late 16th century.

In 1888 Brunei became a British protectorate, and under an agreement of 1906 accepted the appointment of a British Resident as adviser to the sultan. The discovery of large oilfields in the 1920s brought economic prosperity to Brunei.

The country was occupied by the Japanese 1941 and liberated by the Australians 1945, when it was returned to Britain. In 1950 Sir Muda Omar Ali Saiffuddin Saadul Khairi Waddien (1916–1986), popularly known as Sir Omar, became sultan. In 1959, a new constitution gave Brunei internal self-government but made Britain responsible for defence and external affairs; a proposal in 1962 that Brunei should join the Federation of Malaysia was opposed by a revolution, which was put down with British help. As a result the sultan decided to rule by decree. In 1967, he abdicated in favour of his son, Hassanal Bolkiah, but continued to be his chief adviser. In 1971 Brunei gained full internal self-government.

independence achieved In 1984 full independence was achieved, the sultan becoming prime minister and minister of finance and home affairs, presiding over a cabinet of six, three of whom were close relatives. Britain agreed to maintain a small force to protect the gas- and oilfields that make Brunei the wealthiest nation, per head, in Asia.

In 1985, the sultan cautiously allowed the formation of the loyal and reliable Brunei National Democratic Party (BNDP), an organization dominated by business people. A year later, ethnic Chinese and government employees (who were debarred from joining the BNDP) formed, with breakaway members of the other party, the Brunei National United Party (BNUP), which became the country's only political party after the dissolution by the sultan of the BNDP 1988. While loyal to the sultan, the BNUP favours the establishment of an elected prime-ministerial system.

Islamic nationalism Since the death of Sir Omar 1986, the pace of political reform has quickened, with key cabinet portfolios being assigned to nonmembers of the royal family. A more nationalist socioeconomic policy has also begun, with preferential treatment given to native Malays in the commercial sphere rather than the traditional Chinese, and an Islamic state is being constructed.

support for Contras During the US-Iranian arms scandal 1987, it was revealed that the sultan of Brunei donated $10 million to the Nicaraguan Contras (antigovernment guerrillas).

Brüning Heinrich 1885–1970. German politician. Elected to the Reichstag (parliament) 1924, he led the Catholic Centre Party from 1929 and was federal chancellor 1930–32 when political and economic crisis forced his resignation.

Brussels, Treaty of pact of economic, political, cultural, and military alliance established 17 March 1948, for 50 years, by the UK, France, and the Benelux countries, joined by West Germany and Italy 1955. It was the forerunner of the North Atlantic Treaty Organization and the European Community.

Brussilov Aleksei Alekseevich 1853–1926. Russian general, military leader in World War I who achieved major successes against the Austro-Hungarian forces in 1916. Later he was commander of the Red Army 1920, which drove the Poles to within a few miles of Warsaw before being repulsed by them.

Brutus Marcus Junius *c.* 78–42 BC. Roman senator and general, a supporter of ◊Pompey (against ◊Caesar) in the civil war. Pardoned by Caesar and raised to high office by him, he nevertheless plotted Caesar's assassination to restore the purity of the Republic. Brutus committed suicide when he was defeated (with ◊Cassius) by ◊Mark Antony, Caesar's lieutenant, at Philippi 42 BC.

Bryan William Jennings 1860–1925. US politician who campaigned unsuccessfully for the presidency three times: as the Populist and Democratic nominee 1896, as an anti-imperialist Democrat 1900, and as a Democratic tariff reformer 1908. He served as President Wilson's secretary of state 1913–15. In the early 1920s he was a leading fundamentalist and opponent of Clarence ◊Darrow in the ◊Scopes monkey trial.

buccaneer member of any of various groups of seafarers who plundered Spanish ships and colonies on the Spanish American coast in the 17th century. Unlike true pirates, they were acting on (sometimes spurious) commission.

Buchanan James 1791–1868. 15th president of the USA 1857–61, a Democrat. He entered the US House of Representatives 1821–31 and was US minister to Russia 1832–34 when he was elected to the Senate. Adhering to a policy of compromise on the issue of slavery, he left his Senate seat to serve as US secretary of state during the Mexican War (1846–48). Nominated by the Democrats and elected president 1856, he could do little to avert the secession of the South over the issue of slavery, precipitating the outbreak of the Civil War 1861.

Buchenwald site of a Nazi ◊concentration camp 1937–45 at a village NE of Weimar, Germany.

Buckingham George Villiers, 1st Duke of Buckingham 1592–1628. English courtier, adviser to James I and later Charles I. After

Charles's accession, Buckingham attempted to form a Protestant coalition in Europe, which led to war with France, but he failed to relieve the Protestants (◊Huguenots) besieged in La Rochelle 1627. This added to his unpopularity with Parliament, and he was assassinated.

Introduced to the court of James I 1614, he soon became his favourite and was made Earl of Buckingham 1617 and a duke 1623. He failed to arrange the marriage of Prince Charles and the Infanta of Spain 1623, but on returning to England negotiated Charles's alliance with Henrietta Maria, sister of the French king. His policy on the French Protestants was attacked in Parliament, and when about to sail again for La Rochelle he was assassinated in Portsmouth.

Buddha 'enlightened one', title of Prince *Gautama Siddhārtha c.* 563–483 BC. Religious leader, founder of Buddhism, born at Lumbini in Nepal. At the age of 29 he left his wife and son and a life of luxury, to escape from the material burdens of existence. After six years of austerity he realized that asceticism, like overindulgence, was futile, and chose the middle way of meditation. He became enlightened under a bo, or bodhi, tree near Buddh Gaya in Bihar, India. He began teaching at Varanasi, and founded the Sangha, or order of monks. He spent the rest of his life travelling around N India, and died at Kusinagara in Uttar Pradesh.

The life of a creature passes like the torrent in the mountain and the lightning in the sky.

Buddha attributed

Buddhism one of the great world religions, which originated in India about 500 BC. It derives from the teaching of the Buddha, who is regarded as one of a series of such enlightened beings; there are no gods. The chief doctrine is that of *karma*, good or evil deeds meeting an appropriate reward or punishment either in this life or (through reincarnation) a long succession of lives. The main divisions in Buddhism are *Theravāda* (or Hīnayāna) in SE Asia and *Mahāyāna* in N Asia; *Lamaism* in Tibet and *Zen* in Japan are among the many Mahāyāna sects. Its symbol is the lotus. There are over 247.5 million Buddhists worldwide.

Theravāda Buddhism, the School of the Elders, also known as *Hīnayāna* or Lesser Vehicle, prevails in SE Asia (Sri Lanka, Thailand, and Myanmar), and emphasizes the mendicant, meditative life as the way to break the cycle of *samsāra*, or death and rebirth. Its scriptures are written in Pāli, an Indo-Aryan language with its roots in N India. In India itself Buddhism had virtually died out by the 13th century, and was replaced by Hinduism. However, it has 5 million devotees in the 20th century and is growing.

Mahāyāna Buddhism, or Greater Vehicle arose at the beginning of the Christian era. This tradition emphasized the eternal, formless principle of the Buddha as the essence of all things. It exhorts the individual not merely to attain personal nirvana, but to become a trainee Buddha, or *bodhisattva*, and so save others.

Mahāyāna Buddhism prevails in China, Korea, Japan, and Tibet. In the 6th century AD Mahāyāna spread to China with the teachings of Bodhidharma and formed Ch'an, which became established in Japan from the 12th century as *Zen Buddhism*. Zen emphasizes silent meditation with sudden interruptions from a master to encourage awakening of the mind. Japan also has the lay organization *Sōka Gakkai* (Value Creation Society), founded 1930, which equates absolute faith with immediate material benefit; by the 1980s it was followed by more than 7 million households.

Buganda either of two provinces (North and South Buganda) of Uganda, home of the Baganda people and formerly a kingdom from the 17th century. The *kabaka* or king, Edward Mutesa II (1924–1969), was the first president of independent Uganda 1962–66, and his son Ronald Mutebi (1955–) is *sabataka* (head of the Baganda clans) and from 1993 King.

Bukhara or *Bokhara* central city in Uzbekistan. An ancient city in central Asia, it was formerly the capital of the independent emirate of Bukhara, annexed to Russia 1868.

Bukharin Nikolai Ivanovich 1888–1938. Soviet politician and theorist. A moderate, he was the chief Bolshevik thinker after Lenin. Executed on Stalin's orders for treason 1938, he was posthumously rehabilitated 1988.

We might have a two-party system, but one of the two parties would be in office and the other in prison.

Nikolai Bukharin attributed

Bukovina region in SE Europe, divided between the Ukraine and Romania. Part of Moldavia during the Turkish regime, it was ceded by the Ottoman Empire to Austria 1777, becoming a duchy of the Dual Monarchy

1867–1918; then it was included in Romania. N Bukovina was ceded to the USSR 1940 and included in Ukraine as the region of Chernovtsy; the cession was confirmed by the peace treaty 1947, but the question of its return has been raised by Romania. The part of Bukovina remaining in Romania became the district of Suceava.

Bulganin Nikolai 1895–1975. Soviet politician and military leader. His career began in 1918 when he joined the Cheka, the Soviet secret police. He helped to organize Moscow's defence in World War II, became a marshal of the USSR 1947, and was minister of defence 1947–49 and 1953–55. On the fall of Malenkov he became prime minister (chair of Council of Ministers) 1955–58 until ousted by Khrushchev.

Bulgaria country in SE Europe, bounded N by Romania, W by Yugoslavia, S by Greece, SE by Turkey, and E by the Black Sea.

history In the ancient world Bulgaria comprised ◊Thrace and Moesia and was the Roman province of Moesia Inferior. It was occupied in the 6th century AD by the Slavs (from whom the language derives), followed by Bulgars from Asia in the 7th century. In 865 Khan Boris adopted Eastern Orthodox Christianity, and under his son Simeon (893–927), who assumed the title of tsar, Bulgaria became a leading power. It was ruled by ◊Byzantium from the 11th century and, although a second Bulgarian empire was founded after the 14th century, Bulgaria formed part of the ◊Ottoman Empire for almost 500 years, becoming an independent kingdom 1908.

fascism Bulgaria allied itself with Germany during World War I. From 1919 a government of the leftist Agrarian Party introduced land reforms, but was overthrown 1923 by a fascist coup. A monarchical-fascist dictatorship was established 1934 under King ◊Boris III. During World War II Bulgaria again allied itself with Germany, being occupied 1944 by the USSR.

republic In 1946 the monarchy was abolished, and a republic was proclaimed under a communist-leaning alliance, the Fatherland Front, led by Georgi ◊Dimitrov (1882–1949). Bulgaria reverted largely to its 1919 frontiers. The new republic adopted a Soviet-style constitution 1947, with nationalized industries and cooperative farming introduced. Vulko Chervenkov, Dimitrov's brother-in-law, became the dominant political figure 1950–54, introducing a Stalinist regime. He was succeeded by the more moderate Todor ◊Zhivkov, under whom Bulgaria became one of the Soviet Union's most loyal satellites.

haphazard reforms During the 1980s the country faced mounting economic problems, chiefly caused by the rising cost of energy imports. During 1985–89, under the promptings of the Soviet leader Mikhail Gorbachev, a haphazard series of administrative and economic reforms was instituted. This proved insufficient to placate reformists either inside or outside the BCP. In Nov 1989, influenced by the democratization movements sweeping other East European countries and backed by the army and the USSR, the foreign secretary Petar Mladenov ousted Zhivkov. Mladenov became leader of the BCP and president of the state council, and quickly promoted genuine political pluralism. In Dec 1989 legislation was passed to end the BCP's 'leading role' in the state and allow the formation of free opposition parties and trade unions; political prisoners were freed; and the secret-police wing responsible for dissident surveillance was abolished.

relations with Turkey Bulgaria's relations with neighbouring Turkey deteriorated during 1989, following the flight of 300,000 ethnic Turks from Bulgaria to Turkey after the Bulgarian government's violent suppression of their protests at the programme of 'Bulgarianization' (forcing them to adopt Slavic names and resettle elsewhere). The new Mladenov government announced Dec 1989 that the forced assimilation programme would be abandoned; this provoked demonstrations by anti-Turk nationalists (abetted by BCP conservatives) but encouraged the gradual return of most Turkish refugees to Bulgaria, which greatly improved relations with Turkey.

market economy In Feb 1990 Alexander Lilov, a reformer, was elected party chief, and Andrei Lukanov became prime minister. Zhivkov was imprisoned on charges of corruption and abuse of power. A government decree Feb 1990 relegalized private farming and a phased lifting of price controls commenced April 1990 as part of a drive towards a market economy. Huge price rises and food shortages were the result. Also in April, the BCP renamed itself the Bulgarian Socialist Party (BSP). Petar Mladenov resigned as president July 1990, and in Aug the opposition leader Dr Zhelyu Zhelev was elected in his place.

In Nov 1990, after mass demonstrations in Sofia, a general strike, and a boycott of parliament by opposition deputies, the government of Andrei Lukanov resigned. He was replaced in Dec 1990 by a nonparty politician, Dimitur Popov (1927–), heading a caretaker coalition government, and the strikes by workers and students were called off.

end of communist rule A new constitution was adopted in July 1991 which defined the country as a parliamentary republic with a 'democratic, constitutional, and welfare state'. By Oct prices had increased tenfold and unemployment reached 300,000. The Oct general election resulted in a hung parliament and the right-of-centre Union of Democratic Forces (UDF) formed in Nov 1991 a minority government, headed by Filip Dimitrov. This was Bulgaria's first wholly noncommunist government for 46 years. Western economic aid increased significantly and talks on an association agreement with the Economic Community began. Zhan Videnov replaced Lilov as leader of the BSP Dec 1991. In Jan 1992, Zhelyu Zhelev became Bulgaria's first directly elected president, capturing 53% of the vote.

Bulge, Battle of the or *Ardennes offensive* in World War II, Hitler's plan, code-named 'Watch on the Rhine', for a breakthrough by his field marshal ◊Rundstedt aimed at the US line in the Ardennes 16 Dec 1944–28 Jan 1945. There were 77,000 Allied casualties and 130,000 German, including Hitler's last powerful reserve, his Panzer elite. Although US troops were encircled for some weeks at Bastogne, the German counteroffensive failed.

Bull Run, Battles of in the American Civil War, two victories for the Confederate army under General Robert E Lee at *Manassas* Junction, NE Virginia: *First Battle of Bull Run* 21 July 1861; *Second Battle of Bull Run* 29–30 Aug 1862.

Bülow Bernhard, Prince von 1849–1929. German diplomat and politician. He was chancellor of the German Empire 1900–09 under Kaiser Wilhelm II and, holding that self-interest was the only rule for any state, adopted attitudes to France and Russia that unintentionally reinforced the trend towards opposing European power groups: the ◊Triple Entente (Britain, France, Russia) and ◊Triple Alliance (Germany, Austria– Hungary, Italy).

Bunche Ralph 1904–1971. US diplomat. Grandson of a slave, he was principal director of the United Nations Department of Trusteeship 1947–54, and UN undersecretary acting as mediator in Palestine 1948–49 and as special representative in the Congo 1960. He taught at Harvard and Howard universities and was involved in the planning of the United Nations. In 1950 he was awarded the Nobel Prize for Peace, the first awarded to a black man.

Bundelas ◊Rajput clan prominent in the 14th century, which gave its name to the Bundelkhand in N central India. The clan had replaced the ◊Chandelā in the 11th century and continued to resist the attacks of other Indian rulers until coming under British control after 1812.

Bunker Hill, Battle of the first significant engagement in the ◊American Revolution, 17 June 1775, near a small hill in Charlestown (now part of Boston), Massachusetts, USA; the battle actually took place on Breed's Hill. Although the colonists were defeated they were able to retreat to Boston and suffered fewer casualties than the British.

Burgess Guy (Francis de Moncy) 1910–1963. British spy, a diplomat recruited by the USSR as an agent. He was linked with Kim ◊Philby, Donald Maclean (1913–1983), and Anthony Blunt.

burgh (burh or borough) term originating in Germanic lands in the 9th–10th centuries referring to a fortified settlement, usually surrounding a monastery or castle. Later, it was used to mean new towns, or towns that enjoyed particular privileges relating to government and taxation and whose citizens were called *burghers*.

Burgh Hubert de died 1243. English ◊justiciar and regent of England. He began his career in the administration of Richard I, and was promoted to the justiciarship by King John; he remained in that position under Henry III from 1216 until his dismissal. He was a supporter of King John against the barons, and ended French intervention in England by his defeat of the French fleet in the Strait of Dover 1217. He reorganized royal administration and the Common Law.

burgher term used from the 11th century to describe citizens of ◊burghs who were freemen of a burgh, and had the right to participate in its government. They usually had to possess a house within the burgh.

Burghley William Cecil, Baron Burghley 1520–1598. English politician, chief adviser to Elizabeth I as secretary of state from 1558 and Lord High Treasurer from 1572. He was largely responsible for the religious settlement of 1559, and took a leading role in the events preceding the execution of Mary Queen of Scots 1587.

One of Edward VI's secretaries, he lost office under Queen Mary, but on Queen Elizabeth's succession became one of her most trusted ministers. He carefully avoided a premature breach with Spain in the difficult period leading up to the attack by the Spanish Armada 1588, did a great deal towards abolishing monopolies and opening up trade, and was created Baron Burghley 1571.

Burgoyne John 1722–1792. British general and dramatist. He served in the American War of Independence and surrendered 1777 to the colonists at Saratoga, New York State, in one of the pivotal battles of the war.

Burgundy region centred around the valleys of the Rhône and Saône rivers in E France and SW Germany, partly corresponding with modern Bourgogne. Settled by the Teutonic Burgundi around AD 443, and brought under Frankish control 534, Burgundy played a central role in the medieval history of NW Europe. It was divided among various groups between the 9th and 11th centuries, splitting into a duchy in the west, controlled by French ◊Carolingians, while the rest became a county in the ◊Holy Roman Empire. The duchy was acquired by the Capetian king Robert the Pious 1002, and until 1361 it was the most important and loyal fiefdom in the realm. Duchy and county were reunited 1384, and in the 15th century this wealthy region was the glittering capital of European court culture.

Burke Edmund 1729–1797. British Whig politician and political theorist, born in Dublin, Ireland. In Parliament from 1765, he opposed the government's attempts to coerce the American colonists, for example in *Thoughts on the Present Discontents* 1770, and supported the emancipation of Ireland, but denounced the French Revolution, for example in *Reflections on the Revolution in France* 1790.

Burkina Faso (formerly Upper Volta) landlocked country in W Africa, bounded E by Niger, NW and W by Mali, S by Ivory Coast, Ghana, Togo, and Benin.

history The area known from 1984 as Burkina Faso was invaded in the 11th–13th centuries by the Mossi people, whose powerful warrior kingdoms lasted for over 500 years. In the 1890s it became a province of French West Africa, known as Upper Volta.

In 1958 it became a self-governing republic and in 1960 achieved full independence with Maurice Yaméogo as president. A military coup 1966 removed Yaméogo and installed Col Sangoulé Lamizana as president and prime minister. He suspended the constitution, dissolved the national assembly, banned political activity, and set up a supreme council of the armed forces as the instrument of government.

In 1969 the ban on political activity was lifted, and in 1970 a referendum approved a new constitution, based on civilian rule, which was to come into effect after four years of combined military and civilian government. After disagreements between military and civilian members of the government, General Lamizana announced 1974 a return to army rule and dissolved the national assembly.

Lamizana overthrown In 1977 political activity was allowed again, and a referendum approved a constitution that would create a civilian government. In the 1978 elections the Volta Democratic Union (UDV) won a majority in the national assembly, and Lamizana became president. But a deteriorating economy led to strikes, and a bloodless coup led by Col Zerbo overthrew Lamizana 1980. Zerbo formed a government of national recovery, suspended the constitution, and dissolved the national assembly.

country renamed Burkina Faso In 1982 Zerbo was ousted, and Maj Jean-Baptiste Ouédraogo emerged as leader of a military regime, with Capt Thomas Sankara as prime minister. In 1983 Sankara seized power in another coup, becoming president and ruling through a council of ministers. Opposition members were arrested, the national assembly was dissolved, and a National Revolutionary Council (CNR) set up. In 1984 Sankara announced that the country would be known as Burkina Faso ('land of upright men'), symbolizing a break with its colonial past; his government strengthened ties with Ghana and established links with Benin and Libya. Sankara was killed Oct 1987 in a military coup led by a former close colleague, Capt Blaise Compaoré (1951–). In April 1989 a restructuring of the ruling political groupings took place, and in Sept 1989 a plot to oust Compaoré was discovered and foiled.

Compaoré re-elected Throughout 1991 Compaoré resisted calls for a national conference attended by all political parties, but a new constitution was approved. He was re-elected president Dec 1991 but the unusually large number of abstentions in the election reflected his growing unpopularity. Prompted by widespread unrest, multiparty elections were held May 1992. The ruling FP–Popular Front won a clear majority, amid oposition claims of electoral fraud.

Burma former name (to 1989) of ◊Myanmar.

Burma War war 1942–45 during which Burma (now ◊Myanmar) was occupied by Japan. Initially supported by Aung San's Burma National Army, the Japanese captured Rangoon and Mandalay 1942, forcing the withdrawal of

General Alexander's British forces to India. During 1943, ◊Chindit guerrilla resistance was organized and after a year's heavy fighting at Imphal and Kohima, British, Commonwealth, American, and Chinese nationalist troops reopened the 'Burma Road' between India and China Jan 1945. Rangoon was recaptured May 1945.

Burnham Forbes 1923–1985. Guyanese Marxist-Leninist politician. He was prime minister 1964–80, leading the country to independence 1966 and declaring it the world's first cooperative republic 1970. He was executive president 1980–85. Resistance to the US landing in Grenada 1983 was said to be due to his forewarning the Grenadans of the attack.

Burns John 1858–1943. British labour leader, sentenced to six weeks' imprisonment for his part in the Trafalgar Square demonstration on 'Bloody Sunday' 13 Nov 1887, and leader of the strike in 1889 securing the 'dockers' tanner' (wage of 6d per hour). An Independent Labour member of Parliament 1892–1918, he was the first working-class person to be a member of the cabinet, as president of the Local Government Board 1906–14.

Burnside Ambrose Everett 1824–1881. US military leader and politician. He was appointed brigadier general in the Union army soon after the outbreak of the Civil War 1861. Named as George ◊McClellan's successor as commander of the Army of the Potomac, Burnside served briefly in that position before being transferred to the West. He was governor of Rhode Island 1866–69 and US senator 1874–81.

Burr Aaron 1756–1836. US politician, Republican vice president 1800–04, in which year he killed his political rival Alexander ◊Hamilton in a duel. In 1807 Burr was tried and acquitted of treason charges, which implicated him variously in a scheme to conquer Mexico, or part of Florida, or to rule over a seceded Louisiana.

Burundi country in E central Africa, bounded N by Rwanda, W by Zaire, SW by Lake Tanganyika, and SE and E by Tanzania.

history Originally inhabited by the Twa pygmies, Burundi was taken over by Bantu Hutus in the 13th century, and overrun in the 15th century by the Tutsi. In 1890, ruled by a Tutsi king and known as Urundi, it became part of German East Africa and during World War I was occupied by Belgium. Later, as part of Ruanda-Urundi, it was administered by Belgium as a League of Nations (and then United Nations) trust territory.

The 1961 elections, supervised by the UN, were won by UPRONA, a party formed by Louis, one of the sons of the reigning king, Mwambutsa IV. Louis was assassinated after only two weeks as prime minister and was succeeded by his brother-in-law, André Muhirwa. In 1962 Urundi separated from Ruanda and, as Burundi, attained internal self-government and then full independence.

republic In 1966 King Mwambutsa IV, after a 50-year reign, was deposed by another son, Charles, with army help, and the constitution was suspended. Later that year Charles, now Ntare V, was deposed by his prime minister, Capt Michel Micombero, who declared Burundi a republic. Micombero was a Tutsi, whose main rivals were the numerically superior Hutu. In 1972 the deposed Ntare V was killed, allegedly by the Hutu, giving the Tutsi an excuse to massacre large numbers of Hutu.

one-party state In 1973 amendments to the constitution made Micombero president and prime minister and in the following year UPRONA was declared the only political party. In 1976 Micombero was deposed in an army coup led by Col Jean-Baptiste Bagaza, who became president, with a prime minister and a new council of ministers. In 1977 the prime minister announced a return to civilian rule and a five-year plan to eliminate corruption and secure social justice, including promoting some Hutu to government positions.

army massacre In 1978 the post of prime minister was abolished and a new constitution, providing for a national assembly, was adopted 1981 after a referendum. Bagaza was re-elected 1984 (he was the only presidential candidate) but was deposed in a military coup Sept 1987, his government being replaced by a Military Council for National Redemption headed by Maj Pierre Buyoya, believed to be a Tutsi. In Aug 1988 the Tutsi-controlled Burundian army massacred thousands of Hutus in the NE section of the country. Despite Buoya's pledges to end interethnic violence, this massacre was seen by many as a continuation of the strife that began after an abortive Hutu rebellion 1972.

In March 1992 a new constitution, providing for multiparty politics, was approved by referendum by 90% of the electorate in a 97% turnout.

Bush George 1924– . 41st president of the USA 1989–93, a Republican. He was director of the Central Intelligence Agency (CIA) 1976–81 and US vice president 1981–89. As president, his response to the Soviet leader Gorbachev's diplomatic initiatives were initially criticized as inadequate, but his sending of US troops to depose his former ally, General Noriega of Panama, proved a popular move at home. Success in the 1991 Gulf War against Iraq further raised his standing. Domestic economic problems 1991–92 were followed by his defeat in the 1992 presidential elections by Democrat Bill Clinton.

Bush, son of a Connecticut senator, moved to Texas 1948 to build up an oil-drilling company. A congressman 1967–70, he was appointed US ambassador to the United Nations (1971–73) and Republican national chair (1973–74) by President Nixon, and special envoy to China 1974–75 under President Ford.

Bushman former name for the Kung, San, and other hunter-gatherer groups (for example, the Gikwe, Heikom, and Sekhoin) living in and around the Kalahari Desert in southern Africa. They number approximately 50,000 and speak San and other languages of the Khoisan family.

They once occupied a large area, but were driven into the Kalahari Desert in the 18th century by Bantu peoples (Sotho and Nguni). Their early art survives in cave paintings.

bushranger Australian armed robber of the 19th century. The first bushrangers were escaped convicts. The last gang was led by Ned Kelly and his brother Dan in 1878–80. They form the subject of many Australian ballads.

Bustamante (William) Alexander (born Clarke) 1884–1977. Jamaican socialist politician. As leader of the Labour Party, he was the first prime minister of independent Jamaica 1962–67.

Bute John Stuart, 3rd Earl of Bute 1713–1792. British Tory politician, prime minister 1762–63. On the accession of George III in 1760, he became the chief instrument in the king's policy for breaking the power of the Whigs and establishing the personal rule of the monarch through Parliament.

Buthelezi Chief Gatsha 1928– . Zulu leader and politician, chief minister of KwaZulu, a black 'homeland' in the Republic of South Africa from 1970. He is the founder (1975) and president of ◊Inkatha, a paramilitary organization for attaining a nonracial democratic political system. He has been accused of complicity in the factional violence between Inkatha and ◊African National Congress supporters that has continued to rack the townships despite his signing of a peace accord with ANC leader, Nelson Mandela, Sept 1991.

Buthelezi, great-grandson of King ◊Cetewayo, opposed KwaZulu becoming a ◊Black National State, arguing instead for a confederation of black areas, with eventual majority rule over all South Africa under a one-party socialist system.

Butler Josephine (born Gray) 1828–1906. English social reformer. She promoted women's education and the Married Women's Property Act, and campaigned against the Contagious Diseases Acts of 1862–70, which made women in garrison towns suspected of prostitution liable to compulsory examination for venereal disease. Refusal to undergo examination meant imprisonment. As a result of her campaigns the acts were repealed in 1883.

Butler Richard Austen ('Rab'), Baron Butler 1902–1982. British Conservative politician. As minister of education 1941–45, he was responsible for the 1944 Education Act; he was chancellor of the Exchequer 1951–55, Lord Privy Seal 1955–59, and foreign minister 1963–64. As a candidate for the prime ministership, he was defeated by Harold Macmillan in 1957 (under whom he was home secretary 1957–62), and by Alec Douglas-Home in 1963.

Butskellism UK term for political policies tending towards the middle ground in an effort to gain popular support; the term was coined 1954 after R A ◊Butler (moderate Conservative) and Hugh ◊Gaitskell (moderate Labour politician).

Buxar, Battle of battle 1764 at Buxar, in Bihar, NE India, in which the British ◊East India Company secured dominance of N India. It defeated the triple forces of the ◊Mogul emperor Shah Alam II (reigned 1759–1806); Mir Qasim, the recently dispossessed governor of Bengal; and Shuja-ud Daula, governor of the Ganges valley province of Oudh and *wazir* (chief minister) to the emperor.

The *diwani* (revenue-collecting authority) for Bengal, Bihar, and Orissa was transferred to the company by Shah Alam II in Aug 1765 and Oudh became a tributary vassal state.

Byelorussia see ◊Belarus.

Byng George, Viscount Torrington 1663–1733. British admiral. He captured Gibraltar 1704, commanded the fleet that prevented an invasion of England by the 'Old Pretender' James Francis Edward Stuart 1708, and destroyed the Spanish fleet at Messina 1718.

Byng Julian, 1st Viscount of Vimy 1862–1935. British general in World War I, commanding troops in Turkey and France, where, after a victory at Vimy Ridge, he took command of the Third Army.

On Nov 20–Dec 7 1917 he led the successful tank attack on Cambrai. He was governor general of Canada 1921–26, and was made a viscount 1926 and a field marshal 1932.

THE MAKING OF THE BYZANTINE EMPIRE

The making of the Byzantine Empire Roman rule was divided by Diocletian and Maximian AD 286; each chose a subordinate, respectively Constantine and Galerius. Diocletian secured Mesopotamia and settled his court at Nicomedia. His successor Constantine built a new Christian capital 330 at Byzantium, which was renamed Constantinople after him. Constantine, who also convened the Council of Nicaea 325 and established doctrine according to the Nicene Creed, struggled to reconcile different Christian sects in the unity of a new Rome.

Byzantine Empire the *Eastern Roman Empire* 395–1453, with its capital at Constantinople (formerly Byzantium, modern Istanbul).

330 Emperor Constantine converted to Christianity and moved his capital to Constantinople.

The Roman Empire was divided into eastern and western halves.

476 The Western Empire was overrun by barbarian invaders.

527–565 Emperor Justinian I temporarily recovered Italy, N Africa, and parts of Spain.

7th–8th centuries Syria, Egypt, and N Africa were lost to the Muslims, who twice besieged Constantinople (673–77, 718), but the Christian Byzantines maintained their hold on Anatolia.

8th–11th centuries The Iconoclastic controversy brought the emperors into conflict with the papacy, and in 1054 the Greek Orthodox Church broke with the Roman.

867–1056 Under the Macedonian dynasty the Byzantine Empire reached the height of its prosperity; the Bulgars proved a formidable danger, but after a long struggle were finally crushed in 1018 by ◊Basil II ('the Bulgar-

The Byzantine Empire c. 1265–c. 1354 *The Byzantine Empire, already greatly reduced, shrank still further in the 13th and 14th centuries, squeezed between the southward advance of the Serbs to the west and the westward pressure of the Ottomans in W Anatolia. At the end of Mongol rule, the Ottomans advanced into what remained of Byzantine territory, capturing Nicaea 1301 and then Bursa which became the Ottoman capital. Gallipoli was occupied after a violent earthquake 1354, giving the Ottomans a permanent foothold across the Hellespont from which to begin their conquest of the Balkans.*

Slayer'). After Basil's death the Byzantine Empire declined because of internal factions.

1071–73 The Seljuk Turks conquered most of Anatolia.

1204 The Fourth Crusade sacked Constantinople and set Baldwin of Flanders (1171–1205) on the throne of the new Latin (W European) Empire.

1261 The Greeks recaptured the Latin (W European) Empire and restored the Byzantine Empire, but it maintained a precarious existence.

1453 The Turks captured Constantinople and founded the ◊Ottoman Empire.

Byzantium (modern Istanbul) ancient Greek city on the Bosporus, founded as a colony of the Greek city of Megara on an important strategic site at the entrance to the Black Sea in about 660 BC. In AD 330 the capital of the Roman Empire was transferred there by Constantine the Great, who renamed it Constantinople.

Cabal, the (from *kabbala*) group of politicians, the English king ◊Charles II's counsellors 1667–73, whose initials made up the word by coincidence – Clifford (Thomas Clifford 1630–1673), Ashley (Anthony Ashley Cooper, 1st Earl of ◊Shaftesbury), ◊Buckingham (George Villiers, 2nd Duke of Buckingham), Arlington (Henry Bennett, 1st Earl of Arlington 1618–1685), and Lauderdale (John Maitland, Duke of Lauderdale 1616–1682).

cabinet (a small room, implying secrecy) in politics, the group of ministers holding a country's highest executive offices who decide government policy. In Britain the cabinet system originated under the Stuarts. Under William III it became customary for the king to select his ministers from the party with a parliamentary majority. The US cabinet, unlike the British, does not initiate legislation, and its members, appointed by the president, must not be members of Congress. In the USA a cabinet system developed early and the term was used from 1793.

The first British 'cabinet councils' or sub-committees of the ◊Privy Council undertook special tasks. When George I ceased to attend cabinet meetings, the office of prime minister, not officially recognized until 1905, came into existence to provide a chair (Robert Walpole was the first). Cabinet members are chosen by the prime minister; policy is collective and the meetings are secret.

Cabot Sebastian 1474–1557. Italian navigator and cartographer, the second son of Giovanni ◊Caboto. He explored the Brazilian coast and the Rio de la Plata for the Holy Roman Emperor Charles V 1526–30.

He was also employed by Henry VIII, Edward VI, and Ferdinand of Spain. He planned a voyage to China by way of the North-East Passage, the sea route along the N Eurasian coast, encouraged the formation of the Company of Merchant Adventurers of London 1551, and in 1553 and 1556 directed the company's expeditions to Russia, where he opened British trade.

Caboto Giovanni or *John Cabot* 1450–1498. Italian navigator. Commissioned, with his three sons, by Henry VII of England to discover unknown lands, he arrived at Cape Breton Island on 24 June 1497, thus becoming the first European to reach the North American mainland (he thought he was in NE Asia). In 1498 he sailed again, touching Greenland, and probably died on the voyage.

cacique person involved in nepotism or fraud. Originally a word for Indian chiefs in colonial Spanish America, in late 19th-and early 20th-century Spain it came to mean the local political boss who 'delivered' votes to the main parties in Madrid, Spain.

Cade Jack died 1450. English rebel. He was a prosperous landowner, but led a revolt 1450 in Kent against the high taxes and court corruption of Henry VI and demanded the recall from Ireland of Richard, Duke of York. The rebels defeated the royal forces at Sevenoaks and occupied London. After being promised reforms and pardon they dispersed, but Cade was hunted down and killed.

Cadwalader 7th century. Welsh hero. The son of Cadwallon, king of Gwynedd, N Wales, he defeated and killed Eadwine of Northumbria in 633. About a year later he was killed in battle.

Caesar powerful family of ancient Rome, which included Gaius Julius Caesar, whose grand-nephew and adopted son ◊Augustus assumed the name of Caesar and passed it on to his adopted son ◊Tiberius. From then on, it was used by the successive emperors, becoming a title of the Roman rulers. The titles 'tsar' in Russia and 'kaiser' in Germany were both derived from the name Caesar.

Caesar Gaius Julius 100–44 BC. Roman statesman and general. A patrician, Caesar allied himself with the popular party, and when elected to the office of aedile 65, nearly ruined himself with lavish amusements for the Roman populace. Although a free thinker, he was elected chief pontiff 63 and appointed governor of Spain 61. Returning to Rome 60, he formed with Pompey and Crassus the First Triumvirate. As governor of Gaul, he was engaged in its subjugation 58–50, defeating the Germans under Ariovistus and selling thousands of the Belgic tribes into slavery. In 55 he crossed into Britain, returning for a further campaigning visit 54. A revolt by the Gauls under ◊Vercingetorix 52 was crushed 51.

His governorship of Gaul ended 49, and after the death of Crassus, Pompey became his rival. Declaring 'the die is cast', Caesar crossed the Rubicon (the small river separating Gaul from Italy) to meet the army raised against him by Pompey. In the ensuing civil war, he followed Pompey to Greece 48, defeated him at Pharsalus, and followed him to Egypt, where Pompey was murdered.

He was awarded a ten-year dictatorship 46, and with his final victory over the sons of Pompey at Munda in Spain 45, he was awarded the dictatorship for life 44. On 15 March 44 he was stabbed to death by conspirators (led by Brutus and Cassius) at the foot of Pompey's statue in the Senate house. His commentaries on the campaigns and the civil war survive.

caesarism political system similar to ◊Bonapartism, involving dictatorship by an individual supported by the army or a popular movement. The outward trappings of democracy are maintained but manipulated. The term originates with the system created by Julius Caesar that undermined the Roman Republic in the 1st century BC.

Caetano Marcello 1906–1980. Portuguese right-wing politician. Professor of administrative law at Lisbon from 1940, he succeeded the dictator Salazar as prime minister from 1968 until his exile after the military coup of 1974. He was granted political asylum in Brazil.

Cairo (Arabic *El Qahira*) capital of Egypt, on the east bank of the river Nile. El Fustat (Old Cairo) was founded by Arabs about AD 642, Al Qahira about 1000 by the ◊Fatimid ruler Gowhar. Cairo was the capital of the Ayyubid dynasty, one of whose sultans, Saladin, built the Citadel in the late 1100s.

Under the Mamelukes 1250–1517 the city prospered, but declined in the 16th century after conquest by the Turks. It became the capital of the virtually autonomous kingdom of Egypt established by Mehmet Ali 1805. During World War II it was the headquarters of the Allies.

Calcutta largest city of India, on the river Hooghly, the westernmost mouth of the river Ganges, some 130 km/80 mi N of the Bay of Bengal. It is the capital of West Bengal. Calcutta was founded 1686–90 by Job Charnock of the East India Company as a trading post. Captured by Shuja-ud-Daula 1756, during the Anglo-French wars in India, in 1757 it was retaken by Robert Clive. Calcutta served as the seat of government of British India 1773–1912.

calendar division of the year into months, weeks, and days and the method of ordering the years. From year one, an assumed date of the birth of Jesus, dates are calculated backwards (BC 'before Christ' or BCE 'before common era') and forwards (AD, Latin *anno Domini* 'in the year of the Lord', or CE 'common era'). The *lunar month* (period between one new moon and the next) naturally averages 29.5 days, but the Western calendar uses for convenience a *calendar month* with a complete number of days, 30 or 31 (Feb has 28).

All early calendars except the ancient Egyptian were lunar. The word calendar comes from the Latin *Kalendae* or *calendae*, the first day of each month on which, in ancient Rome, solemn proclamation was made of the appearance of the new moon.

The *Western* or *Gregorian calendar* derives from the *Julian calendar* instituted by Julius Caesar 46 BC. It was adjusted by Pope Gregory XIII 1582, who eliminated the accumulated error caused by a faulty calculation of the length of a year and avoided its recurrence by restricting century leap years to those divisible by 400.

The *Chinese calendar* is lunar, with a cycle of 60 years. Both the traditional and, from 1911, the Western calendar are in use in China.

Calhoun John C(aldwell) 1782–1850. US politician; vice president 1825–29 under John Quincy Adams and 1829–33 under Andrew Jackson. Throughout his vice-presidency, he was a defender of strong *states' rights* against an overpowerful federal government and of the institution of slavery. He served in the US Senate 1842–43 and 1845–50, where he continued to espouse the right of states to legislate on slavery.

California Pacific-coast state of the USA. Colonized by Spain 1769; ceded to the USA after the Mexican War 1848; became a state 1850. The discovery of gold in the Sierra Nevada Jan 1848 was followed by the gold rush 1849–56. The completion of the first transcontinental railroad 1869 fostered economic development. The Los Angeles area flourished with the growth of the film industry after 1910, oil discoveries in the early 1920s, and the development of aircraft plants and shipyards during World War II. California became North America's most populous state in 1962.

Caligula Gaius Caesar AD 12–41. Roman emperor, son of Germanicus and successor to Tiberius AD 37. Caligula was a cruel tyrant and was assassinated by an officer of his guard. He is believed to have been mentally unstable.

caliph title of civic and religious heads of the world of Islam. The first caliph was ◊Abu Bakr. Nominally elective, the office became hereditary, held by the Ummayyad dynasty 661–750 and then by the ◊Abbasid dynasty. After the death of the last Abbasid (1258), the title was claimed by a number of Muslim chieftains in Egypt, Turkey, and India. The most powerful of these were the Turkish sultans of the Ottoman Empire.

The title was adopted by the prophet Muhammad's successors. During the 10th century the political and military power passed to the leader of the caliph's Turkish bodyguard; about the same time, an independent ◊Fatimid caliphate sprang up in Egypt. The last of the Turkish caliphs was deposed by Kemal ◊Atatürk in 1924.

When I am starving in the morning, I say to myself that if I were a young man I would emigrate. By the time I am sitting down to breakfast, I ask myself 'Where would I go?'

James Callaghan

Callaghan (Leonard) James, Baron Callaghan 1912– . British Labour politician. As chancellor of the Exchequer 1964–67, he introduced corporation and capital-gains taxes, and resigned following devaluation. He was home secretary 1967–70 and prime minister 1976–79 in a period of increasing economic stress.

Calvert George, Baron Baltimore 1579–1632. English politician who founded the North American colony of Maryland 1632. As a supporter of colonization, he was granted land in Newfoundland 1628 but, finding the climate too harsh, obtained a royal charter for the more temperate Maryland 1632.

Original sin is seen to be a hereditary depravity and corruption of our nature, diffused in to all parts of the soul.

John Calvin
Institutes of the Christian Religion 1536

Calvin John (also known as *Cauvin* or *Chauvin*) 1509–1564. French-born Swiss Protestant church reformer and theologian. He was a leader of the Reformation in Geneva and set up a strict religious community there. His theological system is known as Calvinism, and his church government as Presbyterianism. Calvin wrote (in Latin) *Institutes of the Christian Religion* 1536 and commentaries on the New Testament and much of the Old Testament.

Calvinism Christian doctrine as interpreted by John Calvin and adopted in Scotland, parts of Switzerland, and the Netherlands; by the *Puritans* in England and New England, USA; and by the subsequent Congregational and Presbyterian churches in the USA. Its central doctrine is predestination, under which certain souls (the elect) are predestined by God through the sacrifice of Jesus to salvation, and the rest to damnation.

Cambodia (formerly *Khmer Republic* 1970–76, *Democratic Kampuchea* 1976–79, and *People's Republic of Kampuchea* 1979–89) country in SE Asia, bounded N and NW by Thailand, N by Laos, E and SE by Vietnam, and SW by the Gulf of Thailand.

history The area now known as Cambodia was once occupied by the Khmer empire, an ancient civilization that flourished during the 6th–15th centuries. After this, the region was subject to attacks by the neighbouring Vietnamese and Thai, and in 1863 became a French protectorate. A nationalist movement began in the 1930s, and anti-French feeling was fuelled 1940–41 when the French agreed to Japanese demands for bases in Cambodia, and allowed Thailand to annex Cambodian territory.

During World War II Cambodia was occupied by Japan. France regained control of the country 1946, but it achieved semi-autonomy within the French Union 1949 and full independence 1953. Prince Norodom ◊Sihanouk, who had been elected king 1941, abdicated in favour of his parents and became prime minister as leader of the Popular Socialist Community 1955. When his father died 1960, he became head of state.

Khmer Republic Sihanouk remained neutral during the Vietnam War and was overthrown by a right-wing revolt led by pro-USA Lt-Gen Lon Nol in 1970. Lon Nol first became prime minister (1971–72) and then president (1972–75) of what was termed the new Khmer Republic. His regime was opposed by the exiled Sihanouk and by the communist Khmer Rouge (backed by North Vietnam and China), who merged to form the National United Front of Cambodia. A civil war developed and, despite substantial military aid from the USA during its early stages, Lon Nol's government fell 1975. The country was renamed Kampuchea, with Prince Sihanouk as head of state.

Khmer Rouge regime The Khmer Rouge proceeded ruthlessly to introduce an extreme communist programme, forcing urban groups into rural areas, which led to over 2.5 million deaths from famine, disease, and maltreatment. In 1976 a new constitution removed Prince Sihanouk from power, appointed Khieu Samphan (the former deputy prime minister) president, and placed the Communist Party of Kampuchea, led by ◊Pol Pot, in control. The Khmer Rouge developed close links with China and fell out with its former sponsors, Vietnam and the USSR.

Vietnamese influence In a Vietnamese invasion of Kampuchea launched 1978 in response to border incursions, Pol Pot was overthrown and a pro-Vietnamese puppet government was set up under Heng Samrin. The defeated regime kept up guerrilla resistance under Pol Pot, causing over 300,000 Kampuchean refugees to flee to Thailand in 1979 alone.

resistance movement In 1982 the resistance movement broadened with the formation in Kuala Lumpur, Malaysia, of an anti-Vietnamese coalition and Democratic Kampuchea government in exile with Prince Sihanouk (then living in North Korea) as president, Khieu Samphan (political leader of the now less extreme Khmer Rouge) as vice president, and Son Sann (an ex-premier and contemporary leader of the noncommunist Khmer People's National Liberation Front [KPNLF]) as prime minister. The coalition received sympathetic support from ◊ASEAN countries and China. However, its 60,000 troops were outnumbered by the 170,000 Vietnamese who supported the Heng Samrin government, and the resistance coalition's base camps were overrun 1985. During 1982–91 the USA aided the KPNLF and the Sihanoukist National Army (ANS) – allies of the Khmer Rouge – with millions of dollars in 'humanitarian' aid and secret 'nonlethal' military aid.

Vietnamese troop withdrawal Hopes of a political settlement were improved by the retirement of the reviled Pol Pot as Khmer Rouge military leader 1985 and the appointment of the reformist Hun Sen as prime minister. A mixed-economy domestic approach was adopted and indigenous Khmers promoted to key government posts; at the same time, prompted by the new Soviet leader, Mikhail Gorbachev, the Vietnamese began a phased withdrawal. In spring 1989, after talks with the resistance coalition, the Phnom Penh government agreed to a package of constitutional reforms, including the adoption of Buddhism as the state religion and the readoption of the ideologically neutral name State of Cambodia. Withdrawal of the Vietnamese army was completed Sept 1989.

continued civil war The UN continued to refuse recognition of the Hun Sen government and the civil war intensified, with the Khmer Rouge making advances in the western provinces, capturing the border town of Pailin in Oct 1989. The Phnom Penh government was left with an army of 40,000, backed by a 100,000-strong militia, against the resistance coalition's 45,000 guerrillas, half of whom belonged to the Khmer Rouge. In Sept 1990 the USSR and China reportedly agreed to a mutual cessation of arms supplies to their respective Cambodian clients. In Nov 1990 the five permanent members of the UN Security Council, including the USA, USSR, and China, proposed a peace settlement, but the Phnom Penh government dismissed it, objecting to the establishment of a UN administration within the country.

accord reached Guerrilla fighting intensified Jan 1991 but, for the first time in 12 years, a cease-fire was implemented May–June 1991, and an accord was reached by the all-party Supreme National Council in Pattaya, Thailand, between Prince Sihanouk, the guerrillas' nominal leader, and the Hun Sen government. This breakthrough was brought about, it is believed, by pressure exerted by Vietnam (anxious for Western aid) and China, the respective backers of the Hun Sen regime and the guerrillas. Subsequent meetings in July, Aug, and Sept 1991 added flesh to this accord, including an understanding that the Cambodian government and the Khmer Rouge-led rebel alliance would disband 70% of their armies prior to UN-run elections, which would be held on the basis of proportional representation.

end of civil war On 23 Oct 1991, after nearly four years of intermittent negotiations, Cambodia's four warring factions and 18 interested countries signed a peace agreement in Paris, ending 13 years of civil war. The UN peacekeeping operation provided for a UN Transitional Authority in Cambodia (UNTAC) to be established within six months (preceded by a smaller UN Advance Mission in Cambodia (UNAMIC)). It would administer the country in conjunction with the Supreme National Council (comprising representatives from Cambodia's four warring factions) until the UN-administered general elections in 1993. UNTAC would organize the transportation and resettlement of the 356,000 Cambodian refugees living in camps on the Thai-Cambodian border as well as the 200,000 internally displaced people. It would also attempt the revival of Cambodia's poverty-stricken and moribund economy.

return of Sihanouk and Khmer Rouge The ruling Kampuchean People's Revolutionary Party, anxious to make itself more attractive to voters, formally abandoned its Marxist-Leninist ideology in Oct 1991 and changed its name to the Khmer/Cambodian People's Party. Heng Samrin was replaced as party chair by the powerful Chea Sim and the party endorsed a multiparty democratic system, a free-market economy, and the protection of human rights. It upheld Buddhism as the state religion and declared support for Prince Sihanouk's future candidacy for the state presidency. Prince Sihanouk returned to Phnom Penh on 23 Nov 1991 after a 13-year absence. As the 'legitimate head of state' until the presidential elections, he would administer the country in conjunction with Prime Minister Hun Sen and UNAMIC/UNTAC during the transition period. Khieu Samphan, leader of the Khmer Rouge, also returned to Phnom Penh but was forced to fly back to Thailand after being violently attacked by an angry mob. Despite promises Aug 1992 that the Khmer Rouge would cooperate in the peace process, they were still refusing to disarm in Oct.

restoration of human rights begins In Jan 1992 hundreds of political prisoners began to be released from Cambodia's jails and it was announced that freedom of speech and the formation of new political parties would be allowed.

Cambon Paul 1843–1924. French diplomat who was ambassador to London during the years leading to the outbreak of World War I, and a major figure in the creation of the Anglo-French entente during 1903–04.

Cambrai, Battles of two battles in World War I at Cambrai in NE France:

First Battle Nov–Dec 1917, the town was almost captured by the British when large numbers of tanks were used for the first time.

Second Battle 26 Aug–5 Oct 1918, the town was taken during the final British offensive.

Cambyses 6th century BC. King of Persia 529–522 BC. Succeeding his father Cyrus, he assassinated his brother Smerdis and conquered Egypt in 525 BC. There he outraged many of the local religious customs and was said to have become insane. He died in Syria.

Camelot legendary seat of King ◊Arthur. A possible site is the Iron Age hill fort of South Cadbury Castle in Somerset, England, where excavations from 1967 have revealed remains dating from 3000 BC to AD 1100, including those of a large 6th-century settlement, the time ascribed to Arthur.

Cameroon country in W Africa, bounded NW by Nigeria, NE by Chad, E by the Central African Republic, S by Congo, Gabon, and Equatorial Guinea, and W by the Atlantic.

history The area was first visited by Europeans 1472, when the Portuguese began slave trading in the area. In 1884 Cameroon became a German protectorate. After World War I, France governed about 80% of the area under a League of Nations mandate, with Britain administering the remainder. In 1946 both became United Nations trust territories.

independence In 1957 French Cameroon became a state within the French Community and three years later achieved full independence as the Republic of Cameroon. After a plebiscite 1961, the northern part of British Cameroons merged with Nigeria, and the southern part joined the Republic of Cameroon to form the Federal Republic of Cameroon. The French zone became East Cameroon and the British part West Cameroon.

one-party state Ahmadou Ahidjo, who had been the first president of the republic 1960, became president of the federal republic and was re-elected 1965. In 1966 Cameroon was made a one-party state when the two government parties and most of the opposition parties merged into the Cameroon National Union (UNC). Extreme left-wing opposition to the UNC was crushed 1971. In 1972 the federal system was abolished, and a new national assembly was elected 1973.

Biya's presidency In 1982 Ahidjo resigned, nominating Paul Biya as his successor. In 1983 Biya began to remove Ahidjo's supporters, and in protest Ahidjo resigned the presidency of UNC. Biya was re-elected 1984, while Ahidjo went into exile in France. Biya strengthened his position by abolishing the post of prime minister and reshuffling his cabinet. He also changed the nation's name from the United Republic of Cameroon to the Republic of Cameroon. Many of Ahidjo's supporters were executed after a failed attempt to overthrow Biya. In 1985 UNC changed its name to the Democratic Assembly of the Cameroon People (RDPC), and Biya tightened his control by more cabinet changes. Biya was re-elected president 1988 with 98.75% of the vote.

natural disaster In 1986 a volcanic vent under Lake Nyos released a vast quantity of carbon dioxide and hydrogen sulphide, which suffocated large numbers of people and animals.

constitutional reform In 1990 widespread public disorder resulted from the arrests of lawyers, lecturers, and students. However, Biya granted amnesty to political prisoners. In response to further public unrest, a number of constitutional changes were introduced in Dec 1991, including the lowering of the voting age to 20. Opposition groups complained that most of the changes were designed to help Biya win support in the forthcoming assembly elections. In March 1992 the first multiparty assembly elections in 28 years were held. The ruling RDPC won 89 of the 180 assembly seats, and a coalition of opposition groups 91. A small element in the coalition, holding 6 seats, supported Biya, thus securing a majority for the RDPC. Biya also won the Oct 1992 presidential election, but his victory was challenged by the opposition.

Camillus Marcus Furius died *c.* 365 BC. Roman general and statesman, five times dictator. Following early successes against the ◊Etruscans, he rallied the Romans after the Gallic invasion 387 BC. Camillus was an important leader of the ◊patrician cause in the political crises that followed, and was later victorious in campaigns against the ◊Aequi.

Camorra Italian secret society formed about 1820 by criminals in the dungeons of Naples and continued once they were freed. It dominated politics from 1848, was suppressed 1911, but many members eventually surfaced in the US ◊Mafia. The Camorra still operates in the Naples area.

Campaign for Nuclear Disarmament (CND) nonparty-political British organization advocating the abolition of nuclear weapons worldwide. CND seeks unilateral British initiatives to help start the multilateral process and end the arms race. It was founded 1958.

The movement was launched by the philosopher Bertrand Russell and Canon John Collins and grew out of the demonstration held outside the government's Atomic Weapons Research Establishment at Aldermaston, Berkshire, at Easter 1956. CND held annual marches from Aldermaston to London 1959–63, after the initial march in 1958 which was routed from London to Aldermaston. From 1970 CND has also opposed nuclear power. Its membership peaked in the early 1980s, during the campaign against the presence of US Pershing and cruise nuclear missiles on British soil.

Campbell-Bannerman Henry 1836–1908. British Liberal politician, prime minister 1905–08. It was during his term of office that the South African colonies achieved self-government, and the Trades Disputes Act 1906 was passed.

Camp David official country home of US presidents, situated in the Appalachian mountains, Maryland; it was originally named Shangri-la by F D Roosevelt, but was renamed Camp David by Eisenhower (after his grandson).

Camp David Agreements two framework agreements signed 1978 by Israeli prime minister Begin and Egyptian president Sadat at Camp David, Maryland, USA, under the guidance of US president Carter, covering an Egypt–Israel peace treaty and phased withdrawal of Israel from Sinai, which was completed 1982, and an overall Middle East settlement including the election by the West Bank and Gaza Strip Palestinians of a 'self-governing authority'. The latter issue has stalled repeatedly over questions of who should represent the Palestinians and what form the self-governing body should take.

Camperdown (Dutch *kamperduin*) village on the NW Netherlands coast, off which a British fleet defeated the Dutch 11 Oct 1897 in the Revolutionary Wars.

Campo-Formio, Treaty of peace settlement 1797 during the Revolutionary Wars between Napoleon and Austria, by which France gained the region that is now Belgium and Austria was compensated with Venice and part of an area that now reaches into Slovenia and Croatia.

Canaan ancient region between the Mediterranean and the Dead Sea, called in the Bible the 'Promised Land' of the Israelites. It was occupied as early as the 3rd millennium BC by the Canaanites, a Semitic-speaking people who were known to the Greeks of the 1st millennium BC as Phoenicians. The capital was Ebla (now Tell Mardikh, Syria).

The Canaanite Empire included Syria, Palestine, and part of Mesopotamia. It was conquered by the Israelites during the 13th to 10th centuries BC. Ebla was excavated 1976–77, revealing an archive of inscribed tablets dating from the 3rd millennium BC.

A land flowing with milk and honey ...
On *Canaan* the Bible, Exodus 3:8

Canada country occupying the northern part of the North American continent, bounded S by the USA, N by the Arctic Ocean, NW by Alaska, E by the Atlantic Ocean, and W by the Pacific Ocean.

Canada is a federation of ten provinces: Alberta, British Columbia, Manitoba, New Brunswick, Newfoundland, Nova Scotia, Ontario, Prince Edward Island, Québec, and

Saskatchewan; and two territories: Northwest Territories and Yukon. Each province has a single-chamber assembly, popularly elected; the premier (the leader of the party with the most seats in the legislature) chooses the cabinet. The two-chamber federal parliament consists of the Senate, whose 104 members are appointed by the government for life or until the age of 75 and must be resident in the provinces they represent; and the House of Commons, which has 295 members, elected by universal suffrage in single-member constituencies.

The federal prime minister is the leader of the best-supported party in the House of Commons and is accountable, with the cabinet, to it. Parliament has a maximum life of five years. Legislation must be passed by both chambers and then signed by the governor general.

history Inhabited by indigenous Indian and Inuit (Eskimo) groups, Canada was reached by an English expedition led by John Cabot 1497 and a French expedition under Jacques Cartier 1534. Both countries developed colonies from the 17th century, with hostility between them culminating in the French and Indian Wars (1756–63), in which France was defeated. Antagonism continued, and in 1791 Canada was divided into English-speaking Upper Canada (much of modern Ontario) and French-speaking Lower Canada (much of modern Québec and all of modern mainland Newfoundland). The two were united as Canada Province 1841, when the self-governing Dominion of Canada was founded.

In 1870 the province of Manitoba was added to the confederation, British Columbia joined 1871, and Prince Edward Island 1873. The new provinces of Alberta and Saskatchewan were created from the Northwest Territories 1905. An improving economy led to vast areas of fertile prairie land being opened up for settlement. The discovery of gold and other metals, the exploitation of forests for lumber and paper, the development of fisheries and tourism, and investment from other countries gradually transformed Canada's economy into one of the most important manufacturing and trading nations in the world. World War II stimulated further rapid industrialization, and in the post-war period discovery and exploitation of mineral resources took place on a vast scale. Newfoundland joined the confederation 1949.

Trudeau's era The Progressive Conservatives returned to power 1957, after 22 years of Liberal Party rule. In 1963 the Liberals were reinstated in office under Lester Pearson, who was succeeded by Pierre Trudeau 1968. Trudeau maintained Canada's defensive alliance with the USA but sought to widen its influence internationally. Faced with the problem of Québec's separatist movement, he promised to create equal opportunities for both English- and French-speaking Canadians throughout the country. He won both the 1972 and 1974 elections.

In 1979, with no party having an overall majority in the Commons, the Progressive Conservatives formed a government under Joe Clark. Later that year Trudeau announced his retirement from politics, but when, in Dec 1979, Clark was defeated on his budget proposals, Trudeau reconsidered his decision and won the 1980 general election with a large majority.

Trudeau's third administration was concerned with 'patriation', or the extent to which the British Parliament should determine Canada's constitution. The position was resolved with the passing of the Constitution Act 1982, the last piece of UK legislation to have force in Canada.

In 1983 Clark was replaced as leader of the Progressive Conservatives by Brian Mulroney, a corporate lawyer who had never run for public office, and in 1984 Trudeau retired to be replaced as Liberal Party leader and prime minister by John Turner, a former minister of finance. Within nine days of taking office, Turner called a general election, and the Progressive Conservatives, under Mulroney, won the largest majority in Canadian history.

changing direction Mulroney began an international realignment, placing less emphasis on links established by Trudeau with Asia, Africa, and Latin America, and more on cooperation with Europe and a closer relationship with the USA. The 1988 election was fought on the issue of free trade with the USA, and the Conservatives won with a reduced majority. Although a majority of votes chose parties opposed to free trade, an agreement was signed with the USA 1989.

The 1990s began with the collapse of the Meech Lake Accord, a 1987 compromise between the provinces aimed to getting Québec's acceptance of the 1982 constitutional reforms. Canada joined the coalition against Iraq's invasion of Kuwait 1990-91.

constitutional reform A constitutional reform plan, the Charlottetown Accord, was passed Aug 1992. It gave more autonomy to Québec, increased the powers of provinces, and reformed the Senate. In Nov a national referendum rejected the plan .

Campbell Mulroney resigned his office and was replaced by Kim Campbell June 1993.

In the same month, the parliament ratified the North America Free Trade Agreement with the USA and Mexico. In Oct, the general election resulted in a humiliating defeat for the Conservatives, whose Commons seat tally fell from 189 to 2. Jean Chrétien, Liberal leader, became prime minister. The Bloc Québecois under Lucien Bouchard was the official opposition.

Québec In a 1995 referendum in Québec, voters narrowly rejected a proposal that their province should become sovereign.

In the 1997 general election the Liberal majority was cut substantially.

Candella see ◊Chandelā.

Cannae, Battle of the Romans were defeated by ◊Hannibal 216 BC at Carrhae, now a village in Puglia, Italy.

Canning Charles John, 1st Earl 1812–1862. British administrator, first viceroy of India from 1858. As governor general of India from 1856, he suppressed the Indian Mutiny with a fair but firm hand which earned him the nickname 'Clemency Canning'. He was the son of George Canning.

Canning George 1770–1827. British Tory politician, foreign secretary 1807–10 and 1822–27, and prime minister 1827 in coalition with the Whigs. He was largely responsible, during the Napoleonic Wars, for the seizure of the Danish fleet and British intervention in the Spanish peninsula.

Man, only – rash, refined, presumptuous man,/ Starts from his rank, and mars creation's plan.

        George Canning *Progress of Man*

Canossa ruined castle 19 km/12 mi SW of Reggio, Italy. The Holy Roman emperor Henry IV did penance here before Pope Gregory VII 1077 for having opposed him in the question of investitures.

Cánovas del Castillo Antonio 1828–1897. Spanish politician and chief architect of the political system known as the *turno político* through which his own Conservative party, and that of the Liberals under Práxedes Sagasta, alternated in power. Elections were rigged to ensure the appropriate majorities. Cánovas was assassinated 1897 by anarchists.

Canute *c.* 995–1035. King of England from 1016, Denmark from 1018, and Norway from 1028. Having invaded England 1013 with his father, Sweyn, king of Denmark, he was

acclaimed king on his father's death 1014 by his ◊Viking army. Canute defeated ◊Edmund II Ironside at Assandun, Essex, 1016, and became king of all England on Edmund's death. He succeeded his brother Harold as king of Denmark 1018, compelled King Malcolm to pay homage by invading Scotland about 1027, and conquered Norway 1028. He was succeeded by his illegitimate son Harold I.

Canute VI (*Cnut VI*) 1163–1202. King of Denmark from 1182, son and successor of Waldemar Knudsson. With his brother and successor, Waldemar II, he resisted Frederick I's northward expansion, and established Denmark as the dominant power in the Baltic.

Cao Cao or *Ts'ao Ts'ao* AD 155–220. Chinese general who reunified and pacified N China after the collapse of the ◊Han dynasty. Cao's exploits are recorded in *The Romance of the Three Kingdoms*, China's oldest extant novel, and in other works, in which he appears as a heroic figure. His son Cao Bei (or Ts'ao P'ei) founded the Wei state, one of the ◊Three Kingdoms.

Capet Hugh 938–996. King of France from 987, when he claimed the throne on the death of Louis V. He founded the *Capetian dynasty*, of which various branches continued to reign until the French Revolution, for example, ◊Valois and ◊Bourbon.

Cape Verde group of islands in the Atlantic, W of Senegal (W Africa).

history The Cape Verde islands were first settled in the 15th century by Portugal, the first black inhabitants being slaves imported from W Africa. Over the next five centuries of Portuguese rule the islands were gradually peopled with Portuguese, African slaves, and people of mixed African-European descent who became the majority. The Cape Verdians kept some African culture but came to speak Portuguese or the Portuguese-derived Creole language, and became Catholics.

A liberation movement developed in the 1950s. The mainland territory to which Cape Verde is linked, Guinea-Bissau, achieved independence 1974, and a process began for their eventual union. A transitional government was set up, composed of Portuguese and members of the African Party for the Independence of Portuguese Guinea and Cape Verde (PAIGC).

after independence In 1975 a national people's assembly was elected, and Aristides Pereira, PAIGC secretary general, became president and head of government of Cape Verde. The 1980 constitution provided for the union of the two states but in 1981 this aspect was deleted because of insufficient support, and the PAIGC became the African Party for the Independence of Cape Verde (PAICV). From 1981 to 1990 the PAICV was the only permitted political party. Pereira was re-elected, and relations with Guinea-Bissau improved. Under President Pereira, Cape Verde adopted a nonaligned policy and achieved considerable respect within the region. An opposition party, the Independent Democratic Union of Cape Verde (UCID), operated from Portugal.

end of one-party system In the first multi-party elections, held Jan 1991, a new party, Movement for Democracy (MPD), won a majority in the assembly. After a very low poll the following month, Mascarenhas Monteiro was elected president in succession to Pereira.

capitalism economic system in which the principal means of production, distribution, and exchange are in private (individual or corporate) hands and competitively operated for profit. Many government reforms in the 19th and 20th centuries have brought capitalism increasingly under state control in such areas as monopolies, consumer and employment protection, and health and safety. A *mixed economy* combines the private enterprise of capitalism and a degree of state monopoly, as in nationalized industries.

Capone Al(phonse 'Scarface') 1898–1947. US gangster. During the ◊Prohibition period, he built a formidable criminal organization in Chicago. He was brutal in his pursuit of dominance, killing seven members of a rival gang in the St Valentine's Day massacre. He was imprisoned 1931–39 for income-tax evasion, the only charge that could be sustained against him.

I've been accused of every death except the casualty list of the World War.

Al Capone in a newspaper interview

Caprivi Georg Leo, Graf von 1831–1899. German soldier and politician. While chief of the admiralty (1883–88) he reorganized the German navy. He became imperial chancellor 1890–94 succeeding Bismarck and renewed the Triple Alliance but wavered between European allies and Russia. Although he strengthened the army, he alienated the conservatives.

Caracalla Marcus Aurelius Antoninus AD 186–217. Roman emperor. He succeeded his

father ◊Septimius Severus AD 211 and, with the support of the army, he murdered his brother Geta 212 to become sole ruler of the empire. During his reign, Roman citizenship was given to all subjects of the empire. He was assassinated.

He built on a grandiose scale, and campaigned in Germany and against the ◊Parthians. He was nicknamed after the Celtic cloak (*caracalla*) that he wore.

Caractacus died *c.* AD 54. British chieftain who headed resistance to the Romans in SE England AD 43–51, but was defeated on the Welsh border. Shown in Claudius's triumphal procession, he was released in tribute to his courage and died in Rome.

Carbonari secret revolutionary society in S Italy in the first half of the 19th century that advocated constitutional government. The movement spread to N Italy but support dwindled after the formation of ◊Mazzini's nationalist Young Italy movement, although it helped prove the way for the unification of Italy (see ◊Risorgimento).

Carchemish (now *Karkamis*, Turkey) centre of the ◊Hittite New Empire (*c.* 1400–1200 BC) on the river Euphrates, 80 km/50 mi NE of Aleppo, and taken by Sargon II of Assyria 717 BC. Nebuchadnezzar II of Babylon defeated the Egyptians here 605 BC.

Cárdenas Lázaro 1895–1970. Mexican centre-left politician and general, president 1934–40. A civil servant in early life, Cárdenas took part in the revolutionary campaigns 1915–29 that followed the fall of President Díaz (1830–1915). As president of the republic, he attempted to achieve the goals of the revolution by building schools, distributing land to the peasants, and developing transport and industry. He was minister of defence 1943–45.

Carib member of a group of ◊American Indian people of the northern coast of South America and the islands of the southern West Indies in the Caribbean. Those who moved north to take the islands from the Arawak Indians were alleged by the conquering Spaniards to be fierce cannibals. In 1796, the English in the West Indies deported most of them to Roatan Island, off Honduras.

Carinthia (German *Kärnten*) federal province of Alpine SE Austria, bordering Italy and Slovenia in the S. It was an independent duchy from 976 and a possession of the Habsburg dynasty 1276–1918.

Carlist supporter of the claims of the Spanish pretender Don Carlos de Bourbon (1788–

1855), and his descendants, to the Spanish crown. The Carlist revolt continued, primarily in the Basque provinces, until 1839. In 1977 the Carlist political party was legalized and Carlos Hugo de Bourbon Parma (1930–) renounced his claim as pretender and became reconciled with King Juan Carlos. See also ◊Bourbon.

Carlos I 1863–1908. King of Portugal, of the Braganza-Coburg line, from 1889 until he was assassinated in Lisbon with his elder son Luis. He was succeeded by his younger son Manuel.

Carlos four kings of Spain; see ◊Charles.

Carmelite order mendicant order of friars in the Roman Catholic church. The order was founded on Mount Carmel in Palestine by Berthold, a crusader from Calabria, about 1155, and spread to Europe in the 13th century. The Carmelites have devoted themselves largely to missionary work and mystical theology. They are known as *White Friars* because of the white overmantle they wear (over a brown habit).

Traditionally Carmelites originated in the days of Elijah, who according to the Old Testament is supposed to have lived on Mount Carmel. Following the rule which the patriarch of Jerusalem drew up for them about 1210, they lived as hermits in separate huts. About 1240, the Muslim conquests compelled them to move from Palestine and they spread to the west, mostly in France and England, where the order began to live communally.

Carnot Lazare Nicolas Marguerite 1753–1823. French general and politician. A member of the National Convention in the French Revolution, he organized the armies of the republic. He was war minister 1800–01 and minister of the interior 1815 under Napoleon. His work on fortification, *De la Défense de places fortes* 1810, became a military textbook. Minister of the interior during the Hundred Days, he was proscribed at the restoration of the monarchy and retired to Germany.

Carnot Marie François Sadi 1837–1894. French president from 1887, grandson of Lazare Carnot. He successfully countered the Boulangist anti-German movement (see ◊Boulanger) and in 1892 the scandals arising out of French financial activities in Panama. He was assassinated by an Italian anarchist in Lyon.

Carol I 1839–1914. First king of Romania 1881–1914. A prince of the house of Hohenzollern-Sigmaringen, he was invited to become prince of Romania, then part of the Ottoman Empire, 1866. In 1877, in alliance with Russia, he declared war on Turkey, and the Congress of Berlin 1878 recognized Romanian independence.

Carol II 1893–1953. King of Romania 1930–40. Son of King Ferdinand, he married Princess Helen of Greece and they had a son, Michael. In 1925 he renounced the succession because of his affair with Elena Lupescu and went into exile in Paris. Michael succeeded to the throne 1927, but in 1930 Carol returned to Romania and was proclaimed king. In 1938 he introduced a new constitution under which he practically became an absolute ruler. He was forced to abdicate by the pro-Nazi ◊Iron Guard Sept 1940, went to Mexico, and married his mistress 1947.

Caroline of Brunswick 1768–1821. Queen of George IV of Great Britain, who unsuccessfully attempted to divorce her on his accession to the throne 1820.

Second daughter of Karl Wilhelm, Duke of Brunswick, and Augusta, sister of George III, she married her first cousin, the Prince of Wales, 1795, but after the birth of Princess Charlotte Augusta a separation was arranged. When her husband ascended the throne 1820 she was offered an annuity of £50,000 provided she agreed to renounce the title of queen and to continue to live abroad. She returned forthwith to London, where she assumed royal state. In July 1820 the government brought in a bill to dissolve the marriage, but Lord Brougham's defence led to the bill's abandonment. On 19 July 1821 Caroline was prevented by royal order from entering Westminster Abbey for the coronation. Her funeral was the occasion of popular riots.

Carolingian dynasty Frankish dynasty descending from ◊Pepin the Short (died 768) and named after his son Charlemagne; its last ruler was Louis V of France (reigned 966–87), who was followed by Hugh ◊Capet, first ruler of the Capetian dynasty.

Carolingian Renaissance period of learning which began under ◊Charlemagne.

carpetbagger in US history, derogatory name for any of the entrepreneurs and politicians from the North who moved to the Southern states during ◊Reconstruction 1861–65 after the Civil War, to exploit the chaotic conditions for their own benefit.

With the votes of newly enfranchised blacks and some local white people (called *scalawags*), they won posts in newly created Republican state governments, but were resented by many white Southerners as outsiders and opportunists. The term thus came to mean a corrupt outsider who profits from an area's political instability, although some arrivals had good motives. They were so called because they were supposed to carry their ill-gotten gains in small satchels made of carpeting.

Carrhae, Battle of battle 53 BC in which the invading Roman general Crassus was defeated and killed by the Parthians. The ancient town of Carrhae is near Haran, Turkey.

Carroll Charles 1737–1832. American public official who, as a member of the Continental Congress, was one of the signatories of the Declaration of Independence 1776. He was one of the North American colony of Maryland's first US senators 1789–92.

Carson Edward Henry, Baron Carson 1854–1935. Irish politician and lawyer who campaigned in Ulster during World War I in support of the government, and took office under both Asquith and Lloyd George (attorney general 1915, First Lord of the Admiralty 1916, member of the war cabinet 1917–18). He was a Lord of Appeal in Ordinary 1921–29.

Carson Kit (Christopher) 1809–68. US frontier settler, guide, and Indian agent, who later fought for the Federal side in the Civil War. Carson City, Nevada, was named after him.

Carter Jimmy (James Earl) 1924– . 39th president of the USA 1977–81, a Democrat. In 1976 he narrowly wrested the presidency from Gerald Ford. Features of his presidency were the return of the Panama Canal Zone to Panama, the Camp David Agreements for peace in the Middle East, and the Iranian seizure of US embassy hostages. He was defeated by Ronald Reagan 1980.

We should live our lives as though Christ were coming this afternoon.

Jimmy Carter
speech to Bible class in Plains, Georgia,
March 1976

Carter Doctrine assertion 1980 by President Carter of a vital US interest in the Persian Gulf region (prompted by the Soviet invasion of Afghanistan and instability in Iran): any outside attempt at control would be met by military force if necessary.

Carthage ancient Phoenician port in N Africa founded by colonists from Tyre in the late 9th century BC; it lay 16 km/10 mi N of Tunis, Tunisia. A leading trading centre, it was in conflict with Greece from the 6th century BC, and then with Rome, and was destroyed by Roman

forces 146 BC at the end of the ◊*Punic Wars*. About 45 BC, Roman colonists settled in Carthage, and it became the wealthy capital of the province of Africa. After its capture by the Vandals AD 439 it was little more than a pirate stronghold. From 533 it formed part of the Byzantine Empire until its final destruction by Arabs 698, during their conquest in the name of Islam.

After the capture of Tyre by the Babylonians in the 6th century BC, Carthage became the natural leader of the Phoenician colonies in N Africa and Spain, and there soon began a prolonged struggle with the Greeks, which centred mainly on Sicily, the east of which was dominated by Greek colonies, while the west was held by Carthaginian trading stations. About 540 BC the Carthaginians defeated a Greek attempt to land in Corsica, and 480 BC a Carthaginian attempt to conquer the whole of Sicily was defeated by the Greeks at Himera.

The population of Carthage before its destruction by the Romans in 146 BC is said to have numbered over 700,000. The constitution was an aristocratic republic with two chief magistrates elected annually and a senate of 300 life members. The religion was Phoenician, including the worship of the Moon goddess Tanit, the great Sun god Baal-Ha mmon, and the Tyrian Meklarth; human sacrifices were not unknown. The original strength of Carthage lay in its commerce and its powerful navy; its armies were for the most part mercenaries.

Carthage had not desired to create, but only to enjoy: therefore she left us nothing.

On *Carthage* Hilaire Belloc
Esto Perpetua 1906

Carthusian order Roman Catholic order of monks and, later, nuns, founded by St Bruno 1084 at Chartreuse, near Grenoble, France.

The order was introduced into England about 1178, when the first Charterhouse was founded at Witham in Essex. They were suppressed at the Reformation.

Cartier Georges Étienne 1814–1873. French-Canadian politician. He fought against the British in the rebellion 1837, was elected to the Canadian parliament 1848, and was joint prime minister with John A Macdonald 1858–62. He brought Québec into the Canadian federation 1867.

Cartier Jacques 1491–1557. French navigator who, while seeking a north-west passage to China, was the first European to sail up the St

Lawrence River 1534. He named the site of Montreál.

Casablanca Conference World War II meeting of the US and UK leaders Roosevelt and Churchill, 14–24 Jan 1943, at which the Allied demand for the unconditional surrender of Germany, Italy, and Japan was issued.

Casement Roger David 1864–1916. Irish nationalist. While in the British consular service, he exposed the ruthless exploitation of the people of the Belgian Congo and Peru, for which he was knighted 1911 (degraded 1916). He was hanged for treason by the British for his involvement in the Irish nationalist cause.

In 1914 Casement went to Germany and attempted to induce Irish prisoners of war to form an Irish brigade to take part in a republican insurrection. He returned to Ireland in a submarine 1916 (actually to postpone, not start, the Easter Rising), was arrested, tried for treason, and hanged.

Cassius Gaius died 42 BC. Roman soldier, one of the conspirators who killed Julius ◊Caesar 44 BC. He fought with Pompey against Caesar, and was pardoned after the battle of ◊Pharsalus 48, but became a leader in the conspiracy of 44. After Caesar's death he joined Brutus, and committed suicide after their defeat at ◊Philippi 42.

caste (Portuguese *casta* 'race') stratification of Hindu society into four main groups: *Brahmans* (priests), *Kshatriyas* (nobles and warriors), *Vaisyas* (traders and farmers), and *Sudras* (servants); plus a fifth group, *Harijan* (untouchables). No upward or downward mobility exists, as in classed societies. The system dates from ancient times, and there are more than 3,000 subdivisions.

In Hindu tradition, the four main castes are said to have originated from the head, arms, thighs, and feet respectively of Brahma, the creator; the members of the fifth were probably the aboriginal inhabitants of the country, known variously as Scheduled Castes, Depressed Classes, Untouchables, or Harijan (name coined by Gandhi, 'children of God'). This lowest caste handled animal products, garbage, and human wastes and so was considered to be polluting by touch, or even by sight, to others. Discrimination against them was made illegal 1947 when India became independent, but persists.

Castile kingdom founded in the 10th century, occupying the central plateau of Spain. Its union with ◊Aragon 1479, based on the marriage of ◊Ferdinand and Isabella, effected the foundation of the Spanish state, which at the time was occupied and ruled by the ◊Moors.

Castile comprised the two great basins separated by the Sierra de Gredos and the Sierra de Guadarrama, known traditionally as Old and New Castile. The area now forms the regions of ◊Castilla– León and Castilla–La Mancha.

The kingdom of Castile grew from a small area in the north. In the 11th century, Old Castile was united with León; the kingdom of Toledo was captured from the Moors 1085 and became New Castile, with Toledo the capital of the whole. Castile was united with Aragon 1479, and in 1492, after routing the Moors, Ferdinand and Isabella established the Catholic kingdom of Spain.

Castilla Ramón 1797–1867. President of Peru 1841–51 and 1855–62. He dominated Peruvian politics for over two decades, bringing political stability. Income from guano exports was used to reduce the national debt and improve transport and educational facilities. He abolished black slavery and the head tax on Indians.

castle private fortress of a king or noble. The earliest castles in Britain were built following the Norman Conquest, and the art of castle building reached a peak in the 13th century. By the 15th century, the need for castles for domestic defence had largely disappeared, and the advent of gunpowder made them largely useless against attack.

Castles	
11th century	The motte and bailey castle (the motte was a mound of earth, and the bailey a courtyard enclosed by a wall); the earliest example is on the river Loire in France, dated 1010. The first rectangular keep dates from this time; an example is the White Tower in the Tower of London.
12th century	Development of more substantial defensive systems, based in part on the Crusaders' experiences of sieges during the First Crusade 1096; the first curtain walls with projecting towers were built (as at Framlingham, Suffolk).
13th century	Introduction of the round tower, both for curtain walls (Pembroke, Wales) and for keeps (Conisborough, Yorkshire); concentric planning (in the castles of Wales, such as Beaumaris and Harlech); fortified town walls.
14th century	First use of gunpowder; inclusion of gunports in curtain walls (Bodiam, Sussex).
15th century	Fortified manor houses now adequate for private dwelling.
16th century	End of castle as a practical means of defence; fortified coastal defences, however, continued to be built (Falmouth, Cornwall).

Castlereagh Robert Stewart, Viscount Castlereagh 1769–1822. British Tory politician. As chief secretary for Ireland 1797–1801, he suppressed the rebellion of 1798 and helped the younger Pitt secure the union of England, Scotland, and Ireland 1801. As foreign secretary 1812–22, he coordinated European opposition to Napoleon and represented Britain at the Congress of Vienna 1814–15.

Castro Cipriano 1858–1924. Venezuelan dictator 1899–1908, known as 'the Lion of the Andes'. When he refused to pay off foreign debts 1902, British, German, and Italian ships blockaded the country. He presided over a corrupt government. There were frequent rebellions during his rule, and opponents of his regime were exiled or murdered.

Castro (Ruz) Fidel 1927– . Cuban communist politician, prime minister 1959–76 and president from 1976. He led two unsuccessful coups against the right-wing Batista regime and led the revolution that overthrew the dictator 1959. He raised the standard of living for most Cubans but dealt harshly with dissenters.

Of wealthy parentage, Castro was educated at Jesuit schools and, after studying law at the University of Havana, gained a reputation through his work for poor clients. He opposed the Batista dictatorship, and took part, with his brother Raúl, in an unsuccessful attack on the army barracks at Santiago de Cuba 1953. After some time in exile in the USA and Mexico, Castro attempted a secret landing in Cuba 1956 in which all but 11 of his supporters were killed. He eventually gathered an army of over 5,000 which overthrew Batista on 1 Jan 1959 and he became prime minister a few months later. Raúl Castro was appointed minister of armed forces.

Castro's administration introduced a centrally planned economy based on the production for export of sugar, tobacco, and nickel. He nationalized the property of wealthy Cubans, Americans, and other foreigners 1960, resulting in the severance of relations by the USA, an economic embargo, and US attempts to subvert Cuba's government (see also ◊Bay of Pigs). This enmity came to a head in the ◊Cuban missile crisis 1962. Aid for development was provided by the USSR, which replaced the USA as Cuba's main trading partner, and Castro espoused Marxism-Leninism until, in 1974, he rejected Marx's formula 'from each according to his ability and to each according to his need' and decreed that each Cuban should 'receive according to his work'. He also improved education, housing, and health care for the majority of Cubans but lost the support of the middle

class, hundreds of thousands of whom fled the country. Since 1990, events in E Europe and the disintegration of the USSR have left Castro increasingly isolated.

History will absolve me.

Fidel Castro
after an unsuccessful assault
on army barracks July 1953

Catalaunian Fields plain near Troyes, France, scene of the defeat of Attila the Hun by the Romans and Goths under the Roman general Aëtius 451.

Catalonia (Spanish *Cataluña,* Catalan *Catalunya*) autonomous region of NE Spain. The region has a long tradition of independence. It enjoyed autonomy 1932–39 but lost its privileges for supporting the republican cause in the Spanish ◊Civil War. Autonomy and official use of the Catalan language were restored 1980.

Cat and Mouse Act popular name for the *Prisoners, Temporary Discharge for Health, Act* 1913; an attempt by the UK Liberal government under Herbert Asquith to reduce embarrassment caused by the incarceration of ◊suffragettes accused of violent offences against property.

When the suffragettes embarked on hunger strikes, prison authorities introduced forced feeding, which proved humiliating and sometimes dangerous to the women. Following a public outcry, the hunger strikers were released on a licence that could be revoked without further trial.

Cateau-Cambresis, Treaty of treaty that ended the dynastic wars between the Valois of France and the Habsburg Empire, 2–3 April 1559.

Cathar (medieval Latin 'the pure') member of a sect in medieval Europe usually numbered among the Christian heretics. Influenced by Manichaeism, they started about the 10th century in the Balkans where they were called 'Bogomils', spread to SW Europe where they were often identified with the ◊Albigenses, and by the middle of the 14th century had been destroyed or driven underground by the Inquisition

Catherine I 1684–1727. Empress of Russia from 1725. A Lithuanian peasant, born Martha Skavronsky, she married a Swedish dragoon and eventually became the mistress of Peter the Great. In 1703 she was rechristened Katarina Alexeievna. The tsar divorced his wife 1711 and married Catherine 1712. She accompanied him on his campaigns, and showed tact and shrewdness. In 1724 she was proclaimed empress, and after Peter's death 1725 she ruled capably with the help of her ministers. She allied Russia with Austria and Spain in an anti-English bloc.

Catherine II *the Great* 1729–1796. Empress of Russia from 1762, and daughter of the German prince of Anhalt-Zerbst. In 1745, she married the Russian grand duke Peter. Catherine was able to dominate him; six months after he became Tsar Peter III 1762, he was murdered in a coup and Catherine ruled alone. During her reign Russia extended its boundaries to include territory from wars with the Turks 1768–74, 1787–92, and from the partitions of Poland 1772, 1793, and 1795, as well as establishing hegemony over the Black Sea.

I shall be an autocrat: that's my trade.
And the good Lord will forgive me:
that's his.

           Catherine II (attributed)

Catherine de' Medici 1519–1589. French queen consort of Henry II, whom she married 1533; daughter of Lorenzo de' Medici, Duke of Urbino; and mother of Francis II, Charles IX, and Henry III. At first outshone by Henry's mistress Diane de Poitiers (1490–1566), she became regent 1560–63 for Charles IX and remained in power until his death 1574.

During the religious wars of 1562–69, she first supported the Protestant ◊Huguenots against the Roman Catholic *Guises* to ensure her own position as ruler; she later opposed them, and has been traditionally implicated in the Massacre of ◊St Bartholomew 1572.

Catherine of Aragon 1485–1536. First queen of Henry VIII of England, 1509–33, and mother of Mary I. Catherine had married Henry's elder brother Prince Arthur 1501 and on his death 1502 was betrothed to Henry, marrying him on his accession. She failed to produce a male heir and Henry divorced her without papal approval, thus creating the basis for the English ◊Reformation.

Catherine of Braganza 1638–1705. Queen of Charles II of England 1662–85. Her childlessness and practice of her Catholic faith were unpopular, but Charles resisted pressure for divorce. She returned to Lisbon 1692 after his death.

The daughter of John IV of Portugal (1604–1656), she brought the Portuguese possessions of Bombay and Tangier as her dowry and introduced tea drinking and citrus fruits to England.

Catholic church whole body of the Christian church, though usually referring to the Roman Catholic Church.

Catholic Emancipation in British history, acts of Parliament passed 1780–1829 to relieve Roman Catholics of civil and political restrictions imposed from the time of Henry VIII and the Reformation.

Catholic Monarchs, the term applied to ◊Ferdinand V of Castile and Isabella I, who Catholicized Spain.

Catiline (Lucius Sergius Catilina) *c.* 108–62 BC. Roman politician. Twice failing to be elected to the consulship in 64/63 BC, he planned a military coup, but ◊Cicero exposed his conspiracy. He died at the head of the insurgents.

Cato Marcus Porcius, known as 'the Censor' 234–149 BC. Roman politician. Having significantly developed Roman rule in Spain, Cato was appointed ◊censor 184 BC. He acted severely, taxing luxuries and heavily revising the senatorial and equestrian lists. He was violently opposed to Greek influence on Roman culture and his suspicion of the re-emergence of Carthaginian power led him to remark repeatedly: 'Carthage must be destroyed.'

Cato Street Conspiracy in British history, unsuccessful plot hatched in Cato Street, London, to murder the Tory foreign secretary Robert Castlereagh and all his ministers on 20 Feb 1820. The leader, the Radical Arthur Thistlewood (1770–1820), who intended to set up a provisional government, was hanged with four others.

caucus in the USA, a closed meeting of regular party members; for example, to choose a candidate for office. The term was originally used in the 18th century in Boston, Massachusetts.

In the UK, it was first applied to the organization introduced by the Liberal politician Joseph Chamberlain 1878 and is generally used to mean a local party committee.

caudillo Spanish term for leader, often used for a dictator, which originated during the independence movement in Latin America 1808–26.

At that time civilian institutions were in decline and soldiers, or 'men on horseback', controlled the political system in addition to fighting battles. Post-independence conflicts and wars between neighbour states such as

Peru and Colombia sustained caudillismo. Later it described military strongmen of particular nations who were born in Spain and Latin America, such as Juan Domingo ◊Perón in Argentina or Francisco ◊Franco in Spain.

cavalier horseman of noble birth, but mainly used to describe a male supporter of Charles I in the English Civil War (Cavalier), typically with courtly dress and long hair (as distinct from a Roundhead); also a supporter of Charles II after the Restoration.

Cavell Edith Louisa 1865–1915. British matron of a Red Cross hospital in Brussels, Belgium, in World War I, who helped Allied soldiers escape to the Dutch frontier. She was court-martialled by the Germans and condemned to death.

Standing as I do, in the view of God and eternity I realize that patriotism is not enough. I must have no hatred or bitterness towards anyone.

Edith Cavell to chaplain before her execution by a firing squad 12 Oct 1915

Cavendish Frederick Charles, Lord Cavendish 1836–1882. British administrator, second son of the 7th Duke of Devonshire. He was appointed chief secretary to the lord lieutenant of Ireland in 1882. On the evening of his arrival in Dublin he was murdered in Phoenix Park with Thomas Burke, the permanent Irish undersecretary, by members of the Irish Invincibles, a group of Irish Fenian extremists founded 1881.

Cavour Camillo Benso di, Count 1810–1861. Italian nationalist politician, a leading figure in the Italian ◊Risorgimento. As prime minister of Piedmont 1852–59 and 1860–61, he enlisted the support of Britain and France for the concept of a united Italy achieved 1861; after expelling the Austrians 1859, he assisted Garibaldi in liberating southern Italy 1860.

Cavour was born in Turin, served in the army in early life and entered politics in 1847. From 1848 he sat in the Piedmontese parliament and held cabinet posts 1850–52. As prime minister, he sought to secure French and British sympathy for the cause of Italian unity by sending Piedmontese troops to fight in the Crimean War. In 1858 he had a secret meeting with Napoleon III at Plombières, where they planned the war of 1859 against Austria, which resulted in the union of Lombardy with Pied-

mont. Then the central Italian states joined the kingdom of Italy, although Savoy and Nice were to be ceded to France. With Cavour's approval Garibaldi overthrew the Neapolitan monarchy, but Cavour occupied part of the Papal States which, with Naples and Sicily, were annexed to Italy, to prevent Garibaldi from marching on Rome.

Cayman Islands British island group in the West Indies. The islands were discovered by Chrisopher Columbus 1503; acquired by Britain following the Treaty of Madrid 1670; a dependency of Jamaica 1863, In 1962 the islands became a separate colony, although the inhabitants chose to remain British.

CDU abbreviation for *Christian Democratic Union*, a right-of-centre political party in Germany.

Ceauşescu Nicolae 1918–1989. Romanian politician, leader of the Romanian Communist Party (RCP), in power 1965–89. He pursued a policy line independent of and critical of the USSR. He appointed family members, including his wife *Elena Ceauşescu*, to senior state and party posts, and governed in an increasingly repressive manner, zealously implementing schemes that impoverished the nation. The Ceauşescus were overthrown in a bloody revolutionary coup Dec 1989 and executed.

Cecil Robert, 1st Earl of Salisbury 1563–1612. Secretary of state to Elizabeth I of England, succeeding his father, Lord Burghley; he was afterwards chief minister to James I (James VI of Scotland) whose accession to the English throne he secured. He discovered the ◊Gunpowder Plot, the conspiracy to blow up the King and Parliament 1605. James I created him Earl of Salisbury 1605.

CEDA (acronym for *Confederación* Español de *Derechas* Autónomas) federation of right-wing parties under the leadership of José Maria Gil Robles, founded during the Second Spanish Republic 1933 to provide a right-wing coalition in the Spanish Cortes. Supporting the Catholic and monarchist causes, the federation was uncommitted as to the form of government.

Celt (Greek *Keltoi*) member of an Indo-European people that originated in Alpine Europe and spread to the Iberian peninsula and beyond. They were ironworkers and farmers. In the 1st century BC they were defeated by the Roman Empire and by Germanic tribes and confined largely to Britain, Ireland, and N France.

The Celts' first known territory was in central Europe about 1200 BC, in the basin of the upper Danube, the Alps, and parts of France and S Germany. In the 6th century they spread into Spain and Portugal. Over the next 300 years, they also spread into the British Isles, N Italy (sacking Rome 390 BC), Greece, the Balkans, and parts of Asia Minor, although they never established a united empire.

Between the Bronze and Iron Ages, in the 9th–5th centuries BC, they developed a transitional culture (named the *Hallstatt* culture after its archaeological site SW of Salzburg). They farmed, raised cattle, and were pioneers of ironworking, reaching their peak in the period from the 5th century to the Roman conquest (the *La Tène* culture). Celtic languages survive in Ireland, Wales, Scotland, the Isle of Man, and Brittany, and have been revived in Cornwall.

CENTO abbreviation for the ◊Central Treaty organization.

Central African Federation or (CAF) grouping imposed by the British government 1953, incorporating the territories of Nyasaland and Northern and Southern Rhodesia. Although it established representative government along federal and multiracial lines, an underlying function was to prevent the spread of Afrikaner nationalism into central Africa. It was dismembered 1963 in the face of African demands for independence in Nyasaland and Northern Rhodesia, and the intransigence of the minority white community in Southern Rhodesia.

Central African Republic landlocked country in Central Africa, bordered NE and E by Sudan, S by Zaire and the Congo, W by Cameroon, and NW by Chad.

history A French colony from the late 19th century, the territory of Ubangi-Shari became self-governing within French Equatorial Africa in 1958 and two years later achieved full independence. Barthélémy Boganda, who had founded the Movement for the Social Evolution of Black Africa (MESAN), had been a leading figure in the campaign for independence and became the country's first prime minister. A year before full independence he was killed in an air crash and was succeeded by his nephew, David Dacko, who became president 1960 and 1962 established a one-party state, with MESAN as the only political organization.

Bokassa's rule Dacko was overthrown in a military coup Dec 1965, and the commander in chief of the army, Col Jean-Bédel ◊Bokassa, assumed power. Bokassa annulled the constitution and made himself president for life 1972 and marshal of the republic 1974. An authoritarian regime was established, and in 1976 ex-president Dacko was recalled to be the

president's personal adviser. At the end of that year the republic was restyled the Central African Empire, and in 1977 Bokassa was crowned emperor at a lavish ceremony his country could ill afford. His rule became increasingly dictatorial and idiosyncratic, leading to revolts by students and, in April 1979, by schoolchildren who objected to the compulsory wearing of school uniforms made by a company owned by the Bokassa family. Many of the children were imprisoned, and it is estimated that at least 100 were killed, with the emperor allegedly personally involved.

Dacko's coup In Sept 1979, while Bokassa was in Libya, Dacko ousted him in a bloodless coup, backed by France. The country became a republic again, with Dacko as president. He initially retained a number of Bokassa's former ministers but, following student unrest, they were dropped, and in Feb 1981 a new constitution was adopted, with an elected national assembly. Dacko was elected president for a six-year term in March, but opposition to him grew and in Sept 1981 he was deposed in another bloodless coup, led by the armed forces' Chief of Staff, General André Kolingba.

military government The constitution and all political organizations were suspended, and a military government was installed. Undercover opposition to the Kolingba regime continued, with some French support, but relations with France were improved by an unofficial visit by President Mitterrand in Oct 1982. The leaders of the banned political parties were granted an amnesty, and at the end of the year the French president paid a state visit. In Jan 1985 proposals for a new constitution were announced and in Sept civilians were included in Kolingba's administration. In 1986 Bokassa returned from exile in France, expecting to be returned to power. Instead, he was tried for his part in the killing of the schoolchildren in 1979 and condemned to death; the sentence was commuted to life imprisonment 1988. In 1991, in response to widespread demonstrations calling for a return to a multiparty system, the government announced that it would convene a national conference to discuss the future of the country.

Central America the part of the Americas that links Mexico with the isthmus of Panama, comprising Belize, Costa Rica, El Salvador, Guatemala, Honduras, Nicaragua, and Panama.

It is also an isthmus, crossed by mountains that form part of the Cordilleras. Much of Central America formed part of the Maya civiliza-

Central America to 1532

Toltecs		1517	Hernandez de Córdoba reached Yucatán.
c. 800	Toltecs migrated to Mexico, and established a centre at Tula.	1525	Spanish conquered Guatemala.
		1541	Fall of Yucatán.
c. 900	Toltecs put pressure on the Maya of Yucatán.	1697	Fall of Itzá, last outpost of the Maya.
1168	Tula fell to the Aztecs.	***Aztecs***	
Maya		*c.* 1100	Aztecs migrated from Aztlan.
c. 500 BC– *c.* AD 325	Development of agricultural civilization in Central America. Emergence of hierarchies, and beginning of pyramid building. Origin of calendar and hieroglyphs.	*c.* 1200	Development of small individual states.
		c. 1345	Foundation of Tenochtitlán.
		1358	Foundation of Tlatelolco.
325–625	Early Classic period. Emergence of cult of the stela. Growth of semi-autonomous city states. Cultural development reached a peak in the highlands.	*c.* 1430	League of Tenochtitlán established. Tetzcoco and Tlacopan rulers of Mexico.
		1486–1502	Reign of Ahuitzotl. Aztec influence expanded.
545	Conference of astronomers held at Copán to reform the calendar.	1500	Defensive flooding of Tenochtitlán.
625–800	High point of the Classic period. Hieroglyphics, sculpture, and architecture developed furthest in the lowlands. Increased sophistication in arithmetic and astronomy. Number of religious centres and *stelae* (inscribed pillars) grew.	1502	Accession of Montezuma II. Further expansion of empire.
		1517	Hernandez de Córdoba reached the Mexican coast.
		1518	Juan de Grijalva's expedition reached Mexico.
c. 790	Painting of murals at Bonampak.	1519 February	Hernán Cortés set out for Mexico.
800–925	Collapse of Classic period. Stelae and religious centres abandoned. Migrations to Yucatán, possibly under pressure from the Toltecs. Increasing Mexican influence along W side of Yucatán peninsula.	Nov	Spanish entered Tenochtitlán.
		1520 June	Montezuma II died. Spanish retreated from Tenochtitlán.
		Aug	Tenochtitlán destroyed by Spanish.
925–75	Return to decentralized, agricultural culture. Mexican influence continued to grow.	***Inca***	
		c. 100	Inca hill settlements established at Chavin, Tiahuanaco and Recuay.
975–1200	Mexican period. Itzá settled in Mayapán. Rise of city of Chichen Itzá. Mexican gods worshipped. Wars waged to provide human sacrifices. Priesthood overshadowed by secular princes.	*c.* 500	Coastal centres founded.
		11th century	Cuzco established.
		1438	Accession of Pachacutic. Growth of the Inca empire.
c. 987–1185	League of Mayapán.	1470	Chimu destroyed by Incas.
1194	Rise of Hunac Ceel and the fall of Chichén Itzá.	1471–93	Reign of Tupac Yupanqui saw further advances, and territory acquired as far south as modern Santiago (in Chile).
1200–1541	Mexican culture gradually absorbed into Mayan. Cities developed out of religious centres. Secular authority dominant over that of religion. Artistic decline.	1513	Quito (Ecuador) conquered by Huayna Capac.
1204–1440	Ascendancy of Mayapán in Yucatán. Strong, centralized authority established.	1527	Outbreak of factionalism within the royal family. Sons of Huayna Capac set up rival power bases, Huascar at Cuzco and Atahualpa at Quito.
1441	Xius destroyed Mayapán. Central authority crumbled.	1502	Atahualpa killed by the Spanish under Francisco Pizarro.
1464	Yucatán struck by hurricane.		
1480	Outbreak of plague.	1533	Cuzco conquered.

tion. Spanish settlers married indigenous women, and the area remained out of the mainstream of Spanish Empire history. When the Spanish Empire collapsed in the early 1800s, the area formed the Central American Federa-tion, with a constitution based on that of the USA. Demand for cash crops (bananas, coffee, cotton), especially from the USA, created a strong landowning class controlling a serflike peasantry by military means. There has been

US military intervention in the area, for example in Nicaragua, where the dynasty of General Anastasio Somoza was founded. US president Carter reversed support for such regimes, but in the 1980s, the Reagan and Bush administrations again favoured military and financial aid to right-wing political groups, including the ◊Contras in Nicaragua.

Central Intelligence Agency (CIA) US intelligence organization established 1947. It has actively intervened overseas, generally to undermine left-wing regimes or to protect US financial interests; for example, in the Congo (now Zaire) and Nicaragua. From 1980 all covert activity by the CIA has by law to be reported to Congress.

central planning system by which the state takes complete control over the running of the national economy. For example, in the Soviet Union from the 1920s, targets and strategies were all decided centrally, leaving little or no room for private initiative or enterprise.

Central Powers originally the signatories of the ◊Triple Alliance 1882: Germany, Austria-Hungary, and Italy. During World War I, Italy remained neutral before joining the ◊Allies.

Central Treaty Organization (CENTO) military alliance that replaced the ◊Baghdad Pact 1959; it collapsed when the withdrawal of Iran, Pakistan, and Turkey 1979 left the UK as the only member.

Centre Party (German *Zentrumspartei*) German political party established 1871 to protect Catholic interests. Although alienated by Chancellor Bismarck's ◊*Kulturkampf* 1873–78, in the following years the *Zentrum* became an essential component in the government of imperial Germany. The party continued to play a part in the politics of Weimar Germany before being barred by Hitler in the summer of 1933.

Cetewayo (Cetshwayo) *c.* 1826–1884. King of Zululand, South Africa, 1873–83, whose rule was threatened by British annexation of the Transvaal 1877. Although he defeated the British at Isandhlwana 1879, he was later that year defeated by them at Ulundi. Restored to his throne 1883, he was then expelled by his subjects.

Chaco War conflict between ◊Bolivia and Paraguay 1932–35.

Chad landlocked country in central N Africa, bounded N by Libya, E by Sudan, S by the Central African Republic, and W by Cameroon, Nigeria, and Niger.

history Called Kanem when settled by Arabs in the 7th–13th centuries, the area later became known as Bornu and in the 19th century was conquered by Sudan. From 1913 a province of French Equatorial Africa, Chad became an autonomous state within the French Community 1958, with François Tombalbaye as prime minister.

independence Full independence was achieved 1960, and Tombalbaye became president. He soon faced disagreements between the Arabs of the north, who saw Libya as an ally, and the black African Christians of the south, who felt more sympathy for Nigeria. In the north the Chadian National Liberation Front (Frolinat) revolted against the government. In 1975 Tombalbaye was killed in a coup led by former army Chief of Staff Félix Malloum, who became president of a supreme military council and appealed for national unity. Frolinat continued its opposition, however, supported by Libya, which held a strip of land in the north, believed to contain uranium.

Frolinat expansion By 1978 Frolinat, led by General Goukouni Oueddi, had expanded its territory but was halted with French aid. Malloum tried to reach a settlement by making former Frolinat leader, Hissène Habré, prime minister, but disagreements developed between them. In 1979 fighting broke out again between government and Frolinat forces, and Malloum fled the country. Talks resulted in the formation of a provisional government (GUNT), with Goukouni holding the presidency with Libyan support. A proposed merger with Libya was rejected, and Libya withdrew most of its forces.

civil war The Organization for African Unity (OAU) set up a peacekeeping force but civil war broke out and by 1981 Hissène Habré's Armed Forces of the North (FAN) controlled half the country. Goukouni fled and set up a 'government in exile'. In 1983 a majority of OAU members agreed to recognize Habré's regime, but Goukouni, with Libyan support, fought on.

cease-fire After Libyan bombing, Habré appealed to France for help. Three thousand troops were sent as instructors, with orders to retaliate if attacked. Following a Franco-African summit 1984, a cease-fire was agreed, with latitude 16°N dividing the opposing forces. Libyan president Col Khaddhafi's proposal of a simultaneous withdrawal of French and Libyan troops was accepted. By Dec 1984 all French troops had left, but Libya's withdrawal was doubtful. Habré dissolved the military arm of Frolinat 1984 and formed a new party, the National Union for Independence and Revolution (UNIR), but opposition to his regime grew. In 1987 Goukouni was reported to be under house arrest in Tripoli. Meanwhile Libya intensified its military operations in northern Chad, Habré's government retaliated, and France renewed (if reluctantly) its support.

fall of Habré It was announced March 1989 that France, Chad, and Libya had agreed to observe a cease-fire proposed by the OAU. A meeting July 1989 between Habré and Khaddhafi reflected the improvement in relations between Chad and Libya. Habré was endorsed as president Dec 1989 for another seven-year term under a revised constitution, introduced July 1990. In Dec 1990 the government fell to rebel opposition forces, Hissène Habré was reported killed, and the rebel leader Idriss Deby became president.

towards democracy Between Oct 1991 and Jan 1992, a number of anti-government coups were foiled, sometimes with the help of French troops. In March 1992 the new government moved nearer to multiparty politics when two opposition groups were approved, the Alliance for Democracy and Progress (RDP) and the Union for Democracy and Progress (UPDT).

Chadli Benjedid 1929–   . Algerian socialist politician, president 1979–92. An army colonel, he supported Boumédienne in the overthrow of Ben Bella 1965, and succeeded Boumédienne 1979, pursuing more moderate policies. Chadli resigned Jan 1992 following a victory for Islamic fundamentalists in the first round of assembly elections.

chador (Hindi 'square of cloth') all-enveloping black garment for women worn by some Muslims and Hindus.

The origin of the chador dates to the 6th century BC under Cyrus the Great and the Achaemenian empire in Persia. Together with the purdah (Persian 'veil') and the idea of female seclusion, it persisted under Alexander the Great and the Byzantine Empire, and was adopted by the Arab conquerors of the Byzantines. Its use was revived in Iran in the 1970s by Ayatollah Khomeini in response to the Koranic request for 'modesty' in dress.

Chaka alternative spelling of ◊Shaka, Zulu chief.

Chalcedon, Council of ecumenical council of the early Christian church, convoked 451 by the Roman emperor Marcian, and held at Chalcedon (now Kadiköy, Turkey). The council, attended by over 500 bishops, resulted in the *Definition of Chalcedon*, an agreed doctrine for both the eastern and western churches.

The council was assembled to repudiate the ideas of Eutyches on Jesus' divine nature subsuming the human; it also rejected the Mono-physite doctrine that Jesus had only one nature, and repudiated Nestorianism. It reached a compromise definition of Jesus' nature which it was hoped would satisfy all factions: Jesus was one person in two natures, united 'unconfusedly, unchangeably, indivisibly, inseparably'.

Châlons, Battle of tradition has it that Attila was defeated in his attempt to invade France, at the *Battle of Châlons* 451 by the Roman general Aëtius and the Visigoth Theodoric. Châlons-sur-Marns is the capital of the départment of Marne, NE France.

Chamberlain (Arthur) Neville 1869–1940. British Conservative politician, son of Joseph Chamberlain. He was prime minister 1937–40; his policy of appeasement towards the fascist dictators Mussolini and Hitler (with whom he concluded the ◊Munich Agreement 1938) failed to prevent the outbreak of World War II. He resigned 1940 following the defeat of the British forces in Norway.

In war, whichever side may call itself the victor, there are no winners, but all are losers.

Neville Chamberlain
speech at Kettering 3 July 1938

Chamberlain (Joseph) Austen 1863–1937. British Conservative politician, elder son of Joseph Chamberlain; as foreign secretary 1924–29 he negotiated the Pact of ◊Locarno, for which he won the Nobel Peace Prize 1925, and signed the ◊Kellogg–Briand pact to outlaw war 1928.

Chamberlain Joseph 1836–1914. British politician, reformist mayor of and member of Parliament for Birmingham; in 1886, he resigned from the cabinet over Gladstone's policy of home rule for Ireland, and led the revolt of the Liberal-Unionists.

By 1874 Chamberlain had made a sufficient fortune in the Birmingham screw-manufacturing business to devote himself entirely to politics. He adopted radical views, and took an active part in local affairs. Three times mayor of Birmingham, he carried through many schemes of municipal development. In 1876 he was elected to Parliament and joined the republican group led by Charles Dilke, the extreme left wing of the Liberal Party. In 1880 he entered Gladstone's cabinet as president of the Board of Trade. The climax of his radical period was reached with the unauthorized programme, advocating, among other things, free education, graduated taxation, and smallholdings of 'three acres and a cow'.

As colonial secretary in Salisbury's Conservative government, Chamberlain was responsible for relations with the Boer republics up to the outbreak of war 1899. In 1903 he resigned to campaign for imperial preference or tariff reform as a means of consolidating the empire.

Champlain Samuel de 1567–1635. French pioneer, soldier, and explorer in Canada. Having served in the army of Henry IV and on an expedition to the West Indies, he began his exploration of Canada 1603. In a third expedition 1608 he founded and named Québec, and was appointed lieutenant governor of French Canada 1612.

Chandelā or *Candella* ◊Rajput dynasty that ruled the Bundelkhand region of central India from the 9th to the 11th century. The Chandelās fought against Muslim invaders, until they were replaced by the Bundelas. The Chandelā capital was Khajurāho, the site of 35 sandstone temples, Jain, Buddhist, and Hindu, built in the 10th and 11th centuries.

Chandragupta Maurya ruler of N India c. 325–c. 297 BC, founder of the Mauryan dynasty. He overthrew the Nanda dynasty 325 and then conquered the Punjab 322 after the death of ◊Alexander the Great, expanding his empire west to Persia. He is credited with having united most of India.

Channel Islands group of islands in the English Channel, off the northwest coast of France; they are a possession of the British crown. They comprise the islands of Jersey, Guernsey, Alderney, Great and Little Sark, with the lesser Herm, Brechou, Jethou, and Lihou. The islands came under the same rule as England 1066, and are dependent territories of the British crown. Germany occupied the islands during World War II June 1940–May 1945.

chantry in medieval Europe, a religious foundation in which, in return for an endowment of land, the souls of the donor and the donor's family and friends would be prayed for. A chantry could be held at an existing altar, or in a specially constructed chantry chapel, in which the donor's body was usually buried.

Chantries became widespread in the later Middle Ages, reflecting the acceptance of the doctrine of purgatory, together with the growth of individualistic piety (as in the ◊devotio moderna) and the decline in the popularity of monasteries, to which they were seen as an alternative. Their foundation required the consent of the local bishop and a licence from the king for the

alienation of land in ◊mortmain. They were suppressed in Protestant countries during the Reformation, and abolished in England 1547.

Charge of the Light Brigade disastrous attack by the British Light Brigade of cavalry against the Russian entrenched artillery on 25 Oct 1854 during the Crimean War at the Battle of ◊Balaclava.

Charlemagne Charles I *the Great* 742–814. King of the Franks from 768 and Holy Roman emperor from 800. By inheritance (his father was ◊Pepin the Short) and extensive campaigns of conquest, he united most of W Europe by 804, when after 30 years of war the Saxons came under his control. He reformed the legal, judicial, and military systems; established schools; and promoted Christianity, commerce, agriculture, arts, and literature. In his capital, Aachen, scholars gathered from all over Europe.

Pepin had been mayor of the palace in Merovingian Neustria until he was crowned king by Pope Stephen II (died 757) in 754, and his sons Carl (Charlemagne) and Carloman were crowned as joint heirs. When Pepin died 768, Charlemagne inherited the N Frankish kingdom, and when Carloman died 771, he also took possession of his domains.

He was engaged in his first Saxon campaign when the Pope's call for help against the Lombards reached him; he crossed the Alps, captured Pavia, and took the title of king of the Lombards. The pacification and christianizing of the Saxon peoples occupied the greater part of Charlemagne's reign. From 792 N Saxony was subdued, and in 804 the whole region came under his rule.

In 777 the emir of Zaragoza asked for Charlemagne's help against the emir of Córdoba. Charlemagne crossed the Pyrenees 778 and reached the Ebro but had to turn back from Zaragoza. The rearguard action of Roncesvalles, in which Roland, warden of the Breton March, and other Frankish nobles were ambushed and killed by Basques, was later glorified in the *Chanson de Roland*. In 801 the district between the Pyrenees and the Llobregat was organized as the Spanish March. The independent duchy of Bavaria was incorporated in the kingdom 788, and the ◊Avar people were subdued 791–96 and accepted Christianity. Charlemagne's last campaign was against a Danish attack on his northern frontier 810.

The supremacy of the Frankish king in Europe found outward expression in the bestowal of the imperial title: in Rome, during Mass on Christmas Day 800, Pope Leo III crowned Charlemagne emperor. He enjoyed diplomatic relations with Byzantium, Baghdad,

Charlemagne's Europe *After the partition of the Frankish Kingdom between the sons of Pepin, Charlemagne inherited the entire territory on the death of his brother Carloman. From 772 until his death 814, Charlemagne extended his rule over the Saxons and Slavs to the east, the Avars to the southeast, and the Lombards to the south, but he was successfully resisted by the Muslims in Spain. He was crowned 'Emperor of the Romans' 800.*

Mercia, Northumbria, and other regions. Jury courts were introduced, the laws of the Franks revised, and other peoples' laws written down. A new coinage was introduced, weights and measures were reformed, and communications were improved. Charlemagne also took a lively interest in theology, organized the church in his dominions, and furthered missionary enterprises and monastic reform.

The *Carolingian Renaissance* of learning began when he persuaded the Northumbrian scholar Alcuin to enter his service 781. Charlemagne gathered a kind of academy around him.

Although he never learned to read, he collected the old heroic sagas, began a Frankish grammar, and promoted religious instruction in the vernacular. He died 28 Jan 814 in Aachen, where he was buried. Soon a cycle of heroic legends and romances developed around him, including epics by Ariosto, Boiardo, and Tasso.

Charles (Karl Franz Josef) 1887–1922. Emperor of Austria and king of Hungary from 1916, the last of the Habsburg emperors. He succeeded his great-uncle Franz Josef 1916 but was forced to withdraw to Switzerland 1918, although he refused to abdicate. In 1921 he attempted unsuccessfully to regain the crown of Hungary and was deported to Madeira, where he died.

Charles two kings of Britain:

Charles I 1600–1649. King of Great Britain and Ireland from 1625, son of James I of England (James VI of Scotland). He accepted the ◊petition of right 1628 but then dissolved Parliament and ruled without a parliament 1629–40. His advisers were ◊Strafford and ◊Laud, who persecuted the Puritans and provoked the Scots to revolt. The ◊Short Parliament, summoned 1640, refused funds, and the ◊Long Parliament later that year rebelled. Charles declared war on Parliament 1642 but surrendered 1646 and was beheaded 1649. He was the father of Charles II.

Charles II 1630–1685. King of Great Britain and Ireland from 1660, when Parliament accepted the restoration of the monarchy after the collapse of Cromwell's Commonwealth; son of Charles I. His chief minister Clarendon, who arranged his marriage 1662 with Catherine of Braganza, was replaced 1667 with the ◊Cabal of advisers. His plans to restore Catholicism in Britain led to war with the Netherlands 1672–74 in support of Louis XIV of France and a break with Parliament, which he dissolved 1681. He was succeeded by James II.

This is very true: for my words are my own, and my actions are my ministers.

Charles II in reply to Lord Rochester's observation that the king 'never said a foolish thing, nor ever did a wise one'

Charles ten kings of France, including:

Charles I king of France, better known as the Holy Roman emperor ◊Charlemagne.

Charles II *the Bald* king of France, see ◊Charles II, Holy Roman emperor.

Charles III *the Simple* 879–929. King of France 893–922, son of Louis the Stammerer. He was crowned at Reims. In 911 he ceded what later became the duchy of Normandy to the Norman chief Rollo.

Charles IV *the Fair* 1294–1328. King of France from 1322, when he succeeded Philip V as the last of the direct Capetian line.

Charles V *the Wise* 1337–1380. King of France from 1364. He was regent during the captivity of his father, John II, in England 1356–60, and became king on John's death. He

reconquered nearly all France from England 1369–80.

Charles VI *the Mad* or *the Well-Beloved* 1368–1422. King of France from 1380, succeeding his father Charles V; he was under the regency of his uncles until 1388. He became mentally unstable 1392, and civil war broke out between the dukes of Orléans and Burgundy. Henry V of England invaded France 1415, conquering Normandy, and in 1420 forced Charles to sign the Treaty of Troyes, recognizing Henry as his successor.

Charles VII 1403–1461. King of France from 1429. Son of Charles VI, he was excluded from the succession by the Treaty of Troyes, but recognized by the south of France. In 1429 Joan of Arc raised the siege of Orléans and had him crowned at Reims. He organized France's first standing army and by 1453 had expelled the English from all of France except Calais.

Charles VIII 1470–1498. King of France from 1483, when he succeeded his father, Louis XI. In 1494 he unsuccessfully tried to claim the Neapolitan crown, and when he entered Naples 1495 was forced to withdraw by a coalition of Milan, Venice, Spain, and the Holy Roman Empire. He defeated them at Fornovo, but lost Naples. He died while preparing a second expedition.

Charles IX 1550–1574. King of France from 1560. Second son of Henry II and Catherine de' Medici, he succeeded his brother Francis II at the age of ten but remained under the domination of his mother's regency for ten years while France was torn by religious wars. In 1570 he fell under the influence of the ◊Huguenot leader Gaspard de Coligny (1517–1572); alarmed by this, Catherine instigated his order for the Massacre of ◊St Bartholomew, which led to a new religious war.

Charles X 1757–1836. King of France from 1824. Grandson of Louis XV and brother of Louis XVI and Louis XVIII, he was known as the comte d'Artois before his accession. He fled to England at the beginning of the French Revolution, and when he came to the throne on the death of Louis XVIII, he attempted to reverse the achievements of the Revolution. A revolt ensued 1830, and he again fled to England.

Charles seven rulers of the Holy Roman Empire, including:

Charles I Holy Roman emperor, better known as ◊Charlemagne.

Charles II *the Bald* 823–877. Holy Roman emperor from 875 and (as Charles II) king of France from 843. Younger son of Louis I (the

Pious), he warred against his eldest brother, Emperor Lothair I. The Treaty of Verdun 843 made him king of the West Frankish Kingdom (now France and the Spanish Marches).

Charles III *the Fat* 839–888. Holy Roman emperor 881–87; he became king of the West Franks 885, thus uniting for the last time the whole of Charlemagne's dominions, but was deposed.

Charles IV 1316–1378. Holy Roman emperor from 1355 and king of Bohemia from 1346. Son of John of Luxembourg, king of Bohemia, he was elected king of Germany 1346 and ruled all Germany from 1347. He was the founder of the first German university in Prague 1348.

Charles V 1500–1558. Holy Roman emperor 1519–56. Son of Philip of Burgundy and Joanna of Castile, he inherited vast possessions, which led to rivalry from Francis I of France, whose alliance with the Ottoman Empire brought Vienna under siege 1529 and 1532. Charles was also in conflict with the Protestants in Germany until the Treaty of Passau 1552, which allowed the Lutherans religious liberty.

Charles was born in Ghent and received the Netherlands from his father 1506; Spain, Naples, Sicily, Sardinia, and the Spanish dominions in N Africa and the Americas on the death of his maternal grandfather, Ferdinand V of Castile (1452–1516); and from his paternal grandfather, Maximilian I, the Habsburg dominions 1519, when he was elected emperor. He was crowned in Aachen 1520. From 1517 the empire was split by the rise of Lutheranism, Charles making unsuccessful attempts to reach a settlement at Augsburg 1530 (see Confession of ◊Augsburg), and being forced by the Treaty of Passau to yield most of the Protestant demands. Worn out, he abdicated in favour of his son Philip II in the Netherlands 1555 and Spain 1556. He yielded the imperial crown to his brother Ferdinand I, and retired to the monastery of Yuste, Spain.

Charles VI 1685–1740. Holy Roman emperor from 1711, father of ◊Maria Theresa, whose succession to his Austrian dominions he tried to ensure, and himself claimant to the Spanish throne 1700, thus causing the War of the ◊Spanish Succession.

Charles (Spanish *Carlos*) four kings of Spain, including:

Charles II 1661–1700. King of Spain from 1665. The second son of Philip IV, he was the last of the Spanish Habsburg kings. Mentally handicapped from birth, he bequeathed his dominions to Philip of Anjou, grandson of

Louis XIV, which led to the War of the ◊Spanish Succession.

Charles III 1716–1788. King of Spain from 1759. Son of Philip V, he became duke of Parma 1732 and conquered Naples and Sicily 1734. On the death of his half-brother Ferdinand VI (1713–1759), he became king of Spain, handing over Naples and Sicily to his son Ferdinand (1751–1825). At home, he reformed state finances, strengthened the armed forces, and expelled the Jesuits. During his reign, Spain was involved in the Seven Years' War with France against England. This led to the loss of Florida 1763, which was only regained when Spain and France supported the colonists during the American Revolution.

Charles IV 1748–1819. King of Spain from 1788, when he succeeded his father, Charles III; he left the government in the hands of his wife and her lover, the minister Manuel de Godoy (1767–1851). In 1808 Charles was induced to abdicate by Napoleon's machinations in favour of his son Ferdinand VII (1784–1833), who was subsequently deposed by Napoleon's brother Joseph. Charles was awarded a pension by Napoleon and died in Rome.

Charles (Swedish *Carl*) fifteen kings of Sweden (the first six were local chieftains), including:

Charles VII King of Sweden from about 1161. He helped to establish Christianity in Sweden.

Charles VIII 1408–1470. King of Sweden from 1448. He was elected regent of Sweden 1438, when Sweden broke away from Denmark and Norway. He stepped down 1441 when Christopher III of Bavaria (1418–1448) was elected king, but after his death became king. He was twice expelled by the Danes and twice restored.

Charles IX 1550–1611. King of Sweden from 1604, the youngest son of Gustavus Vasa. In 1568 he and his brother John led the rebellion against Eric XIV (1533–1577); John became king as John III and attempted to Catholicize Sweden, and Charles led the opposition. John's son Sigismund, king of Poland and a Catholic, succeeded to the Swedish throne 1592, and Charles led the Protestants. He was made regent 1595 and deposed Sigismund 1599. Charles was elected king of Sweden 1604 and was involved in unsuccessful wars with Russia, Poland, and Denmark. He was the father of Gustavus Adolphus.

Charles X 1622–1660. King of Sweden from 1654, when he succeeded his cousin Christina. He waged war with Poland and Denmark and in 1657 invaded Denmark by leading his army over the frozen sea.

Charles XI 1655–1697. King of Sweden from 1660, when he succeeded his father Charles X. His mother acted as regent until 1672 when Charles took over the government. He was a remarkable general and reformed the administration.

Charles XII 1682–1718. King of Sweden from 1697, when he succeeded his father, Charles XI. From 1700 he was involved in wars with Denmark, Poland, and Russia.

He won a succession of victories until, in 1709 while invading Russia, he was defeated at Poltava in the Ukraine, and forced to take refuge in Turkey until 1714. He was killed while besieging Fredrikshall, Norway, although it was not known whether he was murdered by his own side or by the enemy.

Charles XIV (Jean Baptiste Jules Bernadotte) 1763–1844. King of Sweden and Norway from 1818. A former marshal in the French army, in 1810 he was elected crown prince of Sweden under the name of Charles John (Carl Johan). Loyal to his adopted country, he brought Sweden into the alliance against Napoleon 1813, as a reward for which Sweden received Norway. He was the founder of the present dynasty.

Charles XV 1826–1872. King of Sweden and Norway from 1859, when he succeeded his father Oscar I. A popular and liberal monarch, his main achievement was the reform of the constitution.

Charles Albert 1798–1849. King of Sardinia from 1831. He showed liberal sympathies in early life, and after his accession introduced some reforms. On the outbreak of the 1848 revolution he granted a constitution and declared war on Austria. His troops were defeated at Custozza and Novara. In 1849 he abdicated in favour of his son Victor Emmanuel and retired to a monastery, where he died.

Charles Edward Stuart the *Young Pretender* or *Bonnie Prince Charlie* 1720–1788. Grandson of James II and son of James, the Old Pretender. In the Jacobite rebellion 1745 Charles won the support of the Scottish Highlanders; his army invaded England to claim the throne but was beaten back by the duke of ◊Cumberland and routed at ◊Culloden 1746. Charles went into exile.

He was born in Rome, and created Prince of Wales at birth. In July 1745 he sailed for Scotland, and landed in Inverness-shire with seven companions. On 19 Aug he raised his father's standard, and within a week had rallied an army of 2,000 Highlanders. He entered Edinburgh almost without resistance, won an easy victory at Prestonpans, invaded England, and by 4 Dec had reached Derby, where his officers insisted on a retreat. The army returned to Scotland and won a victory at Falkirk, but was forced to retire to the Highlands before Cumberland's advance. On 16 April at Culloden Charles's army was routed by Cumberland, and he fled. For five months he wandered through the Highlands with a price of £30,000 on his head before escaping to France. He visited England secretly in 1750, and may have made other visits. In later life he degenerated into a friendless drunkard. He settled in Italy 1766.

Charles Martel c. 688–741. Frankish ruler (Mayor of the Palace) of the E Frankish kingdom from 717 and the whole kingdom from 731. His victory against the Moors at Moussais-la-Bataille near Tours 732 earned him his nickname of Martel, 'the Hammer', because he halted the Islamic advance by the ◊Moors into Europe.

An illegitimate son of Pepin of Heristal (Pepin II, Mayor of the Palace c. 640–714), he was a grandfather of Charlemagne.

Charles the Bold Duke of Burgundy 1433–1477. Son of Philip the Good, he inherited Burgundy and the Low Countries from him 1465. He waged wars attempting to free the duchy from dependence on France and restore it as a kingdom. He was killed in battle.

Charles' ambition was to create a kingdom stretching from the mouth of the Rhine to the mouth of the Rhône. He formed the League of the Public Weal against Louis XI of France, invaded France 1471, and conquered the country as far as Rouen. The Holy Roman emperor, the Swiss, and Lorraine united against him; he captured Nancy, but was defeated at Granson and again at Morat 1476. Nancy was lost, and he was killed while attempting to recapture it. His possessions in the Netherlands passed to the Habsburgs by the marriage of his daughter Mary to Maximilian I of Austria.

Charter 77 Czechoslovak human rights movement founded 1977 to lobby for Czech conformity to UN Declaration of Human Rights; see ◊Czechoslovakia.

Chartism radical British democratic movement, mainly of the working classes, which flourished around 1838–48. It derived its name from the People's Charter, a six-point programme comprising universal male suffrage, equal electoral districts, secret ballot, annual parliaments, and abolition of the property qualification for, and payment of, members of Parliament. Greater prosperity, lack of organization, and rivalry in the leadership led to its demise.

Political power our means, social happiness our end.

Slogan of *Chartism*

Chavez Cesar Estrada 1927–93. US labour organizer who founded the National Farm Workers Association 1962 and, with the support of the AFL-CIO and other major unions, embarked on a successful campaign to unionize California grape workers.

Checheno-Ingush autonomous republic in southern Russia, on the northern slopes of the Caucasus Mountains. It was conquered in the 1850s, and has a large oilfield. The population includes Chechens (53%) and Ingushes (12%). In Oct 1991 the region declared its independence. After a brief, unsuccessful attempt to quell the rebellion, Moscow agreed to enter into negotiations over the republic's future. In March 1992 Checheno-Ingush refused to be party to a federal treaty signed by 18 of Russia's 20 main political subdivisions. By the end of the month at least five people had been killed in clashes between anti- and pro-separatist factions, forcing the republic's parliament to declare a state of emergency.

Checkpoint Charlie Western-controlled crossing point for non-Germans between West Berlin and East Berlin, opened 1961 as the only crossing point between the Allied and Soviet sectors. Its dismantling in June 1990 was seen as a symbol of the ending of the ◊Cold War.

Cheka secret police operating in the USSR 1917–23. It originated from the tsarist Okhrana (the security police under the tsar 1881–1917), and became successively the OGPU (GPU) 1923–34, NKVD 1934–46, MVD 1946–53, and the ◊KGB from 1954.

chemical warfare use in war of gaseous, liquid, or solid substances intended to have a toxic effect on humans, animals, or plants. Various forms of gas, including mustard gas, were used during World War I. Although banned by the Geneva Protocol 1925, they were still used in, for example, the Italian campaign in Abyssinia 1935–36, and the Vietnam War.

Cheng Ho Chinese admiral and emperor, died 1433; see ◊Zheng He.

Chernenko Konstantin 1911–1985. Soviet politician, leader of the Soviet Communist Party (CPSU) and president 1984–85. He was

a protégé of Brezhnev and from 1978 a member of the Politburo.

Cherokee member of a North ◊American Indian people, formerly living in the S Allegheny Mountains of what is now Alabama, the Carolinas, Georgia, and Tennessee. Their scholarly leader Sequoyah (*c.* 1770–1843) devised the syllabary used for writing their language, which belongs to the Macro-Siouan family. In 1829 they were transported to a reservation in Oklahoma by forced march, know n as the Trail of Tears, by order of President Andrew Jackson.

Chetnik member of a Serbian nationalist group that operated underground during the German occupation of Yugoslavia during World War II. Led by Col Draza ◊Mihailović, the Chetniks initially received aid from the Allies, but this was later transferred to the communist partisans led by Tito. The term has also popularly been applied to Serb militia forces in the 1991–92 Yugoslav civil war.

Chiang Ching alternative transliteration of ◊Jiang Qing, Chinese actress, third wife of Mao Zedong.

We shall not talk lightly about sacrifice until we are driven to the last extremity which makes sacrifice inevitable.

Chiang Kai-shek
speech to Fifth Congress of the Guomindang

Chiang Kai-shek (Pinyin *Jiang Jie Shi*) 1887–1975. Chinese nationalist ◊Guomindang (Kuomintang) general and politician, president of China 1928–31 and 1943–49, and of Taiwan from 1949, where he set up a US-supported right-wing government on his expulsion from the mainland by the communist forces.

Chiang took part in the revolution of 1911 that overthrew the Qing dynasty of the Manchus, and on the death of the Guomindang leader Sun Yat-sen was made commander in chief of the nationalist armies in S China 1925. Collaboration with the communists, broken 1927, was resumed after the ◊Xian Incident 1936 when China needed to pool military strength in the struggle against the Japanese invaders of World War II. After the Japanese surrender 1945, civil war between the nationalists and communists erupted, and in Dec 1949 Chiang and his followers took refuge on the island of Taiwan. His son Chiang Ching-kuo (1910–1988) was president of Taiwan 1978–88.

Chibcha member of a South American Indian people of Colombia, whose high chiefdom was conquered by the Spanish in 1538. Their practice of covering their chief with gold dust, during rituals, fostered the legend of the 'Lost City' of El Dorado (the Golden), which was responsible for many failed expeditions into the interior of the continent.

Chicano citizen or resident of the USA of Mexican descent. The term was originally used for those who became US citizens after the ◊Mexican War.

Chifley Ben (Joseph Benedict) 1885–1951. Australian Labor prime minister 1945–49. He united the party in fulfilling a welfare and nationalization programme 1945–49 (although he failed in an attempt to nationalize the banks 1947) and initiated an immigration programme and the Snowy Mountains hydroelectric project.

Chifley was minister of postwar reconstruction 1942–45 under John Curtin, when he succeeded him as prime minister. He crushed a coal miners' strike 1949 by using troops as mine labour. He was leader of the Opposition from 1949 until his death.

Children's Crusade ◊crusade by some 10,000 children from France, the Low Countries, and Germany, in 1212, to recapture Jerusalem for Christianity. Motivated by religious piety, many of them were sold into slavery or died of disease.

Chile South American country, bounded N by Peru and Bolivia, E by Argentina, and S and W by the Pacific Ocean.

history The area now known as Chile was originally occupied by the Araucanian Indians and invaded by the ◊Incas in the 15th century. The first European to reach it was Ferdinand Magellan, who in 1520 sailed through the strait now named after him. A Spanish expedition under Pedro de Valdivia founded Santiago 1541, and Chile was subsequently colonized by Spanish settlers who established an agricultural society, although the Indians continued to rebel until the late 19th century. Becoming independent from Spain 1818, Chile went to war with Peru and Bolivia 1879 and gained considerable territory from them.

'social justice' Most of the 20th century has been characterized by left- versus right-wing struggles. The Christian Democrats under Eduardo Frei held power 1964–70, followed by a left-wing coalition led by Dr Salvador ◊Allende, the first democratically elected Marxist head of state. He promised social justice by constitutional means and began nationalizing industries, including US-owned copper mines.

'authoritarian democracy' The US Central Intelligence Agency painted Allende as a pro-Cuban communist and encouraged opposition to him. In 1973 the army, led by General Augusto Pinochet, overthrew the government. Allende was killed or, as the new regime claimed, committed suicide. Pinochet became president, and his opponents were tortured, imprisoned, or just 'disappeared'. In 1976 Pinochet proclaimed an 'authoritarian democracy' and in 1977 banned all political parties. His policies were 'endorsed' by a referendum 1978.

opposition to government In 1980 a 'transition to democracy' by 1989 was announced, but imprisonment and torture continued. By 1983 opposition to Pinochet had increased, with demands for a return to democratic government. He attempted to placate opposition by initiating public works. In 1984 an antigovernment bombing campaign began, aimed mainly at electricity installations, resulting in a 90-day state of emergency, followed by a 90-day state of siege. In 1985, as opposition grew in the Catholic church and the army as well as among the public, another state of emergency was declared, but the bombings continued, as did the state terror.

pluralist politics In Oct 1988 Pinochet's proposal to remain in office for another eight-year term was rejected in a plebiscite. Another plebiscite Aug 1989 approved constitutional changes leading to a return to pluralist politics and in Dec the moderate Christian Democratic Party (PDC) candidate, Patricio Aylwin, was elected president, his term of office beginning March 1990.

human rights abuses investigated In Jan 1990, the junta approved the disbanding of the secret police of the National Information Centre (CNI), which had replaced the National Information Bureau (DINA) 1977. In Sept 1990 a government commission was set up to investigate some 2,000 political executions 1973–78, 500 political murders 1978–90, and 700 disappearances. In the same month the formerly discredited Salvador Allende was officially recognized by being buried in a marked grave, and President Aylwin censured General Pinochet for trying to return to active politics. In 1991 the official report for President Aylwin revealed 2,279 deaths during Pinochet's term, of which over 2,115 were executions carried out by the secret police. In 1992 the USA announced that a future US–Chilean free-trade agreement would be negotiated.

Chilean Revolution in Chile, the presidency of Salvador ◊Allende 1970–73, the Western hemi-

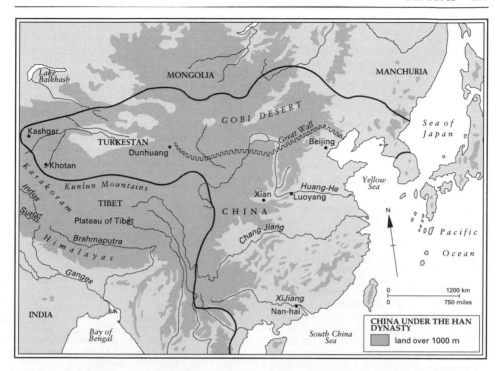

China under the Han dynasty *The Han dynasty marked the heyday of the early Chinese empire. Roughly contemporary with the Roman empire, the Han controlled a larger population and established a comparatively centralized system of administration. At Xian, the capital, a huge Confucianist bureaucracy developed to control the empire's elaborate administrative institutions. Han authority and culture were extended through conquest into S China and N Korea. Westward extension of the Great Wall to Yu-men (Jade Gate) consolidated Han authority in Central Asia.*

sphere's first democratically elected Marxist-oriented president of an independent state.

Chimu South American civilization that flourished on the coast of Peru from about 1250 to about 1470, when it was conquered by the Incas. The Chimu people produced fine work in gold, realistic portrait pottery, savage fanged feline images in clay, and possibly a system of writing or recording by painting patterns on beans. They built aqueducts carrying water many miles, and the huge, mazelike city of Chan Chan, 36 sq km/14 sq mi, on the coast near Trujillo.

China the largest country in E Asia, bounded N by Mongolia; NW by Tajikistan, Kyrgyzstan, Kazakhstan, and Afghanistan; SW by India, Nepal, and Bhutan; S by Myanmar (Burma), Laos, and Vietnam; SE by the South China Sea; E by the East China Sea, North Korea, and Yellow Sea; NE by Russia.

history For early history see ◊China, history (chronology), and Chinese Revolution. In 1949, after their elimination of nationalist resistance on the mainland, the communists inau-

gurated the People's Republic of China, the nationalists having retired to ◊Taiwan.

To begin with, the communist regime concentrated on economic reconstruction. A centralized Soviet-style constitution was adopted 1954, industries were nationalized, and central planning and moderate land reform introduced. The USSR provided economic aid, while China intervened in the ◊Korean War. Development during this period was based on material incentives and industrialization. There was a brief intelletual thaw 1956–57, the Hundred Flowers movement.

Great Leap Forward From 1958, under state president and CCP chair ◊Mao Zedong, China embarked on a major new policy, the ◊Great Leap Forward. This created large self- sufficient agricultural and industrial communes in an effort to achieve classless 'true communism'. The experiment proved unpopular and impossible to coordinate, and over 20 million people died in the floods and famines of 1959–61. The failure of the Great Leap reduced Mao's influence 1962–65, and a successful 'recovery

China: history to 1949

500,000 BC	The oldest human remains found in China were those of 'Peking man' (*Sinanthropus pekinensis*, later known as *Homo erectus*).
25,000 BC	Humans of the Upper Palaeolithic modern type (*Homo sapiens sapiens*) inhabited the region.
5000 BC	A simple Neolithic agricultural society was established.
***c.* 2800– *c.* 2200 BC**	The Sage kings, a period of agricultural development, known only from legend.
***c.* 2200– *c.* 1500 BC**	The Xia dynasty, a Bronze Age early civilization, with further agricultural developments, including irrigation, and the first known use of writing in this area.
***c.* 1500–*c.* 1066 BC**	The Shang dynasty is the first of which we have documentary evidence. Writing became well developed; bronze vases survive in ceremonial burials. The first Chinese calendar was made.
***c.* 1066–221 BC**	During the Zhou dynasty, the feudal structure of society broke down in a period of political upheaval, though iron, money, and written laws were all in use, and philosophers like Confucius flourished. The dynasty ended in the 'Warring States' period (403–221 BC), with the country divided into small kingdoms.
221–206 BC	The Qin dynasty corresponds to the reign of Shi Huangdi, who curbed the feudal nobility and introduced orderly bureaucratic government; he had roads and canals built and began the Great Wall of China to keep out invaders from the north.
206 BC–AD 220	The Han dynasty was a long period of peace, during which territory was incorporated, the keeping of historical records was systematized, and an extensive civil service set up. Art and literature flourished, and Buddhism was introduced. The first census was taken in AD 2, registering a population of 57 million. Chinese caravans traded with the Parthians.
220–581	The area was divided into Three Kingdoms: the Wei, Shu, and Wu. Confucianism was superseded by Buddhism and Taoism; glass was introduced from the West. After prolonged fighting, the Wei became the most powerful kingdom, eventually founding the Western Jin dynasty (265–316), which expanded to take over from the barbarian invaders who ruled much of China at that time, but from 316 to 581 (the Northern and Southern dynasties era) lost the territory they had gained to the Tatar invaders from the north.
581–618	Reunification came with the Sui dynasty: the government was reinstated, the barbarian invasions stopped, and the Great Wall refortified.
618–907	During the Tang dynasty the system of government became more highly developed and centralized, and the empire covered most of SE and much of central Asia. Sculpture, painting, and poetry flourished again, Buddhism spread (8th century) and trade relations were established with the Islamic world and the Byzantine Empire.
907–960	The period known as the Five Dynasties and Ten Kingdoms was characterized by war, economic depression, and loss of territory in N China, central Asia, and Korea, but printing was developed, including the first use of paper money, and porcelain was traded to Islamic lands.
960–1279	The Song dynasty was a period of calm and creativity. Central government was restored, and movable type was invented. At the end of the dynasty, the northern and western frontiers were neglected, and Mongol invasions took place. The Venetian traveller Marco Polo visited the court of the Great Khan in 1275. NE China was controlled by the Liao (945–1125) and Jin (1126–1235) dynasties.
1279–1368	The Yuan dynasty saw the beginning of Mongol rule in China, with Kublai Khan on the throne in Beijing 1293; there were widespread revolts. Marco Polo served the Kublai Khan.
1368–1644	The Mongols were expelled by the first of the native Chinese Ming dynasty, who expanded the empire. Chinese ships sailed to the Sunda Islands 1403, Ceylon 1408, and the Red Sea 1430. Mongolia was captured by the second Ming emperor. Architecture developed and Beijing flourished as the new capital. Portuguese explorers reached Macao 1516 and Canton 1517; other Europeans followed. Chinese porcelain arrived in Europe 1580. The Jesuits reached Beijing 1600.
1644–1912	The last of the dynasties was the Manchu, who were non-Chinese nomads from Manchuria. Initially trade and culture flourished, but during the 19th century it seemed that China would be partitioned among the US and European imperialist nations, since all trade was conducted through treaty ports in their control. The Boxer Rebellion 1900 against Western influence was suppressed by European troops.
1911–12	Revolution broke out, and the infant emperor Henry P'u-i was deposed.

continued

China history: 1912–49 *continued*	
1912	Abdication of the emperor and his government. China became a republic. First parliament met. General Yuan Shih-K'ai became president. Formation of the Guomindang (National People's Party), led by Sun Yat-sen.
1913	Second revolution in Nanjing suppressed.
1916–26	Republic divided by warlordism.
1917	Sun Yat-sen became supreme commander of forces in the S. China entered World War I in an attempt to have treaties with Japan annulled and German treaty ports returned. Very few of these aims were achieved.
1918	Sun Yat-sen resigned and reorganized the Guomindang.
1919	Demonstration of Beijing students led to May 4th movement.
1921	Chinese Communist Party founded in Shanghai. Military government abolished by rump parliament and Sun Yat-sen elected president of new government.
1923	Beginnings of cooperation between Guomindang and communists in order to re-unite China. Guomindang manifesto stated 'Three People's Principles' were platform of the party.
1925	Sun Yat-sen died.
1926	Revolutionary Army led by Chiang Kai-shek attacked warlords in N and central regions. It then took Hengzhou, which became the seat of the National Government Nov.
1927	Shanghai and Nanjing fell to the Revolutionary Army. Chiang Kai-shek broke with the Communist Party and liquidated communists in Shanghai. National Government formed in Nanjing. Suppression of communists and peasant rebellions.
1928	Chiang Kai-shek's forces took Beijing and the unification of China was complete. The Guomindang became the basis for a one-party state. Communist Party created a Red Army in Hunan.
1930–34	Chiang Kai-shek's 'bandit encirclement' campaigns against the communists.
1931	Mukden incident gave pretext for Japanese imperial forces to attack and capture Manchuria.
1932	Japanese set up puppet state of Manchukuo with former emperor P'u-i as head of state. Japanese forces occupied Shanghai.
1933	Armistice with Japan.
1934–35	Red Army undertook Long March from Jiangzi and Fujian provinces in the S to Yanan in the N.
1935	Mao Zedong became effective head of the Chinese Communist Party in Yanan.
1937	Marco Polo Bridge incident provided pretext for further Japanese aggression. The interior of China was attacked, Beijing fell, and the capital was moved to Chungking.
1937–45	Sino-Japanese War. Chiang Kai-shek isolated, but received help from Western powers after Britain and USA entered the war against Japan. Guomindang and communists upheld uneasy truce throughout war.
1943	Chiang Kai-shek met Churchill and Roosevelt in Cairo.
1945	Japanese surrendered in China.
1946	Open warfare between Guomindang, led by Chiang Kai-shek, and communists led by Mao Zedong.
1947	USA failed to organize reconciliation between the two sides. New constitution proclaimed.
1948	Communists took Shanxi and Henan.
1949 Jan	Chiang Kai-shek forced to resign presidency.
Sept	Communists took Beijing. Proclamation of the People's Republic. Chiang Kai-shek and the remainder of the Guomindang forces fled to Formosa (Taiwan).

programme' was begun under President Liu Shaoqi. Private farming plots and markets were reintroduced, communes reduced in size, and income differentials and material incentives restored.

Cultural Revolution Mao struck back against what he saw as a return to capitalism by launching the Great Proletarian Cultural Revolution (1966–69), a 'rectification campaign' directed against 'rightists' in the CCP and seeking to re-establish the supremacy of (Maoist) ideology over economics. During the chaotic campaign, Mao, supported by People's Liberation Army (PLA) chief ◊Lin Biao and the Shanghai-based ◊Gang of Four (led by Mao's wife Jiang Qing) encouraged student (Red Guard) demonstrations against party and government leaders. The chief targets were Liu Shaoqi, ◊Deng Xiaoping (head of the CCP secretariat), and Peng Zhen (mayor of Beijing). All were forced out of office. Government institutions fell into abeyance and new 'Three-Part Revolutionary Committees', comprising Maoist party officials, trade unionists, and PLA commanders, took over administration.

By 1970, Mao sided with pragmatic prime minister ◊Zhou Enlai and began restoring order and a more balanced system. In 1972–73 Deng Xiaoping, finance minister Li Xiannian, and others were rehabilitated, and a policy of détente towards the USA began. This reconstruction movement climaxed in the summoning of the NPC in 1975 for the first time in 11 years to ratify a new constitution and approve an economic plan termed the 'Four Modernizations' – agriculture, industry, armed forces, and science and technology – that aimed at placing China on a par with the West by the year 2000.

after Mao The deaths of Zhou Enlai and Mao Zedong 1976 unleashed a violent succession struggle between the leftist Gang of Four, led by Jiang Qing, and moderate 'rightists', grouped around Vice Premier Deng Xiaoping. Deng was forced into hiding by the Gang; and Mao's moderate protégé ◊Hua Guofeng became CCP chair and head of government 1976. Hua arrested the Gang on charges of treason and held power 1976–78 as a stopgap leader, continuing Zhou Enlai's modernization programme. His authority was progressively challenged, however, by Deng Xiaoping, who returned to office 1977 after campaigns in Beijing.

Deng in power By 1979, after further popular campaigns, Deng had gained effective charge of the government, controlling a majority in the Politburo. State and judicial bodies began to meet again, the late Liu Shaoqi was rehabilitated as a party hero, and economic reforms were introduced. These involved the dismantling of the commune system, the introduction of direct farm incentives under a new 'responsibility system', and the encouragement of foreign investment in 'Special Economic Zones' in coastal enclaves. By June 1981 Deng's supremacy was assured when his protégés ◊Hu Yaobang and ◊Zhao Ziyang had become party chair and prime minister and the Gang of Four were sentenced to life imprisonment. In 1982, Hua Guofeng and a number of senior colleagues were ousted from the Politburo, and the NPC adopted a definitive constitution, restoring the post of state president (abolished since 1975) and establishing a new civil rights code.

modernization The new administration was a collective leadership, with Hu Yaobang in control of party affairs, Zhao Ziyang overseeing state administration, and Deng Xiaoping (a party vice chair and SCMC chair) formulating long-term strategy and supervising the PLA. The triumvirate streamlined the party and state bureaucracies and promoted to power new, younger, and better-educated technocrats. They sought to curb PLA influence by retiring senior commanders and reducing personnel numbers from 4.2 to 3 million. The economy was modernized by extending market incentives and local autonomy and encouraging foreign trade and investment.

prodemocracy movement These economic reforms met with substantial success in the agricultural sector (output more than doubled 1978–85) but had adverse side effects, widening regional and social income differentials and fuelling mass consumerism that created balance-of-payments problems. Contact with the West brought demands for full-scale democratization in China. These calls led in 1986 to widespread student demonstrations, and party chief Hu Yaobang was dismissed 1987 for failing to check the disturbances. Hu's departure imperilled the post-Dengist reform programme, as conservative forces, grouped around the veteran Politburo members Chen Yun and Peng Zhen, sought to halt the changes and re-establish central party control. Chen Yun, Peng Zhen, and Deng Xiaoping all retired from the Politburo in Oct 1987, and soon after Li Peng took over as prime minister, Zhao Ziyang having become CCP chair.

Tiananmen Square massacre With inflation spiralling, an austerity budget was introduced 1989. This provoked urban unrest and a student-led prodemocracy movement, launched in Beijing, rapidly spread to provincial cities. There were mass demonstrations during Soviet leader Mikhail Gorbachev's visit to China in May 1989. Soon after Gorbachev's departure, a brutal crackdown was launched against the demonstrators by Li Peng and President Yang Shangkun, with Deng Xiaoping's support. Martial law was proclaimed and in June 1989 more than 2,000 unarmed protesters were massacred by army troops in the capital's Tiananmen Square. Arrests, executions, martial law, and expulsion of foreign correspondents brought international condemnation and economic sanctions. Communist Party general secretary Zhao Ziyang was ousted and replaced by Jiang Zemin (the Shanghai party chief and new protégé of Deng Xiaoping), a move that consolidated the power of the hardline faction of President Yang Shangkun and Premier Li Peng. Deng officially retired from the last of his party and army posts but remained a dominant figure. A crackdown on dissidents was launched as the pendulum swung sharply away from reform towards conservatism.

foreign affairs In foreign affairs, China's 1960 rift with ◊Khrushchev's Soviet Union over policy differences became irrevocable 1962 when the USSR sided with India during a brief Sino-Indian border war. Relations with the USSR deteriorated further 1969 after border clashes in the disputed Ussuri River region. China pursued a ◊nonaligned strategy, projecting itself as the voice of Third World nations, although it achieved nuclear capability by 1964. During the early 1970s, concern with Soviet expansionism brought rapprochement with the USA, bringing about China's entry to the United Nations 1971 (at ◊Taiwan's expense), and culminating in the establishment of full Sino-American diplomatic relations 1979. In the 1980s there was a partial rapprochement with the USSR, culminating in Gorbachev's visit May 1989. However, a new rift became evident 1990, with the Chinese government denouncing the Soviet leader's 'revisionism'.

Under Deng, relations with the West were warm (except in the aftermath of the Tiananmen massacre), with economic contacts widening. China did not oppose most of the policy of the US-led anti-Iraq alliance during the Persian Gulf crisis of 1990-91, although it abstained in the vote authorizing the war. Jiang Zemin visited the USSR 1991 for talks with Gorbachev, the first visit to the USSR of a CCP leader since 1957. An agreement on the Sino-Soviet border was signed. There were visits to China 1991 by British prime minister John Major and by Vietnamese leaders, who normalised Vietnam's relations with China and signed a trade agreement.

Relations with the USA remained strained because of China's record on human rights and weapon sales. In 1992 China established diplomatic relations with Israel and received the first-ever state visit by a Japanese emperor. In Jan 1996 Li Peng announced that reunificiation with Taiwan would be a priority when Hong Kong (1997) and Macau (1999) were returned to China. Closer relations with Russia were established 1997 with a joint declaration opposing the domination of one superpower (i.e., the USA) in the post-Cold War era.

the economy and Deng By 1992 China's economy, after stalling 1989-90, began to expand again, as the country entered a new phase of economic reform. In March 1996 Li Peng announced to parliament that China's GDP had quadrupled between 1980 and 1995.

Deng Xiaoping, last seen in public in Feb 1994, died Feb 1997, aged 92. His chosen successor was Jiang Zemin. Little change in the current direction, involving a combination of economic reforms with strict political control, was expected.

Chindit member of an Indian division of the British army in World War II that carried out guerrilla operations against the Japanese in Burma (now Myanmar) under the command of Brigadier General Orde Wingate (1903–44). The name derived from the mythical Chinthay

– half lion, half eagle – placed at the entrance of Burmese pagodas to scare away evil spirits.

Chin dynasty hereditary rulers of N China 1122–1234; see ◊Jin dynasty.

Chinese Revolution series of great political upheavals in China 1911–49 that eventually led to Communist Party rule and the establishment of the People's Republic of China.

The Chinese Revolution came about with the collapse of the Manchu dynasty, a result of increasing internal disorders, pressure from foreign governments, and the weakness of central government. A nationalist revolt in 1911–12 led to a provisional republican constitution being proclaimed and a government established in Beijing (Peking) headed by Yuan Shihai. The Guomindang were faced with the problems of restoring the authority of central government and meeting the challenges from militaristic factions (led by ◊warlords) and the growing communist movement.

After 1930, Chiang launched a series of attacks that encircled the communists in SE China and led to an attempt by communist army commander Chu Teh to break out. The resulting Long March to NW China Oct 1934–Oct 1935 reduced the communists' army from over 100,000 to little more than 8,000, mainly as a result of skirmishes with Chiang's forces and the severity of the conditions. During the march, a power struggle developed between Mao Zedong and Chang Kuo T'ao which eventually split the force. Mao's group finally based itself in Yan'an, where it remained throughout the war with the Japanese, forming an uneasy alliance with the nationalists to expel the invaders.

Mao's troops formed the basis of the Red Army that renewed the civil war against the nationalists 1946 and emerged victorious after defeating them at Huai-Hai and Nanjing 1949. As a result, communist rule was established in China under Mao's leadership.

Chirac Jacques 1932–   . French conservative politician, prime minister 1974-76 and 1986-88, and president from 1995. He established the neo-Gaullist Rassemblement pour la République (RPR) 1976.

chivalry code of gallantry and honour that medieval knights were pledged to observe. Its principal virtues were piety, honour, valour, courtesy, chastity, and loyalty. The word originally meant the knightly class of the feudal Middle Ages.

Chivalry originated in feudal France and Spain, spreading rapidly to the rest of Europe and reaching its height in the 12th and 13th

MANCHUKUO
(1932)

REPUBLIC OF MONGOLIA
(1921)

INNER MONGOLIA
(1947)

MANCHURIA

JEHOL
(1933)

Shenyang

Beijing

Yellow
Sea

SHANXI

TIBET

Chiang Jiang

Chongqing

Nanjing

Shanghai

HUNAN

FUJIAN

KOREA

GUANXI ZHUANG

GUANGDONG

Guangzhon

Hong Kong
(British)

Taiwan
(Nationalist China 1949)

Hainan

Pacific

Ocean

South

China

Sea

N

CHINA 1918–49

- - - Area of main Guomindang strength 1927–37
■ Area annexed and occupied by Japanese 1931–33
⬚ Area of communist regrouping after 1932
▨ Main areas of communist support before 1934
—— The Long March of Mao Zedong 1934–35
■ Areas occupied by Japanese 1937–42
- - - Territory occupied by Communists 1947–49

0   800 km
0   500 miles

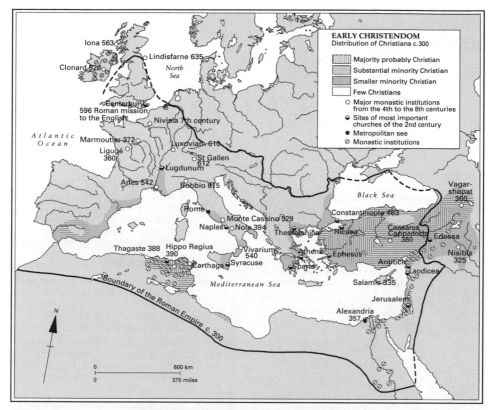

EARLY CHRISTENDOM
Distribution of Christians c.300

- Majority probably Christian
- Substantial minority Christian
- Smaller minority Christian
- Few Christians
- O Major monastic institutions from the 4th to the 8th centuries
- ◑ Sites of most important churches of the 2nd century
- ● Metropolitan see
- ⊘ Monastic institutions

Early Christendom Early Christianity centred around Jerusalem, Antioch, Alexandria, and Rome, with another important centre in the area of Carthage. After intermittent persecution, Christianity was proclaimed the state religion of the Roman Empire 391. Pope Leo I (pope 440–61), asserted the claim of the bishop of Rome to have supreme authority. Christianity survived the fall of the Western Empire 476, and over the following two centuries missionary activity, usually conducted from monasteries, converted most of the Germanic peoples.

centuries. It was strengthened by the Crusades. The earliest orders of chivalry were the Knights Hospitallers and Knights Templars, founded to serve pilgrims to the Holy Land. Secular literature of the period takes knighthood and chivalry as its theme.

Chola dynasty S Indian family of rulers that flourished in the 9th–13th centuries. Based on the banks of the Cauvery River, the Cholas overthrew their ◊Pallava and ◊Pandya neighbours and established themselves as a major

China 1918–49 The years between 1918 and 1949 were a time of internal struggle as Chiang Kai-Shek's nationalist Guomindang and Mao Zedong's Communist party battled for China's 'mandate of heaven' that had been left vacant after the 1912 overthrow of the Qing dynasty. until the Japanese invasion of China in 1937, Chiang Kai-Shek held the upper hand. In 1934–36 he forced the Communists to undertake the Long march from Jiangxi in the south to Shaanxi in the north. However, in 1949 following defeat at Huai-Hai, Chiang and his Guomindang were driven into exile in Taiwan.

pan-regional force. The two greatest Chola kings were Rajaraja I (reigned 985–1014) and his son Rajendra Cholavarma (reigned 1014–44).

During their reigns, Chola military expeditions were sent to the Ganges valley and the Malay archipelago, and magnificent temples were built at Tanjore. The dynasty lasted until c. 1279, but lost much of its territory in west and central India during the 12th century. In addition to making themselves into a maritime power, the Cholas built a system of local government and supported commerce and the arts.

Chou En-lai alternative transliteration of ◊Zhou Enlai.

Christian ten kings of Denmark, including:

Christian I 1426–1481. King of Denmark from 1448, and founder of the Oldenburg dynasty. In 1450 he established the union of Denmark and Norway that lasted until 1814.

Christianity

1st century	The Christian church is traditionally said to have originated at Pentecost, and separated from the parent Jewish religion by the declaration of saints Barnabas and Paul that the distinctive rites of Judaism were not necessary for entry into the Christian church.
3rd century	Christians were persecuted under the Roman emperors SeptimiusSeverus, Decius, and Diocletian.
312	Emperor Constantine established Christianity as the religion of the Roman Empire.
4th century	A settled doctrine of Christian belief evolved, with deviating beliefs condemned as heresies. Questions of discipline threatened disruption within the Church; to settle these, Constantine called the Council of Arles 314, followed by the councils of Nicaea 325 and Constantinople 381.
5th century	Councils of Ephesus 431 and Chalcedon 451. Christianity was carried northwards by such figures as saints Columba and Augustine.
800	Holy Roman Emperor Charlemagne crowned by the pope. The church assisted the growth of the feudal system of which it formed the apex.
1054	The Eastern Orthodox Church split from the Roman Catholic Church.
11th–12th centuries	Secular and ecclesiastical jurisdiction were often in conflict; for example, Emperor Henry IV and Pope Gregory VII, Henry II of England and his archbishop Becket.
1096–1291	The church supported a series of wars in the Middle East, called the Crusades.
1233	The Inquisition was established to suppress heresy.
14th century	Increasing worldliness (against which the foundation of the Dominican and Franciscan monastic orders was a protest) and ecclesiastical abuses led to dissatisfaction and the appearance of the reformers Wycliffe and Huss.
15th–17th centuries	Thousands of women were accused of witchcraft, tortured, and executed.
early 16th century	The Renaissance brought a re-examination of Christianity in N Europe by the humanists Erasmus, More, and Colet.
1517	The German priest Martin Luther started the Reformation, an attempt to return to a pure form of Christianity, and became leader of the Protestant movement.
1519–64	In Switzerland the Reformation was carried out by Calvin and Zwingli.
1529	Henry VIII renounced papal supremacy and proclaimed himself head of the Church of England.
1545-63	The Counter-Reformation was initiated by the Catholic church at the Council of Trent.
1560	The Church of Scotland was established according to Calvin's Presbyterian system.
17th century	Jesuit missionaries established themselves in China and Japan. Puritans, Quakers, and other sects seeking religious freedom established themselves in North America.
18th century	During the Age of Reason, Christian dogmas were questioned, and intellectuals began to examine society in purely secular terms. In England and America, religious revivals occurred among the working classes in the form of Methodism and the Great Awakening. In England the Church of England suffered the loss of large numbers of Nonconformists.
19th century	The evolutionary theories of Darwin and the historical criticism of the Bible challenged the Book of Genesis. Missionaries converted people in Africa and Asia, suppressing indigenous faiths and cultures.
1948	The World Council of Churches was founded as part of the ecumenical movement to reunite various Protestant sects and, to some extent, the Protestant churches and the Catholic church.
1950s–80s	Protestant evangelicism grew rapidly in the USA, spread by television.
1969	A liberation theology of freeing the poor from oppression emerged in South America, and attracted papal disapproval.
1972	The United Reformed Church was formed by the union of the Presbyterian Church in England and the Congregational Church. In the USA, the 1960s–70s saw the growth of cults, some of them nominally Christian, which were a source of social concern.
1980s	The Roman Catholic Church played a major role in the liberalization of the Polish government; and in the USSR the Orthodox Church and other sects were tolerated and even encouraged under Gorbachev.
1989	Barbara Harris, first female bishop, ordained in the USA.
1992	The Church of England General Synod voted in favour of the ordination of women priests.

Christian III 1503–1559. King of Denmark and Norway from 1535. During his reign the Reformation was introduced.

Christian IV 1577–1648. King of Denmark and Norway from 1588. He sided with the Protestants in the Thirty Years' War (1618–48), and founded Christiania (now Oslo, capital of Norway). He was succeeded by Frederick II 1648.

Christian VIII 1786–1848. King of Denmark 1839–48. He was unpopular because of his opposition to reform. His attempt to encourage the Danish language and culture in Schleswig and Holstein led to an insurrection there shortly after his death. He was succeeded by Frederick VII.

Christian IX 1818–1906. King of Denmark from 1863. His daughter Alexandra married Edward VII of the UK and another, Dagmar, married Tsar Alexander III of Russia; his second son, George, became king of Greece. In 1864 he lost the duchies of Schleswig and Holstein after a war with Austria and Prussia.

Christian X 1870–1947. King of Denmark and Iceland from 1912, when he succeeded his father Frederick VIII. He married Alexandrine, Duchess of Mecklenburg-Schwerin, and was popular for his democratic attitude. During World War II he was held prisoner by the Germans in Copenhagen. He was succeeded by Frederick IX.

Christian Democratic Union (CDU) a right-of-centre political party in Germany.

Christianity world religion derived from the teaching of Jesus in the first third of the 1st century, with a present-day membership of about one billion. It is divided into groups or denominations that differ in some areas of belief and practice. Its main divisions are the Roman Catholic, Eastern Orthodox, and Protestant churches.

Christian Socialism a 19th-century movement stressing the social principles of the Bible, and opposed to the untrammelled workings of *laissez-faire* capitalism. Its founders in Britain were F D Maurice (1805-1872), Charles Kingsley, and the novelist Thomas Hughes.

In Europe, the establishment of Christian Socialist parties (the first was in Austria) was a direct response to the threat of socialism and therefore contained many conservative features.

Christina 1626–1689. Queen of Sweden 1632–54. Succeeding her father Gustavus Adolphus at the age of six, she assumed power 1644, but disagreed with the former regent ◊Oxenstjerna. Refusing to marry, she eventu-

ally nominated her cousin Charles Gustavus (Charles X) as her successor. As a secret convert to Roman Catholicism, which was then illegal in Sweden, she had to abdicate 1654, and went to live in Rome, twice returning to Sweden unsuccessfully to claim the throne.

Christophe Henri 1767–1820. West Indian slave, one of the leaders of the revolt against the French 1791, who was proclaimed king of Haiti 1811. His government distributed plantations to military leaders. He shot himself when his troops deserted him because of his alleged cruelty.

Chulalongkorn Rama V 1853–1910. King of Siam (Thailand) from 1868. He studied Western administrative practices and launched an ambitious modernization programme after reaching his majority in 1873. He protected Siam from colonization by astutely playing off French and British interests.

Chun Doo-hwan 1931–   . South Korean military ruler who seized power 1979, president 1981–88 as head of the newly formed Democratic Justice Party.

Chun, trained in Korea and the USA, served as an army commander from 1967 and was in charge of military intelligence 1979 when President Park was assassinated by the chief of the Korean Central Intelligence Agency (KCIA). General Chun took charge of the KCIA and, in a coup, assumed control of the army and the South Korean government. In 1981 Chun was appointed president, and oversaw a period of rapid economic growth, governing in an authoritarian manner. In 1988 he retired to a Buddhist retreat.

Churchill Randolph (Henry Spencer) 1849–1895. British Conservative politician, chancellor of the Exchequer and leader of the House of Commons 1886; father of Winston Churchill.

Churchill Winston (Leonard Spencer) 1874–1965. British Conservative politician, prime minister 1940–45 and 1951–55. In Parliament from 1900, as a Liberal until 1923, he held a number of ministerial offices, including First Lord of the Admiralty 1911–15 and chancellor of the Exchequer 1924–29. Absent from the cabinet in the 1930s, he returned Sept 1939 to lead a coalition government 1940–45, negotiating with Allied leaders in World War II to achieve the unconditional surrender of Germany 1945; he led a Conservative government 1951–55.

In 1911 Asquith appointed him First Lord of the Admiralty. In 1915-16 he served in the trenches in France, but then resumed his parliamentary duties and was minister of munitions under Lloyd George 1917, when he was concerned with the development of the tank. After the armistice he was secretary for war 1918-21 and then as colonial secretary played a leading part in the establishment of the Irish Free State. During the postwar years he was active in support of the Whites (anti-Bolsheviks) in Russia.

In 1922–24 Churchill was out of Parliament. He left the Liberals 1923, and was returned for Epping as a Conservative 1924. Baldwin made him chancellor of the Exchequer, and he brought about Britain's return to the gold standard and was prominent in the defeat of the General Strike 1926. In 1929–39 he was out of office as he disagreed with the Conservatives on India, rearmament, and Chamberlain's policy of appeasement.

On the first day of World War II he went back to his old post at the Admiralty. In May 1940 he was called to the premiership as head of an all-party administration and made a much quoted 'blood, tears, toil, and sweat' speech to the House of Commons. He had a close relationship with US president Roosevelt, and Aug 1941 concluded the ◊Atlantic Charter with him. He travelled to Washington, Casablanca, Cairo, Moscow, and Tehran, meeting the other leaders of the Allied war effort. He met Stalin and Roosevelt in the Crimea Feb 1945 and agreed on the final plans for victory. On 8 May he announced the unconditional surrender of Germany.

The coalition was dissolved 23 May 1945, and Churchill formed a caretaker government drawn mainly from the Conservatives. Defeated in the general election July, he became leader of the opposition until the election Oct 1951, in which he again became prime minister. In April 1955 he resigned.

Never in the field of human conflict was so much owed by so many to so few.

Winston Churchill
speech of 20 Aug 1940

Church of England established form of Christianity in England, a member of the Anglican Communion. It was dissociated from the Roman Catholic Church 1534. There were approximately 1,045,000 regular worshippers in 1995.

2nd century Christianity arrived in England during the Roman occupation.

597 St Augustine became the first archbishop of Canterbury.

1529–34 At the *Reformation* the chief change was political: the sovereign (Henry VIII) replaced the pope as head of the church and assumed the right to appoint archbishops and bishops.

1536–40 The monasteries were closed down.

1549 First publication of the *Book of Common Prayer*, the basis of worship throughout the Anglican church.

1563–1604 The *Thirty-Nine Articles*, the Church's doctrinal basis, were drawn up, enforced by Parliament, and revised.

17th–18th centuries Colonizers took the Church of England to North America (where three US bishops were consecrated after the American Revolution, and whose successors still lead the Episcopal Church in the USA), Australia, New Zealand, and India.

19th century Missionaries were active in Africa. The *Oxford Movement*, led by the academic priests Newman, Keble, and Pusey, eventually developed into Anglo-Catholicism.

20th century There were moves towards reunion with the Methodist and Roman Catholic churches. Modernism, a liberal movement, attracted attention 1963 through a book by a bishop, J A T Robinson. The *ordination of women* was accepted by some overseas Anglican churches, for example, the US Episcopal Church 1976. The Lambeth conference 1978 stated that there was no theological objection to women priests, in Nov 1989 the General Synod accepted in principle, and in 1992 voted in favour, of the ordination of women priests, despite bitter opposition from traditionalists. During the 1980s, 1,000 Anglican churches closed due to declining congregations.

Church of Scotland established form of Christianity in Scotland, first recognized by the state 1560. It is based on the Protestant doctrines of the reformer Calvin and governed on Presbyterian lines. The Church went through several periods of episcopacy in the 17th century, and those who adhered to episcopacy after 1690 formed the Episcopal Church of Scotland, an autonomous church in communion with the Church of England. In 1843, there was a split in the Church of Scotland (the Disruption), in which almost a third of its ministers and members left and formed the Free Church of Scotland. Its membership 1988 was about 850,000.

CIA abbreviation for the ◊Central Intelligence Agency of the US.

Ciano Galeazzo 1903–1944. Italian Fascist politician. Son-in-law of the dictator Mussolini, he was foreign minister and member of the

Fascist Supreme Council 1936–43. He voted against Mussolini at the meeting of the Grand Council July 1943 that overthrew the dictator, but was later tried for treason and shot by the Fascists.

Cicero Marcus Tullius 106–43 BC. Roman orator, writer, and politician. His speeches and philosophical and rhetorical works are models of Latin prose, and his letters provide a picture of contemporary Roman life. As consul 63 BC he exposed the Roman politician Catiline's conspiracy in four major orations.

Born in Arpinium, Cicero became an advocate in Rome, spent three years in Greece studying oratory, and after the dictator Sulla's death distinguished himself in Rome on the side of the popular party. When the First Trium-virate was formed 59 BC, Cicero was exiled and devoted himself to literature. He sided with Pompey during the civil war (49–48) but was pardoned by Julius Caesar and returned to Rome. After Caesar's assassination 44 BC he supported Octavian (the future emperor Augustus) and violently attacked Antony in speeches known as the *Philippics*. On the reconciliation of Antony and Octavian he was executed by Antony's agents.

There is nothing so absurd but some philosopher has said it.

Cicero De Divinatione

Cid, El Rodrigo Díaz de Bivar 1040–1099. Spanish soldier, nicknamed *El Cid* ('the lord') by the ◊Moors. Born in Castile of a noble family, he fought against the king of Navarre and won his nickname *el Campeador* ('the Champion') by killing the Navarrese champion in single combat. Essentially a mercenary, fighting both with and against the Moors, he died while defending Valencia against them, and in subsequent romances became Spain's national hero.

Much of the Cid's present-day reputation is the result of the exploitation of the legendary character as a model Christian military hero by the Nationalists during the Civil War, with Franco presented as a modern equivalent in his reconquest of Spain.

Cincinnatus Lucius Quintus 5th century BC. Roman general. Appointed dictator 458 BC, he defeated the Aequi (an Italian people) in a brief campaign, then resumed life as a yeoman farmer. He became a legend for his republican idealism both in ancient times and in the 18th century.

Cinque Ports group of ports in S England, originally five, Sandwich, Dover, Hythe, Romney, and Hastings, later including Rye, Winchelsea, and others. Probably founded in Roman times, they rose to importance after the Norman conquest and until the end of the 15th century were bound to supply the ships and men necessary against invasion.

CIS abbreviation for ◊*Commonwealth of Independent States*, established 1992 by 11 former Soviet republics.

Cistercian order Roman Catholic monastic order established at Cîteaux 1098 by St Robert de Champagne, abbot of Molesme, as a stricter form of the Benedictine order. Living mainly by agricultural labour, the Cistercians made many advances in farming methods in the Middle Ages. The *Trappists*, so called from the original house at La Trappe in Normandy (founded by Dominique de Rancé 1664), followed a particularly strict version of the rule.

civil disobedience deliberate breaking of laws considered unjust, a form of nonviolent direct action; the term was coined by the US writer Henry Thoreau in an essay of that name 1849. It was advocated by Mahatma ◊Gandhi to prompt peaceful withdrawal of British power from India. Civil disobedience has since been employed by, for instance, the US civil-rights movement in the 1960s and the peace movement in the 1980s.

civil rights rights of the individual citizen. In many countries they are specified (as in the Bill of Rights of the US constitution) and guaranteed by law to ensure equal treatment for all citizens. In the USA, the struggle to obtain civil rights for former slaves and their descendants, both through legislation and in practice, has been a major theme since the Civil War. See *history* under ◊black.

civil-rights movement general term for efforts by American black people to improve their status in society after World War II. Following their significant contribution to the national effort in wartime, they began a sustained campaign for full civil rights which challenged racial discrimination. Despite favourable legislation such as the Civil Rights Act 1964 and the 1965 Voting Rights Act, growing discontent among urban blacks in northern states led to outbreaks of civil disorder such as the Watts riots in Los Angeles, Aug 1965. Another riot in the city 1992, following the acquittal of policemen charged with beating a black motorist, demonstrated continuing problems in American race relations. For full details see *history* under ◊black.

civil service body of administrative staff appointed to carry out the policy of a govern-

American civil-rights campaign 1954–68

1954	In Brown v. Board of Education of Topeka, Kansas, the US Supreme Court ruled that in the field of public education the doctrine of 'separate but equal' has no place'. The decision paved the way for black Americans to challenge the institutions and practices of white supremacism.
1955	Rosa Parks was arrested for defying segregation on city buses in Montgomery, Alabama. A subsequent boycott of buses by the city's black population, which Martin Luther King helped to organize, eventually succeeded in integrating public transport.
1957	Southern Christian Leadership Conference formed under King, coordinating the campaign for civil rights in the southern states. The governor of Arkansas defied a court order to desegregate the central high school in Little Rock, and national guardsmen barred entry to blacks. President Eisenhower was obliged to send in federal paratroopers to secure their access to the school. Civil Rights Act on voting rights and created US Civil Rights Commission.
1960	Civil Rights Act included penalties against mob action.
1961	Congress of Racial Equality sent black and white volunteers on 'freedom rides' to challenge continuing segregation on public transport in southern states.
1962	President Kennedy ordered federal marshals to secure entry of black student James Meredith to whites-only University of Mississippi.
1963 May	During civil rights demonstrations in Birmingham, Alabama, the city police commissioner used dogs, tear gas, and fire hoses to attack campaigners. King was arrested and wrote Letter from Birmingham Jail, a classic affirmation of his belief in non-violent methods to achieve civil rights.
Aug	March on Washington DC by about 250,000 blacks and whites. King delivered 'I have a dream' speech expressing optimism that racial equality and harmony could be achieved.
1964–68	'Long, hot summers' of race riots in American cities, for example Harlem, New York 1964, Watts, Los Angeles 1965, Cleveland, Ohio 1966, Detroit, Michigan and Newark, New Jersey 1967, Washington DC 1968.
1964	As part of President Johnson's 'great society' legislation, Civil Rights Act outlawed racial segregation and discrimination.
1965	Voting Rights Act encouraged registration of black voters, and 250,000 new black voters were enrolled. Malcolm X, Black Muslim leader, was assassinated in New York city. King led march to Montgomery, Alabama, but met violence on the way at Selma.
1968	King assassinated in Memphis, Tennessee. Severe rioting in more than 100 cities.

ment. In Britain, civil servants were originally in the personal service of the sovereign. They were recruited by patronage, and many of them had only nominal duties. The great increase in public expenditure during the Napoleonic Wars led to a move in Parliament for reform of the civil service, but it was not until 1854 that two civil servants, Charles Trevelyan and Stafford Northcote, issued a report as a result of which recruitment by competitive examination, carried out under the Civil Service Commission 1855, came into force. Its recommendations only began to be effective when nomination to the competitive examination was abolished 1870.

civil war war between rival groups within the same country.

Civil War, American also called the *War Between the States* war 1861–65 between the Southern or Confederate States of America and the Northern or Union States. The former wished to maintain certain 'states' rights', in particular the right to determine state law on the institution of slavery, and claimed the right to secede from the Union; the latter fought primarily to maintain the Union, with slave emancipation (proclaimed 1863) a secondary issue.

The war, and in particular its aftermath, when the South was occupied by Northern troops in the period known as the ◊Reconstruction, left behind much bitterness. Industry prospered in the North, while the economy of the South, which had been based on slavery, stagnated for some time.

1861 Seven Southern states set up the Confederate States of America (president Jefferson Davis) 8 Feb; ◊*Fort Sumter,* Charleston, captured 12–14 April; Pierre Beauregard (Confederate) was victorious at the *1st Battle of ◊Bull Run* 21 July.

1862 Battle of *Shiloh* 6–7 April was indecisive. General Grant (Union) captured New Orleans in May, but the Confederates, under General Robert E ◊Lee, were again victorious at the *2nd Battle of ◊Bull Run* 29–30 Aug. Lee's northward advance was then checked by General McClellan at *Antietam* 17 Sept.

1863 The *Emancipation Proclamation* was issued by President Lincoln 1 Jan, freeing the slaves and assuring British and French neutrality; *Battle of Gettysburg* (Union victory) 1–4 July marked the turning point of the war; Grant captured *Vicksburg* 4 July.

1864 In the *Battle of Cold Harbor* near Richmond, Virginia, 1–12 June, Lee delayed Grant in his advance on Richmond. General Sherman (Union) marched through Georgia to the sea, taking *Atlanta* 1 Sept and Savannah 22 Dec, destroying much of the infrastructure as he went. *1865* Lee surrendered to Grant at *Appomattox* courthouse 9 April; Lincoln was assassinated 14 April; the last Confederate troops surrendered 26 May. There were 359,528 Union and 258,000 Confederate dead. The period of ◊Reconstruction began.

Civil War, English the conflict between King Charles I and the Royalists (Cavaliers) on one side and the Parliamentarians (also called Roundheads) under Oliver ◊Cromwell on the other. Their differences centred on the king's unconstitutional acts but became a struggle over the relative powers of crown and Parliament. Hostilities began 1642 and a series of Royalist defeats (Marston Moor 1644, Naseby 1645) culminated in Charles's capture 1647 and execution 1649. The war continued until the final defeat of Royalist forces at Worcester 1651. Cromwell became Protector (ruler) from 1651 until his death 1658. *See chronology.*

Civil War, Spanish war 1936–39 precipitated by a military revolt led by General Franco against the Republican government. Inferior military capability led to the gradual defeat of the Republicans by 1939, and the establishment of Franco's dictatorship.

Franco's insurgents (Nationalists, who were supported by Fascist Italy and Nazi Germany) seized power in the south and northwest, but were suppressed in areas such as Madrid and Barcelona by the workers' militia. The loyalists (Republicans) were aided by the USSR and the volunteers of the International Brigade, which included several writers, among them George Orwell.

1937 Bilbao and the Basque country were bombed into submission by the Nationalists.

The causes of the American Civil War 1861–65

The American Civil War was fought with such ferocity that it cost more lives than all of America's other wars combined. The ferocity of the arguments about its causes reflects the complexity of the forces at work in American antebellum (pre-war) society, which brought on the war after a decade of political crises.

Historians of the war can be divided into two schools. The first considers that it was the unavoidable outcome of conflicting interests between northern and southern states. The second blames it on political leaders for failing to avert an unnecessary war. Analysts are also divided on whether the issue of slavery was the primary cause of the war, or a symptom of other, more critical differences – especially sectional interests and the doctrine of states' rights – between the north and south which had been developing since the formation of the American republic.

The economic split

The fundamental distinction was economic. In the early 1840s the northern states began the process of industrialization, modernizing their society to meet the demands of economic change. In particular, the slogan of Abraham Lincoln's Republican party, 'free labour, free land, free man' encapsulated the ideology of valuing the freedom of individuals to grasp the opportunity for economic self-advancement in a booming, expanding society. The southern states remained stubbornly agrarian both economically and socially. It was a backward-looking way of life of tall white mansions on great plantations, dependent on a labour system which made slaves of approximately four million black Americans.

America was thus divided by economic structure, and was led into fratricidal warfare by a series of political clashes. The most common cause was the future of the west. The crises over California's admission in 1850 and over Kansas-Nebraska in 1854 were typical of the divergent economic interests of north and south in relation to the west. The north wanted free land for independent labour in the same new territories where the south sought to perpetuate its traditional way of life by extending slavery. The issue was not the slavery already practised, but the prospect of its extension into the west. With each clash the politicians saw less of the national view and came to think and speak as regional leaders arousing popular local passions. The birth of a purely northern Republican party in 1854 illustrates the division. Extremists like John Brown stirred up more factionalism, and it was clear that the two groups could no longer live together in the Union.

Infantry ideals

When the war came, there were many in the north who, while unwilling to take up arms for the emancipation of southern black slaves, were willing to fight for the Union which had been shattered by the secession of rebel southern states. Equally, many white southerners who would not fight for slavery were willing to go to war to maintain the right of their state to leave the Union. Others on both sides simply fought for so many dollars a month.

The American Civil War 1861–65

1861 Feb	Having seceded from the Union, seven southern states (S Carolina, Mississippi, Florida, Alabama, Georgia, Louisiana, and Texas) sent representatives to Montgomery, Alabama, to form the rebel Confederate States of America under the presidency of Jefferson Davis. Their constitution legalized slavery.
April	Rebel forces attacked a Federal garrison at Fort Sumter, Charleston, S Carolina, capturing it 14 April. President Lincoln proclaimed a blockade of southern ports.
April–May	Four more states seceded from the Union: Virginia (part remaining loyal, eventually becoming W Virginia), Arkansas, Tennessee, and N Carolina.
July	Battle of Bull Run was first major military engagement of the war, near Manassas Junction, Virginia; Confederate army under generals P G T Bureaugard and Thomas 'Stonewall' Jackson forced Union army to retreat to Washington DC.
1862 Feb	Union general Ulysses S Grant captured strategically located forts Henry and Donelson in Tennessee.
April	Battle of Shiloh, the bloodiest Americans had yet fought, when at terrible cost Grant's army forced rebel troops to withdraw. Confederate government introduced conscription of male white citizens aged 18–35.
June–July	Seven Days' battles in Virginia between Union army under George B McClellan and Confederate forces under generals Jackson and Robert E Lee; McClellan withdrew, but continued to threaten the Confederate capital at Richmond, Virginia.
Aug	At second Battle of Bull Run, Lee's troops forced Union army to fall back again to Washington DC.
Sept	At Battle of Antietam, near Sharpsburg, Maryland, McClellan forced Lee to give up his offensive, but failed to pursue the enemy. Lincoln removed him from his command.
Dec	Lee inflicted heavy losses on Federal forces attacking his position at Battle of Fredericksburg, Virginia.
1863 Jan	Lincoln's Emancipation Proclamation came into effect, freeing slaves in the Confederate states (but not those in border states which had remained loyal to the Union). Some 200,000 blacks eventually served in Union armies.
March	Federal government introduced conscription.
May	Battle of Chancellorsville, Virginia; Lee and Jackson routed Union forces.
July	Lee failed to break through Union lines at decisive Battle of Gettysburg, Pennsylvania, while Grant captured Vicksburg and the W and took control of the Mississippi, cutting the Confederacy in two.
Nov	Grant's victory at Chattanooga, Tennessee, led to his appointment as general in chief by Lincoln (March 1864). Lincoln's Gettysburg Address.
1864 May	Battle of the Wilderness, Virginia. Lee inflicted heavy casualties on Union forces, but Grant continued to move south through Virginia. They clashed again at Battle of Spotsylvania.
June	Battle of Cold Harbor claimed 12,000 casualties in a few hours. Grant wrote: 'I propose to fight it out along this line if it takes all summer'.
Sept	Union general William T Sherman occupied Atlanta, Georgia, and marched through the state to the sea, cutting a wide swathe of destruction.
Nov	Lincoln re-elected president.
Dec	Sherman marched into Savannah, Georgia, continuing over next three months into S and N Carolina.
1865 March	Lee failed to break through Union lines at Battle of Petersburg, Virginia.
April	Lee abandoned Confederate capital at Richmond, Virginia, and surrendered to Grant at Appomattox courthouse, Virginia. John Wilkes Booth assassinated President Lincoln at Ford's Theatre, Washington DC.
May	Last Confederate soldiers laid down their arms. The war had taken the lives of 359,528 Union troops and 258,000 Confederates, and cost $20 billion.

1938 Catalonia was cut off from the main Republican territory.

1939 Barcelona fell in January and Madrid in April, and Franco established a dictatorship.

Clarendon Edward Hyde, 1st Earl of Clarendon 1609–1674. English politician and historian, chief adviser to Charles II 1651-67. A member of Parliament 1640, he joined the Royalist side 1641. The *Clarendon Code*

1661–65, a series of acts passed by the government, was directed at Nonconformists (or Dissenters) and were designed to secure the supremacy of the Church of England.

Clarendon George William Frederick Villiers, 4th Earl of Clarendon 1800–1870. British Liberal diplomat, lord lieutenant of Ireland 1847–52, foreign secretary 1853–58, 1865–66, and 1868–70.

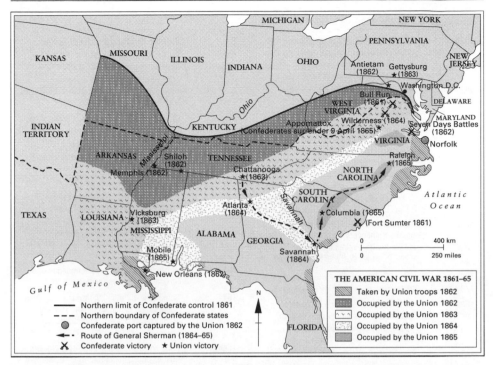

The American Civil War 1861–65 *After the early blockading of southern ports, Union troops pushed gradually into Confederate territory. Only at the Battle of Gettysburg did southern forces come close to launching a counteroffensive into the industrial heartland of the Union states. Simultaneously, the capture of Vicksburg on the Mississippi by Union forces effectively cut the Confederacy in two.*

He was posted to Ireland at the time of the potato famine. His diplomatic skill was shown at the Congress of Paris 1856 and in the settlement of the dispute between Britain and the USA over the *Alabama* cruiser.

Clarendon, Constitutions of in English history, a series of resolutions agreed by a council summoned by Henry II at Clarendon in Wiltshire 1164. The Constitutions aimed at limiting the secular power of the clergy, and were abandoned after the murder of Thomas à Becket. They form an early English legal document of great historical value.

Clark George Rogers 1752–1818. American military leader and explorer. He was made commander of the Virginia frontier militia at the outbreak of the American Revo-lution 1775. During 1778-79 he led an attack on the Indian allies of the British to the west of the Ohio River and founded a settlement at the site of Louisville, Kentucky.

Clark Joe (Joseph) Charles 1939– . Canadian Progressive Conservative politician who became party leader 1976, and May 1979 defeated Pierre ◊Trudeau at the polls to become the youngest prime minister in Canada's history. Following the rejection of his government's budget, he was defeated in a second election Feb 1980. He became secretary of state for external affairs (foreign minister) 1984 in the ◊Mulroney government.

Clark Mark (Wayne) 1896–1984. US general in World War II. In 1942 he became Chief of Staff for ground forces, and deputy to General Eisenhower. He led a successful secret mission by submarine to get information in North Africa to prepare for the Allied invasion, and commanded the 5th Army in the invasion of Italy.

Clarkson Thomas 1760–1846. British philanthropist. From 1785 he devoted himself to a campaign against slavery. He was one of the founders of the Anti-Slavery Society 1823 and was largely responsible for the abolition of slavery in British colonies 1833.

Claudius Tiberius Claudius Nero 10 BC–AD 54. Nephew of ◊Tiberius, made Roman emperor by his troops AD 41, after the murder of his nephew

The English Civil War 1625–49

1625	James I died, succeeded by Charles I, whose first parliament was dissolved after refusing to grant him tonnage and poundage (taxation revenues) for life.	Feb	Bishop's Exclusion Bill passed, barring clergy from secular office and the Lords.
1627	'Five Knights' case in which men who refused to pay a forced loan were imprisoned.	May–June	Irish rebels established supreme council. Militia Ordinance passed, assuming sovereign powers for parliament. Nineteen Propositions rejected by Charles.
1628	Coke, Wentworth, and Eliot presented the Petition of Right, requesting the king not to tax without parliamentary consent, not to billet soldiers in private homes, and not to impose martial law on civilians. Charles accepted this as the price of parliamentary taxation to pay for war with Spain and France. Duke of Buckingham assassinated.	Aug	Charles raised his standard at Nottingham. Outbreak of first Civil War.
		Oct	General Assembly of the Confederate Catholics met at Kilkenny. Battle of Edgehill inconclusive.
1629	Parliament dissolved following disagreement over religious policy, tonnage and poundage, beginning Charles' 'Eleven Years' Tyranny'. War with France ended.	1643	Irish truce left rebels in control of more of Ireland. Solemn League and Covenant, alliance between English Parliamentarians and Scots, pledged to establish Presbyterianism in England and Ireland, and to provide a Scottish army. Scots intervened in Civil War.
1630	End of war with Spain.		
1632	Strafford made lord deputy in Ireland.	1643–49	Westminster Assembly attempted to draw up Calvinist religious settlement.
1633	Laud became archibishop of Canterbury. Savage punishment of puritan William Prynne for his satirical pamphlet *Histriomastix*.	1644	Committee of Both Kingdoms to coordinate Scottish and Parliamentarians' military activities established. Royalists decisively beaten at Marston Moor.
1634	Ship money first collected in London.	1645	Laud executed. New Model Army created. Charles pulled out of Uxbridge negotiations on a new constitutional position. Cromwell and the New Model Army destroyed Royalist forces at Naseby.
1634–37	Laud attempted to enforce ecclesiastical discipline by metropolitan visits.		
1637	Conviction of John Hampden for refusal to pay ship money infringed Petition of Right.	1646	Charles fled to Scotland. Oxford surrendered to parliament. End of first Civil War.
1638	Covenanters in Scotland protested at introduction of Laudian Prayer Book into the Kirk.	1647 May	Charles agreed with parliament to accept Presbyterianism and to surrender control of the militia.
1639	First Bishops' War. Charles sent army to Scotland after its renunciation of episcopacy. Agreement reached without fighting.	June–Aug	Army seized Charles and resolved not to disband without satisfactory terms. Army presented Heads of Proposals to Charles.
1640	Short Parliament April–May voted taxes for the suppression of the Scots, but dissolved to forestall petition against Scottish war. Second Bishops' War ended in defeat for English at Newburn-on-Tyne. Scots received pension and held Northumberland and Durham in Treaty of Ripon. Long Parliament called, passing the Triennial Act and abolishing the Star Chamber. High Commission and Councils of the North and of Wales set up.	Oct–Dec	Army debated Levellers' Agreement of the People at Putney. Charles escaped to the Isle of Wight, and reached agreement with the Scots by Treaty of Newport.
		1648 Jan	Vote of No Addresses passed by Long Parliament declaring an end to negotiations with Charles.
		Aug	Cromwell defeated Scots at Preston. Second Civil War began.
1641	Strafford executed. English and Scots massacred at Ulster. Grand Remonstrance passed appealing to mass opinion against episcopacy and the royal prerogative. Irish Catholic nobility massacred.	Nov–Dec	Army demanded trial of Charles I. Pride's Purge of parliament transferred power to the Rump of independent MPs.
		1649 Jan–Feb	Charles tried and executed. Rump elected Council of State as its executive.
1642 Jan	Charles left Westminster after an unsuccessful attempt to arrest five members of the Commons united both Houses of Parliament and the City against him.	May	Rump declared England a Commonwealth. Cromwell landed in Dublin.
		Sept–Oct	Massacres of garrisons at Drogheda and Wexford by Cromwell.

◊Caligula. Claudius was a scholar, historian, and able administrator. During his reign the Roman empire was considerably extended, and in 43 he took part in the invasion of Britain.

His rule was marked by the increased political power enjoyed by his private secretaries who exercised ministerial functions. Claudius was dominated by his third wife, Messalina, whom he ultimately had executed, and is thought to have been poisoned by his fourth wife, Agrippina the Younger.

Clausewitz Karl von 1780–1831. Prussian officer and writer on war, born near Magdeburg. His book *Vom Kriege/On War* 1833, translated into English 1873, gave a new philosophical foundation to the art of war and put forward a concept of strategy that was influential until World War I.

Claverhouse John Graham, Viscount Dundee 1649–1689. Scottish soldier. Appointed by Charles II to suppress the ◊Covenanters from 1677, he was routed at Drumclog 1679, but three weeks later won the battle of Bothwell Bridge, by which the rebellion was crushed. Until 1688 he was engaged in continued persecution and became known as 'Bloody Clavers', regarded by the Scottish people as a figure of evil. His army then joined the first Jacobite rebellion and defeated the loyalist forces in the pass of Killiecrankie, where he was mortally wounded.

Clay Henry 1777–1852. US politician. He stood unsuccessfully three times for the presidency: as a Democratic-Republican 1824, as a National Republican 1832, and as a Whig 1844. He supported the war of 1812 against Britain, and tried to hold the Union together on the slavery issue by the Missouri Compromise of 1820, and again in the compromise of 1850. He was secretary of state 1825–29, and devised an 'American System' for the national economy.

Clay Lucius DuBignon 1897–1978. US commander in chief of the US occupation forces in Germany 1947-49. He broke the Soviet blockade of Berlin 1948 after 327 days, with an airlift – a term he brought into general use – which involved bringing all supplies into West Berlin by air.

Cleisthenes lived 6th century BC. Athenian statesman, the founder of Atheonian democracy. He was exiled with his family, the ◊Alcmaeonidae, and intrigued and campaigned against the Athenian tyrants, the Pisistratids. After their removal in 510 BC he developed a popular faction in favour of democracy, which was established by his reforms over the next decade.

Clemenceau Georges 1841–1929. French politician and journalist (prominent in the defence of Alfred ◊Dreyfus). He was prime minister 1906–09 and 1917–20. After World War I he presided over the peace conference in Paris that drew up the Treaty of ◊Versailles, but failed to secure for France the Rhine as a frontier.

Clement VII 1478–1534. Pope 1523–34. He refused to allow the divorce of Henry VIII of England and Catherine of Aragon. Illegitimate son of a brother of Lorenzo de' Medici, the ruler of Florence, he commissioned monuments for the Medici chapel in Florence from the Renaissance artist Michelangelo.

Cleon 5th century BC. Athenian politician and general in the ◊Peloponnesian War. He became 'leader of the people' after the death of ◊Pericles to whom he was opposed. He was an aggressive imperialist and advocated a vigorous war policy against the Spartans. He was killed by the Spartans at the battle at Amphipolis 422 BC.

Cleopatra c. 68–30 BC. Queen of Egypt 51–48 and 47–30 BC. When the Roman general Julius Caesar arrived in Egypt, he restored her to the throne from which she had been ousted. Cleopatra and Caesar became lovers and she went with him to Rome. After Caesar's assassination 44 BC she returned to Alexandria and resumed her position as queen of Egypt. In 41 BC she was joined there by Mark Antony, one of Rome's rulers. In 31 BC Rome declared war on Egypt and scored a decisive victory in the naval Battle of ◊Actium off the W coast of Greece. Cleopatra fled with her 60 ships to Egypt; Antony abandoned the struggle and followed her. Both he and Cleopatra committed suicide.

Cleopatra was Macedonian, and the last ruler of the Macedonian dynasty, which ruled Egypt from 323 until annexation by Rome 31. She succeeded her father Ptolemy XII jointly with her brother Ptolemy XIII, and they ruled together from 51 to 49 BC, when she was expelled by him. Her reinstatement in 48 BC by Caesar caused a war between Caesar and her brother, who was defeated and killed. The younger brother, Ptolemy XIV, was elevated to the throne and married to her, in the tradition of the pharaohs, although she actually lived with Caesar and they had a son, Ptolemy XV, known as Caesarion (he was later killed by Octavian).

After Caesar's death, Cleopatra and Mark Antony had three sons, and he divorced in 32 BC his wife Octavia, the sister of Octavian, who then induced the Roman Senate to declare war on Egypt.

Cleveland (Stephen) Grover 1837–1908. 22nd and 24th president of the USA, 1885–89 and 1893–97; the first Democratic president elected after the Civil War, and the only president to hold office for two nonconsecutive terms. He attempted to check corruption in public life, and in 1895 initiated arbitration proceedings that eventually settled a territorial dispute with Britain concerning the Venezuelan boundary.

Clinton Bill (William Jefferson) 1946– . 42nd president of the USA from 1993, a Democrat. He served as governor of Arkansas 1979-81 and 1983-93. As president, he sought to implement a 'New Democrat' programme, combining social reform with economic conservatism as a means of bringing the country out of recession. He introduced legislation to reduce the federal deficit and cut crime, but the loss of both houses of Congress to the Republicans in 1994 presented a serious obstacle to further social reform. However, he successfully repositioned himself on the centre-right to become the first Democrat since F D Roosevelt to be elected for a second term in Nov 1996.

Clive Robert, Baron Clive of Plassey 1725–1774. British soldier and administrator who established British rule in India by victories over French troops at Arcot 1751 and over the nawab of Bengal at Plassey 1757. He was governor of Bengal 1757–60 and 1765–66. On his return to Britain in 1766, his wealth led to allegations that he had abused his power. Although acquitted, he committed suicide.

I feel that I am reserved for some end or other.

Robert Clive after failed suicide attempt

Clovis 465–511. Merovingian king of the Franks from 481. He succeeded his father Childeric as king of the Salian (northern) Franks; defeated the Gallo-Romans (Romanized Gauls) near Soissons 486, ending their rule in France; and defeated the Alemanni, a confederation of Germanic tribes, near Cologne 496. He embraced Christianity and subsequently proved a powerful defender of orthodoxy against the Arian Visigoths, whom he defeated at Poitiers 507. He made Paris his capital.

Clunies-Ross family that established a benevolently paternal rule in the Cocos Islands. John Clunies-Ross, a Scottish seaman, settled on Home Island in 1827. The family's rule ended in 1978 with the purchase of the Cocos by the Australian government.

Cluny town in Saône-et-Loire *département*, France. Its abbey, now in ruins, was the foundation house 910–1790 of the Cluniac order, originally a reformed branch of the Benedictines.

CND abbreviation for ◊*Campaign for Nuclear Disarmament*.

Cnossus alternative form of ◊Knossos, city of ancient Crete.

Cnut IV see ◊Canute VI.

Cobbett William 1763–1835. British Radical politician and journalist, who published the weekly *Political Register* 1802–35. He spent much time in North America. His crusading essays on the conditions of the rural poor were collected as *Rural Rides* 1830.

Cobden Richard 1804–1865. British Liberal politician and economist, co-founder with John Bright of the Anti-Corn Law League 1839. A member of Parliament from 1841, he opposed class and religious privileges and believed in disarmament and free trade.

A typical early Victorian radical, he believed in the abolition of privileges, a minimum of government interference, and the securing of international peace through free trade and by disarmament and arbitration. He opposed trade unionism and most of the factory legislation of his time, because he regarded them as opposed to liberty of contract. His opposition to the Crimean War made him unpopular. He was largely responsible for the commercial treaty with France in 1860.

Cochise c. 1812–1874. American Apache Indian leader who campaigned relentlessly against white settlement of his territory. Unjustly arrested by US authorities 1850, he escaped from custody and took American hostages, whom he later executed. A Chiricahua Apache, Cochise joined forces with the Mimbreno Apache and successfully fought off a large force of California settlers 1862. Finally apprehended by General George Crook 1871, Cochise made peace with the US government the following year.

codex (plural *codices*) book from before the invention of printing: in ancient times wax-coated wooden tablets; later, folded sheets of parchment were attached to the boards, then bound together. The name 'codex' was used for all large works, collections of history, philosophy, poetry, and during the Roman Empire designated collections of laws.

Various codices record Mexican Indian civilizations just after the time of the Spanish Conquest about 1520.

Greek and Roman coinage

The earliest known coins were changing hands just before 600 BC in W Anatolia, in the kingdom of Lydia (modern Turkey). Initiated by King Croesus, they were made from *electrum*, a natural alloy of gold and silver found in the River Pactolus that flowed past Sardis, Lydia's capital. A punch and anvil die was used to stamp the coins with what is assumed to be the Lydian emblem of a lion, or a lion's paws, cutting the metal to reveal its consistency. A major hoard of such coins was discovered in 1904–05 at the sanctuary of Artemis at Ephesus where it may have been left as a dedication.

However, cuneiform documents reveal that from at least the 3rd millennium BC metal was being weighed as bullion for transactions in Mesopotamia (modern Iraq). Coinage itself developed because of the need for relatively small but secure payments from royalty or public sources to artisans, builders, craftsmen, and mercenaries in the increasingly complex world of the Aegean seaboard.

Pure silver coinage

The innovation of coinage was adopted in the 7th century by Greek cities on the Aegean coast, who stamped their own 'types', or images, which were usually gods, but which could also be local products or sometimes a punning symbol. For example a *phoce* (Greek for seal) for the city of Phocaea included the initial letter [PHI]. The real expansion in types, and so in issuing cities and mints, came with the switch from electrum to pure silver coins after 550 BC. Before the end of the 6th century BC, Aegina, Athens, Euboea, Corinth and the Greek cities of Sicily had introduced coinage.

Athens had a puzzling diversity of types, known as *Wappermünzen* or heraldic coins, which was replaced by a prototype of later coinage: an owl, symbol of the goddess Athene, with the opening letters of Athene's name. By the start of the 5th century BC an extraordinarily rich seam of silver was being mined at Lavrion for Athens. Themistocles diverted this source of currency to build the Athenian fleet which defeated the Persians at Salamis in 480 BC.

A spreading influence

Silver and gold coins continued to be stamped by the Persians for use in the Greek world and in the western provinces, but most of the initiative lay with the Greeks, operating on the variable unit-weight of the drachma (handful) and with those who imitated them. The

Athenian coinage was most influential as the empire grew during the 5th century BC, but at Syracuse named and highly skilled designers elaborated types of great finesse, including a chariot for the 4 drachma coin, a horseman and horse for the 2 drachma, and a horseman alone for the unit drachma. Portraiture was slow to arrive on Greek coins, but once introduced it flourished with the increasing emphasis on dynastic rule in the Hellenistic period. The model here was the portrait of Alexander the Great, used by his successors on their coinage to indicate their Macedonian credentials. By now, coinage had spread throughout Asia Minor.

From the beginning of the 4th century BC, bronze was also used. This has been linked with the gradual change away from city-state armies to mercenaries, and a resulting demand for highly localized currencies of low value. This is also illustrated in Athens, where payments for democratic attendance on juries and other forms of public service were made in weights well below that of the standard drachma.

Roman coinage

Coinage first appeared in Rome in about 300 BC, and for some generations was only one method of payment among several, with weighing bullion, bronze bars and discs being used as well as lighter silver and bronze coins. Rome adopted the weight standard of the coins of Naples, and apparently used the coinage heavily in relations with the Greek states in S Italy. The drastic demands and expenditure of the wars against Hannibal prompted the creation of the silver Roman *denarius*, worth ten of the bronze *as* coins. The rate was changed to 16 *asses* in 141 BC, and lasted from then until the 3rd century AD. Gold coinage became widespread under Julius Caesar, with the standard gold coin for much of the imperial period being the *aureus*. Caesar also placed emphasis on portraiture, and the likeness of Augustus was used by Tiberius to underline his succession, on the Hellenistic model. Despite the scale of Roman rule, a closed system of coinage was maintained in the province of Egypt, and local currencies were not abolished. Forgeries and the theft of dies were always a problem, and hoards often contained very large numbers of plated coins. In the 3rd century, Emperor Diocletian put the currency on a gold standard, providing the ancestry for the gold coinage of medieval Europe.

Cody (William Frederick) 'Buffalo Bill' 1846–1917. US scout and performer. From 1883 he toured the USA and Europe with a Wild West show which featured the recreation of Indian attacks and, for a time, the cast included Chief ◊Sitting Bull as well as Annie ◊Oakley. His nickname derives from a time when he had a contract to supply buffalo carcasses to railway labourers (over 4,000 in 18 months).

coin the invention of coinage is attributed to the Chinese in the 2nd millennium BC, the earl-iest types being small-scale bronze reproductions of barter objects such as knives and spades. In the Western world, coinage of stamped, guaranteed weight originated with the Lydians of Asia Minor (early 7th century BC) who used elec-trum, a local natural mixture of gold and silver; the first to issue gold and silver coins was Croe-sus of Lydia in the 6th century BC.

The Cold War

1917 Bolshevik success in Russian Revolution and attempts by Western powers with 'White' Russian forces to defeat them created background of mutual distrust and isolation of the Soviet Union.

1939 Hitler-Stalin (Nazi-Soviet) pact reinforced Western suspicions.

1941 German invasion of Soviet Union created a degree of unity between the 'Big Three' powers.

1942 Disagreements over the post-war reconstruction of Europe began to emerge, a major issue being the future of Poland.

1944 Moscow Conference agreed the division of Germany into zones and the independence of Austria, but no agreement on the rest of Europe.

1945 Feb Yalta Conference produced outline agreement on the future of Poland.

July Potsdam Conference at the end of the war in Europe reinforced the divisions between East and West. USA sought to open up Europe for free capitalist trade. USSR wanted Germany for reparations and E Europe for trade.

1946 Churchill's 'Iron Curtain' speech at Fulton, Missouri, USA.

1947 Zonal partition of Germany created the basis for permanent division as economic conflicts between East and West increased.

March President Truman made Truman Doctrine speech.

April Term 'Cold War' first used by Bernard Baruch in speech referring to the Truman Doctrine.

July USA sponsored Marshall Plan for reconstruction of Europe. Offered to E European states but rejected under Soviet pressure.

Oct Cominform created to direct international communism.

1948 March Western fears of further Soviet encroachment led to Treaty of Brussels between Britain, France, and the Low Countries.

June Yugoslavia expelled from Cominform as Tito pursued separate socialist line.

July Currency reform introduced in the Western zones of Germany and Berlin. USSR retaliated by blocking access to West Berlin. Start of Berlin blockade and Allied airlift (to May 1949). Communist coup in Czechoslovakia.

1949 Jan Establishment of Comecon as economic bloc for Eastern Europe.

April Brussels Treaty extended into North Atlantic Treaty Organization (NATO), which included the US, Canada, Norway, Denmark, Italy, Portugal, Iceland, Greece and Turkey (both 1952), and West Germany (1955). Soviet Union tested its first atomic bomb. Communists won Chinese Civil War and People's Republic founded.

1950 Invasion of South Korea from the N. Early successes led to intervention by United Nations, then Chinese.

1953 Armistice in Korean War left frontiers much the same as in 1950. Death of Stalin.

1954 French driven out of Indochina after defeat at Dien Bien Phu. Vietminh took over in North Vietnam and US-backed capitalist regime ruled in South Vietnam.

1955 Red Army withdrew from Austria. Warsaw Pact formed.

1956 Soviet Union suppressed Hungarian uprising with troops and tanks. Anglo-French and Israeli attack on Egypt, ostensibly to protect the Suez Canal, forced to withdraw under USA and international pressure.

1958 Soviet Union renewed attempts to remove Western forces from Berlin.

1959 Cuban revolution created opportunity for Soviet Union to cultivate an ally in the Caribbean.

1961 East Germans built Berlin Wall to isolate the W sectors of the city.

1962 Cuban missile crisis. USA and USSR in direct confrontation over Soviet missiles sent to Cuba. Resolved when Khrushchev backed down.

1964–75 Direct USA involvement to protect South Vietnam from incursions by communist North Vietnamese and guerrilla Vietcong.

1968 USSR intervened in Czechoslovakia to prevent liberalization.

1972 First Strategic Arms Limitation Treaty (SALT) between US and USSR began process of détente.

1973 US agencies assisted in overthrow of Marxist regime in Chile led by Salvador Allende.

1975 Helsinki Conference on Security and Cooperation in Europe (CSCE) continued the thaw.

1979 USSR invaded Afghanistan.

1980–81 USA gave moral support to liberalization in Poland led by Solidarity movement. President Reagan referred to USSR as 'evil empire'.

1982 USA covert and military intervention in South and Central America increased to prevent supposed communist subversion.

1983 Reagan put forward 'Star Wars' plan for militarization of space.

1985 USA sent troops to Grenada after Marxist coup.

1986 USSR president Gorbachev suggestion to the US of a nuclear disarmament treaty at Reykjavik summit turned down by Reagan.

1989 Collapse of East German state heralded end of Eastern bloc and rapid but unstable liberalization in the USSR. Tiananmen Square massacre in Beijing deepened rifts between Western powers and China.

1990 Formal end of the Cold War declared in Nov signing of CSCE treaty between NATO and Warsaw Pact countries on reduction of conventional forces in Europe. US president Bush announced start of a 'new world order'.

1991 Collapse of USSR into constituent republics.

Coke Edward 1552–1634. Lord Chief Justice of England 1613–17. He was a defender of common law against royal prerogative; against Charles I he drew up the ◊Petition of Right 1628, which defines and protects Parliament's liberties.

For a man's house is his castle.

Edward Coke *Third Institute*

Colbert Jean-Baptiste 1619–1683. French politician, chief minister to Louis XIV, and controller-general (finance minister) from 1665. He reformed the Treasury, promoted French industry and commerce by protectionist measures, and tried to make France a naval power equal to England or the Netherlands, while favouring a peaceful foreign policy.

Colditz town in E Germany, near Leipzig, site of a castle used as a high-security prisoner-of-war camp (Oflag IVC) in World War II. Among daring escapes was that of British Captain Patrick Reid (1910–1990) and others Oct 1942. It became a museum 1989. In 1990 the castle was converted to a hotel.

Cold War ideological, political, and economic tensions 1945–90 between the USSR and Eastern Europe on the one hand and the USA and Western Europe on the other. The Cold War was exacerbated by propaganda, covert activity by intelligence agencies, and economic sanctions; it intensified at times of conflict anywhere in the world. Arms-reduction agreements between the USA and USSR in the late 1980s, and a diminution of Soviet influence in Eastern Europe, symbolized by the opening of the Berlin Wall 1989, led to a reassessment of positions, and the 'war' officially ended 1990.

Colfax Schuyler 1823–1885. US political leader. He was elected to the US House of Representatives 1854 and served as Speaker of the House 1863–69. A radical Republican, Colfax was elected vice president for President Grant's first term 1869–73. He was not renominated because of charges of corruption and financial improprieties.

Coligny Gaspard de 1517–1572. French admiral and soldier, and prominent ◊Huguenot. About 1557 he joined the Protestant party, helping to lead the Huguenot forces during the Wars of Religion. After the Treaty of St Germain 1570, he became a favourite of the young king Charles IX, but was killed on the first night of the Massacre of St ◊Bartholomew.

collective farm (Russian *kolkhoz*) farm in which a group of farmers pool their land, domestic animals, and agricultural implements, retaining as private property enough only for the members' own requirements. The profits of the farm are divided among its members. In cooperative farming, farmers retain private ownership of the land.

Collective farming was first developed in the USSR in 1917, where it became general after 1930. Stalin's collectivization drive 1929–33 wrecked a flourishing agricultural system and alienated the Soviet peasants from the land: 15 million people were left homeless, 1 million of whom were sent to labour camps and some 12 million deported to Siberia. In subsequent years, millions of those peasants forced into collectives died. Collective farming is practised in other countries; it was adopted from 1953 in China, and Israel has a large number of collective farms.

collectivization policy pursued by the Soviet leader Stalin in the USSR after 1928 to reorganize agriculture by taking land into state ownership or creating ◊collective farms. Much of this was achieved during the first two ◊Five-Year Plans but only with much coercion and loss of life among the peasantry.

Collingwood Cuthbert, Baron Collingwood 1748–1810. British admiral who served with Horatio Nelson in the West Indies against France and blockaded French ports 1803–05; after Nelson's death he took command at the Battle of Trafalgar.

Collins Michael 1890–1922. Irish nationalist. He was a Sinn Féin leader, a founder and director of intelligence of the Irish Republican Army 1919, minister for finance in the provisional government of the Irish Free State 1922 (see ◊Ireland, Republic of), commander of the Free State forces in the civil war, and for ten days head of state before being killed by Irishmen opposed to the partition treaty with Britain.

There is no crime in detecting and destroying in war-time, the spy and the informer. They have destroyed without trial. I have paid them back in their own coin.

Michael Collins

Colombia country in South America, bounded N by the Caribbean Sea, W by the Pacific Ocean, NW corner by Panama, E and NE by Venezuela, SE by Brazil, and SW by Peru and Ecuador.

history Until it was conquered by Spain in the 16th century, the area was inhabited by the Chibcha Indians. From 1538 Colombia formed part of a colony known as New Granada, comprising Colombia, Panama, and most of Venezuela. In 1819 the area included Ecuador and became independent as Gran Colombia, a state set up by Simón Bolívar.

The founding president of Colombia, General Francisco de Paula Santander, imposed strong central control over the disparate regions of the new state. Regional rebellions, such as the revolt of the supremos (1839–42), were put down by later rulers. In 1886, President Rafael Núñez imposed a centralist and authoritarian constitution on the nation.

Not until 1930 was there a peaceful change of the party in power, when Enrique Oleya won the presidency.

'La Violencia' In 1948 the left-wing mayor of Bogotá was assassinated, and there followed a decade of near civil war, 'La Violencia', during which it is thought that over 250,000 people died. Left-wing guerrilla activity continued. In 1957, in an effort to halt the violence, the Conservative and Liberal parties formed a National Front, alternating the presidency between them. They were challenged 1970 by the National Popular Alliance (ANAPO), with a special appeal to the working classes, but the Conservative–Liberal coalition continued, and when in 1978 the Liberals won majorities in both chambers of congress and the presidency, they kept the National Front accord.

antidrug campaign In 1982 the Liberals kept their majorities in congress, but Dr Belisario Betancur won the presidency for the Conservatives. He sought a truce with the left-wing guerrillas by granting them an amnesty and freeing political prisoners. When the minister of justice, who had been using harsh measures to curb drug dealing, was assassinated 1984, Betancur reacted by strengthening his antidrug campaign.

In the 1986 elections Liberal Virgilio Barco Vargas won the presidency by a record margin. Three months after taking office, he announced the end of the National Front accord, despite a provision in the constitution that the opposition party always has the opportunity to participate in government if it wishes to. President Vargas declared a new campaign against cocaine traffickers following the assassination in Aug of Luis Carlos Galan, the leading candidate for the 1990 presidential elections. A bombing campaign was undertaken by the cartels in retaliation for confiscation of property and extradition to the USA of leading cartel members, but the Colombian security forces scored a major victory Dec 1989 with the killing in a shoot-out of drug lord José Rodriguez Gacha.

new constitution Assembly elections were held Dec 1990, giving the Liberal Party a five-seat lead over the April 19th movement (M-19). Under President Cesar Gaviria Trujillo a new constitution was adopted July 1991 which included a clause prohibiting the extradition of Colombians for trial in other countries. As a result, several leading drug traffickers surrendered or were arrested 1991, including the head of the Medellín cocaine cartel, Pablo Escobar. In congressional elections held Oct 1991, the Liberal Party retained its control of the senate. In July 1992, Escobar escaped from prison along with several others.

Colombo Plan plan for cooperative economic and social development in Asia and the Pacific, established 1950. The 26 member countries are Afghanistan, Australia, Bangladesh, Bhutan, Cambodia, Canada, Fiji, India, Indonesia, Iran, Japan, South Korea, Laos, Malaysia, Maldives, Myanmar (Burma), Nepal, New Zealand, Pakistan, Papua New Guinea, Philippines, Singapore, Sri Lanka, Thailand, UK, and USA. They meet annually to discuss economic and development plans such as irrigation, hydroelectric schemes, and technical training.

The plan has no central fund but technical assistance and financing of development projects are arranged through individual governments or the International Bank for Reconstruction and Development.

colonialism another name for ◊*imperialism*.

colonial preference programme of tariff reform within the British Empire, also known as ◊imperial preference.

Columbus Christopher (Spanish *Cristóbal Colón*) 1451–1506. Italian navigator and explorer who made four voyages to the New World: 1492 to San Salvador Island, Cuba, and Haiti; 1493–96 to Guadaloupe, Montserrat, Antigua, Puerto Rico, and Jamaica; 1498 to Trinidad and the mainland of South America; 1502–04 to Honduras and Nicaragua.

Believing that Asia could be reached by sailing westwards, he eventually won the support of King Ferdinand and Queen Isabella of Spain and set off on his first voyage from Palos 3 Aug 1492 with three small ships, the *Niña*, the *Pinta*, and his flagship the *Santa Maria*. Land was sighted 12 Oct, probably Watling Island (now San Salvador Island), and within a few weeks he reached Cuba and Haiti, returning to Spain March 1493.

Born in Genoa, Columbus went to sea at an early age, and settled in Portugal 1478. After his third voyage 1498, he became involved in quarrels among the colonists sent to Haiti, and in 1500 the governor sent him back to Spain in chains. Released and compensated by the king, he made his last voyage 1502–04, during which he hoped to find a strait leading to India. He died in poverty in Valladolid and is buried in Seville cathedral.

I must sail on until with the help of our Lord, I discover land.

Christopher Columbus
to crew the day before sighting America 1492 (traditional)

Combination Acts laws passed in Britain 1799 and 1800 making trade unionism illegal, introduced after the French Revolution for fear that the unions would become centres of political agitation. The unions continued to exist, but claimed to be friendly societies or went underground, until the acts were repealed 1824, largely owing to the radical Francis ◊Place.

Comecon (acronym for *Co*uncil for *M*utual *Econ*omic Assistance, or *CMEA*) economic organization 1949–91, linking the USSR with Bulgaria, Czechoslovakia, Hungary, Poland, Romania, East Germany (1950–90), Mongolia (from 1962), Cuba (from 1972), and Vietnam (from 1978), with Yugoslavia as an associated member. Albania also belonged 1949–61. Its establishment was prompted by the ◊Marshall Plan.

Cominform (acronym for *Com*munist *Inform*ation Bureau) organization 1947–56 established by the Soviet politician Andrei Zhdanov (1896–1948) to exchange information between European communist parties. Yugoslavia was expelled 1948. See ◊International.

Comintern acronym from *Com*munist *Intern*ational.

commando member of a specially trained, highly mobile military unit. The term originated in South Africa in the 19th century, where it referred to Boer military reprisal raids against Africans and, in the South African Wars, against the British. Commando units have often carried out operations behind enemy lines.

Committee of Imperial Defence informal group established 1902 to coordinate planning of the British Empire's defence forces. Initially meeting on a temporary basis, it was established

permanently 1904. Members were usually cabinet ministers concerned with defence, military leaders, and key civil servants.

The committee had influence but no executive power. It was taken over by the War Council in wartime.

Commodus Lucius Aelius Aurelius AD 161–192. Roman emperor from 180, son of Marcus Aurelius Antoninus. He was a tyrant, spending lavishly on gladiatorial combats, confiscating the property of the wealthy, persecuting the Senate, and renaming Rome 'Colonia Commodiana'. There were many attempts against his life, and he was finally strangled at the instigation of his mistress and advisers, who had discovered themselves on the emperor's death list.

Common Agricultural Policy (CAP) measures giving financial support to farmers within the ◊European Community.

common land unenclosed wasteland, forest, and pasture used in common by the community at large. Poor people have throughout history gathered fruit, nuts, wood, reeds, roots, game, and so on from common land.

In the UK commons originated in the Middle Ages, when every manor had a large area of unenclosed, uncultivated land from which freeholders had rights to take the natural produce. However, powerful landowners often simply appropriated common land.

Commons, House of the lower but more powerful of the two parts of the British and Canadian ◊parliaments.

commonwealth body politic founded on law for the common 'weal' or good. Political philosophers of the 17th century, such as Thomas Hobbes and John Locke, used the term to mean an organized political community. In Britain it was specifically applied to the regime (*the Commonwealth*) of Oliver ◊Cromwell 1649-60.

Commonwealth conference any consultation between the prime ministers (or defence, finance, foreign, or other ministers) of the sovereign independent members of the British Commonwealth. These are informal discussion meetings, and the implementation of policies is decided by individual governments.

Colonial conferences were instituted 1887, also meeting 1894, 1897, and 1902. The 1907 conference resolved that imperial conferences be held every four years, and these met regularly until 1937 (the most notable being 1926, which defined the relationship of the self-governing members of the Commonwealth). Commonwealth heads of government meetings

(CHOGM) have been held regularly since 1944 when they replaced imperial conferences. Recent Commonwealth conferences have been held in Singapore 1971, the first outside the UK; Sydney 1978, the first regional meeting; Lusaka 1979, the first regular session in Africa; and Vancouver 1987.

Commonwealth Day public holiday celebrated on the second Monday in March in many parts of the Commonwealth. It was called *Empire Day* until 1958 and celebrated on 24 May (Queen Victoria's birthday) until 1966.

Commonwealth Development Corporation organization founded as the Colonial Development Corporation 1948 to aid the development of dependent Commonwealth territories; the change of name and extension of its activities to include those now independent were announced 1962.

Commonwealth Immigration Acts successive acts that attempted to regulate the entry into the UK of British subjects from the Commonwealth. The Commonwealth Immigration Act, passed by the Conservative government 1962, ruled that Commonwealth immigrants entering Britain must have employment or be able to offer required skills.

Commonwealth of Independent States (CIS) successor body to the ◊Union of Soviet Socialist Republics, initially formed as a new commonwealth of Slav republics on 8 Dec 1991 by the presidents of the Russian Federation, Belarus, and Ukraine. On 21 Dec, eight of the nine remaining non-Slav republics – Moldova, Tajikistan, Armenia, Azerbaijan, Turkmenistan, Kazakhstan, Kyrgyzstan, and Uzbekistan – joined the CIS at a meeting held in Kazakhstan's capital, Alma Ata. The CIS formally came into existence in Jan 1992 when President Gorbachev resigned and the Soviet government voted itself out of existence. It has no real, formal political institutions and its role is uncertain. Its headquarters are in Minsk (Mensk), Belarus.

Commonwealth, the (British) voluntary association of 50 countries and their dependencies that once formed part of the ◊British Empire and are now independent sovereign states. They are all regarded as 'full members of the Commonwealth'. Additionally, there are some 20 territories that are not completely sovereign and remain dependencies of the UK or another of the fully sovereign members, and are regarded as 'Commonwealth countries'. Heads of government meet every two years, apart from those of Nauru and Tuvalu; however, Nauru and Tuvalu have the right to participate in all functional activities. The Commonwealth has no charter or constitution, and is founded more on tradition and sentiment than on political or economic factors.

commune group of people or families living together, sharing resources and responsibilities.

Communes developed from early 17th-century religious communities such as the Rosicrucians and Muggletonians, to more radical groups such as the ◊Diggers and the Quakers. Many groups moved to America to found communes, such as the Philadelphia Society (1680s) and the Shakers, which by 1800 had ten groups in North America. The Industrial Revolution saw a new wave of utopian communities associated with the ideas of Robert ◊Owen and Charles Fourier. Communes had a revival during the 1960s, when many small groups were founded. In 1970 it was estimated there were 2,000 communes in the USA, and 100 in England.

The term also refers to a communal division or settlement in a communist country. In China, a policy of Mao Zedong involved the grouping of villages within districts (averaging 30,000 people) and thus, cooperatives were amalgamated into larger units, the communes. 1958 (the ◊Great Leap Forward) saw the establishment of peoples' communes (workers' combines) with shared living quarters and shared meals. Communes organized workers' brigades and were responsible for their own nurseries, schools, clinics, and other facilities.

The term can also refer to the 11th-century to 12th-century association of ◊burghers in north and central Italy. The communes of many cities asserted their independence from the overlordship of either the Holy Roman emperor or the pope, only to fall under the domination of oligarchies or despots during the 13th and 14th centuries.

Commune, Paris two separate periods in the history of Paris 1789–94 and March–May 1871; see ◊Paris Commune.

communism (French *commun* 'common, general') revolutionary socialism based on the theories of the political philosophers Karl Marx and Friedrich Engels, emphasizing common ownership of the means of production and a planned economy. The principle held is that each should work according to their capacity and receive according to their needs. Politically, it seeks the overthrow of capitalism through a proletarian revolution. The first communist state was the USSR after the revolution of 1917. Revolutionary socialist parties and groups united to form communist parties in other countries (in the UK 1920). After World War II, communism was enforced in those countries that came under Soviet occupation. China emerged after 1949 as a potential rival to the USSR in world communist leadership, and other countries attempted to adapt communism to their own needs. The late 1980s saw a movement for more individual freedoms in many communist countries, culminating in the abolition or overthrow of communist rule in Eastern European countries and Mongolia, and further state repression in China. The failed hard-line coup in the USSR against President Gorbachev 1991 resulted in the effective abandonment of communism there.

Many communist parties in capitalist countries, for example, Japan and the *Eurocommunism* of France, Italy, and the major part of the British Communist Party, have since the 1960s or later rejected Soviet dominance.

In the Third World, Libya has attempted to combine revolutionary socialism with Islam; the extreme communist Khmer Rouge devastated Cambodia (then called Kampuchea) 1975–78; Latin America suffers from the US fear of communism in what it regards as its back y ard, with the democratically elected Marxist regime in Chile violently overthrown 1973, and the socialist government of Nicaragua (until it fell 1990) involved in a prolonged civil war against US-backed guerrillas (Contras).

While it looks as if at the moment communism has lost the battle for hearts and minds in Europe, it certainly cannot be said that capitalism as a total world view has won.

On *communism* Robert Runcie in
The Independent Nov 1989

---

community charge a type of ◊poll tax introduced in Scotland 1989 and England and Wales 1991. It was replaced 1993.

Comoros group of islands in the Indian Ocean between Madagascar and the east coast of Africa. Three of them – Njazidja, Nzwani, and Mwali – form the republic of Comoros; the fourth island, Mayotte, is a French dependency.

history Originally inhabited by Asians, Africans, and Indonesians, the Comoros islands were controlled by Muslim sultans until the French acquired them 1841–1909. The islands became a French colony 1912 and were attached to Madagascar 1914–47, when they

were made a French overseas territory. Internal self-government was attained 1961, but full independence not achieved until 1975 because of Mayotte's reluctance to sever links with France. Although the Comoros joined the United Nations 1975, with Ahmed Abdallah as president, Mayotte remained under French administration. Relations with France deteriorated as Ali Soilih, who had overthrown Abdallah, became more powerful as president under a new constitution. In 1978 he was killed by French mercenaries working for Abdallah. Abdallah's use of mercenaries in his return to power led to the Comoros' expulsion from the Organization of African Unity.

one-party state A federal Islamic republic was proclaimed, a new constitution adopted, and Abdallah reconfirmed as president in an election where he was the only candidate. Diplomatic relations with France were restored. In 1979 the Comoros became a one-party state, and government powers were increased. In the same year a plot to overthrow Abdallah was foiled. In 1984 he was re-elected president, and in the following year the constitution was amended, abolishing the post of prime minister and making Abdallah head of government as well as head of state.

In Nov 1989 Abdallah was assassinated during an attack on the presidential palace led by a French mercenary, Col Bob Denard. Denard was subsequently arrested by French army units and returned to France. A provisional military administration was set up, with Said Mohammad Djohar as interim president. In Aug 1990 an attempted antigovernment coup was foiled. The third transitional government in a year was appointed July 1992, and in Sept a coup attempt by army officers was thwarted.

Compromise of 1850 in US history, legislative proposals designed to resolve the sectional conflict between North and South over the admission of California to the Union 1850. Slavery was prohibited in California, but a new fugitive slave law was passed to pacify the slave states. The Senate debate on the compromise lasted nine months; acceptance temporarily revitalized the Union.

concentration camp prison camp for civilians in wartime or under totalitarian rule. The first concentration camps were devised by the British during the Second Boer War in South Africa 1899 for the detention of Afrikaner women and children (with the subsequent deaths of more than 20,000 people). A system of approximately 5,000 concentration camps was developed by the Nazis in Germany and occupied Europe (1933–45) to imprison political and ideological opponents after Hitler became chancellor Jan 1933. Several hundred camps were established in Germany and occupied Europe, the most infamous being the extermination camps of Auschwitz, Belsen, Dachau, Maidanek, Sobibor, and Treblinka. The total number of people who died at the camps exceeded 6 million, and some inmates were subjected to medical experimentation before being killed.

At Oswiecim (Auschwitz-Birkenau), a vast camp complex was created for imprisonment and slave labour as well as the extermination of over 4 million people in gas chambers or by other means. Victims included Jews, Romanies, homosexuals, and other 'misfits' or 'unwanted' people. At Maidanek, about 1.5 million people were exterminated, cremated, and their ashes used as fertilizer. Many camp officials and others responsible were tried after 1945 for war crimes, and executed or imprisoned.

conciliar movement in the history of the Christian church, a 15th-century attempt to urge the supremacy of church councils over the popes, with regard to the ◊Great Schism and the reformation of the church. Councils were held in Pisa 1409, Constance 1414–18, Pavia-Siena 1423–24, Basle 1431–49, and Ferrara-Florence-Rome 1438–47.

After ending the Schism 1417 with the removal of John XXIII (1410–15), Gregory XII (1406–15), and Benedict XIII (1394–1423), and the election of Martin V (1417–31), the movement fell into disunity over questions of reform, allowing Eugenius IV (1431–47) to use the Ferrara-Florence-Rome council to reunite the church and reassert papal supremacy.

concordat agreement regulating relations between the papacy and a secular government, for example, that for France between Pius VII and the emperor Napoleon, which lasted 1801–1905; Mussolini's concordat, which lasted 1929–78 and safeguarded the position of the church in Italy; and one of 1984 in Italy in which Roman Catholicism ceased to be the Italian state religion.

Condé Louis de Bourbon, Prince of Condé 1530–1569. Prominent French ◊Huguenot leader, founder of the house of Condé and uncle of Henry IV of France. He fought in the wars between Henry II and the Holy Roman emperor Charles V, including the defence of Metz.

Condé Louis II 1621–1686. Prince of Condé called the *Great Condé*. French commander who won brilliant victories during the Thirty Years' War at Rocroi 1643 and Lens 1648, but rebelled 1651 and entered the Spanish service.

Pardoned 1660, he commanded Louis XIV's armies against the Spanish and the Dutch.

condominium joint rule of a territory by two or more states, for example, Kanton and Enderbury islands in the South Pacific Phoenix group (under the joint control of Britain and the USA for 50 years from 1939).

Confederacy in US history, popular name for the *Confederate States of America*, the government established by seven (later eleven) Southern states in Feb 1861 when they seceded from the Union, precipitating the American ◊Civil War. Richmond, Virginia, was the capital, and Jefferson Davis the president. The Confederacy fell after its army was defeated 1865 and General Robert E Lee surrendered.

The Confederacy suffered from a lack of political leadership as well as a deficit of troops and supplies. Still, Southern forces won many significant victories. Confederate leaders had hoped to enlist support from Britain and France, but the slavery issue and the Confederacy's uncertain prospects prompted the Europeans to maintain neutrality, although they provided supplies for a time. The Union's blockade and the grinding weight of superior resources made the outcome virtually inevitable 1865. The states of the Confederacy were South Carolina, Georgia, Florida, Alabama, Louisiana, Mississippi, Texas, Virginia, Tennessee, Arkansas, and North Carolina.

Confederation, Articles of in US history, the initial means by which the 13 former British colonies created a form of national government. Ratified 1781, the articles established a unicameral legislature, Congress, with limited powers of raising revenue, regulating currency, and conducting foreign affairs. But because the individual states retained significant autonomy, the confederation was unmanageable. The articles were superseded by the US Constitution 1788.

Conference on Security and Cooperation in Europe (CSCE) international forum attempting to reach agreement in security, economics, science, technology, and human rights. The CSCE first met at the ◊Helsinki Conference in Finland 1975. By the end of March 1992, having admitted the former republics of the USSR, as well as Croatia and Slovenia, its membership had risen to 51 states.

A second conference in Paris Nov 1990 was hailed as marking the formal end of the ◊Cold War. A third conference in Helsinki July 1992 debated the Yugoslav problem and gave the CSCE the power to authorize military responses of the ◊North Atlantic Treaty Organization (NATO), the ◊Western

European Union (WEU), and the ⟡European Community (EC) within Europe.

conference system political system of international conferences in the 19th century promoted principally by the German chancellor Bismarck to ease the integration of a new powerful German state into the 'concert of Europe'.

The conferences were intended to settle great power disputes, mainly related to the Balkans, the Middle East, and the designation of colonies in Africa and Asia. The system fell into disuse with the retirement of Bismarck and the pressures of new European alliance blocks.

Confindustria in European history, a general confederation of industry established in Italy 1920 with the aim of countering working-class agitation. It contributed large funds to the fascist movement, which, in turn, used its *squadristi* against the workers. After Mussolini's takeover of power in 1922, Confindustria became one of the major groups of the fascist corporative state.

Confucianism body of beliefs and practices based on the Chinese classics and supported by the authority of the philosopher Confucius. The origin of things is seen in the union of *yin* and *yang*, the passive and active principles. Human relationships follow the patriarchal pattern. For more than 2,000 years Chinese political government, social organization, and individual conduct was shaped by Confucian principles. In 1912, Confucian philosophy, as a basis for government, was dropped by the state.

The writings on which Confucianism is based include the ideas of a group of traditional books edited by Confucius, as well as his own works, such as the *Analects*, and those of some of his pupils. The *I Ching* is included among the Confucianist texts.

doctrine Until 1912 the emperor of China was regarded as the father of his people, appointed by heaven to rule. The Superior Man was the ideal human and filial piety was the chief virtue. Accompanying a high morality was a kind of ancestor worship.

practices Under the emperor, sacrifices were offered to heaven and earth, the heavenly bodies, the imperial ancestors, various nature gods, and Confucius himself. These were abolished at the Revolution in 1912, but ancestor worship (better expressed as reverence and remembrance) remained a regular practice in the home.

Confucius (Latinized form of *Kong Zi*, 'Kong the master') 551–479 BC. Chinese sage whose name is given to Confucianism. He devoted his life to relieving suffering among the poor through governmental and administrative reform. His emphasis on tradition and ethics

attracted a growing number of pupils during his lifetime. *The Analects of Confucius*, a compilation of his teachings, was published after his death. Within 300 years of the death of Confucius, his teaching was adopted by the Chinese state.

Confucius was born in Lu, in what is now the province of Shangdong, and his early years were spent in poverty. Married at 19, he worked as a minor official, then as a teacher. In 517 there was an uprising in Lu, and Confucius spent the next year or two in the adjoining state of Ch'i. As a teacher he was able to place many of his pupils in government posts but a powerful position eluded him. Only in his fifties was he given an office, but he soon resigned because of the lack of power it conveyed. Then for 14 years he wandered from state to state looking for a ruler who could give him a post where he could put his reforms into practice. At the age of 67 he returned to Lu and devoted himself to teaching. At his death five years later he was buried with great pomp, and his grave outside Qufu has remained a centre of pilgrimage.

Study the past, if you would divine the future.

Confucius

Congo country in W central Africa, bounded N by Cameroon and the Central African Republic, E and S by Zaire, W by the Atlantic Ocean, and NW by Gabon.

history Occupied from the 15th century by the Bakongo, Bateke, and Sanga, the area was exploited by Portuguese slave traders. From 1889 it came under French administration, becoming part of French Equatorial Africa 1910.

The Congo became an autonomous republic within the French Community 1958, and Abbé Fulbert Youlou, a Roman Catholic priest who involved himself in politics and was suspended by the church, became prime minister and then president when full independence was achieved 1960. Two years later plans were announced for a one-party state, but in 1963, after industrial unrest, Youlou was forced to resign.

one-party state A new constitution was approved, and Alphonse Massamba-Débat, a former finance minister, became president, adopting a policy of 'scientific socialism'. The National Revolutionary Movement (MNR) was declared the only political party. In 1968 Capt Marien Ngouabi overthrew Massamba-Débat in a military coup, and the national assembly was replaced by a national council of the revolution. Ngouabi proclaimed a Marxist state but kept economic links with France.

In 1970 the nation became the People's Republic of the Congo, with the Congolese Labour Party (PCT) as the only party, and in 1973 a new constitution provided for an assembly chosen from a single party list. In 1977 Ngouabi was assassinated, and Col Joachim Yhombi-Opango took over. He resigned 1979 and was succeeded by Denis Sassou-Nguessou, who moved away from Soviet influence and strengthened links with France, the USA, and China.

In 1984 Sassou-Nguessou was elected for another five-year term. He increased his control by combining the posts of head of state, head of government, and president of the central committee of the PCT.

communism abandoned In Aug 1990 the ruling PCT announced political reforms, including the abandonment of Marxism-Leninism, the broadening of its membership, and an eventual end of the one-party system; in 1991 the country was renamed the Republic of Congo. A new constitution was approved by referendum March 1992, and multiparty elections were held in Aug. UPADS won the most assembly seats, though no overall majority, and Pascal Lissouba became the country's first democratically elected president. Elections of 1993, won by an UPADS-led coalition, were declared void; an international panel of inquiry 1994 announced a majority for the coalition.

Congo, Democratic Republic of name from 1997 of ◊Zaire

Congregationalism form of church government adopted by those Protestant Christians known as Congregationalists, who let each congregation manage its own affairs. The first Congregationalists were the Brownists, named after Robert Browne, who defined the congregational principle 1580.

Congress national legislature of the USA, consisting of the House of Representatives (435 members, apportioned to the states of the Union on the basis of population, and elected for two-year terms) and the Senate (100 senators, two for each state, elected for six years, one-third elected every two years). Both representatives and senators are elected by direct popular vote. Congress meets in Washington DC, in the Capitol Building. An act of Congress is a bill passed by both houses.

The Congress of the United States met for the first time on 4 March 1789. It was preceded by the Congress of the Confederation representing the several states under the Articles of Confederation from 1781 to 1789.

Congress of Racial Equality (CORE) US nonviolent civil-rights organization, founded in Chicago 1942.

Congress Party Indian political party, founded 1885 as the Indian National Congress. It led the movement to end British rule and was the governing party from independence until 1977, when Indira Gandhi lost the leadership she had held since 1966. The party also held power 1980-89 and 1991-96. Heading a splinter group, known as *Congress (I)*, she achieved an overwhelming victory in the 1980 elections, reducing the main Congress Party to a minority. The I was dropped from the name 1993 after the assassination of Rajiv Gandhi 1991, and small split occurred in the party 1995.

The *Indian National Congress*, founded by the British colonialist Allan Hume (1829-1912), was a moderate body until World War I. Then, under the leadership of Mahatma Gandhi, it began a campaign of nonviolent noncooperation with the British colonizers. It was declared illegal 1932-34, but was recognized as the paramount power in India at the granting of independence in 1947. Dominated in the early years of Indian independence by Prime Minister Nehru, the party won the elections of 1952, 1957, and 1962. Under Indira Gandhi from 1966, it won the elections of 1967 and 1971, but was defeated for the first time 1977.

congress system developed from the Congress of Vienna 1814–15, a series of international meetings in Aachen, Germany, 1818, Troppau, Austria, 1820, and Verona, Italy, 1822. British opposition to the use of congresses by Klemens ◊Metternich as a weapon against liberal and national movements inside Europe brought them to an end as a system of international arbitration, although congresses continued to meet into the 1830s.

Conkling Roscoe 1829–1888. US political leader, one of the founders of the Republican Party 1854. He served in the US House of Representatives 1859–63 and 1865–67, and in the US Senate 1867–81. A radical Republican, Conkling was an active prosecutor in President A ◊Johnson's impeachment trial.

conquistador (Spanish 'conqueror') any of the early Spanish explorers and adventurers in the Americas, such as Hernán Cortés (Mexico) and Francisco Pizarro (Peru).

Conrad five German kings:

Conrad I King of the Germans from 911, when he succeeded Louis the Child, the last of the

German Carolingians. During his reign the realm was harassed by Magyar invaders.

Conrad II King of the Germans from 1024, Holy Roman emperor from 1027. He ceded the Sleswick (Schleswig) borderland, south of the Jutland peninsula, to King Canute, but extended his rule into Lombardy and Burgundy.

Conrad III 1093–1152. German king and Holy Roman emperor from 1138, the first king of the Hohenstaufen dynasty. Throughout his reign there was a fierce struggle between his followers, the ◊*Ghibellines*, and the ◊*Guelphs*, the followers of Henry the Proud, duke of Saxony and Bavaria (1108–1139), and later of his son Henry the Lion (1129–1195).

Conrad IV 1228–1254. Elected king of the Germans 1237. Son of the Holy Roman emperor Frederick II, he had to defend his right of succession against Henry Raspe of Thuringia (died 1247) and William of Holland (1227–56).

Conrad V (Conradin) 1252–1268. Son of Conrad IV, recognized as king of the Germans, Sicily, and Jerusalem by German supporters of the ◊Hohenstaufens 1254. He led ◊Ghibelline forces against Charles of Anjou at the battle of Tagliacozzo, N Italy 1266, and was captured and executed.

conscription legislation for all able-bodied male citizens (and female in some countries, such as Israel) to serve with the armed forces. It originated in France 1792, and in the 19th and 20th centuries became the established practice in almost all European states. Modern conscription systems often permit alternative national service for conscientious objectors.

In Britain conscription was introduced for single men between 18 and 41 in March 1916 and for married men two months later, but was abolished after World War I. It was introduced for the first time in peace April 1939, when all men aged 20 became liable to six months' military training. The National Service Act, passed Sept 1939, made all men between 18 and 41 liable to military service, and in 1941 women also became liable to be called up for the women's services as an alternative to industrial service. Men reaching the age of 18 continued to be called up until 1960.

Conservative Party UK political party, one of the two historic British parties; the name replaced *Tory* in general use from 1830 onwards. Traditionally the party of landed interests, it broadened its political base under Benjamin Disraeli's leadership in the 19th century. The present Conservative Party's free-market capitalism is supported by the world of finance and the management of industry.

Opposed to the *laissez-faire* of the Liberal manufacturers, the Conservative Party supported, to some extent, the struggle of the working class against the harsh conditions arising from the Industrial Revolution. The split of 1846 over Robert Peel's Corn Law policy led to 20 years out of office, or in office without power, until Disraeli 'educated' his party into accepting parliamentary and social change, extended the franchise to the artisan (winning considerable working-class support), launched imperial expansion, and established an alliance with industry and finance.

During 1915–45, except briefly in 1924 and 1929–31, the Conservatives were continually in office, whether alone or as part of a coalition, largely due to the break-up of the traditional two-party system by the rise of Labour.

Narrowly defeated in 1964 under Alec Douglas-Home, the Conservative Party from 1965 elected its leaders, beginning with Edward Heath, who was prime minister 1970–74. Margaret Thatcher replaced Heath and under her leadership the party returned to power 1979. Re-elected 1983 and 1987, she was ousted 1990 after an intra-party challenge by Michael Heseltine. Her successor was John Major, and the party won re-election 1992. By 1995, a clear division had emerged in the party's approach to Europe, with pro-Europeans mainly to the left and 'Eurosceptics' mainly to the right. Eurosceptic John Redwood unsucessfully challenged Major's leadership of the party 1995. In the 1997 general election the party fell to landslide defeat, and John Major immediately announced his resignation a party leader. He was succeeded by William Hague.

Constance, Council of council held by the Roman Catholic church 1414–17 in Constance, Germany. It elected Pope Martin V, which ended the Great Schism 1378–1417 when there were rival popes in Rome and Avignon.

In this sign shalt thou conquer.

Traditional form of words of **Constantine the Great's vision 312**

Constantine the Great c. AD 280–337. First Christian emperor of Rome and founder of Constantinople. He defeated Maxentius, joint emperor of Rome AD 312, and in 313 formally recognized Christianity. As sole emperor of the west of the empire, he defeated Licinius, emperor of the east, to become ruler of the

Roman world 324. He presided over the church's first council at Nicaea 325. Constantine moved his capital to Byzantium on the Bosporus 330, renaming it Constantinople (now Istanbul). In 337 he set out to defend the Euphrates frontier against the Persians but he died before reaching it, at Nicomedia in Asia Minor.

constitution body of fundamental laws of a state, laying down the system of government and defining the relations of the legislature, executive, and judiciary to each other and to the citizens. Since the French Revolution almost all countries (the UK is an exception) have adopted written constitutions; that of the USA (1787) is the oldest.

The constitution of the UK does not exist as a single document but as an accumulation of customs and precedents, together with laws defining certain of its aspects. Among the latter are Magna Carta 1215, the Petition of Right 1628, and the Habeas Corpus Act 1679, limiting the royal powers of taxation and of imprisonment; the Bill of Rights 1689 and the Act of Settlement 1701, establishing the supremacy of ◊Parliament and the independence of the judiciary; and the Parliament Acts 1911 and 1949, limiting the powers of the Lords. The Triennial Act 1694, the Septennial Act 1716, and the Parliament Act 1911 limited the duration of Parliament, while the Reform Acts of 1832, 1867, 1884, 1918, and 1928 extended the electorate.

consul chief magistrate of ancient Rome after the expulsion of the last king 510 BC. The consuls were two annually elected magistrates, both of equal power; they jointly held full civil power in Rome and the chief military command in the field. After the establishment of the Roman Empire the office became purely honorary.

contado in northern and central Italy from the 9th to the 13th century, the territory under a count's jurisdiction. During the 13th century, this jurisdiction passed to the cities, and it came to refer to the rural area over which a city exerted political and economic control.

Contadora Group alliance formed between Colombia, Mexico, Panama, and Venezuela Jan 1983 to establish a general peace treaty for Central America. It was named after Contadora, the island of the Pearl Group in the Gulf of Panama where the first meeting was held.

The process was designed to include the formation of a Central American parliament (similar to the European parliament). Support for the Contadora Group has come from Argentina, Brazil, Peru, and Uruguay, as well as from the Central American states.

Containment US policy (adopted from 1947) that was designed to prevent the spread of communism; first stated by George Kennan, US ambassador to Moscow.

Continental Congress in US history, the federal legislature of the original 13 states, acting as a provisional government during the ◊American Revolution. It was responsible for drawing up the Declaration of Independence, July 1776, and the Articles of ◊Confederation 1777.

The Continental Congress was convened in Philadelphia 1774–89, when the constitution was adopted. The Congress authorized an army to resist the British and issued paper money to finance the war effort.

Continental System system of economic preference and protection within Europe 1806–13 created by the French emperor Napoleon in order to exclude British trade. Apart from its function as economic warfare, the system also reinforced the French economy at the expense of other European states. It failed owing to British naval superiority.

Contra member of a Central American rightwing guerrilla force attempting to overthrow the democratically elected Nicaraguan Sandinista government 1979–90. The Contras, many of them mercenaries or former members of the deposed dictator Somoza's guard (see ◊Nicaraguan Revolution), operated mainly from bases outside Nicaragua, mostly in Honduras, with covert US funding, as revealed by the ◊Irangate hearings 1986–87.

In 1989 US president Bush announced an agreement with Congress to provide $41 million in 'nonlethal' aid to the Contras until Feb 1990. The Sandinista government was defeated by the National Opposition Union, a US-backed coalition, in the Feb 1990 elections. The Contras were disbanded in the same year but, fearing reprisals, a few hundred formed the Re-Contra (officially the 380 Legion) in Feb 1991.

Cook James 1728–1779. British naval explorer. After surveying the St Lawrence 1759, he made three voyages: 1768–71 to Tahiti, New Zealand, and Australia; 1772–75 to the South Pacific; and 1776–79 to the South and North Pacific, attempting to find the Northwest Passage and charting the Siberian coast. He was killed in Hawaii.

In 1768 Cook was given command of an expedition to the South Pacific to witness Venus eclipsing the Sun. He sailed in the *Endeavour* with other scientists, reaching Tahiti in April 1769. He then sailed around New Zealand and made a detailed survey of the east coast of Australia, naming New South Wales and Botany Bay. He returned to England 12 June 1771.

Now a commander, Cook set out 1772 with the *Resolution* and *Adventure* to search for the Southern Continent. The location of Easter Island was determined, and the Marquesas and Tonga Islands plotted. He also went to New Caledonia and Norfolk Island. Cook returned 25 July 1775, having sailed 60,000 mi in three years.

On 25 June 1776, he began his third and last voyage with the *Resolution* and *Discovery*. On the way to New Zealand, he visited several of the Cook or Hervey Islands and revisited the Hawaiian or Sandwich Islands. The ships sighted the North American coast at latitude 45° N and sailed north hoping to discover the Northwest Passage. He made a continuous survey as far as the Bering Strait, where the way was blocked by ice. Cook then surveyed the opposite coast of the strait (Siberia), and returned to Hawaii early 1779, where he was killed in a scuffle with islanders.

Coolidge (John) Calvin 1872–1933. 30th president of the USA 1923-29, a Republican. As governor of Massachusetts 1919, he was responsible for crushing a Boston police strike. As Warren ◊Harding's vice president 1921–23, he succeeded to the presidency on Harding's death (2 Aug 1923). He won the 1924 presidential election, and his period of office was marked by economic growth.

The business of America is business.

Calvin Coolidge
speech 17 Jan 1925

Cooperative Party political party founded in Britain 1917 by the cooperative movement to maintain its principles in parliamentary and local government. A written constitution was adopted 1938. The party had strong links with the Labour Party; from 1946 Cooperative Party candidates stood in elections as Cooperative and Labour Candidates and, after the 1959 general election, agreement was reached to limit the party's candidates to 30.

Coote Eyre 1726–1783. Irish general in British India. His victory 1760 at Wandiwash, followed by the capture of Pondicherry, ended French hopes of supremacy. He returned to India as commander in chief 1779, and several times defeated ◊Hyder Ali, sultan of Mysore.

Copenhagen, Battle of naval victory 2 April 1801 by a British fleet under Sir Hyde Parker (1739–1807) and ◊Nelson over the Danish

fleet. Nelson put his telescope to his blind eye and refused to see Parker's signal for withdrawal.

Copt descendant of those ancient Egyptians who adopted Christianity in the 1st century and refused to convert to Islam after the Arab conquest. They now form a small minority (about 5%) of Egypt's population.

The head of the Coptic church is the Patriarch of Alexandria, currently Shenouda III (1923–), 117th pope of Alexandria. Imprisoned by President Sadat 1981, he is opposed by Muslim fundamentalists.

Before the Arab conquest a majority of Christian Egyptians had adopted Monophysite views (that Christ had 'one nature' rather than being both human and divine). When this was condemned by the Council of Chalcedon 451, they became schismatic and were persecuted by the orthodox party, to which they were opposed on nationalistic as well as religious grounds. They readily accepted Arab rule, but were later subjected to persecution by their new masters. They are mainly town-dwellers, distinguishable in dress and customs from their Muslim compatriots. They rarely marry outside their own sect.

Corday Charlotte 1768–1793. French Girondin (right-wing republican during the French Revolution). After the overthrow of the Girondins by the more extreme Jacobins May 1793, she stabbed to death the Jacobin leader, Jean Paul Marat, with a bread knife as he sat in his bath in July of the same year. She was guillotined.

I have done my task, let others do theirs.

Charlotte Corday on being interrogated for murder July 1793

Corfu incident international crisis 27 Aug–27 Sept 1923 that marked the first assertion of power in foreign affairs by the Italian Fascist government. In 1923 an international commission was determining the frontier between Greece and Albania. On 27 Aug 1923, its chief, Italian general Tellini, was found (with four of his staff) murdered near the Albanian border, but on Greek territory. The Italian government under Benito Mussolini, backed by Italians, Fascist and anti-Fascist, sent an ultimatum to the Greek government demanding compensation, which was rejected. On 31 Aug Mussolini ordered the Italian bombardment and occupation of the Greek island of Corfu. The Greeks appealed to the League of Nations and, under pressure from Britain and France, Mussolini withdrew from Corfu on 27 Sept 1923. Greece had to accept most of the Italian demands, including the payment of a large indemnity.

Corinth (Greek *Kórinthos*) port in Greece, on the isthmus connecting the Peloponnese with the mainland. The rocky isthmus is bisected by the 6.5 km/4 mi Corinth canal, opened 1893. The site of the ancient city-state of Corinth lies 7 km/4.5 mi SW of the port.

Corinth was already a place of some commercial importance in the 9th century BC. At the end of the 6th century BC it joined the Peloponnesian League, and took a prominent part in the ◊Persian and the ◊Peloponnesian Wars. In 146 BC it was conquered by the Romans. The emperor Augustus (63 BC– AD 14) made it capital of the Roman province of Achaea. After many changes of ownership it became part of independent Greece 1822.

Corn Laws in Britain until 1846, laws used to regulate the export or import of cereals in order to maintain an adequate supply for consumers and a secure price for producers. For centuries the Corn Laws formed an integral part of the mercantile system in England; they were repealed because they became an unwarranted tax on food and a hindrance to British exports.

Although mentioned as early as the 12th century, the Corn Laws only became significant in the late 18th century. After the Napoleonic wars, with mounting pressure from a growing urban population, the laws aroused strong opposition because of their tendency to drive up prices. They were modified 1828 and 1842 and, partly as a result of the Irish potato famine, repealed by prime minister Robert Peel 1846.

Cornwallis Charles, 1st Marquess 1738–1805. British general in the ◊American Revolution until 1781, when his defeat at Yorktown led to final surrender and ended the war. He then served twice as governor general of India and once as viceroy of Ireland.

Corregidor island fortress off the Bataan Peninsula at the mouth of Manila Bay, Luzon, the Philippines. On 6 May 1942, Japanese forces captured Corregidor and its 10,000 US and Filipino defenders, completing their conquest of the Philippines. US forces recaptured Corregidor in Feb 1945.

corresponding society in British history, one of the first independent organizations for the working classes, advocating annual parliaments and universal male suffrage. The London Corresponding Society was founded 1792 by politicians Thomas Hardy (1752–1832) and John Horne Tooke (1736–1812). It later established branches in Scotland and the provinces.

Many of its activities had to be held in secret and government fears about the spread of revolutionary doctrines led to its banning 1799.

corsair pirate based on the N African Barbary Coast. From the 16th century onwards the corsairs plundered shipping in the Mediterranean and Atlantic, holding hostages for ransom or selling them as slaves. Although many punitive expeditions were sent against them, they were not suppressed until France occupied Algiers 1830.

Corsica (French *Corse*) island region of France, in the Mediterranean off the west coast of Italy. The Phocaeans of Ionia founded Alalia about 570 BC, and were succeeded in turn by the Etruscans, the Carthaginians, the Romans, the Vandals, and the Arabs. In the 14th century Corsica fell to the Genoese, and in the second half of the 18th century a Corsican nationalist, Pasquale Paoli (1725–1807), led an independence movement.

Genoa sold Corsica to France 1768. In World War II Corsica was occupied by Italy 1942–43. From 1962, French *pieds noirs* (refugees from Algeria), mainly vine growers, were settled in Corsica, and their prosperity helped to fan nationalist feeling, which demands an independent Corsica. This fuelled the National Liberation Front of Corsica (FNLC), banned 1983, which has engaged in some terrorist bombings.

I and my companions suffer from a disease of the heart that can be cured only with gold.

Hernán Cortés message sent to Montezuma 1519

Cortés Hernán (Ferdinand) 1485–1547. Spanish conquistador. He conquered the Aztec empire 1519–21, and secured Mexico for Spain.

Cortés went to the West Indies as a young man and in 1518 was given command of an expedition to Mexico. Landing with only 600 men, he was at first received as a god by the Aztec emperor ◊Montezuma II but was expelled from Tenochtitlán (Mexico City) when he was found not to be 'divine'. With the aid of Indian allies he recaptured the city 1521, and overthrew the Aztec empire. His conquests eventually included most of Mexico and N Central America.

Corunna, Battle of battle Jan 16 1809, during the ◊Peninsular War, to cover embarkation of

British troops after their retreat to Corunna; their commander, John Moore, was killed after ensuring a victory over the French.

Cosgrave Liam 1920– . Irish Fine Gael politician, prime minister of the Republic of Ireland 1973–77. As party leader 1965–77, he headed a Fine Gael–Labour coalition government from 1973. Relations between the Irish and UK governments improved under his premiership.

Cosgrave William Thomas 1880–1965. Irish politician. He took part in the ◊Easter Rising 1916 and sat in the Sinn Féin cabinet of 1919–21. Head of the Free State government 1922–33, he founded and led the Fine Gael opposition 1933–44.

Cossack people of S and SW Russia, Ukraine, and Poland, predominantly of Russian or Ukrainian origin, who took in escaped serfs and lived in independent communal settlements (military brotherhoods) from the 15th to the 19th century. Later they held land in return for military service in the cavalry under Russian and Polish rulers. After 1917, the various Cossack communities were incorporated into the Soviet administrative and collective system.

Costa Rica country in Central America, bounded N by Nicaragua, SE by Panama, E by the Caribbean Sea, and W by the Pacific Ocean.

history Originally occupied by Guaymi Indians, the area was visited by Christopher Columbus 1502 and was colonized by Spanish settlers from the 16th century, becoming independent 1821. Initially part of the ◊Mexican Empire, Costa Rica became – with El Salvador, Guatemala, Honduras, and Nicaragua – part of the ◊United Provinces of Central America 1824–38. After the collapse of the federation, there followed a decade of dictatorships and constitutional conventions before Costa Rica declared itself an independent republic. While the other Central American powers were involved in frequent conflicts at this time, Costa Rica managed to remain aloof, with a few exceptions.

Following the rule of the caudillos (military leaders), the last of whom was Tomás Guardia 1870–82, Costa Rica embarked on a half-century of tranquillity and the consolidation of democracy. The regime of Rafael Calderón 1940–48 saw an attempt to satisfy demands for change through social-security legislation and a new workers' code. Calderón himself was driven into exile after a revolution.

In 1949 a new constitution abolished the army, leaving defence to the Civil Guard. José Figueres, leader of the antigovernment forces in the previous year, became president. He cofounded the National Liberation Party (PLN), nationalized the banks, and introduced a social-security system. He was re-elected 1953.

There followed 16 years of mostly conservative rule, with the reversal of some PLN policies. In 1974 Daniel Oduber won the presidency for the PLN. He returned to socialist policies, extended the welfare state, and established friendly relations with communist states. Communist and left-wing parties were legalized.

In 1978 Rodrigo Carazo of the conservative Unity Coalition (CU) became president. His presidency was marked by economic collapse and allegations of his involvement in illegal arms trafficking between Cuba and El Salvador.

In 1982 Luis Alberto Monge, a former trade-union official and cofounder of the PLN, won a convincing victory in the presidential election. He introduced a 100-day emergency economic programme.

relations with Nicaragua The Monge government came under pressure from the USA to abandon its neutral stance and condemn the left-wing Sandinista regime in Nicaragua. Costa Rica was also urged to re-establish its army. Monge resisted the pressure and in 1983 reaffirmed his country's neutrality, but relations with Nicaragua deteriorated after border clashes between Sandinista forces and the Costa Rican Civil Guard. In 1985 Monge agreed to create a US-trained antiguerrilla guard, increasing doubts about Costa Rica's neutrality.

In 1986 Oscar Arias Sánchez became president on a neutralist platform, defeating the pro-US candidate, Rafael Angel Calderón, of the Christian Socialist Unity Party (PUSC). Arias worked tirelessly for peace in the region, hosting regional summit meetings and negotiating framework treaties. He won the Nobel Prize for Peace 1987 for his efforts. However, Calderón won the 1990 presidential election.

Cottar or *cotter* in feudal times, a free small holder and tenant of a cottage, mainly in S England

Council of Europe body constituted 1949 in Strasbourg, France (still its headquarters), to secure 'a greater measure of unity between the European countries'. The widest association of European states, it has a *Committee* of foreign ministers, a *Parliamentary Assembly* (with members from national parliaments), and a *European Commission* investigating violations of human rights.

Counter-Reformation movement initiated by the Catholic church at the Council of Trent 1545–63 to counter the spread of the ◊Reformation. Extending into the 17th century, its dominant forces included the rise of the Jesuits as an educating and missionary group and the deployment of the Spanish ◊Inquisition in other countries.

Country Party (official name *National Country Party* from 1975) Australian political party representing the interests of the farmers and people of the smaller towns; it holds the power balance between Liberals and Labor. It developed from about 1860, gained strength after the introduction of preferential voting 1918, and has been in coalition with the Liberals from 1949.

county name given by normans in England to Anglo-Saxon shires. Under the local Government Act 1972, which came into effect 1974, the existing English administrative counties were replaced by 45 new county areas of local government, and the 13 Welsh counties were reduced by amalgamation to eight. Under the Local Government (Scotland) Act 1973 the 33 counties of Scotland were amalgamated 1975 in nine new regions and three island areas. Northern Ireland has six geographical counties, but under the Local Government Act 1973 administration is through 26 district councils (single-tier authorities), each based on a main town or centre.

county palatine in medieval England, a county whose lord held particular rights, in lieu of the king, such as pardoning treasons and murders. Under William I there were four counties palatine: Chester, Durham, Kent, and Shropshire.

coup d'état or *coup* forcible takeover of the government of a country by elements from within that country, generally carried out by violent or illegal means. It differs from a revolution in typically being carried out by a small group (for example, of army officers or opposition politicians) to install its leader as head of government, rather than being a mass uprising by the people.

Early examples include the coup of 1799, in which Napoleon overthrew the Revolutionary Directory and declared himself first consul of France, and the coup of 1851 in which Louis Napoleon (then president) dissolved the French national assembly and a year later declared himself emperor. Coups of more recent times include the overthrow of the socialist government of Chile 1973 by a right-wing junta, the military seizure of power in

Surinam Dec 1990, and the short-lived removal of Mikhail Gorbachev from power in the USSR by hardline communists 19–22 Aug 1991.

Courtrai, Battle of defeat of French knights 11 July 1302 by the Flemings of Ghent and Bruges. It is also called the *Battle of the Spurs* because 800 gilt spurs were hung in Courtrai cathedral to commemorate the victory of billmen (soldiers with pikes) over unsupported cavalry.

Covenanter in Scottish history, one of the Presbyterian Christians who swore to uphold their forms of worship in a National Covenant, signed 28 Feb 1638, when Charles I attempted to introduce a liturgy on the English model into Scotland.

A general assembly abolished episcopacy, and the Covenanters signed with the English Parliament the Solemn League and Covenant 1643, promising military aid in return for the establishment of Presbyterianism in England. A Scottish army entered England and fought at Marston Moor 1644. At the Restoration Charles II revived episcopacy in Scotland, evicting resisting ministers, so that revolts followed 1666, 1679, and 1685. However, Presbyterianism was again restored 1688.

Coxey's Army march of the unemployed from Ohio to Washington DC, USA, during the Depression of the mid-1890s, led by businessman Joseph S Coxey (1854–1951). Some 500 marchers demonstrating outside the capital were violently dispersed by police May 1894 and Coxey was arrested.

Craig James 1871–1940. Ulster Unionist politician, the first prime minister of Northern Ireland 1921–40. Craig became a member of Parliament 1906, and was a highly effective organizer of Unionist resistance to Home Rule. As prime minister he carried out systematic discrimination against the Catholic minority, abolishing proportional representation 1929 and redrawing constituency boundaries to ensure Protestant majorities.

Cranmer Thomas 1489–1556. English cleric, archbishop of Canterbury from 1533. A Protestant convert, he helped to shape the doctrines of the Church of England under Edward VI. He was responsible for the issue of the Prayer Books of 1549 and 1552, and supported the succession of Lady Jane Grey 1553.

Condemned for heresy under the Catholic Mary Tudor, he at first recanted, but when his life was not spared, resumed his position and was burned at the stake, first holding to the fire the hand which had signed his recantation.

This was the hand that wrote it, therefore it shall suffer punishment.

Thomas Cranmer
at the stake 21 March 1556

Crassus Marcus Licinius *c.* 108–53 BC. Roman general who crushed the ◊Spartacus uprising 71 BC. In 60 BC he joined with Caesar and Pompey in the First Triumvirate and obtained command in the east 55 BC. Invading Mesopotamia, he was defeated by the Parthians at the battle of Carrhae, captured, and put to death.

Craxi Bettino 1934–   . Italian socialist politician, leader of the Italian Socialist Party (PSI) 1976-93, prime minister 1983–87.

Crazy Horse 1849–1877. Sioux Indian chief, one of the Indian leaders at the massacre of ◊Little Bighorn. He was killed when captured.

Crécy, Battle of first major battle of the Hundred Years' War 1346. Philip VI of France was defeated by Edward III of England at the village of Crécy-en-Ponthieu, now in Somme *département*, France, 18 km/11 mi NE of Abbeville.

Crédit Mobilier scandal US financial scandal 1872 in which more than a dozen US congressmen, including the future president James A Garfield, were implicated. It involved corrupt dealings by the Crédit Mobilier construction company at the expense of shareholders in the Union Pacific Railroad company in the late 1860s. When it broke, the affair tarnished President Ulysses S Grant's second term of office (1873–77).

Creole in the West Indies and Spanish America, originally someone of European descent born in the New World; later someone of mixed European and African descent. In Louisiana and other states on the Gulf of Mexico, it applies either to someone of French or Spanish descent or (popularly) to someone of mixed French or Spanish and African descent.

Crespo Joaquín 1845–1898. Venezuelan president 1884–86, 1892–98. A puppet of Antonia Guzman Blanco during his first term in office, Crespo seized power 1892 and is noted for his involvement in a boundary dispute with Great Britain over Guiana, where gold had been discovered.

Crete largest Greek island in the E Mediterranean Sea. It has remains of the ◊Minoan civilization 3000–1400 BC, (see ◊Knossos) and was successively under Roman, Byzantine, Venetian, and Turkish rule. The island was annexed by Greece 1913.

In 1941 it was captured by German forces from Allied troops who had retreated from the mainland and was retaken by the Allies 1944.

Crimea northern peninsula on the Black Sea, an autonomous republic of ◊Ukraine. Crimea was under Turkish rule 1475–1774; a subsequent brief independence was ended by Russian annexation 1783. Crimea was the republic of Taurida 1917–20 and the Crimean Autonomous Soviet Republic from 1920 until occupied by Germany 1942–1944.

It was then reduced to a region, its Tatar people being deported to Uzbekistan for collaboration. Although they were exonerated 1967 and some were allowed to return, others were forcibly re-exiled 1979. A drift back to their former homeland began 1987 and a federal ruling 1988 confirmed their right to residency. Since 1991 the Crimea has sought to gain independence from the Ukraine; the latter has resisted all secessionist moves.

Crimean War war 1853–56 between Russia and the allied powers of England, France, Turkey, and Sardinia. The war arose from British and French mistrust of Russia's ambitions in the Balkans. It began with an allied Anglo-French expedition to the Crimea to attack the Russian Black Sea city of Sevastopol. The battles of the river Alma, Balaclava (including the Charge of the Light Brigade), and Inkerman 1854 led to a siege which, owing to military mismanagement, lasted for a year until Sept 1855. The war was ended by the Treaty of Paris 1856. The scandal surrounding French and British losses through disease led to the organization of proper military nursing services by Florence Nightingale.

Cripps (Richard) Stafford 1889–1952. British Labour politician, expelled from the Labour Party 1939–45 for supporting a 'Popular Front' against Chamberlain's appeasement policy. He was ambassador to Moscow 1940–42, minister of aircraft production 1942–45, and chancellor of the Exchequer 1947–50.

Crispi Francesco 1819–1907. Italian prime minister 1887–91 and 1893–96. He advocated the ◊Triple Alliance of Italy with Germany and Austria, but was deposed 1896.

Croatia (Serbo-Croatian *Hrvatska*) country in central Europe, bounded N by Slovenia and Hungary, W by the Adriatic Sea, and E by Bosnia-Herzegovina and the Yugoslavian republic of Serbia.

history Part of Pannonia in Roman times, the region was settled by Carpathian Croats in the 7th century. Roman Catholicism was adopted 1054. For most of the 800 years from 1102 Croatia was an autonomous kingdom under the Hungarian crown, but often a battleground between Hungary, Byzantium, and Venice. After 1524, the whole country came under the rule of the Ottoman Empire, returning to the Hungarian crown only after the Peace of Karlovitz 1699.

Croatia was briefly an Austrian crownland 1849 and again a Hungarian crownland 1868. It was included in the kingdom of the Serbs, Croats, and Slovenes formed 1918 (called Yugoslavia from 1929). During World War II a Nazi puppet state, 'Greater Croatia', was established in April 1941 under Ante Pavelic (1889-1959). As many as 500,000 Serbs and 55,000 Jews were massacred by this Croatian regime, which sought to establish a 'pure' Croatian Catholic republic. In Nov 1945 it became a constituent republic within the Yugoslav Socialist Federal Republic, whose dominant figure was Marshal ◊Tito.

Serb–Croat separatism From the 1970s, resentful of perceived Serb dominance of the Yugoslav Federation, a violent separatist movement began to gain ground. Nationalist agitation continued through the 1980s and there was mounting industrial unrest from 1987 as spiralling inflation caused a sharp fall in living standards. In an effort to court popularity and concerned at the Serb chauvinism of Slobodan Milosevic, the Croatia League of Socialists (communists), later renamed the Party of Democratic Renewal (PDR), adopted an increasingly anti-Serb line from the mid-1980s. Following Slovenia's lead, it allowed the formation of rival political parties from 1989. In the multiparty republic elections of April–May 1990, the PDR was comprehensively defeated by the right-wing nationalist Croatian Democratic Union (HDZ). Led by Franjo Tudjman, who had been imprisoned in 1972 for his nationalist activities, the HDZ secured almost a two-thirds assembly majority. Tudjman became president.

secession from Yugoslavia In Feb 1991 the Croatian assembly, along with that of neighbouring Catholic Slovenia, issued a proclamation calling for secession from Yugoslavia and the establishment of a new confederation that excluded Serbia and Montenegro. It also ordered the creation of an independent Croatian army. Concerned at possible maltreatment in a future independent Croatia, Serb militants announced March 1991 the secession from

Croatia of the self-proclaimed 'Serbian Autonomous Region of Krajina', containing 250,000 Serbs. In a May 1991 referendum there was 90% support in Krajina for its remaining with Serbia and Montenegro within a residual Yugoslavia. A week later, Croatia's electors voted overwhelmingly (93%) for independence within a loose confederation of Yugoslav sovereign states. On 26 June 1991 the Croatian government, in concert with Slovenia, issued a unilateral declaration of independence.

civil war From July 1991 there was escalating conflict with the Serb-dominated Yugoslav army and civil war within Croatia. Independent 'governments' were proclaimed in Krajina and E and W Slavonia. A succession of cease-fires ordered by the Yugoslav federal presidency and the European Community passed unobserved and by Sept 1991 at least a third of Croatia had fallen under Serb control, with intense fighting taking place around the towns of Osijek and Vukovar. Croatia's prots were besieged and at least 50,000 people were made refugees. Rich in oil, Croatia retaliated with an oil-supply blockade on Serbia and Oct 1991 severed all official relations with Yugoslavia.

cease-fire A peace plan was successfully brokered Jan 1992 by United Nations (UN) envoy Cyrus Vance. The agreement provided for an immediate cease-fire, the full withdrawal of the Yugoslav army from Croatia, and the deployment of 10,000 UN troops in Krajina and E and W Slavonia until a political settlement was worked out. The accord was disregarded by the breakaway Serb leader in Krajina, Milan Babic, but recognised by the main Serbian and Croatian forces. Under German pressure, Croatia's and Slovenias independence was recognised by the EC, the USA, and then the UN 1992. During March and April 1992 UN peacekeeping forces were drafted into Croatia and gradually took control of Krajina, although Croatian forces continued to shell Krajina's capital, Knin. Tudjman was directly elected president in Aug; the CDU won an overwhelming victory in assembly elections.

Serb-held areas retaken In Jan 1993 Croatia launched an offensive to retake parts of Serb-held Krajina, violating the 1992 accord. An accord was signed 1994 with Bosnia-Herzegovina's Muslim and ethnic-Croat leaders creating a Muslim-Croat federation, eventually to form a loose confederation with Croatia. An offensive by Tudjman 1995 took Krajina and W Slavonia, forcing Croatian Serbs to flee. The CDU won most seats but not a majority in elections. Croatian Serbs agreed to hand back E Slavonia to Croatia over two years. Diplomatic relations were restored between Croatia and Yugoslavia Aug 1996, and Croatia entered the Council of Europe Oct 1996.

Crockett Davy 1786–1836. US folk hero, born in Tennessee, a Democratic Congressman 1827-31 and 1833-35. A series of books, of which he may have been part-author, made him into a mythical hero of the frontier, but their Whig associations cost him his office. He died in the battle of the ◊Alamo during the War of Texan Independence.

Croesus 6th century BC. Last king of Lydia *c.* 560-546 BC, famed for his wealth. Dominant over the Greek cities of the Asia Minor coast, he was defeated and captured by ◊Cyrus the Great and Lydia was absorbed into the Persian empire.

croft small farm in the Highlands of Scotland, traditionally farming common land cooperatively; the 1886 Crofters Act gave security of tenure to crofters. Today, although grazing land is still shared, arable land is typically enclosed.

Cromwell Oliver 1599–1658. English general and politician, Puritan leader of the Parliamentary side in the ◊Civil War. He raised cavalry forces (later called *Ironsides*) which aided the victories at Edgehill 1642 and ◊Marston Moor 1644, and organized the New Model Army, which he led (with General Fairfax) to victory at Naseby 1645. He declared Britain a republic ('the Commonwealth') 1649, following the execution of Charles I. As Lord Protector (ruler) from 1653, Cromwell established religious toleration and raised Britain's prestige in Europe on the basis of an alliance with France against Spain.

Cromwell was born at Huntingdon, NW of Cambridge, son of a small landowner. He entered Parliament 1629 and became active in events leading to the Civil War. Failing to secure a constitutional settlement with Charles I 1646–48, he defeated the 1648 Scottish invasion at Preston. A special commission, of which Cromwell was a member, tried the king and condemned him to death, and a republic, known as 'the Commonwealth', was set up.

The ◊Levellers demanded radical reforms, but he executed their leaders in 1649. He used terror to crush Irish clan resistance 1649–50, and defeated the Scots (who had acknowledged Charles II) at Dunbar 1650 and Worcester 1651. In 1653, having forcibly expelled the corrupt 'Rump' Parliament, he summoned a convention ('Barebone's Parliament'), soon dissolved as too radical, and under a constitution (Instrument of Government) drawn up by the army leaders, became Protector (king in all

but name). The parliament of 1654–55 was dissolved as uncooperative, and after a period of military dictatorship, his last parliament offered him the crown; he refused because he feared the army's republicanism.

A few honest men are better than numbers.

Oliver Cromwell letter Sept 1643

Cromwell Richard 1626–1712. Son of Oliver Cromwell, he succeeded his father as Lord Protector but resigned May 1659, having been forced to abdicate by the army. He lived in exile after the Restoration until 1680, when he returned.

Cromwell Thomas, Earl of Essex *c.* 1485–1540. English politician who drafted the legislation making the Church of England independent of Rome. Originally in Lord Chancellor Wolsey's service, he became secretary to Henry VIII 1534 and the real director of government policy; he was executed for treason.

Cromwell had Henry divorced from Catherine of Aragon by a series of acts that proclaimed him head of the church. From 1536 to 1540 Cromwell suppressed the monasteries, ruthlessly crushed all opposition, and favoured Protestantism, which denied the divine right of the pope. His mistake in arranging Henry's marriage to Anne of Cleves (to cement an alliance with the German Protestant princes against France and the Holy Roman Empire) led to his being accused of treason and beheaded.

Cronje Piet Arnoldus 1835–1911. Boer commander who fought the British in both ◊South African Wars (1881 and 1899–1902). He was defeated and surrendered his 4,000-strong force to Field Marshal Roberts at Paardeberg, Feb 1900.

crown colony any British colony that is under the direct legislative control of the crown and does not possess its own system of representative government. Crown colonies are administered by a crown-appointed governor or by elected or nominated legislative and executive councils with an official majority. Usually the crown retains rights of veto and of direct legislation by orders in council.

crusade European war against non-Christians and heretics, sanctioned by the pope; in particular, the Crusades, a series of wars 1096–1291 undertaken by European rulers to recover Palestine from the Muslims. Motivated by religious zeal, the desire for land, and the trading

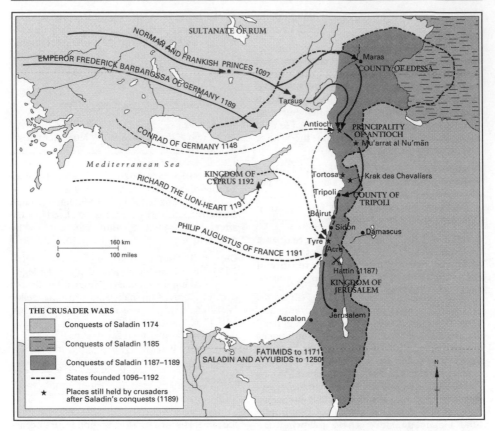

The Crusader Wars *Following a call by Pope Urban II at the Council of Clermont to free the Holy Land from Muslim rule, the first three crusades (1095–99, 1147–49, 1189–92) founded a number of Christian enclaves along the E Mediterranean coast. Jerusalem was captured by the crusaders 1099, but lost to the Muslim leader Saladin in 1187. The Third Crusade ended with a treaty between Richard I of England and Saladin, whereby Christian possessions were recognized and freedom of pilgrimage guaranteed.*

ambitions of the major Italian cities, the Crusades were varied in their aims and effects.

First Crusade 1095–99 led by Baldwin of Boulogne, Godfrey of Bouillon, and Peter the Hermit. Motivated by occupation of Anatolia and Jerusalem by the Seljuk Turks. The crusade succeeded in recapturing Jerusalem and establishing a series of Latin kingdoms on the Syrian coast.

Second Crusade 1147–49 led by Louis VII of France and Emperor Conrad III; a complete failure.

Third Crusade 1189–92 led by Philip II Augustus of France and Richard I of England. Failed to recapture Jerusalem, which had been seized by Saladin 1187.

Fourth Crusade 1202–04 led by William of Montferrata, and Baldwin of Hainault.

Directed against Egypt but diverted by the Venetians to sack and divide Constantinople.

Children's Crusade 1212 thousands of children crossed Europe on their way to Palestine but many were sold into slavery in Marseille, or died of disease and hunger.

Fifth Crusade 1218–21 led by King Andrew of Hungary, Cardinal Pelagius, King John of Jerusalem, and King Hugh of Cyprus. Captured and then lost Damietta, Egypt.

Sixth Crusade 1228–29 led by the Holy Roman emperor Frederick II. Jerusalem recovered by negotiation with the sultan of Egypt, but the city was finally lost 1244.

Seventh and Eighth Crusades 1249–54, 1270–72 both led by Louis IX of France. Acre, the last Christian fortress in Syria, was lost 1291.

Cuba island country in the Caribbean Sea, the largest of the West Indies, off the S coast of Florida and to the E of Mexico.

history The first Europeans to visit Cuba were those of the expedition of Christopher Columbus 1492, who found Arawak Indians there. From 1511 Cuba was a Spanish colony, its economy based on sugar plantations worked by slaves, who were first brought from Africa 1523 to replace the decimated Indian population. Slavery was not abolished until 1886.

Cuba was ceded to the USA 1898, at the end of the ◊Spanish-American War. Under US administration, roads, communications, and health services were improved. A new judicial system was set up on the US model. However, early enthusiasm after independence from Spain soon faded. A republic was proclaimed 1901, but the USA retained its naval base and asserted a right to intervene in internal affairs until 1934.

Batista dictatorship In 1933 an army sergeant, Fulgencio ◊Batista, seized and held power until he retired 1944. In 1952 he regained power in a bloodless coup and began another period of rule that many Cubans found oppressive. In 1953 a young lawyer and son of a sugar planter, Dr Fidel Castro, tried to overthrow him but failed. He went into exile to prepare for another coup in 1956 but was again defeated. He fled to the hills with Dr Ernesto 'Che' ◊Guevara and ten others to form a guerrilla force.

revolution In 1959 Castro's force of 5,000 guerrillas deposed Batista, to great popular acclaim. The 1940 constitution was suspended and replaced by a 'Fundamental Law', power being vested in a council of ministers with Castro as prime minister, his brother Raúl as his deputy, and Che Guevara, reputedly, as the next in command. In 1960 the USA broke off diplomatic relations after all US businesses in Cuba were nationalized without compensation. In 1961 it went further, sponsoring a full-scale (but abortive) invasion, the ◊Bay of Pigs episode. In Dec of that year Castro proclaimed a communist state whose economy would develop along Marxist-Leninist lines.

Cuban missile crisis In 1962 Cuba was expelled from the Organization of American States (OAS), which initiated a full political and economic blockade. Castro responded by tightening relations with the USSR that, in the same year, supplied missiles with atomic warheads for installation in Cuba. The ◊Cuban missile crisis brought the USA and the USSR to the brink of nuclear war, but conflict was averted when the USSR agreed to dismantle the missiles at the US president's insistence.

With Soviet help, Cuba made substantial economic and social progress 1965–72. In 1976 a referendum approved a socialist constitution, and Fidel Castro and his brother were elected president and vice president.

foreign policy During the following five years Cuba played a larger role in world affairs, particularly in Africa, to the disquiet of the USA. Cuban troops played an important role in Angola, supporting the Luanda government against South African-backed rebels.

Re-elected 1981, Castro offered to discuss foreign policy with the USA but Cuba's support for Argentina, against Britain, cooled relations and drew it closer to other Latin American countries. Cuban support of leftist rebels seeking to overthrow the repressive US-backed government of El Salvador caused continuing strains with the USA.

Castro reaffirmed his communist orthodoxy in the light of events in eastern Europe 1989–90. The advent of Soviet leader Gorbachev and the USSR's abandonment of its policy of supporting Third World revolutions led in 1989 to a curtailment of Cuba's foreign military interventions. In Sept 1991 the USSR announced that all Soviet troops were to be withdrawn.

Cuban missile crisis confrontation in international relations 1962 when Soviet rockets were installed in Cuba and US president Kennedy compelled Soviet leader Khrushchev, by an ultimatum, to remove them. The drive by the USSR to match the USA in nuclear weaponry dates from this event.

The USA imposed a naval 'quarantine' around the island, and the two superpowers came closer to possible nuclear war than at any other time. Soviet inferiority in nuclear weapons forced a humiliating capitulation to Kennedy's demands. Some historians maintain that Kennedy's lack of resolve during the ◊Bay of Pigs invasion attempt gave Khrushchev reason to believe that the USA would not resist the introduction of Soviet missiles into Cuba.

Culloden, Battle of defeat 1746 of the ◊Jacobite rebel army of the British prince ◊Charles Edward Stuart by the Duke of Cumberland on a stretch of moorland in Inverness-shire, Scotland. This battle effectively ended the military challenge of the Jacobite rebellion.

Cultural Revolution Chinese mass movement 1966–69 begun by Communist Party chair Mao

Zedong, directed against the upper middle class – bureaucrats, artists, and academics – who were killed, imprisoned, humiliated, or 'resettled'. Intended to 'purify' Chinese communism, it was also an attempt by Mao to renew his political and ideological pre-eminence inside China. Half a million people are estimated to have been killed.

The 'revolution' was characterized by the violent activities of the semimilitary Red Guards, most of them students. Many established and learned people were humbled and eventually sent to work on the land, and from 1966 to 1970 universities were closed. Although the revolution was brought to an end in 1969, the resulting bureaucratic and economic chaos had many long-term effects. The ultra-leftist ◊Gang of Four, led by Mao's wife Jiang Qing and defence minister Lin Biao, played prominent roles in the Cultural Revolution. The chief political victims were ◊Liu Shaoqi and ◊Deng Xiaoping, who were depicted as 'bourgeois reactionaries'. After Mao's death, the Cultural Revolution was criticized officially and the verdicts on hundreds of thousands of people who were wrongly arrested and persecuted were reversed.

Cuman member of a powerful alliance of Turkic-speaking peoples of the Middle Ages, which dominated the steppes in the 11th and 12th centuries and built an empire reaching from the river Volga to the Danube.

For a generation the Cumans held up the Mongol advance on the Volga, but in 1238 a Cuman and Russian army was defeated near Astrakhan, and 200,000 Cumans took refuge in Hungary, where they settled and where their language died out only about 1775. The Mameluke dynasty of Egypt was founded by Cuman ex-slaves. Most of the so-called Tatars of S Russia were of Cuman origin.

I am now in a country so much our enemy that there is hardly any intelligence to be got, and whenever we do procure any it is the business of the country to have it contradicted.

Duke of Cumberland letter from Scotland 1746

Cumberland William Augustus, Duke of Cumberland 1721–1765. British general who ended the Jacobite rising in Scotland with the Battle of Culloden 1746; his brutal repression of the Highlanders earned him the nickname of 'Butcher'.

cuneiform ancient writing system formed of combinations of wedge-shaped strokes, usually impressed on clay. It was probably invented by the Sumerians, and was in use in Mesopotamia as early as the middle of the 4th millennium BC.

It was adopted and modified by the Assyrians, Babylonians, Elamites, Hittites, Persians, and many other peoples with different languages. In the 5th century BC it fell into disuse, but sporadically reappeared in later centuries. The decipherment of cuneiform scripts was pioneered by the German George Grotefend 1802 and the British orientalist Henry Rawlinson 1846.

Cunningham Andrew Browne, 1st Viscount Cunningham of Hyndhope 1883–1963. British admiral in World War II, commander in chief in the Mediterranean 1939–42, maintaining British control; as commander in chief of the Allied Naval Forces in the Mediterranean Feb–Oct 1943 he received the surrender of the Italian fleet.

Cuno Wilhelm 1876–1933. German industrialist and politician who was briefly chancellor of the Weimar Republic 1923.

Cunobelin see ◊Cymbeline.

Curragh 'Mutiny' demand March 1914 by the British general Hubert Gough and his officers, stationed at Curragh, Ireland, that they should not be asked to take part in forcing Protestant Ulster to participate in Home Rule. They were subsequently allowed to return to duty, and after World War I the solution of partition was adopted.

Curtin John 1885–1945. Australian Labor politician, prime minister and minister of defence 1941–45. He was elected leader of the Labor Party 1935. As prime minister, he organized the mobilization of Australia's resources to meet the danger of Japanese invasion during World War II.

Curzon George Nathaniel, 1st Marquess Curzon of Kedleston 1859–1925. British Conservative politician, viceroy of India 1899–1905. During World War I, he was a member of the cabinet 1916–19. As foreign secretary 1919–24, he set up a British protectorate over Persia.

Curzon Line Polish-Soviet frontier proposed after World War I by the territorial commission of the Versailles conference 1919, based on the eastward limit of areas with a predominantly Polish population. It acquired its name after British foreign secretary Lord Curzon suggested in 1920 that the Poles, who had invaded the USSR, should retire to this line pending a Russo-Polish peace conference. The frontier established 1945 generally follows the Curzon Line.

Custer George A(rmstrong) 1839–1876. US Civil War general, the Union's youngest brigadier general as a result of a brilliant war record. He campaigned against the Sioux from 1874, and was killed with a detachment of his troops by the forces of Sioux chief Sitting Bull in the Battle of Little Bighorn, Montana: also called *Custer's last stand*, 25 June 1876.

Cymbeline or *Cunobelin* 1st century AD. King of the Catuvellauni AD 5–40, who fought unsuccessfully against the Roman invasion of Britain. His capital was at Colchester, England.

Cyprus island in the Mediterranean Sea, off the S coast of Turkey and W coast of Syria.

history The strategic position of Cyprus has long made it a coveted territory, and from the 15th century BC it was colonized by a succession of peoples from the mainland. In the 8th century it was within the Assyrian empire, then the Babylonian, Egyptian, and Persian. As part of Ptolemaic Egypt, it was seized by Rome 58 BC. From AD 395 it was ruled by Byzantium, until taken 1191 by England during the Third ◊Crusade. In 1489 it was annexed by Venice, and became part of the Ottoman Empire 1571. It came under British administration 1878 and was annexed by Britain 1914, becoming a crown colony 1925.

enosis In 1955 a guerrilla war against British rule was begun by Greek Cypriots seeking *enosis*, or unification with Greece. The chief organization in this campaign was the National Organization of Cypriot Combatants (EOKA), and its political and military leaders were the head of the Greek Orthodox Church in Cyprus, Archbishop Makarios, and General Grivas. In 1956 Makarios and other enosis leaders were deported by the British government. After years of negotiation, Makarios was allowed to return to become president of a new, independent Greek-Turkish Cyprus, retaining British military and naval bases.

Greek-Turkish conflict In 1963 the Turks withdrew from power-sharing, and fighting began. The following year a United Nations peacekeeping force was set up to keep the two sides apart. After a prolonged period of mutual hostility, relations improved and talks were resumed, with the Turks arguing for a federal state and the Greeks wanting a unitary one.

In 1971 General Grivas returned to the island and began a guerrilla campaign against the Makarios government, which he believed had failed the Greek community. Three years later he died, and his supporters were purged by Makarios, who was himself deposed 1974 by Greek officers of the National Guard and an Enosis extremist, Nicos Sampson, who became president. Makarios fled to Britain.

At the request of the Turkish Cypriot leader Rauf Denktaş, Turkey sent troops to the island 1974, taking control of the north and dividing Cyprus along what became known as the Attila Line, cutting off about a third of the total territory. Sampson resigned, the military regime that had appointed him collapsed, and Makarios returned. The Turkish Cypriots established an independent government for what they called the 'Turkish Federated State of Cyprus' (TFSC), with Denktaş as president.

In 1977 Makarios died and was succeeded by Spyros Kyprianou, who had been president of the house of representatives. In 1980 UN-sponsored peace talks were resumed. The Turkish Cypriots offered to hand back about 4% of the 35% of the territory they controlled and to resettle 40,000 of the 200,000 refugees who had fled to the north, but stalemate was reached on a constitutional settlement.

The Turks wanted equal status for the two communities, equal representation in government, and firm links with Turkey. The Greeks, on the other hand, favoured an alternating presidency, strong central government, and representation in the legislature on a proportional basis.

seeking a solution Between 1982 and 1985 several attempts by the Greek government in Athens and the UN to find a solution failed, and the Turkish Republic of Northern Cyprus (TRNC), with Denktaş as president, was formally declared, but recognized only by Turkey.

In 1985 a meeting between Denktaş and Kyprianou failed to reach agreement, and the UN secretary general drew up proposals for a two-zone federal Cyprus, with a Greek president and a Turkish vice president, but this was not found acceptable. Meanwhile, both Kyprianou and Denktaş had been re-elected.

In 1988 Georgios Vassiliou was elected president of the Greek part of Cyprus, and in Sept talks began between him and Denktaş. However, these were abandoned Sept 1989, reportedly because of Denktaş's intransigence. Peace talks were resumed Aug 1992 under UN auspices in New York, but the dispute between the communities remained unresolved. Because of its strategic importance in the Mediterranean, Cyprus is of international concern.

Cyrenaica area of E Libya, colonized by the Greeks in the 7th century BC; later held by the Egyptians, Romans, Arabs, Turks, and Italians. There are archaeological ruins at Cyrene and Apollonia.

The Greek colonies passed under the rule of the Ptolemies 322 BC, and in 174 BC Cyrenaica became a Roman province. It was conquered by the Arabs in the 7th century AD, by Turkey in the 16th century, and by Italy 1912, when it was developed as a colony. Captured by the British 1942, it remained under British control until it became a province of the new kingdom of Libya from 1951. In 1963 the area was split into a number of smaller divisions under a constitutional reorganization.

Cyrus the Great died 529 BC. Founder of the Persian Empire. As king of Persia, he was originally subject to the ◊Medes, whose empire he overthrew 550 BC. He captured ◊Croesus 546 BC, and conquered ◊Lydia, adding Babylonia (including Syria and Palestine) to his empire 539 BC, allowing exiled Jews to return to Jerusalem. He died fighting in Afghanistan.

Czechoslovakia former country in E central Europe, which came into existence as an independent republic 1918 after the break-up of the ◊Austro-Hungarian empire at the end of World War I. It consisted originally of the Bohemian crownlands (◊Bohemia, ◊Moravia, and part of ◊Silesia) and ◊Slovakia, the area of Hungary inhabited by Slavonic peoples; to this was added as a trust, part of Ruthenia when the Allies and associated powers recognized the new republic under the treaty of St Germain-en-Laye. Besides the Czech and Slovak peoples, the country included substantial minorities of German origin, long settled in the north, and of Hungarian (or Magyar) origin in the south. Despite the problems of welding into a nation such a mixed group of people, Czechoslovakia made considerable political and economic progress until the troubled 1930s. It was the only East European state to retain a parliamentary democracy throughout the interwar period, with five coalition governments (dominated by the Agrarian and National Socialist parties), with Thomas ◊Masaryk serving as president.

Munich Agreement The rise to power of the Nazi leader Hitler in Germany brought a revival of opposition among the German-speaking population, and nationalism among the Magyar speakers. In addition, the Slovak clerical party demanded autonomy for Slovakia. In 1938 the ◊Munich Agreement was made between Britain, France, Germany, and Italy, without consulting Czechoslovakia, resulting in the Sudetenland being taken from Czechoslovakia and given to Germany. Six months later Hitler occupied all Czechoslovakia. A government in exile was established in London under Eduard ◊Beneš until the liberation 1945 by Soviet and US troops. In the same year some 2 million Sudeten Germans were expelled, and Czech Ruthenia was transferred to the Ukraine, USSR.

Elections 1946 gave the left a slight majority, and in Feb 1948 the communists seized power, winning an electoral victory in May. Beneš, who had been president since 1945, resigned. The country was divided into 19 and, in 1960, into 10 regions plus Prague and Bratislava. There was a Stalinist regime during the 1950s, under presidents Klement Gottwald (1948–53), Antonin Zapotocky (1953-57), and Antonin Novotný (1957–68).

Prague Spring Pressure from students and intellectuals brought about policy changes from 1965. Following Novotný's replacement as the Communist Party (CCP) leader by Alexander ◊Dubček and as president by war hero General Ludvík Svoboda (1895-1979), and the appointment of Oldřich Černik as prime minister, a liberalization programme began 1968.

Despite assurances that Czechoslovakia would remain within the ◊Warsaw Pact, the USSR viewed these events with suspicion, and in Aug 1968 sent 600,000 troops from Warsaw Pact countries to restore the orthodox line. Over 70 deaths and some 266 injuries were inflicted by this invasion. After the invasion a purge of liberals began in the CCP, with Dr Gustáv ◊Husák (a Slovak Brezhnevite) replacing Dubček as CCP leader 1969 and Lubomír Štrougal (a Czech) becoming prime minister 1970. Svoboda remained as president until 1975 and negotiated the Soviet withdrawal. In 1973 an amnesty was extended to some of the 40,000 who had fled after the 1968 invasion, signalling a slackening of repression. But a new crackdown commenced 1977, triggered by a human-rights manifesto ('Charter 77') signed by over 700 intellectuals and former party officials in response to the 1975 Helsinki ◊Conference on Security and Cooperation in Europe (CSCE).

protest movement Czechoslovakia under Husák emerged as a loyal ally of the USSR during the 1970s and early 1980s. However, after Mikhail Gorbachev's accession to the Soviet leadership 1985, pressure for economic and administrative reform mounted. In 1987 Husák, while remaining president, was replaced as CCP leader by Miloš Jakeš (1923–), a Czech-born economist. Working with prime minister Ladislav Adamec, a reformist, he began to introduce a reform programme (*prestavba* 'restructuring') on the USSR's perestroika model. His approach was cautious, and dissident activity, which became increasingly widespread 1988–89, was suppressed.

Influenced by events elsewhere in Eastern Europe, a series of initially student-led prodemocracy rallies were held in Prague's Wenceslas Square from 17 Nov 1989. Support for the protest movement rapidly increased after the security forces' brutal suppression of the early rallies; by 20 Nov there were more than 200,000 demonstrators in Prague and a growing number in Bratislava. An umbrella opposition movement, Civic Forum, was swiftly formed under the leadership of playwright and Charter 77 activist Václav ◊Havel, which attracted the support of prominent members of the small political parties that were members of the ruling CCP-dominated National Front coalition.

With the protest movement continuing to grow, Jakeš resigned as CCP leader 24 Nov and was replaced by Karel Urbanek (1941–   ), a South Moravian, and the politburo was purged. Less than a week later, following a brief general strike, the national assembly voted to amend the constitution to strip the CCP of its 'leading role' in the government, and thus of its monopoly on power. Opposition parties, beginning with Civic Forum and its Slovak counterpart, Public Against Violence (PAV), were legalized. On 7 Dec Adamec resigned as prime minister and was replaced by Marián Čalfa, who formed a 'grand coalition' government in which key posts, including the foreign, financial, and labour ministries, were given to former dissidents. Čalfa resigned from the CCP Jan 1990, but remained premier.

reform government On 27 Dec 1989 the rehabilitated Dubček was sworn in as chair of the federal assembly, and on 29 Dec Havel became president of Czechoslovakia. The new reform government immediately extended an amnesty to 22,000 prisoners, secured agreements from the CCP that it would voluntarily give up its existing majorities in the federal and regional assemblies and state agencies, and promised multiparty elections for June 1990. It also announced plans for reducing the size of the armed forces, called on the USSR to pull out its 75,000 troops stationed in the country, and applied for membership of the International Monetary Fund and World Bank. Václav Havel was re-elected president, unopposed, for a further two years by the assembly on 5 July 1990.

moves towards privatization Some devolution of power was introduced 1990 to ameliorate friction between the Czech and Slovak republics. A bill of rights was passed Jan 1991, and moves were made towards price liberalization and privatization of small businesses. In Feb 1991 a bill was passed to return property nationalized after 25 Feb 1948 to its original

owners, the first such restitution measure in Eastern Europe, and legislation was approved May 1991. The name 'Czech and Slovak Federative Republic' was adopted April 1990. In Nov 1990 the Slovak Republic declared Slovak the official language of the republic, a move promoted by the Slovak National Party.

new parties emerge During the opening months of 1991, Civic Forum began to split in two: a centre-right faction under the leadership of finance minister Václav Klaus, designated the Civic Democratic Party April 1991; and a social-democratic group, the Civic Forum Liberal Club, renamed the Civic Movement April 1991, led by foreign minister Jiri Dienstbier and deputy prime minister Pavel Rychetsky. The two factions agreed to work together until the next election. In March 1991 PAV also split when Slovak premier Vladimir Meciar formed a splinter grouping pledged to greater autonomy from Prague. In April 1991 he was dismissed as head of the Slovak government by the presidium of the Slovak National Council (parliament) because of policy differences. Protest rallies were held in the Slovak capital of Bratislava by Meciar supporters. Jan Carnogursky, leader of the Christian Democratic Movement, junior partner in the PAV-led ruling coalition, took over as Slovak premier. In Oct 1991, PAV became a liberal-conservative political party, and was renamed the Civic Democratic Union–Public Action Against Violence (PAV), led by Martin Porubjak. The major political parties were becoming divided into separate Czech and Slovak groups.

foreign relations In July 1991, a month after the final withdrawal of Soviet troops, the USSR agreed to pay the equivalent of US$ 160 million to Czechoslovakia in compensation for damage done to the country since the 1968 Soviet invasion. In Aug, the phased privatization of Czech industry commenced, with 50 of its largest businesses put up for sale on international markets. Friendship treaties were signed with France, Germany, and the USSR in Oct 1991.

Czech and Slovak split A general election was held June 1992. Václav Klaus, leader of the CDP, became prime minister, and President Havel resigned. It was agreed that two separate Czech and Slovak states would be created from Jan 1993, Meciar to be the Czech president and Klaus the Slovak. In Oct 1992 the Slovakia-based political party, Civic Democratic Union–Public Against Violence (PAV), became the Civic Democratic Union (CDU). The Czech Republic and the Slovak Republic became sovereign states 1 Jan 1993.

Dachau site of a Nazi ◊concentration camp during World War II, in Bavaria, Germany.

Dahomey former name (until 1975) of the People's Republic of ◊Benin.

Daimyō (Japanese 'great name') in feudal Japan, a warlord, a large upper-class landowner who employed a body of samurai. In wartime these armed forces had to be put at the disposal of the shogun.

A *daimyō* was a vassal whose landholding was assessed at more than 10,000 *koku* of rice, this being the chief means of exchange. There were 250–300 *daimyō* (the number varied with circumstances). Although they acknowledged the rule of the emperor and shogun, they enforced their own law and did not initially pay tax; however, the costs of maintaining the samurai and other obligatory expenses were very heavy and by 1700 the debts of the *daimyō* were estimated at 100 times the total amount of money in Japan. In 1868–69 the *daimyō* were officially abolished but in most cases became governors of the provinces they had held.

Daladier Edouard 1884–1970. French Radical politician. As prime minister April 1938–March 1940, he signed the ◊Munich Agreement 1938 (by which the Sudeten districts of Czechoslovakia were ceded to Germany) and declared war on Germany 1939. He resigned 1940 because of his unpopularity for failing to assist Finland against Russia. He was arrested on the fall of France 1940 and was a prisoner in Germany 1943-45. Following the end of World War II he was re-elected to the Chamber of Deputies 1946–58.

Daley Richard Joseph 1902–1976. US politician and controversial mayor of Chicago 1955–76. He built a formidable political machine and ensured a Democratic presiden-

tial victory 1960 when J F Kennedy was elected. He hosted the turbulent national Democratic convention 1968.

Dalhousie James Andrew Broun Ramsay, 1st Marquess and 10th Earl of Dalhousie 1812–1860. British administrator, governor general of India 1848–56. In the second Sikh War he annexed the Punjab 1849, and, after the second Burmese War, Lower Burma 1853. He reformed the Indian army and civil service and furthered social and economic progress.

Dalton Hugh, Baron Dalton 1887–1962. British Labour politician and economist. Chancellor of the Exchequer from 1945, he oversaw nationalization of the Bank of England, but resigned 1947 after making a disclosure to a lobby correspondent before a budget speech.

Danby Thomas Osborne, Earl of Danby 1631–1712. British Tory politician. He entered Parliament 1665, acted as Charles II's chief minister 1673–78 and was created earl of Danby 1674, but was imprisoned in the Tower of London 1678–84. In 1688 he signed the invitation to William of Orange to take the throne. Danby was again chief minister 1690–95, and in 1694 was created Duke of Leeds.

Dandolo Venetian family that produced four doges (rulers), of whom the most outstanding, *Enrico* (*c.* 1120–1205), became doge in 1193. He greatly increased the dominions of the Venetian republic and accompanied the crusading army that took Constantinople in 1203.

danegeld in English history, a tax imposed from 991 by Anglo-Saxon kings to pay tribute to the Vikings. After the Norman Conquest the tax continued to be levied until 1162, and the Normans used it to finance military operations.

Danelaw 11th-century name for the area of N and E England settled by the Vikings in the 9th century. Its linguistic influence is still apparent.

Danton Georges Jacques 1759–1794. French revolutionary. Originally a lawyer, during the early years of the Revolution he was one of the most influential people in Paris. He organized the uprising 10 Aug 1792 that overthrew Louis XVI and the monarchy, roused the country to expel the Prussian invaders, and in April 1793 formed the revolutionary tribunal and the *Committee of Public Safety*, of which he was the leader until July of that year. Thereafter he lost power to the ◊Jacobins, and, when he attempted to recover it, was arrested and guillotined.

Danzig German name for the Polish port of ◊Gdánsk.

Danelaw – extent of Danish rule in England By 866 Viking raids on the British Isles and NW Europe, which began in the 8th century and intensified in the 9th, were opposed by the Anglo-Saxons under Alfred the Great. Successive marauding bands settled in N and E England, where their rule and culture (Danelaw) were eventually confined by the power of Mercia and Wessex. Payments (Danegeld) were made by the Saxons to protect their lands. The Danish King Canute ruled England from 1016, and Danish and Norse claims were only resolved by the Norman Conquest 1066.

Darius I *the Great c.* 558–486 BC. King of Persia 521–48 BC. A member of a younger branch of the Achaemenid dynasty, he won the throne from the usurper Gaumata (died 522 BC) and reorganized the government. In 512 BC he marched against the Scythians, a people north of the Black Sea, and subjugated Thrace and Macedonia.

An expedition in 492 BC under his general Mardonius to crush a rebellion in Greece failed, and the army sent into Attica 490 BC was defeated at the battle of Marathon. Darius had an account of his reign inscribed on the mountain at Behistun, Persia.

Darius III see ◊Achaemenid dynasty.

Darlan Jean François 1881–1942. French admiral and politician. He entered the navy 1899, and was appointed admiral and commander in chief 1939. He commanded the French navy 1939–40, took part in the evacuation of Dunkirk, and entered the Pétain cabinet as naval minister. In 1941 he was appointed vice premier, and became strongly anti-British

and pro-German, but in 1942 he was dropped from the cabinet by Laval and sent to N Africa, where he was assassinated.

Darnley Henry Stewart or Stuart, Lord Darnley 1545–1567. British aristocrat, second husband of Mary Queen of Scots from 1565, and father of James I of England (James VI of Scotland). On the advice of her secretary, David ◊Rizzio, Mary refused Darnley the crown matrimonial; in revenge, Darnley led a band of nobles who murdered Rizzio in Mary's presence. Darnley was assassinated 1567.

Darrow Clarence (Seward) 1857–1938. US lawyer, born in Ohio, a champion of liberal causes and defender of the underdog. He defended many trade-union leaders, including Eugene ◊Debs 1894. He was counsel for the defence in the Nathan Leopold and Richard Loeb murder trial in Chicago 1924, and in the ◊Scopes monkey trial. Darrow matched wits in the trial with prosecution attorney William Jennings ◊Bryan. He was an opponent of capital punishment.

When I was a boy I was told that anybody could become President; I'm beginning to believe it.

                                        Clarence Darrow

dauphin title of the eldest son of the kings of France, derived from the personal name of a count, whose lands, known as the *Dauphiné*, traditionally passed to the heir to the throne from 1349 to 1830.

Dauphiné ancient province of France, comprising the modern *départements* of Isère, Drôme, and Hautes-Alpes.

After the collapse of the Roman Empire it belonged to Burgundy, then was under Frankish domination. Afterwards part of Arles, it was sold by its ruler to France in 1349 and thereafter was used as the personal fief of the heir to the throne (the dauphin) until 1560, when it was absorbed into the French kingdom. The capital was Grenoble.

David *c.* 1060–970 BC. Second king of Israel. According to the Old Testament he played the harp for King Saul to banish Saul's melancholy; he later slew the Philistine giant Goliath with a sling and stone. After Saul's death David was anointed king at Hebron, took Jerusalem, and made it his capital.

David two kings of Scotland:

David I 1084–1153. King of Scotland from 1124. The youngest son of Malcolm III

Canmore and St ◊Margaret, he was brought up in the English court of Henry I, and in 1113 married ◊Matilda, widow of the 1st earl of Northampton. He invaded England 1138 in support of Queen Matilda, but was defeated at Northallerton in the Battle of the Standard, and again 1141.

David II 1324–1371. King of Scotland from 1329, son of ◊Robert I (the Bruce). David was married at the age of four to Joanna, daughter of Edward II of England. In 1346 David invaded England, was captured at the battle of Neville's Cross, and imprisoned for 11 years.

Davis Angela 1944– . US left-wing activist for black rights, prominent in the student movement of the 1960s. In 1970 she went into hiding after being accused of supplying guns used in the murder of a judge who had been seized as a hostage in an attempt to secure the release of three black convicts. She was captured, tried, and acquitted. In 1980 she was the Communist vice-presidential candidate.

Davis Jefferson 1808–1889. US politician, president of the short-lived Confederate States of America 1861–65. He was a leader of the Southern Democrats in the US Senate from 1857, and a defender of 'humane' slavery; in 1860 he issued a declaration in favour of secession from the USA. During the Civil War he assumed strong political leadership, but often disagreed with military policy. He was imprisoned for two years after the war, one of the few cases of judicial retribution against Confederate leaders.

Davison Emily 1872–1913. English militant suffragette who died after throwing herself under the king's horse at the Derby at Epsom (she was trampled by the horse). She joined the Women's Social and Political Union in 1906 and served several prison sentences for militant action such as stone throwing, setting fire to pillar boxes, and bombing Lloyd George's country house.

Davitt Michael 1846–1906. Irish nationalist. He joined the Fenians (forerunners of the Irish Republican Army) 1865, and was imprisoned for treason 1870–77. After his release, he and the politician Charles Parnell founded the ◊Land League 1879. Davitt was jailed several times for land-reform agitation. He was a member of Parliament 1895–99, advocating the reconciliation of extreme and constitutional nationalism.

Dawes Charles Gates 1865–1951. US Republican politician. In 1923 he was appointed by the Allied Reparations Commission president of the committee that produced the *Dawes*

Plan, a $200 million loan that enabled Germany to pay enormous war debts after World War I. It reduced tensions temporarily in Europe but was superseded by the ◊Young Plan (which reduced the total reparations bill) 1929. Dawes was made US vice president (under Calvin Coolidge) 1924, received the Nobel Peace Prize 1925, and was ambassador to Britain 1929–32.

Dayan Moshe 1915–1981. Israeli general and politician. As minister of defence 1967 and 1969–74, he was largely responsible for the victory over neighbouring Arab states in the 1967 Six-Day War, but he was criticized for Israel's alleged unpreparedness in the 1973 October War and resigned along with Prime Minister Golda Meir. Foreign minister from 1977, Dayan resigned 1979 in protest over the refusal of the Begin government to negotiate with the Palestinians.

D-day 6 June 1944, the day of the Allied invasion of Normandy under the command of General Eisenhower, with the aim of liberating Western Europe from German occupation.

Dead Sea Scrolls collection of ancient scrolls (rolls of writing) and fragments of scrolls found 1947–56 in caves on the W side of the Jordan, 12 km/7 mi S of Jericho and 2 km/1 mi from the N end of the Dead Sea, at ◊Qumran. They include copies of Old Testament books a thousand years older than those previously known to be extant. The documents date mainly from about 150 BC–AD 68, when the monastic community that owned them, the Essenes, was destroyed by the Romans because of its support for a revolt against their rule.

Deakin Alfred 1856–1919. Australian politician, prime minister 1903–04, 1905–08, and 1909–10. In his second administration, he enacted legislation on defence and pensions.

While there is a lower class, I am in it; while there is a criminal element, I am of it; while there is a soul in prison, I am not free.

Eugene V Debs speech at his trial 1913

Debs Eugene V(ictor) 1855–1926. US labour leader and socialist who organized the Social Democratic Party 1897. He was the founder and first president of the American Railway Union 1893, and was imprisoned for six months in 1894 for defying a federal injunction to end the Pullman strike in Chicago. He was socialist candidate for the presidency in every election from 1900 to 1920, except that of 1916.

Decatur Stephen 1779–1820. US naval hero who, during the war with Tripoli 1801–05, succeeded in burning the *Philadelphia*, which the enemy had captured. During the War of 1812 with Britain, he surrendered only after a desperate resistance 1814. In 1815, he was active against Algerian pirates. Decatur coined the phrase 'our country, right or wrong'. He was killed in a duel.

Decembrist member of one of several Russian secret societies which espoused western liberal ideas and which joined forces to attempt a rebellion against Tsar Nicholas I in December 1825. The rebellion was crushed and five of its leaders executed, but revolutionary activity and increasing police terror continued throughout the century.

Decius Gaius Messius Quintus Traianus 201–251. Roman emperor from 249. He fought a number of campaigns against the ◊Goths but was finally beaten and killed by them near Abritum. He ruthlessly persecuted the Christians.

Declaration of Independence historic US document stating the theory of government on which the USA was founded, based on the right 'to life, liberty, and the pursuit of happiness'. The statement was issued by the ◊Continental Congress 4 July 1776, renouncing all allegiance to the British crown and ending the political connection with Britain.

Following a resolution moved 7 June, by Richard Henry Lee, 'that these United Colonies are, and of right ought to be, free and independent States', a committee including Thomas Jefferson and Benjamin Franklin was set up to draft a declaration; most of the work was done by Jefferson.

The declaration enumerated the grievances the colonists harboured against the British crown, which included his use of Indians to attack colonists, taxation without representation, and denial of civil liberties.

Declaration of Rights in Britain, the statement issued by the Convention Parliament Feb 1689, laying down the conditions under which the crown was to be offered to ◊William III and Mary. Its clauses were later incorporated in the ◊Bill of Rights.

decolonization gradual achievement of independence by former colonies of the European imperial powers which began after World War I. The process of decolonization accelerated after World War II and the movement affected every continent: India and Pakistan

gained independence from Britain 1947; Algeria gained independence from France 1962.

decretal in medieval Europe, a papal ruling on a disputed point, sent to a bishop or abbot in reply to a request or appeal. The earliest dates from Siricius 385. Later decretals were collected to form a decretum.

decretum collection of papal decrees. The best known is that collected by Gratian (died 1159) about 1140, comprising some 4,000 items. The decretum was used as an authoritative source of canon law (the rules and regulations of the church).

Defender of the Faith one of the titles of the English sovereign, conferred on Henry VIII 1521 by Pope Leo X in recognition of the king's treatise against the Protestant Martin Luther. It appears on coins in the abbreviated form *F.D.* (Latin *Fidei Defensor*).

defiance campaign in South Africa, the joint action of non-violent demonstrations and civil disobedience organized by the ◊African National Congress and the Indian ◊Congress Party 1952. Police and press were given notice before trained volunteers trespassed on 'whites-only' areas, broke curfews, or assembled without their passes. The campaigners' aim was to overcrowd the prisons and embarrass the authorities. Over 8,300 arrests were made.

The campaign coincided with the tricentenary celebrations marking the first permanent European settlement established in South Africa by Jan Van Riebeeck. The government response was a draconian Public Safety Bill 1953 allowing it to declare a state of emergency to combat future disorder.

de Gasperi Alcide 1881–1954. Italian politician. A founder of the Christian Democrat Party, he was prime minister 1945–53 and worked for European unification.

de Gaulle Charles André Joseph Marie 1890–1970. French general and first president of the Fifth Republic 1958–69. He organized the ◊Free French troops fighting the Nazis 1940–44, was head of the provisional French government 1944–46, and leader of his own Gaullist party. In 1958 the national assembly asked him to form a government during France's economic recovery and to solve the crisis in Algeria. He became president at the end of 1958, having changed the constitution to provide for a presidential system, and served until 1969.

Born in Lille, he graduated from Saint-Cyr 1911 and was severely wounded and captured by the Germans 1916. In June 1940 he refused

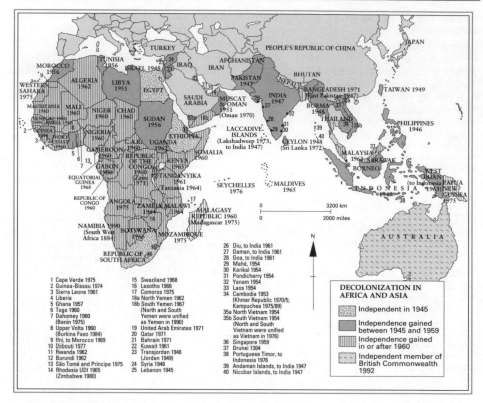

1 Cape Verde 1975
2 Guinea-Bissau 1974
3 Sierra Leone 1961
4 Liberia
5 Ghana 1957
6 Togo 1960
7 Dahomey 1960
(Benin 1975)
8 Upper Volta 1960
(Burkina Faso 1984)
9 Ifni, to Morocco 1969
10 Djibouti 1977
11 Rwanda 1962
12 Burundi 1962
13 São Tomé and Príncipe 1975
14 Rhodesia UDI 1965
(Zimbabwe 1980)

15 Swaziland 1968
16 Lesotho 1966
17 Comoros 1975
18a North Yemen 1962
18b South Yemen 1967
(North and South
Yemen were unified
as Yemen in 1990)
19 United Arab Emirates 1971
20 Qatar 1971
21 Bahrain 1971
22 Kuwait 1961
23 Transjordan 1946
(Jordan 1949)
24 Syria 1946
25 Lebanon 1945

26 Diu, to India 1961
27 Daman, to India 1961
28 Goa, to India 1961
29 Mahé, 1954
30 Karikal 1954
31 Pondicherry 1954
32 Yanam 1954
33 Laos 1954
34 Cambodia 1953
(Khmer Republic 1970/5;
Kampuchea 1975/89)
35a North Vietnam 1954
35b South Vietnam 1954
(North and South
Vietnam were unified
as Vietnam in 1976)
36 Singapore 1959
37 Brunei 1984
38 Portuguese Timor, to
Indonesia 1976
39 Andaman Islands, to India 1947
40 Nicobar Islands, to India 1947

DECOLONIZATION IN AFRICA AND ASIA

Independent in 1945

Independence gained between 1945 and 1959

Independence gained in or after 1960

Independent member of British Commonwealth 1992

Decolonization in Africa and Asia *The withdrawal of European rule from most of Africa and Asia between 1945 and 1975 was swift and largely uninterrupted. The political necessities of rebuilding Europe, the shortage of investment capital, and the expense of maintaining large military forces overseas, accelerated by the rapid growth of African and Asian nationalism, forced the imperial powers to establish a timetable for withdrawal which was completed sooner than anyone had anticipated.*

to accept the new prime minister Pétain's truce with the Germans and became leader of the Free French in England. In 1944 he entered Paris in triumph and was briefly head of the provisional government before resigning over the new constitution of the Fourth Republic 1946. In 1947 he founded the Rassemblement du Peuple Français, a nonparty constitutional reform movement, then withdrew from politics 1953. When national bankruptcy and civil war in Algeria loomed 1958, de Gaulle was called to form a government.

As prime minister he promulgated a constitution subordinating the legislature to the presidency and took office as president Dec 1958. Economic recovery followed, as well as Algerian independence after a bloody war. A nationalist, he opposed 'Anglo-Saxon' influence in Europe.

Re-elected president 1965, he pursued a foreign policy that opposed British entry to the EEC, withdrew French forces from NATO 1966, and pursued the development of a

French nuclear deterrent. He violently quelled student demonstrations May 1968 when they were joined by workers. The Gaullist party, reorganized as Union des Democrates pour la Cinquième République, won an overwhelming majority in the elections of the same year. In 1969 he resigned after the defeat of the government in a referendum on constitutional reform. He retired to the village of Colombey-les-Deux-Eglises in NE France.

If I am not France, what am I doing in your office?

General de Gaulle *making claim to Winston Churchill to lead the Free French 1940*

de Klerk F(rederik) W(illem) 1936– . South African National Party politician, president 1989-94. Projecting himself as a pragmatic conservative who sought gradual reform of the apartheid system, he won the Sept 1989 elections for his party, but with a reduced majority. In Feb 1990 he ended the ban on the ◊African National Congress (ANC) opposition movement and released its effective leader, Nelson ◊Mandela, and by June 1991 he had repealed all racially discriminating laws. He entered into negotiations with the ANC Dec 1991 and in March 1992 a nationwide, whites-only referendum gave him a clear mandate to proceed with plans for major constitutional reform to end white minority rule. After a landslide victory for Mandela and the ANC in the first universal suffrage elections April 1994, de Klerk became second executive deputy president. In May 1995 he withdrew the National Party from the governing coalition. He was awarded the Nobel Prize for Peace jointly with Mandela 1993.

Delcassé Théophile 1852–1923. French politician. He became foreign minister 1898, but had to resign 1905 because of German hostility; he held that post again 1914–15. To a large extent he was responsible for the ◊Entente Cordiale 1904 with Britain.

Delhi sultanate period 1206–1526 of early Muslim rule in north and central India. It saw Delhi become the political capital of northern India, the building of a chain of garrison towns, and the establishment of an immigrant Muslim nobility. The final ruler, Ibrahim Lodi (reigned 1517–1526), attempted to centralize authority, provoking the governor of Punjab to invite Babur, the Mogul chief of Kabul, to invade India. He defeated the sultanate's forces at ◊Panipat 1526.

The sultanate was established after Muhammad Ghuri defeated the Rajput forces of Prithviraja Chauhan. It comprised the Mameluke sultans (1206–90) and then four dynasties: the Khalji Turks (1290–1320), the Tughluqs (1320–1414), the Sayyids (1414–51), and the Afghan Lodis (1451–1526). There was periodic persecution of the Hindu majority and conversion to Islam, but local Indian rulers were accommodated. Muslim influence was extended temporarily into S India during the reign 1296–1316 of the Khalji Ala ud-Din, and that of Muhammad ibn Tughluq 1325–51, who forcibly transferred the capital to Daulatabad in the Deccan 1327–30. However, the sultanate was faced constantly with the danger of internal rebellion and the breakaway of both its Hindu tributaries and Muslim provincial nobility, which eventually led to its demise.

demesne in the Middle Ages in Europe, land kept in the lord's possession, not leased out, but, under the system of ◊villeinage, worked by villeins to supply the lord's household.

Demetrius Donskoi ('of the Don') 1350–1389. Grand prince of Moscow from 1363. In 1380 he achieved the first Russian victory over the Tatars on the plain of Kulikovo, next to the river Don (hence his nickname).

Demirel Suleyman 1924– . Turkish politician, president from 1993. Leader from 1964 of the Justic Party, he was prime minister 1965-71, 1975-77, and 1979-80. He has favoured links with the West and full EU membership.

democracy (Greek *demos* 'the community', *kratos* 'sovereign power') government by the people, usually through elected representatives. In the modern world, democracy has developed from the American and French revolutions.

Representative parliamentary government existed in Iceland from the 10th century and in England from the 13th century, but the British working classes were excluded almost entirely from the vote until 1867, and women were admitted and property qualifications abolished only in 1918.

In *direct democracy* the whole people meet for the making of laws or the direction of executive officers, for example in Athens in the 5th century BC. Direct democracy today is represented mainly by the use of the referendum, as in the UK, France, Switzerland, and certain states of the USA.

In a democracy everyone has a right to be represented, even the jerks.

On *democracy* Chris Patten May 1991

Democratic Party one of the two main political parties of the USA. It tends to be the party of the working person, as opposed to the Republicans, the party of big business, but the divisions between the two are not clear cut. Its stronghold since the Civil War has traditionally been industrial urban centres and the Southern states, but conservative Southern Democrats were largely supportive of Republican positions in the 1980s and helped elect President Reagan.

Originally called Democratic Republicans, the party was founded by Thomas Jefferson 1792 to defend the rights of the individual states against the centralizing policy of the Federalists. The party controlled all the southern states that seceded from the Union 1860–61. In the 20th century, under the presidencies of Franklin D Roosevelt, Harry Truman, John F Kennedy, Lyndon B Johnson, Jimmy Carter, and Bill Clinton, the party has had more liberal social reform policies than the Republicans.

Demosthenes c. 384–322 BC. Athenian orator and politician. From 351 BC he led the party that advocated resistance to the growing power of ◊Philip of Macedon, and in his *Philippics* incited the Athenians to war. This policy resulted in the defeat of Chaeronea 338, and the establishment of Macedonian supremacy. After the death of Alexander he organized a revolt; when it failed, he took poison to avoid capture by the Macedonians.

Deng Xiaoping or *Teng Hsiao-ping* 1904–97. Chinese political leader. A member of the Chinese Communist Party (CCP) from the 1920s, he took part in the Long March 1934–35. He was in the Politburo from 1955 until ousted in the Cultural Revolution 1966–69. Reinstated in the 1970s, he gradually took power and introduced a radical economic modernization programme.

He retired from the Politburo 1987 and from his last official position (as chair of State Military Commission) March 1990, but remained influential behind the scenes.

Deng, born in Sichuan province into a middle-class landlord family, joined the CCP as a student in Paris, where he adopted the name Xiaoping ('Little Peace') 1925, and studied in Moscow 1926. He headed the secretariat during the early 1960s, working closely with President Liu Shaoqi. During the Cultural Revolution Deng was dismissed as a 'capitalist roader' and sent to work in a tractor factory in Nanchang for 're-education'.

Deng was rehabilitated by his patron Zhou Enlai 1973 and served as acting prime minister after Zhou's heart attack 1974. On Zhou's death Jan 1976 he was forced into hiding but returned to office as vice premier July 1977. By Dec 1978, although nominally a CCP vice chair, state vice premier, and Chief of Staff to the PLA, Deng was the controlling force in China. His policy of 'socialism with Chinese characteristics', misinterpreted in the West as a drift to capitalism, had success in rural areas. He helped to oust ◊Hua Guofeng in favour of his protégés ◊Hu Yaobang (later in turn ousted) and ◊Zhao Ziyang.

Denikin Anton Ivanovich 1872–1947. Russian general. He distinguished himself in the ◊Russo-Japanese War 1904–05 and World War I. After the outbreak of the Bolshevik Revolution 1917 he organized a volunteer army of 60,000 Whites (loyalists) but was routed 1919 and escaped to France. He wrote a history of the Revolution and the Civil War.

Denmark peninsula and islands in N Europe, bounded N by the Skagerrak, E by the Kattegat, S by Germany, and W by the North Sea.

history The original home of the Danes was Sweden, and they migrated in the 5th and 6th centuries. Ruled by local chieftains, they terrified Europe by their piratical raids during the 8th–10th centuries, until Harald Bluetooth (c. 940–985) unified Denmark and established Christianity. King Canute (ruled 1014–35) founded an empire embracing Denmark, England, and Norway, which fell apart at his death. After a century of confusion Denmark again dominated the Baltic under Valdemar I, Canute VI, and Valdemar II (1157–1241). Domestic conflict then produced anarchy, until Valdemar IV (1340–1375) restored order. Denmark, Norway, and Sweden were united under one sovereign 1397.

loss of Sweden Sweden broke away 1449 and after a long struggle had its independence recognized 1523. Christian I (1448–1481) secured the duchies of Schleswig and Holstein, fiefs of the Holy Roman Empire, in 1460, and they were held by his descendants until 1863. Christian II (ruled 1513–23) was deposed in favour of his uncle Frederick, whose son Christian III (ruled 1534–59) made Lutheranism the established religion 1536. Attempts to regain Sweden led to disastrous wars with that country 1563–70, 1643–45, and 1657–60; equally disastrous was Christian V's intervention, 1625–29, on the Protestant side of the ◊Thirty Years' War.

policy of neutrality Frederick III (ruled 1648–70) made himself absolute monarch 1665 and ruled through a burgher bureaucracy. Serfdom was abolished 1788. Denmark's adherence 1780 to armed neutrality against Britain resulted in the naval defeat of Copenhagen 1801, and in 1807 the British bombarded Copenhagen and seized the Danish fleet to keep it from the expansionist French emperor Napoleon. This incident drove Denmark into the arms of France, and the Allies at the Congress of ◊Vienna took Norway from Denmark and gave it to Sweden 1815. A liberal movement then arose that in 1848–49 compelled Frederick VII (ruled 1848–63) to grant a democratic constitution. The Germans in Schleswig-Holstein revolted with Prussian support 1848–50, and Prussia seized the provinces 1864 after a short war. North Schleswig was recovered after a plebiscite 1920.

Neutral in World War I, Denmark tried to preserve its neutrality 1939 by signing a pact with Hitler, but was occupied by Germany 1940–45. Although traditionally neutral, Denmark joined the North Atlantic Treaty Organization (◊NATO) 1949 and the ◊European Free Trade Association (EFTA) 1960 but resigned

Causes of the Great Depression

The Wall Street crash of 29 Oct 1929 and the Great Depression that followed were such a shock to most Americans that some early attempts to explain their causes blamed sunspot activity or medieval prophecy. A few held it to be divine retribution on a people who had indulged themselves in a decade of hedonism after World War I and were due for a sobering experience. Others recognized that the 1920s had brought hints of an agricultural recession, amid uninhibited business speculation.

The efforts of economic historians to understand and explain the causes of the Great Depression of the 1930s have been characterized by a degree of 'theological' controversy. This divides adherents of the various economic philosophies, communist and capitalist, monetarist from Keynesian and others. Their lack of consensus in explaining the Great Depression stems from these distinctive philosophical starting points.

The price of 'get rich quick'

In summary, the Wall Street crash was caused by excessive speculation in the stock market during the late 1920s. This was a symptom of the feverish 'get rich quick' mentality that had accompanied almost a decade of growth following post-war reconversion. Then the over-valued commodity markets suddenly lost confidence, and prices tumbled. This set in motion a sequence of disasters that became an economic catastrophe for the richest nation in the world. Banks collapsed, businesses went bankrupt, unemployment soared, welfare organizations could not cope with the rising tide of destitution and politicians seemed powerless to break the vicious downward spiral of American industrial capitalism.

The president at the time of the crach, Herbert Hoover, blamed the calamity in part on international factors. He argued that world trade had deteriorated in the late 1920s because European states had not recovered from the effects of World War I, stating 'the European disease had contaminated the United States'. However, there were other causes closer to home. It went unrecognized that the distribution of national income was not only inequitable but was failing to generate sufficient demand at the broadest level of society to meet the rising levels of supply made possibly by new production technologies. Thus under-consumption was both a cause and a symptom of the Great Depression.

Why it spread across the world

The Wall Street crash need not have led to the severest depression in American history, and a consequent worldwide slump. To understand why a loss of confidence in the New York stock market had such devastating consequences, we must take account of the political actions taken in response to the worsening economic situation after the crash. The Hoover administration was at fault before the crash in allowing the underlying weaknesses of an apparently buoyant economy to go unchecked. Its reaction to the onset of depression failed to restore confidence, through a reluctance to use federal assistance and employ federal controls. President F D Roosevelt's answer in the form of the New Deal from 1933 was to isolate America economically from the rest of a world now infected with depression, and to seek national rather than international recovery. He succeeded in mobilizing massive resources, and his pursuit of prosperity was strengthened by the munitions demands of World War II.

It is a paradox that the Great Depression was caused by abundance rather than the 'iron law' scarcity that governs some economic analyses. American farmers and workers were producing too much. They were too inventive in their modes of production and the enormous power of their economy crushed those of other states. With cruel irony, a surfeit of wealth and power brought disabling poverty.

1973 to join the European Economic Community (EEC). ◊Iceland was part of the Danish kingdom until 1945 and the other parts of non-metropolitan Denmark, the Faroe Islands and Greenland, were given special recognition by a constitution that has been adapted to meet changing circumstances. In 1953 provision was made for a daughter to succeed to the throne in the absence of a male heir, and a system of voting by proportional representation was introduced.

Left-wing policies have dominated Danish politics, and proportional representation (often resulting in minority or coalition governments) has encouraged a moderate approach. In the Dec 1990 general election, the Social Democrats received 37.4% of the vote, the Conservatives 16%, the Liberals 15.8%, Socialist People's Party 8.3%, Progress Party 6.4%. Poul Schlüter continued as prime minister. In a referendum 1992 on European Community policies, the Danish people rejected the Maastricht Treaty, triggering referendums and debates elsewhere in the EC. The Danish government subsequently proposed modifications (codicils) to the treaty prior to a second referendum, planned for 1993.

depression in economics, a period of low output and investment, with high unemployment. Specifically, the term describes two periods of crisis in world economy: 1873–96 and 1929–mid-1930s.

The term is most often used to refer to the world economic crisis precipitated by the Wall Street crash of 29 Oct 1929 when millions of dollars were wiped off US share values in a matter of hours. This forced the closure of many US banks involved in stock speculation and led to the recall of US overseas investments. This loss of US credit had serious repercussions on the European economy, especially that of Germany, and led to a steep fall in the levels of international trade as countries attempted to protect their domestic economies. Although most European countries experienced a slow recovery from this Great Depression during the mid-1930s, the main impetus for renewed economic growth was provided by rearmament programmes later in the decade.

Derby Edward (George Geoffrey Smith) Stanley, 14th Earl of Derby 1799–1869. British politician, prime minister 1852, 1858–59, and 1866–68. Originally a Whig, he became secretary for the colonies 1830, and introduced the bill for the abolition of slavery. He joined the Tories 1834, and the split in the Tory Party over Robert Peel's free-trade policy gave Derby the leadership for 20 years.

dervish in Iran and Turkey, a religious mendicant; throughout the rest of Islam a member of an Islamic religious brotherhood, not necessarily mendicant in character. The Arabic equivalent is *fakir*. There are various orders of dervishes, each with its rule and special ritual. The 'whirling dervishes' claim close communion with the deity through ecstatic dancing; the 'howling dervishes' gash themselves with knives to demonstrate the miraculous feats possible to those who trust in Allah.

Desai Morarji 1896–95. Indian politician. An early follower of Mahatma Gandhi, he was prime minister 1977–79, as leader of the ◊Janata party, after toppling Indira Gandhi. Party infighting led to his resignation of both the premiership and the party leadership.

Desert Rats nickname of the British 8th Army in N Africa during World War II. Their uniforms had a shoulder insignia bearing a jerboa (N African rodent, capable of great leaps). The Desert Rats' most famous victories include the expulsion of the Italian army from Egypt in Dec 1940 when they captured 130,000 prisoners, and the Battle of El Alamein. Their successors, the 7th Armoured Brigade, fought as part of the British 1st Armoured Division in the 1991 Gulf War.

Desmoulins Camille 1760–1794. French revolutionary who summoned the mob to arms on 12 July 1789, so precipitating the revolt that culminated in the storming of the Bastille. A prominent left-wing ◊Jacobin, he was elected to the National Convention 1792. His *Histoire des Brissotins* was largely responsible for the over-

throw of the right-wing ◊Girondins, but shortly after he was sent to the guillotine as too moderate.

A dead king is not a man less.

Camille Desmoulins
voting for the death of Louis XVI

Dessalines Jean Jacques *c.* 1758–1806. Emperor of Haiti 1804–06. Born in Guinea, he was taken to Haiti as a slave, where in 1802 he succeeded ◊Toussaint L'Ouverture as leader of the black revolt against the French. After defeating the French, he proclaimed Haiti's independence and made himself emperor. He was killed when trying to suppress an uprising provoked by his cruelty.

détente (French) reduction of political tension and the easing of strained relations between nations, for example, the ending of the Cold War 1989–90, although it was first used in the 1970s to describe the easing East–West relations, trade agreements, and cultural exchanges.

deterrence underlying conception of the nuclear arms race: the belief that a potential aggressor will be discouraged from launching a 'first strike' nuclear attack by the knowledge that the adversary is capable of inflicting 'unacceptable damage' in a retaliatory strike. This doctrine is widely known as that of *mutual assured destruction (MAD)*. Three essential characteristics of deterrence are: the 'capability to act', 'credibility', and the 'will to act'.

Dettingen, Battle of battle in the Bavarian village of that name where on 27 June 1743, in the War of the Austrian Succession, an army of British, Hanoverians, and Austrians under George II defeated the French under Adrien-Maurice, duc de Noailles (1678–1766).

de Valera Eámon 1882–1975. Irish nationalist politician, prime minister of the Irish Free State/Eire/Republic of Ireland 1932–48, 1951–54, and 1957–59, and president 1959–73. Repeatedly imprisoned, he participated in the Easter Rising 1916 and was leader of the nationalist ◊Sinn Féin party 1917–26, when he formed the republican ◊Fianna Fáil party; he directed negotiations with Britain 1921 but refused to accept the partition of Ireland until 1937.

He was sentenced to death for his part in the Easter Rising, but the sentence was commuted, and he was released under an amnesty 1917. In the same year he was elected member of Parliament for E Clare, and president of Sinn Féin.

He was rearrested May 1918, but escaped to the USA 1919. He returned to Ireland 1920 and directed the struggle against the British government from a hiding place in Dublin. He authorized the negotiations of 1921, but refused to accept the ensuing treaty which divided Ireland into the Free State and the North.

Civil war followed. De Valera was arrested by the Free State government 1923, and spent a year in prison. In 1926 he formed a new party, Fianna Fáil, which secured a majority in 1932. De Valera became prime minister and foreign minister of the Free State, and at once abolished the oath of allegiance and suspended payment of the annuities due under the Land Purchase Acts. In 1938 he negotiated an agreement with Britain, under which all outstanding points were settled. Throughout World War II he maintained a strict neutrality, rejecting an offer by Winston Churchill 1940 to recognize the principle of a united Ireland in return for Eire's entry into the war.

Devolution, War of war waged unsuccessfully 1667–68 by Louis XIV of France to gain Spanish territory in the Netherlands, of which ownership had allegedly 'devolved' on his wife Maria Theresa.

devotio moderna movement of revived religious spirituality which emerged in the Netherlands at the end of the 14th century and spread into the rest of W Europe. Its emphasis was on individual, rather than communal, devotion, including the private reading of religious works.

The movement's followers were drawn from the laity, including women, and clergy. Lay followers formed themselves into associations known as Brethren of the Common Life. Among the followers of *devotio moderna* was Thomas à Kempis, author of *De Imitatio Christi/Imitation of Christ*.

devsirme levy of one in four males aged 10–20 taken by the Ottoman rulers of their Balkan provinces. Those taken were brought to Constantinople and converted to Islam before being trained for the army or the civil service. This practice lasted from the 14th to the mid-17th century.

de Wet Christiaan Rudolf 1854–1922. Boer general and politician. He served in the South African Wars 1880 and 1899. When World War I began, he headed a pro- German rising of 12,000 Afrikaners but was defeated, convicted of treason, and imprisoned. He was sentenced to six years' imprisonment for his part in the uprising, but was released 1915.

Dewey George 1837–1917. US naval officer. Dewey saw action on the Mississippi River and in the blockade of Southern ports during the American Civil War 1861–65. He was appointed chief of the Bureau of Equipment 1889 and of the Board of Inspection and Survey 1895. As commodore, Dewey was dispatched to the Pacific 1896. He destroyed the Spanish fleet in Manila harbour at the outbreak of the Spanish-American War 1898. Dewey was promoted to the rank of admiral of the navy (the highest naval rank ever awarded) 1899. He retired from active service 1900.

Dewey Thomas Edmund 1902–1971. US public official. He was Manhattan district attorney 1937–38 and served as governor of New York 1942–54. Dewey was twice the Republican presidential candidate, losing to F D Roosevelt 1944 and to Truman 1948, the latter race being one of the greatest electoral upsets in US history.

dialectical materialism political, philosophical, and economic theory of the 19th-century German thinkers Karl Marx and Friedrich Engels, also known as ♭Marxism.

Diaspora dispersal of the Jews, initially from Palestine after the Babylonian conquest 586 BC, and then following the Roman sack of Jerusalem AD 70 and their crushing of the Jewish revolt of 135. The term has come to refer to all the Jews living outside Israel.

Díaz Porfirio 1830–1915. Dictator of Mexico 1877–80 and 1884–1911. After losing the 1876 election, he overthrew the government and seized power. He was supported by conservative landowners and foreign capitalists, who invested in railways and mines. He centralized the state at the expense of the peasants and Indians, and dismantled all local and regional leadership. He faced mounting and revolutionary opposition in his final years and was forced into exile 1911.

Díaz del Castillo Bernal *c.* 1495–1584. Spanish soldier and chronicler. He arrived in the New World 1514 with conquistador Pedro Arias de Ávila (*c.* 1440–1531) and took part in the exploration of the Gulf coast of Mexico 1517 and 1518. He served as a common soldier under Pedro de ♭Alvarado during the conquest of Mexico, and is known for his account, *Historia verdadera de la conquista de la Nueva España/True Account of the History of New Spain*.

dictatorship term or office of an absolute ruler, overriding the constitution. (In ancient Rome a dictator was a magistrate invested with emergency powers for six months.) Although dictatorships were common in Latin America during the 19th century, the only European example during this period was the rule of Napoleon III. The crises following World War I produced many dictatorships, including the regimes of Atatürk and Piłsudski (nationalist); Mussolini, Hitler, Primo de Rivera, Franco, and Salazar (all right-wing); and Stalin (Communist).

dictatorship of the proletariat Marxist term for a revolutionary dictatorship established during the transition from capitalism to ◊communism after a socialist revolution.

Diefenbaker John George 1895–1979. Canadian Progressive Conservative politician, prime minister 1957–63; he was defeated after criticism of the proposed manufacture of nuclear weapons in Canada.

Diefenbaker was born in Ontario, and moved to Saskatchewan. A brilliant defence counsel, he became known as the 'prairie lawyer'. He became leader of his party 1956 and prime minister 1957. In 1958 he achieved the greatest landslide in Canadian history. A 'radical' Tory, he was also a strong supporter of Commonwealth unity. He resigned the party leadership 1967, repudiating a 'two nations' policy for Canada. He was known as 'the Chief'.

Dien Bien Phu, Battle of decisive battle in the ◊Indochina War at a French fortress in North Vietnam, near the Laotian border. French troops were besieged 13 March–7 May 1954 by the communist Vietminh. The fall of Dien Bien Phu resulted in the end of French control of Indochina.

diet meeting or convention of the princes and other dignitaries of the Holy Roman (German) Empire, for example, the *Diet of Worms* 1521 which met to consider the question of Luther's doctrines and the governance of the empire under Charles V.

Digger or *True Leveller* member of an English 17th-century radical sect that attempted to seize and share out common land. The Diggers became prominent April 1649 when, headed by Gerrard Winstanley (*c*. 1609–1660), they set up communal colonies near Cobham, Surrey, and elsewhere. These colonies were attacked by mobs and, being pacifists, the Diggers made no resistance. The support they attracted alarmed the government and they were dispersed 1650. Their ideas influenced the early Quakers.

Dimitrov Georgi 1882–1949. Bulgarian communist, prime minister from 1946. He was elected a deputy in 1913 and from 1919 was a member of the executive of the Comintern, an international communist organization (see the ◊International). In 1933 he was arrested in Berlin and tried with others in Leipzig for allegedly setting fire to the parliament building (see ◊Reichstag Fire). Acquitted, he went to the USSR, where he became general secretary of the Comintern until its dissolution in 1943.

Dingaan Zulu chief who obtained the throne in 1828 by murdering his predecessor, Shaka, and became notorious for his cruelty. In warfare with the Boer immigrants into Natal he was defeated on 16 Dec 1838 – 'Dingaan's Day'. He escaped to Swaziland, where he was deposed by his brother Mpande and subsequently assassinated.

Diocletian Gaius Valerius Diocletianus AD 245–313. Roman emperor 284–305, when he abdicated in favour of Galerius. He reorganized and subdivided the empire, with two joint and two subordinate emperors, and in 303 initiated severe persecution of Christians.

Dionysius two tyrants of the ancient Greek city of Syracuse in Sicily. *Dionysius the Elder* (432–367 BC) seized power 405 BC. His first two wars with Carthage further extended the power of Syracuse, but in a third (383–378 BC) he was defeated. He was a patron of ◊Plato. He was succeeded by his son, *Dionysius the Younger*, who was driven out of Syracuse by Dion 356; he was tyrant again 353, but in 343 returned to Corinth.

Diplock court in Northern Ireland, a type of court established 1972 by the British government under Lord Diplock (1907–1985) to try offences linked with guerrilla violence. The right to jury trial was suspended and the court consisted of a single judge, because potential jurors were allegedly being intimidated and were unwilling to serve. Despite widespread criticism, the Diplock courts have remained in operation.

diplomacy process by which states attempt to settle their differences through peaceful means such as negotiation or arbitration.

Directory the five-man ruling executive in France 1795–99. Established by the constitution of 1795, it failed to deal with the political and social tensions in the country and became increasingly unpopular after military defeats. It was overthrown by a military coup 9 Nov 1799 which brought Napoleon Bonaparte to power.

Members of the executive, known as the 'five majesties' included Paul-Jean Barras (1755–1829) and the Abbé Sieyès (1748–1836).

disarmament reduction of a country's weapons of war. Most disarmament talks since World War II have been concerned with nuclear- arms verification and reduction, but biological, chemical, and conventional weapons have also come under discussion at the United Nations and in other forums. Attempts to limit the arms race (initially between the USA and the USSR and since 1992 between the USA and Russia) have included the ◊Strategic Arms Limitation Talks(SALT) of the 1970s and the ◊Strategic Arms Reduction Talks (START) of the 1980s–90s.

Disraeli Benjamin, Earl of Beaconsfield 1804–1881. British Conservative politician and novelist. Elected to Parliament 1837, he was chancellor of the Exchequer under Lord Derby 1852, 1858–59, and 1866–68, and prime minister 1868 and 1874–80. His imperialist policies brought India directly under the crown, and he was personally responsible for purchasing control of the Suez Canal. The central Conservative Party organization is his creation.

Excluded from Peel's government of 1841–46, Disraeli formed his Young England group to keep a critical eye on Peel's Conservatism. Its ideas were expounded in the novel trilogy *Coningsby*, *Sybil*, and *Tancred* 1847. When Peel decided in 1846 to repeal the Corn Laws, Disraeli opposed the measure in a series of witty and effective speeches; Peel's government fell soon after, and Disraeli gradually came to be recognized as the leader of the Conservative Party in the Commons.

During the next 20 years the Conservatives formed short-lived minority governments in 1852, 1858-59, and 1866-68, with Lord Derby as prime minister and Disraeli as chancellor of the Exchequer and leader of the Commons. In 1852 Disraeli first proposed discrimination in income tax between earned and unearned income, but without success. The 1858–59 government legalized the admission of Jews to Parliament, and transferred the government of India from the East India Company to the crown. In 1866 the Conservatives took office after defeating a Liberal Reform Bill, and then attempted to secure the credit of widening the franchise by the Reform Bill of 1867. On Lord Derby's retirement in 1868 Disraeli became prime minister, but a few months later he was defeated by Gladstone in a general election.

In 1874 Disraeli took office for the second time, with a majority of 100. Some useful reform measures were carried, such as the Artisans' Dwelling Act, which empowered local authorities to undertake slum clearance, but the outstanding feature of the government's policy was its imperialism. It was Disraeli's personal initiative that purchased from the Khedive of Egypt a controlling interest in the Suez Canal, conferred on the Queen the title of Empress of India, and sent the Prince of Wales on the first royal tour of that country. He accepted an earldom 1876. The Bulgarian revolt of 1876 and the subsequent Russo-Turkish War of 1877–78 provoked one of many political duels between Disraeli and Gladstone, the Liberal leader, and was concluded by the Congress of Berlin 1878, where Disraeli was the principal British delegate and brought home 'peace with honour' and Cyprus. The government was defeated in 1880, and a year later Disraeli died.

There is no waste of time in life like that of making explanations.

Benjamin Disraeli
speech 1873

dissident in one-party states, a person intellectually dissenting from the official line. Dissidents have been sent into exile, prison, labour camps, and mental institutions, or deprived of their jobs. In the USSR the number of imprisoned dissidents declined from more than 600 in 1986 to fewer than 100 in 1990, of whom the majority were ethnic nationalists. In China the number of prisoners of conscience increased after the 1989 Tiananmen Square massacre, and in South Africa, despite the release of Nelson Mandela in 1990, numerous political dissidents remained in jail.

In the former USSR before the introduction of ◊glasnost, dissidents comprised communists who advocated a more democratic and humanitarian approach; religious proselytizers; Jews wishing to emigrate; and those who supported ethnic or national separatist movements within the USSR (among them Armenians, Lithuanians, Ukrainians, and Tatars). Their views were expressed through samizdat (clandestinely distributed writings) and sometimes published abroad. In the late 1980s Mikhail Gorbachev lifted censorship, accepted a degree of political pluralism, and extended tolerance to religious believers. Almost 100,000 Jews were allowed to emigrate 1985–90.

divine right of kings Christian political doctrine that hereditary monarchy is the system approved by God, hereditary right cannot be forfeited, monarchs are accountable to God alone for their actions, and rebellion against the lawful sovereign is therefore blasphemous.

The doctrine had its origins in the anointing of Pepin in 751 by the pope after Pepin had usurped the throne of the Franks. It was at its peak in 16th- and 17th-century Europe as a weapon against the claims of the papacy – the court of Louis XIV of France pushed this to the limit – and was in 17th-century England maintained by the supporters of the Stuarts in opposition to the democratic theories of the Puritans and Whigs.

Dixie southern states of the USA. The word probably derives from the ◊Mason-Dixon line.

Djibouti country on the E coast of Africa, at the S end of the Red Sea, bounded E by the Gulf of Aden, SE by Somalia, and S, W, and N by Ethiopia.

history During the 9th century missionaries from Arabia converted the Afars inhabiting the area to Islam. A series of wars was fought by the Afar Islamic states and Christian Ethiopia from the 13th to 17th centuries. The French arrived 1862, and in 1884 annexed Djibouti and the neighbouring region as the colony of French Somaliland. In 1967 it was renamed the French Territory of the Afars and the Issas. Opposition to French rule grew during the 1970s, and calls for independence were frequent, sometimes violent.

independence Independence as the Republic of Djibouti was achieved 1977, with Hassan Gouled as president. In 1979 all political parties combined to form the RPP, and the government embarked on the task of uniting the two main ethnic groups: the Issas, who traditionally had strong links with Somalia, and the Afars, who had been linked with Ethiopia.

amicable neutralism In 1981 a new constitution was adopted, making the RPP the only party. President Gouled was re-elected, and in 1982 a chamber of deputies was elected from a list of RPP nominees. Under Gouled, Djibouti pursued a largely successful policy of amicable neutralism with its neighbours, concluding treaties of friendship with Ethiopia, Somalia, Kenya, and Sudan, and tried to assist the peace process in East Africa. Although affected by the 1984–85 droughts, Djibouti managed to maintain stability with European Community aid. Gouled was re-elected 1987 for his final term with 98.71% of the popular vote. In 1991 Amnesty International charged Djibouti's security police with brutality in their treatment of political prisoners. In 1992 Djibouti was elected to the UN Security Counci for the period 1993–95.

Doe Samuel Kenyon 1950–1990. Liberian politician and soldier, head of state 1980–90.

He seized power in a coup. In 1981 he made himself general and army commander in chief. In 1985 he was narrowly elected president, as leader of the newly formed National Democratic Party of Liberia. Having successfully put down an uprising April 1990, Doe was deposed and killed by rebel forces Sept 1990. His human-rights record was poor.

doge chief magistrate in the ancient constitutions of Venice and Genoa. The first doge of Venice was appointed 697 with absolute power (modified 1297), and from his accession dates Venice's prominence in history. The last Venetian doge, Lodovico Manin, retired 1797 and the last Genoese doge 1804.

dollar diplomacy disparaging description of US foreign policy in the early 20th century. The US sought political influence over foreign governments (China 1909 and 1912; Haiti 1910; Nicaragua and Honduras 1911; Dominican Republic 1916) by encouraging American financiers to make loans to countries whose indebtedness could then be used to promote US interests. Dollar diplomacy sometimes resulted in US military intervention (such as marines in Nicaragua 1912-25) to prop up client regimes.

Dollfuss Engelbert 1892–1934. Austrian Christian Socialist politician. He was appointed chancellor in 1932, and in 1933 suppressed parliament and ruled by decree. In Feb 1934 he crushed a protest by the socialist workers by force, and in May Austria was declared a 'corporative' state. The Nazis attempted a coup d'état on 25 July; the Chancellery was seized and Dollfuss murdered.

Domesday Book record of the survey of England carried out 1086 by officials of William the Conqueror in order to assess land tax and other dues, ascertain the value of the crown lands, and enable the king to estimate the power of his vassal barons. The name is derived from the belief that its judgement was as final as that of Doomsday.

Northumberland and Durham were omitted, and also London, Winchester, and certain other towns. The Domesday Book is preserved in two volumes at the Public Record Office, London.

Dominica island in the E Caribbean, between Guadeloupe and Martinique, the largest of the Windward Islands, with the Atlantic Ocean to the E and the Caribbean Sea to the W.

history The island was inhabited by the Amerindian Caribs at the time Christopher Columbus visited it 1493 (since Columbus arrived at the island on a Sunday, he named it Dominica). It became a British possession in the 18th century and was part of the Leeward Islands federation until 1939. In 1940 it was transferred to the Windward Islands and remained attached to that group until 1960, when it was given separate status, with a chief minister and legislative council.

full independence achieved In 1961 the leader of the Dominica Labour Party (DLP), Edward le Blanc, became chief minister; after 13 years in office he retired and was succeeded as prime minister by Patrick John. The DLP held office until full independence was achieved 1978, at which time its leader, John, became the first prime minister under the new constitution. Opposition to John's increasingly authoritarian style of government soon developed, and in the 1980 elections the Dominica Freedom Party (DFP) won a convincing victory on a free-enterprise programme. Its leader, Eugenia Charles, became the Caribbean's first woman prime minister.

antigovernment intrigue In 1981 John was thought to be implicated in a plot against the government, and a state of emergency was imposed. The next year he was tried and acquitted. He was retried 1985, found guilty, and given a 12-year prison sentence. Left-of-centre parties regrouped, making the new Labour Party of Dominica (LPD) the main opposition to the DFP. Eugenia Charles was re-elected 1985 and, with a reduced majority, 1990.

foreign relations Under Eugenia Charles's leadership, Dominica has developed links with France and the USA and in 1983 sent a small force to participate in the US-backed invasion of Grenada. In 1991 representatives of Dominica, St Lucia, St Vincent and the Grenadines, and Grenada proposed that integration with the Windward Islands would benefit the islands politically and economically. Integration would be based on a federal state system, with an elected, executive president and a two-chamber assembly.

Dominican Republic country in the West Indies (E Caribbean), occupying the eastern two-thirds of the island of Hispaniola, with Haiti covering the western third; the Atlantic Ocean is to the E and the Caribbean Sea to the W.

history The island was inhabited by Arawak and Carib Indians when Christopher Columbus arrived 1492, the first European to visit the island. He named it Hispaniola ('Little Spain'). It was divided between France and Spain 1697, and in 1795 the Spanish part (Santo Domingo) was ceded to France. After a revolt it was retaken by Spain 1808. Following a brief period of independence 1821, it was occupied by Haiti

until a successful revolt resulted in the establishment of the Dominican Republic 1844.

From 1845 to 1878 the new republic was dominated by two caudillos (military rulers), Pedro Santana and Buenaventura Báez. Not only was democracy stifled, but the country faced bankruptcy. In an attempt to stabilize the economy and defend the Dominican Republic against attacks by Haiti, in 1861 Santana allowed Spain to annex the country. Four years later, amid growing dissatisfaction, the Spaniards were evicted by General Gregorio Luperón.

The late 19th century saw the country's rulers commit themselves to heavy borrowing from the USA. The years of dictatorship by Ulisses Heureux 1882–99 left the country in a state of political and financial collapse. In 1908, the USA established a customs receivership which managed to reduce the republic's debt. However, domestic politics became so chaotic that in 1916 the USA occupied the Dominican Republic, not withdrawing until 1924.

military coups In 1930 the elected president was overthrown in a military coup, and General Rafael Trujillo Molina became dictator. He was assassinated 1961, and in 1962 Dr Juan Bosch, founder and leader of the left-wing Dominican Revolutionary Party (PRD), who had been in exile for over 30 years, won the country's first free elections. Within a year he was overthrown by the military, who set up their own three-person ruling junta.

democratic constitution An attempt to re-establish Bosch 1965 was defeated with the intervention of US forces, and in 1966 Joaquín Balaguer, a protégé of Trujillo and leader of the Christian Social Reform Party (PRSC), won the presidency. A more democratic constitution was adopted, and Balaguer, despite his links with Trujillo, proved a popular leader, being re-elected 1970 and 1974.

The 1978 election was won by the PRD candidate, Silvestre Antonio Guzmán. The PRD was again successful in the 1982 election, and Salvador Jorge Blanco, the party's left-wing nominee, became president-designate. After allegations of fraud by his family, Guzmán committed suicide before he had finished his term, and an interim president was chosen before the start of Blanco's term.

Blanco steered a restrained course in foreign policy, maintaining good relations with the USA and avoiding too close an association with Cuba. The economy deteriorated, and in 1985 the Blanco administration was forced to adopt harsh austerity measures in return for help from the ◊International Monetary Fund. The PRD became increasingly unpopular, and the PRSC, under Joaquín Balaguer, returned to power 1986. He was re-elected 1990, but by a paper-thin margin, and his party lost its legislative majority.

Dominic, St 1170–1221. Founder of the Roman Catholic Dominican order of preaching friars. Born in Old Castile, Dominic was sent by Pope Innocent III in 1205 to preach to the heretic Albigensian sect in Provence. In 1208 the Pope instigated the Albigensian crusade to suppress the heretics by force, and this was supported by Dominic. In 1215 the Dominican order was given premises at Toulouse; during the following years Dominic established friaries at Bologna and elsewhere in Italy, and by the time of his death the order was established all over W Europe.

Dominions the name formerly applied to the self-governing divisions of the ◊British Empire – for example Australia, New Zealand, Canada, and South Africa.

domino theory idea popularized by US president Eisenhower in 1954 that if one country came under communist rule, adjacent countries were likely to fall to communism as well.

Domitian (Titus Flavius Domitianus) AD 51–96. Roman emperor from AD 81. He finalized the conquest of Britain (see ◊Agricola), strengthened the Rhine–Danube frontier, and suppressed immorality as well as freedom of thought in philosophy religion. His reign of terror led to his assassination.

Donation of Constantine forged 8th-century document purporting to record the Roman emperor Constantine's surrender of temporal sovereignty in W Europe to Pope Sylvester I (314–25).

In the Middle Ages, this document was used as papal propaganda in the struggle between pope and emperor, which was at its most heated during the ◊investiture contest. It was finally exposed as forged by the German philosopher Nicholas of Cusa and Lorenzo Valla in the 15th century.

Dönitz Karl 1891–1980. German admiral, originator of the wolf-pack submarine technique, which sank 15 million tonnes of Allied shipping in World War II. He succeeded Hitler in 1945, capitulated, and was imprisoned 1946–56.

Donner party ill-fated US expedition of pioneers from Missouri to California 1846-47, led by George and Jacob Donner. A group of 87 left the main party and travelled across the Great Salt Desert, reaching the Sierra Nevada mountains too late to cross before the onset of winter. Cut off by snow, they became stranded through the winter of 1846-47. When rescuers reached the party, less than half its members survived, many having died of hypothermia or starvation; the survivors were thought to have resorted to cannibalism when their food ran out.

Don Pacifico Affair incident in 1850 in which British foreign secretary Lord Palmerston was criticized in Parliament and elsewhere in Europe for using British naval superiority to impose his foreign policy. Palmerston sent gunboats to blockade the Greek coast in support of the claim of a Portuguese merchant, David Pacifico, who was born on Gibraltar (and thus a British subject), for compensation from the Greek government after his house was burned down in anti-Semitic riots.

Doomsday Book variant spelling of ◊Domesday Book, the English survey of 1086.

Dorian people of ancient Greece. They entered Greece from the north and took most of the Peloponnese from the Achaeans, perhaps destroying the ◊Mycenaean civilization; this invasion appears to have been completed before 1000 BC. Their chief cities were Sparta, Argos, and Corinth.

Doubleday Abner 1819–1893. American Civil War military leader and reputed inventor of baseball. He served as major general in the Shenandoah Valley campaign and at the Battles of Bull Run and Antietam 1862, and Gettysburg 1863. He retired from active service 1873. In an investigation into the origins of baseball 1907, testimony was given that Doubleday invented the game 1839 in Cooperstown, New York, a claim refuted by sports historians ever since.

Douglas Stephen Arnold 1813–1861. US politician. He served in the US House of Representatives 1843–47 and as senator for Illinois 1847–61. An active Democrat, he urged a compromise on slavery, and debated Abraham Lincoln during the 1858 Senate race winning the election. After losing the 1860 presidential race to Lincoln, Douglas pledged his loyal support to the latter's administration 1861–65.

There are two problems in my life. The political ones are insoluble and the economic ones are incomprehensible.

Alec Douglas-Home
speech Jan 1964

Douglas-Home Alec, Baron Home of the Hirsel 1903–95. British Conservative politician.

cian. He was foreign secretary 1960-63, and succeeded Harold Macmillan as prime minister 1963. He renounced his peerage (as 14th Earl of Home) to fight (and lose) the general election 1964, and resigned as party leader 1965. He was again foreign secretary 1970-74, when he received a life peerage.

Douglass Frederick 1817–1895. US antislavery campaigner active during the American Civil War 1861-65. He issued a call to blacks to take up arms against the South and was instrumental in organizing two black regiments. After the Civil War, he held several US government posts, including minister to Haiti 1889-91. He published appeals for full civil rights for blacks and also campaigned for women's suffrage.

Born a slave in Maryland, Douglass escaped 1838 and fled to Britain to avoid re-enslavement. He returned to the US after he had secured sufficient funds to purchase his freedom. He campaigned relentlessly against slavery, especially through his speeches and his newspaper the *North Star*. His autobiographical *Narrative of the Life of Frederick Douglass* 1845 aroused support for the abolition of slavery.

Doumergue Gaston 1863–1937. French prime minister Dec 1913–June 1914 (during the time leading up to World War I); president 1924–31; and premier again Feb–Nov 1934 of a 'national union' government.

Dowding Hugh Caswall Tremenheere, 1st Baron Dowding 1882–1970. British air chief marshal. He was chief of Fighter Command at the outbreak of World War II in 1939, a post he held through the Battle of Britain 10 July-12 Oct 1940.

Draco 7th century BC. Athenian politician, the first to codify the laws of the Athenian city-state. These were notorious for their severity; hence *draconian*, meaning particularly harsh.

Drake Francis *c.* 1545–1596. English buccaneer and explorer. Having enriched himself as a pirate against Spanish interests in the Caribbean 1567–72, he was sponsored by Elizabeth I for an expedition to the Pacific, sailing round the world 1577–80 in the *Golden Hind*, robbing Spanish ships as he went. This was the second circumnavigation of the globe (the first was by the Portuguese explorer Ferdinand Magellan). Drake also helped to defeat the Spanish Armada 1588 as a vice admiral in the *Revenge*.

Drake was born in Devon and apprenticed to the master of a coasting vessel, who left him the ship at his death. He accompanied his relative, the navigator John Hawkins, 1567 and 1572 to plunder the Caribbean, and returned to England 1573 with considerable booty. After serving in Ireland as a volunteer, he suggested to

Queen Elizabeth I an expedition to the Pacific, and Dec 1577 he sailed in the *Pelican* with four other ships and 166 men towards South America. In Aug 1578 the fleet passed through the Straits of Magellan and was then blown south to Cape Horn. The ships became separated and returned to England, all but the *Pelican*, now renamed the *Golden Hind*. Drake sailed north along the coast of Chile and Peru, robbing Spanish ships as far north as California, and then, in 1579, headed southwest across the Pacific. He rounded the South African Cape June 1580, and reached England Sept 1580. Thus the second voyage around the world, and the first made by an English person, was completed in a little under three years. When the Spanish ambassador demanded Drake's punishment, the Queen knighted him on the deck of the *Golden Hind* at Deptford, London.

In 1581 Drake was chosen mayor of Plymouth, in which capacity he brought fresh water into the city by constructing leats from Dartmoor. In 1584–85 he represented the town of Bosinney in Parliament. In a raid on Cadiz 1587 he burned 10,000 tons of shipping, 'singed the King of Spain's beard', and delayed the invasion of England by the Spanish Armada for a year. He was stationed off the French island of Ushant 1588 to intercept the Armada, but was driven back to England by unfavourable winds. During the fight in the Channel he served as a vice admiral in the *Revenge*. Drake sailed on his last expedition to the West Indies with Hawkins 1595, capturing Nombre de Dios on the N coast of Panama but failing to seize Panama City. In Jan 1596 he died of dysentry off the town of Puerto Bello (now Portobello), Panama.

Dreadnought class of battleships built for the British navy after 1905 and far superior in speed and armaments to anything then afloat. The first modern battleship to be built, it was the basis of battleship design for more than 50 years. The first Dreadnought was launched 1906, with armaments consisting entirely of big guns.

The German Nassau class was begun in 1907, and by 1914, the USA, France, Japan and Austria-Hungary all had battleships of a similar class to the Dreadnought. German plans to build similar craft led to the naval race that contributed to Anglo-German antagonism and the origins of World War II.

Dred Scott Decision US Supreme Court decision 1857 dealing with citizenship and legal rights of slaves. Dred Scott (*c.* 1800–1858), a slave from Missouri, sued for his freedom from his owner John Sanford in the Missouri courts, arguing that he had lived with his owner in Illinois, a free state, and the Wisconsin Territory, where slavery had been outlawed by the Missouri Compromise. After a series of re- versals the case reached the Supreme Court, which ruled (1) black people were not US citizens, (2) slaves did not become free by entering a free state; and (3) the Missouri Compromise was illegal as it interfered with the right to own slaves, guaranteed by the Constitution (this was only the second Congressional act overturned by the Supreme Court). The decision heightened regional tensions as the Civil War neared.

Drees Willem 1886–1988. Dutch socialist politician, prime minister 1948–58. Chair of the Socialist Democratic Workers' Party from 1911 until the German invasion of 1940, he returned to politics in 1947, after being active in the resistance movement. In 1947, as the responsible minister, he introduced a state pension scheme.

Dreikaiserbund (German meaning 'Three Emperors' League') informal alliance from 1872 between the emperors of Russia, Germany, and Austria-Hungary. It was effectively at an end by 1879.

Dresden capital of the state of Saxony, Germany. Under the elector Augustus II the Strong (1694–1733), it became a centre of art and culture. The city was bombed by the Allies on the night 13–14 Feb 1945, 15.5 sq km/6 sq mi of the inner town being destroyed, and deaths being estimated at 35,000–135,000. Following the reunification of Germany 1990 Dresden once again became capital of Saxony.

Dreyfus Alfred 1859–1935. French army officer, victim of miscarriage of justice, anti-Semitism, and cover-up. Employed in the War Ministry, in 1894 he was accused of betraying military secrets to Germany, court-martialled, and sent to the penal colony on ◊Devil's Island, French Guiana. When his innocence was discovered 1896 the military establishment tried to conceal it, and the implications of the Dreyfus affair were passionately discussed in the press until he was exonerated in 1906.

Druse or *Druze* religious sect in the Middle East of some 500,000 people. They are monotheists, preaching that the Fatimid caliph al-Hakim (996-1021) is God; their scriptures are drawn from the Bible, the Koran, and Sufi allegories. Druse militia groups formed one of the three main factions involved in the Lebanese civil war (the others were Amal Shi'ite Muslims and Christian Maronites). The Druse military leader (from the time of his father's assassination 1977) is Walid Jumblatt.

The Druse sect was founded in Egypt in the 11th century, and then fled to Palestine to avoid persecution; today they occupy areas of Syria, Lebanon, and Israel.

Dual Entente alliance between France and Russia that lasted from 1893 until the Bolshevik Revolution of 1917.

Duarte José Napoleon 1925–1990. El Salvadorean politician, president 1980–82 and 1984–88. He was mayor of San Salvador 1964–70, and was elected president 1972, but exiled by the army 1982. On becoming president again 1984, he sought a negotiated settlement with the left-wing guerrillas 1986, but resigned on health grounds.

Dubček Alexander 1921–1992. Czechoslovak politician, chair of the federal assembly from 1989. He was a member of the Slovak ◊resistance movement during World War II, and became first secretary of the Communist Party 1967–69. He launched a liberalization campaign (called the Prague Spring) that was opposed by the USSR and led to the Soviet invasion of Czechoslovakia 1968. He was arrested by Soviet troops and expelled from the party 1970. In 1989 he gave speeches at prodemocracy rallies, and after the fall of the hardline regime, he was elected speaker of the National Assembly in Prague, a position to which he was re-elected 1990. He was fatally injured in a car crash Sept 1992.

Du Bois W(illiam) E(dward) B(urghardt) 1868–1963. US educator and social critic. Du Bois was one of the early leaders of the National Association for the Advancement of Colored People (NAACP) and the editor of its journal *Crisis* 1909-32. As a staunch advocate of black American rights, he came into conflict with Booker T ◊Washington, opposing the latter's policy of compromise on the issue of slavery.

Duce (Italian 'leader') title bestowed on the fascist dictator Benito ◊Mussolini by his followers and later adopted as his official title.

duel fight between two people armed with weapons. A duel is usually fought according to pre-arranged rules with the aim of settling a private quarrel.

In medieval Europe duels were a legal method of settling disputes. By the 16th century the practice had largely ceased but duelling with swords or pistols, often with elaborate ritual, continued unofficially in aristocratic and military circles until the 20th century. Duelling became illegal in the UK 1819.

Dulles John Foster 1888–1959. US politician. Senior US adviser at the founding of the United

Nations, he was largely responsible for drafting the Japanese peace treaty of 1951. As secretary of state 1952–59, he was the architect of US Cold War foreign policy, secured US intervention in South Vietnam after the expulsion of the French 1954, and was critical of Britain during the Suez Crisis 1956.

Duma in Russia, before 1917, an elected assembly that met four times following the short-lived 1905 revolution. With progressive demands the government could not accept, the Duma was largely powerless. After the abdication of Nicholas II, the Duma directed the formation of a provisional government.

Dumbarton Oaks 18th-century mansion in Washington DC, USA, used for conferences and seminars. It was the scene of a conference held 1944 that led to the foundation of the United Nations.

Dumer Paul 1857–1932. French politician. He was elected president of the Chamber in 1905, president of the Senate in 1927, and president of the republic in 1931. He was assassinated by Gorgulov, a White Russian emigré.

Dumouriez Charles François du Périer 1739–1823. French general during the Revolution. In 1792 he was appointed foreign minister, supported the declaration of war against Austria, and after the fall of the monarchy was given command of the army defending Paris. After intriguing with the royalists he had to flee for his life, and from 1804 he lived in England.

Dunkirk (French *Dunkerque*) seaport on the N coast of France, in Nord *département*, on the Strait of Dover. Dunkirk was close to the front line during much of World War I, and in World War II, 337,131 Allied troops (including about 110,000 French) were evacuated from the beaches as German forces approached.

Dupleix Joseph-François, Marquis de 1697–1763. governor general of the French ◊East India Company 1741–54. He wanted to establish an extensive French empire in India and, through skilful diplomacy with local Indian rulers, briefly achieved French domination within the Carnatic (SE India). His wider aims were frustrated by British general Robert ◊Clive, and Dupleix was recalled to France 1754.

Durban riots inter-racial conflict between Zulus and Indians in Durban, South Africa in Jan 1949. The riots, in which 142 people were killed and 1,087 injured, began when a black youth was killed by an Indian shopkeeper. The violence was symptomatic of longstanding social and economic divisions between the two communities. Paradoxically, the riots accelerated cooperation between the ◊African National Congress and Indian leaders.

Durham John George Lambton, 1st Earl of Durham 1792–1840. British politician. Appointed Lord Privy Seal 1830, he drew up the first Reform Bill 1832, and as governor general of Canada briefly in 1837 drafted the Durham Report which led to the union of Upper and Lower Canada.

Dutch East India Company trading monopoly of the 17th and 18th centuries; see ◊East India Company, Dutch.

Duvalier François 1907–1971. Right-wing president of Haiti 1957–71. Known as *Papa Doc*, he ruled as a dictator, organizing the Tontons Macoutes ('bogeymen') as a private security force to intimidate and assassinate opponents of his regime. He rigged the 1961 elections in order to have his term of office extended until 1967, and in 1964 declared himself president for life. He was excommunicated by the Vatican for harassing the church, and was succeeded on his death by his son Jean-Claude Duvalier.

Duvalier Jean-Claude 1951– . Right-wing president of Haiti 1971–86. Known as *Baby Doc*, he succeeded his father François Duvalier, becoming, at the age of 19, the youngest president in the world. He continued to receive support from the USA but was pressured into moderating some elements of his father's regime, yet still tolerated no opposition. In 1986, with Haiti's economy stagnating and with increasing civil disorder, Duvalier fled to France, taking much of the Haitian treasury with him.

Dzungarian Gates ancient route in central Asia on the border of Kazakhstan and Xinjiang Uygur region of China, 470 km/290 mi NW of Urumqi. The route was used in the 13th century by the Mongol hordes on their way to Europe.

Eanes António dos Santos Ramalho 1935– . Portuguese politician. He helped plan the 1974 coup that ended the Caetano regime, and as army chief of staff put down a left-wing revolt Nov 1975. He was president 1976-86.

Early Jubal Anderson 1816–1894. American Confederate military leader. Although long a supporter of the Union, he joined the Confederate army at the outbreak of the American Civil War 1861. After the Battle of Bull Run 1862 he was made general in the army of Northern Virginia, leading campaigns in the Shenandoah Valley 1862 and threatening Washington DC 1864.

Earp Wyatt 1848–1929. US frontier law officer. With his brothers Virgil and Morgan, Doc Holliday, and the legendary Bat ◊Masterson he was involved in the famous gunfight at the OK Corral in Tombstone, Arizona, on 26 Oct 1881. Famous as a scout and buffalo hunter, he also gained a reputation as a gambler and brawler. After leaving Tombstone 1882, he travelled before settling in Los Angeles.

Eastern Front battlefront between Russia and Germany during World War I and World War II.

Eastern question the international and diplomatic problems associated with the weakness and eventual collapse of the Ottoman Empire during the 18th and 19th centuries. Most international disputes arose over the future of the Empire's Balkan possessions, where both Russia and Austria-Hungary were interested parties, and over control of the Bosporus where European naval and Mediterranean powers were anxious to prevent the Russians having access rights for their fleet.

Crises occurred as a result of the Russo-Turkish wars in the 18th century, the Greek War of Independence, and a series of disputes over Egypt and the Balkans. The Congress of Berlin 1878 provided a partial settlement of the Balkan question, but further disputes gave rise to the Bosnian crisis 1908 and the first two Balkan Wars 1912–13. The Ottoman Empire was finally dismantled after its support for the Central Powers and subsequent defeat in World War I.

Easter Rising or *Easter Rebellion* in Irish history, a republican insurrection that began on Easter Monday, April 1916, in Dublin. It was inspired by the Irish Republican Brotherhood (IRB) in an unsuccessful attempt to overthrow British rule in Ireland. It was led by Patrick Pearce of the IRB and James Connolly of Sinn Féin.

Arms from Germany intended for the IRB were intercepted but the rising proceeded regardless with the seizure of the Post Office and other buildings in Dublin by 1,500 volunteers. The rebellion was crushed by the British Army within five days, both sides suffering major losses: 220 civilians, 64 rebels, and 134 members of the Crown Forces were killed during the uprising. Pearce, Connolly, and about a dozen rebel leaders were subsequently executed in Kilmainham Jail. Others, including Éamon de Valera, were spared due to US public opinion, to be given amnesty June 1917.

Eastern Roman Empire alternative name for the ◊Byzantine Empire 395–1453.

East India Company British commercial company 1600–1858 chartered by Queen Elizabeth I and given a monopoly of trade between England and the Far East. In the 18th century, the company became, in effect, the ruler of a large part of India, and a form of dual control by the company and a committee responsible to Parliament in London was introduced by Pitt's India Act 1784. The end of the monopoly of China trade came 1834, and after the ◊Indian Mutiny 1857 the crown took complete control of the government of British India; the India Act 1858 abolished the company.

The East India Company set up factories in Masulipatam, near modern Madras, 1611; on the W coast of India in Surat 1612; on the E coast in Madras 1639; and near Calcutta on the Hooghly (one of the mouths of the Ganges) 1640. By 1652 there were some 23 English factories in India. Bombay came to the British crown 1662, and was granted to the East India Company for £10 a year. The British victory in the Battle of Plassey 1757 gave the company control of Bengal.

East India Company, Dutch (*VOC*, or *Vereenigde Oost-Indische Compagnie*) trading company chartered by the States General (parliament) of the Netherlands, and established in the N Netherlands 1602. It was given a monopoly on Dutch trade in the Indonesian archipelago, and certain sovereign rights such as the creation of an army and a fleet.

East India Company, French trading company set up by France 1664 to compete with the English and Dutch East India companies. It established trading ports at Chandernagore in W Bengal and Pondicherry in SE India.

During the 1740s the French East India Company tried without success to check growing British influence in the subcontinent by making strategic alliances with S Indian rulers. The company foundered during the French Revolution, but France retained control over Chandernagore and Pondicherry until 1952 and 1954 respectively.

East Pakistan former province of ◊Pakistan, now Bangladesh.

East Timor disputed territory on the island of Timor in the Malay Archipelago; prior to 1975, it was a Portuguese colony for almost 460 years. Following Portugal's withdrawal 1975, East Timor was left with a literacy rate of under 10% and no infrastructure. Civil war broke out and the left-wing Revolutionary Front of Independent East Timor (Fretilin) occupied the capital, calling for independence. In opposition, troops from neighbouring Indonesia invaded the territory, declaring East Timor (*Loro Sae*) the 17th province of Indonesia July 1976. This claim is not recognized by the United Nations. (It has long been the aim of Indonesian military rulers to absorb the remaining colonial outposts in the East Indies.)

The war and its attendant famine are thought to have caused more than 100,000 deaths, but starvation had been alleviated by the mid-1980s, and the Indonesian government had built schools, roads, and hospitals. Fretilin guerrillas remained active, claiming to have the support of the population.

Eban Abba 1915– . Israeli diplomat and politician, ambassador in Washington 1950–59 and foreign minister 1966–74.

Ecuador country in South America, bounded N by Colombia, E and S by Peru, and W by the Pacific Ocean.

history The tribes of N highland Ecuador formed the Kingdom of Quito about AD 1000, and it was conquered by the ◊Inca in the 15th century. Ecuador was invaded and colonized by Spain from 1532. It joined Venezuela, Colombia, and Panama in the confederacy of Gran Colombia 1819. After joining other South American colonies in a revolt against Spain, Ecuador was liberated 1822 by Antonio José de ◊Sucre and became fully independent 1830.

With the support of the army, Ecuador was governed by Venezuelan General Juan José Flores 1830–45. However, his lack of understanding of the country led him to hand over power to the revolutionary leader Vicente Rocafuerta 1834–39. Flores was forced into exile 1845. Power passed to a Liberal oligarchy based in Guayaquil. The next 15 years saw the 'nationalization' of both army and government.

During the period 1861–75, Ecuadorian political life was dominated by General Gabriel García Moreno, who promoted education and carried out important public works.

After more than a decade of political instability, the military victory of Eloy Alfaro saw the beginnings of half a century of Liberal hegemony 1895–1944, marked by electoral fraud, military coups, and a lack of respect for basic civil rights. By 1948 some stability was evident, and eight years of Liberal government ensued. In 1956, Dr Camilo Ponce became the first Conservative president for 60 years. Four years later a Liberal, Dr José Maria Velasco (president 1933–35, 1944–47, and 1952–56), was re-elected. He was deposed 1961 by the vice president, who was himself replaced by a military junta the following year. In 1968 Velasco returned from exile and took up the presidency again. Another coup 1972 put the military back in power until in 1978 a new, democratic constitution was adopted.

Economic deterioration caused strikes, demonstrations, and, in 1982, a state of emergency. In the 1984 elections there was no clear majority in the national congress, and the Conservative León Febres Cordero became president on a promise of 'bread, roofs, and jobs'. In 1985 he won a majority in congress when five opposition members shifted their allegiance to him. In 1988 Rodrigo Borja Cevallos was elected president for a moderate left-wing coalition government. In July 1992 the United Republican Party (PUR) leader Sixto Duran Ballen was elected president. The right-wing Social Christian Party (PSC) became the largest party in congress, but without an overall majority.

Eden Anthony, 1st Earl of Avon 1897–1977. British Conservative politician, foreign secretary 1935–38, 1940–45, and 1951–55; prime minister 1955–57, when he resigned after the failure of the Anglo-French military intervention in the ◊Suez Crisis.

Upset by his prime minister's rejection of a peace plan secretly proposed by Roosevelt Jan 1938, Eden resigned as foreign secretary Feb 1938 in protest against Chamberlain's decision to open conversations with the Fascist dictator Mussolini. He was foreign secretary again in the wartime coalition, formed Dec 1940, and in the Conservative government, elected 1951. With the Soviets, he negotiated an interim peace in Vietnam 1954. In April 1955 he succeeded Churchill as prime minister. His use of force in the Suez Crisis led to his resignation Jan 1957, but he continued to maintain that his action was justified.

We are not at war with Egypt. We are in an armed conflict.

Anthony Eden Nov 1956

Edgar known as the Atheling ('of royal blood') *c.* 1050–*c.* 1130. English prince, born in Hungary. Grandson of Edmund Ironside, he was supplanted as heir to Edward the Confessor by William the Conqueror. He led two rebellions against William 1068 and 1069, but made peace 1074.

Edgar the Peaceful 944–975. King of all England from 959. He was the younger son of Edmund I, and strove successfully to unite English and Danes as fellow subjects.

Edgehill, Battle of first battle of the English Civil War. It took place 1642, on a ridge in S Warwickshire, between Royalists under Charles I and Parliamentarians under the Earl of Essex. The result was indecisive.

Edmund II Ironside *c.* 989–1016. King of England 1016, the son of Ethelred II the Unready. He led the resistance to ◊Canute's invasion 1015, and on Ethelred's death 1016 was chosen king by the citizens of London, whereas the Witan (the king's council) elected Canute. In the struggle for the throne, Edmund was defeated by Canute at Assandun (Ashington), Essex, and they divided the kingdom between them; when Edmund died the same year, Canute ruled the whole kingdom.

Edmund, St *c.* 840–870. King of East Anglia from 855. In 870 he was defeated and captured by the Danes at Hoxne, Suffolk, and martyred on refusing to renounce Christianity. He was canonized and his shrine at Bury St Edmunds became a place of pilgrimage.

Edom in the Old Testament, a mountainous area of S Palestine, which stretched from the Dead Sea to the Gulf of Aqaba. Its people were enemies of the Israelites.

Edo, Treaty of 1858 agreement between Japan and the USA, granting trade and diplomatic privileges to the latter. Similar treaties were signed that year with the UK, Russia, the Netherlands, and France. Because the conditions were unfavourable to Japan, the 1858 agreements are counted among the ◊unequal treaties. They were revised in the 1890s.

Under these treaties, foreign nationals in Japan were not subject to Japanese jurisdiction: if they committed offences they could be tried only by the consular courts of the treaty powers. Treaty ports were opened (Nagasaki, Yokohama, and Hakodate from 1859, Niigata from 1860, and Kōe from 1863). The treaties also restricted Japan's power to fix tariff rates. These provisions were resented by the Japanese and there were a number of attempts to revise them in the late 19th century. The extraterritorial jurisdiction provisions were dropped 1899 and the tariff restrictions 1911.

education The earliest known European educational systems were those of ancient Greece. In Sparta the process was devoted mainly to the development of military skills; in Athens, to politics, philosophy, and public speaking, but both were accorded only to the privileged few.

In ancient China, formalized education received impetus from the imperial decree of 165 BC, which established open competitive examinations for the recruitment of members of the civil service, based mainly on a detailed study of literature.

The Romans adopted the Greek system of education and spread it through Western Europe. Following the disintegration of the Roman Empire, widespread education vanished from Europe, although Christian monasteries preserved both learning and Latin. In the Middle Ages, Charlemagne's monastic schools taught the 'seven liberal arts': grammar, logic, rhetoric, arithmetic, geometry, music, and astronomy. These schools produced the theological philosophers of the Scholastic Movement, which in the 11th–13th centuries led to ◊university foundations. The capture of Constantinople, capital of the E Roman Empire, by the Turks 1453 sent the Christian scholars there into exile across Europe, and revived European interest in learning.

Compulsory attendance at primary schools was first established in the mid-18th century in Prussia, and has since spread almost worldwide.

Edward the *Black Prince* 1330–1376. Prince of Wales, eldest son of Edward III of England. The epithet (probably posthumous) may refer to his black armour. During the Hundred

Years' War he fought at the Battle of Crécy 1346 and captured the French king at Poitiers 1356. He ruled Aquitaine 1360–71; during the revolt that eventually ousted him, he caused the massacre of Limoges 1370.

Edward eight kings of England or the UK:

Edward I 1239–1307. King of England from 1272, son of Henry III. Edward led the royal forces against Simon de Montfort in the ◊Barons' War 1264–67, and was on a crusade when he succeeded to the throne. He established English rule over all Wales 1282–84, and secured recognition of his overlordship from the Scottish king, although the Scots (under Wallace and Bruce) fiercely resisted actual conquest. In his reign Parliament took its approximate modern form with the ◊Model Parliament 1295. He was succeeded by his son Edward II.

Edward II 1284–1327. King of England from 1307. Son of Edward I and born at Caernarvon Castle, he was created the first Prince of Wales 1301. His invasion of Scotland 1314 to suppress revolt resulted in defeat at ◊Bannockburn. He was deposed 1327 by his wife Isabella (1292–1358), daughter of Philip IV of France, and her lover Roger de ◊Mortimer, and murdered in Berkeley Castle, Gloucestershire. He was succeeded by his son Edward III.

Edward III 1312–1377. King of England from 1327, son of Edward II. He assumed the government 1330 from his mother, through whom in 1337 he laid claim to the French throne and thus began the ◊Hundred Years' War. He was succeeded by his grandson Richard II.

Edward began his reign by attempting to force his rule on Scotland, winning a victory at Halidon Hill 1333. During the first stage of the Hundred Years' War, English victories included the Battle of Crécy 1346 and the capture of Calais 1347. In 1360 Edward surrendered his claim to the French throne, but the war resumed 1369. During his last years his son John of Gaunt acted as head of government.

Edward IV 1442–1483. King of England 1461–70 and from 1471. He was the son of Richard, Duke of York, and succeeded Henry VI in the Wars of the ◊Roses, temporarily losing the throne to Henry when Edward fell out with his adviser ◊Warwick, but regaining it at the Battle of Barnet 1471. He was succeeded by his son Edward V.

Edward V 1470–1483. King of England 1483. Son of Edward IV, he was deposed three months after his accession in favour of his uncle (◊Richard III), and is traditionally believed to have been murdered (with his brother) in the Tower of London on Richard's orders.

Edward VI 1537–1553. King of England from 1547, son of Henry VIII and Jane Seymour. The government was entrusted to his uncle the Duke of Somerset (who fell from power 1549), and then to the Earl of Warwick, later created Duke of Northumberland. He was succeeded by his sister, Mary I.

Jane Seymour was Henry VIII's third wife, and Edward was his only son. Edward became a staunch Protestant and during his reign the Reformation progressed. He died from tuberculosis.

Edward VII 1841–1910. King of Great Britain and Ireland from 1901. As Prince of Wales he was a prominent social figure, but his mother Queen Victoria considered him too frivolous to take part in political life. In 1860 he made the first tour of Canada and the USA ever undertaken by a British prince.

Edward VIII 1894–1972. King of Great Britain and Northern Ireland Jan–Dec 1936, when he renounced the throne to marry Wallis Warfield Simpson (see ◊abdication crisis). He was created Duke of Windsor and was governor of the Bahamas 1940–45, subsequently settling in France.

Edward the Confessor c. 1003–1066. King of England from 1042, the son of Ethelred II. He lived in Normandy until shortly before his accession. During his reign power was held by Earl ◊Godwin and his son ◊Harold, while the king devoted himself to religion, including the rebuilding of Westminster Abbey (consecrated 1065), where he is buried. His childlessness led ultimately to the Norman Conquest 1066. He was canonized 1161.

Edward the Elder c. 870–924. King of the West Saxons. He succeeded his father ◊Alfred the Great 899. He reconquered SE England and the Midlands from the Danes, uniting Wessex and ◊Mercia with the help of his sister, Athelflad. By the time Edward died, his kingdom was the most powerful in the British Isles. He was succeeded by his son ◊Athelstan.

Edward the Martyr c. 963–978. King of England from 975. Son of King Edgar, he was murdered at Corfe Castle, Dorset, probably at his stepmother Aelfthryth's instigation (she wished to secure the crown for her son, Ethelred). He was canonized 1001.

Edwin c. 585–633. King of Northumbria from 617. He captured and fortified Edinburgh, which was named after him, and was killed in battle with Penda of Mercia 632.

EEC abbreviation for *European Economic Community*; see ◊European Community.

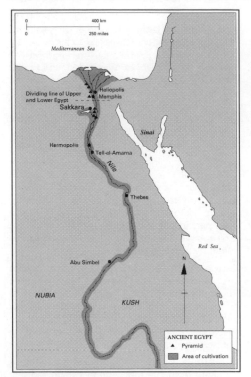

Ancient Egypt Farming communities were established in Egypt by at least 5000 BC. Upper and Lower Egypt were unified by Menes around 3200 with Memphis as capital. The Step Pyramid, designed by Imhotep, was built at Sakkara around 2800. The capital of the New Kingdom (from about 1580) was at Thebes, and briefly at Akhetaton (Tell el Amarna) under the heretic pharaoh Ikhnaton. Ramses II constructed two monumental temples at Abu Simbel which were relocated away from the Aswan Dam 1966–67. After the 8th century BC ancient Egypt was dominated in turn by Libyans, Assyrians, Persians, Greeks, and Romans.

EFTA acronym for ◊*European Free Trade Association*.

Egbert died 839. King of the West Saxons from 802, the son of Ealhmund, an under-king of Kent. By 829 he had united England for the first time under one king.

Egypt country in NE Africa, bounded N by the Mediterranean Sea, E by the Suez Canal and Red Sea, S by Sudan, and W by Libya.

history For early history see ◊chronology: *Ancient Egypt*. After its conquest by ◊Augustus 30 BC, Egypt passed under the rule of Roman, and later Byzantine, governors, and Christianity superseded the ancient religion. The Arabs conquered Egypt AD 639–42, introducing Islam and Arabic to the area, and the country was ruled by successive Arab dynasties until 1250, when the ◊Mamelukes seized power.

Ancient Egypt

5000 BC	Egyptian culture already well established in the Nile Valley, with Neolithic farming villages.
3200	Menes united Lower Egypt (the Delta) with his own kingdom of Upper Egypt.
2800	The architect Imhotep built the step pyramid at Sakkara.
c. **2600**	**Old Kingdom** reached the height of its power and the kings of the 4th dynasty built the pyramids at Giza.
c. **2200–1800**	**Middle Kingdom** under which the unity lost towards the end of the Old Kingdom was restored.
1730	Invading Asian Hyksos people established their kingdom in the Nile Delta.
c. **1580**	**New Kingdom** established by the 18th dynasty following the eviction of the Hyksos, with its capital at Thebes. The high point of ancient Egyptian civilization under the pharaohs Thothmes, Hatshepsut, Amenhotep, Ikhnaton (who moved the capital to Akhetaton), and Tutankhamen.
c. **1321**	19th dynasty: Ramses I built a temple at Karnak, Ramses II the temples at Abu Simbel.
1191	Ramses III defeated the Indo-European Sea Peoples, but after him there was decline, and power within the country passed from the pharaohs to the priests of Ammon.
1090–663	**Late New Kingdom** during this period Egypt was often divided between two or more dynasties; the nobles became virtually independent.
8th–7th centuries	Brief interlude of rule by kings from Nubia.
666	The Assyrians under Ashurbanipal occupied Thebes.
663–609	Psammetichus I restored Egypt's independence and unity.
525	Egypt was conquered by Cambyses and became a Persian province.
c. **405–340**	Period of independence.
332	Conquest by Alexander the Great. On the division of his empire, Egypt went to one of his generals, Ptolemy I, and his descendants, the Macedonian dynasty.
30	Death of Cleopatra, last of the Macedonians, and conquest by the Roman emperor Augustus; Egypt became a province of the Roman empire.
AD 641	Conquest by the Arabs; the Christianity of later Roman rule was for the most part replaced by Islam.

For later history, see ◊ Egypt.

Ancient Egyptian dynasties

c. 3200–2890 BC	1st dynasty established by Menes, who conquered Lower Egypt from Upper Egypt. The capital was located at Memphis. Hieroglyphic script was employed.
c. 2890–2686	2nd dynasty: disputes between Upper and Lower Egypt.
Old Kingdom	
2686–2613	3rd dynasty: Lower Nubia was under Egyptian control. Step Pyramid at Saqqara built by Imhotep for Zoser.
2613–2494	4th dynasty: wars with Nubia and Libya. Great Pyramid of Khufu and Sphinx built at Giza.
2494–2345	5th dynasty: rise of the cult of Ra at Heliopolis.
2345–2181	6th dynasty: reduction in power of pharaohs in favour of regional rulers.
First Intermediate Period	
2160–2040	7th, 8th, 9th, and 10th dynasties: characterized by a lack of unity and dynastic confusion.
Middle Kingdom	
2133–1991	11th dynasty: reunification under Theban rule by Mentuhotep II.
1991–1786	12th dynasty: reigns of Amenhotep I and Sesostris I–III saw expansion into Nubia, Palestine, and Asia, and growth in trade.
Second Intermediate Period	
1786–1633	13th and 14th dynasties: a period of political chaos and division, and the migration of the Hyksos peoples into the Nile Delta area.
1674–1567	15th and 16th dynasties: capture of Memphis led to rule by Hyksos.
1650–1567	17th dynasty founded at Thebes. Upper Egypt liberated from Hyksos.
New Kingdom	
1567–1321	18th dynasty: Hyksos finally defeated by Amosis. Thothmes campaigned in Syria.
	Regency of Hatshepsut *c.* 1500. Thothmes III established Egyptian Asiatic empire in Palestine and Syria. Amenhotep III built temples at Luxor. Reign of Ikhnaton. Tomb of Tutankhamen.
1321–1200	19th dynasty: Ramses I chosen to succeed Horemheb as pharaoh. Resistance to Hittite expansion in Asia. Building programme of Ramses II.
1200–1085	20th dynasty: Ramses III defeated Libyans and Sea Peoples. Territories in Asia lost.
Late Period	
1085–945	21st dynasty: Egypt divided between priest-kings at Thebes and pharaohs at Tanis in the Delta.
950–712	22nd, 23rd, and 24th dynasties: rule by Libyan kings in Upper and Lower Egypt.
712–671	25th dynasty: Ethiopian rule.
666	Thebes captured by Assyrians under Ashurbanipal.
663–525	26th dynasty: Psammetichus of Sais gained control of the Delta.
525	Conquest of Egypt by Cambyses of Persia.
464–454	Athenian attempt to liberate Delta.
405–454	28th, 29th, and 30th dynasties: independence recovered. Greek mercenaries were increasingly used. Egypt re-conquered by Persia.
332	Conquest by Alexander the Great of Macedon. After his death 323 Egypt came under the control of his general, Ptolemy Soter.
304–30	Rule of Macedonian Ptolemies, ending with suicide of Cleopatra. Egypt came under the administration of Rome.
AD 395	Egypt passed into the eastern (Byzantine) half of the divided Roman empire.
641	Arabs conquered Egypt.

Mameluke rule lasted until 1517, when Egypt became part of the Turkish ◊Ottoman Empire.

Contact with Europe began with Napoleon's invasion and the French occupation 1798–1801. A period of anarchy followed, until in 1805 an Albanian officer, Mehemet Ali, was appointed pasha, a title that later became hereditary in his family. Under his successors Egypt met with economic difficulties over the building of the ◊Suez Canal (1859–69), to the extent that an Anglo-French commission was placed in charge of its finances. After subduing a nationalist revolt 1881–82, Britain occupied Egypt, and the government was from then on mainly in the hands of British civilian agents who directed their efforts to the improvement of the Egyptian economy. On the outbreak of World War I in 1914, nominal Turkish suzerainty was abolished, and the country was declared a British protectorate.

independence Postwar agitation by the nationalist Wafd party led to the granting of nominal independence 1922, under King Fuad I. He was succeeded by King Farouk 1936, and

Britain agreed to recognize Egypt's full independence, announcing a phased withdrawal of its forces, except from the Suez Canal, Alexandria, and Port Said, where it had naval bases. The start of World War II delayed the British departure, as did the consequent campaign in Libya that ended in the defeat of the German and Italian forces that had threatened the Canal Zone.

republic In 1946 all British troops except the Suez Canal garrison were withdrawn. In the immediate postwar years a radical movement developed, calling for an end to the British presence and opposing Farouk for his extravagant life style and his failure to prevent the creation of Israel. This led, in 1952, to a bloodless coup by a group of army officers, led by Col Gamal ◊Nasser, who replaced Farouk with a military junta. The 1923 constitution was suspended and all political parties banned. The following year Egypt declared itself a republic, with General Mohammad Neguib as president and prime minister. In 1954 Nasser became prime minister, and an agreement was signed for the withdrawal of British troops from the Canal Zone by 1956.

After a dispute with Neguib, Nasser took over as head of state and embarked on a programme of social reform. He became a major force for the creation of Arab unity and a leader of the ◊nonaligned movement. In 1956 the presidency was strengthened by a new constitution, and Nasser was elected president, unopposed. Later that year, British forces were withdrawn, in accordance with the 1954 agreement.

Suez crisis When the USA and Britain cancelled their offers of financial aid for the Aswan High Dam 1956, Nasser responded by nationalizing the Suez Canal. In a contrived operation, Britain, France, and Israel invaded the Sinai Peninsula 31 Oct 1956, and two days later Egypt was attacked. US pressure brought a cease-fire and an Anglo-French withdrawal 1957. The effect of the abortive Anglo-French operation was to push Egypt towards the USSR and to enhance Nasser's reputation in the Arab world.

In 1958 Egypt and Syria merged to become the United Arab Republic (UAR), with Nasser as president, but three years later Syria withdrew, though Egypt retained the title of UAR until 1971. The 1960s saw several unsuccessful attempts to federate Egypt, Syria, and Iraq. Despite these failures Nasser's prestige grew among his neighbours, while at home, in 1962, he founded the Arab Socialist Union (ASU) as Egypt's only recognized political organization.

Six-Day War In 1967 Egypt led an attack on Israel that developed into the Six-Day War, in which Israel defeated all its opponents, including Egypt. One result of the conflict was the blocking of the Suez Canal, which was not reopened until 1975. After Egypt's defeat, Nasser offered to resign but was persuaded to stay on. In 1970, aged 52, he died and was succeeded by Vice President Col Anwar ◊Sadat.

In 1971 a new constitution was approved, and the title Arab Republic of Egypt adopted. Sadat continued Nasser's policy of promoting Arab unity, but proposals to create a federation of Egypt, Libya, and Syria again failed.

Yom Kippur War In 1973 an attempt was made to regain territory from Israel. After 18 days' fighting, US secretary of state Henry ◊Kissinger arranged a cease-fire, resulting in Israel's evacuation of parts of Sinai, with a UN buffer zone separating the rival armies. This US intervention strengthened ties between the two countries while relations with the USSR cooled.

Camp David agreements In 1977 Sadat went to Israel to address the Israeli parliament and plead for peace. Other Arab states were dismayed by this move, and diplomatic relations with Syria, Libya, Algeria, and the Yemen, as well as the Palestine Liberation Organization (PLO), were severed and Egypt was expelled from the ◊Arab League 1979. Despite this opposition, Sadat pursued his peace initiative, and at the ◊Camp David talks in the USA, he and the Israeli prime minister, Menachem Begin, signed two agreements. The first laid a framework for peace in the Middle East, and the second, a framework for a treaty between the two countries. In 1979 a treaty was signed and Israel began a phased withdrawal from Sinai. As a consequence, Egypt's isolation from the Arab world grew, and the economy suffered from the withdrawal of Saudi subsidies. US aid became vital to Egypt's survival, and links between the two governments grew steadily closer.

position in Arab world In 1981 Sadat was assassinated by a group of Muslim fundamentalists who opposed him and was succeeded by Lt-Gen Hosni ◊Mubarak, who had been vice president since 1975. Just as Sadat had continued the policies of his predecessor, so did Mubarak. In the 1984 elections the National Democratic Party (NDP), formed by Sadat 1948, won an overwhelming victory in the assembly, strengthening Mubarak's position. Although Egypt's treaty with Israel remained intact, relations between the two countries became strained, mainly because of Israel's preemptive activities in Lebanon and the disputed territories. Egypt's relations with other Arab nations improved, and only Libya maintained its trade boycott; the restoration of diplomatic relations with Syria 1989 paved the way for Egypt's resumption of its leadership of the Arab world.

Mubarak has played a growing role in the search for Middle East peace, proposing a ten-point programme to bring about elections in the occupied territories. At home, problems with Muslim fundamentalists increased Mubarak's dependence on military support. In Oct 1987 he was re-elected by referendum for a second term. In the Dec 1990 general election, despite the success of the ruling party (NDP), with 348 seats, independents did well in many areas. Egypt was a member of the UN coalition forces that sought an economic embargo against Iraq 1990 for annexing Kuwait, and its armed forces joined in the military action against Iraq 1991. In Nov 1991, Egypt attended the Middle East peace talks in Spain. From May 1992 outbreaks of violence between Muslim and Christian militants were common.

Egypt is an acquired country, the gift of the river.

On **Egypt** Herodotus *History c.* 460 BC

Eichmann (Karl) Adolf 1906–1962. Austrian Nazi. As an ◊SS official during Hitler's regime (1933-1945), he was responsible for atrocities against Jews and others, including the implementation of genocide. He managed to escape at the fall of Germany 1945, but was discovered in Argentina 1960, abducted by Israeli agents, tried in Israel 1961 for ◊war crimes, and executed.

Eighth Route Army the Chinese *Red Army*, formed 1927 when the communists broke away from the ◊Guomindang (nationalists) and established a separate government in Jiangxi in SE China. When Japan invaded China 1937 the Red Army was recognized as a section of the national forces under the name Eighth Route Army and led by ◊Zhu De.

Eire former name (1937–48) of Southern Ireland, now the Republic of ◊Ireland.

Eisenhower Dwight David ('Ike') 1890–1969. 34th president of the USA 1953–61, a Republican. A general in World War II, he commanded the Allied forces in Italy 1943, then the Allied invasion of Europe, and from Oct 1944 all the Allied armies in the West. As president he promoted business interests at home and conducted the ◊Cold War abroad. His vice president was Richard Nixon.

Eisenhower was born in Texas. A graduate of West Point military academy in 1915, he served in a variety of staff and command posts before World War II. He became commander in chief of the US and British forces for the invasion of North Africa Nov 1942; commanded the Allied invasion of Sicily July 1943; and announced the surrender of Italy 8 Sept 1943. In Dec he became commander of the Allied Expeditionary Force. He served as chair of the joint Chiefs of Staff between 1949 and 1950. He resigned from the army 1952 to campaign for the presidency; he was elected, and re-elected by a wide margin in 1956. A popular politician, Eisenhower held office during a period of domestic and international tension, with the growing civil rights movement at home and the Cold War dominating international politics, although the USA was experiencing an era of postwar prosperity and growth.

El Alamein site of two decisive battles in World War II; see ◊Alamein, El.

El Cid see ◊Cid, El.

El Dorado fabled city of gold believed by the 16th-century Spanish and other Europeans to exist somewhere in the area of the Orinoco and Amazon rivers.

Eleanor of Aquitaine *c.* 1122–1204. Queen of France 1137–51 as wife of Louis VII, and of England from 1154 as wife of Henry II. Henry imprisoned her 1174–89 for supporting their sons, the future Richard I and King John, in revolt against him.

She was the daughter of William X, Duke of Aquitaine, and was married 1137–52 to Louis VII of France, but the marriage was annulled. The same year she married Henry of Anjou, who became king of England 1154.

Eleanor of Castile *c.* 1245–1290. Queen of Edward I of England, the daughter of Ferdinand III of Castile. She married Prince Edward 1254, and accompanied him on his crusade 1270. She died at Harby, Nottinghamshire, and Edward erected stone crosses in towns where her body rested on the funeral journey to London. Several *Eleanor Crosses* are still standing, for example at Northampton.

elector (German *Kurfürst*) any of originally seven (later ten) princes of the Holy Roman Empire who had the prerogative of electing the emperor (in effect, the king of Germany). The electors were the archbishops of Mainz, Trier, and Cologne, the court palatine of the Rhine, the Duke of Saxony, the Margrave of Brandenburg, and the king of Bohemia (in force to 1806). Their constitutional status was formalized 1356 in the document known as the

Golden Bull, which granted them extensive powers within their own domains, to act as judges, issue coins, and impose tolls.

Eliot John 1592–1632. English politician, born in Cornwall. He became a member of Parliament 1614, and with the Earl of Buckingham's patronage was made a vice-admiral 1619. In 1626 he was imprisoned in the Tower of London for demanding Buckingham's impeachment. In 1628 he was a formidable supporter of the ◊petition of right opposing Charles I, and with other parliamentary leaders was again imprisoned in the Tower of London 1629, where he died.

Elizabeth I 1533–1603. Queen of England 1558–1603, the daughter of Henry VIII and Anne Boleyn. Through her Religious Settlement of 1559 she enforced the Protestant religion by law. She had ◊Mary Queen of Scots executed 1587. Her conflict with Roman Catholic Spain led to the defeat of the ◊Spanish Armada 1588. The Elizabethan age was expansionist in commerce and geographical exploration, and arts and literature flourished. The rulers of many European states made unsuccessful bids to marry Elizabeth, and she used these bids to strengthen her power. She was succeeded by James I.

Elizabeth was born at Greenwich, London, 7 Sept 1533. She was well educated in several languages. During her Roman Catholic half-sister Mary's reign, Elizabeth's Protestant sympathies brought her under suspicion, and she lived in seclusion at Hatfield, Hertfordshire, until on Mary's death she became queen. Her first task was to bring about a broad religious settlement.

Many unsuccessful attempts were made by Parliament to persuade Elizabeth to marry or settle the succession. She found courtship a useful political weapon, and she maintained friendships with, among others, the courtiers ◊Leicester, Sir Walter ◊Raleigh, and ◊Essex. She was known as the Virgin Queen.

The arrival in England 1568 of Mary, Queen of Scots, and her imprisonment by Elizabeth caused a political crisis, and a rebellion of the feudal nobility of the north followed 1569. Friction between English and Spanish sailors hastened the breach with Spain. When the Dutch rebelled against Spanish tyranny Elizabeth secretly encouraged them; Philip II retaliated by aiding Catholic conspiracies against her. This undeclared war continued for many years, until the landing of an English army in the Netherlands 1585 and Mary's execution 1587, brought it into the open. Philip's Armada (the fleet sent to invade England 1588) met with total disaster.

The war with Spain continued with varying fortunes to the end of the reign, while events at home foreshadowed the conflicts of the 17th century. Among the Puritans discontent was developing with Elizabeth's religious settlement, and several were imprisoned or executed. Parliament showed a new independence, and in 1601 forced Elizabeth to retreat on the question of the crown granting manufacturing and trading monopolies. Yet her prestige remained unabated, as was shown by the failure of Essex's rebellion 1601.

Anger makes dull men witty, but it keeps them poor.

> *Queen Elizabeth I*
> Francis Bacon *Apophthegms*

Elizabeth II 1926–   . Queen of Great Britain and Northern Ireland from 1952, the elder daughter of George VI. She married her third cousin, Philip, the Duke of Edinburgh, 1947. They have four children: Charles, Anne, Andrew, and Edward.

Princess Elizabeth Alexandra Mary was born in London 21 April 1926; she was educated privately, and assumed official duties at 16. During World War II she served in the Auxiliary Territorial Service, and by an amendment to the Regency Act she became a state counsellor on her 18th birthday. On the death of George VI in 1952 she succeeded to the throne while in Kenya with her husband and was crowned on 2 June 1953.

Elizabeth 1709–1762. Empress of Russia from 1741, daughter of Peter the Great. She carried through a palace revolution and supplanted her cousin, the infant Ivan VI (1730–1764), on the throne. She continued the policy of westernization begun by Peter and allied herself with Austria against Prussia.

Ellis Island island in New York Harbor, USA; area 11 hectares/27 acres. A former reception centre for steerage-class immigrants during the immigration waves between 1892-1943 (12 million people passed through it 1892-1924), it was later used as a detention centre for nonresidents without documentation, or for those who were being deported. It is a National Historic Site (1964) and has the Museum of Immigration (1989).

El Salvador country in Central America, bounded N and E by Honduras, S and SW by the Pacific Ocean, and NW by Guatemala.
history The original inhabitants of the area were Indians, who arrived from Mexico around

3000 BC. From the period of the Maya Indians AD 100 to 1000 remain huge limestone pyramids built by them in western El Salvador. The Pipil Indians were in control of the area at the time of the Spanish conquest 1525. El Salvador and other Central American Spanish colonies broke away from Spanish rule 1821, and became part of the ◊United Provinces of Central America until 1840.

power held by army and oligarchy The history of El Salvador has been marked by a succession of military revolts, with periods of tyrannical rule, violence, and political assassinations. A more orderly form of political succession was established after 1871. Yet governments tended to be dominated by the same economic interests, families, and clans. In general, the army and the planter alike controlled affairs.

guerrilla movement formed After a coup 1961 the conservative National Conciliation Party (PCN) was established, winning all the seats in the national assembly. The PCN stayed in power, with reports of widespread human-rights violations, until challenged 1979 by a socialist guerrilla movement, the Farabundo Martí Liberation Front (FMLN). A civilian-military junta deposed the president.

death squads operate In 1980 the archbishop of San Salvador, Oscar Romero, a champion of human rights, was shot dead in his cathedral. The murder of three US nuns and a social worker prompted US president Jimmy Carter to suspend economic and military aid. In 1980 José Napoleón Duarte, leader of a moderately left-of-centre coalition, returned from exile and became president. The conservative US administration of Ronald Reagan supported him, as an anticommunist, and encouraged him to call elections 1982. The left-wing parties refused to participate, and the elections were held amid great violence, at least 40 people being killed on election day. Although Duarte's Christian Democrats (PDC) won the largest number of assembly seats, a coalition of right-wing parties blocked his continuation as president. A provisional chief executive was selected from a list of candidates acceptable to the military, serving until the 1984 elections, which Duarte won in a runoff against Roberto d'Aubuisson, a rightist suspected of involvement in the death of Archbishop Romero.

guerrilla war In 1984 the president's daughter was abducted by guerrillas, forcing him to negotiate with them, in the face of criticism from opposition parties and the military. In 1985 the anti-imperialist PDC won a convinc-ing victory in the assembly, with 33 seats. The right-wing National Republic Alliance (ARENA) and PCN won 13 and 12 seats respectively, fighting the election on a joint platform. The guerrilla war continued; in Aug 1987 they agreed to meet and discuss the Regional Peace Plan of the ◊Contadora Group with Duarte, but the peace initiative collapsed. The election 1989 of Alfredo Cristiani of D'Aubuisson's ARENA party (amid allegations of ballot-rigging) appeared to herald a return to a hard line against the FMLN rebels.

ballot rigging Following the rigged right-wing victory in the 1989 elections, many activists in trade-union, cooperative, and human-rights organizations were arrested. The guerrillas mounted a surprisingly effective offensive in the wealthy suburbs of San Salvador but in Sept 1989 agreed to peace talks. In 1990 a consistently high level of 'disappearances' was denounced by the country's Human Rights Commission. In the 1991 general election ARENA claimed 43 assembly seats and continued in power.

cost of conflict It was estimated that about 35,000 people were killed 1979–82; some 70,000 between 1980 and 1990. US aid to El Salvador 1981-88 totalled $3.3 billion. During 1982 alone, some 1,600 Salvadorean troops were trained in the USA, and US military advisers were said to be actively involved in the country's internal conflict.

peace accord signed A peace accord initiated by the United Nations, signed by representatives of the government and the FMLN Dec 1991, came into effect Feb 1992. The FMLN subsequently became a political party. The 1994 presidential election was won by Armando Calderón Sol of ARENA.

Emancipation Proclamation in US history, President Lincoln's Civil War announcement, 22 Sept 1862, stating that from the beginning of 1863 all black slaves in states still engaged in rebellion against the federal government would be emancipated. Slaves in border states still remaining loyal to the Union were excluded.

Emmet Robert 1778–1803. Irish nationalist leader. In 1803 he led an unsuccessful revolt in Dublin against British rule and was captured, tried, and hanged. His youth and courage made him an Irish hero.

Empire Day former name (until 1958) of ◊Commonwealth Day.

Empire Settlement Act British act of Parliament 1922 which provided for the first large-scale state-assisted migration programme undertaken by the British government. Over 400,000 people received state subsidies totalling £6million which helped them travel to a variety of imperial destinations, mainly in the dominions, during the inter-war period. The legislation was renewed 1937 and 1952 but operations and costs were on a much smaller scale.

enabling act legislative enactment enabling or empowering a person or corporation to take certain actions. Perhaps the best known example of an Enabling Law was that passed in Germany in March 1933 by the Reichstag and Reichsrat. It granted Hitler's cabinet dictatorial powers until April 1937, and effectively terminated parliamentary government in Germany until 1950. The law firmly established the Nazi dictatorship by giving dictatorial powers to the government.

enclosure appropriation of common land as private property, or the changing of open-field systems to enclosed fields (often used for sheep). This process began in Britain in the 14th century and became widespread in the 15th and 16th centuries. It caused poverty, homelessness, and rural depopulation, and resulted in revolts 1536, 1569, and 1607.

Numerous government measures to prevent depopulation were introduced 1489–1640, including the first Enclosure Act 1603, but were sabotaged by landowning magistrates at local level. A new wave of enclosures by Acts of Parliament 1760–1820 reduced the yeoman class of small landowning farmers to agricultural labourers, or forced them to leave the land. The Enclosure Acts applied to 4.5 million acres or a quarter of England. Some 17 million acres were enclosed without any parliamentary act. From 1876 the enclosure of common land in Britain was limited by statutes. Enclosures occurred throughout Europe on a large scale during the 19th century, often at the behest of governments. The last major Enclosure Act was in 1903.

encomienda in colonial Spanish America, the granting of Indian people to individual conquistadors (settlers) by the Spanish crown.

The system was based on the assignment of Moorish villages to members of the military orders in medieval Castile, but was revived in the colonies, with the idea that native labour was exchanged for protection. Abuses led reformers such as Bartolomé de las Casas (1474–1566) to call for its abolition. It declined steadily after 1550.

Engels Friedrich 1820–1895. German social and political philosopher, a friend of, and collaborator with, Karl ◊Marx on *The Communist Manifesto* 1848 and other key works. His later interpretations of Marxism, and his own philosophical and historical studies such as *Origins of the Family, Private Property, and the State* 1884 (which linked patriarchy with the development of private property), developed such concepts as historical materialism. His use of positivism and Darwinian ideas gave Marxism a scientific and deterministic flavour which was to influence Soviet thinking.

In 1842 Engels's father sent him to work in the cotton factory owned by his family in Manchester, England, where he became involved with ◊Chartism. In 1844 his lifelong friendship with Karl Marx began, and together they worked out the materialist interpretation of history and in 1847–48 wrote the *Communist Manifesto*. Returning to Germany during the 1848–49 revolution, Engels worked with Marx on the *Neue Rheinische Zeitung/New Rhineland Newspaper* and fought on the barricades in Baden. After the defeat of the revolution he returned to Manchester, and for the rest of his life largely supported the Marx family.

Engels's first book was *The Condition of the Working Classes in England* 1845. He summed up the lessons of 1848 in *The Peasants' War in Germany* 1850 and *Revolution and Counter-Revolution in Germany* 1851. After Marx's death Engels was largely responsible for the wider dissemination of his ideas; he edited the second and third volumes of Marx's *Das Kapital* 1885 and 1894. Although Engels himself regarded his ideas as identical with those of Marx, discrepancies between their works are the basis of many Marxist debates.

The State is not 'abolished', it withers away.

Friedrich Engels Anti Dühring

England largest division of the ◊United Kingdom; for earlier history, see ◊Britain, ancient.
history
AD 43 Roman invasion.
5th–7th centuries Anglo-Saxons overran all England except Cornwall and Cumberland, forming independent kingdoms including Northumbria, Mercia, Kent, and Wessex.
c. 597 England converted to Christianity by St Augustine.
829 Egbert of Wessex accepted as overlord of all England.
878 Alfred ceded N and E England to the Danish invaders but kept them out of Wessex.

1066 Norman Conquest; England passed into French hands under William the Conqueror.
1172 Henry II became king of Ireland and established a colony there.
1215 King John forced to sign Magna Carta.
1284 Conquest of Wales, begun by the Normans, completed by Edward I.
1295 Model Parliament set up.
1338–1453 Hundred years' War with France enabled parliament to secure control of taxation and, by impeachment, of the king's choice of ministers.
1348–49 Black Death killed about 30% of the population.
1381 Social upheaval led to the Peasants' Revolt, which was brutally repressed.
1399 Richard II deposed by parliament for absolutism.
1414 Lollard revolt repressed.
1455–85 Wars of the Roses.
1497 Henry VII ended the power of the feudal nobility with the suppression of the Yorkist revolts.
1529 Henry VIII became head of the Church of England after breaking with Rome.
1536–43 Acts of Union united England and Wales after conquest.
1547 Edward VI adopted Protestant doctrines.
1553 Reversion to Roman Catholicism under Mary I.
1558 Elizabeth I adopted a religious compromise.
1588 Attempted invasion of England by the Spanish Armada.
1603 James I united the English and Scottish crowns; parliamentary dissidence increased.
1642–52 Civil War between royalists and parliamentarians, resulting in victory for Parliament.
1649 Charles I executed and the Commonwealth set up.
1653 Oliver Cromwell appointed Lord Protector.
1660 Restoration of Charles II.
1685 Monmouth rebellion.
1688 William of Orange invited to take the throne; flight of James II.
1707 Act of Union between England and Scotland under Queen Anne, after which the countries became known as Great Britain.
For further history, see ◊United Kingdom.

enosis (Greek 'union') movement, developed from 1930, for the union of ◊Cyprus with Greece. The campaign (led by ◊EOKA and supported by Archbishop Makarios) intensified from the 1950s. In 1960 independence from Britain, without union, was granted, and increased demands for union led to its procla-

mation 1974. As a result, Turkey invaded Cyprus, ostensibly to protect the Turkish community, and the island was effectively partitioned.

Entente Cordiale (French 'friendly understanding') agreement reached by Britain and France 1904 recognizing British interests in Egypt and French interests in Morocco. It formed the basis for Anglo-French cooperation before the outbreak of World War I 1914.

Enver Pasha 1881–1922. Turkish politician and soldier. He led the military revolt 1908 that resulted in the Young Turks' revolution (see ◊Turkey). He was killed fighting the Bolsheviks in Turkestan.

EOKA acronym for *Ethnikí Organósis Kipriakóu Agónos* (National Organization of Cypriot Struggle) an underground organization formed by General George ◊Grivas 1955 to fight for the independence of Cyprus from Britain and ultimately its union (*enosis*) with Greece. In 1971, 11 years after the independence of Cyprus, Grivas returned to the island to form EOKA B and to resume the fight for *enosis*, which had not been achieved by the Cypriot government.

Epaminondas *c.* 420–362 BC. Theban general and politician who won a decisive victory over the Spartans at Leuctra 371. He brought independence to Messenia and Arcadia, and consolidated Theban supremacy before dying from wounds received at the battle of Mantinea 362 BC.

Ephor one of the five annually elected magistrates in ancient ◊Sparta. The office was instituted *c.* 700 BC and continued into the 2nd century AD. The ephors exercised considerable control over the dual kingship, and presided over Spartan assemblies.

Equatorial Guinea country in W central Africa, bounded N by Cameroon, E and S by Gabon, and W by the Atlantic Ocean; also five offshore islands including Bioko, off the coast of Cameroon.

history The area was inhabited by Pygmies before the 1200s, followed by various ethnic groups settling the mainland and islands. Reached by Portuguese explorers 1472, the islands came under Spanish rule in the mid-1800s and the mainland territory of Río Muni (now Mbini) 1885, the whole colony being known as Spanish Guinea. From 1959 the territory was a Spanish Overseas Province, with internal autonomy from 1963.

dictatorship After 190 years of Spanish rule, Equatorial Guinea became fully independent

1968, with Francisco Macias Nguema as president with a coalition government. In 1970 he banned all political parties and replaced them with one, the United National Party (PUN). Two years later he declared himself president for life and established a dictatorship, controlling press and radio and forbidding citizens to leave the country. There were many arrests and executions 1976–77. He also established close relations with the Soviet bloc.

military regime In 1979 he was overthrown in a coup by his nephew, Lt-Col Teodoro Obiang Nguema Mbasogo, with at least the tacit approval of Spain. Macias was tried and executed. Obiang expelled the Soviet advisers and technicians and renewed economic and political ties with Spain. He banned the PUN and other political parties and ruled through a supreme military council. Coups against him 1981 and 1983 were unsuccessful, and he was re-elected 1982 and 1989. In 1992 a new constitution was introduced and elections held, but the members of the house of representatives were all nominated by the president and elected unopposed.

Erhard Ludwig 1897–1977. West German Christian Democrat politician, chancellor of the Federal Republic 1963–66. The 'economic miracle' of West Germany's recovery after World War II is largely attributed to Erhard's policy of social free enterprise that he initiated during his period as federal economics minister (1949–63).

Ericsson Leif *c.* AD 1000. Norse explorer, son of Eric the Red, who sailed west from Greenland about 1000 to find a country first sighted by Norsemen 986. Landing with 35 companions in North America, he called it Vinland, because he discovered grape vines growing there.

The story was confirmed 1963 when a Norwegian expedition, led by Helge Ingstad, discovered remains of a Viking settlement (dated about 1000) near the fishing village of L'Anse-aux-Meadows at the northern tip of Newfoundland.

Eric the Red 940–1010. Allegedly the first European to find Greenland. According to a 13th-century saga, he was the son of a Norwegian chieftain, and was banished from Iceland about 982 for murder. He then sailed westward and discovered a land that he called Greenland.

Eritrea province of N Ethiopia. Part of an ancient Ethiopian kingdom until the 7th century; under Ethiopian influence until it fell to the Turks mid-16th century; Italian colony 1889–1941, when it was the base for Italian invasion of Ethiopia; under British administra-

tion from 1941 to 1952, when it became an autonomous part of Ethiopia. Since 1962, when it became a region, various secessionist movements have risen. During the civil war in the 1970s, guerrillas held most of Eritrea; the Ethiopian government, backed by Soviet and Cuban forces, recaptured most towns 1978. Resistance continued throughout the 1980s, aided by conservative Gulf states, and some cooperation with guerrillas in Tigré province. The collapse of Ethiopia's government 1991 led to the recognition of Eritrea's right to seek independence.

Ershad Hussain Mohammad 1930– . Military ruler of Bangladesh 1982-90. He became chief of staff of the Bangladeshi army 1979 and assumed power in a military coup 1982. As president from 1983, Ershad introduced a successful rural-oriented economic programme. He was re-elected 1986 and lifted martial law, but faced continuing political opposition, which forced him to resign Dec 1990. In 1991 he was formally charged with the illegal possession of arms, convicted, and sentenced to ten years' imprisonment. He received a further sentence of three years' imprisonment Feb 1992 after being convicted of corruption.

Esarhaddon King of Assyria from 680 BC, when he succeeded his father ◊Sennacherib. He conquered Egypt 674–671 BC.

escheat (Old French *escheir* 'to fall') in feudal society, the reversion of lands to the lord in the event of the tenant dying without heirs or being convicted for treason. By the late Middle Ages in W Europe, tenants had insured against their lands escheating by granting them to trustees, or feoffees, who would pass them on to the grantor nominated in the will. Lands held directly by the king could not legally be disposed of in this way.

In England, royal officials, called escheators, were appointed to safeguard the king's rights.

Essex Robert Devereux, 2nd Earl of Essex 1566–1601. English soldier and politician. He became a favourite with Queen Elizabeth I from 1587, but was executed because of his policies in Ireland.

Reasons are not like garments, the worse for wearing.

Earl of Essex to Lord Willoughby
1598 or 1599

---

estate in European history, an order of society that enjoyed a specified share in government. In medieval theory, there were usually three estates – the *nobility*, the *clergy*, and the *commons* – with the functions of, respectively, defending society from foreign aggression and internal disorder, attending to its spiritual needs, and working to produce the base with which to support the other two orders.

When parliaments and representative assemblies developed from the 13th century, their organization reflected this theory, with separate houses for the nobility, the commons (usually burghers and gentry), and the clergy.

Estonia country in N Europe, bounded E by Russia, S by Latvia, and N and W by the Baltic Sea.

history Independent states were formed in the area now known as Estonia during the 1st century AD. In the 13th century southern Estonia came under the control of the ◊Teutonic Knights, German crusaders, who converted the inhabitants to Christianity. The Danes, who had taken control of northern Estonia, sold this area to the Teutonic Knights 1324. By the 16th century German nobles owned much of the land. In 1561 Sweden took control of the north, with Poland governing the south; Sweden ruled the whole country 1625–1710. Estonia came under Russian control 1710, but it was not until the 19th century that the Estonians started their movement for independence.

struggle for independence Estonia was occupied by German troops during World War I. The Soviet forces, who tried to regain power 1917, were overthrown by Germany in March 1918, restored Nov 1918, and again overthrown with the help of the British navy May 1919, when Estonia, having declared independence 1918, was established as a democratic republic. A fascist coup 1934 replaced the government.

Soviet republic In 1939 Germany and the USSR secretly agreed that Estonia should come under Russian influence and the country was incorporated into the USSR as the Estonian Soviet Socialist Republic 1940. During World War II Estonia was again occupied by Germany 1941–44, but the USSR subsequently regained control.

renewed nationalism Nationalist dissent grew from 1980. In 1988 Estonia adopted its own constitution, with a power of veto on all Soviet legislation. The new constitution allowed private property and placed land and natural resources under Estonian control. An Estonian popular front (Rahvarinne) was established Oct 1988 to campaign for democratization, increased autonomy, and eventual independence, and held mass rallies. In Nov of the same year Estonia's supreme soviet (state

assembly) voted to declare the republic 'sovereign' and thus autonomous in all matters except military and foreign affairs, although the presidium of the USSR's supreme soviet rejected this as unconstitutional. In 1989 a law was passed replacing Russian with Estonian as the main language and in Nov of that year Estonia's assembly denounced the 1940 incorporation of the republic into the USSR as 'forced annexation'.

multiparty elections Several parties had sprung up by the elections of March 1990 – the Popular Front, the Association for a Free Estonia, and the Russian-oriented International Movement – and a coalition government was formed. A plebiscite in the spring of 1991 voted 77.8% in favour of independence. By the summer the republic had embarked on a programme of privatization. The prices of agricultural products were freed in July 1991.

independence On 20 Aug 1991, in the midst of the attempted anti-Gorbachev coup in the USSR, during which Red Army troops were moved into Tallinn to seize the television transmitter and the republic's main port was blocked by the Soviet navy, Estonia declared its full independence (it had previously been in a 'period of transition') and outlawed the Communist Party. In Sept 1991 this declaration was recognized by the Soviet government and Western nations and the new state was granted membership of the United Nations and also entered the ◊Conference on Security and Cooperation in Europe.

economic problems Prime minister Edgar Savisaar and his cabinet resigned Jan 1992 after failing to alleviate food and energy shortages. Tiit Vahl, the former transport minister, formed a new government which included five key ministers unchanged from the previous cabinet. He proposed the lifting of the state of economic emergency which had recently been imposed by Savisaar. In June a new constitution was approved in a nationwide referendum, but the Sept 1992 presidential election failed to produce a clear winner, putting the onus on the parliament to elect a new head of state. In the parliamentary elections no single party won an overall majority but the right-wing Fatherland Group emerged with the largest number of seats.

ETA separatist movement of the ◊Basques, *Euskadi ta Askatasuna*.

Ethelbert *c.* 552–616. King of Kent 560-616. He was defeated by the West Saxons 568 but later became ruler of England S of the river Humber. Ethelbert received the Christian missionary Augustine 597 and later converted to become the first Christian ruler of Anglo-Saxon

England. He issued the first written code of laws known in England.

Ethelred II *the Unready* c. 968–1016. King of England from 978. He tried to buy off the Danish raiders by paying Danegeld. In 1002, he ordered the massacre of the Danish settlers, provoking an invasion by Sweyn I of Denmark. War with Sweyn and Sweyn's son, Canute, occupied the rest of Ethelred's reign. He was nicknamed the 'Unready' because of his apparent lack of foresight.

Ethiopia country in E Africa, bounded NE by Djibouti and the Red Sea, E and SE by Somalia, S by Kenya, and W and NW by Sudan.

history Long subject to Egypt, the area became independent about the 11th century BC. The kingdom of ◊Aksum flourished 1st–6th centuries AD, reaching its peak about the 4th century with the introduction of Coptic Christianity from Egypt, and declining from the 7th century as Islam expanded. The Arab conquests isolated Aksum from the rest of the Christian world.

During the 10th century there emerged a kingdom that formed the basis of Abyssinia, reinforced 1270 with the founding of a new dynasty. Although it remained independent throughout the period of European colonization of Africa, Abyssinia suffered civil unrest and several invasions from the 16th century, and was eventually reunited 1889 under ◊Menelik II, with Italian support. In 1896 Menelik put down an invasion by Italy, which claimed he had agreed to make the country an Italian protectorate, and annexed Ogaden in the southeast and several provinces to the west.

Ethiopian empire Ethiopia was ruled for over 50 years by ◊Haile Selassie, who became regent 1916, king 1928, and emperor 1930. The country was occupied by Italy 1935–41, and Haile Selassie went into exile in Britain. Ogaden was returned to Somalia, which was also under Italian control. Haile Selassie returned from exile 1941 and ruled until 1974, when he was deposed by the armed forces after famine, high inflation, growing unemployment, and demands for greater democracy. His palace and estates were nationalized, parliament dissolved, and the constitution suspended. Ethiopia was proclaimed a socialist state and rule was established by a Provisional Military Administrative Council (PMAC). Haile Selassie died 1975, aged 83, detained in an apartment in his former palace in Addis Ababa.

secessionist movements General Teferi Benti, who had led the uprising and been made head of state, was killed 1977 by fellow officers and replaced by Col Mengistu Haile Mariam. The Ethiopian empire had been built up by Haile Selassie and Menelik, and annexed regions had made frequent attempts to secede. The 1974 revolution encouraged secessionist movements to increase their efforts, and the military government had to fight to keep Eritrea and Ogaden, where Somalian troops were assisting local guerrillas.

The USSR, having adopted Ethiopia as a new ally, threatened to cut off aid to Somalia, and Cuban troops assisted Mengistu in ending the fighting there. Eritrea and its neighbour, Tigré, continued their struggle for independence.

famine Amid this confusion there was acute famine in the north, including Eritrea, when the rains failed for three successive seasons. In addition to a massive emergency aid programme from many Western nations, the Ethiopian government tried to alleviate the problem by resettling people from the north in the more fertile south. By 1986 more than 500,000 had been forcibly resettled.

Tigré breaks free Meanwhile, the military regime had re-established normal relations with most of its neighbours. In 1987 a new constitution was adopted and Col Mengistu Mariam was elected the country's first president. Tigré province was captured by the Eritrean People's Liberation Front (EPLF) and the Tigré People's Liberation Front (TPLF) Feb 1989, the first time the government had lost control of the entire province. A coup against Mengistu in May 1989 was put down and the military high command subsequently purged. Following a mediation offer by the former US president Jimmy ◊Carter, peace talks with the Eritrean rebels began Aug 1989. At the same time, droughts in the north threatened another widespread famine.

Mengistu ousted Rebel pressure on the Mengistu government increased steadily during early 1991; in May Mengistu fled the country when the Ethiopian People's Revolutionary Democratic Front (EPRDF) occupied Addis Ababa. The EPLF gained virtually complete control of Eritrea and secured the province's capital, Asmara, after 30 years of fighting.

transition period Peace and stability commissions were set up to monitor the end of the civil war. In July 1991 delegates from Ethiopia's political and ethnic groups met to organize a transitional government to administer the country until the elections planned for 1993. The conference also gave regional and ethnic groups the right to form their own countries, and agreed Eritrea's right to seek independence. On 21 July, Meles Zenawi, leader of the EPRDF (which held a majority in Ethiopia's transitional legislature), was elected head of state. In Sept 1991 Isaias Afwerki, leader of the EPLF, became secretary general of the provisional government of Eritrea.

Etruscan member of an ancient people inhabiting Etruria, Italy (modern-day Tuscany and part of Umbria) from the 8th to 4th centuries BC. The Etruscan dynasty of the Tarquins ruled Rome 616-509 BC. At the height of their civilization, in the 6th century BC, the Etruscans achieved great wealth and power from their maritime strength. They were driven out of Rome 509 BC and eventually dominated by the Romans.

Eugène Prince of Savoy 1663–1736. Austrian general who had many victories against the Turkish invaders (whom he expelled from Hungary 1697 in the Battle of Zenta) and against France in the War of the ◊Spanish Succession (battles of Blenheim, Oudenaarde, and Malplaquet).

Eugénie Marie Ignace Augustine de Montijo 1826–1920. Empress of France, daughter of the Spanish count of Montijo. In 1853 she married Louis Napoleon, who had become emperor as ◊Napoleon III. She encouraged court extravagance and Napoleon III's intervention in Mexico, and urged him to fight the Prussians. After his surrender to the Germans at Sedan, NE France, 1870 she fled to England.

Eureka Stockade incident at Ballarat, Australia, when about 150 goldminers, or 'diggers', rebelled against the Victorian state police and military authorities. They took refuge behind a wooden stockade, which was taken in a few minutes by the military on 3 Dec 1854. Some 30 gold diggers were killed, and a few soldiers killed or wounded, but the majority of the rebels were taken prisoner. Among those who escaped was Peter Lalor, their leader. Of the 13 tried for treason, all were acquitted, thus marking the emergence of Australian democracy.

Eurocommunism policy followed by communist parties in Western Europe to seek power within the framework of national political initiative rather than by revolutionary means. In addition, Eurocommunism enabled these parties to free themselves from total reliance on the USSR.

European Atomic Energy Commission (Euratom) organization established by the second Treaty of Rome 1957, which seeks the cooperation of member states of the European Union in nuclear research and the rapid and large-scale development of nonmilitary nuclear energy.

European Community (EC) former name (to 1993) of the ◊European Union (EU).

European Free Trade Association (EFTA) organization established 1960 consisting of Iceland, Norway, Switzerland, and (from 1991) Liechtenstein, previously a nonvoting associate member. There are no import duties between members. Of original EFTA members, Britain and Denmark left (1972) to join the European Community (EC), as did Portugal (1985); Austria, Finland, and Sweden joined the EC's successor, the European Union (EU) 1995.

European Union political and economic alliance consisting of the European Coal and Steel Community (1952), European Economic Community (EEC, popularly called the Common Market, 1957), and the European Atomic Energy Commission (Euratom, 1957). The original six members – Belgium, France, West Germany, Italy, Luxembourg, and the Netherlands – were joined by the UK, Denmark, and the Republic of Ireland 1973, Greece 1981, and Spain and Portugal 1986. East Germany was incorporated on German reunification 1990. Austria, Finland, and Sweden joined 1995. Association agreements, providing for free trade within ten years and the possibility of full membership, were signed with Czechoslovakia, Poland, and Hungary 1991, Romania 1992, and later with Bulgaria and Slovakia. In 1995 there were more than 360 million people in EU countries.

A European Charter of Social Rights (known as the Social Chapter) was approved at the Maastricht summit Dec 1991 by all members except the UK. The same meeting secured agreement on a treaty framework for European union, including political and monetary union, and for a new system of police and military cooperation. After initial rejection by Denmark in a national referendum June 1992, the ◊Maastricht Treaty on European union came into effect 1 Nov 1993 and the designation European Union was adopted, embracing not only the various bodies of its predecessor, the EC, but also two intergovernmental 'pillars', covering common foreign and security policy (CFSP) and cooperation on justice and home affairs. In Sept 1995 the EUs member nations stated their commitment to the attainment of monetary union by 1999, and in Dec 1995 they agreed to call the new currency the euro.

The aims of the EU include the expansion of trade, reduction of competition, the abolition of restrictive trading practices, the encouragement of free movement of capital and labour within the alliance, and the establishment of closer union among European people. A single market with free movement of goods and capital was established Jan 1993.

The EU has the following institutions: the *European Commission* of 20 members pledged to independence of national interests, who initiate Union action (two members each from France, Germany, Italy, Spain, and the UK; and one each from Austria, Belgium, Denmark, Finland, Greece, Ireland, Luxembourg, Netherlands, Portugal, and Sweden); the *Council of Ministers of the European Union*, which makes decisions on the Commission's proposals; the *European Parliament*, directly elected from 1979; the *Economic and Social Committee*, a consultative body; the *Committee of Permanent Representation* (COREPER), consisting of civil servants temporarily seconded by members states to work for the Commission; and the European Court of Justice, to safeguard interpretation of the Rome Treaties (1957) that established the original alliance.

European Court of Justice court to safeguard the interpretation of the Rome Treaties that established the ◊European Union.

European Defence Community supranational western European army planned after World War II and designed to counterbalance the military superiority of the USSR in eastern Europe. Although a treaty was signed 1952, a thaw in East–West relations lessened the need for this force and negotiations were instead directed to the formation of the Western European Union in 1955.

European Free Trade Association (EFTA) organization established 1960 consisting of Austria, Finland, Iceland, Norway, Sweden, Switzerland, and (from 1991) Liechtenstein,

previously a nonvoting associate member. There are no import duties between members.

European Parliament directly elected parliament of the ◊European Union.

Evangelical Movement in Britain, a 19th-century group that stressed basic Protestant beliefs and the message of the four Gospels. The movement was associated with Rev Charles Simeon (1783–1836). It aimed to raise moral enthusiasm and ethical standards among Church of England clergy.

Evesham, Battle of 4 Aug 1265, during the ◊Barons' Wars, Edward, Prince of Wales, defeated Simon de Montfort, who was killed.

Exodus the departure of the Israelites from slavery in Egypt, under the leadership of ◊Moses, for the Promised Land of Canaan. The journey included the miraculous parting of the Red Sea, with the Pharaoh's pursuing forces being drowned as the waters returned.

Exploration *see chronology* (Exploration: 1434–1522) *and feature* (Exploration: the age of disovery).

Eyre Edward John 1815–1901. English explorer who wrote *Expeditions into Central Australia* 1845. He was governor of Jamaica 1864–65. *Lake Eyre* in South Australia is named after him.

Ezekiel lived *c.* 600 BC. Hebrew prophet. Carried into captivity in Babylon by ◊Nebuchadnezzar 597, he preached that Jerusalem's fall was due to the sins of Israel. The book of Ezekiel begins with a description of a vision of supernatural beings.

Ezra a Hebrew scribe who was allowed by Artaxerxes, king of Persia (probably Artaxerxes I, 464–423 BC), to lead his people back to Jerusalem from Babylon 458 BC. He re-established the Mosaic law (laid down by Moses) and forbade intermarriage.

Exploration: the age of discovery

During the 15th and 16th centuries, Europeans broke out of their continent to explore, trade, conquer, and colonize throughout Africa, Asia, and the new continent of America. By 1600, only Australasia remained unknown to Europeans. The explorers' motives were a mixture of greed (there were medieval tales of fabulous wealth in Asia), religious fervour (saving the souls of pagans), desire for fame and glory, and plain curiosity. In essence exploration was an overseas expression of the Renaissance: a new 'human-centred' world ready to conquer and question.

Around the Mediterranean, there was considerable expertise in sailing, navigation, and banking, which was important for financing expeditions. In the Iberian Peninsula the last European strongholds of Islam collapsed (Granada fell in the year of Columbus's first voyage to America), and there was a feeling of triumphalism among the Christian rulers. They believed it was their duty to take the *Reconquista* (Spanish 'reconquest') beyond their own shores, and spread the word of their God into parts unknown – simultaneously extending their secular dominions. Portugal and Spain, best suited geographically, were the pioneers.

Economic demands

These ambitions of church and state provided support for merchants and others who promoted voyages of discovery for economic reasons. Demand for all sorts of commodities was rising as Europe's population recovered from the ravages of the Black Death in the 14th century. Growing trade put pressure on European stocks of gold and silver, from which coins were minted. Nearly all the supplies of these precious metals came from Africa, which was also a source of the slaves which were so important to Mediterranean economies. There was also increasing demand for spices, silk, and other luxury goods from the East.

Problems with the old routes

In the days of Marco Polo (1254–1324), European merchants could travel overland to the Far East to buy silks and spices close to their places of origin. The Mongols allowed Europeans to journey on land all the way to China in relative safety. Trade with North Africa was also fairly easy. However, the 14th and 15th centuries saw the disintegration of the Mongol empire, the expansion of the Ottomans across Asia Minor and the Balkans, and growing isolationism in Ming China. This blocked the direct routes, restricting European traders to the Mediterranean, where they bought at vastly inflated prices from middlemen. An alternative route to the Islamic bloc promised vast fortunes, prompting the race to find a sea route to the East.

The Portuguese were the first to try, with their bid to find a way round the southern tip of Africa. Bartholomew Dias made the breakthrough in 1488, naming the discovery the Cape of Storms (changed by the king of Portugal to the Cape of Good Hope), but it was not until 1497 that Vasco da Gama and his crew became the first Europeans to sail to India. By then the Spanish,

attempting to reach Asia from the W, had stumbled on a new continent.

Encouragement from the past

Educated Europeans had believed the Earth to be round since the time of Aristotle and Plato, but many thought the Atlantic Ocean was unnavigable. This view began to change with the rediscovery in the 15th century of two classical writers previously lost to the Latin Christian tradition, with the translation from Arabic into Latin of works by Ptolemy and Strabo. Ptolemy's *Geography* gave a detailed account of much of Asia and Africa, and he used lines of latitude and longitude to describe locations. He also underestimated the size of the globe by about 25%. Strabo argued that the Atlantic could be crossed, enabling Europeans to reach Asia by sailing west. These theories gave great encouragement to early explorers, including the Genoese Christopher Columbus.

In Oct 1492, sailing under the Spanish flag, Columbus reached San Salvador in the Bahamas, believing it to be the East Indies (hence the common appellation of native Americans as 'Indians'). Further Spanish expeditions followed, and the realization dawned that this was a 'new' continent. At first, the Spanish saw the native Americans as a ready supply of slaves, but this soon changed. Many indigenous peoples were exterminated or decimated by European diseases to which they had no immunity, by the cataclysmic disruption of their traditional cultures, and by the appallingly savage treatment they received which in places amounted to a conscious policy of genocide.

The 'triangular trade'

The casualties were replaced by African slaves, and the 'triangular trade' between Europe, Africa, and the Americas brought misery to millions of Africans from the 16th to the 19th centuries, and vast wealth to some Europeans. American silver helped to turn Spain into the superpower of the 16th century, and over the next 300 years, the exploitation of empires in America, Africa, and Asia allowed European powers to achieve world supremacy.

In the treaties of Tordesillas (1494) and Zaragossa (1529), Spain and Portugal established their monopoly of empire in west and east – Brazil going to Portugal because it would prove to be on the eastern side of the line of longitude dividing the world. France and England were to contest this later in the 16th century. England's challenge was expressed in terms of trade, exploration, and colonization which may be loosely associated with Hawkins' pursuit of slave markets, Drake's voyage round the world, and Raleigh's settlement of Virginia. By the mid 17th century, the Dutch had become an important colonial power as the grip of Portugal in the east began to decline. The Treaty of Utrecht (1713) marked the technical recognition by Spain that her monopolist claims were over, when it conceded to England a formal right to trade in slaves.

Exploration: 1434–1522

1434 Gil Eannes rounded Cape Bojador, opening the way for Portuguese exploration of W Africa.

***c.* 1441** First slaves brought to Europe from W Africa.

1445 Portuguese landed on Cape Verde Islands.

1455 Alvise de Cadamost, a Venetian in Portuguese service, sailed to Africa. Papal bull Pontifex Romanus recognized Portuguese monopoly of African exploration.

1460 Death of Prince Henry of Portugal, 'The Navigator'.

1469 Afonso V of Portugal leased monopoly of W African trade to Fernão Gomes in return for continued exploration.

1474 Paolo Toscanelli's letter encouraged Christopher Columbus of Genoa to sail west.

1478 Abraham Zacuto compiled tables of sun's declination, helping the calculation of latitude.

1479 Spain agreed that Portugal should have monopoly rights in trade with Guinea.

1481 Accession of John II of Portugal. Fort founded at Elmina (in modern Ghana) as base for Portugal's African trade.

1482 Portuguese Diego Cão sailed down W African coast, reaching the Congo and later Angola in search of sea route to India.

1487 John II dispatched Pero de Covilhã to the E in search of Prester John.

1488 Bartolomen Diaz rounded Cape of Good Hope.

1492 Under Spanish patronage, Christopher Columbus reached the West Indies.

1493 Pope Alexander VI issued bulls of demarcation, granting Spanish monopoly of exploration in areas previously controlled by Portugal. Columbus set out to colonize Hispaniola.

1494 Treaty of Tordesillas gave Spain exclusive rights of exploration and exploitation W of a line drawn N-S across the Atlantic. Portugal had similar rights E of this line.

1496 Italian John Cabot, commissioned by Henry VII of England, embarked on first voyage of discovery westwards across the N Atlantic.

1497 Vasco da Gama left Lisbon. Cabot reached Newfoundland on his second voyage.

1498 Da Gama arrived at Calicut, having discovered the sea route to India. Cabot disappeared on his third voyage.

1499 Under Spanish flag, Florentine Amerigo Vespucci and Spaniards Alonso de Hojeda and Juan de la Cosa discovered South America. Christopher and brother Bartholomew Columbus sent back to Spain in chains by Francisco de Bobadilla. Azorean Gaspar Corte Real, sailing for the Portuguese, sighted Greenland.

1500 Portuguese Pedro Alvares Cabral discovered Brazil. Juan de la Cosa produced a world map.

1501 Under Portuguese flag, Vespucci explored the E coast of South America.

1502 Da Gama embarked on second voyage. Columbus set off on his last voyage to search for the Asian mainland.

1504 Columbus returned to Spain. Sebastian Cabot sailed to Newfoundland.

1505 Almeida appointed first viceroy for India, marking the beginning of the Portuguese commercial empire in the East. Spanish conquered Puerto Rico.

1506 Death of Columbus.

1507 First recorded usage of term 'America' to denote the New World, derived from name of explorer Amerigo Vespucci.

1508 Cabot set sail to find the Northwest Passage.

1509 Almeida destroyed Egyptian fleet at Battle of Diu and was then recalled. Albuquerque appointed second viceroy for India.

1510 Portuguese captured Goa from Bijapur. Start of large-scale European trade in African slaves.

1511 Portuguese captured Malacca.

1513 Spaniard Vasco Nuñez de Balboa crossed the isthmus of Darien to reach the Pacific.

1519 Portuguese Ferdinand Magellan and Juan Sebastian del Cano sailed westwards in search of Spice Islands. Hernán Cortés arrived in Mexico.

1521 Siege and capture of Tenochtitlán by Cortés and conquistadores.

1522 Del Cano returned to Spain, having circumnavigated the globe.

Fabian Society UK socialist organization for research, discussion, and publication, founded in London 1884. Its name is derived from the Roman commander ◊Fabius Maximus, and refers to the evolutionary methods by which it hopes to attain socialism by a succession of gradual reforms. Early members included the playwright George Bernard Shaw and Beatrice and Sidney Webb. The society helped to found the Labour Representation Committee in 1900, which became the Labour Party in 1906.

Fabius Maximus Quintus *c.* 260–203 BC. Roman general, known as *Cunctator* or 'Delayer' because of his cautious tactics against Hannibal 217–214 BC, when he continually harassed Hannibal's armies but never risked a set battle.

factory act in Britain, an act of Parliament such as the Health and Safety at Work Act 1974, which governs conditions of work, hours of labour, safety, and sanitary provision in factories and workshops.

In the 19th century legislation was progressively introduced to regulate conditions of work, hours of labour, safety, and sanitary provisions in factories and workshops. The first legislation was the Health and Morals of Apprentices Act 1802. In 1833 the first factory inspectors were appointed. Legislation was extended to offices, shops, and railway premises 1963. All employees are now covered by the Health and Safety at Work Act, which is enforced by the Health and Safety Executive.

Fadden Artie (Arthur) 1895–1973. Australian politician, leader of the Country Party 1941–58 and prime minister Aug–Oct 1941.

Fahd 1921– . King of Saudi Arabia from 1982, when he succeeded his half-brother Khalid. As head of government, he has been active in trying to bring about a solution to the Middle East conflicts.

Fair Deal the social welfare programme advocated by Harry S Truman, president of the USA 1945–53. The Fair Deal proposals, first

Factory Acts in the UK			
1802	Health and Morals of Apprentices Act, a first attempt to regulate conditions for workhouse children in the textile industry.	1901	Minimum working age increased to 12. Trade Boards established to fix minimum wages, extended 1918.
1819	Factory Act prohibited children under nine working in cotton mills. Others were set an 11-hour maximum day.	1909	First Old Age Pensions Act gave five shillings per week to those over 70 with annual incomes less than 31 10 shillings.
1833	Althorp's Factory Act further limited working hours for children in textile factories. Four factory inspectors appointed.	1911	National Insurance Act covered sickness and unemployment in vulnerable trades.
1842	Mines Act prohibited employment of women and children under ten underground. Factory Act reduced hours for children and youths in textile factories.	1931	'Means-tested' unemployment benefit introduced.
		1937	Factory Act limited workers under 16 to a 44-hour week and women to a 48-hour week. New safety regulations introduced.
1847	Factory Act imposed maximum ten-hour day for women and young people in textile factories. Subsequent 1850 Act specified hours as between 6 a.m. and 6 p.m.	1946	National Insurance Act provided comprehensive cover for industrial injuries.
1853	Shift work for children outlawed.	1961	Factories Act extended safety regulations to all workplaces. Graduated pension scheme introduced.
1864 and 1867	Factory Acts extended existing provisions to industries other than textiles and mines, and finally to all places employing over 50 people.	1965	Graduated redundancy payments introduced.
1878	Regulation of conditions in workshops, extended 1891.	1974	Health and Safety at Work legislation extended to cover all workers. Provisions applied to offshore oil and gas workers from 1975.

mooted in 1945 after the end of World War II, aimed to extend the ◊New Deal on health insurance, home ownership, and the laws to maintain farming prices. Although some bills became law – for example a Housing Act, a higher minimum wage, and wider social security benefits – the main proposals were blocked by a hostile Congress.

Fairfax Thomas, 3rd Baron Fairfax of Cameron 1612–1671. English general, commander in chief of the Parliamentary army in the English Civil War. With Oliver Cromwell he formed the ◊New Model Army and defeated Charles I at Naseby. He opposed the king's execution, resigned in protest 1650 against the invasion of Scotland, and participated in the restoration of Charles II after Cromwell's death.

Faisal Ibn Abdul Aziz 1905–1975. King of Saudi Arabia from 1964. He was the younger brother of King Saud, on whose accession 1953 he was declared crown prince. He was prime minister from 1953–60 and from 1962–75. In 1964 he emerged victorious from a lengthy conflict with his brother and adopted a policy of steady modernization of his country. He was assassinated by his nephew.

Faisal I 1885–1933. King of Iraq 1921–33. An Arab nationalist leader during World War I, he was instrumental in liberating the Near East from Ottoman control and was declared king of Syria in 1918 but deposed by the French in 1920. The British then installed him as king in Iraq, where he continued to foster pan-Arabism.

Falange,the (Spanish 'phalanx') also known as Falange Española. Former Spanish Fascist Party, founded 1933 by José Antonio de Rivera (1903–1936), son of military ruler Miguel ◊Primo de Rivera. It was closely modelled in programme and organization on the Italian fascists and on the Nazis. In 1937, when ◊Franco assumed leadership, it was declared the only legal party, and altered its name to Traditionalist Spanish Phalanx.

Falcón Juan Crisóstomo 1820–1870. Venezuelan marshal and president 1863–68. Falcón's rule saw the beginnings of economic recovery after the chaos of the Federal Wars 1858–63. He travelled around the country putting down uprisings while his ministers in Caracas built roads, restored the nation's finances, and established foreign trade links. He fell from power because he was unable to tackle splits in the ruling Liberal party.

Falkland Islands (Spanish *Islas Malvinas*) British crown colony in the S Atlantic. The first European to visit the islands was Englishman John Davis 1592. At the end of the 17th century they were named after Lord Falkland, treasurer of the British navy. West Falkland was settled by the French 1764. The first British settlers arrived 1765; Spain bought out a French settlement 1766, and the British were ejected 1770–71, but British sovereignty was never ceded, and from 1833, when a few Argentines were expelled, British settlement was continuous.

Argentina asserts its succession to the Spanish claim to the 'Islas Malvinas', but the inhabitants oppose cession. Occupied by Argentina April 1982, the islands were recaptured by British military forces in May–June of the same year. In April 1990 Argentina's congress declared the Falkland Islands and other British-held South Atlantic islands part of the new Argentine province of Tierra del Fuego.

Falklands War war between Argentina and Britain over disputed sovereignty of the Falkland Islands initiated when Argentina invaded and occupied the islands 2 April 1982. On the following day, the United Nations Security Council passed a resolution calling for Argentina to withdraw. A British task force was immediately dispatched and, after a fierce conflict in which over 1,000 Argentine and British lives were lost, 12,000 Argentine troops surrendered and the islands were returned to British rule 14–15 June 1982.

The Falklands thing was a fight between two bald men over a comb.

Jorge Luis Borges on the Falklands War in *Time* 1983

Fargo William George 1818–1881. US long-distance transport pioneer. In 1844 he established with Henry Wells (1805–1878) and Daniel Dunning the first express company to carry freight west of Buffalo. Its success led to his appointment 1850 as secretary of the newly established American Express Company, of which he was president 1868–81. He also established *Wells, Fargo & Company* 1851, carrying goods express between New York and San Francisco via Panama.

Farnese Italian family, originating in upper Lazio, who held the duchy of Parma 1545–1731. Among the family's most notable members were Alessandro Farnese (1468–1549), who became Pope Paul III in 1534 and granted his duchy to his illegitimate son Pier Luigi (1503–1547); Elizabeth (1692–1766), niece of the last Farnese duke, married Philip V of Spain and was a force in European politics of the time.

Farouk 1920–1965. King of Egypt 1936–52. He succeeded his father ◊Fuad I. In 1952 a coup headed by General Muhammad Neguib and Colonel Gamal Nasser compelled him to abdicate, and his son Fuad II was temporarily proclaimed in his place.

fasces in ancient Rome, bundles of rods carried in procession by the lictors (minor officials) in front of the chief magistrates, as a symbol of the latter's power over the lives and liberties of the people. An axe was included in the bundle. The fasces were revived in the 20th century as the symbol of ◊fascism.

fascism political ideology that denies all rights to individuals in their relations with the state; specifically, the totalitarian nationalist movement founded in Italy 1919 by ◊Mussolini and followed by Hitler's Germany 1933.

Fascism was essentially a product of the economic and political crisis of the years after World War I. Units called *fasci di combattimento* (combat groups), from the Latin ◊fasces, were originally established to oppose communism. The fascist party, the *Partitio Nazionale Fascista*, controlled Italy 1922–43. Fascism protected the existing social order by forcible suppression of the working-class movement and by providing scapegoats for popular anger such as outsiders who lived within the state: Jews, foreigners, or blacks; it also prepared the citizenry for the economic and psychological mobilization of war.

Fashoda Incident dispute 1898 in the town of Fashoda (now Kodok) situated on the White Nile in SE Sudan, in which a clash between French and British forces nearly led the two countries into war.

Fatah, al- Palestinian nationalist organization founded 1956 to bring about an independent state of Palestine. Also called the Palestine National Liberation Movement, it is the main component of the ◊Palestine Liberation Organization. Its leader is Yassir ◊Arafat.

Fatimid dynasty of Muslim Shi'ite caliphs founded 909 by Obaidallah, who claimed to be a descendant of Fatima (the prophet Muhammad's daughter) and her husband Ali, in N Africa. In 969 the Fatimids conquered Egypt, and the dynasty continued until overthrown by Saladin 1171.

Faulkner Brian 1921–1977. Northern Ireland Unionist politician. He was the last prime minister of Northern Ireland 1971–72 before the Stormont Parliament was suspended.

Fawcett Millicent Garrett 1847–1929. English suffragette, younger sister of Elizabeth Garrett Anderson. A non-militant, she rejected the violent acts of some of her contemporaries in the suffrage movement. She joined the first Women's Suffrage Committee 1867 and became president of the Women's Unionist Association 1889.

Fawkes Guy 1570–1606. English conspirator in the ◊Gunpowder Plot to blow up King James I and the members of both Houses of Parliament. Fawkes, a Roman Catholic convert, was arrested in the cellar underneath the House 4 Nov 1605, tortured, and executed. The event is still commemorated in Britain and elsewhere every 5 Nov with bonfires, fireworks, and the burning of the 'guy', an effigy.

FBI abbreviation for the ◊Federal Bureau of Investigation.

fealty in feudalism, the loyalty and duties owed by a vassal to his lord. In the 9th century fealty obliged the vassal not to take part in any action that would endanger the lord or his property, but by the 11th century the specific duties of fealty were established and included financial obligations and military service. Following an oath of fealty, an act of allegiance and respect (homage) was made by the vassal; when a ◊fief was granted by the lord, it was formalized in the process of investiture.

February Revolution the first of the two political uprisings of the ◊Russian Revolution in 1917 that led to the overthrow of the tsar and the end of the ◊Romanov dynasty.

Federal Bureau of Investigation (FBI) agency of the US Department of Justice that investigates violations of federal law not specifically assigned to other agencies, being particularly concerned with internal security. The FBI was established 1908 and built up a position of powerful autonomy during the autocratic directorship of J Edgar Hoover 1924–72.

Federalist in US history, one who advocated the ratification of the US Constitution 1787–88 in place of the Articles of ◊Confederation. The Federalists became in effect the ruling political party during the presidencies of George Washington and John Adams 1789–1801, legislating to strengthen the authority of the newly created federal government.

Federalist Papers, the in US politics, a series of 85 letters published in the newly independent USA in 1788, attempting to define the relation of the states to the nation, and making the case for a federal government. The papers were signed 'Publius', the joint pseudonym of three leading political figures: Alexander Hamilton, John Jay, and James Madison.

Feijó Diogo Antônio 1784–1843. Brazilian politician, regent of Brazil 1835–37. The illegitimate son of a priest, Feijó trained for the priesthood and was a teacher before his election to the Portuguese Cortes (parliament) 1821. A dedicated liberal and opponent of the slave trade, he was appointed minister of justice after the abdication of Pedro II 1831. A hostile parliament allowed him to accomplish little as regent.

Fenian movement Irish-American republican secret society, founded 1858 and named after the ancient Irish legendary warrior band of the Fianna. The collapse of the movement began when an attempt to establish an independent Irish republic by an uprising in Ireland 1867 failed, as did raids into Canada 1866 and 1870, and England 1867.

Ferdinand II 1452–1516. King of Aragon from 1479, also known as ◊Ferdinand V of Castile.

Ferdinand 1861–1948. King of Bulgaria 1908–18. Son of Prince Augustus of Saxe-Coburg-Gotha, he was elected prince of Bulgaria 1887 and, in 1908, proclaimed Bulgaria's independence of Turkey and assumed the title of tsar. In 1915 he entered World War I as Germany's ally, and in 1918 abdicated.

Ferdinand five kings of Castile, including:

Ferdinand I *the Great* c. 1016–1065. King of Castile from 1035. He began the reconquest of Spain from the Moors and united all NW Spain under his and his brothers' rule.

Let justice be done, though the world perish.

Ferdinand I the Great quoted in M Manlius, *Loci Communes* 1563

Ferdinand V 1452–1516. King of Castile from 1474, *Ferdinand II* of Aragon from 1479, and *Ferdinand III* of Naples from 1504; first king of all Spain. In 1469 he married his cousin Isabella I, who succeeded to the throne of Castile 1474; they were known as *the Catholic Monarchs* because after 700 years of rule by the ◊Moors, they Catholicized Spain. When Ferdinand inherited the throne of Aragon 1479, the two great Spanish kingdoms were brought under a single government for the first time. They introduced the ◊Inquisition 1480; expelled the Jews, forced the final surrender of the Moors at Granada, and financed Columbus' expedition to the Americas, 1492.

Ferdinand three Holy Roman emperors:

Ferdinand I 1503–1564. Holy Roman emperor who succeeded his brother Charles V 1558; king of Bohemia and Hungary from 1526, king of the Germans from 1531. He reformed the German monetary system and reorganized the judicial Aulic council (*Reichshofrat*). He was the son of Philip the Handsome and grandson of Maximilian I.

Ferdinand II 1578–1637. Holy Roman emperor from 1619, when he succeeded his uncle Matthias; king of Bohemia from 1617 and of Hungary from 1618. A zealous Catholic, he provoked the Bohemian revolt that led to the Thirty Years' War. He was a grandson of Ferdinand I.

Ferdinand III 1608–1657. Holy Roman emperor from 1637 when he succeeded his father Ferdinand II; king of Hungary from 1625. Although anxious to conclude the Thirty Years' War, he did not give religious liberty to Protestants.

Ferdinand I 1423–1494. King of Naples 1458–94, known as *Ferrante*. He was the son of Alfonso V of Aragon (1396-1458) and his illegitimacy brought him into conflict with the papacy many times during his reign. His authoritarian rule provoked several baronial revolts, including major ones in 1462 and 1485. He promoted learning and trade, but his hold on his territories was weak. He fought a series of campaigns against the French and Turks to retain his dominions, but the French invaded soon after his death.

Ferdinand III 1452–1516 King of Naples from 1504, also known as ◊Ferdinand V of Castile.

Ferdinand 1865–1927. King of Romania from 1914, when he succeeded his uncle Charles I. In 1916 he declared war on Austria. After the Allied victory in World War I, Ferdinand acquired Transylvania and Bukovina from Austria-Hungary, and Bessarabia from Russia. In 1922 he became king of this Greater Romania. His reign saw agrarian reform and the introduction of universal suffrage.

Ferry Jules François Camille 1832–1893. French republican politician, mayor of Paris during the siege of 1870–71. As a member of the republican governments of 1879–85 (prime minister 1880–81 and 1883–85) he was responsible for the 1882 law making primary education free, compulsory, and secular. He directed French colonial expansion in Tunisia 1881 and Indochina (the acquisition of Tonkin in 1885).

Fertile Crescent region of the Middle East from the Persian Gulf to the Nile Valley,

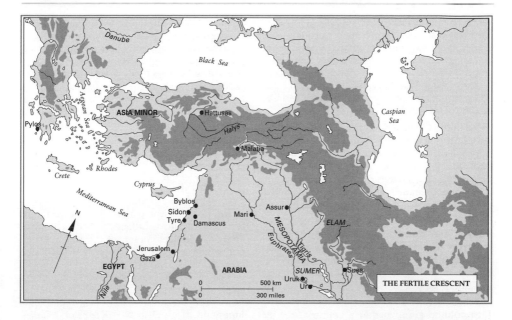

The Fertile Crescent *The Euphrates and Tigris rivers, with the Zagros mountains to the east, Syria and Palestine, and the Anatolian massif, sustained a succession of cultures. Jericho had a defensive wall by 6000 BC. The civilizations of Sumer (from 3200), Assyria (from about 1800), and Persia (capital Susa) followed each other in Mesopotamia and Elam. In Anatolia the Hittites predominated from the 3rd to the 1st millennium BC, with the Minoan and Mycenaean civilizations of Crete and Greece to the west. The Persians conquered Egypt and Phoenicia (Byblos, Tyre, and Sidon) in the later 6th century BC.*

including the Euphrates and Tigris rivers. It was the birthplace of several ancient empires, including Sumer, Assyria, and Persia.

feudalism (Latin *feudem* 'fief', coined 1839) main form of social organization in medieval Europe. A system based primarily on land, it involved a hierarchy of authority, rights, and power that extended from the monarch downwards. An intricate network of duties and obligations linked royalty, nobility, lesser gentry, free tenants, villeins, and serfs. Feudalism was reinforced by a complex legal system and supported by the Christian church. With the growth of commerce and industry from the 13th century, feudalism gradually gave way to the class system as the dominant form of social ranking.

In return for military service the monarch allowed powerful vassals to hold land, and often also to administer justice and levy taxes. They in turn 'sublet' such rights. At the bottom of the system were the serfs, who worked on their lord's manor lands in return for being allowed to cultivate some for themselves, and so underpinned the system. They could not be sold as if they were slaves, but they could not leave the estate to live or work elsewhere without permission. The system declined from the 13th century, partly because of the growth of a money economy, with commerce, trade, and industry, and partly because of the many peasants' revolts 1350–1550. Serfdom ended in England in the 16th century, but lasted in France until 1789 and in the rest of Western Europe until the early 19th century. In Russia it continued until 1861.

Fezzan former province of Libya, a desert region, with many oases. It was captured from Italy 1942, and placed under French control until 1951 when it became a province of the newly independent United Kingdom of Libya. It was split into smaller divisions 1963.

Fianna Fáil (Gaelic 'Soldiers of Destiny') Republic of Ireland political party, founded by the Irish nationalist de Valera 1926. It has been the governing party in the Republic of Ireland 1932–48, 1951–54, 1957–73, 1977–81, 1982, 1987–94 and from 1997. It aims at the establishment of a united and completely independent all-Ireland republic.

Fidei Defensor Latin for the title of 'Defender of the Faith' (still retained by British sovereigns) conferred by Pope Leo X on Henry VIII of England 1521 to reward his writing of a treatise against the Protestant Martin Luther.

fief an estate of lands held by a ◊vassal from his lord, given after the former had sworn homage, or ◊fealty, promising to serve the lord. As a noble tenure, it carried with it rights of jurisdiction.

In the later Middle Ages, it could also refer to a grant of money, given in return for service, as part of ◊bastard feudalism.

Field of the Cloth of Gold site between Guînes and Ardres near Calais, France, where a meeting took place between Henry VIII of England and Francis I of France in June 1520, remarkable for the lavish clothes worn and tent pavilions erected. Francis hoped to gain England's support in opposing the Holy Roman emperor, Charles V, but failed.

Fifteen, the ◊Jacobite rebellion of 1715, led by the 'Old Pretender' ◊James Edward Stuart and the Earl of Mar, in order to place the former on the English throne. Mar was checked at Sheriffmuir, Scotland, and the revolt collapsed.

fifth column group within a country secretly aiding an enemy attacking from without. The term originated 1936 during the Spanish Civil War, when General Mola boasted that Franco supporters were attacking Madrid with four columns and that they had a 'fifth column' inside the city.

Fiji country comprising 844 islands and islets in the SW Pacific Ocean, about 100 of which are inhabited.

history Originally inhabited by Melanesian and Polynesian peoples, Fiji's first European visitor was Abel ◊Tasman 1643. Fiji became a British possession 1874 and achieved full independence within the Commonwealth 1970. Before independence there had been racial tension between Indians, descended from workers brought from India in the late 19th century, and Fijians, so the constitution incorporated an electoral system that would ensure racial balance in the house of representatives.

ethnic divisions Traditionally the Fijians support the Alliance Party (AP), whose leader, Ratu Sir Kamisese Mara, became prime minister at the time of independence and has held office ever since. The Indians support the National Federation Party (NFP), led by Siddiq Koya. The main divisions between the two have centred on land ownership, with the Fijians owning more than 80% of the land and defending their traditional rights, and the Indians demanding greater security of land tenure. The Fijian Labour Party (FLP) was formed 1985 but has so far made little impact at the polls.

republic An attempted coup May 1987, led by Col Sitiveni Rabuka, was abandoned after intervention by the governor general and the Great Council of Chiefs. Another coup by Rabuka in Sept seemed, despite indecision by its leader, more likely to succeed. On this occasion Queen Elizabeth II, at the instigation of the governor general, condemned the coup in an unprecedented fashion. Nevertheless, the coup went ahead and in Oct 1987 the Queen accepted the resignation of the governor general, thereby relinquishing her role as head of state and making Fiji a republic. A new constitution, first drafted Aug 1989, was introduced 1990. It guaranteed indigenous Fijians 37 seats in the new 70-seat parliament; the rest were reserved for native Indians and other national groups. The electoral law of the new constitution would also prevent the army from taking control.

The May 1992 general election resulted in a coalition government. The president named former coup leader Rabuka as prime minister in June.

Fillmore Millard 1800–1874. 13th president of the USA 1850–53, a Whig. Born into a poor farming family in New Cayuga County, New York State, he was Zachary Taylor's vice-president from 1849, and succeeded him on Taylor's death, July 9 1850. Fillmore supported a compromise on slavery 1850 to reconcile North and South.

This compromise pleased neither side, and it contained a harsh fugitive slave act requiring escaped slaves to be returned to their owners. He threatened to enforce this act with troops, if necessary, earning the wrath of the abolitionists. Fillmore failed to be nominated for another term.

final solution (to the Jewish question; German *Endlosung der Judenfrage*) euphemism used by the Nazis to describe the extermination of Jews (and other racial groups or 'undesirables' and opponents of the regime) before and during World War II. See ◊Holocaust.

Fine Gael (Gaelic 'United Ireland') Republic of Ireland political party founded 1933 by W J ◊Cosgrave and led by John Bruton from 1990. It is socially liberal but fiscally conservative.

Finland country in Scandinavia, bounded N by Norway, E by Russia, S and W by the Baltic Sea, and NW by Sweden.

history The nomadic Saami, or Lapps, were the earliest known inhabitants; from about the 1st century BC they were gradually driven north by Finnic nomads from Asia into the far northern region they occupy today. The area was conquered in the 12th–13th centuries by Sweden, and for much of the next 200 years the country was the scene of wars between Sweden and Russia. As a duchy of Sweden, Finland was allowed a measure of autonomy, becoming a grand duchy 1581. In 1809, during the Napoleonic Wars, Finland was invaded and annexed by Russia; nationalist feeling grew, and the country proclaimed its independence during the 1917 Russian revolution. The Soviet regime initially tried to regain control but acknowledged Finland's independence 1920.

Winter War In 1939 the USSR's request for military bases in Finland was rejected, and the USSR invaded Finland. The resulting ◊Winter War lasted for 15 weeks. Finland was defeated and forced to cede territory. In the hope of regaining it, in 1941 it joined Nazi Germany in attacking the USSR, but agreed to a separate armistice 1944. It was again forced to cede territory (12% of its total area) and agree to huge war reparations; in 1948 it signed the Finno-Soviet Pact of Friendship, Co-operation, and Mutual Assistance (the YYA Treaty). War reparations to the USSR were paid off 1952 (amounting to 5% of the gross domestic product 1945–48). In 1955 Finland joined the United Nations and the Nordic Council (which includes Denmark, Iceland, Norway, and Sweden).

neutrality The YYA Treaty was extended 1955, 1970, and 1983. Although the Treaty requires it to repel any attack on the USSR through Finnish territory by Germany or its allies, Finland maintained a policy of strict neutrality. It signed a trade treaty with the EC 1973 and a 15-year trade agreement with the USSR 1977. In 1989 it was admitted into the Council of Europe.

short-term governments Finnish politics have been characterized by instability in governments, over 60 having been formed since independence, including many minority coalitions. The presidency, on the other hand, has been very stable, with only two presidents in over 30 years. Urho Kekkonen was elected president 1956 and re-elected 1962, 1968, and 1978. In 1981 he resigned from office on health grounds and Mauno Koivisto became president Jan 1982; he was re-elected 1988.

The Social Democratic and Centre parties dominated Finland's coalition politics for many years, but the 1987 general election resulted in the Social Democrats entering government in coalition with their archenemies, the Conservatives (KOK), while the Centre Party was forced

into opposition. In the 1991 elections the Centre Party emerged with 55 seats, the Social Democrats 48, the Conservatives 40, the Alliance of the Left 19, and the Greens 10.

In March 1992 the Finnish government agreed to apply formally for membership of the European Community. The economy was hit by the world recession and the disruption of trade with the former USSR; the markka was devalued and cutbacks were made in the extensive welfare system.

Finlandization political term for the tendency of a small state to shape its foreign policy so as to accommodate a much more powerful neighbour, taken from the example of Finland's foreign policy with respect to the USSR.

First World War another name for ◊World War I, 1914–18.

Fisher Andrew 1862–1928. Australian Labor politician. Born in Scotland, he went to Australia 1885, and entered the Australian parliament in 1901. He was prime minister 1908–09, 1910–13, and 1914–15, and Australian high commissioner to the UK 1916–21.

Fisher John Arbuthnot, First Baron Fisher 1841–1920. British admiral, First Sea Lord 1904–10, when he carried out many radical reforms and innovations, including the introduction of the dreadnought battleship.

He served in the Crimean War 1855 and the China War 1859–60. He held various commands before becoming First Sea Lord, and returned to the post 1914, but resigned the following year, disagreeing with Winston Churchill over sending more ships to the Dardanelles, Turkey, in World War I.

The essence of war is violence.
Moderation in war is imbecility.

John Arbuthnot Fisher
quoted in R H Bacon,
Life of Lord Fisher

FitzGerald Garret 1926– . Irish politician. As *Taoiseach* (prime minister) 1981-82 and again 1982–86, he was noted for his attempts to solve the Northern Ireland dispute, ultimately by participating in the Anglo-Irish agreement 1985. He tried to remove some of the overtly Catholic features of the constitution to make the Republic more attractive to Northern Protestants. He retired as leader of the Fine Gael Party 1987.

Five Dynasties and Ten Kingdoms chaotic period in Chinese history 907–960 between the

◊Han and ◊Song dynasties, during which regionally based military dictatorships contested for power. The five dynasties, none of which lasted longer than 16 years, were based mainly in N China and the ten kingdoms in the south.

five-year plan long-term strategic plan for the development of a country's economy. Five-year plans were from 1928 the basis of economic planning in the USSR, aimed particularly at developing heavy and light industry in a primarily agricultural country. They have since been adopted by many other countries.

Flaminius Gaius died 217 BC. Roman consul and general. He constructed the Flaminian Way northward from Rome to Rimini 220 BC, and was killed at the battle of Lake Trasimene fighting ◊Hannibal.

Flanders region of the Low Countries that in the 8th and 9th centuries extended from Calais to the Scheldt and is now covered by the Belgian provinces of Oost Vlaanderen and West Vlaanderen (East and West Flanders), the French *département* of Nord, and part of the Dutch province of Zeeland. The language is Flemish.

It was settled by Salian Franks as Roman allies 358, and in the 6th century, became a province of the Frankish kingdom. Baldwin I (died 879), the son-in-law of Charles the Bald, became its first count 862. During the following 300 years, the county resisted Norman encroachment, expanded its territory, and became a leading centre of the wool industry. In 1194, Philip II married the niece of Count Philip of Alsace (1143–1191), and so began a period of active French involvement in the county.

There was friction within Flemish society between the pro-French bourgeoisie and nobility and the craftworkers in the towns who supported the English, their major partners in the wool trade. In 1302, the craftworkers seized power in Bruges and Ghent and defeated the French at Courtrai, but the pro-French faction regained control of the county 1328. During the Hundred Years' War, Edward III of England put a trade embargo on Flemish wool, which caused serious economic depression, and led to further popular revolts, which were finally put down at the battle of Roosebeke 1382 by the French. The last count, Louis de Male, died 1384, and the county was inherited by his son-in- law, Philip the Bold of Burgundy (1342–1404), to become part of the Burgundian domains.

It underwent a decline under Austrian rule in the 17th to 19th centuries. Fierce battles were fought here in World War I. In World War II the *Battle of Flanders* began with the German breakthrough 10 May 1940 and ended with the British amphibious retreat from Dunkirk 27 May–4 June.

Flodden, Battle of the defeat of the Scots by the English under the Earl of Surrey 9 Sept 1513 on a site 5 km/3 mi SE of Coldstream, Northumberland, England; many Scots, including King James IV, were killed.

Still from the sire, the son shall hear/of the stern strife and carnage drear,/Of Flodden's fatal field,/Where shivered was fair Scotland's spear/and broken was her shield.

On *The Battle of Flodden* Walter Scott
Marmion 1808

Florence (Italian *Firenze*) capital of Tuscany, N Italy. The Roman town of Florentia was founded in the 1st century BC on the site of the Etruscan town of Faesulae. It was besieged by the Goths AD 405 and visited by Charlemagne 786.

In 1052, Florence passed to Countess Matilda of Tuscany (1046–1115), and from the 11th century onwards gained increasing autonomy. In 1198 it became an independent republic, with new city walls, and governed by a body of 12 citizens. In the 13th–14th centuries, the city was the centre of the struggle between the Guelphs (papal supporters) and Ghibellines (supporters of the Holy Roman emperor). Despite this, Florence became immensely prosperous and went on to reach its cultural peak during the 14th–16th centuries.

From the 15th to the 18th century, the ◊Medici family, originally bankers, were the predominant power, in spite of their having been twice expelled by revolutions. In the first of these, in 1493, a year after Lorenzo de' Medici's death, a republic was proclaimed (with ◊Machiavelli as secretary) that lasted until 1512. From 1494 to 1498, the city was under the control of religious reformer ◊Savonarola. In 1527, the Medicis again proclaimed a republic, which lasted through many years of gradual decline until 1737, when the city passed to Maria Theresa of Austria. From 1737 the city was ruled by the Habsburg imperial dynasty. The city was badly damaged in World War II and by floods 1966.

Flores Juan José 1801–1864. Ecuadorian general, president 1830–35, 1839–45. Born in

Venezuela, he joined Simón ◊Bolívar's patriot army in his teens, and soon became one of its most trusted generals. Flores convoked the assembly declaring Ecuador's independence 1830 and was elected its first constitutional president the same year. During his two terms in office Ecuador was an oasis of stability in Spanish America.

Exiled, his attempt to invade Ecuador from Peru 1852 failed, but he was later recalled as a military commander and ended Ecuador's civil war 1860.

FNLA abbreviation for *Front National de Libération de l'Angola* (French 'National Front for the Liberation of Angola').

Foch Ferdinand 1851–1929. Marshal of France during World War I. He was largely responsible for the Allied victory at the first battle of the ◊Marne Sept 1914, and commanded on the NW front Oct 1914–Sept 1916. He was appointed commander in chief of the Allied armies in the spring of 1918, and launched the Allied counter-offensive in July that brought about the negotiation of an armistice to end the war.

Your greatness does not depend upon the size of your command, but on the manner in which you exercise it.

Ferdinand Foch quoted in Aston,
Biography of Foch

Fontenoy, Battle of battle in the War of the ◊Austrian Succession 1745. Marshal Saxe and the French defeated the British, Dutch, and Hanoverians under the duke of Cumberland at a village in Hainaut province, Belgium, SE of Tournai.

Foot Michael 1913– . British Labour politician and writer. A leader of the left-wing Tribune Group, he was secretary of state for employment 1974–76, Lord President of the Council and leader of the House 1976–79, and succeeded James Callaghan as Labour Party leader 1980–83.

Football War popular name for a five-day war between El Salvador and Honduras which began on 14 July 1969, when Salvadorean planes bombed Tegucigelpa. Its army entered Honduras, but the ◊Organization of American States arranged a ceasefire, by which time about 2,000 lives had been lost.

The war is so called because of the mistaken belief that it followed a dispute after a World Cup qualifying match between the two countries. In fact, it arose because of densely populated El Salvador's desire for Honduran territory.

Ford Gerald R(udolph) 1913– . 38th president of the USA 1974–77, a Republican. He was elected to the House of Representatives 1949, was nominated to the vice presidency by Richard Nixon 1973 following the resignation of Spiro Agnew, and became president 1974, when Nixon was forced to resign following the ◊Watergate scandal. He pardoned Nixon and gave amnesty to those who had resisted the draft for the Vietnam War.

Foreign Legion volunteer corps of foreigners within a country's army. The French *Légion Etrangère*, 1831, is one of a number of such forces. Enlisted volunteers are of any nationality (about half are now French), but the officers are usually French. Headquarters until 1962 was in Sidi Bel Abbès, Algeria; the main base is now Corsica, with reception headquarters at Aubagne, near Marseille, France.

The French foreign legion was founded by Louis-Philippe 'to clear France of foreigners' and since then has always taken cast-offs and undesirables, including those from the French army itself. Levels of desertion are relatively high, around 6%.

Formosa alternative name for ◊Taiwan.

Forrest John, 1st Baron Forrest 1847–1918. Australian explorer and politician. He crossed Western Australia W–E 1870, when he went along the southern coast route, and in 1874, when he crossed much further north, exploring the Musgrave Ranges. He was born in Western Australia, and was its first premier 1890–1901.

Forrest Nathan Bedford 1821–1877. American Confederate military leader and founder of the Ku Klux Klan 1866, a secret and sinister society dedicated to white supremacy.

Forster William Edward 1818–1886. British Liberal reformer. In Gladstone's government 1868–74 he was vice president of the council, and secured the passing of the Education Act 1870 and the Ballot Act 1872. He was chief secretary for Ireland 1880–82.

Fort Sumter fort in Charleston Harbor, South Carolina, USA, 6.5 km/4 mi SE of Charleston. The first shots of the US Civil War were fired here 12 April 1861, after its commander had refused the call to surrender made by the Confederate General Beauregard.

Fort Ticonderoga fort in New York State, USA, near Lake Champlain. It was the site of battles between the British and the French 1758–59, and was captured from the British 10

May 1775 by Benedict Arnold and Ethan Allen (leading the ◊Green Mountain Boys).

Forty-Five, the ◊Jacobite rebellion 1745, led by Prince ◊Charles Edward Stuart. With his army of Highlanders 'Bonnie Prince Charlie' occupied Edinburgh and advanced into England as far as Derby, but then turned back. The rising was crushed by the Duke of Cumberland at Culloden 1746.

forum (Latin 'market') in an ancient Roman town, the meeting place and market, like the Greek ◊agora. At Rome the Forum Romanum contained the Senate House, the public speaking platform, covered halls for trading, temples of Saturn, Concord and the Divine Augustus, and memorial arches. Later constructions included the Forum of ◊Caesar (with temple of Venus), the Forum of ◊Augustus (with temple of Mars), and the colonnaded Forum of ◊Trajan, containing Trajan's Column.

Fouché Joseph, duke of Otranto 1759–1820. French politician. He was elected to the National Convention (the post-Revolutionary legislature), and organized the conspiracy that overthrew the ◊Jacobin leader ◊Robespierre. Napolcon cmploycd him as police minister.

Fouquet Nicolas 1615–1680. French politician, a rival to Louis XIV's minister ◊Colbert. Fouquet became *procureur général* of the Paris *parlement* 1650 and *surintendant des finances* 1651, responsible for raising funds for the long war against Spain, a post he held until arrested and imprisoned for embezzlement (at the instigation of Colbert, who succeeded him).

Four Freedoms, the four kinds of liberty essential to human dignity as defined in an address to the US Congress by President F D ◊Roosevelt 6 Jan 1941: freedom of speech and expression, freedom of worship, freedom from want, freedom from fear.

Fourteen Points the terms proposed by President Wilson of the USA in his address to Congress 8 Jan 1918, as a basis for the settlement of World War I. The creation of the League of Nations was one of the points.

Fourth Republic the French constitutional regime that was established between 1944 and 1946 and lasted until 4 Oct 1958: from liberation after Nazi occupation during World War II to the introduction of a new constitution by General de Gaulle.

Fox Charles James 1749–1806. English Whig politician, son of the 1st Baron Holland. He entered Parliament 1769 as a supporter of the court, but went over to the opposition 1774. As secretary of state 1782, leader of the opposition to Pitt, and foreign secretary 1806, he welcomed the French Revolution and brought about the abolition of the slave trade.

How much the greatest event it is that ever happened in the world! And how much the best!

Charles James Fox on the fall of the Bastille

France country in W Europe, bounded NE by Belgium and Germany, E by Germany, Switzerland, and Italy, S by the Mediterranean Sea, SW by Spain and Andorra, and W by the Atlantic Ocean.

history For history before 1945, see ◊*France: history*. A 'united front' provisional government headed by de Gaulle assumed power in the re-established republic before a new constitution was framed and adopted for a Fourth Republic Jan 1946. This provided for a weak executive and powerful National Assembly. With 26 impermanent governments being formed 1946-58, real power passed to the civil service, which, by introducing a new system of 'indicative economic planning', engineered rapid economic reconstruction. Decolonization of French Indochina 1954, Morocco and Tunisia 1956, and entry into the European Economic Community 1957 were also effected.

The Fourth Republic was overthrown 1958 by a political and military crisis over Algerian independence, which threatened to lead to a French army revolt. De Gaulle was recalled from retirement to head a government of national unity and supervised the framing of the new Fifth Republic constitution, which strengthened the president and prime minister.

Fifth Republic De Gaulle, who became president 1959, restored domestic stability and presided over the decolonization of Francophone Africa, including Algerian independence 1962. Close economic links were maintained with former colonies. De Gaulle also initiated a new foreign policy, withdrawing France from military cooperation in the ◊North Atlantic Treaty Organization (NATO) 1966 and developing an autonomous nuclear deterrent force. The de Gaulle era was one of economic growth and large-scale rural–urban migration. Politically, however, there was tight censorship and strong centralization, and in 1967 the public reacted against de Gaulle's paternalism by voting the 'right coalition' a reduced majority.

'May events' In 1968, the nation was paralysed by students' and workers' demonstrations in Paris that spread to the provinces and briefly

threatened the government. De Gaulle called elections and won a landslide victory. In 1969, however, he was defeated in a referendum over proposed Senate and local-government reforms, and resigned. De Gaulle's former prime minister Georges ◊Pompidou was elected president and pursued Gaullist policies until his death 1974.

Pompidou's successor as president, Valéry Giscard d'Estaing, leader of the centre-right Independent Republicans, introduced domestic reforms and played a more active and cooperative role in the EC. Giscard faced opposition, however, from his 'right coalition' partner, Jacques ◊Chirac, who was prime minister 1974–76, and deteriorating international economic conditions. France performed better than many of its European competitors 1974–81, with the president launching a major nuclear power programme to save on energy imports and, while Raymond ◊Barre was prime minister 1976–81, a new liberal 'freer market' economic strategy. During this period the Union for French Democracy party (UDF) was formed to unite several centre-right parties. However, with 1.7 million unemployed, Giscard was defeated by Socialist Party leader François ◊Mitterrand in the 1981 presidential election.

'left coalition' Mitterrand's victory was the first presidential success for the 'left coalition' during the Fifth Republic and was immediately succeeded by a landslide victory for the Socialist Party (PS) and French Communist Party (PCF) in elections to the National Assembly 1981. The new administration introduced a radical programme of social reform, decentralization, and nationalization, and passed a series of reflationary budgets aimed at reducing unemployment.

Financial constraints forced a switch towards a more conservative policy of *rigueur* ('austerity') 1983. A U-turn in economic policy was completed 1984 when Prime Minister Pierre Mauroy was replaced by Laurent Fabius, prompting the resignation of communist members of the cabinet. Unemployment rose to over 2.5 million 1985–86, increasing racial tension in urban areas. The extreme right-wing National Front, led by Jean- Marie ◊Le Pen, benefited from this and gained seats in the March 1986 National Assembly elections. The 'left coalition' lost its majority, the PCF having been in decline in recent years. The PS, however, had emerged as France's single most popular party.

From 1958 to 1986 the president and prime minister had been drawn from the same party coalition, and the president had been allowed to dominate in both home and foreign affairs. In 1986 Mitterrand was obliged to appoint as prime minister the leader of the opposition, Jacques Chirac, who emerged as the dominant force in the 'shared executive'. Chirac introduced a radical 'new conservative' programme of denationalization, deregulation, and 'desocialization', using the executive's decree powers and the parliamentary guillotine to steamroller measures through. His educational and economic reforms encountered serious opposition from militant students and striking workers, necessitating embarrassing policy concessions. Chirac was defeated by Mitterrand in the May 1988 presidential election.

progressive programme In the National Assembly elections June 1988, the socialists emerged as the largest single political party. Mitterrand duly appointed Michel ◊Rocard, a moderate social democrat, as prime minister heading a minority PS government that included several centre-party representatives. Rocard implemented a progressive programme, aimed at protecting the underprivileged and improving the quality of life. In June 1988 he negotiated the Matignon Accord, designed to solve the New Caledonia problem, which was later approved by referendum. Between 1988 and 1990 France enjoyed a strong economic upturn and attention focused increasingly on quality of life, with the Green Party gaining 11% of the national vote in the European Parliament elections of June 1989.

racial tensions The extreme-right National Front continued to do well in municipal elections, pressurizing the government into adopting a hard line against illegal immigration; new programmes were announced for the integration of Muslim immigrants – from Algeria, Tunisia, and other areas with French colonial ties – into mainstream French society. Religious and cultural tensions increased. A commission set up to look at the problems of immigrant integration reported 1991 that France's foreign population was 3.7 million (6.8% of the population), the same as in 1982. However, 10 million citizens were of 'recent foreign origin'.

Gulf War In Sept 1990, after Iraqi violation of the French ambassador's residence in Kuwait, the French government dispatched 5,000 troops to Saudi Arabia. Despite France's previously close ties with Iraq (including arms sales), French military forces played a prominent role within the US-led coalition in the 1991 Gulf War. Defence minister Jean-Pierre Chevenement resigned Feb 1991 in opposition to this strategy, but the majority of people in the country supported the government's stance.

France: history

5th century BC	France, then called Gaul (*Gallia* by the Romans) was invaded by Celtic peoples.
57–51 BC	Conquest by the Roman general Julius Caesar.
1st–5th century AD	During Roman rule the inhabitants of France accepted Roman civilization and the Latin language. As the empire declined, Germanic tribes overran the country and settled.
481–511	A Frankish chief, Clovis, brought the other tribes under his rule, accepted Christianity, and made Paris the capital.
511–751	Under Clovis' successors, the Merovingians, the country sank into anarchy.
741–68	Unity was restored by Pepin, founder of the Carolingian dynasty.
768–814	Charlemagne made France the centre of the Holy Roman Empire.
912	The province of Normandy was granted as a duchy to the Viking leader Rollo, whose invading Norsemen had settled here.
987	The first king of the House of Capet assumed the crown. Under Charlemagne's weak successors the great nobles had become semi-independent. The Capets established rule in the district around Paris but were surrounded by vassals stronger than themselves.
11th–13th centuries	The power of the Capets was gradually extended, with the support of the church and the townspeople.
1337–1453	In the Hundred Years' War Charles VII expelled the English from France, aided by Joan of Arc.
1483	Burgundy and Brittany were annexed. Through the policies of Louis XI the restoration of the royal power was achieved.
1503–1697	Charles VIII's Italian wars initiated a struggle with Spain for supremacy in W Europe that lasted for two centuries.
1592–98	Protestantism (Huguenot) was adopted by a party of the nobles for political reasons; the result was a succession of civil wars, fought under religious slogans.
1589–1610	Henry IV restored peace, established religious toleration, and made the monarchy absolute.
1634–48	The ministers Richelieu and Mazarin, by their intervention in the Thirty Years' War, secured Alsace and made France the leading power in Europe.
1643–1763	Louis XIV embarked on an aggressive policy that united Europe against him; in his reign began the conflict with Britain that lost France its colonies in Canada and India in the War of the Spanish Succession (1701–14), War of the Austrian Succession (1756–58), and Seven Years' War (1756–63).
1789–99	The French Revolution abolished feudalism and absolute monarchy, but failed to establish democracy.
1799–1815	Napoleon's military dictatorship was aided by foreign wars (1792–1802, 1803–15). The Bourbon monarchy was restored 1814 with Louis XVIII.
1830	Charles X's attempt to substitute absolute for limited monarchy provoked a revolution, which placed his cousin, Louis Philippe, on the throne.
1848	In the Feb revolution Louis Philippe was overthrown and the Second Republic set up.
1852–70	The president of the republic, Louis Napoleon, Napoleon I's nephew, restored the empire 1852, with the title of Napoleon III. His expansionist foreign policy ended in defeat in the Franco-Prussian War and the foundation of the Third Republic.
1863–1946	France colonized Indochina, parts of N Africa, and the S Pacific.
1914	France entered World War I.
1936–37	A radical-socialist-communist Popular Front alliance introduced many social reforms.
1939	France entered World War II.
1940	The German invasion allowed the extreme right to set up a puppet dictatorship under Pétain in Vichy, but resistance was maintained by the *maquis* and the Free French under de Gaulle.
1944	Liberation from the Nazis.

For postwar history see ◊France.

Mitterrand to Chirac In 1991 the neo-Gaullist Rally for the Republic (RPR) and the UDF, France's main, usually factious, right-of-centre opposition parties, signed a formal election pact. After disagreements over economic policy, Mitterrand replaced Rocard with Edith Cresson. With the economy in recession, racial tensions increasing, discontent among farmers, militancy among public-sector workers, and financial scandals affecting the PS, Mitterrand's popularity fell, and so did Cresson's. After disappointing results in regional elections, Cresson was replaced by Pierre Bérégovoy 1992.

The PS suffered a heavy defeat in national

assembly elections 1993, held in the midst of recession. Mitterrand appointed Edouard Balladur of the RPR as prime minister. Michel Rocard and then Emmanuelli Henri succeeded Bérégovoy as socialist leader. Balladur was a popular prime minister, but encountered opposition to his tight immigration, privatization and employment policies, and his proposals for local-government funding of private schools. He was at odds with Mitterrand, but was the dominant force in the 'cohabitation' administration as Mitterrand's health failed. He compounded his popularity by engineering an economic recovery and by overseeing a successful humanitarian mission in Rwanda.

A split in the RPR emerged 1995 when both Chirac and Balladur aspired to contest the presidency. Balladur lost out to the populist Chirac, who promised more jobs, higher public-sector wages, and a more relaxed economic policy. At the head of a 'right coalition', Chirac defeated PS candidate Lionel Jospin for the presidency in May. He appointed as prime minister Alain Juppé, and began his presidency with the controversial announcement that nuclear tests would resume in the Pacific. Chirac's popularity suffered due to recession and widespread strikes. In early 1996, the government announced the end of nuclear tests and the future abolition of conscription.

The government announced new spending plans Aug 1996 in an effort to qualify for European Monetary Union membership in 1999, despite high unemployment and poor economic growth. By March 1997, there were improvements in the economy that caused Chirac to call legislative elections in order to win a mandate for his austerity measures. But the elections were won by the PS, and Lionel Jospin became prime minister June 1997.

franchise in politics, the eligibility, right, or privilege to vote at public elections, especially for the members of a legislative body, or parliament. In the UK it was 1918 before all men had the right to vote, and 1928 before women were enfranchised; in New Zealand women were granted the right as early as 1893.

Francia José Gaspar Rodríguez de 1766–1840. Paraguayan dictator 1814–40, known as El Supremo. A lawyer, he emerged as a strongman after independence was achieved 1811, and was designated dictator by congress 1814. Hostile to the Argentine regime, he sealed off the country and followed an isolationist policy.

Francis I 1768–1835. Emperor of Austria 1804, also known as ◊Francis II, Holy Roman emperor.

Francis or *François* two kings of France:

Francis I 1494–1547. King of France from 1515. He succeeded his cousin Louis XII, and from 1519 European politics turned on the rivalry between him and the Holy Roman emperor Charles V, which led to war 1521–29, 1536–38, and 1542–44. In 1525 Francis was defeated and captured at Pavia and released only after signing a humiliating treaty. At home, he developed absolute monarchy.

Francis II 1544–1560. King of France from 1559 when he succeeded his father, Henry II. He married Mary Queen of Scots 1558. He was completely under the influence of his mother, ◊Catherine de' Medici.

Francis two holy Roman Emperors:

Francis I 1708–1765. Holy Roman emperor from 1745, who married ◊Maria Theresa of Austria 1736.

Francis II 1768–1835. Holy Roman emperor 1792–1806. He became Francis I, Emperor of Austria 1804, and abandoned the title of Holy Roman emperor 1806. During his reign Austria was five times involved in war with France, 1792–97, 1798–1801, 1805, 1809, and 1813–14. He succeeded his father Leopold II.

Francisan order Catholic order of friars, *Friars Minor* or *Grey Friars*, founded 1209 by Francis of Assisi. Subdivisions were the strict Observants; the Conventuals, who were allowed to own property corporately; and the Capuchins, founded 1529.

A female order, the *Poor Clares*, was founded by St Clare 1215.

Francis Ferdinand or ◊Franz Ferdinand 1863–1914. Archduke of Austria.

Francis Joseph or ◊Franz Joseph 1830–1916. Emperor of Austria-Hungary.

Franco Francisco (Paulino Hermenegildo Teódulo Bahamonde) 1892–1975. Spanish dictator from 1939. As a general, he led the insurgent Nationalists to victory in the Spanish ◊Civil War 1936-39, supported by Fascist Italy and Nazi Germany, and established a dictatorship. In 1942 Franco reinstated the Cortes (Spanish parliament), which in 1947 passed an act by which he became head of state for life.

In war the heart must be sacrificed.

General Franco, Diario de una Bandera

Franco-Prussian War 1870–71. The Prussian chancellor Bismarck put forward a German candidate for the vacant Spanish throne with the deliberate, and successful, intention of provoking the French emperor Napoleon III into declaring war. The Prussians defeated the French at Sedan, then besieged Paris. The Treaty of Frankfurt May 1871 gave Alsace, Lorraine, and a large French indemnity to Prussia. The war established Prussia, at the head of a newly established German empire, as Europe's leading power.

Frank member of a group of Germanic peoples prominent in Europe in the 3rd to 9th centuries. Believed to have originated in Pomerania on the Black Sea, they had settled on the Rhine by the 3rd century, spread into the Roman Empire by the 4th century, and gradually conquered most of Gaul, Italy, and Germany under the ◊Merovingian and ◊Carolingian dynasties. The kingdom of the W Franks became France, the kingdom of the E Franks became Germany.

The Salian (western) Franks conquered Roman Gaul during the 4th–5th centuries. Their ruler, Clovis, united the Salians with the Ripuarian (eastern) Franks, and they were converted to Christianity. The agriculture of the Merovingian dynasty (named after Clovis's grandfather, Merovech) was more advanced than that of the Romans, and they introduced the three-field system. The Merovingians conquered most of western and central Europe, and lasted until the 8th century when the Carolingian dynasty was founded under Charlemagne. The kingdom of the W Franks was fused by the 9th century into a single people with the Gallo-Romans, speaking the modified form of Latin that became modern French.

Frankfurt Parliament an assembly of liberal politicians and intellectuals that met for a few months in 1848 in the aftermath of the ◊revolutions of 1848 and the overthrow of monarchies in most of the German states. They discussed a constitution for a united Germany, but the restoration of the old order and the suppression of the revolutions ended the parliament.

Franklin Benjamin 1706–1790. US printer, publisher, author, scientist, and statesman. He was the first US ambassador to France 1776-85, and negotiated peace with Britain 1783. As a delegate to the ◊Continental Congress from Pennsylvania 1785-88, he helped to draft the ◊Declaration of Independence and the US Constitution.

Franz Ferdinand or Francis Ferdinand 1863–1914. Archduke of Austria. He became heir to his uncle, Emperor Franz Joseph, in 1884 but while visiting Sarajevo 28 June 1914, he and his wife were assassinated by a Serbian nationalist. Austria used the episode to make unreasonable demands on Serbia that ultimately precipitated World War I.

Franz Joseph or Francis Joseph 1830–1916. Emperor of Austria-Hungary from 1848, when his uncle, Ferdinand I, abdicated. After the suppression of the 1848 revolution, Franz Joseph tried to establish an absolute monarchy but had to grant Austria a parliamentary constitution 1861 and Hungary equality with Austria 1867. He was defeated in the Italian War 1859 and the Prussian War 1866. In 1914 he made the assassination of his heir and nephew Franz Ferdinand the excuse for attacking Serbia, thus precipitating World War I.

Fraser (John) Malcolm 1930– . Australian Liberal politician, prime minister 1975–83; nicknamed 'the Prefect' because of a supposed disregard of subordinates.

Fraser was educated at Oxford University, and later became a millionaire sheep farmer. In March 1975 he replaced Snedden as Liberal Party leader. In Nov, following the Whitlam government's economic difficulties, he blocked finance bills in the Senate, became prime minister of a caretaker government and in the consequent general election won a large majority. He lost to Hawke in the 1983 election.

Fraser Peter 1884–1950. New Zealand Labour politician, born in Scotland. He held various cabinet posts 1935-40, and was prime minister 1940-49.

Frederick V known as *the Winter King* 1596–1632. Elector palatine of the Rhine 1610–23 and king of Bohemia 1619–20 (for one winter, hence the name), having been chosen by the Protestant Bohemians as ruler after the deposition of Catholic emperor ◊Ferdinand II. His selection was the cause of the Thirty Years' War. Frederick was defeated at the Battle of the White Mountain, near Prague, in Nov 1620, by the army of the Catholic League and fled to Holland.

Frederick two Holy Roman emperors:

Frederick I *Barbarossa* ('red-beard') *c.* 1123–1190. Holy Roman emperor from 1152. Originally duke of Swabia, he was elected emperor 1152, and was engaged in a struggle with Pope Alexander III 1159–77, which ended in his submission; the Lombard cities, headed by Milan, took advantage of this to establish their independence of imperial control. Frederick joined the Third Crusade, and was drowned while crossing a river in Anatolia.

Frederick II 1194–1250. Holy Roman emperor from 1212, called 'the Wonder of the World'. He led a crusade 1228–29 that recovered Jerusalem by treaty, without fighting. He quarrelled with the pope, who excommunicated him three times, and a feud began that lasted with intervals until the end of his reign. Frederick, who was a religious sceptic, is often considered the most cultured man of his age. He was the son of Henry VI.

Frederick three kings of Prussia:

Frederick I 1657–1713. King of Prussia from 1701. He became elector of Brandenburg 1688.

Frederick II *the Great* 1712–1786. King of Prussia from 1740, when he succeeded his father Frederick William I. In that year he started the War of the ◊Austrian Succession by his attack on Austria. In the peace of 1745 he secured Silesia. The struggle was renewed in the ◊Seven Years' War 1756–63. He acquired West Prussia in the first partition of Poland 1772 and left Prussia as Germany's foremost state. He was an efficient and just ruler in the spirit of the Enlightenment and a patron of the arts.

My people and I have come to an agreement which satisfies us both. They are to say what they please, and I am to do what I please.

Frederick II the Great (attrib.)

Frederick III 1831–1888. King of Prussia and emperor of Germany 1888. The son of Wilhelm I, he married the eldest daughter (Victoria) of Queen Victoria of the UK 1858 and, as a liberal, frequently opposed Chancellor Bismarck. He died three months after his accession.

Frederick William 1620–1688. Elector of Brandenburg from 1640, 'the Great Elector'. By successful wars against Sweden and Poland, he prepared the way for Prussian power in the 18th century.

Frederick William 1882–1951. Last crown prince of Germany, eldest son of Wilhelm II. During World War I he commanded a group of armies on the western front. In 1918, he retired into private life.

Frederick William four kings of Prussia:

Frederick William I 1688–1740. King of Prussia from 1713, who developed Prussia's military might and commerce.

Frederick William II 1744–1797. King of Prussia from 1786. He was a nephew of Frederick II but had little of his relative's military skill. He was unsuccessful in waging war on the French 1792–95 and lost all Prussia west of the Rhine.

Frederick William III 1770–1840. King of Prussia from 1797. He was defeated by Napoleon 1806, but contributed to his final overthrow 1813–15 and profited by being allotted territory at the Congress of Vienna.

Frederick William IV 1795–1861. King of Prussia from 1840. He upheld the principle of the ◊divine right of kings, but was forced to grant a constitution 1850 after the Prussian revolution 1848. He suffered two strokes 1857 and became mentally debilitated. His brother William (later emperor) took over his duties.

Free French in World War II, movement formed by General Charles ◊de Gaulle in the UK June 1940, consisting of French soldiers who continued to fight against the Axis after the Franco- German armistice. They took the name *Fighting France* 1942 and served in many campaigns, among them General Leclerc's advance from Chad to Tripolitania 1942, the Syrian campaigns 1941, the campaigns in the Western Desert, the Italian campaign, the liberation of France, and the invasion of Germany. Their emblem was the Cross of Lorraine, a cross with two bars.

freeman one who enjoys the freedom of a borough. Since the early Middle Ages, a freeman has been allowed to carry out his craft or trade within the jurisdiction of the borough and to participate in municipal government, but since the development of modern local government, such privileges have become largely honorary.

There have generally been four ways of becoming a freeman: by apprenticeship to an existing freeman; by patrimony, or being the son of a freeman; by redemption, that is, buying the privilege; or, by gift from the borough, the usual method today, when the privilege is granted in recognition of some achievement, benefaction, or special status on the part of the recipient.

freemasonry the beliefs and practices of a group of linked national organizations open to men over the age of 21, united by a common code of morals and certain traditional 'secrets'. Freemasonry is descended from a medieval guild of itinerant masons, which existed in the 14th century and by the 16th was admitting men unconnected with the building trade.

The present order of *Free and Accepted Masons* originated with the formation in London of the first Grand Lodge, or governing body, in 1717, and during the 18th century spread from Britain to the USA, continental Europe, and elsewhere. In France and other European countries, freemasonry assumed a political and anticlerical character; it has been condemned by the papacy, and in some countries was suppressed by the state.

free trade economic system where governments do not interfere in the movement of goods between countries; there are thus no taxes on imports. In the modern economy, free trade tends to hold within economic groups such as the European Union (EU), but not generally, despite such treaties as GATT 1948 and subsequent agreements to reduce tariffs. The opposite of free trade is protectionism.

The case for free trade, first put forward in the 17th century, received its classic statement in Adam Smith's *Wealth of Nations* 1776. The movement towards free trade began with Pitt's commercial treaty with France 1786, and triumphed with the repeal of the Corn Laws 1846. According to traditional economic theory, free trade allows nations to specialize in those commodities which can be produced most efficiently. In Britain, superiority to all rivals as a manufacturing country in the Victorian age made free trade an advantage, but when that superiority was lost the demand for protection was raised, notably by Joseph Chamberlain. The Ottawa Agreements 1932 marked the end of free trade until in 1948 GATT came into operation. A series of resultant international tariff reductions was agreed in the Kennedy Round Conference 1964–67, and the Tokyo Round 1974–79 gave substantial incentives to developing countries.

Frei Edwardo 1911–1982. Chilean president 1964–70. Elected as the only effective anti-Marxist candidate, he pursued a moderate programme of 'Chileanization' of US-owned copper interests. His regime was plagued by inflation and labour unrest, but saw considerable economic development.

He split with the Conservatives 1938 to help found the Falanga Nacional, an anti-fascist Social Christian party, which joined forces with the Social Christian Conservatives 1957. He was a shrewd opposition leader, arguing for reform within a democratic framework.

Frelimo (acronym for *Fr*ont for th*e* *Li*beration of *Mo*zambique) nationalist group aimed at gaining independence for Mozambique from the occupying Portuguese. It began operating from S Tanzania 1963 and continued until victory 1975.

French John Denton Pinkstone, 1st Earl of Ypres 1852–1925. British field marshal. In the second ◊South African War 1899–1902, he relieved Kimberley and took Bloemfontein; in World War I he was Commander in Chief of the British Expeditionary Force in France 1914–15; he resigned after being criticized as indecisive.

It is a solemn thought that at my signal all these fine young fellows go to their death.

Field Marshal John French quoted in Brett, *Journals and Letters of Reginald, Viscount Esher*

French and Indian War also known as the ◊Seven Years' War.

French East India Company see ◊East india Company, French.

French Equatorial Africa federation of French territories in West Africa. Founded 1910, it consisted of Gabon, Middle Congo, Chad, and Ubangi-Shari (now the Central African Republic), and was ruled from Brazzaville. The federation supported the Free French in World War II and was given representation in the French Fourth Republic 1944-58. In 1958, the states voted for autonomy and the federation was dissolved.

French Guiana (French *Guyane Française*) French overseas *département* from 1946, and administrative region from 1974, on the north coast of South America, bounded W by Surinam and E and S by Brazil. First settled by France 1604, the territory became a French possession 1817; penal colonies, including Devil's Island, were established from 1852; by 1945 the shipments of convicts from France ceased.

French Polynesia French Overseas Territory in the S Pacific, consisting of five archipelagos. First visited by Europeans 1595; French Protectorate 1843; annexed to France 1880–82; became an Overseas Territory, changing its name from French Oceania 1958; self-governing 1977. Following demands for independence in ◊New Caledonia 1984–85, agitation increased also in Polynesia.

French Revolution the period 1789–1799 that saw the end of the French monarchy. Although the revolution began as an attempt to create a constitutional monarchy, by late 1792 demands for long-overdue reforms resulted in the proclamation of the First Republic. The violence of the revolution, attacks by other nations, and bitter factional struggles, riots, and counterrevolutionary uprisings consumed the republic. This helped bring the extremists to power, and the bloody Reign of Terror followed. French armies then succeeded in holding off their foreign enemies and one of the generals, ◊Napoleon, seized power 1799.

On 5 May 1789, after the monarchy had attempted to increase taxation and control of affairs, the ◊States General (three 'estates' of nobles, clergy, and commons) met at Versailles to try to establish some constitutional controls. Divisions within the States General led to the formation of a National Assembly by the third (commons) estate 17 June. Repressive measures by ◊Louis XVI led to the storming of the ◊Bastille by the Paris mob 14 July 1789.

On 20 June 1791 the royal family attempted to escape from the control of the Assembly, but Louis XVI was brought back a prisoner from Varennes and forced to accept a new constitution. War with Austria after 20 April 1792 threatened to undermine the revolution, but on 10 Aug the mob stormed the royal palace, and on 21 Sept the First French Republic was proclaimed.

On 21 Jan 1793 Louis XVI was executed. The moderate ◊Girondins were overthrown 2 June by the ◊Jacobins, and control of the country was passed to the infamous Committee of Public Safety, and ◊Robespierre. The mass executions of the Reign of Terror (see ◊Terror, Reign of) began 5 Sept, and the excesses led to the overthrow of the Committee and Robespierre 27 July 1794. The Directory was established to hold a middle course between royalism and Jacobinism. It ruled until Napoleon seized power 1799 as dictator.

French revolutionary calendar the French Revolution 1789 was initially known as the 1st Year of Liberty. When the monarchy was abolished on 21 Sept 1792, the 4th year became 1st Year of the Republic. This calendar was formally adopted in Oct 1793 but its usage was backdated to 22 Sept 1793, which became 1 Vendémiaire. The calendar was discarded from 1 Jan 1806.

French West Africa group of French colonies administered from Dakar 1895–1958. They are now Senegal, Mauritania, Sudan, Burkina Faso, Guinea, Niger, Ivory Coast, and Benin.

Freyberg Bernard Cyril, Baron Freyberg 1889–1963. New Zealand soldier and administrator born in England. He fought in World War I, and during World War II he commanded the New Zealand expeditionary force. He was governor general of New Zealand 1946-52.

Fronde French revolts 1648–53 against the administration of the chief minister ◊Mazarin during Louis XIV's minority. In 1648–49 the Paris *parlement* attempted to limit the royal power, its leaders were arrested, Paris revolted, and the rising was suppressed by the royal army

---

French Revolution 1789–99

1789 (May) Meeting of States-General called by Louis XIV to discuss reform of state finances. Nobility oppose reforms.

(June) Third (commoners) estate demanded end to system where First (noble) estate and Second (church) estate could outvote them; rejected by Louis. Third estate declared themselves a National Assembly and 'tennis court oath' pledged them to draw up new constitution.

(July) Rumours of royal plans to break up the Assembly led to riots in Paris and the storming of the Bastille. Revolutionaries adopted *tricolore* as their flag. Peasant uprisings occurred throughout the country.

1789–91 National Assembly reforms included abolition of noble privileges, dissolution of religious orders, appropriation of church lands, centralization of governments, and limits on the king's power.

1791 (June) King Louis attempted to escape from Paris in order to unite opposition to the Assembly, but was recaptured.

(Sept) The King agreed to a new constitution.

(Oct) New Legislative Assembly met, divided between moderate Girondists and radical

1792 (Jan) Girondists formed a new government but their power in Paris was undermined by the Jacobins. Foreign invasion led to the breakdown of law and order. Hatred of the monarchy increased.

(Aug) The king was suspended from office and the government dismissed

(Sept) National Convention elected on the basis of universal suffrage; dominated by Jacobins. A republic was proclaimed.

(Dec) The king was tried and condemned to death.

1793 (Jan) The king was guillotined.

(April) The National Convention delegated power to the Committee of Public Safety, dominated by Robespierre. The Reign of Terror began.

1794 (July) Robespierre became increasingly unpopular, was deposed and executed.

1795 Moderate Thermidoreans took control of the convention and created a new executive Directory of five members.

1795–99 Directory failed to solve France's internal or external problems and became increasingly unpopular.

1799 Coup d'état overthrew the Directory and a Consulate of three was established, including Napoleon as Chief Consul with special powers.

The French Revolution

In 1789, French royal finances were bankrupt after years of ruinously expensive warfare and uncontrolled domestic spending, while high food prices and shortages were accelerating the economic crisis. King Louis XVI tried to increase his income by reforming the way his revenues were produced. To do this, he was forced to call the States General, a body made up of the three 'estates', which had not met since 1614. When it assembled, the delegates of the First (aristocratic) and Second (clerical) estates were keen to protect their privileged positions. However, the Third (bourgeois) estate wanted far-reaching financial and constitutional reforms.

Thus most of the deputies who assembled at Versailles in June 1789 wanted to set limits on royal power, but for very different reasons. Alarm at royal attempts to halt the proceedings led to members of the Third estate swearing the 'tennis court oath', vowing not to disperse until they had produced a constitution for France. Isolated by lack of support from the nobility, the crown had no choice but to give way and recognize the new body, which became the National, and then the Constituent, Assembly in July.

The storming of the Bastille

Fears of retaliation against the Assembly by the king and the aristocracy caused widespread civil disorder, climaxing in the storming of the Bastille (a state prison) by a Parisian mob, together with the Declaration of Rights of Man and proposals for radical political reform. The limits of royal power, even in the nation's capital, were revealed. Meanwhile in the countryside there was concern about the possibility of aristocratic plots, known as the 'great fear'. This led to attacks on property and records by peasants, and it was clear that forces had been unleashed which even the Assembly could not control. It voted for the abolition of feudalism and introduced many reforms, culminating in the constitution of 1791. Attempts to reconcile the interests of aristocracy, bourgeoisie and peasantry failed and in June 1791, the king tried to escape, but was arrested and returned to Paris. Three months later, he signed the new constitution, marking the end of royal *absolutism* and of the *ancien régime*.

An appetite for war

With the king discredited and the country in turmoil, France was isolated from the rest of Europe. Other monarchs feared that if the French revolution succeeded, their own positions would be threatened next. Within France, an appetite for war developed. The bourgeois Girondins, leaders of the new Legislative Assembly, saw it as a way of achieving nationalist unity and exposing the aristocracy. In contrast, the aristocracy hoped a war would bring about a counter-revolution. War against Austria was declared in April 1792.

A series of military defeats by Austria and Prussia led to the mobilization of the lower classes, but this unleashed a wave of popular demands for equality. On 10 August 1792, an insurrection brought down the Legislative Assembly and the power of the Girondins began to fade. They were replaced by an alliance of the more extreme Montagnards and the working class *sans-culottes*. A new National Convention was elected in September, meeting on the day the revolutionary army won its first major battle against the Prussians at Valmy.

Louis put to the guillotine

The Convention voted to abolish the monarchy and put the king on trial in December 1792, executing him the following month. The Girondins, still trying to defend the principles of property and economic freedom, were swept aside as power passed to the Montagnards. A Committee of Public Safety was set up in Paris, and soon became the main instrument of government, but it failed to reconcile the limited aims of the Montagnards with the aspirations of the *sans-culottes*. From the summer of 1793, ever more radical measures were taken amid constant fear of counter-revolution. Anyone who failed to support the revolution could be arrested and tried, and many were denounced anonymously. Some 40,000 died in this Reign of Terror of 1793–94, relatively few of them aristocrats. Significant figures of the Terror such as Danton and Robespierre fell victim to their own policies during this period. Peasant rebellions against conscription also spread through the country from the Vendée *département*.

The beginning of the end

Despite the success of the revolutionary army in war, domestic conditions worsened as increased state controls were still unable to provide more than the basic necessities for the urban population. The Committee of Public Safety had to deal with extremists who wanted to sweep away the remaining social order, and with the bourgeois who felt the revolution had gone too far already. Repression of militants fuelled the *sans-culottes'* disenchantment with the government. The increasingly centralized regime was tolerated because of the sense of national emergency, but as military success reduced that, so its grip on power slackened. The Thermidorean reaction to the Terror effectively brought the revolution to an end and the influence of the *sans-culottes* was replaced by the ascendancy of the bourgeoisie who had lost control two years before.

Shock waves round the world

The mere narrative of the revolution should not be allowed to disguise its colossal impact. The destruction of the strongest and most centralized absolutist state of the *ancien régime* in the space of a few months sent shock waves around the world. On the one hand, the excesses of the Terror made the revolution a byword for fear among the European aristocracies and property owners. On the other hand, the revolutionaries of 1789 enshrined the ideals of liberty, equality, and fraternity, and laid down principles for future political and social reformers.

under Louis II Condé. In 1650 Condé led a new revolt of the nobility, but this was suppressed by 1653. The defeat of the Fronde enabled Louis to establish an absolutist monarchy in the later 17th century.

Frontenac et Palluau Louis de Buade, Comte de Frontenac et Palluau 1622–1698. French colonial governor. He began his military career 1635, and was appointed governor of the French possessions in North America 1672. Although efficient, he quarrelled with the local bishop and his followers and was recalled 1682. After the Iroquois, supported by the English, won several military victories, Frontenac was reinstated 1689. He defended Québec against the English 1690 and defeated the Iroquois 1696.

Frontier thesis theory concerning the significance of the frontier experience in American historical development, formulated 1893 by US historian Frederick Jackson ◊Turner. Prompted by the 1890 census report's claim that a distinctive frontier line of westward population movement was no longer discernible, Turner argued that the frontier had gone and with it, the first period of American history. His thesis was an attempt to give American history and society distinctive qualities (such as commitment to democratic equality).

front-line states the black nations of southern Africa in the 'front line' of the struggle against the segregationist policies of South Africa: Mozambique, Tanzania, and Zambia, as well as Botswana and Zimbabwe.

Fuad two kings of Egypt:

Fuad I 1868–1936. King of Egypt from 1922. Son of the Khedive Ismail, he succeeded his elder brother Hussein Kiamil as sultan of Egypt 1917; when Egypt was declared independent 1922 he assumed the title of king.

Fuad II 1952– . King of Egypt 1952–53, between the abdication of his father ◊Farouk and the establishment of the republic. He was a grandson of Fuad I.

Fuchs Klaus (Emil Julius) 1911–1988. German spy who worked on atom-bomb research in the USA in World War II, and subsequently at Harwell, UK. He was imprisoned 1950–59 for passing information to the USSR and resettled in eastern Germany.

Führer or *Fuehrer* title adopted by Adolf ◊Hitler as leader of the Nazi Party.

Fujiwara in Japanese history, the ruling clan 858–1185. During that period (the latter part of the ◊Heian), the office of emperor became merely ceremonial, with power exercised by chancellors and regents, who were all Fujiwara and whose daughters in every generation married into the imperial family. There was a Fujiwara in Japanese government as recently as during World War II.

The name Fujiwara dates from 669; the family claimed divine descent. The son of the first Fujiwara became a minister and the grandfather of an emperor, and as this pattern repeated itself for centuries, the clan accumulated wealth and power through the control of government appointments.

In 1868, when the last ◊shogun had been ousted, it was a Fujiwara that the Meiji emperor appointed to the highest government post.

Fula W African empire founded by people of predominantly Fulani extraction. The Fula conquered the Hausa states in the 19th century.

Fulani member of a W African culture from the southern Sahara and Sahel. Traditionally nomadic pastoralists and traders, Fulani groups are found in Senegal, Guinea, Mali, Burkina Faso, Niger, Nigeria, Chad, and Cameroon. The Fulani language is divided into four dialects and belongs to the W Atlantic branch of the Niger-Congo family; it has more than 10 million speakers.

Fulbright (James) William 1905–1995. US Democratic politician. A US senator 1945-75, he was responsible for the *Fulbright Act* 1946, which provided grants for thousands of Americans to study abroad and for overseas students to study in the USA. Fulbright chaired the Senate Foreign Relations Committee 1959–74, and was a strong internationalist and supporter of the United Nations.

Fuller Melville Weston 1833–1910. US jurist and chief justice of the US Supreme Court 1888-1910. Fuller endorsed court options that limited state and federal strengths to regulate private business. He sided with the majority of the Court in *Pollack* v *Farmers Loan and Trust Co* 1895, which held invalid a flat-rate US income tax leading to passage of the 16th Amendment to the Constitution in 1913, authorizing an income tax.

Funj Islamic dynasty that ruled the Sudan from 1505 to the 1820s, when the territory was taken over by the Turkish government of Egypt. During the 16th and 17th centuries the Funj extended their territories westwards and in the 18th century fought a series of wars against Ethiopia. From the late 1600s there were severe internal conflicts when the warrior aristocracy challenged and eventually supplanted the ruling family.

Fusion government South African coalition government formed 1933 which saw the merger of J B M ◊Hertzog's Nationalist Party and J C ◊Smuts' South African Party the following year. The United South African National Party, as it became, attempted to cultivate a broader white unity in South Africa in the face of growing political and economic uncertainty.

fyrd Anglo-Saxon local militia in Britain. All freemen were obliged to defend their shire but, by the 11th century, a distinction was drawn between the *great fyrd*, for local defence, and the *select fyrd*, drawn from better-equipped and experienced warriors who could serve farther afield.

gabelle in French history, term that originally referred to a tax on various items but came to be used exclusively for a tax on salt, first levied by Philip the Fair in 1286 and abolished 1790.

Gabon country in central Africa, bounded N by Cameroon, E and S by the Congo, W by the Atlantic Ocean, and NW by Equatorial Guinea.

history Gabon was colonized by some of its present inhabitants (the Fang and the Omiéné) between the 16th and 18th centuries. Its first European visitors were the Portuguese in the late 15th century. They began a slave trade that lasted almost 400 years. In 1889 Gabon became part of the French Congo and was a province of French Equatorial Africa from 1908.

Gabon achieved full independence 1960. There were then two main political parties, the Gabonese Democratic Bloc (BDG), led by Léon M'ba, and the Gabonese Democratic and Social Union (UDSG), led by Jean-Hilaire Aubame. Although the two parties were evenly matched in popular support, on independence M'ba became president, and Aubame foreign minister.

In 1964 the BDG wanted the two parties to merge, but the UDSG resisted, and M'ba called a general election. Before the elections M'ba was deposed in a military coup by supporters of Aubame but was restored to office with French help. Aubame was tried and imprisoned for treason. The UDSG was outlawed, and most of its members joined the BDG.

Bongo's presidency In 1964 M'ba, although in failing health, was re-elected. He died later that year and was succeeded by Albert-Bernard Bongo who, the following year, established the Gabonese Democratic Party (PDG) as the only legal party. Bongo was re-elected 1973 and was converted to Islam, changing his first name to Omar. In 1979 Bongo, as the sole presidential

candidate, was re-elected for a further seven years.

Gabon's reserves of uranium, manganese, and iron make it the richest country per head in Black Africa, and both M'ba and Bongo have successfully exploited these resources, gaining control of the iron-ore ventures once half-owned by the Bethlehem Steel Corporation of the USA, and concluding economic and technical agreements with China as well as maintaining ties with France. Although President Bongo has operated an authoritarian regime, Gabon's prosperity has diluted any serious opposition to him. He was re-elected Nov 1986, and a coup attempt against him 1989 was defeated by loyal troops. In Sept 1990 the first multiparty elections since 1964 were won by PDG despite claims of widespread fraud, with 553 candidates contesting 120 assembly seats.

Gaddafi alternative form of ◊Khaddhafi, Libyan leader.

Gadsden Purchase in US history, the purchase of approximately 77,700 sq km/30,000 sq mi in what is now New Mexico and Arizona by the USA 1853. The land was bought from Mexico for $10 million in a treaty negotiated by James Gadsden (1788–1858) of South Carolina, to construct a transcontinental railroad route, the Southern Pacific, completed in the 1880s.

Gaitskell Hugh (Todd Naylor) 1906–1963. British Labour politician. In 1950 he became minister of economic affairs, and then chancellor of the Exchequer until Oct 1951. In 1955 he defeated Aneurin Bevan for the succession to Attlee as party leader, and tried to reconcile internal differences on nationalization and disarmament. He was re-elected leader in 1960.

Gall *c.* 1840–1894. American Sioux Indian leader. He became a noted warrior of the Hunkpapa Sioux and a protégé of Chief Sitting Bull. Gall accompanied Sitting Bull to Montana 1876 and led the encirclement and annihilation of General ◊Custer's force at Little Bighorn.

Gallatin Albert 1761–1849. Swiss-born US political leader and diplomat. He served in the US House of Representatives 1795–1801 and was secretary of the treasury 1801–13 during the administrations of Jefferson and Madison. He negotiated the treaty ending the Anglo-American War of 1812–14 and served as US minister to France 1815–22 and to England 1826–27.

Gallatin served in the Pennsylvania state legislature 1790–94. A critic of the Federalists, he helped establish the fiscal power of the US House of Representatives. After the end of his political career, he devoted himself to banking and American Indian ethnology.

Gallegos Rómulo 1884–1969. Venezuelan politician and writer. He was Venezuela's first democratically elected president 1948 before being overthrown by a military coup the same year. He was also a professor of philosophy and literature. His novels include *La trepadora/The Climber* 1925 and *Doña Bárbara* 1929.

Gallic Wars series of military campaigns 58–51 BC in which Julius Caesar, as proconsul of Gaul, annexed Transalpine Gaul (the territory that formed the geographical basis of modern-day France). His final victory over the Gauls led by Vercingetorix 52 BC left him in control of the land area from the Rhine to the Pyrenees and from the Alps to the Atlantic. The final organization of the provinces followed under Augustus.

Gallipoli port in European Turkey, giving its name to the peninsula (ancient name *Chersonesus*) on which it stands. In World War I, at the instigation of Winston Churchill, an unsuccessful attempt was made Feb 1915–Jan 1916 by Allied troops to force their way through the Dardanelles and link up with Russia. The campaign was fought mainly by Australian and New Zealand (◊ANZAC) forces, who suffered heavy losses. An estimated 36,000 Commonwealth troops died during the nine-month campaign.

Galtieri Leopoldo 1926– . Argentine general, president 1981–82. A leading member from 1979 of the ruling right-wing military junta and commander of the army, Galtieri became president in 1981. Under his leadership the junta ordered the seizure 1982 of the Falkland Islands (Malvinas), a British colony in the SW Atlantic claimed by Argentina. After the surrender of his forces he resigned as army commander and was replaced as president. He and his fellow junta members were tried for abuse of human rights and court-martialled for their conduct of the war; he was sentenced to 12 years in prison in 1986.

Gama Vasco da *c.* 1469–1524. Portuguese navigator who commanded an expedition in 1497 to discover the route to India around the Cape of Good Hope in modern South Africa. On Christmas Day 1497 he reached land, which he named Natal. He then crossed the Indian Ocean, arriving at Calicut May 1498, and returning to Portugal Sept 1499.

Da Gama was born at Sines, and chosen by Portuguese King Manoel I for his 1497 expedition. In 1502 he founded a Portuguese colony at Mozambique. In the same year he attacked and plundered Calicut in revenge for the murder of some Portuguese sailors. After 20 years of retirement, he was dispatched to India again as Portuguese viceroy in 1524, but died two months after his arrival in Goa.

Gambetta Léon Michel 1838–1882. French politician, organizer of resistance during the Franco-Prussian War, and founder in 1871 of the Third Republic. In 1881–82 he was prime minister for a few weeks.

Gambia, The country in W Africa, bounded N, E, and S by Senegal and W by the Atlantic Ocean.

history The Gambia was formerly part of the ◊Mali Empire, a Muslim gold-trading empire that flourished in W Africa between the 7th and 15th centuries, and declined at the time of the Portuguese arrival 1455. In the late 16th century commerce was taken over from Portugal by England, and trading posts established on the Gambia River were controlled from Sierra Leone. In 1843 The Gambia was made a crown colony, becoming an independent British colony 1888.

Jawara's presidency Political parties were formed in the 1950s, internal self-government was achieved 1963, and full independence within the Commonwealth 1965, with Dawda Jawara as prime minister. The country declared itself a republic 1970, with Jawara as president, replacing the British monarch as head of state. He was re-elected 1972 and 1977.

With the Progressive People's Party (PPP) the dominant political force, there was pressure to make The Gambia a one-party state, but Jawara resisted this. When an attempted coup against him 1981 was thwarted with Senegalese military aid, ties between the two countries were strengthened to the extent that plans were announced for their merger into a confederation of Senegambia. However, Senegal had doubts about the idea, and in economic terms The Gambia had more to gain. In Sept 1989 it was announced that The Gambia had formally agreed to end the confederation. In 1982 Jawara was re-elected; he was again re-elected 1987. In 1990, The Gambia contributed troops to the multinational force attempting to stabilize Liberia.

Gamelin Maurice Gustave 1872–1958. French commander in chief of the Allied armies in France at the outset of World War II 1939. Replaced by Maxime Weygand after the German breakthrough at Sedan 1940, he was tried by the ◊Vichy government as a scapegoat before the Riom 'war guilt' court 1942. He refused to defend himself and was detained in Germany until released by the Allies 1945.

Ganda member of the Baganda people, the majority ethnic group in Uganda; the Baganda also live in Kenya. Until the 19th century they formed an independent kingdom, the largest in E Africa. It was a British protectorate 1894–1962, and the monarchy was officially overthrown in 1966.

Gandhi Indira (born Nehru) 1917–1984. Indian politician, prime minister of India 1966–77 and 1980–84, and leader of the ◊Congress Party 1966–77 and subsequently of the Congress (I) party. She was assassinated 1984 by members of her Sikh bodyguard, resentful of her use of troops to clear malcontents from the Sikh temple at ◊Amritsar.

Her father, Jawaharlal Nehru, was India's first prime minister. She had two sons, Sanjay Gandhi (1946–1980), who died in an aeroplane crash, and Rajiv ◊Gandhi, who was assassinated 21 May 1991. In 1975 the validity of her re-election to parliament was questioned, and she declared a state of emergency. During this time Sanjay Gandhi implemented a social and economic programme (including an unpopular family-planning policy) which led to her defeat in 1977.

An unjust law is itself a species of violence. Arrest for its breach is more so.

Mahatma Gandhi
Non-Violence in Peace and War

Gandhi Mohandas Karamchand, called *Mahatma* ('Great Soul') 1869–1948. Indian nationalist leader. A pacifist, he led the struggle for Indian independence from the UK by advocating nonviolent noncooperation (*satyagraha*, defence of and by truth) from 1915. He was imprisoned several times by the British authorities and was influential in the nationalist ◊Congress Party and in the independence negotiations 1947. He was assassinated by a Hindu nationalist in the violence that followed the partition of British India into India and Pakistan.

Gandhi was born in Porbandar and studied law in London, later practising as a barrister. He settled in South Africa where until 1914 he led the Indian community in opposition to racial discrimination. Returning to India, he emerged as leader of the Indian National Congress. He organized hunger strikes and events of civil disobedience, and campaigned for social reform, including religious tolerance and an end to discrimination against the so-called untouchable ◊caste.

Gandhi Rajiv 1944–1991. Indian politician, prime minister from 1984 (following his mother Indira Gandhi's assassination) to Nov 1989. As prime minister, he faced growing discontent with his party's elitism and lack of concern for social issues. He was assassinated by a bomb at an election rally.

Elder son of Indira Gandhi and grandson of Nehru, Rajiv Gandhi was born into the Kashmiri Brahmin family that had governed India for all but four years since 1947. He initially displayed little interest in politics and became a pilot with Indian Airlines. But after the death in a plane crash of his brother *Sanjay* (1946–1980), he was elected to his brother's Amethi parliamentary seat 1981. In the Dec 1984 parliamentary elections he won a record majority. His reputation became tarnished by a scandal concerning alleged kickbacks to senior officials from an arms deal with the Swedish munitions firm Bofors and, following his party's defeat in the general election of Nov 1989, Gandhi was forced to resign as premier. He was killed in the middle of the 1991 election campaign at a rally near Madras, while attempting to regain office.

Gang of Four in Chinese history, the chief members of the radical faction that played a key role in directing the ◊Cultural Revolution and tried to seize power after the death of the communist leader Mao Zedong 1976. It included his widow, ◊Jiang Qing; the other members were three young Shanghai politicians: Zhang Chunqiao, Wang Hongwen, and Yao Wenyuan. The coup failed and the Gang of Four were arrested. Publicly tried in 1980, they were found guilty of treason.

gangsterism organized crime, particularly in the USA as a result of the 18th Amendment (◊Prohibition) in 1919.

Bootlegging activities (importing or making illegal liquor) and 'speakeasies' (where alcohol could be illegally purchased) gave rise to rivalry that resulted in hired gangs of criminals (gangsters) and gun battles.

Gardiner Stephen c. 1493–1555. English priest and politician. After being secretary to Cardinal Wolsey, he became bishop of Winchester in 1531. An opponent of Protestantism, he was imprisoned under Edward VI, and as Lord Chancellor 1553–55 under Queen Mary he tried to restore Roman Catholicism.

Garfield James A(bram) 1831–1881. 20th president of the USA 1881, a Republican. A compromise candidate for the presidency, he held office for only four months before being assassinated in Washington DC railway station by a disappointed office-seeker. His short tenure was marked primarily by struggles within the Republican party over influence and cabinet posts.

Garibaldi Giuseppe 1807–1882. Italian soldier who played a central role in the unification of Italy by conquering Sicily and Naples 1860. From 1834 a member of the nationalist Mazzini's ◊Young Italy society, he was forced into exile until 1848 and again 1849–54. He fought against Austria 1848–49, 1859, and 1866, and led two unsuccessful expeditions to liberate Rome from papal rule in 1862 and 1867.

I cannot offer you either wages or honours; I offer you hunger, thirst, forced marches, battles, and death. Anyone who loves his country, follow me.

Giuseppe Garibaldi

Garner John Nance 1868–1967. US political leader and vice president of the USA 1933–41. He served in the US House of Representatives 1903–33. A Democratic leader in the House, he was chosen as Speaker 1931. He later served as vice president during Franklin Roosevelt's first two terms. Opposing Roosevelt's re-election in 1940, Garner retired from public life.

Garrison William Lloyd 1805–1879. US editor and reformer who was an uncompromising opponent of slavery. He founded the abolitionist journal *The Liberator* 1831 and became a leader of the American Anti-Slavery Society. Although initially opposed to violence, he supported the Union cause in the Civil War. After the Emancipation Proclamation, he disbanded the Anti-Slavery Society and devoted his energies to prohibition, feminism, and Indian rights.

Garvey Marcus (Moziah) 1887–1940. Jamaican political thinker and activist, an early advocate of black nationalism. He founded the UNIA (Universal Negro Improvement Association) in 1914, and moved to the USA in 1916, where he established branches in New York and other northern cities. Aiming to achieve human rights and dignity for black people through black pride and economic self-sufficiency, he was considered one of the first militant black nationalists. He led a Back to Africa movement for black Americans to establish a black-governed country in Africa. The Jamaican cult of ◊Rastafarianism is based largely on his ideas.

Gascony ancient province of SW France. With Guienne it formed the duchy of Aquitaine in the 12th century; Henry II of England gained possession of it through his marriage to Eleanor of Aquitaine in 1152, and it was often in English hands until 1451. It was then ruled by the king of France until it was united with the French royal domain 1607 under Henry IV.

GATT acronym for ◊*General Agreement on Tariffs and Trade*.

gaucho part Indian, part Spanish cattle herder of the Argentine and Uruguayan pampas. The gauchos supported Ortiz de Rosas, Argentinian ruler 1835–52.

Gaugamela, Battle of or *Battle of Arbela* decisive defeat in 331 BC of the Persians under Darius III (c. 380–330 BC) by ◊Alexander the Great. The battle took place on the eastern bank of the River Tigris in Upper Mesopotamia (modern Iraq). The defeated Darius fled and was later killed by his own troops.

Gaul member of the Celtic-speaking peoples who inhabited France and Belgium in Roman times; also their territory. Certain Gauls invaded Italy around 400 BC, sacked Rome 387 BC, and settled between the Alps and the Apennines; this district, known as Cisalpine Gaul, was conquered by Rome in about 225 BC.

The Romans annexed S Gaul, from the Alps to the Rhone valley in about 120 BC. This became Gallia Narbonensis. The remaining area, from the Atlantic to the Rhine, was invaded and subjugated by Julius ◊Caesar in the ◊Gallic Wars of 58–51 BC. This was later organized into the three imperial provinces: Aquitania in the W, Belgica in the N, and Lugdunensis in the centre and NW of what is now France.

gaullism political philosophy deriving from the views of Charles ◊de Gaulle but not necessarily confined to Gaullist parties, or even to France. Its basic tenets are the creation and preservation of a strongly centralized state and an unwillingness to enter into international obligations at the expense of national interests.

Gdánsk (German *Danzig*) Polish port. Formerly a member of the ◊Hanseatic League, it was in almo st continuous Prussian possession 1793–1919, when it again became a free city under the protection of the League of Nations. The annexation of the city by Germany marked the beginning of World War II. It reverted to Poland 1945, when the churches and old merchant houses were restored. The Lenin shipyards were the birthplace of Solidarity, the Polish resistance movement to pro-Soviet communism, 1981.

Gelon *c.* 540–478 BC. tyrant of Syracuse. He refused to help the mainland Greeks against ◊Xerxes 480 BC, but later the same year defeated the Carthaginians under Hamilcar Barca at Himera, on the north coast of Sicily, leaving Syracuse as the leading city in the western Greek world.

Gemayel Amin 1942–   . Lebanese politician, a Maronite Christian; president 1982–88. He succeeded his brother, president-elect *Bechir Gemayel* (1947–1982), on his assassination on 14 Sept 1982. The Lebanese parliament was unable to agree on a successor when his term expired, so separate governments were formed under rival Christian and Muslim leaders.

General Agreement on Tariffs and Trade (GATT) organization within the United Nations founded 1948 with the aim of encouraging ◊free trade between nations by reducing tariffs, subsidies, quotas, and regulations that discriminate against imported products. GATT was effectively replaced by the *World Trade Organization* Jan 1995.

During the last round of talks, begun 1986 in Uruguay, the USA opposed European Community (EC) restrictions on agricultural imports, but argued to maintain restrictions on textile imports to the USA. Talks repeatedly stalled over a plan to reduce farm subsidies. Agreement was finally reached 1993. The Final Act was signed 1994 in Marrakesh, Morocco.

General Belgrano Argentine battle cruiser torpedoed and sunk on 2 May 1982 by the British nuclear-powered submarine *Conqueror* during the ◊Falklands War.

general strike refusal to work by employees in several key industries, with the intention of paralysing the economic life of a country. In British history, the General Strike was a nationwide strike called by the Trade Union Congress on 3 May 1926 in support of the miners' union.

Geneva Convention international agreement 1864 regulating the treatment of those wounded in war, and later extended to cover the types of weapons allowed, the treatment of prisoners and the sick, and the protection of civilians in wartime. The rules were revised at conventions held 1906, 1929, and 1949, and by the 1977 Additional Protocols.

Geneva Protocol international agreement 1925 designed to prohibit the use of poisonous gases, chemical weapons, and bacteriological methods of warfare. It came into force 1928 but was not ratified by the USA until 1974.

Genghis Khan *c.* ?1167–1227. Mongol conqueror, ruler of all Mongol peoples from 1206.

He began the conquest of N China 1213, overran the empire of the shah of Khiva 1219–25, and invaded N India, while his lieutenants advanced as far as the Crimea. When he died, his empire ranged from the Yellow Sea to the Black Sea; it continued to expand after his death to extend from Hungary to Korea. Genghis Khan controlled probably a larger area than any other individual in history. He was not only a great military leader, but the creator of a stable political system.

Genji alternative name for ◊Minamoto, an ancient Japanese clan.

genocide deliberate and systematic destruction of a national, racial, religious, or ethnic group defined by the exterminators as undesirable. The term is commonly applied to the policies of the Nazis during World War II (what they called the 'final solution' – the extermination of all 'undesirables' in occupied Europe).

Genscher Hans-Dietrich 1927–   . German politician, chair of the West German Free Democratic Party (FDP) 1974–85, foreign minister 1974–92. A skilled and pragmatic tactician, Genscher became the reunified Germany's most popular politician.

We want not a German Europe but a European Germany.

Hans-Dietrich Genscher
in the *Observer* Dec 1990

gentry the lesser nobility, particularly in England and Wales, not entitled to sit in the House of Lords. By the later Middle Ages, it included knights, esquires, and gentlemen, and after the 17th century, baronets.

George six kings of Great Britain:

George I 1660–1727. King of Great Britain and Ireland from 1714. He was the son of the first elector of Hanover, Ernest Augustus (1629–1698), and his wife Sophia, and a great-grandson of James I. He succeeded to the electorate 1698, and became king on the death of Queen Anne. He attached himself to the Whigs, and spent most of his reign in Hanover, never having learned English.

George II 1683–1760. King of Great Britain and Ireland from 1727, when he succeeded his father, George I. His victory at Dettingen 1743, in the War of the Austrian Succession, was the last battle commanded by a British king. He married Caroline of Anspach 1705. He was succeeded by his grandson George III.

George III 1738–1820. King of Great Britain and Ireland from 1760, when he succeeded his grandfather George II. His rule was marked by intransigence resulting in the loss of the American colonies, for which he shared the blame with his chief minister Lord North, and the emancipation of Catholics in England. Possibly suffering from porphyria, he had repeated attacks of insanity, permanent from 1811. He was succeeded by his son George IV.

George IV 1762–1830. King of Great Britain and Ireland from 1820, when he succeeded his father George III, for whom he had been regent during the king's period of insanity 1811–20. In 1785 he secretly married a Catholic widow, Maria Fitzherbert, but in 1795 also married Princess Caroline of Brunswick, in return for payment of his debts. He was a patron of the arts. His prestige was undermined by his treatment of Caroline (they separated 1796), his dissipation, and his extravagance. He was succeeded by his brother, the duke of Clarence, who became William IV.

George V 1865–1936. King of Great Britain from 1910, when he succeeded his father Edward VII. He was the second son, and became heir 1892 on the death of his elder brother Albert, Duke of Clarence. In 1893, he married Princess Victoria Mary of Teck (Queen Mary), formerly engaged to his brother. During World War I he made several visits to the front. In 1917, he abandoned all German titles for himself and his family. The name of the royal house was changed from Saxe-Coburg-Gotha (popularly known as Brunswick or Hanover) to Windsor.

How is the empire?

George V last words, *The Times* Jan 1936

George VI 1895–1952. King of Great Britain from 1936, when he succeeded after the abdication of his brother Edward VIII, who had succeeded their father George V. Created Duke of York 1920, he married in 1923 Lady Elizabeth Bowes-Lyon (1900–   ), and their children are Elizabeth II and Princess Margaret. During World War II, he visited the Normandy and Italian battlefields.

We're not a family; we're a firm.

George VI

George two kings of Greece:

George I 1845–1913. King of Greece 1863–1913. The son of Christian IX of Denmark, he was nominated to the Greek throne and, in spite of early unpopularity, became a highly successful constitutional monarch. He was assassinated by a Greek, Schinas, at Salonika.

George II 1890–1947. King of Greece 1922–23 and 1935–47. He became king on the expulsion of his father Constantine I 1922 but was himself overthrown 1923. Restored by the military 1935, he set up a dictatorship under Joannis ◊Metaxas, and went into exile during the German occupation 1941–45.

Georgetown, Declaration of call, at a conference in Guyana of nonaligned countries 1972, for a multipolar system to replace the two world power blocs, and for the Mediterranean Sea and Indian Ocean to be neutral.

Georgia, Republic of country in the Caucasus of SE Europe, bounded N by Russia, E by Azerbaijan, S by Armenia, and W by the Black Sea.

history Georgia was converted to Christianity in the 4th century AD. In the 7th century, with the weakening of the Persian and Byzantine empires, an independent Georgian kingdom was created. The kingdom became especially powerful between the late 11th and early 13th centuries. Thereafter the country fell under the sway of Persian, Mongol, and Turkish imperial powers, before being annexed by tsarist Russia in 1801. Tbilisi (Tiflis) developed into an important commercial centre under the tsars; however, the Georgian language and church were gradually suppressed.

under Soviet control In May 1918, amid turmoil in the Russian Empire, Georgia reasserted its independence but, denied economic help from the West, its rebellion was crushed by the Red Army in Feb 1921. In 1922 Georgia entered the USSR as part of the Transcaucasian Federation, along with Armenia and Azerbaijan, before becoming a full republic in 1936. There was rapid industrialization between the 1920s and 1950s, but considerable resistance to rural collectivization, and political purges were instituted by police chief Lavrenti Beria during the 1930s. During World War II, the Soviet dictator Stalin ordered the deportation of 200,000 Meskhetians to Central Asia.

growth of nationalism During the 1950s and 1960s, Georgia's administration became notorious for its laxity and corruption. A drive against crime and corruption was launched 1972–85 by Eduard ◊Shevardnadze, leader of the Georgian Communist Party (GCP), and there was accelerated Russification. This provoked a nationalist backlash, witnessed in the form of mass demonstrations and the founding, in 1974, of the Initiative Group for the Defence of Human Rights in Georgia by the university lecturer Zviad Gamsakhurdia. ◊Glasnost produced an intensification of the nationalist campaign in the later 1980s, with a Georgian Popular Front and separatist group, the National Democratic Party of Georgia, established 1988. This fuelled anti-Georgian feeling among the republic's minorities in ◊Abkhazia and Ossetia. The massacre in Tbilisi of at least 20 peaceful Georgian pro-independence demonstrators by Soviet troops on April 9, 1989 added momentum to the nationalist movement and during 1989–90, with its old-guard leadership purged, the GCP joined the secessionist camp.

After the seven-party Round Table–Free Georgia nationalist coalition triumphed in Georgia's Oct–Nov 1990 supreme soviet elections, Zviad Gamsakhurdia was elected state president. The new parliament voted, in Jan 1991, to establish a republican National Guard and end conscription to the Soviet Army.

independence declared In March 1991 Georgia boycotted the all-Union USSR constitutional referendum. Instead, the republic held a plebiscite on independence, which secured 99% approval. Independence was declared on April 9, 1991 and a campaign of civil disobedience against Soviet interests was launched. On May 26, 1991 Gamsakhurdia became the first republic president in the USSR to be directly elected, winning 87% of the vote and defeating five other candidates. President Gamsakhurdia failed to strongly denounce the anti-Gorbachev coup in Moscow in Aug 1991, prompting the resignation in protest of prime minister Tengiz Sigua. However, the GCP was banned in the wake of the failed Moscow coup.

civil unrest From Sept 1991 the increasingly dictatorial president, arresting political opponents and ordering the closure of pro-opposition newspapers, faced a growing popular protest movement, fuelled further by government troops firing on the crowds. With disorder mounting, Gamsakhurdia declared a state of emergency on Sept 24, 1991. By late Oct 1991 most of the leadership of the nationalist National Democratic Party (NDP), headed by Giorgi Chanturia, had been arrested. The power struggle intensified and Gamsakhurdia was forced to flee to Armenia on Jan 6, 1992. Distracted by these events, Georgia failed to join the new ◊Commonwealth of Independent States (CIS) which was established in Dec 1991.

international recognition In Jan 1992 Georgia was admitted into the ◊Conference on Security and Cooperation in Europe, and in July it became a member of the United Nations (UN).

multiparty elections A military council with Tengiz Sigua as prime minister, having crushed a rebellion by Gamsakhurdia supporters, gave way to a new parliament elected Oct 1992, with Shevardnadze as its chair. There is an exceptionally fragmented multi-party system, riven by clan and regional rivalries, with more than 100 parties competing for power. The new government had to deal with violent unrest in South Ossetia and Akhazia, both of which were seeking autonomy.

Germanicus Caesar 15 BC–AD 19. Roman general. He was the adopted son of the emperor ◊Tiberius and married the emperor ◊Augustus' granddaughter Agrippina. Although he refused the suggestion of his troops that he claim the throne on the death of Augustus, his military victories in Germany made Tiberius jealous. Sent to the Middle East, he died near Antioch, possibly murdered at the instigation of Tiberius. He was the father of ◊Caligula and Agrippina, mother of ◊Nero.

German Spring offensive Germany's final offensive on the Western Front during World War I. By early 1918, German forces outnumbered the Allies on the Western Front. Germany staged three separate offensives, which culminated in the Second Battle of the Marne, fought between 15 July and 6 Aug. It marked the turning point of World War I. After winning the battle the Allies advanced steadily, and by Sept, Germany had lost all the territory it had gained during the spring.

Germany country in central Europe, bounded N by the North and Baltic Seas and Denmark, E by Poland and the Czech Republic, S by Austria and Switzerland, and W by France, Luxembourg, Belgium, and the Netherlands.

history For history before 1949, see: ◊Germany history. In 1949 Germany was divided by the Allied powers and the Soviet Union, forming the German Democratic Republic in the eastern part of the country (formerly the Soviet zone of occupation), and the Federal Republic of Germany in the west (comprising the British, US, and French occupation zones under Allied military control following Germany's surrender 1945). For the next four and a half decades West and East Germany were divided by the policies of the ◊Cold War, with West Germany becoming the strongest European NATO power, and East Germany a vital member of

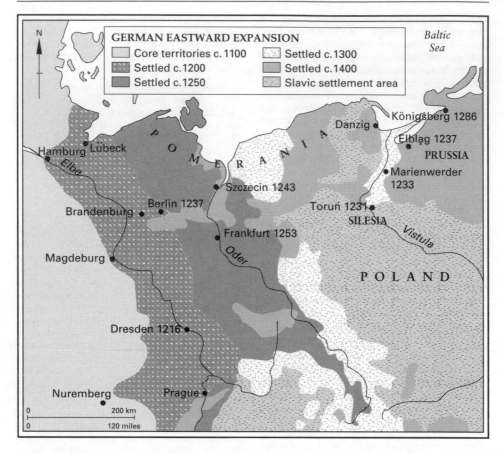

German eastward expansion *In the early 12th century Emperor Lothair II established Marcher lordships along the eastern frontier of his empire to promote expansion into Slavic areas. Colonists introduced three-field agriculture, planned villages and towns based on the German pattern, and imperial law. Generally peaceful, the movement brought great economic benefit to both the empire and its new colonies.*

◊Comecon and the ◊Warsaw Pact during the era of Soviet leader Brezhnev, stationing Soviet medium-range nuclear missiles on its soil.

West Germany under Adenauer In postwar West Germany, a policy of demilitarization, decentralization, and democratization was instituted by the Allied control powers and a new, intentionally provisional, constitution framed, which included eventual German reunification. West ◊Berlin was blockaded by the Soviet Union 1948–49, but survived to form a constituent *Land* in the Federal Republic, after an airlift operation by the Allied powers. Politics during the Federal Republic's first decade were dominated by the Christian Democratic Union (CDU), led by the popular Konrad ◊Adenauer. Chancellor Adenauer and his economics minister, Ludwig ◊Erhard, established a successful approach to economic

management, termed the 'social market economy', which combined the encouragement of free market forces with strategic state intervention on the grounds of social justice. This new approach, combined with aid under the ◊Marshall Plan and the enterprise of the labour force (many of whom were refugees from the partitioned East), brought rapid growth and reconstruction during the 1950s and 1960s, an era termed the 'miracle years'.

During this period, West Germany was also reintegrated into the international community. It gained full sovereignty 1954, entered NATO 1955, emerging as a loyal supporter of the USA, and, under Adenauer's lead, was a founder member of the European Economic Community 1957. Close relations with France enabled the ◊Saarland to be transferred to German sovereignty 1957.

East Germany sovietized East Germany dissolved its five *Länder* (Brandenburg, Mecklenburg–West Pomerania, Saxony, Saxony-Anhalt, and Thuringia) 1952, and its Chamber of States, or upper house, 1958, vesting local authority in 15 *Bezirke*, or administrative districts. Under the 1968 constitution the supreme legislative and executive body in the German Democratic Republic was the Volkskammer (people's chamber), whose 500 members (including 66 from East Berlin) were elected every five years by universal suffrage.

The years immediately after 1949 saw the rapid establishment of a communist regime on the Soviet model, involving the nationalization of industry, the formation of agricultural collectives, and the creation of a one-party political system.

Opposition to such sovietization led, during food shortages, to demonstrations and an uprising 1953, which was suppressed by Soviet troops. East Germany became a sovereign state 1954, recognized at first only by the communist powers.

Brandt and Ostpolitik In 1961, East Germany's construction of the ◊Berlin Wall to prevent refugees from leaving the East created a political crisis that vaulted West Berlin's mayor, Willy ◊Brandt, to international prominence. Domestically, Brandt played a major role in shifting the Social Democratic Party (SPD) away from its traditional Marxist affiliation towards a more moderate position. Support for the SPD steadily increased after this policy switch and the party joined the CDU in a 'grand coalition' 1966–69, before gaining power itself, with the support of the FDP, under Brandt's leadership 1969. As chancellor, Brandt introduced the foreign policy of ◊Ostpolitik, which sought reconciliation with Eastern Europe as a means of improving contacts between East and West Germany.

East Germany saw economic reforms and improved living conditions in the 1960s, and during the next decade a more moderate political stance was adopted, with the replacement of the Stalinist Socialist Unity Party (SED) leader Walter ◊Ulbricht by the pragmatic Erich ◊Honecker. Economic and diplomatic relations with the West were extended.

Schmidt's centrist course West German treaties 1970 normalized relations with the Soviet Union and Poland, and recognized the Oder–Neisse border line, and in 1972 a treaty was effected with East Germany, acknowledging East Germany's borders and separate existence and enabling both countries to enter the United Nations 1973. Brandt resigned as chan-

cellor 1974, after the revelation that his personal assistant had been an East German spy. His successor, the former finance minister, Helmut ◊Schmidt, adhered to Ostpolitik and emerged as a leading advocate of European cooperation.

The CDU is represented in Bavaria by a more right-wing sister party, the Christian Social Union (CSU). A West German SPD–FDP (Free Democratic Party) coalition gained a comfortable victory 1980 when the controversial Franz-Josef ◊Strauss headed the CDU–CSU ticket. Between 1980 and 1982, the left wing of the SPD and the liberal FDP were divided over military policy (in particular the proposed stationing of US nuclear missiles in West Germany) and economic policy.

Kohl's chancellorship Chancellor Schmidt fought to maintain a moderate, centrist course but the FDP eventually withdrew from the federal coalition 1982 and joined forces with the CDU, led by Dr Helmut ◊Kohl, to unseat the chancellor in a 'positive vote of no confidence'. Helmut Schmidt immediately retired from politics and the SPD, led by Hans-Jochen Vögel, was heavily defeated in the Bundestag elections 1983, losing votes on the left to the new environmentalist Green Party. The new Kohl administration, with the FDP's Hans-Dietrich ◊Genscher remaining as foreign minister, adhered closely to the external policy of the previous chancellorship.

At home, a freer market approach was introduced. With unemployment rising to 2.5 million in 1984, problems of social unrest emerged, while violent demonstrations greeted the installation of US nuclear missiles on German soil 1983–84. Internally, the Kohl administration was rocked by scandals over illegal party funding, which briefly touched the chancellor himself. However, a strong recovery in the German economy from 1985 enabled the CDU–CSU–FDP coalition to gain re-election in the federal election 1987.

During 1988–89, after the death of the CSU's Franz-Josef Strauss, support for the far-right Republican party began to climb, and it secured 7% of the vote in the European Parliament elections of June 1989. In 1989–90 events in East Germany and elsewhere in Eastern Europe caused half a million economic and political refugees to enter the Federal Republic, as well as reopening the debate on reunification (*Wiedervereinigung*); this resulted in West German politics becoming more highly charged and polarized. The CDU gave strong support to swift, graduated moves towards 'confederative' reunification, if desired, following free elections in East Germany.

Germany: history

BC–4th century AD	The W Germanic peoples, originating in Scandinavia, moved into the region between the rivers Rhine, Elbe, and Danube, where they were confined by the Roman Empire.
496	The Frankish king Clovis conquered the Alemanni.
768–814	The reign of Holy Roman Emperor Charlemagne, who extended his authority over Germany and imposed Christianity on the Saxons.
814–919	After Charlemagne's death Germany was separated from France under its own kings while the local officials or dukes became virtually independent.
919–1002	Central power was restored by the Saxon dynasty. Otto I, who in 962 revived the title of emperor, began colonizing the Slav lands east of the river Elbe.
1075–1250	A feud between emperors and popes enabled the Germanic princes to recover their independence.
12th century	German expansion eastwards (the *Drang nach Osten*) into lands between the Elbe and the Oder.
1157	Frederick Barbarossa annexed Silesia from Poland.
1493–1519	A temporary revival of imperial power took place under Maximilian I.
1521	The Diet of Worms at which Charles V confronted the Protestant Martin Luther. The Reformation increased Germany's disunity.
1618–48	The Thirty Years' War reduced the empire to a mere name and destroyed Germany's economic and cultural life.
1740–86	The rise of Brandenburg-Prussia as a military power, which had begun in the 17th century, reached its height under Frederick II.
1806	The French emperor Napoleon united W Germany in the Confederation of the Rhine and introduced the ideas and reforms of the French Revolution: his reforms were subsequently imitated in Prussia. The Holy Roman Empire was abolished.
1848	Ideas of democracy and national unity inspired the unsuccessful revolutions of 1848.
1867	The North German Confederation, under the leadership of Prussia, was formed.
1871	Under Chancellor Bismarck's leadership, the German Empire was formed after victorious wars with Austria and France. William I of Prussia became emperor.
1914–18	**World War I**: Germany and other Central Powers at war with Britain, France, and Russia.
1918	A revolution overthrew the monarchy; the social democrats seized power and established the democratic Weimar Republic.
1922–23	Rampant inflation. In 1922 one dollar was worth 50 marks; in 1923 one dollar was worth 2.5 trillion marks.
1929–33	The economic crisis brought Germany close to revolution, until in 1933 the reaction manoeuvred the Nazis into power with Adolf Hitler as chancellor.
1933–39	At home the Nazis solved the unemployment problem by a vast rearmament programme; they suspended the democratic constitution and ruthlessly destroyed all opposition. Abroad, the policy of geopolitical aggression led to war.
1939–45	**World War II**: Germany (from 1940 in an alliance known as the Axis with Italy and Japan) attacked and occupied neighbouring countries, but was defeated by the Allies (the UK and Commonwealth, France 1939–40, the USSR and the USA from 1941, and China).
1945–49	Germany was divided, within its 1937 frontiers, into British, US, French, and Soviet occupation zones.
1949	Germany was partitioned into the communist German Democratic Republic (see ◊Germany, East) and the capitalist German Federal Republic (see ◊Germany, West).

For subsequent history see ◊Germany

exodus to West Germany In East Germany Honecker had been urged by the USSR since 1987 to accelerate the pace of domestic economic and political reform; his refusal to do so increased grassroots pressure for liberalization. In Sept 1989, after the violent suppression of a church and civil-rights activists' demonstration in Leipzig, an umbrella dissident organization, *Neue Forum* (New Forum), was illegally formed. The regime was further destabilized between Aug and Oct 1989 both by the exodus of more than 30,000 of its citizens to West Germany through Hungary (which had opened its borders with Austria in May) and by Honecker's illness during the same period.

reform in East Germany On 6 and 7 Oct the Soviet leader Mikhail Gorbachev visited East Berlin, and made plain his desire to see greater reform. This catalysed the growing reform movement, and a wave of demonstrations (the first since 1953) swept East Berlin, Dresden, Leipzig, and smaller towns. At first, under Honecker's orders, they were violently broken up by riot police. However, the security chief, Egon Krenz, ordered a softer line and in Dresden the reformist Communist Party leader,

Hans Modrow, actually marched with the protesters. Faced with the rising tide of protest and the increasing exodus to West Germany (between 5,000 and 10,000 people a day), which caused grave disruption to the economy, Honecker was replaced as party leader and head of state by Krenz on 18–24 Oct. In an attempt to keep up with the reform movement, Krenz sanctioned far-reaching reforms in Nov 1989 that effectively ended the SED monopoly of power and laid the foundations for a pluralist system. The Politburo was purged of conservative members; Modrow became prime minister and a new cabinet was formed; New Forum was legalized, and opposition parties allowed to form; and borders with the West were opened and free travel allowed, with the Berlin Wall being effectively dismantled.

moves towards reunification In Dec West German Chancellor Kohl announced a ten-point programme for reunification of the two Germanys. While the USA and USSR both called for a slower assessment of this idea, reunification was rapidly achieved on many administrative and economic levels as the governments cooperated on a number of cross-border issues. By mid-Dec the Communist Party had largely ceased to exist as an effective power in East Germany; following revelations of high-level corruption during the Honecker regime, Krenz was forced to resign as SED leader and head of state, being replaced by Gregor Gysi (1948–) and Manfred Gerlach (1928–) respectively. Honecker was placed under house arrest awaiting trial on charges of treason, corruption, and abuse of power, and the Politburo was again purged.

political crisis in East Germany An interim SED–opposition 'government of national responsibility' was formed Feb 1990. The political crisis continued to deepen, with the opposition divided over reunification with West Germany, while the popular reform movement showed signs of running out of control after the storming in Jan of the former security-police (Stasi) headquarters in East Berlin. The East German economy deteriorated further following the exodus of 344,000 people to West Germany in 1989, with a further 1,500 leaving each day, while countrywide work stoppages increased.

East German elections March 1990 were won by the centre-right Alliance for Germany, a three-party coalition led by the CDU. Talks were opened with the West German government on monetary union, concluding with a treaty unifying the economic and monetary systems in July 1990.

reunification Official reunification came about on 3 Oct 1990, with Berlin as the capital (though the seat of government remained in Bonn). In mid-Oct new *Länder* elections were held in former East Germany, in which the conservative parties did well. The first all-German elections since 1932 took place 2 Dec 1990, resulting in victory for Chancellor Kohl and a coalition government composed of the CDU, CSU, and FDP, with only three former East German politicians. In Berlin, which became a *Land*, the ruling SPD lost control of the city council to a new coalition government. The former states of East Germany resumed their status as *Länder*.

social conflict During 1991 divisions grew within the newly united nation as the economy continued to boom in the west, while in the east unemployment rose rapidly. More than 90% of Ossis (easterners) said they felt like second-class citizens, and those in work received less than half the average pay of the Wessis (westerners). Hundreds of racist attacks on foreigners took place, mainly in the east. Public support for Kohl slumped, notably after taxes were raised in order to finance both the rebuilding of the east and the German contribution to the cost of the US-led coalition in the Gulf War against Iraq.

economic crisis in the east Eastern Germany's GDP fell by 15% during 1990 and was projected to decline by 20% during 1991, with a third of the workforce either unemployed or on short time. There were large anti-Kohl demonstrations and outbreaks of right-wing racist violence in eastern cities March–April 1991 as the economic crisis deepened, and the ruling CDU suffered reverses in state elections in western Germany during the of spring 1991 as Wessi voters reacted against Kohl's backtracking on his Dec 1990 election promise not to raise taxes to finance the east's economic development.

Defeat in Kohl's home *Land* of Rhineland-Palatinate April 1991 meant that the CDU lost, to the SPD, the majority it had held in the Bundesrat since Oct 1990. In May 1991 Bjorn Engholm, the minister-president of Schleswig-Holstein since 1988, was elected chair of the SPD. He replaced Hans-Jochen Vögel, who continued as the SPD's leader within the Bundestag. Having previously voted to move from Bonn to Berlin, the Bundesrat voted 5 July 1991 to remain in Bonn, agreeing to reconsider the decision in later years.

racist attacks Throughout 1991 and 1992, neo-Nazis and other far-right groups continued their nationwide campaign against foreigners.

In elections held in Bremen Sept 1991, a shift to the right emerged with support for the CDU and the right-wing, anti-foreigner German People's Union (DVU) rising significantly. Pressure mounted for the government to impose tighter restrictions on refugees: during 1991 250,000 asylum seekers entered Germany. The summer and autumn of 1992 saw numerous violent riots against immigrants by neo-Nazis.

Germany, East (German Democratic Republic, GDR) country 1949–90, formed from the Soviet zone of occupation in the partition of Germany following World War II. East Germany became a sovereign state 1954, and was reunified with West Germany Oct 1990. For history before 1949, see: ◊Germany history; for history after 1949, see ◊Germany.

Germany, West (Federal Republic of Germany) country 1949–90, formed from the British, US, and French occupation zones in the partition of Germany following World War II; reunified with East Germany Oct 1990. For history before 1949, see: ◊Germany history; for history after 1949, see ◊Germany.

Geronimo 1829–1909. Chief of the Chiricahua Apache Indians and war leader. From 1875 to 1885, he fought US federal troops, as well as settlers encroaching on tribal reservations in the Southwest, especially in SE Arizona and New Mexico.

After surrendering to General George Crook March 1886, and agreeing to go to Florida where their families were being held, Geronimo and his followers escaped. Captured again Aug 1886, they were taken to Florida, then to Alabama. The climate proved unhealthy, and they were taken to Fort Sill, Oklahoma, where Geronimo became a farmer.

gerrymander in politics, the rearranging of constituency boundaries to give an unfair advantage to the ruling party. It is now used more generally to describe various kinds of political trickery.

The term derives from US politician Elbridge Gerry (1744–1814), who, while governor of Massachusetts 1812, reorganized an electoral district (shaped like a salamander) in favour of his party.

Gestapo (contraction of *Ge*heime *Sta*ats*polizei*) Nazi Germany's secret police, formed 1933, and under the direction of Heinrich Himmler from 1936.

The Gestapo used torture and terrorism to stamp out anti-Nazi resistance. It was declared a criminal organization at the Nuremberg Trials 1946.

Gettysburg site in Pennsylvania of a decisive battle of the American ◊Civil War 1863, won by the North. The site is now a national cemetery, at the dedication of which President Lincoln delivered the *Gettysburg Address* 19 Nov 1863, a speech in which he reiterated the principles of freedom, equality, and democracy embodied in the US Constitution.

Ghana country in W Africa, bounded N by Burkina Faso, E by Togo, S by the Gulf of Guinea, and W by the Ivory Coast.

history The area now known as Ghana was once made up of several separate kingdoms, including those of the Fanti on the coast and the ◊Ashanti further inland.

The first Europeans to arrive in the region were the Portuguese 1471. Their coastal trading centres, dealing in gold and slaves, flourished alongside Dutch, Danish, British, Swedish, and French traders until about 1800, when the Ashanti, having conquered much of the interior, began to invade the coast. Denmark and the Netherlands abandoned their trading centres, and the Ashanti were defeated by Britain and the Fanti 1874.

the Gold Coast The coastal region became the British colony of the Gold Coast, and after continued fighting, the inland region to the north of Ashanti 1898, and the Ashanti kingdom 1901, were made British protectorates. After 1917 the W part of Togoland, previously governed by Germany, was administered with the Gold Coast. Britain thus controlled both coastal and inland territories, and in 1957 these, together with British Togoland, became independent as Ghana.

Nkrumah's presidency In 1960 Ghana was declared a republic and Dr Kwame ◊Nkrumah, a former prime minister of the Gold Coast, became president. He embarked on a policy of what he called 'African socialism' and established an authoritarian regime. In 1964 he declared Ghana a one-party state, with the Convention People's Party (CPP, which he led) as the only political organization. He then dropped his stance of nonalignment and forged links with the USSR and other communist countries. In 1966, while visiting China, he was deposed in a coup led by General Joseph Ankrah, whose national liberation council released many political prisoners and purged CPP supporters.

In 1969 Ankrah was replaced by General Akwasi Afrifa, who announced plans for a return to civilian government. A new constitution established an elected national assembly and a nonexecutive presidency. The Progress

Party (PP) won a big majority in the assembly, and its leader, Kofi Busia, became prime minister. In 1970 Edward Akufo-Addo became the civilian president.

economic problems and coups Following economic problems, the army seized power again 1972. The constitution was suspended and all political institutions replaced by a National Redemption Council under Col Ignatius Acheampong. In 1976 he too promised a return to civilian rule but critics doubted his sincerity and he was replaced by his deputy, Frederick Akuffo, in a bloodless coup 1978. Like his predecessors, he announced a speedy return to civilian government, but before elections could be held he, in turn, was deposed by junior officers led by Flight-Lt Jerry Rawlings, claiming that previous governments had been corrupt and had mismanaged the economy.

Civilian rule was restored 1979, but two years later Rawlings led another coup, again complaining of the government's incompetence. He established a Provisional National Defence Council with himself as chair, again suspending the constitution, dissolving parliament, and banning political parties. Although Rawlings's policies were initially supported by workers and students, his failure to revive the economy caused discontent, and he has had to deal with a number of demonstrations and attempted coups, including one in Oct 1989. In 1990 the country contributed troops to the multinational force that attempted to stabilize Liberia. A national referendum April 1992 gave overwhelming approval to a proposal for a new, multiparty constitution. In Nov 1992, in the first presidential elections since 1979, Rawlings was elected by a 58.5% majority to head a new civilian government.

Ghana, ancient trading empire that flourished in NW Africa between the 5th and 13th centuries. Founded by the Soninke people, the Ghana Empire was based, like the Mali Empire that superseded it, on the Saharan gold trade. Trade consisted mainly of the exchange of gold from inland deposits for salt from the coast. At its peak in the 11th century, it occupied an area that includes parts of present-day Mali, Senegal, and Mauritania. Wars with the Berber tribes of the Sahara led to its fragmentation and collapse in the 13th century, when much of its territory was absorbed into Mali.

Gheorghiu-Dej Gheorge 1901–1965. Romanian communist politician. A member of the Romanian Communist Party from 1930, he played a leading part in establishing a communist regime 1945. He was prime minister

1952–55 and state president 1961–65. Although retaining the support of Moscow, he adopted an increasingly independent line during his final years.

ghetto separate Jewish quarter in a city; see ◊anti-Semitism.

Ghibelline in medieval Germany and Italy, a supporter of the emperor and member of a rival party to the Guelphs (see ◊Guelph and Ghibelline).

Gibraltar British dependency, situated on a narrow rocky promontory in S Spain. Captured from Spain 1704 by English admiral George Rooke (650–1709), Gibralter was ceded to Britain under the Treaty of Utrecht 1713. A referendum 1967 confirmed the wish of the people to remain in association with the UK, but Spain continues to claim sovereignty and closed the border 1969–85.

Gierek Edward 1913–   . Polish Communist politician. He entered the Politburo of the ruling Polish United Workers' Party (PUWP) in 1956 and was party leader 1970–80. His industrialization programme plunged the country heavily into debt and sparked a series of ◊Solidarity-led strikes.

Gilbert and Ellice Islands former British colony in the Pacific, known since independence 1978 as the countries of ◊Tuvalu and ◊Kiribati.

Gilded Age in US history, a derogatory term referring to the opulence displayed in the post-Civil War decades. It borrows the title of an 1873 political satire by Mark Twain and Charles Dudley Warner (1829–1900), which highlights the respectable veneer of public life covering the many scandals of graft and corruption.

Gilgamesh hero of Sumerian, Hittite, Akkadian, and Assyrian legend, and lord of the Sumerian city of Uruk. The 12 verse books of the *Epic of Gilgamesh* were recorded in a standard version on 12 cuneiform tablets by the Assyrian king Ashurbanipal's scholars in the 7th century BC, and the epic itself is older than Homer's *Iliad* by at least 1,500 years.

The *Epic*'s incident of the Flood is similar to the Old Testament account, since Abraham had been a citizen of the nearby city of Ur in Sumer.

Giolitti Giovanni 1842–1928. Italian liberal politician, born in Mondovi. He was prime minister 1892–93, 1903–05, 1906–09, 1911–14, and 1920–21. He opposed Italian intervention in World War I and pursued a policy of broad coalitions, which proved ineffective in controlling Fascism after 1921.

Girondin member of the right-wing republican party in the French Revolution, so called because a number of their leaders came from the Gironde region. They were driven from power by the ◊Jacobins 1793.

Giscard d'Estaing Valéry 1926– . French conservative politician, president 1974–81. He was finance minister to de Gaulle 1962–66 and Pompidou 1969–74. As leader of the Union pour la Démocratie Française, which he formed in 1978, Giscard sought to project himself as leader of a 'new centre'.

gladiator in ancient Rome, a trained fighter, recruited mainly from slaves, criminals, and prisoners of war, who fought to the death in arenas for the entertainment of spectators. The custom was introduced into Rome from Etruria in 264 BC and continued until the 5th century AD.

Gladstone William Ewart 1809–1898. British Liberal politician, repeatedly prime minister. He entered Parliament as a Tory in 1833 and held ministerial office, but left the party 1846 and after 1859 identified himself with the Liberals. He was chancellor of the Exchequer 1852–55 and 1859–66, and prime minister 1868–74, 1880–85, 1886, and 1892–94. He introduced elementary education 1870 and vote by secret ballot 1872 and many reforms in Ireland, although he failed in his efforts to get a Home Rule Bill passed.

Gladstone was born in Liverpool, the son of a rich merchant. In Peel's government he was president of the Board of Trade 1843–45, and colonial secretary 1845–46. He left the Tory Party with the Peelite group in 1846. He was chancellor of the Exchequer in Aberdeen's government 1852–55 and in the Liberal governments of Palmerston and Russell 1859–66. In his first term as prime minister he carried through a series of reforms, including the disestablishment of the Church of Ireland, the Irish Land Act, and the abolition of the purchase of army commissions and of religious tests in the universities.

Gladstone strongly resisted Disraeli's imperialist and pro-Turkish policy during the latter's government of 1874–80, not least because of Turkish pogroms against subject Christians, and by his Midlothian campaign of 1879 helped to overthrow Disraeli. Gladstone's second government carried the second Irish Land Act and the Reform Act 1884 but was confronted with problems in Ireland, Egypt, and South Africa, and lost prestige through its failure to relieve General ◊Gordon. Returning to office in 1886, Gladstone introduced his first Home Rule Bill, which was defeated by the secession of the Liberal Unionists, and he thereupon resigned. After six years' opposition he formed his last government; his second Home Rule Bill was rejected by the Lords, and in 1894 he resigned. He led a final crusade against the massacre of Armenian Christians in 1896.

All the world over, I will back the masses against the classes.

William Ewart Gladstone

---

glasnost (Russian 'openness') former Soviet leader Mikhail ◊Gorbachev's policy of liberalizing various aspects of Soviet life, such as introducing greater freedom of expression and information and opening up relations with Western countries. *Glasnost* was introduced and adopted by the Soviet government 1986.

Glencoe glen in southern Scotland (modern Strathclyde region), where members of the Macdonald clan were massacred on 13 Febuary 1692. John Campbell, Earl of Breadalbane, was the chief instigator.

Glendower Owen *c.* 1359–*c.* 1416. (Welsh *Owain Glyndwr*) Welsh nationalist leader of a successful revolt against the English in N Wales, who defeated Henry IV in three campaigns 1400–02, although Wales was reconquered 1405–13. Glendower disappeared 1416 after some years of guerrilla warfare.

Glorious Revolution in British history, the events surrounding the removal of James II from the throne and his replacement by Mary (daughter of Charles I) and William of Orange as joint sovereigns in 1689. James had become increasingly unpopular on account of his unconstitutional behaviour and Catholicism. Various elements in England, including seven prominent politicians, plotted to invite the Protestant William to invade. Arriving at Torbay on 5 Nov 1688, William rapidly gained support and James was allowed to flee to France after the army deserted him. William and Mary then accepted a new constitutional settlement, the Bill of Rights 1689, which assured the ascendency of parliamentary power over sovereign rule.

Gobind Singh 1666–1708. Indian religious leader, the tenth and last guru (teacher) of Sikhism, 1675–1708, and founder of the Sikh brotherhood known as the ◊Khalsa. On his death, the Sikh holy book, the *Guru Granth Sahib*, replaced the line of human gurus as the teacher and guide of the Sikh community.

During a period of Sikh persecution Gobind Singh asked those who were willing to die for their faith to join him, the first five willing to risk their lives were named the *pani pyares* 'the faithful ones' by him and proclaimed the first members of the Khalsa. He also introduced the names Singh (lion) for male Sikhs, and Kaur (princess) for female Sikhs.

Godfrey de Bouillon *c.* 1060–1100. French crusader, second son of Count Eustace II of Boulogne. He and his brothers, ◊Baldwin I and Eustace, led 40,000 Germans in the First Crusade 1096. When Jerusalem was taken 1099, he was elected its ruler, but refused the title of king. After his death, Baldwin was elected king.

Godiva Lady *c.* 1040–1080. Wife of Leofric, earl of Mercia (died 1057). Legend has it that her husband promised to reduce the heavy taxes on the people of Coventry if she rode naked through the streets at noon. The grateful citizens remained indoors as she did so, but 'Peeping Tom' bored a hole in his shutters and was struck blind.

Godunov Boris 1552–1605. Tsar of Russia from 1598, elected after the death of Fyodor I, son of Ivan the Terrible. He was assassinated by a pretender to the throne who professed to be Dmitri, a brother of Fyodor and the rightful heir. The legend that has grown up around this forms the basis of Pushkin's play *Boris Godunov* 1831 and Mussorgsky's opera of the same name 1874.

Godwin died 1053. Earl of Wessex from 1020. He secured the succession to the throne in 1042 of ◊Edward the Confessor, to whom he married his daughter Edith, and whose chief minister he became. King Harold II was his son.

Goebbels Paul Josef 1897–1945. German Nazi leader. As minister of propaganda from 1933, he brought all cultural and educational activities under Nazi control and built up sympathetic movements abroad to carry on the 'war of nerves' against Hitler's intended victims. On the capture of Berlin by the Allies, he poisoned himself.

Goering Hermann Wilhelm 1893–1946. Nazi leader, German field marshal from 1938. He was part of Hitler's inner circle, and with Hitler's rise to power was appointed commissioner for aviation from 1933 and built up the Luftwaffe (airforce). He built a vast economic empire in occupied Europe, but later lost favour and was expelled from the party in 1945. Tried at Nuremberg for war crimes, he poisoned himself before he could be executed.

Goering was born in Bavaria. He was a renowned fighter pilot in World War I, and joined the Nazi party in 1922. He was elected to the Reichstag in 1928 and became its president in 1932. In 1936 he took charge of the four-year plan for war preparations.

Gokhale Gopal Krishna 1866–1915. Indian political adviser and friend of Mohandas Gandhi, leader of the Moderate group in the Indian National Congress before World War I.

Gold Coast former name for ◊Ghana, but historically the west coast of Africa from Cape Three Points to the Volta River, where alluvial gold is washed down. Portuguese and French navigators visited this coast in the 14th century, and a British trading settlement developed into the colony of the Gold Coast 1618. With its dependencies of Ashanti and Northern Territories plus the trusteeship territory of Togoland, it became Ghana 1957.

Golden Horde the invading Mongol-Tatar army that first terrorized Europe from 1237 under the leadership of Batu Khan, a grandson of Genghis Khan. ◊Tamerlane broke their power 1395, and ◊Ivan III ended Russia's payment of tribute to them 1480.

gold rush large influx of gold prospectors to an area where gold deposits have recently been discovered. The result is a dramatic increase in population. Cities such as Johannesburg, Melbourne, and San Francisco either originated or were considerably enlarged by gold rushes. Melbourne's population trebled from 77,000 to some 200,000 between 1851 and 1853.

Famous gold rushes	
1848	Sutter's Mill, California (the 'Fortyniners')
1851	New South Wales and Victoria, Australia
1880s	Rhodesia
1886	Fortymile Creek, Yukon, Canada; Johannesburg, Transvaal; Kimberley, West Australia
1890s	Klondike River, Yukon, Canada

gold standard system under which a country's currency is exchangeable for a fixed weight of gold on demand at the central bank. It was almost universally applied 1870–1914, but by 1937 no single country was on the full gold standard. Britain abandoned the gold standard 1931; the USA abandoned it 1971. Holdings of gold are still retained because it is an internationally recognized commodity, which cannot be legislated upon or manipulated by interested countries.

The gold standard broke down in World War I, and attempted revivals were undermined by the Great Depression. After World

War II the par values of the currency units of the ◊International Monetary Fund (which included nearly all members of the United Nations not in the Soviet bloc) were fixed in terms of gold and the US dollar, but by 1976 floating exchange rates (already unofficially operating from 1971) were legalized.

Goldwater Barry 1909– . US Republican politician; presidential candidate in the 1964 election, when he was overwhelmingly defeated by Lyndon ◊Johnson. As a US senator 1953–65 and 1969–87, he voiced the views of his party's right-wing conservative faction. Many of Goldwater's conservative ideas were later adopted by the Republican right, especially the Reagan administration.

Gómez Juan Vicente 1864–1935. Venezuelan dictator 1908–35. The discovery of oil during his rule attracted US, British, and Dutch oil interests and made Venezuela one of the wealthiest countries in Latin America. Gómez amassed a considerable personal fortune and used his well-equipped army to dominate the civilian population.

Gompers Samuel 1850–1924. US labour leader. His early career in the Cigarmakers' Union led him to found and lead the ◊American Federation of Labor 1886. Gompers advocated nonpolitical activity within the existing capitalist system to secure improved wages and working conditions for members.

Gomułka Władysław 1905–1982. Polish Communist politician, party leader 1943–48 and 1956–70. He introduced moderate reforms, including private farming and tolerance for Roman Catholicism.

González Márquez Felipe 1942– . Spanish socialist politician, leader of the Socialist Workers' Party (PSOE), prime minister from 1982–96. His party was re-elected in the 1989 and 1993, but his popularity suffered from economic upheaval and allegations of corruption.

Good Neighbor policy the efforts of US administrations between the two World Wars to improve relations with Latin American and Caribbean states. The phrase was first used by President F D Roosevelt in his inaugural speech March 1933 to describe the foreign policy of his ◊New Deal.

Following a prolonged period of economic and military intervention, Roosevelt withdrew US forces from Nicaragua and Haiti, renouncing any right to intervene, and concluding a treaty (1934) giving Cuba full independence. The goodwill this engendered was to be significant in maintaining the unity of the western hemisphere during World War II.

Gorbachev Mikhail Sergeyevich 1931– . Soviet president, in power 1985-91. He was a member of the Politburo from 1980. As general secretary of the Communist Party (CPSU) 1985-91, and president of the Supreme Soviet 1988–91, he introduced liberal reforms at home (◊*perestroika* and ◊*glasnost*), proposed the introduction of multiparty democracy, and attempted to halt the arms race abroad. He became head of state 1989.

He was awarded the Nobel Peace Prize 1990 but his international reputation suffered in the light of harsh state repression of nationalist demonstrations in the Baltic states. Following an abortive coup attempt by hardliners Aug 1991, international acceptance of independence for the Baltic states, and accelerated moves towards independence in other republics, Gorbachev's power base as Soviet president was greatly weakened and in Dec 1991 he resigned.

Gorbachev, born in the N Caucasus, studied law at Moscow University and joined the CPSU 1952. In 1955–62 he worked for the Komsomol (Communist Youth League) before being apppointed regional agriculture secretary. As Stavropol party leader from 1970 he impressed Andropov, and was brought into the CPSU secretariat 1978.

Gorbachev was promoted into the Politburo and in 1983, when Andropov was general secretary, took broader charge of the Soviet economy. During the Chernenko administration 1984–85, he was chair of the Foreign Affairs Commission. On Chernenko's death 1985 he was appointed party leader. He initiated wide-ranging reforms and broad economic restructuring, and introduced campaigns against alcoholism, corruption, and inefficiency. In the 1988 presidential election by members of the Soviet parliament, he was the sole candidate. Gorbachev radically changed the style of Soviet leadership, despite opposition to the pace of change from both conservatives and radicals but failed both to realize the depth of hostility this aroused against him in the CPSU, and to distance himself from the party.

Early in 1991, Gorbachev shifted to the right in order to placate the conservative wing of the party and appointed some of the hardliners to positions of power. In late spring, he produced a plan for a new union treaty to try to satisfy the demands of reformers. This plan alarmed the hardliners, who, in late summer, temporarily removed him from office. He was saved from this attempted coup mainly by efforts of Boris ◊Yeltsin and the ineptness of the plotters. Soon after his reinstatement, Gorbachev was obliged to relinquish his leadership of the party, renounce communism as a state doctrine, suspend all activities of the Communist Party (including its most powerful organs, the Politburo and the Secretariat), and surrender many of his central powers to the states. During the months that followed, he pressed consistently for an agreement on his proposed union treaty in the hope of preventing a disintegration of the Soviet Union, but was ultimately unable to maintain control and on 25 December 1991 resigned as president, effectively yielding power to Boris ◊Yeltsin.

The policy prevailed of dismembering this country and disuniting the state, with which I cannot agree.

Mikhail Gorbachev
resignation speech 25 Dec 1991.

Gordon Charles (George) 1833–1885. British general sent to Khartoum in the Sudan 1884 to rescue English garrisons that were under attack by the ◊Mahdi, Muhammad Ahmed; he was himself besieged for ten months by the Mahdi's army. A relief expedition arrived 28 Jan 1885 to find that Khartoum had been captured and Gordon killed two days before.

Gordon served in the ◊Crimean War and in China 1864, where he earned his nickname 'Chinese' Gordon in ending the Taiping Rebellion. In 1874 he was employed by the Khedive of Egypt to open the country and 1877–80 was British governor of the Sudan.

Gordon George 1751–1793. British organizer of the so-called *Gordon Riots* of 1778, a protest against removal of penalties imposed on Roman Catholics in the Catholic Relief Act of 1778; he was acquitted on a treason charge. Gordon and the 'No Popery' riots figure in Charles Dickens's novel *Barnaby Rudge*.

Gorton John Grey 1911– . Australian Liberal politician. He was minister for education and science 1966–68, and prime minister 1968–71.

Goth E Germanic people who settled near the Black Sea around the 2nd century AD. There are two branches, the eastern Ostrogoths and the western Visigoths. The *Ostrogoths* were conquered by the Huns 372. They regained their independence 454 and under ◊Theodoric the Great conquered Italy 488–93; they disappeared as a nation after the Byzantine emperor ◊Justinian I reconquered Italy 535–55.

The *Visigoths* migrated to Thrace. Under ◊Alaric they raided Greece and Italy 395–410, sacked Rome, and established a kingdom in S France. Expelled from there by the Franks, they established a Spanish kingdom which lasted until the Moorish conquest of 711.

Gowon Yakubu 1934– . Nigerian politician, head of state 1966–75. He seized power in the military coup of 1966. After the Biafran civil war 1967–70, Gowon reunited the country with his policy of 'no victor, no vanquished'. In 1975 he was overthrown by a military coup.

GPU name (1922–23) for the security service of the Soviet Union; later the ◊KGB.

Gracchus the brothers *Tiberius Sempronius* 163–133 BC and *Gaius Sempronius* 153–121 BC. Roman agrarian reformers. As tribune (magistrate) 133 BC, Tiberius tried to redistribute land away from the large slave-labour farms in order to benefit the poor as well as increase the number of those eligible for military service. He was murdered by a mob of senators. Gaius, tribune 123–122 BC, revived his brother's legislation, and introduced other reforms, but was outlawed by the Senate and killed in a riot.

Gramsci Antonio 1891–1937. Italian Marxist who attempted to unify social theory and political practice. He helped to found the Italian Communist Party 1921 and was elected to parliament 1924, but was imprisoned by the Fascist leader Mussolini from 1926; his *Quaderni di carcere/Prison Notebooks* were published posthumously 1947.

Granada city in the Sierra Nevada in Andalusia, S Spain. Founded by the Moors in the 8th century, it became the capital of an independent kingdom 1236–1492, when it was the last Moorish stronghold to surrender to the Spaniards.

Grand Design in the early 17th century, a plan attributed by the French minister Sully to Henry IV of France (who was assassinated before he could carry it out) for a great Protestant union against the Holy Roman Empire; the term was also applied to President de Gaulle's vision of France's place in a united Europe.

Grandi Dino 1895–1988. Italian politician who challenged Mussolini for leadership of the Italian Fascist Party in 1921 and was subsequently largely responsible for Mussolini's downfall in July 1943.

Grand Remonstrance petition passed by the English Parliament in Nov 1641 that listed all the alleged misdeeds of Charles I and demanded Parliamentary approval for the king's ministers and the reform of the church. Charles refused to accept the Grand Remonstrance and countered by trying to arrest five leading members of the House of Commons

(Pym, Hampden, Holles, Hesilrige, and Strode). The worsening of relations between king and Parliament led to the outbreak of the English Civil War in 1642.

Grange Movement in US history, a farmers' protest in the South and Midwest states against economic hardship and exploitation. The National Grange of the Patrons of Husbandry, formed 1867, was a network of local organizations, employing cooperative practices and advocating 'granger' laws. The movement petered out in the late 1870s.

Grant Ulysses S(impson) 1822–1885. American Civil War general in chief for the Union and 18th president of the USA 1869–77. As a Republican president, he carried through a liberal ◊Reconstruction policy in the South. He failed to suppress extensive political corruption within his own party and cabinet, which tarnished the reputation of his second term.

In 1864 Grant was made commander in chief. He slowly wore down the Confederate general Lee's resistance, and in 1865 received hi s surrender at Appomattox. He was elected president 1868 and re-elected 1872. As president he reformed the civil service andratified the Treaty of Washington with the UK 1871.

I know no method to secure the repeal of bad or obnoxious laws so effective as their stringent execution.

Ulysses S Grant
inaugural address March 1869

Granvelle Antoine Perrenot, de 1517–1586. French diplomat and prelate, adviser to Holy Roman Emperor Charles V and Philip II of Spain. As president of the Netherlands' Council of State (1559-64), he introduced the Inquisition to the Netherlands, where he provoked such hostility that Philip II was obliged to recall him.

He was born in Besançon, eastern France, which was then part of the Holy Roman Empire. He rose to fame as a diplomat in the service of Charles V, became bishop of Arras 1543, and imperial chancellor 1550. In 1554 he helped with the negotiations for the marriage of the future Philip II and Mary I of England. After Charles V's abdication 1555 he served Philip II of Spain, negotiating a number of important treaties and acting as prime minister to the regent in the Low Countries 1559–64. He was made a cardinal 1561. His career after his recall from the Netherlands was less important. He returned from retirement to be viceroy of Naples 1571–75, then president of the supreme council of Italy 1579-84 and later of Castile.

Grattan Henry 1746–1820. Irish politician. He entered the Irish parliament in 1775, led the patriot opposition, and obtained free trade and legislative independence for Ireland 1782. He failed to prevent the Act of Union of Ireland and England in 1805, sat in the British Parliament from that year, and pressed for Catholic emancipation.

Graziani Rodolfo 1882–1955. Italian general. He was commander in chief of Italian forces in North Africa during World War II but was defeated by British forces 1940, and subsequently replaced. Later, as defence minister in the new Mussolini government, he failed to reorganize a republican Fascist army, was captured by the Allies 1945, tried by an Italian military court, and finally released 1950.

Great Awakening religious revival in the American colonies from the late 1730s to the 1760s. It was sparked off by George Whitefield (1714–1770), an itinerant English Methodist preacher whose evangelical fervour and eloquence made many converts. A second 'great awakening' occurred in the first half of the 19th century, establishing the evangelist tradition in US Protestantism.

Great Britain official name for England, Scotland, and Wales, and the adjacent islands (except the Channel Islands and the Isle of Man) from 1603, when the English and Scottish crowns were united under James I of England (James VI of Scotland). With Northern Ireland it forms the ◊United Kingdom.

Great Depression period following the Wall Street crash of 29 Oct 1929; see ◊depression.

Great Exhibition world fair held in Hyde Park, London, UK, in 1851, proclaimed by its originator Prince Albert as 'the Great Exhibition of the Industries of All Nations'. In practice, it glorified British manufacture: over half the 100,000 exhibits were from Britain or the British Empire. Over 6 million people attended the exhibition. The exhibition hall, popularly known as the *Crystal Palace*, was constructed of glass with a cast-iron frame, and designed by Joseph Paxton.

Great Leap Forward change in the economic policy of the People's Republic of China introduced by ◊Mao Zedong under the second five-year plan of 1958–62. The aim was to achieve rapid and simultaneous agricultural and industrial growth through the creation of large new agro-industrial communes. The inefficient and poorly planned allocation of state resources led

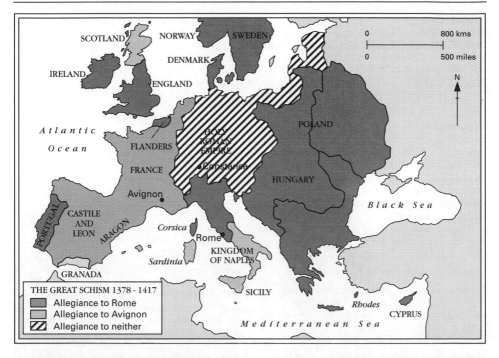

The Great Schism 1378–1417 *The division of Catholic Europe into two camps, one owing allegiance to a Roman pope, the other to a pope in Avignon, began with Pope Urban VI's refusal to accept his deposition as pope in favour of Clement VII, who established himself in Avignon. The schism persisted as the cardinals took sides and continued to elect rival popes. Questions of secular politics tended to determine which camp the various countries of Europe followed. For example, the Avignon papacy was regarded as being under French control and since England was embroiled in the Hundred Years' War with France, English kings recognized the Roman pope. In 1409 the Council of Pisa, called to resolve the schism, further complicated the situation by electing a third pope, Alexander V. The eventual solution came with the Council of Constance 1414–17, and the removal of all three popes in favour of Martin V.*

to the collapse of the strategy by 1960 and the launch of a 'reactionary programme', involving the use of rural markets and private subsidiary plots. More than 20 million people died in the Great Leap famines of 1959–61.

Great Patriotic War (1941–45) war between the USSR and Germany during ◊World War II.

When Germany invaded the USSR in June 1941, the Soviet troops retreated, carrying out a scorched earth policy and relocating strategic industries beyond the Ural Mountains. Stalin remained in Moscow and the Soviet forces, inspired to fight on by his patriotic speeches, launched a counter-offensive. The Allies tried to provide the USSR with vital supplies through Murmansk and Archangel despite German attempts to blockade the ports. In 1942 the Germans failed to take Leningrad and Moscow, and launched an attack towards the river Volga and to capture oil wells at Baku. In Aug 1942 the Germans attacked Stalingrad but it was held by the Russians. A substantial German force was forced to surrender at Stalingrad in Jan 1943.

The Red Army, under the command of Marshal Zhukov, gradually forced the Germans back and by Feb 1945 the Russians had reached the German border. In April 1945 the Russians, who had made tremendous sacrifices (20 million dead and millions more wounded) entered Berlin. In May 1945 the war ended.

Great Power any of the major European powers of the 19th century: Russia, Austria (Austria-Hungary), France, Britain, and Prussia.

Great Schism in European history, the period 1378–1417 in which rival popes had seats in Rome and in Avignon; it was ended by the election of Martin V during the Council of Constance 1414–17.

Great Society political slogan coined 1965 by US President Lyndon B Johnson to describe the ideal society to be created by his administration (1963-69), and to which all other nations would aspire. The programme included extensive social welfare legislation, most of which was subsequently passed by Congress.

Great Trek in South African history, the movement of 12,000–14,000 Boer (Dutch) settlers from Cape Colony 1835 and 1845 to escape British rule. They established republics in Natal and the Transvaal. It is seen by many white South Africans as the main event in the founding of the present republic and also as a justification for continuing whites-only rule.

Great Wall of China continuous defensive wall stretching from W Gansu to the Gulf of Liaodong (2,250 km/1,450 mi). It was once even longer. It was built under the Qin dynasty from 214 BC to prevent incursions by the Turkish and Mongol peoples and extended westwards by the Han dynasty. Some 8 m/25 ft high, it consists of a brick-faced wall of earth and stone, has a series of square watchtowers, and has been carefully restored. It is so large that it can be seen from space.

Great War another name for ◊World War I.

Greece country in SE Europe, comprising the S Balkan peninsula, bounded N by Yugoslavia and Bulgaria, NW by Albania, NE by Turkey, E by the Aegean Sea, S by the Mediterranean Sea, and W by the Ionian Sea.

history For ancient history, see ◊Greece, ancient. From the 14th century Greece came under Ottoman Turkish rule, and except for the years 1686–1715, when the Peloponnese was occupied by the Venetians, it remained Turkish until the outbreak of the War of Independence 1821. British, French, and Russian intervention 1827, which brought about the destruction of the Turkish fleet at Navarino, led to the establishment of Greek independence 1829. Prince Otto of Bavaria was placed on the throne 1832; his despotic rule provoked a rebellion 1843, which set up a parliamentary government, and another 1862, when he was deposed and replaced by Prince George of Denmark. Relations with Turkey were embittered by the Greeks' desire to recover Macedonia, Crete, and other Turkish territories with Greek populations. A war 1897 ended in disaster, but the ◊Balkan Wars 1912–13 won most of the disputed areas for Greece.

In a period of internal conflict from 1914, two monarchs were deposed, and there was a republic 1923-25, when a military coup restored ◊George II, who in the following year established a dictatorship under Joannis ◊Metaxas.

monarchy re-established An Italian invasion 1940 was successfully resisted, but an intensive attack by Germany 1941 overwhelmed the Greeks. During the German occupation of Greece 1941–44, a communist-dominated resistance movement armed and trained a guerrilla army, and after World War II the National Liberation Front, as it was called, wanted to create a socialist state. If the Greek royalist army had not had massive assistance from the USA, under the provisions of the ◊Truman Doctrine, this undoubtedly would have happened. A civil war 1946–49 ended when the royalists defeated the communists. The monarchy was re-established under King Paul, who was succeeded by his son Constantine 1964.

military junta Dissatisfaction with the government and conflicts between the king and his ministers resulted in a coup 1967, replacing the monarchy with a new regime, which, despite its democratic pretensions, was little more than a military dictatorship, with Col George Papadopoulos as its head. All political activity was banned, and opponents of the government were forced out of public life.

republic In 1973 Greece declared itself a republic, and Papadopoulos became president. A civilian cabinet was appointed, but before the year was out another coup brought Lt-Gen Phaidon Ghizikis to the presidency, with Adamantios Androutsopoulos as prime minister. The government's failure to prevent the Turkish invasion of ◊Cyprus led to its downfall, and a former prime minister, Constantine ◊Karamanlis, was recalled from exile to form a new Government of National Salvation. He immediately ended martial law, press censorship, and the ban on political parties, and in the 1974 general election his New Democracy Party (ND) won a decisive majority in parliament.

A referendum the same year rejected the return of the monarchy, and in 1975 a new constitution for a democratic 'Hellenic Republic' was adopted, with Constantine Tsatsos as president. The ND won the 1977 general election with a reduced majority, and in 1980 Karamanlis resigned as prime minister and was elected president. In 1981 Greece became a full member of the European Economic Community (EEC), having been an associate since 1962.

Greek socialism The Panhellenic Socialist Movement (PASOK) won an absolute majority in parliament in the 1981 general election. Its leader, Andreas Papandreou, became Greece's first socialist prime minister. PASOK had been elected on a radical socialist platform, which included withdrawal from the EEC, the removal of US military bases, and a programme of domestic reform. Important social changes, such as lowering the voting age to 18, the legalization of civil marriage and divorce, and an overhaul of the universities and the army, were carried out; but instead of withdrawing from

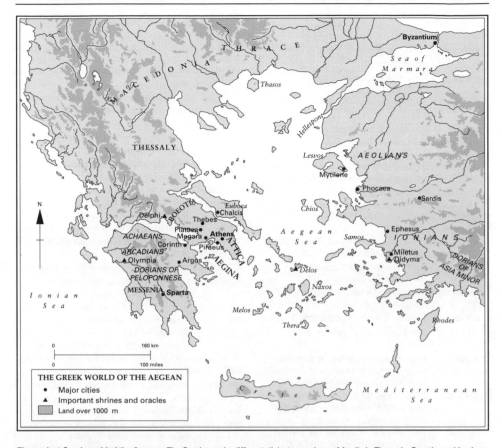

The ancient Greek world of the Aegean *The Greeks spoke different dialects: versions of Aeolic in Thessaly, Boeotia, and Lesbos; Attic Ionic in Athens and cities on the E Aegean coast; and Doric in the SE Aegean and the Peloponnese. Land-based aristocracies or tyrannies were prevalent until the early 5th century BC, when Athens established a democracy reliant on sea-power. Greek cities and communities were drawn into larger leagues: the Delian League (under Athens) and the Peloponnesian League (under Sparta) were most significant in the 5th century.*

Europe, Papandreou was content to obtain a modification of the terms of entry, and, rather than close US bases, he signed a five-year agreement on military and economic cooperation. In 1983 he also signed a ten-year economic-cooperation agreement with the USSR.

Papandreou defeated Despite introducing austerity measures to deal with rising inflation, PASOK won a comfortable majority in the 1985 elections. Criticism of Papandreou grew 1989 when close aides were implicated in a banking scandal. He lost the general elections 1989 and Tzanis Tzannetakis, an ND backbencher, formed Greece's first all-party government for 15 years. However, this soon broke up and after months of negotiation Xenophon Zolotas (PASOK) put together a government of unity, comprising communists, socialists, conservatives, and nonpolitical figures.

Constantine Mitsotakis of the New Democracy Party (ND) was sworn in as the new premier April 1990 and formed a new all-party government after the ND had failed to win an outright majority in the elections. In June Karamanlis was again elected president. Papandreou was cleared of all corruption charges in Jan 1992.

foreign relations An agreement on the siting of US bases in Greece was signed 1990. Greece's refusal to recognize the independence declaration of the breakaway republic of Macedonia under that name won reluctant agreement from the other EC countries 1992. In July 1992 parliament voted by 286 to 14 to ratify the Maastricht Treaty on greater European union.

Greece, ancient the first Greek civilization, known as Mycenaean (*c.* 1600–1200 BC), owed much to the Minoan civilization of Crete and

Ancient Greece from the Mycenaean age to the death of Alexander the Great

1600–1200 BC	Bronze Age Mycenaean civilization flourished, using early written form of Greek language.
1200–1100	Mycenaean centres fell. Use of writing apparently ended.
***c.* 1100**	Dorian Greeks settled in Peloponnese (S Greece).
***c.* 1000**	Ionian Greeks left the mainland for E Aegean area.
***c.* 800**	City wall built at Smyrna (Ionia).
***c.* 750–700**	Greeks colonized areas in Sicily, S Italy, and Black Sea, encouraged by the oracle at Delphi. Writing re-appeared. Sparta pursued war against Messenia. Chalcis and Eretria were rivals in Euboea. Homer's epic poems compiled.
***c.* 680**	Gyges of Lydia began attacks on Ionian Greek cities.
***c.* 670**	Sparta conquered Messenia. Pheidon consolidated power of Argos in NE Peloponnese.
***c.* 665**	Corinthians colonized Corcyra (Corfu), winning the first Greek naval battle.
***c.* 650–585**	Cypselus and his son Periander ruled as tyrants in Corinth.
***c.* 630**	Greek colony established at Cyrene, N Africa.
***c.* 620**	Severe law code of Draco introduced in Athens.
***c.* 600**	Greek colony set up at Massilia (now Marseille). Greek traders established at Naucratis in the Nile Delta. Coinage introduced in Lydia.
594–593	Solon was elected archon (magistrate) at Athens, and achieved economic and political reforms.
560–510	Pisistratus and his sons ruled as tyrants at Athens. Athenian influence established in N Greece and the Dardanelles (Turkey).
556–555	Chilon increased the power of the ephors (senior magistrates) at Sparta.
546	Croesus of Lydia defeated by Cyrus the Great of Persia, who had already subdued the Ionian Greeks.
527	Death of Pisistratus.
514	Hipparchus, son of Pisistratus, assassinated in Athens.
510	Hippias, last of the Pisistratids, was expelled from Athens. The city saw the gradual introduction of democracy by Cleisthenes.
***c.* 510–500**	Formation of the Peloponnesian League, led by Sparta.
499–494	Revolt against Persia by Ionian Greeks, supported by Athens. Miletus was destroyed, and the revolt defeated.
***c.* 494**	Defeat of Argos by Sparta.
493	Themistocles elected archon at Athens, and fortified Piraeus harbour.
492	Persian expedition to N Greece led by Mardonius.
490	Persian campaign against Athens defeated at the Battle of Marathon.
from 483	Athenians started to build warships on the advice of Themistocles.
480–479	Persian invasion of Greece under Xerxes defeated at Battles of Salamis 480 (at sea), and Plataea 479 (on land). Carthaginians defeated by Gelon of Syracuse at Battle of Himera, Sicily 480.
477	Formation of the Delian League by Athens and Ionian Greeks against Persia.
***c.* 465**	Revolt of the Messenians against Sparta.
461	Confirmation of democracy (legal and political) at Athens.
***c.* 450**	Attacks of Delian League on Persian possessions ended.
443–429	Pericles pre-eminent as statesman and general in Athens until his death.
440	Attempted secession of Samos from the Delian League crushed by Athens.
431	Peloponnesian War between Athens and Sparta began.
421	Peace of Nicias signed by Athens and Sparta.
415–413	Athenian expedition against Syracuse defeated. Nicias died.
411	Right-wing coup in Athens failed.
405	Athenian fleet defeated at Battle of Aegospotami by Spartan admiral Lysander.
404	Surrender of Athens. Lysander installed the rule of the Thirty in Athens. Alcibiades died.
403	Democracy re-established at Athens.
395–386	Spartan supremacy challenged in Corinthian War.
382	Thebes garrisoned by Sparta.
371	Sparta defeated by the Thebans under Epaminondas at Battle of Leuctra.
369	City of Messene founded. Messenia became independent of Sparta.
362	Epaminondas died.
358–336	Reign of Philip II of Macedon.
351–338	Expansionist policies of Philip of Macedon opposed by the Athenian orator Demosthenes.
338	Philip of Macedon secured control of mainland Greece at Battle of Chaeronea.
336–323	Reign of Alexander the Great of Macedon.
334	Alexander invaded the Persian empire, winning Battle of Granicus near the Dardanelles.
333	Darius III of Persia defeated at Battle of Ipsus.
332	Persian dockyards destroyed. Siege of Tyre and capture of Egypt by Alexander.
331	Final defeat of Darius at Battle of Gaugamela.
330	Darius III died.
330–327	Campaigns by Alexander in the E Persian provinces.
327–324	Indian expedition by Alexander.
323	Alexander died. Athens and Thessaly revolted against Macedonian supremacy, but were defeated and the Macedonians garrisoned Athens. Demosthenes committed suicide.

may have been produced by the intermarriage of Greek-speaking invaders with the original inhabitants. From the 14th century BC a new wave of invasions began. The Achaeans overran Greece and Crete, destroying the Minoan and Mycenaean civilizations and penetrating Asia Minor; to this period belongs the siege of Troy (c. 1180 BC). The latest of the invaders were the Dorians (c. 1100 BC) who settled in the Peloponnese and founded Sparta. During the years 750–550 BC the Greeks not only became great traders, but founded colonies around the coasts of the Mediterranean and the Black Sea, in Asia Minor, Sicily, S Italy, S France, Spain, and N Africa. The main centres of Greek culture in the 6th century BC were the wealthy Ionian ports of Asia Minor, where Greek philosophy, science, and lyric poetry originated.

Many Greek cities passed from monarchy to the rule of a landowning aristocracy and from there to democracy. Thus Athens passed through the debt reforms of Solon (594 BC), the tyranny of the Pisistratids (560–510 BC), and the establishment of democracy by Cleisthenes (after 510 BC). Sparta remained unique, a state in which a ruling race, organized on military lines, dominated the surrounding population.

After 545 BC the Ionian cities fell under the dominion of the Persian Empire. Aid given them by Athens in an unsuccessful revolt in 499–494 BC provoked Darius of Persia to invade Greece in 490 BC only to be defeated by the Athenians at Marathon and forced to withdraw. Another invasion by the Persian emperor Xerxes, after being delayed by the heroic defence of Thermopylae by 300 Spartans, was defeated at sea off Salamis in 480 BC and on land at Plataea in 479 BC. The Ionian cities were liberated and formed a naval alliance with Athens, the Delian League. Pericles, the democratic leader of Athens 455–429 BC, attempted to convert this into an Athenian empire and to form a land empire in Greece. Mistrust of his ambitions led to the Peloponnesian War (431–404 BC), which destroyed the political power of Athens. In 5th-century Athens, Greek tragedy, comedy, sculpture, and architecture were at their peak.

After the Peloponnesian War, Sparta became the leading Greek power until it was overthrown by Thebes (378–371 BC). The constant wars between the cities gave ◊Philip II of Macedon (359–336 BC) the opportunity to establish his supremacy over Greece. His son ◊Alexander the Great overthrew the Persian Empire, conquered Syria and Egypt, and invaded the Punjab. After his death in 323 BC his empire was divided among his generals, but his conquest had established Greek culture in Asia and Egypt.

Hellenistic period During the 3rd century BC the cities attempted to maintain their independence against Macedon, Egypt, and Rome by forming federations; for example, in the Achaean and Aetolian leagues. Roman intervention began in 214 BC and ended in the annexation of Greece in 146 BC. Under Roman rule Greece remained a cultural centre, until the emperor Justinian closed the university of Athens in AD 529. See also ◊Hellenistic period.

Greeley Horace 1811–1872. US editor, publisher, and politician. One of the founders of the Republican party 1854, Greeley was the unsuccessful presidential candidate of the breakaway Liberal Republicans 1872.

Go West, young man, and grow up with the country.

Horace Greeley Hints toward Reform

Greenham Common site of a continuous peace demonstration 1981–90 on common land near Newbury, Berkshire, UK, outside a US airbase. The women-only camp was established Sept 1981 in protest against the siting of US cruise missiles in the UK. The demonstrations ended with the closure of the base. Greenham Common reverted to standby status, and the last US cruise missiles were withdrawn March 1991.

Greenland (Greenlandic *Kalaalit Nunaat*) world's largest island, lying between the North Atlantic and Arctic Oceans E of North America. Greenland was discovered about 982 by Eric the Red, who founded colonies on the west coast soon after Eskimos from the North American Arctic had made their way to Greenland.

Christianity was introduced to the Vikings about 1000. In 1261 the Viking colonies accepted Norwegian sovereignty, but early in the 15th century all communication with Europe ceased, and by the 16th century the colonies had died out, but the Eskimos had move d on to the E coast. It became a Danish colony in the 18th century, and following a referendum 1979 was granted full internal self-government 1981.

Green Mountain Boys in US history, irregular troops who fought to protect the Vermont part of what was then New Hampshire colony from land claims made by neighbouring New York. In the American Revolution they captured ◊Fort Ticonderoga from the British. Their leader was Ethan Allen (1738-1789), who was later captured by the British. Vermont declared itself an independent republic, refusing to join the Union until 1791. It is popularly known as the Green Mountain State.

Green Party political party aiming to 'preserve the planet and its people', based on the premise that incessant economic growth is unsustainable. The leaderless party structure reflects a general commitment to decentralization. Green parties sprang up in W Europe in the 1970s and in E Europe from 1988. Parties in different countries are linked to one another but unaffiliated with any pressure group. The party had a number of parliamentary seats in 1992: Austria 9, Belgium 13, Finland 8, Italy 20, Luxembourg 2, Republic of Ireland 1, Greece 1, and Germany 2; and 29 members in the European Parliament (Belgium 3, France 8, Italy 7, the Netherlands 2, Spain 1, and Germany 8).

green revolution in agriculture, a popular term for the change in methods of arable farming in Third World countries. The intent has been to provide more and better food for their populations, albeit with a heavy reliance on chemicals and machinery. It was instigated in the 1940s and 1950s, but abandoned by some countries in the 1980s. Much of the food produced is exported as cash crops, so that local diet does not always improve.

Measures include the increased use of tractors and other machines, artificial fertilizers and pesticides, as well as the breeding of new strains of crop plants (mainly rice, wheat, and corn) and farm animals. Much of the work is coordinated by the Food and Agriculture Organization of the United Nations.

The green revolution was initially successful in SE Asia; India doubled its wheat yield in 15 years, and the rice yield in the Philippines rose by 75%. However, yields have levelled off in many areas and some countries, which cannot afford the dams, fertilizers, and machinery required, have adopted intermediate technologies.

Gregory 16 popes, including:

Gregory VII or *Hildebrand* c. 1023–1085. Chief minister to several popes before his election to the papacy 1073. In 1077 he forced the Holy Roman emperor Henry IV to wait in the snow at Canossa for four days, dressed as a penitent, before receiving pardon. He was driven from Rome and died in exile. His feast day is 25 May.

He claimed power to depose kings, denied lay rights to make clerical appointments, and attempted to suppress simony (the buying and selling of church preferments) and to enforce clerical celibacy, making enemies of both rulers and the church.

Grenada island country in the Caribbean, the southernmost of the Windward Islands.

history Prior to the arrival of Christopher Columbus 1498, Grenada was inhabited by ◊Carib Indians. The island was eventually colonized by France 1650 and ceded to Britain 1783. Grenada remained a British colony until 1958, when it joined the Federation of the West Indies until its dissolution 1962. Internal self-government was achieved 1967 and full independence within the Commonwealth 1974. The early political life of the nation was dominated by two figures: Eric Gairy, a trade-union leader who founded the Grenada United Labour Party (GULP) 1950, and Herbert Blaize, of the Grenada National Party (GNP).

after independence On independence in 1974, Gairy was elected prime minister. He was knighted 1977, but his rule became increasingly autocratic and corrupt, and he was replaced 1979 in a bloodless coup by the leader of the left-wing New Jewel Movement (NJM), Maurice Bishop. Bishop suspended the 1974 constitution, established a People's Revolutionary Government, and announced the formation of a people's consultative assembly to draft a new constitution. He promised a nonaligned foreign policy but became convinced that the USA was involved in a plot to destabilize his administration; this was strongly denied.

Grenada's relations with Britain and the USA deteriorated while links with Cuba and the USSR grew stronger. In 1983 Bishop tried to improve relations with the USA and announced the appointment of a commission to draft a new constitution. His conciliatory attitude was opposed by the more left-wing members of his regime, resulting in a military coup, during which Bishop and three of his colleagues were executed.

US-led invasion A Revolutionary Military Council (RMC), led by General Hudson Austin, took control. In response to the outcry caused by the executions, Austin promised a return to civilian rule as soon as possible, but on 25 Oct about 1,900 US troops, accompanied by 300 from Jamaica and Barbados, invaded the island. It was not clear whether the invasion was in response to a request from the governor general or on the initiative of the Organization of Eastern Caribbean States. The RMC forces were defeated and Austin and his colleagues arrested.

new party victory In Nov 1983 the governor general appointed a nonpolitical interim council, and the 1974 constitution was reinstated. Several political parties emerged from hiding, including Eric Gairy's GULP and Herbert Blaize's GNP. After considerable manoeuvring, an informal coalition of centre and left-of-centre parties resulted in the formation of the New National Party (NNP), led by Blaize. In the 1984 general election the NNP won 14 of the 15 seats in the house of representatives and Blaize became prime minister. The USA withdrew most of its forces by the end of 1983 and the remainder by July 1985. In party elections Jan 1989, Blaize lost the leadership of the NNP to the public works minister Keith Mitchell. In Dec 1989 Blaize died and was succeeded by a close colleague, Ben Jones. Elections in 1990 brought Nicholas Braithwaite of the National Democratic Congress to power.

In Sept 1991 representatives of Dominica, St Lucia, St Vincent and the Grenadines, and Grenada proposed that integration with the Windward Islands would benefit the islands politically and economically.

Grenville George 1712–1770. British Whig politician, prime minister, and chancellor of the Exchequer, whose introduction of the ◊Stamp Act 1765 to raise revenue from the colonies was one of the causes of the American Revolution. His government was also responsible for prosecuting the radical John ◊Wilkes.

Grenville Richard 1542–1591. English naval commander and adventurer who died heroically aboard his ship *The Revenge* when attacked by Spanish warships. Grenville fought in Hungary and Ireland 1566–69, and was knighted about 1577. In 1585 he commanded the expedition that founded Virginia, USA, for his cousin Walter ◊Raleigh. From 1586 to 1588 he organized the defence of England against the Spanish Armada.

Grenville William Wyndham, Baron 1759–1834. British Whig politician, foreign secretary from 1791; he resigned along with Prime Minister Pitt the Younger 1801 over George III's refusal to assent to Catholic emancipation. He headed the 'All the Talents' coalition of 1806–07 that abolished the slave trade.

Grey Charles, 2nd Earl Grey 1764–1845. British Whig politician. He entered Parliament 1786, and in 1806 became First Lord of the Admiralty, and foreign secretary soon afterwards. As prime minister 1830–34, he carried the Great Reform Bill that reshaped the parliamentary representative system 1832 and the act abolishing slavery throughout the British Empire 1833.

Grey Edward, 1st Viscount Grey of Fallodon 1862–1933. British Liberal politician, nephew of Charles Grey. As foreign secretary 1905–16 he negotiated an entente with Russia 1907, and backed France against Germany in the ◊Agadir Incident of 1911. In 1914 he said: 'The lamps are going out all over Europe; we shall not see them lit again in our lifetime.'

The moral is obvious: it is that great armaments lead inevitably to war.

> **Edward Grey**, *Twenty-Five Years, 1892–1916* 1925

Grey George 1812–1898. British colonial administrator in Australia and New Zealand, born in Portugal. After several unsuccessful exploratory expeditions in Western Australia, he was appointed governor of South Australia 1840. Autocratic in attitude, he managed to bring the colony out of bankruptcy by 1844. He was lieutenant governor of New Zealand 1845–53, governor of Cape Colony, S Africa, 1854–61, and governor of New Zealand 1861–68. He then entered the New Zealand parliament and was premier 1877–79.

Grey Lady Jane 1537–1554. Queen of England for nine days, 10–19 July 1553, the great-granddaughter of Henry VII. She was married 1553 to Lord Guildford Dudley (died 1554), son of the Duke of ◊Northumberland. Edward VI was persuaded by Northumberland to set aside the claims to the throne of his sisters Mary and Elizabeth. When Edward died on 6 July the same year, Jane reluctantly accepted the crown and was proclaimed queen four days later. Mary, although a Roman Catholic, had the support of the populace, and the Lord Mayor of London announced that she was queen 19 July. She was executed on Tower Green.

Grivas George 1898–1974. Greek Cypriot general who from 1955 led the underground group EOKA's attempts to secure the union (Greek *enosis*) of Cyprus with Greece.

Gromyko Andrei 1909–1989. President of the USSR 1985–88. As ambassador to the USA from 1943, he took part in the Tehran, Yalta, and Potsdam conferences; as United Nations representative 1946–49, he exercised the Soviet veto 26 times. He was foreign minister 1957–85. It was Gromyko who formally nominated Mikhail Gorbachev as Communist Party leader 1985.

Guadeloupe island group in the Leeward Islands, West Indies, an overseas *département* of France. Columbus reached here 1493 and the

Caribs fought against Spanish colonization. A French colony was established 1635.

Guam largest of the Mariana Islands in the W Pacific, an unincorporated territory of the USA. It was ceded by Spain to the USA 1898; occupied by Japan 1941–44. Guam achieved full US citizenship and self-government from 1950. A referendum 1982 favoured the status of a commonwealth, in association with the USA.

Guatemala country in Central America, bounded N and NW by Mexico, E by Belize and the Caribbean Sea, SE by Honduras and El Salvador, and SW by the Pacific Ocean.

history Formerly part of the ◊Maya empire, Guatemala became a Spanish colony 1524. Independent from Spain 1821, it then joined Mexico, becoming independent 1823. It was part of the ◊United Provinces of Central America 1823–40. The military rebellion 1838, led by José Rafael Carrera, set a pattern of long-term dictatorship in Guatemala.

dictatorship Despite frequent ostentatious displays of constitutionalism, the country was ruled by a succession of personal or military dictators. The Indian population, in particular, was ruthlessly exploited, while human rights were ignored or trampled upon.

A revolutionary strike 1944 led to the electoral triumph of Juan José Arévalo. Along with his successor, Jácobo Arbenz, he attempted to curb the power of the army and install political freedoms. Health services and education were expanded. Agrarian reform was also proposed.

era of coups Arbenz's nationalization of the United Fruit Company's plantations 1954 so alarmed the US government that it sponsored a revolution, led by Col Carlos Castillo Armas, who then assumed the presidency. He was assassinated 1963, and the army continued to rule until 1966. There was a brief return to constitutional government until the military returned 1970.

In the 1982 presidential election the government candidate won, but opponents complained that the election had been rigged, and before he could take office there was a coup by a group of young right-wing officers, who installed General Ríos Montt as head of a three-person junta. He soon dissolved the junta, assumed the presidency, and began fighting corruption.

The antigovernment guerrilla movement was growing 1981 and was countered by repressive measures by Montt, so that by 1983 opposition to him was widespread. After several unsuccessful attempts to remove him, a coup led by General Mejía Victores finally succeeded. Mejía Victores declared an amnesty for the guerrillas, the ending of press censorship, and the preparation of a new constitution. After its adoption and elections 1985, the Guatemalan Christian Democratic Party (PDCG) won a majority in the congress as well as the presidency, with Vinicio Cerezo becoming president. In 1989 an attempted coup against Cerezo was put down by the army. By 1989 once more 2% of the population owned over 70% of the land.

deaths and disappearances The army, funded and trained by the USA, destroyed some 440 rural villages and killed more than 100,000 civilians 1980–89; 40,000 people disappeared during the same period. From Jan to Nov 1989 almost 2,000 people were killed and 840 disappeared (representing a six-fold increase over the same period in the preceding year).

In presidential elections Jan 1991, Jorge Serrano Elías of the Solidarity Action Movement (MAS), an ally of Montt, received 68% of the vote and his opponent Jorge Carpio Nicolle of the Centre Party (UCN) 32%. In Sept 1991 diplomatic relations with Belize were established.

Guderian Heinz 1888–1954. German general in World War II. He created the *Panzer* (German 'armour') divisions that formed the ground spearhead of Hitler's ◊*Blitzkrieg* attack strategy, achieving a significant breakthrough at Sedan in Ardennes, France 1940, and leading the advance to Moscow 1941.

We have severely underestimated the Russians, the extent of the country and the treachery of the climate. This is the revenge of reality.

General Heinz Guderian letter 1941

Guelph and Ghibelline rival parties in medieval Germany and Italy, which supported the papal party and the Holy Roman emperors respectively.

They originated in the 12th century as partisans of rival German houses, that of Welf (hence Guelph or Guelf) of the dukes of Bavaria, and that of the lords of ◊Hohenstaufen (whose castle at Waiblingen gave the Ghibellines their name). The Hohenstaufens supplied five Roman emperors: Conrad II (1138–52); Conrad's nephew Frederick Barbarossa (1152–89); Fredericks's son, Henry VI 'The Severe' (1190–97); and Frederick's grandson and great-grandson Frederick II (1212–50) and Conrad IV (1250–54); but the dynasty died out 1268. The Guelphs early became associated with the papacy because of their mutual Hohenstaufen enemy. In Italy, the terms were introduced about 1242 in Florence; the names seem to have been grafted on to pre-existing papal and imperial factions within the city-republics.

guerrilla (Spanish 'little war') irregular soldier fighting in a small unofficial unit, typically against an established or occupying power, and engaging in sabotage, ambush, and the like, rather than pitched battles against an opposing army. Guerrilla tactics have been used both by resistance armies in wartime (for example, the Vietnam War) and in peacetime by national liberation groups and militant political extremists (for example the PLO; Tamil Tigers).

The term was first applied to the Spanish and Portuguese resistance to French occupation during the Peninsular War (1808–14). Guerrilla techniques were widely used in World War II – for example, in Greece and the Balkans. Political activists who resort to violence, particularly **urban guerrillas**, tend to be called 'freedom fighters' by those who support their cause, 'terrorists' by those who oppose it.

Guesdes Jules 1845–1922. French socialist leader from the 1880s who espoused Marxism and revolutionary change. His movement, the Partie Ouvrier Français (French Workers' Party), was eventually incorporated in the foundation of the SFIO (Section Française de l'International Ouvrière/French Section of International Labour) 1905.

Guevara 'Che' Ernesto 1928–1967. Latin American revolutionary. He was born in Argentina and trained there as a doctor, but left his homeland 1953 because of his opposition to the right-wing president Perón. In effecting the Cuban revolution of 1959, he was second only to Castro and Castro's brother Raúl. In 1965 he went to the Congo to fight against white mercenaries, and then to Bolivia, where he was killed in an unsuccessful attempt to lead a peasant rising. He was an orthodox Marxist and renowned for his guerrilla techniques.

In a revolution one wins or dies.

Che Guevara

Guienne ancient province of SW France which formed the duchy of Aquitaine with Gascony in the 12th century. Its capital was Bordeaux. It

became English 1154 and passed to France 1453.

guild or *gild* medieval association, particularly of artisans or merchants, formed for mutual aid and protection and the pursuit of a common purpose, religious or economic. Guilds became politically powerful in Europe but after the 16th century their position was undermined by the growth of capitalism.

Guilds fulfilling charitable or religious functions (for example, the maintenance of schools, roads, or bridges, the assistance of members in misfortune, or the provision of masses for the souls of dead members) flourished in western Europe from the 9th century but were suppressed in Protestant countries at the Reformation.

The earliest form of economic guild, the **guild merchant**, arose during the 11th and 12th centuries; this was an organization of the traders of a town, who had been granted a practical monopoly of its trade by charter. As the merchants often strove to exclude craftworkers from the guild, and to monopolize control of local government, the **craft guilds** came into existence in the 12th and 13th centuries. These, which included journeymen (day workers) and apprentices as well as employers, regulated prices, wages, working conditions, and apprenticeship, prevented unfair practices, and maintained high standards of craft; they also fulfilled many social, religious, and charitable functions. By the 14th century they had taken control of local government, ousting the guild merchant.

guillotine beheading device consisting of a metal blade that descends between two posts. It was common in the Middle Ages and was introduced 1791 in an improved design by physician Joseph Ignace Guillotin (1738–1814) in France. It was subsequently used for executions during the French Revolution. It is still in use in some countries.

Guinea country in W Africa, bounded N by Senegal, NE by Mali, SE by the Ivory Coast, S by Liberia and Sierra Leone, W by the Atlantic Ocean, and NW by Guinea-Bissau.

history Formerly part of the Muslim ◊Mali Empire, which flourished in the region between the 7th and 15th centuries, Guinea's first European visitors were the Portuguese in the mid-15th century, who, together with France and Britain, established the slave trade in the area. In 1849 France proclaimed the Boké region in the east a French protectorate and expanded its territory until by the late 19th century most of W Africa was united under French rule as French West Africa.

Touré's presidency French Guinea became fully independent 1958, under the name of Guinea, after a referendum rejected a proposal to remain a self-governing colony within the French Community. The first president was Sékou Touré, who made the PDG the only political organization and embarked upon a policy of socialist revolution. There were unsuccessful attempts to overthrow him 1961, 1965, 1967, and 1970, and, suspicious of conspiracies by foreign powers, he put his country into virtual diplomatic isolation. By 1975, however, relations with most of his neighbours had returned to normal.

At first rigidly Marxist, crushing all opposition to his policies, Touré gradually moved towards a mixed economy, with private enterprise becoming legal 1979. His regime was nevertheless authoritarian and harsh. He sought closer relations with Western powers, particularly France and the USA, and was re-elected unopposed 1980, but died 1984.

military rule Before the normal machinery for electing his successor could be put into operation, the army staged a bloodless coup, suspending the constitution and setting up a military committee for national recovery, with Col Lansana Conté at its head. Releasing hundreds of political prisoners and lifting press restrictions, he also made efforts to restore his country's international standing through a series of overseas visits. He succeeded in persuading some 200,000 Guineans who had fled the country during the Touré regime to return. In 1985 an attempt to overthrow him while he was out of the country was foiled by loyal troops. In 1990 Guinea contributed troops to the multinational force that attempted to stabilize Liberia. The National Confederation of Guinea Workers (CNTG) called a general strike May 1991 in a campaign against the government.

Guinea-Bissau country in W Africa, bounded N by Senegal, E and SE by Guinea, and SW by the Atlantic Ocean.

history Guinea-Bissau was first reached by Europeans when the Portuguese arrived 1446 and it became a slave-trading centre. Until 1879 it was administered with the Cape Verde Islands, but then became a separate colony under the name of Portuguese Guinea.

Nationalist groups began to form in the 1950s, and PAIGC was established 1956. Portugal refused to grant independence, fighting broke out, and by 1972 PAIGC claimed to control two-thirds of the country. In 1973 the 'liberated areas' were declared independent, a national people's assembly was set up, and Luiz

Cabral was appointed president of a state council. Some 40,000 Portuguese troops were engaged in trying to put down the uprising and suffered heavy losses, but before a clear outcome was reached a coup in Portugal ended the fighting, and PAIGC negotiated independence with the new government in Lisbon.

after independence In 1974 Portugal formally acknowledged Guinea-Bissau as a sovereign nation. PAIGC began to lay the foundations of a socialist state, intended to include Cape Verde, but in 1980, four days before approval of the constitution, Cape Verde withdrew, feeling that Guinea-Bissau was being given preferential treatment. A coup deposed Cabral, and João Vieira became chair of a council of revolution.

At its 1981 congress, PAIGC decided to retain its name, despite Cape Verde's withdrawal, and its position as the only party was confirmed, with Vieira as secretary general. Normal relations between the two countries were restored 1982. In 1984 a new constitution made Vieira head of government as well as head of state. In June 1989 he was re-elected for another five-year term. In Jan 1991 PAIGC approved the introduction of 'integral multipartyism' and in July 1992 a multiparty commission was established to organize assembly and presidential elections in Nov and Dec.

Guise Francis, 2nd Duke of Guise 1519–1563. French soldier and politician. He led the French victory over Germany at Metz 1552 and captured Calais from the English 1558. Along with his brother *Charles* (1527–1574), he was powerful in the government of France during the reign of Francis II. He was assassinated attempting to crush the ◊Huguenots.

Guise Henri, 3rd Duke of Guise 1550–1588. French noble who persecuted the Huguenots and was partly responsible for the Massacre of ◊St Bartholomew 1572. He was assassinated.

Guizot François Pierre Guillaume 1787–1874. French politician and historian, professor of modern history at the Sorbonne, Paris 1812–30. He wrote histories of French and European culture and became prime minister 1847. His resistance to all reforms led to the revolution of 1848.

gulag Russian term for the system of prisons and labour camps used to silence dissidents and opponents of the Soviet regime. In the Stalin era (1920s–1930s), thousands of prisoners died from the harsh conditions of these remote camps.

Gulf War war 16 Jan–28 Feb 1991 between Iraq and a coalition of 28 nations led by the USA. (It is also another name for the ◊Iran–Iraq War).

The invasion and annexation of Kuwait by Iraq on 2 Aug 1990 provoked a build-up of US troops in Saudi Arabia, eventually totalling over 500,000. The UK subsequently deployed 42,000 troops, France 15,000, Egypt 20,000, and other nations smaller contingents. An air offensive lasting six weeks, in which 'smart' weapons came of age, destroyed about one-third of Iraqi equipment and inflicted massive casualties. A 100-hour ground war followed, which effectively destroyed the remnants of the 500,000-strong Iraqi army in or near Kuwait.

A dispute over a shared oilfield and the price of oil was one of the main reasons for Iraq's invasion of Kuwait. Resolutions made in Aug 1990 by the United Nations Security Council for immediate withdrawal of Iraqi troops went unheeded, and a trade embargo and blockade were instituted. In Nov the USA doubled its troop strength in Saudi Arabia to 400,000, and in Dec 1990 the UN Security Council authorized the use of force if Iraq did not withdraw before 15 Jan 1991. Talks between the USA and Iraq failed, as did peace initiatives by the UN and France. By Jan 1991 coalition forces totalled some 725,000. Within 24 hours of the deadline, US and allied forces launched massive air bombardments against Baghdad, hitting strategic targets such as military air bases and communications systems. Saddam Hussein replied by firing missiles at the Israeli cities of Tel Aviv and Haifa (by which tactic he hoped to bring Israel into the war and thus break up the Arab alliance against him), as well as cities in Saudi Arabia; most of these missiles were intercepted.

The ground war started on 24 Feb and the superior range of the US artillery soon devastated the retreating Iraqi forces; by the end of Feb the war was over, Iraq defeated, and Kuwait once more independent, though under a pall of smoke from burning oil wells and facing extensive rebuilding.

Some 90,000 tonnes of ordnance was dropped by US planes on Iraq and occupied Kuwait, of which precision-guided weapons amounted to 7%; of these, 90% hit their targets whereas only 25% of the conventional bombs did so. British forces dropped 3,000 tonnes of ordnance, including 6,000 bombs, of which 1,000 were laser-guided. Napalm and fuel-air explosives were also used by coalition forces, but cluster bombs and multiple-launch rockets were predominant. The cost to the USA of the war was $61.1 billion (£36.3 billion), including $43.1 billion contributed by the allies. Estimates of Iraqi casualties are in the range of 80,000–150,000 troops and 100,000–200,000 civilians; ecological and public-health consequences were expected to cause further deaths

in the months following the war. In May 1991 some 15,000 Iraqi prisoners of war were still in allied custody, and the war created 2-3 million refugees. Severe environmental damage, including oil spills, affected a large area.

gunboat diplomacy the threat of force by one country to achieve its demands. The term arose during the ◊Agadir Incident.

Gunpowder Plot in British history, the Catholic conspiracy to blow up James I and his parliament on 5 Nov 1605. It was discovered through an anonymous letter. Guy ◊Fawkes was found in the cellar beneath the Palace of Westminster, ready to fire a store of explosives. Several of the conspirators were killed, and Fawkes and seven others were executed.

Guomindang Chinese National People's Party, founded 1894 by ◊Sun Yat-sen, which overthrew the Manchu Empire 1912. From 1927 the right wing, led by ◊Chiang Kai-shek, was in conflict with the left, led by Mao Zedong until the Communist victory 1949 (except for the period of the Japanese invasion 1937-45). It survives as the dominant political party of Taiwan, where it is still spelled *Kuomintang*.

Gupta dynasty Indian hereditary rulers that reunified and ruled over much of northern and central India 320–550. The dynasty's stronghold lay in the Magadha region of the middle Ganges valley, with the capital ◊Pataliputra. Gupta influence was extended through military conquest E, W, and S by Chandragupta I, Chandragupta II, and Samudragupta. Hun raids in the NW from the 6th century undermined the Guptas' decentralized administrative structure.

The dynasty grew out of the array of states left from the disintegration c. 200 of the Kushan empire. Its conquest brought about varying degrees of independence and created a prosperous society in which Sanskrit grew out of its religious sphere to become the official language, at least in N India. At the empire's height, the Hindu and Buddhist religions, commerce, and the arts flourished in what is seen as a golden or classical age of Indian civilization.

Gurkha member of a people living in the mountains of Nepal, whose young men have been recruited since 1815 for the British and Indian armies. They are predominantly Tibeto-Mongolians, but their language is Khas, a dialect of a northern Indic language.

Gustaf or **Gustavus** six kings of Sweden, including:

Gustaf V 1858–1950. King of Sweden from 1907, when he succeeded his father Oscar II.

He married Princess Victoria, daughter of the Grand Duke of Baden 1881, thus uniting the reigning Bernadotte dynasty with the former royal house of Vasa.

Gustaf VI 1882–1973. King of Sweden from 1950, when he succeeded his father Gustaf V. He was an archaeologist and expert on Chinese art. He was succeeded by his grandson Carl XVI Gustaf.

Gustavus Adolphus (Gustavus II) 1594–1632. King of Sweden from 1611, when he succeeded his father Charles IX. He waged successful wars with Denmark, Russia, and Poland, and in the ◊Thirty Years' War became a champion of the Protestant cause. Landing in Germany 1630, he defeated the German general Wallenstein at Lützen, SW of Leipzig 6 Nov 1632, but was killed in the battle. He was known as the 'Lion of the North'.

Gustavus Vasa (Gustavus I) 1496–1560. King of Sweden from 1523, when he was elected after leading the Swedish revolt against Danish rule. He united and pacified the country and established Lutheranism as the state religion.

Guyana country in South America, bounded N by the Atlantic Ocean, E by Surinam, S and SW by Brazil, and NW by Venezuela.

history Inhabited by Arawak, Carib, and Warrau Indians when the first Europeans arrived in the late 1500s, the area now known as Guyana was a Dutch colony 1621–1796, when it was seized by Britain. By the Treaty of London 1814, the three Dutch colonies of Essequibo, Demerara, and Berbice were ceded to the UK. In 1831 they were united as British Guiana. However, a Dutch-style constitution prevailed until 1891. The Dutch town of Stabroek was renamed Georgetown and served as the capital.

The abolition of the slave trade 1807 and slavery 1834 brought the ruin of many planters. Between 1838 and 1917, 340,000 immigrants came to the colony from India; this immigration was stopped 1917 under pressure from the government of India.

The transition from colonial to republican status was gradual and not entirely smooth. In 1953 a constitution providing for free elections to an assembly was introduced, and the left-wing People's Progressive Party (PPP), led by Dr Cheddi Jagan, won the popular vote. Within months, however, the UK government suspended the constitution and put in its own interim administration, claiming that the PPP threatened to become a communist dictatorship.

internal self-government In 1957 a breakaway group from the PPP founded a new party, the People's National Congress (PNC), which was supported mainly by Guyanans of African descent, while PPP followers were mainly of Indian descent. Fresh elections, under a revised constitution, were held 1957, and the PPP won again, with Jagan becoming chief minister. Internal self-government was granted 1961 and, with the PPP again the successful party, Jagan became prime minister. Proportional representation was introduced 1963, and in the 1964 elections (under the new voting procedures) the PPP, although winning most votes, did not have an overall majority, resulting in the formation of a PPP–PNC coalition with PNC leader Forbes Burnham as prime minister.

after independence This coalition took the country through to full independence 1966. The PNC won the 1968 and 1973 elections; in 1970 Guyana became a republic within the Commonwealth. In 1980 a new constitution was adopted, making the president head of both state and government, and as a result of the 1981 elections – which opposition parties claimed were fraudulent – Burnham became executive president. The rest of his administration was marked by economic deterioration (necessitating austerity measures) and cool relations with the Western powers, particularly the USA, whose invasion of Grenada he condemned. He died 1985 and was succeeded by Prime Minister Desmond Hoyte.

return of Jagan In the Aug 1992 general election, the PPP had a decisive win and its veteran leader, Cheddi Jagan, became prime minister.

Guzmán Blanco Antonio 1829–1899. Venezuelan dictator and military leader (*caudillo*), who seized power 1870 and remained absolute ruler until 1889. He modernized Caracas to become the political capital; committed resources to education, communications, and agriculture; and encouraged foreign trade.

Haakon seven kings of Norway, including:

Haakon I *the Good* c. 915–961. King of Norway from about 935. The son of Harald Hárfagri ('Finehair') (*c.* 850–930), king of Norway, he was raised in England. He seized the Norwegian throne and tried unsuccessfully to introduce Christianity there. His capital was at Trondheim.

Haakon IV 1204–1263. King of Norway from 1217, the son of Haakon III. Under his rule, Norway flourished both militarily and culturally; he took control of the Faroe Islands, Greenland 1261, and Iceland 1262–64. His court was famed throughout N Europe.

Haakon VII 1872–1957. King of Norway from 1905. Born Prince Charles, the second son of Frederick VIII of Denmark, he was elected king of Norway on separation from Sweden, and in 1906 he took the name Haakon. In World War II he carried on the resistance from Britain during the Nazi occupation of his country. He returned 1945.

habeas corpus (Latin 'you may have the body') in law, a writ directed to someone who has custody of a person, ordering him or her to bring the person before the court issuing the writ and to justify why the person is detained in custody.

Traditional rights to habeas corpus were embodied in the English Habeas Corpus Act 1679. The main principles were adopted in the US Constitution. The Scottish equivalent is the Wrongous Imprisonment Act 1701.

Habsburg or *Hapsburg* European royal family, former imperial house of Austria-Hungary. A Hapsburg, Rudolf I, became king of Germany 1273 and began the family's control of Austria and Styria. They acquired a series of lands and titles, including that of Holy Roman emperor which they held 1273–91, 1298–1308, 1438–1740, and 1745–1806. The Hapsburgs reached the zenith of their power under the emperor Charles V (1519–1556) who divided his lands, creating an Austrian Habsburg line (which ruled until 1918) and a Spanish line (which ruled to 1700).

hacienda large estate typical of most of Spanish colonial and post-colonial Latin America. Typically inherited, haciendas were often built up by the purchase of crown or private lands, or lands traditionally worked by the Indian community. They used cheap, seasonal labour to farm produce, fairly inefficiently, for domestic and export markets. Socially, the hacienda served as a means of control by the ruling oligarchy.

Hadrian AD 76–138. Roman emperor from 117. Born in Spain, he was adopted by his relative, the emperor Trajan, whom he succeeded. He abandoned Trajan's conquests in Mesopotamia and adopted a defensive policy, which included the building of Hadrian's Wall in Britain.

Hadrian's Wall Roman fortification built AD 122–26 to mark England's northern boundary and abandoned about 383; its ruins run 185 km/115 mi from Wallsend on the river Tyne to Maryport, W Cumbria.

Haganah Zionist military organization in Palestine. It originated under the Turkish rule of the Ottoman Empire before World War I to protect Jewish settlements, and many of its members served in the British forces in both world wars. After World War II it condemned guerrilla activity, opposing the British authorities only passively. It formed the basis of the Israeli army after Israel was established 1948.

Haidar Ali (or ◊Hyder Ali) ruler of Mysore, India, from 1761.

Haig Douglas, 1st Earl Haig 1861–1928. British army officer, commander in chief in World War I. His Somme offensive in France in the summer of 1916 made considerable advances only at enormous cost to human life, and his Passchendaele offensive in Belgium from July to Nov 1917 achieved little at a similar loss. He was created field marshal 1917 and, after retiring, became first president of the British Legion 1921.

A national hero at the time of his funeral, Haig's reputation began to fall after Lloyd George's memoirs depicted him as treating soldiers' lives with disdain, while remaining far from battle himself.

Haile Selassie Ras (Prince) Tafari ('the Lion of Judah') 1892–1975. Emperor of Ethiopia

1930–74. He pleaded unsuccessfully to the League of Nations against Italian conquest of his country 1935–36, and lived in the UK until his restoration 1941. He was deposed by a military coup 1974 and died in captivity the following year. Followers of the Rastafarian religion (see ◊Rastafarianism) believe that he was the Messiah, the incarnation of God (Jah).

Haiti country in the Caribbean, occupying the W part of the island of Hispaniola; to the E is the Dominican Republic.

history The island of Hispaniola was once inhabited by ◊Arawak Indians who had died out by the end of the 16th century owing to conquest, warfare, hard labour, and diseases brought in by the Europeans after the arrival of Christopher Columbus 1492. The island was made a Spanish colony under the name of Santo Domingo, but the western part was colonized by France from the mid-17th century. In 1697 the western third of the island was ceded to France by Spain.

independence achieved The period 1790–1804 was fraught with rebellions against France, tension among blacks, whites, and mulattos, and military intervention by France and Britain. In one such rebellion 1791 the island was taken over by slaves, under ◊Toussaint L'Ouverture, and slavery was abolished, but it was then reinstated after he was killed by the French. After independence 1804 the instability continued, with Santo Domingo repossessed by Spain and then by Haiti, and self-proclaimed kings ruling Haiti. In 1844 Haiti and the Dominican Republic became separate states. During the late 19th century Haiti suffered from growing economic and political instability. Several leaders were ousted and murdered.

Duvalier era Friction between Haitians of African descent and mulattos, and the country's political instability, brought a period of US rule 1915–34. In the 1940s and 1950s there were several coups, the last occurring 1956, which resulted in Dr François Duvalier being elected president. After an encouraging start, his administration degenerated into a personal dictatorship, maintained by a private army, the Tontons Macoutes. In 1964 'Papa Doc' Duvalier made himself president for life, with the power to nominate his son as his successor.

On his father's death 1971 Jean-Claude ◊Duvalier came to the presidency at the age of 19 and soon acquired the name of 'Baby Doc'. Although the young Duvalier repeatedly promised a return to democracy, there was little change. In the 1984 elections about 300 government candidates contested the 59 seats, with no opposition at all. In 1985, political parties were legalized, provided they conformed to strict guidelines, but only one party registered, the National Progressive Party (PNP), which supported Duvalier's policies. He was overthrown and exiled to France 1986.

democratization failed The new military regime led by Lt-Gen Henri Namphy offered no protection to the electoral council, and the US government withdrew aid. Elections Nov 1987 were sabotaged by armed gangs of Duvalierists who massacred voters and set fire to polling stations and to vehicles delivering ballot papers in the country. Leslie Manigat, with army support, was made president Feb 1988 but four months later was ousted in a coup led by Namphy, who was in turn replaced by Brig-Gen Prosper Avril in a coup Sept 1988. Avril installed a largely civilian government, but the army was still in control and a coup attempt April 1989 was quickly put down. Early in 1990 opposition to Avril grew, but was suppressed. In Aug and Sept 1990 acting president Ertha Pascal-Trouillot defied calls for her resignation, but elections were held in Dec. Jean-Bertrand Aristide, a Catholic priest, won a landslide victory and in Feb 1991, as president, dismissed the entire army high command, with the exception of General Hérard Abraham, who had earlier permitted Haiti's first free elections.

Aristide ousted A military coup, led by Brig-Gen Raoul Cedras, overthrew Aristide in Sept 1991. In the following month, the army appointed Joseph Nerette as interim president, with Jean Jacques Honorat as prime minister. There was international condemnation of the coup, but efforts to reinstate Aristide failed. Nerette's term of office was extended indefinitely; Marc Bazin replaced Honorat as prime minister in June 1992.

foreign sanctions The USA had resumed food aid to the Avril government Aug 1989. In early 1992 the USA began to modify its 1991 sanctions on Haiti, in an effort to create more jobs there. The Organization of American States (OAS), however, increased its sanctions in May.

hajdule member of a group of Serbian outlaw guerrillas who fought for Christianity against the Turks during the period of Ottoman rule (1459-1878).

Haldane Richard Burdon, Viscount Haldane 1856–1928. British Liberal politician. As secretary for war 1905–12, he sponsored the army reforms that established an expeditionary force, backed by a territorial army and under the unified control of an imperial general staff. He was Lord Chancellor 1912–15 and in the Labour government of 1924. His writings on German philosophy led to accusations of his having pro-German sympathies.

Halifax Edward Frederick Lindley Wood, Earl of Halifax 1881–1959. British Conservative politician, viceroy of India 1926–31. As foreign secretary 1938–40 he was associated with Chamberlain's 'appeasement' policy. He received an earldom 1944 for services to the Allied cause while ambassador to the USA 1941–46.

Hallstatt archaeological site in Upper Austria, SW of Salzburg. In 1846 over 3,000 graves were discovered belonging to a 9th–5th century BC Celtic civilization transitional between the Bronze and Iron Ages.

Halsey William Frederick 1882–1959. US admiral, known as 'Bull'. He was the commander of the Third Fleet in the S Pacific from 1942 during World War II. The Japanese signed the surrender document ending World War II on his flagship, the battleship *Missouri*.

Hamaguchi Osachi, also known as *Hamaguchi Yūkō* 1870–1931. Japanese politician, prime minister 1929–30. His policies created social unrest and alienated military interests. His acceptance of the terms of the London Naval Agreement 1930 was also unpopular. Shot by an assassin Nov 1930, he died of his wounds nine months later.

Hamburg largest inland port of Europe, in Germany, on the river Elbe. In alliance with Lübeck, it founded the ◊Hanseatic League.

Hamilcar Barca c. 270–228 BC. Carthaginian general, father of ◊Hannibal. From 247 to 241 BC in the First ◊Punic War he harassed the Romans in Sicily and Italy and then led an expedition to Spain, where he died in battle.

The interest of the State is in intimate connection with those of the rich individuals belonging to it.
            Alexander Hamilton letter 1781

Hamilton Alexander 1757–1804. US politician who influenced the adoption of a constitution with a strong central government and was the first secretary of the Treasury 1789–95. He led the Federalist Party, and incurred the bitter hatred of Aaron ◊Burr when he voted against Burr and in favour of Thomas Jefferson for the presidency 1801. Challenged to a duel by Burr, Hamilton was wounded and died the next day.

Hamilton James, 1st Duke of Hamilton 1606–1649. Scottish adviser to Charles I. He led an army against the ◊Covenanters (supporters of the National Covenant 1638 to establish Presbyterianism) 1639 and subsequently took part in the negotiations between Charles and the Scots. In the second Civil War he led the Scottish invasion of England, but was captured at Preston and executed.

Hammarskjöld Dag 1905–1961. Swedish secretary general of the United Nations 1953–61. He opposed Britain over the ◊Suez Crisis 1956. His attempts to solve the problem of the Congo (now Zaire), where he was killed in a plane crash, were criticized by the USSR. He was awarded the Nobel Peace Prize 1961.

The only kind of dignity which is genuine is that which is not diminished by the indifference of others.
            Dag Hammarskjöld Markings 1964

Hammurabi king of Babylon from c. 1792 BC. He united his country and took it to the height of its power. He authorized a legal code, of which a copy was found in 1902.

Hampden John 1594–1643. English politician. His refusal in 1636 to pay ◊ship money, a compulsory tax levied to support the navy, made him a national figure. In the Short and Long Parliaments he proved himself a skilful debater and parliamentary strategist. King Charles's attempt to arrest him and four other leading MPs made the Civil War inevitable. He raised his own regiment on the outbreak of hostilities, and on 18 June 1643 was mortally wounded at the skirmish of Chalgrove Field in Oxfordshire, England.

Hancock John 1737–1793. US politician and a leader of the American Revolution. As president of the Continental Congress 1775–77, he was the first to sign the Declaration of Independence 1776. Because he signed it in a large, bold hand (in popular belief, so that it would be big enough for George III to see), his name became a colloquial term for a signature in the USA. He coveted command of the Continental Army, deeply resenting the selection of George ◊Washington. He was governor of Massachusetts 1780–85 and 1787–93.

Han dynasty Chinese ruling family 206 BC–AD 220 established by Liu Bang (256–195 BC) after he overthrew the ◊Qin dynasty, and named after the Han River. There was territorial expansion to the W, SW, and N, including

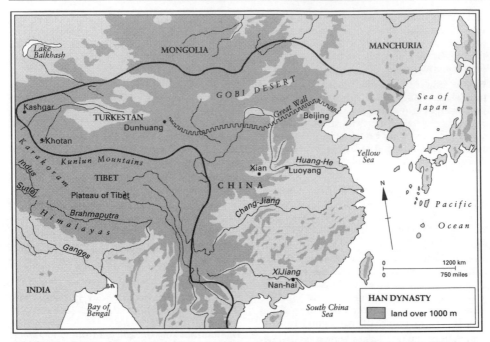

The Han dynasty *The Han dynasty marked the heyday of the early Chinese empire. Roughly contemporary with the Roman empire, the Han controlled a larger population and established a comparatively centralized system of administration. At Xian, the capital, a huge Confucianist bureaucracy developed to control the empire's elaborate administrative institutions. Han authority and culture were extended through conquest into S China and N Korea. Westward extension of the Great Wall to Yu-men (Jade Gate) consolidated Han authority in Central Asia.*

the conquest of Korea by emperor Wudi (Wuti, ruled 141–87 BC) and the suppression of the ◊Xiongnu invaders. Under the Han, a Confucianist-educated civil service was established and Buddhism introduced.

Divided into the eras of the Western Han 206 BC–AD 8 and the Eastern Han 25–220, it was a time of internal peace, except AD 8–25. The building of new canals allowed long-distance trading, while the arts and technologies (including the invention of paper) flourished. The dynasty collapsed under the weight of court intrigues, rebellions, and renewed threat from the Xiongnu, and was replaced by the ◊Three Kingdoms.

Hanging Gardens of Babylon one of the Seven Wonders of the World, constructed in ancient ◊Babylon.

Hannibal 247–182 BC. Carthaginian general from 221 BC, son of Hamilcar Barca. His siege of Saguntum (now Sagunto, near Valencia) precipitated the Second ◊Punic War with Rome. Following a campaign in Italy (after crossing the Alps in 218), Hannibal was the victor at Trasimene in 217 and Cannae in 216, but he failed to take Rome. In 203 he returned to Carthage to meet a Roman invasion but was

defeated at Zama in 202 and exiled in 196 at Rome's insistence.

Hanover, House of German royal dynasty that ruled Great Britain and Ireland 1714–1901. Under the Act of Settlement 1701, the succession passed to the ruling family of Hanover, Germany, on the death of Queen Anne. On the death of Queen Victoria, the crown passed to Edward VII of the house of Saxe-Coburg.

Hanseatic League (German *Hanse* 'group, society') confederation of N European trading cities from the 12th century to 1669. At its height in the late 14th century the Hanseatic League included over 160 cities and towns, among them Lübeck, Hamburg, Cologne, Breslau, and Kraków. The basis of the league's power was its monopoly of the Baltic trade and its relations with Flanders and England. The decline of the Hanseatic League from the 15th century was caused by the closing and moving of trade routes and the development of nation states.

The earliest association had its headquarters in Visby, Sweden; it included over 30 cities, but was gradually supplanted by that headed by Lübeck. Hamburg and Lübeck established their own trading stations in London in 1266 and 1267 respectively, which coalesced in 1282 with that of Cologne to form the so-called Steelyard. There were three other such stations: Bruges, Bergen, and Novgorod. The last general assembly 1669 marked the end of the league.

Hapsburg English form of ◊Habsburg, former imperial house of Austria-Hungary.

Haq Fazlul 1873–1962. Leader of the Bengali Muslim peasantry. He was a member of the Viceroy's Defence Council, established 1941, and was Bengal's first Indian prime minister 1937–43.

Harald III Hardrada or Harald the Ruthless (Norwegian *Harald Hardråde*) 1015–1066. King of Norway 1045–66, ruling jointly with Magnus I 1045–47. He engaged in an unsuccessful attempt to conquer Denmark 1045–62; extended Norwegian rule in Orkney, Shetland, and the Hebrides; and tried to conquer England together with Tostig, Earl of Northumbria. They were defeated by King Harold of England at Stamford Bridge and both died in battle.

Harappa ruined city in the Punjab, NW Pakistan, of a prehistoric culture known as the ◊Indus Valley civilization, which flourished from 2500 to 1600 BC. It is one of two such great cities excavated; the other is ◊Mohenjo Daro.

Hardenberg Karl August von 1750–1822. Prussian politician, foreign minister to King Frederick William III of Prussia during the Napoleonic Wars; he later became chancellor. His military and civic reforms were restrained by the reactionary tendencies of the king.

Hardicanute c. 1019–1042. King of England from 1040. Son of Canute, he was king of Denmark from 1028. In England he was considered a harsh ruler.

Hardie (James) Keir 1856–1915. Scottish socialist, member of Parliament 1892–95 and 1900–15. He worked in the mines as a boy and in 1886 became secretary of the Scottish Miners' Federation. In 1888 he was the first Labour candidate to stand for Parliament; he entered Parliament independently as a Labour member 1892 and was a chief founder of the ◊Independent Labour Party 1893.

Harding Warren G(amaliel) 1865–1923. 29th president of the USA 1921–23, a Republican. He opposed US membership of the League of Nations. There was corruption among members of his cabinet (the ◊Teapot Dome Scandal), with the secretary of the interior later convicted for taking bribes.

Harding was born in Ohio, and entered the US Senate 1914. As president he concluded the peace treaties of 1921 with Germany, Austria, and Hungary, and in the same year called the Washington Naval Conference to resolve conflicting British, Japanese, and US ambitions in the Pacific. He died in office shortly after undeniable evidence of corruption in his administration began to surface.

Hargraves Edward Hammond 1816–1891. Australian prospector, born in England. In 1851 he found gold in the Blue Mountains of New South Wales, thus beginning the first Australian gold rush.

Harley Robert, 1st Earl of Oxford 1661–1724. British Tory politician, chief minister to Queen Anne 1711–14, when he negotiated the Treaty of Utrecht 1713. Accused of treason as a ◊Jacobite after the accession of George I, he was imprisoned 1714–17.

Harold two kings of England:

Harold I died 1040. King of England from 1035. The illegitimate son of Canute, known as *Harefoot*, he claimed the throne 1035 when the legitimate heir Hardicanute was in Denmark. He was elected king 1037.

Harold II c. 1020–1066. King of England from Jan 1066. He succeeded his father Earl Godwin 1053 as earl of Wessex. In 1063 William of Normandy (◊William I) tricked him into swearing to support his claim to the English throne, and when the Witan (a council of high-ranking religious and secular men) elected Harold to succeed Edward the Confessor, William prepared to invade. Meanwhile, Harold's treacherous brother Tostig (died 1066) joined the king of Norway, Harald III Hardrada (1015–1066), in invading Northumbria. Harold routed and killed them at Stamford Bridge 25 Sept. Three days later William landed at Pevensey, Sussex, and Harold was killed at the Battle of Hastings 14 Oct 1066.

Harriman (William) Averell 1891–1986. US diplomat, administrator of ◊lend-lease in World War II, Democratic secretary of commerce in Truman's administration 1946-48, negotiator of the Nuclear Test Ban Treaty with the USSR 1963, and governor of New York 1955–58.

Harris Arthur Travers 1892–1984. British marshal of the Royal Air Force in World War II. Known as 'Bomber Harris', he was commander in chief of Bomber Command 1942–45.

He was an autocratic and single-minded leader, and was criticized for his policy of civilian-bombing of selected cities in Germany;

he authorized the fire-bombing raids on Dresden, in which more than 100,000 died.

Harrison Benjamin 1833–1901. 23rd president of the USA 1889–93, a Republican. He called the first Pan-American Conference, which led to the establishment of the Pan American Union, to improve inter-American cooperation, and develop commercial ties. In 1948 this became the ◊Organization of American States.

Harrison William Henry 1773–1841. 9th president of the US 1841. Elected 1840 as a Whig, he died one month after taking office. His political career was based largely on his reputation as an Indian fighter, and his campaign was constructed to give the impression that he was a man of the people with simple tastes and that the New Yorker, Martin ◊Van Buren, his opponent, was a 'foppish' sophisticate.

Harsha-Vardhana c. 590–647. supreme ruler (*sakala-Uttarapathanatha*) of N India from 606. Through a succession of military victories, he established a large pan-regional empire in N and central India, extending to Kashmir in the NW. It was connected by loose feudalistic tributary ties.

Originally chief of the Pushyabhutis, based in Thanesar near Delhi, he united his throne through a marriage alliance with the Maukharis, whose headquarters at Kanauj, in the upper Ganges valley, became his capital. A devout Buddhist, he was an enlightened and cultured ruler.

Hartford Convention in US history, a meeting of ◊Federalist party delegates from Dec 1814 to Jan 1815 (at the end of the ◊War of 1812) in Hartford, Connecticut. The meeting considered amendments to the US Constitution and the possibility of secession from the union in response to the adverse economic effects of the war on New England. The end of the war forestalled further action.

Hartington Spencer Compton Cavendish 1833–1908. 8th Duke of Devonshire, Marquess of Hartington. British politician, first leader of the Liberal Unionists 1886-1903. As war minister he opposed devolution for Ireland in cabinet and later led the revolt of the Liberal Unionists that defeated Gladstone's Irish Home Rule bill 1886. Hartington refused the premiership three times, 1880, 1886, and 1887, and led the opposition to the Irish Home Rule bill in the House of Lords 1893.

Hasdrubal Barca died 207 BC. Carthaginian general, son of Hamilcar Barca and younger brother of Hannibal. He remained in command in Spain when Hannibal invaded Italy during the Second Punic War and, after fighting there against Scipio until 208, marched to Hannibal's relief. He was defeated and killed in the Metaurus valley, NE Italy.

Hassan II 1929– . King of Morocco from 1961. From 1976 he undertook the occupation of Western Sahara when it was ceded by Spain.

Hastings Warren 1732–1818. British colonial administrator. A protégé of Lord Clive, who established British rule in India, Hastings carried out major reforms, and became governor of Bengal 1772 and governor general of India 1774. Impeached for corruption on his return to England 1785, he was acquitted 1795.

Hastings, Battle of battle 14 Oct 1066 at which William the Conqueror, Duke of Normandy, defeated Harold, King of England. The site is 10 km/6 mi inland from Hastings, at Senlac, Sussex; it is marked by Battle Abbey.

Having defeated an attempt by King Harald Hardrada of Norway at Stamford Bridge, Harold moved south with an army of 9,000 to counter the landing of the duke of Normandy at Pevensey Bay, Kent.

William, having laid a claim to the English throne, dominated the battle with archers supported by cavalry, breaking through ranks of infantry. Both sides suffered heavy losses but the death of Harold allowed William to conquer and become England's king.

Hatshepsut c. 1540–c. 1481 BC. Queen of Egypt during the 18th dynasty. She was the daughter of Thothmes I, with whom she ruled until the accession to the throne of her husband and half-brother Thothmes II. Throughout his reign real power lay with Hatshepsut, and she continued to rule after his death, as regent for her nephew Thothmes III. When she died or was forced to abdicate, Thothmes III defaced her monuments. The ruins of her temple at Deir el-Bahri survive.

Haughey Charles 1925– . Irish Fianna Fáil politician of Ulster descent. Dismissed 1970 from Jack Lynch's cabinet for alleged complicity in IRA gun-running, he was afterwards acquitted. He was prime minister 1979–81, March–Nov 1982, and 1986–92, when he was replaced by Albert Reynolds.

Havel Václav 1936– . Czech dramatist and politician, president of Czechoslovakia 1989-92 and of the Czech Republic from 1993. His plays include *Largo Desolato* 1985, about a dissident intellectual. Havel became widely known as a human-rights activist. He was imprisoned 1979-83 and again 1989 for his support of Charter 77, a human-rights manifesto. As president of Czechoslovakia he sought to preserve a united republic, but resigned in recognition of the breakup of the federation 1992.

I will not disappoint you, but will lead the country into free elections.

Václav Havel addressing the crowds on becoming president, 30 Dec 1989

Hawaii Pacific state of the USA. A Polynesian kingdom from the 6th century until 1893; Hawaii became a republic 1894; ceded itself to the USA 1898, and became a US territory 1900. Japan's air attack on Pearl Harbor 7 Dec 1941 crippled the US Pacific fleet and turned the territory into an armed camp, under martial law, for the remainder of the war. Hawaii became a state 1959.

Hawke Bob (Robert) 1929– . Australian Labor politician, prime minister 1983-91, on the right wing of the party. He was president of the Australian Council of Trade Unions 1970–80. He announced his retirement from politics 1992.

Hawkins John 1532–1595. English navigator, born in Plymouth. Treasurer to the navy 1573–89, he was knighted for his services as a commander against the Spanish Armada 1588.

Hawkins Richard *c.* 1562–1622. English navigator, son of John Hawkins. He held a command against the Spanish Armada 1588, was captured in an expedition against Spanish possessions 1593–94 and released 1602.

Hayden William (Bill) 1933– . Australian Labor politician. He was leader of the Australian Labor Party and of the opposition 1977–83, and minister of foreign affairs 1983. He was governor general 1989–96.

Hayes Rutherford Birchard 1822–1893. 19th president of the USA 1877-81, a Republican. Born in Ohio, he was a major general on the Union side in the Civil War. During his presidency federal troops (see ◊Reconstruction) were withdrawn from the Southern states and the Civil Service reformed.

Haymarket riot notorious episode in US labour history in Chicago's Haymarket Square 4 May 1886. A bomb was thrown at police dispersing a workers' demonstration organized to protest at police brutality against strikers at the nearby International Harvester plant. Seven police officers were killed and many people were wounded. Eight anarchists (mostly German-speaking) were convicted for the bombing, despite lack of evidence, and four of them were executed. Of the others, one committed suicide

and the other three were pardoned 1893 because the trial had been unjust. The affair was a serious setback for the labour movement, associating it in the public mind with anarchism.

Haywood William Dudley 1869–1928. US labour leader. One of the founders of the Industrial Workers of the World (IWW, 'Wobblies') 1905, Haywood was arrested for conspiracy to murder an antiunion politician. His acquittal in 1907 made him a labour hero. Arrested again for sedition during World War I, he spent his later years in exile in the Soviet Union.

Heath Edward (Richard George) 1916– . British Conservative politician, party leader 1965–75. As prime minister 1970–74 he took the UK into the European Community but was brought down by economic and industrial relations crises at home. He was replaced as party leader by Margaret Thatcher 1975, and became increasingly critical of her policies and her opposition to the UK's full participation in the EC. During and after John Major's administration, he continued his attacks on 'Eurosceptic's' within the party.

If politicians lived on praise and thanks, they'd be forced into some other line of business.

Edward Heath 1973

Hebrew member of the Semitic people who lived in Palestine at the time of the Old Testament and who traced their ancestry to ◊Abraham.

hegemony (Greek *hegemonia* 'authority') political dominance of one power over others in a group in which all are supposedly equal. The term was first used for the dominance of Athens over the other Greek city-states, later applied to Prussia within Germany, and, in more recent times, to the USA and the USSR with regard to the rest of the world.

Hegira (or Hijrah) flight from persecution of ◊Muhammad from Mecca to Medina in AD 622, marking the beginning of the Islamic era.

Heian in Japanese history, the period 794–1185, from the foundation of Kyoto as the new capital to the seizure of power by the Minamoto clan. The cutoff date may also be given as 1186, 1192, or 1200. The Heian period was the golden age of Japanese literature and of a highly refined culture at court.

Heike alternative name for ◊Taira, an ancient Japanese clan.

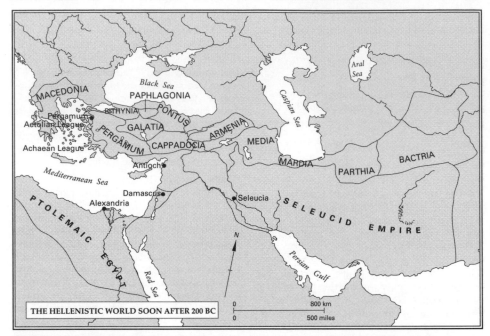

THE HELLENISTIC WORLD SOON AFTER 200 BC

0   800 km
0   500 miles

The Hellenistic world soon after 200 BC The Hellenistic world reflects the conquests of Alexander the Great, with Macedonian dynasties in Egypt and the Seleucid Empire. The Attalid dynasty in Pergamon was begun by a Seleucid officer. In Greece, the Aetolian and Achaean Leagues preserved some independence, but were early allies of Rome. The kingdoms on the northern frontier of the former Persian Empire remained independent, often with administrations influenced by Hellenistic models. The exception was the Celtic state of Galatia.

Hellenic period (from *Hellas*, Greek name for Greece) classical period of ancient Greek civilization, from the first Olympic Games 776 BC until the death of Alexander the Great 323 BC.

Hellenistic period period in Greek civilization from the death of Alexander 323 BC until the accession of the Roman emperor Augustus 27 BC. Alexandria in Egypt was the centre of culture and commerce during this period, and Greek culture spread throughout the Mediterranean region and the near East.

helot member of a class of serfs in ancient Messenia and Sparta who were probably the indigenous inhabitants. Their cruel treatment by the Spartans became proverbial.

Helsinki Conference international meeting 1975 at which 35 countries, including the USSR and the USA, attempted to reach agreement on cooperation in security, economics, science, technology, and human rights. This established the ◊Conference on Security and Cooperation in Europe (CSCE).

Helvetia region, corresponding to W Switzerland, occupied by the Celtic Helvetii 1st century BC–5th century AD. In 58 BC Caesar repulsed their invasion of southern Gaul at Bibracte (near Autun) and Helvetia became subject to Rome.

Hengist 5th century AD. Legendary leader, with his brother Horsa, of the Jutes, who originated in Jutland and settled in Kent about 450, the first Anglo-Saxon settlers in Britain.

Henlein Konrad 1898–1945. Sudeten-German leader of the Sudeten Nazi Party in Czechoslovakia, and closely allied with Hitler's Nazis. He was partly responsible for the destabilization of the Czechoslovak state 1938, which led to the ◊Munich Agreement and secession of the Sudetenland to Germany.

Henrietta Maria 1609–1669. Queen of England 1625–49. The daughter of Henry IV of France, she married Charles I of England 1625. By encouraging him to aid Roman Catholics and make himself an absolute ruler, she became highly unpopular and was exiled 1644–60. She returned to England at the Restoration but retired to France 1665.

Henry Patrick 1736–1799. US politician who in 1775 supported the arming of the Virginia militia against the British by a speech ending, 'Give me liberty or give me death!' He was governor of Virginia 1776–79 and 1784–86.

Henry assisted in the creation of the ◊Continental Congress, of which he was a member. He opposed ratification of the US Constitution on the grounds that it jeopardized states' rights. His influence, however, helped to ensure the passage of ten amendments to it, constituting the ◊Bill of Rights.

Henry eight kings of England:

Henry I 1068–1135. King of England from 1100. Youngest son of William I, he succeeded his brother William II. He won the support of the Saxons by granting them a charter and marrying a Saxon princess. An able administrator, he established a professional bureaucracy and a system of travelling judges. He was succeeded by Stephen.

Henry II 1133–1189. King of England from 1154, when he succeeded ◊Stephen. He was the son of ◊Matilda and Geoffrey of Anjou (1113–1151). He curbed the power of the barons, but his attempt to bring the church courts under control had to be abandoned after the murder of Thomas à ◊Becket. During his reign the English conquest of Ireland began. He was succeeded by his son Richard I.

Henry III 1207–1272. King of England from 1216, when he succeeded John, but he did not rule until 1227. His financial commitments to the papacy and his foreign favourites led to de ◊Montfort's revolt 1264. Henry was defeated at Lewes, Sussex, and imprisoned. He was restored to the throne after the royalist victory at Evesham 1265. He was succeeded by his son Edward I.

Henry IV (Bolingbroke) 1367–1413. King of England from 1399, the son of ◊John of Gaunt. In 1398 he was banished by ◊Richard II for political activity but returned 1399 to head a revolt and be accepted as king by Parliament. He was succeeded by his son Henry V.

He had difficulty in keeping the support of Parliament and the clergy, and had to deal with baronial unrest and ◊Glendower's rising in Wales. In order to win support he had to conciliate the church by a law for the burning of heretics, and to make many concessions to Parliament.

Henry V 1387–1422. King of England from 1413, son of Henry IV. Invading Normandy 1415 (during the Hundred Years' War), he captured Harfleur and defeated the French at ◊Agincourt. He invaded again 1417–19, capturing Rouen. His military victory forced the French into the Treaty of Troyes 1420, which gave Henry control of the French government. He married Catherine of Valois 1420 and gained recognition as heir to the French throne by his father-in-law Charles VI, but died before him. He was succeeded by his son Henry VI.

Henry VI 1421–1471. King of England from 1422, son of Henry V. He assumed royal power 1442 and sided with the party opposed to the continuation of the Hundred Years' War with France. After his marriage 1445, he was dominated by his wife, ◊Margaret of Anjou. The unpopularity of the government, especially after the loss of the English conquests in France, encouraged Richard, Duke of ◊York, to claim the throne, and though York was killed 1460, his son Edward IV proclaimed himself king 1461 (see Wars of the ◊Roses). Henry was captured 1465, temporarily restored 1470, but again imprisoned 1471 and then murdered.

Henry VII 1457–1509. King of England from 1485, son of Edmund Tudor, Earl of Richmond (*c.* 1430–1456), and a descendant of ◊John of Gaunt. He spent his early life in Brittany until 1485, when he landed in Britain to lead the rebellion against Richard III which ended with Richard's defeat and death at ◊Bosworth. By his marriage to Elizabeth of York 1486 he united the houses of York and Lancaster. Yorkist revolts continued until 1497, but Henry restored order after the Wars of the ◊Roses by the ◊Star Chamber and achieved independence from Parliament by amassing a private fortune through confiscations. He was succeeded by his son Henry VIII.

Henry VIII 1491–1547. King of England from 1509, when he succeeded his father Henry VII and married Catherine of Aragon, the widow of his brother. During the period 1513–29 Henry pursued an active foreign policy, largely under the guidance of his Lord Chancellor, Cardinal Wolsey who shared Henry's desire to make England stronger. Wolsey was replaced by Thomas More 1529 for failing to persuade the pope to grant Henry a divorce. After 1532 Henry broke with papal authority, proclaimed himself head of the church in England, dissolved the monasteries, and divorced Catherine. His subsequent wives were Anne Boleyn, Jane Seymour, Anne of Cleves, Catherine Howard, and Catherine Parr. He was succeeded by his son Edward VI.

He divorced Catherine 1533 because she was too old to give him an heir, and married Anne Boleyn, who was beheaded 1536, ostensibly for adultery. Henry's third wife, Jane Seymour, died 1537. He married Anne of Cleves 1540 in pursuance of Thomas Cromwell's policy of allying with the German Protestants, but rapidly abandoned this policy, divorced Anne, and beheaded Cromwell. His fifth wife, Catherine Howard, was beheaded 1542, and the following year he married Catherine Parr, who survived him. Henry never completely lost his popularity, but wars with France and Scotland towards the end of his reign sapped the economy, and in religion he not only executed Roman Catholics, including Thomas More, for refusing to acknowledge his supremacy in the church, but also Protestants who maintained his changes had not gone far enough.

Henry four kings of France:

Henry I 1005–1060. King of France from 1031. He spent much of his reign in conflict with ◊William I the Conqueror, then duke of Normandy.

Henry II 1519–1559. King of France from 1547. He captured the fortresses of Metz and Verdun from the Holy Roman emperor Charles V and Calais from the English. He was killed in a tournament.

In 1526 he was sent with his brother to Spain as a hostage, being returned when there was peace 1530. He married Catherine de' Medici 1533, and from then on was dominated by her, Diane de Poitiers, and Duke Montmorency. Three of his sons, Francis II, Charles IX, and Henry III, became kings of France.

Henry III 1551–1589. King of France from 1574. He fought both the ◊Huguenots (headed by his successor, Henry of Navarre) and the Catholic League (headed by the third Duke of Guise). Guise expelled Henry from Paris 1588 but was assassinated. Henry allied with the Huguenots under Henry of Navarre to besiege the city, but was assassinated by a monk.

Henry IV 1553–1610. King of France from 1589. Son of Antoine de Bourbon and Jeanne, Queen of Navarre, he was brought up as a Protestant and from 1576 led the ◊Huguenots. On his accession he settled the religious question by adopting Catholicism while tolerating Protestantism. He restored peace and strong government to France and brought back prosperity by measures for the promotion of industry and agriculture and the improvement of communications. He was assassinated by a Catholic extremist.

I want there to be no peasant in my kingdom so poor that he is unable to have a chicken in his pot every Sunday.
> **Henry IV** quoted in H de Péréfixe
> *Histoire de Henry le Grand*

Henry seven Holy Roman emperors:

Henry I *the Fowler* c. 876–936. King of Germany from 919, and duke of Saxony from 912.

He secured the frontiers of Saxony, ruled in harmony with its nobles, and extended German influence over the Danes, the Hungarians, and the Slavonic tribes. He was about to claim the imperial crown when he died.

Henry II *the Saint* 973–1024. King of Germany from 1002, Holy Roman emperor from 1014, when he recognized Benedict VIII as pope. He was canonized 1146.

Henry III *the Black* 1017–1056. King of Germany from 1028, Holy Roman emperor from 1039 (crowned 1046). He raised the empire to the height of its power, and extended its authority over Poland, Bohemia, and Hungary.

Henry IV 1050–1106. Holy Roman emperor from 1056, who was involved from 1075 in a struggle with the papacy. Excommunicated twice (1076 and 1080), Henry deposed Gregory and set up the antipope Clement III (died 1191) by whom he was crowned Holy Roman emperor 1084.

Henry V 1081–1125. Holy Roman emperor from 1106. He continued the struggle with the church until the settlement of the ◊investiture contest 1122.

Henry VI 1165–1197. Holy Roman emperor from 1190. As part of his plan for making the empire universal, he captured and imprisoned Richard I of England and compelled him to do homage.

Henry VII 1269–1313. Holy Roman emperor from 1308. He attempted unsuccessfully to revive the imperial supremacy in Italy.

Henry of Blois died 1171. Brother of King Stephen of England, he was bishop of Winchester from 1129, and Pope Innocent II's legate to England from 1139. While remaining loyal to Henry II, he tried to effect a compromise between ◊Becket and the king.

Henry the Lion 1129–1195. Duke of Bavaria 1156-80, duke of Saxony 1142-80, and duke of Lüneburg 1180-85. He was granted the Duchy of Bavaria by the Emperor Frederick Barbarossa. He founded Lübeck and Munich. In 1162 he married Matilda, daughter of Henry II of England. His refusal in 1176 to accompany Frederick Barbarossa to Italy led in 1180 to his being deprived of the duchies of Bavaria and Saxony. Henry led several military expeditions to conquer territory in the East.

Henry the Navigator 1394–1460. Portuguese prince, the fourth son of John I. He set up a school for navigators 1419 and under his patronage Portuguese sailors explored and colonized Madeira, the Cape Verde Islands, and the Azores; they sailed down the African coast almost to Sierra Leone.

heptarchy the seven Saxon kingdoms thought to have existed in England before AD 800: Northumbria, Mercia, East Anglia, Essex, Kent, Sussex, and Wessex. The term was coined by 16th-century historians.

Heraclius c. 575–641. Byzantine emperor from 610. His reign marked a turning point in the empire's fortunes. Of Armenian descent, he recaptured Armenia 622, and other provinces 622–28 from the Persians, but lost them to the Muslims 629–41.

heraldry insignia and symbols representing a person, family, or dynasty. Heraldry originated with simple symbols used on banners and shields for recognition in battle. By the 14th century, it had become a complex pictorial language with its own regulatory bodies (courts of chivalry), used by noble families, corporations, cities, and realms. The world's oldest heraldic court is the English College of Arms founded by Henry V; it was incorporated 1484 by Richard III.

Hereward *the Wake* 11th century. English leader of a revolt against the Normans 1070. His stronghold in the Isle of Ely was captured by William the Conqueror 1071. Hereward escaped, but his fate is unknown.

Herod *the Great* 74–4 BC. King of the Roman province of Judaea, S Palestine, from 40 BC. With the aid of Mark Antony, he established his government in Jerusalem 37 BC. He rebuilt the Temple in Jerusalem, but his Hellenizing tendencies made him suspect to orthodox Jewry. His last years were a reign of terror, and in the New Testament Matthew alleges that he ordered the slaughter of all the infants in Bethlehem to ensure the death of Jesus, whom he foresaw as a rival. He was the father of Herod Antipas.

Herod Agrippa I 10 BC–AD 44. Ruler of Palestine from AD 41. His real name was Marcus Julius Agrippa, erroneously called 'Herod' in the Bible. Grandson of Herod the Great, he was made tetrarch (governor) of Palestine by the Roman emperor Caligula and king by Emperor Claudius AD 41. He put the apostle James to death and imprisoned the apostle Peter. His son was Herod Agrippa II.

Herod Agrippa II c. 40–93 AD. King of Chalcis (now S Lebanon), son of Herod Agrippa I. He was appointed by the Roman emperor Claudius about AD 50, and in AD 60 tried the apostle Paul. He helped the Roman emperor Titus take and sack Jerusalem AD 70, then went to Rome, where he died.

Herod Antipas 21 BC–AD 39. Tetrarch (governor) of the Roman province of Galilee, N Palestine, 4 BC–AD 9, son of Herod the Great. He divorced his wife to marry his niece Herodias, and was responsible for the death of John the Baptist. Jesus was brought before him on Pontius Pilate's discovery that he was a Galilean and hence of Herod's jurisdiction, but Herod returned him without giving any verdict. In AD 38 Herod Antipas went to Rome to try to persuade Emperor Caligula to give him the title of king, but was instead banished.

Herriot Edouard 1872–1957. French Radical socialist politician. An opponent of Poincaré, who as prime minister carried out the French occupation of the Ruhr, Germany, he was briefly prime minister 1924–25, 1926, and 1932. As president of the chamber of deputies 1940, he opposed the policies of the right-wing Vichy government and was arrested and later taken to Germany; he was released 1945 by the Soviets.

Hertzog James Barry Munnik 1866–1942. South African politician, prime minister 1924–39, founder of the Nationalist Party 1913 (the United South African National Party from 1933). He opposed South Africa's entry into both world wars.

Herzl Theodor 1860–1904. Austrian founder of the *Zionist* movement. He was born in Budapest and became a successful playwright and journalist, mainly in Vienna. The ◊Dreyfus case convinced him that the only solution to the problem of anti-Semitism was the resettlement of the Jews in a state of their own. His book *Jewish State* 1896 launched political ◊Zionism, and he became the first president of the World Zionist Organization 1897.

Hess (Walter Richard) Rudolf 1894–1987. German Nazi leader. Imprisoned with Hitler 1924–25, he became his private secretary, taking down *Mein Kampf* from his dictation. In 1932 he was appointed deputy *Führer* to Hitler. On 10 May 1941 he landed by air in the UK with his own compromise peace proposals and was held a prisoner of war until 1945, when he was tried at Nuremberg as a war criminal and sentenced to life imprisonment. He died in ◊Spandau prison, Berlin.

He was effectively in charge of the Nazi party organization until his flight 1941. For the last years of his life he was the only prisoner left in Spandau.

Heydrich Reinhard 1904–1942. German Nazi, head of the party's security service and Heinrich ◊Himmler's deputy. He was instrumental in organizing the ◊final solution, the policy of genocide used against Jews and others. 'Protector' of Bohemia and Moravia from 1941, he was ambushed and killed the following year by three members of the Czechoslovak forces in Britain, who had landed by parachute. Reprisals followed, including several hundred executions and the massacre in ◊Lidice.

Hezekiah in the Old Testament, king of Judah from 719 BC. Against the advice of the prophet Isaiah he rebelled against Assyrian suzerainty in alliance with Egypt, but was defeated by ◊Sennacherib and had to pay out large amounts in indemnities. He carried out religious reforms

Hiawatha 16th-century North American Indian teacher and Onondaga chieftain. He is said to have welded the Five Nations (later joined by a sixth) of the ◊Iroquois into the league of the *Long House*, as the confederacy was known in what is now upper New York State.

Hickok 'Wild Bill' (James Butler) 1837–1876. US pioneer and law enforcer, a legendary figure in the West. In the Civil War he was a sharpshooter and scout for the Union army. He then served as marshal in Kansas, killing as many as 27 people. He was a prodigious gambler and was fatally shot from behind while playing poker in Deadwood, South Dakota.

Hidalgo y Costilla Miguel 1753–1811. Catholic priest, known as 'the Father of Mexican Independence'. He led a violent social protest 1810 against Spanish rule in which his forces swelled to 100,000. During the unrest the Indian population threatened Creoles as well as Spaniards, provoking a counter-revolution by the forces of law and order. Hidalgo attempted to form a separatist government but failed, losing the key battle of Calderón 1811. He was captured and shot by Creole-Spanish forces.

hieroglyphic Egyptian writing system of the mid-4th millennium BC–3rd century AD, which combines picture signs with those indicating letters. The direction of writing is normally from right to left, the signs facing the beginning of the line. It was deciphered 1822 by the French Egyptologist J F Champollion (1790–1832) with the aid of the ◊*Rosetta Stone*, which has the same inscription carved in hieroglyphic, demotic, and Greek.

Hieron died 476 BC. Tyrant of Syracuse after his brother ◊Gelon. He consolidated Syracusan influence in Sicily and extended it to the Italian mainland, defeating the Etruscans at sea. His wealth and prestige made Syracuse second only to Athens as a Greek cultural centre.

Highland Clearances forced removal of tenants from large estates in Scotland during the early 19th century, as landowners 'improved' their estates by switching from arable to sheep farming. It led ultimately to widespread emigration to North America.

Hildebrand name given to ◊Gregory VII c. 1023–1085.

Hill Joe c. 1872–1915. Swedish-born US labour organizer. A member of the Industrial Workers of the World (IWW, 'Wobblies'), he was convicted of murder on circumstantial evidence in Salt Lake City, Utah, 1914. Despite calls by President Wilson and the Swedish government for a re-trial, Hill was executed 1915, becoming a martyr for the labour movement.

Hillsborough Agreement another name for the ◊Anglo-Irish Agreement 1985.

Himera Greek city on the north coast of Sicily, founded c. 649 BC by exiles from Syracuse. In 483 BC Theron of Acragas expelled the ruling tyrant, Terillus, who then looked for support from Carthage. In the *Battle of Himera* 480 BC, Theron and his son-in-law ◊Gelon of Syracuse defeated Terillus and the Carthaginian army. Himera was finally destroyed 409 BC by the Carthaginians, who built another town nearby shortly afterwards.

Himmler Heinrich 1900–1945. German Nazi leader, head of the ◊SS elite corps from 1929, the police and the ◊Gestapo secret police from 1936, and supervisor of the extermination of the Jews in E Europe. During World War II he replaced Goering as Hitler's second-in-command. He was captured May 1945 and committed suicide.

Born in Munich, he joined the Nazi Party in 1925 and became chief of the Bavarian police 1933. His accumulation of offices meant he had command of all German police forces by 1936, which made him one of the most powerful people in Germany. In April 1945 he made a proposal to the Allies that Germany should surrender to the USA and Britain but not to the USSR, which was rejected.

Hindenburg Paul Ludwig Hans von Beneckendorf und Hindenburg 1847–1934. German field marshal and right-wing politician. During World War I he was supreme commander and, with Ludendorff, practically directed Germany's policy until the end of the war. He was president of Germany 1925–33.

Hindenburg Line German western line of World War I fortifications built 1916–17.

Hinduism (Hindu *sanatana dharma* 'eternal tradition') religion originating in N India about 4,000 years ago, which is superficially and in some of its forms polytheistic, but has a concept of the supreme spirit, Brahman, above the many divine manifestations. These include the triad of chief gods (the Trimurti): Brahma, Vishnu, and Siva (creator, preserver, and destroyer). Central to Hinduism are the beliefs in reincarnation and karma (destiny); the oldest scriptures are the *Vedas*. Temple worship is almost universally observed and there are many festivals. There are over 805 million Hindus worldwide. Women are not regarded as the equals of men but should be treated with kindness and respect. Muslim influence in N India led to the veiling of women and the restriction of their movements from about the end of the 12th century.

roots Hindu beliefs originated in the Indus Valley civilization about 4,500 years ago. Much of the tradition that is now associated with Hinduism stems from the ritual and religion of the Aryans who invaded N India about 3,000 years ago.

scriptures The *Veda* collection of hymns, compiled by the Aryans, was followed by the philosophical *Upanishads*, centring on the doctrine of Brahman, and the epics *Rāmāyana* and *Mahābhārata* (which includes the *Bhagavad-Gītā*), all from before the Christian era.

Hirohito (regnal era name *Shōwa*) 1901–1989. Emperor of Japan from 1926, when he succeeded his father Taishō (Yoshihito). After the defeat of Japan in World War II 1945, he was made a figurehead monarch by the US-backed 1946 constitution. He is believed to have played a reluctant role in General ◊Tōjō's prewar expansion plans. He was succeeded by his son Akihito (1933–   ).

We have resolved to endure the unendurable and suffer what is insufferable.

Emperor Hirohito on accepting the Allied terms of surrender, broadcasting to the nation
Aug 1945

Hiroshima industrial city and port on the south coast of Honshu Island, Japan, destroyed by the first wartime use of an atomic bomb 6 Aug 1945. More than 10 sq km/4 sq mi were obliterated, with very heavy damage outside that area. Casualties totalled at least 137,000 out of a population of 343,000: 78,150 were found dead, others died later. The city has largely been rebuilt since the war.

Hispania Roman provinces of Spain and Portugal. The republican provinces were Hispania Citerior ('Nearer', the Ebro region), and Ulterior ('Farther', the Guadalquivir region). Under the empire the peninsula was divided into three administrative areas: Lusitania in the west, Baetica in the south, and Tarraconensis. The Roman emperors Trajan and Hadrian came from Baetica.

hispanidad set of values and attitudes emphasizing the common bonds (blood, language, and culture) between Spain and Spanish-speaking nations.

It was championed by Mexican philosopher and educationalist José Vasconcelos (1881–1958) who stressed the significance to Latin America of Catholicism and the region's Hispanic past.

Hiss Alger 1904–96. US diplomat and liberal Democrat, a former State Department official, imprisoned 1950 for perjury when he denied having been a Soviet spy. There are doubts about the justice of Hiss's conviction.

historical materialism the application of the principles of ◊dialectical materialism to history and sociology. This decrees that the social, political, and cultural superstructure of a society is determined by its economic base and that developments are therefore governed by laws with no room for the influence of individuals. In this theory, change occurs through the meeting of opposing forces (thesis and antithesis) which leads to the production of a higher force (synthesis).

history record of the events of human societies. The earliest surviving historical records are the inscriptions denoting the achievements of Egyptian and Babylonian kings. As a literary form in the Western world, historical writing or *historiography* began with the Greek Herodotus in the 5th century BC, who was first to pass beyond the limits of a purely national outlook.

A generation later, Thucydides brought to history a strong sense of the political and military ambitions of his native Athens. His close account of the ◊Peloponnesian War was continued by ◊Xenophon. Later Greek history and Roman history tended towards rhetoric; Sallust tried to recreate the style of Thucydides, but Livy wrote an Augustan history of his city and its conquests, while Tacitus expressed his cynicism about the imperial dynasty. Medieval history was dominated by a religious philosophy sustained by the Christian church. English chroniclers of this period are Bede, William of Malmesbury, and Matthew Paris. France produced great chroniclers of contemporary events in Froissart and Comines. The Renaissance revived historical writing and the study of history both by restoring classical models and by creating the science of textual criticism. A product of the new secular spirit was Machiavelli's *History of Florence* 1520-23. This critical approach continued into the 17th century but the 18th century Enlightenment disposed of the attempt to explain history in theological terms, and an interpretive masterpiece was produced by Edward Gibbon, *The Decline and Fall of the Roman Empire* 1776-88. An attempt to formulate a *historical method* and a philosophy of history, that of the Italian Giovanni Vico, remained almost unknown until the 19th century. Romanticism left its mark on 19th-century historical writing in the tendency to exalt the contribution of the individual 'hero', and in the introduction of a more colourful and dramatic style and treatment, variously illustrated in the works of the French historian Jules Michelet (1798-1874), and the British writers Carlyle and Macaulay. During the 20th century the study of history has been revolutionized, partly through the contributions of other disciplines, such as the sciences and anthropology. The deciphering of the Egyptian and Babylonian inscriptions was of great importance. Researchers and archaeologists have traced developments in prehistory, and have revealed forgotten civilizations such as that of Crete. Anthropological studies of primitive society and religion, which began with James Frazer's *Golden Bough* 1890, have attempted to analyse the bases of later forms of social organization and belief. The changes brought about by the Industrial Revolution and the accompanying perception of economics as a science forced historians to turn their attention to economic questions. Marx's attempt to find in economic development the most significant, although not the only, determining factor in social change, has influenced many historians. History from the point of view of ordinary people is now recognized as an important element in historical study. Associated with this is the collection of spoken records known as *oral history*. A comparative study of civilizations is offered in A J Toynbee's *Study of History* 1934–54, and on a smaller scale by J M Roberts's *History of the World* 1992. Contemporary historians make a distinction between historical evidence or records, historical writing, and historical method or approaches to the study of history. The study of historical method is also known as *historiography*.

Hitler Adolf 1889–1945. German dictator, born in Austria. He was *Führer* (leader) of the Nazi Party from 1921 and author of *Mein Kampf/ My Struggle* 1925–27. As chancellor of Germany from 1933 and head of state from 1934, he created a dictatorship by playing party and state institutions against each other and continually creating new offices and appointments. His position was not seriously challenged until the 'Bomb Plot' 20 July 1944 (see ◊July Plot) to assassinate him. In foreign affairs, he reoccupied the Rhineland and formed an alliance with the Italian Fascist Mussolini 1936, annexed Austria 1938, and occupied the Sudetenland under the ◊Munich Agreement. The rest of Czechoslovakia was annexed March 1939. The Hitler–Stalin pact was followed in Sept by the invasion of Poland and the declaration of war by Britain and France (see ◊World War II). He committed suicide as Berlin fell.

Born at Braunau-am-Inn, the son of a customs official, he spent his early years in poverty in Vienna and Munich. After serving as a volunteer in the German army during World War I, he was employed as a spy by the military authorities in Munich and in 1919 joined, in this capacity, the German Workers' Party. By 1921 he had assumed its leadership, renamed it the National Socialist German Workers' Party (Nazi Party for short), and provided it with a programme that mixed nationalism with ◊anti-Semitism. Having led an unsuccessful uprising in Munich 1923, he was sentenced to nine months' imprisonment during which he wrote his political testament, *Mein Kampf*. The party did not achieve national importance until the elections of 1930; by 1932, although Field Marshal Hindenburg defeated Hitler in the presidential elections, it formed the largest group in the Reichstag (parliament). As the result of an intrigue directed by Chancellor Franz von Papen, Hitler became chancellor in a Nazi–Nationalist coalition 30 Jan 1933. The opposition was rapidly suppressed, the Nationalists removed from the government, and the Nazis declared the only legal party. In 1934 Hitler succeeded Hindenburg as head of state. Meanwhile, the drive to war began; Germany left the League of Nations, conscription was reintroduced, and in 1936 the Rhineland was reoccupied. Hitler and Mussolini, who were already both involved in Spain, formed an alliance (the Axis) 1936, joined by Japan 1940. Hitler conducted the war in a ruthless but idiosyncratic way, took and ruled most of the neighbouring countries with repressive occupation forces, and had millions of Slavs, Jews, Romanies, homosexuals, and political enemies killed in concentration camps and massacres. He narrowly escaped death 1944 from a bomb explosion at a staff meeting, prepared by high-ranking officers. On 29 April 1945, when

Berlin was largely in Soviet hands, he married his mistress Eva Braun in his bunker under the chancellery building and on the following day committed suicide with her.

The broad mass of a nation ... will more easily fall victim to a big lie than a small one.

Adolf Hitler *Mein Kampf* 1927

Hitler–Stalin pact nonaggression treaty signed by Germany and the USSR 23 Aug 1939. Under the terms of the treaty both countries agreed to remain neutral and to refrain from acts of aggression against each other if either went to war. Secret clauses allowed for the partition of Poland – Hitler was to acquire western Poland, Stalin the eastern part. On 1 Sept 1939 Hitler invaded Poland. The pact ended when Hitler invaded Russia on 22 June 1941. See also ◊World War II.

Hittite member of any of a succession of peoples who inhabited Anatolia and N Syria from the 3rd millennium to the 1st millennium BC. The city of Hattusas (now Boğazköy in central Turkey) became the capital of a strong kingdom which overthrew the Babylonian Empire. After a period of eclipse the *Hittite New Empire* became a great power (about 1400–1200 BC), which successfully waged war with Egypt. The Hittite language is an Indo-European language.

The original Hittites, a people of Armenian/Anatolian type, inhabited a number of city-states in E Anatolia, one of which, Hatti, gained supremacy over the others. An Indo-European people invaded the country about 2000 BC, made themselves the ruling class, and intermarried with the original inhabitants. The Hittites developed advanced military, political, and legal systems. The New Empire concluded a peace treaty with Egypt 1269 BC, but was eventually overthrown by the Sea Peoples. Small Hittite states then arose in N Syria, the most important of which was ◊Carchemish; these were conquered by the Assyrians in the 8th century BC. Carchemish was conquered 717. The Hittites used a cuneiform script, modelled on the Babylonian, for ordinary purposes, and a hieroglyphic script for inscriptions on monuments. The Hittite royal archives were discovered at Hattusas 1906–07 and deciphered 1915.

Hoare–Laval Pact plan for a peaceful settlement to the Italian invasion of Ethiopia in Oct 1935. It was devised by Samuel Hoare (1880–1959), British foreign secretary, and Pierre ◊Laval, French premier, at the request of the ◊League of Nations. Realizing no European country was willing to go to war over Ethiopia, Hoare and Laval proposed official recognition of Italian claims. Public outcry in Britain against the pact's seeming approval of Italian aggression was so great that the pact   had to be disowned and Hoare was forced to resign.

Ho Chi Minh adopted name of Nguyen Tat Thanh 1890–1969. North Vietnamese communist politician, premier and president 1954–69. Having trained in Moscow shortly after the Russian Revolution, he headed the communist ◊Vietminh from 1941 and fought against the French during the ◊Indochina War 1946–54, becoming president and prime minister of the republic at the armistice. Aided by the communist bloc, he did much to develop industrial potential. He relinquished the premiership 1955, but continued as president. In the years before his death, Ho successfully led his country's fight against US-aided South Vietnam in the ◊Vietnam War 1954–75.

Ho Chi Minh Trails North Vietnamese troop and supply routes to South Vietnam via Laos during the ◊Vietnam War 1954-75. In an unsuccessful attempt to disrupt the Trail between 1964 and 1973, the USA dropped 2 million tonnes of bombs in Laos, a country with which it was not at war.

Hodza Milan 1878–1944. Czechoslovak politician, prime minister 1936–38. He and President Beneš were forced to agree to the secession of the Sudeten areas of Czechoslovakia to Germany before resigning 22 Sept 1938 (see ◊Munich Agreement).

Hoess Rudolf 1900–1947. German commandant of Auschwitz concentration camp 1940–43. Under his control, more than 2.5 million people were exterminated. Arrested by Allied military police in 1946, he was handed over to the Polish authorities, who tried and executed him in 1947.

An ego is just imagination. And if a man doesn't have imagination he'll be working for someone else for the rest of his life.

Jimmy Hoffa in *Esquire*

Hoffa Jimmy (James Riddle) 1913–*c.* 1975. US labour leader, president of the International Brotherhood of Teamsters (transport workers) from 1957. He was jailed 1967–71 for attempted bribery of a federal court jury after he was charged with corruption. He was released by President Nixon with the stipulation that he did not engage in union activities, but was evidently attempting to reassert influence when he disappeared. He is generally believed to have been murdered.

Hoffman Abbie (Abbot) 1936–1989. US left-wing political activist, founder of the Yippies (Youth International Party), a political offshoot of the hippies. He was a member of the Chicago Seven, a radical group tried for attempting to disrupt the 1968 Democratic Convention.

Hohenlinden, Battle of in the French ◊Revolutionary Wars, a defeat of the Austrians by the French Dec 1800. Coming after the defeat at ◊Marengo, it led the Austrians to make peace at the Treaty of Lunéville 1801.

Hohenstaufen German family of princes, several members of which were Holy Roman emperors 1138–1208 and 1214–54. They were the first German emperors to make use of associations with Roman law and tradition to aggrandize their office, and included Conrad III; Frederick I (Barbarossa), the first to use the title Holy Roman emperor (previously the title Roman emperor was used); Henry VI; and Frederick II.

The last of the line, Conradin, was executed 1268 with the approval of Pope Clement IV while attempting to gain his Sicilian inheritance. They were supported by the Ghibellines (see ◊Guelph and Ghibelline), who took their name from the family's castle of Waiblingen.

Hohenzollern German family, originating in Württemberg, the main branch of which held the titles of ◊elector of Brandenburg from 1415, king of Prussia from 1701, and German emperor from 1871. The last emperor, Wilhelm II, was dethroned 1918 after the disastrous course of World War I. Another branch of the family were kings of Romania 1881–1947.

Hōjō family regents (*shikken*) and effective rulers of Japan 1203–1333, during most of the Kamakura (◊Minamoto) shogunate. Among its members were Hōjō Yasutoki (regent 1224–42), Hōjō Tokiyori (regent 1245–56), and Hōjō Shigetoki (1198–1261), a high official whose writings on politics were influential.

The Hōjō were related by marriage to Minamoto Yoritomo, the first shogun, and under his successors they held the real power, turning the shoguns into figureheads. The Hōjō ascendancy was confirmed by the Jōkyū War of 1221, when they put down a rebellion led by retired emperor Go-Toba (1180–1239). The Hōjō were also among the last to hold out against the unification of Japan in the 16th century under Toyotomi Hideyoshi. Their cas-

tle of Odawara blocked his access to the Kantō area of central Honshu until 1590 when their ally ◊Tokugawa Ieyasu, to whom they were related by marriage, sided with Hideyoshi and the castle capitulated after a siege.

Holland Sidney George 1893–1961. New Zealand politician, leader of the National Party 1940–57 and prime minister 1949–57.

Holocaust, the the annihilation of more than 16 million people by the Hitler regime 1933–45 in the numerous extermination and ◊concentration camps, most notably Auschwitz, Sobibor, Treblinka, and Maidanek in Poland, and Belsen, Buchenwald, and Dachau in Germany. Of the victims who died during imprisonment or were exterminated, more than 6 million were Jews (over 67% of European Jewry); 10 million were Ukrainian, Polish, and Russian civilians and prisoners of war, Romanies, socialists, homosexuals, and others (labelled 'defectives'). Victims were variously starved, tortured, experimented on, and worked to death. Many thousands were executed in gas chambers, shot, or hanged. It was euphemistically termed the ◊final solution.

Holstein Friedrich von 1839–1909. German diplomat and foreign-affairs expert. He refused the post of foreign minister, but played a key role in German diplomacy from the 1880s until his death.

Holt Harold Edward 1908–1967. Australian Liberal politician, prime minister 1966–67. His brief prime ministership was dominated by the Vietnam War, to which he committed increased Australian troops.

He was minister of labour 1940–41 and 1949–58, and federal treasurer 1958–66, when he succeeded Menzies as prime minister. He was also minister for immigration 1949–56, during which time he made the first modifications to the ◊White Australia Policy, relaxing some restrictions on Asian immigration.

Holy Alliance 'Christian Union of Charity, Peace, and Love' initiated by Alexander I of Russia 1815 and signed by every crowned head in Europe. The alliance became associated with Russian attempts to preserve autocratic monarchies at any price, and served as an excuse to meddle in the internal affairs of other states.

Holyoake Keith Jacka 1904–1983. New Zealand National Party politician, prime minister 1957 (for two months) and 1960–72 during which time he was also foreign minister.

Holy Roman Empire empire of ◊Charlemagne and his successors, and the German Empire 962–1806, both being regarded as the Christian

The Holocaust 1933–45

1933 Jan	Adolf Hitler appointed chancellor of Germany. German Jewish population approximately 500,000.	**1940 April**	Heinrich Himmler ordered the establishment of a concentration camp at Auschwitz.
April	Official boycott of Jewish shops and businesses.	**June**	Commissar Order specified the execution of political commissars attached to Red Army units captured by German forces. Soviet Union invaded, and mass executions of Soviet prisoners of war, civilians and Jews began.
1935 Aug	Sporadic outbursts of anti-Semitic violence in several German cities.		
Sept	Reich Citizenship Law (Nuremberg Law) defined the term 'Jew' and separated Jews from other Germans.	**July**	Hermann Goering issued first order for the liquidation of European Jews.
1936	Olympic Games brought temporary halt to overt measures against Jews.	**Oct–Nov**	First deportations of Jews from Germany. Mass killings of Jews in S Russia.
1938 March	Austrian annexation increased Jewish population of the Greater German Reich by about 200,000.	**1942 Jan**	Mass killings of gypsies from Lodz (Poland) ghetto.
June	Arbitrary arrests of Jews, who were sent to concentration camps.	**July–Sept**	First phase of mass deportations from occupied W Europe to extermination camps in E Poland.
Oct	17,000 East European Jews deported to Poland after its government refused to renew their passports.	**1943 April**	Uprising in Warsaw ghetto. Jewish resistance crushed.
Nov	*Reichskristallnacht* (Crystal Night), anti-Jewish attacks on synagogues and property, in which 91 died and 26,000 were removed to concentration camps.	**June**	Himmler ordered liquidation of all Polish ghettoes.
		Aug–Dec	Deportation of remaining Russian Jews to extermination camps.
Dec	Decree for the compulsory 'Aryanization' of all Jewish businesses.	**1944 April**	Deportation of Greek and Hungarian Jews to extermination camps.
1939 Jan	Special identity cards introduced for Jews, who all had to adopt the name Israel or Sara.	**1945 Jan**	Auschwitz closed.
Oct	Deportations of Jews to ghettoes in the *Generalgouvernement* of Poland.	**May**	Last concentration camp at Mauthausen, Austria, liberated by Allied forces.

(hence 'holy') revival of the Roman Empire. At its height it comprised much of western and central Europe. See ◊Germany, history and ◊Habsburg. *See chronology.*

home front the organized sectors of domestic activity in wartime, mainly associated with World Wars I and II. Features of the UK home front in World War II included the organization of the black-out, evacuation, air-raid shelters, the Home Guard, rationing, and distribution of gas masks. With many men on active military service, women were called upon to carry out jobs previously undertaken only by men.

Home Guard unpaid force formed in Britain May 1940 to repel the expected German invasion, and known until July 1940 as the Local Defence Volunteers.

It consisted of men aged 17–65 who had not been called up, formed part of the armed forces of the crown, and was subject to military law. Over 2 million strong in 1944, it was disbanded 31 Dec 1945, but revived 1951, then placed on a reserve basis 1955, and ceased activities 1957.

homeland or *Bantustan* before 1980, name for the ◊Black National States in the Republic of South Africa.

Homelands Policy South Africa's apartheid policy which set aside ◊Black National States for black Africans.

Home Rule, Irish movement to repeal the Act of ◊Union 1801 that joined Ireland to Britain and to establish an Irish parliament responsible for internal affairs. In 1870 Isaac Butt (1813–1879) formed the Home Rule Association and the movement was led in Parliament from 1880 by Charles ◊Parnell. After 1918 the demand for an independent Irish republic replaced that for home rule.

Gladstone's Home Rule bills 1886 and 1893 were both defeated. A third bill was introduced by the Liberals in 1912, which aroused opposition in Ireland where the Protestant minority in Ulster feared domination by the Catholic majority. Ireland appeared on the brink of civil war but the outbreak of World War I rendered further consideration of Home Rule inopportune. In 1920 the Government of Ireland Act

The Holy Roman Empire

800	Charlemagne crowned Roman emperor in Rome by Pope Leo III.
814	Charlemagne died, succeeded by Louis I (the Pious).
840–43	Civil War culminated in division of Empire between Louis I's sons. Charles got France, Louis got Germany, and Lothar I took Lotharingia and Italy together with the title of emperor.
933	Henry I (the Fowler) defeated the Magyars at Unstrut.
955	Magyars finally beaten by Otto I on the River Lech.
962	Otto I crowned emperor of the Holy Roman Empire of the German nation by Pope John XII.
1046	Henry III reformed papacy at Synod of Sutri.
1059	Selection of pope transferred from emperor to college of cardinals.
1075–1122	War between papacy and empire over (lay) investiture, concluded by the Compromise of Worms.
1077	Henry IV submitted to Pope Gregory VII at Canossa, Italy.
1125	Elective principle for selection of emperors established with accession of Lothar II.
1138	Hohenstaufen dynasty of emperors began with Conrad III.
1158	Frederick I (Barbarossa) began wars against Lombard cities, which were ended by the Peace of Constance 1183
1245	Frederick II deposed by Pope Innocent IV at Council of Lyons.
1268	Last Hohenstaufen prince, Conradin, executed after Battle of Tagliacozzo.
1273	Rudolf I (of Habsburg) became emperor.
1278	Rudolf took Austria from the Bohemians at the Battle of Marchfield.
1356	Charles IV established constitution of the Holy Roman Empire by Golden Bull.
1419–36	(Hussite) Wars against Bohemia ended with compact of Iglau.
1448	Turks began incursions into SE Europe after the Battle of Kossovo.
1495	Diet of Worms failed to introduce effective reforms within the empire.
1519	Charles I of Spain became Emperor Charles V, the last to be crowned by the pope.
1526	Defeat at Battle of Mohacs led to Turkish siege of Vienna 1529.
1530	Rejection of confession of Augsburg led to formation of (Protestant) League of Schmalkalden.
1551	Counter-Reformation instituted in the empire.
1555	Religious settlement of the empire by Peace of Augsburg, allowing freedom of conscience to Catholic and Lutheran princes.
1558	Abdication by Charles V led to division of his territories. Ferdinand became ruler of Habsburg Austrian territories and Holy Roman Emperor, a title held from now on by Austrian Habsburg rulers.
1618	Defenestration of Prague and the beginning of the Thirty Years' War.
1625	Wallenstein became head of imperial forces. He was dismissed 1630.
1632	Battle of Lutzen saw defeat of Wallenstein and death of Gustavus Adolphus of Sweden.
1648	Thirty Years' War ended by the Peace of Westphalia.
1683	Turks finally driven from Vienna.
1701–14	War of Spanish Succession, ended by Treaties of Utrecht 1713 and Rastatt 1714.
1806	Emperor Francis II renounced the imperial crown. Holy Roman Empire abolished by Napoleon.

introduced separate parliaments in the North and South and led to the treaty 1921 that established the Irish Free State.

Home Rule League demand for Indian home rule, established Sept 1916. The Indian demand for home rule was inspired by the unsuccessful ◊Easter rising in Ireland the previous April. It was launched by theosophist and educationalist Annie Besant, who received support from the leading Indian nationalist Bal Gangadhar Tilak (1856–1920), and was briefly interned in Madras 1917. The organization faded after the introduction of the India Act 1919 and the initiation of Mahatma ◊Gandhi's non-cooperation campaign.

Homestead Act in US history, an act of Congress 1862 to encourage settlement of land in the west by offering 65-hectare/160-acre plots cheaply or even free to those willing to cultivate and improve the land for a stipulated amount of time. By 1900 about 32 million hectares/80 million acres had been distributed. Homestead lands are available to this day.

Honduras country in Central America, bounded N by the Caribbean Sea, SE by Nicaragua, S by the Pacific Ocean, SW by El Salvador, and W and NW by Guatemala.

history Originally part of the ◊Maya civilization, the area was reached by Christopher Columbus 1502, and was colonized by Spain from 1526. Becoming independent from Spain 1821, Honduras was part of the ◊United Provinces of Central America until 1840, when it achieved full independence.

independence During the first 30 years after independence, power lay with the cattle barons. Violence and banditry prevailed in the countryside. In 1876, the Liberal Marco Aurelio Soto gained power and imposed order on Honduras. During his presidency, 1876–83, warfare ceased. He introduced the telegraph and supported road building.

After 1900 the Honduran economy became increasingly dependent on the export of bananas. US companies established huge banana plantations. By 1930, through the efforts of the United Fruit company and the Standard Fruit company, Honduras had become the world's leading exporter of bananas. From 1939 to 1949 it was a dictatorship under the leader of the National Party (PN).

civilian rule The government changed in a series of military coups, until the return of civilian rule 1980. The army, however, still controlled security and was able to veto cabinet appointments, and although the 1981 general election was won by the Liberal Party of Honduras (PLH) and its leader, Dr Roberto Suazo, became president, power remained in the hands of General Gustavo Alvarez, the commander in chief of the army. In 1982 Alvarez secured an amendment to the constitution, reducing government control over the armed forces, and was virtually in charge of foreign policy, agreeing 1983 to the establishment of US military bases in the country. The US Central Intelligence Agency was also active in assisting Nicaraguan counter-revolutionary rebels ('Contras') based in Honduras.

tensions with Nicaragua In 1984 Alvarez was ousted by a group of junior officers and the country's close relationship with the USA came under review. In the same year divisions arose in the PLH over selection of presidential candidates and in 1985 the electoral law was changed. Suazo was not eligible for the 1985 presidential elections, and the main PLH candidate was José Azcona. Although the PN nominee won most votes, the revised constitution made Azcona the eventual winner. The presence of Contras on Honduran territory provoked tensions with Nicaragua, which filed a suit against Honduras in the International Court of Justice. The Sandinista government agreed to drop the suit if Contra bases were dismantled and the fighters demobilized, in keeping with the regional peace plan adopted Feb

1989. Thus the presence of the rebels became a distinct political liability for Honduras. In the Nov 1989 presidential election, the PN candidate, Rafael Callejas, was elected; he was inaugurated 1990.

The century-old border dispute with El Salvador, involving 440sq km/170 sq mi, was settled Sept 1992 awarding two-thirds of the territory in question to Honduras. As a result Honduras acquired the region at the delta of the Goascoran River and about four-fifths of two areas along the Negro-Quiagara and the Sazalapa Rivers.

Honecker Erich 1912–94. German communist politician, in power 1973-89, elected chair of the council of state (head of state) 1976. He governed in an outwardly austere and efficient manner and, while favouring East–West détente, was a loyal ally of the USSR. In Oct 1989, following a wave of prodemocracy demonstrations, he was replaced as leader of the Socialist Unity Party (SED) and head of state by Egon Krenz, and in expelled from the Communist Party. He died in exile in Chile.

Hong Kong former British crown colony SE of China, in the South China Sea, comprising Hong Kong Island; the Kowloon Peninsula; many other islands, of which the largest is Lantau; and the mainland New Territories.It reverted to Chinese control 1997.

history Formerly part of China, Hong Kong Island was occupied by Britain 1841, during the first of the ◊Opium Wars, and ceded by China under the 1842 Treaty of Nanking. The Kowloon Peninsula was acquired under the 1860 Beijing (Peking) Convention and the New Territories secured on a 99-year lease from 1898. The colony, which developed into a major centre for Sino-British trade during the late 19th and early 20th centuries, was occupied by Japan 1941–45. The restored British administration promised, after 1946, to increase self-government. These plans were shelved, however, after the 1949 Communist revolution in China. During the 1950s almost 1 million Chinese (predominantly Cantonese) refugees fled to Hong Kong. Immigration continued during the 1960s and 1970s, raising the colony's population from 1 million in 1946 to 5 million in 1980, leading to the imposition of strict border controls during the 1980s. Since 1975, 160,000 Vietnamese boat people have fled to Hong Kong; in 1991 some 61,000 remained. The UK government began forced repatriation 1989.

Hong Kong's economy expanded rapidly during the corresponding period and the colony became one of Asia's major commercial, financial, and industrial centres, boasting the world's busiest container port from 1987. As the date (1997) for the termination of the New Territories' lease approached, negotiations on Hong Kong's future were opened between Britain and China 1982. These culminated in a unique agreement, signed in Beijing 1984, in which Britain agreed to transfer full sovereignty of the islands and New Territories to China 1997 in return for Chinese assurance that Hong Kong's social and economic freedom and capitalist lifestyle would be preserved for at least 50 years.

A borrowed place living on borrowed time.

On *Hong Kong* anonymous, quoted in *The Times* 5 Mar 1981

Hood Samuel, 1st Viscount Hood 1724–1816. British admiral. A masterly tactician, he defeated the French at Dominica in the West Indies 1783, and in the ◊Revolutionary Wars captured Toulon and Corsica.

Hoover Herbert Clark 1874–1964. 31st president of the USA 1929–33, a Republican. He was secretary of commerce 1921–28. Hoover lost public confidence after the stock-market crash of 1929, when he opposed direct government aid for the unemployed in the Depression that followed.

As a mining engineer, Hoover travelled widely before World War I. After the war he organized relief work in occupied Europe; a talented administrator, he subsequently associated with numerous international relief organizations. As president, he failed to prevent the decline of the American economy after the ◊Wall Street crash. In 1933 he was succeeded by ◊F D Roosevelt.

The American system of rugged individualism.

Herbert Hoover campaign speech 1928

Hoover J(ohn) Edgar 1895–1972. US director of the Federal Bureau of Investigation (FBI) from 1924. He built up a powerful network for the detection of organized crime. His drive against alleged communist activities after World War II, and his opposition to the Kennedy administration and others brought much criticism over abuse of power.

Hooverville colloquial term for any shantytown built by the unemployed and destitute in the USA during the Depression 1929–40, named after US president Herbert ◊Hoover whose

policies were blamed for the plight of millions. He also lent his name to 'Hoover blankets' (newspapers) and 'Hoover flags' (turned-out, empty pockets).

Hopewell North American Indian agricultural culture of the central USA, dated about AD 200. The Hopewell built burial mounds up to 12 m/40 ft high and structures such as Serpent Mound in Ohio; see also ◊Moundbuilder.

hoplite in ancient Greece, a heavily armed infantry soldier.

Horn Philip de Montmorency, Count of Horn 1518–1568. Flemish politician. He held high offices under the Holy Roman emperor Charles V and his son Philip II. From 1563 he was one of the leaders of the opposition to the rule of Cardinal Granvella (1517–1586) and to the introduction of the Inquisition. In 1567 he was arrested, together with the Resistance leader Egmont, and both were beheaded in Brussels.

Hornby v. Close UK court case in 1867, in which it was decided that trade unions were illegal associations. The decision, overturned two years later by a special act of Parliament, indirectly led to the full legalization of trade unions under the Trade Union Acts 1871–76.

Horthy Nicholas Horthy de Nagybánya 1868–1957. Hungarian politician and admiral. Leader of the counterrevolutionary White government, he became regent 1920 on the overthrow of the communist Bela Kun regime by Romanian and Czechoslovak intervention. He represented the conservative and military class, and retained power until World War II, trying (although allied to Hitler) to retain independence of action. In 1944 he tried to negotiate a surrender to the USSR but Hungary was taken over by the Nazis and he was deported to Germany. He was released from German captivity the same year by the Western Allies and allowed to go to Portugal, where he died.

Hospitaller member of the Order of ◊St John.

Houphouët-Boigny Félix 1905–93. Ivory Coast right-wing politician, president 1960-93. He held posts in French ministries, and became president of the Republic of the Ivory Coast on independence 1960, maintaining close links with France, which helped to boost an already thriving economy and encourage political stability. Pro-Western and opposed to communist intervention in Africa, Houphouët-Boigny has been strongly criticized for maintaining diplomatic relations with South Africa. He was re-elected for a seventh term 1990 in multiparty elections, amid allegations of ballot rigging and political pressure.

House of Representatives lower house of the US ◊Congress, with 435 members elected at regular two-year intervals, every even year, in Nov.

The House started with fewer than 70 members, but grew as new states joined the Union and the US population increased. Since 1910 the number of members has been fixed at 435.

House Un-American Activities Committee (HUAC) Congressional committee, established 1938, noted for its public investigating into alleged subversion, particularly of communists. It achieved its greatest notoriety during the 1950s through its hearings on communism in the movie industry. It was later renamed the House Internal Security Committee.

Houston Sam 1793–1863. US general who won independence for Texas from Mexico 1836 and was president of the Republic of Texas 1836–45. Houston, Texas, is named after him.

Houston was governor of the state of Tennessee and later US senator for and governor of the state of Texas. He took Indian citizenship when he married a Cherokee.

Hovell William Hilton 1786–1875. English-born explorer in Australia who, with Hamilton ◊Hume, ravelled overland from Gunning, SW of Sydney, to Port Phillip in 1824.

Howard Catherine c. 1520–1542. Queen consort of ◊Henry VIII of England from 1540. In 1541 the archbishop of Canterbury, Thomas Cranmer, accused her of being unchaste before marriage to Henry and she was beheaded 1542 after Cranmer made further charges of adultery.

Hoxha Enver 1908–1985. Albanian Communist politician, the country's leader from 1954. He founded the Albanian Communist Party 1941, and headed the liberation movement 1939–44. He was prime minister 1944–54, combining with foreign affairs 1946–53, and from 1954 was first secretary of the Albanian Party of Labour. In policy he was a Stalinist and independent of both Chinese and Soviet communism.

Hsia dynasty China's first legendary ruling family, c. 2200–c. 1500 bc; see ◊Xia dynasty.

Hua Guofeng or Hua Kuofeng 1920– . Chinese politician, leader of the Chinese Communist Party (CCP) 1976–81, premier 1976–80. He dominated Chinese politics 1976–77, seeking economic modernization without major structural reform. From 1978 he was gradually eclipsed by Deng Xiaoping. Hua was ousted from the Politburo Sept 1982 but remained a member of the CCP Central Committee.

Hua, born in Shanxi into a peasant family, fought under Zhu De, the Red Army leader, during the liberation war 1937–49. He entered the CCP Central Committee 1969 and the Politburo 1973. An orthodox, loyal Maoist, Hua was selected to succeed Zhou Enlai as prime minister Jan 1976 and became party leader on Mao Zedong's death Sept 1976. He was replaced as prime minister by Zhao Ziyang Sept 1980 and as CCP chair by Hu Yaobang June 1981.

Huai-Hai, Battle of decisive campaign 1948–49 in the Chinese Civil War (1946–49). The name is derived from the two main defensive positions held by the nationalist ◊Guomindang force: the Huang (Huai) River in Shandong and Jiangsu provinces, and the Lung Hai railway. Communist forces from the E and W captured Xuzchou (Soochow), a key railway junction, on 1 Dec 1948. On 6 Jan 1949 they secured a crushing victory at Yungchung to the SW, facilitating an advance on Shanghai, which fell in the spring of 1949.

Huáscar c. 1495–1532. King of the Incas. He shared the throne with his half-brother Atahualpa from 1525, but the latter overthrew and murdered him during the Spanish conquest.

Hudson Henry c. 1565–c. 1611. English explorer. Under the auspices of the Muscovy Company 1607–08, he made two unsuccessful attempts to find the Northeast Passage to China. In Sept 1609, commissioned by the Dutch East India Company, he reached New York Bay and sailed 240 km/150 mi up the river that now bears his name, establishing Dutch claims to the area. In 1610, he sailed from London in the *Discovery* and entered what is now the Hudson Strait. After an icebound winter, he was turned adrift by a mutinous crew in what is now Hudson Bay.

Hudson's Bay Company chartered company founded by Prince ◊Rupert 1670 to trade in furs with North American Indians. In 1783 the rival North West Company was formed, but in 1851 this became amalgamated with the Hudson's Bay Company. It is still Canada's biggest fur company, but today also sells general merchandise through department stores and has oil and natural gas interests.

Hughes William Morris 1864–1952. Australian politician, prime minister 1915–23; originally Labor, he headed a national cabinet. After resigning as prime minister 1923, he held many other cabinet posts 1934–41.

Born in London, he emigrated to Australia 1884. He represented Australia in the peace conference after World War I at Versailles.

Huguenot French Protestant in the 16th century; the term referred mainly to Calvinists. Severely persecuted under Francis I and Henry II, the Huguenots survived both an attempt to exterminate them (the *Massacre of ◊St Bartholomew* 24 Aug 1572) and the religious wars of the next 30 years. In 1598 Henry IV (himself formerly a Huguenot) granted them toleration under the *Edict of ◊Nantes*. Louis XIV revoked the edict 1685, attempting their forcible conversion, and 400,000 emigrated. Many settled in North American. Only in 1802 was the Huguenot church again legalized in France.

Hukbalahap movement left-wing Filipino peasant resistance campaign 1942–54. Formed to challenge the Japanese wartime occupation of the Philippines 1942–45, it carried out guerrilla attacks against the Japanese from its base in central Luzon. After World War II, it opposed the Filipino landed elite and its American allies and established an alternative government in Luzon. During the Korean War, a government military campaign 1950–54 defeated the 'Huks'.

Hull Cordell 1871–1955. US Democratic politician. As F D Roosevelt's secretary of state 1933-44, he opposed German and Japanese aggression. He was identified with the Good Neighbor Policy of nonintervention in Latin America. In his last months of office he paved the way for a system of collective security, for which he was called 'father' of the United Nations. He was awarded the Nobel Peace Prize 1945.

Humayun also known as Nasir ud-Din Muhammad 1508–1556. Second Mogul emperor of N India 1530–40 and 1554–56. The son of Babur, he inherited an unsettled empire and faced constant challenges from his three brothers. Following defeat by the Afghan Sher Shad Suri (died 1545), he fled into exile in Persia 1540. Returning to India, he reoccupied Delhi and Agra 1555 but died within a year. He was succeeded by his son ◊Akbar.

Hume Joseph 1777–1855. British Radical politician. Born in Montrose, Scotland, he went to India as an army surgeon 1797, made a fortune, and on his return bought a seat in Parliament. In 1818 he secured election as a Philosophic Radical and supported many progressive measures. His son *Allan Octavian Hume* (1829–1912) was largely responsible for the establishment of the Indian National Congress 1885.

Humphrey Hubert Horatio 1911–1978. US political leader, vice president 1965-69. He was elected to the US Senate 1948, serving for three terms, distinguishing himself an eloquent and effective promoter of key legislation. He was an unsuccessful candidate for the Democratic presidential nomination 1960. Serving as vice president under L B Johnson, he made another unsuccessful run for the presidency 1968. He was re-elected to the Senate in 1970 and 1976.

Hun member of any of a number of nomad Mongol peoples who were first recorded historically in the 2nd century BC, raiding across the Great Wall into China. They entered Europe about AD 372, settled in the area that is now Hungary, and imposed their supremacy on the Ostrogoths and other Germanic peoples. Under the leadership of Attila they attacked the Byzantine Empire, invaded Gaul, and threatened Rome. After Attila's death in 453 their power was broken by a revolt of their subject peoples. The *White Huns*, or Ephthalites, a kindred people, raided Persia and N India in the 5th and 6th centuries.

hundred subdivision of a shire in England, Ireland, and parts of the USA. The term was originally used by Germanic peoples to denote a group of 100 warriors, also the area occupied by 100 families or equalling 100 hides (one hide being the amount of land necessary to support a peasant family). When the Germanic peoples settled in England, the hundred remained the basic military and administrative division of England until its abolition 1867.

Hundred Days in European history, the period 20 March–28 June 1815, marking the French emperor Napoleon's escape from imprisonment on Elba to his departure from Paris after losing the battle of Waterloo 18 June.

Hundred Days' Reform ambitious Westernizing reform programme in China 1898. It sought the modernization of the civil service, the establishment of a national assembly or parliament, and the adoption of a constitutional monarchy. The programme was instigated by scholar-gentry officials, notably Kang Youwei (1858–1927), with the support of Emperor Guangxu (ruled 1875–1908), who attempted to wrest power from Empress Dowager Zi Xi. Her conservative backers rescinded the reforms after 103 days and launched a palace coup, imprisoning Guangxu and forcing Kang Youwei into exile.

Hundred Flowers campaign in Chinese history, a movement 1956–57 of open political and intellectual debate, encouraged by ◊Mao Zedong. The campaign was intended to rouse the bureaucracy and to weaken the position of the Chinese Communist Party's then dominant pro-Soviet 'right wing'. It rapidly got out of hand, resulting in excessive censure of party personnel.

The Hundred Flowers campaign was begun in May 1956, soon after Soviet leader Nikita Khrushchev's 'secret speech' attacking the excesses of Stalinism, and was brought to a close May 1957, with 200,000 intelligentsia critics being exiled to remote rural areas in what became known as the anti-rightist campaign. The name was derived from a slogan from Chinese classical history: 'Let a hundred flowers bloom and a hundred schools of thought contend.'

Hundred Years' War series of conflicts between England and France 1337–1453. Its origins lay with the English kings' possession of Gascony (SW France), which the French kings claimed as their ◊fief, and with trade rivalries over ◊Flanders.

The two kingdoms had a long history of strife before 1337, and the Hundred Years' War has sometimes been interpreted as merely an intensification of these struggles. It was caused by fears of French intervention in Scotland, which the English were trying to subdue, and by the claim of England's ◊Edward III (through his mother Isabel, daughter of Charles IV) to the crown of France.

Hungarian uprising national uprising against Soviet dominance of ◊Hungary in 1956.

Hungary country in central Europe, bounded N by the Slovak Republic, NE by Ukraine, E by Romania, S by Yugoslavia and Croatia, and W by Austria and Slovenia.

history Inhabited by Celts and Slavs, the region became a Roman province. After the Roman era it was overrun at the end of the 4th century AD by Germanic invaders and by Asians who established a Magyar kingdom in the late 9th century, under a chief named Árpád. St Stephen (997–1038) became Hungary's first king; he established a kingdom 1001 and converted the inhabitants to Christianity. After the Árpádian line died out, Hungary was ruled 1308–86 by the ◊Angevins, and subsequently by other foreign princes.

Turkish rule From 1396, successive rulers fought to keep out Turkish invaders but were finally defeated at Mohács 1526, and the south and centre of the country came under Turkish rule for 150 years, while the east was ruled by semi-independent Hungarian princes. By the end of the 17th century the Turks had been driven out by the ◊Habsburgs, bringing Hungary under Austrian rule. After 1815 a national renaissance began, under the leadership of

The Hundred Years' War	
1340	The English were victorious at the naval battle of Sluys.
1346	Battle of Crécy, another English victory.
1347	The English took Calais.
1356	Battle of Poitiers, where Edward the Black Prince defeated the French. King John of France was captured.
late 1350s–early 1360s	France had civil wars, brigandage, and the popular uprising of the Jacquerie.
1360	Treaty of Brétigny-Calais. France accepted English possession of Calais and of a greatly enlarged duchy of Gascony. John was ransomed for £500,000.
1369–1414	The tide turned in favour of the French, and when there was another truce in 1388, only Calais, Bordeaux, and Bayonne were in English hands. A state of half-war continued for many years.
1415	Henry V invaded France and won a victory at Agincourt, followed by conquest of Normandy.
1419	In the Treaty of Toyes, Charles VI of France was forced to disinherit his son, the Dauphin, in favour of Henry V, who was to marry Catherine, Charles's daughter. Most of N France was in English hands.
1422–28	After the death of Henry V his brother Bedford was generally successful.
1429	Joan of Arc raised the siege of Orléans, and the Dauphin was crowned Charles VII at Rheims.
1430–53	Even after Joan's capture and death the French continued their successful counter-offensive, and in 1453 only Calais was left in English hands.

Louis ◊Kossuth. The revolution of 1848–49 proclaimed a Hungarian republic and abolished serfdom, but Austria suppressed the revolt with Russian help.

Austro-Hungarian empire In 1867 the ◊Austro-Hungarian empire was established, giving Hungary self-government. During World War I, Hungary fought on the German side and, after the collapse of the Austro-Hungarian empire, became an independent state 1918. For 133 days in 1919, Hungary was a communist republic under Béla ◊Kun, but this was brought to an end by intervention from Romania and Czechoslovakia. During 1920–44, Hungary was ruled by Admiral ◊Horthy, acting as regent for an unnamed king. After 1933, Horthy fell more and more under German influence and joined Hitler in the invasion of the USSR 1941.

communism Hungary was overrun by the Red Army 1944–45. Horthy fled, and a provisional government, including the communist agriculture minister Imre ◊Nagy, was formed, distributing land to the peasants. An elected assembly inaugurated a republic 1946, but it soon fell under Soviet domination, although only 70 communists had been returned out of a total of 409 deputies. Under Communist Party leader Matyas Rákosi (1892–1971), a Stalinist regime was imposed 1946–53, with a Soviet-style constitution being adopted 1949, industry nationalized, land collectivized, and a wave of secret-police terror launched.

Hungarian national uprising Liberalization in the economic sphere was experienced 1953–55 when Imre Nagy, supported by Soviet premier Malenkov, replaced Rákosi as prime minister. Nagy was removed from office 1955, after the fall of Malenkov, but in 1956, in the wake of ◊Khrushchev's denunciation of Stalin in his 'secret speech', pressure for democratization mounted. Rákosi stepped down as Communist Party leader and, following student and worker demonstrations in Budapest, Nagy was recalled as prime minister, and János ◊Kádár appointed general secretary of the renamed Hungarian Socialist Workers' Party (HSWP). Nagy lifted restrictions on the formation of political parties, released the anticommunist primate Cardinal Mindszenty, and announced plans for Hungary to withdraw from the ◊Warsaw Pact and become a neutral power. These changes were, however, opposed by Kádár, who set up a countergovernment in E Hungary before returning to Budapest with Soviet tanks to overthrow the Nagy government 4 Nov. Some 200,000 fled to the West during the 1956 Hungarian national uprising. After a period of strict repression, Kádár proceeded to introduce pragmatic liberalizing reforms after 1960. Hungary remained, however, a loyal member of the Warsaw Pact and ◊Comecon.

reform Hungary's relations with Moscow significantly improved during the post-Brezhnev era, with Hungary's 'market socialism' experiment influencing Mikhail Gorbachev's *perestroika* programme. Further reforms introduced 1987–88 included additional price deregulation, the establishment of 'enterprise councils', the introduction of value-added tax (VAT), and the creation of a stock market. As elsewhere in Eastern Europe, change came quickly to Hungary from 1988. Kádár, who had become an obstacle to reform, was replaced as general secretary of the ruling HSWP party by Károly Grosz 1988, and was named to a new post, that of party president. Two radical reformers, Rezso Nyers and Imre Pozsgay, were brought into the Politburo. The Hungarian Democratic Forum was formed Sept 1988 as an umbrella movement for opposition groups, and several dozen other political parties were formed 1989–90.

There then began a period of far-reaching political reform in which the rights to demonstrate freely and to form rival political parties and trade unions were ceded. The official verdict on the 1956 events was revised radically, with Nagy being posthumously rehabilitated. In May 1989 the border with Austria was opened, with adverse effects for East Germany as thousands of East Germans escaped to the West through Hungary. Two months later Grosz was forced to cede power to the more radical reformist troika of Nyers (party president), Pozsgay, and Miklos Nemeth (prime minister since Nov 1988), who joined Grosz in a new four-person ruling presidium.

constitutional changes In Oct 1989 a series of constitutional changes, the result of round-table talks held through the summer, were approved by the national assembly. These included the adoption of a new set of electoral rules, the banning of workplace party cells, and the change of the country's name from 'People's Republic' to simply 'Republic'. Also in Oct the HSWP changed its name to the Hungarian Socialist Party (HSP), and adopted Poszgay as its presidential candidate. Conservatives, including Grosz, refused to play an active role in the new party, which had become essentially a social-democratic party committed to multiparty democracy. Despite these changes, the HSP's standing was seriously damaged in the 'Danubegate' scandal of Jan 1990, when it was revealed that the secret police had bugged opposition parties and passed the information obtained to the HSP.

foreign relations In Feb 1990 talks were held with the USSR about the withdrawal of Soviet troops stationed in Hungary. In June 1990 the Hungarian government announced the country's decision no longer to participate in Warsaw Pact military exercises and its intention to withdraw altogether from the Pact. As the Warsaw Pact and Comecon had disbanded by July 1991, the country was able to move towards the West more directly. Hungary joined the Council of Europe in Nov 1990. The last Soviet troops left Hungary, on schedule, June 1991. In Dec 1991 Hungary signed a ten-year association agreement with the European Community (EC) and was awarded trade concessions and a guarantee of economic assistance from the EC. The agreement was effective from March 1992.

privatization As the first step in the privatization programme, a stock exchange was opened in Budapest. In Jan 1991 the forint was devalued by 15% in an effort to boost exports. A Compensation Bill for owners of land and property expropriated under the communist regime was approved by the national assembly June 1991. It was hoped that, by clearing up the uncertainty over ownership, the bill would stimulate the privatization programme and inward foreign investment. Gross national product fell by 7% in 1991, industrial production fell by one-fifth during the first half of 1991, and by the close of 1991 unemployment rose to more than 7%. However, of all the former communist European states, Hungary experienced the smoothest transition towards a market economy. This was credited to the establishment of self-management and privatization before the downfall of the communist regime in 1989.

hunger march procession of the unemployed, a feature of social protest in interwar Britain.

The first took place from Glasgow to London in 1922 and another in 1929. In 1932 the National Unemployed Workers' Movement organized the largest demonstration, with groups converging on London from all parts of the country, but the most emotive was probably the Jarrow Crusade of 1936, when 200 unemployed shipyard workers marched to the capital.

Hunyadi János Corvinus 1387–1456. Hungarian politician and general. Born in Transylvania, reputedly the son of the emperor ◊Sigismund, he won battles against the Turks from the 1440s. In 1456 he defeated them at Belgrade, but died shortly afterwards of the plague.

Huron (French *hure* 'rough hair of the head') nickname for a member of a confederation of five Iroquoian North American Indian peoples living near lakes Huron, Erie, and Ontario in the 16th and 17th centuries. They were almost wiped out by the Iroquois. In the 17th century, surviving Hurons formed a group called Wyandot, some of whose descendants now live in Québec and Oklahoma.

Husák Gustáv 1913–1991. Leader of the Communist Party of Czechoslovakia (CCP) 1969–87 and president 1975–89. After the 1968 Prague Spring of liberalization, his task was to restore control, purge the CCP, and oversee the implementation of a new, federalist constitution. He was deposed in the popular uprising of Nov–Dec 1989 and expelled from the Communist Party Feb 1990.

Husák, a lawyer, was active in the Resistance movement during World War II, and afterwards in the Slovak Communist Party (SCP), and was imprisoned on political grounds 1951–60. Rehabilitated, he was appointed first secretary of the SCP 1968 and CCP leader 1969–87. As titular state president he pursued a policy of cautious reform. He stepped down as party leader 1987, and was replaced as state president by Václav ◊Havel Dec 1989 following the 'gentle revolution'.

huscarl Anglo-Danish warrior in 10th-century Denmark and early 11th-century England. Huscarls formed the bulk of English royal armies until the Norman Conquest.

Huskisson William 1770–1830. British Conservative politician, financier, and advocate of free trade. He served as secretary to the Treasury 1807–09 and colonial agent for Ceylon (now Sri Lanka). He was active in the ◊Corn Law debates and supported their relaxation in 1821.

Huss John (Czech *Jan*) *c.* 1373–1415. Bohemian Christian church reformer, rector of Prague University from 1402, who was excommunicated for attacks on ecclesiastical abuses. He was summoned before the Council of Constance 1414, defended the English reformer John Wycliffe, rejected the pope's authority, and was burned at the stake. His followers were called Hussites.

Hussein ibn Ali *c.* 1854–1931. Leader of the Arab revolt 1916–18 against the Turks. He proclaimed himself king of the Hejaz 1916, accepted the caliphate 1924, but was unable to retain it due to internal fighting. He was deposed 1924 by Ibn Saud.

Hussein ibn Talal 1935– . King of Jordan from 1952. Great-grandson of Hussein ibn Ali, he became king following the mental incapacitation of his father, Talal. By 1967 he had lost all his kingdom west of the river Jordan in the ◊Arab-Israeli Wars, and in 1970 suppressed the ◊Palestine Liberation Organization acting as a guerrilla force against his rule on the remaining East Bank territories. In recent years, he has become a moderating force in Middle Eastern politics. After Iraq's annexation of Kuwait 1990 he attempted to mediate between the opposing sides, at the risk of damaging his relations with both sides.

Hussein Saddam 1937– . Iraqi politician, in power from 1968, president from 1979, progressively eliminating real or imagined opposition factions as he gained increasing dictatorial control. Ruthless in the pursuit of his objectives, he fought a bitter war against Iran

1980–88, with US economic aid, and dealt harshly with Kurdish rebels seeking independence, using chemical weapons against civilian populations. In 1990 he annexed Kuwait, to universal condemnation, before being driven out by a US-dominated coalition army Feb 1991. Iraq's defeat in the ◊Gulf War undermined Saddam's position as the country's leader; when the Kurds rebelled again after the end of the war, he sent the remainder of his army to crush them, bringing international charges of genocide against him and causing hundreds of thousands of Kurds to flee their homes in northern Iraq. His continued bombardment of Shi'ites in southern Iraq caused the UN to impose a 'no-fly zone' in the area.

Hussein joined the Arab Ba'ath Socialist Party as a young man and soon became involved in revolutionary activities. In 1959 he was sentenced to death and took refuge in Egypt, but a coup in 1963 made his return possible, although in the following year he was imprisoned for plotting to overthrow the regime he had helped to install. After his release he took a leading part in the 1968 revolution, removing the civilian government and establishing a Revolutionary Command Council (RCC). At first discreetly, and then more openly, Hussein strengthened his position and in 1979 became RCC chair and state president. In 1977 Saddam Hussein al-Tikriti abolished the use of surnames in Iraq to conceal the fact that a large number of people in the government and ruling party all came from his home village of Tikrit and therefore bore the same surname. The 1990 Kuwait annexation followed a long-running border dispute and was prompted by the need for more oil resources after the expensive war against Iran. Saddam, who had enjoyed US support for being the enemy of Iran and had used poison gas against his own people in Kurdistan without any falling-off in trade with the West, suddenly found himself almost universally condemned. Iraqi assets were frozen and in the UN, Arab, communist, and capitalist nations east and west agreed on a trade embargo and aid to refugees, with the USA and the UK urging aggressive military action. Fears that Saddam might use chemical or even nuclear weapons were raised as predominantly US troops massed on the Saudi Arabian border. With the passing of the UN deadline of 15 Jan 1991 without any withdrawal from Kuwait, allied forces struck Baghdad in a series of air bombardments to which Saddam replied by firing Scud missiles on the Israeli cities of Tel Aviv and Haifa in an unsuccessful effort to bring Israel into the war and thus break up the Arab alliance with the West; he also failed to rally Arab support for a holy war or 'jihad' to eject the Western 'infidels'.

Another potential confrontation with the West was averted 1994. However, in Sept 1996 the US retaliated against Hussein's encroachment into UN protected territories in northern Iraq, carrying out missile attacks on Iraqi military bases in the area.

Hussite follower of John ◊Huss. Opposed to both German and papal influence in Bohemia, the Hussites waged successful war against the Holy Roman Empire from 1419, but Roman Catholicism was finally re-established 1620.

Hu Yaobang 1915–1989. Chinese politician, Communist Party (CCP) chair 1981–87. A protégé of the communist leader Deng Xiaoping, Hu presided over a radical overhaul of the party structure and personnel 1982–86. His death ignited the prodemocracy movement, which was eventually crushed in ◊Tiananmen Square in June 1989.

Hu, born into a peasant family in Hunan province, was a political commissar during the 1934–35 ◊Long March. He was purged as a 'capitalist roader' during the 1966–69 ◊Cultural Revolution and sent into the countryside for 're-education'. He was rehabilitated 1975 but disgraced again when Deng fell from prominence 1976. In Dec 1978, with Deng established in power, Hu was inducted into the CCP Politburo and became head of the revived secretariat 1980 and CCP chair 1981. He was dismissed Jan 1987 for his relaxed handling of a wave of student unrest Dec 1986.

Hyder Ali (or *Haidar Ali*) *c.* 1722–1782. Indian general, sultan of Mysore in SW India from 1759. In command of the army in Mysore from 1749, he became the ruler of the state 1761, and rivalled British power in the area until his triple defeat by Sir Eyre ◊Coote 1781 during the Anglo-French wars. He was the father of Tipu Sultan.

Hyksos ('shepherd kings' or 'princes of the desert') nomadic, probably Semitic people who came to prominence in Egypt in the 18th century BC, and established their own dynasty in the Nile delta, which lasted until 1580 BC. They introduced bronze metallurgy, the wheel, and the use of the horse-drawn chariot.

Ibarruri Dolores, known as *La Pasionaria* ('the passion flower') 1895–1989. Spanish Basque politician, journalist, and orator; she was first elected to the Cortes in 1936. She helped to establish the Popular Front government and was a Loyalist leader in the Civil War. When Franco came to power in 1939 she left Spain for the USSR, where she was active in the Communist Party. She returned to Spain in 1977 after Franco's death and was re-elected to the Cortes (at the age of 81) in the first parliamentary elections for 40 years

---

It is better to die on your feet than to live on your knees.

Dolores Ibarruri speech Sept 1936

Iberia name given by ancient Greek navigators to the Spanish peninsula, derived from the river Iberus (Ebro).

Ibn Saud 1880–1953. First king of Saudi Arabia from 1932. His father was the son of the sultan of Nejd, at whose capital, Riyadh, Ibn Saud was born. In 1891 a rival group seized Riyadh, and Ibn Saud went into exile with his father, who resigned his claim to the throne in his son's favour. In 1902 Ibn Saud recaptured Riyadh and recovered the kingdom, and by 1921 he had brought all central Arabia under his rule. In 1924 he invaded the Hejaz, of which he was proclaimed king in 1926.

Nejd and the Hejaz were united 1932 in the kingdom of Saudi Arabia. Ibn Saud introduced programmes for modernization with revenue from oil, which was discovered 1936.

Iceland island country in the N Atlantic Ocean, situated S of the Arctic Circle, between Greenland and Norway.

history Iceland was first occupied 874 by Norse settlers, who founded a republic and a parliament 930. In 1000 the inhabitants adopted Christianity and about 1263 submitted to the authority of the king of Norway. In 1380 Norway, and with it Iceland, came under Danish rule.

Iceland remained attached to Denmark after Norway became independent 1814. From 1918 it was independent but still recognized the Danish monarch. During World War II Iceland was occupied by British and US forces and voted in a referendum for complete independence 1944.

after independence In 1949 Iceland joined ◊NATO and the ◊Council of Europe, and in 1953 the Nordic Council. Since independence it has been governed by coalitions of the leading parties, sometimes right- and somtimes left-wing groupings, but mostly moderate.

The centre and right-of-centre parties are the Independents and Social Democrats, while those to the left are the Progressives and the People's Alliance. More recent additions have been the Social Democratic Alliance and the Women's Alliance.

overfishing Most of Iceland's external problems have been connected with the overfishing of the waters around its coasts. Domestically governments have been faced with the recurring problem of inflation. In 1985 the Althing unanimously declared the country a nuclear-free zone, banning the entry of all nuclear weapons.

The 1987 elections ended control of the Althing by the Independence and Progressive parties, giving more influence to the minor parties, including the Women's Alliance, which doubled its seat tally. In June 1988 Vigdís Finnbogadóttir was re-elected president for a third four-year term with 92.7% of the vote. Steingrímur Hermannsson became prime minister. Following a general election April 1991, however, he was replaced by Davíd Oddsson, who led a new centre-right coalition of the Independence Party and the Social Democratic Party. In 1992 Iceland announced that it would defy a worldwide ban on whaling in order to resume its own whaling industry.

Iceni ancient people of E England, who revolted against occupying Romans under ◊Boudicca.

iconoclast (Greek 'image-breaker') literally, a person who attacks religious images, originally in obedience to the injunction of the Second Commandment not to worship 'graven images'. Under the influence of Islam and

Judaism, an iconoclastic movement calling for the destruction of religious images developed in the Byzantine empire, and was endorsed by the Emperor Leo III in 726. Fierce persecution of those who made and venerated icons followed, until iconoclasm was declared a heresy in the 9th century.

The same name was applied to those opposing the use of images at the Reformation, when there was much destruction in churches.

Ides in the Roman calendar, the 15th day of March, May, July, and Oct, and the 13th day of all other months (the word originally indicated the full moon); Julius Caesar was assassinated on the Ides of March 44 BC.

Ife town in western Nigeria, traditionally the oldest of the Yoruba kingdoms in the region. Ife was established in the 6th century and became an important Iron-Age town. It was the cultural and religious, though not political, centre of the region, and reached its peak about 1300. Many sculptures in bronze, brass, clay, and ivory have been excavated in and around the town.

Iglesias Pablo 1850–1925. Spanish politician, founder of the Spanish Socialist Party (Partido Socialista Obrero Español, PSOE) in 1879. In 1911 he became the first socialist deputy to be elected to the *Cortes* (Spanish parliament).

Ikhnaton or *Akhenaton* King of Egypt of the 18th dynasty (*c.* 1379–1362 BC), who may have ruled jointly for a time with his father Amenhotep III. He developed the cult of the Sun, Aton, rather than the rival cult of Ammon, and removed his capital to ◊Akhetaton. Some historians believe that his attention to religious reforms rather than imperial defence led to the loss of most of Egypt's possessions in Asia.

Ikhnaton's favourite wife was Nefertiti, and two of their six daughters were married to his successors Smenkhare and Tutankaton (later known as Tutankhamen).

Illyria ancient name for the eastern coastal region on the Adriatic, N of the Gulf of Corinth, conquered by Philip of Macedon. It became a Roman province AD 9. The Albanians are the survivors of its ancient peoples.

imam (Arabic 'leader') in a mosque, the leader of congregational prayer, but generally any notable Islamic leader.

IMF abbreviation for the ◊International Monetary Fund.

impeachment judicial procedure by which government officials are accused of wrongdoing and brought to trial before a legislative body. In the USA the House of Representatives may impeach offenders to be tried before the

Senate, as in the case of President Andrew Johnson 1868. Richard ◊Nixon resigned the US presidency 1974 when threatened by impeachment.

In England the House of Commons from 1376 brought ministers and officers of state to trial before the House of Lords: for example Bacon 1621, Strafford 1640, and Warren Hastings 1788.

imperialism policy of extending the power and rule of a government beyond its own boundaries. A country may attempt to dominate others by direct rule or by less obvious means such as control of markets for goods or raw materials. The latter is often called ◊neocolonialism. In the 19th century imperialism was synonymous with the establishment of colonies (see ◊British Empire).

imperial preference or *colonial preference* programme of tariff reform within the British Empire, advocated by Joseph ◊Chamberlain at the turn of the 20th century. Colonial products would receive preference in Britain's domestic market while duties would be levied on foreign foodstuffs and goods. Likewise, British industry would get favourable treatment in colonial markets at the expense of foreign competition. The revenue generated would pay for social welfare and defence measures. A limited programme was introduced with the ◊Ottawa Agreements 1932.

imperium ((Latin 'command' or 'rule')) in ancient Rome the legal and military power granted to certain magistrates, for example consul, praetor, or dictator. The term also extends to command over a province (◊proconsul). Repeated grants of imperium, with the additional powers of a tribune, became the basis of the principate of Augustus and subsequent emperors. The term was also used for the rule of Rome over the Roman empire.

Inca member of an ancient Peruvian civilization of Quechua-speaking Indians that began in the Andean highlands about 1200; by the time of the Spanish Conquest in the 1530s, the Inca rule d from Ecuador in the north to Chile in the south.

The Inca empire dominated the Andean region militarily. Conquered peoples were transplanted into new homelands near the capital, Cuzco, until they had assimilated Inca culture; they were then resettled. The empire was an agriculturally based theocracy, with priest-rulers at the top of the hierarchy, and with 'the Inca', believed to be a descendant of the Sun, as emperor. An extensive road system united

Imperialism: from Colonialism to Independence

	current name	colonial names and history	colonized	independent
Belgium	Zaïre	Belgian Congo	1885	1960
France	Cambodia	Kampuchea 1970–89	1863	1953
	Laos	French Indochina (protectorate)	1893	1954
	Vietnam	Tonkin, Annam, Conchin-China to 1954 North and South Vietnam 1954–76	1858	1954
	Burkina Faso	Upper Volta to 1984	1896	1960
	Central African Republic	Ubangi-Shari	19th century	1960
	Chad	French Equatorial Africa	19th century	1960
	Côte d'Ivoire	Ivory Coast to 1986	1883	1960
	Madagascar		1896	1960
	Mali	French Sudan	19th century	1960
	Niger		1912	1960
	Algeria		colonized in 19th century – c. 1840	1962 incorporated into France 1881
The Netherlands	Indonesia	Netherlands Indies	17th century	1949
	Suriname	British colony 1650–67	1667	1975
Portugal	Brazil		1532	1822
	Uruguay	province of Brazil	1533	1828
	Mozambique		1505	1975
	Angola		1491	1975
Spain	Paraguay	viceroyalty of Buenos Aires	1537	1811
	Argentina	viceroyalty of Buenos Aires	16th century	1816
	Chile		1541	1818
	Costa Rica		1563	1821
	Mexico	viceroyalty of New Spain	16th century	1821
	Peru		1541	1824
	Bolivia		16th century	1825
	Ecuador	Greater Colombia 1822–30	16th century	1830
	Venezuela	captaincy-general of Caracas to 1822 Greater Colombia 1822–30	16th century	1830
	Honduras	federation of Central America 1821–38	1523	1838
	El Salvador	federation of Central America 1821–39	16th century	1839
	Guatemala	federation of Central America 1821–39	16th century	1839
	Dominican Republic	Hispaniola to 1821	16th century	1844 ruled by Haiti to 1844
	Cuba		1512	1898
	Colombia	viceroyalty of New Granada to 1819 Greater Colombia to 1830	16th century	1903
	Panama	part of Colombia to 1903	16th century	1903
	Philippines	Spain 1565–1898, US 1898–1946	1565	1946

the highland and coastal cities but made them vulnerable to the Spanish, who, after conquest, enslaved the people in mining and food-producing ventures. Today's Quechua-speaking Indians are descendants of the Inca civilization; many still live in the farming villages of the highlands of Peru.

The Inca priesthood allotted labour for irrigation, and built temples and fortresses (made of stone blocks, fitted together without mortar),

Imperialism in Africa: areas of European domination in 1914 *By 1914 five European powers (Britain, France, Germany, the Netherlands, and Portugal), together with the USA and Japan, controlled colonies in Southeast Asia. The Dutch and Portuguese outposts dated back to the 16th century; most of the others were established during the later 19th-century 'High Imperialism' era. The two most significant imperialist powers were Britain and France. Britain controlled a western arc within the region, extending between India and Malaya, while France controlled Indo-China. This enabled Siam (modern Thailand) to retain its formal independence as an intermediate buffer state.*

according to family groups. Produce was collected and similarly distributed; numerical records of stores were kept by means of knotted cords, or 'quipus', writing being unknown. Medicine and advanced surgery was practised and the dead were mummified. The Inca ruin of Machu Picchu, a mountain sanctuary built about 1500, is near Cuzco.

indentured labour work under a restrictive contract of employment for a fixed period in a foreign country in exchange for payment of passage, accommodation, and food. Indentured labour was the means by which many British people emigrated to North America during the colonial era, and in the 19th–early 20th centuries it was used to recruit Asian workers for employment elsewhere in European colonial empires.

Conditions for indentured workers were usually very poor. Many died during the passage, and during the term of indenture (usually between four and seven years) the worker was not allowed to change employer, although the employer could sell the remaining period of indenture, much as a slave could be sold. Indentured labour was widely used as a source of workers from India for employment on sugar plantations in the Caribbean from 1839, following the abolition of slavery.

Independent Labour Party (ILP) British socialist party, founded in Bradford 1893 by the Scottish member of Parliament Keir Hardie. In 1900 it joined with trades unions and Fabians in founding the Labour Representation Committee, the nucleus of the ◊Labour Party. Many members left the ILP to join the Communist Party 1921, and in 1932 all connections with the Labour Party were severed. After World War II the ILP dwindled, eventually becoming extinct. James Maxton (1885–1946) was its chair 1926–46.

India country in S Asia, bounded N by China, Nepal, and Bhutan; E by Myanmar; NW by Pakistan; and SE, S, and SW by the Indian Ocean. Situated in the NE of India, N of the Bay of Bengal, is Bangladesh.

history For history before 1947, see ◊*India subcontinent: history*. Between 1947 and 1949 India temporarily remained under the supervision of a governor general appointed by the British monarch while a new constitution was framed and approved. Former princely states (see ◊India of the Princes; ◊Kashmir) were integrated, and the old British provinces restructured into new states; in 1950 India was proclaimed a fully independent federal republic.

independent republic During its early years the republic faced the problem of resettling refugees from Pakistan and was involved in border skirmishes over Kashmir. Under the leadership of Prime Minister ◊Nehru, land reforms, a new socialist economic programme (involving protectionism), and an emphasis on heavy industries and government planning, were introduced. Sovereignty of parts of India held by France and Portugal was recovered 1950–61.

In foreign affairs, India remained within the ◊Commonwealth, was involved in border clashes with China 1962, and played a leading role in the formation of the ◊nonaligned movement 1961. In 1964, Nehru died and was succeeded as prime minister by Lal Bahadur ◊Shastri. There was a second war with Pakistan over Kashmir 1965.

Indira Gandhi's premiership Indira ◊Gandhi (Nehru's daughter) became prime minister on Shastri's death 1966 and kept broadly to her father's policy programme, but drew closer to the USSR with the signing of a 15-year economic and military assistance agreement 1973. In 1971 Indian troops invaded East Pakistan in support of separatist groups. They defeated Pakistan's troops and oversaw the creation of independent

◊Bangladesh. In 1975, having been found guilty of electoral malpractice during the 1971 election, Indira Gandhi imposed a state of emergency and imprisoned almost 1,000 political opponents. She was cleared of malpractice by the Supreme Court Nov 1975, but the 'emergency' continued for two years, during which period a harsh compulsory birth-control programme was introduced.

The state of emergency was lifted March 1977 for elections in which the opposition Janata Party was swept to power, led by Morarji ◊Desai. The new government was undermined by economic difficulties and internal factional strife. Desai was toppled as prime minister 1979, and a coalition, under Charan Singh, was soon overthrown. In Jan 1980 the Congress (I) Party, led by Indira Gandhi, was returned to power with a landslide victory.

Amritsar massacre The new Gandhi administration was economically successful, but the problems of intercaste violence and regional unrest were such that the Congress (I) Party lost control of a number of states. The greatest unrest was in Punjab, where Sikh demands for greater religious recognition and for resolution of water and land disputes with neighbouring states escalated into calls for the creation of a separate state of 'Khalistan'. In 1984, troops were sent into the Sikhs' most holy shrine, the Golden Temple at Amritsar, to dislodge the armed Sikh extremist leader Sant Jarnail Singh Bhindranwale, resulting in the deaths of Bhindranwale and hundreds of his supporters. The ensuing Sikh backlash brought troop mutinies, culminating in the assassination of Indira Gandhi by her Sikh bodyguards Oct 1984. In Delhi, retaliating Hindus massacred 3,000 Sikhs before the new prime minister, Rajiv ◊Gandhi (Indira's elder son), restored order.

In Dec 1984 Bhopal in central India became the site of a major industrial accident in which more than 2,500 people were killed.

reform In the elections of Dec 1984, Congress (I), benefiting from a wave of public sympathy, gained a record victory. As prime minister, Rajiv Gandhi pledged to modernize and inject greater market efficiency into the Indian economy and to resolve the Punjab, Assam, and Kashmir disputes. Early reforms and the spread of technology, with India launching its first space satellite, augured well. Progress was made towards resolving the ethnic disputes in Assam and the hill areas, with 25 years of rebellion ended in Mizoram, which was made a new state of the Indian Union. However, Gandhi was unable to resolve the Punjab problem, with Sikh-Hindu ethnic conflict continuing, while in

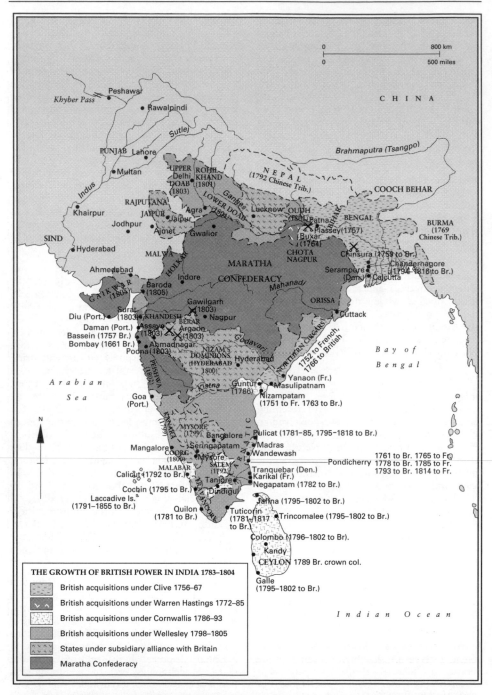

THE GROWTH OF BRITISH POWER IN INDIA 1783–1804

British acquisitions under Clive 1756–67

British acquisitions under Warren Hastings 1772–85

British acquisitions under Cornwallis 1786–93

British acquisitions under Wellesley 1798–1805

States under subsidiary alliance with Britain

Maratha Confederacy

The growth of British power in India The conquest of the vast, populous Indian subcontinent by Britain, a small island nation 12,000 miles distant, was a remarkable phenomenon. It began 1757–64 with the crucial victories at Plassey and Buxar in N India. These were achieved less through the technological and organizational superiority of the East India Company's armies than through the crucial support received from Indian financial and military collaborators. The most significant period of expansion, culminating in the defeat of the rival Maratha Confederacy, occurred under the 'forward Imperialist' Richard Wellesley. However, full extension of the frontiers of the 'Company Raj' was not to be completed until the 19th century.

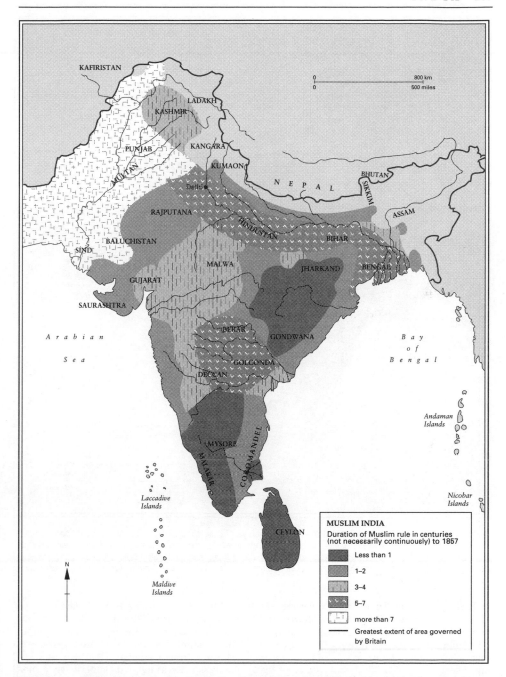

Muslim India *Islam was introduced to India in the 8th century, with the Arab conquest of the Indus valley region of Sind, now modern Pakistan. From 1206, N India's fertile and densely populated Ganges valley zone (Hindustan) was brought under Muslim control by the Delhi Sultanate, which was replaced 1526 by the Mogul empire. It served as a base for military expeditions into western and south-central India, via Malwa. By the late 17th century the greater part of the subcontinent had been brought nominally under Muslim control. Muslim influence was greatest in the northwest and in the grid of Mogul urban and military centres. It was weakest in the predominantly Hindu countryside and south.*

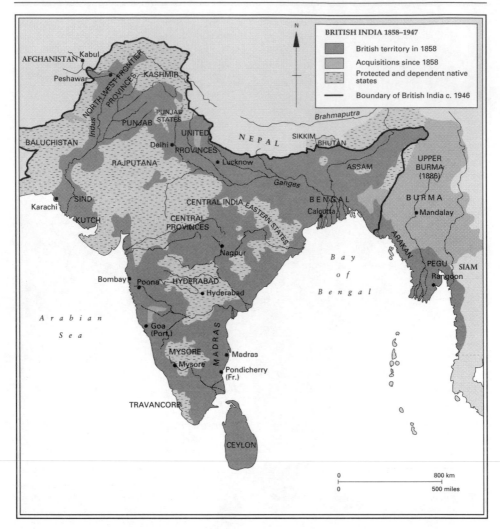

British India 1858–1947 *In 1858, after the Mutiny of the previous year had been suppressed and the East India Company stripped of its administrative role, British India formally came under direct Crown control. With the exception of the annexation of Upper Burma 1886, the period of territorial expansion was over. Stable arrangements with rulers of hundreds of princely states, large and small, left them dependent but in control of more than a third of the subcontinent. Delhi superseded Calcutta 1912 as the political capital of the British Raj.*

N India Hindu-Muslim relations deteriorated. Gandhi's enthusiasm for economic reform also waned from 1986 and his personal reputation was sullied by the uncovering of the 'Bofors scandal' by finance minister V P Singh, involving alleged financial kickbacks received by government-connected organizations from a $1,400-million arms contract with the Swedish Bofors Corporation. In N Sri Lanka, where an Indian Peacekeeping Force (IPKF) had been sent July 1987 as part of an ambitious peace settlement, Indian troops became bogged down in a civil war.

coalition government R Venkataraman was sworn in as president July 1987. Despite bumper harvests 1988–89, Gandhi's popularity continued to fall. V P Singh, who was dismissed from Congress (I) 1987, attacked Gandhi's increasingly dictatorial style and became the recognized leader of the opposition forces, which united under the Janata Dal umbrella Oct 1988. In the general election Nov 1989 a broad anti-Congress electoral pact was forged, embracing the Janata Dal (People's Party), Bharatiya Janata Party (BJP), both factions of the Communist Party, and the

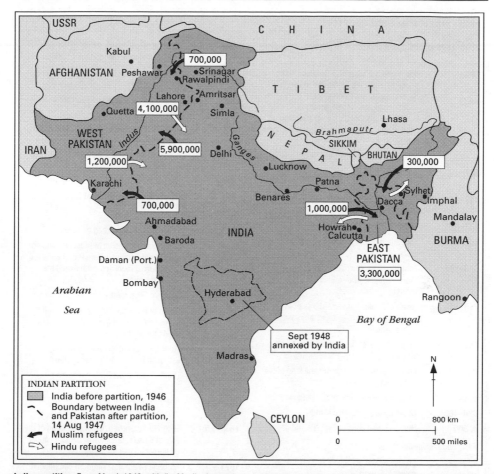

Indian partition *From March 1940, with the Muslim League's commitment to securing statehood for the Muslim community, the Indian subcontinent, united by the British Raj, was set irrevocably on the course of partition. This separation took place on 15 Aug 1947, with power being transferred to the new Dominions of India and Pakistan (East and West). Huge Hindu and Muslim refugee movements ensued. In the Punjab, where the Sikh community had been almost evenly divided by the Radcliffe Boundary award, there was terrible inter-ethnic conflict. In all, the Partition-associated pogroms may have claimed as many as half a million lives.*

regional-level Telugu Desam. This ensured that Congress (I) failed to secure a working majority. V P Singh, widely respected for his incorruptibility, took over at the head of a minority National Front coalition.

separatist violence Singh's main objective was the lowering of racial tensions. However, in Jan 1990 Muslim separatist violence erupted in Kashmir, forcing the imposition of direct rule and leading to a deterioration of relations with Pakistan. Relations were improved with the neighbouring states of Bhutan, Nepal (which had been subject to a partial border blockade by India during 1989), and Sri Lanka, with whom a date (31 March 1990) was agreed for the withdrawal of the IPKF. President's rule was

imposed over Jammu and Kashmir July 1990 and over Assam Nov 1990, as a result of the rising tide of separatist violence. Punjab, where interethnic murders climbed to record heights from Nov, was already under president's rule begun 1983.

During the summer and early autumn of 1990 the Janata Dal government of V P Singh was rocked by a series of events, including the prime minister's decision to employ more low-caste workers in government and public-sector jobs, which resulted in protests by high-caste students and a split in the Janata Dal. Chandra Shekhar, a long-time Singh opponent, emerged as the leader of a rebel faction. Hindu militants (the Vishwa Hindu Parishad) announced that on 30 Oct 1990 they would begin to build a

Indian subcontinent: history to 1947

2500–1500 BC	Harappan civilization of planned, defended cities in the Indus valley.
1500–1200	Aryan peoples invaded from the Iranian plateau and began settlement of the Ganges valley. Brahmanism (an early stage of Hinduism) developed, as did Sanskrit language. Caste system emerged. Iron used in agriculture. Start of India's 'second urbanization'.
c. 600	Rise of Magadha kingdom.
527	Death of Vardhamana Mahavira, founder of the Jain religion.
483	First council of Buddhists held to establish the teachings of Gautama Buddha.
362–321	Nandu dynasty.
327–325	Expedition of Alexander the Great into India.
325–185	First Hindu empire in N India under Chandragupta, who founded the Mauryan dynasty.
268–231	Reign of Asoka, with two-thirds of India under his control. Capital established at Pataliputra.
185	Empire began to break down into smaller kingdoms.
c. AD 78	Accession of Kanishka, Kusana king of the northwest.
c. 240	Kusanas overthrown by Sassanians.
320–480	Gupta dynasty reunited N India.
c. 500	Huns secured control over NW India.

Early and late medieval era

600–42	Establishment of Pallava and Chalukya power in S India.
606–47	Harsha-vardhana ruled as king of Kanauj.
c. 700	Buddhism driven out of India by Hinduism.
712	Arab Muslim invasions of Indus valley began.
740	Chalukyas defeated the Pallavas.
c. 750	Pala dynasty founded in E India by Gopala.
c. 840	Pratiharas rose under King Bhoja.
c. 907	Chola power established in S India.
997–1030	Mahmud the Great of Ghazni mounted campaigns against India and annexed Punjab.
1110	Visnuvardharna and Hoysalas rose in Deccan.
1162–1206	Muhammad Ghuri destroyed the Ghaznavid empire and defeated Prithviraj Chauhan at Battle of Tarain (1192).
1206	Sultanate of Delhi established.
1221	Genghis Khan advanced as far as the Indus.

1296–1316	Alauddin Khalji finally defeated the Rajput princes and repelled Mongol incursions.
1325–51	Sultanate extended by Muhammad ibn Tughluq.
1336	Kingdom of Vijayanagara founded in S India.
1347	Bahmani kingdom founded in Deccan.
1398–99	Tamerlane (or Timur) invaded, annexing Punjab and limiting the power of the sultanate.
1414–50	Rule of the Sayyids at Delhi.
1451	Accession of Bahlol Lodi at Delhi.

Early modern period

1505	First Portuguese trading contacts.
1526	Last Muslim invasion of India culminated in Battle of Panipat, where Babur defeated the sultan of Delhi and established the Mogul empire.
1539	Death of Guru Nanak, founder of Sikhism.
1556–1605	Reign of Emperor Akbar, who pacified N India. Edicts on religious toleration and rights for the Hindu population.
1600	(British) East India company formed to establish trade with the subcontinent.
1609	Dutch expelled the Portuguese from Sri Lanka.
1628–58	Shah Jahan extended the Mogul empire into the Deccan.
1658–1707	Reign of Aurangzeb. Great extension of the Mogul empire, but internal dissent caused by persecution and taxation of Hindus.
1674	Maratha (Mahratta) kingdom established by Sivaji.

Modern era

1725	A Nizamat, largely independent of Moguls, was established at Hyderabad.
1739	Persian king Nadir Shah invaded India and plundered Delhi. With Mogul authority waning, Bengal and Oudh effectively broke away.
1746	Increasing struggle between British and French for influence in India. French success, under Dupleix, was followed by resistance organized by Robert Clive.
1757	British victory over N Indian forces at Battle of Plassey established Clive as governor of Bengal.
1761	Marathas defeated by Afghans at Battle of Panipat. Haidar Ail assumed power in Mysore.
1764	Mogul imperial coalition defeated at Buxar by the East India Company, which secured the dewani (state ruled by a prince) of Bengal 1765.

Indian subcontinent: history to 1947 *continued*

1774–85	East India Company became an administrative agency. Governor General Warren Hastings reorganized the legal and administrative system and defeated the main anti-British coalition of Indian princes.
1799	Ranjit Singh became ruler of a Sikh state in the Punjab. Tipu, sultan of Mysore, killed by British troops.
1803–04	British defeated Maratha coalition in N India.
1813	East India Company's trading monopoly abolished.
1814–16	Gurkha War led to British annexation of Nepal.
1817–18	Third Maratha War. Maratha and Rajput states subjugated.
1824–26	First Burmese War. British annexed Tenasserim, Arakan, and Assam.
1839–42	First Afghan War. British evacuated Punjab.
1849	Britist annexed Punjab.
1852	Second Burmese War. Lower Myanmar annexed by British.
1856	British annexation of Oudh (Awadh).
1857	Anti-British feeling erupted into mutiny of Indian troops in N India and wider civil rebellion. Mogul Bahadur Shah II proclaimed emperor of India in Delhi.
1858	Mutiny suppressed, but reforms took place. East India Company dissolved and India became a viceroyalty under the British crown.

The British Raj

1861	Central provincial legislative councils formed in Bombay and Madras under the Indian Councils Act.
1876–78	Famine killed five million people.
1885	Indian National Congress founded in Bombay as a focus for nationalism.
1896–1900	Series of famines claimed another seven million lives.
1905	Partition of the province of Bengal provoked the Swadeshi movement, an Indian boycott on buying British goods.
1906	All-India Muslim League founded at Dhaka.
1909	Indian Councils Act (Morley-Minto reforms) introduced the elective principle to the central legislative council and provided for separate electorates for Muslims on all councils.
1911	At his coronation durbar (court), George V announced the reunification of Bengal and the transfer of the capital of British India from Calcutta to Delhi.
1915	M K Gandhi returned to India from South Africa.
1918	Influenza pandemic killed 17 million Indians.
1919	Rowlatt Act, enabling the government to try political cases without juries, provoked riots. Amritsar massacre saw 379 killed. Government of India Act (Montagu-Chelmsford reforms) provided for diarchy, with Indians being given a separate legislature, a share in provincial government, and control over certain 'transferred' ministries, including education and health.
1920–22	Gandhi won control of Congress, which became committed to *swaraj* (self-rule), and launched non-cooperation campaign. M A Jinnah, leader of the Muslim League, left Congress.
1922–24	Gandhi imprisoned.
1930	Gandhi arrested after undertaking civil disobedience salt march directed against the Salt Tax.
1935	Government of India Act provided for Indian control of the federal legislature, with defence and external affairs remaining the viceroy's responsibility, and for provincial parliamentary self-government.
1940	Lahore session of Muslim League demanded that India be partitioned along religious lines.
1942	Much of Congress leadership arrested after it commenced a 'Quit India' campaign.
1943–44	Bengal famine claimed 1.5 million lives.
1945	New Labour government in UK sought 'an early realization of self-government in India'.
1947	British India partitioned into the independent dominions of India (predominatly Hindu), and East and West Pakistan (mainly Muslim). Bloody communal riots broke out in Punjab as Hindu, Sikh, and Muslim refugees fled to the new states.

'birthplace' temple dedicated to the warrior god Ram on the site of a mosque in the northern city of Ayodhya. This precipitated serious communal tensions, which the government was unable to quell. On 7 Nov, after troops had fired on Hindu fanatics who were attempting to storm the Ayodhya mosque, the Singh government was voted out of office.

minority government A new minority government was formed by Chandra Shekhar, who led a tiny Janata Dal socialist faction compris-

Gandhi and Indian nationalism

The Indian nationalist movement in 19th-century British India was both a reflection of, and a reaction against, British rule and the spread of Western civilization. Until 1914 Indian nationalism was neither national nor united. Rather it was a caste-based movement promoting sectional interests of traditional Indian religious and ruling elites. For example, membership of Congress was largely drawn from young, English-educated Hindus of high caste seeking employment in the Indian civil service, the legal profession, journalism or education. This imitation of their British masters, together with the lack of any real role in the governing of their country, was at the root of Indian discontent.

Two organizations spearheaded the challenge to foreign rule: the Indian National Congress, founded in 1885; and the Muslim League, established in 1906. Congress was split between moderates led by the liberal Gopal Krishna Gokhale, who worked within the system of British rule, and the revolutionary wing led by Bal Gangadhar Tilak, a Hindu revivalist whose supporters were determined to oust the British by any means, including terrorism. This difference divided Congress, alienated the Muslim minority and heightened communal conflict. By 1907, the two wings were deeply divided, with the moderates gaining the upper hand.

Meanwhile, Lord Curzon, viceroy from 1899 to 1905, followed a policy of centralization in an authoritarian style indifferent to popular opinion. His partition of Bengal in 1905 gave the nationalists the inspiration they badly needed and infused Congress with energy and purpose. The Swadeshi movement, a nationwide boycott of British-made goods with encouragement to buy Indian manufactures instead, also forced the British authorities to introduce the Morley-Minto legislative and administrative reforms designed to conciliate moderate nationalists. Their centrepiece was the Indian Council Act of 1909, which initiated the elective principle to membership of the Indian legislative councils and increased the numbers of Indians serving on them. Indians now had the opportunity to redress their grievances from within the system.

High expectations

Many Indian leaders felt that their country's extensive support for Britain during World War I would be rewarded with dominion status. Nationalists were heartened by the 1917 announcement that the British government would open up every branch of the Indian administration to its people, for it was argued that a policy of 'Indianization' would develop self-governing institutions which would open up a path to responsible government of the country by its people. The tabling of the lengthy Montagu-Chelmsford report (1919) on Indian constitutional reform reinforced this theory.

When the reform package came, it was a disappointment. The Government of India Act (1919), established a dual form of government in which external, financial and judicial matters would remain in official hands, while other portfolios would be controlled by elected representatives. The British expected to satisfy the demands of all but the most ardent nationalists with these measures, particularly the granting of complete control to members at the local level. But Indian expectations were higher than that, and the result was political turbulence made worse by an unsettled economy. Matters worsened with the suppression of mass protest against the repressive Anarchical and Revolutionary Crimes Act (1919), resulting from Justice Rowlatt's committee on sedition. The incident occurred in Amritsar, the provincial capital of Lahore, in April 1919, and proved the spur in revitalizing the nationalist campaign. The shock of the massacre and the ruthlessness of General R E H Dyer horrified many moderate nationalists who now decided to challenge British rule.

The emergence of Gandhi

The most enterprising Congress leader was Mohandas Karamchand Gandhi, who called for a nationwide *satyagraha* or non-cooperation campaign. There were a few attempts to resolve the constitutional deadlock such as the Round Table Conferences, and the Government of India Act (1935) tried to replace diarchy with a federal structure which was unacceptable both to Congress and the Muslim League. Very little had changed by the outbreak of World War II, and if anything the Indian national government was even more split between the Indian princes, the Muslim League, Congress and the isolated Gandhi.

Britain's declaration of war on India's behalf enraged many Congress politicians, and several resigned in protest from the provincial ministries. Gandhi called for yet another non-violent non-cooperation campaign in a bid to paralyse the British administration. It did not work, and the Muslims seized the opportunity to consolidate their positions by taking the posts vacated by their Hindu colleagues. The Japanese invasion of Burma (now Myanmar) in 1942, however, forced the British to seek Congress support for the war against Japan. With this aim, Sir Stafford Cripps was despatched to India in March 1942 but his failure led to deadlock and another mass protest orchestrated by Gandhi in Aug, the Quit India campaign. This was easily contained and for the next two years the Indian political scene was quiet.

Many nationalists hailed the election of Clement Attlee's Labour government in 1945 as the necessary breakthrough, but the transfer of power must be seen also against a backdrop of increased communal violence as Congress and the Muslim League jockeyed for political power. As rioting intensified throughout 1946, the British decided to impose a settlement on the warring factions. The viceroy Lord Mountbatten advanced the British withdrawal from India, forcing both sides to stop the violence, restart negotiations and hold a plebiscite on the future of India. Partition was duly approved, and the British left India on 15 Aug 1947. The subcontinent of India was now independent, but it was still not united, and Pakistan would achieve nationhood within a few months.

ing 56 deputies, and was assured of outside support by the Congress Party of Rajiv Gandhi. Violence continued, with a total of 890 people killed and 4,000 injured in Hindu-Muslim riots and 3,560 people killed in the continuing ethnic strife in Punjab 1990. The higher oil prices due to the crisis in the Persian Gulf badly hit India's economy. At the end of Jan 1991 Shekhar dismissed the opposition-led government of the large southern state of Tamil Nadu, citing the presence of Tamil Tiger rebels from N Sri Lanka. This brought to four the number of states subject to direct rule. In March, Shekhar fell out with his backers, Congress (I), and tendered his resignation, but continued as caretaker premier until elections May 1991.

assassination of Rajiv Gandhi On 21 May 1991, a day after the first round of voting had taken place in the general election, Rajiv Gandhi was assassinated at Sriperumpudur, near Madras, by a bomb strapped to a kamikaze guerrilla. She was one of the Liberation Tigers of Tamil Eelam (LTTE), who resented the presence of Indian forces in Sri Lanka. P V Narasimha Rao, an experienced southerner, became Congress (I) party president.

Congress (I) minority government Gandhi's assassination occurred in the wake of what had been the most violent election campaign in Indian history, with several hundred dying in election-related violence in N India where Hindu, Muslim, and Sikh communal tensions were acute. Fortunately, there was subsequent calm, with polling being delayed until mid-June 1991 in seats not already contested. Benefiting from a sympathy vote, Congress (I) emerged as the largest single party, capturing, along with its allies, around 240 of the 511 seats contested. The BJP, which had performed particularly strongly before Rajiv Gandhi's assassination, captured 125 seats and 25% of the popular vote, V P Singh's National Front and Left Front (Communist Party) allies captured 125 seats, while the Samajwadi Janata Party of the outgoing premier, Chandra Shekhar, captured only five seats. Congress (I) polled well in central and S India, but was defeated by the BJP in its traditional northern Hindu-belt heartland of Uttar Pradesh, where a BJP state government was subsequently formed. The BJP's rise was the most striking development during this election. A Congress (I) minority government was established, headed by P V Narasimha Rao. In a new industrial policy, subsidies were slashed, inward foreign investment encouraged, and industrial licensing scrapped, bringing an end to the 'permit raj'.

violence continues The president's rule was extended over Jammu and Kashmir in Sept 1991 for a further six months and was imposed in Meghalaya in Oct 1991. In Punjab, where killings averaged 600 a month during 1991, the president's rule would remain in force until state elections in Feb 1992. In Sept 1991 a Places of Worship Bill was passed, prohibiting the conversion of any place of worship that existed at the Independence (1947), thus debarring Hindus from converting mosques into temples. Despite the mosque in Ayodhya being exempted from its terms, the bill was opposed by the Hindu-chauvinist BJP.

economic reform Prime Minister Rao continued to introduce reforms designed to make the economy more market-conscious and open it up to greater investment. In Nov 1991, in compliance with the conditions for a loan from the International Monetary Fund of US$ 2.2 billion, it was agreed that fertilizer subsidies should be cut, with small farmers being exempted, and unprofitable factories closed down.

The position of Rao's minority government was strengthened Jan 1992 when a split occurred in the opposition Janata Dal and a number of its deputies left and sought alliance with Congress (I). In elections held Feb 1992 in strife-torn Punjab, Congress (I) won control of the state assembly and a majority in parliament. However, despite heavy security, turnout was only 28%, with the main Sikh nationalist party opponents of Congress boycotting the contest.

foreign relations Despite the break-up of the USSR, economic and military links with Russia remained close. A thaw in relations with China resulted in Dec 1991 after the visit to India of Li Peng, the first Chinese premier to visit India since the border conflict of 1962. In Jan 1992 full diplomatic relations with Israel were established.

Ayodhya clash spreads In Dec 1992 the mosque in Ayodhya was demolished by Hindu activists. Interethnic violence flared up throughout the country, with more than 1,000 casualties in the first week.

India Acts legislation passed 1858, 1919, and 1939 which formed the basis of British rule in India until independence 1947. The 1858 Act abolished the administrative functions of the ◊East India Company, replacing them with direct rule from London. The 1919 Act increased Indian participation at local and provincial levels but did not meet nationalist demands for complete internal self-government (◊Montagu-Chelmsford reforms). The 1939

Act outlined a federal structure but was never implemented.

Indian, American see ◊American Indian.

Indian, Andean see ◊Andean Indian.

Indian Mutiny or *Sepoy Rebellion* or *Mutiny* revolt 1857–58 of Indian soldiers (Sepoys) against the British in India. The uprising was confined to the north, from Bengal to the Punjab, and central India. It led to the end of rule by the ◊East India Company and its replacement by direct British crown administration.

The majority of support for the mutiny came from the army and recently dethroned princes, but in some areas it developed into a peasant uprising and general revolt. It included the seizure of Delhi by the rebels, its siege and recapture by the British, and the defence of Lucknow by a British garrison. One of the rebel leaders was ◊Nana Sahib.

Indian National Congress (INC) official name for the ◊Congress Party of India.

Indian, North American see ◊North American Indian.

India of the Princes the 562 Indian states ruled by princes during the period of British control. They occupied an area of 1,854,347 sq km/715,964 sq mi (45% of the total area of pre-partition India) and had a population of over 93 million. At the partition of British India in 1947 the princes were given independence by the British government but were advised to adhere to either India or Pakistan. Between 1947 and 1950 all except ◊Kashmir were incorporated in either country.

Indochina French former collective name for ◊Cambodia, ◊Laos, and ◊Vietnam, which became independent after World War II.

Indochina War war of independence 1946-54 between the nationalist forces of what was to become Vietnam and France, the occupying colonial power.

In 1945 Vietnamese nationalist communist leader ◊Ho Chi Minh proclaimed an independent Vietnamese republic, which soon began an armed struggle against French forces. France in turn set up a noncommunist state four years later. In 1954, after the siege of ◊Dien Bien Phu, a cease-fire was agreed between France and China that resulted in the establishment of two separate states, North and South Vietnam, divided by the 17th parallel. Attempts at reunification of the country led subsequently to the ◊Vietnam War.

Indonesia country in SE Asia, made up of over 13,000 islands situated on or near the equator, between the Indian and Pacific oceans.

history Between 3000 and 500 BC, immigrants from S China displaced the original Melanesian population of Indonesia. Between AD 700 and 1450, two Buddhist and Hindu empires (Srivijaya and Majapahit) developed, to be superseded by Islam from the 13th century. During the 16th century English and Portuguese traders were active in Indonesia, but in 1595 Holland took over trade in the area (see ◊East India Company, Dutch). In the 17th century the Dutch had still only managed to establish trading centres, while extensive Indonesian kingdoms dominated the region, but by the 18th–19th centuries Dutch control was complete and the islands were proclaimed a Dutch colony 1816.

rise of nationalism A nationalist movement developed during the 1920s under the procommunist Indonesian Nationalist Party (PNI), headed by Achmed ◊Sukarno. This was suppressed by the Dutch, but in 1942, after Japan's occupation of the islands, the PNI was installed in power as an anti-Western puppet government.

'Indonesian Revolution' When Japan surrendered to the Allies 1945, President Sukarno proclaimed Indonesia's independence. The Dutch challenged this by launching military expeditions and imprisoning Sukarno before agreeing, under international pressure, to transfer sovereignty 1949.

republic The new republic was planned as a federation of 16 constituent regions but was made unitary 1950. This led to dominance by Java (which has two-thirds of Indonesia's population), provoking revolts in Sumatra and the predominantly Christian South Moluccas. The paramount political figure in the new republic was President Sukarno, who ruled in an authoritarian manner and pursued an ambitious and expansionist foreign policy. He effected the transfer of Dutch (western) New Guinea (Irian Jaya) to Indonesia 1963.

army massacre With the economy deteriorating, in 1965 a left-wing coup attempt was made against Sukarno. It was put down by army Chief of Staff General ◊Suharto, who coordinated the massacre by the army of between 200,000 and 700,000 people; it was later revealed that US intelligence was directly linked to this massacre, having provided the Indonesian military with lists of around 5,000 alleged members of the Indonesian Communist Party. Suharto then assumed power as emergency ruler 1966.

'New Order' Suharto, president from 1967, instituted a 'New Order'. This involved the concentration of political power in the hands of army and security-force officers, the propaga-

tion of Pancasila, which stressed unity and social justice, the pursuit of a liberal economic programme, and the fierce suppression of communist activity.

Rising oil exports brought significant industrial and agricultural growth to Indonesia during the 1970s, and self-sufficiency in rice production was attained by the 1980s. In addition, its borders were extended by the forcible annexation of the former Portuguese colony of ◊East Timor 1976. Suharto's authoritarian approach met with opposition from left-wing groups, from radical Muslims, and from separatist groups in outlying islands.

resettlement of Javanese In Irian Jaya, following the suppression of a rebellion organized by the Free Papua Movement (OPM), a 'transmigration' programme was instituted by the Suharto government 1986, with the aim of resettling 65 million Javanese there and on other sparsely populated 'outer islands' by 2006. This encountered strong opposition from native Melanesians, prompting the emigration of more than 10,000 refugees to neighbouring Papua New Guinea. Although travel restrictions were partly eased in East Timor 1988, the United Nations refused to recognize Indonesia's sovereignty over the area; an estimated 200,000 were killed or died of starvation in the years since the territory was closed to the outside world.

pro-democracy forums In April 1991, a 45-member Democracy Forum was launched by leading members of the country's religious and cultural intelligentsia, including Abdurrahman Wahid, leader of the Nahdatul Ulama, the country's largest Muslim association. In Aug 1991 a Forum for the Purification of People's Sovereignty (FPPS) was established by General Hartono Resko Dharsono, the country's most prominent dissident, released from prison Sept 1990. The formation of these groups was seen as an attempt to ventilate ideas about freedom in politics in what remains an authoritarian state.

foreign relations Indonesia has pursued a nonaligned foreign policy since the Bandung Conference 1955, and is a member of ◊ASEAN. Under General Suharto, its relations with the West improved.

massacre in East Timor On 12 Nov 1991 soldiers opened fire in Dili, capital of East Timor, at the funeral of a student killed by the police during anti-Indonesian demonstrations two weeks earlier. Up to 180 were massacred and a further 300-400 arrested, with up to 60 executed on 15 Nov 1991. The Netherlands, the former colonial power, announced a suspension of foreign aid in response.

In the June 1992 assembly elections, the ruling Golkar party was returned with a reduced majority.

indulgence in the Roman Catholic church, the total or partial remission of temporal punishment for sins which remain to be expiated after penitence and confession have secured exemption from eternal punishment. The doctrine of indulgence began as the commutation of church penances in exchange for suitable works of charity or money gifts to the church, and became a great source of church revenue. This trade in indulgences roused Luther in 1517 to initiate the Reformation. The Council of Trent 1563 recommended moderate retention of indulgences, and they continue, notably in 'Holy Years'.

Indus Valley civilization one of the four earliest ancient civilizations of the Old World (the other three being the ◊Sumerian civilization 3500 BC; ◊Egypt 3000 BC; and ◊China 2200 BC), developing in the NW of the Indian subcontinent about 2500 BC.

◊Mohenjo Daro and ◊Harappa were the two main city complexes, but many more existed along the Indus valley, now in Pakistan. Remains include grid-planned streets with municipal drainage, public and private buildings, baths, temples, a standardized system of weights and measures – all of which testify to centralized political control. Evidence exists for trade with Sumer and Akkad. The ◊Aryan invasion of about 1500 BC probably led to its downfall.

Industrial Revolution the sudden acceleration of technical and economic development that began in Britain in the second half of the 18th century. The traditional agrarian economy was replaced by one dominated by machinery and manufacturing, made possible through technical advances such as the steam engine. This transferred the balance of political power from the landowner to the industrial capitalist and created an urban working class. From 1830 to the early 20th century, the Industrial Revolution spread throughout Europe and the USA and to Japan and the various colonial empires.

Industrial Workers of the World (IWW) labour movement founded in Chicago, USA 1905, and in Australia 1907, the members of which were popularly known as the *Wobblies*. The IWW was dedicated to the overthrow of capitalism and the creation of a single union for workers, but divided on tactics.

infante and *infanta* title given in Spain and Portugal to the sons (other than the heir

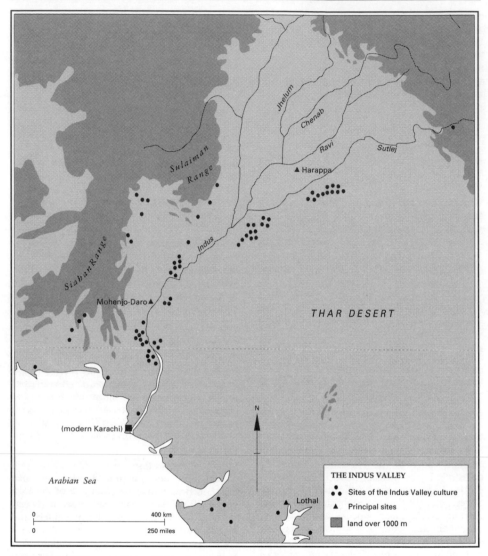

The Indus valley *Between c. 2500 and 1500 BC the lower valley of the river Indus was the site of a highly developed civilization which used copper and bronze, and gave rise to the Indian subcontinent's first truly urban centres: Harappa, Mohenjo Daro, and Lothal. There is evidence of elaborate urban planning, organized collective works, and commercial connections with the Persian Gulf and Mesopotamia. It is still uncertain why the civilization collapsed; flooding, climatic change, overpopulation, and an Aryan invasion are all possible causes.*

apparent) and daughters, respectively, of the sovereign. The heir apparent in Spain bears the title of prince of Asturias.

Inkatha (from the grass coil worn by Zulu women for carrying head loads; its many strands give it strength) South African political organization formed 1975 by Chief Gatsha ◊Buthelezi, leader of 6 million Zulus, the country's biggest ethnic group. Inkatha's avowed aim is to create a nonracial democratic political situation. Inkatha has tried to work with the white regime and, as a result, Buthelezi has been widely regarded as a collaborator. Fighting between Inkatha and African National Congress members cost more than 1,000 lives in the first five months of 1990. In 1991, revelations that Inkatha had received covert financial aid from the South African government during 1989–90 increased the ANC's distrust of its motives.

Inkerman, Battle of battle of the Crimean War, fought on 5 Nov 1854, during which an attack by the Russians on Inkerman Ridge, occupied by the British army besieging Sevastopol, was repulsed.

INLA Abbreviation for ◊Irish National Liberation Army.

Innocent III 1161–1216. Pope from 1198 who asserted papal power over secular princes, in particular over the succession of Holy Roman emperors. He also made King ◊John of England his vassal, compelling him to accept Langton as archbishop of Canterbury. He promoted the fourth Crusade and crusades against the non-Christian Livonians and Letts, and Albigensian heretics of S France.

Inquisition tribunal of the Roman Catholic Church established 1233 to suppress heresy (dissenting views), originally by excommunication. Sentence was pronounced during a religious ceremony, the *auto-da-fé*. The Inquisition operated in France, Italy, Spain, and the Holy Roman Empire, and was especially active following the ◊Reformation; it was later extended to the Americas. Its trials were conducted in secret, under torture, and penalties ranged from fines, through flogging and imprisonment, to death by burning.

During the course of the Spanish Inquisition, until its abolition 1834, some 60,000 cases were tried. The Roman Inquisition was established 1542 to combat the growth of Protestantism. The Inquisition or Holy Office (renamed Sacred Congregation for the Doctrine of the Faith 1965) still deals with ecclesiastical discipline.

intelligentsia in 19th-century Russia, a section of the middle class including lawyers, doctors, teachers, engineers, and some military men, who advocated the adoption of western ideas as a cure for the country's backwardness. They also supported political and social reform but were baulked by an autocratic tsarist regime. This group eventually provided much of the leadership for the revolutionary movements of the early 20th century.

intendant official appointed by the French crown under Louis XIV to administer a territorial *département*. Their powers were extensive but counteracted to some extent by other local officials. The term was also used for certain administrators in Spain, Portugal, and Latin America.

intendencia administrative unit of colonial Spanish America set up during the reign (1759–88) of ◊Charles III. The Bourbon monarchy desired closer supervision of the American population, and intendants were instruments of social control, sent to recover America for Spain after a century of inertia. They reduced the independence of local elites, who regarded them as despotic.

interdict ecclesiastical punishment that excludes an individual, community, or realm from participation in spiritual activities except for communion. It was usually employed against heretics or realms whose ruler was an excommunicant.

Intermediate Nuclear Forces Treaty agreement signed 8 Dec 1987 between the USA and the USSR to eliminate all ground-based nuclear missiles in Europe that were capable of hitting only European targets (including European Russia). It reduced the countries' nuclear arsenals by some 2,000 (4% of the total). The treaty included provisions for each country to inspect the other's bases.

International Bank for Regonstruction and Development specialized agency of the United Nations. Its popular name is the ◊World Bank.

International Brigade international volunteer force on the Republican side in the Spanish ◊Civil War 1936–39.

International Court of Justice main judicial organ of the ◊United Nations, in The Hague, the Netherlands. It hears international law disputes as well as playing an advisory role to UN organs. It was set up by the UN charter 1945 and superseded the World Court.

Internationale international revolutionary socialist anthem; composed 1870 and first sung 1888. The words by Eugène Pottier (1816–1887) were written shortly after Napoleon III's surrender to Prussia; the music is by Pierre Degeyter. It was the Soviet national anthem 1917–44.

International Monetary Fund (IMF) specialized agency of the ◊United Nations, headquarters Washington DC, established under the 1944 ◊Bretton Woods agreement and operational since 1947. It seeks to promote international monetary cooperation and the growth of world trade, and to smooth multilateral payment arrangements among member states. IMF standby loans are available to members in balance-of-payments difficulties (the amount being governed by the member's quota), usually on the basis that the country must agree to take certain corrective measures.

International, the coordinating body established by labour and socialist organizations, including:

First International or *International Working Men's Association* 1864–72, formed in London under Karl ◊Marx.

Second International 1889–1940, founded in Paris.

Third (Socialist) International or *Comintern* 1919–43, formed in Moscow by the Soviet leader Lenin, advocating from 1933 a popular front (communist, socialist, liberal) against the German dictator Hitler.

Fourth International or *Trotskyist International* 1936, somewhat indeterminate, anti-Stalinist.

Revived Socialist International 1951, formed in Frankfurt, Germany, a largely anti-communist association of social democrats.

Interstate Commerce Act in US history, an act of Congress 1887 responding to public concern regarding profiteering and malpractice by railroad companies. It required all charges to be reasonable and fair, and established the Interstate Commerce Commission to investigate railroad management. The act proved difficult to enforce.

Intifada (Arabic 'resurgence' or 'throwing off ') Palestinian uprising; also the title of the involved *Liberation Army of Palestine*, a loosely organized group of adult and teenage Palestinians active since 1987 in attacks on Israeli armed troops in the occupied territories of Palestine. Their campaign for self-determination includes stone-throwing and petrol bombing.

The uprising began Dec 1987 in Gaza. Rumours that a fatal traffic collision had been caused by Israeli security service agents in retaliation for the stabbing of an Israeli the previous week led to demonstrations by teenagers armed with slingshots. It subsequently spread, despite attempts at repression. Some 1,300 Palestinians and 80 Israelis were killed in the uprising up to the end of 1991. Many Palestinian private homes have been dynamited by military order, under a still-valid British emergency regulation promulgated 1946 to put down Jewish guerrillas. The number of soldiers on duty on the West Bank at the beginning of 1989 was said to be more than three times the number needed to conquer it during the Six-Day War.

Invergordon Mutiny incident in the British Atlantic Fleet, Cromarty Firth, Scotland, 15 Sept 1931. Ratings refused to prepare the ships for sea following the government's cuts in their pay; the cuts were consequently modified.

investiture contest conflict between the papacy and the Holy Roman Empire

1075–1122, which centred on the right of lay rulers to appoint prelates (investiture).

It began with the decree of 1075 in which Pope Gregory VII (1021–1085) forbade lay investiture and with Henry IV's excommunication the following year after he refused to accept the ruling. There was a lull in the conflict after Henry's death 1106, but in 1111, Henry V captured Paschal II (*c.* 1050–1118), and forced him to concede that only lay rulers could endow prelates with their temporalities (lands and other possessions). When this was overturned by the Lateran Council of 1112, the church split between pro-papal and pro-imperial factions, and fighting broke out in Germany and Italy. Settlement was reached 1122 at the Diet of Worms, when it was agreed that lay rulers could not appoint prelates but could continue to invest them with their temporalities.

Ionia in Classical times the E coast of the Aegean Sea and the offshore islands, settled about 1000 BC by the Ionians; it included the cities of Ephesus, Miletus, and later Smyrna, and the islands of Chios and Samos.

IRA abbreviation for ◊Irish Republican Army.

Iran country in SW Asia, bounded N by Armenia, Azerbaijan, the Caspian Sea, and Turkmenistan; E by Afghanistan and Pakistan; S and SW by the Gulf of Oman and the Persian Gulf; W by Iraq; and NW by Turkey.

history The name Iran is derived from the Aryan tribes, including the Medes and Persians, who overran Persia (see ◊Persia, ancient) from 1600 BC. ◊Cyrus the Great, who seized the Median throne 550, formed an empire including Babylonia, Syria, and Asia Minor, to which Egypt, Thrace, and Macedonia were later added. It was conquered by Alexander the Great 334–328, then passed to his general Seleucus (*c.* 358–280) and his descendants, until overrun in the 3rd century BC by the Parthians. The Parthian dynasty was overthrown AD 226 by Ardashir, founder of the ◊Sassanian Empire.

During 633–41 Persia was conquered for Islam by the Arabs and then in 1037–55 came under the Seljuk Turks. Their empire broke up in the 12th century and was conquered in the 13th by the Mongols. After 1334 Persia was again divided until its conquest by ◊Tamerlane in the 1380s. A period of violent disorder in the later 15th century was ended by the accession of the Safavid dynasty, who ruled 1499–1736 but were deposed by the great warrior Nadir Shah (ruled 1736–47), whose death was followed by instability until the accession of the Qajar dynasty (1794–1925).

During the 18th century Persia was threatened by Russian expansion, culminating in the loss of Georgia 1801 and a large part of Armenia 1828. Persian claims on Herat, Afghanistan, led to war with Britain 1856–57. Revolutions 1905 and 1909 resulted in the establishment of a parliamentary regime. During World War I the country was occupied by British and Russian forces. An officer, Col Reza Khan, was made minister of war following a coup 1921, and was crowned shah 1925; this allowed him to carry out a massive programme of modernization.

after World War II During World War II, Iran, as it had become known, was occupied by British, US, and Soviet troops until 1946. Anti-British and anti-American feeling grew, and in 1951 the newly elected prime minister, Dr Muhammad Mossadeq, obtained legislative approval for the nationalization of Iran's largely foreign-owned petroleum industry. With US connivance, he was deposed in a 1953 coup, and the dispute over nationalization was settled the following year when oil-drilling concessions were granted to a consortium of eight companies. The shah took complete control of the government, and Iran enjoyed a period of political stability and economic growth 1965–77, based on oil revenue.

Iranian revolution By 1975 the shah had introduced a one-party system, based on the Rastakhis (Iran National Resurgence Party), but opposition to his regime was growing. The most effective opposition came from the religious leader Ayatollah Khomeini, who campaigned from exile in France. He demanded a return to the principles of Islam, and pressure on the shah became so great that in 1979 he left the country, leaving the way open for Khomeini's return. He appointed a provisional government, but power was placed essentially in the hands of the 15-member Islamic Revolutionary Council, controlled by Khomeini.

Islamic republic Iran was declared an Islamic republic, and a new constitution, based on Islamic principles, was adopted. Relations with the USA were badly affected when a group of Iranian students took 63 Americans hostage at the US embassy in Tehran, demanding that the shah return to face trial. Even the death of the shah, in Egypt 1980, did little to resolve the crisis, which ended when all the hostages were released Jan 1981.

Iran–Iraq War In its early years several rifts developed within the new Islamic government. Externally, the war with Iraq, which broke out 1980 after a border dispute, continued with considerable loss of life on both sides. Mean-

while, Islamic law was becoming stricter, with amputation as the penalty for theft and flogging for minor sexual offences. By 1985 the failure to end the ◊Iran–Iraq War and the harshness of the Islamic codes were increasing opposition to Khomeini's regime but his position remained secure. The intervention of the US Navy to conduct convoys through the Gulf 1987–88 resulted in confrontations that proved costly for Iranian forces. Iraq gained the initiative on the battlefield, aided by its use of chemical weapons. By 1987 both sides in the war had increased the scale of their operations, each apparently believing that outright victory was possible. In Aug 1988, under heavy domestic and international pressure, Iran accepted the provisions for a United Nations-sponsored cease-fire. Full diplomatic relations with the UK were restored Dec 1988, but the issuing of a death threat to the author Salman Rushdie caused a severance March 1989.

rebuilding the economy Khomeini's death in June 1989 provoked a power struggle between hardline revolutionaries and so-called pragmatists who recognized a need for trade and cooperation with the West. Revelations in 1989 that Iran had negotiated secret oil sales to Israel reflected Iran's need for hard currency to rebuild its economy as well as a desire to counter Iraq. Struggle for succession began, ending with the confirmation of the former speaker of the Majlis, Hoshemi Rafsanjani, as president with increased powers. Despite his reputation for moderation and pragmatism, Iran's relations with the West were slow to improve. In Aug 1990 Iran accepted Iraq's generous peace terms, which virtually gave back everything it had claimed at the start of the Iran–Iraq War. During the Kurdish refugee crisis that followed the Gulf War, Iran took in nearly 1 million Kurds; it accused the USA and relief agencies of neglecting the Kurds. Iran also condemned the Middle East peace conference held in Spain Nov 1991.

In May 1992 elections supporters of Rafsanjani claimed a majority win, constituting a major setback for Iran's Islamic militants.

Irangate US political scandal 1987 involving senior members of the Reagan administration (called this to echo the Nixon administration's ◊Watergate). Congressional hearings 1986–87 revealed that the US government had secretly sold weapons to Iran in 1985 and traded them for hostages held in Lebanon by pro-Iranian militias, and used the profits to supply right-wing Contra guerrillas in Nicaragua with arms.

Iran–Iraq War or *Gulf War* war between Iran and Iraq 1980–88, claimed by the former to have begun with the Iraqi offensive 21 Sept 1980, and by the latter with the Iranian shelling of border posts 4 Sept 1980. Occasioned by a boundary dispute over the Shatt-al-Arab waterway, it fundamentally arose because of Saddam Hussein's fear of a weakening of his absolute power base in Iraq by Iran's encouragement of the Shi'ite majority in Iraq to rise against the Sunni government. An estimated 1 million people died in the war.

The war's course was marked by offensive and counter-offensive, interspersed with extended periods of stalemate. Chemical weapons were used, cities and the important oil installations of the area were the target for bombing raids and rocket attacks, and international shipping came under fire in the Persian Gulf (including in 1987 the US frigate *Stark*, which was attacked by the Iraqi airforce). Among Arab states, Iran was supported by Libya and Syria, the remainder supporting Iraq. Iran also benefited from secret US arms shipments, the disclosure of which in 1986 led to considerable scandal in the USA, ◊Irangate.

Iraq country in SW Asia, bounded N by Turkey, E by Iran, SE by the Persian Gulf and Kuwait, S by Saudi Arabia, and W by Jordan and Syria.

history The area now occupied by Iraq was formerly ancient ◊Mesopotamia and was the centre of the Sumerian, Babylonian, and Assyrian civilizations 6000 BC–AD 100. It was conquered 114 by the Romans and was ruled 266–632 by the native Sassanids before being invaded 633 by the Arabs. In 1065 the country was taken over by the Turks and was invaded by the Mongols 1258; Baghdad was destroyed 1401 by ◊Tamerlane. Annexed by Suleiman the Magnificent 1533, Iraq became part of the Turkish Ottoman Empire 1638, as the separate *vilayets* (regions) of Basra, Baghdad, and Mosul.

independent kingdom Occupied by Britain in World War I, Iraq was placed under British administration by the League of Nations 1920. In 1932 Iraq became a fully independent kingdom, but until World War II Iraq's increasing formal autonomy masked a continued political and military control by Britain. In 1933 the reigning king, Faisal I, died and was succeeded by his son Ghazi; the leading figure behind the throne was the strongly pro-Western general Nuri-el-Said, who was prime minister 1930–58. In 1939 King Ghazi was killed in an accident, and Faisal II became king at the age of three, his uncle Prince Abdul Ilah acting as regent until 1953 when the king assumed full powers.

In 1955 Iraq signed the ◊Baghdad Pact, a regional collective security agreement, with the USSR seen as the main potential threat, and in 1958 joined Jordan in an Arab Federation, with King Faisal as head of state. In July of that year, a revolution overthrew the monarchy, and King Faisal, Prince Abdul Ilah, and General Nuri were all killed.

republic The constitution was suspended, and Iraq was declared a republic, with Brig Abdul Karim Kassem as head of a left-wing military regime. He withdrew from the Baghdad Pact 1959 and was killed 1963 in a coup led by Col Salem Aref, who established a new government, ended martial law, and within two years had introduced a civilian administration. He died in an air crash 1966, and his brother, who succeeded him, was ousted 1968 and replaced by Maj-Gen Ahmed Hassan al-Bakr. He concentrated power in the hands of a Revolutionary Command Council (RCC) and made himself head of state, head of government, and chair of the RCC.

In 1979 Saddam Hussein, who for several years had been the real power in Iraq, replaced al-Bakr as RCC chair and state president. In 1980 he introduced a National Charter, reaffirming a policy of ◊nonalignment and a constitution that provided for an elected national assembly. The first elections took place that year.

Iran–Iraq War Iraq had, since 1970, enjoyed a fluctuating relationship with Syria, sometimes distant and sometimes close enough to contemplate a complete political and economic union. By 1980, however, the atmosphere was cool. Relations between Iraq and Iran had been tense for some years, with disagreement over their shared border, which runs down the Shatt-al-Arab waterway. The 1979 Iranian revolution made Iraq more suspicious of Iran's intentions, and in 1980 a full-scale war broke out. Despite Iraq's inferior military strength, Iran gained little territory, and by 1986 it seemed as if a stalemate might have been reached. The fighting intensified again in early 1987, by which time hundreds of thousands of lives had been lost on both sides and incalculable damage to industry and property sustained. Following Iranian acceptance of United Nations cease-fire provisions, the war came to an end 1988. Peace talks made little progress on fundamental issues of territory or prisoner-of-war repatriation. Hussein took advantage of the end of hostilities to turn his combat-hardened army against Kurdish separatists, many of whom had sided with Iran. After the war's end, Iraq moved to support Christian forces in Lebanon against

Syrian- and Iranian-backed Muslims. The Iraqis also launched a ballistic missile on a successful test, causing concern about Iraq's suspected nuclear-weapons development. In 1989 an unsuccessful coup attempt against President Hussein was reported.

Gulf War In 1990 Hussein reopened a long-standing territorial dispute with neighbouring Kuwait while seeking to assume leadership of the Arab world. Following increasing diplomatic pressure, on 2 Aug Iraqi troops invaded and annexed Kuwait, installing a puppet government and declaring it part of Iraq. As Iraqi troops massed on his borders, King Fahd of Saudi Arabia requested help from the USA and the UK, and a rapid build-up of US ground and air power and British aircraft began. Meanwhile the UN Security Council condemned the invasion, demanded Iraq's withdrawal, and imposed comprehensive sanctions including an embargo. These were to be enforced by a multinational naval force led by the USA. To make its substantial presence in Saudi Arabia seem more legitimate, the USA sought contributions from other UN members but with only limited success. Unsuccessful attempts to find a peaceful solution to the dispute were made by Egypt, Jordan, France, the USA, the UK, and the UN.

To ensure the safety of his border, President Hussein hastily concluded a permanent peace treaty with Iran, under which he conceded virtually everything for which he had fought the Iran–Iraq War and both countries agreed to release all prisoners of war.

Refusing to withdraw from Kuwait, President Hussein sought to prevent a military strike against him by compelling thousands of non-Iraqi adult males, mainly British and American, living in Iraq to remain there, moving some to unknown strategic locations. Meanwhile, a mass exodus of foreign workers who were allowed to leave created enormous refugee problems in neighbouring Jordan.

In Dec 1990 the UN Security Council set a 15 Jan 1991 deadline for Iraq's withdrawal from Kuwait, after which force could be used. Soon afterwards US president Bush offered talks with Iraq and proposed a UN sponsored international conference to discuss the Middle East's problems. Saddam Hussein then announced that all foreign hostages in Kuwait and Iraq would be allowed to return home. Nevertheless, Iraqi troops were not removed from Kuwait by the deadline and on 16 Jan the US-led Allied forces began the aerial bombardment of Baghdad as the first phase of operation Desert Storm, the military campaign to liberate Kuwait; the

Iraqi military response during the air campaign was largely limited to the firing of Scud missiles into Israel and Saudi Arabia. A last-minute peace initiative by the USSR to avoid a land battle failed, and on 23 Feb the Allied land offensive began, with thousands of Iraqi troops immediately surrendering without a fight to the advancing Allied armies. On 28 Feb 1991, after 100 hours of ground fighting, the Iraqi forces capitulated and agreed to a cease-fire. The total number of Iraqis killed in the war was estimated at around 200,000. By March, Iraq had conceded to peace negotiations.

Various factions in Iraq began uprisings against the government after the withdrawal of the US and allied forces from northern Iraq in July 1991; these were soon quelled by government forces, leading to an immense refugee problem as Kurds in the north and Shi'ites in the south fled from their homes in fear of reprisals. An autonomy agreement offered to the Kurds was rejected in June and subsequent negotiations saw little progress. In Nov 1991 talks were resumed but Iraqi harassment of Kurds continued. After the initial compromise agreement on UN inspection of suspected arms-production sites in July 1991, Saddam Hussein continued to violate the terms of the cease-fire agreement, rejecting UN resolutions on weapons and human rights, and carrying out further obstruction of UN arms inspections. A coup attempt by Iraq's Republican Guard against Saddam Hussein July 1992 was thwarted by officers loyal to him. The conspiracy allegedly received backing from the US and Jordan although the US did not confirm the reports and Jordan denied any role in the plot. In Aug 1992 the UN Security Council imposed a 'no-fly zone' over S Iraq to protect the Shi'ite community.

Ireland: history in prehistoric times Ireland underwent a number of invasions from Europe, the most important of which was that of the Gaels in the 3rd century BC. Gaelic Ireland was divided into kingdoms, nominally subject to an *Ardri* or High King; the chiefs were elected under the tribal or Brehon law, and were usually at war with one another. Christianity was introduced by St Patrick about 432, and during the 5th and 6th centuries Ireland became the home of a civilization which sent out missionaries to Britain and Europe. From about 800 the Danes began to raid Ireland, and later founded Dublin and other coastal towns, until they were defeated by Brian Boru (king from 976) at Clontarf 1014. Anglo-Norman adventurers invaded Ireland 1167, but by the end of the medieval period English rule was still confined to the Pale, the

Ireland 1801–1916

1800	Act of Union established United Kingdom of Great Britain and Ireland. Effective 1801.	1885	Franchise Reform gave Home Rulers 85 seats in new parliament and balance between Liberals and Tories. Home Rule Bill rejected.
1823	Catholic Association founded by Daniel O'Connell to campaign for Catholic political rights.	1886	Home Rule Bill rejected again.
1828	O'Connell elected for County Clare; forced granting of rights for Catholics to sit in Parliament.	1890	Parnell cited in divorce case, which split Home Rule movement.
1829	Catholic Emancipation Act.	1893	Second Home Rule Bill defeated in House of Lords; Gaelic League founded.
1838	Tithe Act (abolishing payment) removed a major source of discontent.	1900	Irish Nationalists reunited under Redmond. 82 MPs elected.
1840	Franchise in Ireland reformed. 'Young Ireland' formed.	1902	Sinn Féin founded by Arthur Griffith.
1846–51	Potato famine resulted in widespread death and emigration. Population reduced by 20%.	1906	Bill for devolution of power to Ireland rejected by Nationalists.
1850	Irish Franchise Act extended voters from 61,000 to 165,000.	1910	Sir Edward Carson led Unionist opposition to Home Rule.
1858	Fenian Brotherhood formed.	1912	Home Rule Bill for whole of Ireland introduced. (Protestant) Ulster Volunteers formed to resist.
1867	Fenian insurrection failed.		
1869	Church of Ireland disestablished.	1913	Home Rule Bill defeated in House of Lords but overridden. (Catholic) Irish Volunteers founded in the South.
1870	Land Act provided greater security for tenants but failed to halt agrarian disorders. Protestant Isaac Butt formed Home Government Association (Home Rule League).		
		1914	Nationalists persuaded to exclude Ulster from Bill for six years but Carson rejected it. Curragh 'mutiny' cast doubt on reliability of British troops against Protestants. Extensive gun-running by both sides. World War I deferred implementation.
1874	Home Rule League won 59 Parliamentary seats and adopted a policy of obstruction.		
1880	Charles Stuart Parnell became leader of Home Rulers, dominated by Catholic groups. 'Boycotts' against landlords unwilling to agree to fair rents.	1916	Easter Rising by members of Irish Republican Brotherhood. Suppressed by troops and leaders executed.
1881	Land Act greeted with hostility. Parnell imprisoned. 'No Rent' movement began.	1919	Irish Republican Army (IRA) formed.
1882	'Kilmainham Treaty' between government and Parnell agreed conciliation. Chief Secretary Cavendish and Under Secretary Burke murdered in Phoenix Park, Dublin.	1921	Partition of Ireland; creation of Irish Free State.
			For subsequent history, see ◊Ireland, Republic of and ◊Ireland, Northern.

territory around Dublin. The Tudors adopted a policy of conquest, confiscation of Irish land, and plantation by English settlers, and further imposed the ◊Reformation and English law on Ireland. The most important of the plantations was that of Ulster, carried out under James I 1610. In 1641 the Irish took advantage of the developing struggle in England between king and Parliament to begin a revolt which was crushed by Oliver ◊Cromwell 1649, the estates of all 'rebels' being confiscated. Another revolt 1689–91 was also defeated, and the Roman Catholic majority held down by penal laws. In 1739–41 a famine killed one-third of the population of 1.5 million.

The subordination of the Irish parliament to that of England, and of Irish economic interests to English, led to the rise of a Protestant patriot party, which in 1782 forced the British government to remove many commercial restrictions and grant the Irish parliament its independence. This did not satisfy the population, who in 1798, influenced by French revolutionary ideas, rose in rebellion, but were again defeated; and in 1800 William ◊Pitt induced the Irish parliament to vote itself out of existence by the Act of ◊Union, effective 1 Jan 1801, which brought Ireland under the aegis of the British crown. During another famine 1846–51, 1.5 million people emigrated, mostly to the USA.

By the 1880s there was a strong movement for home rule for Ireland; Gladstone supported it but was defeated by the British Parliament. By 1914, home rule was conceded but World War I delayed implementation.

The *Easter Rising* took place April 1916, when nationalists seized the Dublin general post office and proclaimed a republic. After a week of fighting, the revolt was suppressed by the British army and most of its leaders executed. From

Northern Ireland from 1967

1967 Northern Ireland Civil Rights Association set up to press for equal treatment for Catholics in the provinces.	SDLP (19%) and Sinn Féin (10%) boycotted the assembly.
1968 Series of civil rights marches sparked off rioting and violence, especially in Londonderry.	**1984** Series of reports from various groups on the future of the province. IRA bomb at Conservative Party conference in Brighton killed five people. Second Anglo-Irish Intergovernmental Council summit meeting agreed to oppose violence and cooperate on security; Britain rejected ideas of confederation or joint sovereignty.
1969 Election results weakened Terence O'Neil's Unionist government. Further rioting led to call-up of (Protestant-based) B-Specials to Royal Ulster Constabulary. Chichester-Clark replaced O'Neil. IRA split into 'official' and 'provisional' wings. RUC disarmed and B-Specials replaced by nonsectarian Ulster Defence Regiment (UDR). British Army deployed in Belfast and Londonderry.	
	1985 Meeting of Margaret Thatcher and Irish premier Garrett Fitzgerald at Hillsborough produced Anglo-Irish agreement on the future of Ulster; regarded as a sell-out by Unionists.
1971 First British soldier killed. Brian Faulkner replaced Chichester-Clark. IRA stepped up bombing campaign.	**1986** Unionist opposition to Anglo-Irish agreement included protests and strikes. Loyalist violence against police and Unionist MPs boycotted Westminster.
1972 'Bloody Sunday' in Londonderry when British Army killed 13 demonstrators. Direct rule from Westminster introduced.	**1987** IRA bombed British Army base in West Germany. Unionist boycott of Westminster ended. Extradition clauses of Anglo-Irish Agreement approved in Eire. IRA bombed Remembrance Day service at Enniskillen – later admitted it to be a 'mistake'.
1974 'Power sharing' between Protestant and Catholic groups tried but failed. IRA extended bombing campaign to UK mainland. Bombs in Guildford and Birmingham caused a substantial number of fatalities.	**1988** Three IRA bombers killed by security forces on Gibraltar.
1976 British Ambassador in Dublin, Christopher Ewart Biggs, assassinated. Peace Movement founded by Betty Williams and Mairead Corrigan.	**1989** After serving fourteen years in prison, the 'Guildford Four' were released when their convictions were ruled unsound by the Court of Appeal.
1978 British MP Airey Neave assassinated by INLA at the House of Commons.	**1990** Anglo-Irish Agreement threatened when Eire refused extraditions. Convictions of 'Birmingham Six' also called into question and sent to the Court of Appeal.
1980 Meeting of Margaret Thatcher and Irish premier Charles Haughey on a peaceful settlement to the Irish question. Hunger strikes and 'dirty protests' started by Republican prisoners in pursuit of political status.	**1991** IRA renewed bombing campaign on British mainland, targetting a meeting of the cabinet in Downing Street and mainline railway stations.
1981 Hunger strikes led to deaths of Bobby Sands and Francis Hughes; Anglo-Irish Intergovernmental Council formed.	**1994** IRA announces cease-fire (broken 1996)
1982 Northern Ireland Assembly created to devolve legislative and executive powers back to the province.	**1997** Cease-fire resumes; multi-party peace talks (started 1996) continue with Sinn Féin.

1918 to 1921 there was guerrilla warfare against the British army, especially by the Irish Republican Army (◊IRA), formed by Michael Collins 1919. This led to a split in the rebel forces, but in 1921 the Anglo-Irish Treaty resulted in partition and the creation of the Irish Free State in S Ireland. For history since that date, see ◊Ireland, Republic of; ◊Ireland, Northern.

Ireland, Northern constituent part of the United Kingdom.

history for history pre-1921, see ◊Ireland, history. The creation of Northern Ireland dates from 1921, when the Irish Free State (subsequently the Republic of Ireland) was established separately from the mainly Protestant counties of Ulster (six out of nine), which were given limited self-government but continued to send members to the House of Commons. Spasmodic outbreaks of violence by the Irish Republican Army (IRA) occurred, but only in 1968-69 were there serious disturbances arising from Protestant political dominance and discrimination against the Roman Catholic minority in employment and housing. British troops were sent 1969 to restore peace and protect Catholics, but disturbances continued and in 1972 the parliament at Stormont was superseded by direct rule from Westminster.

Under the ◊Anglo-Irish Agreement 1985, the Republic of Ireland was given a consultative role (via an Anglo-Irish conference) in Northern Ireland's government, but agreed that there should be no change in its status except by majority consent. All 12 Ulster members of parliament resigned to create a 'referendum' on the proposal through by-elections. A similar boycott of the Northern Ireland Assembly led to its dissolution 1986 by the UK government.

Northern Ireland's political future was debated in talks held in Belfast 1991 – the first direct negotiations between the political parties for 16 years. Follow-up talks between the British government and the main Norther Ireland parties 1992 made little progress. It emerged 1993 that the Catholic nationalist Social Democratic Labour Party (SDLP) and Sinn Féin (political wing of the IRA) had held talks. The British government then engaged in bilateral talks with the main Northern Ireland parties, and, with Dublin, issued a joint peace proposal in Dec, the Downing Street Declaration.

The Provisional IRA announced a unilateral cease-fire Aug 1994, and Sinn Féin engaged in the public talks with British government officials 1995. But there was deadlock over the issue of arms decommissioning. The end of the IRA cease-fire Feb 1996 dealt a severe blow to the peace process, but it was restored 1997 and Sinn Féin joined multi-party peace talks.

Ireland, Republic of country occupying the main part of the island of Ireland, NW Europe. It is bounded E by the Irish Sea, S and W by the Atlantic Ocean, and NE by Northern Ireland.

history For history pre-1921, see ◊Ireland, history. In 1921 a treaty gave Southern Ireland dominion status within the ◊Commonwealth, while six out of the nine counties of Ulster remained part of the UK, with limited self-government. The Irish Free State, as Southern Ireland was formally called 1921, was accepted by IRA leader Michael Collins but not by many of his colleagues, who shifted their allegiance to the Fianna Fáil party leader Éamon ◊de Valera. A civil war ensued, in which Collins was killed. The partition was eventually acknowledged 1937 when a new constitution established the country as a sovereign state under the name of *Eire*.

after independence The IRA continued its fight for an independent, unified Ireland through a campaign of violence, mainly in Northern Ireland but also on the British mainland and, to a lesser extent, in the Irish republic. Eire remained part of the Commonwealth until 1949, when it left, declaring itself the Republic of Ireland, while Northern Ireland remained a constituent part of the UK. In 1973 Fianna Fáil, having held office for over 40 years, was defeated, and Liam Cosgrave formed a coalition of the Fine Gael and Labour parties.

In 1977 Fianna Fáil returned to power, with Jack Lynch as prime minister. In 1979 IRA vio-

lence intensified with the killing of Earl Mountbatten in Ireland and 18 British soldiers in Northern Ireland. Lynch resigned later the same year, and was succeeded by Charles Haughey. His aim was a united Ireland, with considerable independence for the six northern counties. After the 1981 election Garret FitzGerald, leader of Fine Gael, formed another coalition with Labour but was defeated the following year on budget proposals and resigned. Haughey returned to office with a minority government, but he, too, had to resign later that year, resulting in the return of FitzGerald.

Anglo-Irish Agreement In 1983 all the main Irish and Northern Irish political parties initiated the New Ireland Forum as a vehicle for discussion. Its report was rejected by Margaret Thatcher's Conservative government in the UK, but discussions between London and Dublin resulted in the signing of the Anglo-Irish Agreement 1985, providing for regular consultation and exchange of information on political, legal, security, and cross-border matters. The agreement also said that the status of Northern Ireland would not be changed without the consent of a majority of the people. The agreement was criticized by the Unionist parties of Northern Ireland, who asked that it be rescinded. FitzGerald's coalition ended 1986, and the Feb 1987 election again returned Fianna Fáil and Charles Haughey.

relations with UK In 1988 relations with the UK were at a low ebb because of disagreements over extradition decisions. In elections 1989, Haughey failed to win a majority and entered into a coalition with the Progressive Democrats (a breakaway party from Fianna Fáil). In 1990, the left-wing-backed Mary Robinson won the presidential election.

Haughey to Ahern The Progressive Democrats withdrew from the coalition 1992 after allegations against Haughey of illegal telephone tapping. Haughey resigned and was replaced by Albert Reynolds, who led a reconstructed cabinet. In June, a referendum found 69% in favour of the Maastricht Treaty on European union. The results of a general election Nov 1992 were inconclusive. After prolonged negotiations, Reynolds formed a Fianna Fáil-Labour coalition Jan 1993. The new coalition worked closely with the UK government on Northern Ireland, leading to the Downing Street Declaration Dec 1993. An IRA ceasefire was announced 1994 (ending 1996; restored 1997).

Dick Spring, the Labour leader, withdrew from the coalition Nov 1994, and a new coalition was formed with Fine Gael under John Bruton's premiership. The Irish public voted narrowly in a referendum Nov 1995 to legalize divorce. There were further elections in 1997; Bertie Ahern of Fianna Fáil became prime minister and Mary McAleese became president.

Irene, St c. 752–c. 803. Byzantine empress 797–802. The wife of Leo IV (750–80), she became regent for their son Constantine (771–805) on Leo's death. In 797 she deposed her son, had his eyes put out, and assumed the full title of *basileus* ('emperor'), ruling in her own right until deposed and exiled to Lesvos by a revolt in 802. She was made a saint by the Greek Orthodox church for her attacks on iconoclasts.

Ireton Henry 1611–1651. English Civil War general. He joined the parliamentary forces and fought at ◊Edgehill 1642, Gainsborough 1643, and ◊Naseby 1645. After the Battle of Naseby, Ireton, who was opposed to both the extreme republicans and ◊Levellers, strove for a compromise with Charles I, but then played a leading role in his trial and execution. He married his leader Cromwell's daughter in 1646. Lord Deputy in Ireland from 1650, he died after the capture of Limerick.

Irgun short for *Irgun Zvai Leumi* (National Military Society), a Jewish guerrilla group active against the British administration in Palestine 1946–48. Their bombing of the King David Hotel in Jerusalem 22 July 1946 resulted in 91 fatalities.

Irian Jaya western portion of the island of New Guinea, part of Indonesia.

history part of the Dutch East Indies 1828 as Western New Guinea; retained by the Netherlands after Indonesian independence 1949 but ceded to Indonesia 1963 by the United Nations and remained part of Indonesia by an 'Act of Free Choice' 1969. In the 1980s 283,500 hectares/700,000 acres were given over to Indonesia's controversial transmigration programme for the resettlement of farming families from overcrowded Java, causing destruction of rainforests and displacing indigenous people.

Irish Free State former name (1922–37) of Southern Ireland, now the Republic of ◊Ireland.

Irish National Liberation Army (INLA) guerrilla organization committed to the end of British rule in Northern Ireland and the incorporation of Ulster into the Irish Republic. The INLA was a 1974 offshoot of the Irish Republican Army (IRA). Among the INLA's activities was the killing of British politician Airey Neave in 1979.

Irish Republican Army (IRA) militant Irish nationalist organization whose aim is to create a united Irish socialist republic including Ulster. The paramilitary wing of ◊Sinn Féin, it was founded 1919 by Michael ◊Collins and fought a successful war against Britain 1919–21. It came to the fore again 1939 with a bombing campaign in Britain, having been declared illegal in 1936 . Its activities intensified from 1968 onwards, as the civil-rights disorders ('the Troubles') in Northern Ireland developed. In 1970 a group in the north broke away to become the *Provisional IRA*; its objective is the expulsion of the British from Northern Ireland.

The IRA carried out bombings and shootings in Northern Ireland as well as bombings in mainland Britain and in British military bases overseas. In 1979 it murdered Louis ◊Mountbatten, and its bomb attacks in Britain included an attempt to kill UK cabinet members during the 1984 Conservative Party conference in Brighton, Sussex.

The IRA announced a cessation of military activities Aug 1994, in response to a UK-Irish peace initiative. The cease-fire was broken Feb 1996, but restored in July 1997. Sinn Fiin took part in multi-party peace talks from Sept 1997, but participation remained controversial among some in Sinn Fiin and the IRA.

Iron Age developmental stage of human technology when weapons and tools were made from iron. Iron was produced in Thailand by about 1600 BC but was considered inferior in strength to bronze until about 1000 when metallurgical techniques improved and the alloy steel was produced by adding carbon during the smelting process.

Iron Age cultures include *Hallstatt* (named after a site in Austria), *La Tène* (from a site in Switzerland), and *Marnian* (from the Marne region, France).

ironclad wooden warship covered with armour plate. The first to be constructed was the French *Gloire* 1858, but the first to be launched was the British HMS *Warrior* 1859. The first battle between ironclads took place during the American Civil War, when the Union *Monitor* fought the Confederate *Virginia* (formerly the *Merrimack*) 9 March 1862. The design was replaced by battleships of all-metal construction in the 1890s.

Iron Cross medal awarded for valour in the German armed forces. Instituted in Prussia 1813, it consists of a Maltese cross of iron, edged with silver.

Iron Curtain in Europe after World War II, the symbolic boundary of the ◊Cold War between capitalist West and communist East. The term was popularized by the UK prime minister Winston Churchill from 1945.

Iron Guard pro-fascist group controlling Romania in the 1930s. To counter its influence, King Carol II established a dictatorship 1938 but the Iron Guard forced him to abdicate 1940.

Iroquois member of a confederation of NE North American Indians, the Six Nations (Cayuga, Mohawk, Oneida, Onondaga, and Seneca, with the Tuscarora after 1723), traditionally formed by Hiawatha (actually a priestly title) 1570.

irredentist (Latin *redemptus*, bought back) person who wishes to reclaim the lost territories of a state. The term derives from an Italian political party founded about 1878 intending to incorporate Italian-speaking areas into the newly formed state.

Isabella I *the Catholic* 1451–1504. Queen of Castile from 1474, after the death of her brother Henry IV. By her marriage with Ferdinand of Aragon 1469, the crowns of two of the Christian states in the Moorish-held Spanish peninsula were united. In her reign, during 1492, the Moors were driven out of Spain. She introduced the ◊Inquisition into Castile, expelled the Jews, and gave financial encouragement to ◊Columbus. Her youngest daughter was Catherine of Aragon, first wife of Henry VIII of England.

Whosoever hath a good presence and a good fashion, carries continual letters of recommendation.

Isabella I of Spain

Isabella II 1830–1904. Queen of Spain from 1833, when she succeeded her father Ferdinand VII (1784–1833). The Salic Law banning a female sovereign had been repealed by the Cortes (parliament), but her succession was disputed by her uncle Don Carlos de Bourbon (1788–1855). After seven years of civil war, the ◊Carlists were defeated. She abdicated in favour of her son Alfonso XII in 1868.

Isabella of France 1292–1358. Daughter of Philip IV of France, she married Edward II of England 1308, but he slighted and neglected her for his favourites, first Piers Gaveston (died 1312) and later the Despenser family. Supported by her lover Roger Mortimer, Isabella conspired to have Edward deposed and murdered.

Isaurian 8th-century Byzantine imperial dynasty, originating in Asia Minor.

Members of the family had been employed as military leaders by the Byzantines, and they gained great influence and prestige as a result. Leo III acceded in 717 as the first Isaurian emperor, and was followed by Constantine V (718–75), Leo IV (750–80), and Leo's widow Irene, who acted as regent for their son before deposing him 797 and assuming the title of emperor herself. She was deposed 802. The Isaurian rulers maintained the integrity of the empire's borders. With the exception of Irene, they attempted to suppress the use of religious icons.

Islam (Arabic 'submission', that is, to the will of Allah) religion founded in the Arabian peninsula in the early 7th century AD. It emphasizes the oneness of God, his omnipotence, benificence, and inscrutability. The sacred book is the *Koran* of the prophet ◊Muhammad, the Prophet or Messenger of Allah. There are two main Muslim sects: ◊*Sunni* and ◊*Shi'ite*. Other schools include *Sufism*, a mystical movement originating in the 8th century.

Islam began as a militant and missionary religion, and between 711 and 1492 spread east into India, west over N Africa, then north across Gibraltar into the Iberian peninsula. During the Middle Ages, Islamic scholars preserved ancient Greco-Roman learning, while the Dark Ages prevailed in Christian Europe. Islam was seen as an enemy of Christianity by European countries during the Crusades, and Christian states united against a Muslim nation as late as the Battle of Lepanto 1571. Driven from Europe, Islam remained established in N Africa and the Middle East. Islam is a major force in the Arab world and is a focus for nationalism among the peoples of the Central Asian Republics. It is also a significant factor in Pakistan, Indonesia, Malaysia, and parts of Africa.

Islam is the second largest religion in the UK. In 1987 the manifesto *The Muslim Voice* demanded rights in the UK for Muslim views on education (such as single-sex teaching) and on the avoidance of dancing, mixed bathing, and sex education.

Ismail 1830–1895. Khedive (governor) of Egypt 1866–79. A grandson of Mehemet Ali, he became viceroy of Egypt in 1863 and in 1866 received the title of khedive from the Ottoman sultan. He amassed huge foreign debts and in 1875 Britain, at Prime Minister Disraeli's suggestion, bought the khedive's Suez Canal shares for nearly £4 million, establishing Anglo-French control of Egypt's finances. In 1879 the UK and France persuaded the sultan to appoint Tewfik, his son, khedive in his place.

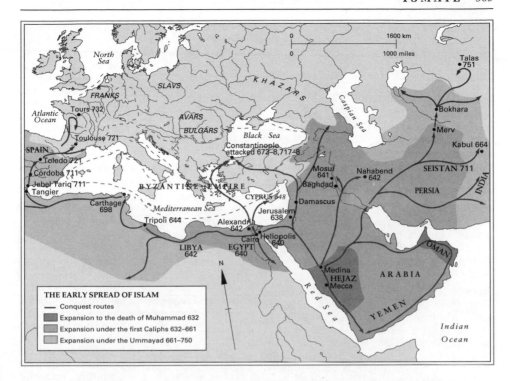

THE EARLY SPREAD OF ISLAM
— Conquest routes
▮ Expansion to the death of Muhammad 632
▮ Expansion under the first Caliphs 632–661
▯ Expansion under the Ummayad 661–750

The early spread of Islam *During Muhammad's lifetime Islam welded together the nomadic peoples of the Arabian peninsula. After his death the nomads, led by their Muslim generals, conquered the Middle East and NE Africa with extraordinary speed. Under the Omayyads there was further expansion into parts of Central Asia and across North Africa into the Iberian peninsula. With the exception of Spain and Portugal these lands have remained the heartlands of Islam.*

Rise of Islam 570–750

570	Birth of prophet Muhammad in Mecca.
	Muhammad and followers took refuge in Christian Abyssinia.
622	*Hijrah* (migration) of Muhammad and followers to Medina.
623–630	Struggle between Medina and Mecca.
624	Muhammad established at Mecca, and instructed his followers (Muslims) to direct their prayers to Mecca rather than Jerusalem.
630	Submission of Mecca to Medina.
632	Death and burial of Muhammad at Mecca.
634–644	Caliphate of Omar.
638	Conquest of Syria.
639	Conquest of Iraq.
640–41	Egypt conquered and Cairo founded. Babylon and Persepolis captured.

644–656	Caliphate of Othman.
649	Cyprus annexed.
658	Moawiya established Omayyad dynasty.
669	Unsuccessful attempt to take Constantinople (repeated 674).
673	Muslims penetrated to Rivers Oxus and Indus.
693	Abd al-Malik introduced Arabic coinage to replace Greek and Persian coins throughout the empire, and reorganized its administration.
710–12	Spain invaded and overwhelmed by Muslim army.
732	Muslim forces repulsed at Poitiers, France, by Charles Martel.
750	Omayyad dynasty ended and was replaced by Abbasids.

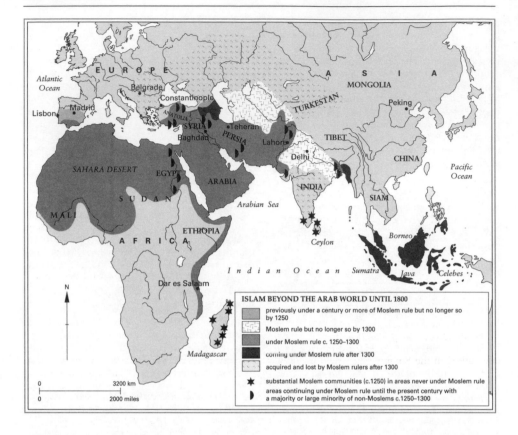

Islam beyond the Arab world until 1800 *After the initial conquests Islam continued to spread, with trade and conquest often preceding religious conversion. As the Islamic lands in Spain gradually fell to the Reconquista, Islamized Turks from Central Asia advanced across Anatolia and into the Balkans, challenging the Byzantine, and, later, the Habsburg Empire. Sufi dervishes followed Muslim merchants to Central Asia, Africa, India, and the Far East, creating converts and the Mogul Sultanate at Delhi. The Moguls later conquered large areas of India.*

Ismail I 1486–1524. Shah of Persia from 1501, founder of the *Safavi dynasty*, who established the first national government since the Arab conquest and Shi'ite Islam as the national religion.

isolationism in politics, concentration on internal rather than foreign affairs; a foreign policy having no interest in international affairs that do not affect the country's own interests.

Israel country in SW Asia, bounded N by Lebanon, E by Syria and Jordan, S by the Gulf of Aqaba, and W by Egypt and the Mediterranean Sea.

history The Zionist movement, calling for an independent community for Jews in their historic homeland of Palestine, began in the 19th century, and in 1917 Britain declared its support for the idea. In 1920 the League of Nations placed Palestine under British administration,

and the British government was immediately faced with the rival claims of Jews who wished to settle there and the indigenous Arabs who opposed them. In 1937 Britain proposed separate Arab and Jewish communities; this was accepted by the Jews but not by the Arabs, and fighting broke out between them. In Europe, the Nazi Holocaust killed about 6 million Jews, and hundreds of thousands tried to get to Palestine before, during, and after World War II 1939–45. Many survivors could no longer live in Europe.

creation of Israel In 1947 the British plan for partition was supported by the United Nations, and when Britain ended its Palestinian mandate 1948, an independent State of Israel was proclaimed, with David ◊Ben-Gurion as prime minister. Neighbouring Arab states sent forces to crush Israel but failed, and when a cease-fire agreement was reached 1949, Israel controlled more land than had been originally allocated to it. The non-Jewish-occupied remainder of Palestine, known as the West Bank, was occupied by Jordan. The creation of Israel encouraged Jewish immigration on a large scale, about 2 million having arrived from all over the world by 1962. Hundreds of thousands of Arab residents fled from Israel to neighbouring countries, such as Jordan and Lebanon. In 1964 a number of Palestinian Arabs in exile founded the ◊Palestine Liberation Organization (PLO), aiming to overthrow Israel.

Arab-Israeli wars During the 1960s there was considerable tension between Israel and Egypt, which, under President ◊Nasser, had become a leader in the Arab world. His nationalization of the ◊Suez Canal 1956 provided an opportunity for Israel, with Britain and France, to attack Egypt and occupy a part of Palestine that Egypt had controlled since 1949, the Gaza Strip, from which Israel was forced by UN and US pressure to withdraw 1957. Ten years later, in the Six-Day War, Israel gained the whole of Jerusalem, the West Bank area of Jordan, the Sinai peninsula in Egypt, and the Golan Heights in Syria. All were placed under Israeli law, although the Sinai was returned to Egypt under the terms of the ◊Camp David Agreements. Ben-Gurion resigned 1963 and was succeeded by Levi Eshkol, leading a coalition government; in 1968 three of the coalition parties combined to form the Israel Labour Party. In 1969 Golda Meir became Labour Party prime minister. In Oct 1973, towards the end of her administration, the Yom Kippur War broke out on the holiest day of the Jewish year. Israel was attacked by Egypt and Syria, and after nearly three weeks of fighting, with heavy losses, a cease-fire was agreed. Golda Meir resigned 1974 and was succeeded by General Yitzhak Rabin, heading a Labour-led coalition.

Camp David Agreements In the 1977 elections the Consolidation Party (Likud) bloc, led by Menachem ◊Begin, won an unexpected victory, and Begin became prime minister. Within five months relations between Egypt and Israel changed dramatically, mainly owing to initiatives by President ◊Sadat of Egypt, encouraged by US president Jimmy ◊Carter. Setting a historical precedent for an Arab leader, Sadat visited Israel to address the Knesset 1977, and the following year the Egyptian and Israeli leaders met at Camp David, in the USA, to sign agreements for peace in the Middle East. A treaty was signed 1979, and in 1980 Egypt and Israel exchanged ambassadors, to the dismay of most of the Arab world.

Israeli forces enter Lebanon Israel withdrew from Sinai by 1982 but continued to occupy the Golan Heights. In the same year Israel, without consulting Egypt, entered Lebanon and surrounded W Beirut, in pursuit of 6,000 PLO fighters who were trapped there. A split between Egypt and Israel was avoided by the efforts of the US special negotiator Philip Habib, who secured the evacuation from Beirut to other Arab countries of about 15,000 PLO and Syrian fighters Aug 1982.

Israel's alleged complicity in massacres in two Palestinian refugee camps increased Arab hostility. Talks between Israel and Lebanon, between Dec 1982 and May 1983, resulted in an agreement, drawn up by US secretary of state George Shultz, calling for the withdrawal of all foreign forces from Lebanon within three months. Syria refused to acknowledge the agreement, and left some 30,000 troops, with about 7,000 PLO members, in the northeast; Israel retaliated by refusing to withdraw its forces from the south.

economic problems During this time Begin faced growing domestic problems, including rapidly rising inflation and opposition to his foreign policies. In 1983 he resigned, and Yitzhak Shamir formed a shaky coalition. Elections July 1984 proved inconclusive, with the Labour Alignment, led by Shimon Peres, winning 44 seats in the Knesset, and Likud, led by Shamir, 41. Neither leader was able to form a viable coalition, but it was eventually agreed that a government of national unity would be formed, with Peres as prime minister for the first 25 months, until Oct 1986, and Shamir as his deputy, and then a reversal of the positions.

Israeli forces withdraw Meanwhile the problems in Lebanon continued. In 1984, under pressure from Syria, President Gemayel of Lebanon abrogated the 1983 treaty with Israel, but the government of national unity in Tel Aviv continued to plan the withdrawal of its forces, although it might lead to outright civil war in S Lebanon. Guerrilla groups of the Shi'ite community of S Lebanon took advantage of the situation by attacking the departing Israeli troops. Israel retaliated by attacking Shi'ite villages. Most of the withdrawal was complete by June 1985. Prime Minister Peres met King Hussein of Jordan secretly in the south of France 1985, and later, in a speech to the UN, Peres said he would not rule out the possibility of an international conference on the Middle East. PLO leader Yassir ◊Arafat also had talks with Hussein and later, in Cairo, renounced PLO guerrilla activity outside Israeli-occupied territory. Domestically, the government of national unity was having

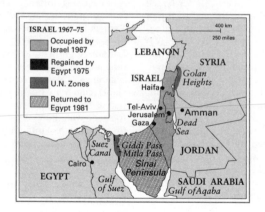

Proposed UN partition of Palestine 1947/Israel 1948–69/Israel 1967–75 The Arab-Israeli conflict is one of the central issues of the modern Middle East. After the British withdrew from Palestine 1948, the Jewish settlers declared the state of Israel, welcoming Jewish refugees from Europe. War broke out almost immediately with neighbouring Arab states. By 1949 the Israelis had consolidated their territory apart from Gaza, the West Bank, and E Jerusalem. Many Palestinians fled, creating a refugee problem. Subsequent wars produced a stalemate with Israel gaining Sinai, Gaza, the West Bank, and the Golan Heights in the Six Day War of 1967. Sinai was returned to Egypt 1982 after the Camp David Agreements of 1978.

some success with its economic policies, inflation falling in 1986 to manageable levels.

political crisis The 1988 general election resulted in a hung parliament. Shamir formed another coalition with the Labour Party, but differences over handling Palestinian issues broke the partnership 1990. Shamir assembled a new coalition including members of Likud and far-right religious and nationalist parties.

occupied territories Egyptian president Hosni Mubarak proposed a plan towards self-rule in the occupied territories. It secured the support of Labour and the USA. Likud accepted some of the provisions but opposed any PLO role in negotiations.

During the Gulf War 1991, Iraq launched Scud missiles against Israel, but Israel did not retaliate. Shamir agreed Aug to an amended Middle East peace plan. In Jan 1992 extreme fundamentalists withdrew support from the coalition over Israel's participation in peace talks. In June elections, Labour defeated Likud and its new leader, Yitzhak Rabin, became prime minister.

peace process The Middle East peace process resumed 1993 with face-to-face talks between Palestinians and Israelis. The process was threatened by Israel's renewal of attacks against southern Lebanon, an attempt to force the Lebanese government to take action against Hezbollah units. But in Sept Rabin and Arafat reached a preliminary peace agreement. Violent outbreaks in the occupied territories stalled further progress, but talks resumed and in May 1994 the first phase of the accord (the Gaza-Jericho agreement) was signed in Cairo. Israeli troops were withdrawn and Arafat became head of an autonomous Palestinian authority in Gaza and Jericho. In Sept 1995 there was the second-phase agreement over the transfer of control of Palestinian areas in the West Bank to the PLO and the holding of elections to a Palestinian coucil. Six weeks later, Rabin was assassinated by a Jewish opponent of the peace accord; he was succeeded by Shimon Peres.

Bombings by the terrorist group Hamas in early 1996 were carried out to lessen Labour's electoral chances, and to damage the peace process. Israel began a campaign in southern Lebanon, including rocket attacks on Beirut. In May Likud leader Binyamin Netanyahu became the first directly elected prime minister. In Dec a new round of peace talks began, reaching agreement on the Israel-Gaza border.

Istanbul city and chief seaport of Turkey. Founded as *Byzantium* about 660 BC, it was renamed *Constantinople* AD 330 and was the capital of the ◊Byzantine Empire until captured by the Turks 1453. As *Istamboul* it was capital of the Ottoman Empire until 1922.

Itagaki Taisuke 1837–1919. Japanese military and political leader, the founder of Japan's first political party, the Jiyūtō (Liberal Party) 1875–81. Involved in the overthrow of the ◊Tokugawa shogunate and the ◊Meiji restoration 1866-68, Itagaki became a champion of democratic principles while continuing to serve in the government for short periods.

After ennoblement in 1887 he retained the leadership of the party and cooperated with ◊Itō Hirobumi in the establishment of parliamentary government in the 1890s.

Italy country in S Europe, bounded N by Switzerland and Austria, E by Slovenia, Croatia, and the Adriatic Sea, S by the Ionian and Mediterranean seas, and W by the Tyrrhenian and Ligurian seas and France. It includes the Mediterranean islands of Sardinia and Sicily.

history The varying peoples inhabiting Italy – Etruscans in Tuscany, Latins and Sabines in middle Italy, Greek colonies in the south and Sicily, and Gauls in the north – were united under Roman rule during the 4th–3rd centuries BC. With the decline of the Roman Empire, and its final extinction AD 476, Italy became exposed to barbarian attacks and passed in turn under the rule of the Ostrogoths and the Lombards. The 8th century witnessed the rise of the papacy as a territorial power, the annexation of the Lombard kingdom by Charlemagne, and his coronation as emperor of the West in 800. From then until 1250 the main issue in Italian history is the relations, at first friendly and later hostile, between the papacy and the Holy Roman Empire. During this struggle the Italian cities seized the opportunity to convert themselves into self-governing republics.

wars and divisions By 1300 five major powers existed in Italy: the city-republics of Milan, Florence, and Venice; the papal states; and the kingdom of Naples. Their mutual rivalries and constant wars laid Italy open 1494–1559 to invasions from France and Spain; as a result Naples and Milan passed under Spanish rule. After 1700 Austria secured Milan and replaced Spain as the dominating power, while Naples passed to a Spanish Bourbon dynasty and Sardinia to the dukes of Savoy. The period of French rule 1796–1814 temporarily unified Italy and introduced the principles of the French Revolution, but after Napoleon's fall Italy was again divided between Austria, the pope, the kingdoms of Sardinia and Naples, and four smaller duchies. Nationalist and democratic ideals nevertheless remained alive and inspired attempts at revolution 1820, 1831, and 1848–49. After this last failure, the Sardinian monarchy assumed the leadership of the national movement.

unification of Italy With the help of Napoleon III, the Austrians were expelled from Lombardy 1859; the duchies joined the Italian kingdom; ◊Garibaldi overthrew the Neapolitan monarchy; and Victor Emmanuel II of Sardinia was proclaimed king of Italy at Turin 1861. Venice and part of Venetia were secured by another war with Austria 1866; in 1870 Italian forces occupied Rome, thus completing the unification of Italy, and the pope ceased to be a temporal ruler until 1929 (see ◊Vatican City State). In 1878 Victor Emmanuel II died and was succeeded by Humbert (Umberto) I, his son, who was assassinated 1900.

colonial empire The formation of a colonial empire began 1869 with the purchase of land on the Bay of Assab, on the Red Sea, from the local sultan. In the next 20 years the Italians occupied all ◊Eritrea, which was made a colony 1889. An attempt to seize Ethiopia was decisively defeated at Adowa 1896. War with Turkey 1911–12 gave Italy Tripoli and Cyrenaica. Italy's intervention on the Allied side in World War I secured it Trieste, the Trentino, and S Tirol.

Fascist era The postwar period was marked by intense political and industrial unrest, culminating 1922 in the establishment of ◊Mussolini's Fascist dictatorship. The regime embraced a policy of aggression with the conquest of Ethiopia 1935–36 and Albania 1939, and Italy entered World War II in 1940 as an ally of Germany. Defeat in Africa 1941–43 and the Allied conquest of Sicily 1943 resulted in Mussolini's downfall; the new government declared war on Germany, and until 1945 Italy was a battlefield of German occupying forces, the Italian underground (partisans), and the advancing Allies.

republic In 1946 Victor Emmanuel III, who had been king since 1900, abdicated in favour of his son Humbert (Umberto) II. The monarchy was abolished after a referendum 1946, and the country became a republic, adopting a new constitution 1948. Between 1946 and 1986 there were nine parliaments and 45 administrations. The Christian Democratic Party was dominant until 1963 and after this participated in most coalition governments. In 1976 the Communists became a significant force, winning over a third of the votes for the chamber of deputies and pressing for what they called the 'historic compromise', a broad-based government with representatives from the Christian Democratic, Socialist, and Communist parties, which would, in effect, be an alliance between Communism and Roman Catholicism. The Christian Democrats rejected this. Apart from a brief period 1977–78, the other parties excluded the Communists from power-sharing, forcing them to join the opposition.

coalition governments In 1980 the Socialists returned to share power with the Christian Democrats and Republicans and participated in a number of subsequent coalitions. In 1983, the leader of the Socialist Party, Bettino Craxi, became the republic's first Socialist prime minister, leading a coalition of Christian Democrats, Socialists, Republicans, Social Democrats, and Liberals. Under Craxi's government, which lasted until 1987, the state of the economy improved, although the north–south divide in productivity and prosperity persists, despite attempts to increase investment in the south. Various short-lived coalition governments followed; in 1989, the veteran Giulio Andreotti put together a new coalition of Christian Democrats, Socialists, and minor parties. In 1990 the Communist Party abandoned Marxism-Leninism and adopted the name Democratic Party of the Left (Partito Democratico della Sinistra). Its leader, Achille Occhetto, was elected secretary general of the renamed party. A referendum held June 1991 overwhelmingly approved reform of the voting procedure in an attempt to eliminate electoral corruption and to reduce the political influence of the Mafia. In Feb 1992 President Cossiga dissolved parliament two months ahead of schedule and set a general election date of 6 April. The election resulted in the ruling coalition losing its majority and the need for the Christian Democrats to forge a new alliance. President Cossiga carried out his threat to resign if a new coalition was not formed within a reasonable time. The election of Oscar Luigi Scalfaro as president in May 1992 was followed in June by the swearing in of Giuliano Amato, leader of the Democratic Party of the Left (PDS), as the new premier. The reshuffled cabinet reflected Amato's intent on reform. In Sept 1992, after unprecedented currency speculation, the government devalued the lira and suspended its membership of the Exchange Rate Mechanism.

foreign relations In foreign affairs Italy has demonstrated its commitment to the European Community (EC) (founder member), NATO, and the United Nations (UN), and in 1983 played an important part in the multinational peacekeeping force in Beirut. Refugees from Albania 1991 strained some towns' resources.

Itō Hirobumi, Prince 1841–1909. Japanese politician, prime minister 1887, 1892–96, 1898, 1900-01. He was a key figure in the modernization of Japan and was involved in the ◊Meiji restoration 1866–68 and in official missions to study forms of government in the USA and Europe in the 1870s and 1880s. As minister for home affairs, he helped draft the Meiji constitution of 1889.

Iturbide Agustín de 1783–1824. Mexican military leader (*caudillo*) who led the conservative faction in the nation's struggle for independence from Spain. In 1822 he crowned himself Emperor Agustín I. His extravagance and failure to restore order led all other parties to turn against him, and he reigned for less than a year (see ◊Mexican Empire).

Ivan six rulers of Russia, including:

Ivan III Ivan the Great 1440–1505. Grand duke of Muscovy from 1462, who revolted against Tatar overlordship by refusing tribute to Grand Khan Ahmed 1480. He claimed the title of tsar, and used the double-headed eagle as the Russian state emblem.

Did I ascend the throne by robbery or armed bloodshed? I was born to rule by the grace of God ... I grew up upon the throne.

Ivan IV the Terrible
letter to Prince Kurbsky Sept 1577

Ivan IV *the Terrible* 1530–1584. Grand duke of Muscovy from 1533; he assumed power 1544 and was crowned as first tsar of Russia 1547. He conquered Kazan 1552, Astrakhan 1556, and Siberia 1581. He reformed the legal code and local administration 1555 and established trade relations with England. In his last years he alternated between debauchery and religious austerities, executing thousands and, in rage, his own son.

Ivan attempted to centralize his rule in Muscovy. He campaigned against the Tatars of Kazan, Astrakhan, and elsewhere, but his policy of forming Russia into an empire led to the fruitless 24-year Livonian war. His regime was marked by brutality, evidenced by the destruction (sacking) of Novgorod.

Ivory Coast (French *Côte d'Ivoire*) country in W Africa, bounded N by Mali and Burkina Faso, E by Ghana, S by the Gulf of Guinea, and W by Liberia and Guinea.

history The area now known as the Ivory Coast/Côte d'Ivoire was once made up of several indigenous kingdoms. From the 16th century the Portuguese, French, and British established trading centres along the coast, dealing in slaves and ivory. During the 19th century France acquired the region by means of treaties with local leaders, eventually incorporating it into ◊French West Africa 1904.

It was given self-government within the French Community 1958 and full independence 1960, when a new constitution was adopted. Félix ◊Houphouët-Boigny is the country's first and only president. He has maintained close links with France since independence, and this support, combined with a good economic growth rate, has given his country a high degree of political stability. He was criticized by some other African leaders for maintaining links with South Africa but defended this policy by arguing that a dialogue between blacks and whites is essential. He has denounced communist intervention in African affairs and has travelled extensively to improve relations with Western powers.

In the Oct and Nov 1990 multiparty elections Houphouët Boigny and the PDCI were re-elected amid widespread criticisms of ballot-rigging and political pressurizing.

Iwo Jima, Battle of intense fighting between Japanese and US forces 19 Feb–17 March 1945 during World War II. In Feb 1945, US marines landed on the island of Iwo Jima, a Japanese air base, intending to use it to prepare for a planned final assault on mainland Japan. The Japanese defences were so strong that 5,000 US marines were killed before the island was captured from the Japanese.

IWW abbreviation for ◊*Industrial Workers of the World*.

J

Jackson Andrew 1767–1845. 7th president of the USA 1829–37, a Democrat. A major general in the War of 1812, he defeated a British force at New Orleans in 1815 (after the official end of the war in 1814) and was involved in the war that led to the purchase of Florida in 1819. The political organization he built as president, with Martin Van Buren, was the basis for the modern ◊Democratic Party. His administration is said to have initiated the ◊spoils system.

Jackson Jesse 1941– . US Democratic politician, a cleric and campaigner for minority rights. He contested his party's 1984 and 1988 presidential nominations in an effort to increase voter registration and to put black issues on the national agenda. Jackson sought to construct what he called a *rainbow coalition* of ethnic-minority and socially deprived groups.

Jackson Stonewall (Thomas Jonathan) 1824–1863. US Confederate general in the American Civil War. He acquired his nickname and his reputation at the Battle of Bull Run, from the firmness with which his brigade resisted the Northern attack. In 1862 he organized the Shenandoah Valley campaign and assisted Robert E ◊Lee's invasion of Maryland. He helped to defeat General Joseph E Hooker's Union army at the battle of Chancellorsville, Virginia, but was fatally wounded by one of his own soldiers in the confusion of battle.

Jacksonian Democracy in US history, the populist, egalitarian spirit pervading the presidencies of Andrew Jackson and Martin Van Buren 1829–1841, which encouraged greater participation in the democratic process. Recent studies have questioned the professed commitment to popular control, emphasizing Jackson's alleged cult of personality.

Jacobin member of an extremist republican club of the French Revolution founded at Versailles 1789, which later used a former Jacobin (Dominican) friary as its headquarters in Paris. Helped by ◊Danton's speeches, they proclaimed the French republic, had the king executed, and overthrew the moderate ◊Girondins 1792–93. Through the Committee of Public Safety, they began the Reign of Terror, led by ◊Robespierre. After his execution 1794, the club was abandoned and the name 'Jacobin' passed into general use for any left-wing extremist.

Jacobite in Britain, a supporter of the royal house of Stuart after the deposition of James II in 1688. They include the Scottish Highlanders, who rose unsuccessfully under ◊Claverhouse in 1689; and those who rose in Scotland and N England under the leadership of ◊James Edward Stuart, the Old Pretender, in 1715, and followed his son ◊Charles Edward Stuart in an invasion of England that reached Derby in 1745–46. After the defeat at ◊Culloden, Jacobitism disappeared as a political force.

Jacquerie French peasant uprising 1358, caused by the ravages of the English army and French nobility during the Hundred Years' War, which reduced the rural population to destitution. The word derives from the nickname for French peasants, Jacques Bonhomme.

Jahangir 'Holder of the World'. Adopted name of Salim 1569–1627. Third Mogul emperor of India 1605–27, succeeding his father ◊Akbar the Great. The first part of his reign was marked by peace, prosperity and a flowering of the arts, but the latter half by rebellion and succession conflicts.

In 1622 he lost Kandahar province in Afghanistan to Persia. His rule was marked by the influence of his Persian wife Nur Jahan and her conflict with Prince Khurran (later ◊Shah Jahan). Jahangir designed the Shalimar Gardens in Kashmir and buildings and gardens in Lahore.

Jainism (Hindi *jaina* 'person who overcomes') ancient Indian religion, sometimes regarded as an offshoot of Hinduism. Jains emphasize the importance of not injuring living beings, and their code of ethics is based on sympathy and compassion for all forms of life. They also believe in karma (destiny) but not in any deity. It is a monastic, ascetic religion. There are two main sects: the Digambaras and the Swetambaras. Jainism practises the most extreme form of nonviolence (*ahimsā*) of all Indian sects, and influenced the philosophy of Mahatma Gandhi. Jains number approximately 6 million; there are Jain communities throughout the world but the majority live in India.

Jainism's sacred books record the teachings of Mahavira (c. 599–527 BC), the last in a line of 24 great masters called Tirthan karas (or *jainas*). Mahavira was born in Vessali (now Bihar), E India. He became an ascetic at the age of 30, achieved enlightenment at 42, and preached for 30 years.

Jakeš Miloš 1922– . Czech communist politician, a member of the Politburo from 1981 and party leader 1987–89. A conservative, he supported the Soviet invasion of Czechoslovakia in 1968. He was forced to resign in Nov 1989 following a series of pro-democracy mass rallies.

Jallianwallah Bagh massacre alternative name for the ◊Amritsar massacre.

Jamaica island in the Caribbean Sea, S of Cuba and W of Haiti.

history Before the arrival of Christopher Columbus 1494, the island was inhabited by ◊Arawak Indians. From 1509 to 1655 it was a Spanish colony, and after this was in British hands until 1959, when it was granted internal self-government, achieving full independence within the ◊Commonwealth 1962.

The two leading political figures in the early days of independence were Alexander Bustamante, leader of the Jamaica Labour Party (JLP), and Norman Manley, leader of the People's National Party (PNP). The JLP won the 1962 and 1967 elections, led by Bustamante's successor, Hugh Shearer, but the PNP, under Norman Manley's son Michael, was successful 1972. He advocated social reform and economic independence from the industrialized world. Despite high unemployment, Manley was returned to power 1976 with an increased majority, but by 1980 the economy had deteriorated, and, rejecting the conditions attached to a loan from the International Monetary Fund, Manley sought support for his policies of economic self-reliance.

The 1980 general election campaign was extremely violent, despite calls by Manley and the leader of the JLP, Edward Seaga, for moderation. The outcome was a decisive victory for the JLP, with 51 of the 60 seats in the house of representatives. Seaga thus received a mandate for a return to a renewal of links with the USA and an emphasis on free enterprise. He severed diplomatic links with Cuba 1981. In 1983 Seaga called an early, snap election, with the opposition claiming they had been given insufficient time to nominate their candidates. The JLP won all 60 seats. There were violent demonstrations when the new parliament was inaugurated, and the PNP said it would continue its opposition

outside the parliamentary arena. In 1989 Manley and the PNP were elected. The new prime minister pledged to pursue moderate economic policies and improve relations with the USA. In March 1992 Manley resigned the premiership on the grounds of ill health. P J Patterson, the former finance minister, was chosen by the PNP as Manley's successor.

James Jesse 1847–1882. US bank and train robber, born in Missouri and a leader, with his brother Frank (1843–1915), of the Quantrill raiders, a Confederate guerrilla band in the Civil War. Frank later led his own gang. Jesse was killed by Bob Ford, an accomplice; Frank remained unconvicted and became a farmer.

James I *the Conqueror* 1208–1276. King of Aragon from 1213, when he succeeded his father. He conquered the Balearic Islands and took Valencia from the ◊Moors, dividing it with Alfonso X of Castile by a treaty of 1244. Both these exploits are recorded in his autobiography *Libre dels feyts/Chronicle*. He largely established Aragon as the dominant power in the Mediterranean.

James two kings of Britain:

James I 1566–1625. King of England from 1603 and Scotland (as *James VI*) from 1567. The son of Mary Queen of Scots and Lord Darnley, he succeeded on his mother's abdication from the Scottish throne, assumed power 1583, established a strong centralized authority, and in 1589 married Anne of Denmark (1574–1619). As successor to Elizabeth I in England, he alienated the Puritans by his High Church views and Parliament by his assertion of ◊divine right, and was generally unpopular because of his favourites, such as ◊Buckingham, and his schemes for an alliance with Spain. He was succeeded by his son Charles I.

James II 1633–1701. King of England and Scotland (as *James VII*) from 1685, second son of Charles I. He succeeded Charles II. James married Anne Hyde 1659 (1637–1671, mother of Mary II and Anne) and Mary of Modena 1673 (mother of James Edward Stuart). He became a Catholic 1671, which led first to attempts to exclude him from the succession, then to the rebellions of ◊Monmouth and ◊Argyll, and finally to the Whig and Tory leaders' invitation to William of Orange to take the throne in 1688. James fled to France, then led an uprising in Ireland 1689, but after defeat at the Battle of the ◊Boyne 1690 remained in exile in France.

James seven kings of Scotland:

James I 1394–1437. King of Scotland 1406–37, who assumed power 1424. He was a cultured and strong monarch whose improvements in the administration of justice brought him popularity among the common people. He was assassinated by a group of conspirators led by the Earl of Atholl.

James II 1430–1460. King of Scotland from 1437, who assumed power 1449. The only surviving son of James I, he was supported by most of the nobles and parliament. He sympathized with the Lancastrians during the Wars of the ◊Roses, and attacked English possessions in S Scotland. He was killed while besieging Roxburgh Castle.

James III 1451–1488. King of Scotland from 1460, who assumed power 1469. His reign was marked by rebellions by the nobles, including his brother Alexander, Duke of Albany. He was murdered during a rebellion supported by his son, who then ascended the throne as James IV.

James IV 1473–1513. King of Scotland from 1488, who married Margaret (1489–1541, daughter of Henry VII) in 1503. He came to the throne after his followers murdered his father, James III, at Sauchieburn. His reign was internally peaceful, but he allied himself with France against England, invaded 1513 and was defeated and killed at the Battle of ◊Flodden. James IV was a patron of poets and architects as well as a military leader.

James V 1512–1542. King of Scotland from 1513, who assumed power 1528. During the long period of his minority, he was caught in a struggle between pro-French and pro-English factions. When he assumed power, he allied himself with France and upheld Catholicism against the Protestants. Following an attack on Scottish territory by Henry VIII's forces, he was defeated near the border at Solway Moss 1542.

James VI of Scotland. See ◊James I of England.

James VII of Scotland. See ◊James II of England.

James Edward Stuart 1688–1766. British prince, known as the *Old Pretender* (for the ◊Jacobites, he was James III). Son of James II, he was born at St James's Palace and after the revolution of 1688 was taken to France. He landed in Scotland in 1715 to head a Jacobite rebellion but withdrew through lack of support. In his later years he settled in Rome.

Jameson Leander Starr 1853–1917. British colonial administrator. In South Africa, early in 1896, he led the *Jameson Raid* from Mafeking into Transvaal to support the non-Boer colonists there, in an attempt to overthrow the government (for which he served some months in prison). Returning to South Africa, he

succeeded Cecil ◊Rhodes as leader of the Progressive Party of Cape Colony, where he was prime minister 1904–08.

Jamestown first permanent settlement in North America, established by Captain John Smith 1607. It was capital of Virginia 1624–99.

janapada in N and W India, any of 16 large territories of kingdoms that were established by *c.* 600 BC. By the 5th century three of these, Kosala, ◊Magadha, and Vatsa, had expanded to become *mahjanapadas*, or large tribal confederacies. From Magadha the ◊Mauryan dynasty later emerged. *Janapadas* were the product of the 'iron revolution', which, through its effect on agriculture, commerce, military technologies, and population densities, made larger state formation possible.

Janata alliance of political parties in India formed 1971 to oppose Indira Gandhi's ◊Congress Party. Victory in the election brought Morarji ◊Desai to power as prime minister but he was unable to control the various groups within the alliance and resigned 1979. His successors fared little better, and the elections of 1980 overwhelmingly returned Indira Gandhi to office.

janissary (Turkish *yeniçeri* 'new force') bodyguard of the Ottoman sultan, the Turkish standing army from the late 14th century until 1826. Until the 16th century janissaries were Christian boys forcibly converted to Islam; after this time they were allowed to marry and recruit their own children. The bodyguard ceased to exist when it revolted against the decision of the sultan in 1826 to raise a regular force. The remaining janissaries were killed in battle or executed after being taken prisoner.

Jansenism Christian teaching of Cornelius Jansen, which divided the Roman Catholic Church in France in the mid-17th century. Emphasizing the more predestinatory approach of Augustine's teaching, as opposed to that of the Jesuits, Jansenism was supported by the philosopher Pascal and Antoine Arnauld (a theologian linked with the abbey of Port Royal). Jansenists were excommunicated 1719.

In 1713 a Jansenist work by Pasquier Quesnel (1634–1719), the leader of the Jansenist party, was condemned by Pope Clement XI as heretical, and after Quesnel's death Jansenism disappeared as an organized movement in France. It survived in the Netherlands, where in 1723 a regular Jansenist church was established under the bishop of Utrecht.

Japan country in NE Asia, occupying a group of islands of which the four main ones are Hokkaido, Honshu, Kyushu, and Shikoku.

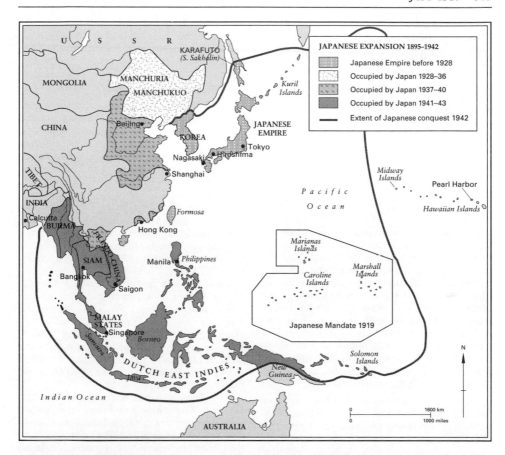

JAPANESE EXPANSION 1895–1942

- Japanese Empire before 1928
- Occupied by Japan 1928–36
- Occupied by Japan 1937–40
- Occupied by Japan 1941–43
- — Extent of Japanese conquest 1942

Japanese expansion 1895–1942 Forced to submit in 1854 and 1858 to the unequal treaties of Kanagawa and Edo and to open itself to foreign commerce, Japan, following the Meiji Restoration 1868, rapidly learned from the West and modernized its military machine. The strength of its navy was first revealed in the 1894–95 and 1904–05 Sino-Japanese and Russo-Japanese wars, and in 1902 an alliance was signed with Britain. Japan's imperialist expansion during and after World War I brought a deterioration in its diplomatic relations with western powers, notably the USA. This culminated in Japan's signing of the Anti-Comintern Pact with Nazi Germany 1936.

Japan is situated between the Sea of Japan (to the W) and the N Pacific (to the E), E of North and South Korea.

history Evidence of early human occupation on the Japanese islands exists in the form of 30,000-year-old tools, but the Japanese nation probably arose from the fusion of two peoples, one from the Malay Peninsula or Polynesia, the other from Asia, who conquered the original inhabitants, the ◊Ainu, and forced them into the northernmost islands. Japanese history remains legendary until the leadership of the first emperor Jimmu was recorded about 660 BC. From 300 BC, agriculture (rice-growing) was introduced, together with bronze, iron, and textile production. During the 4th century AD, the Yamato dynasty unified warring classes in

central Honshu and built huge tombs (the largest being nearly 500 m/1,640 ft). Gradually a feudal society was established. By the 5th century AD, the art of writing had been introduced from Korea. After the introduction of Buddhism, also from Korea, in the 6th century, Chinese culture became generally accepted, but although attempts were made in the 7th century to diminish the power of the nobles and set up a strong centralized monarchy on the Chinese model, real power remained in the hands of the great feudal families (such as Fujiwara, Minamoto, and Taira) until recent times.

shogunates The feudal lords (*daimyō*) organized local affairs. The 12th century saw the creation of a military government (shogunate) – a form that persisted until 1868. Twice during the Kamakura shogunate (1192–1333), Mongol invasions from Korea were repulsed. During the Ashikaga shogunate that followed, the country remained riven by factions. Order was restored towards the end of the 16th century, in the Momoyama period, by three great military leaders, Oda Nobunaga (1534–1582), Toyotomi Hideyoshi (1537–1598), and Tokugawa Ieyasu; at the battle of Sekigahara 1600 Ieyasu defeated his rivals and established the Tokugawa shogunate (1603–1868).

arrival and expulsion of Europeans Contact with Europe began 1542 when Portuguese traders arrived; they were followed by Spanish and in 1609 by Dutch sailors. Christianity was introduced by Francis Xavier 1549. The fear that Roman Catholic propaganda was intended as a preparation for Spanish conquest led to the expulsion of the Spanish 1624 and the Portuguese 1639 and to the almost total extermination of Christianity by persecution; only the Dutch were allowed to trade with Japan, under irksome restrictions, while Japanese subjects were forbidden to leave the country. Firearms, which the highly skilled Japanese swordsmiths had begun to make in imitation of guns introduced by the Europeans, fell largely into oblivion during this period. Arts, crafts, and theatre flourished, as did the internal economy.

opening to the outside world This isolation (*sakoku*) continued until 1853, when the USA insisted on opening trade relations; during the next few years this example was followed by various European powers. Consequently the isolationist party compelled the shogun to abdicate 1868. In law, executive power was vested with the emperor, who moved his capital from Kyoto to Tokyo (as Edo was renamed), but real authority was exercised by a small group of senior politicians, termed *genrō* (among them ◊Itō Hirobumi, ◊Yamagata Aritomo, ◊Matsukata Masayoshi, and ◊Katsura Tarō). During the next 30 years of the Meiji era, the privileges and duties of the ◊samurai class were abolished, a uniform code of law was introduced, the educational system revised, and a constitution on the imperial German model was established 1889. The army was modernized and a powerful navy founded. Industry developed steadily with state support, and a considerable export trade was built up.

Japanese expansionism In 1894 a war with China secured Japanese control of Formosa (Taiwan) and S Manchuria, as well as Korea, which was formally annexed 1910. A victory over Russia 1904–05 gave Japan the southern half of Sakhalin and compelled the Russians to evacuate Manchuria. Japan formed an alliance

with Britain 1902 and joined the Allies in World War I. At the peace settlement it received the German islands in the N Pacific as mandates. The 1920s saw an advance towards democracy and party government, but after 1932 the government assumed a semi-Fascist form.

World War II As a result of successful aggression against China 1931–32, a Japanese puppet monarchy under P'u-i, the last emperor of China, was established in Manchuria (see ◊Manchukuo); war with China was renewed 1937 and continued in Asia until Japan entered World War II with its attack on the US territory of Pearl Harbor 7 Dec 1941. Japan at first won a succession of victories in the Philippines, the Malay Peninsula, Burma (now Myanmar), and the Netherlands Indies. US, Australian, and New Zealand troops retook many of the Pacific islands in battles that resulted in heavy casualties; US, French, and UK troops reclaimed much of SE Asia. Japan was compelled to surrender 15 Aug 1945, after the detonation of atomic bombs by the USA at Hiroshima and Nagasaki. An Allied control commission took charge, and Japan was placed under military occupation by Allied (chiefly US) troops under General Douglas MacArthur until 1952, when the Japanese Peace Treaty came into force and full sovereignty was regained.

After Japan's defeat, Korea was made independent; Manchuria and Formosa (Taiwan) were returned to China; and the islands mandated to Japan after World War I were placed by the United Nations under US trusteeship. Japan regained the Ryukyu Islands 1972 and the Bonin and Volcano Islands 1968 from the USA, and continues to agitate for the return from Russia of the Northern Territories (the islands of the Shikotan and Habomai group) and the southernmost Kuril Islands (Kunashiri and Etorofu).

democratization and reconstruction During Allied rule, Aug 1945–April 1952, a major 'democratization campaign' was launched, involving radical land, social, and educational reform and the framing of a new 'Peace Constitution' 1946 in which Emperor Hirohito (era name Shōwa) renounced his claims to divinity and became a powerless figurehead ruler and the nation committed itself to a pacific foreign policy. Japan concentrated during the early postwar years on economic reconstruction, tending towards neutralism in foreign affairs under the protection provided by the 1951 Security Pact.

Postwar politics in Japan were dominated by the Liberal Democratic Party (LDP), formed 1955 from the merger of existing conservative parties and providing a regular succession of prime ministers. Real decision-making, however, centred around a broader, consensual grouping of politicians, senior civil servants, and directors of the major ◊zaibatsu (finance and industrial houses). Through a paternalist, guided approach to economic development, epitomized by the operations of the Ministry for International Trade and Industry (MITI), the Japanese economy expanded dramatically during the 1950s and 1960s, with gross na-tional product (GNP) increasing by 10% per year.

During this period, Japan was rehabilitated within the international community, entering the UN 1958 and establishing diplomatic relations with Western nations and, following the lead taken by the Nixon presidency, with communist China 1972. Japan's internal politics were rocked 1960 and 1968–69 by violent attacks by the anarchic Red Army guerrilla organization protesting against US domination and in 1974 by the resignation of Prime Minister Kakuei Tanaka after a bribery scandal involving the US Lockheed Corporation. This scandal tarnished the image of the LDP and led to the loss of its absolute majority in the house of representatives 1976.

economic impact abroad Japanese economic growth was maintained during the 1970s, though at a reduced annual rate of 4.5%, and the country made a major impact in the markets of North America and Europe as an exporter of electronics, machinery, and motor vehicles. This created resentment overseas as economic recession began to grip Europe and the USA, and led to calls for Japan to open up its internal market to foreign exporters and to assume a greater share of the defence burden for the Asia–Pacific region. Prime ministers Miki, Fukuda, Ohira, and Suzuki resisted these pressures, and in 1976 the Japanese government placed a rigid limit of 1% of GNP on military spending.

liberalization A review of policy was instituted by Prime Minister Yasuhiro ◊Nakasone, who assumed power 1982. He favoured a strengthening of Japan's military capability, a re-evaluation of attitudes towards the country's past, and the introduction of a more liberal, open-market economic strategy at home. The yen was revalued 1985. His policy departures were controversial and only partly implemented. However, he gained a landslide victory in the 1986 elections, and became the first prime minister since Satō (1964–72) to be re-elected by the LDP for more than one term. Before the defeat 1987 of his plans for tax reform, Nakasone was able to select Noboru ◊Takeshita as his successor.

political scandals Takeshita continued Nakasone's domestic and foreign policies, introducing a 3% sales tax 1988 and lowering income-tax levels to boost domestic consumption. The new sales tax was electorally unpopular, and the government's standing during 1988–89 was further undermined by revelations of insider share-dealing (the Recruit scandal), in which more than 40 senior LDP and opposition figures, including Takeshita and Nakasone, were implicated. Takeshita was forced to resign June 1989. This marked an inauspicious start to the new *Heisei* ('achievement of universal peace') era proclaimed on the death Jan 1989 of Hirohito and the accession of his son Akihito as emperor.

The new prime minister, Sosuke Uno, the former foreign minister, was dogged by a sex scandal and resigned after only 53 days in office. He was replaced by Toshiki Kaifu, a member of the LDP's small scandal-free Komoto faction. included two women. Elections in Feb 1990 were won by the LDP, but with large gains for the Japanese Socialist Party (JSP), led by Ms Takako Doi.

support for Gulf Allies When another insider-trading scandal emerged in the autumn of 1990, it was overshadowed by the crisis in the Persian Gulf, caused by Iraq's annexation of Kuwait. Although Japan is constitutionally debarred from sending troops abroad, the Diet's refusal to pass a bill authorizing the sending of unarmed, noncombatant military personnel damaged Kaifu's standing. However, Japan pledged $13 billion to support the US-led anti-Iraq coalition in the Gulf War. After the war, in 1991, Japan contributed over $2.6 million towards the environmental cleanup, sent teams of experts to help repair desalination plants and remove oil spills, and donated $110 million for the relief of the Kurds and other displaced people.

Kurils In April 1991 Kaifu's government was weakened when a visit by President Gorbachev ended in failure to resolve the conflict over the Kuril Islands, the remaining obstacle to a peace agreement between the USSR and Japan. Russian president Yeltsin's last-minute cancellation of a visit in Sept 1992 was believed to relate to the same issue.

socialists move towards centre In June 1991 Takako Doi, leader of the renamed opposition Social Democratic Party of Japan (SDJP), resigned to take responsibility for her party's crushing defeat in the April 1991 local elections. She was replaced as chair in July by Makoto Tanabe, drawn from the party's right wing and its former vice-chair, who sought to continue the process of moving the SDJP towards the centre that Takako Doi had instituted.

Miyazawa's troubled government In Nov 1991 Kaifu was succeeded as LDP leader, and hence prime minister, by Kiichi Miyazawa, whose government included a surprisingly large number of 'rehabilitated' members tainted by the Lockheed and Recruit scandals. In 1992 the Miyazawa government was rocked by a succession of damaging bribery and corruption scandals, the most serious being centred on the Tokyo Sagawa Kyubin company and its enormous political donations and links with organized crime. More than 100 politicians, a seventh of the Diet membership, were implicated, and in Oct it forced the resignation from the Diet of Shin Kanemaru (1914–), the LDP's deputy chair and most influential figure. A precipitous fall in the stock market in summer 1992 was stopped short in Sept by an economic rescue package of Y10.7 trillion ($87 billion), mainly in extra public spending.

Jarrow Crusade march in 1936 from Jarrow to London, protesting at the high level of unemployment following the closure of Palmer's shipyard in the town.

Jaruzelski Wojciech 1923– . Polish general, communist leader from 1981, president 1985–90. He imposed martial law for the first year of his rule, suppressed the opposition, and banned trade-union activity, but later released many political prisoners. In 1989, elections in favour of the free trade union Solidarity forced Jaruzelski to speed up democratic reforms, overseeing a transition to a new form of 'socialist pluralist' democracy and stepping down as president 1990.

Jaurès Jean Léon 1859–1914. French socialist politician and advocate of international peace. He was a lecturer in philosophy at Toulouse until his election in 1885 as a deputy (member of parliament). In 1893 he joined the Socialist Party, established a united party, and in 1904 founded the newspaper *L'Humanité*, becoming its editor until his assassination.

Capitalism carries within itself war, as clouds carry rain.

> ***Jean Léon Jaurès***
> *Studies in Socialism*

Java or *Jawa* most important island of Indonesia, situated between Sumatra and Bali. In central Java there are ruins of magnificent Buddhist monuments and of the Sivaite temple in Prambanan. The island's last Hindu kingdom, Majapahit, was destroyed about 1520 and followed by a number of short-lived Javanese kingdoms. The Dutch East India company founded a factory 1610. Britain took over during the Napoleonic period, 1811–16, and Java then reverted to Dutch control. Occupied by Japan 1942–45, Java then became part of the republic of ◊Indonesia.

Jay John 1745–1829. US diplomat and jurist, a member of the Continental Congress 1774–89 and its president 1779. With Benjamin Franklin and John Adams, he negotiated the Peace of Paris 1783, which concluded the War of Independence. President Washington named him first chief justice of the US 1789. He negotiated Jay's Treaty with England 1795, averting another war. He was governor of New York 1795–1801.

Jayawardene Junius Richard 1906–96. Sri Lankan politician. Leader of the United Nationalist Party (UNP) from 1970, he became prime minister 1977 and the country's first president 1978–88. Jayawardene embarked on a free market economic strategy, but was confronted with increasing Tamil-Sinhalese ethnic unrest, forcing the imposition of a state of emergency 1983.

Jefferson Thomas 1743–1826. 3rd president of the USA 1801–09, founder of the Democratic Republican Party. He published *A Summary View of the Rights of America* 1774 and as a member of the Continental Congress of 1775–76 was largely responsible for the drafting of the ◊Declaration of Independence. He was governor of Virginia 1779–81, ambassador to Paris 1785–89, secretary of state 1789–93, and vice president 1797–1801.

Jefferson was born in Virginia into a wealthy family. His interests included music, painting, architecture, and the natural sciences; he was very much a product of the 18th-century Enlightenment. His political philosophy of 'agrarian democracy' placed responsibility for upholding a virtuous American republic mainly upon a citizenry of independent yeoman farmers. Ironically, his two terms as president saw the adoption of some of the ideas of his political opponents, the ◊Federalists.

No government ought to be without censors, and where the press is free, no one ever will.

> ***Thomas Jefferson***
> letter to George Washington 9 Sept 1792

Jeffreys George, 1st Baron 1648–1689. Welsh judge, popularly known as the hanging judge. He became Chief Justice of the King's Bench in 1683, and presided over many political trials, notably those of Philip Sidney, Titus Oates, and Richard Baxter, becoming notorious for his brutality.

Jeffreys was born in Denbighshire. In 1685 he was made a peer and Lord Chancellor and, after ◊Monmouth's rebellion, conducted the 'bloody assizes' during which 320 rebels were executed and hundreds more flogged, imprisoned, or transported. He was captured when attempting to flee the country after the revolution of 1688, and died in the Tower of London.

Jehu king of Israel c. 842–815 BC. He led a successful rebellion against the family of ◊Ahab and was responsible for the death of Jezebel.

Jellicoe John Rushworth, 1st Earl 1859–1935. British admiral who commanded the Grand Fleet 1914–16 during World War I; the only action he fought was the inconclusive battle of ◊Jutland. He was First Sea Lord 1916–17, when he failed to push the introduction of the convoy system to combat U-boat attack. Created 1st Earl 1925.

Jena town SE of Weimar, in the state of Thuringia, Germany. On 14 Oct 1806 Napoleon defeated the Prussians here.

Jenkins's Ear, War of war 1739 between Britain and Spain, arising from Britain's illicit trade in Spanish America; it merged into the War of the ◊Austrian Succession 1740–48. The name derives from the claim of Robert Jenkins, a merchant captain, that his ear had been cut off by Spanish coastguards near Jamaica. The incident was seized on by opponents of Robert ◊Walpole who wanted to embarrass his government's antiwar policy and force war with Spain.

Jeremiah 7th–6th century BC. Hebrew prophet, whose ministry continued 626–586 BC. He was imprisoned during ◊Nebuchadnezzar's siege of Jerusalem on suspicion of intending to desert to the enemy. On the city's fall, he retired to Egypt.

Jeroboam 10th century BC. First king of Israel c. 922–901 BC after it split away from the kingdom of Judah.

Jerusalem ancient city of Palestine, divided 1948 between Jordan and the new republic of Israel; area (pre-1967) 37.5 sq km/14.5 sq mi, (post-1967) 108 sq km/42 sq mi, including areas of the West Bank; population (1989) 500,000, about 350,000 Israelis and 150,000 Palestinians. In 1950 the western New City was proclaimed as the Israeli capital, and, having captured from Jordan the eastern Old City 1967, Israel affirmed 1980 that the united city was the country's capital; the United Nations does not recognize the claim.

religions Christianity, Judaism, and Muslim, with Roman Catholic, Anglican, Eastern Orthodox, and Coptic bishoprics. In 1967 Israel guaranteed freedom of access of all faiths to their holy places.

history

1400 BC Jerusalem was ruled by a king subject to Egypt.

c. 1000 BC David made it the capital of a united Jewish kingdom.

586 BC The city was destroyed by Nebuchadnezzar, king of Babylonia, who deported its inhabitants.

539–529 BC Under Cyrus the Great of Persia the exiled Jews were allowed to return to Jerusalem and a new settlement was made.

c. 445 BC The city walls were rebuilt.

333 BC Conquered by Alexander the Great.

63 BC Conquered by the Roman general Pompey.

AD 29 or 30 Under the Roman governor Pontius Pilate, Jesus was executed here.

70 A Jewish revolt led to the complete destruction of the city by the Roman emperor Titus.

135 On its site the emperor Hadrian founded the Roman city of Aelia Capitolina.

615 The city was pillaged by the Persian Chosroës II while under Byzantine rule.

637 It was first conquered by Islam.

1099 Jerusalem captured by the Crusaders and became the Kingdom of Jerusalem under Godfrey of Bouillon.

1187 Recaptured by Saladin, sultan of Egypt.

1516 Became part of the Ottoman Empire.

1917 Britain occupied Palestine.

1922–48 Jerusalem was the capital of the British mandate.

Jervis John, Earl of St Vincent 1735–1823. English admiral who secured the blockage of Toulon, France, 1795 in the Revolutionary Wars, and the defeat of the Spanish fleet off Cape St Vincent 1797, in which Admiral ◊Nelson played a key part. Jervis was a rigid disciplinarian.

Jesuit member of the largest and most influential Roman Catholic religious order (also known as the *Society of Jesus*) founded by Ignatius Loyola 1534, with the aims of protecting Catholicism against the Reformation and carrying out missionary work. During the 16th and 17th centuries Jesuits were missionaries in Japan, China, Paraguay, and among the North American Indians. The order had about 29,000 members (1991).

The Society of Jesus received papal approval 1540. Its main objects were defined as educational work, the suppression of heresy, and missionary work among nonbelievers (its members were not confined to monasteries). Loyola infused into the order a spirit of m ilitary discipline, with long and arduous training. Their political influence resulted in their expulsion during 1759–68 from Portugal, France, and Spain, and suppression by Pope Clement XIV 1773. The order was revived by Pius VII 1814, but has since been expel led from many of the countries of Europe and the Americas, and John Paul II criticized the Jesuits 1981 for supporting revolution in South America.

Jesus c. 4 BC–AD 29 or 30. Hebrew preacher on whose teachings Christianity was founded. According to the accounts of his life in the four Gospels, he was born in Bethlehem, Palestine, son of God and the Virgin Mary, and brought up by Mary and her husband Joseph as a carpenter in Nazareth. After adult baptism, he gathered 12 disciples, but his preaching antagonized the Roman authorities and he was executed by crucifixion. Three days later there came reports of his resurrection and, later, his ascension to heaven.

Through his legal father Joseph, Jesus belonged to the tribe of Judah and the family of David, the second king of Israel, a heritage needed by the Messiah for whom the Hebrew people were waiting. In AD 26/27 his cousin John the Baptist proclaimed the coming of the promised Messiah and baptized Jesus, who then made two missionary journeys through the district of Galilee. His teaching, summarized in the Sermon on the Mount, aroused both religious opposition from the ◊Pharisees and secular opposition from the party supporting the Roman governor, ◊Herod Antipas. When Jesus returned to Jerusalem (probably in AD 29), a week before the Passover festival, he was greeted by the people as the Messiah, and the Hebrew authorities (aided by the apostle Judas) had him arrested and condemned to death, after a hurried trial by the Sanhedrin (supreme Jewish court). The Roman procurator, Pontius Pilate, confirmed the sentence, stressing the threat posed to imperial authority by Jesus' teaching.

Jew follower of ◊Judaism, the Jewish religion. The term is also used to refer to those who claim descent from the ancient Hebrews, a Semitic people of the Middle East. Today, some may recognize their ethnic heritage but not practise the religious or cultural traditions. The term came into use in medieval Europe, based on the Latin name for Judeans, the people of Judah. Prejudice against Jews is termed ◊anti-Semitism.

Jewish Agency administrative body created by the British mandate power in Palestine 1929 to oversee the Jewish population and immigration. In 1948 it took over as the government of an independent Israel.

Jiang Jie Shi alternate transcription of ◊Chiang Kai-shek.

I was Chairman Mao's dog. If he said bite someone, I bit him.

Jiang Qing during her trial

Jiang Qing or *Chiang Ching* 1914–1991. Chinese communist politician, third wife of party leader Mao Zedong. In 1960 she became minister for culture, and played a key role in the 1966–69 Cultural Revolution as the leading member of the Shanghai-based Gang of Four, who attempted to seize power 1976. Jiang was imprisoned 1981.

Jiang was a Shanghai actress when in 1937 she met Mao Zedong at the communist headquarters in Yan'an; she became his wife 1939. She emerged as a radical, egalitarian Maoist. Her influence waned during the early 1970s and her relationship with Mao became embittered. On Mao's death Sept 1976, the ◊Gang of Four, with Jiang as a leading figure, sought to seize power by organizing military coups in Shanghai and Beijing. They were arrested for treason by Mao's successor Hua Guofeng and tried 1980–81. The Gang were blamed for the excesses of the Cultural Revolution, but Jiang asserted during her trial that she had only followed Mao's orders as an obedient wife. This was rejected, and Jiang received a death sentence Jan 1981, which was subsequently commuted to life imprisonment.

jihad (Arabic 'conflict') holy war undertaken by Muslims against nonbelievers. In the *Mecca Declaration* 1981, the Islamic powers pledged a jihad against Israel, though not necessarily military attack.

Jim Crow laws laws designed to deny civil rights to blacks or to enforce the policy of segregation, which existed until Supreme Court decisions and civil-rights legislation of the 1950s and 1960s denied their legality. Jim Crow was originally a derogatory term that white Americans used for a black person.

Jin dynasty or *Chin dynasty* hereditary rulers of N China, including Manchuria and part of Mongolia, 1122–1234, during the closing part of the ◊Song era (960–1279). The dynasty was founded by Juchen (Jurchen) nomad hunters, who sacked the northern Song capital Kaifeng 1126, forcing the Song to retreat south to Hangzhou. The Jin eventually ruled N China as far south as the Huai River. Over time, the Juchen became Sinicized, but from 1214 lost much of their territory to the Mongols led by Genghis Khan.

jingoism blinkered, warmongering patriotism. The term originated in 1878, when the British prime minister Disraeli developed a pro-Turkish policy, which nearly involved the UK in war with Russia. His supporters' war song included the line 'We don't want to fight, but by jingo if we do ... '.

Jinnah Muhammad Ali 1876–1948. Indian politician, Pakistan's first governor general from 1947. He was president of the ◊Muslim League 1916, 1934–48, and by 1940 was advocating the need for a separate state of Pakistan; at the 1946 conferences in London he insisted on the partition of British India into Hindu and Muslim states.

Joan of Arc, St 1412–1431. French military leader. In 1429 at Chinon, NW France, she persuaded Charles VII that she had a divine mission to expel the occupying English from N France (see ◊Hundred Years' War) and secure his coronation. She raised the siege of Orléans, defeated the English at Patay, north of Orléans, and Charles was crowned in Reims. However, she failed to take Paris and was captured May 1430 by the Burgundians, who sold her to the English. She was found guilty of witchcraft and heresy by a tribunal of French ecclesiastics who supported the English. She was burned to death at the stake in Rouen 30 May 1431. In 1920 she was canonized.

Everything that I have done that was good I did by command of my voices.

St Joan of Arc during her trial 1431

Jodl Alfred 1892–1946. German general. In World War II he drew up the Nazi government's plan for the attack on Yugoslavia, Greece, and the USSR. In Jan 1945 he became Chief of Staff and headed the delegation that signed Germany's surrender in Reims 7 May 1945. He was tried for war crimes in Nuremberg 1945–46 and hanged.

Joffre Joseph Jacques Césaire 1852–1931. Marshal of France during World War I. He was chief of general staff 1911. The German invasion of Belgium 1914 took him by surprise, but his stand at the Battle of the ◊Marne resulted in his appointment as supreme commander of all the French armies 1915. His failure to make adequate preparations at Verdun 1916 and the military disasters on the ◊Somme led to his replacement by Nivelle in Dec 1916.

John *Lackland* 1167–1216. King of England from 1199 and acting king from 1189 during his brother Richard I's (the Lion-Heart) absence on the third Crusade. He lost Normandy and almost all the other English possessions in France to Philip II of France by 1205. His repressive policies and excessive taxation brought him into conflict with his barons, and he was forced to seal the ◊Magna Carta 1215. Later repudiation of it led to the first Barons' War 1215–17, during which he died.

John III Sobieski 1624–1696. King of Poland from 1674. He became commander in chief of the army 1668 after victories over the Cossacks and Tatars. A victory over the Turks 1673 helped to get him elected to the Polish throne, and he saved Vienna from the besieging Turks 1683.

John six kings of Portugal, including:

John I 1357–1433. King of Portugal from 1385. An illegitimate son of Pedro I, he was elected by the Cortes (parliament). His claim was supported by an English army against the rival king of Castile, thus establishing the Anglo-Portuguese Alliance 1386. He married Philippa of Lancaster, daughter of ◊John of Gaunt.

John IV 1603–1656. King of Portugal from 1640. Originally duke of Braganza, he was elected king when the Portuguese rebelled against Spanish rule. His reign was marked by a long war against Spain, which did not end until 1668.

John VI 1769–1826. King of Portugal and regent for his insane mother *Maria I* from 1799 until her death 1816. He fled to Brazil when the French invaded Portugal 1807 and did not return until 1822. On his return Brazil declared its independence, with John's elder son Pedro as emperor.

John Bull imaginary figure who is a personification of England, similar to the American Uncle Sam. He is represented in cartoons and caricatures as a prosperous farmer of the 18th century.

The name was popularized by Dr John Arbuthnot's *History of John Bull* 1712, advocating the Tory policy of peace with France.

John of Austria Don 1545–1578. Spanish soldier, the illegitimate son of the Holy Roman emperor Charles V. He defeated the Turks at the Battle of ◊Lepanto 1571.

John captured Tunis 1573 but quickly lost it. He was appointed governor general of the Netherlands 1576 but discovered that real power lay in the hands of William of Orange. John withdrew 1577 and then attacked and defeated the patriot army at Gemblours 31 Jan 1578 with the support of reinforcements from Philip II of Spain. Lack of money stopped him from going any farther. He died of fever.

John of Gaunt 1340–1399. English nobleman and politician, born in Ghent, fourth son of Edward III, Duke of Lancaster from 1362. He distinguished himself during the Hundred Years' War. During Edward's last years, and the years before Richard II attained the age of majority, he acted as head of government, and Parliament protested against his corrupt rule.

Johnson Andrew 1808–1875. 17th president of the USA 1865–69, a Democrat. He was a congressman from Tennessee 1843–53, governor of Tennessee 1853–57, senator 1857–62, and vice president 1865. He succeeded to the presidency on Lincoln's assassination (15 April 1865). His conciliatory policy to the defeated South after the Civil War involved him in a feud with the Radical Republicans, culminating in his impeachment 1868 before the Senate, which failed to convict him by one vote.

Johnson Hiram Warren 1866–1945. US politician. He was the 'Bull Moose' party candidate for vice president in Theodore Roosevelt's unsuccessful bid to regain the presidency 1912. Elected to the US Senate 1917, Johnson served there until his death. He was an unyielding isolationist, opposing US involvement in World War I as well as membership in the League of Nations and World Court.

Johnson Lyndon Baines 1908–1973. 36th president of the USA 1963–69, a Democrat. He was elected to Congress 1937–49 and the Senate 1949–60. Born in Texas, he brought critical Southern support as J F Kennedy's vice-presidential running mate 1960, and became president on Kennedy's assassination.

Following Kennedy's assassination, Johnson pushed civil rights legislation through Congress. However, his foreign policy met wit h considerably less success. After the ◊Tonkin Gulf Incident, which escalated US involvement

in the ◊Vietnam War, support won by Johnson's Great Society legislation (civil rights, education, alleviation of poverty) dissipated, and he declined to run for re-election 1968.

Jonathan Chief (Joseph) Leabua 1914–1987. Lesotho politician. A leader in the drive for independence, Jonathan became prime minister of Lesotho in 1965. His rule was ended by a coup in 1986.

As prime minister, Jonathan played a pragmatic role, allying himself in turn with the South African government and the Organization of African Unity.

Jones John Paul 1747–1792. Scottish-born American naval officer in the War of Independence 1775. Heading a small French-sponsored squadron in the *Bonhomme Richard*, he captured the British warship *Serapis* in a bloody battle off Scarborough 1799.

Jordan country in SW Asia, bounded N by Syria, NE by Iraq, E, SE and S by Saudi Arabia, S by the Gulf of Aqaba, and W by Israel.

history The area forming the kingdom of Jordan was occupied by the independent Nabataeans from the 4th century BC and perhaps earlier, until AD 106 when it became part of the Roman province of Arabia. It was included in the Crusaders' kingdom of Jerusalem 1099–1187. Palestine (partly in the West Bank of present-day Jordan) and Transjordan (the present-day East Bank) were part of the Turkish Ottoman Empire until its dissolution after World War I. Both were then placed under British administration by the League of Nations.

end of British mandates Transjordan acquired greater control of its own affairs than Palestine and separated from it 1923, achieving full independence when the British mandate expired 1946. The mandate for Palestine ran out 1948, whereupon Jewish leaders claimed it for a new state of Israel. Israel was attacked by Arab nations and fought until a cease-fire was agreed 1949. By then Transjordan forces had occupied part of Palestine to add to what they called the new state of Jordan. The following year they annexed the West Bank. In 1952 Hussein ibn Talai came to the Jordanian throne at the age of 17 upon the mental incapacity of his father; he was officially made king 1953. In 1958 Jordan and Iraq formed an Arab Federation, which ended five months later when the Iraqi monarchy was overthrown. In 1967, following the Six-Day War (see ◊Arab-Israeli Wars), Israelis captured the West Bank and have remained in occupation since then.

search for peace King Hussein has survived many upheavals in his own country and neighbouring states, including attempts on his life, and has kept control of Jordan's affairs as well as playing a central role in Middle East affairs. Political parties were banned 1963, partially restored 1971, then banned again 1976. Relations with his neighbours have fluctuated, but he has generally been a moderating influence. After Israel's invasion of Lebanon 1982, Hussein played a key role in attempts to bring peace to the area, establishing a relationship with ◊Palestine Liberation Organization (PLO) leader Yassir ◊Arafat. By 1984 the Arab world was split into two camps, with the moderates represented by Jordan, Egypt, and Arafat's PLO, and the militant radicals by Syria, Libya, and the rebel wing of the PLO. In 1985 Hussein and Arafat put together a framework for a Middle East peace settlement. It would involve bringing together all interested parties, but Israel objected to the PLO being represented. Further progress was hampered by the PLO's alleged complicity in a number of guerrilla operations in that year. Hussein tried to revive the search for peace by secretly meeting the Israeli prime minister in France and persuading Yassir Arafat to renounce publicly PLO violence in territories not occupied by Israel.

greater democratization In response to mounting unrest within Jordan 1989, Hussein promised greater democratization and in Nov elections to an 80-member parliament were held. Soon afterwards the veteran politician Mudar Badran was made prime minister; he announced the lifting of martial law Dec 1989 (imposed since 1967).

Following the Iraqi invasion and annexation of Kuwait Aug 1990, under popular pressure from his own country, Hussein unsuccessfully attempted to act as a mediator. Meanwhile the United Nations trade embargo on Iraq and the exodus of thousands of refugees into Jordan strained Jordan's resources. Jordan attended the historic Middle East peace conference in Spain in Nov 1991. In July 1992 a draft law to legalize political parties was published.

Jörgensen Jörgen 1779–1845. Danish sailor who in 1809 seized control of Iceland, announcing it was under the protection of Britain. His brief reign of corruption ended later the same year when he was captured by a British naval ship. After long imprisonment, in about 1823 he was transported to Van Diemen's Land (Tasmania), where he was pardoned. He wrote a dictionary of Australian Aboriginal dialect.

Joseph Chief c. 1840–1904. American Indian chief of the Nez Percé people. After initially agreeing to leave tribal lands 1877, he later led his people in armed resistance. Defeated, Joseph ordered a mass retreat to Canada, but the Nez Percé were soon caught by General Nelson Miles. They were sent to the Colville Reservation, Washington 1885.

Born in the Wallowa Valley of Oregon, Joseph was the son of a Nez Percé leader who resisted territorial encroachment by the US government. At his father's death in 1873, Joseph assumed the title of chief and was originally an advocate of passive resistance.

Joseph two Holy Roman emperors:

Joseph I 1678–1711. Holy Roman emperor from 1705 and king of Austria, of the house of Habsburg. He spent most of his reign involved in fighting the War of the ◊Spanish Succession.

Joseph II 1741–1790. Holy Roman emperor from 1765, son of Francis I (1708–1765). The reforms he carried out after the death of his mother, ◊Maria Theresa, in 1780, provoked revolts from those who lost privileges.

Josephine Marie Josèphe Rose Tascher de la Pagerie 1763–1814. As wife of ◊Napoleon Bonaparte, she was empress of France 1796–1809. Born on Martinique, she married in 1779 Alexandre de ◊Beauharnais, who played a part in the French Revolution, and in 1796 Napoleon, who divorced her in 1809 because she had not produced children.

Josephus Flavius AD 37–c. 100. Jewish historian and general, born in Jerusalem. He became a Pharisee and commanded the Jewish forces in Galilee in their revolt against Rome from AD 66 (which ended with the mass suicide at Masada). When captured, he gained the favour of the Roman emperor Vespasian and settled in Rome as a citizen. He wrote *Antiquities of the Jews*, an early history to AD 66; *The Jewish War*; and an autobiography.

Josiah c. 647–609 BC. King of Judah. Grandson of Manasseh and son of Amon, he succeeded to the throne at the age of eight. The discovery of a Book of Instruction (probably Deuteronomy, a book of the Old Testament) during repairs of the Temple in 621 BC stimulated thorough reform, which included the removal of all sanctuaries except that of Jerusalem. He was killed in a clash at Megiddo with Pharaoh-nechoh, king of Egypt.

Joubert Petrus Jacobus 1831–1900. Boer general in South Africa. He opposed British annexation of the Transvaal 1877, proclaimed its independence 1880, led the Boer forces in the First ◊South African War against the British 1880–81, defeated ◊Jameson 1896, and fought in the Second South African War.

journeyman in Britain, a man who served his apprenticeship in a trade and worked as a fully qualified employee. The term originated in the regulations of the medieval trade ◊guilds; it derives from the French *journée* ('a day') because journeymen were paid daily.

Each guild normally recognized three grades of worker – apprentices, journeymen, and masters. As a qualified tradesman, a journeyman might have become a master with his own business but most remained employees.

Jovian 331–364. Roman emperor from 363. Captain of the imperial bodyguard, he was chosen as emperor by the troops after ◊Julian's death. He concluded an unpopular peace with the ◊Sassanid empire and restored Christianity as the state religion.

Joyce William 1906–1946. Born in New York, son of a naturalized Irish-born American, he carried on fascist activity in the UK as a 'British subject'. During World War II he made propaganda broadcasts from Germany to the UK, his upper-class accent earning him the nickname *Lord Haw Haw*. He was hanged for treason.

Juárez Benito 1806–1872. Mexican politician, president 1861–65 and 1867–72. In 1861 he suspended repayments of Mexico's foreign debts, which prompted a joint French, British, and Spanish expedition to exert pressure. French forces invaded and created an empire for ◊Maximilian, brother of the Austrian emperor. After their withdrawal in 1867, Maximilian was executed, and Juárez returned to the presidency.

Judah or *Judaea* or *Judea* district of S Palestine. After the death of King Solomon 937 BC, Judah adhered to his son Rehoboam and the Davidic line, whereas the rest of Israel elected Jeroboam as ruler of the northern kingdom. In New Testament times, Judah was the Roman province of Judaea, and in current Israeli usage it refers to the southern area of the West Bank.

Judaism the religion of the ancient Hebrews and their descendants the Jews, based, according to the Old Testament, on a covenant between God and Abraham about 2000 BC, and the renewal of the covenant with Moses about 1200 BC. It rests on the concept of one eternal invisible God, whose will is revealed in the *Torah* and who has a special relationship with the Jewish people. The Torah comprises the first five books of the Bible (the Pentateuch), which contains the history, laws, and guide to life for correct behaviour.

Judith of Bavaria 800–843. Empress of the French. The wife of Louis the Pious (Louis I of France) from 819, she exercised power over her husband to the benefit of their son Charles the Bold.

Jugurtha died 104 BC. King of Numidia, N Africa, who, after a long resistance, was betrayed to the Romans and put to death.

Julian *the Apostate c.* 331–363. Roman emperor. Born in Constantinople, the nephew of Constantine the Great, he was brought up as a Christian but early in life became a convert to paganism. Sent by Constantius to govern Gaul in 355, he was proclaimed emperor by his troops in 360, and in 361 was marching on Constantinople when Constantius' death allowed a peaceful succession. He revived pagan worship and refused to persecute heretics. He was killed in battle against the Persians of the ◊Sassanid empire.

Julius three popes, including:

Julius II 1443–1513. Pope 1503–13. A politician who wanted to make the Papal States the leading power in Italy, he formed international alliances first against Venice and then against France. He began the building of St Peter's Church in Rome 1506 and was the patron of the artists Michelangelo and Raphael.

July Plot or *July Conspiracy* in German history, an unsuccessful attempt to assassinate the dictator Adolf Hitler and to overthrow the Nazi regime 20 July 1944. Colonel von Stauffenberg planted a bomb under the conference table at Hitler's headquarters at Rastenburg, East Prussia. Believing that Hitler had been killed, Stauffenberg flew to Berlin to join Field Marshal von Witzleben and General von Beck to proclaim a government headed by resistance leader and former lord mayor of Leipzig Carl Goerdeler. Hitler was only injured, telephone communications remained intact, and countermeasures were taken in Berlin by Major Ernst Remer. Reprisals were savage: 150 alleged conspirators were executed, while 15 prominent persons, including Field Marshal Rommel, committed suicide and many others were imprisoned.

July Revolution revolution 27–29 July 1830 in France that overthrew the restored Bourbon monarchy of Charles X and substituted the constitutional monarchy of Louis Philippe, whose rule (1830–48) is sometimes referred to as the July Monarchy.

Junker member of the landed aristocracy in Prussia; favoured by Frederick the Great and ◊Bismarck, they controlled land, industry, trade, and the army, and exhibited privilege and arrogance. From the 15th century until the

Judaism

c. 2000 BC Led by Abraham, the ancient Hebrews emigrated from Mesopotamia to Canaan.

18th century –1580 Some settled on the borders of Egypt and were put to forced labour.

13th century They were rescued by Moses, who aimed at their establishment in Palestine. Moses received the Ten Commandments from God and brought them to the people. The main invasion of Canaan was led by Joshua about 1274.

12th–11th centuries During the period of Judges, ascendancy was established over the Canaanites.

c. 1000 Complete conquest of Palestine and the union of all Judea was achieved under David, and Jerusalem became the capital.

10th century Solomon succeeded David and enjoyed a reputation for great wealth and wisdom; but his lack of a constructive policy led, after his death, to the secession of the north of Judea (Israel) under Jeroboam, with only the tribe of Judah remaining under the house of David as the southern kingdom of Judah.

9th–8th centuries Assyria became the dominant power in the Middle East. Israel purchased safety by tribute, but the basis of the society was corrupt, and prophets such as Amos, Isaiah, and Micah predicted destruction. At the hands of Tiglathpileser and his successor Shalmaneser IV, the northern kingdom (Israel) was made into Assyrian provinces after the fall of Samaria 721, although the southern kingdom of Judah was spared as an ally.

586–458 Nebuchadnezzar took Jerusalem and carried off the major part of the population to Babylon. Judaism was retained during exile, and was reconstituted by Ezra on the return to Jerusalem.

520 The Temple, originally built by Solomon, was restored.

c. 444 Ezra promulgated the legal code that was to govern the future of the Jewish people.

4th–3rd centuries After the conquest of the Persian Empire by Alexander the Great, the Syrian Seleucid rulers and the Egyptian Ptolemaic dynasty struggled for Palestine, which came under the government of Egypt, although with a large measure of freedom.

2nd century With the advance of Syrian power, Antiochus IV attempted intervention in the internal quarrels of the Hebrews, even desecrating the Temple, and a revolt broke out 165 led by the Maccabee family.

63 Judaea's near-independence ended when internal dissension caused the Roman general Pompey to intervene, and Roman suzerainty was established.

1st century AD A revolt led to the destruction of the Temple 66-70 by the Roman emperor Titus. Judean national sentiment was encouraged by the work of Rabbi Johanan ben Zakkai (c. 20–90), and following him the president of the Sanhedrin (supreme court) was recognized as the patriarch of Palestinian Jewry.

2nd–3rd centuries Greatest of the Sanhedrin presidents was Rabbi Judah (c. 135–220), who codified the traditional law in the *Mishna*. The Palestinian *Talmud* (c. 375) added the *Gemara* to the *Mishna*.

4th–5th centuries The intellectual leadership of Judaism passed to the descendants of the 6th-century exiles in Babylonia, who compiled the Babylonian *Talmud*.

8th–13th centuries Judaism enjoyed a golden era, producing the philosopher Saadiah, the poet Jehudah Ha-levi (c. 1075–1141), the codifier Moses Maimonides, and others.

14th–17th centuries Where Christianity became the dominant or state religion, the Jews were increasingly segregated from mainstream life and trade by the Inquisition, anti-Semitic legislation, or by expulsion. The Protestant and Islamic states, and their colonies, allowed for refuge. Persecution led to messianic hopes strengthened by the 16th century revival of Kabbalism, culminating in the messianic movement of Shabbatai Sevi in the 17th century.

18th–19th centuries Outbreaks of persecution increased with the rise of European nationalism. Reform Judaism, a rejection of religious orthodoxy and an attempt to interpret it for modern times, began in Germany 1810 and soon was established in England and the USA. In the late 19th century, large numbers of Jews fleeing persecution (pogrom) in Russia and E Europe emigrated to the USA, leading to the development of large Orthodox, Conservative, and Reform communities there. Many became Americanized and lost interest in religion.

20th century Zionism (founded 1896) is a movement dedicated to achieving a secure homeland where the Jewish people would be free from persecution; this led to the establishment of the state of Israel 1948. Liberal Judaism (more radical than Reform) developed in the USA. In 1911 the first synagogue in the UK was founded. The Nazi German regime 1933–45 exterminated 6 million European Jews. Hundreds of thousands of survivors went to Palestine to form the nucleus of the new state of Israel, to the USA, and to other nations. Although most Israeli and American Jews were not affiliated with synagogues after the 1950s, they continued to affirm their Jewish heritage. Both Orthodox and Hasidic Judaism, however, flourished in their new homes and grew rapidly in the 1970s and 1980s.

Judaism in the Ancient World In the Hellenistic age Jewish communities from Babylon as well as Palestine spread throughout the E Mediterranean and to some of the larger cities in the west. There were large communities in Egypt and the Roman province of Asia. In Judaea itself relations with Rome were often violent, and Jerusalem was destroyed AD 70. Revolts and persecutions were followed by greater tolerance within the Roman Empire by the end of the 2nd century AD.

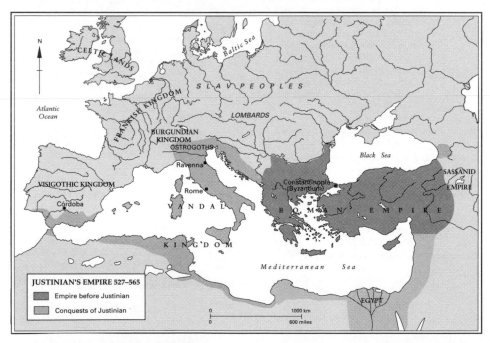

Justinian's empire 527–65 Justinian was made emperor of the East AD 527. He fought campaigns in Syria and Mesopotamia, and on the northern frontier in the Balkans. His general Belisarius conquered the Vandal kingdom in N Africa, occupied Sicily 535, invaded Italy, and in 536 captured Rome from the Ostrogoths, who capitulated at Ravenna 540. Further conquests were made in SE Spain from the Visigoths. However, his attempts to reunify the Christian church in submission to the emperor were frustrated, and the Sassanid Empire remained unsubdued.

1930s they were the source of most of the Prussian civil service and officer corps.

justiciar the chief justice minister of Norman and early Angevin kings, second in power only to the king. By 1265, the government had been divided into various departments, such as the Exchequer and Chancery, which meant that it was no longer desirable to have one official in charge of all.

Examples include Ranalf Glanville and Hubert de ◊Burgh (died 1243). The last justiciar, Hugh Despenser, was killed fighting for the baronial opposition to Henry II at the battle of Evesham 1265.

Justinian I 483–565. Byzantine emperor from 527. He recovered N Africa from the Vandals, SE Spain from the Visigoths, and Italy from the Ostrogoths, largely owing to his great general Belisarius. He ordered the codification of Roman law, which has influenced European jurisprudence; he built the church of St Sophia in Constantinople.

Jute member of a Germanic people who originated in Jutland but later settled in Frankish territory. They occupied Kent, SE England, about 450, according to tradition under Hengist and Horsa, and conquered the Isle of Wight and the opposite coast of Hampshire in the early 6th century.

Jutland, Battle of naval battle of World War I, fought between England and Germany on 31 May 1916, off the W coast of Jutland. Its outcome was indecisive, but the German fleet remained in port for the rest of the war.

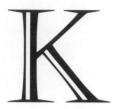

Kádár János 1912–1989. Hungarian Communist leader, in power 1956–88, after suppressing the national uprising. As Hungarian Socialist Workers' Party (HSWP) leader and prime minister 1956–58 and 1961–65, Kádár introduced a series of market-socialist economic reforms, while retaining cordial political relations with the USSR.

kaffir (Arabic *kāfir* 'infidel') South African English term, usually regarded as offensive, for a black person. It was formerly the designation of various Bantu-speaking peoples, including the Xhosa and Pondo of Cape Province, living in much of SE Africa. The term is also used in some countries for an unbeliever; for example, in Pakistan to refer to a Christian.

Kaiser title formerly used by the Holy Roman emperors, Austrian emperors 1806–1918, and German emperors 1871–1918. The word, like the Russian 'tsar', is derived from the Latin *Caesar*.

Kalinin Mikhail Ivanovich 1875–1946. Soviet politician, founder of the newspaper *Pravda*. He was prominent in the 1917 October Revolution, and in 1919 became head of state (president of the Central Executive Committee of the Soviet government until 1937, then president of the Presidium of the Supreme Soviet until 1946).

Kaltenbrunner Ernst 1901–1946. Austrian Nazi leader. After the annexation of Austria 1938 he joined police chief Himmler's staff, and as head of the Security Police (SD) from 1943 was responsible for the murder of millions of Jews (see the ◊Holocaust) and Allied soldiers in World War II. After the war, he was tried at Nuremberg for war crimes and hanged.

Kamenev Lev Borisovich 1883–1936. Russian leader of the Bolshevik movement after 1917 who, with Stalin and Zinoviev, formed a ruling triumvirate in the USSR after Lenin's death 1924. His alignment with the Trotskyists led to his dismissal from office and from the Communist Party by Stalin 1926. Arrested 1934 after Kirov's assassination, Kamenev was secretly tried and sentenced, then retried, condemned, and shot 1936 for allegedly plotting to murder Stalin.

kamikaze (Japanese 'wind of the gods') pilots of the Japanese air force in World War II who deliberately crash-dived their planes, loaded with bombs, usually onto ships of the US Navy.

Kampuchea former name of ◊Cambodia.

Kanaka (Hawaiian 'person') Pacific islander, formerly one kidnapped and taken to Australia or elsewhere in the Pacific as a labourer (see ◊blackbirding); an indigenous Hawaiian.

KANU (acronym for *K*enya *A*frican *N*ational *U*nion) political party founded 1944 and led by Jomo ◊Kenyatta from 1947, when it was the Kenya African Union; it became KANU on independence. The party formed Kenyatta's political power base in 1963 when he became prime minister; in 1964 he became the first president of Kenya.

Karamanlis Constantinos 1907– . Greek politician of the New Democracy Party. A lawyer and an anticommunist, he was prime minister Oct 1955–March 1958, May 1958–Sept 1961, and Nov 1961–June 1963 (when he went into self-imposed exile because of a military coup). He was recalled as prime minister on the fall of the regime of the 'colonels' in July 1974, and was president 1980–85.

Karbala (or ◊Kerbela) holy city of the Shi'ite Muslims in Iraq.

Karelia former independent Finnish state that came under Swedish rule in the 17th century and was annexed by Russia 1721. The greater part of Karelia remaining in Finland after it gained independence 1917 was ceded to Russia 1944. That part still within Finland comprises the E Finnish province of North Karelia, area 21,585 sq km/8,331 sq ft; capital Joensuu; population (1990) 176,800. Folk tales of the Karelian people inspired the Finnish epic *Kalevala*.

Kashmir former part of Jammu state in the north of British India with a largely Muslim population, ruled by a Hindu maharajah, who joined it to the republic of India 1947. There was fighting between pro-India and pro-Pakistan factions, the former being the Hindu ruling class and the latter the Muslim majority, and open war between the two countries 1965–66 and 1971. It is today divided between the Pakistani area of Kashmir and the Indian state of Jammu and Kashmir. Since 1990 it has been riven by Muslim separatist violence.

Kashmir had been under the sway of Hindu India for many centuries when Muslim rule was established by the 14th century. Mogul rule began in the 16th century but was brought to a halt by the Afghan invasion of 1753. This was followed by a period of Sikh overlordship from 1819.

Kassem Abdul Karim 1914–1963. Iraqi politician, prime minister from 1958; he adopted a pro-Soviet policy. Kassem pardoned the leaders of the pro-Egyptian party who tried to assassinate him 1959. He was executed after the 1963 coup.

Katō Kiyomasa 1562–1611. Japanese warrior and politician who was instrumental in the unification of Japan and the banning of Christianity in the country. He led the invasion of Korea 1592, and helped Toyotomi Hideyoshi (1536–1598) and ◊Tokugawa Ieyasu in their efforts to unify Japan.

Katō Taka-akira 1860–1926. Japanese politician, prime minister 1924–26. After a long political career with several terms as foreign minister, Katō led probably the most democratic and liberal regime of the Japanese Empire.

Katsura Tarō 1847–1913. Prince of Japan, army officer, politician, and prime minister (1901-06, 1908–11, 1912–13). He was responsible for the Anglo-Japanese treaty of 1902 (an alliance against Russia), the successful prosecution of the Russo-Japanese war 1904–05, and the annexation of Korea 1910.

Having assisted in the Meiji restoration 1866–68, Katsura became increasingly involved in politics. His support for rearmament, distaste for political parties, and oligarchic rule created unrest; his third ministry Dec 1912–Jan 1913 lasted only seven weeks.

Katyn Forest forest near Smolensk, SW of Moscow, Russia, where 4,500 Polish officer prisoners of war (captured in the German-Soviet partition of Poland 1940) were shot; 10,000 others were killed elsewhere. In 1989 the USSR accepted responsibility for the massacre.

Kaunda Kenneth (David) 1924– . Zambian politician, president 1964–91. Imprisoned in 1958–60 as founder of the Zambia African National Congress, he became in 1964 the first prime minister of Northern Rhodesia, then the first president of independent Zambia. In 1973 he introduced one-party rule. He supported the nationalist movement in Southern Rhodesia, now Zimbabwe, and survived a coup attempt

1980 thought to have been promoted by South Africa. He was elected chair of the Organization of African Unity 1987. In 1990 he was faced with wide anti-government demonstrations, leading to the acceptance of a multiparty political system. He lost the first multiparty election, in Nov 1991, to Frederick Chiluba.

The inability of those in power to still the voices of their own consciences is the great force leading to change.

Kenneth Kaunda in *Observer* July 1965

Kautsky Karl 1854–1938. German socialist theoretician who opposed the reformist ideas of Edouard ◊Bernstein from within the Social Democratic Party. In spite of his Marxist ideas he remained in the party when its left wing broke away to form the German Communist Party (KPD).

Kazakhstan country in central Asia, bounded N by Russia, W by the Caspian Sea, E by China, and S by Turkmenistan, Uzbekistan, and Kyrgyzstan.

history Ruled by the Mongols from the 13th century, the region came under Russian control in the 18th century. Inhabited by the traditionally nomadic but now largely sedentary Kazakh people, it joined the USSR as an autonomous republic in 1920 and became a full union republic in 1936. It was the site of Soviet leader Nikita Khrushchev's ambitious 'virgin lands' agricultural extension programme during the 1950s, which not only led to harvest failures during the early 1960s, but also to a large influx of Russian settlers, turning the Kazakhs into a minority in their own republic. There were violent nationalist riots in the capital in Dec 1986 when the long-serving Kazakh Communist Party (KCP) leader Dinmukahmed Kunayed was effectively sacked by the Soviet leader Mikhail Gorbachev and replaced by an ethnic Russian.

reform under Nazarbayev In June 1989 Nursultan Nazarbayev, a 'reform communist' in favour of nationalism, assumed leadership of the KCP and in Feb 1990 became the republic's president. He embarked on a pragmatic programme of cultural and market-centred economic reform, involving the privatization of the services and housing sectors. During the spring of 1991 President Nazarbayev pressed for the signing of a new USSR Union Treaty and opposed the Aug 1991 coup attempt against Gorbachev in Moscow, describing it as 'illegal and unconstitutional'. Soon after the coup was thwarted, the KCP was abolished. However, Nazarbayev played a key role in ensuring that the 'uncontrolled disintegration' of the USSR was averted.

independence recognized Kazakhstan joined the new ◊Commonwealth of Independent States, formed in Dec 1991, and the republic's independence was recognized by the USA. In Jan 1992 Kazakhstan was admitted into the ◊Conference on Security and Cooperation in Europe (CSCE) and in March into the United Nations (UN). Kazakhstan inherited substantial nuclear forces from the USSR, and the Nazarbayev administration pledged to remove these to become nuclear-free. A trade agreement was signed with the USA May 1992.

Kearny Stephen Watts 1794–1848. US military leader. As brigadier general he was given command of the Army of the West 1846. During the Mexican War 1846–48, he was the military governor of New Mexico and joined in the conquest of California 1847 becoming military governor.

Keitel Wilhelm 1882–1946. German field marshal in World War II, chief of the supreme command from 1938 and Hitler's chief military adviser. He signed Germany's unconditional surrender in Berlin 8 May 1945. Tried at Nuremberg for war crimes, he was hanged.

Kellogg–Briand pact agreement negotiated 1927 between the USA and France to renounce war and seek settlement of disputes by peaceful means. It took its name from the US secretary of state Frank B Kellogg (1856–1937) and the French foreign minister Aristide Briand. Most other nations subsequently signed. Some successes were achieved in settling South American disputes, but the pact made no provision for measures against aggressors and became ineffective in the 1930s, with Japan in Manchuria, Italy in Ethiopia, and Hitler in central Europe.

Kelly Ned (Edward) 1855–1880. Australian ◊bushranger. The son of an Irish convict, he wounded a police officer in 1878 while resisting the arrest of his brother Daniel for horse-stealing. The two brothers escaped and carried out bank robberies. Kelly wore a distinctive home-made armour. In 1880 he was captured and hanged.

Kemal Atatürk Mustafa. Turkish politician; see ◊Atatürk.

Kennedy John F(itzgerald) 'Jack' 1917–1963. 35th president of the USA 1961–63, a Democrat; the first Roman Catholic and the youngest person to be elected president. In foreign policy he carried through the unsuccessful ◊Bay of Pigs invasion of Cuba, and in 1963 secured the withdrawal of Soviet missiles from the island. His programme for reforms at home, called the *New Frontier*, was posthumously executed by Lyndon Johnson. Kennedy was assassinated while on a visit to Dallas, Texas, on 22 Nov 1963 by Lee Harvey Oswald (1939–1963), who was within a few days shot dead by Jack Ruby (1911–1967).

A number of conspiracy theories have been spun around the Kennedy assassination, which was investigated by a special commission headed by Chief Justice Earl Warren. The commission determined that Oswald acted alone, although this is extremely unlikely. A later congressional committee re-examined the evidence and determined that Kennedy 'was probably assassinated as a result of a conspiracy'.

Do you realize the responsibility I carry? I'm the only person standing between Nixon and the White House.

John F Kennedy Oct 1960

Kennedy Joseph Patrick 1888–1969. US industrialist and diplomat; ambassador to the UK 1937–40. A self-made millionaire, he ventured into the film industry, then set up the Securities and Exchange Commission (SEC) for F D Roosevelt. He groomed each of his four sons – Joseph Patrick Kennedy Jr (1915–1944), John F ◊Kennedy, Robert ◊Kennedy, and Edward Kennedy – for a career in politics. His eldest son, Joseph, was killed in action with the naval air force in World War II.

Kennedy Robert (Francis) 1925–1968. US Democratic politician and lawyer. He was presidential campaign manager for his brother John F ◊Kennedy 1960, and as attorney general 1961–64 pursued a racket-busting policy and promoted the Civil Rights Act of 1964. In 1968 he campaigned for the Democratic Party's presidential nomination, but during a campaign stop in California was assassinated by Sirhan Bissara Sirhan (1944–   ), a Jordanian.

Kenneth two kings of Scotland:

Kenneth I *MacAlpin* died 858. King of Scotland from *c.* 844. Traditionally, he is regarded as the founder of the Scottish kingdom (Alba) by virtue of his final defeat of the Picts about 844. He invaded Northumbria six times, and drove the Angles and the Britons over the river Tweed.

Kenneth II died 995. King of Scotland from 971, son of Malcolm I. He invaded Northumbria several times, and his chiefs were in constant conflict with Sigurd the Norwegian over the area of Scotland north of the river Spey. He is believed to have been murdered by his subjects.

Kenya country in E Africa, bounded N by Sudan and Ethiopia, E by Somalia, SE by the Indian Ocean, SW by Tanzania, and W by Uganda.

history Archaeological evidence shows that the area now known as Kenya was first inhabited at least 5 million years ago by early humans. African tribal groups inhabited the area when, in the 8th century, the coast was settled by Arabs, and during the 15th–18th centuries the region was under Portuguese rule.

independence Kenya became a British protectorate 1895 and colony 1920–64, when it achieved full independence within the ◊Commonwealth. There was near civil war during the 20 years before independence, as nationalist groups carried out a campaign of violence. The Kenya African Union (KAU) was founded 1944, and in 1947 Jomo ◊Kenyatta, a member of Kenya's largest ethnic group, the Kikuyu, became its president. Three years later a secret society of young Kikuyu militants was formed, called Mau Mau, which had the same aims as KAU but sought to achieve them by violent means. Although Kenyatta dissociated himself from Mau Mau, the British authorities distrusted him and imprisoned him 1953. By 1956 the guerrilla campaign had largely ended, the state of emergency was lifted and Kenyatta was released.

Kenya was granted internal self-government 1963, and Kenyatta, who had become leader of the Kenya African National Union (KANU), became prime minister and then president after full independence 1964. During his presidency the country achieved considerable stability. When he died in 1978 he was succeeded by Vice President Daniel arap Moi, who built on Kenyatta's achievements. The East Africa Community (EAC), which Kenya joined in 1967 with Tanzania and Uganda, collapsed 1977.

one-party state An attempted coup by junior air-force officers 1982 was foiled and resulted in political detentions and press censorship. The air force and Nairobi University were temporarily dissolved. In the same year the national assembly declared Kenya a one-party state. President Moi was re-elected 1983. He was re-elected unopposed for a third successive presidential term Feb 1988. In June 1989 Moi unexpectedly announced the release of all known political detainees. Kenya led the effort

1989 to ban trading in ivory after poaching of elephants became uncontrollable. The deaths of several US tourists on safari provoked Moi to declare a war against poachers.

calls for political reform In July 1990 there were widespread antigovernment riots while more moderate elements called for a multiparty system. Despite the government's refusal to accept this, former vice president Oginga Odinga launched Feb 1991 a new opposition group, the National Democratic Party. In Dec 1991, after increasing domestic and international pressure for political reform, President Moi announced the imminent introduction of multiparty politics. The Forum for the Restoration of Democracy (FORD) said Jan 1992 that it would reorganize itself as a full political party. In March 1992 the government announced proposals for constitutional changes. An amendment was passed in Aug that was thought to improve Moi's chances of being re-elected. To date, Moi has enjoyed some success in tackling corruption and inefficiency in the public services, but his human-rights record has often been criticized.

In Feb 1992 plans to revive the East Africa co-operation pact were announced.

Kenyatta Jomo. Assumed name of Kamau Ngengi *c.* 1894–1978. Kenyan nationalist politician, prime minister from 1963, as well as the first president of Kenya from 1964 until his death. He led the Kenya African Union from 1947 (*KANU* from 1963) and was active in liberating Kenya from British rule.

A member of the Kikuyu ethnic group, he joined the Kikuyu Central Association (KCA), devoted to recovery of Kikuyu lands from white settlers, and became its president. In 1953 he was sentenced to seven years' imprisonment for his management of the guerrilla organization ◊Mau Mau, though some doubt has been cast on his complicity. Released to exile in N Kenya in 1958, he was allowed t o return to Kikuyuland 1961 and in 1963 became prime minister (also president from 1964) of independent Kenya. His slogans were '*Uhuru na moja*' (Freedom and unity) and '*Harambee*' (Let's get going).

Kerbela or *Karbala* holy city of the Shi'ite Muslims, 96 km/60 mi SW of Baghdad, Iraq. Kerbela is built on the site of the battlefield where Husein, son of ◊Ali and Fatima, was killed 680 while defending his succession to the khalifate.

Kerensky Alexandr Feodorovich 1881–1970. Russian revolutionary politician, prime minister of the second provisional government before its collapse Nov 1917, during the ◊Russian Revolution. He was overthrown by the Bolshevik revolution and fled to France 1918 and to the USA 1940.

Kerr John Robert 1914–1990. Australian lawyer who as governor general 1974–77 controversially dismissed the prime minister, Gough Whitlam, and his government 1975.

Kesselring Albert 1885–1960. German field marshal in World War II, commander of the Luftwaffe (air force) 1939–40, during the invasions of Poland and the Low Countries and the early stages of the Battle of Britain. He later served under Field Marshal Rommel in N Africa, took command in Italy 1943, and was commander in chief on the western front March 1945. His death sentence for war crimes at the Nuremberg trials 1947 was commuted to life imprisonment, but he was released 1952.

KGB secret police of the USSR, the *Komitet Gosudarstvennoy Bezopasnosti*/Committee of State Security, which was in control of frontier and general security and the forced-labour system. KGB officers held key appointments in all fields of daily life, reporting to administration offices in every major town. The KGB was superseded by the Russian Federal Security Agency on the demise of the Soviet Union 1991.

Earlier names for the secret police were *Okhrana* under the tsars; ◊*Cheka* 1918–23; *GPU* or OGPU (*Obedinyonnoye Gosudarstvennoye Polititcheskoye Upravleniye*/Unified State Political Administration) 1923–34; *NKVD* (*Narodny Komisariat Vnutrennykh Del*/People's Commissariat of Internal Affairs) 1934–46; and *MVD* (Ministry of Internal Affairs) 1946–53.

Khaddhafi or *Gaddafi* or *Qaddafi*, Moamer al 1942– . Libyan revolutionary leader. Overthrowing King Idris 1969, he became virtual president of a republic, although he nominally gave up all except an ideological role 1974. He favours territorial expansion in N Africa reaching as far as Zaire, has supported rebels in Chad, and has proposed mergers with a number of countries. His theories, based on those of the Chinese communist leader Mao Zedong, are contained in a *Green Book*.

I am not afraid of anything. If you fear God you do not fear anything else.

Moamer Khaddhafi

---

khaki the dust-coloured uniform of British and Indian troops in India from about 1850, adopted as camouflage during the South African War 1899–1902, and later standard for military uniforms worldwide.

Khalaf Salah, also known as *Abu Iyad* 1933–1991. Palestinian nationalist leader. He became a refugee in 1948 when Israel became independent, and was one of the four founder members–with Yassir Arafat–of the PLO in the 1960s. One of its most senior members, he was involved with the Black September group, and is believed to have orchestrated their campaign of terrorist attacks such as the 1972 killing of 11 Israeli atheletes at the Munich Olympics. He later argued for a diplomatic as well as a terrorist campaign. He was assassinated by an Arab dissident follower of Abu Nidal.

Khalifa Sudanese leader ◊Abd Allah.

Khalsa the brotherhood of the Sikhs, created by Guru Gobind Singh at the festival of Baisakhi in 1699. The Khalsa was originally founded as a militant group to defend the Sikh community from persecution.

Khama Seretse 1921–1980. Botswanan politician, prime minister of Bechuanaland 1965, and first president of Botswana from 1966 until his death.

Khazar member of a people of Turkish origin from the lower Volga basin of Central Asia, who formed a commercial link and a buffer state in the 7th–12th centuries between the Arabs and the Byzantine empire, and later between the Byzantine empire and the Baltic. Their ruler adopted Judaism as the state religion in the 8th century. In the 11th century, Slavonic and nomadic Turks invaded, and by the 13th century the Khazar empire had been absorbed by its neighbours.

khedive title granted by the Turkish sultan to his Egyptian viceroy 1867, retained by succeeding rulers until 1914.

Khe Sanh in the Vietnam War, US Marine outpost near the Laotian border and just south of the demilitarized zone between North and South Vietnam. Garrisoned by 4,000 Marines, it was attacked unsuccessfully by 20,000 North Vietnamese troops 21 Jan–7 April 1968.

Khilafat movement campaign by Indian Muslims after World War I to protect the office of Khalifa from abolition by the British. The Khalifa was the religious and temporal head of the Sunni branch of Islam, and was situated in Constantinople. A strand of the ◊non-cooperation movement in India during the early 1920s, it disappeared when the office was abolished 1924 by the Turkish nationalist Kemal Ataturk.

Khmer or *Kmer* member of the largest ethnic group in Cambodia, numbering about 7 million. Khmer minorities also live in E Thailand and S Vietnam. The Khmer empire, an early SE Asian civilization, was founded AD 616 and came under Indian cultural influence as part of the SE Asian kingdom of Funan. The earliest inscriptions in the Khmer language date from the 7th century AD. The Khmer empire reached its zenith in the 9th–13th centuries, with the building of the capital city and temple complex at Angkor. The Khmers were eventually pushed back by the Thais into the territory they occupy today. The anti-French nationalists of ◊Cambodia adopted the name *Khmer Republic* 1971–75, and the name continues in use by the communist movement called the Khmer Rouge.

Khmer Rouge communist movement in Cambodia (Kampuchea) formed in the 1960s. Controlling the country 1974–78, it was responsible for mass deportations and executions under the leadership of ◊Pol Pot. Since then it has conducted guerrilla warfare, and in 1991 gained representation in the governing body. The leader of the Khmer Rouge from 1985 is Khieu Samphan.

The Khmer Rouge formed the largest opposition group to the US-backed regime led by Lon Nol 1970–75. By 1974 they controlled the countryside, and in 1975 captured the capital, Phnom Penh. Initially former prime minister Prince ◊Sihanouk was installed as head of state, but internal disagreements led to the creation of the Pol Pot government 1976. From 1978, when Vietnam invaded the country, the Khmer Rouge conducted a guerrilla campaign against the Vietnamese forces. Pol Pot retired as military leader 1985 and was succeeded by the more moderate Khieu Samphan. After the withdrawal of Vietnamese forces in 1989, the Khmer Rouge continued its warfare against the Vietnamese-backed government. A UN-brokered peace treaty Oct 1991 between Cambodia's four warring factions failed to win a renunciation of the guerrillas' goal of regaining domination of Cambodia.

Khomeini Ayatollah Ruhollah 1900–1989. Iranian Shi'ite Muslim leader, born in Khomein, central Iran. Exiled for opposition to the Shah from 1964, he returned when the Shah left the country 1979, and established a fundamentalist Islamic republic. His rule was marked by a protracted war with Iraq, and suppression of opposition within Iran, executing thousands of opponents.

Khrushchev Nikita Sergeyevich 1894–1971. Soviet politician, secretary general of the Communist Party 1953–64, premier 1958–64. He emerged as leader from the power struggle following Stalin's death and was the first official to denounce Stalin, in 1956. His de-Stalinization programme gave rise to revolts in Poland and Hungary 1956. Because of problems with the economy and foreign affairs (a breach with China 1960; conflict with the USA in the ◊Cuban missile crisis 1962), he was ousted by Leonid Brezhnev and Alexei Kosygin.

Khufu *c.* 2600 BC. Egyptian king of Memphis, who built the largest of the pyramids, known to the Greeks as the pyramid of Cheops (the Greek form of Khufu).

Kidd 'Captain' (William) *c.* 1645–1701. Scottish pirate. He spent his youth privateering for the British against the French off the North American coast, and in 1695 was given a royal commission to suppress piracy in the Indian Ocean. Instead, he joined a group of pirates in Madagascar. On his way to Boston, Massachusetts, he was arrested 1699, taken to England, and hanged.

Killiecrankie, Battle of during the first ◊Jacobite uprising, defeat on 7 May 1689 of General Mackay (for William of Orange) by John Graham of ◊Claverhouse, a supporter of James II, at Killiecrankie, Scotland. Despite the victory, Claverhouse was killed and the revolt soon petered out; the remaining forces were routed on 21 Aug.

Kilmainham Treaty in Irish history, an informal secret agreement in April 1882 that secured the release of the nationalist Charles ◊Parnell from Kilmainham jail, Dublin, where he had been imprisoned for six months for supporting Irish tenant farmers who had joined the Land League's campaign for agricultural reform.

The British government realized that Parnell could quell violence more easily out of prison than in it. In return for his release, he agreed to accept the Land Act of 1861. The Kilmainham Treaty marked a change in British policy in Ireland from confrontation to cooperation, with the government attempting to conciliate landowners and their tenants, who were refusing to pay rent. This strategy was subsequently threatened by the ◊Phoenix Park murders.

Kim II Sung 1912–94. North Korean communist politician and marshal. He became prime minister 1948 and led North Korea in the Korean War 1950–53. He became president 1972, retaining the presidency of the Communist Worker's party. Known as the 'Great Leader', he campaigned constantly for the reunification of Korea. His son *Kim Jong Il* (1942–), known as the 'Dear Leader', succeeded him.

King Martin Luther Jr 1929–1968. US civil-rights campaigner, black leader, and Baptist minister. He first came to national attention as leader of the ◊Montgomery, Alabama, bus boycott 1955, and was one of the organizers of the massive (200,000 people) march on Washington DC 1963 to demand racial equality. An advocate of nonviolence, he was awarded the Nobel Peace Prize 1964. He was assassinated in Memphis, Tennessee, by James Earl Ray (1928–).

Born in Atlanta, Georgia, son of a Baptist minister, King founded the ◊Southern Christian Leadership Conference 1957. A brilliant and moving speaker, he was the symbol of, and leading figure in, the campaign for integration and equal rights in the late 1950s and early 1960s. In the mid-1960s his moderate approach was criticized by black militants. He was the target of intensive investigation by the federal authorities, chiefly the FBI under J Edgar ◊Hoover. His personal life was scrutinized and criticized by those opposed to his policies. King's birthday (15 Jan) is observed on the third Monday in Jan as a public holiday in the USA.

King William Lyon Mackenzie 1874–1950. Canadian Liberal prime minister 1921–26, 1926–30, and 1935–48. He maintained the unity of the English- and French-speaking populations, and was instrumental in establishing equal status for Canada with Britain.

King's Council in medieval England, a court that carried out much of the monarch's daily administration. It was first established in the reign of Edward I, and became the Privy Council 1534–36.

Kinnock Neil 1942– . British Labour politician, party leader 1983–92. Born and educated in Wales, he was elected to represent a Welsh constituency in Parliament 1970 (Islwyn from 1983). He was further to the left than prime ministers Wilson and Callaghan, but as party leader (in succession to Michael Foot) adopted a moderate position, initiating a major policy review 1988–89. He resigned as party leader after Labour's defeat in the 1992 general election.

Kiribati republic in the W central Pacific Ocean, comprising three groups of coral atolls: the 16 Gilbert Islands, 8 uninhabited Phoenix Islands, 8 of the 11 Line Islands, and the volcanic island of Banaba.

history The first Europeans to visit the area were the Spanish 1606. The 16 predominantly Micronesian-peopled Gilbert Islands and 9 predominantly Melanesian-peopled Ellice Islands became a British protectorate 1892, and then the Gilbert and Ellice Islands Colony (GEIC) 1916. The colony was occupied by Japan 1942-43 and was the scene of fierce fighting between Japanese and US forces.

independence In preparation for self-government, a legislative council was set up 1963, and in 1972 a governor took over from the British high commissioner. In 1974 the legislative council was replaced by an elected house of assembly, and in 1975, when the Ellice Islands separated and became Tuvalu, the GEIC was renamed the Gilbert Islands. The islands achieved internal self-government 1977 and full independence within the ◊Commonwealth 1979, under the name of Kiribati, with Ieremia Tabai as their first president. He was re-elected 1982, 1983, and 1987. He was again re-elected in the general election of May 1991, but was constitutionally prohibited from serving a further term in office. However, he gave his backing to Vice President Teatao Teannaki in the contested presidential election July 1991. Tabai was subsequently appointed environment and natural resources minister in Teannaki's ten-member cabinet.

Banaba The once phosphate-rich island of Banaba campaigned for independence or unification with Fiji in the mid-1970s. However, its environment has been ruined by overmining and its people have been forced to resettle on Rabi Island, 4,160 km/2,600 mi away in the Fiji group.

Kirk Norman 1923–1974. New Zealand Labour politician, prime minister 1972–74. He entered parliament 1957 and led the Labour Party from 1964. During his office as prime minister he withdrew New Zealand troops from the Vietnam War and attempted to block French nuclear tests in the Pacific.

Kirov Sergei Mironovich 1886–1934. Russian Bolshevik leader who joined the party 1904 and played a prominent part in the 1918–20 civil war. As one of ◊Stalin's closest associates, he became first secretary of the Leningrad Communist Party. His assassination, possibly engineered by Stalin, led to the political trials held during the next four years as part of the purge.

Kishi Nobusuke 1896–1987. Japanese politician and prime minister 1957–60. A government minister during World War II and imprisoned 1945, he was never put on trial and returned to politics 1953. During his premiership, Japan began a substantial rearmament programme and signed a new treaty with the USA that gave greater equality in the relationship between the two states.

Kissinger Henry 1923– . German-born US diplomat. After a brilliant academic career at Harvard University, he was appointed national security adviser 1969 by President Nixon, and was secretary of state 1973–77. His missions to the USSR and China improved US relations with both countries, and he took part in negotiating US withdrawal from Vietnam 1973 and in Arab-Israeli peace negotiations 1973–75. Nobel Peace Prize 1973.

Kitchener Horatio Herbert, Earl Kitchener of Khartoum 1850–1916. British soldier and administrator. He defeated the Sudanese dervishes at Omdurman 1898 and reoccupied Khartoum. In South Africa, he was Chief of Staff 1900–02 during the Boer War, and commanded the forces in India 1902–09. He was appointed war minister on the outbreak of World War I, and drowned when his ship was sunk on the way to Russia.

Klondike former gold-mining area in Yukon Canada, named after the river valley where gold was found 1896. About 30,000 people moved there during the following 15 years. Silver is still mined there.

Knesset the Israeli parliament, consisting of a single chamber of 120 deputies elected for a period of four years.

knighthood, order of fraternity carrying with it the rank of knight, admission to which is granted as a mark of royal favour or as a reward for public services. During the Middle Ages in Europe such fraternities fell into two classes, religious and secular. The first class, including the ◊*Templars* and the *Knights of* ◊*St John*, consisted of knights who had taken religious vows and devoted themselves to military service against the Saracens (Arabs) or other non-Christians. The secular orders probably arose from bands of knights engaged in the service of a prince or great noble.

Knights of Labor see ◊Labor, Knights of.

Knights of the Teutonic Order German Christian military order, founded 1190; see ◊Teutonic Knight.

Knights Templar Christian military order, founded in Jerusalem 1119–20; see ◊Templars.

Knossos chief city of ◊Minoan Crete, near present-day Iráklion, 6 km/4 mi SE of Candia. The archaeological site excavated by Arthur ◊Evans 1899–1935, dates from about 2000–1400 BC, and includes the palace throne room, the remains of frescoes, and construction on more than one level.

Knox John c. 1505–1572. Scottish Protestant reformer, founder of the Church of Scotland.

He spent several years in exile for his beliefs, including a period in Geneva where he met John ◊Calvin. He returned to Scotland 1559 to promote Presbyterianism.

Captured by French troops in Scotland 1547, he was imprisoned in France, sentenced to the galleys, and released only by the intercession of the British government 1549. In England he assisted in compiling the Prayer Book, as a royal chaplain from 1551. On Mary's accession 1553 he fled the country and in 1557 was, in his absence, condemned to be burned. In 1559 he returned to Scotland. He was tried for treason but acquitted 1563. He wrote a *History of the Reformation in Scotland* 1586.

Kohl Helmut 1930– . German conservative politician, leader of the Christian Democratic Union (CDU) from 1976, West German chancellor (prime minister) 1982-90, and German chancellor from 1990. He oversaw the reunification of East and West Germany 1989-90 and in 1990 won a resounding victory to become the first chancellor of reunited Germany. After a period of unpopularity due to economic problems, his public esteem improved, and he won a historic fourth election victory 1994.

Kolchak Alexander Vasilievich 1875–1920. Russian admiral, commander of the White forces in Siberia after the Russian Revolution. He proclaimed himself Supreme Ruler of Russia 1918, but was later handed over to the Bolsheviks by his own men and shot.

kolkhoz Russian term for a ◊collective farm, as opposed to a ◊sovkhoz or state-owned farm.

Komsomol Russian name for the All-Union Leninist Communist Youth League of the former Soviet Union. Founded 1918, it acted as the youth section of the Communist Party.

Kongo African kingdom flourishing in the lower Congo region in the 14th–18th centuries. Possessing a sophisticated system of government, its power began to decline early in the 17th century under the impact of intensified slave trading and the interventions of Portuguese merchants and missionaries. In the late 19th century the kingdom was incorporated in the Portuguese colony of Angola. The Kongo people rebelled against colonial rule 1913–17.

Koniev Ivan Stepanovich 1898–1973. Soviet marshal who in World War II liberated Ukraine from the invading German forces 1943 and advanced from the south on Berlin to link up with the British-US forces. He commanded all Warsaw Pact forces 1955–60.

Konoe Fumimaro, Prince 1891–1946. Japanese politician and prime minister 1937–39 and

1940–41. Entering politics in the 1920s, Konoe was active in trying to curb the power of the army in government and preventing an escalation of the war with China. He helped to engineer the fall of the ◊Tōjō government 1944 but committed suicide after being suspected of war crimes.

And do not say, regarding anything, 'I am going to do that tomorrow', but only, 'if God will'.

The Koran 18:23–24

Koran (alternatively transliterated as *Quran*) sacred book of ◊Islam. Written in the purest Arabic, it contains 114 *suras* (chapters), and is stated to have been divinely revealed to the prophet Muhammad about 616.

Korea: history

2333 BC The foundation of the Korean state traditionally dates back to the *Tangun dynasty*.

1122–4th century BC The Chinese Kija dynasty.

AD 688–1000 Korean peninsula unified by Buddhist Shilla kingdom.

10th century After centuries of internal war and invasion, Korea was united within its present boundaries.

1392 Chosun (Yi) dynasty established and Korea became a vassal of China.

16th century Japan invaded Korea for the first time, later withdrawing from a country it had devastated.

1905 Japan began to treat Korea as a protectorate.

1910 Annexed by Japan. Many Japanese colonists settled in Korea, introducing both industrial and agricultural development. However, the enforced adoption of the Japanese language and customs was resented by Koreans.

1945 At the end of World War II, the Japanese in Korea surrendered, but the occupying forces at the cease-fire – the USSR north of the ◊38th parallel, and the USA south of it – created a lasting division of the country as North and South Korea (see ◊Korea, North, and ◊Korea, South, for history since 1945).

Korea, North country in E Asia, bounded NE by Russia, N and NW by China, E by the Sea of Japan, S by South Korea, and W by the Yellow Sea.

history For early history, see ◊Korea, history. The Democratic People's Republic of Korea

was formed from the zone north of the 38th parallel of latitude, occupied by Soviet troops after Japan's surrender 1945. The USSR installed in power an 'Executive Committee of the Korean People', staffed by Soviet-trained Korean communists, before North Korea was declared a People's Republic 1948 under the leadership of the Workers' Party of Korea (KWP), with Kim Il Sung as president. The remaining Soviet forces withdrew 1949.

Korean War In 1950 North Korea, seeking unification of the Korean peninsula, launched a large-scale invasion of South Korea. This began the three-year ◊Korean War which, after intervention by United Nations forces supported by the USA (on the side of the South) and by China (on the side of the North), ended in stalemate. The 38th parallel border between North and South was re-established by the armistice agreement of July 1953, and a UN-patrolled demilitarized buffer zone was created. North Korea has never accepted this agreement and remains committed to reunification.

Despite the establishment 1972 of a North–South coordinating committee to promote peaceful unification relations with the South remained tense and hostile. Border incidents were frequent, and in Oct 1983 four South Korean cabinet ministers were assassinated in Rangoon, Burma (Myanmar), in a bombing incident organized by two North Korean army officers.

economic development Domestically, the years since 1948 have seen economic development in a planned socialist manner. Factories were nationalized and agriculture collectivized in the 1950s, and priority in investment programmes has been given to heavy industry and rural mechanization. North Korean economic growth has, however, lagged behind that of its richer and more populous southern neighbour. In foreign affairs, North Korea adopted a neutral stance in the Sino-Soviet dispute, signing a friendship and mutual assistance treaty with China 1961 while at the same time receiving economic and military aid from the USSR. North Korea remained largely immune from the pluralist or market-socialist wave of reform that swept other communist nations from 1987.

succession question In the 1980s, North Korean politics became dominated by the succession question, with Kim Il Sung seeking to establish his son, Kim Chong-Il (1941–   ), as sole heir designate. His portrait was placed on public display across the country, and in Jan 1992, Kim Chong-Il replaced his father as supreme commander of the armed forces. Elements within the Workers' Party and armed forces appear, however, to oppose Kim's succession aims.

effort to end isolation Recently, North Korea has been anxious to bring to an end its international isolation because of mounting economic shortages. In Sept 1990 Prime Minister Yon Hyong Muk made an unprecedented three-day official visit to South Korea, the highest level official contact since 1948. In Nov–Dec 1990, after four decades of bitter hostility, North Korea had its first formal contact (in Beijing) with the Japanese government. The collapse of communism in the USSR deprived North Korea of considerable military and economic aid and China failed to fill the breach. North Korea was forced to further review its isolationist strategy and began to seek foreign inward investment, especially Japanese. The country was admitted to the United Nations (UN), simultaneously with South Korea, in Sept 1991, and on 13 Dec 1991 a nonaggression pact was signed with South Korea. This provided for the establishment of a military hotline to prevent accidental conflict, the restoration of cross-border communication links, the reunion of divided families, the liberalization of commerce and investment, and the free movement of people and ideas.

In Jan 1992, following an agreement signed with South Korea in Dec banning the production and deployment of nuclear weapons, North Korea also signed the Nuclear Safeguards Agreement, allowing for international inspection of its nuclear facilities.

Korea, South country in E Asia, bounded N by North Korea, E by the Sea of Japan, S by the Korea Strait, and W by the Yellow Sea.

history For early history, see ◊Korea, history. The Republic of Korea was formed out of the zone south of the 38th parallel of latitude that was occupied by US troops after Japan's surrender 1945. The US military government controlled the country until, following national elections, an independent republic was declared 1948. Dr Syngman ◊Rhee, leader of the right-wing Liberal Party, was the nation's first president in a constitution based on the US model. To begin with, the republic had to cope with a massive influx of refugees fleeing the communist regime in the North; then came the 1950–53 ◊Korean War.

President Syngman Rhee, whose regime had been accused of corruption, resigned 1960 as a result of student-led disorder. A new parliamentary-style constitution gave greater power to the legislature, and the ensuing political instability precipitated a military coup led by General ◊Park Chung Hee 1961. A

presidential system of government was re-established, with General Park elected president 1963, and a major programme of industrial development began, involving government planning and financial support. This programme was remarkably successful, with rapid industrial growth during the 1960s and 1970s as South Korea became a major exporter of light and heavy industrial goods.

opposition to government Opposition to the repressive Park regime mounted during the 1970s. In response, martial law was imposed, and in 1972 a new constitution strengthened the president's powers. A clampdown on political dissent, launched 1975, was partially relaxed for the 1978 elections, but brought protests 1979 as economic conditions briefly deteriorated. President Park was assassinated later that year, and martial law was reimposed.

An interim government, led by former prime minister Choi Kyu-Hah, introduced liberalizing reforms, releasing opposition leader Kim Dae Jung 1980. However, as antigovernment demonstrations developed, a new dissident clampdown began, involving the arrest of 30 political leaders, including Kim Dae Jung. After riots in Kim's home city of Kwangju, President Choi resigned 1980 and was replaced by the leader of the army, General Chun Doo Hwan. A new constitution was adopted, and, after Chun Doo Hwan was re-elected president 1981, the new Fifth Republic was proclaimed.

cautious liberalization Under President Chun economic growth resumed, but internal and external criticism of the suppression of civil liberties continued. Cautious liberalization was seen prior to the 1985 assembly elections, with the release of many political prisoners and the return from exile of Kim Dae Jung. After the 1985 election, the opposition parties launched a campaign for genuine democratization, forcing the Chun regime to frame a new, more liberal constitution, which was adopted after a referendum Oct 1987. The ensuing presidential election was won by the ruling party's candidate, Roh Tae Woo, amid opposition charges of fraud. He took over Feb 1988, but in the national assembly elections April 1988 the ruling Democratic Justice Party (DJP) fell well short of an overall majority. Only in Feb 1990, when the DJP merged with two minor opposition parties to form the Democratic Liberal Party (DLP), was a stable governing majority secured.

fear of invasion Since 1953 the perceived threat of invasion from the North has been a key factor in South Korean politics, helping to justify stern rule. South Korea has devoted large resources to modernizing its armed forces, which are supported by (1992) 36,000 US troops, assuring US intervention in the event of an invasion.

further opposition In July 1990 the 80 members of the Party for Peace and Democracy (PPD), led by Kim Dae Jung, all resigned from the national assembly in protest at government attempts to push through new legislation and demanded the calling of a general election. The assembly's speaker refused to accept the resignations, but the opposition deputies continued to boycott parliament when it reconvened in Sept. In the same month full diplomatic relations were established with the USSR.

In Dec 1990 the government launched a 'purification' campaign designed to improve public morals and reduce materialism. In May 1991 at least 250,000 people demonstrated and six attempted suicide in protests triggered by the beating to death of a student by police. Demands for the resignation of the government and the introduction of economic and political reform were met by the replacement of a home-affairs minister and the prime minister (from Dec 1990) Ro Jai Bong by Chung Won Shik, and emergency powers were given to police and security services.

In June 1991, after the new premier was mobbed by students, the authorities instituted a tougher response to student-led protests. In the same month, the ruling DLP secured a sweeping victory in local elections.

foreign affairs South Korea was admitted to the United Nations in Sept 1991. In the same month, the USA announced that all its nuclear weapons in South Korea would be withdrawn and in Nov announced that it planned to reduce its troops in South Korea from 43,000 to 36,000. Despite concerns over North Korea's nuclear aspirations, the prime ministers of the two Koreas met in Seoul on 13 Dec 1991 and signed a nonaggression and confidence-building pact which provided for the restoration of cross-border communications, the reunion of divided families, and the free movement of people and ideas. On 31 Dec 1991 a further pact was signed in Panmunjom in which both states agreed to ban the testing, manufacture, deployment, or possession of nuclear weapons. In Aug 1992 diplomatic relations with China were established.

1992 general election The country's two-party structure was restored in Sept 1991 when the opposition New Democratic Party, led by Kim Dae Jung, and the small Democratic Party, led by Lee Ki Taek, merged to form the Democratic Party, headed jointly by the two

leaders. Chung Ju Yong, founder of the giant Hyundai manufacturing group, established a political party to contest the national assembly elections held in March. The ruling DLP lost its majority; Roh resigned as leader of the DLP in Sept.

Korean War war 1950–53 between North Korea (supported by China) and South Korea, aided by the United Nations (the troops were mainly US). North Korean forces invaded the South 25 June 1950, and the Security Council of the United Nations, owing to a walk-out by the USSR, voted to oppose them. The North Koreans held most of the South when US reinforcements arrived Sept 1950 and forced their way through to the North Korean border with China. The Chinese retaliated, pushing them back to the original boundary Oct 1950; truce negotiations began 1951, although the war did not end until 1953.

By Sept 1950 the North Koreans had overrun most of the South, with the UN forces holding a small area, the Pusan perimeter, in the southeast. The course of the war changed after the surprise landing of US troops later the same month at Inchon on South Korea's NW coast. The troops, led by General Douglas ◊MacArthur, fought their way through North Korea to the Chinese border in little over a month. On Oct 25 1950 Chinese troops attacked across the Yalu River, driving the UN forces below the ◊38th parallel. Truce talks began July 1951, and the war ended two years later, with the restoration of the original boundary on the 38th parallel.

Kornilov Lavr 1870–1918. Russian general, commander in chief of the army, who in Aug 1917 launched an attempted coup, backed by officers, against the revolutionary prime minister, ◊Kerensky. The coup failed, but brought down the provisional government, thus clearing the way for the Bolsheviks to seize power.

Kościuszko Tadeusz 1746–1817. Polish general and nationalist who served with George Washington in the American Revolution (1776–83). He returned to Poland 1784, fought against the Russian invasion that ended in the partition of Poland, and withdrew to Saxony. He returned 1794 to lead the revolt against the occupation, but was defeated by combined Russian and Prussian forces and imprisoned until 1796.

Kosovo or **Kossovo** autonomous region (1974–90) in S Serbia, Yugoslavia. Since it is largely inhabited by Albanians and bordering on Albania, there have been demands for unification with that country, while in the late 1980s

The Korean War 1945–54

1945	Korea part of Japanese empire. Surrender in World War II led to occupation by Russian troops in the N and United States (US) forces in the S, with border at 38th parallel.
1946	Communist government led by Kim Il Sung elected in the North. Right-wing government in the South, led by Syngman Rhee, actively suppressed any left-wing opposition.
1948	Elections to unify country under United Nations (UN) control but Russia refused access to North Korea. Republic of Korea proclaimed in the South, with Syngman Rhee the first president. US troops withdrawn. Korean Democratic People's Republic in the North under Kim Il Sung. Red Army withdrawal continued into 1949.
1950 May	Rhee defeated in elections in South Korea.
June	North Korea invaded South Korea. A UN resolution condemned the attack and called on its members to 'furnish such as assistance as may be necessary' to repel the attack.
July–Aug	North Korean forces advanced rapidly, occupying 90% of South Korea.
Sept	US sent 7th Fleet to Korea and UN land forces under General Douglas MacArthur landed at Inchon. North Korean forces driven back across border and Rhee reinstated.
Oct	UN forces crossed the 38th parallel in an attempt to control all of Korea and were soon close to the Yalu River border with China.
Nov	Chinese army involved in major attacks against UN forces.
1951 Jan	Chinese drove UN forces back and occupied North Korea and up to 33% of South Korea, capturing Seoul.
Feb	UN denounced China as 'wilful aggressor'.
March	Seoul retaken by UN forces.
April	General MacArthur fired as UN commander after seeking to expand the war into China.
July	Peace talks began at Kaesong and moved to Panmunjom in Oct.
1952 May	Syngman Rhee imposed martial law. US considered ousting him.
Dec	President Dwight Eisenhower visited Korea.
1953 Feb	Eisenhower stepped up the campaign by deploying the 7th Fleet.
May	US bombed dams near Pyongyang, causing extensive flooding.
July	Armistice signed. Demilitarized buffer zone created, patrolled by UN.
Oct	Tripartite political talks began at Panmunjom.
Dec	US walked out of talks.
1954	Geneva Convention on Korea.

Serbians agitated for Kosovo to be merged with the rest of Serbia. A state of emergency was declared Feb 1990 after fighting broke out between ethnic Albanians, police, and the Slavonic minority. The parliament and government were dissolved July 1990 and the Serbian parliament formally annexed Kosovo Sept 1990.

In 1991 the Kosovo assembly, though still technically dissolved, organized a referendum on sovereignty which received 99% support. It elected a provisional government, headed by Bujar Bukoshi, which was recognized by Albania Oct 1991. In May 1992 the Albanian majority held unsanctioned elections, chooosing Ibrahim Rugova as president and selecting a 130-member parliament. Serbia regarded the elections as illegal but allowed them to proceed.

Kossuth Lajos 1802–1894. Hungarian nationalist and leader of the revolution of 1848. He proclaimed Hungary's independence of Habsburg rule, became governor of a Hungarian republic 1849, and, when it was defeated by Austria and Russia, fled first to Turkey and then to exile in Britain and Italy.

Kosygin Alexei Nikolaievich 1904–1980. Soviet politician, prime minister 1964–80. He was elected to the Supreme Soviet 1938, became a member of the Politburo 1946, deputy prime minister 1960, and succeeded Khrushchev as premier (while Brezhnev succeeded him as party secretary). In the late 1960s Kosygin's influence declined.

kremlin citadel or fortress of Russian cities. The Moscow kremlin dates from the 12th century, and the name 'the Kremlin' was once synonymous with the Soviet government.

Krishna Menon Vengalil Krishnan 1897–1974. Indian politician who was a leading light in the Indian nationalist movement. He represented India at the United Nations 1952–62, and was defence minister 1957–62, when he was dismissed by Nehru following China's invasion of N India.

Kristallnacht 'night of (broken) glass' 9–10 Nov 1938 when the Nazi Sturmabteilung (SA) militia in Germany and Austria mounted a concerted attack on Jews, their synagogues, homes, and shops. It followed the assassination of a German embassy official in Paris by a Polish-Jewish youth. Subsequent measures included German legislation against Jews owning businesses or property, and restrictions on their going to school or leaving Germany. It was part of the ◊Holocaust.

More than 200,000 Jewish men were arrested and sent to concentration camps, and

91 Jews were killed during the Kristallnacht. The damage to property is estimated at 25 million marks.

This ◊*pogrom* precipitated a rush by Jews for visas to other countries, but restrictive immigration policies throughout the world, and obstructive Nazi regulations at home, made it impossible for most of them to leave.

Kronstadt uprising revolt in March 1921 by sailors of the Russian Baltic Fleet at their headquarters in Kronstadt, outside Petrograd (now St Petersburg). On the orders of the leading Bolshevik, Leon Trotsky, Red Army troops, dressed in white camouflage, crossed the ice to the naval base and captured it on 18 March. The leaders were subsequently shot.

Following a strike by Petrograd workers Feb 1921, the Kronstadt sailors reaffirmed their demands for the rights obtained in theory by the Revolution of 1917. The sailors were thus labelled the 'conscience of the Revolution' for demanding what had been promised, but not delivered, by the Bolsheviks. These perceived them as a threat because of their detection and resentment of the growing Bolshevik monopoly of power.

Kropotkin Peter Alexeivich, Prince Kropotkin 1842–1921. Russian anarchist. Imprisoned for revolutionary activities 1874, he escaped to the UK 1876 and later moved to Switzerland. Expelled from Switzerland 1881, he went to France, where he was imprisoned 1883–86. He lived in Britain until 1917, when he returned to Moscow. Among his works are *Memoirs of a Revolutionist* 1899, *Mutual Aid* 1902, and *Modern Science and Anarchism* 1903.

The word state is identical with the word war.

Peter Kropotkin

Kruger Stephanus Johannes Paulus 1825–1904. President of the Transvaal 1883–1900. He refused to remedy the grievances of the uitlanders (English and other non-Boer white residents) and so precipitated the Second ◊South African War.

Kruger telegram message sent by Kaiser Wilhelm II of Germany to President Kruger of the Transvaal 3 Jan 1896 congratulating him on defeating the ◊Jameson raid of 1895. The text of the telegram provoked indignation in Britain and elsewhere, and represented a worsening of Anglo-German relations, in spite of a German government retraction.

Kubitschek Juscelino 1902–1976. Brazilian president 1956–61. His term as president saw political peace, civil liberty, and rapid economic growth at the cost of high inflation and corruption. He had a strong commitment to public works and the construction of Brasília as the nation's capital.

Kubitschek entered congress 1934, and was governor of Minas Gerais 1951–55, pursuing an active policy of road building, electrification, and industrial development.

Kublai Khan 1216–1294. Mongol emperor of China from 1259. He completed his grandfather ◊Genghis Khan's conquest of N China from 1240, and on his brother Mungo's death 1259 established himself as emperor of China. He moved the capital to Beijing and founded the Yuan dynasty, successfully expanding his empire into Indochina, but was defeated in an attempt to conquer Japan 1281.

Ku Klux Klan US secret society dedicated to white supremacy, founded 1866 in the southern states of the USA to oppose ◊Reconstruction after the American ◊Civil War and to deny political rights to the black population. Members wore hooded white robes to hide their identity, and burned crosses at their night-time meetings.

Its violence led the government to pass the restrictive Ku Klux Klan Acts of 1871. The society re-emerged 1915 in Atlanta, Georgia, and increased in strength during the 1920s as a racist, anti-Semitic, anti-Catholic, and anti-Communist organization. Today the Klan has evolved into a paramilitary extremist group that has forged loose ties with other white supremacist groups.

kulak (Russian) a peasant who could afford to hire labour and often acted as village usurer. The kulaks resisted the Soviet government's policy of collectivization, and in 1930 they were 'liquidated as a class', with up to 5 million being either killed or deported to Siberia.

Kulturkampf (German) a policy introduced by Chancellor Bismarck in Germany 1873 that isolated the Catholic interest and attempted to reduce its power in order to create a political coalition of liberals and agrarian conservatives. The alienation of such a large section of the German population as the Catholics could not be sustained, and the policy was abandoned after 1876 to be replaced by an anti-socialist policy.

Kun Béla 1885–1938. Hungarian politician who created a Soviet republic in Hungary March 1919, which was overthrown Aug 1919 by a Western blockade and Romanian military

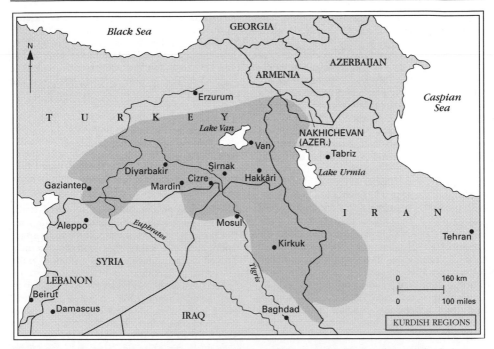

Kurdish regions *The Kurds have inhabited Kurdistan, a mountainous territory southeast of the Armenian mountains, for hundreds of years. Dwelling within the constantly disputed boundaries of states within the Middle East, the Kurds have been the victims of their neighbours' policies of expansion or aggrandizement. Today they dwell uneasily within the political borders of several surrounding nations, their presence in Iraq being a significant factor in that country's relationship with the United Nations.*

actions. The succeeding regime under Admiral Horthy effectively liquidated both socialism and liberalism in Hungary.

Kuomintang original spelling of the Chinese nationalist party, now known (outside Taiwan) as ◊Guomindang.

Kurd member of the Kurdish culture, living mostly in the Taurus and Sagros mountains of W Iran and N Iraq in the region called *Kurdistan*.

References to what may have been the Kurds are found in Sumerian inscriptions dating from 2000 BC. The Greek historian Xenophon also mentions Assyrian battles with the Kurds. During the 13th century, ◊Saladin (Salah-ad-Din), a Kurd, emerged as the foremost leader in the struggle against the Crusaders. There was an ill-fated attempt to set up an autonomous Kurdish state within the Ottoman Empire during the 1880s, and the Treaty of Sèvres 1920 provided a draft scheme for Kurdish independence, which Britain and France reneged on, instead dividing Kurdish territory between their Middle Eastern client states. When in 1922 the Kurds rebelled, they were bombed by the RAF. In 1925 a rebellion of Kurds against the newly

founded Turkish republic was led by Sheik Said, and was savagely put down by the authorities in an attempt to eradicate Kurdish identity, which has persisted to the present. In Turkey until 1991, speaking or writing Kurdish or even owning a recording of Kurdish music was an offence, and 670,000 Kurds were arrested 1981–91. Unlike ethnic Turks, Kurds may by law be held incommunicado for 30 days. Speaking Kurdish was legalized 1991 but publishing or broadcasting in Kurdish remained prohibited. In Iran, the Kurds briefly achieved a Kurdish representative with Soviet backing 1946, were repressed under the shah, and, when they revolted against the regime of Ayatollah Khomeini, were savagely put down 1979–80. It was promised that the four provinces would be united in an autonomous unit; the Kurdish region, however, remains divided. The Kurds of Iraq live in the mountainous NE province of Kirkuk, and were in revolt 1961–75 to obtain a fully autonomous Kurdish state. As a result, they were moved from north to south, a policy that led to revolts 1974–75 and 1977, suppressed with many civilian deaths and the destruction of whole villages. In 1988 Iraq used chemical weapons to drive Kurds into Turkey.

In Nov 1989 the Iraqi army moved an estimated 100,000–500,000 people and again destroyed their villages to create an uninhabited 'security zone' on its borders with Iran and Turkey. In the wake of Iraq's defeat by a US-led alliance in the Gulf War 1991, Iraqi Kurds revolted and briefly controlled many northern Iraqi cities. The Iraqi counterattack forced more than one million Kurds to flee to regions on both sides of Iraq's borders with Turkey and Iran, where thousands died of hunger, exposure, and waterborne diseases. The USA and its allies subsequently stationed a military task force in Turkey to deter Iraqi attacks on the Kurds and, in May 1991, set up a 'safe zone' within which humanitarian aid for the refugees was provided for three months. Following the withdrawal of forces from the safe zone and the return of Kurdish and other Iraqi refugees to their homes, a multi-national force, called 'Operation Poised Hammer', was retained in Turkey until Sept 1991 to protect the Kurds. During April and June 1991, Kurdish leaders and Iraqi government officials held talks on Kurdish autonomy, but no agreement was reached.

Kuropatkin Alexei Nikolaievich 1848–1921. Russian general. He distinguished himself as chief of staff during the Russo-Turkish War 1877–78, was commander in chief in Manchuria 1903, and resigned after his defeat at Mukden 1905 in the ◊Russo-Japanese War. During World War I he commanded the armies on the northern front until 1916.

Kusana dynasty or *Yueh-chih dynasty* N Indian family ruling between the 1st and 2nd centuries AD. The greatest Kusana king was Kaniska (ruled *c.* 78–102). A devout Buddhist and liberal patron of the arts, he extended the empire across central and E India. In decline by 176, the dynasty was overthrown by the ◊Sassanians *c.* 240.

An Indo-European-speaking nomadic people of central Asian descent, the Kusana were forced from China when the Great Wall was extended W by the ◊Han dynasty. Under chief Kujula Kadphises (reigned 15–55), one group of Kusanas secured control over NW India, establishing a capital city at Purushapura (modern Peshawar).

Kūt-al-Imára or *al Kūt* city in Iraq, on the river Tigris. In World War I it was under siege by Turkish forces from Dec 1915 to April 1916, when the British garrison surrendered.

Kutuzov Mikhail Larionovich, Prince of Smolensk 1745–1813. Commander of the Russian forces in the Napoleonic Wars. He commanded an army corps at ◊Austerlitz and the army in its reatreat 1812. After the burning of Moscow that year, he harried the French throughout their retreat and later took command of the united Prussian armies.

Kuwait country in SW Asia, bounded N and NW by Iraq, E by the Persian Gulf, and S and SW by Saudi Arabia.

history The region was part of the Turkish ◊Ottoman Empire from the 16th century; the ruling family founded the sheikdom of Kuwait 1756. The ruler made a treaty with Britain 1899, enabling it to become a self-governing protectorate until it achieved full independence 1961.

discovery of oil Oil was first discovered 1938, and its large-scale exploitation began after 1945, transforming Kuwait City from a small fishing port into a thriving commercial centre. The oil revenues have enabled ambitious public works and education programmes to be undertaken. Sheik Abdullah al-Salem al-Sabah took the title of emir 1961 when he assumed full executive powers. He died 1965 and was succeeded by his brother, Sheik Sabah al-Salem al-Sabah. He, in turn, died 1977 and was succeeded by Crown Prince Jabir, who appointed Sheik Saad al-Abdullah al-Salem al-Sabah as his heir apparent. In Jan 1990 pro-democracy demonstrations were dispersed by the police.

Kuwait used its considerable wealth not only to improve its infrastructure and social services but also attempting to secure its borders, making, for example, substantial donations to Iraq, which in the past had made territorial claims on it. It has also been a strong supporter of the Arab cause generally.

Iran–Iraq War During the 1980–88 Iran–Iraq War, Kuwait was the target of destabilization efforts by the revolutionary Iranian government. Some Shi'ites conducted a terrorist bombing campaign as part of an effort to incite the Shi'ite minority in Kuwait; 17 were arrested 1983 and their freedom was the demand in several hijacking incidents that followed. In 1987 Kuwait sought US protection for its tankers in the wake of attacks on Gulf shipping. Several Kuwaiti tankers were reflagged, and the US Navy conducted convoys through the Gulf. Iranian missiles also struck Kuwaiti installations, provoking fears of an expansion of the conflict. Kuwait released two of the convicted bombers Feb 1989.

Gulf War On 2 Aug 1990 President Saddam Hussein of Iraq reactivated the long-standing territorial dispute and invaded and occupied the country. The emir and most of his family escaped to Saudi Arabia. With more assets outside than in Kuwait, the government in exile was able to provide virtually unlimited financial support to Kuwaitis who had fled and to countries willing to help it regain its territory. On 28 Feb 1991, US-led coalition forces liberated Kuwait. By March 1991 peace negotiations began as part of the effort to restabilize the entire Middle East. In April 1991 the reshuffling of the cabinet provoked criticism from pro-democracy campaigners for leaving power in the hands of the Sabah family.

aftermath of the war About 600 oil wells were sabotaged by the occupying forces; smoke from burning oil created a pall over the whole country. Not until Nov 1991 was Kuwait able to extinguish all the oil-well fires set by the retreating Iraqis. International criticism of a Kuwaiti tribunal which sentenced 21 people to death for alledgedly collaborating with Iraq during the Gulf War resulted in the sentences being reduced to life imprisonment July 1991. Palestinian guest workers who had remained in Kuwait were subjected to reprisals by returning Kuwaitis for alleged collaboration with the Iraqis, and of 350,000 Palestinians in Kuwait before the invasion, only 80,000 remained in 1992. In Oct opposition candidates won a majority of seats in Kuwait's first national-assembly election since 1985.

Kyrgyzstan or *Kirghizia* country in central Asia, bounded N by Kazakhstan, E by China, W by Uzbekistan, and S by Tajikistan.

history Kyrgyzstan is peopled mainly by horse-breeding, mountain-dwelling nomads, the Turkic-speaking descendants of the Mongol invaders who swept across Asia from the 13th century. It was annexed by Russia in 1864. Part of an independent Turkestan republic 1917–24, it then became an autonomous republic within the USSR and, from 1936, a constituent Soviet republic.

end of communism Long viewed as a bastion of conservatism, the republic overwhelmingly endorsed maintenance of the Union in the March 1991 USSR constitutional referendum and its Communist Party (CP) supported the Aug 1991 coup attempt against President Gorbachev in Moscow. However, Askar Akayev, a 'reform communist' who had assumed the republic's presidency in Nov 1990, condemned the coup as unconstitutional. He resigned from the Communist Party of the Soviet Union and ordered the suspension of the republic's CP and the nationalization of its property. He was returned, unchallenged, as Kyrgyzstan's president on 12 Oct 1991 in the republic's first popular election.

foreign relations Kyrgyzstan joined the Commonwealth of Independent States which was formed in Dec 1991. In the same month the USA accorded Kyrgyzstan diplomatic recognition. In Jan 1992 the republic was admitted into the Conference on Security and Cooperation in Europe and in March into the United Nations.

laager term used by the Boers in South Africa to describe an enclosed encampment; now applied derogatively to the siege mentality of sections of the Afrikaner population.

Labor, Knights of in US history, a national labour organization founded by Philadelphia tailor Uriah Stephens in 1869 and committed to cooperative enterprise, equal pay for both sexes, and an eight-hour day. The Knights grew rapidly in the mid-1880s under Terence V Powderly (1849–1924) but gave way to the ◊American Federation of Labor after 1886.

Labor Party in Australia, a political party based on socialist principles. It was founded in 1891 and first held office in 1904. It formed governments 1929–31 and 1939–49, but in the intervening periods internal discord provoked splits, and reduced its effectiveness. It returned to power under Gough Whitlam 1972–75, and again under Bob Hawke 1983-91 and Paul Keating from 1991-96.

Labour Party UK political party founded 1900 on socialist principles, originally formed to represent workers. By 1922 the Labour Party was recognized as the official opposition, and in 1924 formed a minority government (with Liberal support) for a few months under the party's first secretary Ramsay MacDonald. A second minority government in 1929 followed a conservative policy, and in 1931 MacDonald and other leaders, faced with a financial crisis, left the party to support the National government. The first majority Labour government 1945-51 introduced ◊nationalization and the National Health Service, and expanded social security. Labour was again in power 1964-70 and 1974-79. Under Tony Blair, the party regained power 1997.

Labour Representation Committee in British politics, a forerunner 1900–1906 of the Labour Party. The committee was founded in Feb 1900 after a resolution drafted by Ramsay ◊Macdonald and moved by the Amalgamated Society of Railway Workers (now the National Union of Railwaymen) was carried at the 1899 Trades Union Congress (TUC). The resolution called for a special congress of the TUC parliamentary committee to campaign for more Labour members of Parliament. Ramsay MacDonald became its secretary. Following his efforts, 29 Labour members of Parliament were elected in the 1906 general election, and the Labour Representation Committee was renamed the Labour Party.

Lafayette Marie Joseph Gilbert de Motier, Marquis de Lafayette 1757–1834. French soldier and politician. He fought against Britain in the American Revolution 1777–79 and 1780–82. During the French Revolution he sat in the National Assembly as a constitutional royalist and in 1789 presented the Declaration of the Rights of Man. After the storming of the ◊Bastille, he was given command of the National Guard. In 1792 he fled the country after attempting to restore the monarchy and was imprisoned by the Austrians until 1797. He supported Napoleon Bonaparte in 1815, sat in the chamber of deputies as a Liberal from 1818, and played a leading part in the revolution of 1830.

Lafitte Jean *c*. 1780–*c*. 1825. Pirate in America. Suspected of complicity with the British, he was attacked by American forces soon after the outbreak of the Anglo-American War 1812. He proved his loyalty to General Andrew Jackson by his heroic participation in the Battle of New Orleans 1815.

La Guardia Fiorello (Henrico) 1882–1947. US Republican politician; Congressman 1917, 1919, 1923–33; mayor of New York 1933–45. Elected against the opposition of the powerful Tammany Hall Democratic Party organization, he improved the administration, suppressed racketeering, and organized unemployment relief, slum-clearance schemes, and social services. Although nominally a Republican, he supported the Democratic president F D Roosevelt's ◊New Deal. La Guardia Airport, in New York City, is named after him.

Lahore Resolution meeting in Lahore in March 1940 at which the Indian politician Muhammad Ali ◊Jinnah led the Muslim League in demanding the eventual partition of India and the creation of a Muslim state of Pakistan.

laissez faire (French 'let alone') theory that the state should not intervene in economic affairs, except to break up a monopoly. The phrase originated with the Physiocrats, 18th-century French economists whose maxim was *laissez faire et laissez passer*, (literally, 'let go and let pass' – that is, leave the individual alone and let commodities circulate freely). The degree to which intervention should take place is still one of the chief problems of economics. The Scottish economist Adam ◊Smith justified the theory in *The Wealth of Nations*.

Before the 17th century, control by guilds, local authorities, or the state, of wages, prices, employment, and the training of workmen, was taken for granted. As capitalist enterprises developed in the 16th and 17th centuries, entrepreneurs shook off the control of the guilds and local authorities. By the 18th century this process was complete. The reaction against laissez faire began in the mid-19th century and found expression in the factory acts and elsewhere. This reaction was inspired partly by humanitarian protests against the social conditions created by the ◊Industrial Revolution and partly by the wish to counter popular unrest of the 1830s and 1840s by removing some of its causes.

The 20th century has seen an increasing degree of state intervention to promote social benefits, which after World War II in Europe was extended into the field of nationalization of leading industries and services. However, during the 1970s, laissez-faire policies were again pursued in the UK and the USA.

Lancaster House Agreement accord reached in 1979 leading the way to full independence for ◊Zimbabwe.

Lancaster, House of English royal house, a branch of the Plantagenets.

It originated in 1267 when Edmund (died 1296), the younger son of Henry III, was granted the earldom of Lancaster. Converted to a duchy for Henry of Grosmont (died 1361), it passed to John of Gaunt in 1362 by his marriage to Blanche, Henry's daughter. John's son, Henry IV, established the royal dynasty of Lancaster in 1399, and he was followed by two more Lancastrian kings, Henry V and Henry VI.

Land League Irish peasant-rights organization, formed 1879 by Michael ◊Davitt and Charles ◊Parnell to fight against tenant evictions. Through its skilful use of the boycott against anyone who took a farm from which another had been evicted, it forced Gladstone's government to introduce a law in 1881 restricting rents and granting tenants security of tenure.

Lange David (Russell) 1942–   . New Zealand Labour Party prime minister 1983–89. Lange,

a barrister, was elected to the House of Representatives 1977. Labour had a decisive win in the 1984 general election on a non-nuclear military policy, which Lange immediately put into effect, despite criticism from the USA. He introduced a free-market economic policy and was re-elected 1987. He resigned Aug 1989 over a disagreement with his finance minister.

Langobard another name for ◊Lombard, member of a Germanic people.

Langton Stephen *c.* 1150–1228. English priest who was mainly responsible for drafting the charter of rights, the ◊Magna Carta.

Lansbury George 1859–1940. British Labour politician, leader in the Commons 1931–35. He was a member of Parliament for Bow 1910–12 – when he resigned to force a by-election on the issue of votes for women, which he lost – and again 1922–40. In 1921, while mayor of the London borough of Poplar, he went to prison with most of the council rather than modify their policy of more generous unemployment relief.

Lansdowne Henry Charles, 5th Marquis of Lansdowne 1845–1927. British Liberal Unionist politician, governor-general of Canada 1883–88, viceroy of India 1888–93, war minister 1895–1900, and foreign secretary 1900–06. While at the Foreign Office he abandoned Britain's isolationist policy by forming an alliance with Japan and an entente cordiale with France. His letter of 1917 suggesting an offer of peace to Germany created a controversy.

Laos landlocked country in SE Asia, bounded N by China, E by Vietnam, S by Cambodia, W by Thailand, and NW by Myanmar.

history The original SE Asian tribal groups saw a migration from the 4th–5th centuries of people from China. Laos came under Indian influence and adopted Buddhism during the 7th–11th centuries. As part of the ◊Khmer empire from the 11th–13th centuries, it experienced much artistic and architectural activity. From the 12th century, the country was invaded by the Lao from Thailand, who established small independent kingdoms and became Buddhists. Laos became an independent kingdom in the 14th century and was first visited by Europeans in the 17th century, becoming a French protectorate 1893–1945. After a brief period of Japanese occupation, France re-established control 1946 despite opposition from the Chinese-backed Lao Issara (Free Laos) nationalist movement. The country became semi-autonomous 1950, when, under the constitutional monarchy of the king of ◊Luang Prabang, it became an associated state of the French Union.

civil war In 1954, after the Geneva Agreements, Laos gained full independence. Civil war broke out between two factions of former Lao Issara supporters: a moderate, royalist-neutralist group led by Prince Souvanna Phouma, which had supported the 1950 French compromise and was the recognized government for most of the country; and a more extreme communist resistance group, the Pathet Lao ('land of the Lao'), led by ex-Prince Souphanouvong (the half-brother of Prince Souvanna) and supported by China and the ◊Vietminh, which controlled much of N Laos.

A coalition government was established after the 1957 Vientiane Agreement. This soon collapsed, and in 1960 a third, right-wing force emerged when General Phoumi Nosavan, backed by the royal army, overthrew Souvanna Phouma and set up a pro-Western government headed by Prince Boun Gum. A new Geneva Agreement 1962 established a tripartite (right–left–neutral) government under the leadership of Prince Souvanna Phouma. Fighting continued, however, between the North Vietnamese-backed Pathet Lao and the US-backed neutralists and right wing. There was massive aerial bombardment by the US Air Force until the 1973 Vientiane Agreement established a cease-fire line dividing the country NW to SE, giving the communists two-thirds of the country, but giving the Souvanna Phouma government two-thirds of the population. All foreign forces (North Vietnamese, Thai, and US) were to be withdrawn, and both sides received equal representation in Souvanna Phouma's provisional government 1974.

republic In 1975 the communist Pathet Lao (renamed the Lao People's Front) seized power. King Savang Vatthana (1908–1980), who had succeeded 1959, abdicated, and Laos became a People's Democratic Republic under the presidency of Prince Souphanouvong. Prince Souvanna Phouma remained as an 'adviser' to the government, but the real controlling force was now the prime minister and communist party leader, Kaysone Phomvihane.

reform The new administration, which inherited a poor, war-ravaged economy, attempted to reorganize the country along socialist lines, nationalizing businesses and industries and collectivizing agriculture. Faced with a food shortage and the flight of more than 250,000 refugees to Thailand, it modified its approach 1979, introducing production incentives and allowing greater scope for the private sector. Further 'liberalization' followed from 1985 under the prompting of the Soviet leader Mikhail Gorbachev, with a new profit-related 'socialist business accounting system' being adopted. Phoumi Vongvichit became acting president 1986 owing to Souphanouvong's ailing health. In March 1989, multiparty elections were held for the first time since the communists came to power 1975, with the communists retaining political control.

In 1991 the new president, Kaysone Phomvihane, called for acceleration of the pace of replacement of agricultural cooperatives by privately owned farms, as part of economic restructuring. A new constitution was endorsed by the supreme people's assembly in Aug 1991. General Khamtay Siphandon, former vice premier and defence minister, became the new premier.

foreign relations Laos had been closely tied to the USSR. In Aug 1989 party-to-party relations were established with China after a ten-year break. In Nov 1991 the USA upgraded its diplomatic representation in Laos to ambassadorial level for the first time since the communists came to power in 1975. Relations with Thailand, especially commercial links, improved markedly from 1988 when the two countries were involved in a serious border skirmish, but Laos remained closely linked to Vietnam.

A journey of a thousand miles must begin with a single step.

Lao Zi *Tao Tê Ching*

Lao Zi or Lao Tzu *c.* 604–531 BC. Chinese philosopher, commonly regarded as the founder of ◊Taoism, with its emphasis on the Tao, the inevitable and harmonious way of the universe. Nothing certain is known of his life, and he is variously said to have lived in the 6th or the 4th century BC. The *Tao Tê Ching*, the Taoist scripture, is attributed to him but apparently dates from the 3rd century BC.

Largo Caballero Francisco 1869–1946. Spanish socialist and leader of the Spanish Socialist Party (PSOE). He became prime minister of the Popular Front government elected in Feb 1936 and remained in office for the first ten months of the Civil War before being replaced in May 1937 by Juan Negrin (1887–1956).

Las Casas Bartoloméde 1474–1566. Spanish missionary, historian, and colonial reformer, known as *the Apostle of the Indies*. He was one of the first Europeans to call for the abolition of Indian slavery in Latin America. He took part in the conquest of Cuba in 1513, but subsequently worked for American Indian freedom in the Spanish colonies. *Apologetica historia de las Indias* (first published 1875–76) is his account of Indian traditions and his witnessing of Spanish oppression of the Indians.

Las Casas sailed to Hispaniola in the West Indies in 1502 and was ordained priest there in 1512. From Cuba he returned to Spain in 1515 to plead for the Indian cause, winning the support of the Holy Roman emperor Charles V. In what is now Venezuela he unsuccessfully attempted to found a settlement of free Indians. In 1530, shortly before the conquest of Peru, he persuaded the Spanish government to forbid slavery there. In 1542 he became bishop of Chiapas in S Mexico. He returned finally to Spain in 1547.

Lascaux cave system in SW France with prehistoric wall paintings. It is richly decorated with realistic and symbolic paintings of buffaloes, horses, and red deer of the Upper Palaeolithic period, about 18,000 BC. The caves, near Montignac in the Dordogne, were discovered 1940. Similar paintings are found in ◊Altamira, Spain. The opening of the Lascaux caves to tourists led to deterioration of the paintings; the caves were closed 1963 and a facsimile opened 1983.

Lascaux is the Parthenon of prehistory.
On *Lascaux* Cyril Connolly
Ideas and Places 1953

Lassalle Ferdinand 1825–1864. German socialist. He was imprisoned for his part in the ◊revolutions of 1848, during which he met the philosopher Karl ◊Marx, and in 1863 founded the General Association of German Workers (later the Social-Democratic Party). His publications include *The Working Man's Programme* 1862 and *The Open Letter* 1863. He was killed in a duel arising from a love affair.

La Tène prehistoric settlement at the east end of Lake Neuchâtel, Switzerland, which has given its name to a culture of the Iron Age. The culture lasted from the 5th century BC to the Roman conquest.

Lateran Treaties series of agreements that marked the reconciliation of the Italian state with the papacy in 1929. They were hailed as a propaganda victory for the Fascist regime. The treaties involved recognition of the sovereignty of the ◊Vatican City State, the payment of an indemnity for papal possessions lost during unification in 1870, and agreement on the role of the Catholic church within the Italian state in the form of a concordat between Pope Pius XI and the dictator Mussolini.

latifundium (Latin for 'broad' and 'farm') in ancient Rome, a large agricultural estate designed to make maximum use of cheap labour, whether free workmen or slaves.

In present-day Italy, Spain, and South America, the term refers to a large agricultural estate worked by low-paid casual or semiservile labour in the interests of absentee landlords.

Latimer Hugh 1490–1555. English Christian church reformer and bishop. After his conversion to Protestantism in 1524 he was imprisoned several times but was protected by Cardinal Wolsey and Henry VIII. After the accession of the Catholic Mary, he was burned for heresy.

Latvia country in N Europe, bounded E by Russia, N by Estonia, N and NW by the Baltic Sea, S by Lithuania, and SE by Belarus.

history The Vikings invaded the area now known as Latvia in the 9th century and the Russians attacked in the 10th century. The invasion of the ◊Teutonic Knights (German crusaders) in the 13th century was resisted in a lengthy struggle, but Latvia eventually came under their control 1230, converted to Christianity, and was governed by them for more than 200 years. By 1562 Poland and Lithuania had taken over most of the country. Sweden conquered the north 1621 and Russia took over control of this area 1710. By 1800 all of Latvia had come under Russian control. The Latvian independence movement began to emerge in the late 1800s and continued to grow in the early 20th century.

struggle for independence Latvia was partly occupied by the Germans during World War I. The USSR reclaimed control 1917 but was overthrown by Germany Feb 1918, when Latvia declared independence. Soviet rule was restored when Germany withdrew Dec 1918, but Soviet forces were again overthrown by British naval and German forces May–Dec 1919, and democratic rule was established. A coup 1934 replaced the established government. In 1939 a secret German-Soviet agreement assigned Latvia to Soviet rule and in 1940 Latvia was incorporated as a constituent republic of the USSR. During World War II Latvia was again occupied by German forces 1941–44, but the USSR regained control 1944.

As in the other Baltic republics, nationalist dissent grew from 1980, influenced by the Polish example and prompted by an influx of Russian workers and officials. A Latvian Popular Front was established Oct 1988 to campaign for independence and in the same month the prewar flag was readopted and official status given to the Latvian language. In the same year Anatolijs Gorbunov was elected president. In Jan 1990 the Latvian Communist Party (LCP) broke its links with Moscow and in May Latvia followed the lead taken by Lithuania when it unilaterally declared independence from the USSR, subject to a transitional period for negotiation. A multiparty system emerged, the 1990 March–April elections resulting in a Popular Front government. In Jan 1991 Soviet paratroopers seized key installations in Riga, killing one civilian, but began to withdraw later that month after international protests.

A plebiscite in March 1991 voted 73.7% in favour of independence. During the coup attempt against President Gorbachev in the USSR, Soviet troops seized the radio and television station in Riga. In response, on 21 Aug 1991, the republic declared its immediate independence (previously it had been in a 'period of transition') and outlawed the CP. This declaration was recognized by the Soviet government and Western nations Sept 1991 and the new state was granted membership of the United Nations (UN) and admitted into the ◊Conference on Security and Cooperation in Europe (CSCE). In Feb 1992 US Vice President Dan Quayle reopened the US embassy, closed since the Baltic takeover 1940. In March Russia agreed to begin a pullout of ex-Soviet troops from Latvia and in August requested money for that pullout, which they said would be completed by 1994. In July Latvia curbed the rights of non-citizens, prompting Russia to ask the UN for the protection of minorities in that country.

Laud William 1573–1645. English priest; archbishop of Canterbury from 1633. Laud's High Church policy, support for Charles I's unparliamentary rule, censorship of the press, and persecution of the Puritans all aroused bitter opposition, while his strict enforcement of the statutes against enclosures and of laws regulating wages and prices alienated the propertied classes. His attempt to impose the use of the Prayer Book on the Scots precipitated the English ◊Civil War. Impeached by Parliament 1640, he was imprisoned in the Tower of London, summarily condemned to death, and beheaded.

Laurier Wilfrid 1841–1919. Canadian politician, leader of the Liberal Party 1887–1919 and prime minister 1896–1911. The first French-Canadian to hold the office, he encouraged immigration into Canada from Europe and the USA, established a separate Canadian navy, and sent troops to help Britain in the Boer War.

Lausanne, Treaty of peace settlement in 1923 between Greece and Turkey after Turkey refused to accept the terms of the Treaty of Sèvres 1920, which would have made peace with the western Allies. It involved the surrender by Greece of Smyrna (now Izmir) to Turkey and the enforced exchange of the Greek population of Smyrna for the Turkish population of Greece.

Laval Pierre 1883–1945. French right-wing politician. He was prime minister and foreign secretary 1931–32, and again 1935–36. In World War II he joined Pétain's ◊Vichy government as vice-premier in June 1940; dismissed in Dec 1940, he was reinstated by Hitler's orders as head of the government and foreign minister in 1942. After the war he was executed.

If peace is a chimera, I am happy to have caressed her.

Pierre Laval

---

law body of rules and principles under which justice is administered or order enforced in a state or nation. In western Europe there are two main systems: Roman law and English law. US law is a modified form of English law.

Roman legal system of ancient Rome that is now the basis of civil law, one of the main European legal systems.

It originated under the republic, was developed under the empire, and continued in use in the Byzantine Empire until 1453. The first codification was that of the 12 Tables (450 BC), of which only fragments survive. Roman law assumed its final form in the codification of Justinian AD 528–34. An outstanding feature of Roman law was its system of international law (*jus gentium*), applied in disputes between Romans and foreigners or provincials, or between provincials of different states. Church influence led to the adoption of Roman law throughout western continental Europe, and it was spread to E Europe and parts of Asia by the French *Code Napoléon* in the 19th century. Scotland and Québec (because of their French links) and South Africa (because of its link with Holland) also have it as the basis of their legal systems.

English law derives from Anglo-Saxon customs, which were too entrenched to be broken by the Norman Conquest and still form the basis of the common law, which by 1250 had been systematized by the royal judges. Unique to English law is the doctrine of *stare decisis*

(Latin 'to stand by things decided'), which requires that courts abide by former precedents (or decisions) when the same points arise again in litigation. These two concepts are the basis for US law.

Law Andrew Bonar 1858–1923. British Conservative politician. Elected leader of the opposition 1911, he became colonial secretary in Asquith's coalition government 1915–16, chancellor of the Exchequer 1916–19, and Lord Privy Seal 1919–21 in Lloyd George's coalition. He formed a Conservative Cabinet 1922, but resigned on health grounds.

Born in New Brunswick, Canada, he made a fortune in Scotland as a banker and iron-merchant before entering Parliament 1900.

Lawrence T(homas) E(dward), known as *Lawrence of Arabia* 1888–1935. British soldier and writer. Appointed to the military intelligence department in Cairo, Egypt, during World War I, he took part in negotiations for an Arab revolt against the Ottoman Turks, and in 1916 attached himself to the emir Faisal. He became a guerrilla leader of genius, combining raids on Turkish communications with the organization of a joint Arab revolt, described in *The Seven Pillars of Wisdom* 1926.

League of Nations international organization formed after World War I to solve international disputes by arbitration. Established in Geneva, Switzerland, 1920, the league included representatives from states throughout the world, but was severely weakened by the US decision not to become a member, and had no power to enforce its decisions. It was dissolved 1946. Its subsidiaries included the *International Labour Organization* and the *Permanent Court of International Justice* in The Hague, Netherlands, both now under the auspices of the United Nations

---

Why should we kid ourselves? This is a parvenu nation. We never fought for our independence. We never had a state.

On *Lebanon* Edouard Saab (1929–76), quoted in *New York Times* 10 Apr 1976

Lebanon country in W Asia, bounded N and E by Syria, S by Israel, and W by the Mediterranean Sea.

history The area now known as Lebanon was once occupied by ◊Phoenicia, an empire that flourished from the 5th century BC to the 1st century AD, when it came under Roman rule. Christianity was introduced during the Roman

occupation, and Islam arrived with the Arabs 635. Lebanon was part of the Turkish Ottoman Empire from the 16th century, until administered by France under a League of Nations mandate 1920–41. It was declared independent 1941, became a republic 1943, and achieved full autonomy 1944.

Lebanon has a wide variety of religions, including Christianity and many Islamic sects. For many years these coexisted peacefully, giving Lebanon a stability that enabled it, until the mid-1970s, to be a commercial and financial centre. Beirut's thriving business district was largely destroyed 1975–76, and Lebanon's role as an international trader has been greatly diminished.

PLO presence in Lebanon After the establishment of Israel 1948, thousands of Palestinian refugees fled to Lebanon, and the ◊Palestine Liberation Organization (PLO), founded in Beirut 1964, had its headquarters in Lebanon 1971–82 (it moved to Tunis 1982). The PLO presence in Lebanon has been the main reason for Israeli invasions and much of the subsequent civil strife. Fighting has been largely between left-wing Muslims, led by Kamul Jumblatt of the Progressive Socialist Party, and conservative Christian groups, mainly members of the Phalangist Party. There have also been differences between pro-Iranian traditional Muslims, such as the ◊Shi'ites, and and Syrian-backed deviationist Muslims, such as the ◊Druse.

civil war In 1975 the fighting developed into full-scale civil war. A cease-fire was agreed 1976, but fighting began again 1978, when Israeli forces invaded Lebanon in search of PLO guerrillas. The United Nations secured Israel's agreement to a withdrawal and set up an international peacekeeping force, but to little avail. In 1979 Major Saad Haddad, a right-wing Lebanese army officer, with Israeli encouragement, declared an area of about 1,800 sq km/700 sq mi in S Lebanon an 'independent free Lebanon', and the following year Christian Phalangist soldiers took over an area N of Beirut. Throughout this turmoil the Lebanese government was virtually powerless. In 1982 Bachir Gemayel (youngest son of Pierre Gemayel, the founder of the Phalangist Party) became president. He was assassinated before he could assume office and his brother Amin took his place.

efforts to end hostilities In 1983, after exhaustive talks between Lebanon and Israel, under US auspices, an agreement declared an end to hostilities and called for the withdrawal of all foreign forces from the country within three months. Syria refused to recognize the agreement and left about 40,000 troops, with about 7,000 PLO fighters, in N Lebanon. Israel responded by refusing to take its forces from the south. Meanwhile, a full-scale war began between Phalangist and Druse soldiers in the Chouf Mountains, ending in a Christian defeat and the creation of a Druse-controlled ministate. The multinational force was drawn gradually but unwillingly into the conflict until it was withdrawn in the spring of 1984. Attempts were made 1985 and 1986 to end the civil war but rifts within Muslim and Christian groups thwarted them. Meanwhile Lebanon, and particularly Beirut, has seen its infrastructure and earlier prosperity virtually destroyed as it continues to be a battlefield for the rival factions.

The civil war in Beirut pitted the E Beirut 'administration' of General Michel Aoun, backed by Christian army units and Lebanese militia forces (although 30% of them are Muslim), against the W Beirut 'administration' (Muslim) of Premier Selim al-Hoss, supported by Syrian army and Muslim militia allies, including Walid Jumblatt's Progressive Socialist Party (Druse).

In May 1989 the Arab League secured agreement to a cease-fire between Christians and Muslims and in Sept a peace plan was agreed by all except General Aoun, who dissolved the national assembly. The assembly ignored him and in Nov elected the Maronite-Christian René Muawad as president instead of Aoun, but within days he was killed by a car bomb. Elias Hrawi was made his successor and he immediately confirmed the acting prime minister, al-Hoss, in that post. Despite being replaced as army commander in chief, Aoun continued to defy the constituted government.

Western hostages In 1990 it was estimated that 18 Westerners, including eight Americans, were being held hostage in Lebanon by pro-Iranian Shi'ite Muslim groups; many had been held incommunicado for years. In Aug the release of Western hostages began. In Oct government troops, backed by Syria, stormed the presidential palace occupied by General Aoun, who surrendered and took refuge in the French embassy. By Nov the government of Hrawi and al-Hoss had regained control of Beirut and proposals for a new constitution for a Second Republic were being discussed. In Dec Hrawi appointed Umar Karami as prime minister, heading a new government. Following improved relations with Syria and Iran, and strenuous efforts by the UN secretary general, the remaining Western hostages were progressively released; General Aoun was pardoned by the government and allowed to leave his haven in the French embassy. By 1992 all Western hostages had been released.

Faced with increasing economic problems, Prime Minister Karami resigned May 1992 and was replaced by Rashid al-Solh. By that time the 15 years of civil war had left 144,240 dead, 17,415 missing, and 197,505 injured. The Sept 1992 general election was boycotted by many Christians, resulting in the re-election of the pro-Syrian administration, with Rafik a-Hariri as prime minister.

Lebensraum (German 'living space') theory developed by Hitler for the expansion of Germany into E Europe, and in the 1930s used by the Nazis to justify their annexation of neighbouring states on the grounds that Germany was overpopulated.

Lebrun Albert 1871–1950. French politician. He became president of the senate in 1931 and in 1932 was chosen as president of the republic. In 1940 he handed his powers over to Marshal Pétain.

Ledru-Rollin Alexandre Auguste 1807–1874. French politician and contributor to the radical and socialist journal *La Réforme*. He became minister for home affairs in the provisional government formed in 1848 after the overthrow of Louis Philippe and the creation of the Second Republic, but he opposed the elected president Louis Napoleon.

Le Duc Tho 1911–1990. North Vietnamese diplomat who was joint winner (with US secretary of state Kissinger) of the 1973 Nobel Peace Prize for his part in the negotiations to end the Vietnam War. He indefinitely postponed receiving the award.

It is well that war is so terrible, else we would grow too fond of it.

Robert E Lee to a fellow general during the battle of Fredericksburg

---

Lee Robert E(dward) 1807–1870. US Confederate general in the American ◊Civil War, a military strategist. As military adviser to Jefferson ◊Davis, president of the Confederacy, and as commander of the army of N Virginia, he made several raids into Northern territory, but was defeated at ◊Gettysburg and surrendered 1865 at ◊Appomattox.

Lee, born in Virginia, was commissioned 1829 and served in the Mexican War. In 1859 he suppressed John ◊Brown's raid on Harper's

Ferry. On the outbreak of the Civil War 1861 he joined the Confederate army of the Southern States, and in 1862 received the command of the army of N Virginia and won the Seven Days' Battle defending Richmond, Virginia, the Confederate capital, against General McClellan's Union forces. In 1863 Lee won victories at Fredericksburg and Chancellorsville, and in 1864 at Cold Harbor, but was besieged in Petersburg, June 1864–April 1865. He surrendered to General Grant 9 April 1865 at Appomattox courthouse.

Lee Kuan Yew 1923– . Singapore politician, prime minister 1959–90. Lee founded the anticommunist Socialist People's Action Party 1954 and entered the Singapore legislative assembly 1955. He was elected the country's first prime minister 1959, and took Singapore out of the Malaysian federation 1965. He remained in power until his resignation 1990, and was succeeded by Goh Chok Tongo.

Leeward Islands former British colony in the West Indies (1871–1956) comprising Antigua, Montserrat, St Christopher/St Kitts–Nevis, Anguilla, and the Virgin Islands. The Leeward Islands, together with the British Virgin Islands, were members of the Federation of the West Indies 1958–62.

left wing in politics, the socialist parties. The term originated in the French National Assembly of 1789, where the nobles sat in the place of honour to the right of the president, and the commons sat to the left. This arrangement has become customary in European parliaments, where the progressives sit on the left and the conservatives on the right. It is also usual to speak of the right, left, and centre, when referring to the different elements composing a single party.

Legitimist party in France that continued to support the claims of the house of ◊Bourbon after the revolution of 1830. When the direct line became extinct in 1883, the majority of the party transferred allegiance to the house of Orléans.

Legnano, Battle of defeat of Holy Roman emperor Frederick I Barbarossa by members of the Lombard League in 1176 at Legnano, northwest of Milan. It was a major setback to the emperor's plans for imperial domination over Italy and showed for the first time the power of infantry against feudal cavalry.

Leicester Robert Dudley, Earl of Leicester c. 1532–1588. English courtier. Son of the Duke of Northumberland, he was created Earl of Leicester 1564. Queen Elizabeth I gave him command of the army sent to the Netherlands

1585–87 and of the forces prepared to resist the threat of Spanish invasion of 1588. His lack of military success led to his recall, but he retained Elizabeth's favour until his death.

Leicester's good looks attracted Queen Elizabeth, who made him Master of the Horse 1558 and a privy councillor 1559. But his poor performance in the army ended any chance of marrying the queen. He was a staunch supporter of the Protestant cause.

Elizabeth might have married him if he had not been already married to Amy Robsart. When his wife died in 1560 after a fall downstairs, Leicester was suspected of murdering her. In 1576 he secretly married the widow of the Earl of Essex.

Leichhardt Friedrich 1813–1848. Prussianborn Australian explorer. In 1843, he walked 965 km/600 mi from Sydney to Moreton Bay, Queensland, and in 1844 walked from Brisbane to Arnhem Land; he disappeared during a further expedition from Queensland in 1848.

lend-lease in US history, an act of Congress passed in March 1941 that gave the president power to order 'any defense article for the government of any country whose defense the president deemed vital to the defense of the USA'. During World War II, the USA negotiated many Lend-Lease agreements, notably with Britain and the Soviet Union.

Lend-lease was officially stopped in Aug 1945, by which time goods and services to the value of $42 billion had been supplied in this way, of which the British Empire had received 65% and the Soviet Union 23%.

Lenin Vladimir Ilyich. Adopted name of Vladimir Ilyich Ulyanov 1870–1924. Russian revolutionary, first leader of the USSR, and communist theoretician. Active in the 1905 Revolution, Lenin had to leave Russia when it failed, settling in Switzerland in 1914. He returned to Russia after the February revolution of 1917 (see ◊Russian Revolution). He led the Bolshevik revolution in Nov 1917 and became leader of a Soviet government, concluded peace with Germany, and organized a successful resistance to White Russian (protsarist) uprisings and foreign intervention 1918–20. His modification of traditional Marxist doctrine to fit conditions prevailing in Russia became known as *Marxism-Leninism*, the basis of communist ideology.

Lenin was born on 22 April, 1870 in Simbirsk (now renamed Ulyanovsk), on the river Volga, and became a lawyer in St Petersburg. His brother was executed in 1887 for attempting to assassinate Tsar Alexander III. A Marxist from 1889, Lenin was sent to Siberia for spreading revolutionary propaganda 1895–1900. He then edited the political paper *Iskra* ('The Spark') from abroad, and visited London several times. In *What Is to be Done?* 1902 he advocated that a professional core of Social Democratic Party activists should spearhead the revolution in Russia, a suggestion accepted by the majority (*bolsheviki*) at the London party congress 1903. From Switzerland he attacked socialist support for World War I as aiding an 'imperialist' struggle, and wrote *Imperialism* 1917.

After the renewed outbreak of revolution in Feb/March 1917, he returned to Russia in April and called for the transfer of power to the soviets (workers' councils). From the overthrow of the provisional government in Nov 1917 until his death, Lenin effectively controlled the Soviet Union, although an assassination attempt in 1918 injured his health. He founded the Third (Communist) ◊International in 1919. With communism proving inadequate to put the country on its feet, he introduced the private-enterprise ◊New Economic Policy 1921. His embalmed body is in a mausoleum in Red Square, Moscow. In 1898 he married *Nadezhda Konstantinova Krupskaya* (1869–1939), who shared his work and wrote *Memories of Lenin*.

Democracy is a State which recognizes the subjecting of the minority to the majority.

V I Lenin *The State and the Revolution*

Leo III *the Isaurian* c. 680–740. Byzantine emperor and soldier. He seized the throne in 717, successfully defended Constantinople against the Saracens 717–18, and attempted to suppress the use of images in church worship.

Leo thirteen popes, including:

Leo I St *the Great* c. 390–461. Pope from 440 who helped to establish the Christian liturgy. Leo summoned the Chalcedon Council where his Dogmatical Letter was accepted as the voice of St Peter. Acting as ambassador for the emperor Valentinian III (425–455), Leo saved Rome from devastation by the Huns by buying off their king, Attila.

Leo III c. 750–816. Pope from 795. After the withdrawal of the Byzantine emperors, the popes had become the real rulers of Rome. Leo III was forced to flee because of a conspiracy in Rome and took refuge at the court of the Frankish king Charlemagne. He returned to Rome in 799 and crowned Charlemagne emperor on Christmas Day 800, establishing the secular sovereignty of the pope over Rome under the suzerainty of the emperor (who became the Holy Roman emperor).

Leo X Giovanni de' Medici 1475–1521. Pope from 1513. The son of Lorenzo the Magnificent of Florence, he was created a cardinal at 13. He bestowed on Henry VIII of England the title of Defender of the Faith. A patron of the arts, he sponsored the rebuilding of St Peter's Church, Rome. He raised funds for this by selling indulgences (remissions of punishment for sin), a sale that led the religious reformer Martin Luther to rebel against papal authority. Leo X condemned Luther in the bull *Exsurge domine* 1520 and excommunicated him in 1521.

León city in Castilla-León, Spain. It was the capital of the kingdom of León from the 10th century until 1230, when it was merged with Castile.

Leonidas died 480 BC. King of Sparta. He was killed while defending the pass of ◊Thermopylae with 300 Spartans, 700 Thespians, and 400 Thebans against a huge Persian army.

Leopold three kings of the Belgians:

Leopold I 1790–1865. King of the Belgians from 1831, having been elected to the throne on the creation of an independent Belgium. Through his marriage, when prince of Saxe-Coburg, to Princess Charlotte Augusta, he was the uncle of Queen Victoria of Great Britain and had considerable influence over her.

Leopold II 1835–1909. King of the Belgians from 1865, son of Leopold I. He financed the US journalist Henry Stanley's explorations in Africa, which resulted in the foundation of the Congo Free State (now Zaire), from which he extracted a huge fortune by ruthless exploitation.

Leopold III 1901–1983. King of the Belgians 1934–51. He surrendered to the German army in World War II 1940. Postwar charges against his conduct led to a regency by his brother Charles and his eventual abdication 1951 in favour of his son Baudouin.

Leopold two Holy Roman emperors:

Leopold I 1640–1705. Holy Roman emperor from 1658, in succession to his father Ferdinand III. He warred against Louis XIV of France and the Ottoman Empire.

Leopold II 1747–1792. Holy Roman emperor in succession to his brother Joseph II. He was the son of Empress Maria Theresa of Austria. His hostility to the French Revolution led to the outbreak of war a few weeks after his death.

Lepanto, Battle of sea battle 7 Oct 1571, fought in the Mediterranean Gulf of Corinth off Lepanto (Italian name of the Greek port of *Naupaktos*), then in Turkish possession, between the Ottoman Empire and forces from Spain, Venice, Genoa, and the Papal States, jointly commanded by the Spanish soldier Don John of Austria. The combined western fleets overcame Muslim sea power. The Spanish writer Cervantes was wounded in the battle.

Le Pen Jean-Marie 1928–   . French extreme right-wing politician. In 1972 he formed the French National Front, supporting immigrant repatriation and capital punishment; the party gained 14% of the national vote in the 1986 election. Le Pen was elected to the European Parliament in 1984.

Lesotho landlocked country in southern Africa, an enclave within South Africa.

history The area now known as Lesotho was originally inhabited by the San, or Bushmen. During the 18th–19th centuries they were superseded by the Sotho, who were being driven southwards by the Mfecane ('the shaking-up of peoples') caused by the rise of the Zulu nation. Under the name of Basutoland, the Sotho nation was founded by Moshoeshoe I (1790–1870) in 1827, and at his request it became a British protectorate 1868. It achieved internal self-government 1965, with the paramount chief Moshoeshoe II as king, and was given full independence as Lesotho 1966.

The Basotho National Party (BNP), a conservative group favouring limited cooperation with South Africa, held power from independence until 1986. Its leader, Chief Leabua Jonathan, became prime minister 1966 and after 1970, when the king's powers were severely curtailed, the country was effectively under the prime minister's control. From 1975 an organization called the Lesotho Liberation Army (LLA) carried out a number of attacks on BNP members, with alleged South African support. South Africa, while denying complicity, pointed out that Lesotho was allowing the then (until 1990) banned South African nationalist movement, the ◊African National Congress (ANC), to use it as a base.

relations with South Africa Economically, Lesotho has been dependent on South Africa but it has openly rejected the policy of apartheid. In retaliation, South Africa has tightened its border controls, causing food shortages in Lesotho. It has been alleged that South Africa has encouraged BNP dissenters to form a new party, the Basotho Democratic Alliance (BDA), and plotted with the BDA to overthrow the Lesotho government. Lesotho was also under pressure from South Africa to sign a nonaggression pact, similar to the ◊Nkomati Accord between South Africa and Mozambique, but the Lesotho government refused to do so.

In 1986 South Africa imposed a border blockade, cutting off food and fuel supplies to Lesotho, and the government of Chief Jonathan was ousted and replaced in a coup led by General Justin Lekhanya. He announced that all executive and legislative powers would be vested in the king, ruling through a military council chaired by General Lekhanya, and a council of ministers. A week after the coup about 60 ANC members were deported to Zambia, and on the same day the South African blockade was lifted. South Africa denied playing any part in the coup but clearly found the new government more acceptable than the old.

In Nov 1990 the son of the exiled King Moshoeshoe was sworn in as King Letsie III. In 1991 General Lekhanya was ousted in a military coup led by Col Elias Tutsoane Ramaema, and political parties were permitted to operate. Moshoeshoe, the former king, returned from exile in July 1992, but as tribal chief rather than monarch.

lettre de cachet French term for an order signed by the king and closed with his seal (*cachet*); especially an order under which persons might be imprisoned or banished without trial. *Lettres de cachet* were used as a means of disposing of political opponents or criminals of high birth. The system was abolished during the French Revolution.

Levant former name for the E Mediterranean region, or more specifically, the Mediterranean coastal regions of Turkey, Syria, Lebanon, and Israel.

Levellers democratic party in the English Civil War. The Levellers found wide support among Cromwell's New Model Army and the yeoman farmers, artisans, and small traders, and proved a powerful political force 1647–49. Their programme included the establishment of a republic, government by a parliament of one house elected by male suffrage, religious toleration, and sweeping social reforms.

Cromwell's refusal to implement this programme led to mutinies by Levellers in the army, which, when suppressed by Cromwell in 1649, ended the movement. They were led by John ◊Lilburne.

True Levellers (also known as ◊Diggers) were denounced by the Levellers because of their more radical methods.

Lévesque René 1922–1987. French-Canadian politician. In 1968 he founded the Parti Québecois, with the aim of an independent Québec, but a referendum rejected the proposal in 1980. He was premier of Québec 1976–85.

Lewes, Battle of battle in 1264 caused by the baronial opposition to the English King Henry III, led by Simon de Montfort, earl of Leicester (1208–65). The king was defeated and captured at the battle.

The barons objected to Henry's patronage of French nobles in the English court, his weak foreign policy, and his support for the papacy against the Holy Roman Empire. In 1258, they forced him to issue the ◊Provisions of Oxford, and when he later refused to implement them, they revolted. They defeated and captured the king at Lewes in Sussex. Their revolt was broken by de Montfort's death and defeat at Evesham in 1265.

Lewis John L(lewellyn) 1880–1969. US labour leader. President of the United Mine Workers (UMW) 1920–60, he was largely responsible for the adoption of national mining safety standards in the USA. His militancy and the miners' strikes during and after World War II, led to President Truman's nationalization of the mines in 1946.

Lexington town in Massachusetts, USA. The Battle of Lexington and Concord, April 19, 1775, opened the American War of Independence.

Liao dynasty family that ruled part of NE China and Manchuria 945–1125 during the Song era. It was founded by cavalry-based Qidan (Khidan) people, Mongolian speakers who gradually became Sinicized. They were later defeated by the nomadic Juchen (Jurchen) who founded the ◊Jin dynasty.

The dynasty had five capitals, and cabinets for the northern and southern regions. It adopted Chinese ceremonies and writing, but maintained Qidan speech, food, and clothing. The success of barbarian rule over a Chinese population influenced later invaders such as the Mongols and Manchu.

Liaquat Ali Khan Nawabzada 1895–1951. Indian politician, deputy leader of the ◊Muslim League 1940–47, first prime minister of Pakistan from 1947. He was assassinated by objectors to his peace policy with India.

liberalism political and social theory that favours representative government, freedom of the press, speech, and worship, the abolition of class privileges, the use of state resources to protect the welfare of the individual, and international ◊free trade. It is historically associated with the Liberal Party in the UK and the Democratic Party in the USA.

Liberalism developed during the 17th–19th centuries as the distinctive theory of the industrial and commercial classes in their struggle against the power of the monarchy, the church, and the feudal landowners. Economically it was associated with ◊laissez faire, or nonintervention. In the late 19th and early 20th centuries its ideas were modified by the acceptance of universal suffrage and a certain amount of state intervention in economic affairs, in order to ensure a minimum standard of living and to remove extremes of poverty and wealth. The classical statement of liberal principles is found in *On Liberty* and other works of the British philosopher J S Mill.

Liberal Party British political party, the successor to the ◊Whig Party, with an ideology of liberalism. In the 19th century, it represented the interests of commerce and industry. Its outstanding leaders were Palmerston, Gladstone, and Lloyd George. From 1914 it declined, and the rise of the Labour Party pushed the Liberals into the middle ground. The Liberals joined forces with the Social Democratic Party (SDP) as the Alliance for the 1983 and 1987 elections. In 1988, a majority of the SDP voted to merge with the Liberals to form the Social and Liberal Democrats (later theLiberal Democrats).

Liberal Party, Australian political party established 1944 by Robert Menzies after a Labor landslide, derived from the former United Australia Party. After voters rejected Labor'.s large nationalization plans, the Liberals were in power 1949-72, 1975-83, and from 1996 (in coalition with the National Party). It was led by Harold Holt, John Gorton, William McMahon, Billy Snedden, Malcolm Fraser, John Hewson, Alexander Downer, and John Howard.

Liberation Army of Palestine loosely organized Palestinian group active in attacks on Israeli armed troops; see ◊Intifada.

Liberator, the title given to Simón ◊Bolívar, South American revolutionary leader; also a title given to Daniel ◊O'Connell, Irish political leader; and to Bernardo ◊O'Higgins, Chilean revolutionary.

Liberia country in W Africa, bounded N by Guinea, E by the Ivory Coast, S and SW by the Atlantic Ocean, and NW by Sierra Leone.

history The area now known as Liberia was bought by the American Colonization Society, a philanthropic organization active in the first half of the 19th century. The society's aim was to establish a settlement for liberated black slaves from the southern USA. The first settlers arrived 1822, and Liberia was declared an independent republic 1847. The new state suffered from financial difficulties, with bankruptcy 1909 bringing reorganization by US army officers. For almost 160 years the country's leaders were descended from the black American settlers, but the 1980 coup put Africans in power.

military coup William Tubman was president from 1944 until his death 1971 and was succeeded by Vice President William R Tolbert (1913–1980), who was re-elected 1975. In 1980 Tolbert was assassinated in a coup led by Master Sgt Samuel Doe (1952–1990), who suspended the constitution, banned all political parties, and ruled through the People's Redemption Council (PRC). He proceeded to stamp out corruption in the public service, encountering considerable opposition and making enemies who were later to threaten his position.

new constitution A new constitution was approved by the PRC 1983 and by national referendum 1984. Political parties were again permitted, provided they registered with the Special Electoral Commission. In 1984 Doe founded the National Democratic Party of Liberia (NDPL) and announced his intention to stand for the presidency. By 1985 there were 11 political parties, but they complained about the difficulties of the registration process, and only three registered in time for the elections. Doe's party won clear majorities in both chambers, despite alleged election fraud, and he was pronounced president with 51% of the vote. In 1985 there was an unsuccessful attempt to unseat him. Doe alleged complicity by neighbouring Sierra Leone and dealt harshly with the coup leaders.

end of Doe regime A gradual movement towards a pluralist political system, with a number of parties registering in opposition to the ruling NDPL, and growing economic problems threatened the stability of the Doe regime. In July 1990 rebel forces under Charles Taylor and a breakaway faction led by Prince Johnson laid siege to Doe in the presidential palace. Doe refused an offer of assistance by the USA to leave the country. In Sept Doe was captured and killed by rebel forces. In Nov Amos Sawyer became the head of an interim government and in 1991 he was re-elected president. In 1990 a United Nations stabilizing force had been sent to Liberia in an effort to establish peace.

Taylor agreed to work with Sawyer in moves towards peace, and a peace agreement reached Oct 1991, although initially rejected by Raleigh Seekie, leader of the guerrilla group United Liberation Movement of Liberia for Democracy (ULIMO), was finally upheld. However, heavy fighting continued in many areas. In Oct

1992, as fighting increased, Taylor's rebel forces laid siege to Monrovia.

liberty in its medieval sense, a franchise, or collection of privileges, granted to an individual or community by the king, and the area over which this franchise extended.

liberty, equality, fraternity (*liberté, egalité, fraternité*) motto of the French republic from 1793. It was changed 1940–44 under the Vichy government to 'work, family, fatherland'.

Libya country in N Africa, bounded N by the Mediterranean Sea, E by Egypt, SE by Sudan, S by Chad and Niger, and W by Algeria and Tunisia.

history The area now known as Libya was inhabited by N African nomads until it came successively under the domination of Phoenicia, Greece, Rome, the Vandals, Byzantium, and Islam, and from the 16th century was part of the Turkish ◊Ottoman Empire. In 1911 it was conquered by Italy, becoming known as Libya from 1934.

After being the scene of much fighting during World War II, in 1942 it was divided into three provinces: Fezzan, which was placed under French control; Cyrenaica; and Tripolitania, which was placed under British control. In 1951 it achieved independence as the United Kingdom of Libya, Muhammad Idris-as-Sanusi becoming King Idris.

revolution The country enjoyed internal and external stability until a bloodless revolution 1969, led by young nationalist officers, deposed the king and proclaimed a Libyan Arab Republic. Power was vested in a Revolution Command Council (RCC), chaired by Col Moamer al-Khaddhafi, with the Arab Socialist Union (ASU) as the only political party. Khaddhafi soon began proposing schemes for Arab unity, none of which was permanently adopted. In 1972 he planned a federation of Libya, Syria, and Egypt and later that year a merger between Libya and Egypt. In 1980 he proposed a union with Syria and in 1981 with Chad.

Islamic socialism Khaddhafi tried to run the country on socialist Islamic lines, with people's committees pledged to socialism and the teachings of the Koran. The 1977 constitution made him secretary general of the general secretariat of the General People's Congress (GPC), but in 1979 he resigned the post in order to devote more time to 'preserving the revolution'. His attempts to establish himself as a leader of the Arab world have brought him into conflict with Western powers, particularly the USA. The Reagan administration objected to Libya's presence in Chad and its attempts to unseat the

French-US-sponsored government of President Habré. The USA has linked Khaddhafi to worldwide terrorist activities, despite his denials of complicity, and the killing of a US soldier in a bomb attack in Berlin 1986 by an unidentified guerrilla group prompted a raid by US aircraft, some of them British-based, on Tripoli and Benghazi. Libyan terrorists were also blamed for the bombing of Pan American World Airways Flight 103 over Lockerbie, Scotland, in 1988, killing 270 people and for the 1989 bombing of UTA (Union de Transports Aerians) Flight 772 over Niger.

In Jan 1989 Khaddhafi did not respond to the shooting-down of two of his fighters over the Mediterranean off Libya by the US Navy and has worked at improving external relations, particularly in the Arab world, effecting a reconciliation with Egypt Oct 1989.

International sanctions were imposed against Libya in April 1992 after the country had repeatedly refused to extradite six suspects linked to the Lockerbie and UTA bombings. Foreign air links were severed and Libyan diplomatic staff in several countries were expelled and further sanctions were threatened, including the embargo of the country's oil, if Khaddhafi failed to surrender the suspects for trial outside Libya.

Lidice Czechoslovak mining village destroyed by the Nazis on 10 June 1942 as a reprisal for the assassination of Reinhard ◊Heydrich. The men were shot, the women sent to concentration camps, and the children taken to Germany. The officer responsible was hanged in 1946.

Lie Trygve (Halvdan) 1896–1968. Norwegian Labour politician and diplomat. He became secretary of the Labour Party in 1926. During the German occupation of Norway in World War II he was foreign minister in the exiled government 1941–46, when he helped retain the Norwegian fleet for the Allies. He became the first secretary general of the United Nations 1946–53, but resigned over Soviet opposition to his handling of the Korean War.

Liebknecht Karl 1871–1919. German socialist, son of Wilhelm Liebknecht. A founder of the German Communist Party, originally known as the Spartacus League (see ◊Spartacist) 1918, he was one of the few socialists who refused to support World War I. He led an unsuccessful revolt with Rosa Luxemburg in Berlin in 1919 and both were murdered by army officers.

Liebknecht Wilhelm 1826–1900. German socialist. A friend of the communist theoretician Karl Marx, with whom he took part in the ◊revolutions of 1848, he was imprisoned for opposition to the Franco-Prussian War 1870–71. He was one of the founders of the Social Democratic Party 1875. He was the father of Karl Liebknecht.

Liechtenstein landlocked country in W central Europe, bounded E by Austria and W by Switzerland.

history Liechtenstein's history as a sovereign state began 1342; its boundaries have been unchanged since 1434, and it has been known by its present name since 1719. Because of its small population (fewer than 30,000) it has found it convenient to associate itself with larger nations in international matters. For example, since 1923 it formed a customs union with Switzerland, which also 1919–90 represented it abroad. Before this Austria undertook its diplomatic representation.

Liechtenstein is one of the world's richest countries, with an income per head of population greater than that of the USA. Prince Franz Joseph II came to power 1938, and although he retained the title, he passed the duties of prince to his heir, Hans Adam, 1984. Franz Joseph II died Oct 1989.

Liechtenstein was admitted to the United Nations (UN) in Sept 1990. In May 1991, it became the seventh member of the European Free Trade Association.

liege in the feudal system, the allegiance owed by a vassal to his or her lord (the liege lord).

Light Brigade, Charge of the see ◊Charge of the Light Brigade.

Li Hongzhang or *Li Hung-chang* 1823–1901. Chinese politician, promulgator of Western ideas and modernization. He was governor general of Zhili (or Chihli) and high commissioner of the Northern Ports 1870–95, responsible for foreign affairs. He established a modern navy, the Beiyang fleet, 1888, which was humiliatingly destroyed in the ◊Sino-Japanese War.

Li became aware of the need to 'learn from the West' from his association with British general Charles Gordon during the ◊Taiping rebellion 1850–64, which his regional Anhui army helped to suppress. He also negotiated the Boxer protocol with Western powers 1900.

Likud alliance of right-wing Israeli political parties that defeated the Labour Party coalition in the May 1977 election and brought Menachem Begin to power. In 1987 Likud became part of an uneasy national coalition with Labour, formed to solve Israel's economic crisis. In 1989 another coalition was formed under Shamir.

Lilburne John 1614–1657. English republican agitator. He was imprisoned 1638–40 for circulating Puritan pamphlets, fought in the Parliamentary army in the Civil War, and by his advocacy of a democratic republic won the leadership of the Levellers, the democratic party in the English Revolution.

Lima Declaration agreement sponsored by US President F D Roosevelt at the Pan-American Conference Dec 1938 which held that a threat to the peace, security, or territory of any of the American republics would be a source of concern to all the republics. It was designed primarily to safeguard the American continent from the spread of fascism from Europe and provide the USA and other states with a general mandate for intervention if necessary.

Liman von Sanders Otto 1855–1929. German general assigned to the Turkish army to become inspector-general and a Turkish field marshal in Dec 1913. This link between the Turks and the Germans caused great suspicion on the part of the French and Russians.

limes ((Latin 'path' or 'boundary')) Roman border defence, with military road, ditch, fence or wall, and watchtowers, supported by forts. Such defences marked the empire's boundaries in Africa, Germany, and Syria.

In Britain, an earlier *limes* was succeeded by ◊Hadrian's Wall. In southern Germany excavations have revealed a wall over 480 km/300 mi long which passed through Aalen, Bavaria, to link the Rhine and Danube frontiers.

Lin Biao or *Lin Piao* 1907–1971. Chinese politician and general. He joined the communists in 1927, became a commander of ◊Mao Zedong's Red Army, and led the Northeast People's Liberation Army in the civil war after 1945. He became defence minister in 1959, and as vice chair of the party in 1969 he was expected to be Mao's successor. But in 1972 the government announced that Lin had been killed in an aeroplane crash in Mongolia on 17 Sept 1971 while fleeing to the USSR following an abortive coup attempt.

No man is good enough to govern another man without that other's consent.

Abraham Lincoln speech 1854

Lincoln Abraham 1809–1865. 16th president of the USA 1861–65, a Republican. In the American ◊Civil War, his chief concern was the preservation of the Union from which the Confederate (Southern) slave states had seceded on his election. In 1863 he announced the freedom of the slaves with the Emancipation Proclamation. He was re-elected in 1864 with victory for the North in sight, but was assassinated at the end of the war.

Lincoln was born in a log cabin in Kentucky. Self-educated, he practised law from 1837 in Springfield, Illinois. He was a member of the state legislature 1832–42. He joined the new Republican Party in 1856, and was elected president in 1860 on a minority vote. His refusal to concede to Confederate demands for the evacuation of the federal garrison at Fort Sumter, Charleston, South Carolina, precipitated the first hostilities of the Civil War.

Linlithgow John Adrian Louis Hope, 1st Marquess Linlithgow 1860–1908. British administrator, son of the 6th earl of Hopetoun, first governor general of Australia 1900–02.

Lin Piao alternative transliteration of ◊Lin Biao.

Lithuania country in N Europe, bounded N by Latvia, E by Belarus, S by Poland and the Kaliningrad area of Russia, and W by the Baltic Sea.

history Lithuania became a single nation at the end of the 12th century. The ◊Teutonic Knights (German crusaders) who attempted to invade in the 13th century were successfully driven back, and Lithuania extended its boundaries in the 14th century to reach almost as far as Moscow and the Black Sea. In 1386 Lithuania was joined with Poland in a mutually beneficial confederation. The two eventually became a single state 1569, and came under the control of the Russian tsar 1795. Revolts 1831 and 1863 failed to win independence for the state, and a more organized movement for the independence of Lithuania emerged in the 1880s. When self-government was demanded 1905, this was refused by the Russians.

struggle for independence During World War I Lithuania was occupied by German troops. After the war, it declared independence but the USSR claimed Lithuania as a Soviet republic 1918. Soviet forces were overthrown by the Germans, Poles, and nationalist Lithuanians 1919, and a democratic republic was established. This was in turn overthrown by a coup 1926 and the new president, Antanas Smetona, assumed increasing authority. In 1939 Germany took control of part of Lithuania, handing it to the USSR later the same year. In 1940 Lithuania was incorporated as a constituent republic of the USSR, designated the Lithuanian Soviet Socialist Republic. In 1941, when German troops had invaded the USSR, Lithuania revolted against Soviet rule and established its own government. The Germans occupied Lithuania 1941–44, after which Soviet rule was restored.

As in the other Baltic republics, there was strong nationalist dissent from 1980, influenced by the Polish example and prompted by the influx of Russian workers and officials. A popular front, the Sajudis (Lithuanian Restructuring Movement), was formed Oct 1988 to campaign for increased autonomy, and in the same month the republic's supreme soviet (state assembly), to the chagrin of Russian immigrants, decreed Lithuanian the state language and readopted the flag of the independent interwar republic. In Dec 1989 the republic's Communist Party split into two, with the majority wing formally breaking away from the Communist Party of the USSR and establishing itself as a social-democratic, Lithuanian-nationalist body. A multiparty system is in place in the republic, Sadjudis-backed pro-separatist candidates having secured a majority in the Feb–March 1990 elections. In March 1990 Lithuania unilaterally declared independence. The USSR responded by imposing an economic blockade, which was lifted July 1990 after the supreme council agreed to suspend the independence declaration.

Criticized by militant nationalists as being too conciliatory towards Moscow, Prime Minister Kazimiera Prunskiene resigned Jan 1991 and went into exile. She was replaced by Albertas Shiminas. Also in Jan, Soviet paratroopers seized political and communications buildings in Vilnius, killing 13 civilians, but began to withdraw the same month. In July four Lithuanian police and two customs officers were killed at a border post with Byelorussia (now Belarus). The OMON black-beret troops of the Soviet Interior Ministry and KGB were suspected.

independence achieved After the failure of the Aug 1991 anti-Gorbachev coup in the USSR, Lithuania's declaration of independence was recognized by the Soviet government and Western nations Sept 1991 and the new state was granted membership of the United Nations (UN) and admitted into the Conference on Security and Cooperation in Europe (CSCE). At the same time, the Communist Party was outlawed, and Gediminas Vagnorius took over as prime minister. In Feb 1992 President Landsbergis demanded the withdrawal of Russian troops from the Baltic enclave of Kaliningrad, formerly Königsberg. The Lithuanian Supreme Council (parliament) chose Aleksandras Abisala as the new prime minister when Vagnorious received a vote of no confidence in July. In Nov elections the Democratic Labour Party, headed by Algirdas Brazauskas, won the majority vote.

Little Bighorn site in Montana, USA, of General George ◊Custer's defeat by the ◊Sioux Indians 25 June 1876 under their chiefs Crazy Horse and Sitting Bull, known as *Custer's last stand*.

Little Entente series of alliances between Czechoslovakia, Romania, and Yugoslavia 1920–21 for mutual security and the maintenance of existing frontiers. Reinforced by the Treaty of Belgrade 1929, the entente collapsed upon Yugoslav cooperation with Germany 1935–38 and the Anglo-French abandonment of Czechoslovakia in 1938.

Little Red Book book of aphorisms and quotations from the speeches and writings by ◊Mao Zedong, in which he adapted Marxist theory to Chinese conditions. Published 1966, the book was printed in huge numbers and read widely at the start of the ◊Cultural Revolution.

Litvinov Maxim 1876–1951. Soviet politician, commissioner for foreign affairs under Stalin from Jan 1931 until his removal from office in May 1939.

Peace is indivisible.

Maxim Litvinov
speech to League of Nations July 1936

Liu Shaoqi or *Liu Shao-chi* 1898–1969. Chinese communist politician, in effective control of government 1960–65. A Moscow-trained labour organizer, he was a firm proponent of the Soviet style of government based around disciplined one-party control, the use of incentive gradings, and priority for industry over agriculture. This was opposed by ◊Mao Zedong, but began to be implemented by Liu while he was state president 1960–65. Liu was brought down during the ◊Cultural Revolution. He was expelled from the CCP in April 1969 and banished to Kaifeng in Henan province, where he died in Nov 1969 after being locked in a disused bank vault. He was rehabilitated posthumously ten years later.

Liverpool Robert Banks Jenkinson, 2nd Earl Liverpool 1770–1825. British Tory politician. He entered Parliament 1790 and was foreign secretary 1801–03, home secretary 1804–06 and 1807–09, war minister 1809–12, and prime minister 1812–27. His government conducted the Napoleonic Wars to a successful conclusion, but its ruthless suppression of freedom of speech and of the press aroused such opposition that during 1815–20 revolution frequently seemed imminent.

Livia Drusilla 58 BC–AD 29. Roman empress, wife of ◊Augustus from 39 BC, she was the mother by her first husband of ◊Tiberius and engaged in intrigue to secure his succession to the imperial crown. She remained politically active to the end of her life.

Livingstone David 1813–1873. Scottish missionary explorer. In 1841 he went to Africa, reached Lake Ngami 1849, followed the Zambezi to its mouth, saw the Victoria Falls 1855, and went to East and Central Africa 1858–64, reaching Lakes Shirwa and Malawi. From 1866, he tried to find the source of the river Nile, and reached Ujiji in Tanganyika in Oct 1871. British explorer Henry Stanley joined Livingstone in Ujiji.

Men are immortal until their work is done.

> **David Livingstone** letter describing the death of Bishop Mackenzie, March 1862

Livonia former region in Europe on the E coast of the Baltic Sea comprising most of present-day Latvia and Estonia. Conquered and converted to Christianity in the early 13th century by the Livonian Knights, a crusading order, Livonia was independent until 1583, when it was divided between Poland and Sweden. In 1710 it was occupied by Russia, and in 1721 was ceded to Peter the Great, Tsar of Russia.

Llewelyn I 1173–1240. King of Wales from 1194 who extended his rule to all Wales not in Norman hands, driving the English from N Wales 1212, and taking Shrewsbury 1215. During the early part of Henry III's reign, he was several times attacked by English armies. He was married to Joanna, illegitimate daughter of King John.

Llewelyn II ap Gruffydd *c.* 1225–1282. King of Wales from 1246, grandson of Llewelyn I. In 1277 Edward I of England compelled Llewelyn to acknowledge him as overlord and to surrender S Wales. His death while leading a national uprising ended Welsh independence.

The finest eloquence is that which gets things done; the worst is that which delays them.

> **David Lloyd George** speech at Paris Peace Conference Jan 1919

Lloyd George David 1863–1945. Welsh Liberal politician, prime minister of Britain 1916–22. A pioneer of social reform, as chancellor of the Exchequer 1908–15 he introduced old-age pensions 1908 and health and unemployment insurance 1911. High unemployment, intervention in the Russian Civil War, and use of the military police force, the ◊Black and Tans, in Ireland eroded his support as prime minister, and the creation of the Irish Free State in 1921 and his pro-Greek policy against the Turks caused the collapse of his coalition government.

Lloyd George was born in Manchester, became a solicitor, and was member of Parliament for Caernarvon Boroughs from 1890. During the Boer War, he was prominent as a pro-Boer. His 1909 budget (with graduated direct taxes and taxing land values) provoked the Lords to reject it, and resulted in the Act of 1911 limiting their powers. He held ministerial posts during World War I until 1916 when there was an open breach between him and Prime Minister ◊Asquith, and he became prime minister of a coalition government. Securing a unified Allied command, he enabled the Allies to withstand the last German offensive and achieve victory. After World War I he had a major role in the Versailles peace treaty.

In the 1918 elections, he achieved a huge majority over Labour and Asquith's followers. He had become largely distrusted within his own party by 1922, and never regained power.

Lobengula 1836–1894. King of Matabeleland (now part of Zimbabwe) 1870–93. He was overthrown in 1870–83. He was overthrown in 1893 by a military expedition organized by Cecil ◊Rhodes' South African Company.

Locarno, Pact of series of diplomatic documents initialled in Locarno, Switzerland, 16 Oct 1925 and formally signed in London 1 Dec 1925. The pact settled the question of French security, and the signatories – Britain, France, Belgium, Italy, and Germany – guaranteed Germany's existing frontiers with France and Belgium. Following the signing of the pact, Germany was admitted to the League of Nations.

Lodge Henry Cabot 1850–1924. US politician, Republican senator from 1893, and chair of the Senate Foreign Relations Committee after World War I. He influenced the USA to stay out of the ◊League of Nations 1920 as a threat to US sovereignty.

Lollard follower of the English religious reformer John ◊Wycliffe in the 14th century. The Lollards condemned the doctrine of the transubstantiation of the bread and wine of the

Eucharist, advocated the diversion of ecclesiastical property to charitable uses, and denounced war and capital punishment. They were active from about 1377; after the passing of the statute *De heretico comburendo* ('The Necessity of Burning Heretics') 1401 many Lollards were burned, and in 1414 they raised an unsuccessful revolt in London, known as Oldcastle's rebellion.

Lombard or *Langobard* member of a Germanic people who invaded Italy in 568 and occupied Lombardy (named after them) and central Italy. Their capital was Monza. They were conquered by the Frankish ruler Charlemagne in 774.

Lombard league association of N Italian towns and cities (not all of which were in Lombardy) established 1164 to maintain their independence against the Holy Roman emperors' claims of sovereignty. Venice, Padua, Brescia, Milan, and Mantua were among the founders.

Supported by Milan and Pope Alexander III (1105–1181), the league defeated Frederick I Barbarossa at Legnano in N Italy 1179 and effectively resisted Otto IV (1175–1218) and Frederick II, becoming the most powerful champion of the ◊Guelph cause. Internal rivalries led to its dissolution 1250.

Lomé Convention convention in 1975 that established economic cooperation between the European Community and African, Caribbean, and Pacific countries. It was renewed 1979 and 1985.

London, Treaty of secret treaty signed 26 April 1915 between Britain, France, Russia, and Italy. It promised Italy territorial gains (at the expense of Austria-Hungary) on condition that it entered World War I on the side of the Triple Entente (Britain, France, and Russia). Italy's intervention did not achieve the rapid victories expected, and the terms of the treaty (revealed by Russia 1918), angered the USA. Britain and France refused to honour the treaty and, in the post-war peace treaties, Italy received far less territory than promised.

London Working Men's Association (LWMA) campaigning organization for political reform, founded June 1836 by William Lovett and others, who in 1837 drew up the first version of the People's Charter (see ◊Chartism). It was founded in the belief that popular education, achieved through discussion and access to a cheap and honest press, was a means of obtaining political reform. By 1837 the LWMA had 100 members.

Long Huey 1893–1935. US Democratic politician, nicknamed 'the Kingfish', governor of Louisiana 1928–31, US senator for Louisiana 1930–35, legendary for his political rhetoric. He was popular with poor white voters for his programme of social and economic reform, which he called the 'Share Our Wealth' programme. It represented a significant challenge to F D Roosevelt's ◊New Deal economic programme.

Long March in Chinese history, the 10,000 km/6,000 mi trek undertaken 1934–35 by ◊Mao Zedong and his communist forces from SE to NW China, under harassment from the Guomindang (nationalist) army.

Some 100,000 communists left Mao's first headquarters in Jiangxi province in Oct 1934, and only 8,000 lasted the journey to arrive about a year later in Shanxi, which became their new base. The march cemented Mao Zedong's control of the movement.

Long Parliament English Parliament 1640–53 and 1659–60, which continued through the Civil War. After the Royalists withdrew in 1642 and the Presbyterian right was excluded in 1648, the remaining ◊Rump ruled England until expelled by Oliver Cromwell in 1653. Reassembled 1659–60, the Long Parliament initiated the negotiations for the restoration of the monarchy.

López Carlos Antonio 1790–1862. Paraguayan dictator (in succession to his uncle José Francia) from 1840. He achieved some economic improvement, and he was succeeded by his son Francisco López.

López Francisco Solano 1827–1870. Paraguayan dictator in succession to his father Carlos López. He involved the country in a war with Brazil, Uruguay, and Argentina, during which approximately 80% of the population died.

Lord Haw Haw nickname of William ◊Joyce who made propaganda broadcasts during World War II.

Lords, House of upper house of the UK ◊Parliament.

Lorraine, Cross of heraldic cross with double crossbars, emblem of the medieval French nationalist Joan of Arc. It was adopted by the ◊Free French forces in World War II.

Lothair 825–869. King of Lotharingia from 855, when he inherited the region from his father, the Holy Roman emperor Lothair I.

Lothair two Holy Roman emperors:

Lothair I 795–855. Holy Roman emperor from 817 in association with his father Louis I. On Louis's death in 840, the empire was divided between Lothair and his brothers; Lothair took N Italy and the valleys of the rivers Rhône and Rhine.

Lothair II *c.* 1070–1137. Holy Roman emperor from 1133 and German king from 1125. His election as emperor, opposed by the ◊Hohenstaufen family of princes, was the start of the feud between the ◊Guelph and Ghibelline factions, who supported the papal party and the Hohenstaufens' claim to the imperial throne respectively.

Lotharingia medieval region W of the Rhine, between the Jura mountains and the North Sea; the northern portion of the lands assigned to Lothair I when the Carolingian empire was divided. It was called after his son King Lothair, and later corrupted to Lorraine; it is now part of Alsace-Lorraine, France.

Louis eighteen kings of France:

Louis I *the Pious* 778–840. Holy Roman emperor from 814, when he succeeded his father Charlemagne.

Louis II *the Stammerer* 846–879. King of France from 877, son of Charles II, the Bald. He was dominated by the clergy and nobility, who exacted many concessions from him.

Louis III 863–882. King of N France from 879, while his brother Carloman (866–884) ruled S France. He was the son of Louis II. Louis countered a revolt of the nobility at the beginning of his reign, and his resistance to the Normans made him a hero of epic poems.

Louis IV (d'Outremer) 921–954. King of France from 936. His reign was marked by the rebellion of nobles who refused to recognize his authority. As a result of his liberality they were able to build powerful feudal lordships.

He was raised in England after his father Charles III, the Simple, had been overthrown in 922 by Robert I. After the death of Raoul, Robert's brother-in-law and successor, Louis was chosen by the nobles to be king. He had difficulties with his vassal Hugh the Great, and skirmishes with the Hungarians, who had invaded S France.

Louis V 966–987. King of France from 986, last of the ◊Carolingian dynasty (descendants of Charlemagne).

Louis VI *the Fat* 1081–1137. King of France from 1108. He led his army against feudal brigands, the English (under Henry I), and the Holy Roman Empire, temporarily consolidating his realm and extending it into Flanders. He was a benefactor to the church, and his advisers included Abbot ◊Suger.

Louis VII *c.* 1120–1180. King of France from 1137, who led the Second ◊Crusade.

Louis VIII 1187–1226. King of France from 1223, who was invited to become king of England in place of ◊John by the English barons, and unsuccessfully invaded England 1215–17.

Louis IX St 1214–1270. King of France from 1226, leader of the Seventh and Eighth ◊Crusades. He was defeated in the former by the Muslims, spending four years in captivity. He died in Tunis. He was canonized in 1297.

Louis X *the Stubborn* 1289–1316. King of France who succeeded his father Philip IV in 1314. His reign saw widespread discontent among the nobles, which he countered by granting charters guaranteeing seignorial rights, although some historians claim that by using evasive tactics, he gave up nothing.

Louis XI 1423–1483. King of France from 1461. He broke the power of the nobility (headed by ◊Charles the Bold) by intrigue and military power.

Louis XII 1462–1515. King of France from 1499. He was duke of Orléans until he succeeded his cousin Charles VIII to the throne. His reign was devoted to Italian wars.

Louis XIII 1601–1643. King of France from 1610 (in succession to his father Henry IV), he assumed royal power in 1617. He was under the political control of Cardinal ◊Richelieu 1624–42.

Louis XIV *the Sun King* 1638–1715. King of France from 1643, when he succeeded his father Louis XIII; his mother was Anne of Austria. Until 1661 France was ruled by the chief minister, Jules Mazarin, but later Louis took absolute power, summed up in his saying *L'Etat c'est moi* ('I am the state'). Throughout his reign he was engaged in unsuccessful expansionist wars – 1667–68, 1672–78, 1688–97, and 1701–13 (the War of the ◊Spanish Succession) – against various European alliances, always including Britain and the Netherlands. He was a patron of the arts.

The greatest of his ministers was Jean-Baptiste Colbert, whose work was undone by the king's military adventures. Louis attempted 1667–68 to annex the Spanish Netherlands, but was frustrated by an alliance of the Netherlands, Britain, and Sweden. Having detached Britain from the alliance, he invaded the Netherlands in 1672, but the Dutch stood firm (led by William of Orange; see ◊William III of England) and despite the European alliance formed against France, achieved territorial gains at the Peace of Nijmegen 1678.

When war was renewed 1688–97 between Louis and the Grand Alliance (including Britain), formed by William of Orange, the

French were everywhere victorious on land, but the French fleet was almost destroyed at the Battle of La Hogue 1692. The acceptance by Louis of the Spanish throne in 1700 (for his grandson) precipitated the War of the Spanish Succession, and the Treaty of Utrecht 1713 ended French supremacy in Europe.

In 1660 Louis married the Infanta Maria Theresa of Spain, but he was greatly influenced by his mistresses, including Louise de La Vallière, Madame de Montespan, and Madame de Maintenon.

Louis XV 1710–1774. King of France from 1715, with the Duke of Orléans as regent until 1723. He was the great-grandson of Louis XIV. Indolent and frivolous, Louis left government in the hands of his ministers, the Duke of Bourbon and Cardinal Fleury (1653–1743). On the latter's death he attempted to rule alone but became entirely dominated by his mistresses, Madame de Pompadour and Madame Du Barry. His foreign policy led to French possessions in Canada and India being lost to England.

Louis XVI 1754–1793. King of France from 1774, grandson of Louis XV, and son of Louis the Dauphin. He was dominated by his queen, ◊Marie Antoinette, and French finances fell into such confusion that in 1789 the ◊States General (parliament) had to be summoned, and the ◊French Revolution began. Louis lost his personal popularity in June 1791 when he attempted to flee the country, and in Aug 1792 the Parisians stormed the Tuileries palace and took the royal family prisoner. Deposed in Sept 1792, Louis was tried in Dec, sentenced for treason in Jan 1793, and guillotined.

Louis XVII 1785–1795. Nominal king of France, the son of Louis XVI. During the French Revolution he was imprisoned with his parents in 1792 and probably died in prison.

Punctuality is the politeness of kings.

Louis XVIII quoted in J Laffitte, *Souvenirs* 1844

Louis XVIII 1755–1824. King of France 1814–24, the younger brother of Louis XVI. He assumed the title of king in 1795, having fled into exile in 1791 during the French Revolution, but became king only on the fall of Napoleon I in April 1814. Expelled during Napoleon's brief return (the ◊Hundred Days) in 1815, he resumed power after Napoleon's final defeat at Waterloo, pursuing a policy of calculated liberalism until ultra-royalist pressure became dominant after 1820.

Louisiana Purchase purchase by the USA from France 1803 of an area covering about 2,144,000 sq km/828,000 sq mi, including the present-day states of Louisiana, Missouri, Arkansas, Iowa, Nebraska, North Dakota, South Dakota, and Oklahoma.

The purchase, which doubled the size of the USA, marked the end of Napoleon's plans for a colonial empire and ensured free navigation on the Mississippi River for the USA.

Louis–Napoleon name by which ◊Napoleon III (1808–1873) was known.

Louis Philippe 1773–1850. King of France 1830–48. Son of Louis Philippe Joseph, Duke of Orléans 1747–93; both were known as *Philippe Egalité* from their support of the 1792 Revolution. Louis Philippe fled into exile 1793–1814, but became king after the 1830 revolution with the backing of the rich bourgeoisie. Corruption discredited his regime, and after his overthrow, he escaped to the UK and died there.

Loyalist member of approximately 30% of the US population remaining loyal to Britain in the ◊American Revolution. Many Loyalists went to E Ontario, Canada after 1783.

The term also refers to people in Northern Ireland who wish to remain part of the United Kingdom rather than unifying with the Republic of Ireland.

Luang Prabang or *Louangphrabang* Buddhist religious centre in Laos, on the Mekong River at the head of river navigation. It was the capital of the kingdom of Luang Prabang, incorporated in Laos 1946, and the royal capital of Laos 1946–75.

Lucknow city in the state of Uttar Pradesh, India. During the Indian Mutiny against British rule, it was besieged 2 July–16 Nov 1857.

Lucullus Lucius Licinius 110–56 BC. Roman general and consul. As commander against ◊Mithridates of Pontus 74–66 he proved to be one of Rome's ablest generals and administrators, until superseded by Pompey. He then retired from politics.

Luddite one of a group of people involved in machine-wrecking riots in N England 1811–16. The organizer of the Luddites was referred to as General Ludd, but may not have existed. Many Luddites were hanged or transported to penal colonies, such as Australia.

The movement, which began in Nottinghamshire and spread to Lancashire, Cheshire, Derbyshire, Leicestershire, and Yorkshire, was primarily a revolt against the unemployment caused by the introduction of machines in the Industrial Revolution.

Ludendorff Erich von 1865–1937. German general, chief of staff to ◊Hindenburg in World War I, and responsible for the eastern-front victory at the Battle of ◊Tannenberg in 1914. After Hindenburg's appointment as chief of general staff and Ludendorff's as quartermaster-general in 1916, he was also politically influential. He took part in the Nazi rising in Munich in 1923 and sat in the Reichstag (parliament) as a right-wing Nationalist.

Ludwig three kings of Bavaria, including:

Ludwig I 1786–1868. King of Bavaria 1825–48, succeeding his father Maximilian Joseph I. He made Munich an international cultural centre, but his association with the dancer Lola Montez, who dictated his policies for a year, led to his abdication in 1848.

Ludwig II 1845–1886. King of Bavaria from 1864, when he succeeded his father Maximilian II. He supported Austria during the Austro-Prussian War 1866, but brought Bavaria into the Franco-Prussian War as Prussia's ally and in 1871 offered the German crown to the king of Prussia. He was the composer Richard Wagner's patron and built the Bayreuth theatre for him. Declared insane 1886, he drowned himself soon after.

Luftwaffe German air force. In World War I and, as reorganized by the Nazi leader Hermann Goering in 1933, in World War II. The Luftwaffe also covered anti-aircraft defence and the launching of the flying bombs ◊V1 and V2.

Lugard Frederick John Dealtry, 1st Baron Lugard 1858–1945. British colonial administrator. He served in the army 1878–89 and then worked for the British East Africa Company, for whom he took possession of Uganda in 1890. He was high commissioner for N Nigeria 1900–07, governor of Hong Kong 1907–12, and governor general of Nigeria 1914–19.

Lumumba Patrice 1926–1961. Congolese politician, prime minister of Zaire 1960. Imprisoned by the Belgians, but released in time to attend the conference giving the Congo independence in 1960, he led the National Congolese Movement to victory in the subsequent general election. He was deposed in a coup d'état, and murdered some months later.

Lusaka Agreement settlement between ◊Angola and South Africa.

Lusitania ancient area of the Iberian peninsula, roughly equivalent to Portugal. Conquered by Rome in 139 BC, the province of Lusitania rebelled periodically until it was finally conquered by Pompey 73–72 BC.

Lusitania ocean liner sunk by a German submarine on 7 May 1915 with the loss of 1,200 lives, including some US citizens; its destruction helped to bring the USA into World War I.

Luther Martin 1483–1546. German Christian church reformer, a founder of Protestantism. While he was a priest at the University of Wittenberg, he wrote an attack on the sale of indulgences (remissions of punishment for sin) in 95 theses which he nailed to a church door in 1517, in defiance of papal condemnation. The Holy Roman emperor Charles V summoned him to the Diet (meeting of dignitaries of the Holy Roman Empire) of Worms in Germany, in 1521, where he refused to retract his objections. Originally intending reform, his protest led to schism, with the emergence, following the Confession of ◊Augsburg 1530 (a statement of the Protestant faith), of a new Protestant church. Luther is regarded as the instigator of the Protestant revolution, and Lutheranism is now the major religion of many N European countries, including Germany, Sweden, and Denmark.

My conscience is taken captive by God's word, I cannot and will not recant anything. ... Here I stand. I can do no other. God help me. Amen.

Martin Luther at the Diet of Worms 1521

Lutheranism form of Protestant Christianity derived from the life and teaching of Martin Luther; it is sometimes called Evangelical to distinguish it from the other main branch of European Protestantism, the Reformed. The most generally accepted statement of Lutheranism is that of the **Confession of Augsburg** 1530 but Luther's Shorter Catechism also carries great weight. It is the largest Protestant body, including some 80 million persons, of whom 40 million are in Germany, 19 million in Scandinavia, 8.5 million in the USA and Canada, with most of the remainder in central Europe.

The laws of the land [South Africa] virtually criticize God for having created men of colour.

Albert Luthuli
Nobel acceptance speech 1961

Luthuli or *Lutuli* Albert 1899–1967. South African politician, president of the African National Congress 1952–67. Luthuli, a Zulu tribal chief, preached nonviolence and multi-racialism.

Arrested in 1956, he was never actually tried for treason, although he suffered certain restrictions from 1959. He was under suspended sentence for burning his pass (an identity document required of non-white South Africans) when awarded the 1960 Nobel Peace Prize.

Lützen town in Halle county, Germany, SW of Leipzig, where in 1632 Gustavus Adolphus, king of Sweden, defeated the German commander Wallenstein in the Thirty Years' War; Gustavus was killed in the battle. The French emperor Napoleon Bonaparte overcame the Russians and Prussians here in 1813.

Luxembourg landlocked country in W Europe, bounded N and W by Belgium, E by Germany, and S by France.

history Formerly part of the Holy Roman Empire, Luxembourg became a duchy 1354. From 1482 it was under ◊Habsburg control, and in 1797 was ceded, with Belgium, to France. The 1815 ◊Treaty of Vienna made Luxembourg a grand duchy, ruled by the king of the Netherlands. In 1830 Belgium and Luxembourg revolted against Dutch rule; Belgium achieved independence 1839 and most of Luxembourg became part of it, the rest becoming independent in its own right 1848.

role in Europe Although a small country, Luxembourg occupies an important position in W Europe, being a founding member of many international organizations, including the European Coal and Steel Community, the European Atomic Energy Commission, and the European Economic Community. It formed an economic union with Belgium and the Netherlands 1948 (◊Benelux), which became fully effective 1960 and was the forerunner of wider European cooperation.

Grand Duchess Charlotte (1896–1985) abdicated 1964 after a reign of 45 years, and was succeeded by her son, Prince Jean. Proportional representation has resulted in a series of coalition governments. The Christian Social Party headed most of these from 1945 to 1974 when its dominance was challenged by the Socialists. It regained pre-eminence 1979.

In 1991 the European Community (EC) and the European Free Trade Association (EFTA) reached an agreement to establish a Western Europe free-trade area, which would take effect from 1993. The area includes Luxembourg as a member of the EC.

Luxembourg showed its support for the Maastricht Treaty on European union July 1992 when it voted in favour of ratification. However, it sought exemption from the treaty's clause requiring that residents from other EC nations

be allowed to vote in local elections. About one-third of the duchy's population are foreigners.

Luxembourg Accord French-initiated agreement in 1966 that a decision of the Council of Ministers of the European Community may be vetoed by a member whose national interests are at stake.

Luxemburg Rosa 1870–1919. Polish-born German communist. She helped found the Polish Social Democratic Party in the 1890s (which later became the Polish Communist Party). She was a leader of the left wing of the German Social Democratic Party from 1898 and collaborator with Karl Liebknecht in founding the communist Spartacus League 1918 (see ◊Spartacist). She was murdered with him by army officers during the Jan 1919 Berlin workers' revolt.

Freedom is always and exclusively freedom for the one who thinks differently.

Rosa Luxemburg
The Russian Revolution

Lydia ancient kingdom in Anatolia (7th–6th centuries BC), with its capital at Sardis. The Lydians were the first Western people to use standard coinage. Their last king, Croesus, was defeated by the Persians in 546 BC.

Lynch 'Jack' (John) 1917– . Irish politician, prime minister 1966–73 and 1977–79. A Gaelic footballer and a barrister, in 1948 he entered the parliament of the republic as a Fianna Fáil member.

Lyons Joseph Aloysius 1879–1939. Australian politician, founder of the United Australia Party 1931, prime minister 1931–39.

He was born in Tasmania and first elected to parliament in 1929. His wife *Enid Lyons* (1897–   ) was the first woman member of the House of Representatives and of the federal cabinet.

Lysander died 395 BC. Spartan general, politician and admiral. He brought the ◊Peloponnesian War between Athens and Sparta to a successful conclusion by capturing the Athenian fleet at Aegospotami 405 BC, and by starving Athens into surrender in the following year. He set up puppet governments in Athens and its former allies, and tried to secure for himself the Spartan kingship, but was killed in battle with the Thebans 395 BC.

Lytton Edward Robert Bulwer-Lytton, 1st Earl of Lytton 1831–1891. British diplomat, viceroy of India 1876–80, where he pursued a controversial 'forward' policy.

M

Maastricht Treaty treaty on European union which took effect 1 Nov 1993, from which date the European Community (EC) became known as the ◊European Union (EU). Issues covered by the treaty included the EU's decision-making process and the establishment of closer links on foreign and military policy. A European Charter of Social Rights (the 'Social Chapter') was approved by all member states except the UK, but the Labour government elected 1997 was committed to sign it.

The treaty was signed 10 Dec 1991 by leaders of EC nations in Maastricht, the Netherlands. Ratification by the parliaments of member states was preceded by a national referendum in France, Spain, Ireland, and twice in Denmark. Among the aims of the treaty were the strengthening and convergence of the economies of member states so as to establish an economic and monetary union, including a single and stable currency; common citizenship for nationals of member states; a common foreign and security policy, including the eventual framing of a common defence policy; free movement of persons, while ensuring their safety and security; and a closer union among the peoples of Europe in accordance with the principle of 'subsidiarity'. The British government demanded the removal of any reference to federalism.

Macao Portuguese possession on the south coast of China, about 65 km/40 mi W of Hong Kong, from which it is separated by the estuary of the Canton River; it consists of a peninsula and the islands of Taipa and Colôane.

history Macao was first established as a Portuguese trading and missionary post in the Far East 1537, and was leased from China 1557. It was annexed 1849 and recognized as a Portuguese colony by the Chinese government in a

treaty 1887. The port declined in prosperity during the late 19th and early 20th centuries, as its harbour silted up and international trade was diverted to Hong Kong and the new treaty ports. The colony thus concentrated instead on local 'country trade' and became a centre for gambling and, later, tourism.

In 1951 Macao became an overseas province of Portugal, sending an elected representative to the Lisbon parliament. After the Portuguese revolution 1974, it became a 'special territory' and was granted considerable autonomy under a governor appointed by the Portuguese president.

In 1986 negotiations opened between the Portuguese and the Chinese governments over the question of the return of Macao's sovereignty under 'one country, two systems' terms similar to those agreed by China and the UK for ◊Hong Kong. These negotiations were concluded April 1987 by the signing of the Macao Pact, under which Portugal agreed to hand over sovereignty to the People's Republic Dec 1999, and China agreed in return to guarantee to maintain the port's capitalist economic and social system for at least 50 years.

MacArthur Douglas 1880–1964. US general in World War II, commander of US forces in the Far East and, from March 1942, of the Allied forces in the SW Pacific. After the surrender of Japan he commanded the Allied occupation forces there. During 1950 he commanded the UN forces in Korea, but in April 1951, after expressing views contrary to US and UN policy, he was relieved of all his commands by President Truman.

It is fatal to enter any war without the will to win it.

Douglas MacArthur speech at
Republican National Convention 1952

Macbeth died 1057. King of Scotland from 1040. The son of Findlaech, hereditary ruler of Moray, he was commander of the forces of Duncan I, King of Scotia, whom he killed in battle 1040. His reign was prosperous until Duncan's son Malcolm III led an invasion and killed him at Lumphanan.

Maccabees Hebrew family, sometimes known as the *Hasmonaeans*. It was founded by the priest Mattathias (died 166 BC) who, with his sons, led the struggle for independence against the Syrians in the 2nd century BC. Judas (died 161) reconquered Jerusalem 164 BC, and Simon (died 135) established its independence

142 BC. The revolt of the Maccabees lasted until the capture of Jerusalem by the Romans 63 BC. The story is told in four books of the Apocrypha.

McCarthy Joe (Joseph Raymond) 1908–1957. US right-wing Republican politician. His unsubstantiated claim 1950 that the State Department and US army had been infiltrated by communists started a wave of anticommunist hysteria, wild accusations, and blacklists, which continued until he was discredited 1954. He was censured by the US senate for misconduct.

McClellan George Brinton 1826–1885. US Civil War general, commander in chief of the Union forces 1861–62. He was dismissed by President Lincoln when he delayed five weeks in following up his victory over the Confederate General Lee at Antietam (see under ◊Civil War, American). He was the unsuccessful Democrat presidential candidate against Lincoln 1864.

Macdonald Flora 1722–1790. Scottish heroine who rescued Prince Charles Edward Stuart, the Young Pretender, after his defeat at Culloden 1746. Disguising him as her maid, she escorted him from her home in the Hebrides to France. She was arrested, but released 1747.

Society goes on and on and on. It is the same with ideas.

Ramsay MacDonald speech 1935

MacDonald (James) Ramsay 1866–1937. British politician, first Labour prime minister Jan–Oct 1924 and 1929–31. Failing to deal with worsening economic conditions, he left the party to form a coalition government 1931, which was increasingly dominated by Conservatives, until he was replaced by Stanley Baldwin 1935.

MacDonald was born in Scotland, the son of a labourer. He was elected to Parliament 1906, and led the party until 1914, when his opposition to World War I lost him the leadership. This he recovered 1922, and in Jan 1924 he formed a government dependent on the support of the Liberal Party. When this was withdrawn in Oct the same year, he was forced to resign. He returned to office 1929, again as leader of a minority government, which collapsed 1931 as a result of the economic crisis. MacDonald left the Labour Party to form a national government with backing from both Liberal and Conservative parties. He resigned the premiership 1935.

Macdonald John Alexander 1815–1891. Canadian Conservative politician, prime minister 1867–73 and 1878–91. He was born in Glasgow but taken to Ontario as a child. In 1857 he became prime minister of Upper Canada. He took the leading part in the movement for federation, and in 1867 became the first prime minister of Canada. He was defeated 1873 but returned to office 1878 and retained it until his death.

Macedonia ancient region of Greece, forming parts of modern Greece, Bulgaria, and Yugoslavia. Macedonia gained control of Greece after Philip II's victory at Chaeronea 338 BC. His son, ◊Alexander the Great, conquered a vast empire. Macedonia became a Roman province 146 BC.

Macedonia (Greek *Makedhonia*) mountainous region of N Greece, part of the ancient country of Macedonia which was divided between Serbia, Bulgaria, and Greece after the Balkan Wars of 1912–13.

Macedonia landlocked country in SE Europe, bounded N by Serbia, W by Albania, S by Greece, and E by Bulgaria. The ancient region of Macedonia (of which the present-day republic comprises only a part) was originally settled by the Slavs in the 6th century; conquered by the Bulgars in the 7th century, by Byzantium 1014, by Serbia in the 14th century, and by the Ottoman Empire 1355; divided between Serbia, Bulgaria, and Greece after the Balkan Wars 1912-13. After World War I Serbian Macedonia (equivalent to the present-day republic) became part of the federal state of Yugoslavia and demands for greater autonomy were made. During World War II it was occupied by Bulgaria 1941-44 and in the postwar period, as part of Yugoslavia, tensions resurfaced between ethnic Macedonians and the Serb-dominated federal government. In 1992 independence was declared, and the state was admitted to the United Nations 1993.

Machel Samora 1933–1986. Mozambique nationalist leader, president 1975–86. Machel was active in the liberation front ◊Frelimo from its conception 1962, fighting for independence from Portugal. He became Frelimo leader 1966, and Mozambique's first president from independence 1975 until his death in a plane crash near the South African border.

machine politics organization of a local political party to ensure its own election by influencing the electorate, and then to retain power through control of key committees and offices. The idea of machine politics was epitomized in the USA in the late 19th century, where it was used to control individual cities, most notably Chicago and New York.

Mackenzie William Lyon 1795–1861. Canadian politician, born in Scotland. He emigrated to Canada 1820, and led the rebellion of 1837–38, an unsuccessful attempt to limit British rule and establish more democratic institutions in Canada. After its failure he lived in the USA until 1849, and in 1851–58 sat in the Canadian legislature as a Radical. He was grandfather of W L Mackenzie King, the Liberal prime minister.

McKinley William 1843–1901. 25th president of the USA 1897–1901, a Republican. His term as president was marked by the USA's adoption of an imperialist policy, as exemplified by the Spanish-American war 1898 and the annexation of the Philippines. He was first elected to congress 1876. He was assassinated.

McLean John 1785–1861. US jurist. In 1829 he was appointed to the US Supreme Court by President Jackson. During his Court tenure, McLean was an outspoken advocate of the abolition of slavery, writing a passionate dissent in the Dred Scott Case 1857.

MacMahon Marie Edmé Patrice Maurice, Comte de 1808–1893. Marshal of France. Captured at Sedan 1870 during the Franco-Prussian War, he suppressed the ◊Paris Commune after his release, and as president of the republic 1873–79 worked for a royalist restoration until forced to resign.

Jaw-jaw is better than war-war.

Harold Macmillan Jan 1958

Macmillan (Maurice) Harold, 1st Earl of Stockton 1894–1986. British Conservative politician, prime minister 1957–63; foreign secretary 1955 and chancellor of the Exchequer 1955–57. In 1963 he attempted to negotiate British entry into the European Economic Community, but was blocked by French president de Gaulle. Much of his career as prime minister was spent defending the retention of a UK nuclear weapon, and he was responsible for the purchase of US Polaris missiles 1962.

Macmillan was MP for Stockton 1924–29 and 1931–45, and for Bromley 1945–64. As minister of housing 1951–54 he achieved the construction of 300,000 new houses a year. He became prime minister on the resignation of Anthony ◊Eden after the Suez crisis, and led the Conservative Party to victory in the 1959 elections on the slogan 'You've never had it so good' (the phrase was borrowed from a US election campaign). Internationally, his realization of the 'wind of change' in Africa advanced the independence of former colonies. Macmillan's nickname Supermac was coined by the cartoonist Vicky.

Macquarie Lachlan 1762–1824. Scottish administrator in Australia. He succeeded Admiral ◊Bligh as governor of New South Wales 1809, raised the demoralized settlement to prosperity, and did much to rehabilitate ex-convicts. In 1821 he returned to Britain in poor health, exhausted by struggles with his opponents. Lachlan River and Macquarie River and Island are named after him.

MAD abbreviation for *mutual assured destruction*; the basis of the theory of ◊deterrence by possession of nuclear weapons.

Madagascar island country in the Indian Ocean, off the coast of E Africa, about 400 km/280 mi from Mozambique.

history Madagascar was colonized over 2,000 years ago by Africans and Indonesians. They were joined from the 12th century by Muslim traders, and, from 1500, Europeans began to visit the island. Portuguese, Dutch, and English traders having given up, the French established a colony in the mid-17th century but fled after a massacre by local inhabitants. Madagascar was subsequently divided into small kingdoms until the late 18th century when, aided by traders and Christian missionaries, the Merina (the inhabitants of the highland area) united almost all the country under one ruler.

In 1885 the country was made a French protectorate, though French control was not complete until 20 years later.

independence Madagascar remained loyal to Vichy France during World War II, but it was taken by British forces 1942–43 and then handed over to the Free French. During the postwar period nationalist movements became active, and Madagascar became an autonomous state within the French Community 1958 and achieved full independence, as a republic, 1960. Its history since independence has been greatly influenced by the competing interests of its two main ethnic groups, the coastal people, or *cotiers*, and the highland Merina.

The first president of the republic was Philibert Tsiranana, leader of the Social Democratic Party (PSD), which identified itself with the *cotiers*. In 1972 the army, representing the Merina, took control of the government and pursued a more nationalistic line than Tsiranana. This caused resentment among the *cotiers* and, with rising unemployment, led to a government crisis 1975 that resulted in the imposition of martial law under a national military directorate and the banning of all political parties. Later that year a new, socialist constitution was approved and Lt-Comdr Didier Ratsiraka, a *cotier*, was elected president of the Democratic Republic of Madagascar. Political parties were permitted again and in 1976 the Front-Line Revolutionary Organization (AREMA) was formed by Ratsiraka as the nucleus of a single party for the state. By 1977 all political activity was concentrated in FNDR, and all the candidates for the national people's assembly were FNDR nominees.

social and political discontent In 1977 the National Movement for the Independence of Madagascar (MONIMA), a radical socialist party, withdrew from the FNDR and was declared illegal. MONIMA's leader, Monja Jaona, unsuccessfully challenged Ratsiraka for the presidency and, although his party did well in the capital, AREMA won an overwhelming victory in the 1983 elections. Despite this, social and political discontent has continued, particularly among the Merina, who have openly demonstrated their opposition to the government. President Ratsiraka was re-elected with a 62% popular vote March 1989, and in May AREMA won 120 of the 137 assembly seats. Calls for a new constitution and democratic reforms were accompanied by strikes and demonstrations June 1991 and a demand for Ratsiraka's resignation.

Opposition forces formed an 'alternative government' and in response Ratsiraka declared a state of emergency July 1991. Refusal by the opposition to accept the president's concessions resulted in violence and a declaration of 'open war' Aug 1991 by the protesters. Discussions between President Ratsiraka and opposition representatives resulted in the appointment of Guy Razanamasy as prime minister and a widening of the prime minister's powers. In Oct 1991 Ratsiraka, Razanamasy, and opposition representatives signed an agreement for a new unity government. In a referendum Aug 1992 a new constitution, providing for multiparty elections, was approved. Ratsiraka survived a coup attempt the same month.

... one of the greatest and richest isles of the World ...

On *Madagascar* Marco Polo 1320

Madison James 1751–1836. 4th president of the USA 1809–17. In 1787 he became a member of the Philadelphia Constitutional Convention and took a leading part in drawing up the US Constitution and the Bill of Rights. He allied himself firmly with Thomas ◊Jefferson against Alexander ◊Hamilton in the struggle between the more democratic views of Jefferson and the aristocratic, upper-class sentiments of Hamilton. As secretary of state in Jefferson's government 1801–09, Madison completed the ◊Louisiana Purchase negotiated by James Monroe. During his period of office the War of 1812 with Britain took place.

Mafia (Italian 'swank') secret society reputed to control organized crime such as gambling, loansharking, drug traffic, prostitution, and protection; connected with the ◊Camorra of Naples. It originated in Sicily in the late Middle Ages and now operates chiefly there and in countries to which Italians have emigrated, such as the USA and Australia.

It began as a society that avenged wrongs against Sicilian peasants by means of terror and ◊vendetta. In 19th-century Sicily the Mafia was employed by absentee landlords to manage their *latifundia* (landed estates), and through intimidation it soon became the unofficial ruling group. Despite the expropriation and division of the *latifundia* after World War II, the Mafia remains powerful in Sicily. The Italian government has waged periodic campaigns of suppression, notably 1927, when the Fascist leader Mussolini appointed Cesare Mori (1872–?) as prefect of Palermo. Mori's methods were, however, as suspect as those of the people he was arresting, and he was fired 1929. A further campaign was waged 1963–64.

The Mafia grew during ◊Prohibition in the USA. Main centres are New York, Las Vegas, Miami, Atlantic City, and Chicago. Organization is in 'families', each with its own boss, or *capo*. A code of loyalty and secrecy, combined with intimidation of witnesses, makes it difficult to bring criminal charges against its members. However, Al Capone was sentenced for federal tax evasion and Lucky Luciano was deported. Recent cases of the US government versus the Mafia implicated Sicilian-based operators in the drug traffic that plagues much of the Western world (the 'pizza connection'). In 1992 John Gotti, reputedly head of the Gambino 'family' of the Mafia, was convicted.

The Mafia, also known in the USA as *La Cosa Nostra* ('our affair') or the Mob, features frequently in fiction; for example, in the *Godfather* films from 1972 based on a book by Mario Puzo.

Mafikeng former name (until 1980) *Mafeking* town in Bophuthatswana, South Africa. It was the capital of Bechuanaland, and the British officer Robert Baden-Powell held it under Boer siege 12 Oct 1899–17 May 1900.

Magadha kingdom of ancient NE India, roughly corresponding to the middle and southern parts of modern Bihar. It was the scene of many incidents in the life of Buddha and was the seat of the ◊Mauryan dynasty founded in the 3rd century BC. Its capital Pataliputra was a great cultural and political centre.

Magellan Ferdinand 1480–1521. Portuguese navigator. In 1519 he set sail in the *Victoria* from Seville with the intention of reaching the East Indies by a westerly route. He sailed through the *Magellan Strait* at the tip of South America, crossed an ocean he named the Pacific, and in 1521 reached the Philippines, where he was killed in a battle with the islanders. His companions returned to Seville 1522, completing the voyage under del Cano, thus becoming the first circumnavigators of the globe.

Magenta town in Lombardy, Italy, 24 km/15mi W of Milan, where France and Sardinia defeated Austria 1859 during the struggle for Italian independence. Magenta dye was named in honour of the victory.

Maginot Line French fortification system along the German frontier from Switzerland to Luxembourg built 1929–36 under the direction of the war minister, André Maginot. It consisted of semi-underground forts joined by underground passages, and protected by antitank defences; lighter fortifications continued the line to the sea. In 1940 German forces pierced the Belgian frontier line and outflanked the Maginot Line.

Magna Carta (Latin 'great charter') in English history, the charter granted by King John 1215, traditionally seen as guaranteeing human rights against the excessive use of royal power. As a reply to the king's demands for excessive feudal dues and attacks on the privileges of the church, Archbishop Langton proposed to the barons the drawing-up of a binding document 1213. John was forced to accept this at Runnymede (now in Surrey) 15 June 1215.

To no man will we sell, or deny, or delay, right or justice.

Magna Carta 1215

Magyar member of the largest ethnic group in Hungary, comprising 92% of the population.

Magyars are of mixed Ugric and Turkic origin, and they arrived in Hungary towards the end of the 9th century.

Mahdi (Arabic 'he who is guided aright') in Islam, the title of a coming messiah who will establish a reign of justice on Earth. The title has been assumed by many Muslim leaders, notably the Sudanese sheik Muhammad Ahmed (1848–1885), who headed a revolt 1881 against Egypt and 1885 captured Khartoum.

His great-grandson *Sadiq el Mahdi* (1936–), leader of the Umma party in Sudan, was prime minister 1966–67. He was imprisoned 1969–74 for attempting to overthrow the military regime.

Mahmud two sultans of the Ottoman Empire:

Mahmud I 1696–1754. Ottoman sultan from 1730. After restoring order to the empire in Istanbul 1730, he suppressed the Janissary rebellion 1731 and waged war against Persia 1731–46. He led successful wars against Austria and Russia, concluded by the Treaty of Belgrade 1739. He was a patron of the arts and also carried out reform of the army.

Mahmud II 1785–1839. Ottoman sultan from 1808 who attempted to westernize the declining empire, carrying out a series of far-reaching reforms in the civil service and army. The pressure for Greek independence after 1821 led to conflict with Britain, France, and Russia, and he was forced to recognize Greek independence 1830.

In 1826 Mahmud destroyed the janissaries. Wars against Russia 1807–12 resulted in losses of territory. The Ottoman fleet was destroyed at the Battle of Navarino 1827, and the Ottoman forces suffered defeat in the Russo-Turkish war 1828–29. There was further disorder with the revolt in Egypt of ◊Mehemet Ali 1831–32, which in turn led to temporary Ottoman-Russian peace. Attempts to control the rebellious provinces failed 1839, resulting in effect in the granting of Egyptian autonomy.

Mahratta rivals of the Mogul emperors in the 17th and 18th centuries; see ◊Maratha.

Maimonides Moses (Moses Ben Maimon) 1135–1204. Jewish rabbi and philosopher, born in Córdoba, Spain. Known as one of the greatest Hebrew scholars, he attempted to reconcile faith and reason.

He left Spain 1160 to escape the persecution of the Jews and settled in Fez, and later in Cairo, where he was personal physician to Sultan Saladin. His codification of Jewish law is known as the *Mishneh Torah/Torah Reviewed* 1180; he also formulated the *Thirteen*

Principles, which summarize the basic beliefs of Judaism. His philosophical classic *More nevukhim/ The Guide to the Perplexed* 1176–91 helped to introduce Aristotelian thought into medieval philosophy.

Maintenon Françoise d'Aubigné, Marquise de 1635–1719. Second wife of Louis XIV of France from 1684, and widow of the writer Paul Scarron (1610–1660). She was governess to the children of Mme de Montespan by Louis, and his mistress from 1667. She secretly married the king after the death of Queen   Marie Thérèse 1683. Her political influence was considerable and, as a Catholic convert from Protestantism, her religious opinions were zealous.

Majapahit empire last Hindu empire in E ◊Java *c.* 1293–*c.* 1520. Based in the fertile Brantas river valley, it encompassed much of Malaya, Borneo, Sumatra, and Bali, and reached its peak under the ruler Hayam Wuruk (reigned 1350–89).

Major John 1943–   . British Conservative politician, prime minister 1990-1997. He was foreign secretary 1989 and chancellor of the Exchequer. His initial positive approach to European Community (later European Union) matters were hindered from 1991 by divisions within the Conservative Party. Despite continuing public dissatisfaction with the poll tax, the National Health Service, and the recession, Major was returned to power in the 1992 general election. His subsequent handling of a series of domestic crises called into question his ability to govern the country effectively, but he won backing for his launch of a joint UK-Irish peace initiative on Northern Ireland 1993, which led to the general cease-fire 1994. In a desperate bid for party unity, he dramatically resigned the party leadership June 1995, and was re-elected to the post. After a crushing defeat in the 1997 general election, he resigned as leader of the Conservative Party.

major-general after the English Civil War, one of the officers appointed by Oliver Cromwell 1655 to oversee the 12 military districts into which England had been divided. Their powers included organizing the militia, local government, and the collection of some taxes.

Makarios III 1913–1977. Cypriot politician, Greek Orthodox archbishop 1950–77. A leader of the Resistance organization ◊EOKA, he was exiled by the British to the Seychelles 1956–57 for supporting armed action to achieve union with Greece (*enosis*). He was president of the republic of Cyprus 1960–77 (briefly deposed by a Greek military coup July–Dec 1974).

Malawi country in SE Africa, bounded N and NE by Tanzania; E, S, and W by Mozambique; and W by Zambia.

history During the 15th–19th centuries the Malawi empire occupied roughly the southern part of the region that makes up present-day Malawi. The difficulty of the terrain and the warfare between the rival Yao and Ngoni groups long prevented penetration of the region by outsiders, though Scottish explorer David ◊Livingstone reached Lake Malawi 1859. In 1891 Britain annexed the country, making it the British protectorate of Nyasaland from 1907. Between 1953 and 1964 it was part of the Federation of Rhodesia and Nyasaland, which comprised the territory that is now Zimbabwe, Zambia, and Malawi.

republic and one-party state Dr Hastings Banda, through the Malawi Congress Party, led a campaign for independence, and in 1963 the federation was dissolved. Nyasaland became independent as Malawi 1964 and two years later became a republic and a one-party state, with Banda as its first president. He has governed his country in a very individual way, tolerating no opposition, and his foreign policies have at times been rather idiosyncratic. He astonished his black African colleagues 1967 by officially recognizing the Republic of South Africa, and in 1971 became the first African head of state to visit that country. In 1976, however, he also recognized the communist government in Angola. Banda's external policies are based on a mixture of national self-interest and practical reality and have enabled Malawi to live in reasonable harmony with its neighbours.

receiving refugees Malawi adopted an 'open-door' policy towards refugees fleeing the civil war in neighbouring Mozambique; about 70,000 refugees crossed the border Sept 1986. By 1989 the number of refugees had grown to nearly 1 million.

opposition Banda has kept tight control over his government colleagues. In 1977 he released some political detainees and allowed greater press freedom, but human-rights violations and murder of opponents have been reported. His most likely successor was in 1992 tipped to be John Tembo, a minister of state, and his most prominent opponent in Malawi was Chakufwa Chihana, a trade-union leader. There are at least three opposition groups that operate from outside Malawi. During March 1992 the first public calls for multiparty politics were made, and seven high-ranking members of the Roman Catholic church issued a pastoral letter condemning corruption and government censorship and monopoly of the media. In May industrial riots throughout the country resulted in more than 40 deaths. Western nations suspended aid in order to press for greater respect for human rights. In Oct 1992 President Banda announced that a referendum would be held on the issue of multiparty politics.

Malayan Emergency civil conflict in British-ruled Malaya, officially lasting from 1948 to 1960. The Communist Party of Malaya (CPM) launched an insurrection, calling for immediate Malayan independence. Britain responded by mounting a large-scale military and political counter-insurgency operation, while agreeing to eventual independence. In 1957 Malaya became independent and the state of emergency was ended 1960, although some CPM guerrillas continue to operate.

Malaysia country in SE Asia, comprising the Malay Peninsula, bounded N by Thailand, and surrounded E and S by the South China Sea and W by the Strait of Malacca; and the states of Sabah and Sarawak in the northern part of the island of Borneo (S Borneo is part of Indonesia).

history The areas that comprise present-day Malaysia were part of the Buddhist Srivijaya empire in the 9th–14th centuries. This was overthrown by Majapahit, Java's last Hindu kingdom. After this period of Indian influence came the introduction of Islam, and a powerful Muslim empire developed in the area. Its growth was checked by the Portuguese conquest of Malacca 1511. In 1641 the Dutch ousted the Portuguese, and the area came under British control from 1786, with a brief return to Dutch rule 1818–24.

British control British sovereignty was progressively established from the 1820s and a rubber- and tin-based export economy was developed, with Chinese and Indian labourers being imported. Local state chiefs were allowed to retain considerable political autonomy and in 1826 only Singapore, Penang, and Malacca were incorporated in the Straits Settlements colony. British control was extended to Negri Sembilan, Pahang, Perak, and Selangor in 1874, to Johore 1885, and to Kedah, Kelantan, Perlis, and Trengganu between 1910 and 1930. The Federated Malay States was formed 1895. After World War II, with British control being extended over Sarawak, the UK protectorates in Borneo and the Malay Peninsula were unified as the Federation of Malaya crown colony 1948.

Federation of Malaysia The Federation of Malaysia was formed 1963 by the union of the 11 states of the Federation of Malaya with the British crown colonies of N Borneo (then renamed Sabah) and Sarawak, and Singapore, which seceded from the federation 1965. Since 1966 the 11 states on the Malay Peninsula have been known as West Malaysia, and Sabah and Sarawak as East Malaysia. The two regions are separated by 650 km/400 mi of the South China Sea. The establishment of the federation was opposed by guerrillas backed by Sukarno of Indonesia 1963–66, and the Philippines disputed the sovereignty of East Malaysia 1968 through their claim on Sabah.

Tunku Abdul ◊Rahman was Malaysia's first prime minister 1963–69, and his multiracial style of government was successful until anti-Chinese riots in Kuala Lumpur 1969 prompted the formation of an emergency administration. These riots followed a fall in support for the United Malays' National Organization (UMNO) in the federal election and were indicative of Malay resentment of the economic success of the Chinese business community. They provoked the resignation of Rahman 1970 and the creation by his successor, Tun Abdul Razak, of a broader governing coalition, including previous opposition parties in its ranks.

pro-Malay economic policy In addition, a new economic policy was launched 1971, with the aim of raising the percentage of ethnic-Malay-owned businesses from 4% to 30% by 1990 and extending the use of pro-Malay (*bumiputra*) affirmative-action quota systems for university entrance and company employment. During the 1970s Malaysia enjoyed economic growth, but relations with the Chinese community became uneasy later in the decade as a result of the federal government's refusal to welcome Vietnamese refugees. There has also been a revival of fundamentalist Islam in the west and north.

Dr Mahathir bin ◊Mohamad became the new leader of UMNO and prime minister 1981 and pursued a more narrowly Islamic and Malay strategy than his predecessors. He also launched an ambitious industrialization programme, seeking to emulate Japan. He was re-elected 1982 and 1986 but encountered opposition from his Malaysian Chinese Association coalition partners, Christian-Muslim conflict in Sabah, and slower economic growth as a result of the fall in world tin, rubber, and palm-oil prices.

new opposition In 1987, in the wake of worsening Malay-Chinese relations, Mahathir ordered the arrest of more than 100 prominent opposition activists, including the Democratic

Action Party (DAP)'s leader Lim Kit Siang, and a tightening of press censorship. These moves precipitated a rift in UMNO, with former premier Rahman and former trade and industry minister Razaleigh Hamzah leaving to form a new multiracial party grouping, Semangat '46, in 1989. In 1988 a reconstituted new UMNO had been set up by Mahathir. The prime minister also announced some relaxation of the 1971 economic policy that favoured ethnic Malays – Malay equity ownership having reached only 18% by 1987 – as part of a more consensual 'Malay unity' programme.

foreign relations Malaysia joined ◊ASEAN 1967 and originally adopted a pro-Western, anticommunist position. During recent years, while close economic links have been developed with Japan and joint ventures encouraged, relations with the communist powers and with Islamic nations also became closer.

In Oct 1990 federal and state elections were held. Prime Minister Mahathir bin Mohamad's ruling coalition captured 127 of the 180 national assembly seats. The expected strong challenge from Mahathir's rival and former colleague Razaleigh failed to materialize: his Semangat '46 party lost 5 of its 12 seats. However, Islamic (PAS) and Chinese (DAP) party allies polled well locally, with the opposition achieving a clean sweep (and control of the state legislature) in Razaleigh's home state of Kelantan.

economic growth policy The pro-Malay economic policy expired Dec 1990 and was replaced by a new programme, the 'new development policy', which is less discriminatory against non-Malays and aims to achieve an eightfold increase (7% a year) in national income by the year 2020, by which date Malaysia, it is envisaged, will have become a 'fully developed state'.

Malcolm four kings of Scotland, including:

Malcolm III called *Canmore c.* 1031–1093. King of Scotland from 1058, the son of Duncan I (murdered by ◊Macbeth 1040). He fled to England when the throne was usurped by Macbeth, but recovered S Scotland and killed Macbeth in battle 1057. He was killed at Alnwick while invading Northumberland, England.

Malcolm X adopted name of Malcolm Little 1926–1965. US black nationalist leader. While serving a prison sentence for burglary 1946–53, he joined the ◊Black Muslims sect. On his release he campaigned for black separatism, condoning violence in self-defence, but 1964 modified his views to found the Islamic,

socialist Organization of Afro-American Unity, preaching racial solidarity. He was assassinated.

He was born in Omaha, Nebraska, but grew up in foster homes in Michigan, Massachusetts, and New York. Convicted of robbery 1946, he spent seven years in prison, becoming a follower of Black Muslim leader Elijah Muhammad and converting to Islam. In 1952 he officially changed his name to Malcolm X to signify his rootlessness in a racist society. Having become an influential national and international leader, Malcolm X publicly broke with the Black Muslims 1964. A year later he was assassinated by Black Muslim opponents while addressing a rally in Harlem, New York City. His *Autobiography of Malcolm X* was published 1964.

If someone puts his hand on you, send him to the cemetery.

Malcolm X *Malcolm X Speaks*

Maldives group of 1,196 islands in the N Indian Ocean, about 640 km/400 mi SW of Sri Lanka, only 203 of which are inhabited.

history The islands, under Muslim control from the 12th century, came under Portuguese rule 1518. A dependency of Ceylon 1645–1948, they were under British protection 1887–1965 as the Maldive Islands and became a republic 1953. The sultan was restored 1954, and then, three years after achieving full independence as Maldives, the islands returned to republican status 1968.

independence Maldives became fully independent as a sultanate outside the ◊Commonwealth 1965, with Ibrahim Nasir as prime minister. Nasir became president when the sultan was deposed for the second time 1968 and the country became a republic. It rejoined the Commonwealth 1982. Britain had an air-force staging post on the southern island of Gan 1956–75, and its closure meant a substantial loss of income. The president nevertheless refused a Soviet offer 1977 to lease the former base, saying that he did not want it used for military purposes again nor leased to a super power.

In 1978 Nasir announced that he would not stand for re-election, and the Majilis nominated Maumoon Abdul Gayoom, a member of Nasir's cabinet, as his successor. Nasir went to Singapore but was called back to answer charges of misusing government funds. He denied the charges, and attempts to extradite him failed. Despite rumours of a plot to overthrow him, Gayoom was re-elected for a further five years 1983. Under Gayoom economic growth accelerated, helped by an expansion in tourism. Overseas, Gayoom broadly adhered to his predecessor's policy of nonalignment, but also began to develop closer links with the Arab nations of the Middle East, and in 1985 rejoined the Commonwealth and was a founder member of the South Asian Association for Regional Cooperation (SAARC).

coup attempt In Nov 1988, soon after being re-elected for a third term, Gayoom was briefly ousted in an attempted coup led by Abdullah Luthufi, an exiled entrepreneur from the atoll of Adu, which favours secession. Luthufi had recruited a force of 200 Tamil mercenaries in Sri Lanka, and was thought to have the backing of former president Nasir. Gayoom was restored to office after the intervention of Indian paratroops; 17 of those captured, including Luthufi, were sentenced to life imprisonment 1989.

Maldon English market town in Essex, at the mouth of the river Chelmer. It was the scene of a battle in which the East Saxons were defeated by the Danes 991, commemorated in the Anglo-Saxon poem *The Battle of Maldon.*

Malenkov Georgi Maximilianovich 1902–1988. Soviet prime minister 1953–55, Stalin's designated successor but abruptly ousted as Communist Party secretary within two weeks of Stalin's death by ◊Khrushchev, and forced out as prime minister 1955 by ◊Bulganin.

Mali landlocked country in NW Africa, bounded to the NE by Algeria, E by Niger, SE by Burkina Faso, S by the Ivory Coast, SW by Senegal and Guinea, and W and N by Mauritania.

history From the 7th to the 11th century part of the Ghana Empire (see ◊Ghana, ancient), then of the Muslim ◊Mali Empire, which flourished in NW Africa during the 7th–15th centuries, the area now known as Mali came under the rule of the ◊Songhai Empire during the 15th–16th centuries. In 1591 an invasion by Moroccan forces seeking to take over the W Sudanese gold trade destroyed the Songhai Empire and left the area divided into small kingdoms.

Because of its inland position, the region had little contact with Europeans, who were trading around the coast from the 16th century, and it was not until the 19th century that France, by means of treaties with local rulers, established colonies throughout most of NW Africa. As French Sudan, Mali was part of French West Africa from 1895. In 1959, with Senegal, it formed the Federation of Mali. In 1960 Senegal left, and Mali became a fully independent republic.

independence Its first president, Modibo Keita, imposed an authoritarian socialist regime, but his economic policies failed, and he was removed in an army coup 1968. The constitution was suspended, political activity was banned, and government was placed in the hands of a Military Committee for National Liberation (CMLN) with Lt Moussa Traoré as president and head of state. In 1969 he became prime minister as well. He promised a return to civilian rule, and in 1974 a new constitution made Mali a one-party state. A new party, the Malian People's Democratic Union (UDPM), was announced 1976. Despite student opposition to a one-party state and army objections to civilian rule, Traoré successfully made the transition so that by 1979 Mali had a constitutional government, while ultimate power lay with the party and the military establishment.

foreign relations In 1983 Mali and Guinea signed an agreement for eventual economic and political integration. In 1985 a border dispute with Burkina Faso resulted in a five-day conflict that was settled by the International Court of Justice.

multiparty system endorsed Violent demonstrations against one-party rule took place Jan 1991. In March 1991 Traoré was ousted in a coup and replaced by Lt-Col Amadou Toumani Toure. A new multiparty constitution was approved by referendum Jan 1992. In presidential elections April 1992 Toure was defeated and replaced by Alpha Oumar Konare.

Mali Empire Muslim state in NW Africa during the 7th–15th centuries. Thriving on its trade in gold, it reached its peak in the 14th century under Mansa Musa (reigned 1312–37), when it occupied an area covering present-day Senegal, Gambia, Mali, and S Mauritania. Mali's territory was similar to (though larger than) that of the Ghana Empire (see ◊Ghana, ancient), and gave way in turn to the ◊Songhai Empire.

Malik Yakob Alexandrovich 1906–1980. Soviet diplomat. He was permanent representative at the United Nations 1948–53 and 1968–76, and it was his walkout from the Security Council in Jan 1950 that allowed the authorization of UN intervention in Korea (see ◊Korean War).

Malinovsky Ródion Yakolevich 1898–1967. Russian soldier and politician. In World War II he fought at Stalingrad, commanded in the Ukraine, and led the Soviet advance through the Balkans to capture Budapest 1945. He was minister of defence 1957–67.

Malplaquet, Battle of victory 1709 of the British, Dutch, and Austrian forces over the French forces during the War of the ◊Spanish Succession. The village of Malplaquet is in Nord *département*, France.

Malta island in the Mediterranean Sea, S of Sicily, E of Tunisia, and N of Libya.

history Malta was occupied in turn by Phoenicia, Greece, Carthage, and Rome, and fell to the Arabs 870. In 1090 the Norman count Roger of Sicily conquered Malta, and it remained under Sicilian rule until the 16th century, when the Holy Roman emperor Charles V handed it over to the Knights of St John of Jerusalem 1530. After a Turkish attack 1565 the knights fortified the island and held it until 1798, when they surrendered to Napoleon. After requesting British protection, Malta was annexed by Britain 1814 and became a leading naval base. A vital link in World War II, Malta came under heavy attack and was awarded the George Cross decoration.

The island was made self-governing 1947, and in 1955 Dom Mintoff, leader of the Malta Labour Party (MLP), became prime minister. In 1956 the MLP's proposal for integration with the UK was approved by a referendum but opposed by the conservative Nationalist Party, led by Dr Giorgio Borg Olivier. In 1958 Mintoff rejected the British proposals and resigned, causing a constitutional crisis. By 1961 both parties favoured independence, and talks began 1962, with Borg Olivier as prime minister.

independence Malta became a fully independent state within the ◊Commonwealth and under the British crown 1964, having signed a ten-year military and economic aid treaty with the UK. In 1971 Mintoff and the MLP returned to power with a policy of international nonalignment. He declared the 1964 treaty invalid and began to negotiate a new arrangement for leasing the Maltese NATO base and obtaining the maximum economic benefit from it for his country.

republican status agreed A seven-year agreement was signed 1972. Malta became a republic 1974, and in the 1976 general election the MLP was returned with a reduced majority. It again won a narrow majority in the House of Representatives 1981, even though the Nationalists had a bigger share of the popular vote. As a result, Nationalist MPs refused to take their seats for over a year. Relations between the two parties were also damaged by allegations of progovernment bias in the broadcasting service. At the end of 1984 Mintoff announced his retirement, and Dr Mifsud Bonnici succeeded him as MLP leader and prime minister. Three years later, in 1987, the Nationalist Party won the general election and its leader, Edward Fenech Adami, became prime minister. Vincent Tabone was elected president 1989. Malta was the site of the Dec 1989 summit meeting between US president Bush and Soviet president Gorbachev. In Oct 1990 Malta formally applied for European Community (EC) membership. In the Feb 1992 general election the Nationalist Party, under Prime Minister Adami, was returned for another term.

Malta, Knights of another name for members of the military-religious order of the Hospital of ◊St John of Jerusalem.

Mameluke member of a powerful political class that dominated Egypt from the 13th century until their massacre 1811 by Mehemet Ali.

The Mamelukes were originally descended from freed Turkish slaves. They formed the royal bodyguard in the 13th century, and in 1250 placed one of their own number on the throne. Mameluke sultans ruled Egypt until the Turkish conquest of 1517, and they remained the ruling class until 1811.

Manchu or *Qing* last ruling dynasty in China, from 1644 until their overthrow 1912; their last emperor was the infant ◊P'u-i. Originally a nomadic people from Manchuria, they established power through a series of successful invasions from the north, then granted trading rights to the USA and Europeans, which eventually brought strife and the ◊Boxer Rebellion.

Manchukuo former Japanese puppet state in Manchuria and Jehol 1932–45, ruled by the former Chinese emperor Henry ◊P'u-i.

Manchuria European name for the NE region of China, comprising the provinces of Heilongjiang, Jilin, and Liaoning. It was united with China by the Manchu dynasty 1644, but as the Chinese Empire declined, Japan and Russia were rivals for its control. The Russians were expelled after the ◊Russo-Japanese War 1904–05, and in 1932 Japan consolidated its position by creating a puppet state, *Manchukuo*, which disintegrated on the defeat of Japan in World War II.

mandate in history, a territory whose administration was entrusted to Allied states by the League of Nations under the Treaty of Versailles after World War I. Mandated territories were former German and Turkish possessions (including Iraq, Syria, Lebanon, and Palestine). When the United Nations replaced the

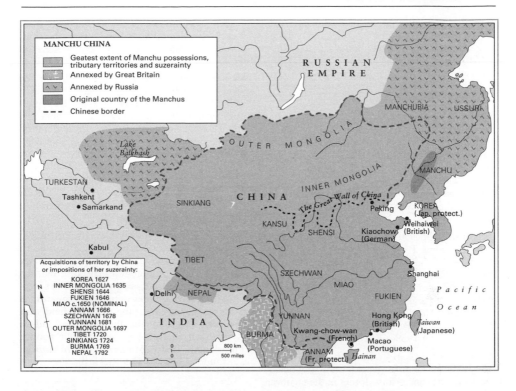

Manchu China *With their homeland in Manchuria, NE of the Great Wall, China's Manchu Qing rulers (1644–1912) were of foreign ethnic origin. This was to be of great significance in the 19th century when, confronted with European commercial and military intrusions, the Qing, in their defence of traditional Chinese values, conservatively resisted calls for administrative and economic modernization. The first century of Qing rule was, however, a period of military success, resulting in tremendous territorial expansion, and of economic and demographic advance.*

League of Nations 1945, mandates that had not achieved independence became known as ◊Trust Territories.

I have cherished the idea of a democratic and free society ... if needs be, it is an ideal for which I am prepared to die.

Nelson Mandela speech Feb 1990

Mandela Nelson (Rolihlahla) 1918– . South African politician and lawyer, president from 1994. He became president of the ◊African National Congress (ANC) 1991. Imprisoned from 1964, as organizer of the then banned ANC, he became a symbol of unity for the worldwide anti-◊apartheid movement. In Feb 1990 he was released, the ban of the ANC having been lifted, and entered into negotiations with the government about a multiracial future for South Africa. In May 1994 he was sworn in as South Africa's first post-apartheid president

1994 after the ANC won 62.65% of the vote in universal-suffrage elections. He shared the Nobel Peace Prize 1993 with South African president F W de Klerk.

Mandela was born near Umbata, S of Lesotho, the son of a local chief. In a trial of several ANC leaders, he was acquitted of treason 1961, but was arrested once more 1964 and given a life sentence on charges of sabotage and plotting to overthrow the government. He married civil-rights activist Winnie Mandela 1955; they separated 1992 and were divorced 1996.

Manhattan Project code name for the development of the ◊atom bomb in the USA in World War II, to which the physicists Enrico Fermi and J Robert Oppenheimer contributed.

Manichaeism religion founded by the prophet Mani (Latinized as Manichaeus, *c.* 216–276). Despite persecution Manichaeism spread and flourished until about the 10th century. Based on the concept of dualism, it held that the material world is evil, an invasion of the spiritual realm of light by the powers of darkness;

particles of divine light imprisoned in evil matter were to be rescued by messengers such as Jesus, and finally by Mani himself.

Mani proclaimed his creed in 241 at the Persian court. Returning from missions to China and India, he was put to death at the instigation of the Zoroastrian priesthood.

manifest destiny in US history, the belief that Americans had a providential mission to extend both their territory and their democratic processes westwards across the continent. The phrase was coined by journalist John L O'Sullivan 1845. Reflecting this belief, Texas and California were shortly afterwards annexed by the USA. (See ◊Mexican War).

Manley Michael (Norman) 1924–97 . Jamaican politician, leader of the socialist People's National Party from 1969, and prime minister 1972–80 and 1989–92. He resigned the premiership because of ill health March 1992 and was succeeded by P J Patterson. Manley left parliament April 1992. His father, *Norman Manley* (1893–1969), was the founder of the People's National Party and prime minister 1959–62.

Mannerheim Carl Gustav Emil von 1867–1951. Finnish general and politician, leader of the conservative forces in the civil war 1917–18 and regent 1918–19. He commanded the Finnish army 1939–40 and 1941–44, and was president of Finland 1944–46.

Manoel two kings of Portugal, including:

Manoel I 1469–1521. King of Portugal from 1495, when he succeeded his uncle John II (1455–1495). He was known as 'the Fortunate', because his reign was distinguished by the discoveries made by Portuguese navigators and the expansion of the Portuguese empire.

manor basic economic unit in ◊feudalism in Europe, established in England under the Norman conquest. It consisted of the lord's house and cultivated land, land rented by free tenants, land held by villagers, common land, woodland, and waste land.

Here and there traces of the system survive in England – the common land may have become an area for public recreation – but the documents sometimes sold at auction and entitling the owner to be called 'lord of the manor' seldom have any rights attached to them.

manumission in medieval England, the act of freeing a villein or serf from his or her bondage. The process took place in a county court and freedom could either be bought or granted as a reward for services rendered.

In Roman times, slaves could become freedmen or freedwomen by being granted manumission by their owner, who let the slave go *(manu misit)*.

Maoism form of communism based on the ideas and teachings of the Chinese communist leader ◊Mao Zedong. It involves an adaptation of ◊Marxism to suit conditions in China and apportions a much greater role to agriculture and the peasantry in the building of socialism, thus effectively bypassing the capitalist (industrial) stage envisaged by Marx. In addition, Maoism places stress on ideological, as well as economic, transformation, based on regular contact maintained between party members and the general population.

Maori member of the indigenous Polynesian people of New Zealand, who numbered 294,200 in 1986, about 10% of the total population. Under the Waitangi Treaty of 1840, the Maoris surrendered their lands to British sovereignty. The Maoris now demand a review of the treaty and claim 70% of the country's land; they have secured a ruling that the fishing grounds of the far north belong solely to local Maori people. The *Maori Unity Movement/Kotahitanga* was founded 1983 by Eva Rickard.

Political power grows out of the barrel of a gun.

Mao Zedong
'Problems of War and Strategy'

Mao Zedong or *Mao Tse-tung* 1893–1976. Chinese political leader and Marxist theoretician. A founder of the Chinese Communist Party (CCP) 1921, Mao soon emerged as its leader. He organized the ◊Long March 1934–35 and the war of liberation 1937–49, following which he established a People's Republic and communist rule in China; he headed the CCP and government until his death. His influence diminished with the failure of his 1958–60 ◊Great Leap Forward, but he emerged dominant again during the 1966–69 ◊Cultural Revolution.

Adapting communism to Chinese conditions, Mao stressed the need for rural rather than urban-based revolutions in Asia, for reducing rural-urban differences, and for perpetual revolution to prevent the emergence of new elites. Mao helped precipitate the Sino-Soviet split 1960 and was a firm advocate of a nonaligned Third World strategy. Since 1978, the leadership of Deng Xiaoping has reinterpreted Maoism and criticized its policy excesses, but many of Mao's ideas remain valued.

Mapai (Miphlegeth Poale Israel) Israeli Workers' Party or Labour Party, founded 1930. Its leading figure until 1965 was David Ben-Gurion. In 1968, the party allied with two other democratic socialist parties to form the Israeli Labour Party, led initially by Levi Eshkol and later by Golda Meir.

Maquis French ◊resistance movement that fought against the German occupation during World War II.

Marat Jean Paul 1743–1793. French Revolutionary leader and journalist. He was elected to the National Convention 1792, where he carried on a long struggle with the right-wing ◊Girondins, ending in their overthrow May 1793. In July he was murdered by Charlotte ◊Corday, a member of the Girondins.

Maratha or *Mahratta* member of a people living mainly in Maharashtra, W India. There are about 40 million speakers of Marathi, a language belonging to the Indo-European family. The Maratha are mostly farmers, and practise Hinduism. In the 17th and 18th centuries the Maratha formed a powerful military confederacy in rivalry with the Mogul emperors. The latter's Afghan allies defeated the Maratha at Panipat 1761, and, after a series of wars with the British 1779–1871, most of their territory was annexed.

The first Marathi kingdom was established by ◊Sivaji 1674, and during the first half of the 18th century, with Mogul influence waning, Maratha authority was extended into central and N India. Politically, the Maratha was a loose confederacy, comprising powerful, independent families, notably the Sindhias, based at Gwalior, and the Holkars, who controlled Malwa in central India. The hereditary Chitpavan Brahmin Peshwas (chief ministers), based at Poona, were unable to control these families.

Marathon, Battle of 490 BC battle in which the Athenians and their allies from Plateae defeated the invading Persians on the plain of Marathon, NE of Athens.

March on Rome, the means by which Fascist leader Benito Mussolini came to power in Italy 1922. A protracted crisis in government and the threat of civil war enabled him to demand the formation of a Fascist government to restore order. On 29 Oct 1922, King Victor Emmanuel III invited Mussolini to come to Rome to take power. The 'march' was a propaganda myth: Mussolini travelled overnight by train from Milan to Rome, where he formed a government the following day, 30 Oct. Some

25,000 fascist Blackshirts were also transported to the city, where they marched in a ceremonial parade 31 Oct.

Marcian 396–457. Eastern Roman emperor 450–457. He was a general who married Pulcheria, sister of Theodosius II, and became emperor at the latter's death. He convened the Council of ◊Chalcedon (the fourth Ecumenical Council of the Christian Church) 451 and refused to pay tribute to Attila the Hun.

Marconi Scandal scandal 1912 in which UK chancellor Lloyd George and two other government ministers were found by a French newspaper to have dealt in shares of the US Marconi company shortly before it was announced that the Post Office had accepted the British Marconi company's bid to construct an imperial wireless chain. A parliamentary select committee, biased towards the Liberal government's interests, found that the other four wireless systems were technically inadequate and therefore the decision to adopt Marconi's tender was not the result of ministerial corruption. The scandal did irreparable harm to Lloyd George's reputation.

Marco Polo see ◊Polo, Marco.

Marco Polo bridge incident conflict 1937 between Chinese and Japanese army troops on the border of Japanese-controlled ◊Manchukuo and China that led to full-scale war between the two states. It lasted until the Japanese surrender 1945.

Marcos Ferdinand 1917–1989. Filipino right-wing politician, president from 1965 to 1986, when he was forced into exile in Hawaii by a popular front led by Corazon ◊Aquino. He was backed by the USA when in power, but in 1988 US authorities indicted him and his wife Imelda Marcos for racketeering, embezzlement.

Marcos was convicted while a law student 1939 of murdering a political opponent of his father, but eventually secured his own acquittal. In World War II he was a guerrilla fighter, survived the Japanese prison camps, and became president 1965. His regime became increasingly repressive, with secret pro-Marcos groups terrorizing and executing his opponents.

Waste no more time arguing what a good man should be. Be one.

Marcus Aurelius
Meditations 2nd century AD

Marcus Aurelius AD 121–180. Roman emperor from 161 and Stoic philosopher. Born in Rome, he was adopted by his uncle, the emperor Antoninus Pius, whom he succeeded in 161. He conceded an equal share in the rule to Lucius Verus (died 169).

Marcus Aurelius spent much of his reign warring against the Germanic tribes and died in Pannonia, where he had gone to drive back the invading Marcomanni.

Mardonius died 479 BC. Persian general who in 492 BC took command of Ionia in western Asia Minor, following the Ionian Revolt. He eased local unrest by replacing tyrants with democracy. The nephew and son-in-law of ◊Darius I, he acted as a leading counsellor and general for ◊Xerxes in the second invasion of Greece 480 BC. He stayed with the army after its defeat by the Greeks at Salamis, and was killed at the Battle of Plataea.

Marengo, Battle of defeat of the Austrians by the French emperor Napoleon on 14 June 1800, as part of his Italian campaign, near the village of Marengo in Piedmont, Italy.

Margaret *the Maid of Norway* 1282–1290. Queen of Scotland from 1285, the daughter of Eric II, king of Norway, and Princess Margaret of Scotland. When only two years old she became queen of Scotland on the death of her grandfather, Alexander III, but died in the Orkneys on the voyage from Norway to her kingdom.

Margaret of Anjou 1430–1482. Queen of England from 1445, wife of ◊Henry VI of England. After the outbreak of the Wars of the ◊Roses 1455, she acted as the leader of the Lancastrians, but was defeated and captured at the battle of Tewkesbury 1471 by Edward IV.

Her one object had been to secure the succession of her son, Edward (born 1453), who was killed at Tewkesbury. After five years' imprisonment Margaret was allowed in 1476 to return to her native France, where she died in poverty.

Margaret, St 1045–1093. Queen of Scotland, the granddaughter of King Edmund Ironside of England. She went to Scotland after the Norman Conquest, and soon after married Malcolm III. The marriage of her daughter Matilda to Henry I united the Norman and English royal houses.

Through her influence, the Lowlands, until then purely Celtic, became largely anglicized. She was canonized 1251 in recognition of her benefactions to the church.

margrave German title (equivalent of marquess) for the 'counts of the march', who guarded the frontier regions of the Holy Roman

Empire from Charlemagne's time. Later the title was used by other territorial princes. Chief among these were the margraves of Austria and of Brandenburg.

Margrethe II 1940– . Queen of Denmark from 1972, when she succeeded her father Frederick IX. In 1967, she married the French diplomat Count Henri de Laborde de Monpezat, who took the title Prince Hendrik. Her heir is Crown Prince Frederick (1968–).

Marianne symbolic figure of the French republic, dating from the Revolution. Statues of her adorn public buildings in France. Her name combines those of the Virgin Mary and St Anne.

Maria Theresa 1717–1780. Empress of Austria from 1740, when she succeeded her father, the Holy Roman emperor Charles VI; her claim to the throne was challenged and she became embroiled, first in the War of the ◊Austrian Succession 1740–48, then in the ◊Seven Years' War 1756–63; she remained in possession of Austria but lost Silesia. The rest of her reign was peaceful and, with her son Joseph II, she introduced social reforms.

Marie Antoinette 1755–1793. Queen of France from 1774. She was the daughter of Empress Maria Theresa of Austria, and married ◊Louis XVI of France 1770. Her reputation for extravagance helped provoke the ◊French Revolution of 1789. She was tried for treason Oct 1793 and guillotined.

Marie de' Medici 1573–1642. Queen of France, wife of Henry IV from 1600, and regent (after his murder) for their son Louis XIII. She left the government to her favourites, the Concinis, until Louis XIII seized power and executed them 1617. She was banished, but after she led a revolt 1619, ◊Richelieu effected her reconciliation with her son. When she attempted to oust him again 1630, she was exiled.

Marie Louise 1791–1847. Queen consort of Napoleon I from 1810 (after his divorce from Josephine), mother of Napoleon II. She was the daughter of Francis I of Austria (see Emperor ◊Francis II) and on Napoleon's fall returned with their son to Austria, where she was granted the duchy of Parma 1815.

Marion Francis *c.* 1732–1795. American military leader. He waged a successful guerrilla war against the British after the fall of Charleston 1780 during the American Revolution. Establishing his field headquarters in inaccessible areas, he became popularly known as the 'Swamp Fox'. He played a major role in the American victory at Eutaw Springs 1781.

Marius Gaius 155–86 BC. Roman general and politician. He was elected consul seven times, the first time in 107 BC. He defeated the Cimbri and the Teutons (Germanic tribes attacking Gaul and Italy) 102–101 BC. Marius tried to deprive ◊Sulla of the command in the east against ◊Mithridates and, as a result, civil war broke out 88 BC. Sulla marched on Rome, and Marius fled to Africa, but later returned and created a reign of terror in Rome.

Mark Antony (Marcus Antonius) 83–30 BC. Roman politician and soldier. He served under Julius ◊Caesar in Gaul, and was consul with him in 44, when he tried to secure for Caesar the title of king. After Caesar's assassination, he formed the Second Triumvirate with Octavian (◊Augustus) and Lepidus. In 42 he defeated Brutus and Cassius at Philippi. He took Egypt as his share of the empire and formed a liaison with ◊Cleopatra, but in 40 he returned to Rome to marry Octavia, the sister of Augustus. In 32 the Senate declared war on Cleopatra, and Mark Antony was defeated by Augustus at the battle of Actium 31 BC. He returned to Egypt and committed suicide.

Markievicz Constance Georgina, Countess Markievicz (born Gore Booth) 1868–1927. Irish nationalist who married the Polish count Markievicz 1900. Her death sentence for taking part in the Easter Rising of 1916 was commuted, and after her release from prison 1917 she was elected to the Westminster Parliament as a Sinn Féin candidate 1918 (technically the first British woman member of Parliament), but did not take her seat.

Marlborough John Churchill, 1st Duke of Marlborough 1650–1722. English soldier, created a duke 1702 by Queen Anne. He was granted the Blenheim mansion in Oxfordshire in recognition of his services, which included defeating the French army outside Vienna in the Battle of ◊Blenheim 1704, during the War of the ◊Spanish Succession.

In 1688 he deserted his patron, James II, for William of Orange, but in 1692 fell into disfavour for Jacobite intrigue. He had married Sarah Jennings (1660–1744), confidante of the future Queen Anne, who created him a duke on her accession. He achieved further victories in Belgium at the battles of ◊Ramillies 1706 and Oudenaarde 1708, and in France at ◊Malplaquet 1709. However, the return of the Tories to power and his wife's quarrel with the queen led to his dismissal 1711 and his flight to Holland to avoid charges of corruption. He returned 1714.

Marne, Battles of the in World War I, two unsuccessful German offensives. In the *First*

Battle 6–9 Sept 1914, von Moltke's advance was halted by the British Expeditionary Force and the French under Foch; in the *Second Battle* 15 July–4 Aug 1918, Ludendorff's advance was defeated by British, French, and US troops under the French general Pétain, and German morale crumbled.

Maronite member of a Christian sect deriving from refugee Monothelites (Christian heretics) of the 7th century. They were subsequently united with the Roman Catholic Church and number about 400,000 in Lebanon and Syria, with an equal number scattered in southern Europe and the Americas.

maroon (Spanish *cimarrón* 'wild, untamed') in the West Indies and Surinam, a freed or escaped African slave. Maroons were organized and armed by the Spanish in Jamaica in the late 17th century and early 18th century. They harried the British with guerrilla tactics.

Marseillaise, La French national anthem; the words and music were composed 1792 as a revolutionary song by the army officer Claude Joseph Rouget de Lisle (1760–1836).

Marshall George Catlett 1880–1959. US general and diplomat. He was army Chief of Staff in World War II, secretary of state 1947–49, and secretary of defence Sept 1950–Sept 1951. He initiated the ◊*Marshall Plan* 1947 and received the Nobel Peace Prize 1953.

Marshall Islands group of islands, the Radak (13 islands) and Ralik (11 islands) chains in the W Pacific. The islands were under German control 1906–19; administered by Japan until 1946, passed to the USA as part of the Pacific Islands Trust Territory 1947. The northern islands of Bikini and Eniwetok were used for atomic bomb tests 1946–63 (the inhabitants were forcibly removed 1946 and 1947 respectively and have demanded compensation); at least 66 US atomic and hydrogen bombs were exploded there between 1946 and 1958. In 1986 a compact of free association with the USA was signed, under which the islands manage their own internal and external affairs but the USA controls military activities in exchange for financial support. In Dec 1990 its membership of the Trust Territory of the Pacific was terminated. It joined the United Nations Sept 1991. The incumbent president Amata Kabua was re-elected 1992 for a further four-year term.

Marshall Plan programme of US economic aid to Europe, set up at the end of World War II, totalling $13,000 billion 1948–52. Officially known as the European Recovery Programme, it was announced by Secretary of State George

C ◊Marshall in a speech at Harvard June 1947, but it was in fact the work of a State Department group led by Dean Acheson. The perceived danger of communist takeover in postwar Europe was the main reason for the aid effort.

Marston Moor, Battle of battle fought in the English Civil War 2 July 1644 on Marston Moor, 11 km/7 mi W of York. The Royalists were conclusively defeated by the Parliamentarians and Scots.

Martí José 1853–1895. Cuban revolutionary. Active in the Cuban independence movement from boyhood, he was deported to Spain 1871, returning 1878. Exiled again for continued opposition, he fled to the United States 1880, from where he organized resistance to Spanish rule. He was killed in battle at Dos Ríos, soon after proclaiming the uprising which led to Cuban independence.

Martí was chief of the Cuban Revolutionary Party formed 1892, and united Cubans in exile. In 1959 Fidel Castro cited him as the 'intellectual author' of the revolution, and he remains a national hero.

Martinet Jean French inspector-general of infantry under Louis XIV whose constant drilling brought the army to a high degree of efficiency – hence the use of his name to mean a strict disciplinarian.

Martinique French island in the West Indies (Lesser Antilles). Martinique was reached by Spanish navigators 1493, and became a French colony 1635; since 1972 it has been a French overseas region.

Marx Karl (Heinrich) 1818–1883. German philosopher, economist, and social theorist whose account of change through conflict is known as historical, or dialectical, materialism (see ◊Marxism). His *Das Kapital/Capital* 1867–95 is the fundamental text of Marxist economics, and his systematic theses on class struggle, history, and the importance of economic factors in politics have exercised an enormous influence on later thinkers and political activists.

Marx was born in Trier, the son of a lawyer, and studied law and philosophy at Bonn and Berlin. During 1842–43, he edited the *Rheinische Zeitung/Rhineland Newspaper* until its suppression. In 1844 he began his life-long collaboration with Friedrich ◊Engels, with whom he developed the Marxist philosophy, first formulated in their joint works, *Die heilige Familie/The Holy Family* 1844 and *Die deutsche Ideologie/German Ideology* 1846 (which contains the theory demonstrating the material basis of

all human activity: 'Life is not determined by consciousness, but consciousness by life'), and Marx's *Misère de la philosophie/Poverty of Philosophy* 1847. Both joined the Communist League, a German refugee organization, and in 1847–48 they prepared its programme, *The Communist Manifesto*. During the 1848 revolution Marx edited the *Neue Rheinische Zeitung/New Rhineland Newspaper*, until he was expelled from Prussia 1849.

He then settled in London, where he wrote *Die Klassenkämpfe in Frankreich/Class Struggles in France* 1849, *Die Achtzehnte Brumaire des Louis Bonaparte/The 18th Brumaire of Louis Bonaparte* 1852, *Zur Kritik der politischen Ökonomie/Critique of Political Economy* 1859, and his monumental work *Das Kapital/Capital*. In 1864 the International Working Men's Association was formed, whose policy Marx, as a member of the general council, largely controlled. Although he showed extraordinary tact in holding together its diverse elements, it collapsed 1872 due to Marx's disputes with the anarchists, including the Russian ◊Bakunin. The second and third volumes of *Das Kapital* were edited from his notes by Engels and published posthumously.

A spectre is haunting Europe – the spectre of communism.

Karl Marx *The Communist Manifesto* 1848

Marxism philosophical system, developed by the 19th-century German social theorists ◊Marx and ◊Engels, also known as *dialectical materialism*, under which matter gives rise to mind (materialism) and all is subject to change (from dialectic). As applied to history, it supposes that the succession of feudalism, capitalism, socialism, and finally the classless society is inevitable. The stubborn resistance of any existing system to change necessitates its complete overthrow in the *class struggle* – in the case of capitalism, by the proletariat – rather than gradual modification.

Social and political institutions progressively change their nature as economic developments transform material conditions. The orthodox belief is that each successive form is 'higher' than the last; perfect socialism is seen as the ultimate rational system, and it is alleged that the state would then wither away. Marxism has proved one of the most powerful and debated theories in modern history, inspiring both dedicated exponents (Lenin, Trotsky, Stalin, Mao) and bitter opponents. It is the basis of ◊communism.

Mary *Queen of Scots* 1542–1587. Queen of Scotland 1542–67. Also known as *Mary Stuart*, she was the daughter of James V. Mary's connection with the English royal line from Henry VII made her a threat to Elizabeth I's hold on the English throne, especially as she represented a champion of the Catholic cause. She was married three times. After her forced abdication she was imprisoned but escaped 1568 to England. Elizabeth I held her prisoner, while the Roman Catholics, who regarded Mary as rightful queen of England, formed many conspiracies to place her on the throne, and for complicity in one of these she was executed.

Mary's mother was the French Mary of Guise. Born in Linlithgow (now in Lothian region, Scotland), Mary was sent to France, where she married the dauphin, later Francis II. After his death she returned to Scotland 1561, which, during her absence, had turned Protestant. She married her cousin, the Earl of ◊Darnley, 1565, but they soon quarrelled, and Darnley took part in the murder of Mary's secretary, ◊Rizzio. In 1567 Darnley was assassinated as the result of a conspiracy formed by the Earl of ◊Bothwell, possibly with Mary's connivance, and shortly after Bothwell married her. A rebellion followed; defeated at Carberry Hill, Mary abdicated and was imprisoned. She escaped 1568, raised an army, and after its defeat at Langside fled to England, only to be imprisoned again. A plot against Elizabeth I devised by Anthony Babington led to her trial and execution at Fotheringay Castle 1587.

In my end is my beginning.

Mary Queen of Scots her motto

Mary Duchess of Burgundy 1457–1482. Daughter of Charles the Bold. She married Maximilian of Austria 1477, thus bringing the Low Countries into the possession of the Habsburgs and, ultimately, of Spain.

Mary two queens of England:

Mary I *Bloody Mary* 1516–1558. Queen of England from 1553. She was the eldest daughter of Henry VIII by Catherine of Aragon. When Edward VI died, Mary secured the crown without difficulty in spite of the conspiracy to substitute Lady Jane ◊Grey. In 1554 Mary married Philip II of Spain, and as a devout Roman Catholic obtained the restoration of papal supremacy and sanctioned the persecution of Protestants. She was succeeded by her half-sister Elizabeth I.

Mary II 1662–1694. Queen of England, Scotland, and Ireland from 1688. She was the Protestant elder daughter of the Catholic ◊James II, and in 1677 was married to her cousin ◊William III of Orange. After the 1688 revolution she accepted the crown jointly with William.

During his absences from England she took charge of the government, and showed courage and resource when invasion seemed possible 1690 and 1692.

Masaryk Jan (Garrigue) 1886–1948. Czechoslovak politician, son of Tomás Masaryk. He was foreign minister from 1940, when the Czechoslovak government was exiled in London in World War II. He returned 1945, retaining the post, but as a result of political pressure by the communists committed suicide.

Masaryk Tomáš (Garrigue) 1850–1937. Czechoslovak nationalist politician. He directed the revolutionary movement against the Austrian Empire, founding with Eduard Beneş and Stefanik the Czechoslovak National Council, and in 1918 was elected first president of the newly formed Czechoslovak Republic. Three times re-elected, he resigned 1935 in favour of Beneş.

Mashonaland eastern ◊Zimbabwe, the land of the Shona people, now divided into three administrative regions (Mashonaland East, Mashonaland Central, and Mashonaland West). Granted to the British South Africa Company 1889, it was included in Southern Rhodesia 1923. The ◊Zimbabwe ruins are here.

Mason–Dixon Line in the USA, the boundary line between Maryland and Pennsylvania, named after Charles Mason (1730–1787) and Jeremiah Dixon (died 1777), English astronomers and surveyors who surveyed it 1763–67. It was popularly seen as dividing the North from the South.

Massasoit also known as Ousamequin, 'Yellow Feather' *c.* 1590–1661. American chief of the Wampanoag, a people inhabiting the coasts of Massachusetts Bay and Cape Cod. He formed alliances with Plymouth Colony 1621 and Massachusetts Bay Colony 1638. After his death, his son Metacomet, known to the English as 'King ◊Philip', took over his father's leadership.

Masséna André 1756–1817. Marshal of France. He served in the French Revolutionary Wars and under the emperor Napoleon was created marshal 1804, duke of Rivoli 1808, and prince of Essling 1809. He was in command in Spain 1810–11 in the Peninsular War and was defeated by British troops under Wellington.

Massey Vincent 1887–1967. Canadian Liberal Party politician. He was the first Canadian to become governor general of Canada (1952–59).

He helped to establish the Massey Foundation 1918 which funded the building of Massey College and the University of Toronto.

Massey William Ferguson 1856–1925. New Zealand politician, born in Ireland; prime minister 1912–25. He led the Reform Party, an offshoot of the Conservative Party, and as prime minister before World War I concentrated on controlling militant unions and the newly formed Federation of Labour.

Matabeleland western portion of ◊Zimbabwe between the Zambezi and Limpopo rivers, inhabited by the Ndebele people.

Mata Hari Stage name of Gertrud Margarete Zelle 1876–1917. Dutch courtesan, dancer, and probable spy. In World War I she had affairs with highly placed military and government officials on both sides and told Allied secrets to the Germans. She may have been a double agent, in the pay of both France and Germany. She was shot by the French on espionage charges.

Mather Increase 1639–1723. American colonial and religious leader. As a defender of the colonial right to self-government, he went to England 1688 to protest revocation of the Massachusetts charter. However, his silence during the Salem witch trials of 1692 lessened his public influence.

Matilda (Empress Maud) 1102–1167. Claimant to the throne of England. On the death of her father, Henry I, 1135, the barons elected her cousin Stephen to be king. Matilda invaded England 1139, and was crowned by her supporters 1141. Civil war ensued until Stephen was finally recognized as king 1153, with Henry II (Matilda's son) as his successor.

Matsudaira Tsuneo 1877–1949. Japanese diplomat and politician who became the first chair of the Japanese Diet (parliament) after World War II. He negotiated for Japan at the London Naval Conference of 1930 and acted as imperial household minister 1936–45, advising the emperor, but was unsuccessful in keeping Japan out of a war with the Western powers.

Matsukata Masayoshi, Prince 1835–1924. Japanese politician, premier 1891–92 and 1896–98. As minister of finance 1881–91 and 1898–1900, he paved the way for the modernization of the Japanese economy.

Matsuoka Yosuke 1880–1946. Japanese politician, foreign minister 1940–41. A fervent nationalist, Matsuoka led Japan out of the League of Nations when it condemned Japan for the seizure of Manchuria. As foreign minister, he allied Japan with Germany and Italy. At the end of World War II, he was arrested as a war criminal but died before his trial.

Matthias Corvinus 1440–1490. King of Hungary from 1458. His aim of uniting Hungary, Austria, and Bohemia involved him in long wars with Holy Roman emperor Frederick III and the kings of Bohemia and Poland, during which he captured Vienna (1485) and made it his capital. His father was János ◊Hunyadi.

Mau Mau Kenyan secret guerrilla movement 1952–60, an offshoot of the Kikuyu Central Association banned in World War II. Its aim was to end British colonial rule. This was achieved 1960 with the granting of Kenyan independence and the election of Jomo Kenyatta as Kenya's first prime minister.

A state of emergency was declared 1952, and by 1956 colonial government forces had killed more than 11,000 Kikuyu. More than 100 Europeans and Asians and 2,000 progovernment Kikuyu were killed by the Mau Mau. The state of emergency was ended 1960, and three years later Kenya achieved independence.

Mauritania country in NW Africa, bounded NE by Algeria, E and S by Mali, SW by Senegal, W by the Atlantic Ocean, and NW by Western Sahara.

history Mauritania was the name of the Roman province of NW Africa, after the Mauri, a ◊Berber people who inhabited it. Berbers occupied the region during the 1st–3rd centuries AD, and it came under the control of the Ghana Empire (see ◊Ghana, ancient) in the 7th–11th centuries. The Berbers were converted to Islam from the 8th century, and Islamic influence continued to dominate as the area was controlled by the ◊Almoravids and then the Arabs. French influence began in the 17th century, with the trade in gum arabic, and developed into colonization by the mid-18th century, when France gained control of S Mauritania.

independence In 1920 Mauritania became a French colony as part of French West Africa. It achieved internal self-government within the French Community 1958 and full independence 1960. Moktar Ould Daddah, leader of the PPM, became president 1961.

Western Sahara conflict In 1975 Spain ceded Western Sahara to Mauritania and Morocco, leaving them to decide how to share it. Without consulting the Saharan people, Mauritania occupied the south, leaving the north to

Morocco. A resistance movement developed against this occupation, the Popular Front for Liberation, or the Polisario Front, with Algerian backing, and Mauritania and Morocco found themselves engaged in a guerrilla war, forcing the two former rivals into a mutual defence pact. The conflict weakened Mauritania's economy, and in 1978 President Daddah was deposed in a bloodless coup led by Col Mohamed Khouna Ould Haidalla. Peace with the Polisario was eventually agreed Aug, allowing diplomatic relations with Algeria to be restored.

PPM banned The only political party, the Mauritanian People's Party (PPM), was banned 1978, and some of its exiled supporters now operate from Paris through the Alliance for a Democratic Mauritania (AMI), or from Dakar, in Senegal, through the Organization of Nationalist Mauritanians.

Taya takes over in military coup In Dec 1984, while Col Haidalla was attending a Franco-African summit meeting in Burundi, Col Maaouia Ould Sid Ahmed Taya, a former prime minister, led a bloodless coup to overthrow him. Diplomatic relations with Morocco were broken 1981 and the situation worsened 1984 when Mauritania formally recognized the Polisario regime in Western Sahara. Normal relations were restored 1985. During 1989 there were a number of clashes with Senegalese in border areas resulting in the death of at least 450 people. The presidents of the two countries met to try to resolve their differences. Citizens of each country were forced to return to their native country, with nearly 50,000 people repatriating by June. In 1991 there were calls for the resignation of President Taya, despite the promise of multiparty elections and the amnesty granted to political prisoners.

multiparty system approved Voters approved a new constitution Aug 1991 that increased political freedom, and opposition parties were legalized. Taya formed the Democratic and Social Republican Party (PRDS) as his main political vehicle. The first multiparty elections for the presidency were held Jan 1992 and for the assembly March 1992. Alleging ballot rigging, the opposition parties boycotted the March 1992 elections, allowing the ruling PRDS a clear win. In April 1992 diplomatic relations with Senegal, severed 1989, were restored.

Mauritius island country in the Indian Ocean, E of Madagascar.

history Uninhabited until the 16th century, the island was colonized on a small scale by the Dutch, who named it Mauricius after Prince Maurice of Nassau. They abandoned it 1710, and in 1715 it was occupied by the French, who imported African slaves to work on their sugarcane plantations. Mauritius was seized by Britain 1810 and was formally ceded by Treaty of ◊Paris 1814. The abolition of slavery 1833 brought about the importation of indentured labourers from India, whose descendants now make up about 70% of the island's population. In 1957 Mauritius achieved internal self-government, and full independence within the Commonwealth 1968.

succession of coalition governments Seewoosagur Ramgoolam, leader of the Mauritius Labour Party (MLP), who had led the country since 1959, became its first prime minister. During the 1970s he led a succession of coalition governments, and even in 1976, when the Mauritius Militant Movement (MMM) became the assembly's largest single party, Ramgoolam formed another fragile coalition. Dissatisfaction with the government's economic policies led to Ramgoolam's defeat and the formation in 1982 of an MMM–Mauritius Socialist Party (PSM) coalition government led by Aneerood Jugnauth. Strains developed within the alliance, 12 MMM ministers resigned 1983, and the coalition was dissolved. Jugnauth then founded the Mauritius Socialist Movement (MSM), and the PSM was incorporated in the new party. A general election later that year resulted in an MSM–MLP–Mauritius Social Democratic Party (PMSD) coalition. Jugnauth became prime minister on the understanding that Sir Seewoosagur Ramgoolam would be president if Mauritius became a republic. When the constitutional change failed to get legislative approval, Sir Seewoosagur Ramgoolam was appointed governor general 1983. He died 1985, and former finance minister Sir Veerasamy Ringadoo replaced him.

On the strength of economic policies that cut inflation and unemployment, Aneerood Jugnauth was re-elected 1987. In Aug 1990 an attempt by Jugnauth to make the country a republic was narrowly defeated in the legislative assembly.

Jugnauth coalition re-elected The ruling coalition headed by Jugnauth secured an overwhelming majority in the Sept 1991 general election. In March 1992 the country became a republic but still remained a member of the Commonwealth. Ringadoo became interim president.

foreign policy Mauritius, which has no standing army, has pursued a moderately nonaligned foreign policy during recent years.

Mauryan dynasty Indian dynasty *c.* 321–*c.* 185 BC, founded by *Chandragupta Maurya* (321–*c.* 279 BC). Under Emperor ◊Asoka most of India was united for the first time, but after his death 232 the empire was riven by dynastic disputes. Reliant on a highly organized aristocracy and a centralized administration, it survived until the assassination of Emperor Brihadratha 185 BC and the creation of the Sunga dynasty.

The empire's core lay in the former ◊janapada of Magadha, situated in the Ganges valley of N India, near plentiful iron ore supplies and with its capital at Pataliputra (now Patna). Chandragupta and his son Bindusara (ruled *c.* 268–231 BC) expanded it to the W and S, and there was consolidation under Asoka. Divided into four provinces, each headed by a prince, the empire was noted for its comparatively advanced bureaucracy, and its encouragement of cultivation and commerce through public works and fiscal measures.

Maximilian 1832–1867. Emperor of Mexico 1864–67. He accepted that title when the French emperor Napoleon III's troops occupied the country, but encountered resistance from the deposed president Benito ◊Juárez. In 1866, after the French troops withdrew on the insistence of the USA, Maximilian was captured by Mexican republicans and shot.

Maximilian I 1459–1519. Holy Roman emperor from 1493, the son of Emperor Frederick III. He had acquired the Low Countries through his marriage to Mary of Burgundy 1477.

May 4th movement Chinese student-led nationalist movement ignited by demonstrations in Beijing 1919. It demanded that China's unpopular warlord government reject the decision by the Versailles peace conference to confirm Japan's rights over the Shandong peninsula that had been asserted in the ◊twenty-one demands 1915.

The students won mass workers' support in Beijing, a boycott of Japanese goods, and stimulated an intellectual revolution, the New Culture movement. Influenced by Marxist and liberal ideas, this stimulated the subsequent creation of the Chinese Communist Party. The 70th anniversary of the May 4th movement was marked by mass prodemocracy demonstrations in ◊Tiananmen Square, Beijing, 1989.

Maya member of an American Indian civilization originating in the Yucatán Peninsula in Central America about 2600 BC, with later sites in Mexico, Guatemala, and Belize, and enjoying a classical period AD 325–925, after which it declined.

Maya civilizations The old empire of the Maya was based on scattered cities in a forested area. The chief of these was Uaxactun, followed in growth and importance by Tikal and Palenque. After 600 years this peaceful federation gave way to the new empire which produced flourishing cities such as Chichén Itzá, with its temple-pyramids, court of 1,000 columns, and observatory tower. The period of the new empire was one in which wars, inter-city strife, and pestilence gradually weakened the Maya, making them easy prey for the first Spanish invaders.

The Maya constructed stone buildings and stepped pyramids without metal tools; used hieroglyphic writing in manuscripts, of which only three survive; were skilled potters, weavers, and farmers; and regulated their rituals and warfare by observations of the planet Venus.

Mayflower the ship in which the ◊Pilgrims sailed 1620 from Plymouth, England, to found Plymouth plantation and Plymouth colony in present-day Massachusetts.

Mayor of the Palace administrator of the royal court of the ◊Merovingian dynasty from 439 to 751. After the death of Dagobert I (605–639) and the subsequent decline of the Merovingian kings, holders of this office became, in effect, rulers of the kingdom and established a hereditary succession until 751, when the Carolingian line began with ◊Pepin the Short.

Mayotte or *Mahore* island group of the ◊Comoros, off the east coast of Africa, a *collectivité territoriale* of France by its own wish. A French colony 1843–1914, and later, with the Comoros, an overseas territory of France. In 1974, Mayotte voted to remain a French dependency.

Mazarin Jules 1602–1661. French politician who succeeded Richelieu as chief minister of France 1642. His attack on the power of the nobility led to the ◊Fronde and his temporary exile, but his diplomacy achieved a successful conclusion to the Thirty Years' War, and, in alliance with Oliver Cromwell during the British protectorate, he gained victory over Spain.

Mazzini Giuseppe 1805–1872. Italian nationalist. He was a member of the revolutionary society, the ◊Carbonari, and founded in exile the nationalist movement Giovane Italia (Young Italy) 1832. Returning to Italy on the outbreak of the 1848 revolution, he headed a republican government established in Rome, but was forced into exile again on its overthrow 1849. He acted as a focus for the movement for Italian unity (see ◊Risorgimento).

Mboya Tom 1930–1969. Kenyan politician, a founder of the Kenya African National Union (◊KANU), and minister of economic affairs from 1964 until his assassination.

Meade George Gordon 1815–1872. US military leader. During the American Civil War, he commanded the Pennsylvania volunteers at the Peninsular Campaign, Bull Run, and Antietam 1862. He led the Army of the Potomac, and the Union forces at Gettysburg 1863. After the war, he served as military governor of Georgia, Alabama, and Florida 1868–69.

Mecca (Arabic *Makkah*) city in Saudi Arabia and, as birthplace of Muhammad, the holiest city of the Islamic world. In the centre of Mecca is the Great Mosque, in the courtyard of which is the Kaaba, the sacred shrine containing the black stone believed to have been given to Abraham by the angel Gabriel.

Mecca Declaration pledge by Islamic powers in 1981 to undertake a ◊Jihad against Israel.

Mede member of a people of NW Iran who in the 9th century BC were tributaries to Assyria, with their capital at Ecbatana (now Hamadán), in the ancient SW Asian country of Media. Allying themselves with Babylon, they destroyed the Assyrian capital of Nineveh 612 BC, and extended their conquests into central Anatolia. In 550 BC they were overthrown by the Persians, with whom they rapidly merged.

Medes and Persians

c. 1400 BC	Settlement of Medes in Iran began.
c. 836	Media and Assyria came into conflict.
c. 700	Beginning of Achaemenian influence in Persia under Median overlordship.
c. 673	Kashtarito united the Medes and made Hamadan their centre.
647–25	Reign of Phraortese. Scythian and Cimmerian incursions.
625–585	Reign of Cyaxares. Median empire founded. Cimmerians and Scythians driven out.
614–12	With Babylonian allies, Cyaxares conquered Assyria.
585	Accession of Astyages, son of Cyaxares. Growth of Zoroastrianism. Frontier with Lydia fixed.
559	Cyrus II, a Persian vassal of the Medes, revolted against Median rule.
550	Death of Astyages. Cyrus now undisputed ruler of Media.
546	Cyrus defeated Croesus of Lydia and extended his influence over W Asia Minor.
539	Cyrus conquered Babylonia.
529	Cyrus killed fighting in E Iran. Cambyses II acceded to the throne.
525	Persians conquered Egypt and advanced into Nubia.
522	Cambyses II died, succeeded by his son-in-law Darius I, who reformed the empire.
494	Greek revolt in W Asia Minor suppressed.
490	Persians defeated by Greeks at Marathon.
486	Darius I died, having subdued Thrace and Macedonia, and extended Persian influence into Egypt, the lower Danube, and the Indus valley. Xerxes I began his reign.
480–79	Failure of Greek campaign led to internal disorder and decrease in centralized power.
464	Xerxes died, succeeded by Artaxerxes I (died 423).
449	Peace of Callias. Persians agreed to leave Asiatic Greeks free and keep out of Aegean.
423–404	Reign of Darius II.
404–358	Reign of Artaxerxes II.
387	Greeks conceded W Asia Minor to Persia.
358–338	Reign of Artaxerxes III.
336–330	Reign of Darius III ended with his assassination and Persia's absorption into the Macedonian empire of Alexander the Great.

Medici noble family of Florence, the city's rulers from 1434 until they died out 1737. Family members included ◊Catherine de' Medici, Pope ◊Leo X, Pope Clement VII, ◊Marie de' Medici.

Medici Cosimo de' 1389–1464. Italian politician and banker. Regarded as the model for Machiavelli's *The Prince*, he dominated the government of Florence from 1434 and was a patron of the arts. He was succeeded by his inept son *Piero de' Medici* (1416–1469).

Medici Cosimo de' 1519–1574. Italian politician, ruler of Florence; duke of Florence from 1537 and 1st grand duke of Tuscany from 1569.

We read that we ought to forgive our enemies; but we do not read that we ought to forgive our friends.

Cosimo de' Medici

Medici Ferdinand de' 1549–1609. Italian politician, grand duke of Tuscany from 1587.

Medici Giovanni de' 1360–1429. Italian entrepreneur and banker, with political influence in Florence as a supporter of the popular party. He was the father of Cosimo de' Medici.

Medici Lorenzo de', *the Magnificent* 1449–1492. Italian politician, ruler of Florence from 1469. He was also a poet and a generous patron of the arts.

Medina (Arabic *Madinah*) Saudi Arabian city, about 355 km/220 mi N of Mecca. It is the second holiest city in the Islamic world, and is believed to contain the tomb of Muhammad. It also contains the tombs of the caliphs or Muslim leaders Abu Bakr, Omar, and Fatima, Muhammad's daughter.

Megiddo site of a fortress town in N Israel, where Thothmes III defeated the Canaanites about 1469 BC; the Old Testament figure Josiah was killed in battle about 609 BC; and in World War I the British field marshal Allenby broke the Turkish front 1918.

Mehemet Ali 1769–1849. Pasha (governor) of Egypt from 1805, and founder of the dynasty that ruled until 1953. An Albanian in the Ottoman service, he had originally been sent to Egypt to fight the French. As pasha, he established a European-style army and navy, fought his Turkish overlord 1831 and 1839, and conquered Sudan.

Meiji Mutsuhito 1852–1912. Emperor of Japan from 1867, under the regnal era name Meiji ('enlightened'). During his reign Japan became a world industrial and naval power. His ministers abolished the feudal system and discrimination against the lowest caste, established state schools, reformed the civil service, and introduced conscription, the Western calendar, and other measures to modernize Japan, including a constitution 1889.

He took the personal name Mutsuhito when he became crown prince 1860. He was the son of Emperor Kōmei (reigned 1846–67), who was a titular ruler in the last years of the Tokugawa shogunate.

Meiji era in Japanese history, the reign of Emperor Meiji 1867–1912. It followed the overthrow of the ◊Tokugawa shogunate and was characterized by the building up of a more centralized and westernized modern state.

Meinhof Ulrike 1934–1976. West German urban guerrilla, member of the ◊*Baader-Meinhof gang* in the 1970s.

Mein Kampf (German 'my struggle') book dictated by Adolf ◊Hitler to Rudolf Hess 1923–24 during Hitler's jail sentence for his part in the abortive 1923 Munich ◊beer-hall putsch. Part autobiography, part political philosophy, the book presents Hitler's ideas of German expansion, anticommunism, and anti-Semitism. It was published in two volumes, 1925 and 1927.

Meir Golda 1898–1978. Israeli Labour (*Mapai*) politician. Born in Russia, she emigrated to the USA 1906, and in 1921 went to Palestine. She was foreign minister 1956–66 and prime minister 1969–74. Criticism of the Israelis' lack of preparation for the 1973 Arab-Israeli War led to election losses for Labour and, unable to form a government, she resigned.

Melanchthon Philip. Assumed name of Philip Schwarzerd 1497–1560. German theologian who helped Luther prepare a German translation of the New Testament. In 1521 he issued the first systematic formulation of Protestant theology, reiterated in the *Confession of* ◊*Augsburg* 1530.

Melbourne William Lamb, 2nd Viscount 1779–1848. British Whig politician. Home secretary 1830–34, he was briefly prime minister in 1834 and again 1835–41. Accused in 1836 of seducing Caroline Norton, he lost the favour of William IV.

Melchite or *Melkite* member of a Christian church in Syria, Egypt, Lebanon, and Israel. The Melchite Church was founded in Syria in the 6th–7th centuries and is now part of the Eastern Orthodox Church.

The Melchites accepted Byzantine rule at the council of Chalcedon 451 (unlike the ◊Maronites). In 1754 some Melchites broke away to form a Uniate Church with Rome.

Melgarejo Mariano c. 1820–1871. Bolivian dictator and most notorious of the ◊caudillos who dominated 19th-century Bolivia. Melgarejo seized power 1864 and survived a series of rebellions before he was overthrown by the last in a series of military uprisings seven years later.

Melgarejo sold disputed land to Brazil, allowed Chilean businessmen to exploit Bolivian nitrate deposits, and seized large tracts of Indian land in the Altiplano (high plateau) to be sold to the highest bidder. This policy deprived virtually all Indians in the area of their land within a few decades.

Mendes Chico (Filho Francisco) 1944–1988. Brazilian environmentalist and labour leader. Opposed to the destruction of Brazil's rainforests, he organized itinerant rubber-tappers into the Workers' Party (PT) and was assassinated by Darci Alves, a cattle rancher's son. Of 488 similar murders in land conflicts in Brazil 1985–89, his was the first to come to trial.

Mendès-France Pierre 1907–1982. French prime minister and foreign minister 1954–55. He extricated France from the war in Indochina, and prepared the way for Tunisian independence.

Mendoza Antonio de c. 1490–1552. First Spanish viceroy of New Spain (Mexico) 1535–51. He attempted to develop agriculture and mining and supported the church in its attempts to convert the Indians. The system he established lasted until the 19th century. He was subsequently viceroy of Peru 1551–52.

Menelik II 1844–1913. Negus (emperor) of Abyssinia (now Ethiopia) from 1889. He defeated the Italians 1896 at ◊Aduwa and thereby retained the independence of his country.

Menéndez de Avilés Pedro 1519–1574. Spanish colonial administrator in America. Philip II of Spain granted him the right to establish a colony in Florida to counter French presence there. In 1565 he founded St Augustine and destroy the French outpost at Fort Caroline.

Menes c. 3200 BC. Traditionally, the first king of the first dynasty of ancient Egypt. He is said to have founded Memphis and organized worship of the gods.

Mennonite member of a Protestant Christian sect, originating as part of the ◊Anabaptist movement in Zürich, Switzerland, 1523. Members refuse to hold civil office or do military service, and reject infant baptism. They were named Mennonites after Menno Simons (1496–1559), leader of a group in Holland. Persecution drove other groups to Russia and North America.

Menshevik (Russian menshinstvo 'minority') member of the minority of the Russian Social Democratic Party, who split from the ◊Bolsheviks 1903. The Mensheviks believed in a large, loosely organized party and that, before socialist revolution could occur in Russia, capitalist society had to develop further. During the Russian Revolution they had limited power and set up a government in Georgia, but were suppressed 1922.

Menzies Robert Gordon 1894–1978. Australian politician, leader of the United Australia (now Liberal) Party and prime minister 1939–41 and 1949–66.

A Melbourne lawyer, he entered politics 1928, was attorney-general in the federal parliament 1934–39, and in 1939 succeeded Joseph Lyons as prime minister and leader of the United Australia Party, resigning 1941 when colleagues were dissatisfied with his leadership of Australia's war effort. In 1949 he became prime minister of a Liberal–Country Party coalition government, and was re-elected 1951, 1954, 1955, 1958, 1961, and 1963; he followed America's lead in committing Australia to the Vietnam War and retired soon after, in 1966. His critics argued that he did not show enough interest in Asia, and supported the USA and white African regimes too uncritically. His defenders argued that he provided stability in domestic policy and national security.

mercantilism economic theory, held in the 16th–18th centuries, that a nation's wealth (in the form of bullion or treasure) was the key to its prosperity. To this end, foreign trade should be regulated to create a surplus of exports over imports, and the state should intervene where necessary (for example, subsidizing exports and taxing imports). The bullion theory of wealth was demolished by Adam Smith in Book IV of *The Wealth of Nations* 1776.

mercenary soldier hired by the army of another country or by a private army. Mercenary military service originated in the 14th century, when cash payment on a regular basis was the only means of guaranteeing soldiers' loyalty. In the 20th century mercenaries have been common in wars and guerrilla activity in Asia, Africa, and Latin America.

Most famous of the mercenary armies was the *Great Company* of the 14th century, which was in effect a glorified protection racket, comprising some 10,000 knights of all nationalities and employing *condottieri*, or contractors, to serve the highest bidder. By the end of the 14th century, condottieri and *freelances* were an institutionalized aspect of warfare. In the 18th century, Swiss cantons and some German states regularly provided the French with troops for mercenary service as a means of raising money; they were regarded as the best forces in the French army. Britain employed 20,000 German mercenaries to make up its numbers during the Seven Years' War 1756–63 and used Hessian forces during the American Revolution 1775–83.

Article 47 of the 1977 Additional Protocols to the Geneva Convention stipulates that 'a mercenary shall not have the right to be a combatant or a prisoner of war' but leaves a party to the Protocols the freedom to grant such status if so wished.

Merchants Adventurers English trading company founded 1407, which controlled the export of cloth to continental Europe. It comprised guilds and traders in many N European ports. In direct opposition to the Hanseatic League, it came to control 75% of English overseas trade by 1550. In 1689 it lost its charter for furthering the traders' own interests at the expense of the English economy. The company was finally dissolved 1806.

Mercia Anglo-Saxon kingdom that emerged in the 6th century. By the late 8th century it dominated all England south of the Humber, but from about 825 came under the power of ♦Wessex. Mercia eventually came to denote an area bounded by the Welsh border, the river Humber, East Anglia, and the river Thames.

Merovingian dynasty Frankish dynasty, named after its founder, *Merovech* (5th century AD). His descendants ruled France from the time of Clovis (481–511) to 751.

Merv oasis in Turkmenistan, a centre of civilization from at least 1200 BC, and site of a town founded by Alexander the Great. Old Merv was destroyed by the emir of Bokhara 1787, and the modern town of Mary, founded by the Russians in 1885, lies 29 km/18 mi to its west.

Meskhetian member of a community of Turkish descent that formerly inhabited Meskhetia, on the then Turkish-Soviet border. They were deported by Stalin 1944 to Kazakhstan and Uzbekistan, and have campaigned since then for a return to their homeland. In June 1989 at least 70 were killed in pogroms directed against their community in the Ferghana Valley of Uzbekistan by the ethnic Uzbeks.

Mesolithic the Middle Stone Age developmental stage of human technology and of ♦prehistory.

Mesopotamia the land between the Tigris and Euphrates rivers, now part of Iraq. Here the civilizations of Sumer and Babylon flourished. Sumer (3500 BC) may have been the earliest urban civilization.

Messalina Valeria *c.* AD 22–48. Third wife of the Roman emperor ♦Claudius. She was notorious for her immorality, forcing a noble to marry her AD 48, although still married to Claudius, who then had her executed.

Metacomet Wampanoag leader better known as King ♦Philip.

Metaxas Ioannis 1870–1941. Greek general and politician, born in Ithaca. He restored ♦George II (1890–1947) as king of Greece, under whom he established a dictatorship as prime minister from 1936, and introduced several necessary economic and military reforms. He led resistance to the Italian invasion of Greece in 1941, refusing to abandon Greece's neutral position.

Methodism evangelical Protestant Christian movement that was founded by John ♦Wesley 1739 within the Church of England, but became a separate body 1795. The Methodist Episcopal Church was founded in the USA 1784. There are over 50 million Methodists worldwide.

Expansion in the 19th century in developing industrial areas enabled people to overcome economic depression or change by spiritual means. Its encouragement of thrift and simple living helped many to raise their economic status. Smaller Methodist groups such as the Primitive Methodists and the Methodist New Connexion provided leadership in early trade unionism in disproportion to their size. Mainstream Wesleyans at first were politically conservative but identified increasingly with Gladstonian liberalism in the second half of the 19th century.

Metternich Klemens (Wenzel Lothar), Prince von Metternich 1773–1859. Austrian politician, the leading figure in European diplomacy after the fall of Napoleon. As foreign minister 1809–48 (as well as chancellor from 1821), he tried to maintain the balance of power in Europe, supporting monarchy and repressing liberalism.

Mexican Empire short-lived empire 1822–23 following the liberation of Mexico from Spain. The empire lasted only eight months, under the revolutionary leader Agustín de ♦Iturbide.

Mesopotamia 4th millennium–539 BC			
c. 4500 BC	Ubaid culture in S Mesopotamia (Iraq).	c. 1500–1350	Mitannian empire established in N Mesopotamia. Assyria was subject to Mitannians.
c. 3500	Sumerian culture superseded Ubaid. Sumerian language appeared in written form.	c. 1380	Subbuliliuma founded New Hittite Kingdom. Beginning of Assyrian independence and expansion under Ashur- uballit.
c. 2800	Earliest Sumerian dynasty. The city of Kish pre-eminent.	c. 1200	Hittite civilization destroyed.
c. 2500	Dynastic rule established at Ur and Lagash. Assyrians settled on the Upper Tigris.	1150–1110	Reign of Nebuchadnezzar I at Babylon.
c. 2350–2200	Empire of Sargon I of Akkad and his dynasty, covering Mesopotamia, parts of Syria, and Elam. Akkadian language replaced Sumerian.	c. 1120–1075	Reign of Tiglath-pileser I in Assyria. Assyrian influence spread to Syria.
c. 2150	Akkadian dynasty finally overthrown by Gutians (from E) and Amorites (from N).	860	Death of Ashurnazirpal II, whose campaigns were commemorated on relief sculptures at Calah.
c. 2050	Akkadian rule restored as the 3rd dynasty of Ur under Ur-Nammu. First legal code introduced.	859–824	Reign of Shalmaneser III of Assyria.
c. 1950	Decline of Ur.	746–728	Under the reign of Tiglath-pileser III, Assyria dominated N Syria, Damascus, and Phoenicia. Assyrian capital established at Nineveh.
c. 1800	Assyrians gained control of territory N of Babylon. Trade with Anatolia.	722–705	Reign of Sargon II of Assyria.
c. 1800–1750	Reign of Hammurabi, during which Babylon unified most of Sumeria. Legal code of Hammurabi.	669	Death of Esarhaddon, whose reign marked the height of Assyrian power.
c. 1640	Labarnas founded the Old Hittite Kingdom.	612	Destruction of Nineveh by the Medes.
c. 1595	Hittites sacked Babylon.	604–562	New Babylonian Empire formed under Nebuchadnezzar II.
c. 1500–1150	Kassites from W became dominant in Babylonia.	587	Babylonians destroyed Jerusalem.
		539	Babylon conquered by Cyrus the Great, and became a province of the Persian empire.

When the French emperor Napoleon I put his brother Joseph on the Spanish throne in 1808, links between Spain and its colonies weakened and an independence movement grew in Mexico. There were several unsuccessful uprisings until, in 1821, General Agustín de Iturbide published a plan promising independence, protection for the church, and the establishment of a monarchy. As no European came forward, he proclaimed himself emperor 1822. Forced to abdicate, he went into exile; on his return to Mexico he was shot by republican leaders Guadalupe Victoria and Santa Anna. Victoria became the first president of Mexico.

Mexican War war between the USA and Mexico 1846–48, begun in territory disputed between Texas (annexed by the USA 1845 but claimed by Mexico) and Mexico. It began when General Zachary Taylor invaded New Mexico after efforts to purchase what are now California and New Mexico failed. Mexico City was taken 1847, and under the Treaty of Guadaloupe Hidalgo that ended the war, the USA acquired New Mexico and California, as well as clear title to Texas in exchange for $15 million.

Mexico country in Central America, bounded N by the USA, E by the Gulf of Mexico, SE by Belize and Guatemala, and SW and W by the Pacific Ocean.

history Mexico was the region of the New World where many civilizations developed, including the Olmec, Maya, Toltec, Mixtec, Zapotec, and the Aztec, who settled on the central plateau and whose last king, Montezuma II, was killed 1520 during the Spanish conquest. The indigenous population was reduced from 21 million in 1519 to 1 million by 1607, with many deaths from Old World diseases to which they had no resistance.

In 1535 Mexico became the viceroyalty of New Spain. Spanish culture and Catholicism were established, and the country's natural resources were exploited. Colonial rule became increasingly oppressive; the struggle for independence began 1810, and Spanish rule was ended 1821. The ◊Mexican Empire followed 1822–23.

Mexican War Mexico's early history as an independent nation was marked by civil and foreign wars and was dominated until 1855 by the dictator Antonio López de ◊Santa Anna.

The US annexation of Texas 1835 brought about the ◊Mexican War 1846-48, in the course of which Mexico suffered further losses, including New Mexico and California. Santa Anna was overthrown 1855 by Benito Juárez, whose liberal reforms included many anticlerical measures.

Habsburg rule In 1861, enticed by the offer of 30% of the proceeds, France planned to intervene in the recovery of 79 million francs owed to a Swiss banker by former Mexican president Miramon, who was overthrown and exiled by Juárez 1860. Seeking to regain power, in 1862 Miramon appealed to Empress Eugénie, consort of Napoleon III, saying that steps must be taken against Juárez and his anti-Christian policies. Eugénie proposed ◊Maximilian, the brother of Emperor Franz-Joseph of Austria. Napoleon agreed, since the plan suited his colonial ambitions, and in 1864 Maximilian accepted the crown offered him by conservative opponents of Juárez. Juárez and his supporters continued to fight against this new branch of the Habsburg empire, and in 1867 the mon-archy collapsed and Maximilian was executed.

gradual reform There followed a capitalist dictatorship under General Porfirio Diaz, who gave the country stability but whose handling of the economy made him unpopular. He was overthrown 1910 by Madero, who re-established a liberal regime but was himself assassinated 1913. The 1910 revolution brought changes in land ownership, labour legislations, and reduction in the powers of the Roman Catholic Church. After a brief period of civil war 1920, Mexico experienced gradual agricultural, political, and social reforms. In 1938 all foreign-owned oil wells were nationalized; compensation was not agreed until 1941. The years after Diaz were marked by political and military strife with the USA, culminating in the unsuccessful US expedition 1916–17 to kill the revolutionary Francisco 'Pancho' Villa (1877–1923).

PRI domination The broadly based Institutional Revolutionary Party (PRI) has dominated Mexican politics since the 1920s, pursuing moderate, left-of-centre policies. Its popularity has been damaged in recent years by the country's poor economic performance and rising international debts. However, despite criticisms from vested-interest groups such as the trade unions and the church, the PRI scored a clear win in the 1985 elections. The government's problems grew worse later that year when an earthquake in Mexico City caused thousands of deaths and made hundreds of thousands homeless.

PRI under challenge The PRI faced its strongest challenge to date in the 1988 elections. Despite claims of fraud during the elections, the PRI candidate, Carlos Salinas de Gortari, was declared president by the electoral college. He subsequently led campaigns against corrupt trade unions and drug traffickers. President Salinas also worked closely with the Bush administration to negotiate debt reductions. In 1991, amid claims of ballot rigging, the PRI decisively won the general elections. In Nov 1991, President Salinas promised widespread constitutional reforms that would affect education, agriculture, and the church. In 1992 public outrage followed a gas sewer-line explosion in Mexico's second largest city, Guadalajara, in April, in which 194 died and 1,400 were injured. In July 1992 state-governor elections, the PRI suffered its second defeat in 63 years in Chihuahua state, losing to a PAN candidate.

foreign policy Mexico's foreign policy has been influenced by its proximity to the USA. At times the Mexican government has criticized US policy in Central America, and as a member, with Colombia, Panama, and Venezuela, of the ◊Contadora Group, has argued for the withdrawal of all foreign advisers from the region.

Mfecane in African history, a series of disturbances in the early 19th century among communities in what is today the eastern part of South Africa. They arose when chief ◊Shaka conquered the Nguni peoples between the Tugela and Pongola rivers, then created by conquest a centralized, militaristic Zulu kingdom from several communities, resulting in large-scale displacement of people.

Michael Mikhail Fyodorovich Romanov 1596–1645. Tsar of Russia from 1613. He was elected tsar by a national assembly, at a time of chaos and foreign invasion, and was the first of the Romanov dynasty, which ruled until 1917.

Middle Ages period of European history between the fall of the Roman Empire in the 5th century and the Renaissance in the 15th. Among the period's distinctive features were the unity of W Europe within the Roman Catholic Church, the feudal organization of political, social, and economic relations, and the use of art for largely religious purposes.

It can be divided into three subperiods:
The *early Middle Ages*, 5th–11th centuries, when Europe was settled by pagan Germanic tribes who adopted the vestiges of Roman institutions and traditions, were converted to Christianity by the church (which had preserved Latin culture after the fall of Rome), and who then founded feudal kingdoms;

The *high Middle Ages*, 12th–13th centuries, which saw the consolidation of feudal states, the expansion of European influence during the ◊Crusades, the flowering of scholasticism and monasteries, and the growth of population and trade;

The *later Middle Ages*, 14th–15th centuries, when Europe was devastated by the ◊Black Death and incessant warfare, ◊feudalism was transformed under the influence of incipient nation-states and new modes of social and economic organization, and the first voyages of discovery were made.

Middle East indeterminate area now usually taken to include the Balkan States, Egypt, and SW Asia. Until the 1940s, this area was generally called the Near East, and the the term Middle East referred to the area from Iran to Burma (now Myanmar).

Middle Kingdom period of Egyptian history embracing the 11th and 12th dynasties (roughly 2040–1786 BC); Chinese term for China and its empire until 1912, describing its central position in the Far East.

Midway Islands two islands in the Pacific, 1,800 km/1,120 mi NW of Honolulu. They were annexed by the USA 1867, and are now administered by the US Navy. The naval *Battle of Midway* 3–6 June 1942, between the USA and Japan, was a turning point in the Pacific in World War II; the US victory marked the end of Japanese expansion in the Pacific.

Mihailović Draza 1893–1946. Yugoslav soldier, leader of the guerrilla ◊Chetniks of World War II against the German occupation. His feud with Tito's communists led to the withdrawal of Allied support and that of his own exiled government from 1943. He turned for help to the Italians and Germans, and was eventually shot for treason.

mikado (Japanese 'honourable palace gate') title until 1867 of the Japanese emperor, when it was replaced by the term *tennō* ('heavenly sovereign').

Milan (Italian *Milano*) capital of Lombardy, Italy. Settled by the Gauls in the 5th century BC, it was conquered by the Roman consul Marcellus 222 BC to become the Roman city of *Mediolanum*. Under Diocletian, in AD 286 Milan was capital of the Western empire. Destroyed by Attila the Hun 452, and again by the Goths 539, the city regained its power through the political importance of its bishops. It became an autonomous commune 1045; then followed a long struggle for supremacy in Lombardy.

The city was taken by ◊Frederick I (Barbarossa) 1162; only in 1176 were his forces finally defeated, at the battle of Legnano. Milanese forces were again defeated by the emperor at the battle of Cortenuova 1237. In the Guelph-Ghibelline struggle the Visconti family emerged at the head of the Ghibelline faction; they gained power 1277, establishing a dynasty which lasted until 1450 when Francesco Sforza seized control and became duke. The Sforza court marked the high point of Milan as a cultural and artistic centre. Control of the city passed to Louis XII of France 1499, and in 1540 it was annexed by Spain, beginning a long decline. The city was ceded to Austria by the Treaty of ◊Utrecht 1714, and in the 18th century began a period of intellectual enlightenment. Milan was in 1796 taken by Napoleon, who made it the capital of the Cisalpine Republic 1799, and in 1805 capital of the kingdom of Italy until 1814, when it reverted to the Austrians. In 1848, Milan rebelled unsuccessfully (the *Cinque Giornate*/Five Days), and in 1859 was joined to Piedmont.

military-industrial complex conjunction of the military establishment and the arms industry, both inflated by Cold War demands. The phrase was first used by US president and former general Dwight D Eisenhower in 1961 to warn Americans of the potential misplacement of power.

militia body of civilian soldiers, usually with some military training, who are on call in emergencies, distinct from professional soldiers. In Switzerland, the militia is the national defence force, and every able-bodied man is liable for service in it. In the UK the *Territorial Army* and in the USA the *National Guard* have supplanted earlier voluntary militias.

In England in the 9th century King Alfred established the first militia, or *fyrd*, in which every freeman was liable to serve. After the Norman Conquest a feudal levy was established in which landowners were responsible for raising the men required. This in turn led to the increasing use of the general levy by English kings to combat the growing power of the barons. In the 16th century, under such threats as the Spanish Armada, plans for internal defence relied increasingly on the militia, or what came to be called 'trained bands', of the general levy.

After the Restoration, the militia fell into neglect, but it was reorganized in 1757, and was relied upon for home defence during the French wars. In the 19th century it extended its activities, serving in the

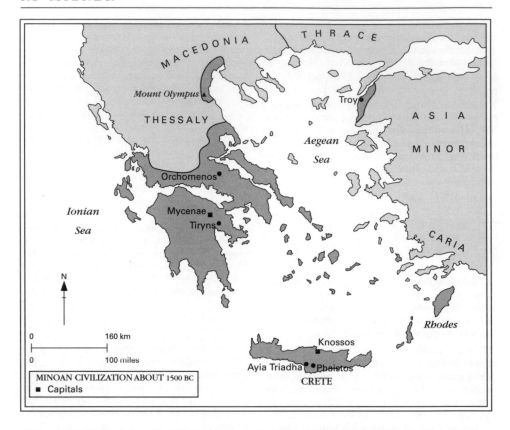

Minoan civilization about 1500 BC *The Minoan civilization lasted c. 3000–1100 BC, and the last period (from c. 1400 BC) was dominated by Mycenae. Both civilizations were agrarian palace cultures of the Bronze Age, with monumental stone citadels prominent in mainland Greece. The deciphering of Linear B tablets proves that the Mycenaeans spoke Greek, and archaeological finds demonstrate that their influence extended by trade and warfare through the Aegean area and beyond.*

Peninsular, Crimean, and South African wars. In 1852 it adopted a volunteer status, and in 1908 it was merged with the Territorial Army and the Special Reserve forces, to supplement the regular army.

Milner Alfred, Viscount Milner 1854-1925. British colonial administrator. He was governor of Cape Colony 1897-1901, governor of the Transvaal and Orange River colonies 1902-05, and joined Lloyd George's war cabinet 1916.

Milošević Slobodan 1941– . Serbian communist politician, party chief and president of Serbia from 1986; re-elected 1990 and 1992 in multiparty elections. Milošević wielded considerable influence over the Serb-dominated Yugoslav federal army during the 1991-92 civil war. He continued to back Serbian militia in BosniaHerzegovina 1992-94, but disclaimed any intention to 'carve up' the newly independent republic. Widely seen as the instigator of the conflict, Milošević changed tactics from

1993, putting pressure on his allies, the Bosnian Serbs, to accept negotiated peace terms; this contributed to the Dayton peace accord for Bosnia-Herzegovina 1995

Minamoto or *Genji* ancient Japanese clan, the members of which were the first ruling shoguns 1192–1219. Their government was based in Kamakura, near present-day Tokyo. After the death of the first shogun, Minamoto Yoritomo (1147–1199), the real power was exercised by the regent for the shogun; throughout the Kamakura period (1192–1333), the regents were of the Hōjō family, a branch of the ⟨∮⟩Taira.

The Minamoto claimed descent from a 9th-century emperor. Minamoto Yoriyoshi (988–1075) was a warlord who built up a power base in the Kanto region when appointed by the court to put down a rebellion there. During the 11th and 12th centuries the Minamoto and the Taira were rivals for power at the court and in the country. The Minamoto emerged victorious in 1185 and Yoritomo received the patent of shogun 1192. Zen teaching and Buddhist sculpture flourished during their shogunate.

Ming dynasty Chinese dynasty 1368–1644, based in Nanjing. During the rule 1402–24 of Yongle (or Yung-lo), there was territorial expansion into Mongolia and Yunnan in the SW. The administrative system was improved, public works were carried out, and foreign trade was developed. Art and literature flourished and distinctive blue and white porcelain was produced.

The Ming dynasty was founded by Zhu Yuanzhang (or Chu Yuan-chang) (1328–1398), a rebel leader who captured the Yuan capital Khanbaligh (modern Beijing) 1368. He set up his headquarters in Nanjing and proclaimed himself Emperor Hong Wu. From the late 16th century, the Ming faced the threat of attack from the NE by Japan, which invaded its tributary Korea 1592. Population pressure also led to peasant rebellions, and decline came with the growth of eunuch power, pressure from Mongols in the N, and an increasing burden of taxes.

Minoan civilization Bronze Age civilization on the Aegean island of Crete. The name is derived from Minos, the legendary king of Crete. The civilization is divided into three main periods: early Minoan, about 3000–2200 BC, middle Minoan, about 2200–1580 BC; and late Minoan, about 1580–1100 BC.

With the opening of the Bronze Age, about 3000 BC, the Minoan culture proper began. Each period was marked by cultural advances in copper and bronze weapons, pottery of increasingly intricate design, frescoes, and the construction of palaces and fine houses at Phaistos and Mallia, in addition to ◊Knossos. About 1400 BC, in the late Minoan period, the civilization was suddenly destroyed by earthquake or war. A partial revival continued until about 1100.

The earlier (Linear A) of two languages used in Crete remains undeciphered; Linear B, which is also found at sites on the mainland of Greece, was deciphered by Michael ◊Ventris.

Minto Gilbert, 4th Earl of 1845–1914. British colonial administrator who succeeded Curzon as viceroy of India, 1905–10. With John Morley, secretary of state for India, he co-sponsored the Morley–Minto reforms of 1909. The reforms increased Indian representation in government at provincial level, but also created separate Muslim and Hindu electorates which, it was believed, helped the British Raj in the policy of divide and rule.

Mintoff Dom(inic) 1916– . Labour prime minister of Malta 1971–84. He negotiated the removal of British and other foreign military bases 1971–79 and made treaties with Libya.

Minuteman a US three-stage intercontinental ballistic missile (ICBM) with a range of about 8,000 km/5,000 mi. In US history the term was applied to members of the citizens' militia in the 1770s. These volunteer soldiers had pledged to be available for battle at a 'minute's notice' during the ◊American Revolution.

mir (Russian 'peace' or 'world') in Russia before the 1917 Revolution, a self-governing village community in which the peasants distributed land and collected taxes.

Mirabeau Honoré Gabriel Riqueti, Comte de 1749–1791. French politician, leader of the National Assembly in the French Revolution. He wanted to establish a parliamentary monarchy on the English model. From May 1790 he secretly acted as political adviser to the king.

Go and tell your master, we are here by the will of the people, and will not leave our places except by the force of bayonets.

Comte de Mirabeau on the States-General being ordered by Louis XVI to leave the hall 1789

---

mission organized attempt to spread a religion. Throughout its history Christianity has been the most assertive of missionary religions; Islam has also played a missionary role. Missionary activity in the Third World has frequently been criticized for its disruptive effects on indigenous peoples and their traditional social, political, and cultural systems.

Missouri Compromise in US history, the solution by Congress (1820–21) of a sectional crisis caused by the 1819 request from Missouri for admission to the union as a slave state, despite its proximity to existing nonslave states. The compromise was the simultaneous admission of Maine as a nonslave state to keep the same ratio.

mita system of forced labour used by Spanish colonies in the Andean regions of South America where Indian communities had to provide labourers to work for the government for fixed periods, most notably in the silver mines where conditions were so bad that many thousands perished.

Mithridates VI Eupator known as *the Great* 132–63 BC. King of Pontus (on the coast of modern Turkey, on the Black Sea), who became the greatest obstacle to Roman expan-

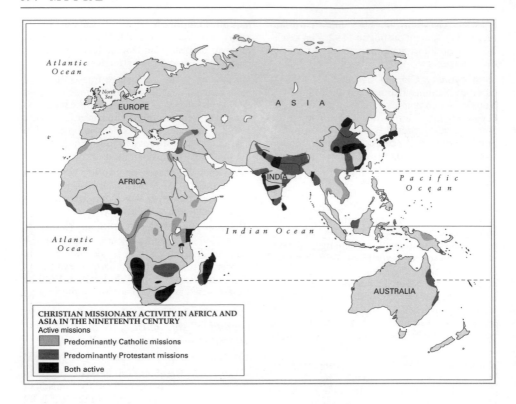

Christian missionary activity in Africa and Asia in the 19th century The 19th century experienced some of the greatest missionary activity, inspired in part by the evangelicalism of the late 18th and early 19th centuries. Missionaries were also helped by the opening of the new trade routes to the interior of Africa and Asia. Great inroads were made in parts of Africa, but in India, SE Asia, and China the already established faiths of Islam, Hinduism, and Buddhism proved more resistant.

sion in the E. He massacred 80,000 Romans in overrunning the rest of Asia Minor and went on to invade Greece. He was defeated by ◊Sulla in the First Mithridatic War 88–84; by ◊Lucullus in the Second 83–81; and by ◊Pompey in the Third 74–64. He was killed by a soldier at his own order.

Mitre Bartólomé 1821–1906. Argentine president 1862–68. In 1852 he helped overthrow the dictatorial regime of Juan Manuel de Rosas, and in 1861 helped unify Argentina. Mitre encouraged immigration and favoured growing commercial links with Europe. He is seen as a symbol of national unity.

Mitterrand François 1916–96. French socialist politician, president 1981–95. He held ministerial posts in 11 governments 1947–58, and founded the French Socialist Party (PS) 1971. In 1985 he introduced proportional representation, allegedly to weaken the growing opposition from left and right. Since 1982 his administrations combined economic orthodoxy with social reform.

Mixtec ancient civilization of pre-colonial Mexico. The Mixtecs succeeded the ◊Zapotecs in the valley of Oaxaca. They founded new towns, including Tilatongo and Teozacualco, and partially rebuilt some Zapotec cities. The Mixtecs produced history books dating from 692 which contain biographies of rulers and noblemen. They were skilled in the use of metals, including gold and silver.

Moab ancient country in Jordan east of the southern part of the river Jordan and the Dead Sea. The inhabitants were closely akin to the Hebrews in culture, language, and religion, but were often at war with them, as recorded in the Old Testament. Moab eventually fell to Arab invaders. The *Moabite Stone*, discovered 1868 at Dhiban, dates from the 9th century BC and records the rising of Mesha, king of Moab, against Israel.

Mobutu Sese Seko Kuku Ngbeandu Wa Za Banga 1930–97. Zairean president 1965-97. He assumed the presidency in a coup, and created a unitary state under a centralized

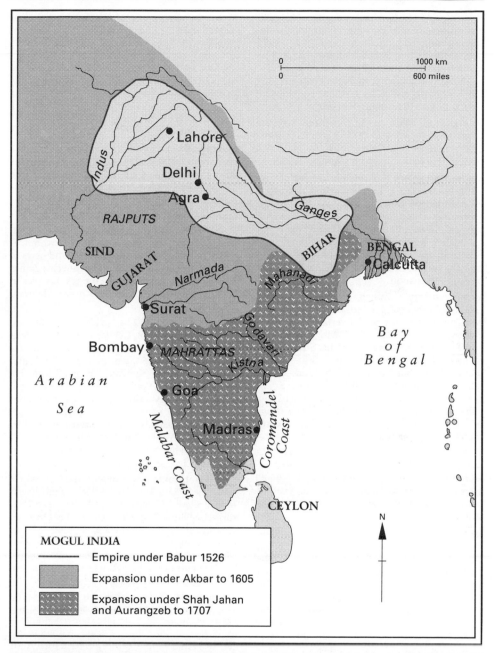

Mogul India *The Mogul empire impressed visiting Europeans through its sheer scale and artistic splendour. Established by Zahir ('Babur'), it was confined initially to the fertile Ganges valley of N India, the core region of the subcontinent. The rich lands of Gujarat in W India were incorporated under Akbar. Further southwards expansion occurred under Shah Jahan and Aurangzeb. Ultimately the empire became politically and militarily overextended and from the late 17th century encountered internal revolts in the Punjab, near Delhi, and a Maratha-led insurrection in the Deccan, east of Bombay.*

government. The harshness of some of his policies and charges of corruption attracted widespread international criticism. In 1991 opposition leaders forced Mobutu to agree formally to give up some of his powers.

Mobutu's tenure as president ended May 1997 when rebels led by Laurent Kabila were poised to take the capital, Kinshasha.

Moche or *Mochica* pre-Inca civilization on the coast of Peru AD 100–800. Remains include cities, massive platform tombs (*adobe*), and pottery that details daily and ceremonial life.

Model Parliament English parliament set up 1295 by Edward I; it was the first to include representatives from outside the clergy and aristocracy, and was established because Edward needed the support of the whole country against his opponents: Wales, France, and Scotland. His sole aim was to raise money for military purposes, and the parliament did not pass any legislation.

Mogul dynasty N Indian dynasty 1526–1858, established by ◊Zahir ud-Din Muhammad, Muslim descendant of Tamerlane, the 14th-century Mongol leader. The Mogul emperors ruled until the last one, ◊Bahadur Shah II, was dethroned and exiled by the British; they included ◊Akbar, ◊Aurangzeb, and ◊Shah Jahan. The Moguls established a more extensive and centralized empire than their ◊Delhi sultanate forebears, and the Mogul era was one of great artistic achievement, urban, and commercial development.

Mohács, Battle of Austro-Hungarian defeat of the Turks 1687, which effectively marked the end of Turkish expansion into Europe. Named after the river port of that name on the Danube in Hungary, which is also the site of a Turkish victory 1526.

Mohamad Mahathir bin 1925– . Prime minister of Malaysia from 1981 and leader of the United Malays' National Organization (UMNO). His 'look east' economic policy emulates Japanese industrialization.

Mahathir bin Mohamad was elected to the House of Representatives 1964 and gained the support of the dominant UMNO's radical youth wing as an advocate of economic help to *bumiputras* (ethnic Malays) and as a proponent of a more Islamic social policy. Mahathir held a number of ministerial posts from 1974 before being appointed prime minister and UMNO leader 1981. He was re-elected 1986 andd 1990, but has alienated sections of UMNO by his authoritarian leadership.

Mohammed alternative form of ◊Muhammad, founder of Islam.

Mohawk member of a North American Indian people, part of the ◊Iroquois confederation, who lived in the Mohawk Valley, New York, and now live on reservations in Ontario, Québec, and New York State, as well as among the general population. Their language belongs to the Macro-Siouan group. In 1990 Mohawks south of Montréal mounted a blockade in a dispute over land with the government of Québec province.

Mohenjo Daro ('mound of the dead') site of a city about 2500–1600 BC on the lower Indus River, Pakistan, where excavations from the 1920s have revealed the ◊Indus Valley civilization, to which the city of ◊Harappa also belongs.

Mohican and Mohegan or *Mahican* two closely related North American Indian peoples, speaking an Algonquian language, who formerly occupied the Hudson Valley and parts of Connecticut, respectively. The novelist James Fenimore Cooper confused the two peoples in his fictional account *The Last of the Mohicans* 1826.

Moi Daniel arap 1924– . Kenyan politician, president from 1978. Leader of Kenya African National Union (KANU), he became minister of home affairs 1964, vice president 1967, and succeeded Jomo Kenyatta as president. He enjoys the support of Western governments but has been widely criticized for Kenya's poor human-rights record. From 1988 his rule became increasingly authoritarian and in 1991, in the face of widespread criticism, he promised an eventual introduction of multiparty politics.

Moldavia former principality in E Europe, on the river Danube, occupying an area divided today between Moldova and Romania. It was independent between the 14th and 16th centuries, when it became part of the Ottoman Empire. In 1861 Moldavia was united with its neighbouring principality Wallachia as Romania. In 1940 the eastern part, Bessarabia, became part of the USSR, whereas the western part remained in Romania.

Moldova or *Moldavia* country in E central Europe, bounded N, S, and E by Ukraine, and W by Romania.

history Formerly a principality in Eastern Europe, occupying an area divided today between the republic of Moldova and modern Romania, the region was independent from the 14th to the 16th century, when it became part of the Ottoman Empire. Its eastern part, Bessarabia, was ruled by Russia 1912–18, but then transferred to Romania. Romania was forced to cede Bessarabia June 1940 and it was joined with part of the Soviet-controlled

Autonomous Moldavian Republic to form the Moldavian Socialist Republic Aug 1940.

nationalist revival Before and after World War II the republic was brutally 'sovietized'. Agriculture was collectivized, private enterprises were taken over by the state, and Russians and Ukrainians settled in the republic. The republic witnessed significant urban and industrial growth from the 1950s. ◊*Glasnost* brought a resurgence of Moldavian nationalism from the late 1980s, and there was pressure for language reform and calls for reversion from the Cyrillic to the Latin alphabet. In 1988 a Moldavian Movement in Support of Perestroika was formed and a year later, in May 1989, the Moldavian Popular Front (MPF) was established. In Aug 1989 the MPF persuaded the republic's government, led since July 1989 by the sympathetic communist president Mircea Snegur, to make Romanian the state language and reinstate the Latin script. This provoked demonstrations and strikes by the republic's Russian speakers and led the Turkish-speaking Gagauz minority, concentrated in the southwest, to campaign for autonomy. In Nov 1989, after MPF radicals had staged a petrol bomb assault on the Interior Ministry headquarters in Chişinău, the Moldavian Communist Party's (MCP) conservative leader, Semyon Grossu, was dismissed and replaced by the more conciliatory Pyotr Luchinsky. In the wake of the Chişinău riots, with inter-ethnic strife worsening, a temporary state of emergency was imposed and a ban placed on public meetings. This restricted campaigning for the Feb 1990 supreme soviet elections, in which, nevertheless, the MPF polled strongly. After this election the movement towards independence gathered momentum, and a 'sovereignty' declaration was made June 1990. In Oct 1990, both the Trans-Dniester region (centred around Tiraspol and around 700,000 strong) and the Gagauz-inhabited region in SW Moldova formed unofficial breakaway republics. Unauthorized elections to an independent parliament by the Gagauz separatists later in Oct and Russian/Moldavian clashes in the Trans-Dniester region in Nov led to states of emergency being declared in both areas.

independence recognized In March 1991 the republic boycotted the USSR referendum on preservation of the Union on the grounds that it might worsen inter-ethnic tensions. During the Aug 1991 anti-Gorbachev attempted coup in Moscow, which was denounced by President Snegur but supported by the Trans-Dniester and Gagauz-inhabited regions, there were large pro-democracy demonstrations in Chişinău. After the coup, MCP activity was banned in

workplaces and on 27 Aug 1991 the republic formally declared its independence. Immediate recognition was accorded by Romania. The republic joined the ◊Commonwealth of Independent States (CIS) Dec 1991. Also in Dec 1991 Snegur was directly elected president; he was unopposed after two challengers withdrew. In Jan 1992 Moldova was admitted into the ◊Conference on Security and Cooperation in Europe (CSCE). United Nations (UN) membership and US diplomatic recognition was granted March 1992.

union with Romania Following pro-unification border rallies, the Moldavian and Romanian presidents met Jan and May 1992 to discuss the possibility of union. President Snegur favoured a gradual approach towards unification with Romania.

Trans-Dniester region violence escalated In March 1992 a state of emergency was declared following an upsurge of fighting in Trans-Dniester region between Moldavian security forces and ethnic Russians and Ukrainians, fearful of the proposed merger with Romania. Between May and July hundreds died in the fighting, with Russian troops present in the republic accused of assisting the Slav separatists. In July President Snegur agreed to deployment of an outside peacekeeping force, and in Aug talks began between Moldova and Russia on implementing an agreement to preserve peace in the Trans-Dniester region and to improve economic ties between the two countries. By mid-August a Russian peacekeeping force was reportedly deployed in the troubled region.

Molly Maguires, the in US history, a secret Irish coalminers' organization in the 1870s that staged strikes and used violence against coal-company officials and property in the anthracite fields of Pennsylvania, prefiguring a long period of turbulence in industrial relations. The movement was infiltrated by Pinkerton agents (detectives), and 1876 trials led to convictions and executions.

The fate of every nation lies in its own strength.

Count von Moltke
speech in the Reichstag 1880

Molotov Vyacheslav Mikhailovich. Assumed name of V M Skriabin 1890–1986. Soviet communist politician. He was chair of the Council of People's Commissars (prime minister) 1930–41 and foreign minister 1939–49 and

1953–56. He negotiated the 1939 nonaggression treaty with Germany (the ◊Hitler–Stalin pact), and, after the German invasion 1941, the Soviet partnership with the Allies. His postwar stance prolonged the Cold War and in 1957 he was expelled from the government for Stalinist activities.

Moltke Helmuth Carl Bernhard, Count von 1800–1891. Prussian general. He became chief of the general staff 1857, and was responsible for the Prussian strategy in the wars with Denmark 1863–64, Austria 1866, and France 1870–71.

Moltke Helmuth Johannes Ludwig von 1848–1916. German general (nephew of Count von Moltke, the Prussian general), chief of the German general staff 1906–14. His use of General Alfred von Schlieffen's (1833–1913) plan for a rapid victory on two fronts failed and he was relieved of command after the defeat at the Marne.

Momoh Joseph Saidu 1937– . Sierra Leone soldier and politician, president 1985–92. An army officer who became commander 1983, with the rank of major-general, he succeeded Siaka Stevens as president when he retired; Momoh was endorsed by Sierra Leone's one political party, the All-People's Congress. He dissociated himself from the policies of his predecessor, pledging to fight corruption and improve the economy. In April 1992 he fled to neighbouring Guinea after a military takeover.

Momoyama in Japanese history, the period 1568–1616 or 1573–1603. During this time three great generals, Oda Nobunaga (1534–1582), Toyotomi Hideyoshi (1537–1598), who invaded Korea 1592, and ◊Tokugawa Ieyasu, successively held power; Ieyasu established the Tokugawa shogunate. Portuguese missionaries and traders were an influence at this time, and Japanese art, architecture (castles), and the tea ceremony flourished. The period is named after a castle built by Hideyoshi in Fushimi, central Honshu.

Mon people of the Irrawaddy delta region of lower Myanmar (Burma). They founded the city of Pegu 573, adopted Theravāda Buddhism, but were conquered by Pagan in the 11th century, by the Toungoo 1539, and by Alaungpaya, founder of the Konbaung dynasty, 1757.

Monaco small sovereign state forming an enclave in S France, with the Mediterranean Sea to the south.

history Formerly part of the Roman Empire, Monaco became a Genoese possession in the 12th century and has been ruled since 1297 by the Grimaldi family. It was a Spanish protectorate 1542–1641, then came under French protection and during the French revolution was annexed by France. The ruling family was imprisoned (one was guillotined) but regained power after the 1814 Treaty of ◊Paris. In 1815 Monaco became a protectorate of Sardinia but reverted to French protection 1861. In 1940 it was occupied by Italy and in 1943 by Germany but was liberated 1945. Prince Rainier III came to the throne 1949 and a male heir, Prince Albert, was born 1958.

Monagas José Tadeo 1784–1868. Venezuelan president 1847–51 and 1855–58, a hero of the independence movement. Monagas wanted to create a separate state in E Venezuela called Oriente, leading to an uprising against President José Antonio Páez 1831. He called it off in return for a pardon for his rebels. The Liberal Monagas clan gained power after the fall 1847 of Páez's Conservative oligarchy. Monagas' brother José Gregorio was president 1851–55, and their 'Liberal oligarchy' was marked by a series of revolts led by Páez' supporters and disillusionment of their Liberal backers. He was forced to resign 1858.

Monck or *Monk* George, 1st Duke of Albemarle 1608–1669. English soldier. During the Civil War he fought for King Charles I, but after being captured changed sides and took command of the Parliamentary forces in Ireland. Under the Commonwealth he became commander in chief in Scotland, and in 1660 he led his army into England and brought about the restoration of Charles II.

If the army will stick by me, I will stick by them.

George Monck
1659

---

monetarism economic policy, advocated by the economist Milton Friedman and the Chicago school of economists, that proposes control of a country's money supply to keep it in step with the country's ability to produce goods, with the aim of curbing inflation. Cutting government spending is advocated, and the long-term aim is to return as much of the economy as possible to the private sector, allegedly in the interests of efficiency.

Monetarist policies were widely adopted in the 1980s in response to the inflation problems caused by spiralling oil prices in 1979.

The Mongol Empire *After Genghis Khan's death 1227 his vast empire was partitioned between his four sons, leading eventually to the formation of the successor states of the Golden Horde under the heirs of Genghis's eldest son Jöchi, the Chagatai Khanate under the second son Chagatai, and the empire of the Great Khan, heirs of Genghis's third son and named successor Ödödei. There also emerged the Il-Khans of Persia, technically vassals of the Chagatai khans. In the 14th century Tamerlane carved out his short-lived empire from the remnants of these two khanates, in an effort to repeat the conquests of Genghis Khan in the name of Islam, but he died while preparing his campaign against China and his empire rapidly collapsed amid internecine squabbles.*

Mongol member of any of the various Mongol (or Mongolian) ethnic groups of Central Asia. Mongols live in Mongolia, Russia, Inner Mongolia (China), Tibet, and Nepal.

During the 13th century AD, under Genghis Khan, the Mongols conquered central Asia and attacked E Europe. Kublai Khan, the grandson of Genghis Khan, was the first emperor of the Yuan dynasty (1279–1368) in China.

Mongol Empire empire established by ◊Genghis Khan, who extended his domains from Russia to N China and became khan of the Mongol tribes 1206. His grandson ◊Kublai Khan conquered China and used foreigners (such as the Venetian traveller Marco ◊Polo) as well as subjects to administer his empire. The Mongols lost China 1367 and suffered defeats in the west 1380; the empire broke up soon afterwards.

Mongolia country in E Central Asia, bounded N by Russia and S by China.

history Inhabited by nomads from N Asia, the area was united under ◊Genghis Khan 1206 and by the end of the 13th century was part of the Mongol Empire that stretched across Asia. From 1689 it was part of China.

After the revolution of 1911–12 Mongolia became autonomous under the Lamaist religious ruler Jebsten Damba Khutukhtu. From 1915 it increasingly fell under Chinese influence and not until 1921, with the support of the USSR, were Mongolian nationalists able to cast off the Chinese yoke.

'Sovietization' In 1924 it adopted the Soviet system of government and, after proclaiming itself a people's republic, launched a programme of 'defeudalization', involving the destruction of Lamaism. In 1931, when two provinces revolted against the Communist Party, religious buildings were destroyed and mass executions carried out on the orders of the Soviet dictator Stalin. An armed uprising by

Expansion of the Mongol Empire

From their homelands in the Siberian steppes, the nomadic Mongols swept across and out of Asia to conquer territories bounded to the E and S by the Pacific, Indochina, and India, and to the W by the Euphrates and the Danube rivers. This vast empire was carved out largely during the lifetime of one man, Temujin (c. 1167–1227). Having proved his military and political prowess in his youth, in 1206 he was elected leader of the Mongols by an assembly of *Kuriltai* (chieftains), adopting the name Genghis Khan, or 'universal ruler'.

He organized the tribes into semi-feudal clans bound together by unquestioning loyalty to the Khan, strict discipline, a law code, and a sophisticated military organization based on the decimal system. To protect himself, Genghis Khan created a 10,000-strong imperial guard. The law code assumed that the Mongols under their Khan were divinely appointed to rule the world and that any attempt to resist them was blasphemy, a crime which justified any atrocity. The immediate objective of these reforms was the creation of an invincible military force, and in this the Mongols all but succeeded, creating the largest empire the world had seen.

Military brilliance

Much of the Mongols' success is due to their military brilliance. Their cavalry armies were fast-moving and well coordinated so that enemies regularly over-estimated their numbers, and were often outflanked or caught off guard. Tight discipline enabled the Mongol forces to execute complicated manoeuvres, such as feigning flight to draw opponents into an ambush, and sheer single-minded determination brought success in apparently superhuman feats of conquest. Their ostensible invincibility and unbridled savagery earned them a fearsome reputation which could demoralize opponents even before battle was joined. Under Genghis and some of his successors the Mongols also proved to be cunning politicians, expert at exploiting the divisions of their neighbours.

The Mongols' reputation for ferocity is certainly justified, for the capture of towns was regularly followed by massacres. These atrocities were not usually committed out of outright savagery, but with political ends in view,

and served as a stark illustration of their authority. This disregard for human life was not unique to the Mongols: massacres of garrisons or sackings of towns were common features of warfare in Europe and much of Asia at this time. The Mongols' fearsome reputation probably stemmed from the scale of their activities, rather than their ruthlessness, for what distinguished them from their contemporaries was their immense success as conquerors.

Absorbed rather than dominant

Genghis Khan died the leader of a people who, despite their unparalleled military successes, were nomads by nature, with very little to teach their subjects about the arts of civilization. Finding themselves the overlords of ancient cultures (including China), it was characteristic for the Mongols to lose their distinctive identity as they were absorbed into their subject populations. Their superior armies assured them of military conquests, but it was the cultures of the vanquished that had the final victory.

Mongols were quick to learn. One of Genghis Khan's and his successor Ögödei's principal advisers, Ye-lui Chu-tsai of the Chinese Khitans, introduced a number of administrative structures based on Chinese precedent, saying 'the empire was won on horseback, but you cannot govern on horseback'. Genghis Khan disregarded the views of his generals in accepting Ye- lui's advice not to exterminate conquered populations, but to allow them to live and work so that their taxes flowed into Mongol coffers. By such arguments the straightforward savagery of the initial expansion gradually diminished. Chinese influence on the empire of the Great Khan culminated in the reign of Kublai, one of Genghis Khan's grandsons, who in 1279 secured control of the whole of China and established himself as the first of the Yuan imperial dynasty. Kublai encouraged foreign trade and among the Europeans welcomed to his court was Marco Polo, who entered his service. But it was the Chinese, not Mongol, features of Kublai's dominion that impressed the Europeans, and which nearly 600 years later inspired Coleridge's *Kubla Khan*.

---

antigovernment forces 1932 was suppressed with Soviet assistance. Marshal Horloogiyn Choybalsan, a former independence fighter, was the effective ruler of the nation until his death in 1952. China recognized its independence 1946, but relations deteriorated as Mongolia took the Soviet side in the Sino-Soviet dispute. In 1966 Mongolia signed a 20-year friendship, cooperation and mutual-assistance pact with the USSR, and some 60,000 Soviet troops based in the country caused China to see it as a Russian colony.

economic change Isolated from the outside world during the 1970s, under the leadership of

Yumjaagiyn Tsedenbal (1916–1991) – the nation's dominant figure from 1958 – Mongolia underwent great economic change as urban industries developed and settled agriculture on the collective system spread, with new areas being brought under cultivation. Tsedenbal was deposed 1984 by Jambyn Batmuntch.

foreign contact and influence After the accession to power in the USSR of Mikhail Gorbachev, Mongolia was encouraged to broaden its outside contacts. Cultural exchanges with China increased, diplomatic relations were established with the USA, and between 1987 and 1990 the number of Soviet troops stationed in the country was reduced from 80,000 to 15,000. Influenced by events in Eastern Europe, an opposition grouping, the Mongolian Democratic Union, was illegally formed Dec 1989 and spearheaded a campaign demanding greater democratization. The Communist Party (MPRP), meanwhile, became committed to political and economic reform.

multiparty politics and market economy
Free multiparty national elections and local municipal and people's hurals were held July 1990. The MPRP secured 83% of the seats of the central parliament and 62% of the seats in the Little Hural. The principal opposition body, the Democratic Party (MDP), led by Erdenijn Bat-Uul, captured only 5% of the seats. In Sept 1990 the new assembly elected the MPRP's Punsalmaagiyn Ochirbat as president and Dashiyn Byambasuren as prime minister. In March 1991 Budragchaa Dashyondon was elected head of the MPRP to replace the allegedly too conservative Gombojavyn Ochirbat. In the wake of the anticommunist repercussions of the failed Aug 1991 anti-Gorbachev coup in the USSR, President Punsalmaagiyn Ochirbat resigned from the MPRP. In Aug 1991 twelve former members of the ruling MPRP were charged with corruption during their terms in office.

The government embarked on an ambitious but, in the short term, painful programme to achieve the transition from central planning to a market economy by 1994. Prices were freed, the currency was massively devalued, a new banking system and stock exchange were established, privatizations began, and the country joined the International Monetary Fund (IMF) and Asian Development Bank.

In June 1991, the word 'Republic' was dropped from the name and in Oct a law was passed providing for the private ownership of land. In Jan 1992 a new constitution came into force. In June parliamentary elections the MPRP won a resounding victory, and in July free-market economist Puntsagiyn Jasray was elected prime minister by an overwhelming majority.

Do not hack me as you did my Lord Russell.

Duke of Monmouth to his executioner

Monmouth James Scott, Duke of Monmouth 1649–1685. Claimant to the English crown, the illegitimate son of Charles II and Lucy Walter. After James II's accession 1685, Monmouth landed in England at Lyme Regis, Dorset, claimed the crown, and raised a rebellion, which was crushed at ◊Sedgemoor in Somerset. He was executed with 320 of his accomplices.

Monroe James 1758–1831. 5th president of the USA 1817–25, a Democratic Republican. He served in the American Revolution, was minister to France 1794–96, and in 1803 negotiated the ◊Louisiana Purchase. He was secretary of state 1811–17. His name is associated with the Monroe Doctrine.

Monroe Doctrine declaration by US president James Monroe 1823 that any further European colonial ambitions in the western hemisphere would be threats to US peace and security, made in response to proposed European intervention against newly independent former Spanish colonies in South America. In return the USA would not interfere in European affairs. The doctrine, subsequently broadened, has been a recurrent theme in US foreign policy, although it has no basis in US or international law.

Mons Graupius, Battle of fought in Scotland in AD 84 by the Romans under their general ◊Agricola.

Montagnard member of a group in the legislative assembly and National Convention convened after the ◊French Revolution. They supported the more extreme aims of the revolution, and were destroyed as a political force after the fall of Robespierre 1794.

Montagu-Chelmsford reforms changes to the constitution of India 1919, whereby Indians obtained greater control in local and some provincial matters such as health, education, and agriculture, while British administrators still controlled finance and law and order. Arguing that the reforms did not go far enough, Indian nationalists organized a concerted non-cooperation campaign 1920–22 in protest.

The reforms were put forward by Edwin Montagu (1879–1924), secretary of state for India, and Lord Chelmsford (1868–1933), viceroy of India. They introduced a two-tier structure to Indian government, with provincial governors presiding over an executive council and a ministry. Indian representation was also conceded on the viceroy's council but central control remained firmly in British hands.

Montcalm Louis-Joseph de Montcalm-Gozon, Marquis de 1712–1759. French general, appointed military commander in Canada 1756. He won a succession of victories over the British during the French and Indian War, but was defeated in 1759 by James ◊Wolfe in Québec on the Plains of Abraham, where both he and Wolfe were killed; this battle marked the end of French rule in Canada.

Montenegro (Serbo-Croatian *Crna Gora*) constituent republic of Yugoslavia. Part of ◊Serbia from the late 12th century, it became independent (under Venetian protectio n) after Serbia was defeated by the Turks 1389. It was forced to accept Turkish suzerainty in the late 15th century, but was never completely subdued by Turkey. It was ruled by bishop princes until 1851, when a monarchy was founded, and became a sovereign principality under the Treaty of Berlin 1878. The monarch used the title of king from 1910 with Nicholas I (1841–1921). Montenegro participated in the Balkan Wars 1912 and 1913. It was overrun by Austria in World War I, and in 1918 voted after the deposition of King Nicholas to become part of Serbia. In 1946 Montenegro became a republic of Yugoslavia. In a referendum March 1992 Montenegrins voted to remain part of the Yugoslav federation; the referendum was boycotted by Montenegro's Muslim and Albanian communities.

The republic held multiparty elections for the first time in Dec 1990; the League of Communists of Montenegro remained in power. A staunch ally of Serbia, Montenegro sided with Serbia in the 1991–92 conflict with Slovenia and Croatia, remaining within the Serb-dominated rump.

Montezuma II 1466–1520. Aztec emperor 1502–20. When the Spanish conquistador Cortés invaded Mexico, Montezuma was imprisoned and killed during the Aztec attack on Cortés's force as it tried to leave Tenochtitlán, the Aztec capital city.

Montfort Simon de Montfort, Earl of Leicester *c.* 1208–1265. English politician and soldier. From 1258 he led the baronial opposition to Henry III's misrule during the second ◊Barons' War and in 1264 defeated and captured the king at Lewes, Sussex. In 1265, as head of government, he summoned the first parliament in which the towns were represented; he was killed at the Battle of Evesham during the last of the Barons' Wars.

Montgomery Bernard Law, 1st Viscount Montgomery of Alamein 1887–1976. British field marshal. At the start of World War II he commanded part of the British Expeditionary Force in France 1939–40 and took part in the evacuation from Dunkirk. In Aug 1942 he took command of the 8th Army, then barring the German advance on Cairo; the victory of El Alamein in Oct turned the tide in N Africa and was followed by the expulsion of Field Marshal Rommel from Egypt and rapid Allied advance into Tunisia. In Feb 1943 Montgomery's forces came under US general Eisenhower's

command, and they took part in the conquest of Tunisia and Sicily and the invasion of Italy. Montgomery was promoted to field marshal in 1944.

Montgomery commanded the Allied armies during the opening phase of the invasion of France in Jun 1944, and from Aug the British and imperial troops that liberated the Netherlands, overran N Germany, and entered Denmark. At his 21st Army Group headquarters on Lüneberg Heath, he received the German surrender on 3 May 1945. He was in command of the British occupation force in Germany until Feb 1946, when he was appointed chief of the Imperial General Staff.

In 1948 he became permanent military chair of the Commanders-in-Chief Committee for W European defence, and 1951–58 was deputy Supreme Commander Europe. Created 1st Viscount Montgomery of Alamein 1946.

Montgomery state capital of Alabama, USA. The *Montgomery Bus Boycott* 1955 began here when a black passenger, Rosa Parks, refused to give up her seat to a white. Led by Martin Luther ◊King Jr, the boycott was a landmark in the civil-rights campaign.

Alabama's bus-segregation laws were nullified by the US Supreme Court 13 Nov 1956. Montgomery was the capital of the Confederacy in the first months of the American Civil War.

Montrose James Graham, 1st Marquess of Montrose 1612–1650. Scottish soldier, son of the 4th earl of Montrose. He supported the ◊Covenanters against Charles I, but after 1640 changed sides. Defeated in 1645 at Philiphaugh, he escaped to Norway. Returning in 1650 to raise a revolt, he survived shipwreck only to have his weakened forces defeated, and (having been betrayed to the Covenanters) was hanged in Edinburgh.

He either fears his fate too much,
Or his deserts are small,
That puts it not unto the touch
To win or lose it all.

    Lord Montrose 'My Dear and Only Love'

Montségur site of the massacre 1244 of the Albigenses as the infamous climax to the pope's 'Albigensian Crusade', organized 1208. After being besieged for ten months in the fortress of Montségur, 255 heretics were burned to death.

Montt Manuel 1809–1800. Chilean president 1851–61. He was a hardliner who promoted economic development, especially railway building, the telegraph, postal services, and gas lighting. His final years in office saw economic recession and political turmoil, including clashes between church and state.

Partly self-educated, Montt became rector of the Instituto Nazional 1835, and while serving as minister of education 1841–45 he offered support to the great reformer Domingo Faustino ◊Sarmiento, then in exile.

Moor any of the NW African Muslims, of mixed Arab and Berber origin, who conquered Spain and ruled its southern part from 711 to 1492. The name (English form of Latin *Maurus*) was originally applied to an inhabitant of the Roman province of Mauritania, in NW Africa.

moot legal and administrative assembly found in nearly every community in medieval England.

Moravia (Czech *Morava*) district of central Europe, from 1960 two regions of Czechoslovakia (now Czech Republic): *South Moravia* (Czech *Jihomoravský*). Part of the Avar territory since the 6th century; conquered by Charlemagne's Holy Roman Empire. In 874 the kingdom of Great Moravia was founded by the Slavic prince Sviatopluk, who ruled until 894. It was conquered by the Magyars 906, and became a fief of Bohemia 1029. It was passed to the Habsburgs 1526, and became an Austrian crown land 1849. It was incorporated in the new republic of Czechoslovakia 1918, forming a province until 1949.

Moray Earl of Moray another spelling of ◊Murray, regent of Scotland 1567–70.

Morazán Francisco 1792–1842. Central American politician, born in Honduras. He was elected president of the United Provinces of Central America in 1830. In the face of secessions he attempted to hold the union together by force but was driven out by the Guatemalan dictator Rafael Carrera. Morazán was eventually captured and executed in 1842.

They [citizens of Utopia] have but few laws ... but they think it against all right and justice that men should be bound to these laws.

Thomas More Utopia 1516

More (St) Thomas 1478–1535. English politician and author. From 1509 he was favoured by ◊Henry VIII and employed on foreign embassies. He was a member of the privy council from 1518 and Lord Chancellor from 1529 but resigned over Henry's break with the pope. For refusing to accept the king as head of the church, he was executed. The title of his political book *Utopia* 1516 has come to mean any supposedly perfect society.

Morelos José María 1765–1815. Mexican priest and revolutionary. A mestizo (person with Spanish American and American Indian parents), Morelos followed independence campaigner Miguel ◊Hidalgo y Costilla, intending to be an army chaplain, but he displayed military genius and came to head his own forces. The independence movement was stalled for five years after his death.

He sought to rescue the revolution from chaos and violence, and to widen its political base. However, the Creoles failed to respond. After four major campaigns against the Spaniards, he was captured, stripped of the priesthood by the Inquisition and executed.

Morgan Henry *c.* 1635–1688. Welsh buccaneer in the Caribbean. He made war against Spain, capturing and sacking Panama 1671. In 1674 he was knighted and appointed lieutenant governor of Jamaica.

Morgenthau Plan proposals for Germany after World War II, originated by Henry Morgenthau Jr (1891–1967), US secretary of the treasury, calling for the elimination of war industries in the Ruhr and Saar basins and the conversion of Germany 'into a country primarily agricultural and pastoral in character'. The plan had already been dropped by the time the Allied leaders Churchill, Roosevelt, and Stalin met at Yalta Feb 1945.

Morley-Minto reforms measures announced 1909 to increase the participation of Indians in their country's government. Introduced by John Morley (1838–1923), secretary of state for India, and Lord Minto (1845–1914), viceroy of India, they did not affect the responsibility of government, which remained in British hands, but did give Indians wider opportunities to be heard.

Mormon or *Latter-day Saint* member of a Christian sect, the *Church of Jesus Christ of Latter-day Saints*, founded at Fayette, New York, in 1830 by Joseph ◊Smith. According to Smith, Mormon was an ancient prophet in North America whose *Book of Mormon*, of which Smith claimed divine revelation, is accepted by Mormons as part of the Christian scriptures. In the 19th century the faction led by Brigham Young was polygamous. It is a missionary church with headquarters in Utah and a worldwide membership of about 6 million.

Moro Aldo 1916–1978. Italian Christian Democrat politician. Prime minister 1963–68 and 1974–76, he was expected to become Italy's president, but he was kidnapped and shot by Red Brigade urban guerrillas.

Moroccan Crises two periods of international tension 1905 and 1911 following German objections to French expansion in Morocco. Their wider purpose was to break up the Anglo-French entente 1904, but both crises served to reinforce the entente and isolate Germany.

Morocco country in NW Africa, bounded N and NW by the Mediterranean Sea, E and SE by Algeria, and S by Western Sahara.

history Originally occupied by ◊Berber tribes, the coastal regions of the area now known as Morocco were under Phoenician rule during the 10th–3rd centuries BC, and became a Roman colony in the 1st century AD. It was invaded in the 5th century by the ◊Vandals, in the 6th century by the Visigoths, and in the 7th century began to be conquered by the Arabs. From the 11th century the region was united under the ◊Almoravids, who ruled a Muslim empire that included Spain, Morocco, and Algeria. They were followed by the ◊Almohads, another Muslim dynasty, whose empire included Libya and Tunisia.

In the 15th century Portugal occupied the Moroccan port of Ceuta but was defeated 1578. Further European influence began in the 19th century and was more lasting, with Morocco being divided 1912 into French and Spanish protectorates. It became fully independent as the Sultanate of Morocco 1956 under Mohammed V (sultan since 1927). The former Spanish protectorate joined the new state, with Tangier, which had previously been an international zone. The sultan was restyled king of Morocco 1957. After his death 1961 he was succeeded by King Hassan II, who has survived several attempted coups and assassinations. Between 1960 and 1972 several constitutions were formulated in an attempt to balance personal royal rule with demands for greater democracy.

Western Sahara dispute Hassan's reign has been dominated by the dispute over ◊Western Sahara, a former Spanish colony seen as historically Moroccan. In 1975 Spain ceded it to Morocco and Mauritania, leaving them to divide it. The inhabitants, who had not been consulted, reacted violently through an independence movement, the Polisario Front. Less than a year later, Morocco and Mauritania were involved in a guerrilla war.

With Algerian support, Polisario set up a government in exile in Algiers, the Sahrahwi Arab Democratic Republic (SADR). This prompted Hassan to sever diplomatic relations with Algeria 1976. In 1979 Mauritania agreed a peace treaty with Polisario, and Morocco annexed the part of Western Sahara that Mauritania had vacated. Polisario reacted by intensifying its operations.

In 1983 the Organization of African Unity (OAU) proposed a cease-fire, direct negotiations between Morocco and Polisario, and a referendum in Western Sahara. Morocco agreed but refused to deal directly with Polisario.

Although the war was costly, it allowed Hassan to capitalize on the patriotism it generated in his country. In 1984 he unexpectedly signed an agreement with Col Khaddhafi of Libya, who had been helping Polisario, for economic and political cooperation and mutual defence. Meanwhile, Morocco was becoming more isolated as the SADR gained wider recognition. Towards the end of 1987 the Polisario guerrillas agreed a cease-fire and in Aug 1988 a United Nations peace plan was accepted by both sides, calling for a referendum to permit the area's inhabitants to choose independence or incorporation into Morocco. Full diplomatic relations with Algeria were restored May 1988, and with Syria Jan 1989.

In 1990–91 Morocco officially opposed Iraq's invasion of Kuwait, although there was much popular support for Iraq. Domestically, the surge in Islamic fundamentalism concerned the government. In Aug 1992 King Hassan appointed the veteran politician Mohamed Lamrani to head a government of independents. In Sept a new constitution was approved by national referendum.

Morris Robert 1734–1806. American political leader. A signatory of the Declaration of Independence 1776, he served in the Continental Congress 1775–78. In 1781 he was appointed superintendent of finance and dealt with the economic problems of the new nation. He served as one of Pennsylvania's first US senators 1789–95.

Morrison Herbert Stanley, Baron Morrison of Lambeth 1888–1965. British Labour politician. He was a founder member and later secretary of the London Labour Party 1915–45, and a member of the London County Council 1922–45. He entered Parliament in 1923, and organised the Labour Party's general election victory in 1945. He was twice defeated in the contest for leadership of the party, once to Clement Attlee in 1932, and then to Hugh

Gaitskell 1955. A skilful organizer, he lacked the ability to unite the party.

He was minister of transport 1929–31, home secretary 1940–45, Lord President of the Council and leader of the House of Commons 1945–51, and foreign secretary March–Oct 1951.

Mortimer Roger de, 8th Baron of Wigmore and 1st Earl of March *c.* 1287–1330. English politician and adventurer. He opposed Edward II and with Edward's queen, Isabella, led a rebellion against him 1326, bringing about his abdication. From 1327 Mortimer ruled England as the queen's lover, until Edward III had him executed.

mortmain lands held by a corporate body, such as the church, in perpetual or inalienable tenure.

In the Middle Ages, alienation in mortmain, usually to a church in return for a ◊chantry foundation, deprived the feudal lord of his future incidents (payments due to him when the land changed ownership) and rights of wardship, and so attempts were often made to regulate the practice.

Moses *c.* 13th century BC. Hebrew lawgiver and judge who led the Israelites out of Egypt to the promised land of Canaan. On Mount Sinai he claimed to have received from Jehovah the oral and written Law, including the *Ten Commandments* engraved on tablets of stone. The first five books of the Old Testament – in Judaism, the *Torah* – are ascribed to him.

According to the Torah, the infant Moses was hidden among the bulrushes on the banks of the Nile when the pharaoh commanded that all newborn male Hebrew children should be destroyed. He was found by a daughter of Pharaoh, who reared him. Eventually he became the leader of the Israelites in their *Exodus* from Egypt and their 40 years' wandering in the wilderness. He died at the age of 120, after having been allowed a glimpse of the Promised Land from Mount Pisgah.

Moslem alternative spelling of *Muslim*, a follower of ◊Islam.

I am not, and never have been, a man of the right. My position was on the left and is now in the centre of politics.

Oswald Mosley,
letter to *The Times* April 1968

Mosley Oswald (Ernald) 1896–1980. British politician, founder of the British Union of Fascists (BUF) 1932. He was a member of Parliament 1918–31, then led the BUF until his

internment 1940–43 during World War His first marriage was to a daughter of the Conservative politician Lord Curzon, his second to Diana Freeman-Mitford, one of the Mitford sisters.

mosque (Arabic *mesjid*) in Islam, a place of worship. Chief features are: the dome; the minaret, a balconied turret from which the faithful are called to prayer; the *mihrab*, or prayer niche, in one of the interior walls, showing the direction of the holy city of Mecca; and an open court surrounded by porticoes.

The earliest mosques were based on the plan of Christian basilicas, although different influences contributed towards their architectural development. Mosques vary a great deal in style in various parts of the world.

Mosquera Tomás Cipriano de 1798–1878. Colombian general and political thinker. Active in the struggle for independence, Mosquera was made intendant (see ◊intendencia) of Guayaquil 1826 by Simón ◊Bolívar. In his first term as president of New Grenada 1845–49 he promoted educational, taxation, and political reforms, but split the ruling class. He called the assembly which created United States of Colombia 1863. Later he took on the Catholic church with a series of anti-clerical policies.

He served in the administration of President José Ignacio de Márquez (1837–41). Exiled 1867 to Peru he returned 1870 and served as governor of Cauca 1871–73, continuing to argue for economic development.

Mossadeq Muhammad 1880–1967. Iranian prime minister 1951–53. A dispute arose with the Anglo-Iranian Oil Company when he called for the nationalization of Iran's oil production, and when he failed in his attempt to overthrow the shah, he was arrested by loyalist forces with support from the USA. From 1956 he was under house arrest.

Moundbuilder member of any of the various North American Indian peoples of the Midwest and the South who built earth mounds, from about 300 BC. The mounds were linear and pictographic in form for tombs, such as the Great Serpent Mound in Ohio, and truncated pyramids and cones for the platforms of chiefs' houses and temples. The ◊Hopewell and Natchez were Moundbuilders.

Mountbatten Louis, 1st Earl Mountbatten of Burma 1900–1979. British admiral and administrator. In World War II he became chief of combined operations 1942 and commander in chief in SE Asia 1943. As last viceroy of India 1947 and first governor general of India until 1948, he oversaw that country's transition to independence. He was killed by an Irish Republican Army bomb aboard his yacht in the Republic of Ireland.

Mounties popular name for the *Royal Canadian Mounted Police*, known for their uniform of red jacket and broad-brimmed hat. Their Security Service, established 1950, was disbanded 1981 and replaced by the independent Canadian Security Intelligence Service.

Mozambique country in SE Africa, bounded N by Zambia, Malawi, and Tanzania; E and S by the Indian Ocean; SW by South Africa and Swaziland; and W by Zimbabwe.

history Mozambique's indigenous peoples are of Bantu origin. By the 10th century the Arabs had established themselves on the coast. The first European to reach Mozambique was Vasco da ◊Gama 1498, and the country became a Portuguese colony 1505. Portugal exploited Mozambique's resources of gold and ivory and used it as a source of slave labour, both locally and overseas. By 1820 the slave trade accounted for 85% of all exports. The trade continued as late as 1912, and 2 million people were shipped to the sugar plantations of Brazil and Cuba; others to neighbouring colonies. In 1891 Portugal leased half the country to two British companies who seized African lands and employed forced labour. In 1895 the last indigenous resistance leader was crushed. From 1926 to 1968 the Portuguese were encouraged to emigrate to Mozambique, where they were given land and use of forced labour. Mozambicans were forbidden by law to trade or run their own business.

Frelimo Guerrilla groups opposed Portuguese rule from the early 1960s, the various left-wing factions combining to form Frelimo. Its leader, Samora Machel, demanded complete independence, and in 1974 internal self-government was achieved, with Joaquim Chissano, a member of Frelimo's central committee, as prime minister.

problems following independence Becoming president of an independent Mozambique 1975, Machel was faced with the emigration of hundreds of thousands of Portuguese settlers, leaving no trained replacements in key economic positions. Two activities had been the mainstay of Mozambique's economy: transit traffic from South Africa and Rhodesia and the export of labour to South African mines. Although Machel supported the African National Congress (ANC) in South Africa and the Patriotic Front in Rhodesia, he knew he must coexist and trade with his two white-governed neighbours. He put heavy pressure

on the Patriotic Front for a settlement of the guerrilla war, and this eventually bore fruit in the 1979 ◊Lancaster House Agreement and the election victory in Zimbabwe of Robert Mugabe, a reliable friend of Mozambique, as leader of the newly independent Zimbabwe.

From 1980 Mozambique was faced with widespread drought, which affected most of southern Africa, and attacks by mercenaries under the banner of the Mozambique National Resistance (MNR), also known as Renamo, who were covertly but strongly backed by South Africa. The attacks concentrated on Mozambique's transport system. MNR forces killed an estimated 100,000 Mozambicans 1982–87; 25% of the population were forced to become refugees. 100,000 people died in the famine between 1983 and 1984.

foreign relations Machel, showing considerable diplomatic skill, had by 1983 repaired relations with the USA, undertaken a successful European tour, and established himself as a respected African leader. In 1984 he signed the ◊Nkomati Accord, under which South Africa agreed to deny facilities to the MNR, and Mozambique in return agreed not to provide bases for the banned ANC. Machel took steps to honour his side of the bargain but was doubtful about South Africa's good faith. In Oct 1986 he died in an air crash near the South African border. Despite the suspicious circumstances, two inquiries pronounced his death an accident.

The following month Frelimo's central committee elected former prime minister Joaquim Chissano as Machel's successor. Chissano immediately pledged to carry on the policies of his predecessor. He strengthened the ties forged by Machel with Zimbabwe and Britain and in 1987 took the unprecedented step of requesting permission to attend the ◊Commonwealth heads-of-government summit that year.

Mozambique's economic problems were aggravated 1987 by food shortages, after another year of drought. The MNR also continued to attack government facilities and kill civilians, by some estimates as many as 100,000. In May 1988, South Africa announced that it would provide training and nonlethal material to Mozambican forces to enable them to defend the Cabora Bassa dam from MNR attack. In 1988 President Chissano met South African state president Botha and later that year, as tension was reduced, Tanzanian troops were withdrawn from the country. In July 1989, at its annual conference, Frelimo offered to abandon Marxism-Leninism to achieve a national consensus and Chissano was re-elected president and party leader.

peace pact signed In Aug 1990 one-party rule was formally ended and in Dec a partial cease-fire was agreed. In 1991 peace talks were held in Rome, and an attempted coup against the government was thwarted. In Aug 1992 a peace accord was agreed, but fighting by right-wing rebels continued; the accord was signed Oct by the opposing factions, but awaited ratification by the Mozambican government. It provided for the two contending armies to be demobilized within six months, with a general election following six months later.

MPLA (abbreviation for *Movimento Popular de Libertaçaõ de Angola*/Popular Movement for the Liberation of Angola) socialist organization founded in the early 1950s that sought to free Angola from Portuguese rule 1961–75 before being involved in the civil war against its former allies ◊UNITA and FNLA 1975–76. The MPLA took control of the country, but UNITA guerrilla activity continues, supported by South Africa.

Mubarak Hosni 1928– . Egyptian politician, president from 1981. Vice president to Anwar Sadat from 1975, Mubarak succeeded him on his assassination. He has continued to pursue Sadat's moderate policies, and has significantly increased the freedom of the press and of political association, while trying to repress the growing Islamic fundamentalist movement.

Mubarak commanded the air force 1972–75 and was responsible for the initial victories in the Egyptian campaign of 1973 against Israel. He led Egypt's opposition to Iraq's 1990 invasion of Kuwait and had an instrumental role in arranging the Middle East peace conference in Nov 1991.

Muckrakers, the movement of US writers and journalists about 1880–1914 who aimed to expose political, commercial, and corporate corruption, and record frankly the age of industrialism, urban poverty, and conspicuous consumption. Novelists included Frank Norris, Theodore Dreiser, Jack London, and Upton Sinclair. The muckrakers were closely associated with ◊Progressivism.

mufti Muslim legal expert who guides the courts in their interpretation. In Turkey the *grand mufti* had supreme spiritual authority until the establishment of the republic in 1924.

Mugabe Robert (Gabriel) 1925– . Zimbabwean politician, prime minister from 1980 and president from 1987. He was in detention in Rhodesia for nationalist activities 1964–74, then carried on guerrilla warfare from Mozambique. As leader of ◊ZANU he was in an uneasy alliance with Joshua ◊Nkomo of ZAPU (Zim-babwe African People's Union) from 1976. The two parties merged 1987. His failure to anticipate and respond to the 1991–92 drought in southern Africa adversely affected his popularity, but was re-elected, unchallenged, 1996.

mugwump (from an Indian word meaning 'chief') in US political history, a colloquial name for the Republicans who voted in the 1884 presidential election for Grover Cleveland, the Democratic candidate, rather than for their Republican nominee, James G Blaine (1830–1893). Blaine was accused of financial improprieties, and the reform-minded mugwumps were partly responsible for his defeat. The term has come to mean a politician who remains neutral on divisive issues.

Muhammad or *Mohammed, Mahomet c.* 570–632. Founder of Islam, born in Mecca on the Arabian peninsula. In about 616 he claimed to be a prophet and that the *Koran* was revealed to him by God (it was later written down by his followers), through the angel Jibra'el. He fled from persecution to the town now known as Medina in 622: the flight, *Hegira*, marks the beginning of the Islamic era.

Originally a shepherd and caravan conductor, Muhammad found leisure for meditation by his marriage with a wealthy widow in 595, and received his first revelation in 610. After some years of secret teaching, in which he taught submission to the will of Allah (Islam), he openly declared himself the prophet of God. The message, originally conveyed to the Arab people, became a universal message, and Muhammad the prophet of humankind. Following persecution from local townspeople, he fled to Medina. After the battle of Badr in 623, he was continuously victorious, entering Mecca as the recognized prophet of Arabia 630. Islam had spread throughout the Arabian peninsula by 632. The succession was troubled.

Mujaheddin (Arabic *mujahid* 'fighters', from ◊*jihad* 'holy war') Islamic fundamentalist guerrillas of contemporary Afghanistan and Iran.

Mukden, Battle of taking of Mukden (now Shenyang), NE China, from Russian occupation by the Japanese 1905, during the ◊Russo-Japanese War. Mukden was later the scene of a surprise attack (the 'Mukden incident') 18 Sept 1931 by the Japanese on the Chinese garrison, which marked the beginning of their invasion of China.

Mulberry Harbour prefabricated floating harbour, used on D-day in World War II, to assist in the assault on the German-held French coast of Normandy.

Muldoon Robert David 1921–1992. New Zealand National Party politician, prime minister 1975–84, during which time he pursued austere economic policies such as a wage-and-price policy to control inflation.

A chartered accountant, he was minister of finance 1967–72, and in 1974 replaced John Marshall as leader of the National Party, after the latter had been criticized as insufficiently aggressive in opposition. He became prime minister in 1975; he sought to introduce curbs on trade unions, was a vigorous supporter of the Western alliance, and a proponent of reform of the international monetary system. He was defeated in the general election of 1984 and was succeeded as prime minister by the Labour Party's David Lange. Muldoon announced his retirement from politics 1992.

Mulroney Brian 1939– . Canadian politician, Progressive Conservative Party leader 1983–1993, prime minister from 1984–1993. He achieved a landslide in the 1984 election, and won the 1988 election on a platform of free trade with the USA, but with a reduced majority. By 1991 his public-opinion standing had fallen to an unprecedented low level.

Munich Agreement pact signed on 29 Sept 1938 by the leaders of the UK (Neville ◊Chamberlain), France (Edouard ◊Daladier), Germany (Hitler), and Italy (Mussolini), under which Czechoslovakia was compelled to surrender its Sudeten-German districts (the ◊*Sudetenland*) to Germany. Chamberlain claimed it would guarantee 'peace in our time', but it did not prevent Hitler from seizing the rest of Czechoslovakia in March 1939.

Municipal Corporations Act English act of Parliament 1835 that laid the foundations of modern local government. The act made local government responsible to a wider electorate of ratepayers through elected councils. Boroughs incorporated in this way were empowered to take on responsibility for policing, public health, and education, and were also subject to regulation and auditing which served to reduce corruption. Similar acts were passed for Scotland (1833) and Ireland (1840).

Munternia Romanian name of ◊Wallachia, a former province of Romania.

Murat Joachim 1767–1815. King of Naples 1808–1815. An officer in the French army, he was made king by Napoleon, but deserted him in 1813 in the vain hope that Austria and Great Britain would recognize him. In 1815 he attempted unsuccessfully to make himself king of all Italy, but when he landed in Calabria in an attempt to gain the throne he was captured and shot.

Muromachi in Japanese history, the period 1392–1568, comprising the greater part of the rule of the ◊Ashikaga shoguns; it is named after the area of Kyoto where their headquarters were sited.

Murray James Stuart, Earl of Murray, or Moray 1531–1570. Regent of Scotland from 1567, an illegitimate son of James V. He was one of the leaders of the Scottish Reformation, and after the deposition of his half-sister ◊Mary Queen of Scots, he became regent. He was assassinated by one of her supporters.

Muscovy anglicized name for both Moscow and Russia in the 16th and 17th centuries. It was also the name of a Russian principality which existed from the 13th to the 16th century; its capital was Moscow.

Museveni Yoweri Kaguta 1945– . Ugandan general and politician, president from 1986. He led the opposition to Idi Amin's regime 1971–78 and was minister of defence 1979–80 but, unhappy with Milton Obote's autocratic leadership, formed the National Resistance Army (NRA). When Obote was ousted in a coup in 1985, Museveni entered into a brief power-sharing agreement with his successor, Tito Okello, before taking over as president. Museveni leads a broad-based coalition government.

Museveni was educated in Uganda and at the University of Dar es Salaam, Tanzania. He entered the army, eventually rising to the rank of general. Until Amin's removal Museveni led the anti-Amin Front for National Salvation, and subsequently the National Resistance Army (NRA), which helped to remove Obote from power.

Muslim or *Moslem*, a follower of ◊Islam.

Muslim Brotherhood movement founded by members of the Sunni branch of Islam in Egypt in 1928. It aims at the establishment of a theocratic Islamic state and is headed by a 'supreme guide'. It is also active in Jordan, Sudan, and Syria.

Muslim League Indian political organization. The All India Muslim League was founded 1906 under the leadership of the Aga Khan. In 1940 the league, led by Muhammad Ali ◊Jinnah, demanded an independent Muslim state. The ◊Congress Party and the Muslim League won most seats in the 1945 elections for an Indian central legislative assembly. In 1946 the Indian constituent assembly was boycotted by the Muslim League. It was partly the activities of the league that led to the establishment of Pakistan.

Mussolini Benito 1883–1945. Italian dictator 1925–43. As founder of the Fascist Movement (see ◊fascism) 1919 and prime minister from 1922, he became known as *Il Duce* ('the leader'). He invaded Ethiopia 1935–36, intervened in the Spanish Civil War 1936–39 in support of Franco, and conquered Albania 1939. In June 1940 Italy entered World War II supporting Hitler. Forced by military and domestic setbacks to resign 1943, Mussolini established a breakaway government in N Italy 1944–45, but was killed trying to flee the country.

For my part I prefer 50,000 rifles to 50,000 votes.

                                    Benito Mussolini 1921

Mustafa Kemal Turkish leader who assumed the name of ◊Atatürk.

mutiny organized act of disobedience or defiance by two or more members of the armed services. In naval and military law, mutiny has always been regarded as one of the most serious of crimes, punishable in wartime by death.

Effective mutinies in history include the ◊Indian Mutiny by Bengal troops against the British 1857 and the mutiny of some Russian soldiers in World War I who left the eastern front for home and helped to bring about the Russian Revolution of 1917. French and British soldiers in the trenches mutinied then, too. Several American units mutinied during the War of American Independence and the War of 1812.

In the UK, as defined in the 1879 Army Discipline Act, the punishment in serious cases can be death; the last British soldier to be executed for mutiny was Private Jim Daly in India in 1920.

Mutsuhito personal name of the Japanese emperor ◊Meiji.

mutual assured destruction (MAD) the basis of the theory of ◊deterrence by possession of nuclear weapons.

I question whether God himself would wish me to hide behind the principles of nonviolence while innocent people are being slaughtered.

                          Bishop Abel Muzorewa 1978

Muzorewa Abel (Tendekayi) 1925– . Zimbabwean politician and Methodist bishop. He was president of the African National Council 1971–85 and prime minister of Rhodesia/Zimbabwe 1979–80. He was detained for a year 1983–84. He was leader of the minority United Africa National Council, which merged with the Zimbabwe Unity Movement (ZUM) 1994.

MVD (abbreviation for the *Soviet Ministry of Internal Affairs*) name (1946–53) of the Soviet secret police; later the ◊KGB.

Myanmar formerly (until 1989) *Burma* country in SE Asia, bounded NW by India and Bangladesh, NE by China, SE by Laos and Thailand, and SW by the Bay of Bengal.

history The Burmese date their era from AD 638, when they had arrived from the region where China meets Tibet. By 850 they had organized a state in the centre of the plain at Pagan, and in the period 1044–1287 maintained a hegemony over most of the area. In 1287 Kublai Khan's grandson Ye-su Timur occupied the region after destroying the Pagan dynasty. After he withdrew, anarchy supervened. From about 1490 to 1750 the Toungoo dynasty maintained itself, with increasing difficulty; in 1752 Alaungpaya reunited the country and founded Rangoon (now Yangon) as his capital.

Burmese wars In a struggle with Britain 1824–26, Alaungpaya's descendants lost the coastal strip from Chittagong to Cape Negrais. The second Burmese War 1852 resulted in the British annexation of Lower Burma, including Rangoon. Thibaw, the last Burmese king, precipitated the third Burmese War 1885, and the British seized Upper Burma 1886. The country was united as a province of India until 1937, when it was made a crown colony with a degree of self-government.

Burma was occupied 1942–45 by Japan, under a government of anti-British nationalists. The nationalists, led by Aung San and U Nu, later founded the Anti-Fascist People's Freedom League (AFPFL). Burma was liberated 1945 and achieved full independence outside the ◊Commonwealth 1948.

republic A parliamentary democracy was established under the Socialist AFPFL led by Prime Minister U Nu. The republic was weakened by civil war between the Karen National Liberation Army (KNLA), communist guerrillas, and ethnic group separatists. Splits within the AFPFL forced the formation of an emergency caretaker government by General Ne Win (1911–) 1958–60, leading to a military coup 1962 and abolition of the parliamentary system. Ne Win became head of a revolutionary council and established a strong one-party state.

In 1974 a new constitution was adopted, the military leaders became civilian rulers, and Ne Win became president. He stepped down to be replaced by U San Yu (1918–) 1981.

Burmese socialism The post-1962 government adopted a foreign policy of neutralist isolationism while at home it pursued its unique, self-reliant, Buddhist-influenced 'Burmese Way towards Socialism', founded on state ownership in the commercial-industrial sector and strict agricultural price control. Internal opposition by armed separatist groups continued after 1962, causing the economy to deteriorate. The Chinese-funded Burmese Communist Party established control over parts of the north; the Karen National Liberation Army in the southeast; and the Kachin Independence Army in the northeast.

opposition movement In 1975 the noncommunist ethnic separatist groups joined together to form the broad National Democratic Front with the aim of creating a federal union. In 1974 and 1976 worsening economic conditions led to a wave of food riots and in Sept 1987 student demonstrations broke out in Rangoon. Workers' riots followed in the spring of 1988. Initially they were violently suppressed, at the cost of several hundred lives, but in mid-1988 San Yu and Ne Win, the leader of the ruling party, were forced to resign, as was the newly appointed president, Brig-Gen Sein Lwin, after the murder of 3,000 unarmed demonstrators. With a mass prodemocracy movement sweeping the nation, the more reformist Maung Maung took over as president and free multiparty elections were promised 'within three months'.

military rule However, in Sept 1988 a military coup was staged by General Saw Maung. Martial law was imposed and authority was transferred to a 19-member state law and order restoration council. The new regime pursued a more liberal economic course. Officially it legalized the formation of political parties, but popular opposition leaders, including Aung San Suu Kyi (the daughter of ◊Aung San) and U Nu, were under house arrest and barred from standing in the elections of May 1990. Behind the scenes, Ne Win remained in control. In June 1989 the country's name was changed to Myanmar.

The May 1990 elections resulted in an overwhelming victory for opposition parties but the military remained in power. An opposition 'parallel government' headed by Dr Sein Win was formed Dec 1990. It was supported by ethnic rebel forces, but denounced by the bulk of the main opposition force. The socialist party headed by U Nu, still under house arrest, was outlawed in 1991.

military crackdown Serious human rights abuses continued. The ruling junta waged military offensives against Karen ethnic insurgents and moved 75,000 troops into Arakan state, in SW Myanmar, in an attempt to stamp out a Muslim-led pro-independence movement. The latter prompted the flight of 50,000 Rohingya Muslims to Bangladesh during late 1991, and as many as 60,000 Muslims fled Myanmar after a further military crackdown on Karen rebels Jan–Feb 1992.

foreign response In Oct 1991 Suu Kyi was awarded the Nobel Peace Prize. The West imposed sanctions against Myanmar. The Association of South East Asian Nations (ASEAN) pursued a more positive policy.

martial law ended In April 1992 Saw Maung stepped down and was succeeded by Than Shwe, the former defence minister. Real power in the junta was said to rest with Khin Nyunt, head of military intelligence, and the former dictator Ne Win. In the same month, U Nu was released from jail along with several other political prisoners but not Suu Kyi, said to be held in circumstances that endanger her life. In Sept 1992 the government ended martial law but the military retained a tight control over political activities. Human-rights abuses continued and Western sanctions remained in force.

Mycenaean civilization Bronze Age civilization that flourished in Crete, Cyprus, Greece, the Aegean Islands, and W Anatolia about 3000–1000 BC. During this period, magnificent architecture and sophisticated artefacts were produced.

Mycenaean civilization was strongly influenced by the ◊Minoan civilization from Crete, from about 1600 BC. It continued to thrive, with its centre at Mycenae, after the decline of Crete in about 1400. It was finally overthrown by the Dorian invasions, about 1100. The system of government was by kings, who also monopolized priestly functions. The Mycenaeans have been identified with the Achaeans of Homer; they may also have been the marauding ◊Sea Peoples of Egyptian records. They used a form of Greek deciphered by Michael Ventris called Linear B, which has been discovered on large numbers of clay tablets containing administrative records. Their palaces were large and luxurious, and their tombs (known as beehive tombs) were massive and impressive monuments. Pottery, frescoes, and metalwork reached a high artistic level. Evidence of the civilization was brought to light by the excavations of Heinrich Schliemann at Troy, Mycenae, and Tiryns (a stronghold on the plain of Argolis) from 1870 onwards, and of Arthur Evans in Crete from 1899.

My Lai massacre killing of 109 civilians in My Lai, a village in South Vietnam, by US troops in March 1968. An investigation in 1969 was followed by the conviction of Lt William Calley, commander of the platoon.

Sentenced to life imprisonment 1971, Calley was later released on parole. His superior officer was acquitted but the trial revealed a US Army policy of punitive tactics against civilians. News of the massacre contributed to domestic pressure for the USA to end its involvement in Vietnam.

N

NAACP abbreviation for ◊*National Association for the Advancement of Colored People*, a US civil rights organization.

Nadir Shah (Khan) *c.* 1880–1933. King of Afghanistan from 1929. Nadir played a key role in the 1919 Afghan War, but was subsequently forced into exile in France. He returned to Kabul in 1929 to seize the throne and embarked on an ambitious modernization programme. This alienated the Muslim clergy and in 1933 he was assassinated by fundamentalists.

Nagasaki industrial port on Kyushu Island, Japan. Nagasaki was the only Japanese port open to European trade from the 16th century until 1859. An atom bomb was dropped on it by the USA 9 Aug 1945.

Three days after ◊Hiroshima, the second atom bomb was dropped here at the end of World War II. Of Nagasaki's population of 212,000, 73,884 were killed and 76,796 injured, not counting the long-term victims of radiation.

Nagorno-Karabakh autonomous region of ◊Azerbaijan An autonomous protectorate after the Russian revolution 1917, Nagorno-Karabakh was annexed to Azerbaijan 1923 against the wishes of the largely Christian-Armenian population. Since the local council declared its intention to transfer control of the region to Armenia 1989, the enclave has been racked by fighting between Armenian and Azeri troops, both attempting to assert control. By Feb 1992, the conflict had caused the loss of at least 1,000 lives (501 during 1991 alone) and the displacement of some 270,000 people, half of them Armenian and half Azeri.

In 1920, inter-ethnic clashes in the Karabakh town of Shusha resulted in the deaths of 30,000 Armenians and 15,000 Azeris. The conflict,

rooted in many centuries of Christian Armenian and Shi'ite Muslim Azeri enmity, re-erupted 1988 and the region has since been the subject of violent disputes between Azerbaijan and neighbouring Armenia.

Nagy Imre 1895–1958. Hungarian politician, prime minister 1953–55 and 1956. He led the Hungarian revolt against Soviet domination in 1956, for which he was executed.

Najibullah Ahmadzai 1947–96. Afghan communist politician, leader of the Peoples Democratic Party of Afghanistan (PDPA) from 1986, and state president 1986-92. Although his government initially survived the withdrawal of Soviet troops Feb 1989, continuing pressure from the Mujaheddin forces resulted in his eventual overthrow. He was executed Sept 1996 by the Talibaan (Islamic student army) who had seized control of most of Afghanistan.

Nakasone Yasuhiro 1917– . Japanese conservative politician, leader of the Liberal Democratic Party (LDP) and prime minister 1982–87. He stepped up military spending and increased Japanese participation in international affairs, with closer ties to the USA. He was forced to resign his party post 1989 as a result of having profited from insider trading in the Recruit scandal. After serving a two-year period of atonement, he rejoined the LDP 1991.

Nakasone was educated at Tokyo University. He held ministerial posts from 1967 and established his own faction within the conservative LDP. In 1982 he was elected president of the LDP and prime minister. He encouraged a less paternalist approach to economic management. Although embarrassed by the conviction of one of his supporters in the 1983 Lockheed corruption scandal, he was re-elected 1986 by a landslide.

Namibia formerly (to 1968) *South West Africa* country in SW Africa, bounded N by Angola and Zambia, E by Botswana and South Africa, and W by the Atlantic Ocean. Walvis Bay, part of South Africa, forms an enclave in Namibia on the Atlantic coast.

history Originally inhabited by the Damara people, it was annexed, with the exception of the British/Cape Colony enclave of Walvis Bay, by Germany 1884; it was occupied in World War I by South African forces under Louis Botha, and was mandated to South Africa 1920.

South African rule South Africa did not accept the termination of the mandate by the United Nations 1966, although briefly accepting the principle of ultimate independence 1978 (UN Security Council Resolution 435);

Napoleonic Europe *The French Revolutionary Wars and later Napoleonic campaigns made Napoleon Bonaparte master of continental Europe. The French Empire was extended to include the Austrian Netherlands and the United Provinces. The German states were amalgamated into the Confederation of the Rhine, and French control was temporarily extended into Spain and much of E Central Europe after Napoleon's victory over Austria at Austerlitz 1805 and during his ultimately unsuccessful Russian campaign 1812.*

in 1968 the UN renamed the territory Namibia. South Africa's apartheid laws were extended to the colony 1966 and in opposition to such racial discrimination Sam ◊Nujoma, an Ovambo, led a political (from 1958) and then (from the mid-1960s) an armed resistance campaign for independence, forming the South-West Africa People's Organization (SWAPO) and the People's Liberation Army of Namibia (PLAN). Following harassment, he was forced into exile 1960, establishing guerrilla bases in Angola and Zambia. Military conflict in Namibia escalated from the mid-1970s as the Pretoria regime

attempted to topple the Marxist government in neighbouring Angola. In 1985 South Africa installed a puppet regime in Namibia, the Transitional Government of National Unity ('TGNU), a multiracial body, but including only one Ovambo minister. It attempted to reform the apartheid system but was internally divided between moderate reformist and conservative wings, and failed to secure UN recognition.

peace settlement In 1988 progress was finally made towards a peace settlement in Namibia as a result of both South Africa and the USSR (via Cuba) tiring of the cost of their proxy military involvement in the civil wars of both the colony and neighbouring Angola. In Aug 1988 the South African and Angolan governments agreed an immediate cease-fire, followed by the rapid withdrawal of South African forces from Angola and, during 1989, the phased withdrawal of Cuba's troops from Angola and South Africa's from Namibia. From April 1989, a UN peacekeeping force was stationed in Namibia to oversee the holding of multiparty elections in Nov. These were won by SWAPO, but its 57% share of the seats in the constituent assembly, which had the task of framing a new 'independence constitution', fell short of the two-thirds majority required for it to dominate the proceedings. As a consequence, a moderate multiparty constitution was adopted Feb 1990. Sam Nujoma was unanimously elected Namibia's first president by the assembly 16 Feb 1990, and was formally sworn in by the UN secretary general on independence day, 21 March 1990. Hage Geingob became prime minister. The retention of the commercially important Walvis Bay by South Africa on Namibia's independence caused tension between the two countries. Inconclusive talks were held in March 1991 over its future possession. However, in Sept 1991 it was announced that South Africa and Namibia had agreed to a joint administration of the enclave; in Aug 1992 it was agreed that a Walvis Bay Joint Administrative Body would be established.

Nanak 1469–c. 1539. Indian guru and founder of Sikhism, a religion based on the unity of God and the equality of all human beings. He was strongly opposed to caste divisions.

At 50, after many years travelling and teaching, he established a new town: Kartarpur, in the Punjab. Here he met his most trusted follower, Lehna. On his death-bed, Guru Nanak announced Lehna as his successor, and gave him the name Guru Angad.

Nana Sahib popular name for Dandhu Panth 1820–c. 1859. The adopted son of a former peshwa (chief minister) of the ◊Maratha people of central India, he joined the rebels in the ◊Indian Mutiny 1857–58, and was respon-sible for the massacre at Kanpur when safe conducts given to British civilians were broken and many women and children massacred. After the failure of the mutiny he took refuge in Nepal.

Nanjing or *Nanking* capital of Jiangsu province, China, 270 km/165 mi NW of Shanghai. The city dates from the 2nd century BC, perhaps earlier. It received the name Nanjing ('southern capital') under the Ming dynasty (1368–1644) and was the capital of China 1368–1403, 1928–37, and 1946–49.

Nanjing, Treaty of 1842 agreement between the UK and China, concluded at the end of the first Opium War, under which Hong Kong was ceded to Britain and five ◊treaty ports, Shanghai, Guangzhou (Canton), Xiamen (Amoy), Fuzhou (Foochow), and Ningbo, were opened to foreign trade. It was the first of the ◊unequal treaties, so called because it was forced on China and was favourable to the UK.

Nantes, Edict of decree by which Henry IV of France granted religious freedom to the ◊Huguenots 1598. It was revoked 1685 by Louis XIV.

Napier Robert Cornelis, 1st Baron Napier of Magdala 1810–1890. British field marshal. Knighted for his services in relieving Lucknow during the ◊Indian Mutiny, he took part in capturing Peking (Beijing) 1860 during the war against China in 1860. He was commander in chief in India 1870–76 and governor of Gibraltar 1876–82.

Naples, Kingdom of the southern part of Italy, alternately independent and united with ◊Sicily in the Kingdom of the Two Sicilies.

Naples was united with Sicily 1140–1282, first under Norman rule 1130–94, then Hohenstaufen 1194–1266, then Angevin from 1268; apart from Sicily, but under continued Angevin rule to 1435; reunited with Sicily 1442–1503, under the house of Aragon to 1501; a Spanish Habsburg possession 1504–1707 and Austrian 1707–35; under Spanish Bourbon rule 1735–99. The *Neapolitan Republic* was established 1799 after Napoleon had left Italy for Egypt, but fell after five months to the forces of reaction under Cardinal Ruffo, with the British admiral Nelson blockading the city by sea; many prominent citizens were massacred after the capitulation. The Spanish Bourbons were restored 1799, 1802–05, and 1815–60, when Naples joined the Kingdom of Italy.

Had I succeeded, I should have died with the reputation of the greatest man that ever lived.

Napoleon I

Napoleon I Bonaparte 1769–1821. Emperor of the French 1804–14 and 1814–15. A general from 1796 in the ◊Revolutionary Wars, in 1799 he overthrew the ruling Directory (see ◊French Revolution) and made himself dictator. From 1803 he conquered most of Europe (the ◊*Napoleonic Wars*) and installed his brothers as puppet kings (see ◊Bonaparte). After the Peninsular War and retreat from Moscow 1812, he was forced to abdicate 1814 and was banished to the island of Elba. In March 1815 he reassumed power but was defeated by British forces at the Battle of ◊Waterloo and exiled to the island of St Helena. His internal administrative reforms and laws are still evident in France.

Napoleon II 1811–1832. Title given by the Bonapartists to the son of Napoleon I and ◊Marie Louise; until 1814 he was known as the king of Rome and after 1818 as the duke of Reichstadt. After his father's abdication 1814 he was taken to the Austrian court, where he spent the rest of his life.

Napoleon III 1808–1873. Emperor of the French 1852–70, known as *Louis-Napoleon*. After two attempted coups (1836 and 1840) he was jailed, then went into exile, returning for the revolution of 1848, when he became president of the Second Republic but proclaimed himself emperor 1852. In 1870 he was manoeuvred by the German chancellor Bismarck into war with Prussia (see ◊Franco-Prussian war); he was forced to surrender at Sedan, NE France, and the empire collapsed.

Hoping to strengthen his regime by military triumphs, he joined in the Crimean War 1854–55, waged war with Austria 1859, winning the Battle of Solferino, annexed Savoy and Nice 1860, and attempted unsuccessfully to found a vassal empire in Mexico 1863–67. In so doing he aroused the mistrust of Europe and isolated France.

At home, his regime was discredited by its notorious corruption; republican and socialist opposition grew, in spite of severe repression, and forced Napoleon, after 1860, to make concessions in the direction of parliamentary government.

Napoleonic Wars 1803–15 a series of European wars conducted by Napoleon I following the ◊Revolutionary Wars, aiming for French conquest of Europe.

1803 Britain renewed the war against France, following an appeal from the Maltese against Napoleon's 1798 seizure of the island.

1805 Napoleon's planned invasion of Britain from Boulogne ended with Nelson's victory at ◊*Trafalgar*. Coalition formed against France by Britain, Austria, Russia, and Sweden. Austria defeated at Ulm; Austria and Russia at ◊*Austerlitz*.

1806 Prussia joined the coalition and was defeated at Jena; Napoleon instituted an attempted blockade, the *Continental System*, to isolate Britain from Europe.

1807 Russia defeated at Eylau and Friedland and, on making peace with Napoleon under the ◊*Treaty of Tilsit*, changed sides, agreeing to attack Sweden, but was forced to retreat.

1808 Napoleon's invasion of Portugal and strategy of installing his relatives as puppet kings led to the ◊*Peninsular War*.

1809 Revived Austrian opposition to Napoleon was ended by defeat at ◊*Wagram*.

1812 The Continental System finally collapsed on its rejection by Russia, and Napoleon made the fatal decision to invade; he reached *Moscow* but was defeated by the Russian resistance and by the bitter winter as he retreated through a countryside laid waste by the retreating Russians (380,000 French soldiers died).

1813 Britain, Prussia, Russia, Austria, and Sweden formed a new coalition, which defeated Napoleon at the *Battle of the Nations*, Leipzig, Germany. He abdicated and was exiled to Elba.

1814 Louis XVIII became king of France, and the Congress of Vienna met to conclude peace.

1815 Napoleon returned to Paris. On 16 June the British commander Wellington defeated the French marshal Ney at Quatre Bras (in Belgium, SE of Brussels), and Napoleon was finally defeated at *Waterloo*, S of Brussels, 18 June.

During the Napoleonic Wars, the annual cost of the British army was between 60% and 90% of total government income. About half of Napoleon's army was made up of foreign mercenaries, mainly Swiss and German.

Narayan Jaya Prakash 1902–1979. Indian politician. A veteran socialist, he was an associate of Vinobha Bham in the Bhoodan movement for rural reforms that took place during the last years of the Raj. He was prominent in the protest movement against Indira Gandhi's emergency regime 1975–77, and acted as umpire in the ◊Janata party leadership contest that followed Indira Gandhi's defeat in 1977.

Narodnik member of a secret Russian political movement, active 1873–76 before its suppression by the tsarist authorities. Narodniks were largely university students, and their main purpose was to convert the peasantry to socialism.

Narses 478–c. 573. Byzantine general. Originally a eunuch slave, he later became an official in the imperial treasury. He was joint commander with the Roman general Belisarius in Italy 538–39, and in 552 destroyed the Ostrogoths at Taginae in the Apennines.

Narváez Pánfilo de *c.* 1480–1525. Spanish conquistador and explorer. Narváez was largely responsible for bringing Cuba under Spanish control 1511. The governor of Cuba sent him to Mexico 1520 to reassert authority over Hernán ◊Cortés. Defeated, he was held captive for two years. He drowned during an expedition to Florida after a fruitless detour for gold split his party.

Naseby, Battle of decisive battle of the English Civil War 14 June 1645, when the Royalists, led by Prince Rupert, were defeated by Oliver Cromwell and General Fairfax. It is named after the nearby village of Naseby, 32 km/20 mi S of Leicester.

Nash Walter 1882–1968. New Zealand Labour politician. He was born in England, and emigrated to New Zealand 1909. He held ministerial posts 1935–49, was prime minister 1957–60, and leader of the Labour Party until 1963.

Nassau agreement treaty signed 18 Dec 1962 whereby the USA provided Britain with Polaris missiles, marking a strengthening in Anglo-American relations.

Nasser Gamal Abdel 1918–1970. Egyptian politician, prime minister 1954–56 and from 1956 president of Egypt (the United Arab Republic 1958–71). In 1952 he was the driving power behind the Neguib coup, which ended the monarchy. His nationalization of the Suez Canal 1956 led to an Anglo-French invasion and the ◊Suez Crisis, and his ambitions for an Egyptian-led union of Arab states led to disquiet in the Middle East (and in the West). Nasser was also an early and influential leader of the nonaligned movement.

Nasser entered the army from Cairo Military Academy, and was wounded in the Palestine War of 1948–49. Initially unpopular after the 1952 coup, he took advantage of demands for change by initiating land reform and depoliticizing the army. His position was secured by an unsuccessful assassination attempt 1954 and his handling of the Suez Crisis 1956.

Abdel Nasser is no more than a transient phenomenon that will run its course and leave.

Gamal Abdel Nasser 1967

Nation Carrie Amelia Moore 1846–1911. US Temperance Movement crusader during the Prohibition 1920–33. Protesting against Kansas state's flagrant disregard for the prohibition law, she marched into illegal saloons with a hatchet, lecturing the patrons on the abuses of alcohol and smashing bottles and bar.

national anthem patriotic song for official occasions. The US national anthem, 'The Star-Spangled Banner', was written during the war of 1812 by Francis Scott Key and was adopted officially in 1931. In Britain 'God Save the King/Queen' has been accepted as such since 1745, although both music and words are of much earlier origin. The German anthem 'Deutschland über Alles/Germany before everything' is sung to music by Haydn. The French national anthem, the ◊'Marseillaise', dates from 1792.

National Association for the Advancement of Colored People (NAACP) US civil-rights organization dedicated to ending inequality and segregation for African-Americans through nonviolent protest. Founded 1910, its first aim was to eradicate lynching. The NAACP campaigned to end segregation in state schools; it funded test cases that eventually led to the Supreme Court decision 1954 outlawing school segregation, although it was only through the ◊civil-rights movement of the 1960s that desegregation was achieved. In 1987 the NAACP had about 500,000 members, black and white.

national debt debt incurred by the central government of a country to its own people and institutions and also to overseas creditors. A government can borrow from the public by means of selling interest-bearing bonds, for example, or from abroad. Traditionally, a major cause of national debt was the cost of war but in recent decades governments have borrowed heavily in order to finance development or nationalization, to support an ailing currency, or to avoid raising taxes.

In Britain the national debt is managed by the Bank of England, under the control of the Treasury. The first issue of government stock in Britain was made in 1693, to raise a loan of £1 million. Historically, increases of the national debt have been caused by wartime expenditure; thus after the War of the Spanish Succession 1701–14 it reached £54 million. By 1900 it reached £610 million but World War I forced it up, by 1920, to £7,828 million and World War II, by 1945, to £21,870,221,651. Since then other factors have increased the national debt, including nationalization expenditure and overseas borrowing to support the pound. However, as a proportion of gross domestic product, the national debt has fallen since 1945 and stabilized at about 40–45%.

The US national debt was $2,436,453,269 in 1870 and $1,132,357,095 in 1905, but had risen to $24,299,321,467 by 1920 and it has since risen almost continuously, reaching $1,823,103 million in 1985.

National Guard ◊militia force recruited by each state of the USA. The volunteer National Guard units are under federal orders in emergencies, and under the control of the governor in peacetime, and are now an integral part of the US Army. The National Guard has been used against demonstrators; in May 1970 at Kent State University, Ohio, they killed four students who were protesting against the bombing of Cambodia by the USA.

National Insurance Act UK act of Parliament 1911, introduced by Lloyd George, Liberal chancellor, which first provided insurance for workers against ill health and unemployment.

nationalism in politics, a movement that consciously aims to unify a nation, create a state, or liberate it from foreign or imperialistic rule. Nationalist movements became a potent factor in European politics during the 19th century; since 1900 nationalism has become a strong force in Asia and Africa and in the late 1980s revived strongly in E Europe.

Stimulated by the French Revolution, movements arose in the 19th century in favour of national unification in Germany and Italy and national independence in Ireland, Italy, Belgium, Hungary, Bohemia, Poland, Finland, and the Balkan states. Revival of interest in the national language, history, traditions, and culture has accompanied and influenced most political movements.

nationalization policy of bringing a country's essential services and industries under public ownership. It was pursued, for example, by the UK Labour government 1945–51. In recent years the trend towards nationalization has slowed and in many countries (the UK, France, and Japan) reversed. Assets in the hands of foreign governments or companies may also be nationalized; for example, Iran's oil industry, the ◊Suez Canal, and US-owned fruit plantations in Guatemala, all in the 1950s.

National Party, Australian Australian political party representing the interests of the farmers and people of the smaller towns. It developed from about 1860 as the *National Country Party*, and holds the power balance between Liberals and Labor. It gained strength following the introduction of proportional representation 1918, and has been in coalition with the Liberals since 1949.

national service ◊conscription into the armed services in peacetime.

National Socialism official name for the ◊Nazi movement in Germany; see also ◊fascism.

Nations, Battle of the defeat of ◊Napoleon I by the coalition of Britain, Prussia, Russia, Austria, and Sweden in 1813.

NATO abbreviation for ◊*North Atlantic Treaty Organization*.

Nauru island country in Polynesia, SW Pacific, W of Kiribati.

history The first Europeans, Britons, arrived 1798 and called it Pleasant Island. The German empire seized it 1888. Nauru was placed under Australian administration by the League of Nations 1920, with the UK and New Zealand as co-trustees. Japan occupied and devastated Nauru 1942–45, destroying its mining facilities and deporting two-thirds of its population to Truk Atoll in Micronesia, 1,600 km/1,000 mi to the northwest. In 1947 Nauru became a United Nations trust territory administered by Australia.

independence Internal self-government was attained 1966, and in 1968, on achieving full independence, Nauru became a 'special member' of the ◊Commonwealth, with no direct representation at meetings of heads of government. The chief of Nauru, Hammer DeRoburt, was elected president 1968 and re-elected until 1983 with one interruption, 1976–78, when Bernard Dowiyogo was president. The Dec 1986 elections resulted in a hung parliament.

In the 1987 elections, DeRoburt secured a narrow majority. This prompted the defeated Kennan Adeang, who had briefly held power 1986, to establish the Democratic Party of Nauru as a formal opposition grouping. In Aug 1989 Adeang secured the ousting of DeRoburt on a vote of no confidence and Kensas Aroi became president, with Adeang as finance minister in the new government. According to Australian government sources, Aroi was DeRoburt's 'unacknowledged natural son'. Four months later Aroi resigned on the grounds of ill health and in the subsequent election was defeated by Bernard Dowiyogo. DeRobert died in Melbourne, Australia, July 1992.

resources Nauru is attempting to sue its former trustees (Australia, New Zealand, and the UK) for removing nearly all the island's phosphate-rich soil 1922–68, leaving it barren. Nauru received $2.5 million for phosphate worth $65 million and had to pay Australia $20 million to keep the remaining soil. Nauru's residual phosphate supplies, which have earned $80 million a year, are due to run out 1995 and an economic diversification programme has been launched.

Navajo or *Navaho* (Tena *Navahu* 'large planted field') member of a North American Indian people related to the Apache, and numbering about 200,000, mostly in Arizona. They speak an Athabaskan language, belonging to the Na-Dené family. The Navajo were traditionally cultivators; many now herd sheep and earn an income from tourism, making and selling rugs, blankets, and silver and turquoise jewellery. Their reservation, created 1868, is the largest in the USA (65,000 sq km/25,000 sq mi), and is mainly in NE Arizona.

Navarino, Battle of decisive naval action 20 Oct 1827 off Pylos in the Greek war of liberation that was won by the combined fleets of the English, French, and Russians under Vice-Admiral Edward Codrington (1770–1851) over the Turkish and Egyptian fleets. Navarino is the Italian and historic name of Pylos Bay, Greece, on the SW coast of the Peloponnese.

Navarre, Kingdom of former kingdom comprising the Spanish province of Navarre and part of what is now the French *département* of Basses-Pyrénées. It resisted the conquest of the ◊Moors and was independent until it became French 1284 on the marriage of Philip IV to the heiress of Navarre. In 1479 Ferdinand of Aragon annexed Spanish Navarre, with French Navarre going to Catherine of Foix (1483–1512), who kept the royal title. Her grandson became Henry IV of France, and Navarre was absorbed in the French crown lands 1620.

Navigation Acts in British history, a series of acts of Parliament passed from 1381 to protect English shipping from foreign competition and to ensure monopoly trading between Britain and its colonies. The last was repealed 1849 (coastal trade exempt until 1853). The Navigation Acts helped to establish England as a major sea power, although they led to higher prices. They ruined the Dutch merchant fleet in the 17th century, and were one of the causes of the ◊American Revolution.

1650 'Commonwealth Ordinance' forbade foreign ships to trade in English colonies.

1651 Forbade the importation of goods except in English vessels or in vessels of the country of origin of the goods. This act led to the Anglo-Dutch War 1652–54.

1660 All colonial produce was required to be exported in English vessels.

1663 Colonies were prohibited from receiving goods in foreign (rather than English) vessels.

Nazca town to the S of Lima, Peru, near a plateau that has geometric linear markings interspersed with giant outlines of birds and animals. The markings were made by American Indians, whose culture dates from the period 200 BC to AD 600, and their function is thought to be ritual rather than astronomical.

Nazca is famous for its pottery, which is often painted with animal, fish, plant, and bird designs in red, white, black, grey, and orange.

Nazi member of the *Nationalsozialistich Deutsche Arbeiterpartei*, usually referred to as the *Nazi Party*. The party was based on the Nazi ideology (◊Nazism).

Nazism ideology based on racism, nationalism, and the supremacy of the state over the individual. The German Nazi party, the *Nationalsozialistiche Deutsche Arbeiterpartei* (National Socialist German Workers' Party), was formed from the German Workers' Party (founded 1919) and led by Adolf ◊Hitler 1921–45.

During the 1930s, many similar parties were created throughout Europe and the USA, although only those of Austria, Hungary, and Sudetenland were of major importance. These parties collaborated with the German occupation of Europe 1939–45. After the Nazi atrocities of World War II (see ◊SS, ◊concentration camp, ◊Holocaust), the party was banned in Germany, but today parties with Nazi or neo-Nazi ideologies exist in many countries.

Nazi-Soviet pact see ◊Hitler–Stalin pact.

Neanderthal hominid of the Mid-Late Palaeolithic, named after the Neander Thal (valley) near Düsseldorf, Germany, where a skeleton was found in 1856. *Homo sapiens neanderthalensis* lived from about 100,000 to 35,000 years ago and was similar in build to present-day people, but slightly smaller, stockier, and heavier-featured with a strong jaw and prominent brow ridges on a sloping forehead.

Neanderthals lived in Europe, the Middle East, and Africa. They looked after their disabled and buried their dead ritualistically. Recent evidence suggests their physical capacity for the sounds of speech. They were replaced throughout Europe by, or possibly interbred with, *Homo sapiens sapiens*, newly arrived from Africa.

Nebuchadnezzar or *Nebuchadrezzar II* king of Babylonia from 604 BC. Shortly before his accession he defeated the Egyptians at Carchemish and brought Palestine and Syria into his empire. Judah revolted, with Egyptian assistance, 596 and 587–586 BC; on both occasions he captured Jerusalem and took many Hebrews into captivity. He largely rebuilt Babylon and constructed the hanging gardens.

Necker Jacques 1732–1804. French politician. As finance minister 1776–81, he attempted reforms, and was dismissed through Queen Marie Antoinette's influence. Recalled 1788, he persuaded Louis XVI to summon the States-General (parliament), which earned him the hatred of the court, and in July 1789 he was banished. The outbreak of the French Revolution with the storming of the Bastille forced his reinstatement, but he resigned Sept 1790.

Nefertiti or *Nofretete* queen of Egypt who ruled *c.* 1372–1350 BC; wife of the pharaoh ◊Ikhnaton.

Nehru Jawaharlal 1889–1964. Indian nationalist politician, prime minister from 1947. Before the partition (the division of British India into India and Pakistan), he led the socialist wing of the nationalist ◊Congress Party, and was second in influence only to Mohandas Gandhi. He was imprisoned nine times by the British 1921–45 for political activities. As prime minister from the creation of the dominion (later republic) of India in Aug 1947, he originated the idea of nonalignment (neutrality towards major powers). His daughter was Prime Minister Indira Gandhi. His sister, Vijaya Lakshmi Pandit (1900–1990) was the UN General Assembly's first female president (1953–54) .

Democracy is good. I say this because other systems are worse.

Jawaharlal Nehru *New York Times* 1961

Nehru Report constitution drafted for India 1928. After Indian nationalists rejected the ◊Simon Commission 1927, an all-party committee was set up, chaired by Motilal Nehru, to map out a constitution. Established to counter British charges that Indians could not find a constitutional consensus among themselves, it advocated that India be given dominion status of complete internal self-government. Many members of the Congress preferred complete independence to dominion status, and in 1929 announced a campaign of civil disobedience to support their demands.

Nelson Horatio, Viscount Nelson 1758–1805. English admiral. He joined the navy in 1770. In the Revolutionary Wars against France he lost the sight in his right eye 1794 and lost his right arm 1797. He became a national hero, and rear admiral, after the victory off Cape St Vincent, Portugal. In 1798 he tracked the French fleet to Aboukir Bay and almost entirely destroyed it in the Battle of the Nile. In 1801 he won a decisive victory over Denmark at the Battle of

◊Copenhagen, and in 1805, after two years of blockading Toulon, another over the Franco-Spanish fleet at the Battle of ◊Trafalgar, near Gibraltar.

England expects every man will do his duty.

Horatio Nelson
at the Battle of Trafalgar 1805

---

neocolonialism disguised form of ◊imperialism, by which a country may grant independence to another country but continue to dominate it by control of markets for goods or raw materials.

Neolithic last period of the ◊Stone Age, characterized by settled communities based on agriculture and domesticated animals, and identified by sophisticated, finely honed stone tools, and ceramic wares. The earliest Neolithic communities appeared about 9000 BC in the Middle East, followed by Egypt, India, and China. In Europe farming began in about 6500 BC in the Balkans and Aegean.

NEP abbreviation for the Soviet leader Lenin's ◊*New Economic Policy*.

Nepal landlocked country in the Himalayan mountain range in Central Asia, bounded N by Tibet (an autonomous region of China), E, S, and W by India.

history From one of a group of small principalities, the Gurkha people emerged to unite Nepal under King Prithivi Narayan Shah 1768. In 1816, after the year-long Anglo-Nepali 'Gurkha War', a British resident (government representative) was stationed in Katmandu and the kingdom became a British-dependent buffer state. The country was recognized as fully independent by Britain 1923 although it remained bound by treaty obligations until 1947, the year of India's independence. Between 1846 and 1951 Nepal was ruled by a hereditary prime minister of the Rana family. The Ranas were overthrown in a revolution led by the Nepali congress, and the monarchy, in the person of King Tribhuvan, was restored to power.

first constitution In 1959 King Mahendra Bir Bikram Shah, who had succeeded his father 1955, promulgated the nation's first constitution and held elections. The Nepali Congress Party leader B P Koirala became prime minister and proceeded to clash with the king over policy. King Mahendra thus dissolved parliament Dec 1960 and issued a ban on political parties Jan 1961. In Dec 1962 he introduced a new, monarch-dominated constitution with an indirectly elected national assembly and tiered system of panchayats (councils).

pressure for reform King Mahendra died 1972. His son Birendra (1945–   ), faced with mounting agitation for political reform led by B P Koirala, held a referendum on the constitution. As a result, it was amended, and the first elections to the national assembly were held May 1981. The new, more independently minded assembly in July 1983 unseated Prime Minister Surya Bahadur Thapa, despite his royal support, and installed in office Lokendra Bahadur Chand. The next assembly elections, in May 1986, returned a majority of members opposed to the partyless panchayat system and resulted in the replacement of Prime Minister Chand.

democratization process In April 1990, following mass prodemocracy demonstrations during which police shot 150 protesters, King Birendra lifted the ban on opposition parties and abolished the panchayat system. In Sept he approved a new constitution that transferred political power from the monarchy to an elected government. In readiness for the 1991 elections, two factions of the Communist Party sank their differences to become the United Nepal Communist Party. Marking the culmination of a 15-month democratization process, on 12 May 1991 the Nepali Congress Party secured a narrow majority of seats in the first pluralist general election since 1959, and Girija Prasad Koirala, brother of former prime minister B P Koirala, became prime minister.

In 1992 communist-led demonstrations in Katmandu and Pátan campaigned for the government's resignation.

foreign affairs In foreign affairs, Nepal has pursued a neutral policy as a member of the ◊nonaligned movement, seeking to create a 'zone of peace' in S Asia between India and China. Increased commercial links with China have been resented by India who, March 1989–June 1990, imposed a partial blockade on Nepal's borders as part of a dispute over the renegotiation of expired transit and trade duties.

Nero Lucius Domitius Ahenobarbus AD 37–68. Roman emperor from 54. In 59 he had his mother Agrippina and his wife Octavia put to death. He patronised the arts and often performed in public. The great fire at Rome in 64 was blamed on the Christians. In 65 a plot against Nero was discovered. In 68 there were further revolts, and Nero committed suicide.

Nerva Marcus Cocceius AD *c.* 35–98. Roman emperor. He was proclaimed emperor on Domitian's death AD 96, and introduced state loans for farmers, family allowances, and allotments of land to poor citizens in his sixteen-month reign.

Netherlands, the country in W Europe on the North Sea, bounded E by Germany and S by Belgium.

history The land south of the Rhine, inhabited by Celts and Germanic peoples, was brought under Roman rule by Julius Caesar as governor of Gaul 51 BC. The ◊Franks followed, and their kings subdued the Frisians and Saxons north of the Rhine in the 7th–8th centuries and imposed Christianity on them. After the empire of ◊Charlemagne broke up, the local feudal lords, headed by the count of Holland and the bishop of Utrecht, became practically independent, although they owed nominal allegiance to the German or Holy Roman Empire. Many Dutch towns during the Middle Ages became prosperous trading centres, usually ruled by small groups of merchants. In the 15th century the Netherlands or Low Countries (Holland, Belgium, Flanders) passed to the dukes of Burgundy, and in 1504 to the Spanish Habsburgs.

war of independence The Dutch opposed the economic demands of the Spanish crown and rebelled from 1568 against the tyranny of the Catholic Philip II of Spain. William the Silent, Prince of Orange, and his sons Maurice (1567–1625) and Frederick Henry (1584–1647) were the leaders of the revolt and of a confederation established by the Union of Utrecht 1579 which created the (seven northern) United Provinces. The south (now Belgium and Luxembourg) was reconquered by Spain, but not the north, and in 1648 its independence as the Dutch Republic was finally recognized under the Treaty of ◊Westphalia. A long struggle followed between the Orangist or popular party, which favoured centralization under the Prince of Orange as chief magistrate or *stadholder*, and the oligarchical or states' rights party. The latter, headed by Johann de ◊Witt, seized control 1650, but William of Orange (◊William III of England) recovered the stadholderate with the French invasion 1672.

Batavian Republic Despite the long war of independence, during the early 17th century the Dutch led the world in trade, art, and science, and founded an empire in the East and West Indies. Commercial and colonial rivalries led to naval wars with England 1652–54,

1665–67, and 1672–74. Thereafter until 1713 Dutch history was dominated by a struggle with France under Louis XIV. These wars exhausted the Netherlands, which in the 18th century ceased to be a great power. The French revolutionary army was welcomed 1795 and created the Batavian Republic. In 1806 Napoleon made his brother Louis king of Holland and 1810–13 annexed the country to France. The Congress of ◊Vienna united N and S Netherlands under King William I (son of Prince William V of Orange), but the south broke away 1830 to become independent Belgium.

cooperation with neighbours Under William I (reigned 1814–40), William II (1840–49), William III (1849–90), and Queen Wilhelmina (1890–1948), the Netherlands followed a path of strict neutrality, but its brutal occupation by Germany 1940–45 persuaded it to adopt a policy of cooperation with its neighbours. It became a member of the Western European Union, the North Atlantic Treaty Organization (NATO), the Benelux customs union, the European Coal and Steel Community, the European Atomic Energy Community (Euratom), and the European Economic Community. In 1980 Queen Juliana, who had reigned since 1948, abdicated in favour of her eldest daughter, Beatrix.

The granting of independence to former colonies (Indonesia 1949, with the addition of W New Guinea 1963; Surinam 1975; increased immigration and unemployment. All governments since 1945 have been coalitions, with the parties differing mainly over economic policies. In the Sept 1989 elections, fought largely on environmental issues, Ruud Lubbers's Christian Democrats won the most parliamentary seats. Lubbers formed a coalition government with the leftist Labour Party.

neutrality the legal status of a country that decides not to choose sides in a war. Certain states, notably Switzerland and Austria, have opted for permanent neutrality. Neutrality always has a legal connotation. In peacetime, neutrality towards the big power alliances is called *nonalignment* (see ◊nonaligned movement).

New Caledonia island group in the S Pacific, a French overseas territory between Australia and the Fiji Islands. New Caledonia was visited by Captain Cook 1774 and became French 1853. A general strike to gain local control of nickel mines 1974 was defeated. In 1981 the French socialist government promised moves towards independence. The 1985 elections resulted in control of most regions by Kanaks, but not the majority of seats. In 1986 the French conservative government reversed the reforms. The Kanaks boycotted a referendum Sept 1987 and a majority were in favour of remaining a French dependency. In 1989 the leader of the Socialist National Liberation front (the most prominent separatist group), Jean-Marie Tjibaou, was murdered.

Newcastle Thomas Pelham-Holles, Duke of Newcastle 1693–1768. British Whig politician, prime minster 1754–56 and 1757–62. He served as secretary of state for thirty years from 1724, then succeeded his younger brother Henry ◊Pelham as prime minister 1754. In 1756 he resigned as a result of setbacks in the Seven Years' War, but returned to office 1757 with ◊Pitt the Elder (1st Earl of Chatham) taking responsibility for the conduct of the war.

New Deal in US history, programme introduced by President F D Roosevelt 1933 to counter the Great ◊Depression, including employment on public works, farm loans at low rates, and social reforms such as old-age and unemployment insurance, prevention of child labour, protection of employees against unfair practices by employers, and loans to local authorities for slum clearance.

Some of the provisions of the New Deal were declared unconstitutional by the Supreme Court 1935–36. The New Deal encouraged the growth of trade-union membership, brought previously unregulated areas of the US economy under federal control, and revitalized cultural life and community spirit. Although full employment did not come until World War II, the New Deal did bring political stability to the industrial-capitalist system.

New Economic Policy (NEP) economic policy of the USSR 1921–29 devised by the Soviet leader Lenin. Rather than requisitioning all agricultural produce above a stated subsistence allowance, the state requisitioned only a fixed proportion of the surplus; the rest could be traded freely by the peasant. The NEP thus reinstated a limited form of free-market trading, although the state retained complete control of major industries.

The NEP was introduced in March 1921 after a series of peasant revolts and the ◊Kronstadt uprising. Aimed at re-establishing an alliance with the peasantry, it began as an agricultural measure to act as an incentive for peasants to produce more food. The policy was ended in 1928 by Stalin's first Five-Year Plan, which began the collectivization of agriculture.

Newfoundland and Labrador Canadian province on the Atlantic Ocean. Colonized by Vikings about AD 1000, Newfoundland was reached by the English, under the Italian navigator Giovanni ◊Caboto 1497. It was the first English colony, established 1583. French settlements made; British sovereignty was not recognized until 1713, although France retained the offshore islands of St Pierre and Miquelon. Internal self-government was achieved 1855. In 1934, as Newfoundland had fallen into financial difficulties, administration was vested in a governor and a special commission. A 1948 referendum favoured federation with Canada and the province joined Canada 1949.

New Frontier programme of US reforms initiated by John F ◊Kennedy.

New Granada viceroyalty, or province, of the Spanish empire in the New World from 1717. It took up the NW region of South America, and was created to defend Cartagena and the Pacific coast. The capital was Sante Fé de Bogotá. New Granada was liberated by Simón ◊Bolívar The viceroyalty was suppressed 1723, but reinstated 1739 because of its strategic position in the war with Great Britain. Towards the end of the 18th century it was a cultural centre of the Spanish empire.

New Guinea island in the SW Pacific, N of Australia, comprising Papua New Guinea and the Indonesian province of West Irian (Irian Jaya area). Part of the Dutch East Indies from 1828, West Irian was ceded by the United Nations to Indonesia 1963.

The western half of New Guinea was annexed by the Dutch 1828. In 1884 the area of Papua on the southeast coast was proclaimed a protectorate by the British, and in the same year Germany took possession of the northeast quarter of New Guinea. Under Australian control 1914–21, German New Guinea was administered as a British mandate and then united with Papua 1945. Papua and New Guinea joint ly gained full independence as Papua New Guinea 1975. The Dutch retained control over the western half of the island (West Irian) after Indonesia gained its independence 1949, but were eventually forced to transfer administrative reponsibility to Indonesia 1963.

Tension between Papua New Guinea and Indonesia has heightened as a result of a growing number of border incidents involving Indonesian troops and Irianese separatist guerrillas. At the same time large numbers of refugees have fled eastwards into Papua New Guinea from West Irian.

New Hebrides former name (until 1980) of ◊Vanuatu, a country in the S Pacific.

Ne Win adopted name of Maung Shu Maung 1911– . Myanmar (Burmese) politician, prime minister 1958–60, ruler from 1962 to 1974, president 1974–81, and chair until 1988 of the ruling Burma Socialist Programme Party (BSPP). His domestic 'Burmese Way to Socialism' policy programme brought the economy into serious decline.

New Ireland Forum meeting between politicians of the Irish Republic and Northern Ireland May 1983. It offered three potential solutions to the Northern Irish problem, but all were rejected by the UK the following year.

newly industrialized country (NIC) country that has in recent decades experienced a breakthrough into manufacturing and rapid export-led economic growth. The prime examples are Taiwan, Hong Kong, Singapore, and South Korea. Their economic development during the 1970s and 1980s was partly due to a rapid increase of manufactured goods in their exports.

New Model Army army created 1645 by Oliver Cromwell to support the cause of Parliament during the English ◊Civil War. It was characterized by organization and discipline. Thomas Fairfax was its first commander.

Newport Riots violent demonstrations by the ◊Chartists in 1839 in Newport, Wales, in support of the Peoples' Charter. It was suppressed with the loss of 20 lives.

New Socialist Destour Party former name (1988–89) of Tunisian political party Democratic Constitutional Rally (RCD).

New Spain viceroyalty, or province, of Spain's American empire established 1536. It comprised present-day Mexico, Central America, the southern half of the United States, the Antilles, and the Philippine Islands. The main sources of wealth were silver mines at Potosí, Bolivia, and Zacatecas, Mexico, and some huge cattle ranches. After a century of decline, New Spain grew steadily from 1770 until it fell to the independence movements 1810–21.

New Style the Gregorian ◊calendar introduced in 1582 and now used throughout most of the Christian world.

New World the Americas, so called by the first Europeans who reached them.

New Zealand or *Aotearoa* country in the SW Pacific Ocean, SE of Australia, comprising two main islands, North Island and South Island, and other small islands.

history New Zealand was occupied by the Polynesian ◊Maoris some time before the 14th century. The Dutch explorer Abel ◊Tasman reached it 1642 but the Maoris would not let him land. The English captain James ◊Cook explored the coasts 1769, 1773, and 1777. British missionaries began to arrive from 1815. By the Treaty of Waitangi 1840 the Maoris accepted British sovereignty; colonization began, and large-scale sheep farming was developed. The colony achieved self-government 1853. The Maoris resented the loss of their land and rose in revolt 1845–47 and 1860–72, until concessions were made, including representation in parliament. George Grey, governor 1845–53 and 1861–70 and Radical prime minister 1877–84, was largely responsible for the conciliation of the Maoris and the introduction of male suffrage.

independence The Conservatives held power 1879–90 and were succeeded by a Liberal government that ruled with trade union support; this government introduced women's suffrage 1893 and old-age pensions 1898, and was a pioneer in labour legislation. After 1912 the Reform (formerly Conservative) Party regained power, and the trade unions broke with the Liberals to form the Labour Party. The Reform and Liberal parties united to become the National Party 1931. New Zealand became a dominion in the British Empire 1907 and was granted full independence 1931. New Zealand troops had served in the Boer War in South Africa, and more than 100,000 fought in World Wars I and II. Independence was formally accepted by the New Zealand legislature 1947.

political stability The country has a record of political stability, with the centrist National Party holding office from the 1930s until it was replaced by a Labour Party administration, led by Norman Kirk, 1972. During this period New Zealand built up a good social security system. The economy was thriving at the time Kirk took office, but growing inflation was aggravated by the 1973–74 energy crisis that resulted in a balance-of-payments deficit. The Labour government's foreign policy line was influenced by the UK's decision to join the European Economic Community, which was likely to affect New Zealand's future exports. It began a phased withdrawal from some of the country's military commitments in SE Asia and established diplomatic relations with China. Norman Kirk died Aug 1974 and was succeeded by the finance minister, Wallace Rowling. The state of the economy worsened, and in 1975 the National Party, led by Robert ◊Muldoon, was returned to power. However, the economy failed to revive, and in 1984 Muldoon introduced controversial labour legislation. To renew his mandate, he called an early election

but was swept out of office by the Labour Party.

non-nuclear military policy The Labour government elected Aug 1987 (with the same majority as in the previous parliament) had fought the election on a non-nuclear military policy, which its leader Prime Minister David Lange immediately put into effect, forbidding any vessels carrying nuclear weapons or powered by nuclear energy from entering New Zealand's ports. This put a strain on relations with the USA, resulting in a suspension of several military-related provisions of the ANZUS pact. In 1985 the trawler *Rainbow Warrior*, the flagship of the environmentalist pressure group Greenpeace, which was monitoring nuclear tests in French Polynesia, was mined in Auckland harbour by French secret service agents, killing a Portuguese photographer aboard. The French prime minister eventually admitted responsibility, and New Zealand demanded compensation.

James McLay was leader of the National Party 1984–86, replaced by James Bolger. In the 1984 general election Labour won 56 seats in the House, and the National Party, 37. In July 1987 the National Party gave its support to the government in a bipartisan non-nuclear policy, and as a result the USA reclassified New Zealand as a 'friendly', rather than an 'allied' country. In Aug Lange was re-elected with a majority of 17. In Aug 1989, Lange resigned, citing health reasons, and was replaced by Geoffrey Palmer. In Sept 1990, faced with a 'no confidence' vote, Prime Minister Palmer resigned and was replaced by a former foreign-affairs minister, Mike Moore. In the Oct 1990 general election the ruling Labour Party was defeated and the National Party leader, Jim Bolger, became the new prime minister. In Nov 1991 Robert Muldoon criticized Bolger's right-wing social policies and announced his planned retirement from parliament for early 1992.

In Dec 1991 New Zealand's traditional two-party party political system was challenged by the formation of the Alliance Party, comprising the Democratic Party, the New Labour Party (NLP), the Green Party, and the (mainly Maori) New Zealand Self-Government Party.

In July 1992 the ban imposed on visits by US warships was lifted and in Sept a referendum approved a change in the voting system, to make it semi-proportional, with effect from 1996.

Ney Michael, Duke of Elchingen, Prince of Ney 1769–1815. Marshal of France under ◊Napoleon I, who commanded the rearguard of the French army during the retreat from

Moscow, and for his personal courage was called 'the bravest of the brave'. When Napoleon returned from Elba, Ney was sent to arrest him, but instead deserted to him and fought at Waterloo. He was subsequently shot for treason.

Soldiers, when I give the command to fire, fire straight at my heart. Wait for the order. It will be my last to you.

Marshal Michael Ney
before his execution by firing squad 1815

Nguyen Van Linh 1914–   . Vietnamese communist politician, member of the Politburo 1976–81 and from 1985; party leader 1986–91. He began economic liberalization and troop withdrawal from Cambodia and Laos.

Nguyen, born in North Vietnam, joined the anti-colonial Thanh Nien, a forerunner of the current Communist Party of Vietnam (CPV), in Haiphong 1929. He spent much of his subsequent party career in the South as a pragmatic reformer. He was a member of CPV's Politburo and secretariat 1976–81, suffered a temporary setback when party conservatives gained the ascendancy, and re-entered the Politburo in 1985, becoming CPV leader in Dec 1986 and resigning from the post June 1991.

Nicaea, Council of Christian church council held in Nicaea (now Iznik, Turkey) in 325, called by the Roman emperor Constantine. It condemned ◊Arianism as heretical and upheld the doctrine of the Trinity in the Nicene Creed.

Nicaragua country in Central America, between the Pacific Ocean and the Caribbean Sea, bounded N by Honduras and S by Costa Rica.

history For early history, see ◊American Indian. The first European to reach Nicaragua was Gil Gonzalez de Avila 1522, who brought it under Spanish rule. It remained Spanish until 1821 and was then briefly united with Mexico. Nicaragua achieved full independence 1838.

foreign investment After two decades of turmoil and invasions from other Central American states, Nicaragua experienced 30 years of relative tranquillity 1863–93 under Conservative rule. This long period of peace led to increasing foreign investment, especially in coffee plantations and railway construction. The Liberal dictator Santos Zelaya, in power 1803–1909, promoted state education, the separation of church and state, and civil marriage

and divorce. He also led the movement for a brief union 1896–98 with El Salvador and Honduras.

US military presence In 1912, at the Nicaraguan government's request, the USA established military bases in the country. Their presence was opposed by a guerrilla group led by Augusto César Sandino. The USA withdrew its forces 1933, but not before it had set up and trained a national guard, commanded by a trusted nominee, General Anastasio Somoza. Sandino was assassinated 1934, but some of his followers continued their guerrilla activity.

Somoza rule The Somoza family began a near-dictatorial rule that was to last for over 40 years. During this time they amassed a huge personal fortune. General Anastasio Somoza was elected president 1936 and stayed in office until his assassination 1956, when he was succeeded by his son Luis. The left-wing Sandinista National Liberation Front (FSLN), named after the former guerrilla leader, was formed 1962 with the object of overthrowing the Somozas by revolution. Luis Somoza was followed by his brother Anastasio, who headed an even more notorious regime. In 1979, after considerable violence and loss of life, Somoza was ousted; see ◊Nicaraguan Revolution.

Sandinista reconstruction The FSLN established a provisional junta of national reconstruction led by Daniel Ortega Saavedra, published a guarantee of civil rights, and appointed a council of state, prior to an elected national assembly and a new constitution; assembly elections held 1984 endorsed the FSLN.

relations with USA Nicaragua's relations with the USA deteriorated rapidly with the election of President Reagan. He froze the package of economic assistance arranged by his predecessor, Jimmy Carter, alleging that the Sandinista government was supporting attempts to overthrow the administration in El Salvador. In March 1982 the Nicaraguan government declared a state of emergency in the wake of attacks on bridges and petroleum installations. The Reagan administration embarked on a policy of destabilizing Nicaragua's government and economy by actively supporting the counter-revolutionary forces (the Contras) – known to have executed prisoners, killed civilians, and engaged in forced conscription – and by covert ◊Central Intelligence Agency operations, including the mining of Nicaraguan harbours 1984.

In Feb 1985 Reagan denounced Ortega's regime, saying that his objective was to 'remove it in the sense of its present structure'. In May 1986 Eden Pastora, a Contra leader, gave up the fight against the Sandinistas and was granted asylum in Costa Rica. The following month the US Congress approved $100 million in overt military aid to the Contras; total US aid to the Contras was $300 million.

Political parties were ostensibly legalized under the terms of a regional peace plan signed by the presidents of El Salvador, Guatemala, Costa Rica, Honduras, and Nicaragua, and peace talks with the Contra rebels had several false starts. In March 1989, 1,900 members of the former National Guard of Anastasia Somoza were released.

Sandinista government defeated Elections held Feb 1990 were won by Violeta Barrios de Chamorro of the US-backed National Opposition Union (UNO). The Bush administration spent $9 million on her election campaign. The USA lifted its economic embargo in March. By the end of June the Contra rebel army had been disbanded and the government had committed itself to reducing armed forces by 50%. In July violent riots occurred as people protested about land rights, inflation, and unemployment.

US pressure continues Chamorro's state visit to the USA in April 1991 was the first by a Nicaraguan president for over 50 years. In exchange for Nicaragua dropping its claim to the damages of $17 billion awarded it by the World Court against the USA, President Bush pledged economic support for Nicaragua, whose total international debt was almost $10 billion. The cost to Nicaragua of the US economic and Contra warfare has been estimated at $15 billion, with 30,000 people killed. US aid was suspended June 1992 due to concern over the extent of Sandinista's influence in Chamorro's government; in an effort to end the suspension, Chamorro dismissed 12 high-level police officers linked with Sandinista.

An earthquake Sept 1992 claimed 116 victims, with more than 150 people declared missing and over 16,000 made homeless.

Nicaraguan Revolution the revolt 1978–79 in Nicaragua, led by the socialist *Sandinistas* against the US-supported right-wing dictatorship established by Anastasio Somoza. His son, President Anastasio (Debayle) Somoza (1925–1980), was forced into exile 1979 and assassinated in Paraguay. The Sandinista National Liberation Front (FSLN) was named after Augusto César Sandino, a guerrilla leader killed by the US-trained National Guard 1934.

Nicholas I 1796–1855. Tsar of Russia from 1825. His Balkan ambitions led to war with Turkey 1827–29 and the Crimean War 1853–56.

Russia has two generals in whom she can confide – generals Janvier and Février.

Nicholas I quoted in *Punch* 1853

Nicholas II 1868–1918. Tsar of Russia 1894–1917. He was dominated by his wife, Tsarina ◊Alexandra, who was under the influence of the religious charlatan ◊Rasputin. His mismanagement of the Russo-Japanese War and of internal affairs led to the revolution of 1905, which he suppressed, although he was forced to grant limited constitutional reforms. He took Russia into World War I in 1914, was forced to abdicate in 1917 after the ◊Russian Revolution and was executed with his family.

Niger landlocked country in NW Africa, bounded N by Algeria and Libya, E by Chad, S by Nigeria and Benin, and W by Burkina Faso and Mali.

history Niger was part of ancient and medieval empires in Africa. European explorers arrived in the late 18th century, and Tuareg people invaded the area from the north. France seized it from the Tuaregs 1904 and made it part of French West Africa, although fighting continued until 1922. It became a French overseas territory 1946 and an autonomous republic within the French Community 1958.

independence Niger achieved full independence 1960, and Hamani Diori was elected president. Maintaining close relations with France, Diori seemed to have established one of the most stable regimes in Africa, and the discovery of uranium deposits promised a sound economic future.

military takeover A severe drought 1968–74 resulted in widespread civil disorder, and in April 1974 Diori was ousted by the army led by the Chief of Staff, Lt-Col Seyni Kountché. Having suspended the constitution and established a military government with himself as president, he tried to restore the economy and negotiated a more equal relationship with France through a cooperation agreement 1977.

Kountché tried to widen his popular support by liberalizing his regime and releasing political prisoners, including former president Hamani Diori. More civilians were introduced into the government with the prospect of an eventual return to constitutional rule. When Kountché died 1987, the supreme military council appointed Col Ali Saibu acting president. He was elected without opposition in elections 1989.

In July 1990 the government announced plans for the introduction of a multiparty political system and in Nov these were endorsed by President Saibu who also agreed to hold a constitutional conference attended by representatives of all political views. The conference opened in July 1991 and in Aug Saibu was stripped of his executive powers, although allowed to retain the title of head of state until a new constitution was agreed. A transitional government consisting of a 15-member High Council of the Republic (HCR) was set up, but collapsed March 1992, leaving an unstable political situation.

Nigeria country in W Africa on the Gulf of Guinea, bounded N by Niger, E by Chad and Cameroon, and W by Benin.

history Nigeria has been inhabited since at least 700 BC. In the 12th–14th centuries civilizations developed in the Yoruba area and, in the Muslim north, Portuguese and British slave traders raided from the 15th century (see ◊slavery).

Lagos was supposedly bought from a chief by British traders 1861; in 1886 it became the colony and protectorate of Lagos. The Niger River valley was developed by the National African Company (later the Royal Niger Company), which ceased 1899, and in 1900 two protectorates were set up: N Nigeria and S Nigeria, with Lagos joined to S Nigeria 1906. Britain's largest African colony, Nigeria, was united 1914.

republic Nigeria became a federation 1954 and achieved full independence, as a constitutional monarchy within the ◊Commonwealth, 1960. In 1963 it became a republic, based on a federal structure so as to accommodate the many different ethnic groups, which included the Ibo, the Yoruba, the Aro, the Angas, and the Hausa. Nigeria's first president was Dr Nnamdi Azikiwe, an Ibo; he was a banker and proprietor of a newspaper group, and had played a leading part in the movement for independence. His chief rival was Abubakar ◊Tafawa Balewa, who was prime minister from 1957 until he was assassinated in a military coup 1966. The coup had been led mainly by Ibo junior officers from the eastern region, which had become richer after the discovery of oil there 1958.

The offices of president and prime minister were suspended, and it was announced that the state's federal structure would be abandoned. Before this could be done, the new military government was overturned in a counter-coup by a mostly Christian group from the north, led by Col Yakubu ◊Gowon.

He re-established the federal system and appointed a military governor for each region. Soon afterwards tens of thousands of Ibos in the north were killed.

civil war In 1967 a conflict developed between Gowon and the military governor of the eastern region, Col Chukwuemeka Odumegwu-Ojukwu, about the distribution of oil revenues, which resulted in Ojukwu's declaration of an independent Ibo state of ◊Biafra. Gowon, after failing to pacify the Ibos, ordered federal troops into the eastern region, and a civil war began, lasting until Jan 1970, when Biafra surrendered to the federal forces. It was the first war among black Africans, and it left the economy gravely weakened. Warfare and famine together took an estimated 1 million lives.

bloodless coups In 1975, while he was out of the country, Gowon was replaced in a bloodless coup led by Brig Murtala Mohammad, but he was killed within a month and replaced by General Olusegun Obasanjo. He announced a gradual return to civilian rule, and in 1979 the leader of the National Party of Nigeria, Shehu Shagari, became president. In Dec 1983, with the economy suffering from falling oil prices, Shagari's civilian government was deposed in another bloodless coup, led by Maj-Gen Muhammadu Buhari. In 1985 another peaceful coup replaced Buhari with a new military government, led by Maj-Gen Ibrahim Babangida, the army Chief of Staff. At the end of the year an attempted coup by rival officers was thwarted.

Babangida reforms In an effort to end the corruption that has existed since independence, President Babangida banned all persons who have ever held elective office from being candidates for the new civilian government. The ban on political activity was also lifted May 1989, but the government has rejected the applications of former political associations for recognition as political parties, instead creating two official parties, one to the left and one to the right of the political spectrum.

The government announced in Aug 1991 the creation of nine new states, bringing the total to 30. In the same month, the total of local government councils increased to 500 with the addition of 47 new ones. The changes were seen as moves towards the decentralization of power. In Dec 1991 the ban prohibiting existing government officials running for office in a new government was lifted. In 1992 it was announced that a system of primary elections, on the US model, was to be introduced to reduce electoral fraud, and that there would be a delay in the return to civilian rule, originally promised for 1992.

social conditions An official population policy encouraging mothers to have no more than four children was ratified 1988. Half the population is under 15. In 1990 inflation was running at 51%. Austerity measures, prescribed by the International Monetary Fund in response to economic assistance, have created widespread dissatisfaction with the government.

Nightingale Florence 1820–1910. English nurse, the founder of nursing as a profession. She took a team of nurses to Scutari (now Üsküdar, Turkey) in 1854 and reduced the ◊Crimean War hospital death rate from 42% to 2%. In 1856 she founded the Nightingale School and Home for Nurses in London.

Night of the Long Knives in World War II, a purge of the German Nazi party to root out possible opposition to Adolf Hitler. On the night of 29–30 June 1934 (and the following two days) the SS units under Heinrich ◊Himmler were used by Hitler to exterminate the Nazi private army Sturm-Abteilung (SA or the Brownshirts) under Captain Ernst Roehm. Others were also executed for alleged conspiracy against Hitler (including Kurt von Schleicher). The Nazi purge enabled Hitler to gain the acceptance of the German officer corps and, when President Hindenburg died five weeks later, to become head of state.

nihilist member of a group of Russian revolutionaries in the reign of Alexander II 1855–81. The name, popularized by the writer Turgenev, means 'one who approves of nothing' (Latin *nihil* 'nothing') belonging to the existing order. In 1878 the Nihilists launched a guerrilla campaign leading to the murder of the tsar Alexander II 1881.

Nijmegen, Treaties of peace treaties 1678–79 between France on the one hand and the Netherlands, Spain, and the Holy Roman Empire on the other, ending the Third Dutch War.

Nile, Battle of the alternative name for the Battle of ◊Aboukir Bay.

Nimitz Chester William 1885–1966. US admiral, commander in chief of the US Pacific fleet. He reconquered the Solomon Islands 1942–43, Gilbert Islands 1943, the Marianas and Marshalls 1944, and signed the Japanese surrender 1945 as the US representative.

Nineteen Propositions demands presented by the English Parliament to Charles I 1642. They were designed to limit the powers of the crown, and their rejection represented the beginning of the Civil War.

ninja (Japanese, from *ninjutsu* 'the art of invisibility') member of a body of trained assassins in feudal Japan, whose martial-arts skills were greatly feared. Popular legend had it that they were able to make themselves invisible.

Nixon Richard (Milhous) 1913–1994. 37th president of the USA 1969–74, a Republican. He attracted attention as a member of the Un-American Activities Committee 1948, and was vice president to Eisenhower 1953–61. As president he was responsible for US withdrawal from Vietnam, and forged new links with China, but at home his culpability in the cover-up of the ◊Watergate scandal and the existence of a 'slush fund' for political machinations during his re-election campaign 1972 led to his resignation 1974 when threatened with ◊impeachment.

In 1969 he formulated the Nixon Doctrine abandoning close involvement with Asian countries, but escalated the war in Cambodia by massive bombing. Re-elected 1972 in a landslide victory over George McGovern, he resigned 1974, the first US president to do so, under threat of impeachment on three counts: obstruction of the administration of justice in the investigation of Watergate; violation of constitutional rights of citizens, for example attempting to use the Internal Revenue Service, Federal Bureau of Investigation, and Central Intelligence Agency as weapons against political opponents; and failure to produce 'papers and things' as ordered by the Judiciary Committee. He was granted a pardon 1974 by President Ford and turned to lecturing and writing.

There can be no whitewash at the White House.

Richard Nixon television speech on Watergate 30 April 1973

Nkomati Accord nonaggression treaty between South Africa and Mozambique concluded 1984, under which they agreed not to give material aid to opposition movements in each other's countries, which in effect meant that South Africa pledged itself not to support the Mozambique National Resistance (Renamo), while Mozambique was committed not to help the then outlawed African National Congress (ANC).

Nkomo Joshua 1917– . Zimbabwean politician, vice-president from 1988. As president of ZAPU (Zimbabwe African People's Union) from 1961, he was a leader of the black nationalist movement against the white

Rhodesian regime. He was a member of Robert ◊Mugabe's cabinet 1980–82 and from 1987.

After completing his education in South Africa, Joshua Nkomo became a welfare officer on Rhodesian Railways and later organizing secretary of the Rhodesian African Railway Workers' Union. He entered politics 1950 and rose to become president of ZAPU. He was soon arrested, with other black African politicians, and was in detention during 1963–74. After his release he joined forces with Robert Mugabe as a joint leader of the Patriotic Front 1976, opposing the white-dominated regime of Ian Smith. Nkomo took part in the Lancaster House Conference, which led to Rhodesia's independence as the new state of Zimbabwe, and became a cabinet minister and vice president.

Western culture is not suitable for us without modification.

Joshua Nkomo in *Observer* Feb 1980

Nkrumah Kwame 1909–1972. Ghanaian nationalist politician, prime minister of the Gold Coast (Ghana's former name) 1952–57 and of newly independent Ghana 1957–60. He became Ghana's first president 1960 but was overthrown in a coup 1966. His policy of 'African socialism' led to links with the communist bloc.

Originally a teacher, he studied later in both Britain and the USA, and on returning to Africa formed the Convention People's Party (CPP) 1949 with the aim of immediate self-government. He was imprisoned in 1950 for incitement of illegal strikes, but was released the same year. As president he established an authoritarian regime and made Ghana a one-party (CPP) state 1964. He then dropped his stance of nonalignment and drew closer to the USSR and other communist countries. Deposed from the presidency while on a visit to Beijing (Peking) 1966, he remained in exile in Guinea, where he was made a co-head of state until his death, but was posthumously 'rehabilitated' 1973.

NKVD (Russian 'People's Commissariat of Internal Affairs') the Soviet secret police 1934–38, replaced by the ◊KGB. The NKVD was reponsible for Stalin's infamous purges.

nobility the ranks of society who originally enjoyed certain hereditary privileges. Their wealth was mainly derived from land. In many societies until the 20th century, they provided the elite personnel of government and the military.

nonaligned movement countries adopting a strategic and political position of neutrality ('nonalignment') towards major powers, specifically the USA and former USSR. Although originally used by poorer states, the nonaligned position was later adopted by oil-producing nations. The 1992 summit in Jakarta was attended by 108 member states. With the ending of the Cold War, the movement's survival was in doubt.

The term was originally used by the Indian prime minister Nehru, and was adopted 1961 at an international conference in Belgrade, Yugoslavia, by the country's president Tito, in general opposition to colonialism, neocolonialism, and imperialism, and to the dominance of dangerously conflicting East and West alliances. However, many members were in receipt of aid from either East or West or both, and some went to war with one another (Vietnam–Cambodia, Ethiopia–Somalia).

non-cooperation movement or *satyagraha* in India, a large-scale civil disobedience campaign orchestrated by Mahatma ◊Gandhi 1920 following the ◊Amritsar massacre April 1919. Based on a policy of peaceful non-cooperation, the strategy was to bring the British administrative machine to a halt by the total withdrawal of Indian support. British-made goods were boycotted, as were schools, courts of law, and elective offices. The campaign made little impression on the British government, since they could ignore it when it was peaceful; when it became violent, Gandhi felt obliged to call off further demonstrations. Its most successful aspect was that it increased political awareness among the Indian people.

Nore mutiny British naval mutiny in 1797, caused by low pay and bad conditions. It took place at anchorage by the Nore in the Thames.

Norman any of the descendants of the Norsemen (to whose chief, Rollo, Normandy was granted by Charles III of France 911) who adopted French language and culture. During the 11th and 12th centuries they conquered England 1066 (under William the Conqueror), Scotland 1072, parts of Wales and Ireland, S Italy, Sicily, and Malta, and took a prominent part in the Crusades.

They introduced feudalism, Latin as the language of government, and Norman French as the language of literature. Church architecture and organization were also influenced by the Normans, although they ceased to exist as a distinct people after the 13th century.

Normandy landings alternative name for ◊D-day.

The Normans

In 911 Charles III, king of the Franks, and known as 'The Simple' because he was reluctant to deceive anyone, gave Rollo, leader of a group of Danish adventurers, the newly- created Duchy of Normandy ('the land of the north men'). He hoped that these Viking poachers would turn gamekeepers and guard the strategic NW approach to the *Île de France* against other adventurers. Rollo and his men were the first Normans.

However, the Normans who conquered England in 1066, and whose activities in the Mediterranean culminated in the creation of the kingdom of Sicily in 1130, do not conform to the popular image of the marauding Viking, except perhaps in their energy and ruthlessness. Indeed, the Normans at the time of the Bayeux tapestry would have been indistinguishable from their French counterparts, while William the Conqueror and Robert Guiscard spoke Old French, not Old Norse. Equally, in S Italy the Normans soon adopted Mediterranean ways, within two generations taking inspiration from Greek or Arabic traditions rather than those of their ancient homeland. So it is doubtful if we should treat 11th- and 12th-century Normandy, England and its Celtic territories, and southern Italy as parts of the same 'Norman' cultural and political sphere.

The merging of the French and Normans

Rollo and his band of followers did not make Normandy politically or culturally 'Scandinavian': the major change they made to the ethnic composition of Normandy was to replace the Frankish elite. Normans everywhere were keen to attract adventurers of any nationality to their service, in the process further diluting their northern blood. By the 11th century, the French and Norman races had virtually merged into one.

The Normans' propaganda may be partly responsible for our habit of seeing them as different from the French. After distancing themselves from the pagan Vikings during the 11th century, Norman writers began to emphasize their links with their Scandinavian forebears in the 12th century, as if to create a separate identity from the French, from whom they were in most respects indistinguishable. Second- and third-generation Normans may have felt a nagging inferiority to their French neighbours, but by the 11th century the cultural gap between Scandinavians and other west Europeans was not great. After

all, one of the most successful rulers of late Saxon England was the Dane King Cnut, while some of the greatest vernacular literature of medieval Europe was written in 11th- and 12th-century Iceland.

Norman government

One distinctive feature of 11th- and 12th-century Normandy was the quality of its government. Its dukes presided over one of the strongest and most centralized administrative systems in continental Europe. The native Frankish nobility had been replaced by rootless adventurers, but when the Normans were surrounded by hostile natives, they learnt the habit of obedience to their duke to avoid being overwhelmed.

William the Conqueror and his followers (many of whom were not Normans at all) found themselves in similar circumstances in 1066. In contrast to the Normandy of the 10th century, England had a more efficient and centralized, better-funded (through national taxation – the *geld*) system of government than any other country in W Europe. It also had a richer and deeper-rooted culture than that of the Normans. Perhaps the misconception that the Normans brought superior civilization to Saxon England is another victory for Norman propaganda.

Historical debate about the Normans

The debate over the extent to which the Normans introduced, rather than adapting existing features of Saxon England, began in the last quarter of the 19th century, when the historian J H Round argued that there had been a 'Norman revolution' which marked a decisive break from 'backward' Saxon culture and dragged the English into the High Middle Ages. This was set against Edward Freeman's gradualist, evolutionary model stressing the elements of continuity after 1066. The argument centres around feudalism and the extent to which this is purely a Norman introduction.

Since the 1950s the general historical consensus has shifted towards the evolutionary view of change in 11th-century England. While not denying the Normans' significant impact, many now see them as a catalyst for changes already in hand. Perhaps the debate tells us as much about historians' perceptions as it does about medieval history.

Norseman early inhabitant of Norway. The term Norsemen is also applied to Scandinavian ◊Vikings who during the 8th–11th centuries raided and settled in Britain, Ireland, France, Russia, Iceland, and Greenland.

The Norse religion (banned 1000) was recognized by the Icelandic government 1973.

North Frederick, 8th Lord North 1732–1792. British Tory politician. He entered Parliament in 1754, became chancellor of the Exchequer in 1767, and was prime minister in a government of Tories and 'king's friends' from 1770. His hard line against the American colonies was sup-

ported by George III, but in 1782 he was forced to resign by the failure of his policy. In 1783 he returned to office in a coalition with Charles ◊Fox, and after its defeat retired from politics.

North Africa Campaign Allied military campaign 1940–42 during World War II. Shortly after Italy declared war on France and Britain June 1940, an Italian offensive was launched from Libya towards Egypt and the Suez Canal. In Dec 1940 Britain launched a successful counter-offensive and captured Cyrenaica. Following agreement between Mussolini and Hitler, the German Afrikakorps was established

0   80 km

0   50 miles

North
Sea

N

NORMAN INVASION OF ENGLAND
▨ Dependency   Battle ⚔
▨ Possessions (England after 1066)

Norman invasion of England After the death of the English king Edward the Confessor 1066, a dispute over the succession between Harold II and William of Normandy led William to mount a seaborne attack on England (Norman Conquest). Harold, having defeated an invading Norwegian army at the Battle of Stamford Bridge, Yorkshire, was forced to rush southwards to meet William's forces a few days later at the Battle of Hastings, 14 Oct 1066. Harold's death and the defeat of his army left William in control of the whole country.

under General Rommel. During 1941 and early 1942 the Axis powers advanced, recaptured Tobruk, and crossed the Egyptian border before halting at El Alamein. The British 8th Army under General Montgomery won a decisive Allied victory against Rommel's forces at El Alamein on 4 Nov 1942, followed by advances across Libya from Tunisia. British and US troops advanced from French NW Africa and the Allied armies in N Africa converged on Tunis. After a last-ditch defence, the Axis forces surrendered in May 1943.

North America third largest of the continents (including Greenland and Central America), and over twice the size of Europe.

North American Indian indigenous inhabitant of North America. Many describe themselves as 'Native Americans' rather than 'American Indians', the latter term having arisen because Columbus believed he had reached the East Indies. See also ◊American Indian.

North Atlantic Treaty Organization (NATO) association set up 1949 to provide for the collective defence of the major W European and North American states against the perceived threat from the USSR. Its chief body is the Council of Foreign Ministers (who have representatives in permanent session), and there is an international secretariat in Brussels, Belgium, and also the Military Committee consisting of the Chiefs of Staff. The military headquarters SHAPE (Supreme Headquarters Allied Powers, Europe) is in Chièvres, near Mons, Belgium. After the E European ◊Warsaw Pact was disbanded 1991, an adjunct to NATO, the *North Atlantic Cooperation Council*, was established, including all the former Soviet republics, with the aim of building greater security in Europe.

Northern and Southern dynasties period in Chinese history 317–581, the last part of the unsettled era known as the ◊Three Kingdoms.

Northern Wei dynasty hereditary Chinese rulers 386–535, in one of the ◊Three Kingdoms.

North–South divide geographical division of the world that theoretically demarcates the rich from the poor. The South includes all of Asia except Japan, Australia, and New Zealand; all of Africa, the Middle East, Central and South

North America: early history	
c. 35,000 BC	American Indians entered North America from Asia.
c. 9000 BC	Marmes man, earliest human remains.
300 BC	Earliest Moundbuilder sites.
c. AD 1000	Leif Ericsson reached North America.
12th–14th centuries	Height of the Moundbuilder and Pueblo cultures.
1492	Columbus first sighted land in the Caribbean 12 Oct.
1497	Giovanni Caboto reached Canada.
1565	First Spanish settlements in Florida.
1585	First attempted English settlement in North Carolina.
1607	First permanent English settlement, Jamestown, Virginia. *For subsequent history see* ◊*Alaska,* ◊*Canada, and* ◊*United States of America.*

America. The North includes Europe, the USA, Canada, and all republics of the former Soviet Union. Newly industrialized countries such as South Korea and Taiwan could, however, be said to have more in common with the industrialized North than with ◊Third World countries.

Northumberland John Dudley, Duke of Northumberland *c.* 1502–1553. English politician, son of the privy councillor Edmund Dudley (beheaded 1510), and chief minister until Edward VI's death 1553. He tried to place his daughter-in-law Lady Jane ◊Grey on the throne, and was executed on Mary I's accession.

Northumbria Anglo-Saxon kingdom that covered NE England and SE Scotland, comprising the 6th-century kingdoms of Bernicia (Forth–Tees) and Deira (Tees–Humber), united in the 7th century. It accepted the supremacy of Wessex 827 and was conquered by the Danes in the late 9th century.

Influenced by Irish missionaries, it was a cultural and religious centre until the 8th century with priests such as Bede, Cuthbert, and Wilfrid.

Northwest Ordinances US Congressional legislation 1784–87 setting out procedures for the sale and settlement of lands still occupied by American Indians. The land, between the Great Lakes and the Mississippi and Ohio rivers, was to be formed into townships and sold at minimum $1 per acre. The sales revenue was the first significant source of income for the new federal government.

The 1787 Ordinance guaranteed freedom of religion for settlers, prohibited slavery in the new territory and outlined procedures for the organization into states for eventual admission to the Union.

Northwest Passage Atlantic–Pacific sea route around the north of Canada. Canada, which owns offshore islands, claims it as an internal waterway; the USA insists that it is an international waterway and sent an icebreaker through without permission 1985.

Early explorers included the Englishmen Martin Frobisher and, later, John Franklin, whose failure to return 1847 led to the organization of 39 expeditions in the next ten years. John Ross reached Lancaster Sound 1818 but mistook a bank of cloud for a range of mountains and turned back. R McClune explored the passage 1850–53 although he did not cover the whole route by sea. The polar explorer Roald Amundsen was the first European to sail through 1903–06.

Northwest rebellion revolt against the Canadian government March–May 1885 by the métis (people of mixed French Canadian and North American Indian descent). Led by their political leader Louis ◊Riel and his military lieutenant Gabriel Dumont (1838–1906), the métis population of what is now Saskatchewan rebelled after a number of economic and political grievances were ignored by the government.

Fearing a full-scale Indian uprising, troops were quickly despatched west along the newly completed transcontinental railway and the rebellion was suppressed. Riel was tried and hanged Nov 1885.

Norway country in NW Europe, on the Scandinavian peninsula, bounded E by Sweden, NE by Finland and Russia, S by the North Sea, W by the Atlantic Ocean, and N by the Arctic Ocean.

history Norway was originally inhabited by the Saami (Lapps) and other nomads and was gradually invaded by ◊Goths. It was ruled by local chieftains until unified by Harald Fairhair (reigned 872–933) as a feudal country. Norway's ◊Vikings raided and settled in many parts of Europe in the 8th–11th centuries. Christianity was introduced by ◊Olaf II in the 11th century; he was defeated 1030 by rebel chiefs backed by ◊Canute, but his son Magnus I regained the throne 1035. Haakon IV (1217–1263) established the authority of the crown over the nobles and the church and made the monarchy hereditary.

◊Denmark and Norway were united by marriage 1380, and in 1397 Norway, Denmark, and Sweden became united under one sovereign. Sweden broke away 1523, but Norway remained under Danish rule until 1814, when it was ceded to Sweden. Norway rebelled, Sweden invaded, and a compromise was reached whereby Norway kept its own parliament but was united with Sweden under a common monarch.

independence Conflict between the Norwegian parliament and the Swedish crown continued until 1905, when the parliament declared Norway completely independent. This was confirmed by plebiscite, and Prince Carl of Denmark was elected king as Haakon VII. He ruled for 52 years until his death 1957. His son Olaf V died 1991 and was succeeded by his only son Harald V.

since World War II The experience of German occupation 1940–45 persuaded the Norwegians to abandon their traditional neutral stance and join the North Atlantic Treaty

Organization (NATO) 1949, the Nordic Council 1952, and the European Free Trade Association (EFTA) 1960. Norway was accepted into membership of the European Economic Community 1972, but a referendum held that year rejected the proposal and the application was withdrawn. Its exploitation of North Sea oil and gas resources have given it a higher income per head of population than most of its European neighbours, and during the Cold War it succeeded in maintaining good relations with the USSR without damaging its commitments in the West.

Norway has enjoyed stability under a series of coalition governments. In Nov 1988 Prime Minister Gro Harlem Brundtland was awarded the annual Third World Prize for her work on environmental issues but in the Sept 1989 election her party lost seats to the far right and the far left. Following a vote of no confidence, she resigned Oct 1989 and was succeeded by the Conservative Jan P Syse. In Oct 1990 the Syse coalition collapsed and Brundtland returned to power, leading a minority Labour government. Olav V died Jan 1991 and was succeeded by his son, Harald V. In 1992, Norway joined Iceland in defying a worldwide ban on whaling in order to resume its own whaling industry.

November criminals name given by right-wing nationalists in post-1918 Germany to the socialist politicians who had taken over the government after the abdication of Kaiser Wilhelm II and had signed the armistice with the Western Allies Nov 1918.

Novgorod industrial city on the Volkhov River, NW Russia; a major trading city in medieval times. Novgorod was the original capital of the Russian state, founded at the invitation of the people of the city by the Viking (Varangian) chieftain Rurik 862. The Viking merchants who went there quickly became fully assimilated into the native Slav population. In 912 the capital of the principality moved to Kiev, but this did little to harm Novgorod. It developed a strong municipal government run by the leaders of the craft guilds and, until the 13th century, flourished as a major commercial centre (with a monopoly on the Russian fur trade) for trade with Scandinavia, the Byzantine Empire, and the Muslim world. (It was known in Russia as 'Lord Novgorod the Great' because of its position on the trade route between the Baltic and Black Seas.) It became one of the principal members of the ◊Hanseatic League, but its economy had already started to decline. This was hastened during the 15th-century rule of the boyars, nobles who had seized power from the guilds 1416. It came under the control of

Ivan the Great III 1478 and was sacked by Ivan the Terrible 1570.

Nu U (Thakin) 1907– . Myanmar politician, prime minister of Burma (now Myanmar) for most of the period from 1948 to the military coup of 1962. Exiled from 1966, U Nu returned to the country 1980 and, in 1988, helped found the National League for Democracy opposition movement.

Formerly a teacher, U Nu joined the Dobhama Asiayone ('Our Burma') nationalist organization during the 1930s and was imprisoned by the British authorities at the start of World War II. He was released 1942, following Japan's invasion of Burma, and appointed foreign minister in a puppet government. In 1945 he fought with the British against the Japanese and on independence became Burma's first prime minister. Excepting short breaks during 1956–57 and 1958–60, he remained in this post until General ◊Ne Win overthrew the parliamentary regime in 1962.

Nubia former African country now divided between Egypt and Sudan; it gives its name to the *Nubian Desert* S of Lake Nasser.

Ancient Egypt, which was briefly ruled by Nubian kings in the 8th–7th centuries BC, knew the north as Wawat and the south as Kush, with the dividing line roughly at Dongola. Egyptian building work in the area included temples at Abu Simbel, Philae, and a defensive chain of forts that established the lines of development of medieval fortification. Nubia's capital about 600 BC–AD 350 was Meroe, near Khartoum. About AD 250–550 most of Nubia was occupied by the X-group people, of whom little is known; their royal mound tombs (mistaken by earlier investigations for natural mounds created by wind erosion) were excavated in the 1930s by W B Emery, and many horses and attendants were found to have been slaughtered to accompany the richly jewelled dead.

Nujoma Sam 1929– . Namibian left-wing politician, president from 1990, founder and leader of ◊SWAPO (the South-West Africa People's Organization) from 1959. He was exiled in 1960 and controlled guerrillas from Angolan bases until the first free elections were held 1989, taking office early the following year.

Numidia ('nomads' land') independent N African kingdom, close to ◊Carthage, which became a Roman province, now E Algeria.

nuncio (Italian 'messenger') diplomatic representative of the pope, from the 16th century, performing the functions of a papal ambassador.

Núñez Rafael 1825–1894. Colombian president 1880–82 and 1884–94, responsible for a new, authoritarian constitution 1886. A doctrinaire Liberal in the 1850s, he held several government posts, and was a foreign diplomat 1863–74. During his terms in office he restored the church's influential position and tried to stimulate economic development with a protective tariff. He also established a central bank, and concluded a concordat with the Vatican 1887.

Nuremberg rallies annual meetings 1933–38 of the German ◊Nazi Party. They were characterized by extensive torchlight parades, marches in party formations, and mass rallies addressed by Nazi leaders such as Hitler and Goebbels.

Nuremberg trials after World War II, the trials of the 24 chief ◊Nazi war criminals Nov 1945–Oct 1946 by an international military tribunal consisting of four judges and four prosecutors: one of each from the USA, UK, USSR, and France. An appendix accused the German cabinet, general staff, high command, Nazi leadership corps, ◊SS, ◊Sturmabteilung, and ◊Gestapo of criminal behaviour.

The main charges in the indictment were: (1) conspiracy to wage wars of aggression; (2) crimes against peace; (3) war crimes, for example, murder and ill-treatment of civilians and prisoners of war, deportation of civilians for slave labour, and killing of hostages; (4) crimes against humanity, for example, mass murder of the Jews and other peoples, and murder and ill-treatment of political opponents.

Nyasaland former name (until 1964) for ◊Malawi.

Nyerere Julius (Kambarage) 1922– . Tanzanian socialist politician, president 1964–85. He devoted himself from 1954 to the formation of the Tanganyika African National Union and subsequent campaigning for independence. He became chief minister 1960, was prime minister of Tanganyika 1961–62, president of the newly formed Tanganyika Republic 1962–64, and first president of Tanzania 1964–85.

He was head of the Organization of African Unity 1984.

OAS abbreviation for ◊*Organization of American States*.

Oastler Richard 1789–1861. English social reformer. He opposed child labour and the ◊poor law 1834, which restricted relief, and was largely responsible for securing the Factory Act 1833 and the Ten Hours Act 1847. He was given the nickname of the 'Factory King' for his achievements on behalf of workers.

Oates Titus 1649–1705. English conspirator. A priest, he entered the Jesuit colleges at Valladolid, Spain, and St Omer, France, as a spy 1677–78, and on his return to England announced he had discovered a 'Popish Plot' to murder Charles II and re-establish Catholicism. Although this story was almost entirely false, many innocent Roman Catholics were executed during 1678–80 on Oates's evidence.

In 1685 Oates was flogged, pilloried, and imprisoned for perjury. He was pardoned and granted a pension after the revolution of 1688.

OAU abbreviation for ◊*Organization of African Unity*.

Obote (Apollo) Milton 1924– . Ugandan politician who led the independence movement from 1961. He became prime minister 1962 and was president 1966–71 and 1980–85, being overthrown by first Idi ◊Amin and then by Lt-Gen Tito Okello.

Obrenovich Serbian dynasty that ruled 1816–42 and 1859–1903. The dynasty engaged in a feud with the rival house of Karageorgevich, which obtained the throne by the murder of the last Obrenovich 1903.

O'Connell Daniel 1775–1847. Irish politician, called 'the Liberator'. Although ineligible, as a Roman Catholic, to take his seat, he was elected member of Parliament for County Clare 1828 and so forced the government to grant Catholic emancipation. In Parliament he cooperated with the Whigs in the hope of obtaining concessions until 1841, when he launched his campaign for repeal of the union.

O'Connor Feargus 1794–1855. Irish parliamentarian, a follower of Daniel ◊O'Connell. He sat in Parliament 1832–35, and as editor of the *Northern Star* became an influential figure of the radical working-class Chartist movement (see ◊Chartism).

Octavian original name of ◊Augustus, the first Roman emperor.

October Revolution second stage of the ◊Russian Revolution 1917, when, on 24 Oct (6 Nov in the Western calendar), the Bolshevik forces under Trotsky, and on orders from Lenin, seized the Winter Palace and arrested members of the Provisional Government. The following day the Second All-Russian Congress of Soviets handed over power to the Bolsheviks.

October War the surprise attack on Israel October 1973 by Egypt and Syria; see ◊Arab-Israeli Wars.

Octobrists group of Russian liberal constitutional politicians who accepted the reforming October Manifesto instituted by Tsar Nicholas II after the 1905 revolution and rejected more radical reforms.

Oder-Neisse Line border between Poland and East Germany agreed at the Potsdam Conference 1945 at the end of World War II, named after the two rivers that formed the frontier.

Odoacer 433–493. King of Italy from 476, when he deposed Romulus Augustulus, the last Roman emperor. He was a leader of the barbarian mercenaries employed by Rome. He was overthrown and killed by Theodoric the Great, king of the Ostrogoths.

Odo of Bayeux c. 1030–1097. French bishop, co-regent of England, who probably commissioned the Bayeux Tapestry. He was the son of Duke ◊Robert I of Normandy and half-brother of ◊William I the Conqueror, from whom he received his bishopric 1049. His service at the Battle of ◊Hastings won him the earldom of Kent 1067 and vast English estates, making him one of the richest men in Europe. During William's absence in Normandy 1067 he shared the regency of England with William Fitzosborne and remained prominent in the royal administration until 1082.

Offa died 796. King of Mercia, England, from 757. He conquered Essex, Kent, Sussex, and Surrey; defeated the Welsh and the West Saxons; and established Mercian supremacy over all England south of the river Humber.

Ogaden desert region in Harar province, SE Ethiopia, that borders on Somalia. It is a desert plateau, rising to 1,000 m/3,280 ft, inhabited mainly by Somali nomads practising arid farming. The area became one of five new autonomous provinces created in Ethiopia 1987.

A claim to the area was made by Somalia in the 1960s, resulting in guerrilla fighting and major Somali advances during 1977. By 1980 Ethiopia, backed by the USSR and Cuba, was again in virtual control of the area, but armed clashes continued. In 1988 diplomatic relations were restored between Ethiopia and Somalia and troops were withdrawn from their shared border. Internal troubles in Somalia 1990 created a large refugee population in E Ogaden.

OGPU name 1923–34 of the Soviet secret police, later the ◊KGB.

O'Higgins Bernardo 1778–1842. Chilean revolutionary, known as 'the Liberator of Chile'. He was a leader of the struggle for independence from Spanish rule 1810–17 and head of the first permanent national government 1817–23.

Okinawa largest of the Japanese Ryukyu Islands in the W Pacific. It was captured by the USA in the *Battle of Okinawa* 1 April–21 June 1945, with 47,000 US casualties (12,000 dead) and 60,000 Japanese (only a few hundred survived as prisoners). During the invasion over 150,000 Okinawans, mainly civilians, died; many were massacred by Japanese forces. The island was returned to Japan 1972.

Ōkubo Toshimichi 1831–1878. Japanese samurai leader from Satsuma province in S Japan, whose opposition to the Tokugawa shogunate made him a leader in the ◊Meiji restoration 1866–88. He served as finance and home minister in the Meiji government, but was assassinated by a former samurai from Satsuma in May 1878.

Okuma Shigenobu 1838–1922. Japanese politician and prime minister 1898 and 1914–16. He presided over Japanese pressure for territorial concessions in China, before retiring 1916.

Olaf five kings of Norway, including:

Olaf I Tryggvesson 969–1000. King of Norway from 995. He began the conversion of Norway to Christianity and was killed in a sea battle against the Danes and Swedes.

Olaf II Haraldsson 995–1030. King of Norway from 1015. He offended his subjects by his centralizing policy and zeal for Christianity, and was killed in battle by Norwegian rebel chiefs backed by ◊Canute of Denmark. He was declared the patron saint of Norway 1164.

Oldenbarneveldt Johan van 1547–1619. Dutch politician, a leading figure in the Netherlands' struggle for independence from Spain, who helped William the Silent negotiate the Union of Utrecht 1579.

Old Pretender nickname of ◊James Edward Stuart, the son of James II of England.

Old Style qualification, often abbreviated to 'OS', of dates before the year 1752 in England as quoted in later writings. In that year the ◊calendar in use in England was reformed by the omission of 11 days, in order to bring it into line with the more exact Gregorian system, and the beginning of the year was put back from 25 March to 1 Jan.

Olivares Count-Duke of (born Gaspar de Guzmán) 1587–1645. Spanish prime minister 1621–43. He overstretched Spain in foreign affairs and unsuccessfully attempted domestic reform. He committed Spain to recapturing the Netherlands and to involvement in the Thirty Years' War 1618–48, and his efforts to centralize power led to revolts in Catalonia and Portugal, which brought about his downfall.

Olmec first civilization of Mesoamerica and thought to be the mother culture of the Mayans. It developed in the coastal zone S of Vera Cruz and in adjacent Tabasco 1200–400 BC. The Olmecs built a large clay pyramid and several smaller mounds on the island of La Venta. Some gigantic stone heads, vestiges of their religion, also remain. The naturalistic Olmec art had a distinctive and influential style, often using the 'were-jaguar' motif of a scaless figure with fangs.

Olympia sanctuary in the W Peloponnese, ancient Greece, with a temple of Zeus, and the stadium (for foot races, boxing, wrestling) and hippodrome (for chariot and horse races), where the original Olympic games were held.

Oman country at the SE end of the Arabian peninsula, bounded W by the United Arab Emirates, Saudi Arabia, and Yemen, SE by the Arabian Sea, and NE by the Gulf of Oman.

history For early history, see ◊Arabia. The city of Muscat has long been a trading post. The country was in Portugal's possession 1508–1658 and was then ruled by Persia until 1744. By the early 19th century, the state of Muscat and Oman was the most powerful in Arabia: it ruled Zanzibar until 1861 and also coastal parts of Persia and Pakistan.

independent sultanate In 1951 it became the independent Sultanate of Muscat and Oman and signed a treaty of friendship with Britain. Said bin Taimur, who had been sultan since 1932, was overthrown by his son, Qaboos bin Said, in a bloodless coup 1970, and the country was renamed the Sultanate of Oman. Qaboos embarked on a more liberal and expansionist policy than his father. The Popular Front for the Liberation of Oman has been fighting to overthrow the sultanate since 1965.

Oman's wealth is based on a few oilfields. Conflicts in nearby countries, such as Yemen, Iran, Iraq, Kuwait, and Afghanistan, have not only emphasized the country's strategic importance but put its own security at risk. The sultan has tried to follow a path of ◊nonalignment, while maintaining close ties with the USA and other NATO countries. In 1991, as part of the Gulf Cooperation Council, Oman troops fought in Operation Desert Storm against Iraqi troops occupying Kuwait.

Omar 581–644. Adviser of the prophet Muhammad. In 634 he succeeded Abu Bakr as caliph (civic and religious leader of Islam), and conquered Syria, Palestine, Egypt, and Persia. He was assassinated by a slave. The Mosque of Omar in Jerusalem is attributed to him.

Omayyad dynasty Arabian dynasty of the Islamic empire who reigned as caliphs (civic and religious leaders of Islam) 661–750, when they were overthrown by Abbasids. A member of the family, Abd al-Rahmam, escaped to Spain and in 756 assumed the title of emir of Córdoba. His dynasty, which took the title of caliph in 929, ruled in Córdoba until the early 11th century.

Omdurman, Battle of battle on 2 Sept 1898 in which the Sudanese, led by the Khalifa, were defeated by British and Egyptian troops under General Kitchener.

O'Neill Terence, Baron O'Neill of the Maine 1914–1990. Northern Irish Unionist politician. In the Ulster government he was minister of finance 1956–63, then prime minister 1963–69. He resigned when opposed by his party on measures to extend rights to Roman Catholics, including a universal franchise.

OPEC acronym for ◊*Organization of Petroleum-Exporting Countries*.

open-door policy economic philosophy of equal access by all nations to another nation's markets.

Opium Wars two wars, the First Opium War 1839–42 and the Second Opium War 1856–60, waged by Britain against China to enforce the opening of Chinese ports to trade in opium. Opium from British India paid for Britain's imports from China, such as porcelain, silk, and, above all, tea.

The *First Opium War*, between Britain and China, resulted in the cession of Hong Kong to Britain and the opening of five treaty ports. Other European states were also subsequently given concessions. The *Second Opium War* followed between Britain and France in alliance against China, when there was further Chinese resistance to the opium trade. China was forced to give the European states greater trading privileges, at the expense of its people.

Orange Free State province of the Republic of South Africa, 127,993 sq km/49,405 sq mi in area.

Original settlements from 1810 were complemented by the ◊Great Trek, and the state was recognized by Britain as independent 1854. Following the South African, or Boer, War 1899–1902, it was annexed by Britain until it entered the union as a province 1910.

Orange, House of royal family of the Netherlands. The title is derived from the small principality of Orange in S France, held by the family from the 8th century to 1713. They held considerable possessions in the Netherlands, to which, after 1530, was added the German county of Nassau.

From the time of William, Prince of Orange, the family dominated Dutch history, bearing the title of stadholder (magistrate) for the greater part of the 17th and 18th centuries. The son of Stadholder William V became King William I 1815.

Orangeman member of the Ulster Protestant *Orange Society* established 1795 in opposition to the United Irishmen and the Roman Catholic secret societies. It was a revival of the Orange Institution 1688, formed in support of William (III) of Orange, whose victory over the Catholic James II at the Battle of the Boyne 1690 is commemorated annually by Protestants in parades on 12 July.

Orange, Project in South Africa, 1980 plan for a white 'homeland' (Projek Oranje) to be established on the border between ◊Orange Free State and the Northern Cape. No black person would be allowed to live or work there.

ordeal, trial by in tribal societies and in Europe in medieval times, a method of testing guilt of an accused person based on the belief in heaven's protection of the innocent. Examples of such ordeals are walking barefoot over heated iron, dipping the hand into boiling water, and swallowing consecrated bread (causing the guilty to choke).

In Europe the practice originated with the Franks in the 8th century, and survived until the 13th century. In another ordeal, the accused would be bound and thrown into cold water; if he or she sank, it would prove innocence, but remaining afloat showed guilt.

Orford, 1st Earl of title of British politician Robert ◊Walpole.

Organisation de l'Armée Secrète (OAS) guerrilla organization formed 1961 by French settlers devoted to perpetuating their own rule in Algeria (Algérie Française). It collapsed on the imprisonment 1962–68 of its leader, General Raoul Salan.

Organization for Economic Cooperation and Development (OECD) international organization of 24 industrialized countries that provides a forum for discussion and coordination of member states' economic and social policies. Founded 1961, with its headquarters in Paris, the OECD superseded the Organization for European Economic Cooperation, which had been established 1948 to implement the ◊Marshall Plan.

Organization of African Unity (OAU) association established 1963 to eradicate colonialism and improve economic, cultural, and political cooperation in Africa. Its membership expanded to 51 countries when Namibia joined after independence 1990. The secretary general is Salim Ahmed Salim of Tanzania. Its headquarters are in Addis Ababa, Ethiopia.

Organization of American States (OAS) association founded 1948 by a charter signed by representatives of 30 North, Central, and South American states. It aims to maintain peace and solidarity within the hemisphere, and is also concerned with the social and economic development of Latin America.

Organization of Petroleum-Exporting Countries (OPEC) body established 1960 to coordinate price and supply policies of oil-producing states. Its concerted action in raising prices in the 1970s triggered worldwide recession but also lessened demand so that its influence was reduced by the mid-1980s. OPEC members in 1991 were: Algeria, Ecuador, Gabon, Indonesia, Iran, Iraq, Kuwait, Libya, Nigeria, Qatar, Saudi Arabia, the United Arab Emirates, and Venezuela.

OPEC also aimed to improve the position of Third World states by forcing Western states to open their markets to the resultant products.

Orlando Vittorio Emanuele 1860–1952. Italian politician, prime minister 1917–19. He attended the Paris Peace Conference after World War I, but dissatisfaction with his handling of the Adriatic settlement led to his resignation. He initially supported Mussolini but

was in retirement 1925–46, when he returned to the assembly and then the senate.

Orleanists French monarchist group that supported the Orléans branch of the royal family in opposition to the Bourbon Legitimists. Both groups were united 1883 when the Bourbon line died out.

Ormonde James Butler, Duke of Ormonde 1610–1688. Irish general. He commanded the Royalist troops in Ireland 1641–50 during the Irish rebellion and the English Civil War, and was lord lieutenant 1644–47, 1661–69, and 1677–84. He was created a marquess 1642 and a duke 1661.

Orsini Felice 1819–1858. Italian political activist, a member of the ◊Carbonari secret revolutionary group, who attempted unsuccessfully to assassinate Napoleon III in Paris Jan 1858. He was subsequently executed, but the Orsini affair awakened Napoleon's interest in Italy and led to a secret alliance with Piedmont at Plombières 1858, directed against Austria.

Osborne Judgement UK legal ruling of 1909 that prevented ◊trade unions from using membership subscriptions to finance the Labour Party. In 1913 the judgement was negated by the Trade Union Act, which permitted them to raise political levies and provide financial support to the Labour Party. Individual trade unionists could 'contract out' of the political levy by signing a form saying they did not wish to pay.

Oscar II 1829–1907. King of Sweden and Norway 1872–1905, king of Sweden until 1907. He was the younger son of Oscar I, and succeeded his brother Charles XV. He tried hard to prevent the separation of his two kingdoms but relinquished the throne of Norway to Haakon VII 1905.

Osman I or *Othman I* 1259–1326. Turkish ruler from 1299. He began his career in the service of the Seljuk Turks, but in 1299 he set up a kingdom of his own in Bithynia, NW Asia, and assumed the title of sultan. He conquered a great part of Anatolia, so founding a Turkish empire. His successors were known as 'sons of Osman', from which the term ◊Ottoman Empire is derived.

Ootpolitik German foreign policy intoduced by Willy ◊Brandt which sought reconciliation with Eastern Europe as a means of improving contacts between East and West Germany.

Ostrogoth member of a branch of the E Germanic people, the ◊Goths.

Oswiecim (German ◊*Auschwitz*) town in S Poland, site of the World War II extermination and ◊concentration camp.

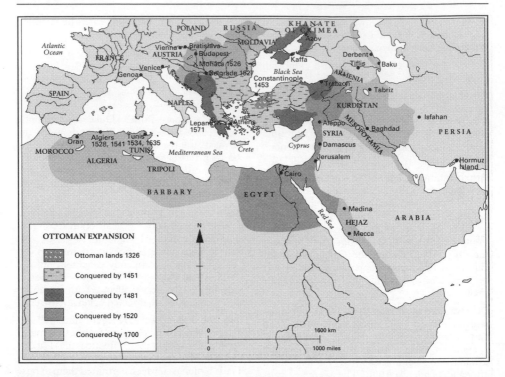

Expansion of the Ottoman Empire *The Ottomans expanded westwards into Byzantine and later Balkan territory and eastwards across Anatolia. Constantinople was captured 1453 by Mehmet II the Conqueror. Selim I overthrew the Mamelukes in Egypt and Syria, and Suleiman II the Magnificent overran much of Hungary in the 16th century. By the end of the century the limits of Ottoman expansion had been set, with Vienna in the west and Tabriz in the east remaining outside their empire.*

Othman *c.* 574–656. Third caliph (leader of the Islamic empire) from 644, a son-in-law of the prophet Muhammad. Under his rule the Arabs became a naval power and extended their rule to N Africa and Cyprus, but Othman's personal weaknesses led to his assassination. He was responsible for the compilation of the authoritative version of the Koran, the sacred book of Islam.

Othman I another name for the Turkish sultan ◊Osman I.

Ottawa agreements trade agreements concluded at the Imperial Economic Conference, held in Ottawa 1932, between Britain and its dependent territories, lowering tariffs on British manufactured goods and increasing duties on non-Dominion produce.

Otto four Holy Roman emperors, including:

Otto I 912–973. Holy Roman emperor from 936. He restored the power of the empire, asserted his authority over the pope and the nobles, ended the Magyar menace by his victory at the Lechfeld 955, and refounded the East Mark, or Austria, as a barrier against them.

Otto IV *c.* 1182–1218. Holy Roman emperor, elected 1198. He engaged in controversy with Pope Innocent III, and was defeated by the pope's ally, Philip of France, at Bouvines 1214.

Ottoman Empire Muslim empire of the Turks 1300–1920, the successor of the ◊Seljuk Empire. It was founded by ◊Osman I and reached its height with ◊Suleiman in the 16th century. Its capital was Istanbul (formerly Constantinople).

At its greatest extent the Ottoman empire's boundaries were Europe as far as Hungary, part of S Russia, Iran, the Palestinian coastline, Egypt, and N Africa. From the 17th century it was in decline. There was an attempted revival and reform under the Young Turk party 1908, but the regime crumbled when Turkey sided with Germany in World War I. The sultanate was abolished by Kemal Atatürk 1922; the last sultan was Muhammad VI.

Oudenaarde, Battle of victory by the British, Dutch, and Austrians over the French 1708 during the War of the ◊Spanish Succession. Oudenaarde is a town of E Flanders, W Belgium, 28 km/18mi SSW of Ghent.

Ottoman Empire 1805–1923			
1805	Mehemet (Mohammad) Ali acclaimed pasha in Egypt.	1877–78	Russo-Turkish war ended in Treaty of San Stefano. Romania, Serbia, Montenegro, and Bulgaria given independence.
1807	Reforming sultan Selim III attempted representative government but was deposed by janissaries and killed.	1878	Congress of Berlin reinforced some aspects of San Stefano but returned some Bulgarian territory to Turkish control. Austria given administrative rights over Bosnia-Herzegovina.
1811	Mehemet Ali massacred the Mamelukes.		
1821–29	Greek War of Independence.		
1826	Janissaries massacred and abolished in army reforms.	1890–97	Uprisings by Christians in Armenia brutally suppressed, discrediting the regime.
1827	Turkish-Egyptian fleet destroyed by British, French, and Russian navies in Battle of Navarino.	1896–97	Turks defeated Greeks in dispute over Crete.
		1908	Military uprisings in Arabia, Albania, and, led by Enver Pasha, Salonika.
1828–29	Russo-Turkish War.	1909	Abdul Hamid II deposed and replaced by Mohammad V.
1830	London Conference recognized Greek independence.	1911–13	Tripolitania Wars against Italy. Libyan territory lost. Young Turk Party came to political prominence. Turkish armies defeated in First and Second Balkan Wars.
1831	Mehemet Ali declared war on sultan.		
1833	Treaty of Unkiar-Skelessi after Russian help against Mehemet Ali reinforced Russian influence over Turkish Empire.		
		1914	German-Turkish defensive alliance brought Turkey into World War I. Egypt became a British protectorate.
1839–61	Sultanate of Abdul Mejid I. Attempts at administrative and judicial reform.	1915	Allied offensive against Gallipoli repulsed.
1839	Sultan declared war on Mehemet Ali. Egyptian victory at Nazib provoked British, Russian, and Prussian action.	1916	Turkish troops thwarted British offensive on Mesopotamia. Beginnings of the Arab Revolt.
		1918	British breakthrough in Palestine prompted Turks to request an armistice.
1840	Mehemet Ali recognized as hereditary ruler of Egypt but forced to make peace.	1918–23	Growth of Turkish nationalist movement led by Mustafa Kemal (Atatürk).
1841	Straits Convention (Dardanelles Treaty) closed the Straits (Bosporus) to all warships in time of peace.	1919	National congresses at Erzurum and Sivas demanded a Turkish nation-state.
1853–56	Crimean War. Turkish state and economy increasingly indebted and under European control.	1920	Ottoman government refused demands of National Congress. Empire signed peace treaty with Allies at Sèvres but ratification refused.
1875	State bankruptcy.	1920–21	Turks suppressed Armenian separatist state.
1875–76	Uprisings in Turkish Balkan possessions. Serbo-Turkish War. First constitution gave all religious creeds and nationalities equal rights.	1922	Mustafa Kemal defeated the Greeks in Anatolia and abolished sultanate.
1876–1909	Sultan Abdul Hamid II set constitution aside and ruled as despot.	1923	Peace of Lausanne. Boundaries of new Turkish state defined and Mustafa Kemal became first president of the Turkish Republic.

outlawry in medieval England, a declaration that a criminal was outside the protection of the law, with his or her lands and goods forfeited to the Crown, and all civil rights being set aside. It was a lucrative royal 'privilege'; ◊Magna Carta restricted its use, and under Edward III it was further modified. Some outlaws, such as Robin Hood, became popular heroes.

overlander one of the Australian drovers in the 19th century who opened up new territory by driving their cattle through remote areas to new stations, or to market, before the establishment of regular stock routes.

Overlord, Operation Allied invasion of Normandy 6 June 1944 (D-day) during World War II.

Owen Robert 1771–1858. British socialist, born in Wales. In 1800 he became manager of a mill at New Lanark, Scotland, where by improving working and housing conditions and providing schools he created a model community. His ideas stimulated the cooperative movement

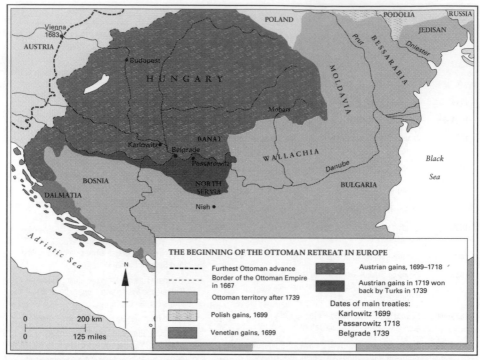

The beginning of Ottoman retreat in Europe *After centuries of expansion, an unsuccessful siege of Vienna 1683 finally halted the Ottoman advance into SE Europe. In the following years the Austrians captured Hungary and after a battle at Mohács 1687 the Ottomans lost most of their territory above the Danube. The Treaty of Karlowitz confirmed European gains. A brief success against the Russians followed by further defeats at the hands of the Austrians who acquired parts of Hungary, Serbia, and Wallachia by the Treaty of Passarowitz 1718. Further wars after 1736 brought Russian victories and Austrian defeats. The Ottomans regained some lost territories under the Treaty of Belgrade 1739, but had to concede some ground to Russia.*

(the pooling of resources for joint economic benefit).

From 1817 Owen proposed that 'villages of cooperation', self-supporting communities run on socialist lines, should be founded; these, he believed, would ultimately replace private ownership. His later attempt to run such a community in the USA failed.

Oxenstjerna Axel Gustafsson, Count Oxenstjerna 1583–1654. Swedish politician, chancellor from 1612. He pursued Gustavus Adolphus's foreign policy, acted as regent for Queen Christina, and maintained Swedish interests during and after the Thirty Years' War.

Oxford and Asquith, Earl of title of British Liberal politician Herbert Henry ♢Asquith.

Pacific War war 1879–83 fought by an alliance of Bolivia and Peru against Chile. Chile seized Antofagasta and the coast between the mouths of the rivers Loa and Paposo, rendering Bolivia landlocked, and also annexed the southern Peruvian coastline from Arica to the mouth of the Loa, including the nitrate fields of the Atacama Desert.

pacifism belief that violence, even in self-defence, is unjustifiable under any conditions and that arbitration is preferable to war as a means of solving disputes. In the East, pacifism has roots in Buddhism, and nonviolent action was used by Mahatma ◊Gandhi in the struggle for Indian independence.

Pacifist sentiment in Europe before and during World War I persuaded many to become conscientious objectors and refuse to fight, even when conscripted. They were imprisoned and in some cases executed. As a result of the carnage in the war, pacifism became more acceptable in the 1920s and 1930s, and organizations like the Peace Pledge Union in Britain were initiated. During World War II, conscientious objectors who refused to bear arms were often placed in noncombatant units such as the British Pioneer Corps, or in medical units.

pact of steel military alliance between Nazi Germany and Fascist Italy, instituted 1939.

Page Earle (Christmas Grafton) 1880–1961. Australian politician, leader of the Country Party 1920–39 and briefly prime minister in April 1939. He represented Australia in the British war cabinet 1941–42 and was minister of health 1949–55.

Pahlavi dynasty Iranian dynasty founded by Reza Khan (1877–1944), an army officer who seized control of the government 1921 and was

proclaimed shah 1925. During World War II, Britain and the USSR were nervous about his German sympathies and occupied Iran 1941–46. They compelled him to abdicate 1941 in favour of his son Muhammad Reza Shah Pahlavi, who took office in 1956, with US support, and was deposed in the Islamic revolution of 1979.

Paine Thomas 1737–1809. English left-wing political writer, active in the American and French revolutions. His pamphlet *Common Sense* 1776 ignited passions in the American Revolution; others include *The Rights of Man* 1791 and *The Age of Reason* 1793. He advocated republicanism, deism, the abolition of slavery, and the emancipation of women.

Government, even in its best state, is but a necessary evil; in its worst state, an intolerable one.

Thomas Paine *Common Sense*

Pakistan country in S Asia, stretching from the Himalayas to the Arabian Sea, bounded W by Iran, NW by Afghanistan, NE by China, and E by India.

history For history before 1947, see ◊Indus Valley Civilization and ◊India. The name 'Pakistan' for a Muslim division of British India was put forward 1930 by Choudhary Rahmat Ali (1897–1951) from names of the Muslim parts of the subcontinent: *P*unjab, the *A*fghan NW Frontier, *K*ashmir, *S*ind, and Baluchi*stan*. *Pak* means 'pure' in Urdu and *stan* means 'land'. Fear of domination by the Hindu majority in India led in 1940 to a serious demand for a separate Muslim state, which delayed India's independence for some years. In 1947 British India was divided into two dominions, India and Pakistan.

republic After the death of its leader ◊Jinnah 1948, Pakistan remained a dominion with the British monarch as head of state until a republic was declared 1956. Its new constitution was abrogated 1958, and military rule was imposed through a coup by General Muhammad ◊Ayub Khan. The country experienced rapid economic growth during the 1960s, but regional tension mounted between demographically dominant East Pakistan and West Pakistan, where political and military power was concentrated. After serious strikes and riots 1969, General Ayub Khan was replaced by General Agha Muhammad Yahya Khan.

civil war Pakistan's first elections with universal suffrage were held 1970 to elect an assembly to frame a new constitution. Sheik Mujib ur-Rahman's Awami League, which proposed autonomy, gained a majority of seats in East Pakistan, and the Pakistan People's Party (or PPP) in West Pakistan. East Pakistan declared its independence from the West 1971, precipitating a civil war. India intervened on East Pakistan's side, and the independent republic of ◊Bangladesh emerged.

parliamentary government General Yahya Khan resigned, passing power in (W) Pakistan to the People's Party leader Zulfiqar Ali ◊Bhutto, who introduced a new federal parliamentary constitution 1973 and a socialist economic programme of land reform and nationalization. From the mid-1970s the Sind-based Bhutto faced deteriorating economic conditions and growing regional opposition, particularly from Baluchistan and from Pathans campaigning for an independent Pakhtoonistan.

martial law Bhutto won a majority in the 1977 assembly elections but was accused of ballot-rigging. Riots ensued, and after four months of unrest, the Punjabi Muslim army Chief of Staff, General ◊Zia ul-Haq, seized power in a bloodless coup 1977. Martial law was imposed; Bhutto was imprisoned for alleged murder and hanged 1979.

Islamization programme General Zia imposed severe restrictions on political activity. He introduced a broad Islamization programme aimed at deepening his support base and appeasing Islamic fundamentalists. This was opposed by middle-class professionals and by the Shi'ite minority. In 1981, nine banned opposition parties, including the People's Party of Pakistan, formed the Movement for the Restoration of Democracy alliance to campaign for a return to parliamentary government. The military government responded by arresting several hundred opposition politicians. A renewed democracy campaign 1983 resulted in considerable anti-government violence in Sind province. From 1982, however, General Zia slowly began enlarging the civilian element in his government and in 1984, he held a successful referendum on the Islamization process, which was taken to legitimize his continuing as president for a further five-year term.

civilian government In 1985, direct elections were held to the national and provincial assemblies, but on a nonparty basis. A new civilian cabinet was formed and an amended constitution adopted. Martial law and the ban on political parties were lifted, military courts were abolished, and military administrators stepped down in favour of civilians. A government was formed by the Pagaro faction of the Pakistan Muslim League (PML) led by Mohammad Khan Junejo, which was subservient to General Zia. Benazir Bhutto, the daughter of Zulfiqar Ali Bhutto and leader of the PPP, returned 1986 from self-exile in London to launch a popular campaign for immediate open elections. Riots erupted in Lahore, Karachi, and rural Sind, where troops were sent in, and PPP leaders were arrested.

Islamic law introduced In 1988, concerned with the deteriorating state of the economy and anxious to accelerate the Islamization process, President Zia dismissed the Junejo government and dissolved the national assembly and provincial legislatures, promising fresh elections within 90 days. Ruling by ordinance, Zia decreed that the Shari'a, the Islamic legal code, would immediately become the country's supreme law. A month later he was killed, along with senior army officers, in a military air crash near Bahawalpur. Sabotage was suspected. Ghulam Ishaq Khan, the Senate's elderly chair, succeeded as president. In subsequent multi-party elections, the PPP, which had moved towards the centre in its policy stance, emerged as the largest single party.

Benazir Bhutto's government After forging a coalition with the Mohajir National Movement (MQM), Benazir Bhutto was sworn in as prime minister Nov 1988, and Ghulam Ishaq Khan was elected president. The new Bhutto administration pledged itself to a free-market economic programme, support of the Afghan mujaheddin, and to leave untouched the military budget. In Oct 1989 the MQM withdrew from the ruling coalition and allied itself with the opposition Islamic Democratic Alliance (IDA). The Bhutto government narrowly survived a vote of no confidence a month later.

Sharif's government Benazir Bhutto's government was dismissed from office by president Ghulam Ishaq Khan Aug 1990 on accusations of incompetence, corruption, and abuse of power. The national assemblies were also dissolved. In Oct 1990 the opposition swept to victory and Nawaz Sharif, Bhutto's former chief minister of Punjab province, became prime minister. Sharif had headed the IDA, which incorporated the PML (led by former premier Mohammad Khan Junejo). The IDA captured 105 of the 207 parliamentary seats contested to the 45 of Bhutto's PPP. It also secured control of three of the four provincial assemblies, Bhutto's Sind stronghold being the exception. Sharif promised to pursue a free-market economic programme and was supported by the military, state bureaucracy, and mullahs.

Islamic law enforced In May 1991 a Shari'a bill, enforcing Islamic law and designed to create an 'Islamic welfare state' was enacted. The opposition PPP, though welcoming parts of the social reform programme, unsuccessfully voted against the bill. Nawaz Sharif also launched a privatization and deregulation programme, but these reforms were soon upset by labour unrest and terrorist incidents and by the uncovering of a financial scandal involving Nawaz Sharif's family and members of the government.

foreign affairs In foreign affairs, Pakistan's relations with India have been strained since independence, with border wars over Kashmir 1965 and East Pakistan 1971. It left the Commonwealth 1972, when the new state of Bangladesh was accepted, but rejoined 1989. As a result of shared hostility to India, Pakistan has been allied with China since the 1950s; during the 1970s it developed close relations with the USA, providing support for the US-backed Afghan rebels, while joining the ◊nonaligned movement 1979 and drawing closer to the Islamic states of the Middle East and Africa. During the Persian Gulf crisis and war against Iraq of 1990–91, Pakistan sent 11,000 troops to Saudi Arabia to guard Islamic shrines, but there was considerable anti-Americanism within the country and popular support for Saddam Hussein.

nuclear capability The USA suspended military aid in Oct 1990 after learning that Pakistan was seeking to develop nuclear weapons. (Benazir Bhutto admitted Sept 1991 that Pakistan did have the ability to build a nuclear weapon rapidly.)

Pala dynasty NE Indian hereditary rulers, influential between the 8th and 13th centuries. Based in the agriculturally rich region of Bihar and Bengal, the dynasty was founded by Gopala, who had been elected king, and reached its peak under his son Dharmapala (reigned *c.* 770–810).

Palaeolithic earliest stage of human technology and development of the Stone Age; see ◊prehistory.

Palatinate (called the *Pfalz* in Germany) historic division of Germany, dating from before the 8th century. It was ruled by a *count palatine* (a count with royal prerogatives) and varied in size.

When the Palatinate was attached to Bavaria 1815 it consisted of two separate parts: Rhenish (or Lower) Palatinate on the Rhine (capital Heidelberg), and Upper Palatinate (capital Amberg on the Vils) 210 km/130 mi to the east. In 1946 Rhenish Palatinate became an administrative division of the *Land* (German region) of Rhineland-Palatinate with its capital at Neustadt; Upper Palatinate remained an administrative division of Bavaria with its capital at Regensburg.

Palau former name (until 1981) of the Republic of ◊Belau.

Palestine (Arabic *Falastin* 'Philistine') geographical area at the eastern end of the Mediterranean sea, also known as the Holy Land because of its historic and symbolic importance for Jews, Christians and Muslims. In ancient times Palestine extended E of the river Jordan. Early settlers included the Canaanites, Hebrews, and Philistines. Over the centuries it became part of the Egyptian, Assyrian, Macedonian, Ptolemaic, Seleucid, Roman, Byzantine, Arab, and Ottoman empires. Today it comprises parts of modern Israel, and Jordan.

Under the 1993 Oslo accord, interim Palestinian self-rule was introduced in the Gaza strip and Jericho; a permanent pact on self-rule began with an agreement signed 1995 in Cairo. Yassir Arafat, leader of the Palestinian Liberation Organization (PLO), was elected president of the Palestinian National Council 1996.

Palestine Liberation Organization (PLO) Arab organization founded 1964 to bring about an independent state of Palestine. It consists of several distinct groupings, the chief of which is al-◊Fatah, led by Yassir ◊Arafat, the president of the PLO from 1969. The PLO has pursued diplomatic initiatives, but also operates as a guerrilla army.

Beirut, Lebanon, became PLO headquarters 1970–71 after its defeat in the Jordanian civil war. In 1974 the PLO became the first non-governmental delegation to be admitted to a session of the UN General Assembly. When Israel invaded Lebanon 1982 the PLO had to abandon its headquarters there; it moved on to Tunis, Tunisia and in 1986 to Baghdad, Iraq. PLO members who remained in Lebanon after the expulsion were later drawn into the internal conflict (see ◊Arab-Israeli Wars). In 1986 Jordan suspended 'political coordination' with the PLO and expelled Arafat's deputy, dealing instead directly with Palestinians in Israeli-occupied territories. In 1988, the Palestine National Council voted to create a state of Palestine, but at the same time endorsed United Nations resolution 242, recognizing Israel's right to exist.

Palestine Wars another name for the ◊Arab-Israeli Wars.

Pallava dynasty hereditary Hindu kings that dominated SE India between the 4th and 9th centuries. The dynasty's greatest rulers

Palestine history	
c. 1000 BC	Hebrew leader King David formed a united Kingdom of Israel.
922	Kingdom of Israel split into Israel in the north and Judah in the south after the death of King Solomon.
722	Israel conquered by Assyrians.
586	Judah conquered by Babylonians who destroyed Jerusalem and forced many Jews into exile in Babylon.
539	Palestine became part of Persian empire.
536	Jews allowed to return to Jerusalem.
332	Conquest by Alexander the Great.
168	Maccabean revolt against Seleucids restored independence.
63	Conquest by Roman empire.
AD 70	Romans destroyed Jerusalem following Jewish revolt.
636	Conquest by the Muslim Arabs made Palestine a target for the Crusades.
1516	Conquest by the Ottoman Turks.
1880–1914	Jewish immigration increased sharply as a result of pogroms in Russia and Poland.
1897	At the first Zionist Congress, Jews called for a permanent homeland in Palestine.
1909	Tel Aviv, the first all-Jewish town in Palestine was founded.
1917	The Balfour Declaration expressed the British government's support for the establishment of a Jewish national homeland in Palestine.
1917–18	The Turks were driven out by the British under field marshal Allenby in World War I.
1922	A League of Nations mandate (which incorporated the Balfour Declaration) placed Palestine under British administration.
1936–39	Arab revolt took place, fuelled by Jewish immigration (300,000 people 1920–39).
1937	The Peel Commission report recommended the partition of Palestine into Jewish and Arab states.
1939–45	Arab and Jewish Palestinians served in the Allied forces in World War II.
1946	Resentment of immigration restrictions led to acts of anti-British violence by Jewish guerrilla groups.
1947	The United Nations (UN) approved Britain's plan for partition.
1948	A Jewish state of Israel was proclaimed 14 May (eight hours before Britain's renunciation of the mandate was due). A series of Arab-Israeli Wars resulted in Israeli territorial gains and the occupation of other parts of Palestine by Egypt and Jordan. Many Palestinian Arabs were displaced.
1964	The Palestinian Liberation Organization (PLO) was formed and a guerrilla war was waged against the Jewish state.
1974	The PLO became the first nongovernmental delegation to be admitted to a plenary session of the UN General Assembly.
1987	The Intifada, a popular uprising against Israeli occupation, began.
1988	PLO leader Yassir Arafat renounced terrorism; the USA agreed to meetings.
1989	Israeli prime minister Yitzhak Shamir proposed Palestinian elections in the West Bank/Gaza Strip.
1991	Gulf War against Iraq's annexation of Kuwait caused diplomatic reconsideration of a Palestinian state in an effort to stabilize the Middle East. A peace conference in Spain in Nov included Israel and Arab states.
1993	Historic accord of mutual recognition signed by Israel and PLO, outlining plans for interim Palestinian self-rule in Gaza Strip and West Bank town of Jericho and for phased withdrawal of Israeli troops from occupied territories.

were Simhavisnu (ruled c. 575–600) and Narasimhavarman I (ruled 630–668). Their capital was Kanchi, SW of Madras.

Under the Pallavas, maritime trade with Sri Lanka and SE Asia flourished, as did music, painting, literature, and architecture. Structural stone temples replaced rock buildings, the most impressive example being the sculptured Shore Temple at the seaport of Mahabalipuram, dedicated to the god Shiva.

Palme (Sven) Olof 1927–1986. Swedish social-democratic politician, prime minister 1969–76 and 1982–86. As prime minister he carried out constitutional reforms, turning the Riksdag into a single-chamber parliament and stripping the monarch of power, and was widely respected for his support of Third World Countries. He was assassinated Feb 1986.

Palmerston Henry John Temple, 3rd Viscount Palmerston 1784–1865. British politician. Initially a Tory, in Parliament from 1807, he was secretary-at-war 1809–28. He broke with the Tories 1830 and sat in the Whig cabinets of 1830–34, 1835–41, and 1846–51 as foreign secretary. He was prime minister 1855–58 (when he rectified Aberdeen's mismanagement of the Crimean War, suppressed the ◊Indian Mutiny, and carried through the Second Opium War) and 1859–65 (when he almost involved Britain in the American Civil War on the side of the South).

Palmerston succeeded to an Irish peerage 1802. He served under five Tory prime ministers before joining the Whigs. His foreignj policy was marked by distrust of France and Russia, against whose designs he backed the independence of Belgium and Turkey. He became home secretary in the coalition government of 1852, and prime minister on its fall, and was responsible for the warship *Alabama* going to the Confederate side in the American Civil War. He was popular with the people and made good use of the press, but his high handed attitude annoyed Queen Victoria and other ministers.

Pan-Africanist Congress (PAC) militant black South African nationalist group, which broke away from the African National Congress (ANC) 1959. More radical than the ANC, the Pan-Africanist Congress has a black-only policy for Africa. PAC was outlawed from 1960 to 1990. Its military wing is called Poqo ('we alone').

In March 1960, the PAC organized a campaign of protest against South African pass laws, which resulted in the ◊Sharpeville massacre; the following month, the PAC was declared an illegal organization by the South

African government. It continued guerrilla activities against South Africa from bases in Botswana until its legalization was restored 1990.

Panama country in Central America, on a narrow isthmus between the Caribbean and the Pacific Ocean, bounded W by Costa Rica and E by Colombia.

history For early history, see ◊American Indian. Panama was visited by Christopher Columbus 1502. Vasco Núñez de ◊Balboa found the Pacific from the Darien isthmus 1513. Spanish settlements were sacked by Francis ◊Drake 1572–95 and Henry Morgan 1668–71; Morgan destroyed the old city of Panama, which dated from 1519. Remains of Fort St Andrews, built by Scottish settlers 1698–1701, were discovered 1976. Panama remained part of the viceroyalties of Peru and New Granada until 1821, when it gained independence from Spain; it joined Gran Colombia 1822.

independence Panama achieved full independence 1903 with US support. At the same time the USA bought the rights to build the Panama Canal and was given control of a strip of territory 16 km/10 mi wide, known as the Canal Zone, in perpetuity. Panama was guaranteed US protection and an annuity. In 1939 Panama's protectorate status was ended by mutual agreement, and in 1977 two treaties were signed by Panama's president (1968–78), General Omar Torrijos Herrera, and US president Carter. One transferred ownership of the canal to Panama effective 1999 and the other guaranteed its subsequent neutrality, with the conditions that only Panamanian forces would be stationed in the zone, and that the USA would have the right to use force to keep the canal open if it became obstructed.

deterioration of economy The 1980s saw a deterioration in the state of Panama's economy, with opposition to the austerity measures that the government introduced to try to halt the decline. The centre-right National Democratic Union (Unade) won 40 seats in the 1984 general election; the centre-left Democratic Opposition Alliance (ADO) won 27 seats. After a very close result, Dr Nicolás Ardito Barletta, the Democratic Revolutionary Party (PRD) candidate, was declared president, but in 1985 he resigned, amid speculation that he had been forced to do so by the commander of the National Guard. Relations between Panama and the USA deteriorated with the departure of President Barletta, and the Reagan administration cut and later suspended its financial aid.

Barletta was succeeded by Eric Arturo del Valle, but the country was, from 1983, effectively ruled by the army commander in chief, General Manuel Noriega. Although the 1977 Torrijos–Carter Canal Treaties specified that US forces in Panama were present purely to defend the canal, Noriega cooperated in allowing the US to use Panama as an intelligence, training, resupply, and weapons base for the Reagan administration's campaigns in Nicaragua and El Salvador.

accusations against Noriega In 1987 Noriega was accused of corruption, election rigging, involvement in the cocaine trade, and the murder of a political opponent. Noriega's forces were allegedly responsible for up to a dozen political killings between 1983 and 1989. Political parties, labour and student unions, and business groups united as the National Civic Crusade to campaign for his removal; demonstrations were suppressed by riot police. In July 1987 Noriega successfully resisted calls for his removal, despite the suspension of US military and economic aid. He declared the May 1989 assembly elections invalid and in Sept Francisco Rodríguez, with army backing, was made president. In the following month an attempted coup against Noriega was put down.

US invasion In Dec 1989, after mounting harassment of Americans in the Canal Zone, US president Bush ordered troops to invade the country with the declared object of arresting Noriega and bringing him to trial. Several hundred people were killed and more were made homeless in the US invasion. The US and Panamanian forces raided newspaper offices and rounded up hundreds of dissidents, many of whom were imprisoned without charge. Noriega sought refuge in the Vatican embassy but eventually surrendered and was taken to the USA, where he was convicted 1992 of charges relating to drug trafficking. Guillermo Endara became president and worked to balance Panama's aims against pressures from the USA, its most important partner, in such areas as banking. In Oct 1991 an attempted antigovernment coup by former officers loyal to Noriega was thwarted. In Dec 1991 the army was formally abolished. Noriega was tried in a US court April 1992 and found guilty of drug offences.

Panama Canal canal across the Panama isthmus in Central America, connecting the Pacific and Atlantic oceans; length 80 km/50 mi, with 12 locks. Built by the USA 1904–14 after an unsuccessful attempt by the French, it was formally opened 1920. The *Panama Canal Zone* was acquired 'in perpetuity' by the USA

1903, comprising land extending about 5 km/3 mi on either side of the canal. The zone passed to Panama 1979, and control of the canal itself was ceded to Panama by the USA Jan 1990 under the terms of the Panama Canal Treaty 1977. The Canal Zone has several US military bases.

It is the greatest liberty that Man has ever taken with Nature.

On the *Panama Canal*
James Bryce *South America* 1912

Pan-American Union former name (1910–48) of the ◊Organization of American States.

Pandya dynasty S Indian hereditary rulers 3rd century BC–16th century AD. Based in the region around its capital Madurai, the dynasty extended its power into Kerala (SW India) and Sri Lanka during the reigns of kings Kadungon (ruled 590–620), Arikesar Maravarman (670–700), Varagunamaharaja I (765–815), and Srimara Srivallabha (815–862). The Pandya peak came under Jatavarman Sundara's reign 1251–1268. After Madurai was invaded by the ◊Delhi sultanate 1311, the Pandyas faded to become merely local rulers.

Pan-Germanism movement that developed during the 19th century to encourage unity between German- and Dutch-speaking peoples in Austria, the Netherlands, Flanders, Luxembourg, and Switzerland. Encouraged by the unification of Germany after 1871, the movement had an increasingly high profile in the period up to 1914.

Panipat, Battles of three decisive battles: 1526, when Babur, great-grandson of the Mongol conqueror Tamerlane, defeated the emperor of Delhi and founded the Mogul empire; 1556, won by his descendant ◊Akbar; 1761, when the ◊Marathas were defeated by Ahmad Shah Durrani of Afghanistan. The town of Panipat is in Punjab, India, 80 km/50 mi west of Delhi.

Pankhurst Emmeline (born Goulden) 1858–1928. English suffragette. Founder of the Women's Social and Political Union 1903, she launched the militant suffragette campaign 1905. In 1926 she joined the Conservative Party and was a prospective Parliamentary candidate.

She was supported by her daughters *Christabel Pankhurst* (1880–1958), political leader of the movement, and *Sylvia Pankhurst* (1882–1960). The latter was imprisoned nine times under the 'Cat and Mouse Act', and was a pacifist in World War I.

Women had always fought for men, and for their children. Now they were ready to fight for their own human rights. Our militant movement was established.

Emmeline Pankhurst *My Own Story*

Panzer (German 'armour') divisions of World War II created by Heinz ◊Guderian.

Papa Doc nickname of François ◊Duvalier, right-wing president of Haiti 1957–71.

Papal States area of central Italy in which the pope was temporal ruler from 756 until the unification of Italy 1870.

Papandreou Andreas 1919– 96. Greek socialist politician, founder of the Pan-Hellenic Socialist Movement (PASOK); prime minister 1981-89 and again 1993-96. He lost the 1989 election after being implicated in an alleged embezzlement scandal, involving the diversion of funds to the Greek government from the Bank of Crete, headed by George Koskotas. In Jan 1992 a trial cleared Papandreou of all corruption charges.

Papen Franz von 1879–1969. German right-wing politician. As chancellor 1932, he negotiated the Nazi-Conservative alliance that made Hitler chancellor 1933. He was envoy to Austria 1934–38 and ambassador to Turkey 1939–44. Although acquitted at the ◊Nuremberg trials, he was imprisoned by a German denazification court for three years.

Papineau Louis Joseph 1786–1871. Canadian politician. He led a mission to England to protest against the planned union of Lower Canada (Québec) and Upper Canada (Ontario), and demanded economic reform and an elected provincial legislature. In 1835 he gained the cooperation of William Lyon ◊Mackenzie in Upper Canada, and in 1837 organized an unsuccessful rebellion of the French against British rule in Lower Canada. He fled the country, but returned 1847 to sit in the United Canadian legislature until 1854.

Papua New Guinea country in the SW Pacific, comprising the eastern part of the island of New Guinea, the Bismarck Archipelago, and part of the Solomon Islands.

history New Guinea has been inhabited for at least 50,000 years, probably by people arriving from the E Indonesian islands. Agricultural economy dates back some 6,000 years. In the

Western Highlands, a permanent system with drainage and garden tools was established 2,500 years ago. The sweet potato, introduced 1,200 years, ago became the staple crop of the highlands, the yam and taro being grown in lowland areas. The first European to reach New Guinea was probably the Portuguese explorer Jorge de Menezes in about 1526, who named it 'Ilhas dos Papuas'. It was visited by several Dutch traders in the 17th century, and by the Englishman William Dampier 1700, who named the island of New Britain. French explorer Louis Antoine de Bougainville was in the arca 1768. The Dutch East India Company took control of the western half of the island, and in 1828 it became part of the Dutch East Indies. In 1884 the southeast was claimed by Britain, the northeast by Germany. The British part, Papua, was transferred to Australia 1905. The German part was transferred after World War I, when Australia was granted a League of Nations mandate and then a trusteeship over the area.

independence Freed from Japanese occupation 1945, the two territories were jointly administered by Australia and, after achieving internal self-government as Papua New Guinea, became fully independent within the Commonwealth 1975. The first prime minister after independence was Michael Somare, leader of the PP. Despite allegations of incompetence, he held office until 1980, when Julius Chan, leader of the PPP, succeeded him. Somare returned to power 1982, but in 1985 he lost a no-confidence motion in parliament and was replaced by Paias Wingti, leader of the breakaway PDM, with former prime minister Chan as his deputy. In 1987 Prime Minister Wingti returned to power with a slender majority of three votes. He announced a more independent foreign policy of good relations with the USSR, USA, Japan, and China.

six-party coalition In 1988, following shifts in coalition alliances, Wingti lost a no-confidence vote and was replaced as prime minister by the former foreign minister and PP's new leader, Rabbie Namaliu. Somare became foreign minister in the new six-party coalition government. Faced with deteriorating internal law and order – soldiers rioting in Port Moresby in Feb 1989 over inadequate pay increases – the government imposed a state of emergency on Bougainville island from June 1989 because of the growing strength there of the guerrilla separatist movement, which had forced the closure a month earlier of the island's Panguna copper and gold mine, which provided 40% of the country's export revenue. The

government withdrew its troops from the island March 1990. In May 1990 the secessionist Bougainville Revolutionary Army (BRA) issued a unilateral declaration of independence, to which the government responded by imposing a blockade. An interim peace accord – the 'Endeavour Accord' – Aug 1990 was followed by a peace accord signed Jan 1991, and intended to be permanent.

In Oct 1991 the governor general Vincent Serei Eri was removed after his refusal to dismiss deputy prime minister Ted Diro who was found guilty of corruption in Oct. On 11 Nov 1991 Wiwa Korowi was elected to replace Eri. In April 1992 an outlawed Bougainville separatist group were responsible for the deaths of a peace negotiator and six others, damaging chances of a negotiated peace settlement. In July Wingti was elected premier for a second term.

economic slump After a slump during 1989–90 caused by the closure of the Bougainville mine and falling world prices for its coffee and cocoa exports, Papua New Guinea has enjoyed an economic boom, with gold production doubling 1990–92 as a result of the discovery of huge new deposits.

Paraguay landlocked country in South America, bounded NE by Brazil, S by Argentina, and NW by Bolivia.

history For early history, see ◊American Indian. The Guaraní Indians had a settled agricultural civilization before the arrival of Europeans: Sebastian ◊Cabot 1526–30, followed by Spanish colonists, who founded the city of Asunción 1537. From about 1600 until 1767, when they were expelled, Jesuit missionaries administered much of the country. It became a province subordinate to the Spanish viceroyalty of Peru, then from 1776 part of the viceroyalty of Buenos Aires.

independence In 1811 Paraguay declared its independence. The first president was J G R Francia (ruled 1816–40), a despot; he was followed by his nephew C A López and in 1862 by his son F S López, who involved Paraguay in a war with Brazil, Argentina, and Uruguay. Paraguay was invaded and López killed at Aquidabán 1870. When the war was finally over, the population consisted mainly of women and children. Recovery was slow, with many revolutions. Continuing disputes with Bolivia over the frontier in the torrid Chaco zone of the north flared up into war 1932–35; arbitration by the USA and five South American republics reached a peace settlement 1938.

military governments Since 1940 Paraguay has been mostly under the control of military governments led by strong, autocratic leaders. General Morínigo was president 1940–48 and General Alfredo Stroessner 1954–89. During the US presidency of Jimmy ◊Carter the Stroessner regime came under strong criticism for its violation of human rights, and this resulted in a tempering of the general's iron rule. Stroessner maintained his supremacy by ensuring that the armed forces and business community shared in the spoils of office and by preventing opposition groups from coalescing into a credible challenge. In the 1983 Congress elections the National Republican Party (Colorado Party), led by the president, with the largest number of votes, automatically secured 20 Senate and 40 Chamber seats. The Radical Liberal Party was placed second, with six Senate and 13 Chamber seats.

Stroessner sought and won an eighth consecutive term only to be ousted, in Feb 1989, by General Andrés Rodríguez who, in May 1989, was elected president. The Colorado Party was also successful in the congressional elections. During 1989–90, Rodríguez made progress on economic growth and political democracy. In Dec 1991 the Colorado Party won 58% of the vote for an assembly to write a new constitution.

Paris Commune two periods of government in France:

The Paris municipal government 1789–94 was established after the storming of the ◊Bastille and remained powerful in the French Revolution until the fall of Robespierre 1794.

The provisional national government 18 March–May 1871 was formed while Paris was besieged by the Germans during the Franco-Prussian War. It consisted of socialists and left-wing republicans, and is often considered the first socialist government in history. Elected after the right-wing National Assembly at Versailles tried to disarm the National Guard, it fell when the Versailles troops captured Paris and massacred 20,000–30,000 people 21–28 May.

parish in Britain, a subdivision of a county often coinciding with an original territorial subdivision in Christian church administration, served by a parish church. In the US, the parish is an ecclesiastical unit committed to one minister or priest.

The origins of the parish lie in early medieval Italian cities, and by the 12th century, most of Christian Europe was divided into parishes. The parish has frequently been the centre of community life, especially in rural areas.

Paris, Treaty of any of various peace treaties signed in Paris, including: *1763* ending the ◊Seven Years' War; *1783* recognizing American independence; *1814* and *1815* following the abdication and final defeat of ◊Napoleon I; *1856* ending the ◊Crimean War; *1898* ending the ◊Spanish-American War; *1919–20* the conference preparing the Treaty of ◊Versailles at the end of World War I was held in Paris; *1946* after World War II, the peace treaties between the ◊Allies and Italy, Romania, Hungary, Bulgaria, and Finland; *1951* treaty signed by France, West Germany, Italy, Belgium, Netherlands and Luxembourg, embodying the Schuman Plan to set up a single coal and steel authority; *1973* ending US participation in the ◊Vietnam War.

Park Chung Hee 1917–1979. President of South Korea 1963–79. Under his rule South Korea had one of the world's fastest-growing economies, but recession and his increasing authoritarianism led to his assassination 1979.

Parker Bonnie 1911–1943. US criminal; see ◊Bonnie and Clyde.

Parkes Henry 1815–1896. Australian politician, born in the UK. He promoted education and the cause of federation, and suggested the official name 'Commonwealth of Australia'. He was five times premier of New South Wales 1872–91. Parkes, New South Wales, is named after him.

parliament (French 'speaking') legislative body of a country. The world's oldest parliament is the Icelandic Althing which dates from about 930. The UK Parliament is usually dated from 1265. The legislature of the USA is called ◊Congress and comprises the ◊House of Representatives and the ◊Senate.

In the UK, Parliament is the supreme legislature, comprising the *House of Commons* and the *House of Lords*. The origins of Parliament are in the 13th century, but its powers were not established until the late 17th century. The powers of the Lords were curtailed 1911, and the duration of parliaments was fixed at five years, but any parliament may extend its own life, as happened during both world wars. The UK Parliament meets in the Palace of Westminster, London.

history Parliament originated under the Norman kings as the Great Council of royal tenants-in-chief, to which in the 13th century representatives of the shires were sometimes summoned. The Parliament summoned by Simon de Montfort 1265 (as head of government in the Barons' War) set a precedent by including representatives of the boroughs as

Parliamentary reform in the UK

1822 Lord John Russell proposed a redistribution of seats. Whig Party espoused cause of reform.

1830 Duke of Wellington resigned as prime minister bringing in Whig ministry under Lord Grey, committed to reform. (Electorate 516,000 = 2% of population.)

1832 Reform Act involved redistribution of parliamentary seats from 'rotten boroughs' to urban constituencies. Franchise extended to householders paying £10 per year rent in towns and 40-shilling freeholders in counties. (Electorate 813,000 = 3% of population.)

1867 Reform Act involved further redistribution of seats and extension of franchise to all ratepayers in boroughs. (Electorate 2,500,000 = 8% of population.)

1872 Ballot Act introduced secret ballots for elections.

1883 Corrupt and Illegal Practices Act set limits to election expenses.

1884 Reform Act again involved redistribution of seats and equalization of franchise for boroughs and counties, to include all householders and ratepayers. (Electorate 5,600,000 = 16% of population.)

1885 Further redistribution of parliamentary seats.

1918 Representation of the People Act gave the vote to all men over 21 and all women ratepayers (or wives of ratepayers) over 30.

1928 Representation of the People (Equal Franchise) Act gave the vote to all women over 21.

1948 Plural voting abolished. Permanent Boundary Commission established.

1970 Voting age reduced to 18.

1979 Constituencies established for direct election to European Parliament in Strasbourg.

well as the shires. Under Edward III the burgesses and knights of the shires began to meet separately from the barons, thus forming the House of Commons. By the 15th century Parliament had acquired the right to legislate, vote, and appropriate supplies, examine public accounts, and impeach royal ministers. The powers of Parliament were much diminished under the Yorkists and Tudors but under Elizabeth I a new spirit of independence appeared. The revolutions of 1640 and 1688 established parliamentary control over the executive and judiciary, and finally abolished all royal claim to tax or legislate without parliamentary consent. During these struggles the two great parties (Whig and Tory) emerged, and after 1688 it became customary for the sovereign to choose ministers from the party dominant in the Commons. The English Parliament was united with the Scottish 1707, and with the Irish

1801–1922. The ◊franchise was extended to the middle classes 1832, to the urban working classes 1867, to agricultural labourers 1884, and to women 1918 and 1928. The duration of parliaments was fixed at three years 1694, at seven 1716, and at five 1911. Payment of MPs was introduced 1911. A *public bill* that has been passed is an act of Parliament.

You choose a member indeed; but when you have chosen him, he not a member of Bristol, but a member of parliament.

On *parliament* Edmund Burke, speech at Bristol 1774

Parnell Charles Stewart 1846–1891. Irish nationalist politician. He supported a policy of obstruction and violence to attain ◊Home Rule, and became the president of the Nationalist Party 1877. In 1879 he approved the ◊Land League, and his attitude led to his imprisonment 1881. His career was ruined 1890 when he was cited as co-respondent in a divorce case.

These Englishmen despise us because we are Irish, but we must stand up to them. That's the only way to treat an Englishman – stand up to him.

Charles Stewart Parnell letter to his brother

Parr Catherine 1512–1548. Sixth wife of Henry VIII of England. She had already lost two husbands when in 1543 she married Henry VIII. She survived him, and in 1547 married Lord Seymour of Sudeley (1508–1549).

Parthia ancient country in W Asia in what is now NE Iran, capital Ctesiphon. Parthian ascendancy began with the Arsacid dynasty in 248 BC, and reached the peak of its power under Mithridates I in the 2nd century BC; the region was annexed to Persia under the Sassanids AD 226.

Parthian horse riders feigned retreat and shot their arrows unexpectedly backwards, hence the use of 'Parthian shot' to mean a remark delivered in parting. Parthian administration was influenced by the Seleucid empire in Syria and later they successfully resisted the Romans.

partisan member of an armed group that operates behind enemy lines or in occupied territories during wars. The name 'partisans' was first given to armed bands of Russians who operated against Napoleon's army in Russia during 1812, but has since been used to describe

Russian, Yugoslav, Italian, Greek, and Polish Resistance groups against the Germans during World War II. In Yugoslavia the communist partisans under their leader, Tito, played a major role in defeating the Germans.

Passchendaele village in W Flanders, Belgium, near Ypres. The Passchendaele ridge before Ypres was the object of a costly and unsuccessful British offensive in World War I, between July and Nov 1917; British casualties numbered nearly 400,000.

pass laws South African laws that required the black population to carry passbooks (identity documents) at all times and severely restricted freedom of movement. The laws, a major cause of discontent, formed a central part of the policies of ◊apartheid. They were repealed 1986.

Pataliputra ancient N Indian city, founded *c.* 490 BC as a small fort (Pataligrama) near the river Ganges within the ◊Magadha ◊*janapada*. It became the capital for both the Mauryan dynasty under Chandragupta and, later, of the imperial Guptas. During the reign of Emperor Asoka in the 3rd century BC, it was the world's largest city, with a population of 150,000–300,000. As *Patna*, it remains an important regional centre.

Patel Sardar Vallabhbhai 1875–1950. Indian political leader. A fervent follower of Mahatma ◊Gandhi and a leader of the Indian National Congress, he was deputy prime minister 1947–50, after independence. Patel participated in the ◊satyagraha in Kaira in 1918. He was a member of the right wing of the Indian National Congress.

patrician member of a privileged class in ancient Rome, which originally dominated the ◊Senate. During the 5th and 4th centuries BC many of the rights formerly exercised by the patricians alone were extended to the plebeians, and patrician descent became a matter of prestige.

patronage power to give a favoured appointment to an office or position in politics, business, or the church; or sponsorship of the arts. Patronage was for centuries bestowed mainly by individuals (in Europe often royal or noble) or by the church. In the 20th century, patrons have tended to be political parties, the state, and – in the arts – private industry and foundations.

In Britain, where it was nicknamed 'Old Corruption', patronage existed in the 16th century, but was most common from the Restoration of 1660 to the 19th century, when it was used to manage elections and ensure party support. Patronage was used not only for the preferment of friends, but also as a means of social justice,

often favouring, for example, the families of those in adversity. Political patronage has largely been replaced by a system of meritocracy (in which selection is by open competition rather than by personal recommendation).

In war nothing is impossible, provided you use audacity.
    George S Patton *War As I Knew It* 1947

Patton George (Smith) 1885–1945. US general in World War II, known as 'Blood and Guts'. He was appointed to command the 2nd Armored Division 1940 and became commanding general of the First Armored Corps 1941. In 1942 he led the Western Task Force that landed at Casablanca, Morocco. After commanding the 7th Army, he led the 3rd Army across France and into Germany, and in 1945 took over the 15th Army.

Paulus Friedrich von 1890–1957. German field marshal in World War II, commander of the forces that besieged Stalingrad (now Volgograd) in the USSR 1942–43; he was captured and gave evidence at the Nuremberg trials before settling in East Germany.

Pavia, Battle of battle 1525 between France and the Holy Roman Empire. The Habsburg emperor Charles V defeated and captured Francis I of France; the battle marked the beginning of Habsburg dominance in Italy.

Paz (Estenssoro) Victor 1907– . President of Bolivia 1952–56, 1960–64, and 1985–89. He founded and led the Movimiento Nacionalista Revolucionario (MNR) which seized power 1952. His regime extended the vote to Indians, nationalized the country's largest tin mines, embarked on a programme of agrarian reform, and brought inflation under control.

After holding a number of financial posts Paz entered politics in the 1930s and in 1942 founded the MNR. In exile in Argentina during one of Bolivia's many periods of military rule, he returned in 1951 and became president in 1952. He immediately embarked on a programme of political reform, retaining the presidency until 1956 and being re-elected 1960–64 and again in 1985, returning from near-retirement at the age of 77. During his long career he was Bolivian ambassador to London 1956–59 and a professor at London University 1966. Following an indecisive presidential contest 1989, Paz was replaced by Jaime Paz Zamora of the Movement of the Revolutionary Left (MIR). The latter was elected by congress after entering into a power-sharing agreement with former military dictator, Hugo Banzer Suarez.

peace movement collective opposition to war. The Western peace movements of the late 20th century can trace their origins to the pacifists of the 19th century and conscientious objectors during World War I. The campaigns after World War II have tended to concentrate on nuclear weapons, but there are numerous organizations devoted to peace, some wholly pacifist, some merely opposed to escalation.

Pearl Harbor US Pacific naval base in Oahu, Hawaii, USA, the scene of a Japanese aerial attack 7 Dec 1941, which brought the USA into World War II. More than 2,000 members of US armed forces were killed, and a large part of the US Pacific fleet was destroyed or damaged.

Pearse Patrick Henry 1879–1916. Irish poet prominent in the Gaelic revival, a leader of the ◊Easter Rising 1916. Proclaimed president of the provisional government, he was court-martialled and shot after its suppression.

We may make mistakes and shoot the wrong people, but bloodshed is a cleansing and a sanctifying thing, and the nation which regards it as the final horror has lost its manhood.

Patrick Pearse

Pearson Lester Bowles 1897–1972. Canadian politician, leader of the Liberal Party from 1958, prime minister 1963–68. As foreign minister 1948–57, he represented Canada at the United Nations, playing a key role in settling the ◊Suez Crisis 1956. Nobel Peace Prize 1957.

Pearson served as president of the General Assembly 1952–53 and helped to create the UN Emergency Force (UNEF) that policed Sinai following the Egypt–Israel war of 1956. As prime minister, he led the way to formulating a national medicare (health insurance) law.

peasant country-dweller engaged in small-scale farming. A peasant normally owns or rents a small amount of land, aiming to be self-sufficient and to sell surplus supplies locally.

In the UK, the move towards larger farms in the 18th century resulted in the disappearance of the independent peasantry, although small-scale farming survives in smallholdings and Scottish crofts. Landowners in countries such as France, Spain, and Italy showed less direct interest in agriculture, so the tradition of small

independent landholding remains a distinctive way of life today. See also ◊commune.

Peasants' Revolt the rising of the English peasantry in June 1381, the culminative result of economic, social, and political disillusionment. It was sparked off by the imposition of a new poll tax, three times the rates of those imposed in 1377 and 1379. Led by Wat ◊Tyler and John ◊Ball, rebels from SE England marched on London and demanded reforms. The revolt was put down by deceit and force by the authorities.

Following the plague of the Black Death, a shortage of agricultural workers led to higher wages. The Statute of Labourers, enacted 1351, attempted to return wages to pre-plague levels. When the third poll tax was enforced 1381, riots broke out all over England, especially in Essex and Kent. Wat Tyler and John Ball emerged as leaders and the rebels went on to London, where they continued plundering, burning John of Gaunt's palace at the Savoy, and taking the prisons at Newgate and Fleet. The young king Richard II attempted to appease the mob, who demanded an end to serfdom and feudalism. The rebels then took the Tower of London and murdered Archbishop Sudbury and Robert Hales. Again the king attempted to make peace at Smithfield, but Tyler was stabbed to death by William Walworth, the Lord Mayor of London. The king made concessions to the rebels, and they dispersed, but the concessions were revoked immediately.

Pedro two emperors of Brazil:

Pedro I 1798–1834. Emperor of Brazil 1822–31. The son of John VI of Portugal, he escaped to Brazil on Napoleon's invasion, and was appointed regent 1821. He proclaimed Brazil independent 1822 and was crowned emperor, but abdicated 1831 and returned to Portugal.

Pedro II 1825–1891. Emperor of Brazil 1831–89. He proved an enlightened ruler, but his antislavery measures alienated the landowners, who compelled him to abdicate.

Peel Robert 1788–1850. British Conservative politician. As home secretary 1822–27 and 1828–30, he founded the modern police force and in 1829 introduced Roman Catholic emancipation. He was prime minister 1834–35 and 1841–46, when his repeal of the ◊Corn Laws caused him and his followers to break with the party.

Peel, born in Lancashire, entered Parliament as a Tory 1809. After the passing of the Reform Bill of 1832, which he had resisted, he reformed the Tories under the name of the Conservative

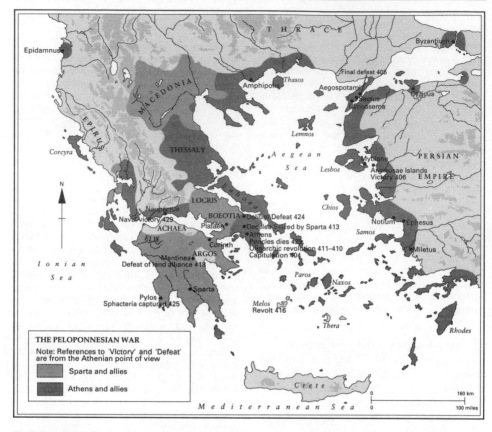

The Peloponnesian War *The Peloponnesian War, fought 431–404 BC between Athens and Sparta and their respective allies, was caused by disputes between Athens and Corinth, and by Spartan fear of Athenian power. The Athenian-led Delian League was based on sea-power in the Aegean and beyond. Only Achaea and Argos remained neutral, although Argos finally fought against Sparta at Mantinea 418. The Persian Empire provided finance for the rival navies after 413, and Athens was defeated at Aegospotami 405.*

Party, on a basis of accepting necessary changes and seeking middle-class support. He fell from prime ministerial office because his repeal of the Corn Laws 1846 was opposed by the majority of his party. He and his followers then formed a third party standing between the Liberals and Conservatives; the majority of the Peelites, including Gladstone, subsequently joined the Liberals.

Peipus, Lake (Estonian *Peipsi*, Russian *Chudskoye*) lake forming the boundary between Estonia and Pskov'oblast', an administrative region of Russia. Alexander Nevski defeated the Teutonic Knights on its frozen surface 1242.

Peking see ◊Beijing.

Peking man Chinese representative of an early species of human, found as fossils, 500,000–750,000 years old, in the cave of Choukoutien 1927 near Beijing (Peking). Peking man used chipped stone tools, hunted game, and used fire. Similar varieties of early human have been found in Java and E Africa. Their classification is disputed: some anthropologists classify them as *Homo erectus*, others as *Homo sapiens pithecanthropus*.

Pelham Henry 1696–1754. British Whig politician. He held a succession of offices in Robert Walpole's cabinet 1721–42, and was prime minister 1743–54. His brother Thomas Pelham-Holles, 1st Duke of ◊Newcastle, succeeded him as prime minister.

Peloponnesian War conflict between Athens and Sparta and their allies, 431–404 BC, originating in suspicions about the ambitions of the Athenian leader Pericles. It was ended by the Spartan general Lysander's capture of the

The Peloponnesian War 431–404 BC

The Peloponnesian War was a 27-year, intermittent conflict between a land army (the Peloponnesian League), and a sea force (the Athenian empire), in a bid to become the undisputed leading Greek power. The Athenian empire had developed out of the Delian League, and comprised Athens and the scattered Ionian islands and states on the E coast of the Aegean. The Peloponnesian League was led by Sparta, and included cities in the Peloponnese (the peninsula forming the S part of Greece), on and around the Isthmus of Corinth, and mainland Greece, notably Thebes in Boeotia, neighbour to Athens and which separated it from its mainland allies.

Territorial tensions

The leading powers were divided ideologically, with Athens acclaiming popular sovereignty and democracy, while Sparta stood for oligarchical and separatist attitudes. Simmering Spartan fear of the growth of Athenian power made war at some stage inevitable, but two major sources of tension between Athens and Corinth, raised the temperature. First, Corcyra (Corfu) quarrelled with Corinth, of which it was a colony, in 435 BC. It was accepted into the Athenian alliance in 433 BC because of the strength of its navy, and its strategically important position as a port of call on the sea routes to S Italy and Sicily. Second, the small N Grecian city of Potidaea attempted to leave the Delian League in 432 BC following an increase in payments demanded towards League expenses by Athens. Another cause of dissatisfaction within the Delian League was the Megarian decree, which excluded Megarians (Megara is a Greek mainland city) from the Athenian agora and from the harbours of the empire.

Indecisive war on land

After the failure of embassies between Athens and Sparta to start negotiations, the fighting began in 431 BC. Its pattern was set by the Athenian statesman Pericles, who suggested that the Athenians abandon some territory to the superior Peloponnesian land forces and rely on their formidable walls and fleet of over 200 triremes (great warships) for protection, supported by the empire and its wealth. It was an effective strategy which ensured ten years' deadlock. For the first six years, Peloponnesian invaders destroyed Athenian crops every spring in an unsuccessful attempt to starve them out. The beleaguered Athenians had to crush a serious revolt on the island of Lesbos in 427 BC, the year their allies the Plataeans were treacherously destroyed by the Spartans. However, two years later, the Athenians landed at Pylos in the W Peloponnese, captured a Spartan force on the island of Sphacteria, and encouraged the Messenians to revolt. They prevented further invasions by using their captives as hostages, but defeats by the Boeotians in 424 BC at Delium and in N Greece by the Spartan Brasidas led to the fragile truce of the Peace of Nicias in 421 BC.

The sea proves decisive

After their bid to support an alliance of Peloponnesian states against Sparta was ended at the Battle of Mantinea in 418 BC, the Athenians turned to imperialist expansion by sea. They destroyed the Spartan colony on the small island of Melos in the S Aegean in the winter of 416 BC, and the following year opted for an ambitious naval expedition against Syracuse, the most important colony of Corinth and a major commercial rival. The pursuit of this rich prize decided the outcome of the war. After two years of failure under the indecisive command of Nicias, the huge expeditionary force was annihilated in 413 BC, and the Athenian empire was further weakened as many of its cities withdrew from the alliance. Sparta immediately established a permanent base in Athenian territory, while in Athens the democracy itself was harshly criticized, surviving a coup in 411 BC. The Athenian navy, based on the island of Samos, fought hard to re-establish its control in the Aegean under the command of Alcibiades, but was dealt a final death blow in 405 BC. The Peloponnesian fleet, with Lysander as its admiral and partly financed by Persia, caught the Athenian ships on the beach at Aegospotami in the N Aegean. Athens surrendered the following year. The war stimulated a cultural, rather than political, awareness among Athenians, and the great age of philosophers followed. Our knowledge of the war itself is heavily reliant on the historian Thucydides.

Athenian fleet in 405, and his starving the Athenians into surrender in 404. Sparta's victory meant the destruction of the political power of Athens.

penal colony settlement established to receive transported convicts and built in part through convict labour. Examples include a British settlement in New South Wales, Australia, 1788–1857; Devil's Island, a former French penal colony off the South American coast; and the Soviet gulags.

Penda c. 577–654. King of Mercia, an Anglo-Saxon kingdom in England, from about 632. He raised Mercia to a powerful kingdom, and defeated and killed two Northumbrian kings, Edwin 632 and Oswald 641. He was killed in battle by Oswy, king of Northumbria.

Pendleton Act in US history, a civil service reform bill 1883 sponsored by senator George Pendleton (1825–1889) of Ohio that was designed to curb the power of patronage exercised by new administrations over a swelling federal bureaucracy. Initially about 10% of civil service appointments were made subject to competitive examinations administered by an independent Civil Service Commission.

Peninsular War war 1808–14 caused by the French emperor Napoleon's invasion of Portugal and Spain.

1807 Portugal was occupied by the French.

1808 Napoleon placed his brother Joseph Bonaparte on the Spanish throne. Armed revolts followed all over Spain and Portugal. A British force under Sir Arthur Wellesley was sent to Portugal and defeated the French at Vimeiro; Wellesley was then superseded, and the French were allowed to withdraw.

1809 Wellesley took a new army to Portugal, and advanced on Madrid, but after defeating the French at Talavera had to retreat.

1810–11 Wellesley (now Viscount Wellington) stood on the defensive.

1812 Wellington won another victory at Salamanca, occupied Madrid, and forced the French to evacuate S Spain.

1813 Wellington's victory at Vittoria drove the French from Spain.

1814 Wellington invaded S France. The war was ended by Napoleon's abdication.

Penn William 1644–1718. English member of the Society of Friends (Quakers), born in London. He joined the Society 1667, and in 1681 obtained a grant of land in America (in settlement of a debt owed by the king to his father) on which he established the colony of Pennsylvania as a refuge for persecuted Quakers.

Pentagon Papers top-secret US Defense Department report on the history of US involvement in the Vietnam War that was leaked to the *New York Times* by Defense Department employee Daniel Ellsberg June 1971, fuelling the antiwar movement. President Nixon tried to stop publication, but the Supreme Court ruled in favour of the press.

People's Budget in UK history, the Liberal government's budget of 1909 to finance social reforms and naval rearmament. The chancellor of the Exchequer David Lloyd George proposed graded and increased income tax and a 'supertax' on high incomes. The budget aroused great debate and precipitated a constitutional crisis.

The People's Budget was passed in the House of Commons but rejected by the House of Lords. The prime minister Herbert Henry Asquith denounced the House of Lords for a breach of the constitution over the finance bill and obtained the dissolution of Parliament. The Liberals were returned to power in the general election of 1910. In 1911 the Parliament Act greatly reduced the power of the House of Lords.

People's Charter the key document of ◊Chartism, a movement for reform of the British political system in the 1830s. It was used to mobilize working-class support following the restricted extension of the franchise specified by the 1832 Reform Act. It was drawn up in Feb 1837.

The campaign failed but within 70 years four of its six objectives: universal male suffrage, abolition of property qualifications for members of Parliament, payment of MPs, and voting by secret ballot had been realized.

Pepin *the Short* c. 714–c. 768. King of the Franks from 751. The son of ◊Charles Martel, he acted as ◊Mayor of the Palace to the last Merovingian king, Childeric III, deposed him and assumed the royal title himself, founding the ◊Carolingian dynasty. He was ◊Charlemagne's father.

Perceval Spencer 1762–1812. British Tory politician. He became chancellor of the Exchequer 1807 and prime minister 1809. He was shot in the lobby of the House of Commons 1812 by a merchant who blamed government measures for his bankruptcy.

Percy Henry 'Hotspur' 1364–1403. English soldier, son of the 1st Earl of Northumberland. In repelling a border raid, he defeated the Scots at Homildon Hill in Durham 1402. He was killed at the battle of Shrewsbury while in revolt against Henry IV.

Peres Shimon 1923– . Israeli socialist politician, prime minister 1984-86 and 1995-96. Peres was prime minister, then foreign minister, under a power-sharing agreement with the leader of the Consolidation Party (Likud), Yitzhak ◊Shamir. He was finance minister in a Labour-Likud coalition 1989-90. As foreign minister in Yitzhak Rabin's Labour government from 1992, he negotiated the 1993 peace agreement with the Palestine Liberation Organization (PLO). He was awarded the 1994 Nobel Peace Prize jointly with Israeli prime minister, Rabin, and PLO leader, Yassir Arafat.

perestroika (Russian 'restructuring') in Soviet politics, the wide-ranging economic and political reforms initiated from 1985 by Mikhail Gorbachev, finally leading to the demise of the Soviet Union. Originally, in the economic sphere, *perestroika* was conceived as involving 'intensive development' concentrating on automation and improved labour efficiency. It evolved to attend increasingly to market indicators and incentives ('market socialism') and the gradual dismantling of the Stalinist central-planning system, with decision-taking being devolved to self-financing enterprises.

Pérez Jiménez Marcos 1914– . Venezuelan president 1952–58 who led the military junta which overthrew the Acción Democrática government of Rómulo Gallegos 1948. Pérez Jiménez was made provisional president 1952 and approved as constitutional president by Congress 1953. His regime had a reputation as the most repressive in Venezuelan history. It also encouraged European immigration and undertook massive public works in the capital Caracas.

Pericles c. 495–429 BC. Athenian politician who was effective leader of the city from 443 BC and under whom Athenian power reached its height. His policies helped to transform the Delian League iinto an Athenian empire, but the disasters of the ◊Peloponnesian War led to his removal from office 430 BC. Although quicky reinstated, he died soon after.

One's sense of honour is the only thing that does not grow old.

Pericles, funeral oration to the Athenian dead, 431 BC

Perón (María Estela) Isabel (born Martínez) 1931– . President of Argentina 1974–76, and third wife of Juan Perón. She succeeded him after he died in office, but labour unrest, inflation, and political violence pushed the country to the brink of chaos. Accused of corruption, she was held under house arrest for five years. She went into exile in Spain.

Perón Evita (María Eva) (born Duarte) 1919–1952. Argentine populist leader. A successful radio actress, she married Juan ◊Perón in 1945. When he became president the following year, she became his chief adviser and virtually ran the health and labour ministries, devoting herself to helping the poor, improving education, and achieving women's suffrage. She was politically astute and sought the vice-presidency 1951, but was opposed by the army and withdrew.

If I had not been born Perón I would have liked to be Perón.

Juan Perón in The *Observer* Feb 1960

Perón Juan (Domingo) 1895–1974. Argentine politician, dictator 1946–55 and from 1973 until his death. His populist appeal to the poor was enhanced by the charisma and political work of his second wife Eva (Evita) Perón.

After her death in 1952 his popularity waned and he was deposed in a military coup 1955. He returned from exile to the presidency 1973, but died in office 1974, and was succeeded by his third wife Isabel Perón.

A professional army officer, Perón took part in the right-wing military coup that toppled Argentina's government 1943 and his popularity with the *descamisados* ('shirtless ones') led to his election as president 1946. He instituted social reforms, but encountered economic difficulties.

Perry Matthew (Calbraith) 1794–1858. US naval officer, commander of the expedition of 1853 that reopened communication between Japan and the outside world after 250 years' isolation. Evident military superiority enabled him to negotiate the Treaty of Kanagawa 1854, giving the USA trading rights with Japan.

Persepolis ancient royal city of the Persian Empire, 65 km/40 mi NE of Shiraz. It was burned down after its capture in 331 BC by Alexander the Great.

Pershing John Joseph 1860–1948. US general. He served in the Spanish War 1898, the Philippines 1899–1903, and Mexico 1916–17. He commanded the US Expeditionary Force sent to France 1917–18.

Persia, ancient kingdom in SW Asia. The early Persians were a nomadic Aryan people who migrated through the Caucasus to the Iranian plateau.

7th century BC The Persians were established in the present region of Fars, which then belonged to the Assyrians.

549 BC Cyrus the Great overthrew the empire of the Medes, to whom the Persians had been subject, and founded the Persian Empire.

539 BC Having conquered all Anatolia, Cyrus added Babylonia (including Syria and Palestine) to his empire.

525 BC His son and successor Cambyses conquered Egypt.

521–485 BC Darius I organized an efficient centralized system of administration and extended Persian rule east into Afghanistan and NW India and as far north as the Danube, but the empire was weakened by internal dynastic struggles.

499–449 BC The Persian Wars with Greece ended Persian domination of the Aegean seaboard.

331 BC Alexander the Great drove the Persians under Darius III (died 330 BC) into retreat at Gaugmela on the Tigris, marking the end of the

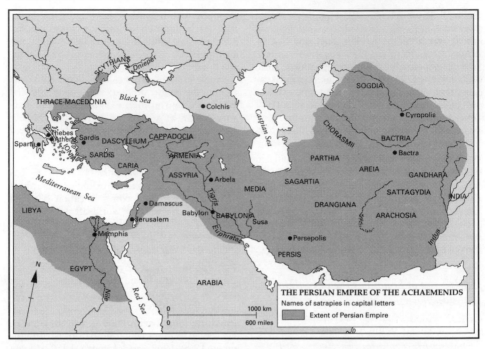

The Persian Empire of the Achaemenids *The original Persian kingdom was the region of modern Fars in SW Iran. Cyrus the Great of the Achaemenid dynasty supplanted the Medes 549 BC and brought Persian rule into Anatolia, Babylonia, Syria, and Palestine. His successor Cambyses conquered Egypt 525 and Darius I extended the Persian Empire to the Indus valley and campaigned in Europe. Imperial provinces were known as satrapies, linked to the capital (Susa) by roads and a royal messenger system. The dynasty ended with the victories of Alexander the Great of Macedon 331.*

Persian Empire and the beginning of the Hellenistic period under the Seleucids.

250 BC–AD 230 The Arsacid dynasty established Parthia as the leading power in the region.

224 The Sassanian Empire was established in Persia and annexed Parthia.

637 Arabs took the capital, Ctesiphon, and introduced Islam in place of Zoroastrianism.

For modern history see ◊Iran.

Persian Wars series of conflicts between Greece and Persia 499–449 BC. The eventual victory of Greece marked the end of Persian domination of the ancient world and the beginning of Greek supremacy.

499 BC Revolt of the Ionian Greeks against Persian rule.

490 BC Darius I of Persia defeated at Marathon.

480 BC Xerxes I victorious at Thermopylae (narrow pass from Thessaly to Locris, which Leonidas, King of Sparta, and 1,000 men defended to the death against the Persians);

Athens was captured, but the Greek navy was victorious at ◊Salamis.

479 BC Greeks under Spartan general Pausanias (died *c.* 470) victorious at Plataea, driving the Persians from the country.

Peru country in South America, on the Pacific, bounded N by Ecuador and Colombia, E by Brazil and Bolivia, and S by Chile.

history For early history, see ◊American Indian. The ◊Chimu culture flourished from about 1200 and was gradually superseded by the ◊Inca empire, building on 800 years of Andean civilization and covering a large part of South America. Civil war had weakened the Incas when the conquistador ◊Pizarro arrived from Spain 1531 and began raiding, looting, and enslaving the people. He executed the last of the Inca emperors, Atahualpa, 1533. Before Pizarro's assassination 1541, Spanish rule was firmly established.

independence A native revolt by Tupac Amaru 1780 failed, and during the successful rebellions by the European settlers in other Spanish possessions in South America

1810–22, Peru remained the Spanish government's headquarters; it was the last to achieve independence 1824. It attempted union with Bolivia 1836–39. It fought a naval war against Spain 1864–66, and in the Pacific War against Chile 1879–83 over the nitrate fields of the Atacama Desert, Peru was defeated and lost three provinces (one, Tacna, was returned 1929). Other boundary disputes were settled by arbitration 1902 with Bolivia, 1927 with Colombia, and 1942 with Ecuador. Peru declared war on Germany and Japan Feb 1945.

dictatorships Peru was ruled by right-wing dictatorships from the mid-1920s until 1945, when free elections returned. Although Peru's oldest political organization, (the American Popular Revolutionary Alliance (APRA)), was the largest party in Congress, it was constantly thwarted by smaller conservative groups, anxious to protect their business interests. APRA was founded in the 1920s to fight imperialism throughout South America, but Peru was the only country where it became established.

military rule In 1948 a group of army officers led by General Manuel Odría ousted the elected government, temporarily banned APRA, and installed a military junta. Odría became president 1950 and remained in power until 1956. In 1963 military rule ended, and Fernando Belaúnde Terry, the joint candidate of the Popular Action (AP) and Christian Democrats (PDC) parties, won the presidency, while APRA took the largest share of the Chamber of Deputies seats.

After economic problems and industrial unrest, Belaúnde was deposed in a bloodless coup 1968, and the army returned to power led by General Velasco Alvarado. Velasco introduced land reform, with private estates being turned into cooperative farms, but he failed to return any land to Indian peasant communities, and the Maoist guerrillas of Sendero Luminoso ('Shining Path') became increasingly active in the Indian region of S Peru.

economic and social crisis Another bloodless coup, 1975, brought in General Morales Bermúdez. He called elections for the presidency and both chambers of Congress 1980, and Belaúnde was re-elected. Belaúnde embarked on a programme of agrarian and industrial reform, but at the end of his presidency, in 1985, the country was again in a state of economic and social crisis. His constitutionally elected successor was the young Social Democrat, Alan García Pérez, who embarked on a programme to cleanse the army and police of the old guard. By 1986 about 1,400 had elected to retire. After trying to expand the

economy with price and exchange controls, in 1987 he announced his intention to nationalize the banks and insurance companies but delayed the move, after a vigorous campaign against the proposal.

In 1989 the International Development Bank suspended credit to Peru because it was six months behind in debt payments. The annual inflation rate to April was 4,329%. García Pérez declared his support for the Sandinista government in Nicaragua and criticized US policy throughout Latin America. The party of García Pérez, constitutionally barred from seeking re-election, saw its popularity slip in the Nov 1989 municipal elections. Novelist Mario Vargas Llosa, the candidate of the centre-right Democratic Front coalition, was long considered the favourite to succeed García Pérez. However, Alberto Fujimori, the son of Japanese immigrants and leader of a new party, Change 90, forced a run-off in April elections. A political novice, Fujimori won a substantial victory in June. Soon after taking office he instituted a drastic economic adjustment programme in an attempt to halt Peru's inflation and to pay foreign debt. In Aug 1990 an attempt to assassinate the president, by means of a car filled with dynamite ramming the presidential palace, failed.

opposition to Fujimori With mounting opposition to the government and fears of a military coup, Fujimori allied himself April 1992 with the army, suspended the assembly, and sacked half of the country's top judges, declaring them to be corrupt. The move, which he announced as a crackdown on rebel leaders and drug traffickers, brought international criticism (including a suspension of US humanitarian aid) and a challenge from his deputy, Maximo San Roman, who branded him a dictator. Fujimori said he would return to democratic rule within a year.

rebel leader arrested Shining Path terrorists stepped up their campaign in response to the crackdown, with renewed attacks on property in Lima reported July 1992. In Sept police arrested Shining Path leader, Abimael Guzman Reynoso, along with several other high-ranking members of the group. All received life sentences Oct; terrorist attacks intensified in response.

Pétain Henri Philippe 1856–1951. French general and right-wing politician. His defence of Verdun 1916 during World War I made him a national hero. In World War II he became prime minister June 1940 and signed an armistice with Germany. Removing the seat of government to Vichy, a health resort in central

France, he established an authoritarian regime. On the Allied invasion he was taken to Germany, but returned 1945 and was sentenced to death for treason, the sentence being commuted to life imprisonment.

> *To make a union with Great Britain would be a fusion with a corpse.*
>
> Henri Philippe Pétain in response to Churchill's proposal of an Anglo-French union 1940

Peter three tsars of Russia:

Peter I *the Great* 1672–1725. Tsar of Russia from 1682 on the death of his brother Tsar Feodor; he assumed control of the government 1689. He attempted to reorganize the country on Western lines; the army was modernized, a fleet was built, the administrative and legal systems were remodelled, education was encouraged, and the church was brought under state control. On the Baltic coast, where he had conquered territory from Sweden, Peter built his new capital, St Petersburg.

After a successful campaign against the Ottoman Empire 1696, he visited Holland and Britain to study Western techniques, and worked in Dutch and English shipyards. In order to secure an outlet to the Baltic, Peter undertook a war with Sweden 1700–21, which resulted in the acquisition of Estonia and parts of Latvia and Finland. A war with Persia 1722–23 added Baku to Russia.

Peter II 1715–1730. Tsar of Russia from 1727. Son of Peter the Great, he had been passed over in favour of Catherine I 1725 but succeeded her 1727. He died of smallpox.

Peter III 1728–1762. Tsar of Russia 1762. Weak-minded son of Peter I's eldest daughter, Anne, he was adopted 1741 by his aunt ◊Elizabeth, Empress of Russia, and at her command married the future Catherine II 1745. He was deposed in favour of his wife and probably murdered by her lover, Alexius Orlov.

Peter I 1844–1921. King of Serbia from 1903. He was the son of Prince Alexander Karageorgevich and was elected king when the last Obrenovich king was murdered 1903. He took part in the retreat of the Serbian army 1915, and in 1918 was proclaimed first king of the Serbs, Croats, and Slovenes (renamed Yugoslavia in 1921).

Peter II 1923–1970. King of Yugoslavia 1934–45. He succeeded his father, Alexander I, and assumed the royal power after the overthrow of the regency 1941. He escaped to the UK after the German invasion, and married Princess Alexandra of Greece 1944. He was dethroned 1945 when Marshal Tito came to power and the Soviet-backed federal republic was formed.

Peterloo massacre the events in St Peter's Fields, Manchester, England, 16 Aug 1819, when an open-air meeting in support of parliamentary reform was charged by yeomanry and hussars. Eleven people were killed and 500 wounded. The name was given in analogy with the Battle of Waterloo.

Peter the Hermit 1050–1115. French priest whose eloquent preaching of the First ◊Crusade sent thousands of peasants marching against the Turks, who massacred them in Asia Minor. Peter escaped and accompanied the main body of crusaders to Jerusalem.

petition of right in British law, the procedure whereby, before the passing of the Crown Proceedings Act 1947, a subject petitioned for legal relief against the crown, for example for money due under a contract, or for property of which the crown had taken possession.

An example is the petition of right presented by Parliament and accepted by Charles I in 1628, declaring illegal taxation without parliamentary consent, imprisonment without trial, billeting of soldiers on private persons, and use of martial law.

Pfalz German name of the historic division of Germany, the ◊Palatinate.

Phalangist member of a Lebanese military organization (*Phalanges Libanaises*), since 1958 the political and military force of the ◊Maronite Church in Lebanon. The Phalangists' unbending right-wing policies and resistance to the introduction of democratic institutions helped contribute to the civil war in Lebanon.

The Phalanges Libanaises was founded 1936 by Pierre Gemayel after seeing the discipline and authoritarianism of Nazi Germany. Its initial aim was to protect the Maronite position in Lebanon; in 1958 it entered the political arena to oppose growing Arab nationalism.

The Phalangists today form the largest Lebanese political group.

phalanx in ancient Greece and Macedonia a battle formation using up to 16 lines of infantry with pikes about 4 m/13 ft long, protected to the sides and rear by cavalry. It was used by Philip II and Alexander the Great of Macedon, and though more successful than the conventional ◊hoplite formation, it proved inferior to the Roman legion.

Pharaoh Hebrew form of the Egyptian royal title Per-'o. This term, meaning 'great house', was originally applied to the royal household, and after about 950 BC to the king.

Pharisee (Hebrew 'separatist') member of a conservative Jewish sect that arose in the 2nd century BC in protest against all movements favouring compromise with Hellenistic culture. The Pharisees were devout adherents of the law, both as found in the Torah and in the oral tradition known as the Mishnah.

They were opposed by the Sadducees on several grounds: the Sadducees did not acknowledge the Mishnah; the Pharisees opposed Greek and Roman rule of their country; and the Pharisees held a number of beliefs – such as the existence of hell, angels, and demons, the resurrection of the dead, and the future coming of the Messiah – not found in the Torah.

The Pharisees rejected political action, and in the 1st century AD the left wing of their followers, the *Zealots*, broke away to pursue a revolutionary nationalist policy. After the fall of Jerusalem, Pharisee ideas became the basis of orthodox Judaism as the people were dispersed throughout the W Roman empire.

Pharsalus, Battle of battle in which Julius ◊Caesar defeated ◊Pompey and the Roman senatorial army 48 BC. It was fought near the site of the ancient city of Pharsalus, N central Greece.

Philadelphia ('the city of brotherly love') industrial city and port on the Delaware River in Pennsylvania, USA. Founded 1682 by William Penn, it was the first capital of the USA 1790–1800. The Declaration of Independence was adopted in the city's Independence Hall.

Philby Kim (Harold) 1912–1988. British intelligence officer from 1940 and Soviet agent from 1933. He was liaison officer in Washington 1949–51, when he was confirmed to be a double agent and asked to resign. Named in 1963 as having warned Guy Burgess and Donald Maclean (similarly double agents) that their activities were known, he fled to the USSR and became a Soviet citizen and general in the KGB. A fourth member of the ring was Anthony Blunt.

To betray you must first belong.

Kim Philby in the *New York Times* 1967

Philip 'King'. Name given to Metacomet by the English *c.* 1639–1676. American chief of the Wampanoag people. During the growing tension over Indian versus settlers' land rights, Philip was arrested and his people were disarmed 1671. Full-scale hostilities culminated in 'King Philip's War' 1675, and Philip was defeated and murdered 1676. Although costly to the English, King Philip's War ended Indian resistance in New England.

Born in Rhode Island, Metacomet was the son of Wampanoag chieftain ◊Massasoit. In 1662, after the death of his father and elder brother, he assumed power and was called 'King Philip' by the English colonists.

Philip six kings of France, including:

Philip II (Philip Augustus) 1165–1223. King of France from 1180. As part of his efforts to establish a strong monarchy and evict the English from their French possessions, he waged war in turn against the English kings Henry II, Richard I (with whom he also went on the Third Crusade), and John (against whom he won the decisive battle of Bouvines in Flanders 1214).

Philip IV *the Fair* 1268–1314. King of France from 1285. He engaged in a feud with Pope Boniface VIII and made him a prisoner 1303. Clement V (1264–1314), elected pope through Philip's influence 1305, moved the papal seat to Avignon 1309 and collaborated with Philip to suppress the ◊Templars, a powerful order of knights. Philip allied with the Scots against England and invaded Flanders.

Philip VI 1293–1350. King of France from 1328, first of the house of Valois, elected by the barons on the death of his cousin, Charles IV. His claim was challenged by Edward III of England, who defeated him at Crécy 1346.

Philip II of Macedon 382–336 BC. King of ◊Macedonia from 359 BC. He seized the throne from his nephew, for whom he was regent, defeated the Greek city-states at the battle of Chaeronea (in central Greece) 338 and formed them into a league whose forces could be united against Persia. He was assassinated while he was planning this expedition, and was succeeded by his son ◊Alexander the Great.

Philip's tomb was discovered at Vergina, N Greece, in 1978.

Philip five kings of Spain, including.

Philip II 1527–1598. King of Spain from 1556. He was born at Valladolid, the son of the Habsburg emperor Charles V, and in 1554 married Queen Mary of England. On his father's abdication 1556 he inherited Spain, the Netherlands, and the Spanish possessions in Italy and the Americas, and in 1580 he annexed Portugal. His intolerance and lack of understanding of the Netherlanders drove them into revolt. Political and religious differences combined to involve him in war with England and, after 1589, with France.

Philip V 1683–1746. King of Spain from 1700. A grandson of Louis XIV of France, he was the first Bourbon king of Spain. He was not recognized by the major European powers until 1713. See ◊Spanish Succession, War of the.

Philippi ancient city of Macedonia founded by Philip of Macedon 358 BC. Near Philippi, Mark Antony and Augustus defeated Brutus and Cassius 42 BC.

Philippines country in SE Asia, on an archipelago of more than 7,000 islands W of the Pacific Ocean and S of the SE Asian mainland.

history The people of the Philippine islands probably came from the Malay Peninsula. They were semi-nomadic and lived by hunting and fishing when the first Europeans, ◊Magellan's crew, arrived 1521, followed by conquering Spanish forces 1565. Roman Catholicism was introduced during the reign of Philip II (after whom the islands were named), replacing Islam, which had been spread by Arab traders and missionaries.

During the 19th century there was a series of armed nationalist revolts. In 1898, during the Spanish-American War, the USA sank the Spanish armada in Manila Bay. Philippine nationalists proclaimed their independence, but were put down by US forces who killed 200,000 Filipinos (one-fifth of the population), most of them civilians; 4,000 US soldiers also died before the war ended in 1901. The revolts continued after the islands were ceded by Spain to the USA 1898, and increasing self-government was granted 1916 and 1935.

republic The Philippines were occupied by Japan 1942–45, before becoming a fully independent republic 1946. A succession of presidents drawn from the islands' wealthy estate-owning elite followed, doing little to improve the lot of the peasants, who had formed a left-wing guerrilla movement, the Hukbalahap.

In 1965 President Diosdado Macapagal was defeated by Ferdinand ◊Marcos, the leader of the Nationalist Party. Marcos initiated rapid economic development and some land reform. He was re-elected 1969, but encountered growing opposition from communist insurgents and Muslim separatists in the south. A high rate of population growth aggravated poverty and unemployment.

martial law Some months before his second term was completed, Marcos declared martial law 1972, suspended the constitution, and began to rule by decree. Intermittent referenda allowed him to retain power. Marcos's authoritarian leadership was criticized for corruption, and in 1977 the opposition leader, Benigno Aquino, was jailed under sentence of death for alleged subversion. In 1978 martial law was relaxed, the 1972 ban on political parties was lifted, and elections for an interim national assembly were held, resulting in an overwhelming victory for Marcos.

partial return to democracy In 1981 martial law was lifted completely, and hundreds of political prisoners released. Marcos then won approval, by referendum, for a partial return to democratic government with himself as president, working with a prime minister and executive council. Political and economic conditions deteriorated, communist guerrilla insurgency escalated, unemployment climbed to over 30% and the national debt increased. In 1983 Benigno Aquino, returning from self-imposed exile in the USA, was shot dead at Manila airport. Marcos was widely suspected of involvement in a conspiracy to murder Aquino.

National assembly elections were held 1984, and although the government party stayed in power, the opposition registered significant gains. Then early in 1986 the main anti-Marcos movement, United Nationalist Democratic Organization (UNIDO), chose Corazón ◊Aquino, Benigno's widow, despite her political inexperience, to contest new presidential elections that Marcos had been persuaded to hold as a means of maintaining vital US economic and diplomatic support. The campaign resulted in over 100 deaths, and large-scale electoral fraud was witnessed by international observers. The national assembly declared Marcos the winner, a result disputed by an independent electoral watchdog.

'people's power' Corazón Aquino began a nonviolent protest, termed 'people's power', which gathered massive popular support, backed by the Roman Catholic church; President Marcos came under strong international pressure, particularly from the USA, to step down. The army, led by Chief of Staff Lt-Gen Fidel Ramos and defence minister Juan Enrile, declared its support for Aquino, and Marcos left for exile in Hawaii.

On assuming the presidency, Corazón Aquino dissolved the pro-Marcos national assembly. She proceeded to govern in a conciliatory fashion, working with a coalition cabinet team comprising opposition politicians and senior military figures. She freed 500 political prisoners and granted an amnesty to the New People's Army (NPA) communist guerrillas in an effort to end the 17-year-old insurgency and introduced a rural-employment economic programme with some land reforms, though these were opposed by property owners.

coup attempts The new administration endured a series of attempted coups by pro-Marcos supporters and faced serious opposition from Juan Enrile, dismissed Nov 1986. In Feb 1987 a new 'freedom constitution' was overwhelmingly approved in a national plebiscite. This gave Aquino a mandate to rule as president until 30 June 1992. In the subsequent congressional elections, Aquino's People's Power coalition won over 90% of the elected seats. However, a coup attempt in Aug 1987 led by Col Gregorio 'Gringo' Honasan, an army officer closely linked with Enrile, claimed 53 lives. There was a shift to the right in the government's policy. Tougher measures were instituted against the NPA, and the Land Reform Act 1988 was diluted.

relations with USA US economic and military aid to the Philippines between 1985 and 1989 was approximately $1.5 billion. In addition, US air support was provided to help foil a further Honasan-planned coup attempt in Dec 1989. Aquino declared a state of emergency, and survived another coup attempt Oct 1990.

Mount Pinatubo eruption At least 343 people were killed and 100,000–200,000 made homeless when the Mount Pinatubo volcano, dormant for 600 years and situated 90 km/56 mi NW of Manila, erupted June 1991. The US Clark Field and Subic Bay military bases, 15 and 40 km/9 and 25 mi away, had to be temporarily evacuated, and much rice-growing land was covered in up to 3 m/10 ft of volcanic ash.

US evicted from Subic Bay The senate of the Philippines voted Sept 1991 to reject a renewal of the US lease for its Subic Bay naval base. Renewal of the lease would have given the Philippines over $2 billion in aid over a ten-year period and the provision of up to 45,000 jobs. Although Aquino supported renewal of the lease, opposition was overwhelming. Critics of the base claimed that its existence contravened a clause in the constitution which banned nuclear weapons, and that the presence of the military personnel had encouraged prostitution.

In Nov 1991 Imelda Marcos returned to the Philippines after almost six years in exile. She immediately posted bail against seven charges of tax evasion, and subsequently declared herself a presidential candidate.

Ramos elected president In Jan 1992 President Aquino confirmed that she would not contest the presidential elections. The elections took place in May, and in June Fidel Ramos was announced as Aquino's successor.

Philip the Good 1396–1467. Duke of Burgundy from 1419. He engaged in the Hundred Years' War as an ally of England until he made peace with the French at the Council of Arras 1435. He made the Netherlands a centre of art and learning.

Philistine member of a seafaring people of non-Semitic origin who founded city-states on the Palestinian coastal plain in the 12th century BC, adopting a Semitic language and religion. They were at war with the Israelites in the 11th–10th centuries BC (hence the pejorative use of their name in Hebrew records for anyone uncivilized in intellectual and artistic terms). They were largely absorbed into the kingdom of Israel under King David, about 1000 BC, and later came under Assyrian rule.

Phillip Arthur 1738–1814. British vice admiral, founder and governor of the convict settlement at Sydney, Australia, 1788–92, and hence founder of New South Wales.

Philosophes the leading intellectuals of pre-revolutionary 18th-century France, including Condorcet, Diderot, Rousseau, and Voltaire. Their role in furthering the principles of the enlightenment and extolling the power of human reason made them question the structures of the *ancien régime*, and they were held responsible by some for influencing the revolutionaries of 1789.

Phoenicia ancient Greek name for N ◊Canaan on the E coast of the Mediterranean. The Phoenician civilization flourished from about 1200 until the capture of Tyre by Alexander the Great in 332 BC. Seafaring traders and artisans, they are said to have circumnavigated Africa and established colonies in Cyprus, N Africa (for example Carthage), Malta, Sicily, and Spain. Their cities (Tyre, Sidon, and Byblos were the main ones) were independent states ruled by hereditary kings but dominated by merchant ruling classes. Their exports included Tyrian purple dye and cloth, furniture (from the timber of Lebanon), and jewellery.

Phoenix Park Murders the murder of several prominent members of the British government in Phoenix Park, Dublin, Ireland, on 6 May 1882. The murders threatened the cooperation between the Liberal government and the Irish nationalist members at Westminster which had been secured by the ◊Kilmainham Treaty.

phoney war the period in World War II between Sept 1939, when the Germans had occupied Poland, and April 1940, when the invasions of Denmark and Norway took place. During this time there were few signs of hostilities in Western Europe; indeed, Hitler made some attempts to arrange a peace settlement with Britain and France.

Phrygia former kingdom of W Asia covering the Anatolian plateau. It was inhabited in ancient times by an Indo-European people and achieved great prosperity in the 8th century BC under a line of kings bearing in turn the names Gordius and Midas, but then fell under Lydian rule. From Phrygia the cult of the Earth goddess Cybele was introduced into Greece and Rome.

physiocrat member of a school of 18th-century French economists including François Quesnay (1694–1774) and Mirabeau who believed in the bounty of nature and the inherent goodness of man. They held that governments should intervene in society only where individuals' liberties were infringed. Otherwise there should be a *laissez-faire* system with free trade between states. Adam Smith was much influenced by their ideas.

Pict Roman term for a member of the peoples of N Scotland, possibly meaning 'painted' (tattooed). Of pre-Celtic origin, and speaking a non-Celtic language, the Picts are thought to have inhabited much of England before the arrival of the Celtic Britons. They were united with the Celtic Scots under the rule of Kenneth MacAlpin 844.

Pieck Wilhelm 1876–1960. German communist politician. He was a leader of the 1919 ♢Spartacist revolt and a founder of the Socialist Unity Party 1946. He opposed both the Weimar Republic and Nazism. From 1949 he was president of East Germany; the office was abolished on his death.

Pierce Franklin 1804–1869. 14th president of the USA, 1852–56. A Democrat, he held office in the US House of Representatives 1833–37, and the US Senate 1837–42. Chosen as a compromise candidate of the Democratic party, he was elected president 1852. Despite his expansionist foreign policy, North–South tensions grew more intense, and Pierce was denied renomination 1856.

Pilate Pontius early 1st century AD. Roman procurator of Judea AD 26–36. The New Testament Gospels describe his reluctant ordering of Jesus' crucifixion, but there has been considerable debate about his actual role in it.

Pilate was unsympathetic to the Jews; his actions several times provoked riots, and in AD 36 he was recalled to Rome to account for the brutal suppression of a Samaritan revolt. The Greek historian Eusebius says he committed suicide after Jesus' crucifixion, but another tradition says he became a Christian, and he is regarded as a saint and martyr in the Ethiopian Coptic and Greek Orthodox churches.

pilgrimage journey to sacred places inspired by religious devotion. For Hindus, the holy places include Varanasi and the purifying river Ganges; for Buddhists, the places connected with the crises of Buddha's career; for the ancient Greeks, the shrines at Delphi and Ephesus among others; for Jews, the sanctuary at Jerusalem; and for Muslims, Mecca.

Among Christians, pilgrimages were common by the 2nd century, and as a direct result of the growing frequency and numbers of pilgrimages there arose numerous hospices catering for pilgrims, the religious orders of knighthood, and the Crusades. The great centres of Christian pilgrimages have been, or still are, Jerusalem, Rome, the tomb of St James of Compostela in Spain, the shrine of Becket in Canterbury, England, and the holy places at La Salette and Lourdes in France.

Pilgrimage of Grace rebellion against Henry VIII of England 1536–37, originating in Yorkshire and Lincolnshire. The uprising was directed against the policies of the monarch (such as the dissolution of the monasteries and the effects of the enclosure of common land).

Pilgrims the emigrants who sailed from Plymouth, Devon, England, in the *Mayflower* on 16 Sept 1620 to found the first colony in New England at New Plymouth, Massachusetts. Of the 102 passengers fewer than a quarter were Puritan refugees.

The Pilgrims (also known as the Pilgrim Fathers) landed at Cape Cod in Dec, and about half their number died over the winter before they received help from the Indians.

Pilsudski Józef (Klemens) 1867–1935. Polish nationalist politician, dictator from 1926. Born in Russian Poland, he founded the Polish Socialist Party 1892 and was twice imprisoned for anti-Russian activities. During World War I he commanded a Polish force to fight for Germany but fell under suspicion of intriguing with the Allies and was imprisoned by the Germans 1917–18. When Poland became independent 1919, he was elected chief of state, and led an unsuccessful Polish attack on the USSR 1920. He retired 1923, but in 1926 led a military coup that established his dictatorship until his death.

Pinkie, Battle of battle on 10 Sept 1547 near Musselburgh, Lothian, Scotland, in which the Scots were defeated by the English under the Duke of Somerset.

Pinochet (Ugarte) Augusto 1915–   . Military ruler of Chile from 1973, when a coup backed by the US Central Intelligence Agency ousted and killed President Salvador Allende. Pinochet took over the presidency and governed ruthlessly, crushing all opposition. He was voted out of power when general elections were held in Dec 1989 but remains head of the armed forces until 1997.

In 1990 Pinochet's attempt to reassert political influence was firmly censured by President Patricio Aylwin.

The army sees no reason to say sorry for having taken part in this patriotic task.

General Pinochet in response to a report on human-rights abuses under his regime
March 1991

Pisistratus *c.* 605–527 BC. Athenian politician. Although of noble family, he assumed the leadership of the peasant party, and seized power 561 BC. He was twice expelled, but recovered power from 541 BC until his death.

Unlimited power is apt to corrupt the minds of those who possess it.

William Pitt the Elder
House of Lords, 9 Jan 1770

Pitt William, *the Elder*, 1st Earl of Chatham 1708–1778. British Whig politician, 'the Great Commoner'. As paymaster of the forces 1746–55, he broke with tradition by refusing to enrich himself; he was dismissed for attacking the duke of Newcastle, the prime minister. He served effectively as prime minister in coalition governments 1756–61 (successfully conducting the Seven Years' War) and 1766–68.

Entering Parliament 1735, Pitt led the Patriot faction opposed to the Whig prime minister Robert Walpole and attacked Walpole's successor, Carteret, for his conduct of the War of the Austrian Succession. Recalled by popular demand to form a government on the outbreak of the Seven Years' War 1756, he was forced to form a coalition with Newcastle 1757. A 'year of victories' ensued 1759, and the French were expelled from India and Canada. In 1761 Pitt wished to escalate the war by a declaration of war on Spain, George III disagreed

and Pitt resigned, but was again recalled to form an all-party government 1766. He championed the Americans against the king, though rejecting independence, and collapsed during his last speech in the House of Lords – opposing the withdrawal of British troops – and died a month later.

Pitt William, *the Younger* 1759–1806. British Tory prime minister 1783–1801 and 1804–06. He raised the importance of the House of Commons, clamped down on corruption, carried out fiscal reforms, and effected the union with Ireland. He attempted to keep Britain at peace but underestimated the importance of the French Revolution and became embroiled in wars with France from 1793; he died on hearing of Napoleon's victory at Austerlitz.

Son of William Pitt the Elder, he entered Cambridge University at 14 and Parliament at 22. He was the Whig Shelburne's chancellor of the Exchequer 1782–83, and with the support of the Tories and king's friends became Britain's youngest prime minister 1783. He reorganized the country's finances and negotiated reciprocal tariff reduction with France. In 1793, however, the new French republic declared war and England fared badly. Pitt's policy in Ireland led to the 1798 revolt, and he tried to solve the Irish question by the Act of Union 1800, but George III rejected the Catholic emancipation Pitt had promised as a condition, and Pitt resigned 1801.

On his return to office 1804, he organized an alliance with Austria, Russia, and Sweden against Napoleon, which was shattered at Austerlitz. In declining health, he died on hearing the news, saying: 'Oh, my country! How I leave my country!' He was buried in Westminster Abbey.

Pius 12 popes, including:

Pius IV 1499–1565. Pope from 1559, of the ◊Medici family. He reassembled the Council of Trent (see Counter-Reformation under ◊Reformation) and completed its work 1563.

Pius V 1504–1572. Pope from 1566. He excommunicated Elizabeth I of England, and organized the expedition against the Turks that won the victory of ◊Lepanto.

Pius VII 1742–1823. Pope from 1800. He concluded a concordat (papal agreement) with France 1801 and took part in Napoleon's coronation, but relations became strained. Napoleon annexed the papal states, and Pius was imprisoned 1809–14. After his return to Rome 1814, he revived the Jesuit order.

Pius XII (Eugenio Pacelli) 1876–1958. Pope from 1939. He was conservative in doctrine and politics, and condemned Modernism. He proclaimed the dogma of the bodily assumption of the Virgin Mary 1950 and in 1951 restated the doctrine (strongly criticized by many) that the life of an infant must not be sacrificed to save a mother in labour. He was criticized for failing to speak out against atrocities committed by the Germans during World War II and has been accused of collusion with the Nazis.

Pizarro Francisco *c.* 1475–1541. Spanish conquistador who took part in the expeditions of Vasco Núñez de Balboa and others. He explored the NW coast of South America in 1526–27, and conquered Peru 1531 with 180 followers. The Inca king Atahualpa was seized and murdered. In 1535 Pizarro founded the Peruvian city of Lima. Internal feuding led to Pizarro's assassination.

His half-brother *Gonzalo Pizarro* (*c.* 1505–1548) explored the region east of Quito 1541–42. He made himself governor of Peru 1544, but was defeated and executed.

Plaatje Solomon Tshekiso 1876–1932. Pioneer South African black community leader who was the first secretary general and founder of the ◊African National Congress 1912.

Place Francis 1771–1854. English Radical. He showed great powers as a political organizer, and made Westminster a centre of pro-labour union Radicalism. He secured the repeal of the anti-union Combination Acts 1824.

plague disease transmitted by fleas (carried by the black rat) which infect the sufferer with the bacillus *Pasteurella pestis*. An early symptom is swelling of lymph nodes, usually in the armpit and groin; such swellings are called 'buboes', hence *bubonic* plague. It causes virulent blood poisoning and the death rate is high.

Other and even more virulent forms of plague are *septicaemic* and *pneumonic*; the latter was fatal before the introduction of sulpha drugs and antibiotics. Outbreaks of plague still occur, mostly in poor countries, but never to the extent seen in the late Middle Ages. After the ◊Black Death in the 14th century, plague remained endemic for the next three centuries, the most notorious outbreak being the Great Plague of London in 1665, when about 100,000 of the 400,000 inhabitants died.

Plaid Cymru (Welsh 'Party of Wales') Welsh nationalist political party established 1925, dedicated to an independent Wales. In 1966 the first Plaid Cymru member of Parliament was elected.

Plains Indian member of any of the North American Indian peoples of the Great Plains, which extend over 3,000 km/2,000 mi from Alberta to Texas. The Plains Indians were drawn from diverse linguistic stocks fringing the Plains but shared many cultural traits, especially the nomadic hunting of bison herds once horses became available in the 18th century. The various groups include Blackfoot, Cheyenne, Comanche, Pawnee, and Dakota or Sioux.

Plantagenet English royal house, reigning 1154–1399, whose name comes from the nickname of Geoffrey, Count of Anjou (1113–1151), father of Henry II, who often wore in his hat a sprig of broom, *planta genista*. In the 1450s, Richard, Duke of York, took 'Plantagenet' as a surname to emphasize his superior claim to the throne over Henry VI's.

Plassey, Battle of victory in India 23 June 1757, for the British under Robert ◊Clive, which brought Bengal under British rule.

Clive defeated Suraj-ud-Dowlah, nawab of Bengal, near a village in W Bengal. Although outnumbered, he used the support of his Indian banker allies to buy the defection of Suraj's general Mir Jafar, who became nawab.

Plataea, Battle of battle 479 BC, in which the Greeks defeated the Persians during the ◊Persian Wars.

plebeian Roman citizen who did not belong to the privileged class of the ◊patricians. During the 5th–4th centuries BC, plebeians waged a long struggle to win political and social equality with the patricians, eventually securing admission to the offices formerly reserved for patricians.

Plekhanov Georgi Valentinovich 1857–1918. Russian Marxist revolutionary and theorist, founder of the ◊Menshevik party. He led the first populist demonstration in St Petersburg, became a Marxist and, with Lenin, edited the newspaper *Iskra* (spark). In 1903 his opposition to Lenin led to the Bolshevik-Menshevik split.

PLO abbreviation for the ◊Palestine Liberation Organization founded 1964 to bring about an independent state of Palestine.

Pocahontas *c.* 1595–1617. American Indian alleged to have saved the life of English colonist John Smith when he was captured by her father, Powhatan. She was kidnapped 1613 by an Englishman, Samuel Argall, and later married colonist John Rolfe (1585–1622) and was entertained as a princess at the English court.

Pocahontas's marriage and conversion to Christianity brought about a period of peaceful relations between Indians and settlers. She died of smallpox after her return to Virginia.

podesta in the Italian ◊communes, the highest civic official, appointed by the leading citizens, and often holding great power.

pogrom (Russian 'destruction') unprovoked violent attack on an ethnic group, particularly Jews, carried out with official sanction. The Russian pogroms against Jews began 1881, after the assassination of Tsar Alexander II, and again in 1903–06; persecution of the Jews remained constant until the Russian Revolution. Later there were pogroms in E Europe, especially in Poland after 1918, and in Germany under Hitler (see ◊Holocaust).

Poincaré Raymond Nicolas Landry 1860–1934. French politician, prime minister 1912–13, president 1913–20, and again prime minister 1922–24 (when he ordered the occupation of the Ruhr, Germany) and 1926–29.

Poindexter John Marlan 1936– . US rear admiral and Republican government official. In 1981 he joined the Reagan administration's National Security Council (NSC) and became national security adviser 1985. As a result of the ◊Irangate scandal, Poindexter was forced to resign 1986, along with his assistant, Oliver North.

Poitevin in English history, relating to the reigns of King John and King Henry III. The term is derived from the region of France south of the Loire (Poitou), which was controlled by the English for most of this period.

Poitiers capital of Poitou-Charentes, W France; population (1990) 82,500. Products include chemicals and clothing. The Merovingian king Clovis defeated the Visigoths under Alaric here 507; ◊Charles Martel stemmed the Saracen advance 732, and ◊Edward the Black Prince of England defeated the French 1356.

Poland country in E Europe, bounded N by the Baltic Sea, E by Lithuania, Belarus, and Ukraine, S by the Czech and Slovak Republics, and W by Germany.

history In the 10th century the Polish tribes were first united under one Christian ruler, Mieczyslaw. Mongols devastated the country 1241, and thereafter German and Jewish refugees were encouraged to settle among the ◊Slav population. The first parliament met 1331, and Casimir the Great (1333–1370) raised the country to a high level of prosperity. Under the Jagiellonian dynasty (1386–1572) Poland became a great power, the largest country in Europe when it was united with Lithuania (1569–1776). Elected kings followed the death of the last Jagiello, a reactionary nobility wielded much power, and Poland's strength

declined. But Stephen Báthory defeated Ivan the Terrible of Russia 1581, and in 1683 John III Sobieski forced the Turks to raise their siege of Vienna. In the mid-17th century a war against Russia, Sweden, and Brandenburg ended in the complete defeat of Poland, from which it was never allowed to recover.

Wars with the Ottoman Empire, dissension among the nobles, quarrels at the election of every king, the continuance of serfdom, and the persecution of Protestants and Greek Orthodox Catholics laid the country open to interference by Austria, Russia, and Prussia, ending with partition 1772, and again 1793, when Prussia and Russia seized further areas. A patriotic uprising led by Tadeusz Kościusko was defeated, and Russia, Austria, and Prussia occupied the rest of the country 1795. The Congress of ◊Vienna rearranged the division 1815 and reconstituted the Russian portion as a kingdom under the tsar. Uprisings 1830 and 1863 led to intensified repression and an increased attempt to Russify the population.

independent republic Poland was revived as an independent republic 1918 under the leadership of Józef Pilsudski, who took advantage of the USSR's internal upheaval to advance into Lithuania and the Ukraine before the Polish troops were driven back by the Red Army. Poland and the USSR then agreed on a frontier east of the ◊Curzon Line. Politically, the initial post-independence years were characterized by instability, 14 multiparty coalition governments holding power 1918–26. Pilsudski seized complete power in a coup and proceeded to govern in an increasingly authoritarian manner until his death in 1935. He was succeeded by a military regime headed by Edward Śmigly-Rydz.

World War II In April 1939 the UK and France concluded a pact with Poland to render military aid if it was attacked, and at the beginning of Sept Germany invaded (see ◊World War II). During the war, western Poland was incorporated into the Nazi Reich, while the remainder, after a brief Soviet occupation of the east (1940–41), was treated as a colony. The country endured the full brunt of Nazi barbarism: a third of the educated elite were 'liquidated' and, in all, 6 million Poles lost their lives, half of them Jews slaughtered in concentration camps.

people's republic A treaty between Poland and the USSR Aug 1945 (ratified 1946) established Poland's eastern frontier at the Curzon Line. Poland lost 181,350 sq km/70,000 sq mi in the east to the USSR but gained 101,000 sq km/39,000 sq mi in the west from Germany.

After elections, a 'people's republic' was established 1947, and Poland joined ◊Comecon 1949 and the ◊Warsaw Pact 1955, remaining under close Soviet supervision, with the Soviet marshal Rokossovsky serving as minister for war 1949–56. A harsh Stalinist form of rule was instituted under the leadership of Boleslaw Bierut (1892–1956), involving rural collectivization, the persecution of Catholic church opposition, and the arrest of Cardinal Stefan Wyszyński 1953.

civil unrest In 1956, serious strikes and riots, leading to 53 deaths, broke out in Poznań in opposition to Soviet 'exploitation' and food shortages. The more pragmatic Wladyslaw ◊Gomułka took over as leader of the Polish United Workers' Party (PUWP) (Communist Party), reintroduced private farming, and released Cardinal Wyszyński.

A further outbreak of strikes and rioting in Gdańsk, Gdynia, and Szczecin 1970 followed sudden food-price rises. This led to Gomulka's replacement as PUWP leader by the Silesia party boss Edward ◊Gierek, whose programme aimed at raising living standards and consumer-goods production. The country's foreign debt grew, and food prices again triggered strikes and demonstrations 1976. Opposition to the Gierek regime, which was accused of corruption, mounted 1979 after a visit to his homeland by the recently elected Pope John Paul II.

rise of Solidarity Strikes in Warsaw 1980, following a poor harvest and meat-price increases, rapidly spread across the country. The government attempted to appease workers by entering into pay negotiations with unofficial strike committees, but at the Gdańsk shipyards demands emerged for permission to form free, independent trade unions. The government conceded the right to strike, and in Gdańsk 1980 the ◊Solidarity (Solidarność) union was formed under the leadership of Lech ◊Wałesa. In 1980 the ailing Gierek was replaced as PUWP leader by Stanislaw Kania, but unrest continued as the 10-million-member Solidarity campaigned for a five-day working week and established a rural section.

martial law With food shortages mounting and PUWP control slipping, Kania was replaced as PUWP leader 1981 by the prime minister, General Wojciech ◊Jaruzelski; the Soviet army was active on Poland's borders; and martial law was imposed Dec 1981. Trade-union activity was banned, the leaders of Solidarity arrested, a night curfew imposed, and the Military Council of National Salvation established, headed by Jaruzelski. Five months of severe repression ensued, resulting in 15 deaths and 10,000 arrests. The USA imposed economic sanctions.

In June 1982, curfew restrictions were eased, prompting further serious rioting in Aug. In Nov Wałesa was released, and in Dec 1982 martial law was suspended (lifted 1983). The pope visited Poland 1983 and called for conciliation. The authorities responded by dissolving the Military Council and granting an amnesty to political prisoners and activists. In 1984, 35,000 prisoners and detainees were released on the 40th anniversary of the People's Republic, and the USA relaxed its economic sanctions.

slow improvements The Jaruzelski administration pursued pragmatic reform, including liberalization of the electoral system. Conditions remained tense, however, strained by the continued ban on Solidarity and by a threat (withdrawn 1986) to try Wałesa for slandering state electoral officials. Economic conditions and farm output slowly improved, but Poland's foreign debt remained huge. During 1988 the nation's shipyards, coalmines, ports, and steelworks were paralysed by a wave of Solidarity-led strikes for higher wages to offset the effect of recent price rises. With its economic strategy in tatters, the government of prime minister Zbigniew Messner resigned, being replaced Dec 1988 by a new administration headed by the reformist communist Mieczyslaw F Rakowski, and the PUWP's politburo was infused with a new clutch of technocrats.

socialist pluralism After six weeks of PUWP–Solidarity–church negotiations, a historic accord was reached April 1989 under whose terms Solidarity was relegalized, the formation of opposition political associations tolerated, legal rights conferred on the Catholic church, the state's media monopoly lifted, and a new 'socialist pluralist' constitution drafted.

In the subsequent national assembly elections, held June 1989, Solidarity captured all but one of the Sejm and Senate seats for which they were entitled to contest (most seats were reserved for PUWP-backed candidates). Jaruzelski was elected president by parliament July 1989.

market economy In Sept 1989 a 'grand coalition' was formed with Tadeusz Mazowiecki, editor of Solidarity's newspaper, who became prime minister. Jaruzelski continued as president, and was re-elected in July. The new government, which attracted generous financial aid from Western powers, proceeded to dismantle the command economy and encourage the private sector. A tough austerity programme approved by the International Monetary Fund (IMF) was also instituted to solve the problem of hyperinflation, which ran at 550% in 1989.

In Jan 1990 the PUWP voted to disband and re-formed as the Social Democracy Party. Censorship was abolished in April. During 1990 living standards in Poland fell by 40%. The number of unemployed rose to over 1 million. In July 1990, 40 members of the 259-strong Solidarity caucus, under the leadership of Zbigniew Bujak and Wladyslaw Frasyniuk, established the Citizens' Movement–Democratic Action Party (ROAD) to provide a credible alternative to the Wałesa-oriented Solidarity Centre Alliance (SCA) established in May.

split in Solidarity Wałesa accused the government of delaying political and economic reform and forcing workers to bear the brunt of the austerity programme. In July 100 SCA deputies and senators petitioned Jaruzelski to stand down to make way for Wałesa. In Sept the Sejm passed a bill establishing a presidential term of five years. In the first round of presidential elections, held 25 Nov 1990, the rupture within Solidarity was exposed by both Prime Minister Mazowiecki and Lech Wałesa contesting for the position. Having run a populist campaign, Wałesa topped the poll with a 40% vote share, and Mazowiecki, defending an unpopular government, finished in third position, with 18% of the vote, behind Stanislaw Tymiński, a previously obscure, right-wing, returned emigré Canadian entrepreneur, who captured 23% of the vote. In the second round, held 9 Dec, Wałesa defeated Tymiński.

Wałesa becomes president In Dec 1990 the defeated Mazowiecki resigned as prime minister. Wałesa resigned the Solidarity chair and was sworn in as president. He chose for prime minister an economist and former Solidarity activist, Jan Krzysztof Bielecki (1951–   ), and the new government included the IMF-backed finance minister Leszek Balcerowicz and other ministers from the outgoing administration. They pledged to consolidate the free market they had introduced, and the first privatization share sales were held Jan 1991, with mixed success.

foreign relations Poland's relations with the USSR deteriorated in early 1991 over the issue of Soviet troop withdrawals: there were some 50,000 stationed on Polish territory, and the Poles wanted them to leave by the end of the year, coinciding with withdrawals from Hungary and Czechoslovakia. Told that it would take three years, Wałesa refused to allow Soviet troops to pass through Poland on their way back to the USSR from other countries. In Oct

1991 a treaty was signed providing for the withdrawal of all Soviet combat troops by 15 Nov 1992 and the remainder by the end of 1993.

In June 1991 a treaty of good-neighbourliness and friendly cooperation was signed with Germany, confirming the Oder–Neisse border and recognizing the rights of the 500,000-strong German minority in Poland to their own culture, language, and religion.

new political parties Three new political parties were formed March–April 1991. The Centre Alliance was a right-of-centre, Christian Democratic grouping supported by Wałesa and the Polish episcopate, and favouring a modern market economy. The Democratic Social Movement was a successor to ROAD. Led by Zbingniew Bujak, it appealed to workers and farmers, called for complete separation of church and state and was viewed as the chief future electoral rival of the SCA. Party X was formed by Stanislaw Tymiński, the Dec 1990 presidential contender.

public discontent The IMF approved further major loans April 1991 in support of the Polish government's economic reform programme. There was growing public discontent at the decline in living standards brought about by currency reform and the deepening recession. This led to industrial unrest as unemployment reached 1.5 million (8.4% of the working population) by June 1991.

political deadlock Bielecki offered his resignation at the end of Aug 1991, complaining that he no longer enjoyed the support of a Sejm that still contained many communists. Parliament refused to accept either the resignation or the government's crucial proposed budget cuts. President Wałesa urged it to confer emergency powers to enable the government to rule by decree until the general election. This plea was rejected, creating an impasse, although Bielecki agreed to stay as prime minister until the elections.

first multiparty election The Oct 1991 general election was Poland's first post-communist, fully free, multiparty contest. No dominant party emerged from the voting, and Wałesa proposed that he should combine the positions of president and prime minister for two years, heading a 'national unity' grand coalition government. However, this failed to gain broad support. An attempt was then made to construct a left-of-centre coalition led by Broneslaw Geremek. This foundered, and in Dec 1991 Wałesa reluctantly allowed Jan Olszewski, a former Solidarity defence lawyer and a representative of the Centre Alliance, to set about forming a five-party, centre-right coalition government. This government pledged to pursue a more gradual approach to market-oriented reform and, in particular, to slow down the privatization programme by concentrating instead on helping ailing state industries.

In April 1992 Wałesa called for greater powers as president. In June Olszewski was ousted on a vote of no confidence; Waldemar Pawlak succeeded him but proved unable to hold together a workable coalition. In July Wałesa nominated Hanna Suchocka as Pawlak's successor and Poland's first woman premier.

economic problems At the close of 1991 Poland's foreign debt stood at US $42 billion. GNP fell during 1990 and 1991 by 12% and 17% respectively and employment rose to more than 11%, with more than 2 million out of work. However, the annual rate of inflation fell from 684% in early 1990 to 60% at the end of 1991.

Pole Reginald 1500–1558. English cardinal from 1536 who returned from Rome as papal legate on the accession of Mary. He succeded Cranmer as archbishop of Canterbury 1556.

polis (Greek 'city') in ancient Greece, a city-state, the political and social centre of most larger Greek communities. Originally a citadel on a rock or hill, in classical times the polis consisted of a walled city with adjoining land, which could be extensive. Membership of a polis as a citizen, participation in its cults and festivals, and the protection of its laws formed the basis of classical Greek civilization, which was marked by intense inter-city rivalries and conflicts until the ◊Hellenistic period.

Polish Corridor strip of land designated under the Treaty of ◊Versailles 1919 to give Poland access to the Baltic. It cut off East Prussia from the rest of Germany. When Poland took over the southern part of East Prussia 1945, it was absorbed.

Politburo contraction of 'political bureau', the executive committee (known as the Presidium 1952–66) of the Supreme Soviet in the USSR, which laid down party policy. It consisted of about 12 voting and 6 candidate (nonvoting) members.

Polk James Knox 1795–1849. 11th president of the USA 1845–49, a Democrat, born in North Carolina. He allowed Texas admission to the Union, and forced the war on Mexico that resulted in the annexation of California and New Mexico.

poll tax tax levied on every individual, without reference to income or property. Being simple to administer, it was among the earliest sorts of tax (introduced in England 1377), but because of its indiscriminate nature (it is a regressive tax, in that it falls proportionately more on poorer people) it has often proved unpopular. The *community charge*, a type of poll tax, was introduced in Scotland by the British government April 1989, and in England and Wales 1990, replacing the property-based local taxation. Its unpopularity led to the announcement 1991 of a replacement, a 'council tax', based both on property values and on the size of households, introduced 1993–94.

The poll tax of 1377 contributed to the ◊Peasants' Revolt of 1381 and was abolished in England 1698. In the USA it survived until 1964 when its use was declared unconstitutional in federal elections because of its frequent abuse as a tool for disenfranchising blacks.

Polo Marco 1254–1324. Venetian traveller and writer. He travelled overland to China 1271–75, and served the emperor Kublai Khan until he returned to Europe by sea 1292–95. He was captured while fighting for Venice against Genoa, and, while in prison 1296–98, dictated an account of his travels.

After his father (Niccolo) and uncle (Maffeo) returned from a trading journey to China 1260–69, Marco began his own trip overland to China. Once there, he learned Mongolian and served the emperor Kublai Khan, returning nearly 20 years later by sea to his native country. His accounts of his travels remained the primary source of information about the Far East until the 19th century.

I have not told half of what I saw.

Marco Polo last words

Pol Pot (also known as *Saloth Sar, Tol Saut,* and *Pol Porth*) 1925– . Cambodian politician and leader of the Khmer Rouge communist movement that overthrew the government 1975. After widespread atrocities against the civilian population, his regime was deposed by a Vietnamese invasion 1979. Pol Pot continued to help lead the Khmer Rouge despite his official resignation. He was captured in 1997.

Pol Pot was a member of the anti-French resistance under Ho Chi Minh in the 1940s. In 1975 he proclaimed Democratic Kampuchea with himself as premier. His policies were to evacuate cities and put people to work in the countryside. The Khmer Rouge also carried out a systematic extermination of the Western-influenced educated and middle classes (1–4 million).

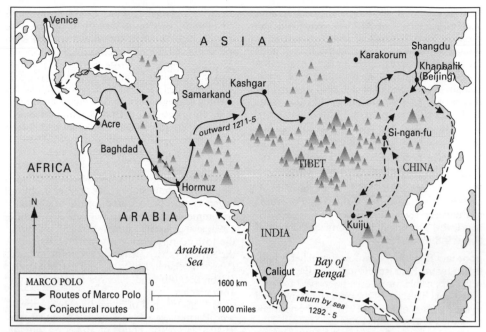

Venice
ASIA
Karakorum
Shangdu
Khanbalik (Beijing)
Kashgar
Samarkand
Acre
outward 1271-5
Si-ngan-fu
Baghdad
AFRICA
TIBET
CHINA
Hormuz
N
ARABIA
Kuiju
INDIA
Arabian
Sea
Bay of
Bengal
Calicut

MARCO POLO
→ Routes of Marco Polo
- -→ Conjectural routes
0   1600 km
0   1000 miles
return by sea
1292 - 5

Marco Polo *Following the traditional Silk Road from China to the Levant, the Venetian Marco Polo journeyed 1271–75 through Central Asia, via Samarkand, to the Mongol capital at Karakorum. Only a teenager, he travelled with his father and uncle, both merchants, who had earlier visited and been well received by the great Mongol prince, Kublai Khan. Marco was noticed by the Great Khan and his later travels through Asia were as the Mongol emperor's envoy. He returned to Venice by land and sea, with his father and uncle, 1292–95.*

Poltava city in Ukraine. Peter the Great defeated Charles XII of Sweden here 1709.

Pompadour Jeanne Antoinette Poisson, Marquise de Pompadour 1721–1764. Mistress of ◊Louis XV of France from 1744, born in Paris. She largely dictated the government's ill-fated policy of reversing France's anti-Austrian policy for an anti-Prussian one. She acted as the patron of the Enlightenment philosophers Voltaire and Diderot.

Pompey *the Great* (Gnaeus Pompeius Magnus) 106–48 BC. Roman soldier and politician. From 60 to 53 BC he was a member of the First Triumvirate with Julius ◊Caesar and Crassus.

Originally a supporter of ◊Sulla, Pompey became consul with Crassus in 70 BC. He defeated ◊Mithridates VI Eupator of Pontus, and annexed Syria and Palestine. He married Caesar's daughter Julia (died 54 BC) in 59 BC. When the Triumvirate broke down after 53 BC, Pompey was drawn into leadership of the senatorial faction. On the outbreak of civil war 49 BC he withdrew to Greece, was defeated by Caesar at Pharsalus 48 BC, and was murdered in Egypt.

Pompidou Georges 1911–1974. French conservative politician, president 1969–74. He negotiated a settlement with the Algerians 1961 and, as prime minister 1962–68, with the students in the revolt of May 1968.

A statesman is a politician who places himself at the service of the nation. A politician is a statesman who places the nation at his service.

Georges Pompidou in *The Observer*
Dec 1973

Ponce de León Juan *c.* 1460–1521. Spanish soldier and explorer. He is believed to have sailed with Columbus 1493, and served 1502–04 in Hispaniola. He conquered Puerto Rico 1508, and was made governor 1509. In 1513 he was the first European to reach Florida.

He returned to Spain 1514 to report his 'discovery' of Florida (which he thought was an island), and was given permission by King Ferdinand to colonize it. In the attempt, he received an arrow wound of which he died in Cuba.

Pontiac c. 1720–1769. North American Indian, chief of the Ottawa from 1755. Allied with the French forces during the French and Indian War, Pontiac was hunted by the British after the French withdrawal. He led the 'Conspiracy of Pontiac' 1763–64 in an attempt to resist British persecution. He achieved remarkable success against overwhelming odds, but eventually signed a peace treaty 1766.

Pontus kingdom of NE Asia Minor on the Black Sea from about 300–65 BC when its greaest ruler, ◊Mithridates VI Eupator, was defeated by the Roman General ◊Pompey

Pony Express in the USA, a system of mail-carrying by relays of horse riders that operated in the years 1860–61 between St Joseph, Missouri, and Sacramento, California, a distance of about 2,896 km/1,800 mi.

poor law English system for poor relief, established by the Poor Relief Act 1601. Each parish was responsible for its own poor, paid for by a parish tax. The care of the poor was transferred to the Ministry of Health 1918, but the poor law remained in force until 1930.

Poor law was reformed in the 19th century. After the Royal Commission on the Poor Law 1834, 'outdoor' relief for able-bodied paupers was abolished and replaced by ◊workhouses run by unions of parishes. Conditions in such workhouses were designed to act as a deterrent for all but the genuinely destitute, but the Andover workhouse scandal 1847 removed some of the greatest corruptions and evils of the system.

Popish Plot supposed plot to murder Charles II; see under Titus ◊Oates.

popular front political alliance of liberals, socialists, communists, and other centre and left-wing parties. This policy was propounded by the Communist International 1935 against fascism and was adopted in France and Spain, where popular-front governments were elected 1936; that in France was overthrown 1938 and the one in Spain fell with the defeat of the Republic in the Spanish Civil War 1939.

Populism in US history, a late 19th-century political movement that developed out of farmers' protests against economic hardship. The Populist, or People's Party was founded 1892 and ran several presidential candidates. It failed, however, to reverse increasing industrialization and the relative decline of agriculture in the USA.

Portland William Henry Cavendish Bentinck, 3rd Duke of Portland 1738–1809. British politician, originally a Whig, who in 1783 became nominal prime minister in the Fox–North coalition government. During the French Revolution he joined the Tories, and was prime minister 1807–09.

Portugal country in SW Europe, on the Atlantic Ocean, bounded N and E by Spain.

history Portugal originated in the 11th century as a country subject to ◊León, while the south was ruled by the ◊Moors. It became an independent monarchy in the reign of Afonso I (1128–1185), who captured Lisbon 1147. Afonso III (1248–1279) expelled the Moors. During the 13th century the Cortes, an assembly representing nobles, clergy, and cities, began to meet and secured control of taxation. A commercial treaty with England was signed 1294, and an alliance established 1373. During the 15th century Portuguese mariners explored the African coast, opened the sea route to India (Vasco da Gama, 1497–98), and reached Brazil (Cabral, 1500), and colonists followed in the 16th century.

In 1580 Philip II of Spain seized the crown. The Portuguese rebelled against Spanish rule 1640, placed the house of Braganza on the throne, and aftcr a long war forced Spain to recognize their independence 1668. Portugal fought as the ally of Britain in the War of the ◊Spanish Succession. France invaded Portugal 1807–11 (see ◊Peninsular War). A strong democratic movement developed, and after a civil war 1828–34, constitutional government was established.

republic Carlos I was assassinated 1908; his son Manuel II was driven from the country by a revolution 1910, and a republic was proclaimed. Portugal remained economically weak and corrupt until the start of the dictatorship of Dr Antonio de Oliveira ◊Salazar, prime minister from 1928. Social conditions were improved at the cost of personal liberties. Salazar was succeeded as prime minister 1968 by Dr Marcello Caetano, who proved unable to liberalize the political system or deal with the costly wars in Portugal's colonies of Angola and Mozambique.

military coup Criticisms of his administration led to a military coup April 1974 to 'save the nation from government'. The Junta of National Salvation was set up, headed by General António Ribeiro de Spínola. He became president a month later, with a military colleague replacing the civilian prime minister. After disagreements within the junta, Spínola resigned Sept 1974 and was replaced by General Francisco da Costa Gomes. In 1975 there was a swing to the left among the military and President Gomes narrowly avoided a communist coup by collaborating with the leader of the moderate Socialist Party (PS), Mario ◊Soares.

free elections In 1976 Portugal's first free assembly elections in 50 years were held. The PS won 36% of the vote, and Soares formed a minority government. The army chief, General António Ramalho ◊Eanes, won the presidency, with the support of centre and left-of-centre parties. After surviving precariously for over two years, Soares resigned 1978. A period of political instability followed, with five prime ministers in two and a half years, until, in Dec 1980, President Eanes invited Dr Francisco Balsemão, a co-founder of the Social Democratic Party (PSD), to form a centre-party coalition.

new constitution Dr Balsemão survived many challenges to his leadership, and in 1982 the assembly approved his new constitution, which would reduce the powers of the president and move the country to a fully civilian government. In 1985 a minority government was formed by the former finance minister Professor Aníbal Cavaco Silva of the PSD. He has increased economic growth and raised living standards, and favours a free market and privatization. In the 1986 presidential election Soares became Portugal's first civilian president for 60 years.

Portugal entered the European Community 1986 and is a member of NATO.

socialism abandoned In July 1987 the PSD won an absolute majority in parliament, with the PRD and Communists both losing seats. In June 1989 the parliament approved a series of measures that denationalized major industries and renounced the socialist economy. In Jan 1991, Soares was re-elected to a five-year term, while in the Oct 1991 general election the PSD was re-elected with a slightly reduced majority.

Potemkin Grigory Aleksandrovich, Prince Potemkin 1739–1791. Russian politician. He entered the army and attracted the notice of Catherine II, whose friendship he kept throughout his life. He was an active administrator who reformed the army, built the Black Sea Fleet, conquered the Crimea 1783, developed S Russia, and founded the Kherson arsenal 1788 (the first Russian naval base on the Black Sea).

Potsdam Conference conference held in Potsdam, Germany, 17 July–2 Aug 1945 between representatives of the USA, the UK, and the USSR. They established the political and economic principles governing the treatment of Germany in the initial period of Allied control at the end of World War II.

poujadist member of an extreme right-wing political movement in France led by Pierre Poujade (1920–   ), which was prominent in French politics 1954–58. Known in France as the *Union de Défense des Commerçants et Artisants*, it won 52 seats in the national election of 1956. Its voting strength came mainly from the lower-middle-class and petit-bourgeois sections of society but the return of ◊de Gaulle to power 1958, and the foundation of the Fifth Republic led to a rapid decline in the movement's fortunes.

POUM acronym for *Partido Obrero de Unificación Marxista* ('Workers' Marxist Union Party') a small Spanish anti-Stalinist communist party led by Andrés Nin and Joaquín Maurín, prominent during the Spanish Civil War. Since Republican Spain received most of its external help from the USSR, the Spanish communist party used this to force the suppression of POUM in 1937. POUM supporters included the English writer George Orwell, who chronicled events in his book *Homage to Catalonia*.

praemunire three English acts of Parliament passed 1353, 1365, and 1393, aimed to prevent appeal to the pope against the power of the king, and therefore an early demonstration of independence from Rome. The statutes were opposed by English bishops.

praetor in ancient Rome, a magistrate, elected annually, who assisted the ◊consuls (the chief magistrates) and presided over the civil courts. After a year in office, a praetor would act as a provincial governor for a further year. The number of praetors was finally increased to eight. The office declined in importance under the emperors.

Prague Spring the 1968 programme of liberalization, begun under a new Communist Party leader in Czechoslovakia. In Aug 1968 Soviet tanks invaded Czechoslovakia and entered the capital Prague to put down the liberalization movement initiated by the prime minister Alexander Dubček, who had earlier sought to assure the Soviets that his planned reforms would not threaten socialism. Dubček was arrested but released soon afterwards. Most of the Prague Spring reforms were reversed.

Prasad Rajendra 1884–1963. Indian politician. He was national president of the Indian National Congress several times between 1934 and 1948 and India's first president after independence 1950–62.

Prasad was trained as a lawyer, and was a loyal follower of Mahatma ◊Gandhi.

prefect French government official who, under the centralized Napoleonic system 1800–1984, was responsible for enforcing government policy in each *département* and *région*. In 1984 prefects were replaced by presidents of elected councils.

prehistory human cultures before the use of writing. A classification system was devised 1816 by Danish archaeologist Christian Thomsen, based on the predominant materials used by early humans for tools and weapons: ◊Stone Age, ◊Bronze Age, ◊Iron Age, the Three Age system.

Stone Age Stone was predominant for tools and weapons. The Stone Age is divided into:

Old Stone Age (Palaeolithic) 3,500,000–8500 BC. Tools were chipped into shape by early humans, or hominids, from Africa, Asia, the Middle East, and Europe as well as later Neanderthal and Cro-Magnon people; the only domesticated animals were dogs. Some Asians crossed the Bering land bridge to inhabit the Americas. Cave paintings were produced from 20,000 years ago in many parts of the world; for example, Altamira, Spain; Lascaux, France; India; and Australia.

Middle Stone Age (Mesolithic) and *New Stone Age* (Neolithic). Stone and bone tools were used. In Neolithic times, agriculture and the domestication of goats, sheep, and cattle began. Stone Age cultures survived in the Americas, Asia, Africa, Oceania, and Australia until the 19th and 20th centuries.

Bronze Age Bronze tools and weapons began approximately 5000 BC in the Far East, and continued in the Middle East until about 1200 BC; in Europe this period lasted from about 2000 to 500 BC.

Iron Age Iron was hardened (alloyed) by the addition of carbon, so that it superseded bronze for tools and weapons; in the Old World generally from about 1000 BC.

Prempeh I chief of the Ashanti people in W Africa. He became king 1888, and later opposed British attempts to take over the region. He was deported and in 1900 the Ashanti were defeated. He returned to Kumasi (capital of the Ashanti region, now in Ghana) 1924 as chief of the people.

press gang method used to recruit soldiers and sailors into the British armed forces in the 18th and early 19th centuries. In effect it was a form of kidnapping carried out by the services or their agents, often with the aid of armed men. This was similar to the practice of 'shanghaiing' sailors for duty in the merchant marine, especially in the Far East.

Prester John legendary Christian prince. During the 12th and 13th centuries, Prester John was believed to be the ruler of a powerful empire in Asia. From the 14th to the 16th century, he was generally believed to be the king of Abyssinia (now Ethiopia) in N E Africa.

Prestonpans, Battle of battle 1745 in which Prince ◊Charles Edward Stuart's Jacobite forces defeated the English. Named after the nearby town of Prestonpans in Lothian Region, E Scotland.

Pretoria administrative capital of the Republic of South Africa from 1910 and capital of Transvaal province from 1860; Founded 1855, it was named after Boer leader Andries Pretorius (1799-1853).

Pride's purge the removal of about 100 Royalists and Presbyterians of the English House of Commons from Parliament by a detachment of soldiers led by Col Thomas Pride (died 1658) in 1648. They were accused of negotiating with Charles I and were seen as unreliable by the army. The remaining members were termed the ◊Rump and voted in favour of the king's trial.

Primitive Methodism Protestant Christian movement, an offshoot of Wesleyan ◊Methodism, that emerged in England 1811 when evangelical enthusiasts organized camp meetings at places such as Mow Cop 1807. Inspired by American example, open-air sermons were accompanied by prayers and hymn singing. In 1932 the Primitive Methodists became a constituent of a unified Methodist church.

Hugh Bourne (1772–1852) and William Clowes, who were both expelled from the Wesleyan Methodist circuit for participating in camp meetings, formed a missionary campaign that led to the development of Primitive Methodist circuits in central, eastern and northern England. They gained a strong following in working-class mining and agricultural communities, and concentrated on villages and towns rather than major urban centres. Primitive Methodism as a separate sect was exported to the USA in 1829 and then to Canada, Australia, New Zealand, South Africa, and Nigeria.

Primo de Rivera Miguel 1870–1930. Spanish soldier and politician, dictator from 1923 as well as premier from 1925. He was captain-general of Catalonia when he led a coup against the ineffective monarchy and became virtual dictator of Spain with the support of Alfonso XIII. He resigned 1930.

principate (from Latin *princeps* 'first') in ancient Rome, an unofficial title for the rule of ◊Augustus and his successors, designating the emperor as the leading citizen.

Prithviraja Chauhan III died 1192. Hindu ruler of Delhi and king of the Chauhan ◊Rajputs, who controlled the Delhi-Ajmer region of N central India. He commanded a coalition of Rajput forces which sought to halt Muhammad Ghuri's Turk-Muslim army at Tarain. Victorious in the first conflict 1191, he died heroically in the second Battle of Tarain 1192. He is immortalized in Hindi ballads and folk literature as a figure of romance and chivalry.

privateer privately owned and armed ship commissioned by a state to attack enemy vessels. The crews of such ships were, in effect, legalized pirates; they were not paid but received a share of the spoils. Privateering existed from ancient times until the 19th century, when it was declared illegal by the Declaration of Paris 1856.

Privy Council council composed originally of the chief royal officials of the Norman kings in Britain; under the Tudors and early Stuarts it became the chief governing body. It was replaced from 1688 by the ◊cabinet, originally a committee of the council, and the council itself now retains only formal powers in issuing royal proclamations and orders-in-council. Cabinet ministers are automatically members, and it is presided over by the Lord President of the Council.

Privy Seal, Lord until 1884, the UK officer of state in charge of the royal seal to prevent its misuse. The honorary title is now held by a senior cabinet minister who has special non-departmental duties.

proconsul Roman ◊consul (chief magistrate) who went on to govern a province when his term as consul ended.

Profumo John (Dennis) 1915– . British Conservative politician, secretary of state for war from 1960 to June 1963, when he resigned on the disclosure of his involvement with Christine Keeler, mistress also of a Soviet naval attaché.

Progressivism in US history, the name of both a reform movement and a political party, active in the two decades before World War I. Mainly middle-class and urban-based, Progressives secured legislation at national, state, and local levels to improve the democratic system, working conditions, and welfare provision.

Prohibition in US history, the period 1920–33 when alcohol was illegal, representing the culmination of a long campaign by church and women's organizations, temperance societies, and the Anti-Saloon League. This led to bootlegging (the illegal distribution of liquor, often illicitly distilled), to the financial advantage of organized crime, and public opinion insisted on repeal 1933.

proletariat in Marxist theory, those classes in society that possess no property, and therefore depend on the sale of their labour or expertise (as opposed to the capitalists or bourgeoisie, who own the means of production, and the petty bourgeoisie, or working small-property owners). They are usually divided into the industrial, agricultural, and intellectual proletariat.

The term is derived from Latin *proletarii*, 'the class possessing no property', whose contribution to the state was considered to be their offspring, *proles*.

protectorate formerly in international law, a small state under the direct or indirect control of a larger one. The 20th-century equivalent was a ◊Trust Territory. In English history the rule of Oliver and Richard ◊Cromwell 1653–59 is referred to as *the Protectorate*.

Protestantism one of the main divisions of Christianity, which emerged from Roman Catholicism at the ◊Reformation. The chief denominations are the Anglican Communion (Episcopalian in the USA), Baptists, Lutherans, Methodists, Pentecostals, and Presbyterians, with a total membership of about 300 million.

Protestantism takes its name from the protest of Martin Luther and his supporters at the Diet of Spires 1529 against the decision to reaffirm the edict of the Diet of Worms against the Reformation. The first conscious statement of Protestantism as a distinct movement was the Confession of Augsburg 1530. The chief characteristics of original Protestantism are the acceptance of the Bible as the only source of truth, the universal priesthood of all believers, and forgiveness of sins solely through faith in Jesus Christ. The Protestant church minimalises the liturgical aspects of Christianity and emphasizes the preaching and hearing of the word of God before sacramental faith and practice. The many interpretations of doctrine and practice are reflected in the various denominations. The ecumenical movement of the 20th century has unsuccessfully attempted to reunite various Protestant denominations and, to some extent, the Protestant churches and the Catholic church.

Protocols of Zion forged document containing supposed plans for Jewish world conquest, alleged to have been submitted by Theodor ◊Herzl to the first Zionist Congress at Basel 1897, and published in Russia 1905. Although proved to be a forgery 1921, the document was used by Hitler in his anti-Semitic campaign 1933–45.

provincia in ancient Rome, region of authority of a magistrate holding power in Italy or elsewhere. In the republic, provinces were determined by the ◊senate for the consuls and praetors. Under the empire, they were divided into senatorial and imperial, for which the emperor himself made the appointments. Additions to the provinces of the Roman empire effectively stopped after ◊Trajan died AD 117.

Provisional IRA breakaway group of the ◊Irish Republican Army which uses force in its objective to expel the British from Northern Ireland.

Provisions of Oxford provisions issued by Henry III of England 1258 under pressure from Simon de Montfort and the baronial opposition. They provided for the establishment of a baronial council to run the government, carry out reforms, and keep a check on royal power.

War is the national industry of Prussia.

On *Prussia* Comte de Mirabeau

Prussia N German state 1618–1945 on the Baltic coast. It was an independent kingdom until 1867, when it became, under Otto von ◊Bismarck, the military power of the North German Confederation and part of the German Empire 1871 under the Prussian king Wilhelm I. West Prussia became part of Poland under the Treaty of ◊Versailles, and East Prussia was largely incorporated into the USSR after 1945.

1618 Formed by the union of Brandenburg and the duchy of Prussia (established 1525).

1640–88 The country's military power was founded by Frederick William, the 'Great Elector'.

1701 Prussia became a kingdom under Frederick I.

1713–40 Frederick William I expanded the army.

1740–86 Silesia, East Frisia, and West Prussia were annexed by Frederick II the Great.

1806 Frederick William III was defeated at Jena by Napoleon Bonaparte.

1815 After the Congress of Vienna Prussia regained its lost territories and also acquired lands in the Rhineland and Saxony.

1848 The revolutions of 1848 overthrew the government but it was restored the following year.

1864 War with Denmark resulted in the acquisition of Schleswig.

1866 After the defeat of Austria, Prussia acquired Holstein and formed the North German Confederation with the territories of Hanover, Nassau, Frankfurt-am-Main, and Hesse-Cassel.

1871 After Prussia's victory in the Franco-Prussian War, the German Empire was proclaimed, under Bismarck's chancellorship, for Wilhelm I.

1918 Prussia became a republic after World War I.

1932 Prussia lost its local independence in Hitler's Germany and came under the control of the Reich.

1946 After World War II the Allies abolished Prussia altogether, dividing its territories among East and West Germany, Poland, and the USSR.

Ptolemy dynasty of kings of Macedonian origin who ruled Egypt over a period of 300 years; they included:

Ptolemy I *c.* 367–283 BC. Ruler of Egypt from 323 BC, king from 304. He was one of ◊Alexander the Great's generals, and established the dynasty and Macedonian organization of the state in Alexandria.

It is more kingly to enrich others than to enjoy wealth oneself.

Ptolemy I

Ptolemy XIII 63–47 BC. Joint ruler of Egypt with his sister-wife ◊Cleopatra in the period preceding the Roman annexation of Egypt. He was killed fighting against Julius ◊Caesar.

Public Health Acts 1848, 1872, 1875 in the UK, legislation enacted by Parliament to deal with squalor and disease and to establish a code of sanitary law. The first act, in 1848, established a central board of health with three members who were responsible to Parliament to impose local boards of health in districts where the death rate was above the national average and made provision for other local boards of health to be established by petition. The 1872 act made it obligatory for every local authority to appoint a medical officer of health. The 1875 act consolidated previous acts and provided a comprehensive code for public health.

Puerto Rico the Commonwealth of; easternmost island of the Greater Antilles, situated between the US Virgin Islands and the

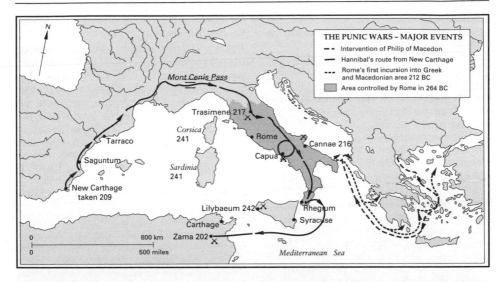

THE PUNIC WARS – MAJOR EVENTS
- - Intervention of Philip of Macedon
— Hannibal's route from New Carthage
--- Rome's first incursion into Greek and Macedonian area 212 BC
▨ Area controlled by Rome in 264 BC

The Punic Wars – major events *The First Punic War 264–241 BC was confined to Sicily, which had long been under Carthaginian influence, and ended in victory for Rome. In the Second Punic War Hannibal invaded Italy from Spain, crossing the Alps and winning victories at Cannae and Trasimene 217. His alliance with Philip V of Macedon drew Rome into conflict with Greece, and in Spain the Romans took New Carthage. Forced into S Italy, Hannibal withdrew to Carthage and was defeated at Zama in 202. The Third Punic War 149–146, took place in Africa and ended in the sack of Carthage.*

Dominican Republic. It visited 1493 by Columbus; annexed by Spain 1509; ceded to the USA after the ◊Spanish-American War 1898; achieved commonwealth status with local self-government 1952.

This was confirmed in preference to independence by a referendum 1967, but there is both an independence movement and one preferring incorporation as a state of the USA. Although legislation in favour of a further referendum was proposed and discussed 1990–91, it was later shelved.

P'u-i (or *Pu-Yi*) Henry 1906–1967. Last emperor of China (as Hsuan Tung) from 1908 until his deposition 1912; he was restored for a week 1917. After his deposition he chose to be called Henry. He was president 1932–34 and emperor 1934–45 of the Japanese puppet state of Manchukuo (see ◊Manchuria).

Pullman strike US rail strike 1894 involving George Pullman's Palace Car Company workers at Pullman, Illinois, and the American Railway Union led by Eugene ◊Debs. Strikers protested May 1894 against lay-offs and wage cuts of 25–40%. Midwestern railways were paralysed by July, but President Grover Cleveland sent federal troops to the Chicago strike centre, ostensibly to protect the US mail trains, crushing the strike. Debs was jailed for six months for defying an injunction not to impede the mail trains by continuing the strike.

Punic (Latin *Punicus* 'a Phoenician') relating to ◊Carthage, ancient city in N Africa founded by the Phoenicians.

The Romans boldly aspired to universal dominion and, what is more, achieved what they aimed at.

On the *Punic Wars* Polybius *Histoires* II, 38

Punic Wars three wars between ◊Rome and ◊Carthage:

First 264–241 BC, resulted in the defeat of the Carthaginians under ◊Hamilcar Barca and the cession of Sicily to Rome

Second 218–201 BC, Hannibal invaded Italy, defeated the Romans at Trebia, Trasimene, and at Cannae (under ◊Fabius Maximus), but was finally defeated himself by Scipio Africanus Major at Zama (now in Algeria)

Third 149–146 BC, ended in the destruction of Carthage, and its possessions becoming the Roman province of Africa.

Punjab (Sanskrit 'five rivers': the Indus tributaries Jhelum, Chenab, Ravi, Beas, and Sutlej) former state of British India, now divided between India and Pakistan. Punjab was annexed by Britain 1849, after the Sikh Wars 1845–46 and 1848–49, and formed into a province with its capital at Lahore. Under the British, W Punjab was extensively irrigated, and land was granted to Indians who had served in the British army. The current Punjab state of NW India has been the site of Sikh–Hindu inter-ethnic violence since the early 1980s.

Punjab massacres in the violence occurring after the partition of India 1947, more than a million people died while relocating in the Punjab. The eastern section became an Indian state, while the western area, dominated by the Muslims, went to Pakistan. Violence occurred as Muslims fled from eastern Punjab, and Hindus and Sikhs moved from Pakistan to India.

Puritan from 1564, a member of the Church of England who wished to eliminate Roman Catholic survivals in church ritual, or substitute a presbyterian for an episcopal form of church government. The term also covers the separatists who withdrew from the church altogether. The Puritans were identified with the parliamentary opposition under James I and Charles I, and after the Restoration were driven from the church, and more usually known as Dissenters or Nonconformists.

putsch Swiss German term for a violent seizure of political power, such as Adolf Hitler and Erich von Ludendorff's abortive Munich ◊beer-hall putsch Nov 1923, which attempted to overthrow the Bavarian government.

Pu-Yi alternative transliteration of the name of the last Chinese emperor, Henry ◊P'u-i.

Pylos port in SW Greece where the Battle of ◊Navarino was fought 1827.

Pym John 1584–1643. English Parliamentarian, largely responsible for the ◊petition of right 1628. As leader of the Puritan opposition in the ◊Long Parliament from 1640, he moved the impeachment of Charles I's advisers the Earl of Strafford and William Laud, drew up the ◊Grand Remonstrance, and was the chief of five members of Parliament Charles I wanted arrested 1642. The five hid themselves and then emerged triumphant when the king left London.

Pyrrhus *c.* 318–272 BC. King of Epirus, Greece, from 307, who invaded Italy 280, as an ally of the Tarentines against Rome. He twice defeated the Romans but with such heavy losses that a *Pyrrhic victory* has come to mean a victory not worth winning. He returned to Greece 275 after his defeat at Benevento, and was killed in a riot in Argos.

One more such victory and we are lost.

Pyrrhus after defeating the Romans
at Asculum, 279 BC

Qaboos bin Said 1940– . Sultan of Oman, the 14th descendant of the Albusaid family. Opposed to the conservative views of his father, he overthrew him 1970 in a bloodless coup and assumed the sultanship. Since then he has followed more liberal and expansionist policies, while maintaining his country's position of international nonalignment.

My parliament is the street. I myself talk to my Omanis ... I do not want a parliament of coffee drinkers, who steal my precious time and only talk.

Qaboos bin Said 1979

Qaddafi alternative form of ◊Khaddhafi, Libyan leader.

Qadisiya, Battle of battle fought in S Iraq 637. A Muslim Arab force defeated a larger Zoroastrian Persian army and ended the ◊Sassanian Empire. The defeat is still resented in Iran, where Muslim Arab nationalism threatens to break up the Iranian state.

Qatar country in the Middle East, occupying Qatar peninsula in the Arabian Gulf, bounded SW by Saudi Arabia and S by United Arab Emirates.

history For early history, see ◊Arabia. Qatar, which used to be under ◊Bahrain's control, has had a treaty with Britain since 1868. It was part of the ◊Ottoman Empire from 1872 until World War I. The British government gave formal recognition 1916 to Sheik Abdullah al-Thani as Qatar's ruler, guaranteeing protection in return for an influence over the country's external affairs.

In 1968 Britain announced its intention of withdrawing its forces from the Persian Gulf

area by 1981, and Qatar, having failed in an attempt to form an association with other Gulf states, became fully independent 1 Sept 1971. A new treaty of friendship with the UK replaced the former protectorate.

after independence In 1972, while the emir, Sheik Ahmad, was out of the country, his cousin, the crown prince, Sheik Khalifa, led a bloodless coup; already prime minister, he declared himself also emir. He embarked on an ambitious programme of social and economic reform, curbing the extravagances of the royal family. Qatar has good relations with most of its neighbours and is regarded as one of the more stable and moderate Arab states, although it devotes more than 43% of GNP to defence. Development programmes are hampered by a lack of skilled workers. In the 1991 ◊Gulf War, Qatar's forces fought with the UN coalition against the Iraqi occupiers of Kuwait.

Qin dynasty China's first imperial dynasty 221–206 BC. It was established by ◊Shi Huangdi, ruler of the Qin, the most powerful of the Zhou era warring states. The power of the feudal nobility was curbed and greater central authority exerted over N central China, which was unified through a bureaucratic administrative system.

Writing and measurement systems were standardized, state roads and canals built, and border defence consolidated into what became known as the ◊Great Wall of China. On the debit side, the dynasty is identified with injustice, oppression, and a literary inquisition which came to be known as 'the burning of the books'.

Quadruple Alliance in European history, three military alliances of four nations:

Quadruple Alliance 1718 Austria, Britain, France, and the United Provinces (Netherlands) joined forces to prevent Spain from annexing Sardinia and Sicily;

Quadruple Alliance 1813 Austria, Britain, Prussia, and Russia allied to defeat the French emperor Napoleon; renewed 1815 and 1818. See Congress of ◊Vienna.

Quadruple Alliance 1834 Britain, France, Portugal, and Spain guaranteed the constitutional monarchies of Spain and Portugal against rebels in the Carlist War.

quaestor Roman magistrate whose duties were mainly concerned with public finances. The quaestors originated as assistants to the consuls. Both urban and military quaestors existed, the latter being attached to the commanding generals in the provinces.

Quantrill William Clarke 1837–1865. US proslavery outlaw who became leader of an irregular unit on the Confederate side in the American Civil War. Frank and Jesse ◊James were members of his gang (called Quantrill's Raiders).

Quatre Bras, Battle of battle fought 16 June 1815 during the Napoleonic Wars, in which the British commander Wellington defeated French forces under Marshal Ney. It is named after a hamlet in Brabant, Belgium, 32 km/20 mi SE of Brussels.

Québec capital and industrial port of Québec province, on the St Lawrence River, Canada. The city was founded by the French explorer Samuel de Champlain 1608, and was a French colony 1608–1763. The British, under General ◊Wolfe, captured Québec 1759 after a battle on the nearby Plains of Abraham; both Wolfe and the French commander ◊Montcalm were killed.

Québec province of E Canada. Known as New France 1534–1763; captured by the British and became province of Québec 1763–90, Lower Canada 1791–1846, Canada East 1846–67; one of the original provinces 1867. Nationalist feelings 1960s (despite existing safeguards for Québec's French-derived civil law, customs, religion, and language) were encouraged by French president de Gaulle's exclamation '*Vive le Québec libre/Long live free Québec*' on a visit to the province, and led to the foundation of the Parti Québecois by René Lévesque 1968.

The Québec Liberation Front (FLQ) separatists had conducted a bombing campaign in the 1960s and fermented an uprising 1970; Parti Québecois won power 1976; a referendum on 'sovereignty-association' (separation) was defeated 1980. In 1982, when Canada severed its last legal ties with the UK, Québec opposed the new Constitution Act as denying the province's claim to an absolute veto over constitutional change. Robert Bourassa and Liberals returned to power 1985 and enacted restrictive English-language legislation. The right of veto was proposed for all provinces of Canada 1987, but the agreement failed to be ratified by its 1990 deadline and support for independence grew. The Parti Québecois was defeated by the Liberal Party 1989.

By 1995, the Parti Québecois held power again under Lucien Bouchard when a referendum on soveriety was narrowly rejected (50.6% to 49.4%)

Québec Conference two conferences of Allied leaders in the city of Québec during World War II. The *first conference*1943 approved British admiral Mountbatten as supreme Allied commander in SE Asia and made plans for the invasion of France, for which US general Eisenhower was to be supreme commander. The *second conference* Sept 1944 adopted plans for intensified air attacks on Germany, created a unified strategy against Japan, and established a postwar policy for a defeated Germany.

Quechua or *Quichua* or *Kechua* member of the largest group of South American Indians. The Quechua live in the Andean region. Their ancestors included the Inca, who established the Quechua language in the region.

Quiberon peninsula and coastal town in Brittany, NW France; in 1759 the British admiral ◊Hawke defeated a French fleet (under Conflans) in Quiberon Bay.

Qing last ruling dynasty in China (from 1644); see ◊Manchu.

Quisling Vidkun 1887–1945. Norwegian politician. Leader from 1933 of the Norwegian Fascist Party, he aided the Nazi invasion of Norway 1940 by delaying mobilization and urging non-resistance. He was made premier by Hitler 1942, and was arrested and shot as a traitor by the Norwegians 1945. His name became a generic term for a traitor who aids an occupying force.

Quit India movement campaign against British rule in India led by Mahatma ◊Gandhi begun Aug 1942. In March 1942 Sir Stafford ◊Cripps tried unsuccessfully to persuade the Congress Party of the need for it to participate in the war effort against Japan. Instead, Gandhi called on the British to leave India and let Indians deal with the Japanese by non-violent means. Calls to 'Quit India' were met with the arrest of Gandhi and other Congress leaders, which led to bloodshed, violence, and suppression.

Quran (or ◊Kerbela) sacred book of Islam.

Rabin Yitzhak 1922–1995. Israeli Labour politician, prime minister 1974–77 and 1992–95. His support of Palestinian self-government in the occupied territories contributed to his party's success 1992. In Sept 1993 he signed a peace agreement with the Palestinian Liberation Organization (PLO), providing for a phased withdrawal of Israeli forces. He was the joint recipient of the 1994 Nobel Peace Prize. He was shot dead at a peace rally in Nov 1995.

race-relations acts UK acts of Parliament 1965, 1968, and 1976 to combat discrimination. The Race Relations Act 1976 prohibits discrimination on the grounds of colour, race, nationality, or ethnic origin. Indirect as well as direct discrimination is prohibited in the provision of goods, services, facilities, employment, accommodation, and advertisements. The Commission for Racial Equality was set up under the act to investigate complaints.

Radić Stjepan 1871–1928. Yugoslav nationalist politician, founder of the Croatian Peasant Party 1904. He led the Croat national movement within the Austro-Hungarian Empire and advocated a federal state with Croatian autonomy. His opposition to Serbian supremacy within Yugoslavia led to his assassination.

Radical in Britain, supporter of parliamentary reform before the Reform Bill 1832. As a group the Radicals later became the progressive wing of the Liberal Party. During the 1860s (led by Cobden, Bright, and J S Mill) they campaigned for extension of the franchise, free trade, and ◊laissez faire, but after 1870, under the leadership of Joseph Chamberlain and Charles Dilke, they adopted a republican and semi-socialist programme. With the growth of ◊socialism in the later 19th century, Radicalism ceased to exist as an organized movement.

In France, the Radical Party was a major force in the politics of the Third Republic, 1871–1940.

Raeder Erich 1876–1960. German admiral. Chief of Staff in World War I, he became head of the navy 1928, but was dismissed by Hitler in 1943 because of his failure to prevent Allied Arctic convoys from reaching the USSR. Sentenced to life imprisonment at the Nuremberg trials of war criminals, he was released 1955 on grounds of ill health.

Raffles Thomas Stamford 1781–1826. British colonial administrator, born in Jamaica. He served in the British ◊East India Company, took part in the capture of Java from the Dutch 1811, and while governor of Sumatra 1818–23 was responsible for the acquisition and founding of Singapore 1819.

Rafsanjani Hojatoleslam Ali Akbar Hashemi 1934– . Iranian politician and cleric, president 1989-97. When his former teacher Ayatollah ◊Khomeini returned after the revolution of 1979–80, Rafsanjani became the speaker of the Iranian parliament and, after Khomeini's death, state president and effective political leader.

Rafsanjani was born near Kerman, SE Iran, to a family of pistachio farmers. At 14 he went to study Islamic jurisprudence with Khomeini in the to Shi'ites holy city of Qom and qualified as an *alim* (Islamic teacher). During the period 1964–78, he acquired considerable wealth through his construction business but kept in touch with his exiled mentor and was repeatedly imprisoned for fundamentalist political activity. His attitude became more moderate in the 1980s.

Raglan FitzRoy James Henry Somerset, 1st Baron Raglan 1788–1855. English general. He took part in the Peninsular War under Wellington, and lost his right arm at Waterloo. He commanded the British forces in the Crimean War from 1854. The *raglan sleeve*, cut right up to the neckline with no shoulder seam, is named after him.

Don't carry away that arm till I have taken off my ring.

Lord Raglan

Rahman Sheik Mujibur 1921–1975. Bangladeshi nationalist politician, president 1975. He was arrested several times for campaigning for the autonomy of East Pakistan. He won the elections 1970 as leader of the Awami League but was again arrested when negotiations with the Pakistan government broke down. After the civil war 1971, he became prime minister of the newly independent Bangladesh. He was presidential dictator Jan–Aug 1975, when he was assassinated.

Rahman Tunku Abdul 1903–1990. Malaysian politician, first prime minister of independent Malaya 1957–63 and of Malaysia 1963–70.

Born at Kuala Keda, the son of the sultan and his sixth wife, a Thai princess, the Tunku studied law in England. After returning to Malaya he founded the Alliance Party 1952. The party was successful in the 1955 elections, and the Tunku became prime minister of Malaya on gaining independence 1957, continuing when Malaya became part of Malaysia 1963. His achievement was to bring together the Malay, Chinese, and Indian peoples within the Alliance Party, but in the 1960s he was accused of showing bias towards Malays. Ethnic riots followed in Kuala Lumpur 1969 and, after many attempts to restore better relations, the Tunku retired 1970. In his later years he voiced criticism of the authoritarian leadership of Mahathir bin Mohamad.

Rajput member of a Hindu people, predominantly soldiers and landowners, widespread over N India. The Rajput states of NW India are now merged in Rajasthan. The Rana family (ruling aristocracy of Nepal until 1951) was also Rajput. Rajastani languages belong to the Indo-Iranian branch of the Indo-European family.

history Rajput clans are descended from 5th–7th-century warrior tribes of central Asia. By the 9th century they controlled much of the arid region of Rajasthan in W central India and later migrated east into Haryana and the upper Ganges valley, pressurized by Muslim incursions from the NW. During the early medieval period, numbers of Rajput clans challenged for supremacy in central and N India, resulting in incessant local warfare. ◊Prithviraja briefly secured unity, but was defeated at Tarain by the Muslim invaders. The subsequent Delhi sultanate and Mogul periods of Muslim rule witnessed periodic Rajput rebellions. During this time Rajput chiefs retained considerable authority at the local level and participated in central and provincial administration. This continued during the British period, when many Rajput Princely States in Rajasthan retained nominal independence.

Raleigh or *Ralegh* Walter c. 1552–1618. English adventurer. He made colonizing and exploring voyages to North America 1584–87 and South America 1595, and naval attacks on Spanish ports. His aggressive actions against Spanish interests brought him into conflict with the pacific James I. He was imprisoned for treason 1603–16 and executed on his return from an unsuccessful final expedition to South America.

Tis a sharp remedy, but a sure one for all ills.

> **Walter Raleigh** feeling the edge of the axe before his execution

Rameses alternative spelling of ◊Ramses, name of kings of ancient Egypt.

Ramillies, Battle of battle in which British commander Marlborough defeated the French 23 May 1706, during the War of the ◊Spanish Succession, at a village in Brabant, Belgium, 21 km/13 mi N of Namur.

Ramses or *Rameses* 11 kings (pharoahs) of ancient Egypt, including:

Ramses II or *Rameses II* king of Egypt about 1304–1236 BC, the son of Seti I. He campaigned successfully against the Hittites, and built two rock temples at Abu Simbel in Upper Egypt.

Ramses III or *Rameses III* king of Egypt about 1200–1168 BC. He won victories over the Libyans and the ◊Sea Peoples and asserted his control over Palestine.

Randolph Asa Philip 1889–1979. US labour and civil rights leader. Devoting himself to the cause of unionization, especially among black Americans, he was named a vice president of the American Federation of Labor and Congress of Industrial Organizations (AFL-CIO) 1957. He was one of the organizers of the 1963 civil rights march on Washington.

Ranjit Singh 1780–1839. Indian maharajah. He succeeded his father as a minor Sikh leader 1792, and created a Sikh army that conquered Kashmir and the Punjab. In alliance with the British, he established himself as 'Lion of the Punjab', ruler of the strongest of the independent Indian states.

Rapacki Plan plan put to the United Nations 2 Oct 1957 by Polish Foreign Minister Adam Rapacki, proposing a zone closed to the manufacture or deployment of nuclear weapons in Poland, Czechoslovakia, East and West Germany. The ban was to be enforced by NATO and Warsaw Pact observers. The USA and Britain rejected the plan as it gave the USSR advantages due to its superiority in conventional forces.

Rapallo, Treaties of treaties were signed here 1920 (settling the common frontiers of Italy and Yugoslavia) and 1922 (cancelling German and Russian counterclaims for indemnities for World War I). German soldiers were also permitted to train in the USSR, in defiance of the Treaty of ◊Versailles. Rapallo is a port and winter resort in Liguria, NW Italy.

rapprochement improvement of relations between two formerly antagonistic states, such as the agreement between Britain and France in 1904 which ended decades of colonial rivalry.

Rashdun the 'rightly guided ones', the first four caliphs (heads) of Islam: Abu Bakr, Omar, Othman, and Ali.

Rasputin (Russian 'dissolute') Grigory Efimovich 1871–1916. Siberian Eastern Orthodox mystic who acquired influence over the tsarina ◊Alexandra, wife of ◊Nicholas II, and was able to make political and ecclesiastical appointments. His abuse of power and notorious debauchery (reputedly including the tsarina) led to his murder by a group of nobles.

Rastafarianism religion originating in the West Indies, based on the ideas of Marcus ◊Garvey, who called on black people to return to Africa and set up a black-governed country there. When Haile Selassie (*Ras Tafari*, 'Lion of Judah') was crowned emperor of Ethiopia 1930, this was seen as a fulfilment of prophecy and some Rastafarians acknowledged him as an incarnation of God (*Jah*), others as a prophet.

Raatatt, Treaty of in 1714, agreement signed by Austria and France that supplemented the Treaty of ◊Utrecht and helped to end the War of the ◊Spanish Succession.

Rathenau Walther 1867–1922. German politician. He was a leading industrialist and was appointed economic director during World War I, developing a system of economic planning in combination with capitalism. After the war he founded the Democratic Party, and became foreign minister 1922. The same year he signed the Rapallo Treaty of Friendship with the USSR, cancelling German and Soviet counterclaims for indemnities for World War I, and soon after was assassinated by right-wing fanatics.

Rayburn Samuel Taliaferro 1882–1961. US political leader. A Democrat, he was elected to the US Congress 1912. He supported President Roosevelt's New Deal programme 1933, and was elected majority leader 1937 and Speaker of the House 1940. With the exception of two terms, he served as Speaker until his death. His tenure in the House 1912–61 was the longest on record.

Reagan Ronald (Wilson) 1911– . 40th president of the USA 1981–89, a Republican. He was governor of California 1966–74, and a former Hollywood actor. Reagan was a hawkish and popular president. He adopted an aggressive policy in Central America, attempting to overthrow the government of Nicaragua, and invading Grenada 1983. In 1987, ◊Irangate was investigated by the Tower Commission; Reagan admitted that USA–Iran negotiations had become an 'arms for hostages deal', but denied knowledge of resultant funds being illegally sent to the Contras in Nicaragua. He increased military spending (sending the national budget deficit to record levels), cut social programmes, introduced deregulation of domestic markets, and cut taxes. His ◊Strategic Defense Initiative, announced 1983, proved controversial owing to the cost and unfeasibility. He was succeeded by George Bush.

You know, by the time you reach my age, you've made plenty of mistakes if you've lived your life properly.
Ronald Reagan Observer 1987

realpolitik (German *Realpolitik* 'politics of realism') belief that the pragmatic pursuit of self-interest and power, backed up by force when convenient, is the only realistic option for a great state. The term was coined 1859 to describe ◊Bismarck's policies.

Reconquista (Spanish 'reconquest') the Christian defeat of the ◊Moors 9th–15th centuries, and their expulsion from Spain.

Spain was conquered by the Muslims between 711 and 728, and its reconquest began with Galicia, Leon, and Castile. By the 13th century, only Granada was left in Muslim hands, but disunity within the Christian kingdoms left it unconquered until 1492, when it fell to ◊Ferdinand and Isabella.

Reconstruction in US history, the period 1865–77 after the Civil War during which the nation was reunited under the federal government after the defeat of the Southern Confederacy.

Amendments to the US constitution, and to Southern state constitutions, conferred equal civil and political rights on blacks, although many Southern states, still opposed to these radical Republican measures, still practised discrimination and segregation. During Reconstruction, industrial and commercial projects restored the economy of the South but failed to ensure racial equality, and the former slaves remained, in most cases, landless labourers.

Red Army name of the army of the USSR until 1946; later known as the *Soviet Army*. It developed from the Red Guards, volunteers who carried out the Bolshevik revolution, and received its name because it fought under the red flag. The Chinese revolutionary army was also called the Red Army.

Red Army Faction left-wing guerilla group also known as the ◊Baader-Meinhof gang.

Red Brigades (Italian *Brigate rosse*) extreme left-wing guerrilla groups active in Italy during the 1970s and early 1980s. They were implicated in many kidnappings and killings, some later attributed to right-wing *agents provocateurs*, including that of Christian Democrat leader Aldo Moro 1978.

Red Cloud (Sioux name *Mahpiua Luta*) 1822–1909. American Sioux Indian leader. Paramount chief of the Oglala Sioux from 1860, he led the armed resistance to the advance of white settlers along the Bozeman Trail. He signed the Fort Laramie Treaty 1869 which gave the Indians a large area in the Black Hills of Dakota. He resisted any involvement in the war which culminated in the Battle of Little Bighorn 1876.

The white man made us many promises, more than I can remember, but they never kept but one; they promised to take our land and they took it.

> Red Cloud quoted in Dee Brown
> *Bury My Heart at Wounded Knee*

Red Cross international relief agency founded by the Geneva Convention 1864 at the instigation of the Swiss doctor Henri Dunant to assist the wounded and prisoners in war. Its symbol is a symmetrical red cross on a white ground. In addition to dealing with associated problems of war, such as refugees and the care of the disabled, the Red Cross is increasingly concerned with victims of natural disasters – floods, earthquakes, epidemics, and accidents.

Prompted by war horrors described by Dunant, the Geneva Convention laid down principles to ensure the safety of ambulances, hospitals, stores, and personnel distinguished by the Red Cross emblem. The Muslim equivalent is the *Red Crescent*.

Red Guard one of the school and college students, wearing red armbands, active in the ◊Cultural Revolution in China 1966–69. The armed workers who took part in the ◊Russian Revolution of 1917 were also called Red Guards.

Redmond John Edward 1856–1918. Irish politician, Parnell's successor as leader of the Nationalist Party 1890–1916. The 1910 elections saw him holding the balance of power in the House of Commons, and he secured the introduction of a ◊Home Rule bill, which was opposed by Protestant Ulster.

Red Scare in US history, campaign against radicals and dissenters which took place in the aftermath of World War I and the Russian Revolution, during a period of labour disorders in the USA. A wave of strikes in 1919 was seen as a prelude to revolution and violently suppressed. Thousands of people were arrested on suspicion, and communists were banned from entry to the country.

Some labour organizations, notably the ◊Industrial Workers of the World, had advocated violence, and there were anarchist bombing incidents. Soon all socialists were perceived as threats to the state. Spymaster J Edgar ◊Hoover was enlisted to track subversives, and a nationwide roundup of suspects on 2 Jan 1920 led to 556 deportations. Many of the left-wing leaders were immigrants, and fear of foreigners played a large part in the Red Scare. It was after this that the system of immigration quotas was established.

reducciones mission villages in Spanish Latin American colonies which were used to concentrate the indigenous Indian populations and convert them to Christianity. Similar villages in Portuguese colonies were called reduçoẽs.

reeve in Anglo-Saxon England, an official charged with the administration of a shire or burgh, fulfilling functions similar to those of the later sheriff. After the Norman Conquest, the term tended to be restricted to the person elected by the villeins to oversee the work of the manor and to communicate with the manorial lord.

referendum procedure whereby a decision on proposed legislation is referred to the electorate for settlement by direct vote of all the people. It is most frequently employed in Switzerland, the first country to use it, but has become increasingly widespread. In 1992 several European countries (Ireland, Denmark, France) held referenda on whether or not to ratify the ◊Maastricht Treaty on closer European economic and political union. A referendum was held in the UK for the first time 1975 on the issue of membership of the European Community.

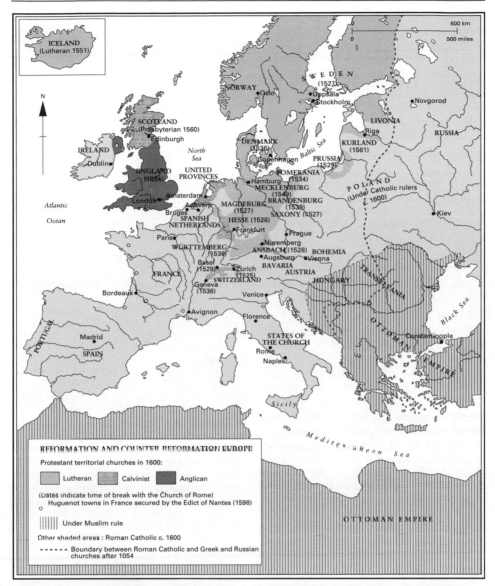

Reformation and Counter-Reformation in Europe *The Protestant Reformation began 1517 with Martin Luther and spread through Central and N Europe during the 16th century when individuals and congregations took up the new teachings. In many cases a state's religion was determined by that of its ruler, and the spread of Protestantism in Germany was often due to rulers' efforts to distance themselves from control by the Holy Roman Empire. The decision to break with the papacy in England owed more to Henry VIII's secular concerns than to his religious convictions. The Wars of Religion in France ultimately secured freedom of worship for the Protestant Huguenots but elsewhere religious toleration was the exception rather than the norm. By the 16th century, Christianity was also facing threats from the growth of the Ottoman Empire in the Balkans and SE Europe.*

Reform Acts UK acts of Parliament 1832, 1867, and 1884 that extended voting rights and redistributed parliamentary seats; also known as ◊Representation of the People Acts.

The 1832 act abolished pocket and ◊rotten boroughs, which had formed unrepresentative constituencies, redistributed seats on a more equitable basis in the counties, and formed some new boroughs. The franchise was extended to male householders in property worth £10 a year or more in the boroughs and to owners of freehold property worth £2 a year, £10 copyholders, or £50 leaseholders in the counties. The 1867 act redistributed seats from corrupt and small boroughs to the counties and large urban areas. It also extended the franchise in boroughs to adult male heads of households, and in counties to males who owned, or held on long leases, land worth £5 a year, or who occupied land worth £12 on which they paid poor rates. The 1884 act extended the franchise to male agricultural labourers.

Reformation religious and political movement in 16th-century Europe to reform the Roman Catholic church, which led to the establishment of Protestant churches. Anticipated from the 12th century by the Waldenses, Lollards, and Hussites, it was set off by German priest Martin ◊Luther 1517, and became effective when the absolute monarchies gave it support by challenging the political power of the papacy and confiscating church wealth.

1517 Martin Luther's protest against the sale of indulgences began the Reformation in Europe.

1519 Ulrich Zwingli led the Reformation in Switzerland.

1529 The term 'Protestant' was first used.

1533 Henry VIII renounced papal supremacy and proclaimed himself head of the Church of England.

1541 The French theologian John Calvin established Presbyterianism in Geneva, Switzerland.

1559 The Protestant John Knox returned from exile to found the Church of Scotland.

1545–1563 The *Counter-Reformation* was initiated by the Roman Catholic Church at the *Council of Trent*. It aimed at reforming abuses and regaining the lost ground by using moral persuasion and extending the Spanish Inquisition to other countries.

1648 By the end of the Thirty Years' War, the present European alignment had been reached, with the separation of Catholic and Protestant churches.

We permit those of the so-called Reformed Religion to live and abide in all the towns and districts of this our realm ... free from inquisition, molestation or compulsion to do anything ... against their Conscience.

On the *Reformation* Henry IV of France, the Edict of Nantes 1598

---

refugee person fleeing from oppressive or dangerous conditions (such as political, religious, or military persecution) and seeking refuge in a foreign country. In 1991 there were an estimated 17 million refugees worldwide, whose resettlement and welfare were the responsibility of the United Nations High Commission for Refugees (UNHCR).

The term was originally applied to the French Huguenots who came to England after toleration of Protestantism was withdrawn with the revocation of the Edict of Nantes in 1685. Major refugee movements in 20th-century Europe include: Jews from the pogroms of Russia 1881–1914 and again after the Revolution; White Russians from the USSR after 1917; Jews from Germany and other Nazi-dominated countries 1933–45; the displaced people of World War II; and from 1991 victims of the the civil wars in Croatia and Bosnia-Herzegovina.

Many Chinese fled the mainland after the communist revolution of 1949, especially to Taiwan and Hong Kong; many Latin Americans fled from Cuba, Colombia, Brazil, Chile, Argentina, and Central America when new governments took power; and many boat people left Vietnam after the victory of the North over the South. Refugee movements created by natural disasters and famine have been widespread, most notably in Ethiopia and Sudan, where civil war has also contributed. Between 1985 and 1989 the number of refugees doubled worldwide, and the Gulf War 1991 created 1.5 million refugees, though many were later able to return to their homes.

A distinction is usually made by Western nations between 'political' refugees and so-called 'economic' refugees, who are said to be escaping from poverty rather than persecution, particularly when the refugees come from low-income countries. The latter group often becomes illegal immigrants. International law recognizes the right of the persecuted to seek asylum but does not oblige states to provide it. Only 0.17% of W Europe's population are refugees.

Since 1920, international organizations have been set up to help refugees, including the Nansen Office for Russian refugees in the 1920s, and the United Nations High Commission for Refugees in 1945. In 1970 there were 2.5 million refugees worldwide, in 1985 10 million, in 1990 15 million.

Regency in Britain, the years 1811–20 during which ◊George IV (then Prince of Wales) acted as regent for his father ◊George III.

Rehoboam king of Judah about 932–915 BC, son of Solomon. Under his rule the Jewish nation split into the two kingdoms of Israel and

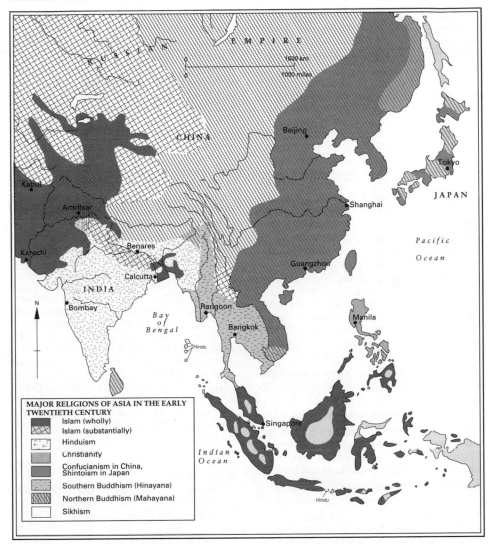

Major religions of Asia in the early 20th century *Asia has been the birthplace of great national religions, notably Confucianism in China, Hinduism and Sikhism in India, and Shintoism in Japan, as well as the great ancient international religion, Buddhism. Through trading and missionary links, it was later exposed to Islam, brought to NW India from the 8th century and to Indonesia from the 13th century. Roman Catholicism was introduced to the East Indies and Philippines in the 16th century by the Portuguese and Spanish. 19th-century European imperialism was associated with a further wave of Christian missionary activity.*

Judah. Ten of the tribes revolted against him and took Jeroboam as their ruler, leaving Rehoboam only the tribes of Judah and Benjamin.

Reich (German 'empire') three periods in European history. The First Reich was the Holy Roman Empire 962–1806, the Second Reich the German Empire 1871–1918, and the ◊Third Reich Nazi Germany 1933–45.

Reichstag German parliament building and lower legislative house during the German Empire 1871–1918 and Weimar Republic 1919–33.

Reichstag Fire burning of the German parliament building in Berlin 27 Feb 1933, less than a month after the Nazi leader Hitler became chancellor. The fire was used as a justification for the suspension of many constitutional guarantees and also as an excuse to attack the communists. There is still debate over whether the Nazis were involved in this crime, of which they were the main beneficiaries.

Reims (English *Rheims*) capital of Champagne-Ardenne region, France; population (1990) 185,200. It is the centre of the champagne industry and has textile industries. It was known in Roman times as *Durocortu-rum*. From 987 all but six French kings were crowned here. Ceded to England 1420 under the Treaty of Troyes, it was retaken by Joan of Arc, who had Charles VII consecrated in the 13th-century cathedral. In World War II, the German High Command formally surrendered here to US general Eisenhower 7 May 1945.

religion (Latin *religare* 'to bind') code of belief or philosophy, which often involves the worship of a God or gods. Belief in a supernatural power is not essential (absent in, for example, Buddhism and Confucianism), but faithful adherence is usually considered to be rewarded, for example by escape from human existence (Buddhism), by a future existence (Christianity, Islam), or by worldly benefit (Sōka Gakkai Buddhism). Among the chief religions are:

ancient and pantheist religions of Babylonia, Assyria, Egypt, Greece, and Rome;

oriental Hinduism, Buddhism, Jainism, Parseeism, Confucianism, Taoism, and Shinto;

'religions of a book' Judaism, Christianity (the principal divisions are Roman Catholic, Eastern Orthodox, and Protestant), and Islam (the principal divisions are Sunni and Shi'ite);

combined derivation such as Baha'ism, the Unification Church, and Mormonism.

Religion, Wars of series of civil wars 1562–89 in France between Catholics and (Protestant) Huguenots. Each side was led by noble families which competed for influence over a weakened monarchy. The most infamous event was the Massacre of ◊St Bartholomew 1572, carried out on the orders of the Catholic faction led by ◊Catherine de' Medici and the Duke of Guise. After 1584, the heir apparent to the French throne was the Huguenot Henry of Navarre. This prompted further hostilities, but after his accession as Henry IV 1589, he was able to maintain his hold on power, partly through military victory and partly by converting to Catholicism 1593. He introduced the Edict of Nantes 1598, guaranteeing freedom of worship throughout his kingdom.

remittance man in the 19th century, man living in a British colony (often Australia) on money sent (remitted) to him from England, on condition that he did not return. This exile was imposed by the family because of some transgression.

Renaissance period and intellectual movement in European cultural history that is traditionally seen as ending the Middle Ages and beginning modern times. The Renaissance started in Italy in the 14th century and flourished in W Europe until about the 17th century.

The aim of Renaissance education was to produce the 'complete human being' (*Renaissance man*), conversant in the humanities, mathematics and science (including their application in war), the arts and crafts, and athletics and sport; to enlarge the bounds of learning and geographical knowledge; to encourage the growth of scepticism and free thought, and the study and imitation of Greek and Latin literature and art. The revival of interest in classical Greek and Roman culture inspired artists such as Leonardo da Vinci, Michelangelo, and Dürer, architects such as Brunelleschi and Alberti, writers such as Petrarch and Boccaccio. Scientists and explorers proliferated as well.

The beginning of the Italian Renaissance is usually dated in the 14th century with the writers Petrarch and Boccaccio. The invention of printing (mid-15th century) and geographical discoveries helped spread the new spirit. Exploration by Europeans opened Africa, Asia, and the New World to trade, colonization, and imperialism. Biblical criticism by the Dutch humanist Erasmus and others contributed to the Reformation, but the Counter-Reformation almost extinguished the movement in 16th-century Italy.

Figures of the Renaissance include the politician Machiavelli, the poets Ariosto and Tasso, the philosopher Bruno, the physicist Galileo, and the artists Michelangelo, Cellini, and Raphael in Italy; the writers Rabelais and Montaigne in France, Cervantes in Spain, and Camoëns in Portugal; the astronomer Copernicus in Poland; and the politicians More and Bacon, and the writers Sidney, Marlowe, and Shakespeare in England.

reparation compensation paid by countries that start wars in which they are defeated, as by Germany in both world wars. Iraq is required to pay reparations, under the terms of a United Nations resolution, after its defeat in the 1991 Gulf War.

repartimiento term for the 'distribution' of the native Indian population among conquistadors or settlers in colonial Spanish America (16th to 19th centuries). It forced the Indians into financial dependence.

The system was widespread in Mexico, Oaxaca, Zatatecas, and Yucatán. It was imposed with particular brutality in Peru, where it contributed to the Tupas Amaru rebellion 1780.

Representation of the People Acts series of UK acts of Parliament from 1867 that extended voting rights, creating universal suffrage in 1928.

The 1867 and 1884 acts are known as the second and third ◊Reform Acts. The 1918 act gave the vote to men over the age of 21 and women over the age of 30, and the 1928 act extended the vote to women over the age of 21. Certain people had the right to more than one vote; this was abolished by the 1948 act. The 1969 act reduced the minimum age of voting to 18.

Representatives, House of lower house of the US ◊Congress; see ◊House of Representatives.

Republican Party one of the USA's two main political parties, formed 1854. It is more conservative than the Democratic Party, favouring capital and big business and opposing state subvention and federal controls. In the late 20th century most presidents have come from the Republican Party, but in Congress Republicans were outnumbered until 1994.

The party was founded by a coalition of slavery opponents, who elected their first president, Abraham Lincoln, in 1860. The early Republican Party supported protective tariffs and homestead legislation for western settlers. Towards the end of the century the Republican Party was identified with US imperialism and industrial expansion. After an isolationist period before World War II, the party adopted an active foreign policy under Richard Nixon. It then enjoyed landslide presidential victories for Ronald Reagan but his successor George Bush lost power to the Democrats 1992.

residencia in Spanish history, the debriefing of an official after a term of office in the American colonies. The procedure was designed to ensure that officials remained answerable to the crown and carried out its policies efficiently.

resistance movement opposition movement in a country occupied by an enemy or colonial power, especially in the 20th century; for example, the French resistance to Nazism in World War II.

During World War II, resistance in E Europe took the form of ◊guerrilla warfare, for example in Yugoslavia, Greece, Poland, and by ◊partisan bands behind the German lines in the USSR. In more industrialized countries, such as France (where the underground movement was called the *maquis*), Belgium, and Czecho-

slovakia, sabotage in factories and on the railways, propaganda, and the assassination of Germans and collaborators were the main priorities.

Most resistance movements in World War II were based on an alliance of all anti-fascist parties, but there was internal conflict between those elements intent only on defeat of the enemy, and those who aimed at establishing communist governments, as in Yugoslavia and Greece.

After World War II the same methods were used in Palestine, South America, and European colonial possessions in Africa and Asia to unsettle established regimes.

Restoration in English history, the period when the monarchy, in the person of Charles II, was re-established after the English Civil War and the fall of the ◊Protectorate 1660.

Retz Jean François Paul de Gondi, Cardinal de Retz 1614–1679. French politician. A priest with political ambitions, he stirred up and largely led the insurrection known as the ◊Fronde. After a period of imprisonment and exile he was restored to favour 1662 and created abbot of St Denis.

A man who doesn't trust himself can never really trust anyone else.
Cardinal de Retz *Mémoires* 1718

Réunion French island of the Mascarenes group, in the Indian Ocean, 650 km/400 mi E of Madagascar and 180 km/110 mi SW of Mauritius. It was explored by Portuguese (the first European visitors) 1513; annexed by Louis XIII of France 1642; overseas *département* of France 1946; overseas region 1972.

revanche (French 'revenge') in French history, those who, following the Franco-Prussian War 1870-71, favoured a foreign policy directed towards the recapture of Alsace-Lorraine from Germany.

Revere Paul 1735–1818. American revolutionary, a Boston silversmith, who carried the news of the approach of British troops to Lexington and Concord (see ◊American Revolution) on the night of 18 April 1775. On the next morning the first shots of the Revolution were fired at Lexington.

revolution any rapid, far-reaching, or violent change in the political, social, or economic structure of society. It is usually applied to political change: examples include the American Revolution, where colonists broke free

Revolutionary Wars

1791	Emperor Leopold II and Frederick William II of Prussia issued the Declaration of Pillnitz inviting the European powers to restore the French king Louis XVI to power.
1792	France declared war on Austria, which formed a coalition with Prussia, Sardinia, and (from 1793), Britain, Spain, and the Netherlands; victories for France at Valmy and Jemappes.
1793	French reverses until the reorganization by Lazare Carnot.
1795	Prussia, the Netherlands, and Spain made peace with France.
1796	Sardinia was forced to make peace by the Italian campaign of Napoleon I, then a commander.
1797	Austria was compelled to make peace with France under the Treaty of Campo-Formio.
1798	Napoleon's fleet, after its capture of Malta, was defeated by the British admiral Nelson in Egypt at the Battle of the Nile (Aboukir Bay), and Napoleon had to return to France without his army; William Pitt the Younger, Britain's prime minister, organized a new coalition with Russia, Austria, Naples, Portugal, and Turkey.
1798–99	The coalition mounted its major campaign in Italy (under the Russian field marshal Suvorov), but dissension led to the withdrawal of Russia.
1799	Napoleon, on his return from Egypt, reorganized the French army.
1800	Austrian army defeated by Napoleon at Marengo in NW Italy 14 June, and again 3 Dec (by General Moreau) at Hohenlinden near Munich; the coalition collapsed.
1801	Austria made peace under the Treaty of Lunéville; Sir Ralph Abercromby defeated the French army by land in Egypt at the Battle of Alexandria, but was himself killed.
1802	Treaty of Amiens truce between France and Britain, followed by the Napoleonic Wars.

from their colonial ties and established a sovereign, independent nation; the French Revolution, where an absolute monarchy was overthrown by opposition from inside the country and a popular uprising; and the Russian Revolution, where a repressive monarchy was overthrown by those seeking to institute widespread social and economic changes based on a socialist model.

While political revolutions are often associated with violence, other types of change can have just as much impact on society. Most notable is the Industrial Revolution of the mid-18th century, which caused massive economic and social changes. In the 1970s and 1980s a high-tech revolution based on the silicon chip took place, facilitating the widespread use of computers.

Revolutionary Wars series of wars 1791–1802 between France and the combined armies of England, Austria, Prussia, and others, during the period of the ◊French Revolution.

revolutions of 1848 series of revolts in various parts of Europe against monarchical rule. While some of the revolutionaries had republican ideas, many more were motivated by economic grievances. The revolution began in France with the overthrow of Louis Philippe and then spread to Italy, the Austrian Empire, and Germany, where the short-lived ◊Frankfurt Parliament put forward ideas about political unity in Germany. None of the revolutions enjoyed any lasting success, and most were violently suppressed within a few months.

revolutions of 1989 popular uprisings in many countries of Eastern Europe against communist rule, prompted by internal reforms in the USSR that permitted dissent within its sphere of influence. By 1990 nearly all the Warsaw Pact countries had moved from one-party to pluralist political systems, in most cases peacefully but with growing hostility between various nationalist and ethnic groups.

Until the late 1980s, any discontent, however widespread, had been kept in check by the use or threat of military force controlled from Moscow. Mikhail Gorbachev's official encouragement of *perestroika* (radical restructuring) and *glasnost* (greater political openness), largely for economic reasons, allowed popular discontent to boil over. Throughout the summer and autumn of 1989 the Eastern European states broke away from the communist bloc, as the Soviet republics were to do during the next two years. Bulgaria, Czechoslovakia, and Hungary achieved bloodless coups; Poland held free elections; East Germany took the first steps towards reunification with West Germany; Romania's revolution was short and bloody; Yugoslavia held multiparty elections 1990 but then broke up into civil war. Albania held elections 1991.

Reynaud Paul 1878–1966. French prime minister in World War II, who succeeded Edouard Daladier in March 1940 but resigned in June after the German breakthrough. He was imprisoned by the Germans until 1945, and again held government offices after the war.

Rhee Syngman 1875–1965. Korean right-wing politician. A rebel under Chinese and Japanese rule, he became president of South Korea from 1948 until riots forced him to resign and leave the country 1960.

Rhineland province of Prussia from 1815. Its unchallenged annexation by Nazi Germany 1936 was a harbinger of World War II.

Under the terms of the Treaty of Versailles 1919, following World War I, the Rhineland was to be occupied by Allied forces for 15 years, with a permanent demilitarized zone. Demilitarization was reaffirmed by the Treaties of Locarno, but German foreign minister Gustav Stresemann achieved the removal of the British forces 1926 and French forces 1930. Both treaties were violated when Adolf Hitler's troops marched into the demilitarized zone of the Rhineland 1936. Britain and France merely protested, and it remained under German occupation. It was the scene of heavy fighting 1944, and was recaptured by US troops 1945, becoming one of the largest states of West Germany after the end of the war.

Rhodes (Greek *Ródhos*) Greek island, largest of the Dodecanese, in the E Aegean Sea. Rhodes was settled by the Greeks about 1000 BC; the Colossus of Rhodes (fell 224 BC), was one of the ◊Seven Wonders of the World; held by the Knights Hospitallers of St John 1306–1522; taken from Turkish rule by the Italian occupation 1912; ceded to Greece 1947.

Rhodes Cecil (John) 1853–1902. South African politician, born in the UK, prime minister of Cape Colony 1890–96. Aiming at the formation of a South African federation and the creation of a block of British territory from the Cape to Cairo, he was responsible for the annexation of Bechuanaland (now Botswana) in 1885. He formed the British South Africa Company in 1889, which occupied Mashonaland and Matabeleland, thus forming *Rhodesia* (now Zambia and Zimbabwe).

He entered the Cape legislature 1881, and became prime minister 1890, but the discovery of his complicity in the Jameson Raid forced him to resign 1896. Advocating Anglo-Afrikaner cooperation, he was less alive to the rights of black Africans, despite the final 1898 wording of his dictum: 'Equal rights for every civilized man south of the Zambezi.'

So little done, so much to do.

Cecil Rhodes last words

Rhodesia former name of ◊Zambia (Northern Rhodesia) and ◊Zimbabwe (Southern Rhodesia), in S Africa.

Ribbentrop Joachim von 1893–1946. German Nazi politician and diplomat, foreign minister 1938–45, during which time he negotiated the Non-Aggression Pact between Germany and the USSR. He was tried at Nuremberg as a war criminal 1946 and hanged.

Ribbentrop was born in the Rhineland. Awarded the Iron Cross in World War I, he became a wine merchant in 1919. He joined the Nazi party 1932 and acted as Hitler's adviser on foreign affairs; he was German ambassador to Britain 1936–38. A political lightweight, he was useful to Hitler since he posed no threat.

Richard three kings of England:

Richard I *the Lion-Heart* (French *Coeur-de-Lion*) 1157–1199. King of England from 1189, who spent all but six months of his reign abroad. He was the third son of Henry II, against whom he twice rebelled. In the third ◊Crusade 1191–92 he won victories at Cyprus, Acre, and Arsuf (against ◊Saladin), but failed to recover Jerusalem. While returning overland he was captured by the Duke of Austria, who handed him over to the emperor Henry VI, and he was held prisoner until a large ransom was raised. He then returned briefly to England, where his brother John I had been ruling in his stead. His later years were spent in warfare in France, where he was killed.

As regards his kingdom and rank he was inferior to the king of France but he outstripped him in wealth, in valour, and in fame as a soldier.

On *Richard I* Beha al-Din 1190

Richard II 1367–1400. King of England from 1377, effectively from 1389, son of Edward the Black Prince. He reigned in conflict with Parliament; they executed some of his associates 1388, and he executed some of the opposing barons 1397, whereupon he made himself absolute. Two years later, forced to abdicate in favour of ◊Henry IV, he was jailed and probably assassinated.

Richard was born in Bordeaux. He succeeded his grandfather Edward III when only ten, the government being in the hands of a council of regency. His fondness for favourites resulted in conflicts with Parliament, and in 1388 the baronial party headed by the Duke of Gloucester had many of his friends executed. Richard recovered control 1389, and ruled moderately until 1397, when he had Gloucester murdered and his other leading opponents executed or banished, and assumed absolute power. In 1399 his cousin Henry Bolingbroke, Duke of Hereford (later Henry IV), returned from exile to lead a revolt; Richard II was deposed by Parliament and imprisoned in Pontefract Castle, where he died mysteriously.

Richard III 1452–1485. King of England from 1483. The son of Richard, Duke of York, he was created duke of Gloucester by his brother Edward IV, and distinguished himself in the Wars of the ◊Roses. On Edward's death 1483 he became protector to his nephew Edward V, and soon secured the crown for himself on the plea that Edward IV's sons were illegitimate. He proved a capable ruler, but the suspicion that he had murdered Edward V and his brother undermined his popularity. In 1485 Henry, Earl of Richmond (later ◊Henry VII), raised a rebellion, and Richard III was defeated and killed at ◊Bosworth.

Richelieu Armand Jean du Plessis de 1585–1642. French cardinal and politician, chief minister from 1624. He aimed to make the monarchy absolute; he ruthlessly crushed opposition by the nobility and destroyed the political power of the ◊Huguenots, while leaving them religious freedom. Abroad, he sought to establish French supremacy by breaking the power of the Habsburgs; he therefore supported the Swedish king Gustavus Adolphus and the German Protestant princes against Austria and in 1635 brought France into the Thirty Years' War.

Born in Paris of a noble family, he entered the church and was created bishop of Luçon 1606 and a cardinal 1622. Through the influence of ◊Marie de' Medici he became ◊Louis XIII's chief minister 1624, a position he retained until his death. His secretary Père ◊Joseph was the original Grey Eminence.

Nothing is as dangerous for the state as those who would govern kingdoms with maxims found in books.

Cardinal Richelieu *Political Testament* 1687

Ridley Nicholas *c.* 1500–1555. English Protestant bishop. He became chaplain to Henry VIII 1541, and bishop of London 1550. He took an active part in the Reformation and supported Lady Jane Grey's claim to the throne. After Mary's accession he was arrested and burned as a heretic.

Riel Louis 1844–1885. French-Canadian rebel, a champion of the Métis (an Indian-French people); he established a provisional government in Winnipeg in an unsuccessful revolt 1869–70 and was hanged for treason after leading a second revolt in Saskatchewan 1885.

Rienzi Cola di *c.* 1313–1354. Italian political reformer. In 1347, he tried to re-establish the forms of an ancient Roman republic. His second attempt seven years later ended with his assassination.

Riff revolt Moroccan revolt against French and Spanish invaders. See ◊Abd el-Krim.

Rights of Man and the Citizen, Declaration of historic French document. According to the statement of the French National Assembly 1789, these rights include representation in the legislature; equality before the law; equality of opportunity; freedom from arbitrary imprisonment; freedom of speech and religion; taxation in proportion to ability to pay; and security of property. In 1946 were added equal rights for women; right to work, join a union, and strike; leisure, social security, and support in old age; and free education.

right wing the more conservative or reactionary section of a political party or spectrum. It originated in the French national assembly 1789, where the nobles sat in the place of honour on the president's right, whereas the commons were on his left (hence ◊left wing).

Rinzai (Chinese *Lin-ch'i*) school of Zen Buddhism introduced to Japan from China in the 12th century by the monk Eisai and others. It emphasizes rigorous monastic discipline and sudden enlightenment by meditation on a *kōan* (paradoxical question).

Riot Act in the UK, act of Parliament passed 1714 to suppress the ◊Jacobite disorders. If three or more persons assembled unlawfully to the disturbance of the public peace, a magistrate could read a proclamation ordering them to disperse ('reading the Riot Act'), after which they might be dispersed by force. It was superseded by the Public Order Act 1986.

Risorgimento movement for Italian national unity and independence from 1815. Leading figures in the movement included ◊Cavour, ◊Mazzini, and ◊Garibaldi. Uprisings 1848–49 failed, but with help from France in a war against Austria – to oust it from Italian provinces in the north – an Italian kingdom was founded 1861. Unification was finally completed with the addition of Venetia 1866 and the Papal States 1870.

Rivadavia Bernardino 1780–1845. Argentine politician, first president of Argentina 1826–27. During his rule he made a number of social reforms including extending the franchise to all males over 20 and encouraging freedom of the press. Unable to control the provincial ◊caudillos, he was forced to resign and spent most of his remaining years in exile in Europe.

Rivadavia was secretary to the revolutionary junta 1811–12 and a minister in the Rodríguez administration 1820–23. War with Brazil over Uruguay 1825–28 forced him to call the congress which wrote the central constitution 1826, and elected him to the presidency. An enigmatic and controversial figure, he is variously regarded as a democrat, republican, monarchist, and traitor.

Rivera José Fructuoso *c.* 1788–1854. Uruguayan general and politician, president 1830–34, 1839–43. Rivera fought under José ◊Artigas and submitted to Brazilian occupation before rejoining the revolution 1825. When he became president his financial mismanagement and favouritism provoked open dissent. He led a revolt 1836 against his successor Manuel Oribe (1792–1857), during which he became the focus of the Colorado Party. During his second term in office he declared war on Argentina, and besieged Montevideo, but was exiled following dissent within his own party 1847.

Rivonia trial court proceedings begun Oct 1963 in South Africa against a group of ten people, including Walter ◊Sisulu and Nelson ◊Mandela. They were accused of sabotage and conspiracy to overthrow the South African government, and nine were found guilty and sentenced to life imprisonment June 1964.

The accused, senior ◊African National Congress officials and leaders of the multi-racial terrorist organization Umkhonto we Sizwe (Spear of the Nation), an offshoot of the African National Congress, were arrested July 1963 at Lilliesleaf Farm outside Rivonia near Johannesburg.

Rizzio David 1533–1566. Italian adventurer at the court of Mary Queen of Scots. After her marriage to ◊Darnley, Rizzio's influence over her incited her husband's jealousy, and he was murdered by Darnley and his friends.

Robert two dukes of Normandy:

Robert I *the Devil* died 1035. Duke of Normandy from 1027. Also known as *The Magnificent*, he was the father of William the Conqueror, and was legendary for his cruelty. He became duke after the death of his brother Richard III, in which he may have been implicated.

Robert II *c.* 1054–1134. Eldest son of ◊William I (the Conqueror), succeeding him as duke of Normandy (but not on the English throne) 1087. His brother ◊William II ascended the English throne, and they warred until 1096, after which Robert took part in the First Crusade. When his other brother ◊Henry I claimed the English throne 1100, Robert contested the claim and invaded England unsuccessfully 1101. Henry invaded Normandy 1106, and captured Robert, who remained a prisoner in England until his death.

Robert three kings of Scotland:

Robert I *Robert the Bruce* 1274–1329. King of Scotland from 1306, and grandson of Robert de ◊Bruce. He shared in the national uprising led by William ◊Wallace, and, after Wallace's execution 1305, rose once more against Edward I of England, and was crowned at Scone 1306. He defeated Edward II at ◊Bannockburn 1314. In 1328 the treaty of Northampton recognized Scotland's independence and Robert as king.

Robert II 1316–1390. King of Scotland from 1371. He was the son of Walter (1293–1326), steward of Scotland, who married Marjory, daughter of Robert I. He was the first king of the house of Stuart.

Robert III *c.* 1340–1406. King of Scotland from 1390, son of Robert II. He was unable to control the nobles, and the government fell largely into the hands of his brother, Robert, Duke of Albany (*c.* 1340–1420).

Robert Guiscard *c.* 1015–1085. Norman adventurer and duke of Apulia. Robert, also known as 'the wizard', carved out a fiefdom centred on Apulia in southern Italy, of which he became duke 1059. By 1071 he had forced the Byzantines from southern Italy and the ◊Arabs from Sicily, establishing his younger brother Roger as count and laying the foundations for the Norman kingdom of Sicily. He imposed a centralized feudal state over an ethnically diverse realm, and was a great patron of the Catholic church.

Any institution that does not suppose the people good, and the magistrate corruptible, is evil.

Maximilien Robespierre
Déclaration des Droits de l'Homme 1793

Roberts Frederick Sleigh ('Bobs'), 1st Earl Roberts 1832–1914. British field marshal. During the Afghan War of 1878–80 he occupied Kabul, and during the Second South African War 1899–1902 he made possible the annexation of the Transvaal and Orange Free State.

Born in India, Roberts joined the Bengal Artillery in 1851, and served through the ◊Indian Mutiny, receiving the VC, and the Abyssinian campaign of 1867–68. After serving in Afghanistan and making a victorious march to Kandahar, he became commander in chief in India 1885–93 and in Ireland 1895–99. He then received the command in South Africa, where he occupied Bloemfontein and Pretoria.

Robespierre Maximilien François Marie Isidore de 1758–1794. French politician in the ◊French Revolution. As leader of the ◊Jacobins in the National Convention, he supported the execution of Louis XVI and the overthrow of the right-wing republican Girondins, and in July 1793 was elected to the Committee of Public Safety. A year later he was guillotined; many believe that he was a scapegoat for the Reign of ◊Terror since he ordered only 72 executions personally.

Robespierre, a lawyer, was elected to the National Assembly of 1789–91. His defence of democratic principles made him popular in Paris, while his disinterestedness won him the nickname of 'the Incorruptible'. His zeal for social reform and his attacks on the excesses of the extremists made him enemies on both right and left; a conspiracy was formed against him, and in July 1794 he was overthrown and executed by those who actually perpetrated the Reign of Terror.

Rob Roy nickname of Robert MacGregor 1671–1734. Scottish Highland ◊Jacobite outlaw. After losing his estates, he lived by cattle theft and extortion. Captured, he was sentenced to transportation but pardoned 1727. He is a central character in Walter Scott's historical novel *Rob Roy* 1817.

Rockingham Charles Watson Wentworth, 2nd Marquess of Rockingham 1730–1782. British Whig politician, prime minister 1765–66 and 1782 (when he died in office); he supported the American claim to independence.

Rodney George Brydges Rodney, Baron Rodney 1718–1792. British admiral. In 1762 he captured Martinique, St Lucia, and Grenada from the French. In 1780 he relieved Gibraltar by defeating a Spanish squadron off Cape St Vincent. In 1782 he crushed the French fleet under Count de Grasse off Dominica, for which he was raised to the peerage.

Roger II 1095–1154. King of Sicily from 1130. The second son of Count Roger I of Sicily (1031–1101), by the time he was crowned king on the authority of Pope Innocent II (died 1143) he had achieved mastery over the whole of Norman Italy. He used his navy to conquer Malta and territories in North Africa, and to harass Byzantine possessions in the eastern Mediterranean. His Palermo court was a major cultural centre where Latin, Greek, and Arab scholars mixed freely.

Röhm Ernst 1887–1934. German leader of the Nazi Brownshirts, the SA (◊Sturmabteilung). On the pretext of an intended SA *Putsch* (uprising) by the Brownshirts, the Nazis had some hundred of them, including Röhm, killed 29–30 June 1934. The event is known as the ◊Night of the Long Knives.

Rollo First duke of Normandy *c.* 860–932. Viking leader. He left Norway about 875 and marauded, sailing up the Seine to Rouen. He besieged Paris 886, and in 912 was baptized and granted the province of Normandy by Charles III of France. He was its duke until his retirement to a monastery 927. He was an ancestor of William the Conqueror.

Roman Britain period in British history from the mid-1st century BC to the mid-4th century AD. England was rapidly Romanized, but north of York fewer remains of Roman civilization have been found. Roman towns include London, York, Chester, St Albans, Colchester, Lincoln, Gloucester, and Bath. The most enduring mark of the occupation was the system of military roads radiating from London.

Roman relations with Britain began with Caesar's invasions of 55 and 54 BC, but the actual conquest was not begun until AD 43. After several unsuccessful attempts to conquer Scotland the northern frontier was fixed at ◊Hadrian's Wall. During the 4th century Britain was raided by the Saxons, Picts, and Scots.

Roman Catholicism one of the main divisions of the Christian religion, separate from the Eastern Orthodox Church from 1054, and headed by the pope. For history and beliefs, see ◊Christianity. Membership is about 585 million worldwide, concentrated in S Europe, Latin America, and the Philippines.

Romania country in SE Europe, bounded N and E by Ukraine, E by Moldova, SE by the Black Sea, S by Bulgaria, SW by Yugoslavia, and NW by Hungary.

history The earliest known inhabitants merged with invaders from ◊Thrace. Ancient Rome made it the province of Dacia; the poet Ovid was one of the settlers, and the people and language were Romanized. After the withdrawal of the Romans AD 275, Romania was occupied by ◊Goths, and during the 6th–12th centuries was overrun by ◊Huns, Bulgars, ◊Slavs, and other invaders. The principalities of Wallachia in the south, and Moldavia in the east, dating from the 14th century, fell to the ◊Ottoman Empire in the 15th and 16th centuries.

Turkish rule was exchanged for Russian protection 1829–56. In 1859 Moldavia and Wallachia elected Prince Alexander Cuza, under whom they were united as Romania from 1861. He was deposed 1866 and Prince Charles of Hohenzollern-Sigmaringen elected. After the Russo-Turkish war 1877–78, in which Romania sided with Russia, the great powers recognized Romania's independence, and in 1881 Prince Charles became King Carol I.

after independence Romania fought against Bulgaria in the Second ◊Balkan War 1913 and annexed S Dobruja. It entered World War I on the Allied side 1916, was occupied by the Germans 1917–18, but received Bessarabia from Russia and ◊Bukovina and ◊Transylvania from the dismembered Habsburg empire under the 1918 peace settlement, thus emerging as the largest state in the Balkans. During the late 1930s, to counter the growing popularity of the fascist ◊Iron Guard movement, ◊Carol II abolished the democratic constitution of 1923 and established his own dictatorship.

World War II In 1940 he was forced to surrender Bessarabia and N Bukovina to the USSR, N Transylvania to Hungary, and S Dobruja to Bulgaria, and abdicated when Romania was occupied by Germany in Aug. Power was assumed by Ion Antonescu (1882–1946, ruling in the name of Carol's son King ◊Michael), who signed the Axis Pact Nov 1940 and declared war on the USSR June 1941. In Aug 1944, with the Red Army on Romania's borders, King Michael supported the ousting of the Antonescu government by a coalition of left and centre parties, including the communists. Romania subsequently joined the war against Germany and in the Paris peace treaties 1947 recovered Transylvania but lost Bessarabia and N Bukovina to the USSR (they were included in Moldavia and the Ukraine) and S Dobruja to Bulgaria.

republic In the elections 1946 a Communist-led coalition achieved a majority and proceeded to force King Michael to abdicate. The new Romanian People's Republic was proclaimed Dec 1947 and dominated by the Romanian Communist Party, then termed the Romanian Workers' Party (RWP). Soviet-style constitutions were adopted 1948 and 1952; Romania joined ◊Comecon 1949 and co-signed the ◊Warsaw Pact 1955; and a programme of nationalization and agricultural collectivization was launched. After a rapid purge of opposition leaders, the RWP became firmly established in power, enabling Soviet occupation forces to leave the country 1958.

Ceauşescu era The dominant political personality 1945–65 was RWP leader and state president Gheorghe ◊Gheorghiu- Dej. He was succeeded by Nicolae ◊Ceauşescu, who placed greater emphasis on national autonomy and proclaimed Romania a socialist republic. Under Ceauşescu, Romania adopted a foreign-policy line independent of the USSR, condemned the 1968 invasion of Czechoslovakia, and refused to participate directly in Warsaw Pact manoeuvres or allow Russian troops to enter the country. Ceauşescu called for multilateral nuclear disarmament and the creation of a Balkan nuclear-weapons-free zone and maintained warm relations with China. He was created president 1974.

austerity programme At home, the secret police (Securitate) maintained a tight Stalinist rein on dissident activities, while a Ceauşescu personality cult was propagated, with almost 40 members of the president's extended family, including his wife Elena and son Nicu, occupying senior party and state positions. Economic difficulties mounted as Ceauşescu, pledging himself to repay the country's accumulated foreign debt (achieved 1989), embarked on an austerity programme. This led to food shortages and widespread power cuts in the winters from 1985 onwards; the army occupied power plants and brutally crushed workers' demonstrations in Braşov 1987.

relations with neighbours From 1985 Ceauşescu refused to follow the path of political and economic reform laid by Soviet leader Mikhail Gorbachev, even calling in the spring of 1989 for Warsaw Pact nations to intervene to prevent the opposition Solidarity movement from assuming power in Poland. Romania's relations with Hungary also reached crisis point 1988– 89 as a result of a Ceauşescu 'systematization plan' to demolish 7,000 villages and replace them with 500 agro-industrial complexes, in the process forcibly resettling and assimilating Transylvania-based ethnic Hungarians.

overthrow of Ceauşescu The unexpected overthrow of the Ceauşescu regime began Dec 1989. It was sparked off by the government's plans to exile a dissident Protestant pastor, László Tökes (1952–   ), to a remote village. Ethnic Hungarians and Romanians joined forces in the city of Timişoara to form an anti-Ceauşescu protest movement. Hundreds of demonstrators were killed in the state's subsequent crackdown on 17 Dec. Four days later, an officially sponsored rally in Bucharest backfired when the crowd chanted anti-Ceauşescu slogans. Divisions between the military and Securitate rapidly emerged and on 22 Dec the army Chief of Staff, General Stefan Gusa, turned against the president and called on his soldiers to 'defend the uprising'. Ceauşescu attempted to flee, but was caught and summarily tried and executed on Christmas Day.

National Salvation Front Battles between Ceauşescu-loyal Securitate members and the army ensued in Bucharest, with several thousand being killed, but the army seizing the upper hand. A National Salvation Front was established, embracing former dissident intellectuals, reform communists, and military leaders. At its head was Ion Iliescu (1930–), a Moscow-trained communist; Petre Roman (1947–), an engineer without political experience, was appointed prime minister. The Front's council proceeded to relegalize the formation of alternative political parties and draft a new constitution. Faced with grave economic problems, it initiated a ban on the export of foodstuffs, the abandonment of the 'systematization programme', the dissolution of the Securitate (a new intelligence service, accountable to parliament, was set up in its place), the abolition of the RCP's leading role, and the relegalization of small-plot farming and abortion (all contraception had been banned by Ceauşescu). It legalized the Eastern Orthodox Church, and the Vatican re-established diplomatic relations.

market economy In May 1990 Ion Iliescu won the country's first free elections since World War II. Moving towards a legal market economy, the government cut subsidies, the leu was devalued, and prices were allowed to float. Industrial exports slumped and strikes and protests increased until the government agreed to postpone its price-liberalization programme. Refugees continued to leave the country and there were demonstrations against the government during Dec 1990 and Jan 1991, especially in Timişoara and Bucharest.

The second stage of price liberalization commenced April 1991, despite trade-union protests against the sharply rising cost of living and level of unemployment (over one million). At the same time the leu was devalued by 72% to meet the loan conditions set by the International Monetary Fund. President Iliescu signed a law in Aug to allow for the privatization of all state enterprises except utilities. In Nov 1991 the leu was made internally convertible. Prices rose 400% during 1991 and hundreds of thousands were on short-time work. GNP fell during 1991 to 12%.

In late Sept 1991 prime minister Petre Roman resigned after three days of riots in Bucharest by thousands of striking miners, protesting against soaring prices and a fall in their living standards. Theodor Stolojan, the finance minister and a proponent of accelerated price liberalization, was appointed prime minister. He formed a new, cross-party coalition government in Oct 1991.

A new treaty on cooperation and good-neighbourliness was signed 1991 with the USSR, which obliged the two states 'not to take part in any type of alliance directed against either of them'.

new constitution A national referendum Dec 1991 overwhelmingly endorsed a new constitution which guaranteed pluralism, human rights, and a free market. This cleared the path for a general election in 1992, which Iliescu won despite more than 3 million votes being declared invalid.

Romanov dynasty rulers of Russia from 1613 to the ◊Russian Revolution 1917. Under the Romanovs, Russia developed into an absolutist empire.

Rome (Italian *Roma*) capital of Italy and of Lazio region, on the river Tiber, 27 km/17 mi from the Tyrrhenian Sea. (For early history see ◊Rome, ancient.)

After the deposition of the last emperor, Romulus Augustulus 476, the papacy became the real ruler of Rome and from the 8th century was recognized as such. As a result of the French Revolution, Rome temporarily became a republic 1798-99, and was annexed to the French Empire 1808–14, until the pope returned on Napoleon's fall. During the 1848–49 revolution, a republic was established under Mazzini's leadership but, in spite of Garibaldi's defence, was overthrown by French troops.

In 1870 Rome became the capital of Italy, the pope retiring into the Vatican until 1929 when the Vatican City was recognized as a sovereign state. The occupation of Rome by the Fascists 1922 marked the beginning of Mussolini's rule, but in 1943 Rome was occupied by Germany and then captured by the Allies 1944.

Rome, ancient civilization based in Rome, which lasted for about 800 years. Traditionally founded 753 BC, Rome became a republic 510 BC. From then, its history is one of almost continual expansion until the murder of Julius ◊Caesar and foundation of the empire under ◊Augustus and his successors. At its peak under ◊Trajan, the Roman Empire stretched from Britain to Mesopotamia and the Caspian Sea. A long train of emperors ruling by virtue of military, rather than civil, power marked the beginning of Rome's long decline; under ◊Diocletian, the empire was divided into two parts – East and West – although temporarily reunited under ◊Constantine, the first emperor

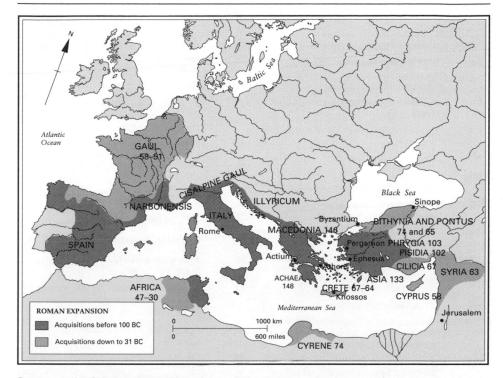

Roman expansion Sicily became the first Roman province 227 BC. In 197 two provinces were acquired in Spain. The defeat of Macedon in 168 led finally to the incorporation of Greece, and the Attalids bequeathed Pergamum to Rome 133. Roman involvement in Gaul began with the tribes in the Po valley, and extended to the Rhone valley. Julius Caesar conquered Gaul 58–51. The break-up of the eastern Seleucid Empire resulted in further conquests after 163. Cyrene was bequeathed by Egypt to Rome, and Crete later united to it. Caesar increased the empire's African possessions by adding Numidia to Carthage.

formally to adopt Christianity. The end of the Roman Empire is generally dated by the deposition of the last emperor in the west AD 476. The Eastern Empire continued until 1453 (see ◊Byzantine Empire).

The civilization of ancient Rome occupied first the Italian peninsula, then most of Europe, the Middle East, and North Africa. It influenced the whole of western Europe throughout the Middle Ages, the Renaissance, and beyond, in the fields of art and architecture, literature, law, and engineering, and through continued use by scholars of its language, Latin.

Rome–Berlin Axis another name for the ◊Axis.

Rome–Berlin–Tokyo Axis another name for the ◊Axis.

Rome, Sack of AD 410. The invasion and capture of the city of Rome by the Goths, generally accepted as marking the effective end of the Roman Empire.

Rome, Treaties of two international agreements signed 25 March 1957 by Belgium, France, West Germany, Italy, Luxembourg,

and the Netherlands, which established the European Economic Community (◊European Community) and the European Atomic Energy Commission (EURATOM).

The terms of the economic treaty, which came into effect 1 Jan 1958, provided for economic cooperation, reduction (and eventual removal) of customs barriers, and the free movement of capital, goods, and labour between the member countries, together with common agricultural and trading policies. Subsequent new members of the European Community have been obliged to accept these terms.

The ordinary soldier has a surprisingly good nose for what is true and what is false.

Field Marshal Erwin Rommel

Rommel Erwin 1891–1944. German field marshal. He served in World War I, and in World War II he played an important part in the

Ancient Rome

753 BC According to tradition, Rome was founded.

510 The Etruscan dynasty of the Tarquins was expelled and a republic established, with power concentrated in patrician hands.

450 Publication of the law code contained in the Twelve Tables.

396 Capture of Etruscan Veii, 15 km/9 mi N of Rome.

387 Rome sacked by Gauls.

367 Plebeians gained the right to be consuls (the two chief magistrates, elected annually).

343–290 Sabines to the N, and the Samnites to the SE, were conquered.

338 Cities of Latium formed into a league under Roman control.

280–272 Greek cities in S Italy subdued.

264–241 First Punic War against Carthage, ending in a Roman victory and the annexation of Sicily.

238 Sardinia seized from Carthage.

226–222 Roman conquest of Cisalpine Gaul (Lombardy, Italy). More conflict with Carthage, which was attempting to conquer Spain.

218 Second Punic War. Hannibal crossed the Alps and invaded Italy, winning a series of brilliant victories.

202 Victory of General Scipio Africanus Major over Hannibal at Zama was followed by the surrender of Carthage and relinquishing of its Spanish colonies.

188 Peace of Apamea confined the rule of the Seleucid king Antiochus the Great to Asia.

168 Final defeat of Macedon by Rome.

146 After a revolt, Greece became in effect a Roman province. Carthage was destroyed and its territory annexed.

133 Tiberius Gracchus suggested agrarian reforms and was murdered by the senatorial party. Roman province of Asia formed from the kingdom of Pergamum, bequeathed to Rome by the Attalid dynasty.

123 Tiberius' policy adopted by his brother Gaius Gracchus, who was likewise murdered.

91–88 Social War: revolt by the Italian cities forced Rome to grant citizenship to all Italians.

87 While Sulla was repelling an invasion of Greece by King Mithridates of Pontus (in Asia Minor), Marius seized power.

82–79 Sulla returned and established a dictatorship ruled by terror.

70 Sulla's constitutional changes were reversed by Pompey and Crassus.

66–63 Pompey defeated Mithridates and annexed Syria.

60 The First Triumvirate was formed, an alliance between Pompey and the democratic leaders Crassus and Caesar.

51 Caesar conquered Gaul as far as the Rhine.

49 Caesar crossed the Rubicon, returned to Italy and a civil war between him and Pompey's senatorial party began.

48 Pompey defeated at Pharsalus.

44 Caesar's dictatorship ended by his assassination.

43 Second Triumvirate formed by Octavian, Mark Antony and Lepidus.

32 War between Octavian and Mark Antony.

31 Mark Antony defeated at Actium.

30 Egypt was annexed after the deaths of Mark Antony and Cleopatra.

27 Octavian took the name Augustus. He was by now absolute ruler, though in title he was only *princeps* (first citizen).

AD 14 Augustus died. Tiberius proclaimed as his successor.

43 Claudius added Britain to the empire.

70 Jerusalem sacked by Titus.

96–180 The empire enjoyed a golden age under the Flavian and Antonine emperors Nerva, Trajan, Hadrian, Antoninus Pius, and Marcus Aurelius.

115 Trajan conquered Parthia, achieving the peak of Roman territorial expansion.

180 Marcus Aurelius died, and a century of war and disorder followed, with a succession of generals being put on the throne by their armies.

212 Caracalla granted citizenship to the communities of the empire.

284–305 Diocletian reorganized the empire, dividing power between himself and three others (the Tetrarchy).

313 Constantine I recognized the Christians' right to freedom of worship by the Edict of Milan.

330 Constantine made Constantinople his new imperial capital.

395 The empire divided into eastern and western parts.

410 Visigoths sacked Rome. Roman legions withdrew from Britain.

451–52 Huns raided Gaul and Italy.

455 Vandals sacked Rome.

476 Last Western emperor, Romulus Augustulus, deposed.

invasions of central Europe and France. He was commander of the N African offensive from 1941 (when he was nicknamed 'Desert Fox') until defeated in the Battles of El Alamein.

Rommel was commander in chief for a short time against the Allies in Europe 1944 but (as a sympathizer with the ◊Stauffenberg plot against Hitler) was forced to commit suicide.

Romulus Augustulus born *c.* AD 461. last Roman emperor in the West. He was made emperor by his father the patrician Orestes, about 475 but was compelled to abdicate 476 by Odoacer, leader of the barbarian mercenaries, who nicknamed him Augustulus. The date of his death is unknown.

rōnin (Japanese 'wave man') in Japanese history, a ◊samurai who had no allegiance to a feudal lord. Especially numerous in the 16th century, many of them engaged in brigandage and in 1651 they were were responsible for an unsuccessful rebellion.

Roosevelt (Anna) Eleanor 1884–1962. US social worker, lecturer, and First Lady; her newspaper column 'My Day' was widely syndicated. She influenced ◊New Deal policies, especially supporting desegregation. She was a delegate to the UN general assembly and chair of the UN commission on human rights 1946–51, and helped to draw up the Declaration of Human Rights at the UN 1945. She was married to President Franklin Roosevelt.

Roosevelt Franklin D(elano) 1882–1945. 32nd president of the USA 1933–45, a Democrat. He served as governor of New York 1929–33. Becoming president during the Great ◊Depression, he launched the ◊*New Deal* economic and social reform programme, which made him popular with the people. After the outbreak of World War II he introduced ◊lend-lease for the supply of war materials and services to the Allies and drew up the ◊Atlantic Charter of solidarity. Once the USA had entered the war 1941, he spent much time in meetings with Allied leaders (see ◊Québec, ◊Tehran, and ◊Yalta conferences).

When he first became president 1933, Roosevelt inculcated a new spirit of hope by his skilful 'fireside chats' on the radio and his inaugural-address statement: 'The only thing we have to fear is fear itself.' Surrounding himself by a 'Brain Trust' of experts, he immediately launched his reform programme. Banks were reopened, federal credit was restored, the gold standard was abandoned, and the dollar devalued. During the first hundred days of his administration, major legislation to facilitate industrial and agricultural recovery

was enacted. In 1935 he introduced the Utilities Act, directed against abuses in the large holding companies, and the Social Security Act, providing for disability and retirement insurance. The presidential election 1936 was won entirely on the record of the New Deal. During 1935–36 Roosevelt was involved in a conflict over the composition of the Supreme Court, following its nullification of major New Deal measures as unconstitutional. In 1938 he introduced measures for farm relief and the improvement of working conditions.

In his foreign policy, Roosevelt endeavoured to use his influence to restrain Axis aggression, and to establish 'good neighbor' relations with other countries in the Americas. Soon after the outbreak of war, he launched a vast rearmament programme, introduced conscription, and provided for the supply of armaments to the Allies on a 'cash-and-carry' basis. In spite of strong isolationist opposition, he broke a long- standing precedent in running for a third term; he was re-elected 1940. He announced that the USA would become the 'arsenal of democracy'. Roosevelt was eager for US entry into the war on behalf of the Allies. In addition to his revulsion for Hitler, he wanted to establish the USA as a world power, filling the vacuum he expected to be left by the breakup of the British Empire. He was restrained by isolationist forces in Congress, and some argued that he welcomed the Japanese attack on Pearl Harbor.

Public opinion, however, was in favour of staying out of the war, so Roosevelt and the military chiefs deliberately kept back the intelligence reports received from the British and others concerning the imminent Japanese attack on the naval base at Pearl Harbor in Hawaii.

The deaths at Pearl Harbor 7 Dec 1941 incited public opinion, and the USA entered the war. From this point on, Roosevelt concerned himself solely with the conduct of the war. He participated in the Washington 1942 and ◊Casablanca 1943 conferences to plan the Mediterranean assault, and the conferences in Québec, Cairo, and Tehran 1943, and Yalta 1945, at which the final preparations were made for the Allied victory. He was re-elected for a fourth term 1944, but died 1945.

We must be the great arsenal of democracy.

    Franklin D Roosevelt speech 1940

Roosevelt Theodore 1858–1919. 26th president of the USA 1901–09, a Republican. After serving as governor of New York 1898–1900 he became vice president to ◊McKinley, whom he succeeded as president on McKinley's assassination 1901. He campaigned against the great trusts (associations of enterprises that reduce competition), while carrying on a jingoist foreign policy designed to enforce US supremacy over Latin America.

At age 42, Roosevelt was the youngest man to become president of the USA. In office he became more liberal. He tackled business monopolies, initiated measures for the conservation of national resources, and introduced the Pure Food and Drug Act. He won the Nobel Peace Prize 1906 for his part in ending the Russo-Japanese war. Alienated after his retirement by the conservatism of his successor Taft, Roosevelt formed the Progressive or 'Bull Moose' Party. As their candidate he unsuccessfully ran for the presidency 1912. During World War I he strongly advocated US intervention.

Rosas Juan Manuel de 1793–1877. Argentine soldier, gaucho (cowboy) and dictator 1835–52. Rosas used his private gaucho army to overthrow the Liberal regime of Bernardino ◊Rivadavia 1827. A Buenos Aires Federalist, he was governor of that city 1829–32 and, when he was also dictator of Argentina, presided over a reign of terror. While appealing to the urban masses, huge land sales at absurdly low prices benefited the landed aristocracy, including Rosas' wealthy Creole family. A manipulative and ruthless operator against centralists, once he became dictator Rosas began a cult of personality which included his image being displayed on church altars. Rosas supported the Uruguayan Blancos led by Manuel Oribe (1792– 1857) by besieging Montevideo for nine years from 1843. This led to his downfall when a key henchman, Justo José de Urquiza, changed sides and relieved the city 1852. Rosas spent the rest of his life in Britain.

Rosebery Archibald Philip Primrose, 5th Earl of Rosebery 1847–1929. British Liberal politician. He was foreign secretary 1886 and 1892–94, when he succeeded Gladstone as prime minister, but his government survived less than a year. After 1896 his imperialist views gradually placed him further from the mainstream of the Liberal Party.

Rosenberg Alfred 1893–1946. German politician, born in Tallinn, Estonia. He became the chief Nazi ideologist and was minister for eastern occupied territories 1941–44. He was tried at ◊Nuremberg 1946 as a war criminal and hanged.

Rosenberg Julius 1918–53 and Ethel Greenglass 1915–53 US married couple, convicted of being leaders of a nuclear-espionage ring passing information from Ethel's brother via courier to the USSR. The Rosenbergs were executed after much public controversy and demonstration. They were the only Americans executed for espionage during peacetime.

Roses, Wars of the civil wars in England 1455–85 between the houses of ◊Lancaster (badge, red rose) and ◊York (badge, white rose), both of whom claimed the throne through descent from the sons of Edward III. As a result of ◊Henry VI's lapse into insanity 1453, Richard, Duke of York, was installed as protector of the realm. Upon his recovery, Henry forced York to take up arms in self-defence.

1455 Opened with battle of St Albans 22 May, a Yorkist victory.

1459–61 War renewed. Richard, Duke of York, killed in 1460, but his son Edward IV, having been proclaimed king, confirmed his position by a victory at Towton 29 March 1461.

1470 Warwick (who had helped Edward to the throne) allied instead with Henry VI's queen, Margaret of Anjou; Henry VI restored to the throne.

1471 Edward returned, defeated Warwick at Barnet 14 April and Margaret at Tewkesbury 4 May, her son killed, and her forces destroyed. Henry VI was murdered in the Tower of London.

1485 Yorkist regime ended with the defeat of Richard III by the future Henry VII at Bosworth 22 Aug.

The name Wars of the Roses was given in the 19th century by novelist Walter Scott.

Rosetta Stone slab of basalt with inscriptions from 197 BC, found near the town of Rosetta, Egypt, 1799. Giving the same text in three versions – Greek, hieroglyphic, and demotic script – it became the key to deciphering other Egyptian inscriptions.

Discovered during the French Revolutionary Wars by one of Napoleon's officers in the town now called Rashid, in the Nile delta, the Rosetta Stone was captured by the British 1801, and placed in the British Museum 1802. Demotic is a cursive script (for quick writing) derived from Egyptian hieratic, which in turn is a more easily written form of hieroglyphic.

rotten borough English parliamentary constituency, before the Great Reform Act 1832, that returned members to Parliament in spite of having small numbers of electors. Such a borough could easily be manipulated by those with sufficient money or influence.

Roundhead member of the Parliamentary party during the English Civil War 1640–60, opposing the royalist Cavaliers. The term referred to the short hair then worn only by men of the lower classes.

Rousseau Jean-Jacques 1712–1778. French social philosopher and writer whose *Du Contrat social*/*Social Contract* 1762, emphasizing the rights of the people over those of the government, was a significant influence on the French Revolution. In the novel *Emile* 1762 he outlined a new theory of education.

I hate books, for they only teach people to talk about what they do not understand.

Jean-Jacques Rousseau *Emile* 1762

Rowbotham Sheila 1943–   . British socialist, feminist, historian, lecturer, and writer. Her pamphlet *Women's Liberation and the New Politics* 1970 laid down fundamental approaches and demands of the emerging women's movement. Rowbotham taught in schools and then became involved with the Workers' Educational Association.

Rowlatt Bills in India 1919, peacetime extensions of restrictions introduced during World War I to counter the perceived threat of revolution. The planned legislation would inhibit individual rights and allow the Indian administration to arrest and detain people without a warrant. The bills were vigorously opposed by Indian nationalists, and the young Congress Party leader Mohandas ◊Gandhi called for a nationwide campaign for their repeal. Only one of the two bills was enacted, but it was never used and was later repealed.

Rowntree Benjamin Seebohm 1871–1954. British entrepreneur and philanthropist. Much of the money he acquired as chair (1925–41) of the family firm of confectioners, H I Rowntree, he used to fund investigations into social conditions. His writings include *Poverty, A Study of Town Life* 1900. The three *Rowntree Trusts*, which were founded by his father *Joseph Rowntree* (1836–1925) in 1904, fund research into housing, social care, and social policy, support projects relating to social justice, and give grants to pressure groups working in these areas.

Roy Manabendra Nakh 1887–1954. Founder of the Indian Communist Party in exile in Tashkent 1920. Expelled from the Comintern 1929, he returned to India and was imprisoned for five years. A steadfast communist, he finally became disillusioned after World War II and developed his ideas on practical humanism.

Rozwi Empire or *Changamire* highly advanced empire in southeast Africa, located S of the Zambezi river and centred around the stone city of Great Zimbabwe. It replaced the gold-trading empire of Mwene Mutapa from the 15th century. The Rozwi Empire survived until the ◊Mfecane of the 1830s, when overpopulation to the south drove the Nguni and Ndebele people northwards into Rozwi territory in search of more land.

Roy Manabendra Nakh 1887–1954. Founder of the Indian Communist Party in exile in Tashkent 1920. Expelled from the Comintern 1929, he returned to India and was imprisoned for five years. A steadfast communist, he finally became disillusioned after World War II and developed his ideas on practical humanism.

Rubicon ancient name of the small river flowing into the Adriatic which, under the Roman Republic, marked the boundary between Italy proper and Cisalpine Gaul. When ◊Caesar led his army across it 49 BC he therefore declared war on the republic. The Rubicon is believed to be the present-day *Fiumicino*, which flows into the Adriatic just N of Rimini.

Rudolph 1858–1889. Crown prince of Austria, the only son of Emperor Franz Joseph. In 1889 he and his mistress, Baroness Marie Vetsera, were found shot in his hunting lodge at Mayerling, near Vienna. The official verdict was suicide, although there were rumours that it was perpetrated by Jesuits, Hungarian nobles, or the baroness's husband.

Rudolph two Holy Roman emperors:

Rudolph I 1218–1291. Holy Roman emperor from 1273. Originally count of Habsburg, he was the first Habsburg emperor and expanded his dynasty by investing his sons with the duchies of Austria and Styria.

Rudolph II 1552–1612. Holy Roman emperor from 1576, when he succeeded his father Maximilian II. His policies led to unrest in Hungary and Bohemia, which led to the surrender of Hungary to his brother Matthias 1608 and religious freedom for Bohemia.

Rump, the English parliament formed between Dec 1648 and Nov 1653 after ◊Pride's purge of the ◊Long Parliament to ensure a majority in favour of trying Charles I. It was dismissed

1653 by Cromwell, who replaced it with the ◊Barebones Parliament.

Reinstated after the Protectorate ended 1659 and the full membership of the Long Parliament restored 1660, the Rump dissolved itself shortly afterwards and was replaced by the Convention Parliament, which brought about the restoration of the monarchy.

Rum Rebellion military insurrection in Australia 1808 when the governor of New South Wales, William ◊Bligh, was deposed by George Johnston, commander of the New South Wales Corps. This was a culmination of attempts by successive governors to curb the power and economic privileges of the Corps, which rested partly on the officers' trade in liquor. Bligh had particularly clashed with John Macarthur and had arrested him on a charge of anti-government incitation. Johnston was persuaded to release Macarthur and then imprisoned the governor.

Rundstedt Karl Rudolf Gerd von 1875–1953. German field marshal in World War II. Largely responsible for the German breakthrough in France 1940, he was defeated on the Ukrainian front 1941. As commander in chief in France from 1942, he resisted the Allied invasion 1944 and in Dec launched the temporarily successful Ardennes offensive.

Rupert Prince 1619–1682. English Royalist general and admiral, born in Prague, son of the Elector Palatine Frederick V (1596–1632) and James I's daughter Elizabeth. Defeated by Cromwell at ◊Marston Moor and ◊Naseby in the Civil War, he commanded a privateering fleet 1649–52, until routed by Admiral Robert Blake, and, returning after the Restoration, was a distinguished admiral in the Dutch Wars. He founded the ◊Hudson's Bay Company.

Rush Benjamin 1745–1813. American physician and public official. Committed to the cause of the American Revolution 1775–83, he was a signatory of the Declaration of Independence 1776 and was named surgeon general of the Continental army 1777.

Russell John, 1st Earl Russell 1792–1878. British Liberal politician, son of the 6th Duke of Bedford. He entered the House of Commons 1813 and supported Catholic emancipation and the Reform Bill. He held cabinet posts 1830–41, became prime minister 1846–52, and was again a cabinet minister until becoming prime minister again 1865–66. He retired after the defeat of his Reform Bill 1866.

As foreign secretary in Aberdeen's coalition 1852 and in Palmerston's second government 1859–65, Russell assisted Italy's struggle for

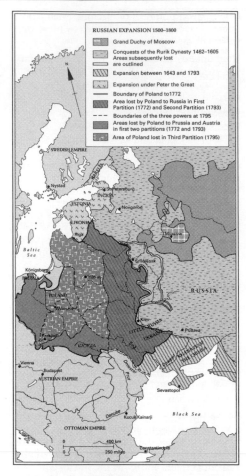

Russian expansion 1500–1800 *The Russian Empire originated in the 15th century with the Grand Duchy of Moscow and was extended by conquest in all directions. Tsar Ivan IV (the Terrible) added Kazan 1552, Astrakhan 1556, and parts of Siberia 1581. Peter the Great added the Baltic states (Livonia, Estonia, and part of Finland) 1721. There was considerable expansion in the late 18th century under the rule of Catherine II (the Great). The Crimea was detached from Ottoman rule and then annexed 1783; the kingdom of Poland was reduced 1772 and absorbed into the empire 1795.*

unity, although his indecisive policies on Poland, Denmark, and the American Civil War provoked much criticism. He had a strained relationship with Palmerston.

Russia originally the pre-revolutionary Russian Empire (until 1917), now accurately restricted to the ◊Russian Federation.

Russian civil war bitter conflict of nearly three years (1918–21) which followed Russian setbacks in World War I and the upheavals of the 1917 Revolution. In Dec 1917 counterrevolu-

Russia: history

9th–10th centuries	Viking chieftains established their own rule in Novgorod, Kiev, and other cities.
10th–12th centuries	Kiev temporarily united the Russian peoples into an empire. Christianity was introduced from Constantinople 988.
13th century	The Mongols (the Golden Horde) overran the southern steppes 1223, compelling the Russian princes to pay tribute.
14th century	Byelorussia and Ukraine came under Polish rule.
1462–1505	Ivan III ('the Great'), prince of Moscow, threw off the Mongol yoke and united the northwest.
1547–84	Ivan IV ('the Terrible') assumed the title of tsar and conquered Kazan and Astrakhan. During his reign the colonization of Siberia began.
1613	The first Romanov tsar, Michael, was elected after a period of chaos.
1667	Following a Cossack revolt, E Ukraine was reunited with Russia.
1682–1725	Peter I ('the Great') modernized the bureaucracy and army. He founded a navy and a new capital, St Petersburg; introduced Western education; and wrested the Baltic seaboard from Sweden. By 1700 the colonization of Siberia had reached the Pacific.
1762–96	Catherine II ('the Great') annexed the Crimea and part of Poland and recovered W Ukraine and White Russia.
1798–1814	Russia intervened in the Revolutionary and Napoleonic Wars (1798–1801, 1805–07) and after repelling Napoleon's invasion, took part in his overthrow (1812–14).
1827–29	War with Turkey resulted from Russian attempts to dominate the Balkans.
1853–56	The Crimean War.
1861	Serfdom was abolished (on terms unfavourable to the peasants). A rapid growth of industry followed, a working-class movement developed, and revolutionary ideas spread, culminating in the assassination of Alexander II 1881.
1898	The Social Democratic Party was founded.
1904–05	The occupation of Manchuria resulted in war with Japan (see Russo-Japanese War).
1905	A revolution, although suppressed, compelled the tsar to accept a parliament (the Duma) with limited powers.
1914	Russo-German rivalries in the Balkans, which had brought Russia into an alliance with France 1895 and Britain 1907, were one of the causes of the outbreak of World War I.
1917	During World War I, the Russian Revolution began.

For subsequent history until 1991, see ◊ Union of Soviet Socialist Republics.

tionary armies, the 'Whites' began to organise resistance to the October Revolution of 1917. The Red Army (Bolsheviks), improvised by Leon Trotsky, opposed them and civil war resulted. Hostilities continued for nearly three years with the Bolsheviks being successful.

The war was fought in the regions of the Caucasus and southern Russia, the Ukraine, the Baltic, northern Russia, and Siberia. The Bolsheviks also had to fight against the armies of Latvia, Lithuania, Estonia, and Finland. In N Russia the British and French landed troops at Murmansk in June 1918, seized Archangel, and set up a puppet government. They continued outbursts of fighting against the Bolsheviks until Oct 1919. In Siberia, Admiral Kolchak, with the assistance of a Czech legion (composed of prisoners of war) and of Japanese forces that had landed at Vladivostok established a 'White' government at Omsk. Kolchak was captured and executed by the Bolsheviks Feb 1920. While each of the 'White' armies was engaged in an isolated operation, the Soviet forces were waging a single war. Trotsky was an active agent for the Bolsheviks in all the crucial operations of the war. The Bolsheviks put down peasant risings in 1920 and a mutiny by sailors at Kronstadt in 1921. The Bolsheviks were far superior to the Whites in both organization and propaganda. The last foreign forces left Soviet soil in 1922 when the Japanese evacuated Vladivostok. The Soviet government was recognized by Britain in 1924, and by the USA in 1933.

Russian Federation or *Russia* country in N Asia and E Europe, bounded N by the Arctic Ocean, E by the Bering Sea and the Sea of Okhotsk, W by Norway, Finland, the Baltic States, Belarus, and Ukraine, and S by China, Mongolia, Georgia, Azerbaijan, and Kazakhstan.

history For pre-1990 history see ◊ Russia, history and ◊ Union of Soviet Socialist Republics. The Russian Federation declared its economic and political sovereignty in June 1990 and began to challenge Soviet authority. The republic held back revenue from the centre, embarked on a strategy of market reform, and established its own independent security and communications structures.

Commonwealth of Independent States formed After the defeat of the coup attempt against Soviet president Gorbachev Aug 1991, the Russian Federation, led by Boris Yeltsin, Russia's first ever popularly elected leader, moved swiftly to break the political-institutional structures that had held together the USSR, in particular the Communist Party of the Soviet

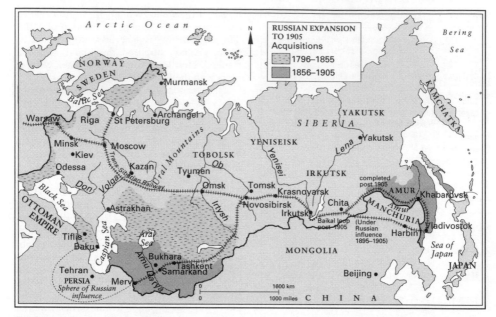

Russian expansion to 1905 *The Russian Empire began an expansion beyond the Ural Mountains into Asiatic Siberia and Central Asia in the 19th century. The opening up of these territories was consolidated at the end of the century by the Trans-Siberian Railway. Expansion to the Pacific brought disputes with the Chinese Empire in Manchuria, and with Japan, a conflict which led to the disastrous Russo-Japanese war of 1904–05. Expansion southwards towards Afghanistan engendered rivalry with the British in India. The formal control established over N Asia allowed for the exploitation of vast economic resources in Russia's quest for industrial growth.*

Union (CPSU). Russia sought to maintain some sort of confederal structure in order that economic ties might continue and territorial disputes be avoided, but was wary of Gorbachev's plan for a reorganized federation. Instead, after Ukraine's independence referendum on 1 Dec 1991, Russia proposed the ◊Commonwealth of Independent States (CIS). The USA officially acknowledged Russia's independence in the same month and accorded it diplomatic recognition, as did the European Community, and admission to the United Nations was granted.

the newly independent republic The Russian Federation contains almost half the population of the former USSR and around 70% of its agricultural and industrial output. It is a vast federation, spanning 11 time zones, stretching 3,000 km/2,000 mi from the Arctic Ocean to China and containing 16 'autonomous republics', five 'autonomous regions' and ten 'autonomous districts', each catering for a distinct non-Russian ethnic group, including Tatars, Chechens, Chuvash, Dagestanis, Buryats, Yakuts, Kalmyks, and Chuchi, and each with its own parliament and laws. After 1990 many of these made sovereignty or independence declara-

tions, most conspicuously the oil-rich and predominantly Muslim Tataria (Tatarstan), where Russia's largest ethnic minority resides, gas-rich Bashkir, Siberian Yakutia, and Checheno-Ingush in the SW, which made integration into the new federation difficult despite Russia's pledge to concede considerable autonomy. The Russian Federation also faced the threat of territorial claims and border conflicts with neighbouring republics.

The new Russian Federation, despite the weakness of its economy, remained a 'great power'. It inherited much of the former USSR's strategic and diplomatic assets, including a permanent seat on the United Nations Security Council (taken up 1992), embassies overseas, and a considerable conventional and nuclear military arsenal. It was admitted into the ◊Conference on Security and Cooperation (CSCE) in Europe Jan 1992.

Despite growing internal frictions, a federal treaty between Yeltsin and the leaders of 18 of Russia's 20 main political subdivisions was signed in March 1992 giving regional governments broad autonomy within a loose Russian Federation. Checheno-Ingush and Tatarstan refused to sign, the latter voting in a referendum for sovereignty within Russia, a move opposed by Yeltsin.

the economy Russia's immediate concern was an economic crisis, leading to riots in nearly a dozen cities Jan 1992. International Monetary Fund (IMF) loans were agreed in 1992, 1993, and 1996 as market reforms continued.

In the first Russian-American summit June 1992, Yeltsin and George Bush agreed a major reduction in strategic nuclear weapons, signing the START-II arms-reduction treaty Dec.

A power struggle between Yeltsin and the Congress of People's Deputies led to Yeltsin's dissolution of parliament Sept 1993. An attempted coup against Yeltsin was foiled. In Dec, parliamentary elections saw large gains by the extremists, but a new constitution, with greater presidential powers, won approval.

defence In 1994, Russia joined NATO's partnership for peace programme. In Dec, Russia invaded the breakaway republic of Chechnya. A peace deal was signed July 1995, but fighting continued. Voter disillusionment in Yeltsin was reflected in parliamentary elections Dec 1995. But boosted by a fresh peace agreement for Chechnya, Yeltsin was re-elected president July 1996. In early 1997 the last Russian troops withdrew from Chechnya.

Russian Revolution two revolutions of Feb and Oct 1917 (Julian ◊calendar) that began with the overthrow of the Romanov dynasty and ended with the establishment of a communist soviet (council) state, the Union of Soviet Socialist Republics (USSR).

The *February Revolution* (March by the Western calendar) arose because of food and fuel shortages, the ongoing repressiveness of the tsarist government, and military incompetence in World War I. Riots in Petrograd (as St Petersburg was named 1914–24) led to the abdication of Tsar Nicholas II and the formation of a provisional government under Prince Lvov. They had little support as troops, communications, and transport were controlled by the Petrograd workers' and soldiers' council. ◊Lenin returned to Russia in April as head of the ◊Bolsheviks. Kerensky replaced Lvov as head of government in July. During this period, the Bolsheviks gained control of the soviets and advocated land reform (under the slogan 'All power to the Soviets') and an end to their involvement in World War I.

The *October Revolution* was a coup on the night of 25–26 Oct (6–7 Nov Western calendar). Bolshevik workers and sailors seized the government buildings and the Winter Palace, Petrograd. The second All-Russian Congress of Soviets, which met the following

---

Russian Revolution (Western calendar)

1894	Beginning of the reign of Tsar Nicholas II.
1898	Formation of the Social Democratic Party among industrial workers under the influence of Plekhanov and Lenin.
1901	Formation of the Socialist Revolutionary Party.
1903	Split in Social Democratic Party at the party's second congress (London Conference) into Bolsheviks and Mensheviks.
1905	**Jan:** 'Bloody Sunday', where repression of workers in St Petersburg led to widespread strikes and the '1905 Revolution'. **Oct:** strikes and the first 'soviet' (local revolutionary council) in St Petersburg. October constitution provided for new parliament (Duma). **Dec:** insurrection of workers in Moscow. Punitive repression by the 'Black Hundreds'.
1914	**July:** outbreak of war between Russia and the Central Powers.
1917	**March:** outbreak of riots in Petrograd (St Petersburg). Tsar Nicholas abdicated. Provisional government established under Prince Lvov. Power struggles between government and Petrograd soviet. **April:** Lenin arrived in Petrograd. He demanded the transfer of power to soviets; an end to the war; the seizure of land by the peasants; control of industry by the workers. **July:** Bolsheviks attempted to seize power in Petrograd. Trotsky arrested and Lenin in hiding. Kerensky became head of a provisional government. **Sept:** Kornilov coup failed owing to strike by workers. Kerensky's government weakened. **Nov:** Bolshevik Revolution. Military revolutionary committee and Red Guards seized government offices and the Winter Palace, arresting all the members of the provisional government. Second All-Russian Congress of Soviets created the Council of Peoples Commissars as new governmental authority. Led by Lenin, with Trotsky as commissar for war and Stalin as commissar for national minorities. Land Decree ordered immediate distribution of land to the peasants. Banks were nationalized and national debt repudiated. Elections to the Constituent Assembly gave large majority to the Socialist Revolutionary Party. Bolsheviks a minority.
1918	**Jan:** Constituent Assembly met in Petrograd but almost immediately broken up by Red Guards **March:** Treaty of Brest-Litovsk marked the end of the war with the Central Powers but with massive losses of territory. **July:** murder of the tsar and his family.
1918-20	Civil War in Russia between Red Army led by Trotsky and White Russian forces. Red Army ultimately victorious.
1923	**6 July:** constitution of USSR adopted.

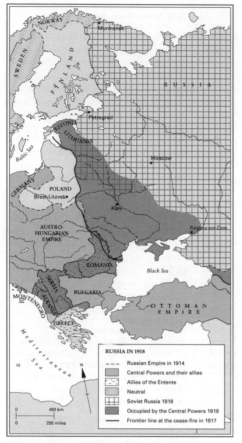

RUSSIA IN 1918
- - - Russian Empire in 1914
Central Powers and their allies
Allies of the Entente
Neutral
Soviet Russia 1918
Occupied by the Central Powers 1918
Frontier line at the cease-fire in 1917

Russia in 1918 *After the second (Bolshevik) revolution in Russia, Lenin was obliged to stand by his promise to end Russian involvement in the Great War. This brought substantial territorial and material losses. The Treaty of Brest-Litovsk 1918 conceded much of European Russia to the Central Powers. Although the treaty was reversed by the Paris peace conference 1919, the Bolsheviks had to deal with opposition from pro-tsarist White Russian forces and Polish attempts to establish the eastern borders of their newly formed state.*

day, proclaimed itself the new government of Russia, and Lenin became leader. Bolsheviks soon took control of the cities, established worker control in factories, and nationalized the banks. The ◊Cheka (secret police) was set up to silence the opposition. The government concluded peace with Germany early in 1918 through the Treaty of ◊Brest-Litovsk, but civil war broke out in that year when anti-Bolshevik elements within the army attempted to seize power. The war lasted until 1922, when the Red Army, organized by ◊Trotsky, finally overcame 'White' (Tsarist) opposition, but with huge losses, after which communist con-

trol was complete. Some 2 million refugees fled during these years.

Russian revolution, 1905 political upheaval centred in and around St Petersburg, Russia 1905–06, leading up to the February and October revolutions of 1917. On 22 Jan 1905 thousands of striking unarmed workers marched to Tsar Nicholas II's Winter Palace in St Petersburg, to ask for reforms. Government troops fired on the crowd, killing many people. After this 'Bloody Sunday' slaughter the revolution gained strength, culminating in a general strike which paralysed the whole country in Oct 1905. Revolutionaries in St Petersburg formed a 'soviet' (council) called the Soviet of Workers' Deputies. Nicholas II then granted the Duma (parliament) the power to pass or reject proposed laws. Although these measures satisfied the liberal element, the revolution continued to gain ground and came to a head when the army crushed a serious uprising in Dec 1905.

Russo-Japanese War war between Russia and Japan 1904–05, which arose from conflicting ambitions in Korea and ◊Manchuria, specifically, the Russian occupation of Port Arthur (modern Dalian) 1896 and of the Amur province 1900. Japan successfully besieged Port Arthur May 1904–Jan 1905, took Mukden (modern Shenyang, see ◊Mukden, Battle of) on 29 Feb–10 March, and on 27 May defeated the Russian Baltic fleet, which had sailed halfway around the world to Tsushima Strait. A peace was signed 23 Aug 1905. Russia surrendered its lease on Port Arthur, ceded S Sakhalin to Japan, evacuated Manchuria, and recognized Japan's interests in Korea.

What this country needs is a short victorious war to stem the tide of revolution.

Vyacheslav Plehve, shortly before the *Russo-Japanese War*

Ruyter Michael Adrianszoon de 1607–1676. Dutch admiral who led his country's fleet in the wars against England. On 1–4 June 1666 he forced the British fleet under Rupert and Albemarle to retire into the Thames, but on 25 July was heavily defeated off the North Foreland, Kent. In 1667 he sailed up the Medway, burning three men-of-war at Chatham, and capturing others.

Rwanda landlocked country in central Africa, bounded N by Uganda, E by Tanzania, S by Burundi, and W by Zaire.

history The population comprises two ethnic groups: the Hutu majority were dominated by the Tutsi minority; there is also a pygmy minority, the Twa.

Rwanda was linked to the neighbouring state of Burundi, 1891–1919, within the empire of German East Africa, then under Belgian administration as a League of Nations mandate, and then as a United Nations trust territory.

In 1961 the monarchy was abolished, and Ruanda, as it was then called, became a republic. It achieved full independence 1962 as Rwanda, with Grégoire Kayibanda as its first president. Fighting broke out 1959 between the Hutu and the Tutsi, resulting in the loss of some 20,000 lives before an uneasy peace was agreed 1965.

after independence Kayibanda was re-elected president 1969, but by the end of 1972 the civil warfare had resumed, and in 1973 the head of the National Guard, Maj-Gen Juvenal Habyarimana, led a bloodless coup, ousting Kayibanda and establishing a military government. Meetings of the legislature were suspended, and the MRND was formed as the only legally permitted political organization. A referendum held at the end of 1978 approved a new constitution, but military rule continued until 1980, when civilian rule was adopted. In Oct 1990, in response to an attack by the Rwandan Patriotic Army, the government promised to reform the constitution after an invasion from Uganda of Tutsi refugees was contained. In April 1994, President Habyarimana and Burundian president Cyprien Ntaryamira were killed in an air crash. Fighting renewed between government forces and the FPR, and escalated quickly. Hundreds of thousands of Rwandans, mostly civilians, were killed, and many more fled to neighbouring countries. Genocide was carried out by Hutu terror bands ('machetti') on Tutsi civilians.

French troops were drafted in June 1994 as part of humanitarian mission, creating a 'safe zone'. In July 1994 the FPR, in control of most of the country, announced a cease-fire and established a transitional coalition government, including many moderate Hutus. Pasteur Bizimungu became head of state.

In Oct 1996 Rwanda and Zaire were near war as Rwanda supported the massacre of Hutus by Tutsis in Zaire. A massive refugee problem was averted when most refugees were allowed to return peacefully to Rwanda, but violence began again Jan 1997 when Hutu extremists embarked on a wave of Tutsi killings.

Rye House Plot conspiracy 1683 by English Whig extremists against Charles II for his Roman Catholic leanings. They intended to murder Charles and his brother James, Duke of York, at Rye House, Hoddesdon, Hertfordshire, but the plot was betrayed. The Duke of ◊Monmouth was involved, and alleged conspirators, including Lord William Russell (1639–1683) and Algernon Sidney (1622–1683), were executed for complicity.

S

SA the *Sturmabteilung* (Storm Troops) of the German Nazi Party, also known as ◊Brownshirts.

Saarland (French *Sarre*) *Land* (state) of Germany. In 1919, the Saar district was administered by France under the auspices of the League of Nations; a plebiscite returned it to Germany 1935; Hitler gave it the name Saarbrücken. Part of the French zone of occupation 1945, it was included in the economic union with France 1947. It was returned to Germany 1957.

Sabah Jabir al Ahmadal Jabir al- 1928– . Emir of Kuwait from 1977. He suspended the national assembly 1986, after mounting parliamentary criticism, ruling in a feudal, paternalistic manner. On the invasion of Kuwait by Iraq 1990 he fled to Saudi Arabia, returning to Kuwait in March 1991.

Sabine member of an ancient people of central Italy, conquered by the Romans and amalgamated with them in the 3rd century BC.

Sacco-Vanzetti case murder trial in Massachusetts, USA, 1920–21. Italian immigrants Nicola Sacco (1891–1927) and Bartolomeo Vanzetti (1888–1927) were convicted of murder during an alleged robbery. The conviction was upheld on appeal, with application for retrial denied. Prolonged controversy delayed execution until 1927. In 1977 the verdict was declared unjust because of the judge's prejudice against the accuseds' anarchist views.

Sadat Anwar 1918–1981. Egyptian politician. Succeeding ◊Nasser as president 1970, he restored morale by his handling of the Egyptian campaign in the 1973 war against Israel. In 1974 his plan for economic, social, and political reform to transform Egypt was unanimously adopted in a referendum. In 1977 he visited Israel to reconcile the two countries, and shared the Nobel Peace Prize with Israeli prime minister Menachem Begin 1978. He was assassinated by Islamic fundamentalists.

Sadowa, Battle of or *Battle of Königgrätz* Prussian victory over the Austrian army 13 km/8 mi NW of Hradec Kralove (German Königgrätz) 3 July 1866, ending the ◊Seven Weeks' War. It confirmed Prussian hegemony over the German states and led to the formation of the North German Confederation 1867. It is named after the nearby village of Sadowa (Czech Sadová) in the Czech Republic.

Sage Kings legendary rulers of China *c.* 2800–*c.* 2200. Of the three sovereigns and five emperors based in the Huang He (Yellow River) region, Huang-tu (reigned *c.* 2697 BC) is credited with defeating the barbarians. The era has been associated with the domestication of animals, agricultural development, the gradual replacement of stone implements with bronze, and the formation of larger tribal confederacies.

Sahel (Arabic *sahil* 'coast') marginal area to the S of the Sahara, from Senegal to Somalia, where the desert is gradually encroaching. The desertification is partly due to climatic change but has also been caused by the pressures of a rapidly expanding population, which have led to overgrazing and the destruction of trees and scrub for fuelwood. In recent years many famines have taken place in the area.

Saigō Takamori 1827–1877. Japanese general and conservative politician who helped in the ◊Meiji restoration and then rebelled against it. He became commander in chief 1872 and one of the leading figures in the Meiji government, but resigned 1873 to lead the ill-fated Satsuma rebellion 1877.

Saigō was a minor official from Satsuma in Kyushu, a province traditionally at odds with the shogunate. With ◊Ōkubo Toshimichi, he led the successful samurai rebellion 1867–68 against the Tokugawa shogunate. Saigō became a government minister 1871 and field marshal 1873. Disapproving of the Meiji government and in particular the introduction of conscription, which threatened the samurai way of life, he resigned 1873 after his plan for a war of redemption against Korea had been rejected. He committed suicide after leading the unsuccessful revolt in Satsuma, whose defeat meant the end of the samurai class.

Saigon, Battle of during the Vietnam War, battle 29 Jan–23 Feb 1968, when 5,000 Vietcong were expelled by South Vietnamese and US forces. The city was finally taken by North Vietnamese forces 30 April 1975, after South Vietnamese withdrawal from the central highlands.

St Albans, Battle of first battle in the English Wars of the ◊Roses, on 22 May 1455 at St Albans, Hertfordshire; a victory for the house of York.

St Bartholomew, Massacre of slaughter of ◊Huguenots (Protestants) in Paris, 24 Aug–17 Sept 1572, and until 3 Oct in the provinces. About 25,000 people are believed to have been killed. When ◊Catherine de' Medici's plot to have Admiral ◊Coligny assassinated failed, she resolved to have all the Huguenot leaders killed, persuading her son Charles IX it was in the interest of public safety.

Catherine received congratulations from all the Catholic powers, and the pope ordered a medal to be struck.

St Christopher (St Kitts)–Nevis country in the West Indies, in the E Caribbean Sea, part of the Leeward Islands.

history The original ◊American Indian inhabitants were Caribs. St Christopher (then called Liamuiga) and Nevis were named by Christopher ◊Columbus 1493. St Christopher became Britain's first West Indian colony 1623, and Nevis was settled soon afterwards. France also claimed ownership until 1713. Sugar plantations were worked by slaves.

The islands were part of the Leeward Islands Federation 1871–1956 and a single colony with the British Virgin Islands until 1960. In 1967 St Christopher, Nevis, and Anguilla attained internal self-government within the Commonwealth as associated states, and Robert Bradshaw, leader of the Labour Party, became the first prime minister. In 1970 the Nevis Reformation Party (NRP) was formed, calling for separation for Nevis, and the following year Anguilla, disagreeing with the government in St Christopher, chose to return to being a British dependency.

Bradshaw died 1978 and was succeeded by his deputy, Paul Southwell. He died the following year, to be replaced by Lee L Moore. The 1980 general election produced a hung assembly, and, although Labour won more than 50% of the popular vote, a People's Action Party (PAM)–NRP coalition government was formed, with the PAM leader, Dr Kennedy Simmonds, as prime minister.

independence On 1 Sept 1983 St Christopher and Nevis became independent. In the 1984 general election the PAM–NRP coalition was decisively returned to office. In the 1989 general election, PAM won 6 of the 11 elective seats in the national asssembly and Dr Kennedy Simmonds continued in office.

St John, Order of (full title *Knights Hospitallers of St John of Jerusalem*) oldest order of Christian chivalry, named from the hospital at Jerusalem founded about 1048 by merchants of Amalfi for pilgrims, whose travel routes the knights defended from the Muslims. Today there are about 8,000 knights (male and female), and the Grand Master is the world's highest ranking Roman Catholic lay person.

On being forced to leave Palestine, the knights went to Cyprus 1291, to Rhodes 1309, and to Malta (granted to them by Emperor Charles V) 1530. Expelled by Napoleon (on his way to Egypt) 1798, they established their headquarters in Rome (Palazzo di Malta).

Saint-Just Louis Antoine Léon Florelle de 1767–1794. French revolutionary. A close associate of ◊Robespierre, he became a member of the Committee of Public Safety 1793, and was guillotined with Robespierre.

Elected to the National Convention in 1792, he was its youngest member at 25 and immediately made his mark by a radical speech condemning King Louis XVI ('one cannot reign without guilt'). His later actions confirm the tone of his book *The Spirit of the Revolution* 1791 in which he showed his distrust of the masses and his advocacy of repression. On his appointment to the Committee of Public Safety he was able to carry out his theories by condemning 'not merely traitors, but the indifferent', including Danton and Lavoisier, although his own death was to follow within weeks.

St Lucia country in the West Indies, in the E Caribbean Sea, one of the Windward Islands.

history The original inhabitants were Carib Indians. ◊Columbus arrived 1502. The island was settled by the French 1635, who introduced ◊slavery, and ceded to Britain 1803. It became a crown colony 1814.

independence St Lucia was a colony within the Windward Islands federal system until 1960, and acquired internal self-government 1967 as a West Indies associated state. The leader of the United Workers' Party (UWP), John Compton, became prime minister. In 1975 the associated states agreed to seek independence separately, and in Feb 1979, after prolonged negotiations, St Lucia achieved full independence within the ◊Commonwealth, with Compton as prime minister.

The St Lucia Labour Party (SLP) came to power 1979 led by Allan Louisy, but a split developed within the party, and in 1981 Louisy was forced to resign, being replaced by the attorney general, Winston Cenac. Soon afterwards George Odlum, who had been Louisy's deputy, left with two other SLP members to form a new party, the Progressive Labour Party

(PLP). For the next year the Cenac government had to fight off calls for a change of government that culminated in a general strike. Cenac eventually resigned, and in the general election 1982 the UWP won a decisive victory, enabling John Compton to return as prime minister. In new elections April 1987, Compton's UWP was only narrowly returned by a 9:8 majority over the SLP.

In Sept 1991 representatives of Dominica, St Lucia, St Vincent and the Grenadines, and Grenada proposed that integration with the Windward Islands would benefit the islands politically and economically. Integration would be based on a federal state system, with an elected, executive president and a two-chamber assembly.

St Valentine's Day Massacre the murder in Chicago, USA, of seven unarmed members of the 'Bugs' Moran gang on 14 Feb 1929 by members of Al Capone's gang disguised as police. The killings testified to the intensity of gangland warfare for the control of the trade in illicit liquor during ◊Prohibition.

St Vincent and the Grenadines country in the West Indies, in the E Caribbean Sea, part of the Windward Islands.

There is a single-chamber legislature, the House of Assembly, with 19 members, of which 13 are elected by universal suffrage, 4 appointed by the governor general on the advice of the prime minister, and 2 on the advice of the leader of the opposition. The assembly has a life of five years.

history The original inhabitants were Carib Indians. ◊Columbus landed on St Vincent 1498. Claimed and settled by Britain and France, with African labour (see ◊slavery), the islands were ceded to Britain 1783.

independence Collectively known as St Vincent, the islands of St Vincent and the islets of the northern Grenadines were part of the West Indies Federation until 1962 and acquired internal self-government 1969 as an associated state. They achieved full independence, within the ◊Commonwealth, as St Vincent and the Grenadines, Oct 1979.

Until the 1980s two parties dominated politics in the islands, the St Vincent Labour Party (SVLP) and the People's Political Party (PPP). Milton Cato, SVLP leader, was prime minister at independence but his leadership was challenged 1981 when a decline in the economy and his attempts to introduce new industrial-relations legislation resulted in a general strike. Cato survived mainly because of divisions in the opposition parties, and in 1984 the centrist New Democratic Party (NDP), led by an SVLP defector and former prime minister, James Mitchell, won a surprising victory. He was re-elected 1989, his party winning all the assembly seats.

In Sept 1991 representatives of Dominica, St Lucia, St Vincent and the Grenadines, and Grenada proposed that integration with the Windward Islands would benefit the islands politically and economically. Integration would be based on a federal state system, with an elected, executive president and a two-chamber assembly.

Saladin or *Sala-ud-din* 1138–1193. Born a Kurd, sultan of Egypt from 1175, in succession to the Atabeg of Mosul, on whose behalf he conquered Egypt 1164–74. He subsequently conquered Syria 1174–87 and precipitated the third ◊Crusade by his recovery of Jerusalem from the Christians 1187. Renowned for knightly courtesy, Saladin made peace with Richard I of England 1192.

Salamanca, Battle of victory of the British commander Wellington over the French army in the ◊Peninsular War, 22 July 1812.

Salamis, Battle of naval battle off the coast of the island of Salamis in which the Greeks defeated the Persians 480 BC.

Salazar Antonio de Oliveira 1889–1970. Portuguese prime minister 1932–68 who exercised a virtual dictatorship. During World War II he maintained Portuguese neutrality but fought long colonial wars in Africa (Angola and Mozambique) that impeded his country's economic development as well as that of the colonies.

A corporative constitution on the Italian model was introduced 1933, and until 1945 Salazar's National Union, founded 1930, remained the only legal party. Salazar was also foreign minister 1936–47.

Salic law a law adopted in the Middle Ages by several European royal houses, excluding women from succession to the throne. The name derives mistakenly from the Salian or northern division of the Franks, who supposedly practised it.

In Sweden 1980 such a provision was abrogated to allow Princess Victoria to become crown princess.

Salisbury Robert Cecil, 1st Earl of Salisbury. Title conferred on Robert ◊Cecil, secretary of state to Elizabeth I of England.

Salisbury Robert Arthur Talbot Gascoyne-Cecil, 3rd Marquess of Salisbury 1830–1903. British Conservative politician. He entered the Commons 1853 and succeeded to his title 1868.

As foreign secretary 1878–80, he took part in the Congress of Berlin, and as prime minister 1885–86, 1886–92, and 1895–1902 gave his main attention to foreign policy, remaining also as foreign secretary for most of this time.

No lesson seems to be so deeply inculcated by the experience of life as that you should never trust experts.

3rd Marquess of Salisbury

Salt March demonstration 11 March–4 May 1930 during the period of Indian nationalist agitation against British rule, forming part of Mahatma Gandhi's campaign of ▷civil disobedience.

On 11 March 1930 Gandhi and his followers set out to walk 241 mi/150 km to Dandi, to campaign against the salt tax imposed by the British government, which maintained its monopoly by making it illegal for Indians to make their own salt. After arriving at Dandi on 6 April, Gandhi and his followers defied the British government by making their own salt. On 4 May Gandhi announced that the government-owned Dharasana saltworks were to be taken over on behalf of the Indian people. Gandhi was arrested but his followers advanced on the saltworks as planned. As the marchers moved forward in columns they were beaten to the ground, offering no resistance.

Samaria region of ancient Israel. The town of Samaria (now Sebastiyeh) on the west bank of the river Jordan was the capital of Israel in the 10th–8th centuries BC. It was renamed Sebaste in the 1st century BC by the Roman administrator Herod the Great.

samizdat (Russian 'self-published') in the USSR and eastern Europe before the 1989 uprisings, written material circulated underground to evade state censorship; for example, reviews of Solzhenitzyn's banned novel *August 1914* 1972.

Samoa, American group of islands 4,200 km/2,610 mi S of Hawaii, administered by the USA. The islands were acquired by the USA Dec 1899 by agreement with Britain and Germany under the Treaty of Berlin. A constitution was adopted 1960 and revised 1967.

Samoa, Western country in the SW Pacific Ocean, in Polynesia, NE of Fiji.

history The original inhabitants were Polynesians, and the first Europeans to reach the island group of Samoa, 1722, were Dutch. In the 19th century Germany, the UK, and the

USA had conflicting interests in the islands and administered them jointly 1889–99, when they were divided into American Samoa and Western Samoa. Western Samoa was a German colony until World War I and from 1920 was administered by New Zealand, first as a League of Nations mandate and from 1946 as a United Nations trust territory.

independence Western Samoa was granted internal self-government gradually until it achieved full independence, within the Commonwealth, 1 Jan 1962. The office of head of state was held jointly by two traditional rulers, but on the death of one of them, the other, Malietoa Tanumafili II, became the sole head of state for life. The prime minister at the time of independence was Fiame Mata Afa Mulinu'u. He lost power 1970 but regained it 1973 until his death 1975. In 1976 the first prime minister who was not of royal blood was elected, Tupuola Taisi Efi.

In 1979 the opposition politicians came together to form the Human Rights Protection Party (HRPP) which won the 1982 election, Va'ai Kolone becoming prime minister. Later that year he was replaced by Tupuola Efi. Efi resigned a few months later when his budget was not approved and was replaced by the new HRPP leader, Tofilau Eti Alesana. The HRPP won a decisive victory Feb 1985, and Tofilau Eti Alesana continued as prime minister. At the end of the year he resigned and Va'ai Kolone returned to lead a government of independents and members of Tupuola Taisi Efi's (now known as Tupua Tamasese Efi) new formed Christian Democratic Party (CDP). The general election Feb 1988 produced a hung parliament with Tofilau Eti Alesana emerging as premier. Following the introduction of universal adult suffrage 1990, Tofilau Eti Alesana was returned for a further three-year term in the April 1991 general election, and Va'ai Kolone resumed leadership of the opposition. Tofilau Eti Alesana made wholesale changes to his cabinet May 1991, bringing in Fiame Naomi as the first woman to serve in a Western Samoan cabinet.

Samuel 11th–10th centuries BC. In the Old Testament, the last of the judges who ruled the ancient Hebrews before their adoption of a monarchy, and the first of the prophets; the two books bearing his name cover the story of Samuel and the reigns of kings Saul and David.

samurai member of the military caste in Japan from the mid-12th century until 1869, when the feudal system was abolished and all samurai pensioned off by the government. A samurai was an armed retainer of a *daimyō* (large landowner) with specific duties and privileges and a strict code of honour. A *rōnin* was a samurai without feudal allegiance.

From the 16th century, commoners were not allowed to carry swords, whereas samurai had two swords, and the higher class of samurai were permitted to fight on horseback. It is estimated that 8% of the population belonged to samurai families. A financial depression from about 1700 caused serious hardship to the samurai, beginning a gradual disintegration of their traditions and prestige, accelerated by the fall of the Tokugawa shogunate 1868, in which they had assisted. Under the new ◊Meiji emperor they were stripped of their role, and many rebelled. Their last uprising was the *Satsuma Rebellion* 1877–78, in which 40,000 samurai took part.

sanction economic or military measure taken by a state or number of states to enforce international law. The first use of sanctions was the attempted economic boycott of Italy (1935–36) during the Abyssinian War by the League of Nations.

Other examples of sanctions are the economic boycott of Rhodesia, after its unilateral declaration of independence 1965, by the United Nations; the call for measures against South Africa on human-rights grounds by the UN and other organizations from 1985; and the economic boycott of Iraq 1990 in protest over its invasion of Kuwait, following resolutions passed by the UN.

Sandinista member of the socialist movement that carried out the ◊Nicaraguan Revolution.

San Francisco chief Pacific port of the USA, in California. In 1578 Sir Francis Drake's flagship, the *Golden Hind*, stopped near San Francisco on its voyage around the world. A Spanish fort and mission were established 1776. The original Spanish village was called Yerba Buena; its name was changed to San Francisco 1846. In the same year the town was occupied during the war with Mexico. When gold was discovered 1848 its population increased from about 800 to about 25,000 in two years. In 1906 the city was almost destroyed by an earthquake and subsequent fire that killed 452 people. It was the site of the drawing up of the United Nations Charter 1945 and of the signing of the peace treaty between the Allied nations and Japan 1951.

San Francisco conference conference attended by representatives from 50 nations who had declared war on Germany before March 1945; held in San Francisco, California, USA. The conference drew up the United Nations Charter, which was signed 26 June 1945.

San Martín José de 1778–1850. South American revolutionary leader. He served in the Spanish army during the Peninsular War, but after 1812 he devoted himself to the South American struggle for independence, playing a large part in the liberation of Argentina, Chile, and Peru from Spanish rule.

sans-culotte (French 'without knee breeches') in the French Revolution, a member of the working classes, who wore trousers, as opposed to the aristocracy and bourgeoisie, who wore knee breeches.

Santa Anna Antonio López de 1795–1876. Mexican revolutionary who became general and dictator of Mexico for most of the years between 1824 and 1855. He led the attack on the ◊Alamo fort in Texas 1836.

A leader in achieving independence from Spain in 1821, he pursued a chequered career of victory and defeat and was in and out of office as president or dictator for the rest of his life.

Santa Cruz Andrés 1792–1865. President of Bolivia 1829–34, 1839, 1841–44, and 1853–55. Strongwilled and conservative, he dabbled in political intrigue before and after his intermittent rule as dictator. He established order in the new state and increased expenditure on education and road building.

Santa Cruz was made a grand marshal after his part in the Battles of Junin and Ayacucho which brought about the independence of Peru 1824. Two years later Simón ◊Bolívar named him president of Peru's council of ministers, but the Peruvian congress rejected him. As president, he formed the Peru-Bolivian Confederation 1836 but its economic and strategic power threatened Chile and Argentina who forced its break-up 1839.

Sānusī Sidi Muhammad ibn Ali as-c. 1787–1859. Algerian-born Muslim religious reformer. He preached a return to the puritanism of early Islam and met with much success in Libya, where he founded the sect named after him. He made Jaghbub his centre.

São Tomé e Príncipe country in the Gulf of Guinea, off the coast of W Africa.

history The islands were uninhabited until the arrival of the Portuguese 1471, who brought convicts and exiled Jews to work on sugar plantations. Later ◊slavery became the main trade, and in the 19th century forced labour was used on coffee and cocoa plantations.

independence As a Portuguese colony, São Tomé e Príncipe acquired internal self-government 1973. After the military coup in Portugal 1974, the new government in Lisbon formally recognized the liberation movement, MLSTP, led by Dr Manuel Pinto da Costa, as the sole representative of the people of the islands and granted full independence July 1975. Dr da Costa became the first president, and in Dec a national people's assembly was elected. During the first few years of his presidency there were several unsuccessful attempts to depose him, and small opposition groups still operate from outside the country, mainly from Lisbon.

international links With a worsening economy, da Costa began to reassess his country's international links, which had made it too dependent on the Eastern bloc and, in consequence, isolated from the West. In 1984 he proclaimed that in future São Tomé e Príncipe would be a nonaligned state, and the number of Angolan, Cuban, and Soviet advisers in the country was sharply reduced. Gradually São Tomé e Príncipe has turned towards nearby African states such as Gabon, Cameroon, and Equatorial Guinea, as well as maintaining its links with Lisbon. In 1987 the constitution was amended, making the president subject to election by popular vote, and in March 1988 an attempted coup against him was foiled. In Sept 1990 a new constitution, introducing multiparty politics, was approved by referendum. In Jan 1991 multiparty elections were held for the assembly, resulting in the party losing its majority. In March the country's first free election led to the election of Miguel Trovoada after President Manuel Pinto da Costa withdrew.

Saracen ancient Greek and Roman term for an Arab, used in the Middle Ages by Europeans for all Muslims. The equivalent term used in Spain was ◊Moor.

Saragossa city in Aragon, Spain; see ◊Zaragoza.

Saratoga Springs city and spa in New York State, USA. In 1777 the British general John Burgoyne was defeated in two engagements nearby during the American Revolution.

Sarawak state of Malaysia, on the northwest corner of the island of Borneo. Sarawak was granted by the Sultan of Brunei to English soldier James Brooke 1841, who became 'Rajah of Sarawak'. It was a British protectorate from 1888 until captured by the Japanese in World War II. It was a crown colony 1946–63, when it became part of Malaysia.

Sardinia (Italian *Sardegna*) mountainous island, special autonomous region of Italy. After centuries of foreign rule, it became linked 1720 with Piedmont, and this dual kingdom became the basis of a united Italy 1861.

Sargon two Mesopotamian kings:

Sargon I king of Akkad *c.* 2334–2279 BC, and founder of the first Mesopotamian empire. Like Moses, he was said to have been found floating in a cradle on the local river, in his case the Euphrates.

Sargon II died 705 BC. King of Assyria from 722 BC, who assumed the name of his predecessor. To keep conquered peoples from rising against him, he had whole populations moved from their homelands, including the Israelites from Samaria.

Sarmiento Domingo Faustino 1811–1888. Argentina's first civilian president 1868–74, regarded as one of the most brilliant Argentines of the 19th century. An outspoken critic of the dictator Juan Manuel de ◊Rosas, Sarmiento spent many years in exile. As president, he doubled the number of schools, creating the best education system in Latin America, and encouraged the establishment of libraries and museums. He also expanded trade, extended railroad building, and encouraged immigration.

Sassanian Empire Persian empire founded AD 224 by Ardashir, a chieftain in the area of what is now Fars, in Iran, who had taken over ◊Parthia; it was named after his grandfather, Sasan. The capital was Ctesiphon, near modern Baghdad, Iraq. After a rapid period of expansion, when it contested supremacy with Rome, it was destroyed in 637 by Muslim Arabs at the Battle of ◊Qadisiya.

Satō Eisaku 1901–1975. Japanese conservative politician, prime minister 1964–72. He ran against Hayato Ikeda (1899–1965) for the Liberal Democratic Party leadership and succeeded him as prime minister, pledged to a more independent foreign policy. He shared a Nobel Prize for Peace in 1974 for his rejection of nuclear weapons. His brother *Nobosuke Kishi* (1896–1987) was prime minister of Japan 1957–60.

satrap title of a provincial governor in ancient Persia. Under Darius I, the Persian Empire was divided between some 20 satraps, each owing allegiance only to the king.

satyagraha (Sanskrit 'insistence on truth') nonviolent resistance to British rule in India, as employed by Mahatma ◊Gandhi from 1918 to press for political reform.

Satsuma Rebellion last uprising of the ◊samurai, in 1877–78.

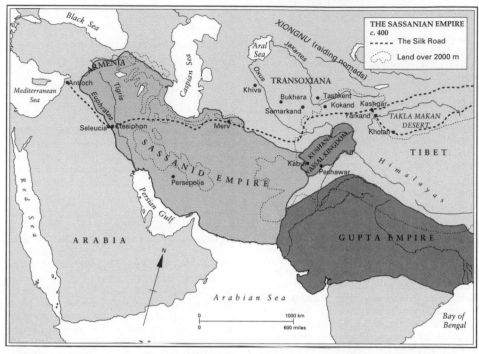

The Sassanian Empire *The Sassanian Empire was founded AD 224 by Ardashir in succession to the Persian and Parthian empires of the Achaemenids and Arsacids. The Sassanians were in constant conflict with Rome, and threatened the Roman limes (frontier defences) in Mesopotamia. Roman resistance to the west forced an energetic Sassanian expansion eastwards as far as India. The empire finally collapsed after defeat by the Arabs at Qadisiya in S Iraq AD 637.*

Saudi Arabia country on the Arabian peninsula, stretching from the Red Sea in the W to the Arabian Gulf in the E, bounded N by Jordan, Iraq, and Kuwait; E by Qatar and United Arab Emirates; SE by Oman; and S by Yemen.

history For early history, see ◊Arabia. The sultanate of Nejd in the interior came under Turkish rule in the 18th century. Present-day Saudi Arabia is almost entirely the creation of King Ibn Saud who, after the dissolution of the ◊Ottoman Empire 1918, fought rival Arab rulers until, in 1926, he had established himself as the undisputed king of the Hejaz and sultan of Nejd. In 1932 Nejd and Hejaz became the United Kingdom of Saudi Arabia.

economic prosperity Oil was discovered in the 1930s, commercially exploited from the 1940s, and became the basis of the country's prosperity. Ibn Saud died 1953 and was succeeded by his eldest son, Saud. During King Saud's reign relations between Saudi Arabia and Egypt became strained, and in 1964 he abdicated in favour of his brother Faisal. Under King Faisal, Saudi Arabia became a leader among Arab oil producers.

In 1975 Faisal was assassinated and his half-brother, Khalid, succeeded him. Khalid was in failing health and increasingly relied on his brother Fahd to perform the duties of government. King Khalid died 1982 and was succeeded by Fahd.

Middle East affairs Saudi Arabia has drawn up proposals for a permanent settlement of the Arab–Israeli dispute. It gave financial support to Iraq in its war with Iran. The ◊Iran–Iraq War also prompted Saudi Arabia to buy advanced missiles from the USA. Islamic fundamentalists staged demonstrations in ◊Mecca 1979 and 1987, leading to violence and worsening relations with Iran. In 1989 Saudi Arabia assumed a leading role in the search for a settlement of the Lebanese civil war, hosting a constitutional convention of Lebanese legislators in Taif.

On 2 Aug 1990 Iraq invaded and occupied neighbouring Kuwait, threatening the security of Saudi Arabia. King Fahd turned to the USA and UK for protection and a massive build-up of ground and air strength began, alongside Saudi Arabia's own forces, culminating in the ◊Gulf War 1991 and Iraq's forced withdrawal from Kuwait. In return, King Fahd agreed to increase his oil output to offset the loss of Kuwaiti and Iraqi production, and to pay a substantial part of the cost of maintaining US and British forces. During the Gulf War, Saudi Arabia served as the staging ground for the air and ground assaults on Iraqi forces. The country was hit by Iraqi missile strikes but suffered no serious damage. In May 1991 religious leaders demanded the creation of a 'consultative council' to assist in the government of the kingdom, as proposed by King Fahd a month earlier. In Nov 1991, Saudi Arabia was one of the main participants in the historic Middle East peace conference in Spain. The formation of a 'consultative council' March 1992, as a move towards more representative government, was viewed with cynicism by some observers.

Saul in the Old Testament, the first king of Israel. He was anointed by Samuel and warred successfully against the neighbouring Ammonites and Philistines, but fell from God's favour in his battle against the Amalekites. He became jealous and suspicious of David and turned against him and Samuel. After being wounded in battle with the Philistines, in which his three sons died, he committed suicide.

Savimbi Jonas 1934– . Angolan soldier and right-wing revolutionary, founder and leader of the National Union for the Total Independence of Angola (UNITA). From 1975 UNITA, under Savimbi's leadership, tried to overthrow the government. A peace agreement was signed 1994; Savimbi rejected the offer of vice presidency in a coalition government 1996.

The struggle for independence from Portugal escalated 1961 into a civil war. In 1966 Savimbi founded the right-wing UNITA, which he led against the left-wing People's Movement for the Liberation of Angola (MPLA), led by Agostinho Neto. Neto, with Soviet and Cuban support, became president when independence was achieved 1975, while UNITA, assisted by South Africa, continued its fight. A cease-fire was agreed June 1989, but fighting continued, and the truce was abandoned after two months. A truce was finally signed May 1991. Civil violence between government and UNITA supporters re-erupted Sept 1992 following an election victory for the ruling party, a result which Savimbi disputed.

Savonarola Girolamo 1452–1498. Italian reformer, a Dominican friar and an eloquent preacher. His crusade against political and religious corruption won him popular support, and in 1494 he led a revolt in Florence that expelled the ruling Medici family and established a democratic republic. His denunciations of Pope ◊Alexander VI led to his excommunication in 1497, and in 1498 he was arrested, tortured, hanged, and burned for heresy.

Savoy area of France between the Alps, Lake Geneva, and the river Rhône. A medieval duchy, it was made into the *départements* of Savoie and Haute-Savoie, in the Rhône-Alpes region. Savoy was a duchy from the 14th century, with the capital Chambéry. In 1720 it became a province of the kingdom of Sardinia which, with Nice, was ceded to France in 1860 by Victor Emmanuel II (king of Italy from 1861) in return for French assistance in driving the Austrians from Italy.

Saxe-Coburg-Gotha Saxon duchy. Albert, the Prince Consort of Britain's Queen Victoria, was a son of the 1st Duke, Ernest I (1784–1844), who was succeeded by Albert's elder brother, Ernest II (1818–1893). It remained the name of the British royal house until 1917, when it was changed to Windsor.

Saxon member of Germanic tribe in the Danish peninsula and northern Germany. The Saxons migrated from their homelands, under pressure from the Franks, and spread into various parts of Europe, including Britain (see ◊Anglo-Saxon). They also undertook piracy in the North Sea and English Channel.

Saxony (German *Sachsen*) administrative *Land* (state) of Germany. Conquered by Charlemagne 792, Saxony became a powerful medieval German duchy. The electors of Saxony were also kings of Poland 1697–1763. Saxony was part of East Germany 1946–90, forming a region with Anhalt.

Saxony takes its name from the early Saxon inhabitants whose territories originally reached as far west as the Rhine. The duchy of Saxony was divided 1260 but reconstituted in 1424 when a new electorate embracing Thuringia, Meissen, and Wittenberg was formed. The northern part of Saxony became a province of Prussia 1815, its king having sided with Napoleon. In 1946 Saxony was joined with Anhalt as a region of East Germany and in 1952 it was split into the districts of Leipzig, Dresden, and Chemnitz (later named Karl-Marx-Stadt). The state of Saxony was restored 1990 following German reunification and the abolition of the former East German districts.

scalawag white supporter in the American South during the ◊Reconstruction 1861–65, associated with the ◊carpetbaggers.

Scapa Flow expanse of sea in the Orkney Islands, Scotland, until 1957 a base of the Royal Navy. It was the main base of the Grand Fleet during World War I and in 1919 was the scene

Saxony: history	
792	Saxony was conquered by Charlemagne.
814	When Charlemagne's empire broke up after his death, Saxony became a dukedom.
13th century	It became an electorate (that is, ruled by an elector).
1483	Martin Luther was born in Saxony, and the Reformation originated here.
1618–48	Saxony suffered much in the Thirty Years' War.
18th century	Saxony became a kingdom.
1815	Because Saxony had supported Napoleon I, half the kingdom was given to Prussia by the Congress of Vienna, becoming the Prussian province of Saxony.
1866	The remaining kingdom joined the North German Confederation.
1871	Incorporated in the German Empire.
1918	At the end of World War I, the king abdicated and Saxony became one of the federal states of the German Republic.
1946	After World War II, Saxony was made part of a new administrative region of East Germany as Saxony-Anhalt.
1952	Saxony-Anhalt was divided into Leipzig, Dresden, and Chemnitz regions.
1990	Saxony was restored as a state of the Federal Republic of Germany.

of the scuttling of 71 surrendered German warships.

Scheer Reinhard 1863–1928. German admiral in World War I, commander of the High Sea Fleet in 1916 at the Battle of ◊Jutland.

schism formal split over a doctrinal difference between religious believers, as in the ◊Great Schism in the Roman Catholic Church; over the doctrine of papal infallibility, as with the Old Catholics in 1879; and over the use of the Latin Tridentine mass 1988.

Schleswig-Holstein *Land* (state) of Germany. Schleswig (Danish *Slesvig*) and Holstein were two duchies held by the kings of Denmark from 1460, but were not part of the kingdom; a number of the inhabitants were German, and Holstein was a member of the Confederation of the Rhine formed 1815. Possession of the duchies had long been disputed by Prussia, and when Frederick VII of Denmark died without an heir 1863, Prussia, supported by Austria, fought and defeated the Danes 1864, and in 1866 annexed the two duchies. A plebiscite held 1920 gave the northern part of Schleswig to Denmark, which made it the province of

Haderslev and Aabenraa; the rest, with Holstein, remained part of Germany.

Schlieffen Plan military plan produced Dec 1905 by German chief of general staff, General Count Alfred von Schlieffen (1833–1913), that formed the basis of German military planning before World War I, and inspired Hitler's plans for the conquest of Europe in World War II. It involved a simultaneous attack on Russia and France, the object being to defeat France quickly and then deploy all available resources against the Russians.

Schmidt Helmut 1918– . German socialist politician, member of the Social Democratic Party (SPD), chancellor of West Germany 1974–83. As chancellor, Schmidt introduced social reforms and continued Brandt's policy of Ostpolitik. With the French president Giscard d'Estaing, he instigated annual world and European economic summits. He was a firm supporter of NATO and of the deployment of US nuclear missiles in West Germany during the early 1980s.

Schuman Robert 1886–1963. French politician. He was prime minister 1947–48, and as foreign minister 1948–53 he proposed in May 1950 a common market for coal and steel (the *Schuman Plan*), which was established as the European Coal and Steel Community 1952, the basis of the European Community.

Schuschnigg Kurt von 1897–1977. Austrian chancellor 1934–38, in succession to ◊Dollfuss. He tried in vain to prevent Nazi annexation (Anschluss) but in Feb 1938 he was forced to accept a Nazi minister of the interior, and a month later Austria was occupied and annexed by Germany. He was imprisoned in Germany until 1945, when he went to the USA; he returned to Austria 1967.

Scipio Africanus Major 237–*c.* 183 BC. Roman general. He defeated the Carthaginians in Spain 210–206, invaded Africa 204, and defeated Hannibal at Zama 202.

Scipio Africanus Minor *c.* 185–129 BC. Roman general, the adopted grandson of Scipio Africanus Major, also known as *Scipio Aemilianus*. He destroyed Carthage 146, and subdued Spain 133. He was opposed to his brothers-in-law, the Gracchi (see ◊Gracchus).

Scipio Publius Cornelius died 211 BC. Roman general, father of Scipio Africanus Major. Elected consul 218, during the Second ◊Punic War, he was defeated by Hannibal at Trebia and killed by the Carthaginians in Spain.

SCLC abbreviation for US civil-rights organiza-tion ◊*Southern Christian Leadership Conference*.

Scone site of ancient palace where most of the Scottish kings were crowned on the Stone of Destiny (now in the Coronation Chair at Westminster, London). The village of Scone is in Tayside, Scotland, N of Perth.

Scopes monkey trial trial held in Dayton, Tennessee, USA, 1925. John T Scopes, a science teacher at the high school, was accused of teaching, contrary to a law of the state, Darwin's theory of evolution. He was fined $100, but this was waived on a technical point. The defence counsel was Clarence Darrow and the prosecutor William Jennings ◊Bryan.

Scotland the northernmost part of Britain, formerly an independent country, now part of the UK. See chronology *Scotland: history.*

Scullin James Henry 1876–1953. Australian Labor politician. He was leader of the Federal Parliamentary Labor Party 1928–35, and prime minister and minister of industry 1929–31.

scutage in medieval Europe, a feudal tax imposed on knights as a substitute for military service. It developed from fines for non-attendance at musters under the Carolingians, but in England by the 12th century it had become a purely fiscal measure designed to raise money to finance mercenary armies, reflecting the decline in the military significance of feudalism.

Scythia region north of the Black Sea between the Carpathian mountains and the river Don, inhabited by the Scythians 7th–1st centuries BC. From the middle of the 4th century, they were slowly superseded by the Sarmatians. The Scythians produced ornaments and vases in gold and electrum with animal decoration. Although there is no surviving written work, there are spectacular archaeological remains, including vast royal burial mounds which often contain horse skeletons.

Sea Peoples unidentified seafaring warriors who may have been Achaeans, Etruscans, or ◊Philistines, who ravaged and settled the Mediterranean coasts in the 12th–13th centuries BC. They were defeated by Ramses III of Egypt 1191 BC.

Second Front in World War II, battle line opened against Germany on 6 June 1944 by the Allies (Britain and the USA). See ◊D-day.

Second Moroccan Crisis alternative name for the ◊Agadir Incident.

Second World War alternative name for ◊World War II, 1939–45.

secularization the process through which religious thinking, practice, and institutions lose their religious and/or social significance. The concept is based on the theory, held by some sociologists, that as societies become industrialized their religious morals, values, and institutions give way to secular ones and some religious traits become common secular practices.

Sedan town on the river Meuse, in Ardennes département, NE France. In 1870 Sedan was the scene of Napoleon III's surrender to Germany during the ◊Franco-Prussian War. It was the focal point of the German advance into France 1940.

Seddon Richard John 1845–1906. New Zealand Liberal politician, prime minister 1893–1906.

Sedgemoor, Battle of in English history, a battle 6 July 1685 in which Monmouth's rebellion was crushed by the forces of James II, on a tract of marshy land 5 km/3 mi SE of Bridgwater, Somerset.

Seleucus I Nicator *c.* 358–280 BC. Macedonian general under Alexander the Great and founder of the *Seleucid Empire.* After Alexander's death 323 BC, Seleucus became governor and then (312 BC) ruler of Babylonia, founding the city of Seleucia on the river Tigris. He conquered Syria and had himself crowned king 306 BC, but his expansionist policies brought him into conflict with the Ptolemies of Egypt, and he was assassinated. He was succeeded by his son Antiochus I.

self-strengthening movement military, political, and economic reform campaign 1861–95. A reaction to defeat in the ◊Opium Wars, it was mainly concerned with military modernization, under the slogan 'learn the superior barbarian (Western) techniques to control the barbarians'. The inadequacy of the reforms was made clear by China's naval and military defeat by Meiji Japan in the ◊Sino-Japanese War.

Seljuk Empire empire of the Turkish people (converted to Islam during the 7th century) under the leadership of the invading Tatars or Seljuk Turks. The Seljuk Empire 1055–1243 included Iran, Iraq, and most of Anatolia and Syria. It was a loose confederation whose centre was in Iran, jointly ruled by members of the family led by a great sultan exercising varying degrees of effective power. It was succeeded by the ◊Ottoman Empire.

Semiramis lived *c.* 800 BC. Greek name for *Sammuramat,* an Assyrian queen, later identified with the chief Assyrian goddess Ishtar.

Senanayake Don Stephen 1884–1952. First prime minister of independent Sri Lanka (formerly Ceylon) 1947–52. Active in politics from

Scotland: history

c. 3,000 BC	Neolithic settlements include Beaker People and Skara Brae remains on Orkney.
1st millennium BC	The Picts reached Scotland from mainland Europe.
1st century AD	More than 400 brochs, thick-walled circular towers, built in far N regions.
79–84	Roman invasion by Julius Agricola; defeat of Caledonians at Mons Graupius, E Scotland.
122–128	Hadrian's Wall built to keep the northern tribes out of England.
c. 142	Antonine Wall from Forth to the Clyde, a stone and turf wall, built by Roman general Lollius Urbicus as a forward defence.
c. 185	Antonine Wall abandoned.
297	First reference to Picts in Latin documents.
c. 500	The Scots, Gaelic-speaking Irish immigrants, led by Fergus, son of Erc, settled in Kingdom of Dalriada (modern Argyll), with capital at Dunadd.
563	St Columba founded Iona and began the conversion of the Picts to Christianity.
9th century	Norsemen conquered Orkney, Shetland, Western Isles, and much of Highlands.
c. 843	Unification of Picts, Scots, Britons, and Angles under Kenneth I MacAlpine.
1018	At the Battle of Carham Malcolm II defeated Northumbrian army, bringing Lothian under Scottish rule.
1034	Duncan became king of United Scotland.
1040	Duncan murdered by Macbeth.
1069	Malcolm III (Ceann Mor) married English Princess Margaret, who introduced several reforms to Scottish Church.
1263	Battle of Largs: defeat by Scots of Norwegian king Haakon.
1295	First treaty between Scotland and France (the 'Auld Alliance').
1296	Edward I of England invaded and declared himself King of Scotland.
1297	William Wallace and Andrew Moray defeated English at Battle of Stirling Bridge.
1314	Robert Bruce defeated English under Edward II at the Battle of Bannockburn.
1326	Parliament at Cambuskenneth the first to be attended by nobles, clergy, and burghs.
1328	Scottish independence under Robert Bruce recognized by England.
1371	Robert II, the first Stuart king, crowned.
1513	Scots defeated by English (and King James IV killed) at Battle of Flodden.
1542	Mary Queen of Scots succeeded to throne when less than a week old.
1544	Henry VIII laid waste to Edinburgh and the Borders (the 'Rough Wooing').
1557	The First Covenant signed, pledging to break with Rome.
1559	John Knox returned permanently to Scotland, to participate in shift of Scottish Church to Protestantism.
1567	Mary forced to abdicate and the following year fled to England.
1603	Crowns of England and Scotland united under James VI who became James I of England.
1638	National Covenant condemned Charles I's changes in Church ritual; Scottish rebellion.
1643	Solemn League and Covenant: Scottish Covenanters ally with English Parliament against Charles I.
1651	Cromwell invaded Scotland and defeated Scots at Dunbar and Inverkeithing.
1689	At Killiecrankie Jacobite forces under Graham of Claverhouse, Viscount Dundee, defeated William of Orange's army, but Dundee mortally wounded.
1692	Massacre of Glencoe: William of Orange ordered the MacDonalds of Glencoe murdered in their sleep.
1707	Act of Union united Scottish and English parliaments.
1715	The 'Fifteen': Jacobite rebellion in support of James Edward Stuart, 'James VII'.
1745	The 'Fortyfive': Charles Edward Stuart landed in Scotland and marched as far south as Derby before turning back.
1746	Jacobites defeated at Battle of Culloden by English forces under Duke of Cumberland.
1767	Creation of Edinburgh New Town, planned by James Craig (1749–1795).
1843	The Disruption: 400 ministers left the Church of Scotland to form the Free Church of Scotland.
1886	Crofters Act provided security of tenure for crofters.
1888	James Keir Hardie founded the Scottish Labour Party.
1926	Secretary for Scotland became a British Cabinet post.
1928	National Party of Scotland formed (became Scottish National Party 1934).
1975	Scottish counties replaced by nine regions and three island areas.
1979	Referendum rejected proposal for directly elected Scottish assembly.
1997	Referendum accepted proposal for Scottish parliament.

1915, he became leader of the United National Party and negotiated independence from Britain 1947. A devout Buddhist, he promoted Sinhalese–Tamil racial harmony and rural development.

senate in ancient Rome, the 'council of elders'. Originally consisting of the heads of patrician families, it was recruited from ex-magistrates and persons who had rendered notable public service, but was periodically purged by the censors. Although nominally advisory, it controlled finance and foreign policy.

Seneca Falls Convention in US history, a meeting in New York State July 1848 of women campaigning for greater rights. A Declaration of Sentiments, paraphrasing the US Declaration of Independence, called for female suffrage, equal educational and employment opportunities, and more legal rights.

Senegal country in W Africa, on the Atlantic Ocean, bounded N by Mauritania, E by Mali, S by Guinea and Guinea-Bissau, and enclosing the Gambia on three sides.

history Portuguese explorers arrived in the 15th century, and French settlers in the 17th. Senegal had a French governor from 1854, became part of French West Africa 1895, and a territory 1902.

independence Senegal became an independent republic Sept 1960, with Léopold Sédar ◊Senghor, leader of the Senegalese Progressive Union (UPS), as its first president. Senghor was also prime minister 1962–70. The UPS was the only legal party from 1966 until in Dec 1976 it was reconstituted as the Senegalese Socialist Party (PS) and two opposition parties were legally registered. In 1978 Senghor was decisively re-elected.

Senghor retired at the end of 1980 and was succeeded by Abdou Diouf, who declared an amnesty for political offenders and permitted more parties to register. In the 1983 elections the PS won 111 of the assembly seats and the main opposition, the Senegalese Democratic Party (PDS), eight seats. Later that year Diouf tightened control of his party and the government, abolishing the post of prime minister. This met open, sometimes violent, opposition, but he and the PS remained firmly in power.

Senegambia confederation In 1980 Senegal sent troops to the Gambia to protect it against a suspected Libyan invasion, and it intervened again 1981 to thwart an attempted coup. As the two countries came closer together, they agreed on an eventual merger, and the confederation of Senegambia came into being Feb 1982. Senegal has always maintained close links with

France, allowing it to retain military bases. In the Feb 1988 elections Diouf was re-elected president with 73% of the vote, but his ruling party had a slightly reduced majority in the national assembly. In April 1989 border disputes led to a severance of diplomatic relations with neighbouring Mauritania, with more than 450 people killed during violent clashes between Senegalese and Mauritanians. Over 50,000 people were repatriated from both countries May 1989. In Aug 1989 formal recognition was given of the ending of the unsuccessful federation of Senegambia.

Constitutional changes were proposed Sept 1991, including the reduction of the voting age from 21 to 18 and the limitation of the presidential mandate to two terms. Diplomatic relations with Mauritania, severed 1989, were restored April 1992.

Senghor Léopold (Sédar) 1906– . Senegalese politician and writer, first president of independent Senegal 1960–80. He was Senegalese deputy to the French National Assembly 1946–58, and founder of the Senegalese Progressive Union. He was also a well-known poet and a founder of *négritude*, a black literary and philosophical movement.

Sennacherib died 681 BC. King of Assyria from 705 BC. Son of ◊Sargon II, he rebuilt the city of Nineveh on a grand scale, sacked Babylon 689, and defeated Hezekiah, king of Judah, but failed to take Jerusalem. He was assassinated by his sons, and one of them, Esarhaddon, succeeded him.

sepoy Indian soldier in the service of the British or Indian army in the days of British rule in India. The ◊Indian Mutiny 1857–58 was thus also known as the Sepoy Rebellion or Mutiny.

Sepoy Rebellion alternative name for the ◊Indian Mutiny, a revolt of Indian soldiers against the British in India 1857-58.

Septimius Severus Lucius 146–211. Roman emperor. He held a command on the Danube when in 193 the emperor Pertinax was murdered. Proclaimed emperor by his troops, Severus proved an able administrator. He was born in N Africa, and was the only African to become emperor. He died at York while campaigning in Britain against the Caledonians.

Serbia (Serbo-Croatian *Srbija*) constituent republic of Yugoslavia, which includes Kosovo and Vojvodina. The Serbs settled in the Balkans in the 7th century and became Christians in the 9th century. They were united as one kingdom about 1169; the Serbian hero Stephan Dushan (1331–1355) founded an empire covering most of the Balkans. After their defeat at Kosovo 1389 they came under the domination of the Turks, who annexed Serbia 1459. Uprisings 1804–16, led by Kara George and Milosh Obrenovich, forced the Turks to recognize Serbia as an autonomous principality under Milosh. The assassination of Kara George on Obrenovich's orders gave rise to a long feud between the two houses. After a war with Turkey 1876–78, Serbia became an independent kingdom. On the assassination of the last Obrenovich 1903 the Karageorgevich dynasty came to the throne.

The two Balkan Wars 1912–13 greatly enlarged Serbia's territory at the expense of Turkey and Bulgaria. Serbia's designs on Bosnia-Herzegovina, backed by Russia, led to friction with Austria, culminating in the outbreak of war 1914. Serbia was overrun 1915–16 and was occupied until 1918, when it became the nucleus of the new kingdom of the Serbs, Croats, and Slovenes, and subsequently ◊Yugoslavia. Rivalry between Croats and Serbs continued within the republic. During World War II Serbia was under a puppet government set up by the Germans; after the war it became a constituent republic of Yugoslavia.

From 1986 Slobodan Milosević as Serbian party chief and president waged a populist campaign to end the autonomous status of the provinces of Kosovo and Vojvodina. Despite a violent Albanian backlash in Kosovo 1989–90 and growing pressure in Croatia and Slovenia to break away from the federation, Serbia formally annexed Kosovo Sept 1990. Milosević was re-elected by a landslide majority Dec 1990, but in March 1991 there were anticommunist and anti-Milosević riots in Belgrade. The 1991 civil war arose from the Milosevic government attempting the forcible annexation of Serb-dominated regions in Croatia, making use of the largely Serbian federal army. In Oct 1991 Milosevic renounced claims to Croatia under threats of European Community (EC) and United Nations (UN) sanctions but fighting continued until a cease-fire Jan 1992. EC recognition of Slovenian, Croatian, and Bosnia-Herzegovinan independence left Serbia dominating a depleted 'rump' Yugoslavia. A successor Yugoslavia, announced by Serbia and Montenegro April, was rejected by the USA and EC. Despite demonstrations 1992 in Belgrade demanding the ousting of Milosevic and an end to the war in Bosnia-Herzegovina, Milosevic was re-elected Dec.

During the winter of 1996-97 there was pro-democracy unrest in Belgrade. Authorities initially refused to recognize opposition victories in Nov 1996 municipal elections, but Milosevic accepted them Feb 1997. In July Milosevic was elected to the Yugoslav presidency.

serfdom the legal and economic status of peasants under ◊feudalism. Serfs could not be sold like slaves, but they were not free to leave their master's estate without his permission. They had to work the lord's land without pay for a number of days every week and pay a percentage of their produce to the lord every year. They also served as soldiers in the event of conflict. Serfs also had to perform extra labour at harvest time and other busy seasons; in return they were allowed to cultivate a portion of the estate for their own benefit. In England serfdom died out between the 14th and 17th centuries, but it lasted in France until 1789, in Russia until 1861, and in most other European countries until the early 19th century.

Settlement, Act of in Britain, a law passed 1701 during the reign of King William III, designed to ensure a Protestant succession to the throne by excluding the Roman Catholic descendants of James II in favour of the Protestant House of Hanover. Elizabeth II still reigns under this act.

Seven Weeks' War war 1866 between Austria and Prussia, engineered by the German chancellor ◊Bismarck. It was nominally over the possession of ◊Schleswig-Holstein, but it was actually to confirm Prussia's superseding Austria as the leading German state. The Prussian victory at the Battle of ◊Sadowa was the culmination of General von Moltke's victories.

Seven Wonders of the World in antiquity, the pyramids of Egypt, the hanging gardens of Babylon, the temple of Artemis at Ephesus, the statue of Zeus at Olympia, the Mausoleum at Halicarnassus, the Colossus of Rhodes, and the Pharos (lighthouse) at Alexandria.

Seven Years' War (in North America known as the *French and Indian War*) war 1756–63 arising from the conflict between Austria and Prussia, and between France and Britain over colonial supremacy. Britain and Prussia defeated France, Austria, Spain, and Russia; Britain gained control of India and many of France's colonies, including Canada. Spain ceded Florida to Britain in exchange for Cuba. Fighting against great odds, Prussia was eventually successful in becoming established as one of the great European powers. The war ended with the Treaty of Paris 1763, signed by Britain, France, and Spain.

Severus Alexander AD 208–235. Roman emperor from 222, when he succeeded his cousin Heliogabalus. He attempted to involve the Senate more closely in administration, and was the patron of the jurists Ulpian and Paulus, and the historian Cassius Dio. His campaign against the Persians 232 achieved some success, but in 235, on his way to defend Gaul against German invaders, he was killed in a mutiny.

Sèvres, Treaty of the last of the treaties that ended World War I. Negotiated between the Allied powers and the Ottoman Empire, it was finalized Aug 1920 but never ratified by the Turkish government.

The treaty reduced the size of Turkey by making concessions to the Greeks, Kurds, and Armenians, as well as ending Turkish control of Arab lands. Its terms were rejected by the newly created nationalist government and the treaty was never ratified. It was superseded by the Treaty of ◊Lausanne in 1923.

Seward William Henry 1801–1872. US public official. A leader of the Republican party, he was appointed secretary of state by President Lincoln 1860. Although seriously wounded in the 1865 assassination of Lincoln, Seward continued to serve as secretary of state under President Andrew Johnson to 1868, purchasing Alaska for the USA from Russia for $7.2 million 1867.

Seychelles country in the Indian Ocean, off E Africa, N of Madagascar.

history The islands were probably visited by the Portuguese about 1500 and became a French colony 1744. Seychelles was ceded to Britain by France 1814 and was ruled as part of ◊Mauritius until it became a crown colony 1903.

independence In the 1960s several political parties were formed, campaigning for independence, the most significant being the Seychelles Democratic Party (SDP), led by James Mancham, and the Seychelles People's United Party (SPUP), led by France-Albert René. René demanded complete independence, while Mancham favoured integration with Britain. In 1975 internal self-government was agreed. The two parties then formed a coalition government with Mancham as prime minister. In June 1976 Seychelles became an independent republic within the Commonwealth, with Mancham as president and René as prime minister.

one-party state The following year René staged an armed coup while Mancham was attending a Commonwealth conference in London, and declared himself president. A new constitution was adopted, creating a one-party state, with the SPUP being renamed the Seychelles People's Progressive Front (SPPF). René, as the only candidate, was formally elected president 1979 and then re-elected 1984 and 1989. There have been several unsuccessful attempts to overthrow him, the last reported 1987.

René followed a policy of nonalignment and prohibited the use of port facilities to vessels carrying nuclear weapons. He maintained close links with Tanzania, which provided military support. The demise of the USSR and the consequential loss of economic support considerably weakened René's position.

multiparty election In 1992 James Mancham, the former president, returned from exile in the UK announcing that he hoped to contest the presidency. A multiparty election, the first since 1974, was held in July 1992 and was won by the SPPF. The election was to a 20-member commission to draft a new, democratic constitution.

Seymour Jane *c.* 1509–1537. Third wife of Henry VIII, whom she married in 1536. She died soon after the birth of her son Edward VI.

Sforza Italian family that ruled the duchy of Milan 1450–99, 1512–15, and 1522–35. Its court was a centre of Renaissance culture and its rulers prominent patrons of the arts.

The family's original name was Attendoli but it took the name Sforza (Italian 'force') in the early 13th century. Francesco Sforza (1401–1466) obtained Milan by marriage 1441 to the ◊Visconti heiress; then his son Galeazzo (1444–1476) ruled and became a patron of the arts. After his assassination, his brother Ludovico (1451–1508) seized power, made Milan one of the most powerful Italian states, and became a great patron of artists, especially Leonardo da Vinci. He was ousted by Louis XII of France 1499, restored 1512–15, then ousted again. His son Francesco (1495–1535) was re-established 1522 by Emperor Charles V. Francesco had no male heirs, and Milan passed to Charles 1535.

Shaftesbury Anthony Ashley Cooper, 1st Earl of Shaftesbury 1621–1683. English politician, a supporter of the Restoration of the monarchy. He became Lord Chancellor in 1672, but went into opposition in 1673 and began to organize the ◊Whig Party. He headed the Whigs' demand for the exclusion of the future James II from the succession, secured the passing of the Habeas Corpus Act 1679, then, when accused of treason 1681, fled to Holland.

Shaftesbury Anthony Ashley Cooper, 7th Earl of Shaftesbury 1801–1885. British Tory politician. He strongly supported the Ten Hours Act of 1847 and other factory legislation, including the 1842 act forbidding the employment of women and children underground in mines. He was also associated with the movement to provide free education for the poor.

shah (more formally, *shahanshah* 'king of kings') traditional title of ancient Persian rulers, and also of those of the recent ◊Pahlavi dynasty in Iran.

Shah Jahan 1592–1666. Mogul emperor of India from 1628, under whom the dynasty reached its zenith. Succeeding his father ◊Jahangir, he extended Mogul authority into the Deccan plateau (E India), subjugating Ahmadnagar, Bijapur, and Golconda 1636, but lost Kandahar in the NW to the Persians 1653. On falling seriously ill 1658 he was dethroned and imprisoned by his son ◊Aurangzeb.

Shaka or *Chaka* c. 1787–1828. Zulu chief who formed a Zulu empire in SE Africa. He seized power from his half-brother 1816 and then embarked on a bloody military campaign to unite the Zulu clans. He was assassinated by his two half-brothers.

His efforts to unite the Zulu peoples of Nguni (the area that today forms the South African province of Natal) initiated the period of warfare known as the ◊Mfecane.

Shaker member of the Christian sect of the *United Society of Believers in Christ's Second Appearing*, called Shakers because of their ecstatic shakings in worship. The movement was founded by James and Jane Wardley in England about 1747, and taken to North America 1774 by Ann Lee (1736–1784). They anticipated modern spiritualist beliefs, but their doctrine of celibacy led to their virtual extinction.

Shalmaneser five Assyrian kings including:

Shalmaneser III king of Assyria 859–824 BC who pursued an aggressive policy and brought Babylon and Israel under the domination of Assyria.

Our image has undergone a change from David fighting Goliath to being Goliath.

Yitzhak Shamir on Israel in
the *Observer* Jan 1989

Shamir Yitzhak 1915– . Polish-born Israeli right-wing politician; prime minister 1983–84 and 1986–92; leader of the Likud (Consolidation Party). He was foreign minister under Menachem Begin 1980–83, and again foreign minister in the ◊Peres unity government 1984–86.

In Oct 1986, he and Peres exchanged positions, Shamir becoming prime minister and Peres taking over as foreign minister. Shamir was re-elected 1989 and formed a new coalition government with Peres; this broke up 1990 and

Shamir then formed a government without Labour membership and with religious support. He was a leader of the ◊Stern Gang of guerrillas (1940–48) during the British mandate rule of Palestine.

Shan people of the mountainous borderlands between Myanmar (Burma), Thailand, and China. The Shan entered Burma in the 13th century and founded a powerful kingdom at Ava 1360, which lasted until Upper Burma was unified by the ◊Toungoo dynasty from 1531. Shan-Myanmar enmity has endured, despite the Shan having adopted Theravāda Buddhism and much Burmese culture. The Shan state was largely independent of Burma until it was officially incorporated after the military coup 1962.

Shang dynasty or *Yin dynasty* China's first fully authenticated dynasty, c. 1500–c. 1066 BC, which saw the start of the Bronze Age. Shang rulers dominated the Huang He (Yellow River) plain of N China, developing a complex agricultural civilization which introduced a written language.

The dynasty's existence was verified in the 1920s by the discovery of inscribed oracle bones ('dragon bones') at its capital situated at Anyang, N Henan.

Shaoshan the birthplace in the Chinese province of Hunan of the communist leader ◊Mao Zedong.

Shari'a the law of ◊Islam believed by Muslims to be based on divine revelation, and drawn from a number of sources, including the Koran, the Hadith, and the consensus of the Muslim community. Under this law, *qisās*, or retribution, allows a family to exact equal punishment on an accused; *diyat*, or blood money, is payable to a dead person's family as compensation.

From the latter part of the 19th century, the role of the Shari'a courts in the majority of Muslim countries began to be taken over by secular courts, and the Shari'a to be largely restricted to family law. Modifications of Koranic maxims have resulted from the introduction of Western law; for example, compensation can now be claimed only after a conviction by a criminal court.

Sharpeville black township in South Africa, 65 km/40 mi S of Johannesburg and N of Vereeniging; 69 people were killed here when police fired on a crowd of anti-apartheid demonstrators 21 March 1960.

The massacre took place during a campaign launched by the Pan-Africanist Congress against the pass laws (laws requiring nonwhite

South Africans to carry identity papers). On the anniversary of the massacre in 1985, during funerals of people who had been killed protesting against unemployment, 19 people were shot by the police at Langa near Port Elizabeth.

Shastri Lal Bahadur 1904–1966. Indian politician, prime minister 1964–66. He campaigned for national integration, and secured a declaration of peace with Pakistan at the Tashkent peace conference 1966.

Before independence, he was imprisoned several times for civil disobedience. Because of his small stature, he was known as 'the Sparrow'.

Shays Daniel *c.* 1747–1825. American political agitator. In 1786 he led Shays Rebellion, an armed uprising of impoverished farmers, against the refusal of the state government to offer economic relief. The riot was suppressed 1787 by a Massachusetts militia force, but it drew public attention to the plight of the western farmers and the need for a stronger central government. Shays was pardoned 1788.

Sheffield Outrages in British history, sensational reports in the national press 1866 exemplifying summary justice exercised by trade unions to secure subscriptions and obtain compliance with rules by threats, removal of tools, sabotage of equipment at work, and assaults.

sheik leader or chief of an Arab family or village.

Sheridan Philip Henry 1831–1888. Union general in the American ◊Civil War. Recognizing Sheridan's aggressive spirit, General Ulysses S ◊Grant gave him command of his cavalry in 1864, and soon after of the Army of the Shenandoah Valley, Virginia. Sheridan laid waste to the valley, cutting off grain supplies to the Confederate armies. In the final stage of the war, Sheridan forced General Robert E ◊Lee to retreat to Appomattox and surrender.

sheriff (Old English *scīr* 'shire', *gerēfa* 'reeve') in England and Wales, the crown's chief executive officer in a county for ceremonial purposes; in Scotland, the equivalent of the English county-court judge, but also dealing with criminal cases; and in the USA the popularly elected head law-enforcement officer of a county, combining judicial authority with administrative duties. In England, the office (elective until Edward II) dates from before the Norman Conquest.

Sherman Roger 1721–1793. American public official. He was one of the signatories of the Declaration of Independence 1776, the Articles of Confederation 1781, and the US Constitution 1788. A supporter of American independence, he was a member of the Continental Congress 1774–81 and 1783–84. At the Constitutional Convention 1787 he introduced the 'Connecticut Compromise', providing for a bicameral federal legislature. Sherman served in the US House of Representatives 1789–91 and the US Senate 1791–93.

Sherman William Tecumseh 1820–1891. Union general in the American ◊Civil War. In 1864 he captured and burned Atlanta; continued his march eastward, to the sea, laying Georgia waste; and then drove the Confederates northward. He was US Army chief of staff 1869-83.

There is many a boy here today who looks on war as all glory, but, boys, it is all hell.

General Sherman speech
Aug 1880

Sherman Anti-Trust Act in US history, an act of Congress 1890, named after senator John Sherman (1823–1900) of Ohio, designed to prevent powerful corporations from monopolizing industries and restraining trade for their own benefit. Relatively few prosecutions of such trusts were successful under the act.

Shevardnadze Edvard 1928– . Georgian politician, Soviet foreign minister 1985–91, head of state of Georgia from 1992. A supporter of ◊Gorbachev, he was first secretary of the Georgian Communist Party from 1972 and an advocate of economic reform. In 1985 he became a member of the Politburo, working for détente and disarmament. In July 1991, he resigned from the Communist Party (CPSU) and, along with other reformers and leading democrats, established the Democratic Reform Movement. In March 1992 he was chosen as chair of Georgia's ruling military council, and in Oct elected speaker of parliament.

Shiah or ◊*Shi'ite* member of one of the two main sects of ◊Islam.

Shidehara Kijuro 1872–1951. Japanese politician and diplomat, prime minister 1945–46. As foreign minister 1924–27 and 1929–31, he promoted conciliation with China, and economic rather than military expansion. After a brief period as prime minister 1945–46, he became speaker of the Japanese Diet (parliament) 1946–51.

Shi Huangdi or *Shih Huang Ti* 259–210 BC. Emperor of China who succeeded to the throne of the state of Qin in 246 BC and reunited China as an empire by 228 BC. He burned almost all existing books in 213 BC to destroy ties with the past; rebuilt the ◊Great Wall of China; and was buried in Xian, Shaanxi province, in a tomb complex guarded by 10,000 life-size terracotta warriors (excavated in the 1980s).

He had so overextended his power that the dynasty and the empire collapsed with the death of his weak successor in 207 BC.

Shi'ite or *Shiah* member of a sect of Islam who believe that ◊Ali was ◊Muhammad's first true successor. They are doctrinally opposed to the Sunni Muslims. They developed their own law differing only in minor directions, such as inheritance and the status of women. Holy men have greater authority in the Shi'ite sect than in the Sunni sect. They are prominent in Iran, the Lebanon, and Indo-Pakistan, and are also found in Iraq and Bahrain.

Breakaway sub-sects include the *Alawite* sect, to which the ruling party in Syria belongs; and the *Ismaili* sect, with the Aga Khan IV (1936–) as its spiritual head. The term Shi'ite originally referred to shi'a ('the partisans') of Ali.

In the aftermath of the Gulf War 1991, many thousands of Shi'ites in Iraq were forced to take refuge in the marshes of S Iraq, after unsuccessfully rebelling against Saddam Hussein. Shi'ite sacred shrines were desecrated and atrocities committed by the armed forces on civilians.

Shimonoseki, Treaty of peace agreement 1895 ending the First ◊Sino-Japanese War, under which Japan received from China the Pescadores Islands, Taiwan, and the Liaodong peninsula.

Shinto (Chinese *shin tao* 'way of the gods') the indigenous religion of Japan. It combines an empathetic oneness with natural forces and loyalty to the reigning dynasty as descendants of the Sun goddess, Amaterasu-Omikami. Traditional Shinto followers stressed obedience and devotion to the emperor, and an aggressive nationalistic aspect was developed by the Meiji rulers. Today Shinto has discarded these aspects.

Shinto is the Chinese transliteration of the Japanese *Kami-no-Michi*. Shinto ceremonies appeal to the kami, the mysterious forces of nature manifest in topographical features such as mountains, trees, stones, springs, and caves. Shinto focuses on purity, devotion, and sincerity.

Shinto's holiest shrine is at Ise, near Kyoto, where in the temple of the Sun goddess is preserved the mirror that she is supposed to have given to Jimmu, the legendary first emperor, in the 7th century BC.

ship money tax for support of the navy, levied on the coastal districts of England in the Middle Ages. Ship money was declared illegal by Parliament 1641.

shire administrative area formed in Britain for the purpose of raising taxes in Anglo-Saxon times. By AD 1000 most of southern England had been divided into shires with fortified strongholds at their centres. The Midland counties of England are still known as *the Shires*; for example Derbyshire, Nottinghamshire, and Staffordshire.

shogun in Japanese history, title of a series of military strongmen 1192–1868 who relegated the emperor's role to that of figurehead. Technically an imperial appointment, the office was treated as hereditary and was held by the ◊Minamoto clan 1192–1219, by the ◊Ashikaga 1336-1573, and by the ◊Tokugawa 1603–1868. The shogun held legislative, judicial, and executive power.

The emperor had been a national and religious figurehead rather than a direct ruler since the rise of the Fujiwara clan in the 9th century, but the exercise of power had been by officials of the court rather than of the army. The title of *seii-tai-shōgun*, 'barbarian-subduing commander', first given 794 to one of the imperial guards appointed to lead an expedition against the Ainu people, had before 1192 entailed only temporary military command. The *bakufu* (shogunate), the administrative structure set up by the first Minamoto shogun, gradually extended its area of operations to all aspects of government.

Shona member of a Bantu-speaking people of southern Africa, comprising approximately 80% of the population of Zimbabwe. They also occupy the land between the Save and Pungure rivers in Mozambique, and smaller groups are found in South Africa, Botswana, and Zambia. The Shona are mainly farmers, living in scattered villages. The Shona language belongs to the Niger-Congo family.

Short Parliament the English Parliament that was summoned by Charles I on 13 April 1640 to raise funds for his war against the Scots. It was succeeded later in the year by the ◊Long Parliament.

show trial public and well-reported trial of people accused of crimes against the state. In the USSR in the 1930s and 1940s, Stalin carried out show trials against economic saboteurs, Communist Party members, army officers, and even members of the Bolshevik leadership.

shuttle diplomacy in international relations, the efforts of an independent mediator to achieve a compromise solution between belligerent parties, travelling back and forth from one to the other.

The term came into use in the 1970s. In 1990–91 shuttle diplomacy was practised by US secretary of state James Baker in the period leading up to, and following, the ◊Gulf War.

Siberia Asian region of Russia, extending from the Ural Mountains to the Pacific Ocean. Overrun by Russia in the 17th century, Siberia was used from the 18th century to exile political and criminal prisoners. The first *Trans-Siberian Railway* 1892–1905 from St Petersburg (via Omsk, Novosibirsk, Irkutsk, and Khabarovsk) to Vladivostok, approximately 8,700 km/5,400 mi, began to open it up. A popular front was formed 1988, campaigning for ecological and political reform.

Sicily (Italian *Sicilia*) the largest Mediterranean island, an autonomous region of Italy. Conquered by most of the major powers of the ancient world, Sicily flourished under the Greeks who colonized the island during the 8th–5th centuries BC. It was invaded by Carthage and became part of the Roman empire 241 BC–AD 476. In the Middle Ages it was ruled successively by the Arabs; the Normans 1059–1194, who established the *Kingdom of the Two Sicilies* (that is, Sicily and the southern part of Italy); the German emperors; and then the Angevins, until the popular revolt known as the *Sicilian Vespers* 1282. Spanish rule was invited and continued in varying forms, with a temporary displacement of the Spanish Bourbons by Napoleon, until ◊Garibaldi's invasion 1860 resulted in the two Sicilies being united with Italy 1861.

Siegfried Line in World War I, a defensive line established 1918 by the Germans in France; in World War II, the Allies' name for the West Wall, a German defensive line established along its western frontier, from the Netherlands to Switzerland.

Sierra Leone country in W Africa, on the Atlantic Ocean, bounded N and E by Guinea and SE by Liberia.

history Freetown, the capital, was founded by Britain 1787 for homeless Africans rescued from ◊slavery. Sierra Leone became a British colony 1808.

independence Sierra Leone achieved full independence as a constitutional monarchy within the ◊Commonwealth 1961, with Sir Milton Margai, leader of the Sierra Leone People's Party (SLPP), as prime minister. He died 1964 and was succeeded by his half-brother, Dr Albert Margai. The 1967 general election was won by the APC, led by Dr Siaka Stevens, but the result was disputed by the army, which assumed control and forced the governor general to leave the country.

one-party state In 1968 another army revolt brought back Stevens as prime minister, and in 1971, after the constitution had been changed to make Sierra Leone a republic, he became president. He was re-elected 1976, and the APC, having won the 1977 general election by a big margin, began to demand the creation of a one-party state. To this end, a new constitution was approved by referendum 1978, and Stevens was sworn in as president.

Stevens did not run 1985, and the APC endorsed the commander of the army, Maj-Gen Joseph Momoh, as the sole candidate for the party leadership and presidency. Momoh appointed a civilian cabinet and dissociated himself from the policies of his predecessor, who had been criticized for failing to prevent corruption within his administration. The last elections for the House of Representatives were held May 1982 but annulled because of alleged irregularities. It was reported Oct 1989 that an attempted coup against the government had been put down. In Aug 1991 a move towards multiparty politics was approved by referendum. Subsequently six political parties decided to combine to form the United Front of Political Movements (UNIFORM). The parties are the National Action Party (NAP), Sierra Leone People's Party (SLPP), Democratic People's Party (DPP), National Democratic Alliance (NDA), National Democratic Party (NDP), and the Civic Development Education Movement (CDM).

In April 1992 the army took over the government and President Momoh fled to neighbouring Guinea. An interim National Provisional Ruling Council (NPRC) was set up, led by Capt Valentine Strasser that consisted of eighteen army officers and four civilians. Capt Strasser pledged to restore civilian rule and multiparty politics.

Sigismund 1368–1437. Holy Roman emperor from 1411. He convened and presided over the council of Constance 1414–18, where he promised protection to the religious reformer ◊Huss, but imprisoned him after his condemnation for heresy and acquiesced in his burning. King of Bohemia from 1419, he led the military campaign against the ◊Hussites.

Sihanouk Norodom 1922– .Cambodian politician, king 1941–55 and from 1993, prime minister 1955–70, when his government was overthrown by a military coup led by Lon Nol.

With Pol Pot's resistance front, he overthrew Lon Nol 1975 and again became prime minister 1975–76, when he was forced to resign by the ◊Khmer Rouge. He returned from exile Nov 1991 under the auspices of a United Nations-brokered peace settlement to head the Supreme National Council, a new coalition comprising all Cambodia's warring factions, including the Khmer Rouge. He was crowned King 1993.

Sikhism religion professed by 14 million Indians, living mainly in the Punjab. Sikhism was founded by Nanak (1469–c. 1539). Sikhs believe in a single God who is the immortal creator of the universe and who has never been incarnate in any form, and in the equality of all human beings; Sikhism is strongly opposed to caste divisions.

On Nanak's death he was followed as guru by a succession of leaders who converted the Sikhs (the word means 'disciple') into a military confraternity which established itself as a political power. The last of the gurus, Guru Gobind Singh (1666–1708), instituted the *Khanda-di-Pahul* and established the Khalsa. Gobind Singh was assassinated by a Muslim 1708, and since then the holy book *Guru Granth Sahib* has taken the place of a leader.

Upon the partition of India many Sikhs migrated from W to E Punjab, and in 1966 the efforts of Sant Fateh Singh (c. 1911–72) led to the creation of a Sikh state within India by partition of the Punjab. However, the Akali separatist movement agitates for a completely independent Sikh state, Khalistan, and a revival of fundamentalist belief, and was headed from 1978 by Sant Jarnail Singh Bhindranwale (1947–84), killed in the siege of the Golden Temple, ◊Amritsar. In retaliation for this, the Indian prime minister Indira Gandhi was assassinated in Oct of the same year by her Sikh bodyguards. Heavy rioting followed, in which 1,000 Sikhs were killed.

Sikh Wars two wars in India between the Sikhs and the British:

The *First Sikh War 1845–46* followed an invasion of British India by Punjabi Sikhs. The Sikhs were defeated and part of their territory annexed.

The *Second Sikh War 1848–49* arose from a Sikh revolt in Multan. They were defeated, and the British annexed the Punjab.

Sikorski Wladyslaw 1881–1943. Polish general and politician; prime minister 1922–23, and 1939–43 of the Polish government in exile in London during World War II. He was killed in an aeroplane crash near Gibraltar in controversial circumstances.

Silesia region of Europe that has long been disputed because of its geographical position, mineral resources, and industrial potential; now in Poland and the Czech Republic. Dispute began in the 17th century with claims on the area by both Austria and Prussia. It was seized by Prussia's Frederick the Great, which started the War of the ◊Austrian Succession; this was finally recognized by Austria 1763, after the Seven Years' War. After World War I, it was divided in 1919 among newly formed Czechoslovakia, revived Poland, and Germany, which retained the largest part. In 1945, after World War II, all German Silesia east of the Oder–Neisse line was transferred to Polish administration; about 10 million inhabitants of German origin, both there and in Czechoslovak Silesia, were expelled.

Silk Road ancient and medieval overland route of about 6,400 km/4,000 mi by which silk was brought from China to Europe in return for trade goods; it ran west via the Gobi Desert, Samarkand, and Antioch to Mediterranean ports in Greece, Italy, the Middle East, and Egypt. Buddhism came to China via this route, which was superseded from the 16th century by sea trade.

Simon John Allsebrook, Viscount Simon 1873–1954. British Liberal politician. He was home secretary 1915–16, but resigned over the issue of conscription. He was foreign secretary 1931–35, home secretary again 1935–37, chancellor of the Exchequer 1937–40, and lord chancellor 1940–45.

Simon Commission or *Indian Statutory Commission* all-party group set up Nov 1927 to examine the working of government in India and recommend future policy. Chaired by the Liberal Sir John Simon (1873–1954), it was entirely drawn from the British ruling classes. This exclusion of Indian representatives prompted an immediate boycott by the Indian National Congress and later the ◊Muslim League.

In 1928, in response to British charges that Indians could not agree among themselves what constitutional changes were needed, Motilal Nehru set up and chaired an all-party committee which drafted an Indian constitution and demanded free dominion status.

Sinai, Battle of battle 6–24 Oct 1973 during the Yom Kippur War between Israel and Egypt. It was one of the longest tank battles in history. Israeli troops crossed the Suez canal 16 Oct, cutting off the Egyptian 3rd Army.

Sind province of SE Pakistan, mainly in the Indus delta, its capital and chief is the seaport Karachi. Annexed 1843, Sind became a province of British India, and part of Pakistan on independence. There is agitation for its creation as a separate state, Sindhudesh.

Singapore (Sanskrit *Singa pura* 'city of the lion') country in SE Asia, off the tip of the Malay Peninsula.

history For early history, see ◊Malaysia. Singapore was leased as a trading post 1819 from the sultan of Johore by the British East India Company at a time when it was a swampy jungle. It passed to the crown 1858 and formed part of the ◊Straits Settlements 1867–1942.

During World War II, Singapore functioned as a vital British military base in the Far East. Designed to be invulnerable to naval attack, it was invaded by land and occupied by Japan Feb 1942– Sept 1945. Singapore became a separate British crown colony 1946 and fully self-governing, with ◊Lee Kuan Yew as prime minister, from 1959. It joined the Federation of ◊Malaysia 1963 but seceded 1965, alleging discrimination against the federation's Chinese members. A new independent republic of Singapore, within the ◊Commonwealth, was thus formed Sept 1965.

rapid development The new republic's internal political affairs were dominated by Prime Minister Lee Kuan Yew's People's Action Party (PAP), which gained a monopoly of all parliamentary seats in the elections between 1968 and 1980. Under Lee's stewardship, Singapore developed rapidly as a commercial and financial entrepôt and as a centre for new export industries. Today its inhabitants enjoy the highest standard of living in Asia outside Japan and Brunei.

During the early 1980s, as the pace of economic growth briefly slowed, opposition to the Lee regime began to surface, with support for the PAP falling from 76% to 63% in the Dec 1984 election and two opposition deputies winning parliamentary seats for the first time. Lee responded by taking a firmer line against dissent, with J B Jeyaretnam, the Workers' Party leader, being conveniently found guilty of perjury Nov 1986 and deprived of his parliamentary seat. Support for the PAP held steady, at 62%, in the Sept 1988 election and the opposition won only one seat. In Nov 1990 Lee resigned, handing over to his deputy, Goh Chok Tong, but remaining a senior member of the cabinet. The PAP was returned to power with 61% of the vote in the general election held, ahead of schedule, Aug 1991.

foreign policy Singapore allied itself closely with the USA 1965–74. Since the mid-1970s, however, it has pursued a neutralist foreign policy and improved its relations with China. It is a member of the Association of South East Asian Nations.

... the second doorway of the wide world's trade ...

On *Singapore* Rudyard Kipling 'The Song of the Cities' 1893

Sinhalese member of the majority ethnic group of Sri Lanka (70% of the population). Sinhalese is the official language of Sri Lanka; it belongs to the Indo-Iranian branch of the Indo-European family, and is written in a script derived from the Indian Pali form. The Sinhalese are Buddhists. Since 1971 they have been involved in a violent struggle with the Tamil minority, who are seeking independence.

Sinn Féin ('We ourselves') Irish nationalist party founded by Arthur Griffith (1872–1922) in 1905; in 1917 Eamon ◊de Valera became its president. It is the political wing of the Irish Republican Army, and is similarly split between comparative moderates and extremists. In 1985 it gained representation in 17 out of 26 district councils in Northern Ireland.

Sino-Japanese Wars two wars waged by Japan against China 1894–95 and 1931–45 to expand to the mainland. Territory gained in the First Sino-Japanese War (Korea) and in the 1930s (Manchuria, Shanghai) was returned at the end of World War II.

First Sino-Japanese War 1894–95. Under the treaty of Shimonoseki, Japan secured the 'independence' of Korea, cession of Taiwan and the nearby Pescadores Islands, and the Liaodong peninsula (for a naval base). France, Germany, and Russia pressured Japan into returning the last-named, which Russia occupied 1896 to establish Port Arthur (now Lüda); this led to the Russo-Japanese War 1904–05.

Second Sino-Japanese War 1931–45:

1931–32 The Japanese occupied Manchuria, which they formed into the puppet state of Manchukuo. They also attacked Shanghai, and moved into NE China.

1937 Chinese leaders Chiang Kai-shek and Mao Zedong allied to fight the Japanese; war was renewed as the Japanese overran NE China and seized Shanghai and Nanjing.

1938 Japanese capture of Wuhan and Guangzhou was followed by the transfer of the

Chinese capital to Chongqing; a period of stalemate followed.

1941 Japanese attack on the USA (see ◊Pearl Harbor) led to the extension of lend-lease aid to China and US entry into war against Japan and its allies.

1944 A Japanese offensive threatened Chongqing.

1945 The Chinese received the Japanese surrender at Nanjing in Sept, after the Allies had concluded World War II.

Sino-Soviet split period of strained relations between the two major communist powers, China and the USSR, during the early 1960s, thus dividing the communist world. The tension was based partly on differences in ideology but also involved rivalry for leadership and old territorial border claims. The Chinese Communists also criticized the USSR for supplying aircraft to India and for withdrawing technical and military aid to China in 1960. The USSR supported India in its border warfare with China between 1961 and 1962.

Sioux a member of a group of North American ◊Plains Indians, now living on reservations in South Dakota and Nebraska, and in American society. Their language belongs to the Macro-Siouan family.

When gold was discovered in their treaty territory, the USA sent in troops to remove them 1876. Under chiefs Crazy Horse and Sitting Bull they defeated General George Custer at Little Bighorn, Montana; as a result, Congress abrogated the Fort Laramie Treaty of 1868 (which had given the Sioux a large area in the Black Hills of Dakota).

Siraj-ud-Daula 1728–1757. Nawab of Bengal, India, from April 1756. He captured Calcutta from the British in June 1756 and imprisoned some of the British in the ◊Black Hole of Calcutta (a small room in which a number of them died), but was defeated in 1757 by Robert ◊Clive, and lost Bengal to the British at the Battle of ◊Plassey. He was killed in his capital, Murshidabad.

Sisulu Walter 1912–   . South African civil-rights activist, one of the first full-time secretary generals of the African National Congress (ANC), in 1964, with Nelson Mandela. He was imprisoned following the 1964 Rivonia Trial for opposition to the apartheid system and released, at the age of 77, as a gesture of reform by President F W ◊De Klerk 1989. In 1991, when Mandela became ANC president, Sisulu became his deputy.

Sitting Bull *c.* 1834–1893. North American Indian chief who agreed to ◊Sioux resettlement 1868. When the treaty was broken by the USA, he led the Sioux against Lieutenant Colonel ◊Custer at the Battle of the ◊Little Bighorn 1876.

He was pursued by the US Army and forced to flee to Canada. He was allowed to return 1881, and he toured in the Wild West show of 'Buffalo Bill' ◊Cody. He settled on a Dakota reservation and was killed during his arrest on suspicion of involvement in Indian agitations.

Sivaji or Shivaji 1627–1680. founder of the ◊Maratha state in W India, which lasted until 1818. Drawn from a Maratha noble family, he gained a reputation as a skilled warrior and defender of Hindu interests in successful confrontations with the Muslim rulers of Bijapur and the emperor Aurangzeb. He was crowned raja (king) 1674 and remains a Hindu hero.

Sivaji was a superb organizer, setting up an equitable land system which helped to finance his military exploits. He was an innovative fighter, using guerrilla tactics of speed and surprise.

Six Acts in British history, acts of Parliament passed 1819 by Lord Liverpool's Tory administration to curtail political radicalism in the aftermath of the ◊Peterloo massacre and during a period of agitation for reform when ◊habeas corpus was suspended and the powers of magistrates extended.

Six Articles act introduced by Henry VIII in England in 1539 to settle disputes over dogma in the English church.

The articles affirmed belief in transubstantiation, communion in one kind only, auricular confession, monastic vows, celibacy of the clergy, and private masses; those who rejected transubstantiation were to be burned at the stake. The act was repealed in 1547, replaced by 42 articles in 1551, and by an act of Thirty-Nine Articles in 1571.

Six-Day War another name for the third ◊Arab–Israeli War.

Slav member of an Indo-European people in central and E Europe, the Balkans, and parts of N Asia, speaking closely related Slavonic languages. The ancestors of the Slavs are believed to have included the Sarmatians and ◊Scythians. Moving west from Central Asia, they settled in E and SE Europe during the 2nd and 3rd millennia BC.

slavery the enforced servitude of one person (a slave) to another or one group to another. A

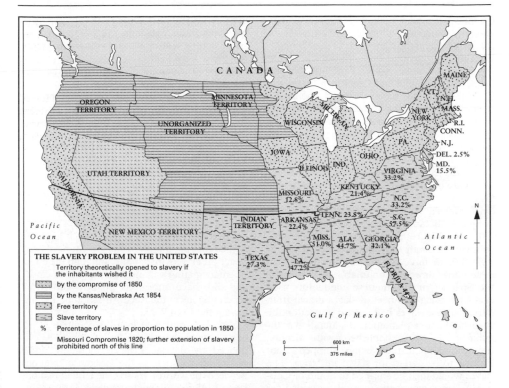

THE SLAVERY PROBLEM IN THE UNITED STATES
Territory theoretically opened to slavery if the inhabitants wished it
- by the compromise of 1850
- by the Kansas/Nebraska Act 1854
- Free territory
- Slave territory
- % Percentage of slaves in proportion to population in 1850
- Missouri Compromise 1820; further extension of slavery prohibited north of this line

The slavery problem in the United States The road to the American Civil War was marked with a series of political compromises between the northern states which had abolished slavery within their borders, and the southern states which continued to use slave labour. At issue in the compromises of 1820 and 1850 was the future of slavery in new territory: would slavery be prohibited or practised in the new western states joining the Union? Both North and South had economic and political reasons for claiming the new lands in the west.

slave has no personal rights and is the property of another person through birth, purchase, or capture. Slavery goes back to prehistoric times but declined in Europe after the fall of the Roman Empire. During the imperialism of Spain, Portugal, and Britain in the 16th–18th centuries and in the American South in the 17th–19th centuries, slavery became a mainstay of an agricultural factory economy, with millions of Africans sold to work on plantations in North and South America. Millions more died in the process, but the profits from this trade were enormous. Slavery was abolished in the British Empire 1833 and in the USA at the end of the Civil War 1863–65 (see ◊abolitionism) , but continues illegally in some countries.

Chattel slavery involves outright ownership of the slave by a master, but there are forms of partial slavery where an individual is tied to the land, or to another person, by legal obligations, as in ◊serfdom or ◊indentured labour.

As a social and economic institution, slavery originated in the times when humans adopted sedentary farming methods of subsistence rather than more mobile forms of hunting and gathering. It was known in Shang dynasty China (*c.* 1500–*c.* 1066 BC) and ancient Egypt, and is recorded in the Babylonian code of Hammurabi (*c.* 1750 BC), the Sanskrit Laws of Manu (c. 600 BC), and the Bible. Slave labour became commonplace in ancient Greece and Rome, when it was used to cultivate large estates and to meet the demand for personal servants in the towns. Slaves were created through the capture of enemies, through birth to slave parents, through sale into slavery by free parents, and as a means of punishment.

After the fall of the Roman Empire in the 5th century, slavery persisted in Arab lands and in central Europe, where many Slavs were captured and taken as slaves to Germany (hence the derivation of the word). Historically, slave-owning societies included the Ottoman Empire, the Crimean Khanate, the Inca Empire (Peru), and the Sokoto Caliphate and the Hausa (Nigeria). Central Asians such as the Mongols, Kazakhs, and various Turkic groups also kept slaves, as did some Native American peoples (such as Comanche and Creek). In Spain and Portugal, where the reconquest of the peninsula from the Moors in the 15th century created an acute shortage of labour, captured Muslims were enslaved. They were soon followed by slaves from Africa, imported by the Portuguese prince Henry the Navigator after 1444. Slaves were used for a wide range of tasks, and a regular trade in slaves was established between the Guinea Coast and the slave markets of the Iberian peninsula.

Slavery became of major economic importance after the 16th century with the European conquest of South and Central America. Needing a labour force but finding the indigenous inhabitants unwilling or unable to cooperate, the Spanish and Portuguese conquerors used ever-increasing numbers of slaves drawn from Africa. These slaves had a great impact on the sugar and coffee plantations. A lucrative triangular trade was established with alcohol, firearms, and textiles being shipped from Europe to be traded for slaves in Africa. The slaves would then be shipped to South or Central America where they would be traded for staples such as molasses and later raw cotton. In 1619 the first black slaves landed in an English colony in North America (Virginia).

The vast profits became a major element in the British economy and the West Indian trade in general. It has been estimated that the British slave trade alone shipped 2 million slaves from Africa to the West Indies between 1680 and 1786. The total slave trade to the Americas in the single year of 1790 may have exceeded 70,000. According to another estimate, during the nearly 400 years of the slave trade, a total of 15 million slaves were delivered to buyers and some 40 million Africans lost their lives in the notorious 'middle passage'.

Anti-slavery movements and changes in the political and economic structure of Europe helped to bring about the abolition of slavery in most of Europe during the later 18th and early 19th century, followed by abolition in overseas territories somewhat later.

Only in the Southern states of the USA did slavery persist as a major, if not essential, component of the economy—providing the labour force for the cotton and other plantations. While the Northern states abolished slavery in the 1787–1804 period, the Southern states insisted on protecting the institution. Slavery became an issue in the economic struggles between Southern plantation owners and Northern industrialists in the first half of the 19th century, a struggle that culminated in the American Civil War.

Despite the common perception to the contrary, the war was not fought primarily on the slavery issue. Abraham Lincoln, however, saw the political advantages of promising freedom for Southern slaves, and the Emancipation Proclamation was enacted in 1863. This was reinforced after the war by the 13th, 14th, and 15th amendments to the US constitution (1865, 1868, and 1870), which abolished slavery altogether and guaranteed citizenship and civil rights to former slaves. Apart from the moral issues, there has also been a good deal of debate on the economic efficiency of slavery as a system of production in the USA. It has been argued that plantation owners might have been better off employing labour, although the effect of emancipating vast numbers of slaves could, and did, have enormous political and social repercussions in the Reconstruction period following the Civil War.

Although outlawed in most countries, various forms of slavery continue to exist—as evidenced by the steps taken by international organizations such as the League of Nations between the world wars and the United Nations since 1945 to curb such practices.

No one shall be held in slavery or servitude; slavery and the slave trade shall be prohibited in all their forms.

On *slavery* United Nations Universal Declaration of Human Rights, article four 1948

Slavophile intellectual and political group in 19th-century Russia that promoted the idea of an Eastern orientation for the empire in opposition to those who wanted the country to adopt Western methods and ideas of development.

Slim William Joseph, 1st Viscount 1891–1970. British field marshal in World War II. He commanded the 1st Burma Corps 1942–45, stemming the Japanese invasion of India, and then forcing them out of Burma (now Myanmar). He was governor general of Australia 1953–60.

In a battle nothing is ever as good or as bad as the first reports of excited men would have it.

William Joseph Slim *Unofficial History*

Slovakia one of the two republics that formed the Federative Republic of Czechoslovakia. Settled in the 5th–6th centuries by Slavs; it was occupied by the Magyars in the 10th century, and was part of the kingdom of Hungary until 1918, when it became a province of Czechoslovakia. Slovakia was a puppet state under German domination 1939–45, and was abolished as an administrative division in 1949. Its capital and chief town is Bratislava. It was re-established as a sovereign state after the breakup of the Czechoslovak Republic in 1993.

Slovenia or *Slovenija* country in S central Europe, bounded N by Austria, E by Hungary, W by Italy, and S by Croatia.

history Settled by the Slovenes in the 6th century, the region came under Frankish rule 788, and then under Hungarian domination 907–55. It was controlled by the Habsburgs from 1335. It formed part of the Austrian crownlands of Carniola, Styria, and Carinthia prior to its incorporation 1918 into the kingdom of the Serbs, Croats, and Slovenes, which became part of Yugoslavia 1928. Unlike neighbouring Croatia, there were few Slovenian demands for autonomy during the 1930s. During World War II the region was occupied by Germany and Italy; it was made a constituent republic within the Yugoslav Socialist Federal Republic in Nov 1945. It was the most economically advanced and politically liberal republic within the federation, helping to subsidize the poorer republics.

nationalist unrest From the 1980s there was economic decline and increasing nationalist unrest. The leadership of the ruling Slovene League of Communists (LCS) responded by pressing for greater autonomy within the federation to enable the republic to pursue a strategy of economic liberalization and political pluralism. In 1989 opposition parties were legalized and a free, multiparty election was held in April 1990. Despite renaming themselves the Party of Democratic Reform (PDR) and adopting a social democratic programme, the communists were convincingly defeated by the six-party Democratic Opposition of Slovenia (DEMOS), a nationalist, centre-right coalition, which campaigned for independence within a year. However, the PDR's reformist leader was popularly elected state president, renouncing his party membership once installed in office. The new government promoted the formation of a new loose Yugoslav confederation, but this was resisted by Serbia.

secession from Yugoslavia With overwhelming support given to a referendum on independence held in Dec 1990, plans were made for secession. An independent army, the Slovenian Territorial Defence Force, was established in the spring of 1991. Following the announcement on 8 May 1991 that secession of both Slovenia and Croatia from the federation would take place on 26 June 1991, more than 100 were killed in clashes around newly established Slovene border posts. The European Community (EC) brokered a cease-fire, based upon a three-month suspension of Slovenia's declaration of independence and the withdrawal of the Yugoslav National Army (JNA) from the republic. This was successfully implemented as the focus of the Serb-dominated JNA's activity switched to Croatia, with its much larger Serb minority. On 23 Dec 1991 Slovenia adopted a new constitution. Slovenia, whose independence was formally recognized by the European Community (EC) and the USA Jan 1992. A vote of no confidence in the government April 1992 led to the appointment of Janez Drnovsek as prime minister designate. He formed a new Executive Council and promised early elections. Slovenia was admitted to the United Nations (UN) May 1992.

Sluis, Battle of (or *Sluys*) 1340 naval victory for England over France which marked the beginning of the Hundred Years' War. England took control of the English Channel and seized 200 great ships from the French navy of Philip IV; there were 30,000 French casualties.

Smith Ian (Douglas) 1919– . Rhodesian politician. He was a founder of the Rhodesian Front 1962 and prime minister 1964–79. In 1965 he made a unilateral declaration of Rhodesia's independence and, despite United Nations sanctions, maintained his regime with tenacity. In 1979 he was succeeded as prime minister by Bishop Abel Muzorewa, when the country was renamed Zimbabwe. He was suspended from the Zimbabwe parliament April 1987 and resigned in May as head of the white opposition party.

Smith John 1938–94. British Labour politician, party leader 1992-94. He was secretary of state for trade 1978–79 and from 1979 held various shadow cabinet posts, culminating in shadow chancellor 1978–92.

A trained lawyer, Smith distinguished himself as a public speaker at an early age. He entered parliament 1970 and served in the administrations of Harold Wilson and James Callaghan. He succeeded Neil Kinnock as party leader July 1992.

smuggling illegal import or export of prohibited goods or evasion of customs duties on dutiable goods. Smuggling has a long tradition in most border and coastal regions; goods smuggled include tobacco, spirits, diamonds, gold, and illegal drugs.

Restrictions on imports, originally a means of preventing debasement of coinage (for example, in 14th-century England), were later used for raising revenue, mainly on luxury goods, and led to a flourishing period of smuggling during the 18th century in such goods as wine, brandy, tea, tobacco, and lace.

Smuts Jan Christian 1870–1950. South African politician and soldier; prime minister 1919–24 and 1939–48. He supported the Allies in both world wars and was a member of the British imperial war cabinet 1917–18.

During the Second ◊South African War (1899–1902) Smuts commanded the Boer forces in his native Cape Colony. He subsequently worked for reconciliation between the Boers and the British. On the establishment of the Union of South Africa, he became minister of the interior 1910–12 and defence minister 1910–20. During World War I he commanded the South African forces in E Africa 1916–17. He was prime minister 1919–24 and minister of justice 1933–39; on the outbreak of World War II he succeeded General Hertzog as premier.

Snowden Philip, 1st Viscount Snowden 1864–1937. British right-wing Labour politician, chancellor of the Exchequer 1924 and 1929–31. He entered the coalition National Government in 1931 as Lord Privy Seal, but resigned in 1932.

Soares Mario 1924– . Portuguese socialist politician, president 1986-96. Exiled 1970, he returned to Portugal 1974, and, as leader of the Portuguese Socialist Party, was prime minister 1976–78. He resigned as party leader 1980, but in 1986 he was elected Portugal's first socialist president.

Sobieski John. Alternative name for John III, king of Poland.

socage Anglo-Saxon term for the free tenure of land by the peasantry. Sokemen, holders of land by this tenure, formed the upper stratum of peasant society at the time of the ◊Domesday Book.

social contract the idea that government authority derives originally from an agreement between ruler and ruled in which the former agrees to provide order in return for obedience from the latter. It has been used to support both absolutism (Hobbes) and democracy (Locke, Rousseau).

The term was revived in the UK in 1974 when a head-on clash between the Conservative government and the trade unions resulted in a general election which enabled a Labour government to take power. It now denotes an unofficial agreement (hence also called 'social compact') between a government and organized labour that, in return for control of prices, rents, and so on, the unions would refrain from economically disruptive wage demands.

social credit theory, put forward by Canadian C H Douglas (1879–1952), that economic crises are caused by bank control of money, which leads to shortage of purchasing power. His remedy was payment of a 'social dividend'. There have been provincial social-credit governments in Canada, but the central government has always vetoed the plan.

social democracy political ideology or belief in the gradual evolution of a democratic ◊socialism within existing political structures. The earliest was the German Sozialdemokratische Partei (SPD) 1891, which had been created after 1875 by the amalgamation of other groups including August Bebel's earlier German Social Democratic Workers' Party, founded 1869. Parties along the lines of the German model were founded in the last two decades of the 19th century in a number of countries, including Austria, Belgium, the Netherlands, Hungary, Poland, and Russia. The British Labour Party is in the social democratic tradition.

Social Democratic Federation (SDF) in British history, a socialist society, founded as the Democratic Federation in 1881 and renamed in 1884. It was led by H M Hyndman (1842–1921), a former conservative journalist and stockbroker who claimed Karl ◊Marx as his inspiration without obtaining recognition from his mentor. In 1911 it became the British Socialist Party.

The SDF organized meetings and marches for the unemployed that led to some clashes with police in central London in 1886 and 1887.

social history branch of history that documents the living and working conditions of people rather than affairs of state. In recent years television programmes, books, and museums have helped to give social history a wide appeal.

History became a serious branch of study in the 18th century, but was confined to ancient civilizations and to recent political and religious history. Only in the early 20th century did historians begin to study how people lived and worked in the past.

socialism movement aiming to establish a classless society by substituting public for private ownership of the means of production, distribution, and exchange. The term has been used to describe positions as widely apart as anarchism and social democracy. Socialist ideas appeared in classical times; in early Christianity; among later Christian sects such as the ◊Anabaptists and ◊Diggers; and, in the 18th and early 19th centuries, were put forward as systematic political aims by Jean-Jacques Rousseau, Claude Saint-Simon, François Fourier, and Robert Owen, among others. See also Karl ◊Marx and Friedrich ◊Engels.

The late 19th and early 20th centuries saw a division between those who reacted against Marxism leading to social-democratic parties and those who emphasized the original revolutionary significance of Marx's teachings. Weakened by these divisions, the second ◊International (founded in 1889) collapsed in 1914, right-wing socialists in all countries supporting participation in World War I while the left opposed it. The Russian Revolution took socialism from the sphere of theory to that of practice, and was followed in 1919 by the foundation of the Third International, which completed the division between right and left. This lack of unity, in spite of the temporary successes of the popular fronts in France and Spain in 1936–38, facilitated the rise of fascism and Nazism.

After World War II socialist and communist parties tended to formal union in Eastern Europe, although the rigid communist control that ensued was later modified in some respects in, for example, Poland, Romania, and Yugoslavia. Subsequent tendencies to broaden communism were suppressed in Hungary (1956) and Czechoslovakia (1968). In 1989, however, revolutionary change throughout Eastern Europe ended this rigid control; this was followed in 1991 by the disbanding of the Soviet Communist Party and the ensuing disintegration of the Soviet Union. In Western Europe a communist takeover of the Portuguese revolution failed 1975–76, and elsewhere, as in France under François Mitterrand, attempts at socialist-communist cooperation petered out. Most countries in W Europe have a strong socialist party; for example, the Social Democratic Party in Germany.

> *Under socialism all will govern in turn and will soon become accustomed to no one governing.*
>
> On *socialism* V I Lenin
> *The State and Revolution*

'**socialism in one country**' concept proposed by ◊Stalin in 1924. In contrast to ◊Trotsky's theory of the permanent revolution, Stalin suggested that the emphasis be changed away from promoting revolutions abroad to the idea of building socialism, economically and politically, in the USSR without help from other countries.

social mobility movement of groups and individuals up and down the social scale in a classed society. The extent or range of social mobility varies in different societies. Individual social mobility may occur through education, marriage, talent, and so on; group mobility usually occurs through change in the occupational structure caused by new technological or economic developments.

The caste system of India and the feudalism of medieval Europe are cited as examples of closed societies, where little social mobility was possible; the class system of Western industrial societies is considered relatively open and flexible.

Solferino, Battle of Napoleon III's victory over the Austrians 1859 at a village near Verona, N Italy, 8 km/5 mi S of Lake Garda.

Solidarity (Polish *Solidarność*) national confederation of independent trade unions in Poland, formed under the leadership of Lech ◊Wałesa Sept 1980. An illegal organization from 1981 to 1989, it was then elected to head the Polish government. Divisions soon emerged in the leadership. Solidarity had 2.8 million members in 1991.

Solomon *c.* 974–*c.* 937 BC. In the Old Testament, third king of Israel, son of David by Bathsheba. During a peaceful reign, he was famed for his wisdom and his alliances with Egypt and Phoneicia. The much later biblical Proverbs, Ecclesiastes, and Song of Songs are attributed to him. He built the temple in Jerusalem with the aid of heavy taxation and forced labour, resulting in the revolt of N Israel.

Solomon Islands country in the SW Pacific Ocean, E of New Guinea, comprising many hundreds of islands, the largest of which is Guadalcanal.

history The islands were inhabited by Melanesians, and were sighted by a 1568 expedition from Peru led by the Spanish navigator Alvaro de Mendaña. They became a British protectorate in the 1890s.

independence The Solomon Islands acquired internal self-government 1976, with Peter Kenilorea, leader of the Solomon Islands

United Party (SIUPA), as chief minister. He became prime minister when they achieved full independence within the Commonwealth 1978. In 1981 he was replaced by Solomon Mamaloni of the People's Progressive Party. Kenilorea had been unable to devolve power to the regions while preserving the unity of the state, but Mamaloni created five ministerial posts specifically for provincial affairs.

In the 1984 general election SIUPA won 13 seats and the opposition, now the People's Alliance Party (PAP), 12. Sir Peter Kenilorea, as he had become, returned to office at the head of a coalition government. He immediately abolished the five provincial ministries. Kenilorea, after narrowly surviving a series of no-confidence motions, resigned again as prime minister Dec 1986, following allegations that he had accepted US $47,000 of French aid to repair cyclone damage to his home village in Malaita province. Kenilorea remained in the cabinet of his successor, Ezekiel Alebua, a fellow SIUPA member, and became deputy prime minister from Feb 1988. In the general election of Feb 1989 support for the SIUPA halved to six seats and the PAP, led by Mamaloni, re-emerged, with 14 seats, as the dominant party. Mamaloni formed a coalition government which included members of the opposition. The coalition government promised to reform the constitution so as to establish a republic and also to reduce the influence of 'foreign aid personnel'. In Oct 1990 Mamaloni resigned as leader of the ruling PAP after a receiving a vote of no confidence. He continued as head of government and as a result both the PAP and the opposition parties splintered into personality-based factions.

foreign relations In its external relations, the Solomon Islands, under the SIUPA administrations, has pursued a moderate pro-Western course. However, during the 1981–84 Mamaloni administration relations with the USA were strained by the government's refusal to allow nuclear-powered warships within the islands' territorial waters. In pursuit of a new, broader 'Pacific strategy', the Solomon Islands joined Papua New Guinea and Vanuatu in forming the Spearhead Group, March 1988, with the aim of preserving Melanesian cultural traditions and securing independence for the French dependency of New Caledonia.

Solon *c.* 638–558 BC. Athenian statesman. As one of the chief magistrates about 594 BC, he carried out the cancellation of all debts from which land or liberty was the security and the revision of the constitution that laid the foundations of Athenian democracy.

If things are going well, religion and legislation are beneficial; if not, they are of no avail.

Solon

Solyman or ◊Suleiman 1494–1566. Ottoman sultan from 1520.

Somalia country in NE Africa (the Horn of Africa), on the Indian Ocean, bounded NW by Djibouti, W by Ethiopia, and SW by Kenya.

history Somalia developed around Arab trading posts that grew into sultanates. A British protectorate of Somaliland was established 1884–87, and Somalia, an Italian protectorate, 1889. The latter was a colony from 1927 and incorporated into Italian East Africa 1936; it came under British military rule 1941–50, when as a United Nations trusteeship it was again administered by Italy.

independence Somalia became a fully independent republic 1960 through a merger of the two former colonial territories. Since then, Somalia has been involved in disputes with its neighbours because of its insistence on the right of all Somalis to self-determination, wherever they have settled. This has frequently applied to those living in the Ogaden district of Ethiopia and in NE Kenya. A dispute over the border with Kenya resulted in a break in diplomatic relations with Britain 1963–68. The dispute with Ethiopia led to an eight-month war 1978, in which Somalia was defeated by Ethiopian troops assisted by Soviet and Cuban weapons and advisers. Some 1.5 million refugees entered Somalia, and guerrilla fighting continued in Ogaden until its secession 1991. There was a rapprochement with Kenya 1984 and, in 1986, the first meeting for ten years between the Somali and Ethiopian leaders.

The first president of Somalia was Aden Abdullah Osman, who was succeeded 1967 by Dr Abdirashid Ali Shermarke of the Somali Youth League (SYL), which had become the dominant political party. In Oct 1969, President Shermarke was assassinated, and the army seized power under Maj-Gen Mohamed Siad Barre. He suspended the 1960 constitution, dissolved the national assembly, banned all political parties, and formed a military government. In 1970 he declared Somalia a socialist state.

one-party state In 1976, the junta transferred power to the newly created SRSP, and three years later the constitution for a one-party state was adopted. Over the next few years Barre consolidated his position by increasing the influence of his own clan and reducing that of his northern rival, despite often violent opposition.

opposition and repression In 1982 the antigovernment Somali National Movement (SNM) was formed. Oppressive counter measures by the government led to an estimated 50,000–60,000 civilian deaths by 1990 and 400,000 refugees fleeing to Ethiopia. All post was censored in the north, identity cards were necessary for travel within the country, and contact with foreigners was discouraged.

Barre was re-elected Jan 1987, although the Somali National Movement had taken control of large parts of the north and east of the country. In riots June 1989 an estimated 400 people were killed by government troops; the government claimed only 24 people died. Government soldiers, pursuing refugees believed to be SNM rebels, crossed into Kenya Sept 1989 and killed four Kenyan policemen. Kenya threatened reprisals even as Prime Minister Samantar announced the release of all political prisoners. He ruled out talks with the SNM.

rebel coup In Jan 1991 President Barre survived an attempted coup but fled the capital as rebels captured it. After discussions with different political and social groups, Ali Mahdi Mohammed was named president. The secession of NE Somalia, as the Somaliland Republic, was announced May 1991. A cease-fire signed June 1991 between four rival Somali factions (United Somali Congress (USC), Somali Salvation Democratic Front (SSDF), Somali Patriotic Movement (SPM), and Somali Democratic Movement (SDM)), failed to hold. In Sept 1991 the outbreak of severe fighting with many casualties was reported in Mogadishu, the capital. The fighting continued in the succeeding months and 20,000 people were reported to have been killed or injured by the year's end.

It was revealed April 1992 that Mohamed Siad Barre had given up his attempt to return to power and had taken his family and the remnants of his army into exile in Kenya.

famine The widespread famine of 1992, caused in most part by the civil war, was estimated by the International Red Cross to have affected more than a quarter of Somalia's 6 million people. In order to alleviate this disaster, the US organized its largest relief operation to Africa in Aug. Other Western nations also contributed to the airlift and the UN sent troops to guard the food shipments. Even so, relief efforts were hampered by the political instability, and on 9 Dec a contingent of 1,800 US Marines landed in Mogadishu and seized control of the harbour and airport. They were the first of a planned US military presence of 30,000; France and Italy also committed themselves to sending troops. Two days later the two dominant warlords in the area, Ali Mahdi Mohammed and General Mohammed Farah Aideed, both of the USC, agreed a truce.

Somerset Edward Seymour, 1st Duke of Somerset *c.* 1506–1552. English politician. Created Earl of Hertford after Henry VIII's marriage to his sister Jane, he became Duke of Somerset and protector (regent) for Edward VI in 1547. His attempt to check ◊enclosure (the transfer of land from common to private ownership) offended landowners and his moderation in religion upset the Protestants, and he was beheaded on a fake treason charge in 1552.

If we had heroes in previous wars, today we have them not in thousands but in half millions.

On the *Battle of the Somme*
Captain Reginald Leetham, diary 1916

Somme, Battle of the Allied offensive in World War I July–Nov 1916 at Beaumont-Hamel-Chaulnes, on the river Somme in N France, during which severe losses were suffered by both sides. It was planned by the Marshal of France, Joseph Joffre, and UK commander in chief Douglas Haig; the Allies lost over 600,000 soldiers and advanced 32 km/20 mi. It was the first battle in which tanks were used. The German offensive around St Quentin March–April 1918 is sometimes called the Second Battle of the Somme.

Somoza García Anastasio 1896–1956. Nicaraguan soldier and politician, president 1937–47 and 1950–56. A protégé of the USA, who wanted a reliable ally to protect their interests in Central America, he was virtual dictator of Nicaragua from 1937 until his assassination in 1956. He exiled most of his political opponents and amassed a considerable fortune in land and businesses. Members of his family retained control of the country until 1979, when they were overthrown by popular forces.

Song dynasty or *Sung dynasty* Chinese imperial family 960–1279, founded by northern general Taizu (Zhao Kuangyin 928–76). A distinction is conventionally made between the Northern Song period 960–1126, when the capital lay at Kaifeng, and Southern Song 1127–1279, when it was at Hangzhou (Hangchow). A stable government was supported by a thoroughly centralized administration. The dynasty was eventually ended by Mongol invasion.

During the Song era, such technology as shipbuilding, firearms, clock-making, and the use of the compass, was far ahead of western Europe. Painting, poetry, and ceramics flourished, as did economic development, particularly in the rice-growing SE. NE China remained independent of the Song, being ruled by the◊Liao and ◊Jin dynasties.

Songhai Empire former kingdom of NW Africa, founded in the 8th century, which developed into a powerful Muslim empire under the rule of Sonni Ali (reigned 1464–92). It superseded the ◊Mali Empire and extended its territory, occupying an area that included parts of present-day Guinea, Burkina Faso, Senegal, Gambia, Mali, Mauritania, Niger, and Nigeria. In 1591 it was invaded and overthrown by Morocco.

Sons of Liberty in American colonial history, the name adopted by those colonists opposing the ◊Stamp Act of 1765. Merchants, lawyers, farmers, artisans, and labourers joined what was an early instance of concerted resistance to British rule, causing the repeal of the act in March 1766.

Sophia Electress of Hanover 1630–1714. Twelfth child of Frederick V, elector palatine of the Rhine and king of Bohemia, and Elizabeth, daughter of James I of England.

Soult Nicolas Jean de Dieu 1769–1851. Marshal of France. He held commands in Spain in the Peninsular War, where he sacked the port of Santander 1808, and was Chief of Staff at the Battle of ◊Waterloo. He was war minister 1830–40.

Souphanouvong Prince 1912–95. Laotian politician, president 1975–86. After an abortive revolt against French rule in 1945, he led the guerrilla organization Pathet Lao, and in 1975 became the first president of the Republic of Laos.

South Africa country on the southern tip of Africa, bounded N by Namibia, Botswana, and Zimbabwe and NE by Mozambique and Swaziland.

history The area was originally inhabited by Kung and Khoikhoi. Bantu-speaking peoples, including Sotho, Swazi, Xhosa, and Zulu, settled there before the 17th century. The Cape of Good Hope was rounded by Bartolomeu Diaz 1488; the coast of Natal was sighted by Vasco da Gama 1497. The Dutch East India Company founded Cape Town 1652 as a port of call

on the way to the Indies. Occupied by Britain 1795 and 1806, Cape Town and the hinterland were purchased by Britain 1814 for £6 million. Britons also settled in Natal, on the coast near Durban, 1824. In 1836 some 10,000 Dutch, wishing to escape from British rule, set out north on the Great Trek and founded the republic of Transvaal and the Orange Free State; they also settled in N Natal, which became part of Cape Colony 1844 and a separate colony 1856. The Orange Free State was annexed by Britain 1848 but became independent 1854.

Boer War The discovery of diamonds at Kimberley, Cape Colony, 1867, and of gold in Transvaal 1886, attracted prospectors, who came into conflict with the Dutch farmers, the ◊Boers. Britain attempted to occupy Transvaal 1877–81 but withdrew after a severe defeat at Majuba in the first of the ◊South African Wars. Denial of citizenship rights to the migrant miners (uitlanders) in Transvaal, and the imperialist ambitions of Cecil ◊Rhodes and others, led to the Jameson Raid (see L S ◊Jameson) and the Boer War 1899–1902.

Union of South Africa In 1910 the Union of South Africa was formed, comprising the provinces of Cape of Good Hope, Natal, Orange Free State, and Transvaal. A Boer rebellion on the outbreak of World War I was speedily crushed by Jan ◊Smuts. South Africa occupied German SW Africa (now Namibia). Between the wars the union was alternately governed by the republican nationalists under James ◊Hertzog and the South African Party under Smuts, who supported the Commonwealth connection. Hertzog wanted South Africa to be neutral in World War II, but Smuts took over as premier, and South African troops fought with the Allies.

introduction of apartheid The National Party (NP) came to power 1948 and has ruled South Africa ever since. Its leader, Daniel Malan, initiated the policy of apartheid, attempting to justify it as 'separate but equal' development. In fact, all but the white minority are denied a voice in the nation's affairs. In the 1950s the ◊African National Congress (ANC) led a campaign of civil disobedience until it and other similar movements were declared illegal 1960, and in 1964 the ANC leader Nelson Mandela was sentenced to life imprisonment for alleged sabotage. He became a central symbol of black opposition to the apartheid regime, remaining in prison until 1990.

'homelands' established Malan was succeeded 1958 by Hendrik ◊Verwoerd, who with-

drew from the Commonwealth rather than abandon apartheid, and the Union became the Republic of South Africa 1961. Verwoerd was assassinated 1966, but his successor, B J ◊Vorster, pursued the same policy. Pass laws restricting the movement of blacks within the country had been introduced, causing international outrage, and ten 'homelands' (Bantustans; see ◊Black National State) were established to contain particular ethnic groups. By the 1980s thousands of the apartheid regime's opponents had been imprisoned without trial and more than 3,000,000 people had been forcibly resettled in black townships. International condemnation of police brutality followed the news of the death in detention of the black community leader Steve Biko 1977.

constitutional reform In 1978 Vorster resigned and was succeeded by Pieter W ◊Botha. He embarked on constitutional reform to involve coloureds and Asians, but not blacks, in the governmental process. This led to a clash within the NP, and in March 1982 Dr Andries Treurnicht, leader of the hardline (*verkrampte*) wing, and 15 other extremists were expelled. They later formed a new party, the Conservative Party of South Africa (CPSA). Although there were considerable doubts about Botha's proposals in the coloured and Indian communities as well as among the whites, they were approved by 66% of the voters in an all-white referendum and came into effect Sept 1984. In 1985 a number of apartheid laws were amended or repealed, including the ban on sexual relations or marriage between people of different races and the ban on mixed racial membership of political parties, but the underlying inequalities in the system remained and dissatisfaction of the black community grew. In the 1986 cabinet of 21, including Botha, there were 19 whites, 1 coloured, and 1 Indian. The National Party continued to increase its majority at each election, with the white opposition parties failing to unseat the NP. Both the Conservative Party (CP) and the Democratic Party (DP) made gains in the Sept 1989 elections, with the ruling NP losing one-quarter of its seats. Its new total was only nine seats more than was required for a majority, its worst electoral showing since coming to power 1948.

state of emergency In May 1986 South Africa attacked what it claimed to be guerrilla strongholds in Botswana, Zambia, and Zimbabwe. The exiled ANC leader Oliver ◊Tambo was receiving increasing moral support in meetings with politicians throughout the world, and Winnie Mandela, during her husband's continuing imprisonment, was 'banned' repeatedly

for condemning the system publicly. Nonviolent resistance was advocated by Bishop ◊Tutu, the ◊Inkatha movement, and others. A state of emergency was declared June 1986, a few days before the tenth anniversary of the first ◊Soweto uprising, marked by a strike in which millions of blacks participated. Serious rioting broke out in the townships and was met with police violence, causing hundreds of deaths. Between 1980 and 1990 some 1,070 people were judicially executed.

sanctions imposed Abroad, calls for economic sanctions against South Africa grew during 1985 and 1986. At the Heads of Commonwealth conference 1985 the Eminent Persons' Group (EPG) of Commonwealth politicians was conceived to investigate the likelihood of change in South Africa without sanctions. In July 1986 the EPG reported that there were no signs of genuine liberalization. Reluctantly, Britain's prime minister, Margaret Thatcher, agreed to limited measures. Some Commonwealth countries, notably Australia and Canada, took additional independent action. The US Congress eventually forced President Reagan to move in the same direction. Between 1988 and 1990 economic sanctions cost the South African treasury more than $4 billion in lost revenue. The decisions by individual multinational companies to close down their South African operations may, in the long term, have the greatest effect.

promise of reform At the end of 1988 South Africa signed a peace agreement with Angola and Cuba, which included the acceptance of Namibia's independence, and in 1989, under UN supervision, free elections took place there. In Feb 1989 state president Botha suffered a stroke that forced him to give up the NP leadership and later the presidency. He was succeeded in both roles by F W de Klerk, who promised major constitutional reforms. Meanwhile the nonracialist Democratic Party was launched, advocating universal adult suffrage, and made significant progress in the Sept 1989 whites-only assembly elections. Despite de Klerk's release of the veteran ANC activist, Walter Sisulu, and some of his colleagues Oct 1989, the new president's promises of political reform were treated with scepticism by the opposition until he announced the lifting of the ban on the ANC, followed by the release of Mandela 11 Feb 1990. In Sept President de Klerk declared membership of the National Party open to all races. In Dec ANC president Tambo returned triumphantly and in Jan 1991 after a meeting between Nelson Mandela and Zulu leader Chief Buthelezi both urged their followers to end attacks on one other. Mandela was subsequently elected ANC president, but revelations of government financial support and police funding for Inkatha political activities, for example to counter the ANC and foment division among blacks, threatened ANC cooperation.

abandonment of apartheid announced In Feb 1991 President de Klerk announced the intended repeal of all remaining apartheid laws. In March he announced legislation to abolish all racial controls on land ownership, enabling all South Africans to purchase land anywhere.

In June 1991 all the remaining racially discriminating laws were repealed. As a result the USA lifted its trade and investment sanctions against South Africa in July and the country was readmitted into international sport by the International Olympic Committee. In Sept President de Klerk announced a draft constitution, giving black people the franchise but providing strong safeguards for the white minority. It was immediately criticized by the ANC because it served to perpetuate the white hegemony. However, the ANC agreed to negotiate and it joined with the Pan-Africanist Congress (PAC) to form a united front against the government.

South African Wars and aftermath			
1867	Diamonds discovered in Griqualand.	June	Pretoria captured.
1871	Diamond fields annexed by British, and administered by Cape Colony.	Aug	Buller defeated Louis Botha at Bergendal in last set-piece battle of the war. Refugee camps established, which were later transformed into notorious concentration camps.
1877	First annexation of the Transvaal, also known as the South African Republic (SAR).		
1879	Zulu War. British forces invaded and annexed Zululand.	Sept	Roberts formally annexed Transvaal and declared the war over.
1880–81	First South African (Boer) War against Afrikaners led by Paul Kruger. British defeated at Majuba Hill (Feb 1881). Pretoria Convention restoreed limited independence to SAR.	Oct	Kruger sailed for France and Buller returned to England. Formal proclamation at Pretoria of annexation of Transvaal.
1886	Large gold deposits found on the Witwatersrand.	Nov	Kitchener succeeded Roberts as commander in chief in South Africa and initiated farm-burning policy to deprive Boer rebels of essential supplies. Administration of concentration camps transferred from military to civilian authorities. Roberts returned to England.
1890	Cecil Rhodes became prime minister of Cape Colony.		
1895–96	Jameson Raid failed to overthrow SAR. Rhodes implicated and resigned as Cape prime minister.	Dec	Guerrilla war began as Boers retook initiative and 'invaded' the Cape. War of attrition began.
1897	Sir Alfred Milner appointed as British high commissioner at the Cape.		
1899 Oct	Outbreak of the (second) Boer War. Boer sieges of Kimberley, Mafeking, and Ladysmith began.	1901 Jan	Modderfontein captured by Boer general Jan Smuts. Africans massacred.
Dec	'Black week': British commander in chief Sir Redvers Buller suffered defeats at Stormberg, Magersfontein, and Colenso. Lord Roberts replaced Buller and appointed Kitchener as Chief of Staff.	Feb	Abortive peace talks at Middelburg between Kitchener and Botha.
		May	Milner sailed for England. Military situation unresolved throughout the rest of year. Anti-guerrilla tactics of using large numbers of mounted troops to sweep areas cordoned by barbed wire and blockhouses only partially successful.
1900 Jan	Roberts and Kitchener arrived in Cape Town. Battle of Spion Kop.		
Feb	Roberts began march through the Cape. Kimberley relieved. Battle of Paardeberg and surrender of Piet Cronje's force of commandos. Buller finally relieved Ladysmith.	1902 March	Cecil Rhodes died.
		April–May	Meeting of Boer peace delegates at Pretoria, who then met British officials at Vereeniging to finalize surrender terms. War ended.
March	Roberts captured Bloemfontein, capital of Orange Free State.	1905	Liberal Party elected to office in Britain.
		1907	Transvaal received self-government.
May	Mafeking relieved and Johannesburg captured.	1910	Unification of South African colonies and creation of the dominion of South Africa.

In Dec, however, PAC withdrew, claiming that the planning of the negotiations was undemocratic. Chief Buthelezi also withdrew, but Inkatha remained. A whites-only referendum held March 1992 gave de Klerk a clear mandate to proceed with plans for the new constitution which would end white minority rule.

massacre at Boipatong More than 40 people were killed in the black township of Boipatong by Inkatha, aided and abetted by police, June 1992. The ANC called a halt to the constitutional talks until the government took steps to curb township violence.

The Boers said the war was for liberty. The British said it was for equality. The majority of the inhabitants, who were not white at all, gained neither liberty nor equality.

On the second *South African War* (Boer War) Rayne Kruger 1959

South African Wars two wars between the Boers (settlers of Dutch origin) and the British; essentially fought for the gold and diamonds of the Transvaal.

The *War of 1881* was triggered by the attempt of the Boers of the ◊Transvaal to reassert the independence surrendered 1877 in return for British aid against African peoples. The British were defeated at Majuba, and the Transvaal again became independent.

The *War of 1899–1902*, also known as the *Boer War*, was preceded by the armed Jameson Raid into the Boer Transvaal; a failed attempt, inspired by the Cape Colony prime minister Rhodes, to precipitate a revolt against Kruger, the Transvaal president. The *uitlanders* (non-Boer immigrants) were still not given the vote by the Boers, negotiations failed, and the Boers invaded British territory, besieging Ladysmith, Mafeking (now Mafikeng), and Kimberley. The war ended with the Peace of Vereeniging following the Boer defeat.

British commander ◊Kitchener countered Boer guerrilla warfare by putting the noncombatants who supported them into concentration camps, where about 26,000 women and children died of sickness.

South America fourth largest of the continents, nearly twice as large as Europe (13% of the world's land surface), extending S from ◊Central America.

history (for the archaic and later American Indian cultures, see ◊American Indian):

16th century Arrival of Europeans, with the Spanish (Pizarro) and Portuguese conquest; the local people were mainly killed, assimilated, or, where considered unsuitable for slave labour, replaced by imported slaves from Africa.

18th century Revolt of Túpac Amaru.

19th century Napoleon's toppling of the Spanish throne opened the way for the liberation of its colonies (led by Simón Bolívar and José de San Martín). Brazil became independent peacefully. Large-scale European immigration took place (Hispanic, Italian, and German). Interstate wars took a heavy toll—for example, the Paraguay War and Pacific War.

20th century Rapid industrialization and high population growth. In the 1980s heavy indebtedness incurred to fund economic expansion led to an inability to meet interest payments in the world slump.

1946–55 Juan Perón was president in Argentina.

1952 Revolution in Bolivia limited large landowners, nationalized tin mines.

1970–73 Elected socialist government under Salvador Allende in Chile ended in military coup backed by the US Central Intelligence Agency.

1982 Falklands War between the UK and Argentina.

1985 Brazil inaugurated its first civilian president since 1964.

1989 Democratic transition of power in Argentina. Initial steps taken towards reestablishment of relations with Britain.

Southampton Insurrection US slave revolt in Southampton County, Virginia, 1831 led by Nat ◊Turner.

Southeast Asia Treaty Organization (SEATO) collective military system 1954–77 established by Australia, France, New Zealand, Pakistan, the Philippines, Thailand, the UK, and the USA, with Vietnam, Cambodia, and Laos as protocol states. After the Vietnam War, SEATO was phased out.

Its nonmilitary aspects were assumed by the ◊Association of Southeast Asian Nations (ASEAN).

Southern Christian Leadership Conference (SCLC) US civil-rights organization founded 1957 by Martin Luther ◊King, Jr, and led by him until his assassination 1968. It advocated nonviolence and passive resistance, and it sponsored the 1963 march on Washington DC that focused national attention on the civil-rights movement. Its nonviolent philosophy

EL SALVADOR
1838
HONDURAS 1838
NICARAGUA 1838

MOSQUITO COAST
(TO NICARAGUA 1860)

Caribbean Sea

COSTA RICA
1838
•Panama
PANAMA 1903

Caracas

VENEZUELA
1830

Georgetown
BRITISH
DUTCH
Paramaribo• •Cayenne
FRENCH

GUIANA

•Bogotá
COLOMBIA
1831
(name taken in 1861)

•Quito
ECUADOR
1830

Amazon

•Lima

PERU
1821

B R A Z I L
1 8 2 2
(Empire until 1889)

•Brasília

La Paz•
BOLIVIA
1825

Pacific

Ocean

Rio de Janeiro•
PARAGUAY
1811
São Paulo•
•Asunción

ARGENTINA
1810
(Argentine
Confederation
until 1853)

URUGUAY
1828

Buenos
Aires•
•Montevideo

•Santiago

Plate

CHILE
1818

Atlantic

Ocean

N

Falkland Islands
(to UK 1833)

SOUTH AMERICA AFTER INDEPENDENCE

Main blocks of territory disputed
and changing hands during the
wars of the nineteenth century

European possessions

Peru and Bolivia were confederated 1836–39

0		1600 km
0		1000 miles

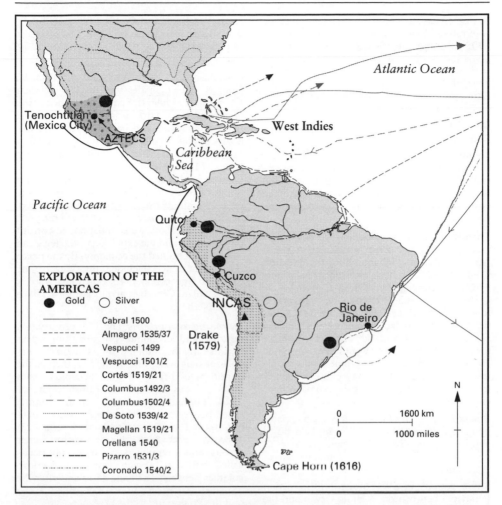

EXPLORATION OF THE AMERICAS

- ● Gold
- ○ Silver

————	Cabral 1500
--------	Almagro 1535/37
— — — —	Vespucci 1499
— — — —	Vespucci 1501/2
— — — —	Cortés 1519/21
·············	Columbus1492/3
— — — —	Columbus1502/4
·············	De Soto 1539/42
————	Magellan 1519/21
—·—·—·	Orellana 1540
— —·— —	Pizarro 1531/3
——————	Coronado 1540/2

Drake (1579)

Exploration of the Americas Spain's encounter with the New World began with Columbus's first voyage of 1492. The Spanish conquest of Mexico and Peru was hastened by the help the conquistadors received from discontented subjects of the ruling Aztecs and Incas. By 1560 silver, obtained largely with slave labour from the local Indians, was the Spanish colonies' chief export. In 1500 Pedro Cabral established Portugal's link with modern-day Brazil, which during the next hundred years was established as the world's biggest producer of sugar.

was increasingly challenged by militants, and it lost its central position in the movement.

The Rev Jesse ◊Jackson began his association with the civil-rights movement with King at the SCLC.

South America after independence Although the Wars of Liberation date from 1808, when Napoleon's armies invaded Spain, to 1826, many of the existing South American nations did not gain their independence until later in the century. Brazil, which broke with Portugal 1822, retained a monarchy while all other South American nations chose to become republics.

South Sea Bubble financial crisis in Britain in 1720. The South Sea Company, founded 1711, which had a monopoly of trade with South America, offered in 1719 to take over more than half the national debt in return for further concessions. Its 100 shares rapidly rose to 1,000, and an orgy of speculation followed. When the 'bubble' burst, thousands were ruined. The discovery that cabinet ministers had been guilty of corruption led to a political crisis.

South West Africa former name (to 1968) of ◊Namibia.

soviet (Russian 'council') originally a strike committee elected by Russian workers in the 1905 revolution; in 1917 these were set up by peasants, soldiers, and factory workers. The soviets sent delegates to the All-Russian Congress of Soviets to represent their opinions to a future government. They were later taken over by the ◊Bolsheviks.

Soviet Union see ◊Union of Soviet Socialist Republics.

sovkhoz Soviet state-owned farm where the workers were state employees (such farms are still widespread in ex-Soviet republics). The sovkhoz differs from the *kolkhoz* where the farm is run by a collective (see ◊collective farm).

Soweto (acronym for *South West Township*) racially segregated urban settlement in South Africa, SW of Johannesburg; population (1983) 915,872. It has experienced civil unrest because of the ◊apartheid regime.

It began as a shanty town in the 1930s and is now the largest black city in South Africa, but until 1976 its population could have status only as temporary residents, serving as a workforce for Johannesburg. There were serious riots June 1976, sparked by a ruling that Afrikaans be used in African schools there. Reforms followed, but riots flared up again 1985 and have continued into the 1990s.

Spaak Paul-Henri 1899–1972. Belgian socialist politician. From 1936 to 1966 he held office almost continuously as foreign minister or prime minister. He was an ardent advocate of international peace.

Spain country in SW Europe, on the Iberian Peninsula between the Atlantic Ocean and the Mediterranean Sea, bounded N by France and W by Portugal.

history Pre-Roman Spain was inhabited by Iberians, Basques, Celts, and Celtiberians. Greece and Phoenicia established colonies on the coast from the 7th century BC; Carthage dominated from the 5th century, trying to found an empire in the southeast. This was conquered by ancient Rome about 200 BC, and after a long struggle all Spain was absorbed into the Roman Empire. At the invitation of Rome the Visigoths (see ◊Goths) set up a kingdom in Spain from the beginning of the 5th century AD until the invasion by the ◊Moors 711. Christian resistance held out in the north, and by 1248 they had reconquered all Spain except ◊Granada. During this struggle a number of small kingdoms were formed, all of which by the 13th century had been absorbed by ◊Castile and ◊Aragon. The marriage of Ferdinand of

Aragon to Isabella of Castile 1469 united their domains on their accession 1479. The conquest of Granada 1492 completed the unification of Spain.

world power Under Ferdinand and Isabella, Charles I (see ◊Charles V of the Holy Roman Empire), and Philip II, Spain became one of the greatest powers in the world. The discoveries of Columbus, made on behalf of Spain, were followed by the conquest of most of Central and South America. Naples and Sicily were annexed 1503, Milan 1535, Portugal 1580, and Charles I inherited the Netherlands, but with the revolt in the Netherlands from 1568 and the defeat of the Armada 1588, Spain's power began to decline. The loss of civil and religious freedom, constant wars, inflation, a corrupt bureaucracy, and the expulsion of the Jews and Moors undermined the economy. By the peace of Utrecht that concluded the War of the ◊Spanish Succession 1713, Spain lost Naples, Sicily, Milan, Gibraltar, and its last possessions in the Netherlands.

wars and revolutions The 18th century saw reforms and economic progress, but Spain became involved in the ◊Revolutionary and ◊Napoleonic wars, first as the ally, then as the opponent of France. France occupied Spain 1808 and was expelled with British assistance 1814. Throughout the 19th century conflict raged between monarchists and liberals; revolutions and civil wars took place 1820–23, 1833–39, and 1868, besides many minor revolts, and a republic was temporarily established 1873–74. Spain lost its American colonies between 1810 and 1830 and after the ◊Spanish–American War 1898 ceded Cuba and the Philippines to the USA.

Spanish Civil War Republicanism, socialism, and anarchism grew after 1900; ◊Primo de Rivera's dictatorship 1923–30 failed to preserve the monarchy under ◊Alfonso XIII, and in 1931 a republic was established. In 1936 the Popular Front, a centre-left alliance, took office and introduced agrarian and other reforms that aroused the opposition of the landlords and the Catholic church. A military rebellion led by General Francisco ◊Franco resulted in the Spanish ◊Civil War 1936–39. Franco, who was supported by the German Nazis and Italian Fascists, won the war, establishing a military dictatorship.

monarchy restored In 1947 Franco allowed the revival of a legislature with limited powers and announced that after his death the monarchy would be restored, naming the grandson of the last monarch, Prince Juan Carlos de

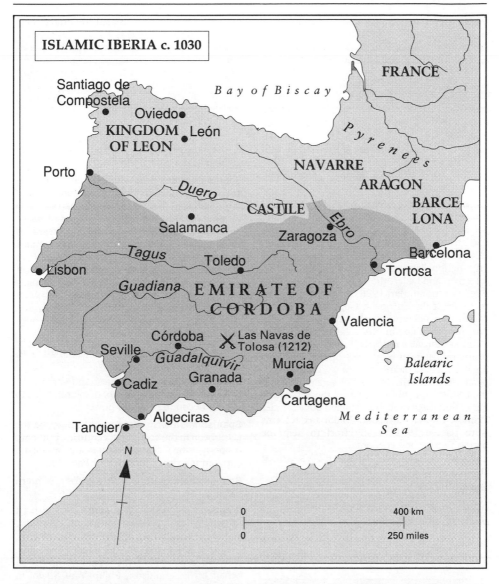

ISLAMIC IBERIA c. 1030

Santiago de Compostela
Oviedo
KINGDOM OF LEON
León
Porto
NAVARRE
ARAGON
BARCE-LONA
Duero
CASTILE
Ebro
Salamanca
Zaragoza
Barcelona
Tagus
Toledo
Tortosa
Lisbon
Guadiana
EMIRATE OF CÓRDOBA
Valencia
Córdoba
Las Navas de Tolosa (1212)
Seville
Guadalquivir
Murcia
Balearic Islands
Cadiz
Granada
Cartagena
Algeciras
Mediterranean Sea
Tangier
N

Bay of Biscay
FRANCE
Pyrenees

0   400 km
0   250 miles

Islamic Iberia c.1030 *The Omayyads took most of Iberia from the Visigoths between 711 and 718. The emirate of Córdoba was consequently established as a brilliant centre of Islamic civilization, considerably more advanced than its neighbouring Christian states of Navarre, Aragón, Castile, Barcelona, and León. Civil strife within Islamic Iberia allowed the Christians to begin the process of driving back the Moors known as the Reconquista. The Almohad army was destroyed at Navas de Tolosa 1212, and by 1248 only Granada remained in Muslim hands.*

Bourbon, as his successor. Franco died 1975, and King Juan Carlos became head of state. There followed a slow but steady progress to democratic government, with the new constitution endorsed by referendum 1978.

regional demands and right-wing threat
Spain faced two main internal problems: the

demands for independence by regional extremists and the possibility of a right-wing military coup. The leader of the ruling Democratic Centre Party (UCD), Adolfo Suárez, suddenly resigned 1981 and was succeeded by his deputy, Leopoldo Calvo Sotelo. He was immediately confronted with an attempted army coup in Madrid, while at the same time the military commander of Valencia declared a state of emergency there and sent tanks out on the streets. Both uprisings failed, and the two leaders were tried and imprisoned.

Sotelo's decision to take Spain into NATO was widely criticized, and he was forced to call a general election Oct 1982. The result was a sweeping victory for the Socialist Workers' Party (PSOE), led by Felipe González. The ♢Basque separatist organization, ETA, had stepped up its campaign for independence with widespread terrorist activity, spreading in 1985 to the Mediterranean holiday resorts and threatening Spain's lucrative tourist industry.

González administration The PSOE had fought the 1982 election on a policy of taking Spain out of NATO and carrying out extensive nationalization. Once in office, however, González showed himself to be a pragmatist. His nationalization programme was highly selective, and he left the decision on NATO to a referendum. In Jan 1986 Spain became a full member of the European Community, and in March the referendum showed popular support for remaining in NATO. In the July 1986 election González returned for another term as prime minister. In Nov 1988 Spain, with Portugal, became a member of the ♢Western European Union. In the Nov 1989 general election the PSOE won only 175 seats in the 350-member national assembly but retained power under Prime Minister González. Major tax reforms were passed 1991 in an effort to help the nation's struggling economy.

After an unofficial truce, ETA's armed struggle resumed Aug 1992.

Spain flourished as a province, and has declined as a kingdom.

On *Spain* Edward Gibbon
The Decline and Fall of the Roman Empire
1776–88

Spandau suburb of Berlin, Germany. The chief war criminals condemned at the Nuremberg Trials 1946 were imprisoned in the fortress there. The last of them was the Nazi leader Rudolf Hess, and the prison was demolished after his death 1987.

Spanish-American War brief war 1898 between Spain and the USA over Spanish rule in Cuba and the Philippines; the complete defeat of Spain made the USA a colonial power. The Treaty of Paris ceded the Philippines, Guam, and Puerto Rico to the USA; Cuba became independent. The USA paid $20

million to Spain. Thus ended Spain's colonial presence in the Americas.

The war began in Cuba when the US battleship *Maine* was blown up in Havana harbour, allegedly by the Spanish. Other engagements included the Battle of Manila Bay, in which Commander George Dewey's navy destroyed the Spanish fleet in the Philippines; and the taking of the Cuban port cities of El Caney and San Juan Heights (in which Theodore Roosevelt's regiment, the Rough Riders, was involved), destroying the Spanish fleet there.

Spanish Armada fleet sent by Philip II of Spain against England in 1588. Consisting of 130 ships, it sailed from Lisbon and carried on a running fight up the Channel with the English fleet of 197 small ships under Howard of Effingham and Francis ♢Drake. The Armada anchored off Calais but fireships forced it to put to sea, and a general action followed off Gravelines. What remained of the Armada escaped around the N of Scotland and W of Ireland, suffering many losses by storm and shipwreck on the way. Only about half the original fleet returned to Spain.

Spanish Civil War 1936–39. See ♢Civil War, Spanish.

Spanish Empire the conquest and annexation of territories from the time of ♢Columbus led to ♢Spain becoming a world power.

Spanish Main term often used to describe the Caribbean in the 16th–17th centuries, but more properly the South American mainland between the river Orinoco and Panama.

Spanish Sahara former name for ♢Western Sahara.

Spanish Succession, War of the war 1701–14 of Britain, Austria, the Netherlands, Portugal, and Denmark (the Allies) against France, Spain, and Bavaria. It was caused by Louis XIV's acceptance of the Spanish throne on behalf of his grandson, Philip V of Spain, in defiance of the Partition Treaty of 1700, under which it would have passed to Archduke Charles of Austria (later Holy Roman emperor Charles VI).

Peace was made by the Treaties of Utrecht 1713 and Rastatt 1714. Philip V was recognized as king of Spain, thus founding the Spanish branch of the Bourbon dynasty. Britain received Gibraltar, Minorca, and Nova Scotia; and Austria received Belgium, Milan, and Naples.

1704 The French marched on Vienna to try to end the war, but were defeated at *Blenheim* by the Duke of Marlborough and Eugène of Savoy.

1705 The Allies invaded Spain, twice occupying Madrid but failing to hold it.

1706 Marlborough was victorious over the French (under Villeroi) at *Ramillies* 23 May, in Brabant, Belgium.

1708 Marlborough and Eugène were victorious over the French (under the Duke of Burgundy and Vendôme) at *Oudenaarde* (near Ghent, Belgium) 30 June–11 July.

1709 Marlborough was victorious with Eugène over the French (under Villars) at *Malplaquet* 11 Sept.

1713 Treaties of Utrecht and *1714* Rastat under which the Allies recognized Philip as King of Spain, but Gibraltar, Minorca, and Nova Scotia were ceded to Britain, and Belgium, Milan, and Naples to Austria.

Sparta ancient Greek city-state in the S Peloponnese, developed from Dorian settlements in the 10th century BC. The Dorians formed the ruling race in Sparta, the original inhabitants being divided into *perioeci* (tributaries without political rights) and helots or serfs. The state was ruled by two hereditary kings, and under the constitution attributed to Lycurgus all citizens were trained for war from childhood. As a result, the Spartans became proverbial for their indifference to pain or death, their contempt for luxury and the arts, and their harsh treatment of the helots. They distinguished themselves in the ◊Persian and ◊Peloponnesian wars, but defeat by the Thebans in 371 BC marked the start of their decline. The ancient city was destroyed by the Visigoths in 396 AD.

They resisted to the last, with their swords if they had them, and, if not, with their hands and teeth.

On the defeat of *Sparta* at the battle of Thermopylae, Herodius *Histories* VII 227

Spartacist member of a group of left-wing radicals in Germany at the end of World War I, founders of the *Spartacus League*, which became the German Communist Party in 1919. The league participated in the Berlin workers' revolt of Jan 1919, which was suppressed by the Freikorps on the orders of the socialist government. The agitation ended with the murder of Spartacist leaders Karl ◊Liebknecht and Rosa ◊Luxemburg.

Spartacus died 71 BC. Thracian gladiator who in 73 BC led a revolt of gladiators and slaves in Capua, near Naples and swept through southern Italy and Cisalpine Gaul. He was eventually caught by Roman general Crassus 71 BC and Spartacus and his followers were crucified.

Special Areas Acts UK acts of Parliament 1936 and 1937, aimed at dealing with high unemployment in some regions of Britain. These areas, designated 'special areas', attracted government assistance in the form of loans and subsidies to generate new employment. Other measures included setting up industrial and trading estates that could be leased at subsidized rates. The acts were an early example of regional aid.

special relationship belief that ties of common language, culture, and shared aims of the defence of democratic principles should sustain a political relationship between the USA and the UK, and that the same would not apply to relationships between the USA and other European states.

Close cooperation in the sharing of nuclear-weapons technology has usually been cited as evidence of this bond, whereas the belated entry of the USA into both world wars in support of the UK has been interpreted as proof of its limitations in the light of political realities. Despite the special relationship, differences of opinion have occurred, largely reflecting the role of the USA as a superpower with concomitant global views compared to that of Britain as an increasingly European-oriented state.

Speenhamland system method of poor relief in England started by Berkshire magistrates in 1795, whereby wages were supplemented from the poor-rates. However, it encouraged the payment of low wages and was superseded by the 1834 ◊Poor Law.

Speer Albert 1905–1981. German architect and minister in the Nazi government during World War II.

spoils system in the USA, the granting of offices and favours among the supporters of a party in office. The spoils system, a type of ◊patronage, was used by President Jackson in the 1830s in particular, and by Republican administrations after the civil war. The practice remained common in the 20th century in US local government.

SPQR abbreviation for *Senatus Populusque Romanus*, Latin 'the Senate and the Roman People'.

Spurs, Battle of the alternative name for the Battle of ◊Courtrai.

Sri Lanka island in the Indian Ocean, off the SE coast of India.

history The aboriginal people, the Vedda, were conquered about 550 BC by the Sinhalese from India under their first king, Vijaya. In the 3rd century BC the island became a world centre of Buddhism. The spice trade brought Arabs, who called the island Serendip, and Europeans, who called it Ceylon. Portugal established settlements 1505, taken over by the Netherlands 1658 and by Britain 1796. Ceylon was ceded to Britain 1802 and became a crown colony.

Sinhalese/Tamil conflict Under British rule Tamils (originally from S India but long settled in the north and east) took up English education and progressed rapidly in administrative careers. Many more Tamils immigrated to work on new tea and rubber plantations in central Sri Lanka. Conflicts between the Sinhalese majority and the Tamils surfaced during the 1920s as nationalist politics developed. In 1931, universal suffrage was introduced for an elected legislature and executive council in which power was shared with the British, and in Feb 1948 independence was achieved.

dominion status Between 1948 and 1972, Sri Lanka remained a dominion within the British Commonwealth with a titular governor general. The United National Party (UNP), led consecutively by Don and Dudley ◊Senanayake, held power until 1956, when the radical socialist and more narrowly Sinhalese Sri Lanka Freedom Party (SLFP), led by Solomon ◊Bandaranaike, gained electoral victory and established Sinhalese rather than English as the official language to be used for entrance to universities and the civil service. This precipitated Tamil riots, culminating in the prime minister's assassination Sept 1959. Bandaranaike's widow, Sirimavo, became prime minister and held office until 1977, except for UNP interludes 1960 and 1965–70. She implemented a radical economic programme of nationalization and land reform, a pro-Sinhalese educational and employment policy, and an independent foreign policy as part of the ◊nonaligned movement.

Tamil separatist movement In 1972 the new national name Sri Lanka ('Resplendent Island') was adopted. Economic conditions deteriorated, while Tamil complaints of discrimination bred a separatist movement calling for the creation of an independent Tamil state (Eelam) in the north and east. The Tamil United Liberation Front (TULF) coalition was formed 1976 to campaign for this goal and emerged as the second-largest party in parliament from the elections July 1977, easily won by the UNP led by Junius Jayawardene. The new government introduced a new, freer-market economic programme and a presidentialist constitution. In Oct 1980 Sirimavo Bandaranaike was deprived of her civil rights for six years for alleged abuses of power. The guerrilla activities of the Liberation Tigers of Tamil Eelam (LTTE) in the north and east provoked the frequent imposition of a state of emergency. In 1982 Jayawardene was re-elected president, and the life of parliament was prolonged by referendum.

civil war The violence escalated 1983, causing the deaths of over 400 people, mainly Tamils in the Jaffna area. This prompted legislation outlawing separatist organizations, including the TULF. The near civil war has cost thousands of lives and blighted the country's economy; the tourist industry has collapsed, foreign investment dried up, and aid donors have become reluctant to prop up a government seemingly bent on imposing a military solution.

Colombo Accord All-party talks with Indian mediation repeatedly failed to solve the Tamil dispute, but in July 1987, amid protest riots, President Jayawardene and the Indian prime minister Rajiv Gandhi signed a peace pact. It proposed to make Tamil and English official languages, create a semi-autonomous homeland for the Tamils in the north and east, recognize the Tigers (once disarmed) as their representatives, and hold a referendum 1988 in the eastern province, which has pockets of Sinhalese and 32% Muslims. To police this agreement, a 7,000-strong Indian peacekeeping force (IPKF) was despatched to the Tiger-controlled Jaffna area. The Tamil Tigers put down their weapons and agreed to talks with the Sri Lankan government April 1989.

continued fighting The employment of Indian troops fanned unrest among the Sinhala community, who viewed the Colombo Accord as a sell-out to Tamil interests. Protest riots erupted in the south and senior UNP politicians, including President Jayawardene, were targeted for assassination by the resurfaced Sinhala-Marxist People's Liberation Front (JVP). In the north, the IPKF failed to capture the Tigers' leader Velupillai Prabhakaran, who continued to wage a guerrilla war from fresh bases in the rural east.

reconciliation attempts Prime Minister Ranasinghe Premadasa stood for the governing party in the presidential election of Dec 1989 and defeated the SLFP's Sirimavo Bandaranaike, who called for the immediate withdrawal of the IPKF in a campaign that was marred by JVP-induced violence. In the general elections Feb 1989 the UNP secured a narrow overall majority. Finance minister D B Wijetunge was appointed prime minister. Roundtable negotiations were held with Tiger leaders June 1989 and India withdrew its troops March 1990. Despite these reconciliatory moves, the civil war, with its two fronts in the north and south, continued, with the death toll exceeding 1,000 a month, and around 100 people a week being detained under the emergency laws. In Aug 1991 the Sri Lankan army secured a major victory against the Tamil Tigers at Elephant Pass, the gateway between the Tigers' stronghold of Jaffna peninsula and the Sri Lankan mainland, killing 2,552 Tiger guerrillas for the loss of 153 soldiers. There was some evidence that the Tamil Tigers were disintegrating but there remained an average of 150 people killed per day in inter-ethnic violence.

new party In Dec 1991 a new party, the Democratic United National Front, was formed by UNP dissidents.

foreign relations Sri Lanka is a member of the Commonwealth and ◊nonaligned movement and joined the South Asian Association for Regional Cooperation 1985.

SS Nazi elite corps (German *Schutz-Staffel* 'protective squadron') established 1925. Under ◊Himmler its 500,000 membership included the full-time *Waffen-SS* (armed SS), which fought in World War II, and 'honorary' members. The SS performed state police duties and was brutal in its treatment of the Jews and others in the concentration camps and occupied territories. It was condemned at the Nuremberg Trials of war criminals.

stadholder or *stadtholder* leader of the United Provinces of the Netherlands from the 15th to the 18th century.

Originally provincial leaders appointed by the central government, stadholders were subsequently elected in the newly independent Dutch republic. For much of their existence they competed with the States General (parliament) for control of the country. The stadholders later became dominated by the house of Orange-Nassau. In 1747 the office became hereditary, but was abolished in 1795.

Stahlhelm German paramilitary and ex-soldiers' organization prominent in the 1920s and 1930s and associated with the German National People's Party (DNVP) and German People's Party (DVP).

Stakhanov Aleksei 1906–1977. Soviet miner who exceeded production norms; he gave his name to the *Stakhanovite* movement of the 1930s, when workers were offered incentives to simplify and reorganize work processes in order to increase production.

Stalin Joseph. Adopted name (Russian 'steel') of Joseph Vissarionovich Djugashvili 1879–1953. Soviet politician. A member of the October Revolution Committee 1917, Stalin became general secretary of the Communist Party 1922. After ◊Lenin's death 1924, Stalin sought to create 'socialism in one country' and clashed with ◊Trotsky, who denied the possibility of socialism inside Russia until revolution had occurred in W Europe. Stalin won this ideological struggle by 1927, and a series of five-year plans was launched to collectivize industry and agriculture from 1928. All opposition was eliminated in the Great Purge 1936–38. During World War II, Stalin intervened in the military direction of the campaigns against Nazi Germany. His role was denounced after his death by Khrushchev and other members of the Soviet regime.

Born in Georgia, the son of a shoemaker, Stalin was educated for the priesthood but was expelled from his seminary for Marxist propaganda. He became a member of the Social Democratic Party 1898, and joined Lenin and the Bolsheviks 1903. He was repeatedly exiled to Siberia 1903–13. He then became a member of the Communist Party's ◊Politburo, and sat on the October Revolution committee. Stalin rapidly consolidated a powerful following (including Molotov); in 1921 he became commissar for nationalities in the Soviet government, responsible for the decree granting equal rights to all peoples of the Russian Empire, and was appointed general secretary of the Communist Party 1922. As dictator in the 1930s, he disposed of all real and imagined enemies. In recent years increasing evidence has been uncovered revealing Stalin's anti-Semitism, for example, the execution of 19 Jewish activists in 1952 for a 'Zionist conspiracy'.

The export of revolution is nonsense. Every country makes its own revolution if it wants to, and if it does not there will be no revolution.

Joseph Stalin interview 1936

Stamp Act UK act of Parliament in 1765 that sought to raise enough money from the American colonies to cover the cost of their defence. Refusal to use the required tax stamps and a blockade of British merchant shipping in the colonies forced repeal of the act the following year. It helped to precipitate the ◊American Revolution.

The act provoked vandalism and looting in America, and the *Stamp Act Congress* in Oct of that year (the first intercolonial congress) declared the act unconstitutional, with the slogan 'No taxation without representation', because the colonies were not represented in the British Parliament.

The act taxed (by requiring an official stamp) all publications and legal documents published in British colonies.

Standish Miles *c.* 1584–1656. American colonial military leader. As military adviser to the Pilgrim Fathers, he arrived in New England 1621 and obtained a charter for Plymouth Colony from England 1925. Although one of the most influential figures in colonial New England, he is best remembered through US poet Henry Longfellow's *The Courtship of Miles Standish* 1863.

Stanton Elizabeth Cady 1815–1902. US feminist who, with Susan B ◊Anthony, founded the National Woman Suffrage Association 1869, the first women's movement in the USA and was its first president. She and Anthony wrote and compiled the *History of Women's Suffrage* 1881–86. Stanton also worked for the abolition of slavery.

staple in medieval Europe, a riverside town where merchants had to offer their wares for sale before proceeding to their destination, a practice that constituted a form of toll; such towns were particularly common on the Rhine.

In English usage, it referred to a town appointed as the exclusive market for a particular commodity, especially wool. The wool staple was established by the English crown in Calais 1353. This form of monopoly trading was abandoned 1617.

Star Chamber in English history, a civil and criminal court, named after the star-shaped ceiling decoration of the room in the Palace of Westminster, London, where its first meetings were held. Created in 1487 by Henry VII, the Star Chamber comprised some 20 or 30 judges. It was abolished 1641 by the ◊Long Parliament.

The Star Chamber became notorious under Charles I for judgements favourable to the king and to Archbishop ◊Laud (for example, the branding on both cheeks of William Prynne in 1637 for seditious libel). Under the Thatcher government 1979–90 the term was revived for private ministerial meetings at which disputes between the Treasury and high-spending departments were resolved.

States General former French parliament that consisted of three estates: nobility, clergy, and commons. First summoned 1302, it declined in importance as the power of the crown grew. It was not called at all 1614–1789 when the crown needed to institute fiscal reforms to avoid financial collapse. Once called, the demands made by the States General formed the first phase in the ◊French Revolution. States General is also the name of the Dutch parliament.

States' Rights interpretation of the US constitution which emphasizes the powers retained by individual states and minimizes those given to the federal government. The dividing line between state and national sovereignty was left deliberately vague in the Philadelphia convention devising the constitution 1787.

In 1832 South Carolina developed the doctrine of nullification, claiming the right to overrule federal laws against its own interests. The practice of slavery was claimed to be among a state's rights in the years leading up to the American Civil War, and the right to secede from the union was claimed by those southern states forming the Confederacy at its outbreak. More recently, federal support for civil rights campaigns during the 1950s and 1960s was sometimes inhibited by a reluctance to challenge states' rights.

Statute of Westminster British act of Parliament 1931 which gave the dominions of the British Empire complete autonomy in their conduct of exter-nal affairs. It made them self-governing states whose only allegiance was to the British Crown.

Stauffenberg Claus von 1907–1944. German colonel in World War II who, in a conspiracy to assassinate Hitler, planted a bomb in the dictator's headquarters conference room in the Wolf's Lair at Rastenburg, East Prussia, 20 July 1944. Hitler was merely injured, and Stauffenberg and 200 others were later executed by the Nazi regime.

Stephen *c.* 1097–1154. King of England from 1135. A grandson of William I, he was elected king 1135, although he had previously recognized Henry I's daughter ◊Matilda as heiress to the throne. Matilda landed in England 1139, and civil war disrupted the country until 1153, when Stephen acknowledged Matilda's son, Henry II, as his own heir.

Stephen I, St 975–1038. King of Hungary from 997, when he succeeded his father. He completed the conversion of Hungary to Christianity and was canonized in 1803.

Stern Gang formal name *Fighters for the Freedom of Israel* Zionist guerrilla group founded 1940 by Abraham Stern (1907–1942). The group carried out anti-British attacks during the UK mandate rule in Palestine, both on individuals and on strategic targets. Stern was killed by British forces in 1942, but the group survived until 1948, when it was outlawed with the creation of the independent state of Israel.

Stevens Siaka Probin 1905–1988. Sierra Leone politician, president 1971–85. He was the leader of the moderate left-wing All People's Congress (APC), from 1978 the country's only legal political party.

Stevens became prime minister in 1968 and in 1971, under a revised constitution, became Sierra Leone's first president. He created a one-party state based on the APC, and remained in power until his retirement at the age of 80.

Stevenson Adlai 1900–1965. US Democrat politician. As governor of Illinois 1949–53 he campaigned vigorously against corruption in public life, and as Democratic candidate for the presidency 1952 and 1956 was twice defeated by Eisenhower. In 1945 he was chief US delegate at the founding conference of the United Nations.

Stilicho Flavius AD 359–408. Roman general, of ◊Vandal origin, who campaigned successfully against the Visigoths and Ostrogoths. He virtually ruled the western empire as guardian of Honorius (son of ◊Theodosius I) from 395, but was later executed on Honorius's orders.

Stirling James 1791–1865. Scottish naval officer and colonial administrator, the first governor of Western Australia 1828–39. Having explored the west coast of Australia in 1827, he persuaded the government to proclaim Western Australia a British colony (originally under the name of the Swan River Colony), and returned there with the first settlers in 1829.

Stock Market Crash panic selling on the New York Stock Exchange Oct 1929, also known as the ◊Wall Street crash.

Stone Age the developmental stage of humans in ◊prehistory before the use of metals, when tools and weapons were made chiefly of stone. The Stone Age is subdivided into the Old or Palaeolithic, the Middle or Mesolithic, and the New or Neolithic. The people of the Old Stone Age were hunters and gatherers, whereas the Neolithic people took the first steps in agriculture, the domestication of animals, weaving, and pottery.

Strafford Thomas Wentworth, 1st Earl of Strafford 1593–1641. English politician, originally an opponent of Charles I, but from 1628 on the Royalist side. He ruled despotically as

Lord Deputy of Ireland 1632–39, when he returned to England as Charles's chief adviser and received an earldom. He was impeached in 1640 by Parliament, abandoned by Charles as a scapegoat, and beheaded.

straits question international and diplomatic debate in the 19th and 20th centuries over Russian naval access to the Mediterranean from the Black Sea via the Bosporus.

Straits Settlements former province of the ◊East India Company 1826–58, a British crown colony 1867–1946; it comprised Singapore, Malacca, Penang, Cocos Islands, Christmas Island, and Labuan.

Stralsund, Peace of in 1369, the peace between Waldemar IV of Denmark and the Hanseatic League (association of N German trading towns) that concluded the Hanse war 1362–69.

Denmark had unsuccessfully attempted to reduce the power of the Hanseatic League in Scandinavia, and by this peace, Waldemar had to recognize the league's trading rights in his territories and assent to an enlargement of its privileges.

Star Wars attempt by the USA to develop a defence system against nuclear missiles, also called the ◊Strategic Defence Initiative (SDI).

Strategic Arms Limitation Talks (SALT) series of US-Soviet discussions 1969–79 aimed at reducing the rate of nuclear-arms build-up (as opposed to *disarmament*, which would reduce the number of weapons, as discussed in ◊Strategic Arms Reduction Talks (START). Treaties in the 1970s sought to prevent the growth of nuclear arsenals.

Strategic Arms Reduction Talks (START) phase in US-Soviet peace discussions dealing with disarmament. START began with talks in Geneva 1983, leading to the signing of the ◊Intermediate Nuclear Forces (INF) Treaty 1987. Reductions of about 30% in strategic nuclear weapons systems were agreed 1991.

Strategic Defense Initiative (SDI) also called *Star Wars*, attempt by the USA to develop a defence system against incoming nuclear missiles, based in part outside the Earth's atmosphere. It was announced by President Reagan in March 1983, and the research had by 1990 cost over $16.5 billion.

Strauss Franz-Josef 1915–1988. German conservative politician, leader of the West German Bavarian Christian Social Union (CSU) party 1961–88, premier of Bavaria 1978–88.

Born and educated in Munich, Strauss, after military service 1939–45, joined the CSU and was elected to the *Bundestag* (parliament) in 1949. He held ministerial posts during the 1950s and 1960s and became leader of the CSU 1961. In 1962 he lost his post as minister of defence when he illegally shut down the offices of *Der Spiegel* for a month, after the magazine revealed details of a failed NATO exercise. In the 1970s, Strauss opposed Ostpolitik (the policy of reconciliation with the East). He left the *Bundestag* to become premier of Bavaria in 1978, and was heavily defeated in 1980 as chancellor candidate. From 1982 Strauss sought to force changes in economic and foreign policy of the coalition under Chancellor Kohl.

Stresa Front summit meeting 11–14 April 1935 between the prime ministers of Britain, France, and Italy (Ramsay MacDonald, Pierre Flandin, and Benito Mussolini) with the aim of forming a common front against Germany. The 'front' soon broke up: in Oct 1935 Italy was severely criticized for launching an Abyssinian War 1935–36 to establish an east African Italian empire, and on 2 Nov 1936 Benito Mussolini proclaimed the Rome–Berlin Axis, which brought Germany and Italy into close collaboration between 1936 and 1945.

Stresemann Gustav 1878–1929. German politician, chancellor in 1923 and foreign minister from 1923 to 1929 of the Weimar Republic. During World War I he was a strong nationalist but his views became more moderate under the Weimar Republic. His achievements included reducing the amount of war reparations paid by Germany after the Treaty of Versailles 1919; negotiating the Locarno Treaties 1925; and Germany's admission to the League of Nations. He shared the 1926 Nobel Peace Prize with Aristide Briand.

Stroessner Alfredo 1912– . Military leader and president of Paraguay 1954–89. As head of the armed forces from 1951, he seized power in a coup in 1954 sponsored by the right-wing ruling Colorado Party. Accused by his opponents of harsh repression, his regime spent heavily on the military to preserve his authority. Despite criticisms of his government's civil-rights record, he was re-elected seven times and remained in office until ousted in an army-led coup 1989.

Stuart or *Stewart* royal family who inherited the Scottish throne in 1371 and the English throne in 1603, holding it until 1714, when Queen Anne died without heirs and the house of Stuarts was replaced by the house of ◊Hanover.

Stuart John McDouall 1815–1866. Scottish-born Australian explorer. He went with Charles Sturt on his 1844 expedition, and in 1860, after two unsuccessful attempts, crossed the centre of Australia from Adelaide in the southeast to the coast of Arnhem Land. He almost lost his life on the return journey.

Sturmabteilung (SA) German militia, also known as *Brownshirts*, of the ◊Nazi Party, established 1921 under the leadership of Ernst Röhm, in charge of physical training and political indoctrination.

Stuyvesant Peter 1610–1672. Dutch colonial leader in America. Appointed director general of New Netherland 1646, he arrived there in 1647. He reorganized the administration of the colony and established a permanent boundary with Connecticut by the Treaty of Hartford 1650. Forced to surrender the colony to the British 1664, Stuyvesant remained there for the rest of his life.

Suárez González Adolfo 1932– . Spanish politician, prime minister 1976–81. A friend of King Juan Carlos, he was appointed by the king to guide Spain into democracy after the death of the fascist dictator Franco.

Sucre Antonio José de 1795–1830. South American revolutionary leader. As chief lieutenant of Simón ◊Bolívar, he won several battles in freeing the colonies of Ecuador and Bolivia from Spanish rule, and in 1826 became president of Bolivia. After a mutiny by the army and invasion by Peru, he resigned in 1828 and was assassinated in 1830 on his way to join Bolívar.

Sudan country in NE Africa, bounded N by Egypt, NE by the Red Sea, E by Ethiopia, S by Kenya, Uganda, and Zaire, W by the Central African Republic and Chad, and NW by Libya. It is the largest country in Africa.

history In ancient times, the region was known as ◊Nubia and was taken over by the kingdoms of Upper and Lower Egypt. The Nubians were later converted to Coptic Christianity in the 6th century and to Islam in the 15th century when Arabs invaded. Sudan was again ruled by Egypt from 1820. A revolt began 1881, led by a sheik who took the title of ◊Mahdi and captured Khartoum 1885. It was subdued by an Anglo-Egyptian army under Lord ◊Kitchener 1896-98 and administered as an Anglo-Egyptian condominium from 1899.

independent republic The Sudan, as it was called, achieved independence as a republic 1956. Two years later a coup ousted the civil administration, and a military government was set up; in 1964 this was overthrown and civilian rule was reinstated. Five years later the army returned in a coup led by Col Gaafar Mohammed Nimeri. All political bodies were abolished, the Revolutionary Command Council (RCC) set up, and the country's name changed to the Democratic Republic of Sudan. Close links were soon established with Egypt, and in 1970 an agreement in principle was reached for eventual union. In 1972 this should have become, with the addition of Syria, the Federation of Arab Republics, but internal opposition blocked both developments. In 1971 a new constitution was adopted, Nimeri confirmed as president, and the Sudanese Socialist Union (SSU) declared the only party.

regional problems The most serious problem confronting Nimeri was open aggression between the Muslim north and the chiefly Christian south, which had started as long ago as 1955. At a conference in Addis Ababa 1972 he granted the three southern provinces a considerable degree of autonomy, but fighting continued. Nimeri had come to power in a left-wing revolution but soon turned to the West, and the USA, for support. By 1974 he had established a national assembly, but his position still relied on army backing. In 1983 he was re-elected for a third term, but his regional problems persisted. By sending more troops south against the Sudan People's Liberation Army he alienated the north and then caused considerable resentment in the south by replacing the penal code with strict Islamic law. His economic policies contributed to the widespread unrest.

military takeover In March 1985 a general strike was provoked by a sharp devaluation of the Sudanese pound and an increase in bread prices. Nimeri was in the USA when army mutiny threatened. One of his supporters, General Swar al-Dahab, took over in a bloodless coup. He set up a transitional military council and held elections for a legislative assembly April 1986, contested by more than 40 parties, the three most significant being the New National Umma Party (NNUP), which won 99 seats; the Democratic Unionist Party (DUP), 63 seats; and the National Islamic Front, 51 seats. A coalition government was formed, with Ahmed Ali el-Mirghani (DUP) as president of the Supreme Council and Sadiq al-Mahdi (NNUP) as prime minister. Strikes and shortages persisted, with inflation running at about 100% and the highest national debt in Africa, and in July 1987 a state of emergency was declared. In Oct 1987 the prime minister announced the break-up of the government of national unity and the formation of a new coalition. In Dec 1988 the signing of a peace agreement with the Sudan People's Liberation Movement (SPLM), led by John Garang, threatened to split the coalition government and eventually led to a military takeover by General Ahmed el-Bashir July 1989. El-Bashir established a 15-man revolutionary council with himself as head of state and government. Just weeks before the successful coup, the military foiled the second attempt in six months to restore former strongman, Gaafar Nimeri, to power. Bashir's government arrested al-Mahdi and announced that its first priority was to bring an end to the six-year war between the Muslim north and the Christian and animist south. As part of an effort to end the civil war, which remained a problem in 1991, the government announced the division of the country into nine provinces, to be governed under a federal system.

Sudetenland mountainous region of N Czechoslovakia (now the Czech Republic), annexed by Germany under the ◊Munich Agreement 1938; it was returned to Czechoslovakia 1945.

Suez Canal artificial waterway, 160 km/100 mi long, from Port Said to Suez, linking the Mediterranean and Red seas, separating Africa from Asia, and providing the shortest eastwards sea route from Europe. It was opened 1869, nationalized 1956, blocked by Egypt during the Arab–Israeli War 1967, and not re-opened until 1975.

The French Suez Canal Company was formed 1858 to execute the scheme of Ferdinand de Lesseps. The canal was opened 1869, and in 1875 British prime minister ◊Disraeli acquired a major shareholding for Britain from the khedive of Egypt. The 1888 Convention of Constantinople opened it to all nations. The Suez Canal was admininstered by a company with offices in Paris controlled by a council of 33 (10 of them British) until 1956 when it was forcibly nationalized by President ◊Nasser of Egypt.

It cannot be made, it shall not be made; but if it were made there would be a war between England and France for the possession of Egypt.

On the **Suez Canal** Lord Palmerston 1851

Suez Crisis military confrontation Oct–Dec 1956 following the nationalization of the Suez Canal by President Nasser of Egypt. In an attempt to reassert international control of the canal, Israel launched an attack, after which

British and French troops landed. Widespread international censure forced the withdrawal of the British and French. The crisis resulted in the resignation of British prime minister Eden.

At a London conference of maritime powers the Australian prime minister, Robert Menzies, was appointed to negotiate a settlement in Cairo. His mission was unsuccessful. The military intervention met Soviet protest and considerable domestic opposition, and the USA did not support it. British, French, and Australian relations with the USA were greatly strained during this period.

suffragette or *suffragist* woman fighting for the right to vote. In the UK, women's suffrage bills were repeatedly introduced and defeated in Parliament between 1886 and 1911, and a militant campaign was launched 1906 by Emmeline ◊Pankhurst and her daughters. In 1918 women were granted limited franchise; in 1928 it was extended to all women over 21. In the USA the 19th amendment to the constitution 1920 gave women the vote in federal and state elections.

Many suffragettes were imprisoned and were force-fed when they went on hunger strike; under the notorious 'Cat and Mouse Act' of 1913 they could be repeatedly released to regain their health and then rearrested. The struggle was called off on the outbreak of World War I.

suffragist US term for suffragette.

Suharto Raden 1921– . Indonesian politician and general. He ousted Sukarno to become president 1967. He ended confrontation with Malaysia, invaded East Timor 1975, and reached a cooperation agreement with Papua New Guinea 1979. His authoritarian rule has met with domestic opposition from the left. He was re-elected 1973, 1978, 1983, and 1988. He became head of the ◊nonaligned movement 1992.

Sui dynasty Chinese ruling family 581–618 which reunited China after the strife of the ◊Three Kingdoms era. There were two Sui emperors: Yang Qien (Yang Chien, 541–604), and Yangdi (Yang-ti, ruled 605–17). Though short-lived, the Sui re-established strong centralized government, rebuilding the ◊Great Wall and digging canals which later formed part of the Grand Canal system. The Sui capital was Chang'an.

Sukarno Achmad 1901–1970. Indonesian nationalist, president 1945–67. During World War II he cooperated in the local administration set up by the Japanese, replacing Dutch rule. After the war he became the first president of the new Indonesian republic, becoming president-for-life in 1966; he was ousted by ◊Suharto.

Suleiman or *Solyman* or *Suleyman* 1494–1566. Ottoman sultan from 1520, known as *the Magnificent* and *the Lawgiver*. Under his rule, the Ottoman Empire flourished and reached its largest extent. He made conquests in the Balkans, the Mediterranean, Persia, and N Africa, but was defeated at Vienna in 1529 and Valletta (on Malta) in 1565. He was a patron of the arts, a poet, and an administrator.

Suleiman captured Belgrade in 1521, the Mediterranean island of Rhodes in 1522, defeated the Hungarians at Mohács in 1526, and was halted in his advance into Europe only by his failure to take Vienna, capital of the Austro-Hungarian Empire, after a siege Sept–Oct 1529. In 1534 he turned more successfully against Persia, and then in campaigns against the Arab world took almost all of N Africa and the Red Sea port of Aden. Only the Knights of Malta inflicted severe defeat on both his army and fleet when he tried to take Valletta in 1565.

Sulla Lucius Cornelius 138–78 BC. Roman general and politician, a leader of the senatorial party. Forcibly suppressing the democrats by marching on Rome in 88 BC, he departed for a successful campaign against ◊Mithridates VI of Pontus. The democrats seized power in his absence, but on his return in 82 Sulla captured Rome and massacred all opponents. The reforms he introduced as dictator, which strengthened the Senate, were conservative and short-lived. He retired 79 BC.

Sully Maximilien de Béthune, Duc de Sully 1560–1641. French politician, who served with the Protestant ◊Huguenots in the wars of religion, and, as Henry IV's superintendent of finances 1598–1611, aided French recovery.

Sumerian civilization the world's earliest civilization, dating from about 3200 BC and located at the confluence of the Tigris and Euphrates rivers in lower Mesopotamia (present-day Iraq). It was a city-state with priests as secular rulers. After 2300 BC, Sumer declined.

Sumerian culture was based on the taxation of the surplus produced by agricultural villagers to support the urban ruling class and its public-works programme, which included state-controlled irrigation. Cities included Lagash, Eridu, and Ur. Centralized control over the region (an empire) was first asserted by neighbouring Akkad, about 2300 BC. Trade with Egypt and the Indus Valley may have influenced the formation of the ancient civilizations there.

SURINAM 551

US-Soviet summits

1969	SALT talks began in Helsinki.
1972	US president Nixon and Soviet president Brezhnev signed SALT I accord.
1973	Brezhnev met Nixon in Washington DC.
1974	Nixon met Brezhnev in Moscow; US president Ford met Brezhnev in Vladivostok.
1975	Ford and Brezhnev attended 35-nation meeting in Helsinki.
1979	US president Carter and Brezhnev signed SALT II accord in Vienna.
1983	Strategic Arms Reduction Talks (START) held in Geneva.
1986	US president Reagan and Soviet president Gorbachev met in Reykyavik.
1987	Intermediate Nuclear Forces treaty signed in Washington DC.
1989	Cuts in short-range missiles in Europe proposed conditional on reduction of conventional forces.
1991	US president Bush and Gorbachev met in Moscow. START treaty signed, designed to reduce by approximately one-third the number of long-range nuclear warheads held by the USA and the USSR.

summit conference in international diplomacy, a personal meeting between heads of state to settle international crises and other matters of general concern. The term was first coined by Winston Churchill in 1950 although it could be applied to the meetings between himself, Roosevelt, and Stalin at Tehran and Yalta during World War II.

Sumner Charles 1811–1874. US political leader. Elected to the US Senate as a FreeSoil Democrat 1852, he was defeated by South Carolina congressman Preston Brooks 1856 for his uncompromising abolitionist views on the issue of slavery. During the American Civil War 1861–65, he was a Republican leader in Congress. A supporter of Radical Reconstruction, he opposed President Grant's renomination 1872.

Sunderland Robert Spencer, 2nd Earl of Sunderland 1640–1702. English politician, a sceptical intriguer who converted to Roman Catholicism to secure his place under James II, and then reverted with the political tide. In 1688 he fled to Holland (disguised as a woman), where he made himself invaluable to the future William III. Now a Whig, he advised the new king to adopt the system, which still prevails, of choosing the government from the dominant party in the Commons.

Sung dynasty Chinese imperial family 960–1279; see ◊Song dynasty.

Sunni member of the larger of the two main sects of ◊Islam, with about 680 million adherents. Sunni Muslims believe that the first three caliphs were all legitimate successors of the prophet Muhammad, and that guidance on belief and life should come from the Koran and the Hadith, and from the Shari'a, not from a human authority or spiritual leader. Imams in Sunni Islam are educated lay teachers of the faith and prayer leaders. The name derives from the *Sunna*, Arabic 'code of behaviour', the body of traditional law evolved from the teaching and acts of Muhammad.

Sun Yat-sen or *Sun Zhong Shan* 1867–1925. Chinese revolutionary leader, founder of the ◊Guomindang (nationalist party) 1894, and provisional president of the Republic of China 1912 after playing a vital part in deposing the emperor. He was president of a breakaway government from 1921.

Sun Yat-sen was the son of a Christian farmer. After many years in exile he returned to China during the 1911 revolution that overthrew the Manchu dynasty. In an effort to bring unity to China, he resigned as provisional president 1912 in favour of the military leader Yuan Shikai. As a result of Yuan's increasingly dictatorial methods, Sun established an independent republic in S China based in Canton 1921. He was criticized for lack of organizational ability, but his 'three people's principles' of nationalism, democracy, and social reform are accepted by both the nationalists and the Chinese communists.

In the construction of a country it is not the practical workers, but the planners and idealists that are difficult to find.

Sun Yat-sen

Sun Zhong Shan Pinyin transliteration of ◊Sun Yat-sen.

superpower term used to describe the USA and the USSR from the end of World War II 1945, when they emerged as significantly stronger than all other countries.

Supremacy, Acts of two UK acts of Parliament 1534 and 1559, which established Henry VIII and Elizabeth I respectively as head of the English church in place of the pope.

Surinam country on the N coast of South America, bounded W by French Guiana, S by Brazil, E by Guyana, and N by the Atlantic Ocean.

history For early history, see ◊American Indian. Founded as a colony by the English 1650, Surinam became Dutch 1667. Except for two interregnums, 1795–1802 and 1814–16, Surinam remained a Dutch possession until 1975. The slave trade was abolished 1814; however, large numbers of slaves were brought in illegally to work on the sugar, coffee, and cotton plantations. After the abolition of slavery in the Dutch colonies 1863, India provided large numbers of migrant workers: 34,000 entered Surinam 1873–1916.

independence The Netherlands Constitution Act 1922 made Surinam an integrated territory of the Kingdom of the Netherlands. Political tensions increased, culminating in a suspension of relations during World War II. In 1954, as Dutch Guiana, the country was made an equal member of the Kingdom of the Netherlands, with internal self-government. Full independence was achieved 1975, with Dr Johan Ferrier as president and Henck Arron, leader of the Surinam National Party (NPS), as prime minister.

military coup In 1980 Arron's government was overthrown in an army coup, but President Ferrier refused to recognize the military regime and appointed Dr Henk Chin A Sen, of the Nationalist Republican Party, to head a civilian administration. Five months later the army staged another coup, and President Ferrier was replaced by Dr Chin A Sen. The new president announced details of a draft constitution that would reduce the army's role in government, whereupon the army, led by Lt Col Desi Bouterse, dismissed Dr Chin A Sen and set up the Revolutionary People's Front.

instability There followed months of confusion in which a state of siege and then martial law were imposed. From Feb 1980 to Jan 1983 there were six attempted coups by different army groups. Because of the chaos and killings of opposition leaders, Netherlands and US aid was stopped, and Bouterse turned to Libya and Cuba for assistance. The partnership between the army, the trade unions, and business, which had operated since 1981, broke up 1985, and Bouterse turned to the traditional parties that had operated before the 1980 coup: the NPS, the left-wing Indian Progressive Reform Party (VHP), and the Indonesian Party for National Unity and Solidarity (KTPI). The ban on political activity was lifted, and leaders of the three main parties were invited to take seats on the Supreme Council, with Wym Udenhout as prime minister. The Nov 1987 election was won by the three-party Front for Democracy and Development (FDD) and Ramsewak

Shankar was elected president of the national assembly. In March 1989 a new constitution was approved prior to an election in Nov.

A bloody coup by the army Dec 1990 removed President Shankar, Bouterse denying any involvement. In Jan 1991 the assembly elected Johan Kraag as caretaker president. In national elections held May 1991 the New Front for Democracy (NF) won 29 seats in the 51-seat National Assembly. Ronald Venetiaan was elected president in Sept. In Aug 1992 the government reached an agreement with the two largest guerrilla groups, the Surinamese Liberation Army and the Tucayana Amazonas, to end hostilities.

suttee Hindu custom whereby a widow committed suicide by joining her husband's funeral pyre, often under public and family pressure. Banned in the 17th century by the Mogul emperors, the custom continued even after it was made illegal under British rule 1829. There continue to be sporadic revivals.

Suzuki Zenkō 1911– . Japanese politician. Originally a socialist member of the Diet in 1947, he became a conservative (Liberal Democrat) in 1949, and was prime minister 1980–82.

Swabia (German *Schwaben*) historic region of SW Germany, an independent duchy in the Middle Ages. It includes Augsburg and Ulm and forms part of the *Länder* (states) of Baden-Württemberg, Bavaria, and Hessen.

Swadeshi movement (Bengali 'from one's own country') in India, a boycott of foreign-made goods orchestrated by Indian nationalists in response to the partition of Bengal 1905. Huge bonfires of imported cloth, especially Lancashire cotton, were lit throughout Bengal. Protesters vowed to use only domestic (Swadeshi) cottons, and other goods manufactured in India. The boycott spread throughout the subcontinent, providing a stimulus to indigenous Indian industry and nationalist protest.

SWAPO (*South West Africa People's Organization*) organization formed 1959 in South West Africa (now ◊Namibia) to oppose South African rule. SWAPO guerrillas, led by Sam Nujoma, began attacking with support from Angola. In 1966 SWAPO was recognized by the United Nations as the legitimate government of Namibia, and won the first independent election 1989.

Swarajiya or *Self-Government Party* political party established in India in 1922 as an attempt to reinforce the position of the Congress Party in the Indian legislature. In 1923, it became the largest party in the central assembly and also in some provincial assemblies, but its tactics of obstruction against British colonial rule were only partially successful. Recognized by the Congress Party in 1924, Swarajiya continued until 1929 and was revived to help the Congress Party to contest the 1934 elections.

swastika (Sanskrit *svastika*) cross in which the bars are extended at right angles in the same clockwise or anticlockwise direction. An ancient good-luck symbol in both the New and the Old World and an Aryan and Buddhist mystic sign, it was adopted by Hitler as the emblem of the Nazi Party and incorporated into the German national flag 1935–45.

Swazi kingdom S African kingdom, established by Sobhuza I (died 1839), and named after his successor Mswati (ruled 1840–75). The kingdom was established by Sobhuza as a result of the ◊Mfecane disturbances.

Swaziland country in SE Africa, bounded E by Mozambique and SE, S, W, and N by South Africa.

history For early history, see ◊South Africa. The region's original autonomy was guaranteed by Britain and the Transvaal, and Swaziland became a special High Commission territory 1903. The South African government repeatedly asked for Swaziland to be placed under its jurisdiction, but this call was resisted by the British government as well as the people of Swaziland. In 1967 the country achieved internal self-government and in 1968 full independence within the Commonwealth, with King Sobhuza II as head of state. In 1973 the king suspended the constitution and assumed absolute powers. In 1978 the new constitution was announced.

power struggles over accession King Sobhuza died 1982, and the role of head of state passed to the queen mother, Dzeliwe, until the king's heir, Prince Makhosetive, should reach the age of 21 in 1989, but a power struggle developed within the royal family. Queen Dzeliwe was ousted by another of King Sobhuza's wives, Ntombi, who became queen regent Oct 1983, and in April 1986 the crown prince was formally invested as King Mswati III. He has a supreme advisory body, the Liqoqo, all of whose 11 members are appointed by him. By June 1987 a power struggle had developed between the Liqoqo and Queen Ntombi over the accession of her son Mswati III. He dissolved parliament and a new government was elected in the same year, with Sotsha Dlamini as prime minister. Following demands for greater freedom and complaints of government hostility towards trade unions, King Mswati called for the creation of an *indaba* (popular parliament) Aug 1990, in which people's views could be expressed. There were doubts about whether this was a genuine move towards democratic reform. There was agitation for further democratic reforms Oct 1991.

Sweden country in N Europe, bounded W by Norway, NE by Finland and the Gulf of Bothnia, SE by the Baltic Sea, and SW by the Kattegat.

The prime minister is nominated by the speaker of the Riksdag and confirmed by a vote of the whole house. The prime minister chooses a cabinet, and all are then responsible to the Riksdag. The king or queen now has a purely formal role; the normal duties of a constitutional monarch, such as dissolving parliament and deciding who should be asked to form an administration, are undertaken by the speaker.

history S Sweden has been inhabited since about 6000 BC. The Swedish Vikings in AD 800–1060 sailed mainly to the east and founded the principality of ◊Novgorod. In the mid-12th century the Swedes in the north were united with the Goths in the south and accepted Christianity. A series of crusades from the 12th to the 14th centuries brought Finland under Swedish rule. Sweden, Norway, and Denmark were united under a Danish dynasty 1397–1520. ◊Gustavus Vasa was subsequently elected king of Sweden. The Vasa line ruled until 1818, when the French marshal Bernadotte established the present dynasty.

Sweden's territorial ambitions led to warfare in Europe from the 16th to the 18th centuries (see ◊Gustavus Adolphus, ◊Thirty Years' War, ◊Charles X, ◊Charles XII) which left the country impoverished. Science and culture flourished under Gustavus III 1771–91. Sweden lost Finland to Russia 1809 but annexed Norway 1814, a union dissolved 1905.

Sweden has a long tradition of neutrality and political stability, and a highly developed social welfare system. The office of ombudsman is a Swedish invention, and Sweden was one of the first countries to adopt a system of open government.

constitutional reform The Social Democratic Labour Party (SAP) was continuously in power 1951–76, usually in coalition. In 1969 Olof Palme became prime minister. He carried out two major reforms of the constitution, reducing the chambers in parliament from two to one 1971 and in 1975 removing the last of the monarch's constitutional powers. In the general election 1976 he was defeated over the issue of the level of taxation needed to fund the welfare system.

controversy over nuclear power Thorbjörn Fälldin, leader of the Centre Party, formed a centre-right coalition government. The Fälldin administration fell 1978 over its wish to follow a non-nuclear energy policy, and was replaced by a minority Liberal government. Fälldin returned 1979, heading another coalition, and in a referendum the following year there was a narrow majority in favour of continuing with a limited nuclear-energy programme.

prime minister assassinated Fälldin remained in power until 1982, when the Social Democrats, with Olof Palme, returned with a minority government. Palme was soon faced with deterioriating relations with the USSR, arising from suspected violations of Swedish territorial waters by Soviet submarines. The situation had improved substantially by 1985.

In Feb 1986, Olof Palme was murdered by an unknown assailant. Palme's deputy, Ingvar Carlsson, took over as prime minister and leader of the SAP.

economic problems In the Sept 1988 general election Carlsson and the SAP were re-elected with a reduced majority. The Green Party won enough votes to gain representation in the Riksdag. In Feb 1990, with mounting opposition to its economic policies, the government resigned, leaving Carlsson as a caretaker prime minister. In Dec 1990 the Riksdag supported the government's decision to apply for European Community membership. Elections in Sept 1991 led to the defeat of Carlsson's government. He was succeeded as prime minister by Carl Bildt who led a minority coalition comprising the Moderate Party (M), the Liberals (Fp), the Centre Party (C), and the Christian Democratic Community Party (KdS). In Sept 1992 it was announced that an unprecedented agreement between the Conservatives and Social Democrats had been reached to work together to attack the country's economic problems.

Sweyn I died 1014. King of Denmark from about 986, nicknamed 'Forkbeard'. He raided England, finally conquered it in 1013, and styled himself king, but his early death led to the return of ◊Ethelred II.

Switzerland landlocked country in W Europe, bounded N by Germany, E by Austria and Liechtenstein, S by Italy, and W by France.

history The region was settled by peoples that the Romans called Helvetians or Transalpine Gauls, and it became a province of the Roman Empire after Julius Caesar's conquest. In 1291 the cantons of Schwyz, Uri, and Lower Unterwalden formed the Everlasting League to defend their liberties against their ◊Habsburg overlords. More towns and districts joined them, and there were 13 cantons by 1513. The Reformation was accepted during 1523-29 by Zürich, Berne, and Basel, but the rural cantons remained Catholic. Switzerland gradually won more freedom from Habsburg control until its complete independence was recognized by the Treaty of ◊Westphalia 1648.

democratic federation A peasant uprising 1653 was suppressed. A French invasion 1798 established the Helvetic Republic with a centralized government; this was modified by Napoleon's Act of Mediation 1803, which made Switzerland a democratic federation. The Congress of ◊Vienna 1815 guaranteed Swiss neutrality, and Switzerland received Geneva and other territories, increasing the number of cantons to 22. After a civil war between the Sonderbund (a union of the Catholic cantons Lucerne, Zug, Freiburg, and Valais) and the Liberals, a revised federal constitution, giving the central government wide powers, was introduced 1848; a further revision 1874 increased its powers and introduced the principle of the referendum.

international role Switzerland, for centuries a neutral country, has been the base for many international organizations and the host of many international peace conferences. A referendum 1986 rejected the advice of the government and came out overwhelmingly against membership of the United Nations. Its domestic politics have been characterized by coalition governments and a stability that has enabled it to become one of the world's richest countries (per person).

After the Oct 1987 election, the four-party coalition continued in power, although there was a significant increase in the number of seats held by the Green Party. In 1989, a referendum found widespread dissatisfaction with the national militia and military service requirements. In Aug 1991 the country celebrated its 700th anniversary. The Oct 1991 national elections, in which 18-year-olds were allowed to vote for the first time, saw little change in the resulting seat distribution, with the four-party coalition retaining control. In Jan 1992 René Felber became president and Adolf Ogi vice president. Switzerland decided to apply for full membership of the European Community.

syndicalism (French *syndicat* 'trade union') political movement in 19th-century Europe that rejected parliamentary activity in favour of direct action, culminating in a revolutionary general strike to secure worker ownership and control of industry. After 1918 syndicalism was absorbed in communism, although it continued to have an independent existence in Spain until the late 1930s.

Syria country in W Asia, on the Mediterranean Sea, bounded N by Turkey, E by Iraq, S by Jordan, and SW by Israel and Lebanon.

history Ancient Syria was inhabited by various small kingdoms that fought against Israel and were subdued by the Assyrians. It was subsequently occupied by Babylonia, Persia, and Macedonia but gained prominence under Seleucus Nicator, founder of ◊Antioch 300 BC, and ◊Antiochus III the Great. After forming part of the Roman and Byzantine empires, it was conquered by the Saracens 636. During the Middle Ages, Syria was the scene of many battles between Muslims and European Crusaders.

Syria was part of the ◊Ottoman Empire 1516–1918. It was occupied by British and French troops 1918–19 and in 1920 placed under French mandate. Syria became independent 1946 and three years later came under military rule.

military coup In 1958 Syria merged with Egypt to become the United Arab Republic (UAR), but after an army coup 1961 Syria seceded, and the independent Syrian Arab Republic was established. In 1963 a government was formed, mainly from members of the Arab Socialist Renaissance (Ba'ath) Party, but three years later the army removed it. In 1970 the moderate wing of the Ba'ath Party, led by Lt-Gen Hafez al-Assad, secured power in a bloodless coup, and in the following year Assad was elected president. He also became head of government, secretary general of the Ba'ath Arab Socialist Party, and president of the National Progressive Front (NPF), an umbrella organization for the five main socialist parties. Syria is therefore in reality, if not in a strictly legal sense, a one-party state.

Middle East affairs Externally Syria has played a leading role in Middle East affairs. In the Six-Day War 1967 it lost territory to Israel, and after the Yom Kippur War 1973 Israel formally annexed the Golan Heights, which had previously been part of Syria. During 1976 Assad increasingly intervened in the civil war in

Lebanon, eventually committing some 50,000 troops to the operations. Relations between Syria and Egypt cooled after President Sadat's Israel peace initiative 1977 and the subsequent ◊Camp David agreements. Assad consistently opposed US-sponsored peace moves in Lebanon, arguing that they infringed upon Lebanese sovereignty. He also questioned Yassir Arafat's leadership of the Palestine Liberation Organization (PLO) and supported opposition to him.

leaning towards the West In 1984 President Assad and the Lebanese president Amin Gemayel approved plans for a government of national unity in Lebanon, which would give equal representation to Muslims and Christians, and secured the reluctant agreement of Nabih Berri of the Shi'ite Amal Militia and Walid Jumblatt, leader of the ◊Druse. Fighting still continued, and Assad's credibility suffered, but in 1985 his authority proved sufficient to secure the release of 39 US hostages from an aircraft hijacked by the extremist Shi'ite group Hezbollah. In Nov 1986 Britain broke off diplomatic relations after claiming to have proof of Syrian involvement in international terrorism, when a Syrian citizen attempted to blow up an Israeli plane at Heathrow, London. In July 1987 Syria instigated a crackdown on the pro-Iranian Hezbollah party.

Syria has been leaning to the West, its policies in Lebanon in direct conflict with Iran's dream of an Islamic republic, and its crumbling economy has been promised Arab aid if Damascus switches allegiance. In June 1987, following a private visit by former US president Jimmy ◊Carter, Syria's relations with the USA began to improve, and efforts were made to arrange the release of Western hostages in Lebanon, a process that continued through 1991. After Iraq's invasion of Kuwait Aug 1990, Syria sided with other Arab states and the UN coalition against Iraq, contributing troops for the ◊Gulf War. In Nov 1990 full diplomatic relations with Britain were resumed, and in 1991 President Assad agreed to a US Middle East peace plan. In Dec Assad was re-elected, unopposed, for a fourth term.

Tafawa Balewa Alhaji Abubakar 1912–1966. Nigerian politician, prime minister from 1957 to 1966, when he was assassinated in a coup d'état.

Tafawa Balewa entered the House of Representatives 1952, was minister of works 1952–54, and minister of transport 1954–57.

Taff Vale judgement decision 1901 by the British law lords that trade unions were liable for their members' actions, and could hence be sued for damages in the event of a strike, picketing, or boycotting an employer. It resulted in a rapid growth of union membership, and was replaced by the Trades Disputes Act 1906.

Taft Robert Alphonso 1889–1953. US right-wing Republican senator from 1939, and a candidate for the presidential nomination 1940, 1944, 1948, and 1952. He sponsored the Taft–Hartley Labor Act 1947, restricting union power. He was the son of President William Taft.

Taft William Howard 1857–1930. 27th president of the USA 1909–13, a Republican. He was secretary of war 1904–08 in Theodore Roosevelt's administration, but as president his conservatism provoked Roosevelt to stand against him in the 1912 election. Taft served as chief justice of the Supreme Court 1921–30.

taille in pre-revolutionary France, either of two forms of taxation. The *personal taille*, levied from the 15th century, was assessed by tax collectors on the individual's personal wealth. Nobles, clerics, and many other groups were exempt from this tax and its burden fell disproportionately on the peasantry. During a similar period the *'real' taille* was levied on common land in central and south-western France and produced more revenue for the crown.

Taiping rebellion popular revolt 1850–64 that undermined China's Qing dynasty. By 1853 the rebels had secured control over much of the central and lower Chang Jiang valley region, instituting radical, populist land reforms. Civil war continued until 1864, when the Taipings, weakened by internal dissension, were overcome by the provincial Hunan army of ◊Zeng Guofan and the Ever-Victorious Army, led by American F T Ward and British soldier Charles ◊Gordon.

The rebellion was triggered by the famine of 1849–50, and was led by Hong Xiuquan (Hung Hsui-ch'an, 1813–1864). The most serious and widespread of a number of mid-19th century rebellions, it began in the southern province of Guangxi, where the Hakka community had been partly Christianized. Hong Xiuquan declared himself to be the younger brother of Jesus Christ. Many of his followers were drawn from marginal mining, charcoal-burning, boating, and secret-society communities. Nanjing was made capital for 'Heavenly King' Hong Xiuquan, and he committed suicide when the city came under siege.

Taira or *Heike* in Japanese history, a military clan prominent in the 10th–12th centuries and dominant at court 1159–85. Their destruction by their rivals, the ◊Minamoto, 1185 is the subject of the 13th-century literary classic *Heike Monogatari/The Tale of the Heike*.

Taiwan country in E Asia, officially the Republic of China, occupying the island of Taiwan between the E China Sea and the S China Sea, separated from the coast of China by the Formosa Strait.

history Taiwan, then known as Formosa ('the beautiful'), was settled by China from the 15th century, briefly occupied by the Dutch during the mid-17th century, and annexed by the Chinese Manchu dynasty 1683. It was ceded to Japan under the terms of the Treaty of Shimonoseki after the 1895 Sino-Japanese war and not regained by China until the Japanese surrender Aug 1945.

Chinese nationalist government In Dec 1949 Taiwan became the refuge for the Chinese nationalist government forces of ◊Chiang Kai-shek which were compelled to evacuate the mainland after their defeat by the communist troops of Mao Zedong. Chiang and his nationalist followers dominated the island and maintained an army of 600,000 in the hope of reconquering the mainland, over which they still claimed sovereignty. They continued to be recognized by the USA as the legitimate government of China, and occupied China's United Nations and Security Council seats until Oct 1971, when they were expelled and replaced by the People's Republic.

economic growth Taiwan was protected by US naval forces during the Korean War 1950–53 and signed a mutual defence treaty with the USA 1954. Benefiting from such security, the country enjoyed a period of rapid economic growth during the 1950s and 1960s, emerging as an export-oriented, newly industrialized country. Political power during these years was concentrated in the hands of the Kuomintang (◊Guomindang) and the armed forces led by President Chiang Kai-shek, with martial law imposed and opposition activity outlawed.

external changes During the 1970s the Taiwanese government was forced to adjust to rapid external changes as the USA adopted a new policy of détente towards Communist China. In Jan 1979 this culminated in the full normalization of Sino-US relations, the severing of Taiwanese-US diplomatic contacts, and the annulment of the USA's 1954 security pact. Other Western nations followed suit in ending diplomatic relations with Taiwan during the 1970s and early 1980s.

democratization and 'Taiwanization' These developments, coupled with generational change within the Kuomintang, prompted a slow review of Taiwanese policies, both domestic and external. Chiang Kai-shek died in April 1975 and his son Chiang Ching-kuo (1910-1988) became party chair and, from 1978, state president. Under his stewardship, a programme of gradual democratization and 'Taiwanization' was adopted, with elections being held for 'vacated seats' within the national assembly and Legislative Yuan and native Taiwanese being more rapidly inducted into the Kuomintang. In the Dec 1986 elections a formal opposition party, the Democratic Progressive Party (DPP), led by Chiang Peng-chien, was tolerated and captured 22% of the vote to the Kuomintang's 69%. In July 1987 martial law was lifted and replaced with a national security law under which demonstrations and the formation of opposition parties were legalized, provided they forswore communism, and press restrictions were lifted.

accelerating reform President Chiang was succeeded on his death by Lee Teng-hui, the Taiwanese-born vice president from 1984. The new president accelerated the pace of reform. Many 'old guard' figures were retired 1988–89 and a plan for phasing out by 1992, through voluntary retirement, up to 200 mainland constituencies and replacing them with Taiwanese deputies was approved. In the Dec 1989 Legislative Yuan elections the Kuomintang's vote share fell to 59% and from Sept 1990 the 'ancient guard' Chinese-born Kuomintang members became a minority within Taiwan's parliament.

relations with China normalized On 1 May 1991 President Lee Teng-hui officially declared an end to the 42 years of 'civil war' ('Period of Communist Rebellion') between the Kuomintang government of the Republic of China (Taiwan) and the People's Republic of China. For the first time, the existence of a Communist Party-led government in Beijing was officially recognized and on 28 April 1991 the first formal Taiwanese delegation visited Beijing.

calls for independence rejected In Oct 1991 the opposition party, DPP, introduced a new clause into its charter which advocated Taiwanese independence and called for a plebiscite on the issue, despite the fact that calling for independence remained a seditious offence.

At the end of 1991 the 566 last remaining 'life members' formally resigned from their legislative posts. In Dec 1991 a new national assembly was elected and became the first to be controlled by Taiwan-elected members. The KMT won a landslide victory when it captured 71% of the vote and 254 of the 325 seats at stake, thus securing the required majority to push through fundamental reform of the constitution. The DPP was damaged by its technically illegal pro-independence stance; the Taiwanese remained concerned that a declaration of independence might prompt invasion by mainland China or by internal factional divisions.

foreign relations Following the diplomatic pact between China and South Korea signed Aug 1992, Taiwan severed relations with the latter. South Africa was left as the only major country with full diplomatic links with Taiwan.

Tajikistan or *Tadzhikistan* country in central Asia, bounded N by Kyrgyzstan and Uzbekistan, E by China, and S by Afghanistan and Pakistan.

history The Tajiks are descended from the Mongol invaders who swept across Asia from the 13th century. Conquered by Tsarist Russia 1877–1900, and formed 1924 from the Tajik areas of Bokhara and Turkestan, it became a constituent republic of Soviet Union 1929. Its people speak a Persian language.

growth of nationalism From the late 1980s there was a resurgence in Tajik consciousness. In 1989 a Rastakhiz ('Revival") Popular Front was established and during 1990 there were serious inter-ethnic clashes in Dushanbe.

independence declared The Communist Party of Tajikistan (CPT), led by the conservative

Kakhar Makhkamov, initially supported the Aug 1991 anti-Gorbachev attempted coup in Moscow. However, after pro-democracy demonstrations in Dushanbe and a vote of no confidence, Makhkamov was forced to resign on 31 Aug 1991. Under acting president Kadreddin Aslonov, a declaration of independence was made on 9 Sept 1991, and the activities of the CPT, now renamed the Socialist Party of Tajikstan (SPT), were banned on 22 September. A day later, at a special session of the supreme soviet, this ban was overturned. Aslonov was replaced as president by Rakhman Nabiyev, the former Brezhnev-appointed CPT leader who had been removed by Mikhail ◊Gorbachev in 1985, and a three-month state of emergency was imposed. However, after more than a week of popular protest, hunger strikes, and civil disobedience, orchestrated by the opposition Union of Democratic Forces, Nabiyev agreed to re-suspend the SPT, lift the state of emergency, legalize the opposition parties, step down as president, and hold direct elections on 24 Nov 1991. Nabiyev comfortably secured election, capturing 58% of the vote. However, the opposition, and outside observers, claimed that voting had been rigged.

CIS membership Tajikstan joined the ◊Commonwealth of Independent States in Dec 1991. It was admitted into the ◊Conference on Security and Cooperation in Europe (CSCE) in Jan 1992 and, two months later, became a member of the United Nations (UN). In Feb Tajikstan joined the Economic Cooperation Organization (ECO) founded by Iran, Pakistan, and Turkey 1975, which aimed to reduce customs tariffs and eventually form a customs union. US diplomatic recognition was also given at this time. In May 1992, because of public unrest, President Nabiyev was forced into a coalition with opposition leaders and in Sept of the same year he was forced to resign.

Taj Mahal erected as a tomb by 1650 in ◊Agra, India, for the emperor's wife Mumtaz Mahal.

Takeshita Noboru 1924– . Japanese rightwing politician. Elected to parliament as a Liberal Democratic Party (LDP) deputy 1958, he became president of the LDP and prime minister Oct 1987. He and members of his administration were shown in the Recruit scandal to have been involved in insider-trading and he resigned April 1989.

tallage English tax paid by cities, boroughs, and royal ◊demesnes, first levied under Henry II as a replacement for ◊danegeld. It was abolished 1340 after it had been superseded by grants of taxation voted by Parliament.

Talleyrand-Perigord Charles Maurice de 1754–1838. French politician and diplomat. As bishop of Autun 1789–91 he supported moderate reform during the ◊French Revolution, was excommunicated by the pope, and fled to the USA during the Reign of Terror (persecution of anti-revolutionaries). He returned and became foreign minister under the Directory 1797–99 and under Napoleon 1799–1807. He represented France at the Congress of ◊Vienna 1814–15.

Speech was given to man to disguise his thoughts.

Charles de Talleyrand-Perigord

Tambo Oliver 1917–1993. South African nationalist politician, in exile 1960–90, president of the African National Congress (ANC) 1977–91. Because of poor health, he was given the honorary post of national chair July 1991, and Nelson ◊Mandela resumed the ANC presidency.

Tambo was expelled from teacher training for organizing a student protest, and joined the ANC 1944. He set up a law practice with Mandela in Johannesburg 1952. In 1956 Tambo, with other ANC members, was arrested on charges of treason; he was released the following year. When the ANC was banned 1960, he left South Africa to set up an external wing. He became acting ANC president 1967 and president 1977, during Mandela's imprisonment. In Dec 1990 he returned to South Africa.

Tamerlane or *Tamburlaine* or *Timur i Leng* ('Timur the Lame') 1336–1405. Mongol ruler of Samarkand, in Uzbekistan, from 1369 who conquered Persia, Azerbaijan, Armenia, and Georgia. He defeated the ◊Golden Horde 1395, sacked Delhi 1398, invaded Syria and Anatolia, and captured the Ottoman sultan in Ankara 1402; he died invading China. He was a descendant of the Mongol leader Genghis Khan and the great-grandfather of Babur, founder of the Mogul Empire.

Tamil member of the majority ethnic group living in the Indian state of Tamil Nadu (formerly Madras). Tamils also live in S India, N Sri Lanka, Malaysia, Singapore, and South Africa, totalling 35–55 million worldwide. Tamil belongs to the Dravidian family of languages; written records in Tamil date from the 3rd century BC. The 3 million Tamils in Sri Lanka are predominantly Hindu, unlike the Sinhalese majority, who are mainly Buddhist. The *Tamil Tigers*, most prominent of the various Tamil groupings, are attempting to create a separate homeland in N Sri Lanka through both political and military means.

The Dravidian ancestors of the Tamils settled in S India well before the arrival of the Aryans from the NW. Although they share the Hindu religion with their northern neighbours, the Tamils retain a distinct culture. During the 19th century the British encouraged Tamils to move to work on plantations in Sri Lanka, where there was already a Tamil population, and Malaysia.

Tammany Hall Democratic Party organization in New York. It originated 1789 as the Society of St Tammany, named after an American Indian chief. It was dominant from 1800 until the 1930s and gained a reputation for corruption and rule by bosses; its domination was broken by Mayor ◊La Guardia in the 1930s and Mayor Koch in the 1970s.

Tanaka Kakuei 1918– . Japanese right-wing politician, leader of the dominant Liberal Democratic Party (LDP) and prime minister 1972–74. In 1976 he was charged with corruption and resigned from the LDP but remained a powerful faction leader.

In the Diet (Japanese parliament) from 1947, Tanaka was minister of finance 1962–65 and of international trade and industry 1971–72, before becoming LDP leader. In 1974 he had to resign the premiership because of allegations of corruption and 1976 he was arrested for accepting bribes from the Lockheed Corporation while premier. He was found guilty 1983, but remained in the Diet as an independent deputy pending appeal. He was also implicated in the 1988–89 Recruit scandal of insider trading.

Tanganyika a German colony from 1884 to 1914, and now part of ◊Tanzania.

Tanganyika African National Union (TANU) moderate socialist national party organized by Tanzanian politician Julius ◊Nyerere in the 1950s. TANU won electoral successes 1958 and 1960, ensuring that Nyerere was recognized as prime minister on 1 May 1961, when Tanganyika prepared for independence from Britain.

Tang dynasty the greatest of China's imperial dynasties, which ruled 618–907. Founded by the Sui official Li Yuan (566–635), it extended Chinese authority into central Asia, Tibet, Korea, and Annam, establishing what was then the world's largest empire. The dynasty's peak was reached during the reign (712–56) of Emperor Minghuang (Hsuan-tsung).

The Tang dynasty set up a centralized administrative system based on the ◊Han examination model. Buddhism continued to spread and the arts and science flourished. Printing was invented, gunpowder first used, and seaborne and overland trade and cultural contacts were widened.

Tannenberg, Battle of two battles, named after a village now in N Poland:

1410 the Poles and Lithuanians defeated the Teutonic Knights, establishing Poland as a major power;

1914 during World War I, when Tannenberg was part of East Prussia, ◊Hindenburg defeated the Russians.

Tantrism forms of Hinduism and Buddhism that emphasize the division of the universe into male and female forces that maintain its unity by their interaction; this gives women equal status with men.

Tantric Buddhism, practised in medieval India, depended on the tuition of teachers and the use of yoga, mantras, and meditation to enable its followers to master themselves and gain oneness with the universe.

Tanzania country in E Africa, bounded N by Uganda and Kenya; S by Mozambique, Malawi, and Zambia; W by Zaire, Burundi, and Rwanda; and E by the Indian Ocean.

history For early history, see ◊Africa. Zanzibar was under Portuguese control during the 16th–17th centuries. In 1822 it was united with the nearby island of Pemba. It was a British protectorate 1890–1963, when it became an independent sultanate, an uprising followed, and the sultan was overthrown 1964.

independence Tanganyika was a German colony 1884–1914, until conquered by Britain during World War I; it was a British League of Nations mandate 1920–46 and came under United Nations (UN) trusteeship 1946–62. It achieved full independence within the ◊Commonwealth, 1961, with Julius ◊Nyerere as prime minister. He gave up the post some six weeks after independence to devote himself to the development of the Tanganyika African National Union (TANU), but in Dec 1962, when Tanganyika became a republic, he returned to become the nation's first president.

United Republic of Tanzania Tanzania was founded by the union of Tanganyika and Zanzibar April 1964. Nyerere became president of the new United Republic of Tanzania and dominated the nation's politics for the next 20 years, being re-elected 1965, 1970, 1975, and 1980. Known throughout Tanzania as Mwalimu ('teacher'), he established himself as a Christian socialist who attempted to put into practice a philosophy that he believed would secure his country's future. He committed himself in the Arusha Declaration of 1967 (the name comes from the N Tanzanian town where he made his historic statement) to building a socialist state for the millions of poor peasants through a series of village cooperatives (*ujamas*). Nyerere became one of Africa's most respected politicians. In the final years of his presidency economic pressures, domestic and international, forced him to compromise his ideals and accept a more capitalistic society than he would have wished, but his achievements have included the best public health service on the African continent, according to UN officials, and a universal primary school system.

foreign relations Relations between Tanzania and its neighbours have been variable. The East Africa Community (EAC) of Tanzania, Kenya, and Uganda, formed 1967, broke up 1977, and relations between Tanzania and the more capitalistic Kenya became uneasy. In 1979 Nyerere sent troops to support the Uganda National Liberation Front in its bid to overthrow President Idi Amin. This enhanced Nyerere's reputation but damaged his country's economy. Tanzania also supported the liberation movements in Mozambique and Rhodesia.

In 1977 TANU and the Afro-Shirazi Party of Zanzibar merged to become the Revolutionary Party of Tanzania (CCM), and this was made the only legal political organization. Nyerere retired from the presidency at the end of 1985 but remained as CCM chair. The president of Zanzibar, Ali Hassan Mwinyi, was adopted as the sole presidential candidate by the CCM congress Dec 1985. In May 1990 Julius Nyerere announced his retirement as party chair and in Aug 1990 he was replaced by President Mwinyi.

end of one-party rule In Feb 1992 the governing CCM party endorsed a proposal to introduce multiparty politics; Mwinyi's government had tolerated the formation of at least five opposition groups since 1991. Also in Feb, it was announced that the East Africa cooperation agreement with Kenya and Uganda would be revived.

Taoism Chinese philosophical system, traditionally founded by the Chinese philosopher Lao Zi 6th century BC. He is also attributed authorship of the scriptures, *Tao Te Ching*, although these were apparently compiled 3rd century BC. The 'tao' or 'way' denotes the hidden principle of the universe, and less stress is laid on good deeds than on harmonious interaction with the environment, which automati-

cally ensures right behaviour. The magical side of Taoism is illustrated by the *I Ching* or *Book of Changes*, a book of divination.

beliefs The universe is believed to be kept in balance by the opposing forces of yin and yang that operate in dynamic tension between themselves. This magical, ritualistic aspect of Taoism developed from the 2nd century AD and was largely responsible for its popular growth; it stresses physical immortality, and this was attempted by means ranging from dietary regulation and fasting to alchemy. By the 3rd century, worship of gods had begun to appear, including that of the stove god Tsao Chun. From the 4th century, rivalry between Taoists and Mahāyāna Buddhists was strong in China, leading to persecution of one religion by the other; this was resolved by mutual assimilation, and Taoism developed monastic communities similar to those of the Buddhists.

Tariff Reform League organization set up 1903 as a vehicle for the ideas of the Liberal politician Joseph ◊Chamberlain on protective tariffs. It aimed to unify the British Empire by promoting imperial preference in trade.

This policy was unacceptable to dominion governments as it would constrict their economic policies and put a tax on foodstuffs imported into Britain. Consequently, the league's objective became the introduction of protection for British goods against competition from Germany and the USA.

Tarquinius Superbus (Tarquin the Proud) lived 6th century BC. Last king of Rome 534–510 BC. According to legend, he was deposed when his son Sextus raped Lucretia.

Tartar see ◊Tatar.

Tasman Abel Janszoon 1603–1659. Dutch navigator. In 1642, he was the first European to see Tasmania. He also made the first European sightings of New Zealand, Tonga, and Fiji.

He called Tasmania Van Diemen's Land in honour of the governor general of the Netherlands Indies; it was subsequently renamed in his honour 1856.

Tatar or *Tartar* member of a Turkic people, the descendants of the mixed Mongol and Turkic followers of ◊Genghis Khan, called the Golden Horde because of the wealth they gained by plunder. The vast Tatar state was conquered by Russia 1552. The Tatars now live mainly in the Russian autonomous republic of Tatarstan, W Siberia, Turkmenistan, and Uzbekistan (where they were deported from the Crimea 1944). There are over 5 million speakers of the Tatar language, which belongs to the Turkic branch of the Altaic family. The

Tatar people are mainly Muslim, although some have converted to the Orthodox Church.

Tatarstan formerly *Tatar Autonomous Republic* autonomous republic of E Russia. A territory of Volga-Kama Bulgar state from the 10th century when Islam was introduced; conquered by the Mongols 1236; the capital of the powerful Khanate of Kazan until conquered by Russia 1552; an autonomous republic from 1920. In recent years the republic (mainly Muslim and an important industrial and oil-producing area) has seen moves towards increased autonomy. In Aug 1990 the republic's assembly upgraded Tatarstan to full republic status, proclaiming its economic and political 'sovereignty', and in April 1991 there were popular demonstrations in support of this action. In June 1991 it refused to participate in the Russian presidential election, and in March 1992 declined to be party to a federal treaty, signed in Moscow by 18 of Russia's other 20 main political subdivisions. A referendum 21 March 1992 favoured Tatarstan becoming a sovereign state within Russia.

Taylor Zachary 1784–1850. 12th president of the USA 1849–50. A veteran of the War of 1812 and a hero of the Mexican War (1846–48), he was nominated for the presidency by the Whigs in 1848 and was elected. He died less than one and a half years into his term, during the congressional debate on California's admission to the Union. He was succeeded by Vice President Millard Fillmore.

Teapot Dome Scandal US political scandal that revealed the corruption of President ◊Harding's administration. It centred on the leasing of naval oil reserves 1921 at Teapot Dome, Wyoming, without competitive bidding, as a result of bribing the secretary of the interior, Albert B Fall (1861–1944). Fall was tried and imprisoned 1929.

Tecumseh 1768–1813. North American Indian chief of the Shawnee. He attempted to unite the Indian peoples from Canada to Florida against the encroachment of white settlers, but the defeat of his brother *Tenskwatawa*, 'the Prophet', at the battle of Tippecanoe in Nov 1811 by W H Harrison, governor of the Indiana Territory, largely destroyed the confederacy built up by Tecumseh. He was commissioned a brigadier general in the British army during the War of 1812, and died in battle.

Tehran Conference conference held 1943 in Tehran, Iran, the first meeting of World War II Allied leaders Churchill, Roosevelt, and Stalin. The chief subject discussed was coordination of Allied strategy in W and E Europe.

temperance movement societies dedicated to curtailing the consumption of alcohol by total prohibition, local restriction, or encouragement of declarations of personal abstinence ('the pledge'). Temperance movements were first set up in the USA, Ireland, and Scotland, then in the N of England in the 1830s.

The proponents of temperance were drawn from evangelical or nonconformist Christians, trade unionists, Chartists, members of cooperatives, the self-help movement, and the Church of England. After 1871 the movement supported the ◊Liberal Party in its attempts to use the licensing laws to restrict the consumption of alcoholic beverages.

Templars or *Knights Templar* or *Order of Poor Knights of Christ and of the Temple of Solomon* military religious order founded in Jerusalem 1119–20 to protect pilgrims travelling to the Holy Land. They played an important part in the ◊Crusades of the 12th and 13th centuries. Innocent II placed them under direct papal authority 1139, and their international links allowed them to adapt to the 13th-century decline of the Crusader states by becoming Europe's bankers. The Templars' independence, power, and wealth, rather than their alleged heresy, probably motivated ◊Philip IV of France, helped by the Avignon Pope Clement V, to suppress the order 1307–14.

Ten Commandments laws engraved on tablets of stone which were given to ◊Moses on Mount Sinai.

Teng Hsiao-ping see ◊Deng Xiaoping.

Ten Hours Act 1847 British act of Parliament that restricted the working day of all workers except adult males. It was prompted by the public campaign (the 'Ten Hours Movement') set up 1831. Women and young people were restricted to a $10\frac{1}{2}$ hour day, with $1\frac{1}{2}$ hours for meals, between 6 am and 6 pm.

Tennessee Valley Authority (TVA) US government corporation founded 1933 to develop the Tennessee river basin (an area of some 104,000 sq km/40,000 sq mi) by building hydroelectric power stations, producing and distributing fertilizers, and similar activities. The TVA was associated with President F D Roosevelt's ◊New Deal, promoting economic growth by government investment.

terrorism systematic violence in the furtherance of political aims, often by small ◊guerrilla groups, such as the Fatah Revolutionary Council led by Abu Nidal, a splinter group that split from the Palestine Liberation Organization 1973.

Terror, Reign of period of the ◊French Revolution when the Jacobins were in power (Oct 1793–July 1794) under ◊Robespierre and instituted mass persecution of their opponents. About 1,400 were executed, mainly by guillotine, until public indignation rose and Robespierre was overthrown in July 1794.

Test Act act of Parliament passed in England 1673, more than 100 years after similar legislation in Scotland, requiring holders of public office to renounce the doctrine of transubstantiation and take the sacrament in an Anglican church, thus excluding Catholics, Nonconformists, and non-Christians from office. Its clauses were repealed 1828–29. Scottish tests were abolished 1889. In Ireland the Test Act was introduced 1704 and English legislation on oaths of allegiance and religious declarations were made valid there 1782. All these provisions were abolished 1871.

Test Ban Treaty agreement signed by the USA, the USSR, and the UK 5 Aug 1963 contracting to test nuclear weapons only underground. In the following two years 90 other nations signed the treaty, the only major nonsignatories being France and China, which continued underwater and ground-level tests.

Tet Offensive in the Vietnam War, a prolonged attack mounted by the ◊Vietcong against Saigon (now Ho Chi Minh City) and other South Vietnamese cities and hamlets, including the US Marine base at ◊Khe Sanh, which began 30 Jan 1968. Although the Vietcong were finally forced to withdraw, the Tet Offensive brought into question the ability of the South Vietnamese army and their US allies to win the war and added fuel to the antiwar movement in both the USA and Australia. Of 84,000 communist Vietcong who took part in the offensive, 32,000 were killed by mid-Feb.

Teutonic Knight member of a German Christian military order, the *Knights of the Teutonic Order*, founded 1190 by Hermann of Salza in Palestine. They crusaded against the pagan Prussians and Lithuanians from 1228 and controlled Prussia until the 16th century. Their capital was Marienburg (now Malbork, Poland).

The Teutonic Knights were originally members of the German aristocracy who founded an order of hospitallers in Acre 1190 and became a military order 1198. They wore white robes with black crosses. They were based in Palestine until 1268 when they were expelled by the Mamelukes (rulers of Egypt), after which they concentrated on taking Roman Catholicism into E Europe under the control of the pope.

They were prevented from expanding into Russia by ◊Alexander Nevski at the battle of Lake Peipus 1243, but they ruthlessly colonized Prussia 1226–83. By the 15th century, pressure from neighbouring powers and the decline of the crusader ideal led to their containment within E Prussia. Their influence ended 1525 when their grand master Albert of Brandenburg was converted to Lutheranism and declared Prussia to be a secular duchy.

Texas state in southwestern USA. It was settled by the 1682; part of Mexico 1821–36; Santa Anna massacred the Alamo garrison 1836, but was defeated by Sam Houston at San Jacinto the same year; Texas became an independent republic 1836–45, with Houston as president; in 1845 it became a state of the USA. Texas is the only state in the USA to have previously been an independent republic.

Thailand country in SE Asia on the Gulf of Siam, bounded E by Laos and Cambodia, S by Malaysia, and W by Myanmar (Burma).

Far-left parties, such as the Communist Party, are outlawed, as are parties that field candidates in fewer than half the nation's constituencies. Effective political power in Thailand remains ultimately with the army leadership.

history Thailand has an ancient civilization, with Bronze Age artefacts from as early as 4000 BC. Siam, as it was called until 1939 (and 1945–49), has been united as a kingdom since 1350; the present dynasty dates from 1782. It was reached by Portuguese traders 1511, followed by the British East India Company and the Dutch in the 17th century. Treaties of friendship and trade 1826 and 1855 established Britain as the paramount power in the region and opened Siam to foreign commerce. Under King Rama Chulalongkura 1868–1910, there was a measure of economic modernization. Anglo-French diplomatic agreements of 1896 and 1904 established Siam as a neutral buffer kingdom between British Burma and French Indochina.

After World War I, a movement for national renaissance developed, which culminated in a coup against the absolute monarch King Prajadhipok and the establishment instead of a representative system of government 1932. The name of Muang Thai ('land of the free') was adopted 1939. Thailand was occupied by Japan 1941-44. The government collaborated, but there was a guerrilla resistance movement. A period of instability followed the Japanese withdrawal, King Ananda Mahidol was assassinated 1946, and the army assumed power in a coup 1947 led by Field Marshal Pibul Songgram.

military junta rule The army retained control during the next two decades, with the leader of the military junta periodically changed by a series of bloodless coups: Field Marshal Pibul Songgram 1947–57, Field Marshal Sarit Thanarat 1957–63, and General Thanom Kittikachorn 1963–73. The monarch, King Bhumibol Adulyadej, was only a figurehead, and experiments with elected assemblies were undertaken 1957–58 and 1968–71. During this era of junta rule, Thailand allied itself with the USA and encountered serious communist guerrilla insurgency along its borders with Laos, Cambodia, and Malaysia. Despite achievements in the economic sphere, the junta was overthrown by violent student riots Oct 1973. Free elections were held 1975 and 1976. A series of coalition governments lacked stability, and the military assumed power again 1976–77.

The army supreme commander, General Kriangsak Chomanan, held power 1977–80 and established a mixed civilian and military form of government under the monarch's direction. Having deposed Kriangsak Oct 1980, General Prem Tinsulanonda (1920–) formally relinquished his army office and headed an elected civilian coalition government.

rapid economic growth Attempted coups April 1983 and Sept 1985 were easily crushed by Prime Minister Prem, who ruled in a cautious apolitical manner. With an economic growth averaging 9%-10% a year, Thailand emerged as an export- oriented, newly industrializing country.

military coup Chatichai Choonhavan, leader of the Thai Nation party, was elected prime minister 1988. In Feb 1991 he was overthrown in a bloodless coup led by General Sunthorn Kongsompong, the supreme military commander, and army chief General Suchinda Kraprayoon. It was the country's 17th coup or attempted putsch since the abolition of the absolute monarchy 1932. A civilian, Anand Panyarachun, was appointed interim prime minister, subject to the ultimate control of the military junta, but after new elections March 1992 he was replaced by General Suchinda. His appointment sparked the largest street demonstrations for two decades, forcing him to resign.

In May 1992 the ruling coalition agreed to a package of constitutional reforms, including the proviso that the prime minister should not come from the ranks of the military. Anand was made interim prime minister in June. The Sept 1992 general election gave a Democratic coalition 185 seats in the 360-member parliament and Chuan Leekpai became prime minister.

foreign affairs The civil war in Cambodia and Laos, which resulted in the flight of more than 500,000 refugees to Thailand 1975-90, provided justification for continued quasi- military rule and the maintenance of martial law until May 1991. Thailand drew closer to its allies in the Association of South East Asian Nations, who jointly supported the Cambodian guerrilla resistance to the Vietnamese-imposed government, and its relations improved. Thailand was drawn more deeply into the Cambodian civil war with the shelling July 1989 of a refugee camp in Thailand, but tensions eased after the Cambodian peace agreement 1991.

thane or *thegn* Anglo-Saxon hereditary nobleman rewarded by the granting of land for service to the monarch or a lord.

Thant, U 1909–1974. Burmese diplomat, secretary general of the United Nations 1962–71. He helped to resolve the US-Soviet crisis over the Soviet installation of missiles in Cuba, and he made the controversial decision to withdraw the UN peacekeeping force from the Egypt–Israel border 1967 (see ◊Arab–Israeli Wars).

Thatcher Margaret Hilda (born Roberts), Baroness Thatcher of Kesteven 1925– . British Conservative politician, prime minister 1979–90. She was education minister 1970–74 and Conservative Party leader from 1975. In 1982 she sent British troops to recapture the Falkland Islands from Argentina. She confronted trade-union power during the miners' strike 1984–85, sold off majority stakes in many public utilities to the private sector, and reduced the influence of local government through such measures as the abolition of metropolitan councils, the control of expenditure through 'rate-capping', and the introduction of the community charge, or ◊poll tax, from 1989. In 1990 splits in the cabinet over the issues of Europe and consensus government forced her resignation. An astute Parliamentary tactician, she tolerated little disagreement, either from opposition or from within her own party.

To those waiting with bated breath for that favourite media catch-phrase, the U-turn, I have only one thing to say. You turn if you want to. The lady's not for turning.

Margaret Thatcher speech to the Conservative Party Conference 1980

Thebes capital of Boeotia in ancient Greece. In the Peloponnesian War it was allied with Sparta against Athens. For a short time after 371 BC when Thebes defeated Sparta at Leuctra, it was the most powerful state in Greece. Alexander the Great destroyed it 336 BC and although it was restored, it never regained its former power.

thegn alternative spelling of ◊thane.

Themistocles c. 525–c. 460 BC. Athenian soldier and politician. Largely through his success in persuading the Athenians to build a navy, Greece was saved from Persian conquest. He fought with distinction in the Battle of ◊Salamis 480 BC during the Persian War. About 470 he was accused of embezzlement and conspiracy against Athens, banished and fled to Asia, where Artaxerxes, the Persian king, received him with favour.

Theodora 500–548. Byzantine empress from 527. She was originally the mistress of Emperor Justinian before marrying him in 525. She earned a reputation for charity, courage, and championing the rights of women.

The daughter of a bear-keeper, Theodora became an actress and prostitute. Despite her many detractors, she became immensely influential, since Justinian consulted her on all affairs of state.

Theodoric the Great c. 455–526. King of the Ostrogoths from 474 in succession to his father. He invaded Italy 488, overthrew King Odoacer (whom he murdered) and established his own Ostrogothic kingdom there, with its capital in Ravenna. He had no strong successor, and his kingdom eventually became part of the Byzantine Empire of Justinian.

Theodosius I 'the Great' c. AD 346–395. Roman emperor. Appointed Emperor of the East in 379, he fought against the ◊Goths successfully, and established Christianity throughout the region. He invaded Italy in 393, restoring unity to the empire and died in Milan. He was buried in Constantinople.

A pious Christian and adherent of the Nicene creed, he dealt severely with heretics, ordering the death penalty from some extreme sects.

Theodosius II 401–450. Byzantine emperor from 408 who defeated the Persians 421 and 441, and from 441 bought off ◊Attila's Huns with tribute.

Thermidor 11th month of the French Revolutionary calendar, which gave its name to the period after the fall of the Jacobins and the proscription of Robespierre by the National Convention 9 Thermidor 1794.

Thermopylae, Battle of battle during the ◊Persian Wars 480 BC when Leonidas, king of Sparta, and 1,000 men defended the pass of Thermopylae to the death against a much greater force of Persians. The pass led from Thessaly to Phocis in central Greece.

Thessaly (Greek *Thessalia*) region of E central Greece, on the Aegean. It was an independent state in ancient Greece and later formed part of the Roman province of ◊Macedonia. It was Turkish from the 14th century until incorporated in Greece 1881.

Thiers Louis Adolphe 1797–1877. French politician and historian, first president of the Third Republic 1871–73. He held cabinet posts under Louis Philippe, led the parliamentary opposition to Napoleon III from 1863, and as head of the provisional government 1871 negotiated peace with Prussia and suppressed the briefly autonomous ◊Paris Commune.

thing assembly of freemen in the Norse lands (Scandinavia) during the medieval period. It could encompass a meeting of the whole nation (*Althing*) or of a small town or community (*Husthing*).

third estate or *tiers état* in pre-revolutionary France, the order of society comprising the common people as distinct from members of the first (noble) or the second (clerical) estates. All three met collectively as the ◊States General.

Third Reich (Third Empire) term used by the Nazis to describe Germany during the years of Hitler's dictatorship after 1933. The idea of the Third Reich was based on the existence of two previous German empires, the medieval Holy Roman Empire and the second empire 1871–1918.

The term was coined by German writer Moeller van den Bruck (1876–1925) in the 1920s.

Third World or *developing world* those countries that are less developed than the industrialized free-market countries of the West (First World) and the industrialized former Communist countries (Second World). Third World countries are the poorest, as measured by their income per head of population, and are concentrated in Asia, Africa, and Latin America.

They are divided into low-income countries, including China and India; middle-income countries, such as Nigeria, Indonesia, and Bolivia; and upper-middle-income countries, such as Brazil, Algeria, and Malaysia. The Third World has 75% of the world's population but consumes only 20% of its resources. In 1990 the average income per head of population in the northern hemisphere was $12,500, which is 18 times higher than that in the southern hemisphere.

Thirteen Colonies 13 American colonies that signed the ◊Declaration of Independence from Britain 1776. Led by George Washington, the Continental Army defeated the British army in the ◊American Revolution 1776–81 to become the original 13 United States of America: Connecticut, Delaware, Georgia, Maryland, Massachusetts, New Hampshire, New Jersey, New York, North Carolina, Pennsylvania, Rhode Island, South Carolina, and Virginia. They were united first under the Articles of ◊Confederation and from 1789, the US constitution.

38th parallel demarcation line between North (People's Democratic Republic of) and South (Republic of) Korea, agreed at the Yalta Conference 1945 and largely unaltered by the Korean War 1950–53.

Thirty Years' War major war 1618–48 in central Europe. Beginning as a German conflict between Protestants and Catholics, it gradually became transformed into a struggle to determine whether the ruling Austrian Habsburg family would gain control of all Germany. The war caused serious economic and demographic problems in central Europe.

1618–20 A Bohemian revolt against Austrian rule was defeated. Some Protestant princes continued the struggle against Austria.

1625–27 Denmark entered the war on the Protestant side.

1630 Gustavus Adolphus of Sweden intervened on the Protestant side, overrunning N Germany.

1631 The Catholic commander Tilly stormed Magdeburg.

1632 Tilly was defeated at Breitenfeld and the river Lech, and was killed. The German general Wallenstein was defeated at the Battle of Lützen; Gustavus Adolphus killed.

1634 When the Swedes were defeated at Nördlingen, ◊Richelieu brought France into the war to inflict several defeats on Austria's Spanish allies. Wallenstein was assassinated.

1648 The *Treaty of Westphalia* gave France S Alsace, and Sweden got certain Baltic provinces, the emperor's authority in Germany becoming only nominal. The mercenary armies of Wallenstein, Tilly, and Mansfeld devastated Germany.

Thothmes four Egyptian kings of the 18th dynasty, including:

Thothmes I king of Egypt 1540–1501 BC. He campaigned in Syria.

Thothmes III king of Egypt c. 1500–1446 BC. He extended the empire to the river Euphrates, and conquered Nubia. He was a grandson of Thothmes I.

thousand days period of office of US president John F Kennedy from 20 Jan 1961 to his assassination on 22 Nov 1963.

Thrace (Greek *Thráki*) ancient region of the Balkans, SE Europe, formed by parts of modern Greece and Bulgaria. The area was conquered by Persia 6th–5th centuries BC and by Macedonia 4th–2nd centuries BC. From AD 46 it was a Roman province, then part of the Byzantine Empire, and Turkish from the 15th century until 1878; it was then subject to constant dispute until after World War I, when it was divided (in 1923) into western Thrace (the Greek province of Thráki) and eastern Thrace (European Turkey).

three-day week in the UK, policy adopted by Prime Minister Edward Heath Jan 1974 to combat an economic crisis and coal miners' strike. A shortage of electrical power led to the allocation of energy to industry for only three days each week. A general election was called Feb 1974, which the government lost.

'Three Emperors' League' an alliance of emperors from 1872, known in German as ◊Dreikaiserbund.

Three Kingdoms in China 220–581, an era of disruptive, intermittent warfare between three powers. Sometimes the term is used to cover the period 220–280 following the end of the ◊Han dynasty when the Wei, Shu, and Wu fought for supremacy.

From 265 the Wei established their preeminence and united the country under the Western Jin (Ch'in) dynasty until 316. N China fell under the control of the Sixteen Dynasties 317– 386, before the rise of the Northern Wei 386–535, founded by the barbarian Xianbi (Hsien-pi), a proto-Mongol people who established their capital at Luoyang (Lo-yang). The period 317–581, known as the era of the Northern and Southern dynasties, was characterized by political decentralization and the growing influence of Buddhism.

Thucydides c. 455–400 BC. Athenian historian who exercised military command in the ◊Peloponnesian War with Sparta, but was banished from Athens in 424. In his *History of the Peloponnesian War*, he gave a detailed account of the conflict down to 411.

Thule Greek and Roman name for the northernmost land known. It was applied to the Shetlands, the Orkneys, and Iceland, and by later writers to Scandinavia.

Tiahuanaco or *Tihuanaco* site of a Peruvian city, 24 kim/15 mi S of Lake Titicaca in the Andes, which gave its name to the 8th–14th-century civilization that preceded the Inca and built many of the roads the Inca are credited with building.

Dating from *c*.600, Tiahuanaco was situated 4,000 m/13,000 ft above sea level. According to Indian legend, it was built in one night by a race of giants.

Tiananmen Square (Chinese 'Square of Heavenly Peace') paved open space in central Beijing (Peking), China, the largest public square in the world (area 0.4 sq km/0.14 sq mi). On 3–4 June 1989 more than 1,000 unarmed protesters were killed by government troops in a massacre that crushed China's emerging prodemocracy movement.

Hundreds of thousands of demonstrators had occupied the square from early May, calling for political reform and the resignation of the communist leadership. They were led by students, 3,000 of whom staged a hunger strike in the square. The massacre that followed was sanctioned by the old guard of leaders, including Deng Xiaoping.

Tianjin, Treaty of agreement 1858 between China and Western powers, signed at the end of the second Opium (Arrow) War. It was one of the ◊unequal treaties forced on China by the West. A further ten treaty ports, mainly along the Chang Jiang, were opened to Britain, France, Russia, and the USA.

Tiberius Claudius Nero 42 BC–AD 37. Roman emperor, the stepson, adopted son, and successor of Augustus from AD 14. He was a cautious ruler whose reign was marred by the heavy incident of trials for treason or conspiracy. Tiberius fell under the influence of Sejanus who encouraged the emperor's fear of assassination and was instrumental in Tiberius' departure from Rome to Capreae (Capri). He never returned to Rome.

It is the part of a good shepherd to shear his flock, not flay it.

Claudius Nero Tiberius AD 2

Tibet autonomous region of SW China (Pinyin form *Xizang*) Tibet was an independent kingdom from the 5th century AD. It came under nominal Chinese rule about 1700. Independence was regained after a revolt 1912. China regained control 1951 when the historic ruler and religious leader, the Dalai Lama, was driven from the country and the monks (who formed 25% of the population) were forced out of the monasteries. Between 1951 and 1959 the Chinese People's Liberation Army (PLA) controlled Tibet, although the Dalai Lama returned as nominal spiritual and temporal head of state. In 1959 a Tibetan uprising spread from bordering regions to Lhasa and was supported by Tibet's local government. The rebellion was suppressed by the PLA, prompting the Dalai Lama and 9,000 Tibetans to flee to India. The Chinese proceeded to dissolve the Tibet local government, abolish serfdom, collectivize agriculture, and suppress Lamaism. In 1965 Tibet became an autonomous region of China. Chinese rule continued to be resented, however, and the economy languished.

From 1979, the leadership in Beijing adopted a more liberal and pragmatic policy towards Tibet. Traditional agriculture, livestock, and trading practices were restored (under the 1980 slogan 'relax, relax, and relax again'), a number of older political leaders and rebels were rehabilitated or pardoned, and the promotion of local Tibetan cadres was encouraged. In addition, a somewhat more tolerant attitude towards Lamaism has been adopted (temples damaged during the 1965–68 Cultural Revolution are being repaired) and attempts, thus far unsuccessful, have been made to persuade the Dalai Lama to return from exile.

Pro-independence demonstrations erupted in Lhasa in Sept–Oct 1987, again throughout 1988, and in March 1989. These were forcibly suppressed by Chinese troops.

Tigré or *Tigray* region in the northern highlands of Ethiopia; area 65,900 sq km/25,444 sq mi. The chief town is Mekele. The region had an estimated population of 2.4 million in 1984, at a time when drought and famine were driving large numbers of people to fertile land in the S or into neighbouring Sudan. Since 1978 a guerrilla group known as the Tigré People's Liberation Front (TPLF) has been fighting for regional autonomy. In 1989 government troops were forced from the province, and the TPLF advanced towards Addis Ababa, playing a key role in the fall of the Ethiopian government May 1991.

Tilly Jan Tserklaes, Count von Tilly 1559–1632. Flemish commander of the army of the Catholic League and imperial forces in the ◊Thirty Years' War. Notorious for his storming of Magdeburg, E Germany, 1631, he was defeated by the Swedish king Gustavus Adolphus at Breitenfeld and at the river Lech in SW Germany, where he was mortally wounded.

Tilsit, Treaty of agreement between Russia and France (under ◊Napoleon I) on 7 July 1807. Another treaty on 9 July 1807 was between Prussia and France.

Timbuktu or *Tombouctou* town in Mali. A camel caravan centre from the 11th century on the fringe of the Sahara, since 1960 it has been surrounded by the southward movement of the desert, and the former canal link with the river Niger is dry.

Timur i Leng alternative spelling of ◊Tamerlane, Mongol ruler.

Tipu Sultan *c.* 1750–1799. Sultan of Mysore (now Karnataka) in SW India from the death of his father, ◊Hyder Ali, 1782. He died of wounds when his capital, Seringapatam, was captured by the British. His rocket brigade led Sir William Congreve (1772–1828) to develop the weapon for use in the ◊Napoleonic Wars.

Tirpitz Alfred von 1849–1930. German admiral. As secretary for the navy 1897–1916, he created the German navy and planned the World War I U-boat campaign.

tithe formerly, payment exacted from the inhabitants of a parish for the maintenance of the church and its incumbent; some religious groups continue the practice by giving 10% of members' incomes to charity.

It was originally the grant of a tenth of all agricultural produce made to priests in Hebrew society. In the Middle Ages the tithe was adopted as a tax in kind paid to the local parish church, usually for the support of the incumbent, and stored in a special tithe barn; as such, it survived into contemporary times in Europe and Britain. In Protestant countries, these payments were often appropriated by lay landlords.

Tito adopted name of Josip Broz 1892–1980. Yugoslav communist politician, in power from 1945. In World War II he organized the National Liberation Army to carry on guerrilla warfare against the German invasion 1941, and was created marshal 1943. As prime minister 1946–53 and president from 1953, he followed a foreign policy of 'positive neutralism'.

Born in Croatia, Tito served in the Austrian army during World War I, was captured by the Russians, and fought in the Red Army during the civil wars. Returning to Yugoslavia 1923, he became prominent as a communist and during World War II as ◊partisan leader against the Nazis. In 1943 he established a provisional government and gained Allied recognition (previously given to the ◊Chetniks), and with Soviet help proclaimed the federal republic 1945. As prime minister, he settled the Yugoslav minori-

ties question on a federal basis, and in 1953 took the newly created post of president (for life from 1974). In 1948 he was criticized by the USSR and other communist countries for his successful system of decentralized profit-sharing workers' councils, and became a leader of the ◊nonaligned movement.

Any movement in history that attempts to perpetuate itself becomes reactionary.

Marshal Tito

Titus Flavius Sabinus Vespasianus AD 39–81. Roman emperor from AD 79. Eldest son of ◊Vespasian, he captured Jerusalem 70 to end the Jewish revolt in Roman Palestine. He completed the Colosseum, and helped to mitigate the suffering from the eruption of Vesuvius in 79, which destroyed Pompeii and Herculaneum.

Tlatelolco, Treaty of international agreement signed 1967 in Tlatelolco, Mexico, prohibiting nuclear weapons in Latin America.

Tobruk Libyan port. Occupied by Italy 1911, it was taken by Britain 1941 during World War II, and unsuccessfully besieged by Axis forces April–Dec 1941. It was captured by Germany June 1942 after the retreat of the main British force to Egypt, and this precipitated the replacement of Auchinleck by Montgomery as British commander.

Democratic institutions generally give men a lofty notion of their country and themselves.

Alexis de Tocqueville
Democracy in America 1835

Tocqueville Alexis de 1805–1859. French politician and political scientist, author of the first analytical study of the US constitution, *De la Démocratie en Amérique/Democracy in America* 1835, and of a penetrating description of France before the Revolution, *L'Ancien Régime et la Révolution/The Old Regime and the Revolution* 1856.

Elected to the Chamber of Deputies 1839, Tocqueville became vice president of the Constituent Assembly and minister of foreign affairs 1849. He retired after Napoleon III's coup 1851.

Togliatti Palmiro 1893–1964. Italian politician who was a founding member of the Italian

Communist Party 1921 and effectively its leader for almost 40 years from 1926 until his death. In exile 1926–44, he returned after the fall of the Fascist dictator Mussolini to become a member of Badoglio's government and held office until 1946.

Togo country in W Africa, on the Atlantic Ocean, bounded N by Burkina Faso, E by Benin, and W by Ghana.

history Called Togoland, the country was a German protectorate 1885–1914, when it was captured by Anglo-French forces. It was divided between Britain and France 1922 under a League of Nations mandate and continued under United Nations trusteeship from 1946. In 1956 British Togoland voted for integration with Ghana, where it became Volta region 1957.

independence French Togoland voted to become an autonomous republic within the French union. The new Togolese republic achieved internal self-government 1956 and full independence 1960. Sylvanus Olympio, leader of the United Togolese (UT) party, became president in an unopposed election April 1961. In 1963 Olympio was killed in a military coup and his brother-in-law Nicolas Grunitzky, who had gone into exile, was recalled to become president.

gradual democratization In 1967 Grunitzky was, in turn, deposed in a bloodless military coup, led by Lt-Gen Etienne Gnassingbé Eyadéma. The new constitution was suspended; Eyadéma assumed the presidency and banned all political activity. Six years later he founded a new party, the socialist, nationalist RPT, and declared it the only legal political organization. Between 1967 and 1977 there were several attempts to overthrow him but by 1979 Eyadéma felt sufficiently secure to propose a new coalition and embark on a policy of gradual democratization. An attempt to overthrow him Oct 1986, by mercenaries from Burkina Faso and Ghana, was easily thwarted. In 1991, in response to pressure from demonstrators, Eyadéma announced the introduction of a multiparty system. In April he legalized opposition parties, freed political prisoners, and granted amnesty to those implicated in the 1986 attempted coup. In a pro-democracy conference in August, Eyadéma's presidential power was substantially reduced and an interim government was formed, headed by premier Joseph Kokou Koffigoh. Between Oct and Nov 1991, three attempts by Eyadéma's troops to oust the interim government all failed. However, in Aug 1992 the Koffigoh administration agreed to return to President Eyadéma much of

the power they had taken away in 1991. In a referendum Sept 1992 there was overwhelming support for a new, multiparty constitution.

Tōgō Heihachirō 1846–1934. Japanese admiral who commanded the fleet at the battle of ◊Tsushima 1905, when Japan defeated the Russians and effectively ended the Russo-Japanese War of 1904–05.

Tōjō Hideki 1884–1948. Japanese general and premier 1941–44 during World War II. Promoted to Chief of Staff of Japan's Guangdong army in Manchuria 1937, he served as minister for war 1940–41. He was held responsible for defeats in the Pacific 1944 and forced to resign. After Japan's defeat, he was hanged as a war criminal.

Tokugawa military family that controlled Japan as ◊shoguns 1603–1868. *Tokugawa Ieyasu* (1542–1616) was the Japanese general and politician who established the Tokugawa shogunate. The Tokugawa were feudal lords who ruled about one-quarter of Japan. Undermined by increasing foreign incursions, they were overthrown by an attack of provincial forces from Chōshū, Satsuma, and Tosa, who restored the ◊Meiji emperor to power.

Tokyo capital of Japan, on Honshu Island. Founded in the 16th century as *Yedo* (or *Edo*), it was renamed when the emperor moved his court there from Kyoto 1868. An earthquake 1923 killed 58,000 people and destroyed much of the city, which was again severely damaged by Allied bombing in World War II.

Tokyo trials war-crimes trials 1946–48 of Japan's wartime leaders, held during the Allied occupation after World War II. Former prime minister Tōjō was among the seven sentenced to death by an international tribunal, while 16 were given life imprisonment. Political considerations allowed Emperor Showa (Hirohito) to escape trial.

Tolpuddle Martyrs six farm labourers of Tolpuddle, a village in Dorset, SW England, who were transported to Australia in 1834 for forming a trade union. After nationwide agitation they were pardoned two years later. They returned to England and all but one migrated to Canada.

Toltec member of an ancient American Indian people who ruled much of Mexico in the 10th–12th centuries, with their capital and religious centre at Tula, NE of Mexico City. They also constructed a similar city at Chichén Itzá in Yucatán. After the Toltecs' fall in the 13th century, the Aztecs took over much of their former territory, except for the regions regained by the Maya.

Tommy Atkins or *Tommy* popular name for the British soldier.

Tone (Theobald) Wolfe 1763–1798. Irish nationalist, prominent in the revolutionary society of the United Irishmen. In 1798 he accompanied the French invasion of Ireland, was captured and condemned to death, but slit his own throat in prison.

That Ireland was not able of herself to throw off the yoke, I know; I therefore sought for aid wherever it was to be found.

Wolfe Tone
speech at court martial Nov 1798

Tonga country in the SW Pacific Ocean, in Polynesia.

history The original inhabitants were Polynesians, and the first European visitors to the islands were Dutch, 1616 and 1643 (Abel Tasman). Captain Cook dubbed them the Friendly Islands 1773. The contemporary Tongan dynasty was founded 1831 by Prince Taufa'ahau Tupou, who assumed the designation King George Tupou I when he ascended the throne. He consolidated the kingdom by conquest, encouraged the spread of Christianity, and granted a constitution. Tonga became a British protectorate from 1900, but under the terms of revised treaties of 1958 and 1967 recovered increased control over its internal affairs.

Queen Salote Tupou III died 1965 and was succeeded by her son, Prince Tupouto'a Tungi, who as King Tupou IV led his nation to full independence, within the Commonwealth, 1970.

In the Feb 1990 elections for nine elected representatives of the people in the Legislative Assembly, three pro-democracy candidates were successful. They attempted to secure support for some dilution of the absolute power of the king.

Tonkin Gulf Incident clash that triggered US entry into the Vietnam War in Aug 1964. Two US destroyers (USS *C Turner Joy* and USS *Maddox*) reported that they were fired on by North Vietnamese torpedo boats. It is unclear whether hostile shots were actually fired, but the reported attack was taken as a pretext for making air raids against North Vietnam. On 7 Aug the US Congress passed the *Tonkin Gulf Resolution*, which formed the basis for the considerable increase in US military involvement in the Vietnam War. The resolution

allowed President Johnson to 'take all necessary steps, including the use of armed forces' to help SEATO (South-East Asia Treaty Organization) members 'defend their freedom'. This resolution formed the basis for the considerable increase in US military involvement in the Vietnam War; it was repealed 1970 in the light of evidence that the Johnson administration contrived to deceive Congress about the incident.

tonnage and poundage duties granted in England 1371–1787 by Parliament to the crown on imports and exports of wine and other goods. They were levied by Charles I in 1626 without parliamentary consent, provoking controversy.

Tonton Macoute member of a private army of death squads on Haiti. The Tontons Macoutes were initially organized by François ◊Duvalier, president of Haiti 1957–71, and continued to terrorize the population under his successor J C Duvalier. It is alleged that the organization continued to operate after Duvalier's exile to France.

Tordesillas, Treaty of agreement reached 1494 when Spain and Portugal divided the uncharted world between themselves. An imaginary line was drawn 370 leagues W of the Azores and the Cape Verde Islands, with Spain receiving all lands discovered to the W, and Portugal those to the E.

The treaty was negotiated because Portugal was unhappy with Spanish pope Alexander VI's four papal bulls of 1493 about a monopoly of navigation and conquest, which were more favourable to Spain.

Torquemada Tomás de 1420–1498. Spanish Dominican monk, confessor to Queen Isabella I. In 1483 he revived the ◊Inquisition on her behalf, and at least 2,000 'heretics' were burned; Torquemada also expelled the Jews from Spain 1492, with a resultant decline of the economy.

Tory Party the forerunner of the British ◊Conservative Party from about 1680 to 1830. It was the party of the squire and parson, as opposed to the Whigs (supported by the trading classes and Nonconformists). The name is still applied colloquially to the Conservative Party. In the USA a Tory was an opponent of the break with Britain in the War of American Independence 1775–83.

total history alternative name for the ◊Annales school of historians

totalitarianism government control of all activities within a country, overtly political or otherwise, as in fascist or communist dictatorships. Examples of totalitarian regimes are Italy under Benito ◊Mussolini 1922–45; Germany under Adolph ◊Hitler 1933–45; the USSR under Joseph ◊Stalin from the 1930s until his death in 1953; more recently Romania under Nicolae ◊Ceauşescu 1974–89.

Totenkopfverbände the 'death's head' units of the Nazi ◊SS organization. Originally used to guard concentration camps after 1935, they became an elite fighting division attached to the Waffen-SS during World War II.

Totila died 522. King of the Ostrogoths, who warred with the Byzantine emperor Justinian for Italy, and was killed by General Narses at the battle of Taginae 552 in the Apennines.

Toungoo dynasty Burmese family of rulers 1539–1752 that reunified the country (now Myanmar) after the collapse of Pagan. The dynasty was founded by Tabinshweti and its most famous king was Bayinnaung. Its capital was at Pegu until 1634, then at Ava, which was captured 1752 by the ◊Mon people as they overthrew the dynasty.

Tours city on the river Loire, W central France. It has a 13th–15th-century cathedral. An ancient city and former capital of Touraine, it was the site of the French defeat of the Arabs 732 under ◊Charles Martel. Tours became the French capital for four days during World War II.

Toussaint L'Ouverture Pierre Dominique *c.* 1743–1803. Haitian revolutionary leader, born a slave. He joined the insurrection of 1791 against the French colonizers and was made governor by the revolutionary French government. He expelled the Spanish and British, but when the French emperor Napoleon reimposed slavery he revolted, was captured, and died in prison in France. In 1983 his remains were returned to Haiti.

Townshend Charles 1725–1767. British politician, chancellor of the Exchequer 1766–67. The *Townshend Acts*, designed to assert Britain's traditional authority over its colonies, resulted in widespread resistance. Among other things they levied taxes on imports (such as tea, glass, and paper) into the North American colonies. Opposition in the colonies to taxation without representation (see ◊Stamp Act) precipitated the American Revolution.

Townshend Charles, 2nd Viscount Townshend (known as 'Turnip' Townshend) 1674–1738. English politician and agriculturalist. He was secretary of state under George I 1714–17, when dismissed for opposing the king's foreign policy, and 1721–30, after which he retired to his farm and did valuable work in developing crop rotation and cultivating winter feeds for cattle (hence his nickname).

Toynbee Arnold 1852–1883. English economic historian who coined the term 'industrial revolution' in his *Lectures on the Industrial Revolution*, published 1884.

Toyotomi Hideyoshi. Adopted name of Kinoshita Tōkichirō 1537–1598. Japanese warlord, one of the three military leaders who unified Japan in the 16th century (◊Momoyama period). Successful military campaigns and alliances gave him control of central and SW Japan by 1587 and E Japan by 1590. His invasion of Korea 1592–98 was, however, defeated.

Skilled in siege strategy, Hideyoshi rose in the service of Oda Nobunaga (1534–1582), the first of the three great Momoyama warlords, and on the death of Nobunaga took over the leadership of his troops, subduing Kyushu island in the SW. He reached an agreement with his main rival, ◊Tokugawa Ieyasu, in E central Honshu, and had himself appointed regent (*kanpaku*) by the emperor 1585, chancellor (*dajōdaijin*) 1586, and retired regent (*taiko*) 1592, the last being the title by which he is still known in Japan; he did not take the title of shogun. He was an able administrator, introducing new land and tax systems and ordering the disarmament of all but the samurai class. He instigated land surveys and in 1590 a population census.

trade union organization of employed workers formed to undertake collective bargaining with employers and to try to achieve improved working conditions for its members.

history, UK Trade unions of a kind existed in the Middle Ages as artisans' guilds, and combinations of wage earners were formed at the time of industrialization in the 18th century; but trade unions did not formally (or legally) come into existence in Britain until the Industrial Revolution in the 19th century. The early history of trade unions is one of illegality and of legislation to prevent their existence. Five centuries of repressive legislation in Britain culminated in the passing of the ◊Combination Laws 1799 and 1800 which made unions illegal. The repeal of these 1824–25 enabled organizations of workers to engage in collective bargaining, although still subject to legal restrictions and with no legal protection for their funds until the enactment of a series of Trade Union Acts 1871–76. In 1868, 34 delegates representing 118,000 trade unionists met at a 'congress' in Manchester; the Trades Union Congress (TUC) gradually became accepted as the central organization for trade unions.

Under the Trade Union Act of 1871 unions became full legal organizations and union funds were protected from dishonest officials. Successive acts of Parliament enabled the

British trade unions	
1799 The Combination Act outlawed organizations of workers combining for the purpose of improving conditions or raising wages. The act was slightly modified 1800.	**1871** The Trade Union Act gave unions legal recognition.
	1888 Beginnings of 'new unionism' and the organization of unskilled workers.
1811 Luddite machine-breaking campaign against hosiers began; it was ended by arrests and military action 1812.	**1901** Taff Vale case re-established union liability for damage done by strikes; this was reversed by the Trade Disputes Act 1906.
1818 Weavers and spinners formed the General Union of Trades in Lancashire.	**1909** Osborne judgements ruled against unions using funds for political purposes; this was reversed by the Trade Union Act 1913.
1824 The Combination Act repealed most of the restrictive legislation but an upsurge of violent activity led to a further act 1825. Trade unions could only bargain peacefully over working hours and conditions.	**1918–20** Widespread industrial unrest on return to a peacetime economy.
	1926 A general strike was called by the TUC in support of the miners.
1830 The General Union of Trades became the National Association for the Protection of Labour; it collapsed 1832.	**1930–34** Union membership fell as a result of economic recession. The Transport and General Workers replaced the Miners Federation as the largest single union.
1834 Formation of the Grand National Consolidated Trade Union, which lasted only a few months. Six agricultural labourers from Tolpuddle, Dorset, were convicted of swearing illegal oaths and transported to Australia.	**1965** The Trade Disputes Act gave unions further immunities.
	1969 The TUC successfully stopped the Labour government White Paper *In Place of Strife*.
1842 The 'Plug Plot' (removing plugs from boilers) took on the appearance of a general strike in support of a People's Charter.	**1971** The Conservative government passed the Industrial Relations Act, limiting union powers.
1851 The foundation of the Amalgamated Society of Engineers marked the beginning of the 'New Model Unionism' of skilled workers.	**1973–74** 'Winter of Discontent'. Strikes brought about electoral defeat for the Conservative government. Labour introduced the 'Social Contract'.
1866 The 'Sheffield outrages' (attacks on nonunion labour) led to a Royal Commission. The Hornby v. Close case cast doubt on the legal status of unions.	**1980** The Conservatives introduced the Employment Act, severely restricting the powers of unions to picket or enforced closed shop; this was extended 1982.
1867 Amendments to the Master and Servant Act gave more scope for trade unions, and the Royal Commission recommended they be given formal legal status.	**1984** The miners' strike led to widespread confrontation and divisions within the miners' union.
1868 The first Trades Union Congress (TUC) was held in Manchester.	**1984–90** The Conservative government continued to limit the powers of trade unions through various legislative acts.

unions to broaden their field of action; for example, the Trade Disputes Act of 1906 protected the unions against claims for damages by their employers (see ◊Taff Vale judgement); and the 1913 Trade Union Act allowed the unions to raise a political levy (see ◊Osborne Judgement). The Trades Union Congress was for many years representative mainly of unions of skilled workers, but in the 1890s the organization of unskilled labour spread rapidly. Industrial unionism (the organization of all workers in one industry or trade) began about this time, but characteristic of the so-called New Unionism at the time of the 1889 dock strike was the rise of general labour unions (for example, the Dock Workers and General Labourers in the gas industry).

During World War I the leading trade unions cooperated with the employers and the government, and by 1918 were stronger than ever before with a membership of 8 million. In 1926, following a protracted series of disputes in the coal industry, the TUC called a general strike in support of the miners; this collapsed and after nine days it was called off, leaving the miners' union to continue the strike alone for a further six months. Under the Trade Disputes and Trade Union Act of 1927 general strikes or strikes called in sympathy with other workers were made illegal.

During World War II a number of trade-union leaders served in the coalition government and membership of trade unions had again risen to 8 million by 1944. The restrictive 1927 Act was repealed under the Labour government in 1946. The postwar period was marked by increased unionism among white-collar workers. From the 1960s onwards there were confrontations between the government and the trade unions, and unofficial, or wildcat, strikes set public opinion against the trade-union movement. The Labour governments' (1964– 70) attempts to introduce legislative reform of the unions was strongly opposed   and eventually abandoned in 1969. The   Conservative government's Industrial Relations Act 1971 (including registration of   trade unions, legal enforcement of collective agreements, compulsory cooling-off periods, and strike   ballots) was repealed by the succeeding Labour government 1974, and voluntary wage restraint attempted under a ◊social contract.

The Thatcher government, in the Employment Acts of 1980 and 1982, restricted the closed shop, picketing, secondary action against anyone other than the employer in dispute, immunity of trade unions in respect of unlawful activity by their officials, and the definition of a trade dispute, which must be between workers and employers, not between workers. The Trade Union Act 1984 made it compulsory to have secret ballots for elections and before strikes.

history, US The great growth of US trade unionism, apart from the abortive Knights of Labor 1869–86 (see also ◊American Federation of Labor), came in the post-Depression years. Employers and the US government have historically been more opposed to trade unionism than those in Britain, often using police and armed guards to harass pickets and protect strike breakers, which has led to episodes of violence and bitter confrontation. US legislation includes the Taft–Hartley Act 1947, which among other measures outlaws the closed shop.

Trafalgar, Battle of battle 21 Oct 1805 in the ◊Napoleonic Wars. The British fleet under Admiral Nelson defeated a Franco-Spanish fleet; Nelson was mortally wounded. The victory laid the foundation for British naval supremacy throughout the 19th century. It is named after Cape Trafalgar, a low headland in SW Spain, near the western entrance to the Straits of Gibraltar.

trainbands in English history, a civil militia first formed in 1573 by Elizabeth I to meet the possibility of invasion. Trainbands were used by Charles I against the Scots in 1639, but their lack of training meant they were of dubious military value.

Trajan (Marcus Ulpius Trajanus) AD 52–117. Roman emperor and soldier, born in Seville. He was adopted as heir by ◊Nerva, whom he succeeded AD 98. He conquered Dacia (Romania) 101–07 and much of ◊Parthia (113–17), bringing the empire to its greatest extent. *Trajan's Column*, erected in the Forum he had constructed, commemorates his Dacian victories.

Transjordan part of the former Turkish Ottoman Empire and now part of ◊Jordan (the present-day East Bank).

Transkei largest of South Africa's Bantustans, or homelands, extending NE from the Great Kei River, on the coast of Cape Province, to the border of Natal; area 43,808 sq km/16,910 sq mi. It became self-governing 1963, and achieved full 'independence' 1976. It is governed by a military council since a 1987 coup (military leader Maj-Gen H B Holomisa from 1987).

transportation punishment of sending convicted persons to overseas territories either for life or for shorter periods. It was introduced in England towards the end of the 17th century and was abolished 1857 after many thousands had been transported, mostly to Australia. It was also used for punishment of criminals by France until 1938.

Transvaal province of NE South Africa, bordering Zimbabwe to the N. It was settled by *Voortrekkers*, Boers who left Cape Colony in the Great Trek from 1831. Independence was recognized by Britain 1852, until the settlers' difficulties with the conquered Zulus led to British annexation 1877. It was made a British colony after the South African War 1899–1902, and in 1910 became a province of the Union of South Africa.

Transylvania mountainous area of central and NW Romania, bounded to the S by the Transylvanian Alps (an extension of the Carpathian Mountains), formerly a province, with its capital at Cluj. It was part of Hungary from about 1000 until its people voted to unite with Romania 1918.

Trappist monk of the ◊Cistercian order who followed a particularly strict version of the rule.

treaty written agreement between two or more states. Treaties take effect either immediately on signature or, more often, on ratification. Ratification involves a further exchange of documents and usually takes place after the internal governments have approved the terms of the treaty. Treaties are binding in international law, the rules being laid down in the Vienna Convention on the Law of Treaties 1969.

treaty port port in Asia where the Western powers had special commercial privileges in the 19th century. As a result of the enforced ◊unequal treaties, treaty ports were established mainly in China, from 1842, and Japan, 1854–99. Foreigners living in 'concessions' in the ports were not subject to local taxes or laws.

On the eve of the republican revolution 1911 there were more than 50 treaty ports in China, mainly on the E seaboard and along the Chang Jiang. They were dynamic focuses for Westernization and industrialization. Although resented by the ◊Guomindang government, foreign privileges in the treaty ports lasted until 1943.

trench warfare hostilities conducted from defensive long, narrow, deeply dug trenches, which were first used widely during the American Civil War in 1864. Trenches were commonly used from the advent of mechanized war until increased mobility provided by the aeroplane and the motor car enabled attacking armies to avoid such large-scale, immobile forms of defence.

Trent, Council of conference held 1545–63 by the Roman Catholic Church at Trento, N Italy initiating the ◊Counter-Reformation; see also ◊Reformation.

Treurnicht Andries Petrus 1921–1993. South African Conservative Party politician. A former minister of the Dutch Reformed Church, he was elected to the South African parliament as a National Party member 1971 but left it 1982 to form a new right-wing Conservative Party, opposed to any dilution of the ◊apartheid system.

Triad secret society, founded in China as a Buddhist cult AD 36. It became known as the Triad because the triangle played a significant part in the initiation ceremony. Today it is reputed to be involved in organized crime (drugs, gambling, prostitution) among overseas Chinese. Its headquarters are alleged to be in Hong Kong.

In the 18th century the Triad became political, aiming at the overthrow of the Manchu dynasty, and backed the Taiping Rebellion 1851 and Sun Yat-sen's establishment of a republic 1912.

trial by ordeal in the Middle Ages, a test of guilt or innocence; see ◊ordeal, trial by.

tribune Roman magistrate of ◊plebeian family, elected annually to defend the interests of the common people; only two were originally chosen in the early 5th century BC, but there were later ten. They could veto the decisions of any other magistrate.

tricolour (French *tricouleur*) the French national flag of three vertical bands of red, white, and blue. The red and blue were the colours of Paris and the white represented the royal house of Bourbon. The flag was first adopted on 17 July 1789, three days after the storming of the Bastille during the French Revolution.

Trinidad and Tobago country in the West Indies, off the coast of Venezuela.

Tobago was given its own house of assembly 1980. It has 15 members, 12 popularly elected and 3 chosen by the majority party.

history For early history, see ◊American Indian. The islands of Trinidad and Tobago were visited by Columbus 1498. Trinidad was colonized by Spain from 1532 and ceded to Britain 1802, having been captured 1797. Tobago was settled by the Netherlands in the 1630s and subsequently occupied by various countries before being ceded to Britain by France 1814. Trinidad and Tobago were amalgamated 1888 as a British colony.

independence Trinidad and Tobago's first political party, the People's National Movement (PNM), was formed 1956 by Dr Eric Williams, and when the colony achieved internal self-government 1959 he became the first chief minister. Between 1958 and 1961 it was a member of the Federation of the West Indies but withdrew and achieved full independence, within the Commonwealth, 1962, Williams becoming the first prime minister.

republic A new constitution was adopted 1976 that made Trinidad and Tobago a republic. The former governor general, Ellis Clarke, became the first president and Williams continued as prime minister. Williams died March 1981 without having nominated a successor, and the president appointed George Chambers; the PNM formally adopted him as leader May 1981. The opposition, a moderate left-wing party grouping led by Arthur Robinson, was during the next few years reorganized as the National Alliance for Reconstruction (NAR), until in the 1986 general election it swept the PNM from power and Arthur Robinson became prime minister.

An attempted coup July 1990 resulted in the capture of Prime Minister Robinson by a former policeman, Abu Bakr. In Aug 1990 the rebels surrendered and an injured Robinson was released. Robinson was defeated in the Dec 1991 general election and was succeeded as prime minister by Patrick Manning, leader of the PNM. NAR won only two of the 36 assembly seats, compared with PNM's 21.

Triple Alliance pact from 1882 between Germany, Austria-Hungary, and Italy to offset the power of Russia and France. It was last renewed 1912, but during World War I Italy's initial neutrality gradually changed and it denounced the alliance 1915. The term also refers to other alliances: 1668 – England, Holland, and Sweden; 1717 – Britain, Holland, and France (joined 1718 by Austria); 1788 – Britain, Prussia, and Holland; 1795 – Britain, Russia, and Austria.

Triple Entente alliance of Britain, France, and Russia 1907–17. In 1911 this became a military alliance and formed the basis of the Allied powers in World War I against the Central Powers, Germany and Austria-Hungary.

Tripoli (Arabic *Tarabolus al-Gharb*) capital and chief port of Libya. Tripoli was founded about the 7th century BC by Phoenicians from Oea (now Tripoli in Lebanon). It was a base for Axis powers during World War II. In 1986 it was bombed by the US Air Force in retaliation for international guerrilla activity.

Tripolitania former province of Libya, stretching from Cyrenaica in the E to Tunisia in the W. It came under Turkish rule in the 16th century; Italy captured it from Turkey 1912, and the British captured it from Italy 1942 and controlled it until it was incorporated into the newly independent United Kingdom of Libya, established 1951. In 1963 Tripolitania was subdivided into administrative divisions.

trireme ancient Greek warship with three banks of oars as well as sails, 38 m/115 ft long. They were used at the battle of ◊Salamis and by the Romans until the 4th century AD.

triumph in ancient Rome, the victory procession of a returning general. The senate and the victorious army accompanied the crowned victor, displaying spoils taken from the enemy, together with important captives who were usually executed on the Capitoline Hill. Roman emperors assumed the right to celebrate triumphs.

triumvir one of a group of three administrators sharing power in ancient Rome, as in the *First Triumvirate* 60 BC: Caesar, Pompey, Crassus; and *Second Triumvirate* 43 BC: Augustus, Antony, and Lepidus.

Tromp Maarten Harpertszoon 1597–1653. Dutch admiral. He twice defeated the occupying Spaniards 1639. He was defeated by English admiral Blake May 1652, but in Nov triumphed over Blake in the Strait of Dover. In Feb–June 1653 he was defeated by Blake and Monk, and was killed off the Dutch coast. His son, *Cornelius Tromp* (1629–1691), also an admiral, fought a battle against the English and French fleets in 1673.

Trotsky Leon. Adopted name of Lev Davidovitch Bronstein 1879–1940. Russian revolutionary. He joined the Bolshevik party and took a leading part in the seizure of power 1917 and raising the Red Army that fought the Civil War 1918–20. In the struggle for power that followed ◊Lenin's death 1924, ◊Stalin defeated Trotsky, and this and other differences with the Communist Party led to his exile 1929. He settled in Mexico, where he was assassinated with an ice pick at Stalin's instigation. Trotsky believed in world revolution and in permanent revolution, and was an uncompromising, if liberal, idealist.

Patriotism to the Soviet State is a duty, whereas patriotism to a bourgeois state is treachery.

Leon Trotsky

Trotskyism form of Marxism advocated by Leon Trotsky. Its central concept is that of *permanent revolution*. In his view a proletarian revolution, leading to a socialist society, could not be achieved in isolation, so it would be necessary to spark off further revolutions throughout Europe and ultimately worldwide. This was in direct opposition to the Stalinist view that socialism should be built and consolidated within individual countries.

Truck Acts UK acts of Parliament introduced 1831, 1887, 1896, and 1940 to prevent employers misusing wage-payment systems to the detriment of their workers. The legislation made it illegal to pay wages with goods in kind or with tokens for use in shops owned by the employers.

Trudeau Pierre (Elliott) 1919– . Canadian Liberal politician. He was prime minister 1968–79 and 1980–84. In 1980, having won again by a landslide on a platform opposing Québec separatism, he helped to defeat the Québec independence movement in a referendum. He repatriated the constitution from Britain 1982, but by 1984 had so lost support that he resigned.

True Leveller or *Digger* member of a radical Puritan group which flourished 1649–50.

Trujillo Molina Rafael (Leónidas) 1891–1961. Dictator of the Dominican Republic from 1930. As commander of the Dominican Guard, he seized power and established a ruthless dictatorship. He was assassinated.

Truman Harry S 1884–1972. 33rd president of the USA 1945–53, a Democrat. In Jan 1945 he became vice president to F D Roosevelt, and president when Roosevelt died in April that year. He used the atom bomb against Japan, launched the ◊Marshall Plan to restore W Europe's economy, and nurtured the European Community and NATO (including the re-armament of West Germany).

Truman Doctrine US president Harry Truman's 1947 declaration that the USA would 'support free peoples who are resisting attempted subjugation by armed minorities or by outside pressures'. It was used to justify sending a counterinsurgency military mission to Greece after World War II and sending US troops abroad (for example, to Korea).

Trust Territory country or area formerly held under the United Nations trusteeship system to be prepared for independence, either former mandates, territories taken over by the Allies in World War II, or those voluntarily placed under the UN by the administering state.

Ts'ao Ts'ao chinese general AD 155–220; see ◊Cao Cao.

tsar the Russian imperial title 1547-1721 (although it continued in popular use to 1917), derived from Latin *caesar*.

Tsushima Japanese island between Korea and Japan in *Tsushima Strait*; area 702 sq km/271 sq mi. The Russian fleet was destroyed by the Japanese here 27 May 1905 in the ◊Russo-Japanese War, and 12,000 Russians were killed. The chief settlement is Izuhara.

Tuareg Arabic name given to nomadic stock-breeders from west and central Sahara and Sahel (Algeria, Libya, Mali, Niger, and Burkina Faso).

In the 19th century the Tuareg became involved in trans-Saharan trade and sometimes raided desert caravans. Traditionally they live in handwoven or goatskin tents and herd goats and camels, though many Tuareg have settled in urban areas.

Tubman Harriet Ross 1821–1913. US abolitionist. Born a slave in Maryland, she escaped to Philadelphia (where slavery was outlawed) 1849. She set up the *Underground Railroad*, a secret network of sympathizers, to help slaves escape to the North and Canada. During the American ◊Civil War she spied for the Union army. She spoke against slavery and for women's rights, and founded schools for emancipated slaves after the Civil War.

Tubman William V S 1895–1971. Liberian politician. The descendant of US slaves, he was a lawyer in the USA. After his election to the presidency of Liberia 1944 he concentrated on uniting the various ethnic groups. Re-elected several times, he died in office of natural causes, despite frequent assassination attempts.

Tudor dynasty English dynasty 1485-1603, descended from the Welsh Owen Tudor (*c.* 1400–1461), second husband of Catherine of Valois (widow of Henry V of England). Their son Edmund married Margaret Beaufort (1443–1509), the great-granddaughter of ◊John of Gaunt, and was the father of Henry VII, who became king by overthrowing Richard III 1485. The dynasty ended with the death of Elizabeth I 1603.

The Tudors were portrayed in a favourable light in Shakespeare's history plays.

Tukulor empire Muslim theocracy founded by al-Hajj Umar (*c.* 1797–1864). Stretching from the western Sudan to Senegal, it flourished for most of the 19th century, but its power was sapped by continuous internal disorder.

Tunisia country in N Africa, on the Mediterranean Sea, bounded SE by Libya and W by Algeria.

history Founded as ◊Carthage by the Phoenicians in the 8th century BC, Tunisia was under Arab rule from the 7th century AD until it became part of the ◊Ottoman Empire 1574. It harboured the ◊Barbary Coast pirates until the 19th century. It became a French protectorate 1881.

The Destour Socialist Party (PSD), founded 1934 by Habib Bourguiba, led Tunisia's campaign for independence from France. The country achieved internal self-government 1955 and full independence 1956, with Bourguiba as prime minister. A year later the monarchy was abolished, and Tunisia became a republic, with Bourguiba as president. A new constitution was adopted 1959, and the first national assembly elected. Between 1963 and 1981 the PSD was the only legally recognized party, but since then others have been allowed. In Nov 1986 the PSD won all the assembly seats, while other parties boycotted the elections.

foreign affairs President Bourguiba followed a distinctive foreign policy, establishing links with the Western powers, including the USA, but joining other Arab states in condemning the US-inspired Egypt–Israel treaty. He allowed the Palestine Liberation Organization (PLO) to use Tunis as its headquarters, and this led to an Israeli attack 1985 that strained relations with the USA. Diplomatic links with Libya were severed 1985.

Bourguiba's firm and paternalistic rule, and his long period in Tunisian politics, made him a national legend, evidenced by the elaborate mausoleum that was built in anticipation of his death. However, in Nov 1987 he was deposed and replaced by Zine el-Abidine Ben Ali. In July 1988, a number of significant constitutional changes were announced, presaging a move to more pluralist politics, but in the April 1989 elections the renamed PSD, the Constitutional Democratic Rally (RCD), won all 141 assembly seats. During the Gulf War Jan–Feb 1991 which followed Iraq's invasion of Kuwait, there were anti-US protests in Tunisia.

Ben Ali's active repression of Islamic fundamentalists provoked criticism from Western nations Jan 1992. Hundreds of supporters of the fundamentalist al-Nahda party, whose aim was to turn the country into an Islamic state, were alleged to have been tortured during their detention since 1990. The West saw the crackdown as a major setback in Tunisia's progress towards democracy.

Túpac Amarú adopted name of José Gabriel Condorcanqui c. 1742–1781. Peruvian Indian revolutionary leader, executed for his revolt against Spanish rule 1780; he claimed to be descended from the last chieftain of the Incas.

Tupamaros urban guerrilla movement operating in Uruguay, aimed at creating a Marxist revolution, largely active in the 1960s–70s, named after 18th-century revolutionary Túpac Amarú. It was founded by Raul Sendic (died 1989); he served more than 13 years in prison.

Turenne Henry de la Tour d'Auvergne, Vicomte de Turenne 1611–1675. French marshal under Louis XIV, known for his siege technique. He fought for the Protestant alliance during the Thirty Years' War, and on both sides during the wars of the Fronde.

God is always on the side of the big battalions.

Henri, Vicomte de Turenne

Turkey country between the Black Sea to the N and the Mediterranean Sea to the S, bounded E by Armenia, Georgia, and Iran, SE by Iraq and Syria, W by Greece and the Aegean Sea, and NW by Bulgaria.

history The Turks originally came from Mongolia and spread into Turkestan in the 6th century AD. During the 7th century they adopted Islam. In 1055 the Seljuk Turks secured political control of the caliphate and established an empire in Asia Minor. The Ottoman Turks, driven from central Asia by the Mongols, entered the service of the Seljuks, and Osman I founded a kingdom of his own 1299. Having overrun Asia Minor, the Ottomans began their European conquests by seizing Gallipoli 1354; they captured Constantinople 1453 and by 1480 were masters of the Balkans. By 1550 they had conquered Egypt, Syria, Arabia, Mesopotamia, Tripoli, and most of Hungary; thereafter the empire ceased to expand, although Cyprus was taken 1571 and Crete 1669.

decline of Ottoman Empire The Christian counter-offensive opened 1683 with the defeat of the Turks before Vienna; in 1699 the Turks lost Hungary, and in 1774 Russia ousted them from Moldavia, Wallachia, and the Crimea. In the Balkans there was an unsuccessful revolt in Serbia 1804, but Greece threw off Turkish rule 1821–29. Russia's attempts to exploit this situation were resisted by Britain and France, which in the Crimean War (1854–56) fought on the Turkish side. The Bulgarian uprising of 1876 led to a new war between Turkey and Russia, and by the Treaty of Berlin 1878 Turkey lost Bulgaria, Bosnia, and Herzegovina. A militant nationalist group, the Young Turks, secured the grant of a constitution 1908; Italy took advantage of the ensuing crisis to seize Tripoli 1911–12, while the Balkan states expelled the Turks from Albania and Macedonia 1912–13. Turkey entered World War I on the German side 1914, only to lose Syria, Arabia, Mesopotamia, and its nominal suzerainty in Egypt.

independent republic The Greek occupation of Izmir 1919 provoked the establishment of a nationalist congress with Mustafa Kemal (◊Atatürk) as president. Having defeated Italian and French forces, he expelled the Greeks 1922. Peace was concluded 1923 with the Treaty of ◊Lausanne and Turkey was proclaimed an independent republic with Kemal as its first president. He introduced a policy of westernization and a new legal code. He died 1938, but his People's Party remained in power.

series of governments Turkey's first free elections were held 1950 and won by the Democratic Party (DP), led by Celal Bayar and Adnan Menderes. Bayar became president and Menderes prime minister. In 1960, after a military coup, President Bayar was imprisoned and Menderes executed. A new constitution was adopted 1961 and civilian rule restored, but with the leader of the coup, General Cemal

OTTOMAN DECLINE AND THE EMERGENCE OF MODERN TURKEY 1683–1923

Areas lost 1683–1812		Areas lost 1879–1914	
Areas lost 1813–78		Ottoman Empire 1914	
– – – Boundaries of independent Balkan States 1914		—— Turkish border after Treaty of Lausanne 1923	

Some of the shaded areas lost include tributary peoples over whom the Ottomans claimed suzerainty as well as areas of direct Ottoman rule.

The emergence of modern Turkey 1683–1923 *The Ottoman retreat was a slow process spanning over two centuries. It was due initially to military developments in Europe and Russia's expansion southwards. The loss of Egypt and Greece at the beginning of the 19th century was, however, more the result of internal weaknesses and European intervention. By 1914 only the Arab and Anatolian heartlands remained under direct control. After World War I Anatolia became the nation state of Turkey. Syria, Iraq, and Palestine were placed under French and British mandates.*

Gürsel, as president. There followed a series of civilian governments, led mainly by the veteran politician Ismet Inonu until 1965, when the Justice Party (JP), led by Suleyman Demirel, came to power. Prompted by strikes and student unrest, the army forced Demirel to resign 1971, and for the next two years the country came under military rule again.

effective partition of Cyprus A civilian government was restored 1973, a coalition led by Bulent Ecevit. The following year Turkey sent troops to Cyprus to protect the Turkish-Cypriot community, resulting in the effective partition of the island. Ecevit's government fell when he refused to annex N Cyprus, and in 1975 Suleyman Demirel returned at the head of a right-wing coalition. Elections held 1977 were inconclusive, and Demirel precariously held on to power until 1978 when Ecevit returned, leading another coalition. He was faced with a deteriorating economy and outbreaks of sectional violence and by 1979 had lost his working majority and resigned.

international pressure Demirel returned in Nov, but the violence continued and in Sept 1980 the army stepped in and set up a national security council, with Bulent Ulusu as prime minister. Martial law was imposed, political activity suspended, and a harsh regime established. Strong international pressure was put on Turkey to return to a more democratic system of government, and in May 1983 political parties were allowed to operate again. The old parties reformed under new names and in Nov three of them contested the assembly elections: the conservative Motherland Party (ANAP), the Nationalist Democracy Party (MDP), and the Populist Party (SDPP). The ANAP won a large majority and its leader, Turgut Özal, became prime minister. Ethnic Kurds suffer from discrimination; since 1984 there has been guerrilla fighting in ◊Kurdistan, and a separatist Kurdish Workers' Party (PKK) is active. In 1989 Özal was elected president, with Yildirim Akbulut as prime minister. In 1991 Mesut Yilmaz replaced Akbulut as head of the ANAP and became prime minister.

EC membership refused After World War II Turkey felt itself threatened by the USSR and joined a number of military alliances, including NATO 1952 and the Baghdad Pact 1955, which became the Central Treaty Organization 1959 and was dissolved 1979. Turkey strengthened Western links and by 1987 was making overtures to the European Community. Turkey has long been criticized for the harshness of its penal system and its violations of human rights. Its future role will depend on its willingness and ability to create a more humane and fully democratic system of government, but, despite significant advances since 1983, at the end of 1989 it learned that its application for membership of the European Community had been refused and would not be considered again until at least the mid-1990s. During the 1990–91 Gulf War, Turkey supported the US-led forces, allowing use of vital bases in the country.

Demirel regains premiership Following the inconclusive general election held in Oct 1991, Suleyman Demirel eventually formed a coalition government Nov 1991 with the support of the Social Democratic Populist Party. Demirel became premier for the seventh time.

earthquake causes chaos Two earthquakes March 1992 killed thousands of people and destroyed numerous buildings, bridges, and roads. The worst-hit areas centred around Tunceli and Erzincan; the latter was the site of a major earthquake in 1939 which left more than 30,000 dead.

Turkmenistan country in central Asia, bounded N by Kazakhstan and Uzbekistan, W by the Caspian Sea, and S by Iran and Afghanistan.

history The principal Turkmen tribes are the Tekkes of Merv and Attok, the Ersaris, the Yomuds, and the Gokluns, all speaking varieties of a Turkic language and descended from the Mongol invaders who swept across Asia in the 13th century. Conquered by Tsarist Russia 1877–1900, the region became part of the Turkestan Soviet Socialist Autonomous Republic 1921, and a constituent republic of the USSR 1925. The Soviet-built Kara Kum canal brought millions of acres of desert to life, although living standards remained very low.

independence achieved Turkmenistan's nationalist movement was more muted than in other former Soviet Central Asian republics. In Aug 1990 Turkmenistan's supreme soviet declared its 'sovereignty'; however, in the March 1991 USSR constitutional referendum the population voted to maintain the Union, and the anti-Gorbachev attempted coup in Moscow in Aug 1991 was initially supported by President Niyazov. However, in the Oct 1991 referendum there was an overwhelming (94%) vote in favour of independence, duly declared.

Turkmenistan joined the ◊Commonwealth of Independent States (CIS) in Dec 1991. It was admitted into the ◊Conference on Security and Cooperation in Europe (CSCE) in Jan 1992 and into the United Nations March 1992. In the same month US diplomatic recognition was achieved. In Feb Turkmenistan had joined the Economic Cooperation Organization (ECO), founded by Iran, Pakistan, and Turkey 1975, which aimed to reduce customs tariffs and eventually form a customs union. A new constitution was introduced May 1992 but the republic's political system remained dominated by communists.

Turkoman or *Turkman* member of the majority ethnic group in Turkmenistan. They live to the E of the Caspian Sea, around the Kara Kum desert, and along the borders of Afghanistan and Iran. Traditionally the Turkomen were tent-dwelling pastoral nomads, though the majority are now sedentary farmers. Their language belongs to the Turkic branch of the Altaic family. They are predominantly Sunni Muslims.

Turner John Napier 1929– . Canadian Liberal politician, prime minister 1984. He was elected to the House of Commons 1962 and served in the cabinet of Pierre Trudeau until resigning 1975. He succeeded Trudeau as party leader and prime minister 1984, but lost the 1984 and 1988 elections. Turner resigned as leader 1989, and returned to his law practice. He was replaced as Liberal Party chief by Herbert Gray in Feb 1990.

Turner Nat 1800–1831. US slave and Baptist preacher. Believing himself divinely appointed, he led 60 slaves in a revolt – the *Southampton Insurrection* of 1831 – in Southampton County, Virginia. Before he and 16 of the others were hanged, at least 55 slave-owners had been killed.

Tutankhamen king of Egypt of the 18th dynasty, about 1360–1350 BC. A son of Ikhnaton (also called Amenhotep IV), he was about 11 at his accession. In 1922 his tomb was discovered by British archaeologists Lord Carnarvon and Howard Carter in the Valley of the Kings at Luxor, almost untouched by tomb robbers.

Tutsi member of a minority ethnic group living in Rwanda and Burundi. Although fewer in number, they have traditionally been politically dominant over the Hutu majority and the Twa (or Pygmies). The Tutsi are traditionally farmers; they also hold virtually all positions of importance in Burundi's government and army. They have carried out massacres in response to Hutu rebellions, notably in 1972 and 1988. In Rwanda the balance of power is more even.

Tutu Desmond (Mpilo) 1931– . South African priest, Anglican archbishop of Cape Town 1986-96 and general secretary of the South African Council of Churches 1979–84. One of the leading figures in the struggle against apartheid in South Africa, he was awarded the 1984 Nobel Prize for Peace.

We don't want apartheid liberalized. We want it dismantled. You can't improve something that is intrinsically evil.

Desmond Tutu speech June 1986

Tuvalu country in the SW Pacific Ocean; formerly (until 1976) the Ellice Islands; part of Polynesia.

history The islands were inhabited by Melanesians, and were invaded and occupied by Samoans during the 16th century. They were first reached by Europeans 1765. During the mid-19th century European slave traders captured indigenous Melanesians for forced labour on plantations in South America. As a result of this, and the importation of European diseases,

the population declined from an estimated 20,000 to barely 3,000. Originally known as the Ellice Islands, they were a British protectorate 1892–1915 and part of the Gilbert and Ellice Islands colony 1915–75, when they became a separate British colony.

special member of Commonwealth In 1978 the Ellice Islands became fully independent within the Commonwealth, reverting to their old name of Tuvalu, meaning 'eight standing together' (there are nine, but one is very small). Because of its small size, Tuvalu is a 'special member' of the Commonwealth and does not have direct representation at meetings of heads of government. Its first prime minister was Toaripi Lauti, replaced 1981 as a result of his alleged involvement in an investment scandal, by Dr Tomasi Puapua, who was re-elected 1985. In 1986 a poll was taken to decide whether Tuvalu should remain a constitutional monarchy or become a republic. Only one atoll favoured republican status. Following new elections Sept 1989, Puapua was replaced as prime minister by Bikenibeu Paeniu, whose new administration pledged to reduce the country's dependence on foreign aid, which contributes more than a quarter of gross domestic product.

Tweed William Marcy ('Boss') 1823–1878. US politician. He held office in the US House of Representatives 1853-55. In various municipal offices, and from 1867 in New York state senate, he controlled government spending and accumulated a fortune estimated at somewhere between $45 million and $200 million. He was convicted of forgery and larceny and sent to jail 1873-75, when he escaped to Spain.

Twelver member of a Shi'ite Muslim sect who believes that the 12th imam (Islamic leader) did not die, but is waiting to return towards the end of the world as the Mahdi, the 'rightly guided one', to establish a reign of peace and justice on Earth.

Twelve Tables in ancient Rome, the earliest law code, drawn from religious and secular custom. It was published on tablets of bronze or wood at the Roman ◊forum *c.* 450 BC, and though these were destroyed in the sack of Rome by Celts 387 BC, the code survived to have influence into the later republic.

Twenty-One demands Japanese attempt 18 Jan 1915 to make China a virtual protectorate if 21 'outstanding questions' were not resolved. China's president ◊Yuan Shikai submitted to the extension of Japanese power in Manchuria, Shandong, the Chang Jiang valley, and the SE, but refused to appoint Japanese political and financial advisers to his government.

Japan threatened war in issuing the demands as it exploited the favour it had earned with the Allies by its seizure of the German territory of Kiaochow in Nov 1914 during World War I, and Republican China's debilitation by civil war. The incident aroused nationalist resentment, witnessed in the ◊May 4th movement 1919, and American concern at Japanese expansionism.

Tyler John 1790–1862. 10th president of the USA 1841–45, succeeding Benjamin ◊Harrison, who died after only a month in office. Tyler's government annexed Texas 1845.

Tyler was the first US vice president to succeed to the presidency. Because he was not in favour of many of the Whig Party's policies, he was constantly at odds with the cabinet and Congress until elections forced the Whigs from power.

Tyler Wat died 1381. English leader of the ◊Peasants' Revolt of 1381. He was probably born in Kent or Essex, and may have served in the French wars. After taking Canterbury he led the peasant army to Blackheath and occupied London. At Mile End King Richard II met the rebels and promised to redress their grievances, which included the imposition of a poll tax. At a further conference at Smithfield, Tyler was murdered.

Tzu-Hsi alternative transliteration of ◊Zi Xi, dowager empress of China.

U-2 US military reconnaissance aeroplane, used in secret flights over the USSR from 1956 to photograph military installations. In 1960 a U-2 was shot down over the USSR and the pilot, Gary Powers, was captured and imprisoned. He was exchanged for a US-held Soviet agent two years later. In 1962 U-2 flights revealed the construction of Soviet missile bases in Cuba.

U-boat (German *Unterseeboot* 'undersea boat') German submarine. The title was used in both world wars.

UDI acronym for ◊*Unilateral Declaration of Independence*.

Uganda landlocked country in E Africa, bounded N by Sudan, E by Kenya, S by Tanzania and Rwanda, and W by Zaire.

history Uganda was a British protectorate 1894-1962. It became an independent member of the ◊Commonwealth 1962, with Dr Milton Obote, leader of the Uganda People's Congress (UPC), as prime minister. In 1963 it was proclaimed a federal republic; King Mutesa II became president, ruling through a cabinet. King Mutesa was deposed in a coup 1966, and Obote became executive president. One of his first acts was to end the federal status. After an attempt to assassinate him 1969, Obote banned all opposition and established what was effectively a one-party state.

Idi Amin's regime In 1971 Obote was overthrown in an army coup led by Maj-Gen Idi ◊Amin Dada, who suspended the constitution and all political activity and took legislative and executive powers into his own hands. Obote fled to Tanzania. Amin proceeded to wage what he called an 'economic war' against foreign domination, resulting in the mass expulsion of people of Asian ancestry, many of whom settled in Britain. In 1976 Amin claimed that large tracts of Kenya historically belonged to Uganda and accused Kenya of cooperating with the Israeli government in a raid on Entebbe airport to free hostages held in a hijacked aircraft. Relations with Kenya became strained, and diplomatic links with Britain were severed. During the next two years the Amin regime carried out a widespread campaign against any likely opposition, resulting in thousands of deaths and imprisonments. The East African Community (EAC) consisting of Tanzania, Kenya, and Uganda, formed 1967, collapsed 1977.

military coups In 1978, when Amin annexed the Kagera area of Tanzania, near the Uganda border, the Tanzanian president, Julius Nyerere, sent troops to support the Uganda National Liberation Army (UNLA), which had been formed to fight Amin. Within five months Tanzanian troops had entered the Uganda capital, Kampala, forcing Amin to flee, first to Libya and then to Saudi Arabia. A provisional government, drawn from a cross-section of exiled groups, was set up, with Dr Yusuf Lule as president. Two months later Lule was replaced by Godfrey Binaisa who, in turn, was overthrown by the army. A military commission made arrangements for national elections, which were won by the UPC, and Milton Obote came back to power.

Obote's government was soon under pressure from a range of exiled groups operating outside the country and guerrilla forces inside, and he was only kept in office by the presence of Tanzanian troops. When they were withdrawn June 1982 a major offensive was launched against the Obote government by the National Resistance Movement (NRM) and the National Resistance Army (NRA), led by Dr Lule and Yoweri Museveni. By 1985 Obote was unable to control the army, which had been involved in indiscriminate killings, and he was ousted in July in a coup led by Brig Tito Okello. Obote fled to Kenya and then Zambia, where he was given political asylum.

national reconciliation Okello had little more success in controlling the army and, after a brief period of power-sharing with the NRA, fled to Sudan Jan 1986. Museveni was sworn in as president and announced a policy of national reconciliation, promising a return to normal parliamentary government within three to five years. He formed a cabinet in which most of Uganda's political parties were represented, including the NRM, which is the political wing of the NRA, the Democratic Party, the Conservative Party, the UPC, and the Uganda Freedom Movement. He worked at consolidating his hold domestically, reviving the economy, and improving African relations, as in the nonaggression treaty signed with Sudan 1990.

foreign relations In Feb 1992 it was announced that EAC, the East Africa cooperation pact, would be revived.

Uganda Martyrs 22 Africans, of whom 12 were boy pages, put to death 1885–87 by King Mwanga of Uganda for refusing to renounce Christianity. They were canonized as the first African saints of the Roman Catholic Church 1964.

uitlander (Dutch 'foreigner') in South African history, term applied by the Boer inhabitants of the Transvaal to immigrants of non-Dutch origin (mostly British) in the late 19th century. The uitlanders' inferior political position in the Transvaal led to the Second ◊South African War 1899–1902.

UK abbreviation for the ◊*United Kingdom*.

Ukraine country in E central Europe, bounded E by Russia, N by Belarus, S by Moldova, Romania, and the Black Sea, and W by Poland, the Slovak Republic, and Hungary.

history The Ukraine formed the heartland of the medieval state of Kievan Rus which emerged in the 9th century. Uniting Ukrainians, Russians (Muscovites), and Belorussians, it became the leading power in eastern Europe, before being destroyed by Mongol invasion in the 13th century. Christianity was adopted from Byzantium 988. It came under Catholic Polish rule from the 14th century, with the peasantry reduced to serfdom. In 1648 there was a revolt against Polish oppression led by Cossacks, composed originally of runaway serfs, and a militarist state was established by hetman (elected leader) Bohdan Khmelnytsky (d. 1657). East and West Ukraine were partitioned between Muscovy and Poland in 1667.

Tsarist rule Under Tsar ◊Peter I the publication of Ukrainian books was banned in 1720 and serfdom was introduced into E Ukraine ('Little Russia') in 1783. In the late 18th century, Russia also secured control over all of W Ukraine, except Galicia, which was annexed by Austria in 1772. The 19th century witnessed a Ukrainian cultural revival and the establishment of secret nationalist organizations, especially in Galicia. During the late 19th and early 20th centuries there was rapid economic development and urbanization, but under the late Tsars suppression of Ukraininan culture and 'Russification' intensified.

World War I and II After the overthrow of the Tsar, an independent Ukrainian People's Republic was proclaimed in 1918, which allied itself with the ◊Central Powers. The Germans installed a conservative hetman regime, which was popularly overthrown at the close of World War I. After two years of civil war, W Ukraine (Galicia-Volhymia) was transferred to Polish rule, while the remainder came under Soviet control, becoming a constituent republic of the USSR in 1922. In the mid-1920s a conciliatory policy of Ukrainization was pursued; however, during the 1930s there was a mass purge of intellectuals, kulaks ('rich farmers') and the destruction of the Ukrainian Orthodox Church. During the 'collectivization famine' of 1932–33 at least 7 million peasants died. Polish-controlled W Ukraine was occupied by the Red Army from Sept 1939 until the Nazi German invasion of the USSR in June 1941, followed by mass deportations and exterminations of more than 5 million Ukrainians and Ukrainian Jews. In 1944 Moscow ordered the deportation en masse to Central Asia of Crimean Tatars, who were accused of collaboration.

sovietization After World War II, Soviet-ruled Ukraine was enlarged to include territories formerly under Polish (W Ukraine), Czechoslovak (Transcarpathian Ukraine), and Romanian (N Bukovina and part of Bessarabia) control and became a founding member of the United Nations. W Ukraine remained the site of partisan resistance by the Ukrainian Insurgent Army (UPA) until the early 1950s and, as part of a 'sovietization' campaign, there were mass arrests and deportations to Siberia of 500,000 people and inward migration of Russians.

dissident movement After Soviet leader Stalin's death in 1953, Ukraine was treated in a more conciliatory fashion by his successor Nikita Khrushchev, who had been Ukrainian Communist Party (UCP) leader 1938–47. In Feb 1954, to 'celebrate' the 300th anniversary of Slavic 'fraternal union', Crimea was transferred back to Ukraine's jurisdiction and in the 1960s there was a Ukrainian literary revival and growth of the dissident movement. In 1972–73 a crackdown on dissent was launched and the Brezhnevite Vladimir Shcherbitsky replaced the more liberal Petro Shelest as UCP leader. However, from the mid-1970s Helsinki Monitoring Groups became active and the officially abolished Uniate Church continued to operate underground in W Ukraine. In the wake of the Chernobyl nuclear power-plant accident in 1986, a popular environmentalist movement, Green World, emerged in Ukraine.

nationalism intensifies Emboldened by ◊*glasnost*, nationalist and pro-reform demonstrations increased, led by the People's Movement of Ukraine for Restructuring (Rukh), established Feb 1989. Shcherbitsky was ousted as CP leader Sept 1989, the Uniate Church was allowed to re-register Dec 1989, and in the March 1990 republic supreme-soviet election, 'reform communist' and Rukh candidates in the Democratic Bloc polled strongly in a number of areas. In July 1990 the new parliament declared the republic's economic and political sovereignty.

declaration of independence Ukraine's president, Leonid Kravchuk, was slow to condemn the Aug 1991 anti- Gorbachev attempted coup in Moscow, which had provoked a series of Rukh-led pro-democracy rallies in Lviv (Lvov). However, after the coup's failure, Kravchuk swiftly donned nationalist colours, banning the UCP and declaring the republic's provisional independence on 24 Sept 1991, pending a referendum in Dec, which came out 90% in favour of independence. Simultaneously, Kravchuk was popularly elected president, capturing 61% of the vote.

CIS membership Ukraine joined the ◊Commonwealth of Independent States, formed Dec 1991, and its independence was immediately recognized by Canada, home to around 1 million Ukrainians, as well as by Ukraine's central European neighbours. In the same month its independence was recognized by the USA, who also accorded it full diplomatic recognition, and by the European Community. In Jan 1992, Ukraine was admitted into the ◊Conference on Security and Cooperation in Europe.

economic reforms A programme of market-centred economic reform and privatization was launched, with prices freed Jan 1992 but 'temporarily' re-regulated in Feb. A pipeline deal completed with Iran helped to reduce Ukraine's dependence on Russia for oil. Coupons were introduced as a secondary currency to the rouble, pending the creation of an independent currency, the grivna. However, the continued strength of ex-communist apparatchiks threatened to frustrate the programme.

military reorganization Ukraine inherited a substantial nuclear arsenal, but pledged to become a nuclear-free state by 1994, while establishing an independent 200,000–400,000-strong army. In March it suspended agreed tactical-arms shipments to Russia, claiming that there was no assurance that Russia was dismantling them. Post-independence quarrels with Russia over the division of military forces continued; agreement was reached Aug 1992 on joint control of the Black Sea fleet until 1995, after which time it would probably be divided between the two countries.

Crimean demands for recognition The Crimea, which, despite the return of 150,000 Tatars since 1989, is 70% Russian, declared its independence Sept 1991 but confirmed that it would remain part of the Ukraine. In May 1992 a declaration of sovereignty was made but subsequently rescinded after Ukraine threatened to use 'all available means' to prevent the republic's secession.

Ulbricht Walter 1893–1973. East German communist politician, in power 1960–71. He lived in exile in the USSR during Hitler's rule 1933–45. A Stalinist, he became first secretary of the Socialist Unity Party in East Germany 1950 and (as chair of the Council of State from 1960) was instrumental in the building of the Berlin Wall 1961. He established East Germany's economy and recognition outside the Eastern European bloc.

Ulm, Battle of battle in 1805 during the ◊Napoleonic Wars which took place at Ulm on the Danube, in southwest Germany. General Mack (1752-1828), commanding an Austrian army of 33,000 men, allowed himself to be surrounded by Napoleon's forces and had to surrender. This paved the way for the occupation of Vienna and a crushing French victory at Austerlitz 2 Dec 1805.

Ulster former kingdom in Northern Ireland, annexed by England 1461, from Jacobean times a centre of English, and later Scottish, settlement on land confiscated from its owners; divided 1921 into Norther ◊Ireland (counties Antrim, Armagh, Down, Fermanagh, Londonderry, and Tyrone) and the Republic of ◊Ireland (counties Cavan, Donegal, and Monaghan).

Umar 2nd caliph (head) of Islam, a strong disciplinarian. Under his rule Islam spread to Egypt and Persia. He was assassinated in Medina.

Umayyad alternative spelling of ◊Omayyad dynasty.

Umkhonto we Sizwe military wing of the ◊African National Congress.

UN abbreviation for the ◊*United Nations*.

Underground Railroad in US history, a network established in the North before the American ◊Civil War to provide sanctuary and assistance for escaped black slaves. Safe houses, transport facilities, and 'conductors' existed to lead the slaves to safety in the North and Canada.

unequal treaties series of agreements drawn up 1842–58 through which Western powers won diplomatic privileges and territorial concessions in China and Japan (see ◊Edo, Treaty of). Under the threat of coercion, the enfeebled Chinese Qing dynasty was forced to sign the agreements, which established the ◊treaty ports. Nationalist resentment at this fuelled the ◊Boxer movement 1900.

The first unequal treaty was the Treaty of Nanjing 1842, concluded at the end of the first ◊Opium War, under which Hong Kong was ceded to Britain and five ◊treaty ports, Shanghai, Guangzhou (Canton), Xiamen (Amoy), Fuzhou (Foochow), and Ningbo, were opened to foreign trade. Further treaty ports were opened by the Treaty of ◊Tianjin (Tientsin) 1858. Unequal treaties were also forced on the Tokugawa shogunate in Japan by the USA with the treaties of Kanagawa 1854 and Edo 1858, but the Western powers had to surrender their special treaty-port privileges in Japan 1899.

Uniformity, Acts of two acts of Parliament in England. The first in 1559 imposed the Prayer Book on the whole English kingdom; the second in 1662 required the Prayer Book to be used in all churches, and some 2,000 ministers who refused to comply were ejected.

Unilateral Declaration of Independence (UDI) unnegotiated severing of relations with a colonial power; especially, the declaration made by Ian Smith's Rhodesian Front government 11 Nov 1965, announcing the independence of Rhodesia (now Zimbabwe) from Britain.

Smith unilaterally declared Rhodesia an independent state, to resist sharing power with the black African majority. It was a move condemned by the United Nations and by the UK, who imposed sanctions (trade restrictions and an oil embargo). With the support of the UN, Britain also imposed a naval blockade, but this was countered by the South African government breaking sanctions. Negotiations between British prime minister Harold Wilson and Smith foundered. It was not until April 1980 that the Republic of Zimbabwe was proclaimed.

Union, Act of 1707 Act of Parliament that brought about the union of England and Scotland; that of 1801 united England and Ireland. The latter was revoked when the Irish Free State was constituted 1922.

Union of Soviet Socialist Republics (USSR or Soviet Union) former country in N Asia and E Europe that reverted to independent states following the resignation of Mikhail Gorbachev 1991; see ◊Armenia, ◊Azerbaijan, ◊Belarus, ◊Estonia, ◊Georgia, ◊Kazakhstan, ◊Kyrgyzstan, ◊Latvia, ◊Lithuania, ◊Moldova, ◊Russian Federation, ◊Tajikistan, ◊Turkmenistan, ◊Ukraine, and ◊Uzbekistan.

Stalin's socialism Trotsky was expelled 1927, and Stalin's policy of socialism in one country adopted. During the first two five-year plans 1928–39, heavy and light industries were developed, and agriculture collectivized. The country was transformed as industry grew at an annual (official) rate of 16% with, as a consequence, the size of the manual workforce quadrupling and the urban population doubling. However, the social cost was enormous, with millions dying in the Ukraine and Kazakhstan famine of 1932–34, as well as in the political purges and liquidations launched during the 1920s and 1930s. Leading party figures, including Nikolai Bulkharin, Lev Kamenev, and Grigory Zinoviev were victims of these 'show trial' purges. In the process, the Soviet political system was deformed, as inner-party democracy gave way to autocracy based around a Stalinist personality cult.

From 1933 the USSR put forward a policy of collective resistance to aggression. In 1939 it concluded a nonaggression pact with Germany, and Poland was invaded and divided between them. The USSR invaded Finland 1939 but signed a brief peace 1940. For events 1941–45, see ◊World War II. Some 25 million Russians perished during this 'Great Patriotic War'.

Cold War During the immediate postwar years the USSR concentrated on consolidating its empire in Eastern Europe and on providing indirect support to anticolonial movements in the Far East. Relations with the West, particularly the USA, sharply deteriorated. On the death of Stalin in March 1953, a collective leadership, including Nikita Khrushchev (CPSU first or general secretary 1953–64), Georgi Malenkov (prime minister 1953–55), Nikolai Bulganin (prime minister 1955–58), Vyacheslav Molotov (foreign minister 1953–56), and Lazar Kaganovich, assumed power. They combined to remove the secret-police chief Lavrenti Beria in Dec 1953, and introduced a new legal code that regularized the political system. Strong differences emerged within the collective leadership over future political and economic reform, and a fierce succession struggle developed.

Khrushchev's 'liberalization policy' Khrushchev emerged dominant from this contest, ousting Malenkov, Molotov, and Kaganovich (the 'antiparty' group) June 1957 and Bulganin June 1958 to combine the posts of prime minister and party first secretary. At the 1961 Party Congress, Khrushchev introduced a new party programme for rapid agricultural, industrial, and technological development to enable the USSR to move ahead of the USA in economic terms by 1980 and attain full communism. He launched a 'virgin lands' cultivation campaign in Kazakhstan, increased rural incentives, and decentralized industrial management through the creation of new regional economic councils (*sovnarkhozy*). In addition, Khrushchev introduced radical party rule changes, sanctioned a cultural thaw, and devised the principle of 'peaceful coexistence' with the West to divert resources from the military sector. These reforms enjoyed initial success; having exploded its first hydrogen bomb 1953 and launched a space satellite (Sputnik I) 1957, the USSR emerged as a serious technological rival to the USA. But Khrushchev's liberalization policy and his denunciation of the errors and crimes of the Stalin era at the Feb 1956 Party Congress had serious repercussions among the USSR's satellites – a nationalist revolt in Hungary and a breach in relations with Yugoslavia and China – while his administrative reforms were fiercely opposed by senior party and state officials. After a series of poor harvests in overcropped Kazakhstan and the ◊Cuban missile crisis 1962, these opponents succeeded in ousting Khrushchev at the Central Committee meeting Oct 1964.

A new and conservative collective leadership, based around the figures of Leonid Brezhnev (CPSU general secretary 1964–82), Alexei Kosygin (prime minister 1964–80), Nikolai Podgorny (state president 1965–77), and Mikhail Suslov (ideology secretary 1964–82), assumed power and immediately abandoned Khrushchev's *sovnarkhozy* and party reforms and reimposed strict censorship in the cultural sphere. Priority was now given to the expansion and modernization of the Soviet armed forces, including the creation of a naval force with global reach. This, coupled with the Warsaw Pact invasion of Czechoslovakia 1968, resulted in a renewal of the ◊Cold War 1964–70.

the Brezhnev doctrine During the later 1960s, Leonid Brezhnev emerged as the dominant figure. He governed in a cautious and consensual manner and brought into the Politburo leaders from all the significant centres of power, including the ◊KGB (Yuri Andropov), the army (Marshal Andrei Grechko), and the diplomatic service (Andrei Gromyko). Working with Prime Minister Kosygin, Brezhnev introduced a series of minor economic reforms and gave new priority to agricultural and consumer-goods production. He oversaw the framing of a new constitution 1977 where the limits for internal dissent were clearly set out and the 'Brezhnev doctrine' was also promulgated 1968, establishing the power of the USSR to intervene to 'preserve socialism' in E Europe as it did in Czechoslovakia.

era of détente Brezhnev, who became the new state president May 1977, emerged as an international figure during the 1970s, frequently meeting Western leaders during a new era of détente. The landmarks of this period were the SALT I and SALT II Soviet-US arms-limitation agreements of 1972 and 1979 (see ◊Strategic Arms Limitation Talks) and the Helsinki Accord 1975, which brought Western recognition of the postwar division of Eastern Europe. Another cultural thaw resulted in the emergence of a vocal dissident movement. The political and military influence of the USSR was extended into Africa with the establishment of new communist governments in Mozambique 1974, Angola and Ethiopia 1975, and South Yemen 1978. The détente era was brought to an end by the Soviet invasion of Afghanistan in Dec 1979 and the Polish crisis 1980–81. The final years of the Brezhnev administration were ones of hardening policy, mounting corruption, and economic stagnation.

Andropov and Chernenko Yuri Andropov, the former KGB chief, was elected CPSU leader on Brezhnev's death Nov 1982 and began energetically to introduce a series of radical economic reforms aimed at streamlining and decentralizing the planning system and inculcating greater labour discipline. Andropov also launched a campaign against corrupt and complacent party and state bureaucrats. These measures had a perceptible impact on the Soviet economy during 1983, but when Andropov died Feb 1984 he was succeeded by the cautious and elderly Brezhnev supporter Konstantin Chernenko. Chernenko held power as a stop-gap leader for 13 months, his sole initiative being a renewed search for détente with the USA that was rejected by the hardline Reagan administration.

Gorbachev's 'market socialism' On Chernenko's death in March 1985, power was transferred to a new generation led by Mikhail Gorbachev, at 54 the CPSU's youngest leader since Stalin. Gorbachev introduced a number of reforms. He began to free farmers and factory managers from bureaucratic interference and to increase material incentives in a 'market socialist' manner. Working with Ideology Secretary Yegor Ligachev and Prime Minister Nikolai Ryzhkov, he restructured party and

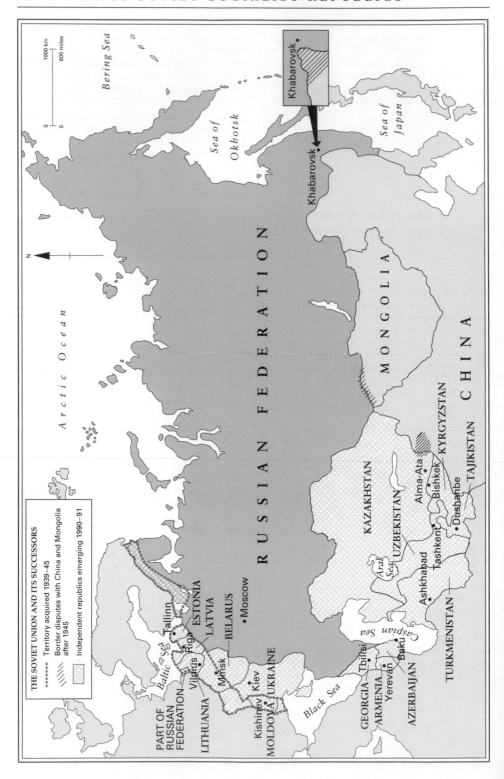

THE SOVIET UNION AND ITS SUCCESSORS

≈≈≈≈≈≈≈ Territory acquired 1939–45

//////// Border disputes with China and Mongolia
         after 1945

▒▒▒▒   Independent republics emerging 1990–91

1000 km
600 miles

N

Bering Sea

Sea of Okhotsk

Sea of Japan

Arctic Ocean

Khabarovsk

Khabarovsk

RUSSIAN FEDERATION

MONGOLIA

CHINA

KAZAKHSTAN

Alma-Ata

Bishkek   KYRGYZSTAN

Dushanbe   TAJIKISTAN

UZBEKISTAN

Tashkent

Aral Sea

Ashkhabad

TURKMENISTAN

Caspian Sea

Baku

AZERBAIJAN

Yerevan

ARMENIA

GEORGIA

Tbilisi

Black Sea

Moscow

PART OF
RUSSIAN
FEDERATION

Baltic Sea

Tallinn   ESTONIA

Riga   LATVIA

BELARUS

Vilnius

LITHUANIA

Minsk

Kiev

Kishinev   UKRAINE

MOLDOVA

state bureaucracies and replaced cautious Brezhnevites with ambitious technocrats. Ligachev soon became the leading voice for the conservative wing of the Politburo and was increasingly considered an obstacle to Gorbachev's policies of *glasnost* ('openness'). Ligachev was demoted to the agriculture portfolio, and he was openly ridiculed and accused of corruption. Gorbachev made explicit his renunciation of the 'Brezhnev doctrine' 1989.

These changes were not lost on the opposition leaders in the Baltic republics or on Communist deputies in the newly assertive Soviet Parliament. Lithuania declared it would permit free elections, then the Lithuanian Communist Party declared its independence from Moscow. By Jan 1990, Gorbachev was faced with growing calls for secession from the Soviet Union, and he had been forced to reconsider his earlier opposition to a multiparty system in the USSR itself. He also was provoked to declare a state of emergency and despatch troops to quell warfare between Armenians and Azerbaijanis, fighting each other for religious and territorial reasons.

détente initiative Working with Foreign Secretary Eduard Shevardnadze, Gorbachev made skilful use of the foreign media to put the case against space weapons and nuclear testing. He met US president Reagan in Geneva and Reykjavik in Nov 1985 and Oct 1986, and, at the Washington summit of Dec 1987, he concluded a treaty designed to eliminate medium-range Intermediate Nuclear Forces (INF) from European soil. This treaty was ratified at the Moscow summit of May–June 1988. As part of the new détente initiative, the USSR also withdrew all its troops from Afghanistan in Feb 1989 and made broad cutbacks in the size of its conventional forces 1989-90.

glasnost and perestroika Gorbachev pressed for an acceleration (*uskoreniye*) of his domestic, economic, and political programme of restructuring (*perestroika*) from 1987, but faced growing opposition both from conservatives grouped around Ligachev and radicals led by Boris

---

The Soviet Union and its successors The failure of Gorbachev's reforms to hold the USSR together led in 1990–91 to the rapid growth and expression of nationalist feeling in its constituent republics. The Baltic states (Latvia, Lithuania, and Estonia) were among the first to make their claim for independence, followed by Georgia, Belarus, and the Ukraine. Disputes over territory (as in the rival Azerbaijani and Armenian claims to Nagorno-Karabakh) and matériel (the division of the former Soviet navy between the Russian Republic and the Ukraine) promptly threatened the peaceful evolution of the new states.

Yeltsin. Gorbachev's *glasnost* policy helped fan growing nationalist demands for secession among the republics of the Baltic and Transcaucasia. To add momentum to the reform process, in June 1988 Gorbachev convened a special 4,991 member All-Union Party Conference, the first since 1941. At this meeting a radical constitutional overhaul was approved. A new 'super-legislature', the Congress of the USSR People's Deputies (CUPD), was created, from which a full-time working parliament was subsequently to be elected, headed by a state president with increased powers. The members of this CUPD were to be chosen in competition with one another. The authority of the local soviets was enhanced and their structures made more democratic, while, in the economic sphere, it was agreed to re-introduce private leasehold farming, reform the price system, and allow part-time private enterprise in the service and small-scale industry sectors.

'socialist pluralism' The June 1988 reforms constituted the most fundamental reordering of the Soviet policy since the 'Stalinist departure' of 1928, entailing the creation of a new type of 'socialist democracy', as well as a new mixed economic system. The CUPD elections of March–April 1989 showed clear opposition to conservative *apparatchiks*. In May 1989, the CUPD elected Gorbachev as its chair, and thus as state president. During 1989 this movement towards 'socialist pluralism' was furthered by Gorbachev's abandonment of the ◊Brezhnev doctrine and his sanctioning of the establishment of noncommunist and 'reform communist' governments elsewhere in Eastern Europe. This led to the ruling regimes of Poland, Czechoslovakia, and Romania being overthrown in a wave of 'people's power'. Responding to these developments in Feb 1990, the CPSU Central Committee agreed to create a new directly elected state executive presidency on US and French models. In March 1990 the Soviet Parliament authorized private ownership of the means of production, forbidden since the 1920s. Further constitutional amendments made 1990 supported the right of self-determination, including secession of republics, and ended the CPSU's monopoly of power.

popular discontent The Gorbachev reform programme showed signs of running out of control 1989-90 as a result both of growing nationalist tensions (which in April 1989 and Jan 1990 had prompted the despatch of troops to the Caucasus region, first to break up demonstrations in Tbilisi, Georgia, and then to attempt to quell a civil war between Armenia and Azerbaijan over the disputed enclave of

◊Nagorno-Karabakh) and mounting popular discontent over the failure of *perestroika* to improve living standards.

end of Cold War In their Dec 1989 summit meeting in Malta, Gorbachev and US president Bush declared an end to the Cold War, opening the possibility of most-favoured-nation trading status with the USA, membership of ◊General Agreement on Tariffs and Trade (GATT), and an influx of Western investment. A Gorbachev trip to Canada and the USA followed May–June 1990 and a ◊Conference on Security and Cooperation in Europe (CSCE) in Paris Nov 1990.

moves towards independence in the republics Throughout 1990 the political and economic situation deteriorated. In pluralist elections held at local and republic levels, anti-communist, nationalist, and radical deputies polled strongly, particularly in the Baltic republics and cities. Their new governments issued declarations of republican sovereignty and, in the case of the Baltics, independence. These Moscow refused to recognize, and imposed a temporary economic blockade on Lithuania. As the year progressed, a 'war of laws' developed between the centre and the republics, who kept back funds (leading to a worsening federal budget deficit), and the system of central economic planning and resource distribution began to break down. As a consequence, with crime and labour unrest also increasing, the USSR's national income fell by at least 4% during 1990 and was to decline by a further 15% during 1991. Indeed, despite a bumper, but ill-collected, harvest, mounting food shortages led to rationing and an emergency international airlift of food aid during the winter of 1990–91.

break-up of the CPSU The CPSU also began to fracture during 1990 as a result of nationalist challenges within the republics and divisions among conservatives (grouped in the Soyuz and Communists for Russia bodies), liberals (Communists for Democracy), and radicals (Democratic Platform) over the direction and pace of economic and political reform. A split was formalized at the 28th CPSU Congress July 1990, when Boris Yeltsin, the new indirectly elected president of the RSFSR, and Gavriil Popov and Anatoly Sobchak, radical mayors of Moscow and Leningrad, resigned their party membership. Earlier, in the RSFSR, a new Russian Communist Party had been formed.

Gorbachev's swing to the right In Dec 1990, concerned at the gathering pace of economic and political disintegration and ethnic strife, Gorbachev persuaded the Soviet parliament to vote him increased emergency presidential powers and approve a new federalized political structure. Subsequently, under pressure from the Soyuz group, the military, and the KGB, a clear rightward shift in policy became apparent. This was manifested by the appointment of the conservative Valentin Pavlov as prime minister, Gennady Yanayev as vice president, and Boris Pugo as interior minister; by the resignation of foreign minister, Shevardnadze, who warned of an impending dictatorship; by the dispatch of paratroopers to Vilnius and Riga to seize political and communications buildings; and by retightening of press and television censorship. In protest, striking miners called for Gorbachev's resignation.

proposed new union treaty From the spring of 1991, after his proposal to preserve the USSR as a 'renewed federation of equal sovereign republics' secured public approval in a union-wide referendum (though boycotted by six republics), Gorbachev again attempted to reconstruct a centre-left reform alliance with liberals and radicals. In April 1991 a pact aimed at achieving stable relations between the federal and republican governments and concerned with economic reform (price liberalization, progressive privatization, and the control of political strikes) was signed by the presidents of nine republics; the Baltic States, Armenia, Georgia, and Moldova refused to sign. Two months later, the draft of a new Union Treaty, entailing a much greater devolution of authority and the establishment of a new two-chamber federal legislature and a directly elected executive president, was also approved by nine republics. In July 1991 Gorbachev's standing was further enhanced by his attendance, as an invited guest, at the Group of Seven (G7) summit of the leaders of the chief industrialized Western countries, held in London, and the signing, in Moscow, of a Strategic Arms Reduction Treaty (START), to reduce the number of US and Soviet long-range nuclear missiles. At home, however, Boris Yeltsin, who was popularly elected as the RSFR's president June 1991, pressed for even greater reform and in July 1991 Communist Party cells were banned from operating in factories, farms, and government offices in the Russian Republic. In the same month a Democratic Reform Movement was formed by Eduard Shevardnadze, Alexander Yakovlev, and the mayors of Moscow and Leningrad, Anatoly Sobchak and Gavriil Popov.

abortive anti-Gorbachev coup These liberal-radical initiatives raised disquiet among CPSU conservatives and in June 1991 Prime Minister Pavlov unsuccessfully attempted to persuade the Soviet parliament to vote him extra powers. Two months later, on Monday 19 Aug 1991, a day before the new union treaty was to be signed, an attempted coup was launched by a reactionary alliance of leaders of the Communist Party *apparatchiki*, the military-industrial complex, the KGB, and the armed forces. It was declared in the early hours of the morning that President Gorbachev was ill and that Vice President Gennady Yanayev would take over as president, as part of an eight-person emergency committee, which also included Prime Minister Pavlov, Defence Minister Dmitri Yazov, KGB Chief Vladimir Kryuchkov, and Interior Minister Boris Pugo. The committee assumed control over radio and television, banned demonstrations and all but eight newspapers, imposed a curfew, and sent tanks into Moscow. They failed, however, to arrest the Russian president Boris Yeltsin, who defiantly stood out as head of a democratic 'opposition state' based at the Russian Parliament, the so-called 'White House', where external telephone links remained in operation. Yeltsin called for a general strike and the reinstatement of President Gorbachev. On Wednesday morning, having failed to wrest control of the 'White House' and win either international or unionwide acknowledgement of the change of regime, and having endured large demonstrations in Moscow, St Petersburg (formerly Leningrad), Chişinău (Moldova), and Lvov (Ukraine) on Tuesday, the coup disintegrated. The junta's leaders were arrested and in the early hours of Thursday 22 Aug President Gorbachev, fully reinstated, arrived back in Moscow. There were 15 fatalities during the crisis.

aftermath of the coup In the wake of the failed coup, established communist structures, as well as the union itself, rapidly disintegrated, faced by a popular backlash which resulted in such icons of communism as the Felix Dzerzhinsky statue outside the KGB headquarters in Moscow being toppled and the Red Flag burned, being replaced by traditional, in some cases tsarist, symbols. President Gorbachev initially misjudged the changed mood, intimating his continued faith in the popularly discredited Communist Party and seeking to keep to a minimum of changes in personnel and institutions. However, forced by pressure exerted by the public and by Boris Yeltsin, whose stature both at home and abroad had been hugely enhanced, a succession of far-reaching reforms were instituted which effectively sounded the death knell of Soviet communism and resulted in the frac-

turing of the union and its subsequent refounding on a much changed and truncated basis.

The new union cabinet was effectively selected by Yeltsin and staffed largely with radical democrats from the Russian Republic – the Russian prime minister Ivan Silaev became the Soviet prime minister. Yeltsin also declared himself to have assumed charge of the armed forces within the Russian Republic and, at a heated session of the Russian Parliament, pressurized President Gorbachev into signing a decree suspending the activities of the Russian Communist Party. In addition, a new Russian national guard was established and control assumed over all economic assets in the republic. Recognizing the changed realities, Gorbachev announced 24 Aug 1991 that he was immediately resigning as general secretary of the Communist Party of the Soviet Union and ordered its Central Committee to dissolve itself.

republics declare independence The attempted coup also speeded up the movement towards dissolution of the Soviet Union. During the coup, when Red Army tanks were sent into their capitals with orders to seize radio and television stations, the Estonian and Latvian parliaments followed the earlier example of Lithuania and declared independence. After the coup the largely conservative-communist controlled republics of Azerbaijan, Belarus, and Uzbekistan, as well as the key republic of Ukraine, also joined the Baltics, Georgia, Moldova, and Armenia in declaring their independence. Their governments acted partly in the hope of shoring up their authority and privileges and partly because they feared Russian domination of the existing USSR and possible future territorial disputes.

new union treaty signed At an emergency session of the Congress of People's Deputies, the union was partially salvaged through the negotiation of a new union treaty in which each republic was to be allowed to decide its own terms of association, with much greater power being devolved from the centre in what represented a new loose confederation, or 'Union of Sovereign States', though with the armed forces retained under a single military command. Ten republics – the three Baltics, Georgia, and Moldova being the exceptions – declared a willingness to sign this agreement. The Congress also voted 5 Sept 1991 to establish a new system of government in which it would be abolished and its powers would be assumed by a revamped, two-chamber supreme soviet, with its upper chamber chosen by the republics and its decisions ratified by the latter; a state council (government), comprising President

Soviet Union: history

1917	Revolution: provisional democratic government established by Mensheviks. Communist takeover by Bolsheviks under Lenin.
1922	Soviet Union established.
1924	Death of Lenin.
1928	Stalin emerged as absolute ruler after ousting Trotsky.
1930s	Purges of Stalin's opponents took place.
1939	Nonaggression pact signed with Germany.
1941–45	Great Patriotic War against Germany.
1949	Comecon created.
1953	Stalin died. Beria removed. 'Collective leadership' in power.
1955	Warsaw Pact created.
1956	Khrushchev made February 'secret speech'. Hungarian uprising.
1957–58	Ousting of 'antiparty' group and Bulganin.
1960	Sino-Soviet rift.
1962	Cuban missile crisis.
1964	Khrushchev ousted by new 'collective leadership'.
1968	Czechoslovakia invaded.
1969	Sino-Soviet border war.
1972	Salt I arms-limitation agreed with USA.
1977	Brezhnev elected president.
1979	Salt II. Soviet invasion of Afghanistan.
1980	Kosygin replaced as prime minister by Tikhonov.
1980–81	Polish crisis.
1982	Deaths of Suslov and Brezhnev. Andropov became Communist Party leader.
1984	Chernenko succeeded Andropov.
1985	Gorbachev succeeded Chernenko and introduced wide-ranging reforms. Gromyko appointed president.
1986	Gorbachev's power consolidated at 27th Party Congress. Chernobyl nuclear disaster.
1987	USSR and USA agreed to scrap intermediate-range nuclear missiles. Boris Yeltsin, Moscow party chief, dismissed for criticizing slow pace of reform.
1988	Nationalists challenged in Kazakhstan, Baltic republics, Armenia, and Azerbaijan. Earthquake killed thousands in Armenia. Constitution radically overhauled; private sector encouraged at Special All-Union Party Conference. Gorbachev replaced Gromyko as head of state.
1989	Troops withdrew from Afghanistan. General election held, with candidate choice for new congress of People's deputies. Nationalist riots in Georgia. 74 members of (25%) CPSU Central Committee removed. Gorbachev elected state president; conservative communist regimes in Eastern Europe overthrown. Relations with Chinese normalized. Lithuania allowed multiparty elections. Gorbachev renounced 'Brezhnev doctrine'; Soviet Union admitted invasion of Afghanistan and intervention in Czechoslovakia to have been mistakes; Gorbachev opposed calls to modify Soviet constitution; Lithuanian Communist Party declared independence from Moscow.
1990	Troops sent to Azerbaijan during civil war with Armenia. CPSU Central Committee agreed to end one-party rule. Increased powers voted to state president by CUPD. Gorbachev opposed independence of Baltic republics; sanctions imposed on Lithuania; elections showed strength of liberal Communists. Boris Yeltsin elected president of Russian republic by RSFSR parliament and left the Communist Party.
1991	Plan to preserve USSR as 'renewed federation of equal sovereign republics' approved in unionwide referendum, though boycotted by six republics. June: Yeltsin elected president of Russian Republic in direct, popular election and issued decree banning Communist Party cells in the RSFSR. Shevardnadze left CPSU and, with other liberal reformers, formed Democratic Reform Movement. New Union treaty approved by nine republics. Aug: coup by hardline communists, led by Yanayev and Pavlov, removed Gorbachev from power; Gorbachev restored but position undermined by Yeltsin who initiated a rapid dissolution of communist rule, the KGB, and existing communist structures. In wake of failed coup several republics declared independence. Sept: independence of the republics of Latvia, Lithuania, and Estonia formally acknowledged. Nov: Efforts to form a new 'Union of Sovereign States' failed. Dec: Gorbachev resigned; new federated arrangement emerged, the Commonwealth of Independent States (CIS); Soviet parliament voted USSR out of existence.

Gorbachev and the heads of the ten republics; and an interrepublican economic committee with equal representation from all 15 republics and chaired by Ivan Silaev. It also acknowl-edged the rights of republics to secede, opening the way 6 Sept 1991 for President Gorbachev to formally recognize the independence of the Baltic states by decree.

decentralization and new realities The possibility of forging a new, decentralized union receded as 1991 progressed. Concerned at the accumulation of political and economic authority by Russia, several of the republics began to seek full independence so as to escape Russian domination, refusing to sign new economic and political agreements. Participation in the new supreme soviet and state council was patchy, their gatherings attracting members from, at most, ten republics. Although a declaration of intent to maintain a 'common economic zone' of interrepublican free trade and to uphold existing factory ties was initialled Oct 1991, along with a civic and interethnic accord, the republics proved unable to agree on specific details of a proposed new economic and political union. As a consequence, President Gorbachev occupied the position of a figurehead leader, possessing little real authority, although his position was slightly strengthened by the return of Shevardnadze to head the foreign relations ministry Nov 1991. Instead, the pre-eminent leader in the new USSR, governing significantly from the former office of the CPSU Politburo, was Russia's president, Boris Yeltsin. In Nov 1991 the Russian Republic took over control of the Soviet money supply and exchange rate, and began implementing a market-centred economic reform programme. On 14 Nov preliminary agreement was reached on the formation of a new 'Union of Sovereign States', but in a subsequent meeting on 25 Nov the republican delegations that attended refused to initial the treaty.

The growing power of the individual republics became apparent in late Nov when the Group of Seven (G7) industrial countries reached a Soviet debt-deferral agreement with the USSR and included eight of the republics as signatories. On 8 Dec 1991 the most powerful of the republics – Russia, Belarus, and Ukraine – agreed to form the ◊Commonwealth of Independent States (CIS), a development denounced by Gorbachev. By mid-Dec, the five Central Asian republics (Kazakhstan, Kyrgyzstan, Tajikistan, Turkmenistan, and Uzbekistan) had announced that they would join the CIS, and Gorbachev had agreed on a transfer of power from the centralized government to the CIS. The remaining republics (Armenia, Azerbaijan, and Moldova) except Georgia, torn by civil war, joined the others in signing agreements on 21 Dec to establish the commonwealth, formally designated an alliance of independent states. The formal dissolution of the USSR came on 25 Dec when Gorbachev resigned as president.

UNITA (acronym for *União Nacional para a Independencia Total de Angola*/National Union for the Total Independence of Angola) Angolan nationalist movement backed by South Africa, which continued to wage guerrilla warfare against the ruling MPLA regime after the latter gained control of the country in 1976. The UNITA leader Jonas ◊Savimbi founded the movement 1966. A peace agreement ending the civil war between MPLA–PT and UNITA was signed May 1991, but fighting broke out again Sept 1992 after Savimbi disputed an election victory for the ruling party. UNITA forces rapidly took control of more than half the country, including northern diamond areas.

Unitarianism Christian-derived sect that rejects the orthodox doctrine of the Trinity, asserts the fatherhood of God and the brotherhood of humanity, and gives a pre-eminent position to Jesus as a religious teacher, while denying his divinity. Unitarianism is widespread in England and North America.

United Arab Emirates federation in SW Asia, on the Arabian Gulf, bounded NW by Qatar, SW by Saudi Arabia, and SE by Oman.

There is a federal national council of 40 members appointed by the emirates for a two-year term, and this operates as a consultative assembly. There are no political parties.

history For early history, see ◊Arabia. In 1952 the seven sheikdoms of Abu Dhabi, Ajman, Dubai, Fujairah, Ras al Khaimah, Sharjah, and Umm al Qaiwain set up, on British advice, the Trucial Council, consisting of all seven rulers, with a view to eventually establishing a federation. In the 1960s the Trucial States, as they were known, became very wealthy through the exploitation of oil deposits.

The whole area was under British protection, but in 1968 the British government announced that it was withdrawing its forces within three years. The seven Trucial States, with Bahrain and Qatar, formed the Federation of Arab Emirates, which was intended to become a federal state, but in 1971 Bahrain and Qatar seceded to become independent nations. Six of the Trucial States then combined to form the United Arab Emirates. The remaining sheikdom, Ras al Khaimah, joined Feb 1972. Sheik Sultan Zayed bin al-Nahayan, the ruler of Abu Dhabi, became the first president.

In 1976 Sheik Zayed, disappointed with the slow progress towards centralization, was persuaded to accept another term as president only with assurances that the federal government would be given more control over such activities as defence and internal security. In recent years the United Arab Emirates has played an increasingly prominent role in Middle East affairs, and in 1985 it established diplomatic and economic links with the USSR and China.

In 1990–91, the UAE opposed Iraq's invasion of Kuwait and contributed troops and economic support to the UN coalition that defeated Iraq in the ◊Gulf War. The international financial scandal surrounding the 1991 collapse of the Bank of Commerce and Credit International (BCCI) had serious implications for the UAE because Abu Dhabi's ruler held a controlling interest in the bank.

United Australia Party Australian political party formed by Joseph ◊Lyons 1931 from the right-wing Nationalist Party. It was led by Robert Menzies after the death of Lyons. Considered to have become too dominated by financial interests, it lost heavily to the Labor Party 1943, and was reorganized as the ◊Liberal Party 1944.

United Democratic Front moderate multiracial political organization in South Africa, founded 1983. It was an important focus of anti-apartheid action in South Africa until 1989, when the African National Congress and Pan-Africanist Congress were unbanned.

United Irishmen society formed 1791 by Wolfe ◊Tone to campaign for parliamentary reform in Ireland. It later became a secret revolutionary group.

Inspired by the republican ideals of the French Revolution, the United Irishmen was initially a debating society, calling for reforms such as the right of Catholics to vote in Irish elections, but after an attempt to suppress it in 1793, the organization became secret, looking to France for military aid. An attempted insurrection 1798 was quickly defeated and the leaders captured.

United Kingdom (UK) country in NW Europe off the coast of France, consisting of England, Scotland, Wales, and Northern Ireland.

history For early history, see ◊Britain, ancient; ◊England, history; ◊Scotland, history; ◊Wales, history; ◊Ireland, history. The term 'United Kingdom' became official 1801, but was in use from 1707, when the Act of Union combined Scotland and England into the United Kingdom of Great Britain. Cabinet government developed under Robert Walpole, in practice the first prime minister (1721–42). Two ◊Jacobite rebellions sought to restore the Stuarts to the throne until the Battle of ◊Culloden 1746, after which the Scottish Highlanders were brutally suppressed. The American colonies that became the USA were lost in the ◊American Revolution.

The Act of Ireland 1801 united Britain and Ireland. This was the time of the ◊Industrial Revolution, the mechanization of production that shifted the balance of political power from the landowner to the industrial capitalist and created an exploited urban working class. In protest, the ◊Luddites destroyed machinery. Agricultural ◊enclosures drove small farmers off the land. The alliance of the industrialists with the ◊Whigs produced a new party, the Liberals, with an ideology of ◊free trade and nonintervention in economic affairs. In 1832 they carried a Reform Bill transferring political power from the aristocracy to the middle classes and for the next 40 years the Liberal Party was a major force. The working classes, who had no vote, created their own organizations in the trade unions and ◊Chartism; their attempts to seek parliamentary reform were brutally suppressed (at the ◊Peterloo massacre 1819). The Conservative prime minister Robert Peel introduced a number of domestic reforms, including the repeal of the Corn Laws 1846.

After 1875 the UK's industrial monopoly was challenged by Germany and the USA. To seek new markets and sources of raw materials, the Conservatives under Disraeli launched the UK on a career of imperialist expansion in Egypt, South Africa, and elsewhere. Canada, Australia, and New Zealand became self-governing dominions.

World War I and the Depression The domestic issues after 1900 were social reform and home rule for Ireland; the Labour Party emerged from an alliance of trade unions and small socialist bodies 1900; the ◊suffragettes were active until ◊World War I. After the war a wave of strikes culminated in the general strike 1926; three years later a world economic crisis precipitated the Depression that marked the 1930s and brought to power a coalition government 1931.

The following years were dominated by unemployment, which reached almost 3 million in 1933. The death of George V Jan 1936 brought Edward VIII to the throne, closely followed by the ◊abdication crisis precipitated by his desire to marry US divorcee Wallis Simpson. In Dec 1936, Edward VIII abdicated, and George VI came to the throne.

World War II In 1939 Germany invaded Poland, and Britain entered ◊World War II by declaring war on Germany. In 1940 Winston Churchill became prime minister, leader of the Conservative Party, and head of a coalition government. The country sustained intensive bombardment in the 'Battle of Britain' July–Oct

---

1940, and the Blitz of night bombing which affected especially London and Coventry. After the defeat of Germany 1945, the Labour Party, led by Clement Attlee, gained power.

reform and renewal In 1945 the UK was still nominally at the head of an empire that covered a quarter of the world's surface and included a quarter of its population, and, although two world wars had gravely weakened it, many of its citizens and some of its politicians still saw it as a world power. The reality of its position soon became apparent when the newly elected Labour government confronted the problems of rebuilding the war-damaged economy. This renewal was greatly helped, as in other W European countries, by support from the USA through the ◊Marshall Plan. Between 1945 and 1951 the Labour government carried out an ambitious programme of public ownership and investment and laid the foundations of a national health service and welfare state. During the same period the dismemberment of the British Empire, restyled the British ◊Commonwealth, was begun, a process that was to continue into the 1980s.

Suez Crisis When in 1951 the Conservative Party was returned to power, under Winston Churchill, the essential features of the welfare state and the public sector were retained. In 1955 Churchill, in his 81st year, was succeeded by the foreign secretary, Anthony Eden. In 1956 Eden found himself confronted by the takeover of the Suez Canal by the president of Egypt, Gamal Nasser. Eden's perception of the threat posed by Nasser was not shared by everyone, even within the Conservative Party. The British invasion of Egypt, in conjunction with France and Israel, brought widespread criticism and was abandoned in the face of pressure from the USA and the United Nations. Eden resigned, and the Conservatives chose Harold Macmillan as their new leader and prime minister.

Supermac The Conservatives won the 1959 general election with an increased majority. By the early 1960s, the economy had improved, living standards had risen, and Prime Minister Harold Macmillan was known as 'Supermac'. Internationally, he established working relationships with the US presidents Eisenhower and Kennedy. He also did much for the Commonwealth, but was sufficiently realistic to see that the UK's long-term economic and political future lay in Europe. The framework for the European Economic Community (EEC) had been created by the mid-1950s, with the UK an onlooker rather than a participant, and in 1961 the first serious attempt was made to join the

EEC, only to have it blocked by the French president, Charles de Gaulle.

poor economic performance Despite rising living standards, the UK's economic performance was not as successful as that of many of its competitors, such as West Germany and Japan. There was a growing awareness that there was insufficient investment in industry, that young talent was going into the professions or financial institutions rather than manufacturing, and that training was poorly planned and inadequately funded. It was against this background that Macmillan unexpectedly resigned 1963, on the grounds of ill health, and was succeeded by the foreign secretary, Lord Home, who immediately renounced his title to become Alec Douglas-Home.

Wilson government In the general election 1964 the Labour Party won a slender majority and its leader, Harold Wilson, became prime minister. The election had been fought on the issue of the economy. Wilson created the Department of Economic Affairs (DEA) to challenge the short-term conservatism of the Treasury, and brought in a leading trade unionist to head a new Department of Technology. In an early general election 1966 Wilson increased his Commons majority, but his promises of fundamental changes in economic planning, industrial investment, and improved work practices were not fulfilled. The DEA was disbanded 1969 and an ambitious plan for the reform of industrial relations was dropped in the face of trade-union opposition.

Heath's 'counter-revolution' In 1970 the Conservatives returned to power under Edward Heath. He, too, saw institutional change as one way of achieving industrial reform and created two new central departments (Trade and Industry, Environment) and a think tank to advise the government on long-term strategy, the Central Policy Review Staff. He attempted to change the climate of industrial relations through a long and complicated Industrial Relations Bill. He saw entry into the EEC as the 'cold shower of competition' that industry needed, and membership was negotiated 1972.

miners' strike Heath's 'counter-revolution', as he saw it, was frustrated by the trade unions, and the sharp rise in oil prices 1973 forced a U-turn in economic policy. Instead of abandoning 'lame ducks' to their fate, he found it necessary to take ailing industrial companies, such as Rolls-Royce, into public ownership. The introduction of a statutory incomes policy precipitated a national miners' strike in the winter of 1973–74 and Heath decided to challenge the unions by holding an early general election 1974. The result was a hung Parliament, with Labour winning the biggest number of seats but no single party having an overall majority. Heath tried briefly to form a coalition with the Liberals and, when this failed, resigned.

Wilson's 'social contract' Harold Wilson returned to the premiership, heading a minority government, but in another general election later the same year won enough additional seats to give him a working majority. He had taken over a damaged economy and a nation puzzled and divided by the events of the previous years. He turned to Labour's natural ally and founder, the trade-union movement, for support and jointly they agreed on a 'social contract': the government pledged itself to redress the imbalance between management and unions created by the Heath industrial-relations legislation, and the unions promised to cooperate in a voluntary industrial and incomes policy. Wilson met criticism from a growing left-wing movement within his party, impatient for radical change. In March 1976 Wilson, apparently tired and disillusioned, retired in midterm.

financial crisis Wilson was succeeded by the political veteran James Callaghan. In the other two parties, Heath had unexpectedly been ousted by Margaret Thatcher, and the Liberal Party leader, Jeremy Thorpe, had resigned after a personal scandal and been succeeded by the young Scottish MP David Steel. Callaghan was now leading a divided party and a government with a dwindling parliamentary majority. Later in 1976 an unexpected financial crisis arose from a drop in confidence in the overseas exchange markets, a rapidly falling pound, and a drain on the country's foreign reserves. After considerable debate within the cabinet, both before and afterwards, it was decided to seek help from the International Monetary Fund and submit to its stringent economic policies. Within weeks the crisis was over and within months the economy was showing clear signs of improvement.

Lib–Lab Pact In 1977, to shore up his slender parliamentary majority, Callaghan entered into an agreement with the new leader of the Liberal Party, David Steel. Under the 'Lib–Lab Pact' Labour pursued moderate, nonconfrontational policies in consultation with the Liberals, who, in turn, voted with the government, and the economy improved dramatically. The Lib–Lab Pact had effectively finished by the autumn of 1978, and soon the social contract with the unions began to disintegrate. Widespread and damaging strikes in the public sector badly affected essential services during what became

known as the 'winter of discontent'. At the end of March 1979 Callaghan lost a vote of confidence in the House of Commons and was forced into a general election.

Conservatives under Thatcher The Conservatives returned to power under the UK's first woman prime minister, Margaret Thatcher. She inherited a number of inflationary public-sector pay awards that, together with a budget that doubled the rate of value-added tax, resulted in a sharp rise in prices and interest rates. The Conservatives were pledged to reduce inflation and did so by mainly monetarist policies, which caused the number of unemployed to rise from 1.3 million to 2 million in the first year. Thatcher had experience in only one government department, and it was nearly two years before she made any major changes to the cabinet she inherited from Heath. In foreign affairs Zimbabwe became independent 1980 after many years, and without the bloodshed many had feared.

creation of SDP Meanwhile, changes were taking place in the other parties. Callaghan resigned the leadership of the Labour Party 1980 and was replaced by the left-winger Michael Foot, and early in 1981 three Labour shadow-cabinet members, David Owen, Shirley Williams, and William Rodgers, with the former deputy leader Roy Jenkins (collectively dubbed the 'Gang of Four'), broke away to form a new centrist group, the Social Democratic Party (SDP). The new party made an early impression, winning a series of by-elections within months of its creation. From 1983 to 1988 the Liberals and the SDP were linked in an electoral pact, the Alliance. They advocated the introduction of a system of proportional representation, which would ensure a fairer parity between votes gained and seats won.

Falklands War Unemployment continued to rise, passing the 3-million mark Jan 1982, and the Conservatives and their leader were receiving low ratings in the public-opinion polls. An unforeseen event rescued them: the invasion of the Falkland Islands by Argentina. Thatcher's decision to send a battle fleet to recover the islands paid off. The general election 1983 was fought with the euphoria of the Falklands victory still in the air and the Labour Party, under its new leader, divided and unconvincing. The Conservatives had a landslide victory, winning more Commons seats than any party since 1945, although with less than half the popular vote. Thatcher was able to establish her position firmly, replacing most of her original cabinet.

domestic problems The next three years were marked by rising unemployment and growing dissent: a dispute at the government's main intelligence-gathering station, GCHQ; a bitter and protracted miners' strike; increasing violence in Northern Ireland; an attempted assassination of leading members of the Conservative Party during their annual conference; and riots in inner-city areas of London, Bristol, and Liverpool. The government was further embarrassed by its own prosecutions under the Official Secrets Act and the resignations of two prominent cabinet ministers. With the short-term profits from North Sea oil and an ambitious privatization programme, the inflation rate continued to fall and by the winter of 1986-87 the economy was buoyant enough to allow the chancellor of the Exchequer to arrange a pre-election spending and credit boom.

party leadership changes Leadership changes took place by 1987 in two of the other parties. Michael Foot was replaced by his Welsh protégé Neil Kinnock; Roy Jenkins was replaced by David Owen as SDP leader, to be succeeded in turn by Robert MacLennan Sept 1987, when the SDP and Liberal parties voted to initiate talks towards a merger. Despite high unemployment and Thatcher's increasingly authoritarian style of government, the Conservatives were re-elected June 1987.

The merger of the Liberal and Social Democratic parties was an acrimonious affair, with the SDP, led by David Owen, refusing to join the merged party and operating as a rival group. Paddy Ashdown emerged as the leader of the new party.

In a cabinet reshuffle July 1989, Geoffrey Howe was replaced as foreign secretary by John Major. In Oct 1989 the chancellor of the Exchequer, Nigel Lawson, resigned because of disagreements with the prime minister, and Major replaced him. Douglas Hurd took over the foreign office. The government was widely criticized for its decisions forcibly to repatriate Vietnamese 'boat people' and to give right of abode in the UK to the families of 50,000 'key' Hong Kong citizens after the transfer of the colony to China 1997. David Owen announced that the SDP would no longer be able to fight in all national constituencies and would only operate as a 'guerrilla force'. The Green Party polled 2 million votes in the European elections.

Thatcher challenged In Sept 1990 the House of Commons was recalled for an emergency debate that endorsed the government's military activities in the Persian Gulf. In Oct the government announced that it was joining the European exchange-rate mechanism (ERM). In Nov the deputy prime minister, Geoffrey Howe, gave a dramatic resignation speech, strongly critical of Thatcher. Michael Heseltine then announced his candidacy for the leadership of the Conservative Party. Having failed to gain a clear victory in the first ballot of the leadership election, Thatcher was persuaded by her colleagues to withdraw from the contest. In the subsequent second ballot John Major won, becoming party leader and prime minister.

Major's leadership Major experienced initial popularity due to his consensual style of leadership, but dissatisfaction with the poll tax continued. A hastily constructed replacement for the poll tax did little to repair the damage done to the Conservative Party, which suffered heavy losses in local elections 1991. The deterioration of the National Health Service was also an issue. Despite the government's apparently waning popularity and almost two years of economic recession, the party won its fourth consecutive victory April 1992, with a reduced majority. Neil Kinnock resigned as Labour leader and was replaced by John Smith.

Europe and the Conservatives With a deepening recession and international pressure on the pound, the government was forced to devalue Sept 1992 and leave the ERM. Parliament ratified the ◊Maastricht treaty for closer European union July 1993. But disagreements about Europe continued to plague the Conservative Party. The party was suffering from low public popularity, demonstrated by poor election results. It was also the subject of a series of personal scandals. Faced with a right-wing 'Eurosceptic' rebellion over his policies on Europe, Major resigned the party leadership and was re-elected to the post in summer 1995.

Northern Ireland In Dec 1993 Major and Irish premier Albert Reynolds issued a joint peace proposal for Northern Ireland, the Downing Street Declaration, offering all-party constitutional talks in return for a cessation of violence. The Irish Republican Army (IRA) announced a cease-fire Aug 1994, but the cease-fire was interrupted 1996-97.

Labour John Smith died May 1994, and Tony Blair became the new Labour leader. Already enjoying great success, the popularity of the Labour party was boosted still further under Blair's young and articulate leadership.

Conservatives defeated The country went to the polls May 1997. Opinion polls, predicting a clear win for Labour, were accurate. Blair and his party won a Commons majority of 179. The Conservative Party had its lowest share of the vote since 1832 and the smallest number of seats since 1906. The new government took office determined to 'hit the ground running', and announced a number of policy initiatives, derived from its election manifesto, and a significant change in its attitude towards Europe.

United Nations (UN) association of states for international peace, security, and cooperation, with its headquarters in New York. The UN was established 1945 by 41 states as a successor to the ◊League of Nations, and has played a role in many areas, such as refugees, development assistance, disaster relief, cultural cooperation, and peacekeeping. The name 'United Nations' was coined by US president F D Roosevelt.

Our instrument and our hope is the United Nations, and I see little merit in the impatience of those who would abandon this imperfect world instrument because they dislike our imperfect world.
On the *United Nations* J F Kennedy
Jan 1962

United Provinces federation of states in the northern Netherlands 1579–1795. Established by the Union of Utrecht 1579, it aimed to assert independence from the Spanish crown. It comprised Holland, Zeeland, Friesland, Gelderland, Utrecht, Overijssel, and Groningen.

United Provinces of Central America political union 1823–38 established by the Central American states of Costa Rica, El Salvador, Guatemala, Honduras, and Nicaragua. The union followed the break-up of the Spanish empire and was initially dominated by Guatemala. Its unity was more apparent than real, and the federation fell apart in 1838. Subsequent attempts at reunification foundered.

United States of America (USA) country in North America, extending from the Atlantic Ocean in the east to the Pacific Ocean in the west, bounded north by Canada and south by Mexico, and including the outlying states of Alaska and Hawaii.

history For early history, see ◊American Indian. The Spanish first settled in Florida 1565. The first permanent English settlement was at Jamestown, Virginia, 1607. In 1620 English ◊Pilgrims landed at Plymouth and founded the colony of Massachusetts and, later, Connecticut. English Catholics founded Maryland 1634; English Quakers founded Pennsylvania 1682. A Dutch settlement 1614 on Manhattan Island, named New Amsterdam 1626, was

renamed New York after it was taken by England 1664. In the 18th century the English colonies were threatened by French expansion from the Great Lakes to Louisiana until the English won the French and Indian War (in Europe called the Seven Years' War 1756–63).

American Revolution In 1775, following years of increasing tension, the 13 colonies (Connecticut, Delaware, Georgia, Maryland, Massachusetts, New Hampshire, New Jersey, New York, North Carolina, Pennsylvania, Rhode Island, South Carolina, and Virginia) rose against the British government, assembled at the Continental Congress, and fought British troops in Massachusetts, at Lexington and Concord. Meeting in Philadelphia in 1776, they declared themselves to be 'free and independent states'. Led by General George Washington, they defeated George III's armies in the ◊American Revolution. By the Treaty of Paris 1783 Britain recognized the independence of the 13 colonies. The constitution came into force 1789. Washington was unanimously elected as the first president.

The ◊Louisiana territory was bought from Napoleon 1803, and Florida acquired from Spain 1819. Napoleon's trade blockade of British shipping led indirectly to the Anglo-American War 1812–14. Expansion to the west, under the slogan of '◊manifest destiny', reached the Pacific, and the Mexican War 1846–48 secured the areas of Arizona, California, part of Colorado and Wyoming, Nevada, Utah, New Mexico, and Texas. ◊Alaska was purchased from Russia 1867. Hawaii ceded itself to the USA 1898.

The ◊Civil War 1861-65 put an end to slavery but left ill feeling between north and south. It stimulated industrial development in the north, as well as the construction of roads and railways westwards.

international involvement The USA had traditionally followed a policy of isolationism. Involvement in international affairs really began with the Spanish-American War 1898, which involved the USA in Guam, Puerto Rico, and the Philippines. The Panama Canal Zone rights were leased 1903. After trying to maintain an isolationist stance, under President Woodrow Wilson, the USA entered ◊World War I 1917; it was not a party to the Treaty of Versailles but made peace by separate treaties 1921. A period of isolationism followed. The country's economic expansion was brought to a halt by the stock-market crash 1929, which marked the start of the ◊Depression. President Franklin Roosevelt's ◊New Deal 1933 did not solve the problem, and only preparations for

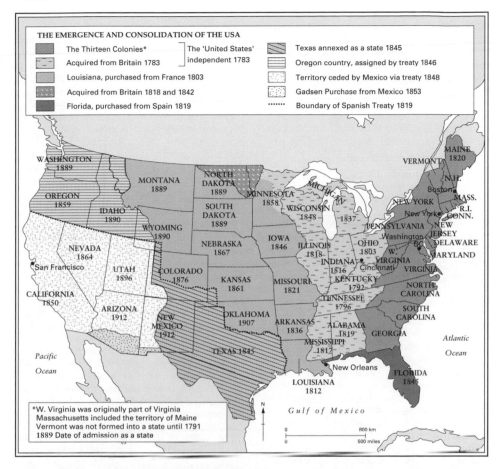

THE EMERGENCE AND CONSOLIDATION OF THE USA

The Thirteen Colonies*

Acquired from Britain 1783 / The 'United States' independent 1783

Louisiana, purchased from France 1803

Acquired from Britain 1818 and 1842

Florida, purchased from Spain 1819

Texas annexed as a state 1845

Oregon country, assigned by treaty 1846

Territory ceded by Mexico via treaty 1848

Gadsen Purchase from Mexico 1853

Boundary of Spanish Treaty 1819

WASHINGTON 1889
OREGON 1859
IDAHO 1890
NEVADA 1864
San Francisco
CALIFORNIA 1850
UTAH 1896
ARIZONA 1912
MONTANA 1889
WYOMING 1890
COLORADO 1876
NEW MEXICO 1912
NORTH DAKOTA 1889
SOUTH DAKOTA 1889
NEBRASKA 1867
KANSAS 1861
OKLAHOMA 1907
TEXAS 1845
MINNESOTA 1858
IOWA 1846
MISSOURI 1821
ARKANSAS 1836
MICHIGAN
WISCONSIN 1848
ILLINOIS 1818
INDIANA 1816
KENTUCKY 1792
TENNESSEE 1796
MISSISSIPPI 1817
ALABAMA 1819
LOUISIANA 1812
New Orleans
OHIO 1803
W. Cincinnati
VIRGINIA
NORTH CAROLINA
SOUTH CAROLINA
GEORGIA
FLORIDA 1845
PENNSYLVANIA
Washington DC
NEW YORK
New York
MAINE 1820
VERMONT
N.H.
Boston MASS.
R.I.
CONN.
NEW JERSEY
DELAWARE
MARYLAND

Pacific Ocean

Atlantic Ocean

Gulf of Mexico

*W. Virginia was originally part of Virginia
Massachusetts included the territory of Maine
Vermont was not formed into a state until 1791
1889 Date of admission as a state

0 800 km
0 500 miles

The emergence and consolidation of the USA *A fundamental feature of American history was the rapid expansion westwards of its territory. British efforts to stop the westward migration of its American colonists (by a royal proclamation 1763) were a contributory cause of the Revolution and War of Independence. Thereafter the USA expanded its territory across the continent at dramatic speed, acquiring land by negotiation, purchase, and conquest.*

◊World War II brought full employment. The USA declared war when Japan attacked the Pearl Harbor naval base on Honolulu Dec 1941.

the Truman doctrine The USA, having emerged from the war as a superpower, remained internationalist during the prosperity of the postwar era. Under the presidency of Harry S Truman (Democrat), a doctrine of intervention in support of endangered 'free peoples' and of 'containing the spread of communism' was devised by secretaries of state George Marshall and Dean Acheson. This led to the USA's intervention in Greece and support for Nationalist Taiwan 1949 and its participation in the ◊Korean War 1950–53. The USA, in addition, helped to create new global

and regional bodies designed to maintain the peace – the United Nations (UN) 1945, the Organization of American States (OAS) 1948, the North Atlantic Treaty Organization (NATO) 1949, the South-East Asia Treaty Organization (SEATO) 1954 – and launched the ◊Marshall Plan 1947 to strengthen the capitalist economies of its allies while standing off similar strategies of the USSR-dominated Eastern Bloc. This began the Cold War. Truman's foreign policy was criticized as being 'soft on communism' between 1950 and 1952, as a wave of anti- Soviet hysteria, spearheaded by Senator Joseph McCarthy, swept the nation.

Eisenhower and Cold War prosperity This rightward shift in the public mood brought Republican victory in the congressional and presidential elections 1952, with popular military commander General Dwight D Eisenhower becoming president. He was re-elected by an increased margin Nov 1956. Eisenhower adhered to the Truman–Acheson doctrine of 'containment of communism', while at home he pursued a policy of 'progressive conservatism' designed to encourage business enterprise. The Eisenhower era was one of economic growth, involving the migration of southern blacks to the northern industrial cities and rapid expansion in the educational sector.

King and Kennedy In the southern states, where racial segregation and discrimination were openly practised, a new civil-rights movement developed under the leadership of Dr Martin Luther King, Jr. Promising a 'New Frontier' programme of social reform, John F Kennedy (Democrat) won the presidential election Nov 1960 and emerged as an active supporter of civil rights and space exploration and an opponent of communism abroad (see ◊Bay of Pigs). He was assassinated Nov 1963.

Johnson's 'Great Society' It was left to his vice president and successor, Lyndon B Johnson, to oversee the passage of additional liberal reforms, called the 'Great Society' by Johnson. These measures, which included the Equal Opportunities, Voting Rights, Housing, and Medicare acts, guaranteed blacks their civil rights and extended the reach and responsibilities of the federal government. The black migration to the northern cities went into reverse from 1970, stimulated by new economic opportunity in American sunbelt states, new black political influence, and a feeling of returning to earlier roots.

Vietnam War Abroad, President Johnson escalated US involvement in the ◊Vietnam War 1964–75, which polarized public opinion and deeply divided the Democratic Party into 'hawks' and 'doves'. Johnson declined to run for re-election Nov 1968, and his vice president, Hubert Humphrey, was defeated by Republican Richard Nixon. Working with National Security Adviser Henry ◊Kissinger, Nixon escalated the Vietnam conflict by invading neighbouring Cambodia before he began a gradual disengagement, launching a policy of détente that brought an improvement in relations with the USSR (with ◊Strategic Arms Limitation Talks) and a visit to communist China 1973.

Watergate scandal Nixon, faced with a divided opposition led by the liberal George McGovern, had gained re-election by an overwhelming margin Nov 1972, but during the campaign, Nixon's staff had broken into the Democratic Party's ◊Watergate headquarters. When this and the attempts at cover-up came to light, the scandal forced the resignation of the president Aug 1974, just short of impeachment. Watergate shook the US public's confidence in the Washington establishment. Gerald Ford, who had been appointed vice president when Spiro Agnew was forced to step down Dec 1973, pardoned Nixon and kept the services of Kissinger and the policy of détente when he became president. He faced a hostile, Democrat-dominated Congress that introduced legislation curbing the unauthorized power of the presidency, attempting to mend fences both at home and abroad. He also had to deal with the economic recession and increased OPEC oil prices that began under Nixon 1973.

Carter presidency Ford ran in the presidential election Nov 1976, but was defeated by Washington outsider and Democrat Jimmy Carter, who promised open and honest government. Carter was a fiscal conservative but social liberal, who sought to extend welfare provision through greater administrative efficiency. He substantially ended the fuel crisis through enforced conservation in the energy bills 1978 and 1980. In foreign relations President Carter emphasized human rights. In the Middle East, he moved close to a peace settlement 1978–79 (the ◊Camp David Agreements) and in Jan 1979 the USA's diplomatic relations with communist China were fully normalized. The Carter presidency was, however, brought down by two foreign-policy crises 1979–80: the fall of the shah of Iran and the Soviet invasion of Afghanistan. The president's leadership style, military economies, and moralistic foreign policy were blamed by the press for weakening US influence abroad. There was a swell of anticommunist feeling and mounting support for a new policy of rearmament and selective interventionism. President Carter responded to this new mood by enunciating the hawkish ◊Carter Doctrine 1980 and supporting a new arms-development programme, but his popularity plunged during 1980 as economic recession gripped the country and US embassy staff members were held hostage by Shi'ite Muslim fundamentalists in Tehran.

Reagan administration The Republican Ronald Reagan benefited from Carter's difficulties and was elected Nov 1980, when the Democrats also lost control of the Senate. The new president had risen to prominence as an effective, television-skilled campaigner. He purported to believe in a return to traditional Christian and family values and promoted a domestic policy of supply-side economics, decentralization, and deregulation. The early years of the Reagan presidency witnessed substantial reductions in taxation, with cutbacks in federal welfare programmes that created serious hardships in many sectors as economic recession gripped the nation. Reagan rejected détente and spoke of the USSR as an 'evil empire' that needed to be checked by a military build-up and a readiness to employ force. This led to a sharp deterioration in Soviet-US relations, ushering in a new cold war during the Polish crisis 1981. He was re-elected on a wave of optimistic patriotism Nov 1984, defeating the Democrat ticket of Walter Mondale and Geraldine Ferraro by a record margin. A radical tax-cutting bill passed in Congress, and in 1986 a large budget and trade deficit developed (as a spending economy was developed to control Congress). At home and overseas the president faced mounting public opposition to his interventions in Central America. The new Soviet leader Mikhail Gorbachev pressed unsuccessfully for arms reduction during superpower summits in Geneva (Nov 1985) and Reykjavik (Oct 1986), but a further summit Dec 1987, with an agreement to scrap intermediate-range nuclear missiles, appeared to promise a new détente.

Irangate scandal In Nov 1986 the Republican Party lost control of the Senate in the midterm elections, just before the disclosure of a scandal concerning US arms sales to Iran in return for hostages held in Beirut, with the profits illegally diverted to help the Nicaraguan 'Contra' (anti-communist) guerrillas. The ◊Irangate scandal briefly dented public confidence in the administration and forced the dismissal and resignation of key cabinet members. During the last two years of his presidency, a more consensual Reagan was on view and, helped by his Dec 1987 arms reduction deal, he left office with much of his popular affection restored.

Bush in power Reagan's popularity transferred itself to Vice President George Bush who, despite selecting the inexperienced Dan Quayle as his running-mate and despite opposition charges that he had been indirectly involved in the Irangate proceedings, defeated the Democrats' candidate Michael Dukakis in the presidential election of Nov 1988. Bush came to power, after six years of economic growth, at a time of uncertainty. Reagan's tax-cutting policy had led to mounting federal trade and budget deficits, which had served to turn the USA into a debtor nation for the first time

American colonial history 1607–1773	
1607	First British colony founded at Jamestown, Virginia.
1614	Dutch established a trading post on Manhattan island. It became the settlement of New Amsterdam from 1624.
1620	*Mayflower* landed English settlers (the Piligrim Fathers) at New Plymouth, Massachusetts.
1630	Massachusetts Bay colony founded.
1634	Maryland colony founded.
1636	Connecticut colony founded.
1638	New Haven and New Hampshire colonies founded.
1660	First Navigation Act passed, by which Britain controlled trade with the new colonies.
1664	Dutch forced to cede their New Netherland colony to Britain. It became New York.
1681	Pennsylvania colony founded.
1692	Witch trials in Salem, Massachusetts.
1696	British Board of Trade and Plantations set up to regulate colonial commerce.
1700	Population of British colonies roughly 250,000.
1732	Georgia founded.
1734–39	Great Awakening, religious revival around colonies, began.
1740–48	England involved in War of Austrian Succession (King George's War).
1754–63	Anglo-French War (from 1756, Seven Years' War).
1763	Treaty of Paris confirmed supremacy of the 13 British colonies in N America. George III's proclamation sought to define western boundaries for new settlements.
1764–67	Legislation passed designed to strengthen royal and parliamentary control over the British colonies: Sugar Act and Currency Act 1764; Stamp Act 1765 (repealed 1766); Declaratory Act 1766; Townshend Acts 1767 (repealed 1770 except for tea tax).
1770	Boston massacre: British troops killed five protestors outside customs house.
1773	Tea Act passed, designed to save East India Company from bankruptcy, but widely regarded by colonies as another attempt to tax them, prompting Boston Tea Party (Dec).

in its history and had precipitated a stock-market crash Oct 1987. Retrenchment was concentrated 1989-90 in the military sphere, helped by continuing Soviet moves towards reductions in both conventional and nuclear forces. Domestically, Bush spoke of the need to create a 'kinder, gentler nation', and unveiled minor initiatives in the areas of education, drug control, and the environment, where problems

Growth of the USA 1773–1890

1773	Boston Tea Party protested against trading restrictions and taxation imposed by British parliament on American colonies.	**1836**	Secession of Texas from Mexico after the Battle of the Alamo.
1774	First Continental Congress of all colonies except Georgia, which produced a Declaration of Rights and Grievances.	**1845**	Texas and Florida admitted to the Union.
		1846	Oregon Treaty defined US–Canadian border along 49th parallel. US declared war on Mexico.
1775	British decided to restore order in Massachusetts. Skirmish in Lexington and battle at Concord. Second Continental Congress raised troops to oppose British. American Revolution began.	**1848**	In the Treaty of Guadalupe-Hidalgo, Mexico ceded all territory N of the Rio Grande to the US.
		1848–49	Californian gold rush.
		1850	California admitted to Union.
1776	Declaration of Independence signed at Philadelphia.	**1853**	S Arizona sold by Mexico to the US in Gadsden purchase.
1777	Battles at Brandy Wine and Germantown, Pennsylvania and Saratoga, New York. Articles of Confederation presented to Congress, but not put into operation until 1781.	**1860**	Lincoln elected president.
		1861–65	Civil War.
		1862	Homestead Act encouraged settlement in the west.
1781	General Washington captured Yorktown.	**1862–69**	First transcontinental railroad built.
1782	British acknowledged American independence.	**1865**	Slavery abolished. Lincoln assassinated.
1783	Treaty of Paris ended war.	**1866**	Southern states formally readmitted to Union in first stage of Reconstruction.
1787	Convention in Philadelphia drafted new constitution to replace Articles of Confederation.	**1867**	US bought Alaska from Russian empire for $7.2 million.
1789	George Washington elected first president of United States.	**1870s**	Frontier warfare between American Indians and encroaching settlers, supported by US army.
1803	Louisiana purchased from the French for $15 million.	**1877**	End of reconstruction attempts to reform the southern states after their defeat in the Civil War.
1812–14	War with Britain, arising from commercial disputes caused by Britain's struggle with Napoleon.	**1887**	Dawes Act sought to reform Indian society.
1819	Acquisition of Florida from the Spanish crown.	**1890**	Battle of Wounded Knee, S Dakota, marked end of Indian warfare. Census report noted disappearance of frontier line of settlement in the W, the 'closing of the frontier'.
1823	Monroe Doctrine, designed to limit European influence in the Americas.		

had surfaced during the Reagan years. (In 1990, almost 500,000 children were suffering from malnutrition and at least 100,000 people were homeless.) The start of his presidency was marred by the Senate's rejection of his nomination for Defense Secretary, John Tower, following criticisms of Tower's lifestyle and his links to military contractors. With his overthrowing of the corrupt Panamanian leader, General Manuel Noriega, Dec 1989, Bush began to establish his presidency.

In Sept 1990 the Senate confirmed David Souter, a conservative jurist from New Hampshire who had been nominated by President Bush, as a new Supreme Court justice. He replaced Justice William Brennan, a veteran liberal, who resigned in July. Souter's appointment appeared likely to strengthen the conservative majority that had been established within the Court, as did the confirmation in 1991 of Clarence Thomas after long and bitter Congressional hearings.

Gulf War The USA responded to Iraq's invasion and annexation of Kuwait 2 Aug 1990 by coordinating, in the UN, the passage of a series of resolutions demanding Iraq's unconditional withdrawal and imposing comprehensive economic sanctions. By late Nov the USA had sent more than 230,000 troops and support personnel to Saudi Arabia to form the core of a 400,000-strong Western and Arab 'desert shield' with the object of defending the Saudi frontier and, if necessary, dislodging Iraq from Kuwait. A further 150,000 US troops were sent early Dec and the ◊Gulf War was fought in Jan–Feb 1991.

US reaction to demise of USSR In July 1991 Bush and Gorbachev held the first superpower summit since the end of the Cold War and signed the long-awaited START treaty (see ◊Strategic Arms Reduction Talks). The USA condemned the attempted Moscow coup Aug 1991 which briefly removed Gorbachev, and backed efforts to restore him. Bush reacted to later developments with initial caution.

Bush followed US success in the Gulf War by convening a Middle East peace conference 1991. At home, the recession continued, and Bushs approval rating slumped.

Clinton Bill Clinton defeated Bush and independent Ross Perot in the 1992 presidential election. He campaigned on health-care reform, cautious state intervention in the economy, environmental protection, and defence of minority rights. In 1993, he won passage of his medium-term budget intended to reduce the federal budget deficit, of the North American Free Trade Agreement, and of wide-ranging anti-crime measures. A US-led offensive against forces of Somali warlord General Aidid was the subject of international criticism.

Republican gains Allegations about Clinton's involvement in irregular financial dealings of the 1980s (the Whitewater affair) became the subject of investigations from 1994. As 1994 progressed, there was increasing opposition to, and ultimately rejection of, health-care reform proposals. In the Nov 1994 midterm elections, both chambers of Congress were won by the Republicans. Newt Gingrich became House speaker and effective leader of the opposition.

Clinton versus the Republicans In 1995, the Republicans fought to secure passage of their manifesto, 'Contract with America', with an array of radical populist measures. Despite success in the lower chamber, many faced opposition in the Senate and by Clinton. In foreign policy, Clinton oversaw further progress in negotiations about Palestinian self-rule and brokered the Dayton peace agreement for Bosnia-Herzegovina.

Despite continuing allegations of personal and financial scandals, Clinton won re-election 1996 against Perot and Republican Bob Dole.

university institution of higher learning for those who have completed primary and secondary ◊education.

The first European university was Salerno in Italy, established in the 9th century, followed by Bologna, Paris, Oxford, and Cambridge in the 12th century, and Montpellier and Toulouse in the 13th century. The universities of Prague, Vienna, Heidelberg, and Cologne were established in the 14th century as well as many French universities including those at Avignon, Orléans, Cahors, Grenoble, Angers, and Orange. The universities of Aix, Dole, Poitiers, Caen, Nantes, Besançon, Bourges, and Bordeaux were established in the 15th century. St Andrews, the first Scottish university, was founded in 1411, and Trinity College, Dublin,

in 1591. In the UK, a number of universities were founded in the 19th and earlier 20th centuries mainly in the large cities. These became known as the 'redbrick' universities, as opposed to the ancient stone of Oxford and Cambridge. After World War II, many more universities were founded.

The USA has both state universities (funded by the individual states) and private universities. The oldest universities in the USA are all private: Harvard 1636, William and Mary 1693, Yale 1701, Pennsylvania 1741, and Princeton 1746.

Upington town in Transvaal, South Africa, 800 km/500 mi W of Pretoria. In Nov 1985 it was the scene of a demonstration against high rents that resulted in the death of a police officer and the subsequent arrest of 25 people. The 'Upington 25', as they came to be known, were later found guilty of murder under the law of common purpose. On appeal 1991, the death sentences were set aside and the prison sentences, for all but one of the original 25 people convicted, were reduced.

Urban eight popes, including:

Urban II *c.* 1042–1099. Pope 1088–99. He launched the First ◊Crusade at the Council of Clermont in France 1095.

Urban VIII Maffeo Barberini 1568–1644. Pope 1623–44. His policies during the ◊Thirty Years' War were designed more to maintain the balance of forces in Europe and prevent one side from dominating the papacy than to further the ◊Counter-Reformation. He extended the papal dominions and improved their defences. During his papacy, Galileo was summoned 1633 to recant the theories that the Vatican condemned as heretical.

Urquiza Justo José de 1801–1870. Argentine president 1854–60, regarded as the organizer of the Argentine nation. Governor of Entre Ríos from 1841, he set up a progressive administration. Supported by Brazil and Uruguay, he defeated the unpopular dictator Juan Manuel de ◊Rosas in the Battle of Caseros 1852. As president he fostered internal economic development and created the Argentine Confederation 1853 which united the country's provinces, but he failed to bring Buenos Aires into it.

Uruguay country in South America, on the Atlantic coast, bounded N by Brazil and W by Argentina.

history For early history, see ◊American Indian. The area was settled by both Spain 1624 and Portugal 1680, but Spain secured the whole in the 18th century. In 1814 Spanish rule was

European universities founded before 1500 *Universities originated as urban associations of teachers and students from the 11th century. Gradually they acquired legal identities and privileges to emerge as universities ('corporations'), beginning with Salerno, then Bologna, Paris, Montpellier, and Oxford, all in the 12th century. They trained men for the church, the law, and royal service.*

overthrown under the leadership of José Artigas, dictator until driven out by Brazil 1820. Disputed between Argentina and Brazil 1825–28, Uruguay declared its independence 1825, although it was not recognized by its neighbours until 1853.

The names of Uruguay's two main political parties, the liberal Colorado (the Reds) and the conservative Blanco (the Whites), are derived from the colours of the flags carried in the civil war 1836. The assumption of power by General Vinancia Flores 1865 led to a period of uninterrupted rule by the Colorado party until the next century, though civil war and revolutionary upheavals were frequent. After the civil war of 1896, the Colorados struck a deal with the Blancos that gave the latter control of six of the country's 18 departments. This political stability encouraged large-scale foreign investment in livestock farming and infrastructural development.

The rule of José Battle 1903–07 and 1911–15 brought peace and prosperity. Uruguay gained a reputation as a modern, democratic nation, Latin America's first welfare state.

From 1951 to 1966 there was a collective leadership called 'collegiate government', and then a new constitution was adopted and a single president elected, the Blanco candidate, Jorge Pacheco Areco. His presidency was marked by high inflation, labour unrest, and growing guerrilla activity by the ◊Tupamaros.

repressive regime In 1972 Pacheco was replaced by the Colorado candidate, Juan Maria Bordaberry Arocena. Within a year the Tupamaros had been crushed, and all other left-wing groups banned. Bordaberry now headed a repressive regime, under which the normal democratic institutions had been dissolved. In 1976 he refused any movement towards constitutional government, was deposed by the army, and Dr Aparicio Méndez Manfredini was made president. Despite promises to return to democratic government, the severe repression continued, and political opponents were imprisoned.

'Programme of National Accord' In 1981 the deteriorating economy made the army anxious to return to constitutional government, and a retired general, Gregorio Alvarez Armellino, was appointed president for an interim period. Discussions between the army and the main political parties failed to agree on the form of constitution to be adopted, and civil unrest, in the shape of strikes and demonstrations, grew. By 1984 antigovernment activity had reached a crisis point, and eventually all the main political leaders signed an agreement for a 'Programme of National Accord'. The 1966 constitution, with some modifications, was restored, and in 1985 a general election was held. The Colorado Party won a narrow majority, and its leader, Dr Julio Maria Sanguinetti, became president. The army stepped down, and by 1986 President Sanguinetti was presiding over a government of national accord in which all the main parties – Colorado, Blanco, and the left-wing Broad Front – were represented. In the Nov 1989 elections Luis Lacalle Herrera (Blanco), was narrowly elected president, with 37% of the vote compared with 30% for his Colorado opponent. After his inauguration in 1990, he concentrated his efforts on economic problems.

USSR abbreviation for the former ◊*Union of Soviet Socialist Republics*.

Ustaše or **Ustashi** Croatian nationalist terrorist organization founded 1929 and led by Ante Pavelić against the Yugoslav state. It was responsible for the murder of King Alexander of Yugoslavia in France in 1934 but came to prominence during World War II through collaboration with the Italian and German forces occupying Yugoslavia. It achieved some success in establishing a puppet Croatian state led by Pavelić under German tutelage, but carried out widespread atrocities against ethnic minorities in its territories. The state was destroyed by the Axis defeat in 1945 and Pavelić fled to South America where he died. The organization persisted underground during the communist period and some of its members re-emerged to play a role in the formation of a separate Croatian state after the collapse of Yugoslavia 1990–92.

usury former term for charging interest on a loan of money. In medieval times, usury was held to be a sin, and Christians were forbidden to lend (although not to borrow).

The practice of charging interest is still regarded as usury in some Muslim countries.

Under English law, usury remained forbidden until the 13th century, when trade and the need for credit was increased; for example, Jews were absolved from the ban on usury by the Fourth Lateran Council of 1215.

Utrecht, Treaty of treaty signed 1713 that ended the War of the ◊Spanish Succession. Philip V was recognized as the legitimate king of Spain, thus founding the Spanish branch of the Bourbon dynasty and ending the French king Louis XIV's attempts at expansion; the Netherlands, Milan, and Naples were ceded to Austria; Britain gained Gibraltar; the duchy of Savoy was granted Sicily.

Utrecht, Union of in 1579, the union of seven provinces of the N Netherlands – Holland, Zeeland, Friesland, Groningen, Utrecht, Gelderland, and Overijssel – that became the basis of opposition to the Spanish crown and the foundation of the present-day Dutch state.

Uzbekistan country in central Asia, bounded N by Kazakhstan and the Aral Sea, E by Kyrgyzstan and Tajikistan, S by Afghanistan, and W by Turkmenistan.

history The Turkmen are Turkic-speaking descendants of the Mongol invaders who swept across Asia from the 13th century. Part of Turkestan, Turkmenistan was conquered by Tsarist Russia 1865–76, with the emir of Bukhara becoming a vassal. The Tashkent soviet gradually extended its power 1917–24, with the emir of Bukhara deposed 1920. Uzbekistan became a constituent republic of the USSR 1925, although guerrilla resistance continued for a number of years. Some 160,000 ◊Meskhetian Turks were forcibly transported from their native Georgia to Uzbekistan by Stalin 1944. After World War II Uzbekistan became a major cotton-growing region, producing two-thirds of Soviet output. The Uzbek Communist Party (UCP) leadership, who controlled the republic like a feudal fief, were both notorious for the extent of their corruption and for their obedience to Moscow. In return, Uzbekistan received large subsidies.

growth of nationalism From the late 1980s there was an upsurge in Islamic consciousness provoking violent clashes with Meskhetian, Armenian, and Kyrgyz minority communities, particularly in the Ferghana Valley, which had become a hotbed for ◊Wahabi Islamic militancy. In Sept 1989 an Uzbek nationalist organization, the Birlik ('Unity') People's Movement, was formed. The UCP, under the leadership of Islam Karimov, responded by declaring the republic's 'sovereignty' in June 1990 and replacing Russian administrators with Uzbeks.

independence recognized President Karimov did not immediately condemn the Aug 1991 anti-Gorbachev attempted coup in Moscow. However, once the coup was defeated, the UCP broke its links with the Communist Party of the Soviet Union and on 31 Aug 1991 the republic declared its independence. Uzbekistan joined the new ◊Commonwealth of Independent States in Dec 1991. On 29 Dec Karimov was directly elected president, capturing 86% of the vote. Uzbekistan was admitted to the ◊Helsinki Conference on Security and Cooperation in Europe (CSCE) in Jan 1992. In Feb it also joined the Economic Cooperation Organization (ECO), founded by Iran, Pakistan, and Turkey 1975, which aimed to reduce customs tariffs and eventually form a customs union. Admission to the United Nations was granted March 1992; US diplomatic recognition was also achieved at this point.

President Karimov embarked on a strategy of gradualist market-centred economic reform.

However, political authoritarianism continued. Communist Party cells were banned from the armed forces, the police, and civil service and the UCP changed its designation. Nevertheless, the former UCP apparatus and personnel remained very much in control, with opposition groups either harassed or, in the case of the Islamic Renaissance Party, banned. A coalition of clergymen, led by the ◊mufti of Tashkent, called for fresh multiparty elections and an end to Communist Party activity. Ethnic Russians, formerly preponderant in the industrial workforce and bureaucracy, began to leave the republic, with adverse economic consequences. In Jan 1992 several people died in student-led food riots in Tashkent after prices had been liberalized. Aided by an inflow of funds from Saudi Arabia and despite the secularist stance of President Karimov, a revival of Islamic teaching and studies commenced.

V1, V2 (German *Vergeltungswaffe* 'revenge weapons') German flying bombs of World War II, launched against Britain in 1944 and 1945. The V1, also called the doodlebug and buzz bomb, was an uncrewed monoplane carrying a bomb, powered by a simple kind of jet engine called a pulse jet. The V2, a rocket bomb with a preset guidance system, was the first long-range ballistic ◊missile. It was 14 m/47 ft long, carried a 1-tonne warhead, and hit its target at a speed of 5,000 kph/3,000 mph.

Valdemar alternative spelling of ◊Waldemar, four kings of Denmark.

Valera Éamon de. Irish politician; see ◊de Valera.

Valle José Cecilio del 1776–1834. Central American Conservative politician. Valle was elected mayor of Guatemala city 1820 towards the end of Spanish colonial rule. To avert social revolution, he joined the provisional junta which took control of Central America 1821, and led its annexation into Agustin de ◊Iturbide's Mexican empire. When this fell 1824, he was elected first president of the Federation of Central America, but was denied the post on a technicality. He died as the votes that would have made him president were being counted.

Valley Forge site in Pennsylvania 32 km/20 mi NW of Philadelphia, USA, where George Washington's army spent the winter of 1777–78 in great hardship during the ◊American Revolution. Of the 10,000 men there, 2,500 died of disease and the rest suffered from lack of rations and other supplies; many deserted.

Valmy, Battle of battle in 1792 in which the army of the French Revolution under General ◊Dumouriez defeated the Prussians at a French village in the Marne *département*. See ◊Revolutionary Wars.

Valois branch of the Capetian dynasty, originally counts of Valois (see Hugh ◊Capet) in France, members of which occupied the French throne from Philip VI 1328 to Henry III 1589.

Van Buren Martin 1782–1862. Eighth president of the US 1837–41, a Democrat, who had helped establish the ◊Democratic Party. He was secretary of state 1829–31, minister to Britain 1831–33, vice president 1833–37, and president during the Panic of 1837, the worst US economic crisis until that time, caused by land speculation in the West. Refusing to intervene, he advocated the establishment of an independent treasury, one not linked to the federal government, worsening the depression and losing the 1840 election.

Vandal member of a Germanic people related to the ◊Goths. In the 5th century AD the Vandals invaded Roman Gaul and Spain, many settling in Andalusia (formerly Vandalitia) and others reaching N Africa 429. They sacked Rome 455 were defeated by Belisarius general of the emperor ◊Justinian, in the 6th century.

Van Diemen's Land former name (1642–1855) of Tasmania, Australia. It was named by Dutch navigator Abel Tasman after the governor general of the Dutch East Indies, Anthony van Diemen. The name Tasmania was used from the 1840s and became official 1855.

Vane Henry 1613–1662. English politician. In 1640 elected a member of the ◊Long Parliament, he was prominent in the impeachment of Archbishop ◊Laud and in 1643–53 was in effect the civilian head of the Parliamentary government. At the Restoration of the monarchy he was executed.

Vanuatu group of islands in the SW Pacific Ocean, part of Melanesia.

history Originally settled by Melanesians, the islands were reached from Europe 1606 by the Portuguese navigator Pedro Fernandez de Queiras. Called the New Hebrides, they were jointly administered by France and Britain from 1906. Vanuatu escaped Japanese occupation during World War II.

In the 1970s two political parties were formed, the New Hebrides National Party, supported by British interests, and the Union of New Hebrides Communities, supported by France. Discussions began in London about eventual independence, and they resulted in the election of a representative assembly Nov 1975. Independence was delayed because of objections by the National Party, which had changed its name to the Vanua'aku Party (VP). A government of national unity was formed Dec 1978 with Father Gerard Leymang as chief minister and the VP leader, Father Walter Lini, as his deputy. In 1980 a revolt by French settlers and plantation workers on the island of Espíritu Santo was put down by British, French, and Papua New Guinean troops.

independence Later in 1980 the New Hebrides became independent, within the Commonwealth, as the Republic of Vanuatu. The first president was George Kalkoa, who adopted the name Sokomanu, and the first prime minister was Father Lini.

Lini pursued a left-of-centre, nonaligned foreign policy, which included support for the Kanak separatist movement in New Caledonia. This soured relations with France and provoked mounting opposition within parliament. Despite the VP retaining its majority after the Nov 1987 general election, this opposition continued, prompting Lini in July 1988 to expel from parliament his rival Barak Sope. Lini was then dismissed as prime minister and parliament dissolved by President Sokomanu, who appointed his nephew Sope head of an interim government. However, the Supreme Court ruled these actions unconstitutional and security forces loyal to Lini arrested the president, Sope, and opposition leader Maxime Carlot and reinstated the former prime minister. Fred Timakata, formerly minister of health, was elected president in Jan 1989.

In Aug 1991 the VP voted to replace Lini as its leader, and thus as prime minister, with Donald Kalpokas, a former education and foreign minister and fellow founder of the party. The reason appeared to be opposition to Lini's autocratic leadership style. Lini initially refused to stand down. However, in Sept he agreed to do so, but expected to return as premier after the Nov 1991 general election.

coalition formed In the Dec 1991 general election none of the parties won an overall majority. The Union of Moderate Parties (UMP) and the Vanuatu National United Party (VNUP), formed by Lini, finally agreed to form a coalition government under Maxime Carlot on the understanding that Lini would not be a member of the new government.

role in Pacific region Externally, since independence, Vanuatu has sought to promote greater cooperation among the states of the Pacific region. As part of this strategy, along with Papua New Guinea and the Solomon Islands, it formed, in March 1988, the 'Spearhead Group', whose aim is to preserve Melanesian cultural tradition and campaign for New Caledonia's independence.

Varangian member of a widespread Swedish Viking people in E Europe and the Balkans; more particularly a member of the Byzantine imperial guard founded 988 by Vladimir of Kiev (955–1015), which lasted until the fall of Constantinople 1453.

From the late 11th century, the Byzantine guard included English and Norman mercenaries, as well as Scandinavians. It was feared and respected as an elite military force, and occasionally dabbled in politics.

Vargas Getúlio 1883–1954. President of Brazil 1930–45 and 1951–54. He overthrew the republic 1930 and in 1937 set up a totalitarian, pro-fascist state known as the *Estado Novo*. Ousted by a military coup 1945, he returned as president 1951 but, amid mounting opposition and political scandal, committed suicide 1954.

Vasa dynasty Swedish royal house founded by ◊Gustavus Vasa. He liberated his country from Danish rule 1520–23 and put down local uprisings of nobles and peasants. By 1544 he was secure enough to make his title hereditary. His grandson, ◊Gustavus Adolphus, became king 1611 and led the armies of the Protestant princes in the ◊Thirty Years' War until his death. The dynasty ended 1809 when Gustavus IV was deposed by a revolution and replaced by his uncle Charles XIII. With no heir to the throne, the crown was offered 1810 to one of Napoleon's generals, Bernadotte, who became King Charles John until his death in 1844.

vassal in medieval Europe, a person who paid feudal homage to a superior lord (see ◊feudalism), and who promised military service and advice in return for a grant of land. The term was used from the 9th century.

The relationship of vassalage was the mainstay of the feudal system and declined along with it during the transition to ◊bastard feudalism.

Vatican City State sovereign area within the city of Rome, Italy. The pope has traditionally been based in Rome, where the Vatican has been a papal residence since 1377.

The Vatican City State came into being through the Lateran Treaty of 1929, under which Italy recognized the sovereignty of the pope over the city of the Vatican. The 1947 Italian constitution reaffirmed the Lateran Treaty, and under its terms, Roman Catholicism became the state religion in Italy, enjoying special privileges. This remained so until, under a new 1984 Concordat (ratified 1985), Catholicism ceased to be the state religion.

Vendée, Wars of the in the French Revolution, a series of peasant uprisings against the

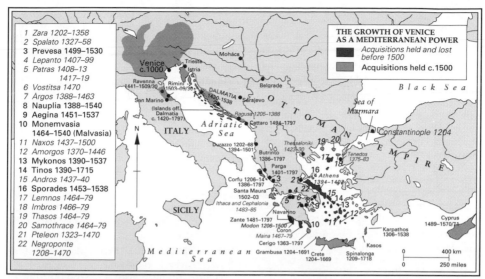

1 Zara 1202–1358
2 Spalato 1327–58
3 **Prevesa 1499–1530**
4 Lepanto 1407–99
5 Patras 1408–13
 1417–19
6 Vostitsa 1470
7 Argos 1388–1463
8 Nauplia 1388–1540
9 Aegina 1451–1537
10 Monemvasia
 1464–1540 (Malvasia)
11 Naxos 1437–1500
12 Amorgos 1370–1446
13 Mykonos 1390–1537
14 Tinos 1390–1715
15 Andros 1437–40
16 Sporades 1453–1538
17 Lemnos 1464–79
18 Imbros 1466–79
19 Thasos 1464–79
20 Samothrace 1464–79
21 Pteleon 1323–1470
22 Negroponte
 1208–1470

**THE GROWTH OF VENICE
AS A MEDITERRANEAN POWER**
Acquisitions held and lost
before 1500
Acquisitions held c.1500

The growth of Venice as a Mediterranean power The Venetian Republic reached its peak between the 12th and 15th centuries. The decline of the Byzantine Empire allowed enterprising Venetian merchants to establish trading ports and settlements along the Adriatic coast and in the Aegean Islands. Although some territories were gained in the 15th century, the city became increasingly involved in disputes with other Italian states and had to face new threats from the emerging Ottoman Empire, eventually leading to the loss of most colonies by the 16th century.

revolutionary government that began in the Vendée *département*, W France 1793, and spread to other areas of France, lasting until 1795.

Vendôme Louis Joseph, Duc de Vendôme 1654–1712. Marshal of France under Louis XIV, he lost his command after defeat by the British commander Marlborough at Oudenaarde, Belgium, 1708, but achieved successes in the 1710 Spanish campaign during the War of the ◊Spanish Succession.

Venezuela country in northern South America, on the Caribbean Sea, bounded E by Guyana, S by Brazil, and W by Colombia.

history For early history, see ◊American Indian. Columbus visited Venezuela 1498, and there was a Spanish settlement from 1520. In 1811 a rebellion against Spain began, led by Simón Bolívar, and Venezuela became independent 1830.

dictatorship Venezuela's first president, General José Antonio Páez, established 1830–48 the pattern of dictatorial rule. The claims of competing caudillos (military leaders) kept the country in a state of constant turmoil.

greater stability Venezuela adopted a new constitution 1961, and three years later Rómulo Betancourt became the first president to have served a full term of office. He was succeeded by Dr Raúl Leoni 1964 and by Dr Rafael

Caldera 1969. The latter did much to bring economic and political stability, although underground abductions and assassinations still occurred. In 1974 Carlos Andrés Pérez, of the Democratic Action Party (AD), became president, and stability increased. In 1979 Dr Luis Herrera, leader of the Social Christian Party (COPEI), was elected.

austerity policies Against a background of growing economic problems, the 1984 general election was contested by 20 parties and 13 presidential candidates. It was a bitterly fought campaign and resulted in the election of Dr Jaime Lusinchi as president and a win for the Democratic Action Party (AD) in with an absolute majority in congress. President Lusinchi's austere economic policies were unpopular, and he tried to conclude a social pact among the government, trade unions, and business. He reached an agreement with the government's creditor bankers for a rescheduling of Venezuela's large public debt.

In 1988 Venezuela suspended payment on its foreign debt, which had grown due to a drop in oil prices since the 1970s. In Feb 1989, newly elected president Carlos Andrés Pérez instituted price increases and other austerity measures designed to satisfy $4.3 billion loan terms imposed by the International Monetary Fund. Riots followed in which at least 300 people were killed. In May a general strike was declared to protest against the austerity programme. Elections held in Dec were boycotted by the main opposition groups.

At a meeting in Caracas in May 1991, the leaders of the Andean Common market countries agreed to create a Latin American free-trade zone.

Throughout 1990 and 1991 dissatisfaction with the austerity plan increased, resulting in more violent demonstations, especially by students. In Feb 1992 an attempted coup by a group of army officers was foiled by troops loyal to the president, who acted quickly to remove a number of senior commanders. Pressured by mounting public unrest, Pérez promised major constitutional reforms and approval by referendum.

Venice (Italian *Venezia*) city-port on the Adriatic coast of Italy. In 1991 archaeologist Ernesto Canal established that the city was founded by the Romans in the 1st century AD; it was previously thought to have been founded by mainlanders fleeing from the Barbarians in AD 421. Venice became a wealthy independent trading republic in the 10th century, stretching by the mid-15th century to the Alps and including Crete. It was governed by an aristocratic oligarchy, the Council of Ten, and a senate, which appointed the doge 697–1797. Venice helped defeat the Ottoman Empire in the naval battle of Lepanto 1571 but the republic was overthrown by Napoleon 1797. It passed to Austria 1815 but finally became part of the kingdom of Italy 1866.

Venizelos Eleutherios 1864–1936. Greek politician born in Crete, leader of the Cretan movement against Turkish rule until the union of the island with Greece in 1905. He later became prime minister of the Greek state on five occasions, 1910–15, 1917–20, 1924, 1928–32, and 1933, before being exiled to France in 1935.

Every enterprise that does not succeed is a mistake.

Eleutherios Venizelos

Vercingetorix Gallic chieftain. Leader of a revolt of all the tribes of Gaul against the Romans 52 BC; he lost, was captured, displayed in Julius Caesar's triumph 46 BC, and later executed. This ended the Gallic resistance to Roman rule.

Vernon Edward 1684–1757. English admiral who captured Portobello from the Spanish in the Caribbean in 1739, with a loss of only seven men.

Versailles city in N France, on the outskirts of Paris. It grew up around the palace of Louis XIV, built 1661–87 on the site of Louis XIII's hunting lodge, and became France's seat of government 1682–1789.

Versailles, Treaty of peace treaty after World War I between the Allies and Germany, signed 28 June 1919. It established the League of Nations. Germany surrendered Alsace-Lorraine to France, and large areas in the east to Poland, and made smaller cessions to Czechoslovakia, Lithuania, Belgium, and Denmark. The Rhineland was demilitarized, German rearmament was restricted, and Germany agreed to pay reparations for war damage. The treaty was never ratified by the USA, which made a separate peace with Germany and Austria 1921.

Verwoerd Hendrik (Frensch) 1901–1966. South African right-wing Nationalist Party politician, prime minister 1958–66. As minister of native affairs 1950–58, he was the chief promoter of apartheid legislation (segregation by race). He made the country a republic 1961. He was assassinated 1966.

An emperor should die standing.

Vespasian from Suetonius
Twelve Caesars

Vespasian (Titus Flavius Vespasianus) AD 9–79. Roman emperor from AD 69. Proclaimed emperor by his soldiers while he was campaigning in Palestine, he reorganized the eastern provinces, and was a capable administrator. He was responsible for the construction of the Colosseum in Rome, which was completed by his son ◊Titus.

Vespucci Amerigo 1454–1512. Florentine merchant. The Americas were named after him as a result of the widespread circulation of his accounts of his explorations. His accounts of the voyage 1499–1501 indicate that he had been to places he could not possibly have reached (the Pacific Ocean, British Columbia, Antarctica).

veto (Latin 'I forbid') exercise by a sovereign, branch of legislature, or other political power, of the right to prevent the enactment or operation of a law, or the taking of some course of action.

In the UK the sovereign has a right to refuse assent to any measure passed by Parliament, but this has not been exercised since the 18th century; the House of Lords also has a suspensory veto on all legislation except finance measures, but this is comparatively seldom exercised. In the USA, the president may veto legislation, but this can be overruled by a two-thirds majority in Congress. At the United Nations, members of the Security Council can exercise a veto on resolutions.

viceroy chief official representing a sovereign in a colony, dominion or province, as in many Spanish and Portuguese American colonies and as in the British administration of India.

Vichy government in World War II, the right-wing government of unoccupied France after the country's defeat by the Germans June 1940, named after the spa town of Vichy, France, where the national assembly was based under Prime Minister Pétain until the liberation 1944. *Vichy France* was that part of France not occupied by German troops until Nov 1942. Authoritarian and collaborationist, the Vichy regime cooperated with the Germans even after they had moved to the unoccupied zone Nov 1942. It imprisoned some 135,000 people, interned another 70,000, deported some 76,000 Jews, and sent 650,000 French workers to Germany.

Victor Emmanuel II 1820–1878. First king of united Italy from 1861. He became king of Sardinia on the abdication of his father Charles Albert 1849. In 1855 he allied Sardinia with France and the UK in the Crimean War. In 1859 in alliance with the French he defeated the Austrians and annexed Lombardy. By 1860 most of Italy had come under his rule, and in 1861 he was proclaimed king of Italy. In 1870 he made Rome his capital.

Victor Emmanuel III 1869–1947. King of Italy from the assassination of his father, Umberto I, 1900. He acquiesced in the Fascist regime of Mussolini from 1922 and, after the dictator's fall 1943, relinquished power to his son Umberto II, who cooperated with the Allies. Victor Emmanuel formally abdicated 1946.

Victoria 1819–1901. Queen of the UK from 1837, when she succeeded her uncle William IV, and empress of India from 1876. In 1840 she married Prince ◊Albert of Saxe-Coburg and Gotha. Her relations with her prime ministers ranged from the affectionate (Melbourne and Disraeli) to the stormy (Peel, Palmerston, and Gladstone). Her golden jubilee 1887 and diamond jubilee 1897 marked a waning of republican sentiment, which had developed with her withdrawal from public life on Albert's death 1861.

Only child of Edward, Duke of Kent, fourth son of George III, she was born 24 May 1819 at Kensington Palace, London. She and Albert had four sons and five daughters. After Albert's death 1861 she lived mainly in retirement. Nevertheless, she kept control of affairs, refusing the Prince of Wales (Edward VII) any active role.

Victory British battleship, 2,198 tonnes/2,164 tons, launched 1765, and now in dry dock in Portsmouth harbour, England. It was the flagship of Admiral Nelson at Trafalgar.

Vienna, Congress of international conference held 1814–15 that agreed the settlement of Europe after the Napoleonic Wars. National representatives included the Austrian foreign minister Metternich, Alexander I of Russia, the British foreign secretary Castlereagh and military commander Wellington, and the French politician Talleyrand.

Its final act created a kingdom of the Netherlands, a German confederation of 39 states, Lombardy-Venetia subject to Austria, and the kingdom of Poland. Monarchs were restored in Spain, Naples, Piedmont, Tuscany, and Modena; Louis XVIII was confirmed king of France.

Vietcong (Vietnamese 'Vietnamese communists') in the Vietnam War 1954–75, the members of the National Front for the Liberation of South Vietnam, founded 1960, who fought the South Vietnamese and US forces. The name was coined by the South Vietnamese government to differentiate these communist guerrillas from the ◊Vietminh.

Vietminh the Vietnam Independence League, founded 1941 to oppose the Japanese occupation of Indochina and later directed against the French colonial power. The Vietminh were instrumental in achieving Vietnamese independence through military victory at Dien Bien Phu 1954.

Vietnam country in SE Asia, on the South China Sea, bounded N by China and W by Cambodia and Laos.

The dominating force in Vietnam is the Communist Party. It is controlled by a politburo, and is prescribed a 'leading role' by the constitution.

history Originally settled by SE Asian hunters and agriculturalists, Vietnam was founded 208 BC in the Red River delta in the north, under Chinese overlordship. Under direct Chinese rule 111 BC–AD 939, it was thereafter at times nominally subject to China. It annexed land to the south and defeated the forces of Mongol emperor Kublai Khan 1288. European traders arrived in the 16th century. The country was united under one dynasty 1802.

France conquered Vietnam between 1858–84, and it joined Cambodia, Laos, and

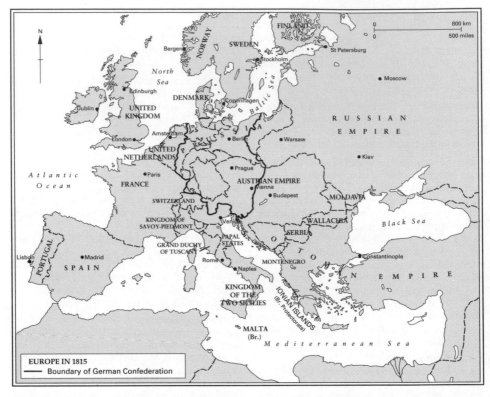

Europe in 1815 at the time of the Congress of Vienna *The victorious Allied powers, Austria, Prussia, Russia, and the United Kingdom, met in Vienna to reconstruct the continent after the final defeat of Napoleon 1815. Spain, Austria, and many of the Italian states were restored to their previous rulers and boundaries. The former Austrian Netherlands and United Provinces were amalgamated into the kingdom of the United Netherlands. Poland was divided between the Russian Empire and an enlarged Prussian state. The German states, including Austria and Prussia, were incorporated into a loose German Confederation.*

Annam as the French colonial possessions of Indochina. French Indochina was occupied by Japan 1940–45.

north/south division ◊Ho Chi Minh, who had built up the Vietminh (Independence) League, overthrew the Japanese-supported regime of Bao Dai, the former emperor of Annam, Sept 1945. French attempts to regain control and restore Bao Dai led to bitter fighting 1946–54, and final defeat of the French at Dien Bien Phu. At the 1954 Geneva Conference the country was divided along the 17th parallel of latitude into communist North Vietnam, led by Ho Chi Minh, with its capital at Hanoi, and pro-Western South Vietnam, led by Ngo Dinh Diem, with its capital at Saigon.

Vietnam War Within South Vietnam, the communist guerrilla National Liberation Front, or Vietcong, gained strength, being supplied with military aid by North Vietnam and China. The USA gave strong backing to the incumbent

government in South Vietnam and became, following the Aug 1964 ◊Tonkin Gulf incident, actively embroiled in the ◊Vietnam War. The years 1964–68 witnessed an escalation in US military involvement to 500,000 troops. From 1969, however, as a result of mounting casualties and domestic opposition, the USA gradually began to withdraw its forces and sue for peace. A cease-fire agreement was negotiated Jan 1973 but was breached by the North Vietnamese, who moved south, surrounding and capturing Saigon (renamed Ho Chi Minh City) in April 1975.

socialist republic The Socialist Republic of Vietnam was proclaimed July 1976, and a programme to integrate the south was launched. The new republic encountered considerable problems. The economy was in ruins, the two decades of civil war having claimed the lives of more than 2 million; it had maimed 4 million, left more than half the population homeless,

The Vietnam War 1945–75

1945	Japanese surrendered in French Indochina. Northern zone under Chinese control allowed establishment of Democratic Republic of Vietnam under Ho Chi Minh.
1946	French reoccupied southern zone but failed to defeat Vietminh forces under General Giap.
1948	Attempt to form alternative government under Bao Dai failed to halt civil war.
1953	Vietminh invaded Laos.
1954	French suffered colossal military defeat at Dien Bien Phu. Geneva Conference of foreign ministers agreed partition of Indochina into four states: Laos, Cambodia, North Vietnam, and South Vietnam.
1955	Bao Dai deposed and replaced by American-backed Ngo Dinh Diem, who used dictatorial methods and refused a referendum on government in South Vietnam.
1957	Insurgent Vietcong began an offensive against the south. US provided limited amounts of indirect aid.
1963	Military coup overthrew and killed Diem.
1964	Tonkin Gulf incident, when US destroyers were reportedly attacked by North Vietnamese, triggered US entry into the war.
1965 Jan	Major defeat of government forces at Binh-Gia, E of Saigon, by communists.
March	US began regular bombing of North Vietnam.
July	US began to send in combat troops.
1966	President Johnson increased numbers of US ground forces.
1967	US troops invaded the Demilitarized Zone (DMZ).
1968 Jan	Vietcong began Tet Offensive with attacks around Saigon, Hue, and Khe Sanh.
March	My Lai massacre by US troops.
May	Peace talks between US and North Vietnam began in Paris.
Nov	US bombing of North Vietnam halted.
1969 Jan	Paris peace talks included Vietcong/NLF and South Vietnam.
Sept	President Nixon announced phased withdrawal of 550,000 American troops in an attempt to 'Vietnamize' the war. Death of Ho Chi Minh, succeeded by Ton Duc Thang.
Nov–Dec	Widespread anti-Vietnam War demonstrations in US.
1970	Fighting extended to Cambodia in an attempt to eliminate communist bases. Government of Prince Sihanouk overthrown and a republic proclaimed.
1971	South Vietnamese forces moved into Laos with US air support, in a further bid to cut off communist supply lines. US broke off peace talks in Paris.
1972 March	Major North Vietnamese offensive only halted by US bombing campaign and shelling of North Vietnam. US ground forces did not participate.
1973 Jan	Ceasefire agreement and withdrawal of remaining US forces.
1973–74	South Vietnamese forces gradually overwhelmed.
1975	North Vietnamese captured Saigon (renamed Ho Chi Minh City).

and resulted in the destruction of 70% of the country's industrial capacity.

foreign relations In Dec 1978 Vietnam was at war again, toppling the pro-Chinese Khmer Rouge government in Kampuchea (now Cambodia) led by Pol Pot and installing a puppet administration led by Heng Samrin. A year later, in response to accusations of maltreatment of ethnic Chinese living in Vietnam, China mounted a brief, largely unsuccessful, punitive invasion of North Vietnam 17 Feb–16 March 1979. These actions, coupled with campaigns against private businesses in the south, induced the flight of about 700,000 Chinese and middle-class Vietnamese from the country 1978–79, often by sea (the 'boat people'). Economic and diplomatic relations with China were severed as Vietnam became closer to the USSR, being admitted into the East-bloc economic organization Comecon June 1978.

economic reform Despite considerable economic aid from the Eastern bloc, Vietnam did not reach its planned growth targets 1976–85. This forced policy adjustments 1979 and 1985. Further economic liberalization followed the death of Le Duan (1907–1986), effective leader since 1969, and the retirement of other prominent 'old guard' leaders 1986. Under the pragmatic lead of Nguyen Van Linh (1914–), a 'renovation' programme was launched. The private marketing of agricultural produce and formation of private businesses were now permitted, agricultural cooperatives were partially dismantled, foreign 'joint venture' inward investment was encouraged, and more than 10,000 political prisoners were released. Economic reform was most successful in the south. In general, however, the country faced a severe economic crisis from 1988, with inflation, famine conditions in rural areas, and rising urban unemployment inducing a further flight of 'boat people' refugees 1989–90, predominantly to Hong Kong; some of these were forcibly repatriated beginning Dec 1989.

Nguyen Van Linh resigned from his leadership of the Communist Party at the congress held June 1991 and Do Muoi, a supporter of Linh's policies, was elected the party's new general secretary. Vo Van Kiet, a leading advocate of capitalist-style reform, replaced him as prime minister Aug 1991.

improved foreign relations In 1989 Vietnam had withdrawn the last of its troops from Cambodia. The signing of the Cambodian peace agreement in Oct 1991 helped improve Vietnam's external image. Relations with China were normalized, after a 12-year breach, in Nov 1991, when Do Muoi and Vo Van Kiet paid a state visit to Beijing and signed a series of commercial and diplomatic agreements. Commercial links have also been established with members of the Association of South East Asian States. The US embargo on trade with and investment in Vietnam, imposed in 1975, remains in force, as does the veto on International Monetary Fund loans.

Vietnam War 1954–75. War between communist North Vietnam and US-backed South Vietnam. 200,000 South Vietnamese soldiers, 1 million North Vietnamese soldiers, and 500,000 civilians were killed. 56,555 US soldiers were killed 1961–75, a fifth of them by their own troops. The war destroyed 50% of the country's forest cover and 20% of agricultural land. Cambodia, a neutral neighbour, was bombed by the US 1969–75, with 1 million killed or wounded.

vigilante in US history, originally a member of a 'vigilance committee', a self-appointed group to maintain public order in the absence of organized authority, especially in Western frontier communities. The vigilante tradition continues with present-day urban groups patrolling streets and subways to deter muggers and rapists.

Vijayanagar the capital of the last extensive Hindu empire in India between the 14th and 17th centuries, situated on the river Tungabhadra, S India. The empire attained its peak under the warrior Krishna Deva Raya (reigned 1509–65), when the city had an estimated population of 500,000. Thereafter it came under repeated attack by the Deccani Muslim kingdoms of Ahmadnagar, Bijapur, and Golconda.

The empire was established by Harihara I (reigned 1336–57), a warrior chief from the Sangama dynasty, and was extended to the S

and NE by his brother Bukka (reigned 1344–77) and by Devaraya II (reigned 1422–46). The Sangama dynasty was overthrown 1485 by provincial governor Saluva Narasimha (reigned 1486–91), and the Saluvas were replaced by the Tiluvas *c.* 1505–65. The city was destroyed after defeat at the Battle of Talikota 1565.

Viking or *Norseman* medieval Scandinavian sea warrior. They traded with and raided Europe in the 8th–11th centuries, and often settled there. In France the Vikings were given Normandy. Under Sweyn I they conquered England 1013, and his son Canute was king of England as well as Denmark and Norway. In the east they established the first Russian state and founded ◊Novgorod. They reached the Byzantine Empire in the south, and in the west sailed the seas to Ireland, Iceland, Greenland, and North America; see ◊Eric the Red, Leif ◊Ericsson, ◊Vinland.

In their narrow, shallow-draught, highly manoeuvrable longships, the Vikings penetrated far inland along rivers. They plundered for gold and land, and the need for organized resistance accelerated the growth of the feudal system. In England and Ireland they were known as 'Danes'. They created settlements, for example in York, and greatly influenced the development of the English language. The Vikings had a sophisticated literary culture, and an organized system of government with an assembly (◊thing). As ◊'Normans' they achieved a second conquest of England 1066.

The Swedish *Varangians* were invited to settle differences among the Slav chieftains in Russia 862. The Varangians also formed the imperial guard in Constantinople.

vilayet administrative division of the Ottoman Empire under a law of 1864, with each vilayet, or province, controlled by a *vali*; some were subdivided into sanjaks. The vilayet system was an attempt by the Ottoman rulers to gain more power over the provinces, but many retained a large degree of autonomy.

villeinage system of serfdom that prevailed in Europe in the Middle Ages. A villein was a peasant who gave dues and services to his lord in exchange for land. In France until the 13th century, 'villeins' could refer to rural or urban non-nobles, but after this, it came to mean exclusively rural non-noble freemen. In Norman England, it referred to free peasants of relatively high status.

Their social position declined until, by the early 14th century, their personal and juridicial status was close to that of serfs. After the mid-14th century, as the effects of the Black Death

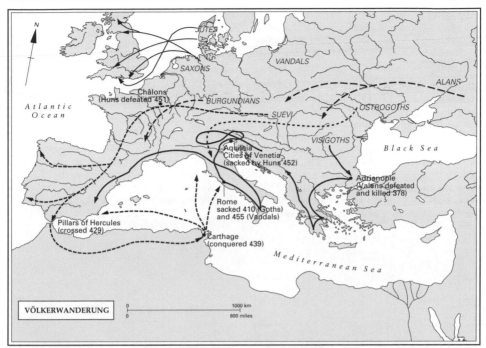

Völkerwanderung *The Germanic peoples originated in Scandinavia and present-day Schleswig. They moved south because of environmental changes, population pressures, and the temptations presented by the wealth of the Roman Empire. By the 1st century AD they covered most of Europe beyond the northeastern frontier of the Roman Empire. Between c. 370 and c. 570, the westward movement of the Huns caused further Germanic migration which the Romans were unable to contain. This led to pressure on Byzantine possessions and the collapse of the Western Empire.*

led to a severe labour shortage, their status improved. By the 15th century villeinage had been supplanted by a system of free tenure and labour in England, but it continued in France until 1789.

At the time of the Domesday Book, the villeins were the most numerous element in the English population, providing the labour force for the manors.

Vimy Ridge hill in N France, taken in World War I by Canadian troops during the battle of Arras, April 1917, at the cost of 11,285 lives. It is a spur of the ridge of Nôtre Dame de Lorette, 8 km/5 mi NE of Arras.

Vinland Norse name for the area of North America, probably the coast of Nova Scotia or New England, which the Norse adventurer and explorer Leif ◊Ericsson visited about 1000. It was named after the wild grapes that grew there and is celebrated in an important Norse saga.

Visconti dukes and rulers of Milan 1277–1447. They originated as north Italian feudal lords who attained dominance over the city as a result of alliance with the Holy Roman emperors. Despite papal opposition, by the mid-14th cen-

tury they ruled 15 other major towns in northern Italy. The duchy passed to the ◊Sforzas 1450, after a short-lived republic.

They had no formal title until Gian Galeazzo (1351–1402) bought the title of duke from Emperor Wenceslas IV (1361–1419). On the death of the last male Visconti, Filippo Maria 1447, the duchy was passed to the Sforzas 1450 after a short-lived republic.

Visigoth member of the western branch of the ◊Goths, an E Germanic people.

Vittorio Veneto town in Veneto, NE Italy. It was the site of the final victory of Italy and its allies over Austria Oct 1918.

Vladimir I St 956–1015 Russian saint, prince of Novgorod, and grand duke of Kiev. Converted to Christianity 988, he married Anna, Christian sister of the Byzantine emperor ◊Basil II, and established the Byzantine rite of Orthodox Christianity as the Russian national faith.

Völkerwanderung (German 'nations wandering') migration of peoples, usually with reference to the Slavic and Germanic movement in Europe in the 1st–11th centuries AD.

Volgograd formerly (until 1925) *Tsaritsyn* and (1925–61) *Stalingrad*, city in SW Russia, on the river Volga. Its successful defence 1942–43 against Germany was a turning point in World War II.

Voroshilov Klement Efremovich 1881–1969. Marshal of the USSR. He joined the Bolsheviks 1903 and was arrested many times and exiled, but escaped. He became a Red Army commander in the civil war 1918–20, a member of the central committee 1921, commissar for war 1925, member of the Politburo 1926, and marshal 1935. He was removed as war commissar 1940 after defeats on the Finland front and failing to raise the German siege of Leningrad. He was a member of the committee for defence 1941–44 and president of the Presidium of the USSR 1953–60.

Vorster Balthazar Johannes 1915–1983. South African Nationalist politician, prime minister 1966–78, and president 1978–79. During his term as prime minister some elements of apartheid were allowed to lapse, and attempts were made to improve relations with the outside world. He resigned the presidency because of a financial scandal.

Vyshinsky Andrei 1883–1954. Soviet politician. As commissar for justice, he acted as prosecutor at Stalin's treason trials 1936–38. He was foreign minister 1949–53 and often represented the USSR at the United Nations.

Wafd (Arabic 'deputation') the main Egyptian nationalist party between World Wars I and II. Under Nahas Pasha it formed a number of governments in the 1920s and 1930s. Dismissed by King Farouk in 1938, it was reinstated by the British 1941. The party's pro-British stance weakened its claim to lead the nationalist movement, and the party was again dismissed by Farouk 1952, shortly before his own deposition. Wafd was banned in Jan 1953.

Wagner Robert F(erdinand) 1877–1953. US Democratic senator 1927–49, a leading figure in the development of welfare provision in the USA, especially in the ◊New Deal era. He helped draft much new legislation, including the National Industrial Recovery Act 1933, the Social Security Act 1936, and the National Labor Relations Act 1935, known as the Wagner Act.

Wagram, Battle of battle July 1809 when French troops under Emperor Napoleon won an important victory over the Austrian army under Archduke Charles near the village of Wagram, NE of Vienna, Austria. The outcome forced Austria to concede general defeat to the French.

Wahabi puritanical Saudi Islamic sect founded by Muhammad ibn-Abd-al-Wahab (1703–1792), which regards all other sects as heretical. By the early 20th century it had spread throughout the Arabian peninsula; it still remains the official ideology of the Saudi Arabian kingdom.

Waitangi, Treaty of treaty negotiated in New Zealand 1840 between the British government and the indigenous Maoris. The treaty guaranteed Maoris their own territory and gave them British citizenship. The British claimed sovereignty over the territory and the treaty is seen as the establishment of modern New Zealand.

Wakefield West Yorkshire, England. The Lancastrians defeatd the Yorkists here 1460, during the Wars of the ◊Roses.

Wakefield Edward Gibbon 1796–1862. British colonial administrator. He was imprisoned 1826–29 for abducting an heiress, and became manager of the South Australian Association, which founded a colony 1836. He was an agent for the New Zealand Land Company 1839–46, and emigrated there in 1853. His son *Edward Jerningham Wakefield* (1820–1879) wrote *Adventure in New Zealand* 1845.

Walachia alternative spelling of ◊Wallachia, part of Romania.

Waldemar or *Valdemar* four kings of Denmark, including:

Waldemar I *the Great* 1131–1182. King of Denmark from 1157, who defeated rival claimants to the throne and overcame the ◊Wends on the Baltic island of Rügen 1169.

Waldemar II *the Conqueror* 1170–1241. King of Denmark from 1202. He was the second son of Waldemar I and succeeded his brother Canute VI. He gained control of land north of the river Elbe (which he later lost), as well as much of Estonia, and he completed the codification of Danish law.

Waldemar IV 1320–1375. King of Denmark from 1340, responsible for reuniting his country by capturing Skåne (S Sweden) and the island of Gotland 1361. However, the resulting conflict with the ◊Hanseatic League led to defeat by them, and in 1370 he was forced to submit to the Peace of Stralsund.

Waldheim Kurt 1918– . Austrian politician and diplomat, president 1986–92. He was secretary general of the United Nations 1972–81, having been Austria's representative there 1964–68 and 1970–71. He was elected president of Austria despite revelations that during World War II he had been an intelligence officer in an army unit responsible for transporting Jews to death camps. His election therefore led to some diplomatic isolation of Austria, and in 1991 he announced that he would not run for re-election.

Wales (Welsh *Cymru*) Principality of; constituent part of the United Kingdom, in the west between the British Channel and the Irish Sea.

history
c. 400 BC Wales occupied by Celts from central Europe.

AD 50–60 Wales became part of the Roman Empire.

c. 200 Christianity adopted.

c. 450–600 Wales became the chief Celtic stronghold in the west since the Saxons invaded and settled in S Britain. The Celtic tribes united against England.

8th century Frontier pushed back to Offa's Dyke.

9th–11th centuries Vikings raided the coasts. At this time Wales was divided into small states organized on a clan basis, although princes such as Rhodri (844–878), Howel the Good (*c.* 904–949), and Griffith ap Llewelyn (1039–1063) temporarily united the country.

11th–12th centuries Continual pressure on Wales from the Normans across the English border was resisted, notably by Llewelyn I and II.

1277 Edward I of England accepted as overlord by the Welsh.

1284 Edward I completed the conquest of Wales that had been begun by the Normans.

1294 Revolt against English rule put down by Edward I.

1350–1500 Welsh nationalist uprisings against the English; the most notable was that led by Owen Glendower.

1485 Henry Tudor, a Welshman, became Henry VII of England.

1536–43 Acts of Union united England and Wales after conquest under Henry VIII. Wales sent representatives to the English Parliament; English law was established in Wales; English became the official language.

18th century Evangelical revival made Nonconformism a powerful factor in Welsh life. A strong coal and iron industry developed in the south.

19th century The miners and ironworkers were militant supporters of Chartism, and Wales became a stronghold of trade unionism and socialism.

1893 University of Wales founded.

1920s–30s Wales suffered from industrial depression; unemployment reached 21% 1937, and a considerable exodus of population took place.

post-1945 Growing nationalist movement and a revival of the language, earlier suppressed or discouraged.

1966 Plaid Cymru, the Welsh National Party, returned its first member to Westminster.

1979 Referendum rejected a proposal for limited home rule.

1997 Referendum accepted a proposal for a separate Welsh assembly with limited powers.

For other history, see ◊United Kingdom.

Wałesa Lech 1943– . Polish trade-union leader and president of Poland 1990–95, founder of ◊Solidarity (Solidarność) in 1980, an organization, independent of the Communist Party, which forced substantial political and economic concessions from the Polish government 1980–81 until being outlawed. He was awarded the Nobel Prize for Peace 1983.

Wales, Church in the Welsh Anglican Church, independent from the ◊Church of England.

The Welsh church became strongly Protestant in the 16th century, but in the 17th and 18th centuries declined from being led by a succession of English-appointed bishops. It was disestablished by an act of Parliament 1920, with its endowments appropriated.

Walker William 1824–1860. US adventurer who for a short time established himself as president of a republic in NW Mexico, and was briefly president of Nicaragua 1856–57. He was eventually executed and is now regarded as a symbol of US imperialism in Central America.

Wallace George Corley 1919– . US politician who was opposed to integration; he was governor of Alabama 1963–67, 1971–79, and 1983–87. He contested the presidency in 1968 as an independent (the American Independent Party) and in 1972 campaigned for the Democratic nomination but was shot at a rally and became partly paralysed.

Wallace William 1272–1305. Scottish nationalist who led a revolt against English rule 1297, won a victory at Stirling, and assumed the title 'governor of Scotland'. Edward I defeated him at Falkirk 1298, and Wallace was captured and executed.

Wallachia independent medieval principality, founded 1290, with allegiance to Hungary until 1330 and under Turkish rule 1387–1861, when it was united with the neighbouring principality of Moldavia to form Romania.

Wallenstein Albrecht Eusebius Wenzel von 1583–1634. German general who, until his defeat at Lützen 1632, led the Habsburg armies in the Thirty Years' War. He was assassinated.

Wall Street crash 1929 (or *Stock Market Crash*) panic selling on the New York Stock Exchange following an artificial boom 1927–29 fed by speculation. On 24 Oct 1929, 13 million shares changed hands, with further heavy selling on 28 Oct and the disposal of 16 million shares on 29 Oct. Many shareholders were ruined, banks and businesses failed, and in the ◊Depression that followed, unemployment rose to approximately 17 million.

The repercussions of the Wall Street crash, experienced throughout the USA, were also felt in Europe, worsened by the reduction of US loans. A world economic crisis followed the crash, bringing an era of depression and unemployment.

Walpole Robert, 1st Earl of Orford 1676–1745. British Whig politician, the first 'prime minister' as First Lord of the Treasury and chancellor of the Exchequer 1715–17 and 1721–42. He encouraged trade and tried to avoid foreign disputes (until forced into the War of Jenkins's Ear with Spain 1739).

Opponents thought his foreign policies worked to the advantage of France. He held favour with George I and George II, struggling against ◊Jacobite intrigues, and received an earldom when he eventually retired 1742.

Walsingham Francis c. 1530–1590. English politician who, as secretary of state from 1573, both advocated a strong anti-Spanish policy and ran the efficient government spy system that made it work.

Walter Hubert died 1205. Archbishop of Canterbury 1193–1205. As justiciar (chief political and legal officer) 1193–98, he ruled England during Richard I's absence and introduced the offices of coroner and justice of the peace.

war act of force, usually on behalf of the state, intended to compel a declared enemy to obey the will of the other. The aim is to render the opponent incapable of further resistance by destroying its capability and will to bear arms in pursuit of its own aims. War is therefore a continuation of politics carried on with violent and destructive means, as an instrument of policy.

The estimated figure for loss of life in Third World wars since 1945 is 17 million.

Types of war include:

guerrilla war the waging of low-level conflict by irregular forces against an occupying army or against the rear of an enemy force. Examples include Mao Zedong's campaign against the Nationalist Chinese and T E Lawrence's Arab revolt against the Turks.

low-intensity conflict US term for its interventions in the Third World (stepped up in the 1980s), ranging from drug-running to funding and training guerrillas, and fought with political, economic, and cultural weapons as well as by military means.

civil war the waging of war by opposing parties, or members of different regions, within a state. The American Civil War 1861–65, the English Civil War of the 17th century, and the Spanish Civil War 1936–39 are notable examples.

limited war the concept that a war may be limited in both geographical extent and levels of force exerted and have aims that stop short of achieving the destruction of the enemy. The Korean War 1950–53 falls within this category.

total war the waging of war against both combatants and noncombatants, taking the view that no distinction should be made between them. The Spanish Civil War marked the beginning of this type of warfare, in which bombing from the air included both civilian and military targets.

Warbeck Perkin c. 1474–1499. Flemish pretender to the English throne. Claiming to be Richard, brother of Edward V, he led a rising against Henry VII in 1497, and was hanged after attempting to escape from the Tower of London.

war crime offence (such as murder of a civilian or a prisoner of war) that contravenes the internationally accepted laws governing the conduct of wars, particularly The Hague Convention 1907 and the Geneva Convention 1949. A key principle of the law relating to such crimes is that obedience to the orders of a superior is no defence. In practice, prosecutions are generally brought by the victorious side.

War crimes became a major issue in the aftermath of World War II. The United Nations War Crimes Commission was set up 1943 to investigate German atrocities against Allied nationals. Leading Nazis were tried in ◊Nuremberg 1945–46. High-ranking Japanese defendants were tried in the ◊Tokyo trials before the International Military Tribunal, and others by the legal section of the Allied supreme command.

warlord in China, any of the provincial leaders who took advantage of central government weakness, after the death of the first president of republican China 1912, to organize their own private armies and fiefdoms. They engaged in civil wars until the nationalist leader Chiang Kai-shek's Northern Expedition against them 1926, and they exerted power until the communists seized control under Mao Zedong 1949.

War of 1812 war between the USA and Britain caused by British interference with US trade (shipping) as part of the economic warfare against Napoleonic France. Tensions with the British in Canada led to plans for a US invasion but these were never realized and success was limited to the capture of Detroit and a few notable naval victories. In 1814, British forces occupied Washington DC and burned the

White House and the Capitol. A treaty signed in Ghent, Belgium, Dec 1814 ended the conflict.

US sailors were impressed from American ships, and a blockade was imposed on US shipping by Britain. In North America, British assistance was extended to Indians (such as ◊Tecumseh harassing the NW settlements. President Madison authorized the beginning of hostilities against the British on the high seas and in Canada; US forces failed twice in attempts to invade British-held Canada. After the peace treaty had been signed in Ghent, but before news of it reached the USA, American troops under Andrew ◊Jackson defeated the British at New Orleans 1815.

War Powers Act legislation passed 1973 enabling the US president to deploy US forces abroad for combat without prior Congressional approval. The president is nevertheless required to report to both Houses of Congress within 48 hours of having taken such action.

Warsaw (Polish *Warszawa*) capital of Poland, on the river Vistula. Founded in the 13th century, it replaced Kraków as capital 1595. Its university was founded 1818. Between the mid-nineteenth century and 1940, a third of the population were Jews. It was taken by the Germans 27 Sept 1939, and 250,000 Poles were killed during two months of street fighting that started 1 Aug 1944. It was finally liberated 17 Jan 1945. The old city was virtually destroyed in World War II but has been reconstructed.

Warsaw Pact or *Eastern European Mutual Assistance Pact* military alliance 1955–91 between the USSR and East European communist states, originally established as a response to the admission of West Germany into NATO. Its military structures and agreements were dismantled early in 1991; a political organization remained until the alliance was officially dissolved July 1991.

Warwick Richard Neville, Earl of Warwick 1428–1471. English politician, called *the Kingmaker*. During the Wars of the ◊Roses he fought at first on the Yorkist side against the Lancastrians, and was largely responsible for placing Edward IV on the throne. Having quarrelled with him, he restored Henry VI in 1470, but was defeated and killed by Edward at Barnet, Hertfordshire.

Washington George 1732–1799. First president of the USA 1789–97. As a strong opponent of the British government's policy, he sat in the ◊Continental Congresses of 1774 and 1775, and on the outbreak of the War of

◊American Independence was chosen commander in chief. After the war he retired to his Virginia estate, Mount Vernon, but in 1787 he re-entered politics as president of the Constitutional Convention.   He was elected president of the USA 1789 and re-elected 1793, but refused to serve a third term, setting a precedent that was followed until 1940. He scrupulously avoided overstepping the constitutional boundaries of presidential power. In his farewell address 1796, he maintained that the USA should avoid European quarrels and entangling alliances. He is buried at Mount Vernon.

There is nothing so likely to produce peace as to be well prepared to meet an enemy.

> **George Washington**,
> letter to Elbridge Gerry 1780

Washington DC (District of Columbia) national capital of the USA, on the Potomac River. The District of Columbia, initially land ceded from Maryland and Virginia, was established by Act of Congress 1790–91, and was first used as the seat of Congress 1800. The right to vote in national elections was not granted to residents until 1961. Local self-rule began 1975.

Watergate US political scandal, named after the building in Washington DC that housed the Democrats' campaign headquarters in the 1972 presidential election. Five men, hired by the Republican Committee to Re-elect the President (CREEP), were caught after breaking into the Watergate with complex electronic surveillance equipment. Investigations revealed that the White House was implicated in the break-in, and that there was a 'slush fund', used to finance unethical activities. In Aug 1974, President ◊Nixon was forced by the Supreme Court to surrender to Congress tape recordings of conversations he had held with administration officials, which indicated his complicity in a cover-up. Nixon resigned rather than face impeachment for obstruction of justice and other crimes.

Waterloo, Battle of battle on 18 June 1815 in which British forces commanded by Wellington defeated the French army of Emperor Napoleon near the village of Waterloo, 13 km/8 mi S of Brussels, Belgium. Napoleon found Wellington's army isolated from his allies and began a direct offensive to smash them, but the British held on until joined by the Prussians

N

NORWAY

North Sea

DENMARK

SWEDEN

FINLAND

Baltic Sea

ESTONIA

LATVIA

LITHUANIA

Kaliningrad (Königsberg)

WHITE RUSSIA

●Hamburg
Bremen
UK   Berlin●
WEST   EAST
GERMANY
(GDR)
●Cologne
Bonn● ●Frankfurt
FR.   *GERMANY*
FRANCE
FR.   USA
Munich●
SWITZ.

POLAND   Warsaw●   ●Brest-Litovsk

●Prague

CZECHOSLOVAKIA

UKRAINE

●Vienna
AUSTRIA
●Budapest
HUNGARY
●Zagreb

ROMANIA

ITALY

Adriatic Sea

Belgrade●

YUGOSLAVIA

BULGARIA

● Sofia

POST-WAR GERMANY AND CENTRAL EUROPE

- - - -   Pre-war boundary of Germany and
Poland

Post-war USSR

Warsaw Pact member-states 1955

Hatched areas show the German zones
occupied by the Allies (1945–55)

The three western zones constitute the
former Federal Republic, the Russian zone
being the German Democratic Republic (East)

Berlin remained under four-power occupation

ALBANIA

GREECE

0   400 km
0   250 miles

Warsaw Pact countries *The Soviet army controlled most of E Europe at the end of World War II. Its continuing presence, coupled with the activities of indigenous communist parties, led to communist takeovers in Poland, Czechoslovakia, Hungary, Romania, and Bulgaria in the years 1945–49. Austria and Yugoslavia were reconstituted as independent states and Germany was
divided between the four Allied powers, but economic and political differences between the USSR and the West led to the isolation of the Soviet zone and its establishment as a separate state, the German Democratic Republic (East Germany). In 1955 all
these states joined the Warsaw Pact, a security organization set up in opposition to NATO. Albania was also a member until its
ideological split from Soviet-style communism 1961. The Warsaw Pact and the communist regimes remained intact until the collapse of East Germany 1989–90 and the end of Soviet control in E Europe.*

under General Blücher. Four days later Napoleon abdicated for the second and final time.

Wellington had 68,000 soldiers (of whom 24,000 were British, the remainder being German, Dutch, and Belgian) and Napoleon had 72,000. The French casualties numbered about 37,000, the British 13,000, and the Prussians 7,000.

The next misfortune to losing a battle is to gain such a victory as this.

On the *Battle of Waterloo*
Duke of Wellington 1815

Wavell Archibald, 1st Earl 1883–1950. British field marshal in World War II. As commander in chief Middle East, he successfully defended Egypt against Italy July 1939. He was transferred as commander in chief India in July 1941, and was viceroy 1943–47.

Weimar Republic the constitutional republic in Germany 1919–33, which was crippled by the election of antidemocratic parties to the ◊Reichstag (parliament), and then subverted by the Nazi leader Hitler after his appointment as chancellor 1933. It took its name from the city where in Feb 1919 a constituent assembly met to draw up a democratic constitution.

Weizmann Chaim 1874–1952. Zionist leader, the first president of Israel (1948–52), and a chemist. He conducted the negotiations leading up to the Balfour Declaration, by which Britain declared its support for an independent Jewish state.

Born in Russia, he became a naturalized British subject, and as director of the Admiralty laboratories 1916–19 discovered a process for manufacturing acetone, a solvent. He became head of the Hebrew University in Jerusalem, then in 1948 became the first president of the new republic of Israel.

Welensky Roy 1907–1991. Rhodesian politician. He was instrumental in the creation of a federation of North Rhodesia (now Zambia), Southern Rhodesia (now Zimbabwe), and Nyasaland (now Malawi) in 1953 and was prime minister 1956–63, when the federation was disbanded. His Southern Rhodesian Federal Party was defeated by Ian Smith's Rhodesian Front in 1964. In 1965, following Smith's Rhodesian unilateral declaration of Southern Rhodesian independence from Britain, Welensky left politics.

welfare state political system under which the state (rather than the individual or the private sector) has responsibility for the welfare of its citizens. Services such as unemployment and sickness benefits, family allowances and income supplements, pensions, medical care, and education may be provided and financed through state insurance schemes and taxation.

Wellesley Richard Colley, Marquess of Wellesley 1760–1842. British administrator; brother of the Duke of Wellington. He was governor general of India 1798–1805, and by his victories over the Mahrattas of W India greatly extended the territory under British rule. He was foreign secretary 1809–12, and lord lieutenant of Ireland 1821–28 and 1833–34.

Wellington Arthur Wellesley, 1st Duke of Wellington 1769–1852. British soldier and Tory politician. As commander in the ◊Peninsular War, he expelled the French from Spain 1814. He defeated Napoleon Bonaparte at Quatre-Bras and Waterloo 1815, and was a member of the Congress of Vienna. As prime minister 1828–30, he was forced to concede Roman Catholic emancipation.

Wells, Fargo & Company transport organization for carrying goods in the US between New York and San Francisco, established by William George ◊Fargo, Henry Wells and associates in 1851.

Weltpolitik (German 'world politics') term applied to German foreign policy after about 1890, which represented Emperor Wilhelm II's attempt to make Germany into a world power through an aggressive foreign policy on colonies and naval building combined with an increase in nationalism at home.

Wends NW Slavonic peoples who settled east of the rivers Elbe and Saale in the 6th–8th centuries. By the 12th century most had been forcibly Christianized and absorbed by invading Germans; a few preserved their identity and survive as the Sorbs of Lusatia (E Germany/Poland).

Wentworth William Charles 1790–1872. Australian politician and newspaper publisher. In 1855 he was in Britain to steer the New South Wales constitution through Parliament, and campaigned for Australian federalism and self-government. He was the son of D'Arcy Wentworth (c. 1762–1827), surgeon of the penal settlement on Norfolk Island.

wergild or *wergeld* in Anglo-Saxon and Germanic law during the Middle Ages, the compensation paid by a murderer to the relatives of the victim, its value dependent on the

Welfare State: social reform in Britain

1597 and 1601	Elizabethan Poor Laws made parishes responsible for the poor, and allowed for 'indoor' relief (in the workhouse) and 'outdoor' relief (in the home).	1911	National Insurance Act established contributory scheme for workers in industries where unemployment was common, with payments to be made by employees, employers, and the government.
1691	Registration of recipients of poor relief introduced. Settlement Act allowed greater mobility for those seeking work.	1918	Ministry of Health established.
		1925	Widow's Pension Act provided contributory pensions for widows, orphans, and the elderly.
1722	'Knatchbull's Act' allowed for the creation of parish 'unions' to assist in the building of workhouses.	1929	Local Government Act transferred responsibility for the poor from Boards of Guardians to Public Assistance Committees of local authorities.
1795	Speenhamland system established by magistrates in Berkshire to create a sliding scale of relief to offset inflation problems during the French Revolutionary Wars.	1931	Introduction of 'means-tested' unemployment benefit.
1819	Poor Relief Act gave those paying for poor relief a greater say in its administration.	1942	Beveridge Report advocated system of comprehensive national insurance and welfare schemes.
1834	Poor Law Amendment Act attempted to create a uniform system of relief, overseen by three commissioners.	1944	White Papers on a National Health Service, employment policy, and social insurance paved the way for the welfare state.
1845	Lunacy Act empowered inspection of asylums and homes for the mentally ill.	1946	National Insurance Act established welfare state system.
1847	Poor Law Commission replaced by Poor Law Board directly responsible to government after a scandal at Andover workhouse.	1948	National Assistance Act removed remaining provisions of Poor Law and instituted cash payments for those in need.
1848	Public Health Act created local Boards of Health and Public Health Inspectorate.	1961	Graduated pension scheme introduced.
1872 and 1875	Public Health Acts dealt with sanitation, drainage, and water supply.	1967	Abortion Act.
		1971	Abolition of free school milk.
1906	Local authorities permitted to provide school meals.	1985	Reform of social security system.
		1986	Social Security Act modified provision of state benefits in favour of personal private schemes.
1909	Old age pensions introduced for those over 70.		

social rank of the deceased. It originated in European tribal society as a substitute for the blood feud (essentially a form of ◊vendetta), and was replaced by punishments imposed by courts of law during the 10th and 11th centuries.

Wesley John 1703–1791. English founder of ◊Methodism. When the pulpits of the Church of England were closed to him and his followers, he took the gospel to the people. For 50 years he rode about the country on horseback, preaching daily, largely in the open air. His sermons became the doctrinal standard of the Wesleyan Methodist Church.

Wessex the kingdom of the West Saxons in Britain, said to have been founded by Cerdic about AD 500, covering present-day Hampshire, Dorset, Wiltshire, Berkshire, Somerset, and Devon. In 829 Egbert established West Saxon supremacy over all England. Thomas Hardy used the term Wessex in his novels for the SW counties of England.

West, American the Great Plains region of the USA to the east of the Rocky Mountains from Canada to Mexico.

West Bank area (5,879 sq km/2,270 sq mi) on the west bank of the river Jordan. The West Bank was taken by the Jordanian army 1948 at the end of the Arab–Israeli war that followed the creation of the state of Israel, and was captured by Israel during the Six-Day War 5–10 June 1967. The continuing Israeli occupation and settlement of the area has created tensions with the Arab population.

In 1988 King Hussein announced that Jordan was cutting 'legal and administrative ties' with the West Bank, leaving responsibility for Arabs in the region to the ◊Palestine Liberation Organization (which was already the position in practice).

Western European Union (WEU) organization established 1955 as a consultative forum for military issues among the W European governments: Belgium, France, the Nether-

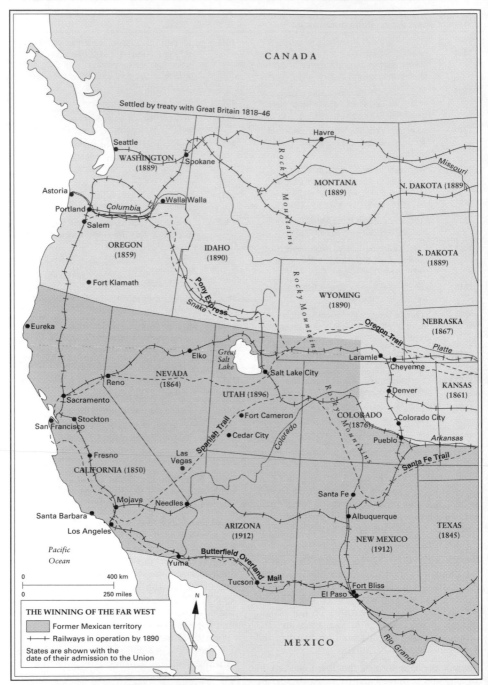

American West: the winning of the far west *During the second half of the 19th century Mexican territory from Texas to California was incorporated as new states of the USA, and the far west from Canada to Mexico was opened up to settlement. The extension of the transcontinental railway to the Pacific coast from 1869 was of vital importance in the economic development of the far west.*

lands, Italy, Luxembourg, the UK, Germany, and (from 1988) Spain and Portugal.

Western Front battle zone in World War I between Germany and its enemies France and Britain, extending as lines of trenches from Nieuport on the Belgian coast through Ypres, Arras, Albert, Soissons, and Rheims to Verdun, constructed by both Germany and the Allies.

For over three years neither side advanced far from their defensive positions. During the period of trench warfare there were a number of significant changes. Poison gas was used by Germany at Ypres, Belgium April 1915 and tanks were employed by Britain on the River Somme in Sept 1916. A German offensive in the spring of 1918 enabled the troops to reach the Marne River. By summer the Allies were advancing all along the front and the Germans were driven back into Belgium.

Western Jin or *Western Ch'in* in Chinese history, the period 265–316 when the Wei dynasty established its pre-eminence and united the country. The Western Jin falls in the ◊Three Kingdoms era.

Western Sahara formerly *Spanish Sahara* disputed territory in NW Africa bounded to the N by Morocco, to the W and S by Mauritania, and to the E by the Atlantic Ocean.

This 1,000-km-long Saharan coastal region was designated a Spanish 'sphere of influence' 1884 because it lies opposite the Spanish-ruled Canary Islands. On securing its independence 1956, Morocco laid claim to and invaded this 'Spanish Sahara' territory, but was repulsed. Moroccan interest was rekindled from 1965, following the discovery of rich phosphate resources at Bou-Craa, and with in Spanish Sahara a pro-independence nationalist movement developed, spearheaded by the Popular Front for the Liberation of Saguia al Hamra and Rio de Oro (Polisario), established 1973.

partition After the death of the Spanish ruler General Franco, Spain withdrew and the territory was partitioned between Morocco and Mauritania. Polisario rejected this partition, declared their own independent Saharan Arab Democratic Republic (SADR), and proceeded to wage a guerrilla war, securing indirect support from Algeria and, later, Libya. By 1979 they had succeeded in their struggle against Mauritania, which withdrew from their southern sector and concluded a peace agreement with Polisario, and in 1982 the SADR was accepted as a full member of the ◊Organization of African Unity. By the end of 1990, 70 coun-

American West	
1250	An unidentified epidemic weakened the American Indian civilization.
1550	Horses were introduced by the Spanish. Francisco Coronado made his expedition into the southwest.
1775	Wilderness Road was opened by Daniel Boone.
1804	Meriwether Lewis and William Clark explored the Louisiana Purchase lands for President Jefferson.
1805	Zebulon Pike (after whom Pikes Peak was named) explored the Mississippi.
1819	Major Stephen Long, a US government topographical engineer, explored the Great Plains.
1822	The Santa Fe Trail was established.
1824	The Great Salt Lake was discovered by Jim Bridger, 'mountain man', trapper, and guide.
1836	Davy Crockett and other Texans were defeated by Mexicans at the Battle of the Alamo.
1840–60	The Oregon Trail was in use.
1846	The Mormon trek was made to Utah under Brigham Young.
1846–48	The Mexican War.
1849–56	The California gold rush.
1860	The Pony Express (St Joseph, Missouri–San Francisco, California) was in operation 3 April–22 Oct; it was superseded by the telegraph.
1863	On 1 Jan the first homestead was filed; this was followed by the settlement of the Western Prairies and Great Plains.
1865–90	Wars were fought against the Indians, accompanied by the rapid extermination of the buffalo, upon which much of Great Plains and Indian life depended.
1867–80s	Period of the 'cattle kingdom', and cow trails such as the Chisholm Trail from Texas to the railheads at Abilene, Wichita, and Dodge City.
1869	The first transcontinental railroad was completed by Central Pacific company, building eastward from Sacramento, California, and Union Pacific company, building westward from Omaha, Nebraska.
1876	The Battle of Little Bighorn fought between General Custer and Plains Indians.
1890	The Battle of Wounded Knee; official census declaration that the West no longer had a frontier line.

tries had granted diplomatic recognition to the SADR.

defensive wall Morocco, which occupied the Mauritanian-evacuated zone, still retained control over the bulk of the territory, including the key towns and phosphate mines, which they protected with an 'electronic defensive wall' 4,000 km/2,500 mi long, completed 1987.

EUROPE
(TREATY OF WESTPHALIA 1648)

Brandenburg-Prussia
Austrian Habsburg
Spanish Habsburg
Swedish possessions
Venetian possessions
Ottoman Empire
Boundary of the
Holy Roman Empire

RUSSIA

POLAND

Kiev

UKRAINE

CRIMEA

MOLDAVIA

TRANSYLVANIA

WALLACHIA

Black Sea

Budapest

HUNGARY

Belgrade

MONTENEGRO

OTTOMAN EMPIRE

Constantinople

Crete

Ionian Islands

Mediterranean Sea

ESTONIA

LIVONIA

Königsberg
Duchy of
Prussia

Warsaw

Stockholm

Baltic
Sea

S W E D E N

N O R W A Y

Copenhagen

DENMARK

North
Sea

MORAVIA

Vienna

AUSTRIA

BOHEMIA

STYRIA

CARINTHIA

CARNIOLA

VENETIAN REPUBLIC

PAPAL
STATES

Rome

Naples

KINGDOM OF THE
TWO SICILIES

Palermo

SILESIA

POMERANIA

BRANDENBURG

Hamburg

Bremen

SAXONY

BAVARIA

TYROL

MILAN

Genoa

Corsica

Sardinia

Münster

WEST-
PHALIA

Heidelberg

PALATINATE

Amsterdam

Antwerp

UNITED
PROVINCES

SPANISH
NETHERLANDS

SWITZERLAND

Geneva

SAVOY

PIEDMONT

Paris

F R A N C E

SCOTLAND

Edinburgh

ENGLAND

London

IRELAND

Atlantic
Ocean

PORTUGAL

Madrid

S P A I N

800 km

500 miles

N

0

0

From the mid-1980s this wall was gradually extended outwards as Libya and Algeria reduced their support for Polisario and drew closer to Morocco. In 1988, Morocco and the Polisario Front agreed to United Nations-sponsored plans for a cease-fire and a referendum in Western Sahara, based on 1974 voting rolls, to decide the territory's future. However, subsequent divisions over the terms of the referendum resulted in continued fighting.

Western Samoa see ◊Samoa, Western.

West Indies, Federation of the federal union 1958–62 comprising Antigua, Barbados, Dominica, Grenada, Jamaica, Montserrat, St Christopher (St Kitts)–Nevis and Anguilla, St Lucia, St Vincent, and Trinidad and Tobago. This federation came to an end when first Jamaica and then Trinidad and Tobago withdrew.

West Pakistan a province of ◊Pakistan.

Westphalia independent medieval duchy, incorporated in Prussia by the Congress of Vienna 1815, and made a province 1816 with Münster as its capital. Since 1946 it has been part of the German *Land* (region) of North Rhine-Westphalia.

Westphalia included the Ruhr, the chief industrial area of Germany, and was the scene of violent fighting during the last stages of World War II. The kingdom of Westphalia, created by the French emperor Napoleon 1807–13, did not include the duchy, but was made up of Prussian lands W of the Elbe, Hessen, Brunswick, and Hanover.

Westphalia, Treaty of agreement 1648 ending the ◊Thirty Years' War. The peace marked the end of the supremacy of the Holy Roman Empire and the emergence of France as a dominant power. It recognized the sovereignty of the German states, Switzerland, and the Netherlands; Lutherans, Calvinists, and Roman Catholics were given equal rights.

Weygand Maxime 1867–1965. French general. In 1940, as French commander in chief, he advised surrender to Germany, and was subsequently high commissioner of N Africa 1940–41. He was a prisoner in Germany 1942–45, and was arrested after his return to France; he was released 1946, and in 1949 the sentence of national infamy was quashed.

Whig Party in the UK, predecessor of the Liberal Party. The name was first used of rebel ◊Covenanters and then of those who wished to exclude James II from the English succession (as a Roman Catholic). They were in power continuously 1714–60 and pressed for industrial and commercial development, a vigorous foreign policy, and religious toleration. During the French Revolution, the Whigs demanded parliamentary reform in Britain, and from the passing of the Reform Bill in 1832 became known as Liberals.

Whig Party in the USA, political party opposed to the autocratic presidency of Andrew Jackson from 1834. The Whig presidents were W H Harrison, Taylor, and Fillmore. The party diverged over the issue of slavery: the Northern Whigs joined the Republican party and the Southern or 'Cotton' Whigs joined the Democrats. The title was taken from the British Whig Party which supported Parliament against the king. During the American Revolution, colonial patriots described themselves as Whigs, while those remaining loyal to Britain were known as Tories.

Whitby, Synod of council summoned by King Oswy of Northumbria 664, which decided to adopt the Roman rather than the Celtic form of Christianity for Britain.

White counter-revolutionary, especially during the Russian civil wars 1917–21. Originally the term described the party opposing the French Revolution, when the royalists used the white lily of the French monarchy as their badge.

White Byron Raymond 1917– . US jurist. He worked to elect John F Kennedy to the presidency 1960 and was appointed by him as associate justice of the Supreme Court 1962– . He was a moderate conservative, usually dissenting on the rights of criminals, but upholding the right of accused citizens to trial by jury.

Born in Fort Collins, Colorado, USA, White graduated from the University of Colorado 1938. He studied at Oxford University, UK, as a Rhodes scholar 1939 and entered Yale Law

---

Europe at the Treaty of Westphalia 1648 Thirty years of war in Europe were brought to an end by the Treaty of Westphalia 1648. The war had been started by the attempts of the Holy Roman emperor Ferdinand II to reimpose Catholicism throughout the empire. After initial successes in Bohemia and the Palatinate he was opposed 1625 by a Protestant League of England, the United Provinces, and Denmark. They were joined by Sweden 1630. A series of major, non-decisive battles followed, including Lützen 1632, where the Swedish king Gustavus Adolphus was killed. After five years of negotiations at Osnabrück, the treaty was signed, recognizing three religions: Catholicism, Lutheranism, and Calvinism. There was to be no further persecution on the grounds of religious faith. Sweden and France gained some territory under the settlement and the independence of Switzerland and the United Provinces was universally recognized. Within the Holy Roman Empire individual states obtained a greater degree of freedom from the emperor.

School 1940. He graduated from Yale 1946 after service with the US navy in World War II. He served as deputy attorney general 1961–62, before being appointed to the Supreme Court. He served as law clerk 1946–47 to Supreme Court associate justice Fred M Vinson.

White Australia Policy Australian government policy of immigration restriction, mainly aimed at non-Europeans, which began in the 1850s in an attempt to limit the number of Chinese entering the Australian goldfields and was official until 1945.

White terror general term used by socialists and Marxists to describe a right-wing counterrevolution: for example, the attempts by the Chinese Guomindang to massacre the communists 1927–31; see ◊White.

Whitlam Gough (Edward) 1916– . Australian politician, leader of the Labor Party 1967–78 and prime minister 1972–75. He cultivated closer relations with Asia, attempted redistribution of wealth, and raised loans to increase national ownership of industry and resources.

When the opposition blocked finance bills in the Senate, following a crisis of confidence, Whitlam refused to call a general election, and was dismissed by the governor general (Sir John Kerr). He was defeated in the subsequent general election by Malcolm ◊Fraser.

Wilberforce William 1759–1833. English reformer who was instrumental in abolishing slavery in the British Empire. He entered Parliament 1780; in 1807 his bill for the abolition of the slave trade was passed, and in 1833, largely through his efforts, slavery was abolished throughout the empire.

Wilkes John 1727–1797. British Radical politician, imprisoned for his political views; member of Parliament 1757–64 and from 1774. He championed parliamentary reform, religious toleration, and US independence.

Willem Dutch form of ◊William.

William four kings of England:

William I *the Conqueror* c. 1027–1087. King of England from 1066. He was the illegitimate son of Robert I the Magnificent and succeeded his father as duke of Normandy 1035. Claiming that his relative King Edward the Confessor had bequeathed him the English throne, William invaded the country 1066, defeating ◊Harold II at Hastings, Sussex, and was crowned king of England.

He was crowned in Westminster Abbey on Christmas Day 1066. He completed the establishment of feudalism in England, compiling detailed records of land and property in the Domesday Book, and kept he barons firmly under control. He died in Rouen after a fall from his horse and is buried in Caen, France. He was succeeded by his son William II.

William II *Rufus, the Red* c. 1056–1100. King of England from 1087, the third son of William I. He spent most of his reign attempting to capture Normandy from his brother ◊Robert II, duke of Normandy. His extortion of money led his barons to revolt and caused confrontation with Bishop Anselm. He was killed while hunting in the New Forest, Hampshire, and was succeeded by his brother Henry I.

William III *William of Orange* 1650–1702. King of Great Britain and Ireland from 1688, the son of William II of Orange and Mary, daughter of Charles I. He was offered the English crown by the parliamentary opposition to James II. He invaded England 1688 and in 1689 became joint sovereign with his wife, ◊Mary II. He spent much of his reign campaigning, first in Ireland, where he defeated James II at the battle of the Boyne 1690, and later against the French in Flanders. He was succeeded by Mary's sister, Anne.

Born in the Netherlands, William was made *stadtholder* (chief magistrate) 1672 to resist the French invasion. He forced Louis XIV to make peace 1678 and then concentrated on building up a European alliance against France. In 1677 he married his cousin Mary, daughter of the future James II. When invited by both Whig and Tory leaders to take the crown from James, he landed with a large force at Torbay, Devon. James fled to France, and his Scottish and Irish supporters were defeated at the battles of Dunkeld 1689 and the Boyne 1690.

William IV 1765–1837. King of Great Britain and Ireland from 1830, when he succeeded his brother George IV; third son of George III. He was created duke of Clarence 1789, and married Adelaide of Saxe-Meiningen (1792–1849) 1818. During the Reform Bill crisis he secured its passage by agreeing to create new peers to overcome the hostile majority in the House of Lords. He was succeeded by Victoria.

William two emperors of Germany:

William I 1797–1888. King of Prussia from 1861 and emperor of Germany from 1871; the son of Frederick William III. He served in the Napoleonic Wars 1814–15 and helped to crush the 1848 revolution. After he succeeded his brother Frederick William IV to the throne of Prussia, his policy was largely dictated by his chancellor ◊Bismarck, who secured his proclamation as emperor.

William II 1859–1941. Emperor of Germany from 1888, the son of Frederick III and Victoria, daughter of Queen Victoria of Britain. In 1890 he forced Chancellor Bismarck to resign and began to direct foreign policy himself, which proved disastrous. He encouraged warlike policies and built up the German navy. In 1914 he first approved Austria's ultimatum to Serbia and then, when he realized war was inevitable, tried in vain to prevent it. In 1918 he fled to Holland, after Germany's defeat and his abdication.

William three kings of the Netherlands:

William I 1772–1844. King of the Netherlands 1815–40. He lived in exile during the French occupation 1795–1813 and fought against the emperor Napoleon at Jena and Wagram. The Austrian Netherlands were added to his kingdom by the Allies 1815, but secured independence (recognized by the major European states 1839) by the revolution of 1830. William's unpopularity led to his abdication 1840.

William II 1792–1849. King of the Netherlands 1840–49, son of William I. He served with the British army in the Peninsular War and at Waterloo. In 1848 he averted revolution by conceding a liberal constitution.

William III 1817–1890. King of the Netherlands 1849–90, the son of William II. In 1862 he abolished slavery in the Dutch East Indies.

William *the Lion* 1143–1214. King of Scotland from 1165. He was captured by Henry II while invading England 1174, and forced to do homage, but Richard I abandoned the English claim to suzerainty for a money payment 1189. In 1209 William was forced by King John to renounce his claim to Northumberland.

William *the Silent* 1533–1584. Prince of Orange from 1544. Leading a revolt against Spanish rule in the Netherlands from 1573, he briefly succeeded in uniting the Catholic south and Protestant northern provinces, but the former provinces submitted to Spain while the latter formed a federation 1579 (Union of Utrecht) which repudiated Spanish suzerainty 1581.

William, brought up at the court of Charles V, was appointed governor of Holland by Philip II of Spain 1559, but joined the revolt of 1572 against Spain's oppressive rule and, as a Protestant from 1573, became the national leader and first ◊stadholder. He was known as 'the Silent' because of his absolute discretion. He was assassinated by a Spanish agent.

Williams Roger *c.* 1603–1683. American colonist, founder of the Rhode Island colony 1636, based on democracy and complete religious freedom. He tried to maintain good relations with the Indians of the region, although he fought against them in the Pequot War and King Philip's War.

William the Marshal 1st Earl of Pembroke *c.* 1146–1219. English knight, regent of England from 1216. After supporting the dying Henry II against Richard (later Richard I), he went on a crusade to Palestine, was pardoned by Richard, and was granted an earldom 1189. On King John's death he was appointed guardian of the future Henry III, and defeated the French under Louis VIII to enable Henry to gain the throne.

Wilson (James) Harold, Baron Wilson of Rievaulx 1916–95. British Labour politician, party leader from 1963, prime minister 1964–70 and 1974–76. His premiership was dominated by the issue of UK admission to membership of the European Community, the social contract (unofficial agreement with the trade unions), and economic difficulties.

Wilson (Thomas) Woodrow 1856–1924. 28th president of the USA 1913–21, a Democrat. He kept the USA out of World War I until 1917, and in Jan 1918 issued his 'Fourteen Points' as a basis for a just peace settlement. At the peace conference in Paris he secured the inclusion of the ◊League of Nations in individual peace treaties, but these were not ratified by Congress, so the USA did not join the League. Nobel Peace Prize 1919.

The world must be made safe for democracy.

Woodrow Wilson speech in 1917

Windsor, House of official name of the British royal family since 1917, adopted in place of Saxe-Coburg-Gotha. Since 1960 those descendants of Elizabeth II not entitled to the prefix HRH (His/Her Royal Highness) have borne the surname Mountbatten-Windsor.

Wingate Orde Charles 1903–1944. British soldier. In 1936 he established a reputation for unorthodox tactics in Palestine. In World War II he served in the Middle East, and later led the Chindits, the 3rd Indian Division, in guerrilla operations against the Japanese army in Burma (now Myanmar).

Winter King, the name given to ◊Frederick V (1596–1632) because he was king of Bohemia for one winter (1619–20).

winter of discontent the winter of 1978–79 in Britain, marked by a series of strikes that contributed to the defeat of the Labour government in the general election of spring 1979. The phrase is from Shakespeare's *Richard III*: 'Now is the winter of our discontent/Made glorious summer by this sun of York.'

Winter War the USSR's invasion of Finland 30 Nov 1939–12 March 1940, also called the Russo-Finnish War.

The USSR set up a Finnish puppet government in E Karelia, but their invasion forces were at first repulsed by the greatly outnumbered Finnish troops under Marshal Mannerheim. In Feb 1940 the Finnish lines were broken by a million-strong Soviet offensive. In the March armistice Finland ceded part of Karelia to the USSR.

Winthrop John 1588–1649. American colonist and first governor of the Massachusetts Bay Colony. A devout Puritan and one of the founders of the Massachusetts Bay Company 1620 and served as Massachusetts governor or deputy governor until his death. He departed for New England with a large group of settlers 1630. He was a founder of the city of Boston the same year.

Witan or *Witenagemot* council of the Anglo-Saxon kings, the forerunner of Parliament, but including only royal household officials, great landowners, and top churchmen.

Witt Johann de 1625–1672. Dutch politician, grand pensionary of Holland and virtual prime minister from 1653. His skilful diplomacy ended the Dutch Wars of 1652–54 and 1665–67, and in 1668 he formed a triple alliance with England and Sweden against Louis XIV of France. He was murdered by a rioting mob.

Wittelsbach Bavarian dynasty, who ruled Bavaria as dukes from 1180, electors from 1623, and kings 1806–1918.

Wolfe James 1727–1759. British soldier who served in Canada and commanded a victorious expedition against the French general Montcalm in Québec on the Plains of Abraham, during which both commanders were killed. The British victory established their supremacy over Canada.

Wolsey Thomas *c.* 1475–1530. English cleric and politician. In Henry VIII's service from 1509, he became archbishop of York 1514, cardinal and lord chancellor 1515, and began the dissolution of the monasteries. His reluctance to further Henry's divorce from Catherine of Aragon, partly because of his ambition to be

Women's movement: UK	
1562	The Statute of Artificers made it illegal to employ men or women in a trade before they had served seven years' apprenticeship. (It was never strictly enforced for women, as many guilds still allowed members to employ their wives and daughters in workshops.)
1753	Lord Hardwick's Marriage Act brought marriage under state control and created a firmer distinction between the married and unmarried.
1803	Abortion was made illegal.
1836	Marriage Act reform permitted civil weddings and enforced the official registration of births, deaths, and marriages.
1839	The Custody of Infants Act allowed mothers to have custody of their children under seven years old.
1840s	A series of factory acts limited the working day and occupations of women and children. A bastardy amendment put all the responsibility for the maintenance of an illegitimate child onto its mother.
1857	The Marriage and Divorce Act enabled a man to obtain divorce if his wife had committed adultery. (Women were only eligible for divorce if their husband's adultery was combined with incest, sodomy, cruelty, etc.)
1857–82	The Married Women's Property Acts allowed them to own possessions of various kinds for the first time.
1861	Abortion became a criminal offence even if performed as a life-saving act or done by the woman herself.
1862–70	The Contagious Diseases Acts introduced compulsory examination of prostitutes for venereal disease.
1860s	Fathers could be named and required to pay maintenance for illegitimate children.
1864	Schools Enquiry Commission recommendations led to the establishment of high schools for girls.
1867	The Second Reform Act enfranchised the majority of male householders. The first women's suffrage committee was formed in Manchester.
1869	Women ratepayers were allowed to vote in municipal (local) elections.
1871	Newnham College, Cambridge, was founded for women.
1872	The Elizabeth Garrett Anderson Hospital for women opened in London.
1874	The London School of Medicine for women was founded.
1878	Judicial separation of a married couple became possible. Maintenance orders could be enforced in court. *(continued)*

women's movement: UK (continued)

1880	The Trades Union Congress (TUC) adopted the principle of equal pay for women.
1882	The Married Women's Property Act gave wives legal control over their own earned income.
1883	The Contagious Diseases Acts were repealed.
1885	The age of consent was raised to 16.
1887	The National Union of Women's Suffrage Societies became a nationwide group under Millicent Fawcett.
1903	The Women's Social and Political Union (WSPU) was founded by Emmeline and Christabel Pankhurst.
1905–10	Militant campaigns split the WSPU. Sylvia Pankhurst formed the East London Women's Federation.
1918	The Parliament (Qualification of Women) Act gave the vote to women householders over 30.
1923	Wives were given equal rights to sue for divorce on the grounds of adultery.
1925	The Guardianship of Infants Act gave women equal rights to the guardianship of their children.
1928	The 'Flapper' Vote: all women over 21 were given the vote.
1937	The Matrimonial Causes Act gave new grounds for divorce including desertion for three years and cruelty.
1944	The Butler Education Act introduced free secondary education for all.
1946	A Royal Commission on equal pay was formed.
1948	Cambridge University allowed women candidates to be awarded degrees.
1960	Legal aid became available for divorce cases.
1967	The Abortion Law Reform Act made abortion legal under medical supervision and within certain criteria.
1969	Divorce reform was introduced that reduced the time a petitioner needed to wait before applying for a divorce.
1973	The Matrimonial Causes Act provided legislation to enable financial provision to be granted on divorce.
1975	The Sex Discrimination and Equal Pay Acts were passed. The National and Scottish Women's Aid Federations were formed.
1976	The Domestic Violence and Matrimonial Proceedings Act came into effect. The Sexual Offences (Amendment) Act attempted to limit a man's defence of consent in rape cases.
1977	The employed married women's option to stay partially out of the National Insurance system was phased out. Women qualified for their own pensions.
1980	The Social Security Act allowed a married woman to claim supplementary benefit and family income supplement if she was the main wage earner.
1983	The government was forced to amend the 1975 Equal Pay Act to conform to European Community directives.
1984	The Matrimonial and Family Proceedings Act made it less likely for a woman to be granted maintenance on divorce. It also reduced the number of years a petitioner must wait before applying for a divorce to one.
1986	The granting of invalid-care allowance was successfully challenged in the European Court of Justice. The Sex Discrimination Act (Amendment) allowed women to retire at the same age as men, and lifted legal restrictions preventing women from working night shifts in manufacturing industries. Firms with less than five employees were no longer exempt from the act.
1990	The legal limit for abortion was reduced to 24 weeks.
1991	Rape within marriage became a prosecutable offence in the UK.

pope, led to his downfall 1529. He was charged with high treason 1530 but died before being tried.

> *Had I but served God as diligently as I have done the King, He would not have given me over in my grey hairs.*
>
> **Thomas Wolsey**
> of his own career and sudden downfall

Women's Land Army organization founded 1916 for the recruitment of women to work on farms during World War I. At its peak Sept 1918 it had 16,000 members. It re-formed June 1939, before the outbreak of World War II.

Many 'Land Girls' joined up to help the war effort and, by Aug 1943, 87,000 were employed in farm work.

women's movement the campaign for the rights of women, including social, political, and economic equality with men. Early European campaigners of the 17th–19th centuries fought for women's right to own property, to have access to higher education, and to vote (see ◊suffragette). Once women's suffrage was achieved in the 20th century, the emphasis of the movement shifted to the goals of equal social and economic opportunities for women, including employment.

Pioneer 19th-century feminists, considered radical for their belief in the equality of the sexes, include Mary Wollstonecraft and Emmeline Pankhurst in the UK, and Lucy Stone, Susan B Anthony and Elizabeth Cady Stanton in the USA. The women's movement gained worldwide impetus after World War II with such theorists as Simone de Beauvoir, Betty Friedan, Kate Millett, Gloria Steinem, and Germaine Greer, and the founding of the National Organization of Women (NOW) in New York 1966.

women's services the organized military use of women on a large scale, a 20th-century development. First, women replaced men in factories, on farms, and in noncombat tasks during wartime; they are now found in combat units in many countries, including the USA, Cuba, the UK, and Israel.

The USA has a separate Women's Army Corps (WAC), established 1948, which developed from the Women's Army Auxiliary Corps (WAAC); but in the navy and air force women are integrated into the general structure. There are separate nurse corps for the three services.

In Britain there are separate corps for all three services: *Women's Royal Army Corps* (WRAC) created 1949 to take over the functions of the Auxiliary Territorial Service, established 1938 – its World War I equivalent was the Women's Army Auxiliary Corps (WAAC); *Women's Royal Naval Service* (WRNS) 1917–19 and 1939 onwards, allowed in combat roles on surface ships from 1990; and the *Women's Royal Air Force* (WRAF) established 1918 but known 1939–48 as the Women's Auxiliary Air Force (WAAF). There are also nursing services.

Women's Social and Political Union (WSPU) British political movement founded 1903 by Emmeline ◊Pankhurst to organize a militant crusade for female suffrage.

In 1909, faced with government indifference, the WSPU embarked on a campaign of window smashing, painting slashing, telephone-wire cutting, and arson of public buildings. This civil disobedience had little result and was overtaken by the outbreak of World War I. In Nov 1917, the WSPU became the *Women's Party* led by Christabel Pankhurst.

workhouse in the UK, a former institution to house and maintain people unable to earn their own living. Groups of parishes in England combined to build workhouses for the poor, the aged, the disabled, and orphaned children from about 1815 until about 1930.

Sixteenth-century poor laws made parishes responsible for helping the poor within their boundaries. The 19th-century parish unions found workhouses more cost-effective. An act of Parliament 1834 improved supervision of workhouses, where conditions were sometimes harsh, and a new welfare legislation in the early 20th century made them redundant.

working men's club social club set up in the 19th century to cater for the education and recreation of working men. Educational institutes for working men were a feature of most industrial towns in Britain by the early 19th century. In 1852 the Collonade Workingmens's Club in London became the first to provide purely recreational facilities.

Works Progress Administration (WPA, renamed *Works Projects Administration* 1939) in US history, a government initiative to reduce unemployment during the Depression (11 million in 1934). Formed 1935, it provided useful work for 8.5 million people during its eight-year existence, mainly in construction projects, at a total cost of $11 billion, and was discontinued only in 1943 when the change to a war economy eliminated unemployment. The WPA was an integral part of President Roosevelt's ◊New Deal.

World Bank popular name for the *International Bank for Reconstruction and Development* specialized agency of the United Nations that borrows in the commercial market and lends on commercial terms. It was established 1945 under the 1944 Bretton Woods agreement, which also created the International Monetary Fund. The *International Development Association* is an arm of the World Bank.

World War I 1914–1918. War between the Central European Powers (Germany, Austria-Hungary, and allies) on one side and the Triple Entente (Britain and the British Empire, France, and Russia) and their allies, including the USA (which entered 1917), on the other side. An estimated 10 million lives were lost and twice that number were wounded. It was fought on the eastern and western fronts, in the Middle East, Africa, and at sea. Towards the end of the war Russia withdrew because of the Russian Revolution 1917. The peace treaty of Versailles 1919 was the formal end to the war.

1914 outbreak On 28 June the heir to the Austrian throne was assassinated in Sarajevo, Serbia; on 28 July Austria declared war on Serbia; as Russia mobilized, Germany declared war on Russia and France, taking a short cut in the west by invading Belgium; on 4 Aug Britain declared war on Germany; dominions within the Empire, including Australia, were automatically involved.

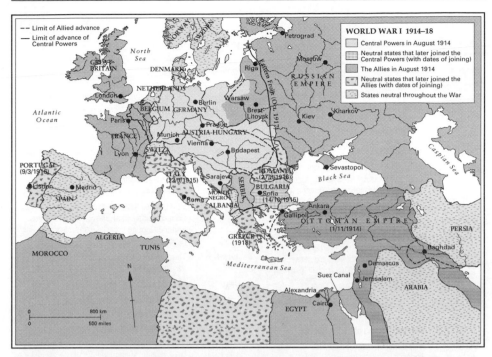

Limit of Allied advance
Limit of advance of Central Powers

WORLD WAR I 1914–18
- Central Powers in August 1914
- Neutral states that later joined the Central Powers (with dates of joining)
- The Allies in August 1914
- Neutral states that later joined the Allies (with dates of joining)
- States neutral throughout the War

World War I 1914–18 In the course of 20 days in July and August 1914, the major European countries were engulfed in war, largely because of the alliances which had committed them to support each other in the event of threats to their security or interests. Later that year Turkey joined the Central Powers and became a theatre of war in which the Allies suffered reverses at Suvla Bay and Gallipoli in the following year. Despite pre-war treaty agreements with the Central Powers, in 1915 Italy joined the Allies. Bulgaria joined the Central Powers in the same year. Only the neutrals stood apart from a conflict which embraced mainland Europe and the E Mediterranean and would later involve Japan and the USA.

Western Front The German advance reached within a few miles of Paris, but an Allied counterattack at the Marne drove them back to the Aisne River, the opposing lines then settled into trench warfare.

Eastern Front The German commander Hindenburg halted the Russian advance through the Ukraine and across Austria-Hungary at the Battle of Tannenberg in E Prussia.

Africa By Sept most of Germany's African colonies were in Allied hands; guerrilla warfare centred in Cameroon until 1916 and military operations in German East Africa until November 1918.

Middle East On 1 Nov Turkey entered the war on the side of the Central Powers and soon attacked Russia in the Caucasus Mountains.

1915 **Western Front** Several offensives on both sides resulted in insignificant gains. At Ypres, Belgium, the Germans used poison gas for the first time.

Eastern Front The German field marshals Mackensen and Hindenburg drove back the Russians and took Poland.

The lamps are going out all over Europe; we shall not see them lit again in our lifetime.

On the outbreak of *World War I*
Edward Grey

Middle East British attacks against Turkey in Mesopotamia (Iraq), the Dardanelles, and at Gallipoli (where 7,600 Anzacs were killed) were all unsuccessful.

Italy Italy declared war on Austria; Bulgaria joined the Central Powers.

war at sea Germany declared all-out U-boat war, but the sinking of the British ocean liner *Lusitania* (with Americans among the 1,198 lost) led to demands that the USA enter the war.

1916 **Western Front** The German attack at Verdun was countered by the Allies on the river Somme, where tanks were used for the first time.
Eastern Front Romania joined the Allies but was soon overrun by Germany.

World War I

1914 June	Assassination of Archduke Franz Ferdinand of Austria 28 June.
July	German government issued 'blank cheque' to Austria, offering support in war against Serbia. Austrian ultimatum to Serbia. Serbs accepted all but two points. Austria refused to accept compromise and declared war. Russia began mobilization to defend Serbian ally. Germany demanded Russian demobilization.
Aug	Germany declared war on Russia. France mobilized to assist Russian ally. Germans occupied Luxembourg and demanded access to Belgian territory, which was refused. Germany declared war on France and invaded Belgium. Britain declared war on Germany, then on Austria. Dominions within the Empire, including Australia, automatically involved. Battle of Tannenburg between Central Powers and Russians. Russian army encircled.
Sept	British and French troops halted German advance just short of Paris, and drove them back. First Battle of the Marne, and of the Aisne. Beginning of trench warfare.
Oct–Nov	First Battle of Ypres. Britain declared war on Turkey.
1915 April–May	Gallipoli offensive launched by British and dominion troops against Turkish forces. Second Battle of Ypres. First use of poison gas by Germans. Italy joined war against Austria. German submarine sank ocean liner *Lusitania* 7 May, later helping to bring USA into the war.
Aug–Sept	Warsaw evacuated by the Russians. Battle of Tarnopol. Vilna taken by the Germans. Tsar Nicholas II took supreme control of Russian forces.
1916 Jan	Final evacuation of British and dominion troops from Gallipoli.
Feb	German offensive against Verdun began, with huge losses for little territorial gain.
May	Naval battle of Jutland between British and German imperial fleets ended inconclusively, but put a stop to further German naval participation in the war.
June	Russian (Brusilov) offensive against the Ukraine began.
July–Nov	First Battle of the Somme, a sustained Anglo-French offensive which won little territory and lost a huge number of lives.
Aug	Hindenburg and Ludendorff took command of the German armed forces. Romania entered the war against Austria but was rapidly overrun.
Sept	Early tanks used by British on Western Front.
Nov	Nivelle replaced Joffre as commander of French forces. Battle of the Ancre on the Western Front.
Dec	French completed recapture of Verdun fortifications. Austrians occupied Bucharest.
1917 Feb	Germany declared unrestricted submarine warfare. Russian Revolution began and tsarist rule overthrown.
March	British seizure of Baghdad and occupation of Persia.
March–April	Germans retreated to Siegfried Line (Arras–Soissons) on Western Front.
April–May	USA entered the war against Germany. Unsuccessful British and French offensives. Mutinies among French troops. Nivelle replaced by Pétain.
July–Nov	Third Ypres offensive including Battle of Passchendaele.
Sept	Germans occupied Riga.
Oct–Nov	Battle of Caporetto saw Italian troops defeated by Austrians.
Dec	Jerusalem taken by British forces under Allenby.
1918 Jan	US President Woodrow Wilson proclaimed 'Fourteen Points' as a basis for peace settlement.
March	Treaty of Brest-Litovsk with Central Powers ended Russian participation in the war, with substantial concessions of territory and reparations. Second Battle of the Somme began with German spring offensive.
July–Aug	Allied counter-offensive, including tank attack at Amiens, drove Germans back to the Siegfried Line.
Sept	Hindenburg and Ludendorff called for an armistice.
Oct	Armistice offered on the basis of the 'Fourteen Points'. German naval and military mutinies at Kiel and Wilhelmshaven.
Nov	Austria-Hungary signed armistice with Allies. Kaiser Wilhelm II of Germany went into exile. Provisional government under social democrat Friedrich Ebert formed. Germany agreed armistice. Fighting on Western Front stopped.
1919 Jan	Peace conference opened at Versailles.
May	Demands presented to Germany.
June	Germany signed peace treaty, followed by other Central Powers: Austria (Treaty of St Germain-en-Laye, Sept), Bulgaria (Neuilly, Nov), Hungary (Trianon, June 1920), and Turkey (Sèvres, Aug 1920).

Middle East Kut-al-Imara, Iraq, was taken from the British by the Turks.

war at sea The Battle of Jutland between England and Germany, although indecisive, put a stop to further German naval participation in the war.

1917 The USA entered the war in April. British and Empire troops launched the third battle at Ypres and by Nov had taken Passchendaele.

1918 Eastern Front On 3 March Soviet Russia signed the Treaty of Brest-Litovsk with Germany, ending Russian participation in the war (the Russian Revolution 1917 led into their civil war 1918–21).

Western Front Germany began a final offensive. In April the Allies appointed the French marshal Foch supreme commander, but by June (when the first US troops went into battle) the Allies had lost all gains since 1915, and the Germans were on the river Marne. The battle at Amiens marked the launch of the victorious Allied offensive.

Italy At Vittorio Veneto the British and Italians finally defeated the Austrians.

German capitulation This began with naval mutinies at Kiel, followed by uprisings in the major cities. Kaiser Wilhelm II abdicated, and on 11 Nov the armistice was signed.

1919 18 June, peace treaty of Versailles. (The USA signed a separate peace accord with Germany and Austria 1921.)

Europe during World War II 1939–45 *The German armies had remarkable success in overrunning Poland 1939, W Europe 1940, and the western USSR 1941 before their advance reached its limits Nov 1942 and was checked by the Soviet army. German rule in occupied Europe varied: in the west existing administrations continued to function under German control with coercion increasing as Nazi demands grew and the war situation deteriorated; in the east the policy was one of brutal exploitation and the immediate implementation of Nazi racial policies. Victories in North Africa 1942–43 allowed the Allies to invade Italy from the south, but this campaign failed to provide a complete breakthrough. The Soviet victory at the Battle of Stalingrad Dec 1942–Jan 1943 marked the turning point in the war and this was reinforced by the Anglo-Canadian-American landing in Normandy June 1944. The Allied policy towards Germany of unconditional surrender meant their armies overran and then occupied the country 1945, bringing the war to an end.*

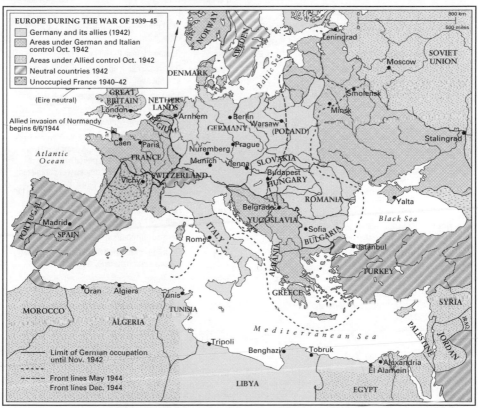

World War II

1939 Sept	German invasion of Poland; Britain and France declared war on Germany; the USSR invaded Poland; fall of Warsaw (Poland divided between Germany and USSR).	**May**	End of Axis resistance in N Africa.
		July	A coup by King Victor Emmanuel and Marshal Badoglio forced Mussolini to resign.
Nov	The USSR invaded Finland.	**Aug**	Beginning of the campaign against the Japanese in Burma (now Myanmar); US Marines landed on Guadalcanal, Solomon Islands.
1940 March	Soviet peace treaty with Finland.		
April	Germany occupied Denmark, Norway, the Netherlands, Belgium, and Luxembourg. In Britain, a coalition government was formed under Churchill.	**Sept**	Italy surrendered to the Allies; Mussolini was rescued by the Germans who set up a Republican Fascist government in N Italy; Allied landings at Salerno; the USSR retook Smolensk.
May	Germany outflanked the defensive French Maginot Line.	**Oct**	Italy declared war on Germany.
May–June	Evacuation of 337,131 Allied troops from Dunkirk, France, across the Channel to England.	**Nov**	The US Navy defeated the Japanese in the Battle of Guadalcanal.
June	Italy declared war on Britain and France; the Germans entered Paris; the French prime minister Pétain signed an armistice with Germany and moved the seat of government to Vichy.	**Nov–Dec**	The Allied leaders met at the Tehran Conference.
		1944 Jan	Allied landing in Nazi-occupied Italy: Battle of Anzio.
July–Oct	Battle of Britain between British and German air forces.	**March**	End of the German U-boat campaign in the Atlantic.
Sept	Japanese invasion of French Indochina.	**May**	Fall of Monte Cassino, S Italy.
Oct	Abortive Italian invasion of Greece.	**6 June**	D-day: Allied landings in Nazi-occupied and heavily defended Normandy.
1941 April	Germany occupied Greece and Yugoslavia.	**July**	The bomb plot by German generals against Hitler failed.
June	Germany invaded the USSR; Finland declared war on the USSR.	**Aug**	Romania joined the Allies.
July	The Germans entered Smolensk, USSR.	**Sept**	Battle of Arnhem on the Rhine; Soviet armistice with Finland.
Dec	The Germans came within 40 km/25 mi of Moscow, with Leningrad (now St Petersburg) under siege. First Soviet counteroffensive. Japan bombed Pearl Harbor, Hawaii, and declared war on the USA and Britain. Germany and Italy declared war on the USA.	**Oct**	The Yugoslav guerrilla leader Tito and Soviets entered Belgrade.
		Dec	German counter-offensive, Battle of the Bulge.
1942 Jan	Japanese conquest of the Philippines.	**1945 Feb**	The Soviets reached the German border; Yalta conference; Allied bombing campaign over Germany (Dresden destroyed); the US reconquest of the Philippines was completed; the Americans landed on Iwo Jima, south of Japan.
June	Naval battle of Midway, the turning point of the Pacific War.		
Aug	German attack on Stalingrad (now Volgograd), USSR.	**April**	Hitler committed suicide; Mussolini was captured by Italian partisans and shot.
Oct–Nov	Battle of El Alamein in N Africa, turn of the tide for the Western Allies.	**May**	German surrender to the Allies.
Nov	Soviet counteroffensive on Stalingrad.	**June**	US troops completed the conquest of Okinawa (one of the Japanese Ryukyu Islands).
1943 Jan	The Casablanca Conference issued the Allied demand of unconditional surrender; the Germans retreated from Stalingrad.	**July**	The Potsdam Conference issued an Allied ultimatum to Japan.
March	The USSR drove the Germans back to the river Donetz.	**Aug**	Atom bombs were dropped by the USA on Hiroshima and Nagasaki; Japan surrendered.

World War II 1939–1945. War between Germany, Italy, and Japan (the Axis powers) on one side, and Britain, the Commonwealth, France, the USA, the USSR, and China (the Allied powers) on the other. An estimated 55 million lives were lost, 20 million of them citizens of the USSR. The war was fought in the Atlantic and Pacific theatres. In 1945, Germany surrendered (May) but Japan fought on until the USA dropped atomic bombs on Hiroshima and Nagasaki (Aug).

The power of Germany must be broken in the battlefields of Europe

Franklin D Roosevelt 1941

Worms industrial town in Rhineland-Palatinate, Germany, on the river Rhine. The Protestant reformer Martin Luther appeared before the *Diet* (Assembly) *of Worms* 1521 and was declared an outlaw by the Roman Catholic church.

Wounded Knee site on the Oglala Sioux Reservation, South Dakota, USA, of a confrontation between the US Army and American Indians. Chief Sitting Bull was killed, supposedly resisting arrest, on 15 Dec 1890, and on 29 Dec a group of Indians involved in the Ghost Dance Movement (aimed at resumption of Indian control of North America with the aid of the spirits of dead braves) were surrounded and 153 killed.

In 1973 the militant American Indian Movement, in the siege of Wounded Knee 27 Feb–8 May, held hostages and demanded a government investigation of the Indian treaties.

Wrangel Peter Nicolaievich, Baron von 1878–1928. Russian general, born in St Petersburg. He commanded a division of Cossacks in World War I, and in 1920, after succeeding Anton Denikin as commander in chief of the White Army, defeated by the Bolsheviks in the Crimea.

Wycliffe John *c.* 1320–1384. English religious reformer. Allying himself with the party of John of Gaunt, which was opposed to ecclesiastical influence at court, he attacked abuses in the church, maintaining that the Bible rather than the church was the supreme authority. He criticized such fundamental doctrines as priestly absolution, confession, and indulgences, and set disciples to work on translating the Bible into English.

under the Zhou dynasty (1066–221 BC); under the Han dynasty (206 BC–AD 220), when it was called *Changan* ('long peace'); and under the Tang dynasty 618–907 as *Siking* ('western capital'). The Manchus called it *Sian* ('western peace'), now spelled Xian. It reverted to Changan 1913–32, was Siking 1932–43, and again Sian from 1943. It was here that the imperial court retired after the Boxer Rebellion 1900.

Xian Incident kidnapping of the Chinese generalissimo and politician ◊Chiang Kai-shek in Xian 12 Dec 1936, by one of his own generals, to force his cooperation with the communists against the Japanese invaders.

Xenophon *c*. 430–354 BC. Greek historian, philosopher, and soldier. In 401 he joined a Greek mercenary army aiding the Persian prince Cyrus, and on the latter's death took command. His *Anabasis* describes how he led 10,000 Greeks on a 1,600-km/1,000-mile march home across enemy territory. His other works include *Memorabilia*, *Apology*, and *Hellenica/A History of My Times*.

Xerxes *c*. 519–465 BC. King of Persia from 485 BC when he succeeded his father Darius. In 480, at the head of a great army which was supported by the Phoenician navy, he crossed the Dardanelles over a bridge of boats. He captured and burned Athens, but the Persian fleet was defeated at Salamis and Xerxes was forced to retreat. His general Mardonius remained behind in Greece, but was defeated by the Greeks at Plataea 479. Xerxes was eventually murdered in a court intrigue.

Xia dynasty or *Hsia dynasty* China's first legendary ruling family, *c*. 2200–*c*. 1500 BC, reputedly founded by the model emperor Yu the Great. He is believed to have controlled floods by constructing dykes. Archaeological evidence suggests that the Xia dynasty really did exist, as a Bronze Age civilization where writing was being developed, with its capital at Erlidou (Erh-li-t'ou) in Henan (Honan).

Xian industrial city and capital of Shaanxi province, China. It was the capital of China

Xinjiang Uygur or *Sinkiang Uighur* autonomous region of NW China. The region was under Manchu rule from the 18th century. Large sections were ceded to Russia 1864 and 1881; China has raised the question of their return and regards the frontier between Xinjiang Uygur and Tajikistan, which runs for 480 km/300 mi, as undemarcated.

Xiongnu or *Hsiung-nu* Turkish-speaking nomad horseriding people from central Asia who founded an extensive Chinese steppe empire and harried N Chinese states in the 3rd century BC. Originating from Mongolia and S Siberia, they were forced back to the Gobi desert 119 BC by China's Han-dynasty emperor Wudi (Wu-ti, reigned 141–87 BC) through a bloody war of attrition. The ◊Great Wall of China was then extended to strengthen defences against them. The Xiongnu later became vassals of China, being employed as frontier troops.

XYZ Affair in American history, an incident 1797–98 in which the French as represented by foreign minister ◊Talleyrand were accused of demanding a $250,000 bribe before agreeing to negotiate with US envoys in Paris. Three French agents (referred to by President John Adams 1797 as X, Y, and Z) held secret talks with the envoys over the money. Publicity fuelled anti-French feelings in the USA and led to increased military spending.

Yahya Khan Agha Muhammad 1917–1980. Pakistani president 1969–71. His mishandling of the Bangladesh separatist issue led to civil war, and he was forced to resign.

Yahya Khan fought with the British army in the Middle East during World War II, escaping German capture in Italy. Later, as Pakistan's chief of army general staff, he supported General Ayub Khan's 1958 coup and in 1969 became military ruler. Following defeat by India 1971, he resigned and was under house arrest 1972–75.

Yalta Conference in 1945, a meeting at which the Allied leaders Churchill (UK), Roosevelt (USA), and Stalin (USSR) completed plans for the defeat of Germany in World War II and the foundation of the United Nations. It took place in Yalta, a Soviet holiday resort in the Crimea.

Yamagata Aritomo 1838–1922. Japanese soldier, politician, and prime minister 1889–91 and 1898–1900. As war minister 1873 and chief of the imperial general staff 1878, he was largely responsible for the modernization of the military system. He returned as chief of staff during the Russo-Japanese War 1904–05 and remained an influential political figure until he was disgraced in 1921 for having meddled in the marriage arrangements of the crown prince.

Yamamoto Gombei 1852–1933. Japanese admiral and politician. As prime minister 1913–14, he began Japanese expansion into China and initiated political reforms. He became premier again 1923 but resigned the following year.

Yamato ancient name of Japan and particularly the province of W Honshu where Japanese civilization began and where the early capitals were located; also the clan from which all emperors of Japan are descended, claiming the sun-goddess as ancestor. The Yamato period is often taken as AD 539–710 (followed by the Nara period).

According to legend, the Japanese empire dates from the conquest of the Yamato region by Emperor Jimmu 660 BC. Two chronicles, the *Kojiki/Record of Ancient Matters* 7th century and the *Nihon shoki* 720, give creation myths and annals of legendary and early historical reigns. The 29th emperor, Kimmei (reigned 539–71), is regarded as the first fully historical emperor. In the era of Prince Shōtoku Taishi (574–622) and the Taika reform period 645–50, the Yamato rulers became greatly influenced by the culture of ◊Tang dynasty China, notably Buddhism, Confucianism, and China's bureaucratic system. In the mid-9th century the emperors ceded effective control of government to the ◊Fujiwara clan and hardly ever ruled in their own right until the Meiji restoration 1868.

Yanayev Gennady 1937– . Soviet communist politician, leader of the failed Aug 1991 anti-Gorbachev coup, after which he was charged with treason but was released 1994. He was vice president of the USSR 1990–91.

Yankee colloquial (often disparaging) term for an American. Outside the USA the term is applied to any American.

During the American Civil War, the term was applied by Southerners to any Northerner or member of the Union Army and is still used today to refer to Northerners.

Yedo or *Edo* former name of ◊Tokyo, Japan, until 1868.

You can erect a throne of bayonets, but you cannot sit on it for long.

Boris Yeltsin 20 Aug 1991

Yeltsin Boris Nikolayevich 1931– . Russian politician, president of the Russian Soviet Federative Socialist Republic (RSFSR) 1990-91, and president of the Russian Federation from 1991. He directed the Federation's secession from the USSR and the formation of a new, decentralized confederation, the ◊Commonwealth of Independent States, with himself as the most powerful leader. A referendum 1993 supported his policies of price deregulation and accelerated privatization, despite severe economic problems and civil unrest. He survived a coup attempt later the same year, but was subsequently forced to compromise on the pace of his reforms after far-right electoral gains, and lost considerable support. Despite poor health, he secured re-election 1996.

Yemen country in SW Asia, bounded N by Saudi Arabia, E by Oman, S by the Gulf of Aden, and W by the Red Sea.

history North Yemen was a kingdom in the 2nd millennium BC, followed by successive periods of rule by Egypt, Rome, and Ethiopia. North Yemen adopted Islam 628, formed part of the ◊Ottoman Empire 1538–1630, and was occupied by Turkey in the 19th century.

For the early history of South Yemen, see ◊Arabia.

North Yemen declared a republic The last king of North Yemen, Imam Muhammad, was killed in a military coup 1962. The declaration of the new Yemen Arab Republic (YAR) provoked a civil war between royalist forces, assisted by Saudi Arabia, and republicans, helped by Egypt. By 1967 the republicans, under Marshal Abdullah al-Sallal, had won. Later that year Sallal was deposed while on a foreign visit, and a Republican Council took over.

South Yemen republic founded The People's Democratic Republic of Yemen (South Yemen) was founded 1967 by the union of ◊Aden and the Federation of South Arabia, both of which had been under British rule or protection. Before Britain withdrew, two rival factions fought for power, the Marxist National Liberation Front (NLF) and the Front for the Liberation of Occupied South Yemen (FLOSY). The NLF eventually won and assumed power as the National Front (NF). On the third anniversary of independence, 1 Nov 1970, the country was renamed the People's Democratic Republic of Yemen, and a provisional Supreme People's Council (SPC) was set up 1971 as the nation's parliament.

The accession of the left-wing NF government caused hundreds of thousands of people to flee to North Yemen, where a more moderate regime was in power. This resulted in clashes between the South Yemen government and mercenaries operating from North Yemen, and war broke out 1971. The Arab League arranged a cease-fire 1972, and the two countries signed an agreement to merge, but the agreement was not honoured.

In North Yemen the pro-Saudi Col Ibrahim al-Hamadi seized power 1974, and by 1975 there were rumours of an attempt to restore the monarchy. In 1977 Hamadi was assassinated and Col Ahmed ibn Hussein al-Ghashmi, another member of the Military Command Council which Hamadi had set up 1974, took over. In 1978 a gradual move towards a more constitutional form of government was started, with the appointment of the Constituent People's Assembly, the dissolution of the Military Command Council, and the installation of Ghashmi as president. In 1978 Ghashmi was killed when a bomb exploded in a suitcase carried by an envoy from South Yemen, and Col Ali Abdullah Saleh took over as president.

In the aftermath of Ghashmi's death, the South Yemen president Rubayi Ali was deposed and executed. Two days later the three political parties of South Yemen agreed to merge to form a 'Marxist–Leninist vanguard party', the Yemen Socialist Party (YSP), and Abdul Fattah Ismail became its secretary general. In Dec 1978 Ismail was appointed head of state but four months later resigned and went into exile in the USSR. He was succeeded by Ali Nasser Muhammad.

In 1979 South Yemen's neighbours became concerned when a 20-year Treaty of Friendship and Cooperation was signed, allowing the USSR to station troops in the country, and three years later an aid agreement between the two countries was concluded. A subsequent aid agreement with Kuwait helped to reduce anxieties.

two Yemens at war War broke out again between the two Yemens after the assassination of President Ghashmi of North Yemen. The Arab League again intervened to arrange a cease-fire 1979, and for the second time the two countries agreed to unite. This time definite progress was made so that by 1983 a joint Yemen council was meeting at six-monthly intervals, and in March 1984 a joint committee on foreign policy sat for the first time in Aden.

In North Yemen President Saleh was re-elected for a further five years 1983, and again 1988, while in South Yemen Ali Nasser Muhammad was re-elected secretary general of the YSP and its political bureau for another five years 1985. He soon began taking steps to remove his opponents, his personal guard killing three bureau members. This led to a short civil war and the dismissal of Ali Nasser from all his posts in the party and the government. A new administration was formed, headed by Haydar Abu Bakr al-Attas, which immediately committed itself to eventual union with North Yemen.

unification A draft constitution of the unified state of Yemen was published Dec 1989 and in Jan 1990 the border between the two countries was opened to allow free movement for all citizens. The unification was proclaimed 22 May, with Ali Abdullah Saleh as leader of the new Republic of Yemen and Sana'a as its capital. The new constitution was approved May 1991 and a general election was promised for Nov 1992.

yeoman in England, a small landowner who farmed his own fields – a system that formed a bridge between the break-up of feudalism and the agricultural revolution of the 18th–19th centuries.

Yeomen of the Guard English military corps, popularly known as *Beefeaters*, the sovereign's bodyguard since the corps was founded by Henry VII 1485. Its duties are now purely ceremonial.

Yezidi Islamic sect originating as disciples of the Sufi saint Sheik Adi ibn Musafir (12th century). The beliefs of its adherents mingle folk traditions with Islam, also incorporating features of Judaism and Christianity (they practise circumcision and baptism), and include a cult of the Fallen Angel who has been reconciled with God. Their chief centre is near Mosul, Iraq.

Yin dynasty start of the Bronze Age in China, *c.* 1500–*c.* 1066 BC, also known as the ◊Shang dynasty.

Yippie in the USA, a member of the *Youth International Party* (YIP), led by Abbie ◊Hoffmann and Jerry Rubin (1938–94), who mocked the US political process during the 1960s.

Yom Kippur War the surprise attack on Israel October 1973 by Egypt and Syria; see ◊Arab–Israeli Wars. It is named after the Jewish national holiday on which it began, the holiest day of the Jewish year.

York English dynasty founded by Richard, Duke of York (1411–60). He claimed the throne through his descent from Lionel, Duke of Clarence (1338–1368), third son of Edward III, whereas the reigning monarch, Henry VI of the rival house of Lancaster, was descended from the fourth son. The argument was fought out in the Wars of the ◊Roses. York was killed at the Battle of Wakefield 1460, but next year his son became King Edward IV, in turn succeeded by his son Edward V and then by his brother Richard III, with whose death at Bosworth the line ended. The Lancastrian victor in that battle was crowned Henry VII and consolidated his claim by marrying Edward IV's eldest daughter, Elizabeth.

York Alvin Cullum 'Sergeant' 1887–1964. US war hero. Although a conscientious objector, York was drafted as a private in the 82nd Infantry Division in World War I and promoted to the rank of sergeant. At the Battle of the Argonne Forest 8 Oct 1918 during World War I, York led a charge against a German position in which he and his comrades captured 132 prisoners and 35 machine guns.

York Frederick Augustus, Duke of York 1763–1827. Second son of George III. He was an unsuccessful commander in the Netherlands 1793–99 and British commander in chief 1798–1809.

Yoruba member of the majority ethnic group living in SW Nigeria; there is a Yoruba minority in E Benin. They number approximately 20 million in all, and their language belongs to the Kwa branch of the Niger-Congo family. The Yoruba established powerful city states in the 15th century, known for their advanced culture which includes sculpture, art, and music.

Yoshida Shigeru 1878–1967. Japanese conservative (Liberal Party) politician who served as prime minister of US-occupied Japan for most of the post-World War II period 1946–54. He was foreign minister 1945–46.

Young Ireland Irish nationalist organization, founded 1840 by William Smith O'Brien (1803–1864), who attempted an abortive insurrection of the peasants against the British in Tipperary 1848. O'Brien was sentenced to death, but later pardoned.

Young Italy Italian nationalist organization founded 1831 by Giuseppe ◊Mazzini while in exile in Marseille. The movement, which was immediately popular, was followed the next year by Young Germany, Young Poland, and similar organizations. All the groups were linked by Mazzini in his Young Europe movement, but none achieved much practical success; attempted uprisings by Young Italy 1834 and 1844 failed miserably. It was superseded in Italy by the ◊Risorgimento.

Young Plan scheme devised by US entrepreneur Owen D Young to reschedule German payments of war reparations 1929.

Young Pretender nickname of ◊Charles Edward Stuart, claimant to the Scottish and English thrones.

Young Turk member of a reformist movement of young army officers in the Ottoman Empire founded 1889. The movement was instrumental in the constitutional changes of 1908 and the abdication of Sultan ◊Abdul-Hamid II 1909. It gained prestige during the Balkan Wars 1912–13 and encouraged Turkish links with the German empire. Its influence diminished after 1918. The term is now used for a member of any radical or rebellious faction within a party or organization.

Ypres (Flemish *Ieper*) Belgian town in W Flanders, 40 km/25 mi S of Ostend, a site of three major battles 1914–1917 fought in World War I. The Menin Gate 1927 is a memorial to British soldiers lost in these battles.

Oct–Nov 1914 the Germans launched an assault on British defensive positions and captured the Messines Ridge, but failed to take Ypres.

April to May 1915 the Germans launched a renewed attack using poison gas and chlorine (the first recorded use in war), in an unsuccessful attempt to break the British line.

July to Nov 1917 (known also as Passchendaele), an allied offensive, including British, Canadian, and Australian troops, was launched under British commander-in-chief Douglas Haig, in an attempt to capture ports on the Belgian coast held by Germans. The long and bitter battle, fought in appalling conditions of driving rain and waterlogged ground, achieved an advance of only 8 km/5 mi of territory that was of no strategic significance. The allied attack resulted in more than 300,000 casualties.

Ypres, 1st Earl of title of Sir John ◊French, British field marshal.

Yuan dynasty ◊Mongol rulers of China 1279–1368 after ◊Kublai Khan defeated the Song dynasty. Much of Song China's administrative infrastructure survived and internal and foreign trade expanded. The Silk Route to the west was re-established and the Grand Canal extended north to Beijing to supply the court with grain.

The Mongol conquest was particularly brutal, and relations with the Chinese were never easy, resulting in the recruitment of foreigners such as central Asian Muslims to act as officials. The Venetian traveller Marco ◊Polo also served at the court. After the death of Temur (ruled 1294–1307), there was increasing internal disorder and economic discontent. This was the first dynasty to control territories S of the Chang Jiang.

Yuanmingyuan palace outside Beijing, China, begun in the 18th century by Emperor Kangxi, but mostly built 1747–59 by his grandson Qianlong. The palace was burned down by Lord Elgin Oct 1860 as revenge for cruelty shown to Western prisoners taken during the advance on Beijing the preceding month. The palace, from its destruction, became a symbol of national humiliation.

Yuan Shikai 1859–1916. Chinese soldier and politician, leader of Republican China 1911–16. He assumed dictatorial powers 1912, dissolving parliament and suppressing Sun Yatsen's ◊Guomindang. He died soon after proclaiming himself emperor.

Although committed to military reform, Yuan betrayed the modernizing emperor Guangxu and sided with the Empress Dowager ◊Zi Xi during the Hundred Days' Reform 1898. With a power base in N China, he was appointed prime minister and commander in chief after the 1911 revolution against the Manchu Qings and was made president 1912. He lost credibility after submitting to Japan's ◊21 demands 1915, ceding territory to Japan.

Yugoslavia country in SE Europe, with a SW coastline on the Adriatic Sea, bounded W by Bosnia-Herzegovina, NW by Croatia, E by Romania and Bulgaria, and S by Greece and Albania.

history Originally inhabited by nomadic peoples from the central Asian plateau, and later by Slavs, the country came under the rule of the Greek and then Roman empires. During the early medieval period the present-day republics of Yugoslavia existed as substantially independent bodies, the most important being the kingdom of Serbia. During the 14th and 15th centuries much of the country was conquered by the Turks and incorporated into the Ottoman Empire, except for mountainous Montenegro, which survived as a sovereign principality, and Croatia and Slovenia in the NW, which formed part of the Austro-Hungarian Habsburg empire.

Kingdom of the Serbs, Croats, and Slovenes Anti-Ottoman uprisings secured Serbia a measure of autonomy from the early 19th century and full independence from 1878, and the new kingdom proceeded to enlarge its territory, at Turkey and Bulgaria's expense, during the Balkan Wars 1912–13. However, not until the collapse of the Austro-Hungarian empire at the end of World War I were Croatia and Slovenia liberated from foreign control. A new 'Kingdom of the Serbs, Croats, and Slovenes' was formed Dec 1918, with the Serbian Peter Karageorgevic at its helm, to which Montenegro acceded following its people's deposition of its own ruler, King Nicholas.

Peter I died 1921 and was succeeded by his son Alexander, who renamed the country Yugoslavia ('nation of the South Slavs') and who, faced with opposition from the Croatians at home and from the Italians abroad, established a military dictatorship 1929. He was assassinated Oct 1934. Alexander's young son ◊Peter II succeeded, and a regency under the latter's uncle Paul (1893–1976) was set up that came under increasing influence from Germany and Italy. The regency was briefly overthrown by pro-Allied groups March 1941, precipitating an invasion by German troops.

Peter II fled, while two guerrilla groups – pro-royalist, Serbian-based Chetniks, led by General Draza ◊Mihailović, and communist partisans, led by Josip Broz (Marshal ◊Tito) – engaged in resistance activities.

Yugoslav Republic under Tito Tito established a provisional government at liberated Jajce in Bosnia-Herzegovina Nov 1943 and proclaimed the Yugoslav Federal Republic Nov 1945 after the expulsion, with Soviet help, of the remaining German forces. Elections were held, a communist constitution on the Soviet model was introduced, and remaining royalist opposition crushed. Tito broke with Stalin 1948 and, with the constitutional law of 1953, adopted a more liberal and decentralized form of communism centred around workers' self-management and the support of private farming. Tito became the dominating force in Yugoslavia and held the newly created post of president from 1953 until his death May 1980.
regional discontent In foreign affairs, the country sought to maintain a balance between East and West and played a leading role in the creation of the ◊nonaligned movement 1961. Domestically, the nation experienced continuing regional discontent, in particular in ◊Croatia where a violent separatist movement gained ground in the 1970s. To deal with these problems, Tito encouraged further decentralization and devolution of power to the constituent republics. A system of collective leadership and regular rotation of office posts was introduced to prevent the creation of regional cliques. However, the problems of regionalist unrest grew worse during the 1980s, notably in Kosovo (see ◊Serbia) and ◊Bosnia), where Albanian and Islamic nationalism respectively were strong.

economic austerity This regionalist discontent was fanned by a decline in living standards from 1980, caused by mounting foreign debt, the service of which absorbed more than 10% of GNP, and a spiralling inflation rate, which reached 200% in 1988 and 700% in 1989. From 1987 to 1988 the federal government under the leadership of Prime Minister Branko Mikulić, a Bosnian, instituted a 'market socialist' programme of prices and wages decontrol and the greater encouragement of the private sector and foreign 'inward investment'. The short-term consequence of this restructuring programme was a period of increased economic austerity and a rise in the unemployment rate to 15%. Following a wave of strikes and mounting internal disorder, Mikulić was replaced as prime minister Jan 1989 by Ante Marković, a reformist Croatian.

multiparty elections The unity of the ruling Communist Party began to crumble 1988–90 as both personal and ideologically based feuds developed between the leaders of its republican branches. Slobodan Milošević, the hardline Serbian party chief, waged a populist campaign against Kosovo's and Vojvodina's autonomous status securing their reintegration within Serbia. This led to a violent ethnic Albanian backlash in Kosovo 1989–90 and to growing pressure in more liberal, propluralist Croatia and Slovenia for their republics to break away from the federation. The schism within the Communist Party was confirmed Jan 1990 when its congress had to be abandoned after a walkout by the Slovene delegation. In Sept Kosovo and Vojvodina were effectively stripped of their autonomy when a new multiparty constitution came into effect in Serbia.

In multiparty elections held in Serbia Dec 1990, Slobodan Milošević was elected president and his Serbian Socialist Party (the renamed communists) achieved an assembly majority. In Bosnia-Herzegovina the League of Communists was voted out and the three Muslim, Serb, and Croat nationalist parties formed a coalition. In Macedonia the multiparty election held Nov 1990 resulted in a hung parliament. In Montenegro, the League of Communists held on to power. Concerned at the rising tide of ethnic conflict and political disintegration, Prime Minister Marković founded the Alliance of Reform Forces July 1990 which aimed to preserve Yugoslav unity within a pluralist federation.

Slovenia's call for secession In July 1990 the Slovenian assembly proclaimed full sovereignty and in Feb 1991 called for secession from Yugoslavia.

Croatian assertion of autonomy In Croatia, ethnic tension between majority Croat and minority Serb populations increased following the election April–May 1990 of a right-wing Croat nationalist government led by Franjo Tudjman. Fearing a resurgence of ethnic persecution, Serbs held, in Aug, an unofficial referendum on the issue of cultural autonomy. In the same month there was an anti-Croat uprising in the Serb-dominated town of Knin in the west. In Feb 1991 the Croatian assembly called for secession from Yugoslavia on the same terms as Slovenia. Serb militants in Krajina in turn demanded secession from Croatia and held a referendum, a week ahead of a referendum on sovereignty throughout Croatia. In Krajina, 90% of electors voted 'to remain part of Yugoslavia with Serbia and Montenegro and others who want to preserve Yugoslavia'. In

Croatia, 93% voted for the republic to become a sovereign and independent country.

In March 1991 there were anticommunist and anti-Milošević riots in Belgrade, spreading to Novi Sad in Vojvodina. On 15 March 1991 the state president, Borisav Jović, a Serbian, dramatically resigned, after his plan to introduce martial law failed to gain support. There were fears that his departure might presage a military takeover in Yugoslavia. Croatia's representative on the state presidency, Stipe Mesic, a noncommunist committed to the abolition of the federal structure, was formally elected to the collective state presidency June 1991 after three months of political uncertainty. In Bosnia-Herzegovina, there was increasing civil disorder from the spring of 1991.

Slovenia and Croatia declare independence On 25 June 1991 both Slovenia and Croatia issued declarations of independence from Yugoslavia. The lack of recognition from other nations precipitated, from June 1991, bloody military confrontations between the federal army and republican forces. A European Community (EC) delegation of foreign ministers brokered a cease-fire at the end of June but it soon fell apart when the Slovenian parliament overruled the decision of the republic's president, Milan Kučan, to suspend independence for a three-month period. However, threatened with the suspension of EC monetary aid to Yugoslavia it was agreed that the Yugoslav national army would withdraw from Slovenia, which seemed set to secure its independence. But between July and Sept 1991 civil war intensified in ethnically mixed Croatia.

It became uncertain who (politicians or the military) now controlled Yugoslavia at the federal level. Furthermore, the Yugoslav national army had become factionalized, with many units refusing to heed President Mesic's call for a return to barracks.

calls for cease-fire A new cease-fire was ordered by the federal presidency 7 Aug 1991, after the EC, which viewed Serbia as the real aggressor, threatened to apply economic sanctions against the republic. However, the cease-fire again failed to hold and by Sept around a third of Croatia was under Serb control. Oil-rich Croatia responded by imposing an oil supply blockade on Serbia and attacked federal army barracks within the republic. Another EC-brokered cease-fire 2 Sept 1991 collapsed. Both Serbia and Croatia called for international peacekeeping troops to be deployed and further efforts (including an economic embargo) were made by the EC to achieve a settlement Nov 1991.

other republics call for independence In Aug 1991 Serbia revealed plans to annex the SE part of Bosnia-Herzegovina, causing ethnic clashes within the republic. From Sept 1991 border areas began to fall to the Serbs who established autonomous enclaves. In Oct 1991 the republic's sovereignty was declared but this was resisted by the Serbs. In Macedonia a referendum on independence held Sept 1991 received overwhelming support, despite being boycotted by the Albanian and Serbian minorities. In Kosovo, an unofficial referendum on sovereignty held Sept 1991 received overwhelming support.

collapse of federal government Between Sept and Oct 1991 Croat and Slovene representatives resigned from federal bodies and Bosnian and Macedonian representatives withdrew from the federal presidency. In effect, Serbia was left dominating a 'rump' Yugoslavia. On 5 Dec 1991 Stipe Mesic resigned from the presidency, declaring that 'Yugoslavia no longer exists'. On 20 Dec the federal prime minister, Ante Marković, also resigned.

cease-fire in Croatia In early Jan 1992 a UN peace plan was successfully brokered in Sarajevo which provided for an immediate cease-fire in Croatia. This accord was disregarded by the breakaway Serb leader in Krajina, Milan Babić, but recognized by the main Croatian and Serbian forces. Croatia's and Slovenia's independence was recognized by the EC and the USA on 15 Jan 1992.

Bosnia-Herzegovina and Macedonia In Bosnia-Herzegovina, Muslims and Croats held a referendum Feb 1992 and voted overwhelmingly in favour of seeking EC recognition of independence, despite a boycott by the Serbs. Official recognition was granted by the EC and the USA in April 1992. Serb opposition to independence continued, with several hundred people killed in violent clashes. Macedonia declared its independence Jan 1992 and immediate recognition was accorded by Bulgaria, but not by Serbia or neighbouring Greece. In an unofficial referendum held in the same month, Macedonia's Albanian community voted for autonomy.

Concern for ethnic minorities in Serbia and Serbia's attempted 'carve-up' of the newly independent Bosnian republic prompted the EC and the USA to deny recognition of a new Yugoslavia, announced by Serbia and Montenegro April 1992. The UN withdrew its ambassadors from Belgrade May 1992 and the US demand for Yugoslavia's expulsion from the ◊Conference on Security and Cooperation in Europe (CSCE) was met July 1992. In Sept Yugoslavia's membership of the UN was suspended because of Serbia's alleged backing of atrocities carried out by Bosnian Serbs against Muslims and Croats, the policy of 'ethnic cleansing' carried out by means of enforced evacuations, and the suspected existence of Serbian-run concentration camps in Bosnia.

In Dec 1992 Milošević was re-elected Serbian president, defeating opposition leader Milan Panić, who was subsequently ousted on a vote of no confidence. Radoje Kontić was named prime minister of Yugoslavia in Feb 1993. In April Macedonia was awarded UN membership under the provisional name of the Former Yugoslav Republic of Macedonia. In June 1993 Cosić was removed from office by the Yugoslav parliament, reputedly at the instigation of Milošević, and replaced by Zoran Lilić.

international sanctions Yugoslavias economy was badly affected by international sanctions. Industrial production contracted sharply and by Oct 1993 inflation had reached a monthly rate of 2000%, with fuel in increasingly short supply. Despite this hardship, President Milošević's Socialist Party secured a slim majority in parliamentary elections Dec 1993. In Oct 1994 international sanctions against Serbia and Montenegro after Milošević, responding to UN pressure, ordered a blockade of Bosnian Serbs. Appeals for military aid from the respective leaders of the Bosnian and Krajina Serbs were rejected in Aug 1995, and from Sept Serbia played a key role in negotiations leading up to the US-brokered Dayton peace accord for Bosnia-Herzegovina, finally agreeing to recognize the separate existence of Croatia and Bosnia-Herzegovina in Nov 1995. The following month the USA lifted its economic sanctions against Serbia. In Aug 1996

Serbiaand Croatia agreed to restore diplomatic relations. In Oct the UN Security Council voted to end economic sanctions against Serbia. In Oct 1996 full diplomatic relations were opened with Bosnia-Herzegovina.

In early Nov 1996 the ruling Socialist Party of Serbia (SPS)-dominated United List secured victory in elections to the 138-member Chamber of Citizens, the lower house of the two Chamber Federal Assembly. The List won 64 seats and the allied Social Democratic Party of Montenegro (SDPCG) 20 seats. Concurrent elections to the Republican Assembly in Montenegro were won by the SDPCG, with 45 seats out of 71.

From late Nov 1996 there were mounting mass demonstrations, particularly in Belgrade, involving students, academics, and trade unionists, against the government of Slobodan Milošević. They were a result of government-sanctioned malpractices in the Nov municipal elections to prevent the Zajedno (Together) opposition alliance winning in 14 of the republic's 18 largest cities, including Belgrade. The nationalist Serbian Renewal Movement (SPO), led by Vuk Drašković and part of Zajedno, spearheaded the protests. 250,000 marched in Belgrade in Dec 1996, but from late Dec riot police launched a crackdown. Marches were officially banned, but daily student-led protests continued throughout Jan 1997. In Dec 1996 a report by a delegation from the Organization for Security and Cooperation in Europe (OSCE) called on the government to accept Zajedno's victories in the municipal elections. The Serbian parliament responded Feb 1997 by passing legislation to recognise the Zajedno municipal victories. This brought opposition demonstrations to an end.

In July 1997 elections Slobodan Milošević was elected to the Yugoslav presidency despite the protests of the pro-democratic movement.

Z

Zadar (Italian *Zara*) port and resort in Croatia. The city was sacked by the army of the Fourth Crusade 1202, which led to the Crusade being excommunicated by Pope Innocent III. It was alternately held and lost by the Venetian republic from the 12th century until its seizure by Austria 1813. It was the capital of Dalmatia 1815–1918 and part of Italy from 1920 until 1947, when it became part of Yugoslavia; it now belongs to independent Croatia.

Zahir ud-Din Muhammad 1483–1530. First Great Mogul of India from 1526, called *Babur* (arabic 'lion'). He was the great-grandson of the Mongol conqueror Tamerlane and, at the age of 11, succeeded his father, Omar Sheik Mirza, as ruler of Ferghana (Turkestan). In 1526 he defeated the emperor of Delhi at Panipat in the Punjab, captured Delhi and ◊Agra (the site of the Taj Mahal), and established a dynasty that lasted until 1858.

za'im in Lebanon, a political leader, originally the holder of a feudal office. The office is largely hereditary; an example is the Jumblatt family, traditional leaders of the Druse party. The pattern of Lebanese politics has been that individual *za'im*, rather than parties or even government ministers, wield effective power.

Zaire country in central Africa, bounded W by Congo, N by the Central African Republic and Sudan, E by Uganda, Rwanda, Burundi, and Tanzania, SE by Zambia, and SW by Angola. There is a short coastline on the Atlantic Ocean.

history The area was originally peopled by central African hunters and agriculturalists. The name Zaire (from *Zadi* 'big water') was given by Portuguese explorers who arrived on the country's Atlantic coast in the 15th century. The great medieval kingdom of Kongo, centred on the banks of the Zaïre River, was then in

decline, and the subsequent slave trade weakened it further. The interior was not explored by Europeans until the arrival of Stanley and ◊Livingstone in the 1870s, partly financed by Leopold II of Belgium, who established the Congo Free State under his personal rule 1885. Local resistance was suppressed, and the inhabitants were exploited. When the atrocious treatment of local labour was made public, Belgium annexed the country as a colony, the Belgian Congo, 1908, and conditions were marginally improved.

independence Zaire was given full independence June 1960 as the Republic of the Congo. The new state was intended to be governed centrally from Leopoldville by President Joseph Kasavubu and Prime Minister Patrice Lumumba, but Moise Tshombe immediately declared the rich mining province of Katanga (renamed Shaba 1972) independent under his leadership. Fighting broke out, which was not quelled by Belgian troops, and the United Nations (UN) Security Council agreed to send a force to restore order and protect lives. Meanwhile, disagreements between Kasavubu and Lumumba on how the crisis should be tackled prompted the Congolese army commander, Col Joseph-Désiré ◊Mobutu, to step in and temporarily take over the government. Lumumba was imprisoned and later released, and five months later power was handed back to Kasavubu. Soon afterwards Lumumba was murdered and the white mercenaries employed by Tshombe were thought to be responsible. The outcry that followed resulted in a new government being formed, with Cyrille Adoula as prime minister.

During the fighting between Tshombe's mercenaries and UN forces the UN secretary general, Dag ◊Hammarskjöld, flew to Katanga province to mediate and was killed in an air crash on the border with Northern Rhodesia. The attempted secession of Katanga was finally stopped 1963 when Tshombe went into exile, taking many of his followers with him to form the Congolese National Liberation Front (FNLC). In July 1964 Tshombe returned from exile, and President Kasavubu appointed him interim prime minister until elections for a new government could be held. In Aug the country was renamed the Democratic Republic of the Congo.

'second republic' A power struggle soon developed between Kasavubu and Tshombe, and again the army, under Mobutu, intervened, establishing a 'second republic' Nov 1965. A new constitution was adopted 1967, Tshombe died in captivity 1969, and Mobutu was elected

president for a seven-year term 1970. The following year the country became the Republic of Zaire, and the Popular Movement of the Revolution (MPR) was declared the only legal political party 1972. In the same year the president became known as Mobutu Sese Seko.

reform and stability Mobutu, re-elected 1977, carried out a large number of political and constitutional reforms. He gradually improved the structure of public administration and brought stability to what had once seemed an ungovernable country, although he faced two revolts in Shaba province. The first in March 1977 was put down with the support of Moroccan forces airlifted to Zaire by France. The second in May 1978 was repulsed by French and Belgian paratroopers. Both invasions were instigated by the Congolese National Liberation Front, operating from bases in Angola. However, the harshness of some of his policies brought international criticism and in 1983 he offered amnesty to all political exiles. Marshal Mobutu, as he was now called, was re-elected 1984 for a third term.

Because of mounting pressures, Mobutu promised multiparty elections for 1992, and after countrywide rioting agreed to share power with the opposition 1991. The agreement failed due to disagreements between Mobutu and prime minister Etienne Tshisekedi. Widespread rioting re-erupted Oct 1992. In 1994 an interim parliament elected Kengo Wa Dondo prime minister. Mobutu accepted this, but opposed reform initiatives; a new constitution was nevertheless adopted 1994.

In Oct 1996 Zaire and Rwanda were on the brink of war following mass killings of Hutus by Tutsis; it was averted when thousands of Hutus were allowed to return to Zaire. Meanwhile the Alliance of Democratic Forces for the Liberation of Zaire-Congo (ADFL) made advances under Laurent Kabila. Mobutu resigned as president May 1997 when the rebels were poised to take the capital, Kinshasha. Kabila, the new president, renamed Zaire the Democratic Republic of Congo.

Zama, Battle of battle fought in 202 BC in Numidia (now Algeria), in which the Carthaginians under Hannibal were defeated by the Romans under Scipio, so ending the Second ◊Punic War.

Zambia landlocked country in S central Africa, bounded N by Zaire and Tanzania, E by Malawi, S by Mozambique, Zimbabwe, Botswana, and Namibia, and W by Angola.

history For early history, see ◊Africa. The country was visited by the Portuguese in the late 18th century and by ◊Livingstone 1851. As Northern Rhodesia it became a British protectorate 1924, together with the former kingdom of Barotseland (now Western Province), taken under British protection at the request of its ruler 1890.

independent republic From 1953 the country, with Southern Rhodesia (now Zimbabwe) and Nyasaland (now Malawi), was part of the Federation of Rhodesia and Nyasaland, dissolved 1963. Northern Rhodesia became the independent Republic of Zambia 1964, within the Commonwealth, with Dr Kenneth ◊Kaunda, leader of the United National Independence Party (UNIP), as its first president. Between 1964 and 1972, when it was declared a one-party state, Zambia was troubled with frequent outbreaks of violence because of disputes within the governing party and conflicts among the country's more than 70 tribes.

relations with Rhodesia Zambia was economically dependent on neighbouring white-ruled Rhodesia but tolerated liberation groups operating on the border, and relations between the two countries deteriorated. The border was closed 1973, and in 1976 Kaunda declared his support for the Patriotic Front, led by Robert Mugabe and Joshua Nkomo, which was fighting the white regime in Rhodesia. Despite his imposition of strict economic policies, Kaunda was re-elected 1983 and again Oct 1988, unopposed, for a sixth consecutive term.

end of Kaunda presidency In 1990, in response to the growing strength of the opposition Movement for Multiparty Democracy (MMD), President Kaunda announced that a multiparty system would be introduced by Oct 1991. The MMD applied for formal registration as a political party and the formation of the National Democratic Alliance (Nada) was announced. Elections were held Oct 1991 and the MMD won an overwhelming victory. Frederick Chiluba was sworn in as Zambia's new president 2 Nov 1991, bringing to an end the 27-year leadership of Kaunda.

drought As a result of the worst drought experienced by South Africa in the 20th century, Zambia suffered dire food and water shortages in 1992.

ZANU (acronym for **Zimbabwe African National Union**) political organization founded in 1963 by the Reverend Ndabaningi Sithole and later led by Robert Mugabe. It was banned 1964 by Ian Smith's Rhodesian Front government, against which it conducted a guerrilla war from Zambia until the free elections of

1980, when the ZANU Patriotic Front party, led by Mugabe, won 63% of the vote. In 1987 it merged with ◊ZAPU in preparation for making Zimbabwe a one-party state.

Zanzibar island region of Tanzania. It was settled by Arab traders in the 7th century; occupied by the Portugues e in the 16th century; became a sultanate in the 17th century; under British protection 1890–1963. Together with the island of Pemba, some nearby islets, and a strip of mainland territory, it became a republic 1963. It merged with Tanganyika as Tanzania 1964.

Zapata Emiliano 1879–1919. Mexican Indian revolutionary leader. He led a revolt against dictator Porfirio Díaz (1830–1915) from 1911 under the slogan 'Land and Liberty', to repossess for the indigenous Mexicans the land taken by the Spanish. By 1915 he was driven into retreat, and was assassinated.

Many of them, so as to curry favour with tyrants, for a fistful of coins, or through bribery or corruption, are shedding the blood of their brothers.

Emiliano Zapata Plan de Ayala

Zapotec member of a North American Indian people of S Mexico, now numbering approximately 250,000, living mainly in Oaxaca. The ancient Zapotec built the ceremonial centre of Monte Albán in 1000–500 BC; developing one of the classic Mesoamerican civilizations by AD 300, but declined under pressure from the ◊Mixtecs from 900 until the Spanish Conquest 1530s.

ZAPU (acronym **Zimbabwe African People's Union**) political organization founded by Joshua Nkomo 1961 and banned 1962 by the Rhodesian government. It engaged in a guerrilla war in alliance with ◊ZANU against the Rhodesian regime until late 1979. In the 1980 elections ZAPU was defeated and was then persecuted by the ruling ZANU Patriotic Front party. In 1987 the two parties merged.

Zaragoza (English *Saragossa*) city in Aragon, Spain. A Celtic settlement known as *Salduba* was captured by the Romans in the 1st century BC, they named it *Caesarea Augusta*, after their leader; later it was captured by Visigoths and Moors and was taken 1118 by Alfonso the Warrior, King of Navarre and Aragon, after a nine-month siege. It remained the capital of Aragon until the end of the 15th century. From June 1808 to Feb 1809, in the Peninsular War,

it resisted a French siege. Maria Augustin (died 1859), known as the 'Maid of Zaragoza', became a national hero for her part in the defence.

Zealot member of a revolutionary Jewish nationalist group in Roman Palestine which had broken away from the ◊Pharisees in the 1st century AD.

zemstvo Russian provincial or district councils established by Tsar Alexander II 1864. They were responsible for local administration until the revolution of 1917.

Zeng Guofan or *Tseng Kuo-fan* 1811–1872. Chinese imperial official who played a crucial role in crushing the ◊Taiping rebellion. He raised the Hunan army 1852 to organize resistance to this revolt, eventually capturing Nanjing 1864. The regional influence he acquired made him in some ways a forerunner of the 20th-century Chinese warlords.

Fearful that Zeng's provincial army might grow too powerful, the government refused him money, forcing him to extract local financial support. He became a supporter of the ◊self-strengthening movement for military modernization, and was governor general of Liangjiang in E central China 1860–65, setting up the Jiangnan Arsenal in Shanghai for the manufacture of modern weapons and the study of Western science and technology.

Zentrumspartei German name for the ◊Centre Party 1871–1933.

Communists should be the first to be concerned about their people and country and the last to enjoy themselves.

Zhao Ziyang in Observer March 1988

Zhao Ziyang 1918– . Chinese politician, prime minister 1980–87 and secretary of the Chinese Communist Party 1987–89. His reforms included self-management and incentives for workers and factories. He lost his secretaryship and other posts after the Tiananmen Square massacre in Beijing June 1989.

Zhao was appointed prime minister 1980 and assumed, in addition, the post of CCP general secretary Jan 1987. His economic reforms were criticized for causing inflation, and his liberal views of the prodemocracy demonstrations that culminated in the student occupation of Tiananmen Square led to his downfall.

Zheng He or *Cheng Ho* died 1433. Chinese admiral and emperor during the ◊Ming dynasty. A Muslim court eunuch, he undertook maritime expeditions 1405–33 to India, the Persian Gulf, and E Africa, demonstrating China's early command of the compass and shipbuilding techniques.

About 60 vessels were used in the first voyage, to India 1405–07, and Zheng undertook seven journeys in all, involving 28,000 persons. The expeditions ceased 1433, probably because of their expense and the Ming government's indifference to foreign trade.

Zhivkov Todor 1911– . Bulgarian Communist Party leader 1954–89, prime minister 1962–71, president 1971–89. His period in office was one of caution and conservatism. In 1992 he was convicted of gross embezzlement.

Zhou dynasty or *Chou dynasty* Chinese succession of rulers *c.* 1066–256 BC during which cities emerged and philosophy flourished. It was established by the Zhou, a semi-nomadic people from the Wei Valley region, W of the great bend in the Huang He (Yellow River). Zhou influence waned from 403 BC, as the Warring States era began.

The founder was Wu Wang, 'the Martial', who claimed that ◊Shang dynasty misrule justified the transfer of the 'mandate of heaven'. Under the Zhou, agriculture and commerce developed further, iron implements and metal coins came into use, cities formed, and the philosophies of Confucius, Lao Zi, Mencius, and Taoism flowered. The Western Zhou controlled feudal vassal states in the Wei Valley, basing their capital at Hao, near Xian, until 771 BC. A new capital was later set up at Luoyang, to serve the Eastern Zhou. Zhou society had a very similar structure to later feudal European and Japanese periods, with strict divisions and hereditary classes.

Zhou Enlai or *Chou En-lai* 1898–1976. Chinese politician. Zhou, a member of the Chinese Communist Party (CCP) from the 1920s, was prime minister 1949–76 and foreign minister 1949–58. He was a moderate Maoist and weathered the Cultural Revolution.

Born into a declining mandarin gentry family near Shanghai, Zhou studied in Japan and Paris, where he became a founder member of the overseas branch of the CCP. He adhered to the Moscow line of urban-based revolution in China, organizing communist cells in Shanghai and an abortive uprising in Nanchang 1927. In 1935 Zhou supported the election of Mao Zedong as CCP leader and remained a loyal ally during the next 40 years. He served as liaison officer 1937–46 between the CCP and Chiang Kai-shek's nationalist Guomindang government. In 1949 he became prime minister, an office he held until his death Jan 1976.

Zhou, a moderator between the opposing camps of Liu Shaoqi and Mao Zedong, restored orderly progress after the Great Leap Forward (1958–60) and the Cultural Revolution (1966–69), and was the architect of the Four Modernizations programme 1975. Abroad, Zhou sought to foster Third World unity at the Bandung Conference 1955, averted an outright border confrontation with the USSR by negotiation with Prime Minister Kosygin 1969, and was the principal advocate of détente with the USA during the early 1970s.

Zhu De or *Chu Teh* 1886–1976. Chinese Red Army leader from 1931. He devised the tactic of mobile guerrilla warfare and organized the ◊Long March to Shaanxi 1934–35. He was made a marshal 1955.

The son of a wealthy Sichuan landlord, Zhu served in the Chinese Imperial Army before supporting Sun Yat-sen in the 1911 revolution. He studied communism in Germany and Paris 1922–25 and joined the Chinese Communist Party (CCP) on his return, becoming commander in chief of the Red Army. Working closely with Mao Zedong, Zhu organized the Red Army's Jiangxi break-out 1931 and led the 18th Route Army during the liberation war 1937–49. He served as head of state (chair of the Standing Committee of the National People's Congress) 1975–76.

History shows that risks should be taken but not blindly.

Marshal Zhukov 1965

Zhukov Georgi Konstantinovich 1896–1974. Marshal of the USSR in World War II and minister of defence 1955–57. As chief of staff from 1941, he defended Moscow 1941, counterattacked at Stalingrad (now Volgograd) 1942, organized the relief of Leningrad (now St Petersburg) 1943, and led the offensive from the Ukraine March 1944 which ended in the fall of Berlin.

Zia ul-Haq Mohammad 1924–1988. Pakistani general, in power from 1977 until his death, probably an assassination, in an aircraft explosion. He became army chief of staff 1976, led the military coup against Zulfiqar Ali ◊Bhutto 1977, and became president 1978. Zia introduced a fundamentalist Islamic regime and restricted political activity.

Zia was a career soldier from a middle-class Punjabi Muslim family. As army chief of staff, his opposition to the Soviet invasion of Afghanistan 1979 drew support from the USA, but his refusal to commute the death sentence imposed on Zulfiqar Ali Bhutto was widely condemned. He lifted martial law 1985.

If the Court sentences the blighter to hang, then the blighter will hang.

General Zia ul-Haq of the death sentence imposed on former president Zulfiqar Ali Bhutto 1979

Zimbabwe or **Great Zimbabwe** extensive stone architectural ruins near Victoria in Mashonaland, Zimbabwe. The structure was probably the work of the Shona people who established their rule about AD 1000 and who mined minerals for trading. The word *zimbabwe* means 'house of stone' in Shona language. The new state of Zimbabwe took its name from these ruins.

Zimbabwe landlocked country in S central Africa, bounded N by Zambia, E by Mozambique, S by South Africa, and W by Botswana.

history There was a Bantu-speaking civilization in the area before AD 300. By 1200 ◊Mashonaland, now E Zimbabwe, was a major settlement of the Shona people, who had moved in from the north and erected stone buildings. The name Zimbabwe means 'stone house' in Bantu. In the 15th century the Shona empire, under Mutota, expanded across Zimbabwe before it fell to the Rozwi, who ruled until the 19th century. Portuguese explorers reached the area in the early 16th century. In 1837 the Matabele, a Bantu people, in retreat after unsuccessful battles with the ◊Boers, settled in W Zimbabwe. Mashonaland and ◊Matabeleland, together with what is now Zambia, were granted to the British South Africa Company 1889, and the whole was named Rhodesia 1895 in honour of Cecil ◊Rhodes. King Lobengula of Matabeleland accepted British protection 1888 but rebelled 1893; he was defeated, but in 1896 after the Jameson Raid the Matabele once more unsuccessfully tried to regain their independence. The portion of the area south of the Zambezi River, then known as Southern Rhodesia, became self-governing 1923 and a member of the Federation of Rhodesia and Nyasaland 1953.

African nationalists were campaigning for full democracy, and the African National Congress (ANC), which had been present since 1934, was reconvened 1957 under the leadership of Joshua Nkomo. It was banned 1959, and Nkomo went into exile to become leader of the National Democratic Party (NDP), which had been formed by some ANC members. When the NDP was banned 1961, Nkomo created the Zimbabwe African People's Union (ZAPU); this was banned 1962. In 1963 a splinter group developed from ZAPU, the Zimbabwe African National Union (ZANU), led by the Rev Ndabaningi Sithole, with Robert ◊Mugabe as its secretary general.

unilateral declaration of independence After the dissolution of the Federation of Rhodesia and Nyasaland 1963 the leader of the Rhodesian Front party (RF), Winston Field, became the first prime minister of Rhodesia. The RF was a group of white politicians committed to maintaining racial segregation. In April 1964 Field resigned and was replaced by Ian ◊Smith, who rejected terms for independence proposed by Britain that required clear progress towards majority rule. Four months later ZANU was banned, and Nkomo and Mugabe imprisoned. In Nov 1965, after further British attempts to negotiate a formula for independence, Smith annulled the 1961 constitution and unilaterally announced Rhodesia's independence. Britain broke off diplomatic and trading links and the United Nations initiated economic sanctions, but these were bypassed by many multinational companies. The British prime minister, Harold Wilson, had abortive talks with Smith 1966 and 1968.

disputed independence arrangements In 1969 Rhodesia declared itself a republic and adopted a new constitution, with white majority representation in a two-chamber legislature. Armed South African police at times supported the Smith regime against ZAPU and ZANU guerrillas. In 1972 another draft agreement for independence was rejected by the British government as not acceptable to the Rhodesian people 'as a whole'. A conference in Geneva 1975 was attended by deputations from the British government, the Smith regime, and the African nationalists, represented by Bishop Abel ◊Muzorewa, president of the African National Council, which had been formed 1971 to oppose the earlier independence arrangements, and Robert Mugabe and Joshua Nkomo, who had been released from detention and had jointly formed the Patriotic Front (PF).

At the beginning of 1979 Smith produced a new 'majority rule' constitution, which contained an inbuilt protection for the white minority but which he had managed to get Muzorewa to accept. In June 1979 Bishop Muzorewa was pronounced prime minister of what was to be called Zimbabwe Rhodesia. The new constitution was denounced by Mugabe and Nkomo as another attempt by Smith to perpetuate the white domination, and they continued to lead the Zimbabwe African National Liberation Army from bases in neighbouring Mozambique.

In Aug 1979 the new British prime minister Margaret ◊Thatcher under the influence of her foreign secretary Lord Carrington and President Kaunda of Zambia, agreed to the holding of a constitutional conference in London at which all shades of political opinion in Rhodesia would be represented. The conference, Sept 1979, resulted in what became known as the Lancaster House Agreement and paved the way for full independence. A member of the British cabinet, Lord Soames, was sent to Rhodesia as governor general to arrange a timetable for independence. Economic and trade sanctions were lifted. A small Commonwealth monitoring force supervised the disarming of the thousands of guerrilla fighters who brought their weapons and ammunition from all parts of the country.

independent state achieved A new constitution was adopted, and elections were held, under independent supervision, Feb 1980. They resulted in a decisive win for Robert Mugabe's ZANU–PF party. The new state of Zimbabwe became fully independent April 1980, with the Rev Canaan Banana as president and Robert Mugabe as prime minister. During the next few years a rift developed between Mugabe and Nkomo and between ZANU PF and ZAPU supporters. Nkomo was accused of trying to undermine Mugabe's administration and was dismissed from the cabinet. Fearing for his safety, he spent some months in the UK. ZAPU was opposed to the 1984 proposal by the ZANU–PF for the eventual creation of a one-party socialist state.

Mugabe's party increased its majority in the 1985 elections with 63 seats against 15 and early in 1986 he announced that the separate seats for the whites in the assembly would be abolished within a year. Relations between the two parties and the two leaders eventually improved and by 1986 discussions of a merger were under way. When President Banana retired 1987, Mugabe combined the posts of head of state and prime minister. In Dec 1989 a draft constitution was drawn up that renounced Marxism–Leninism as the state ideology and created a one-party state, fusing the governing party and opposition groups; the ZANU–PF abandoned its Marxist ideology 1991. A new opposition group headed by former Mugabe ally, Edgar Tekere, was launched 1989, with the intention to challenge the

ZANU– PF in the 1990 elections. Tekere announced that his Zimbabwe Unity Movement would advocate capitalism and multiparty democracy. However, the ZANU–PF won a comfortable victory March 1990 and Mugabe was re-elected president. The state of emergency, in force since 1965, was ended July 1990. Mugabe's proposals Aug 1990 for a one-party state were strongly opposed. In July 1992 Rev Sithole and Ian Smith formed a United Front to oppose the ZANU–PF.

Zinoviev Grigory 1883–1936. Russian communist politician whose name was attached to a forgery, the *Zinoviev letter*, inciting Britain's communists to rise, which helped to topple the Labour government 1924.

A prominent Bolshevik, Zinoviev returned to Russia 1917 with Lenin and played a leading part in the Revolution. He became head of the Communist ◊International 1919. As one of the 'Old Bolsheviks', he was seen by Stalin as a threat. He was accused of complicity in the murder of the Bolshevik leader Sergei Kirov 1934, and was tried and shot.

Zion Jebusite (Amorites of Canaan) stronghold in Jerusalem captured by King David, and the hill on which he built the Temple, symbol of Jerusalem and of Jewish national life.

Zionism political movement advocating the re-establishment of a Jewish homeland in Palestine, the 'promised land' of the Bible, with its capital Jerusalem, the 'city of Zion'.

1896 As a response to European ◊anti-Semitism, Theodor Herzl published his *Jewish State*, outlining a scheme for setting up an autonomous Jewish commonwealth under Ottoman suzerainty.

1897 The World Zionist Congress was established in Basel, Switzerland, with Herzl as its first president. *Hatikva* (The Hope) was adopted as the Zionist anthem, which was the unofficial anthem of Palestine until 1948 when it was sung at the proclamation of the State of Israel on May 14.

1917 The ◊Balfour Declaration was secured from Britain by Chaim Weizmann. It promised the Jews a homeland in Palestine.

1940–48 Jewish settlement in the British mandate of Palestine led to armed conflict between militant Zionists (see ◊Irgun, ◊Stern Gang) and both Palestinian Arabs and the British.

1947 In Nov the United Nations (UN) divided Palestine into Jewish and Arab states, with Jerusalem as an international city.

1948 The Jews in Palestine proclaimed the State of Israel on May 14, but the Arab states rejected both the partition of Palestine and the existence of Israel. The armies of Iraq, Syria, Lebanon, Trans-Jordan, Saudi Arabia, Yemen, and Egypt crossed Israel's borders and attacked en masse but were defeated by the Israeli army (*Haganah*).

1948–73 In addition to constant border sniping and clashes, one or more Arab nations have attacked Israel in the on-going ◊Arab-Israeli wars of 1956, 1967, and 1973.

1975 The General Assembly of the UN condemned Zionism as 'a form of racism and racial discrimination'; among those voting against the resolution were the USA and the members of the European Community.

1991 Attacked during Gulf War by Iraqi missiles and criticized for its adamant attitude against Palestinian aspirations, Israel met with Arab nations for the first time in a historic Middle East peace conference held in Spain. The UN General Assembly repealed its 1975 resolution condemning Zionism.

Zi Xi or *Tz'u-hsi* c. 1834–1908. Empress dowager of China. She was presented as a concubine to the emperor Xianfeng. On his death 1861 she became regent for her young son Tongzhi (1856–1875) until 1873 and, after his death, for her nephew Guangxu (1871–1908) until 1889. A ruthless conservative, she blocked the Hundred Days' Reform launched in 1898 and assumed power again, having Guangxu imprisoned. Her policies helped deny China a peaceful transition to political and economic reform.

Zoë c. 978–1050. Byzantine empress who ruled from 1028 until 1050. She gained the title by marriage to the heir apparent Romanus III Argyrus, but was reputed to have poisoned him (1034) in order to marry her lover Michael. He died 1041 and Zoë and her sister Theodora were proclaimed joint empresses. Rivalry led to Zoë marrying Constantine IX Monomachus with whom she reigned until her death.

Zog Ahmed Beg Zogu 1895–1961. King of Albania 1928–39. He became prime minister of Albania 1922, president of the republic 1925, and proclaimed himself king 1928. He was driven out by the Italians 1939 and settled in England.

Zollverein 19th-century German customs union, begun under Prussian auspices 1828; the union included most German-speaking states except Austria by 1834.

Although designed to remove tariff barriers and facilitate trade within the German confederation, the Zollverein also had a political effect in isolating Austria. The Austrians were committed to trade tariffs to protect their agriculture and industry; thus their inability to join the Zollverein served to increase Prussian power in the confederation.

Zongli Yamen (alternatively transcribed as Tsung Li Yamen) advisory body created in China after 1861 to deal with foreign affairs and other state modernization projects. It consisted of national and provincial state officials but was limited by a lack of power and the creation of an admiralty in 1885 and a formal foreign office after 1901.

Zoroaster or *Zarathustra* 6th century BC. Persian prophet and religious teacher, founder of Zoroastrianism. Zoroaster believed that he had seen God, Ahura Mazda, in a vision. His first vision came at the age of 30 and, after initial rejection and violent attack, he converted King Vishtaspa. Subsequently, his teachings spread rapidly, becoming the official religion of the kingdom.

Zoroastrianism pre-Islamic Persian religion founded by the Persian prophet Zoroaster in the 6th century BC, and still practised by the Parsees in India. The *Zendavesta* are the sacred scriptures of the faith. The theology is dualistic, *Ahura Mazda* or *Ormuzd* (the good God) being perpetually in conflict with *Ahriman* (the evil God), but the former is assured of eventual victory. There are approximately 100,000 (1991) Zoroastrians worldwide.

Zulu member of a group of southern African peoples mainly from Natal, South Africa. Their present homeland, KwaZulu, represents the nucleus of the once extensive and militaristic Zulu kingdom. Today many Zulus work in the industrial centres around Johannesburg and Durban. The Zulu language, closely related to Xhosa, belongs to the Bantu branch of the Niger-Congo family.

Zwingli Ulrich 1484–1531. Swiss Protestant, born in St Gallen. He was ordained a Roman Catholic priest 1506, but by 1519 was a Reformer and led the Reformation in Switzerland with his insistence on the sole authority of the Scriptures. He was killed in a skirmish at Kappel during a war against the cantons that had not accepted the Reformation.

In the things of this life, the labourer is most like to God.

Ulrich Zwingli 1525

Appendix 1
Political and Religious Leaders

Prime ministers of Australia from 1901

term	name	party
1901–03	Sir Edmund Barton	Protectionist
1903–04	Alfred Deacon	Protectionist
1904	John Watson	Labor
1904–05	Sir G Reid	Free Trade–Protectionist coalition
1905–08	Alfred Deakin	Protectionist
1908–09	Andrew Fisher	Labor
1909–10	Alfred Deakin	Fusion
1910–13	Andrew Fisher	Labor
1913–14	Sir J Cook	Liberal
1914–15	Andrew Fisher	Labor
1915–23	William Morris Hughes	Labor (National Labor from 1917)
1923–29	J H Scullin	Labor
1932–39	Joseph Aloysius Lyons	United Australia–Country coalition
1939–41	R G Menzies	United Australia
1941	A W Fadden	Country–United Australia coalition
1941–45	John Curtin	Labor
1945	F M Forde	Labor
1945–49	J B Chifley	Labor
1949–66	R G Menzies	Liberal–Country coalition
1966–67	Harold Holt	Liberal–Country coalition
1967–68	John McEwen	Liberal–Country coalition
1968–71	J G Gorton	Liberal–Country coalition
1971–72	William McMahon	Liberal–Country coalition
1972–75	Gough Whitlam	Labor
1975–83	Malcolm Fraser	Liberal–National coalition
1983–91	Robert Hawke	Labor
1991–96	Paul Keating	Labor
1996–	John Howard	Liberal-National coalition

Aztec emperors

reign*	name
1372–91	Acamapichtli (chieftain at Tenochtitlán; traditional founder of Aztec royal house)
1391–1416	Huitzilihuitl (son)
1416–27	Chimalpopoca (son)
1427–40	Itzcoatl (son of Acamapichtli)
1468–81	Axayacatl (grandson of Itzcoatl)
1481–86	Tizoc (brother)
1486–1502	Ahuitzotl (brother)
1502–20	Montezuma II, Xocoyotzin (son of Axayacatl)
1520	Cuitlahuac (brother)
1520–21	Cuauhtemoc (son of Ahuitzotl)

* Dates before 1468 are approximate.

Presidents of Brazil from 1914

term	name	party
1945–46	José Linhares	independent
1946–51	Eurico Dutra	Social Democratic
1951–54	Getúlio Vargas	Brazil Labor
1954–55	Joco Café	Social Progressive
1955	Carlos da Luz	independent
1955–56	Nereu Ramos	independent
1956–61	Juscelino Kubitschek	Social Democratic
1961	Jânio Quadros	Christian Democratic/Democratic National
1961–64	João Goulart	Brazil Labor
1964	Ranieri Mazzili	independent
1964–67	Humberto Branco	military
1967–69	Arthur da Costa e Silva	military
1968–74	Emilio Medici	military
1974–79	Ernesto Geisel	military
1979–85	João Figueiredo	military
1985–89	José Sarney	Social Democratic
1989–92	Fernando Collor de Mello	National Reconstruction
1992-94	Itamar Franco	National Reconstruction
1995-	Fernando Henrique Cardoso	Social Democratic

Prime Ministers of Canada from 1867

term	name	party
1867–73	John A Macdonald	Conservative
1873–78	Alexander Mackenzie	Liberal
1878–91	John A Macdonald	Conservative
1891–92	John J Abbott	Conservative
1892–94	John S D Thompson	Conservative
1894–96	Mackenzie Bowell	Conservative
1896	Charles Tupper	Conservative
1896–1911	Wilfred Laurier	Liberal
1911–20	Robert L Borden	Conservative
1920–21	Arthur Meighen	Conservative
1921–26	William L M King	Liberal
1926	Arthur Meighen	Conservative
1926–30	William L M King	Liberal
1930–35	Richard B Bennett	Conservative
1935–48	William L M King	Liberal
1948–57	Louis S St Laurent	Liberal
1957–63	John G Diefenbaker	Conservative
1963–68	Lester B Pearson	Liberal
1968–79	Pierre E Trudeau	Liberal
1979–80	Joseph Clark	Progressive Conservative
1980–84	Pierre E Trudeau	Liberal
1984	John Turner	Liberal
1984–93	Brian Mulroney	Progressive Conservative
1993	Kim Campbell	Progressive Conservative
1993–	Jean Chrétien	Liberal

Ming-Dynasty Emperors of China

reign	name	born
1368–98	Hongwu	1328
1398–1402	Jianwen	1377
1402–24	Yongle	1360
1424–25	Hongxi	1378
1425–35	Xuande	1399
1435–49	Zhengtong	1427*
1449–57	Jingtai	1428
1457–64	Tianshun	1427
1464–87	Chenghua	1447
1487–1505	Hongzhi	1470
1505–21	Zhengde	1491
1521–67	Jiajing	1507
1567–72	Longqing	1537
1572–1620	Wanli	1563
1620	Taichang	1582
1620–27	Tianqi	1605
1627–44	Chongzhen	1611

* Zhengtong was deposed in 1449 and held captive. He was restored, as Tianshun, in 1457.

Qing-Dynasty Emperors of China

reign	name	born
1644–61	Shunzhi	1638
1661-1722	Kangxi	1645
1722–35	Yongzheng	1678
1735–96	Qianlong	1711
1796–1820	Jiaqing	1760
1820–50	Daoguang	1782
1850–61	Xianfeng	1831
1861–75	Tongzhi	1856
1875–1908	Guangxu	1871
1908–12	Xuantong*	1906

* Personal name: P'u-i

People's Republic of China: Prime Ministers and Communist Party Leaders

prime ministers		Communist Party leaders	
term	name	term	name
1949–76	Zhou Enlai	1935–76	Mao Zedong
1976–80	Hua Guofeng	1976–81	Hua Guofeng
1980–88	Zhao Ziyang	1981–87	Hu Yaobang
1988–	Li Peng	1987–89	Zhao Ziyang
		1989–	Jiang Zemin

English Sovereigns from 900

reign	name	relationship

West Saxon kings
901–25	Edward the Elder	son of Alfred the Great
925–40	Athelstan	son of Edward I
940–46	Edmund	half-brother of Athelstan
946–55	Edred	brother of Edmund
955–59	Edwy	son of Edmund
959–75	Edgar	brother of Edwy
975–78	Edward the Martyr	son of Edgar
978–1016	Ethelred II	son of Edgar
1016	Edmund Ironside	son of Ethelred

Danish kings
1016–35	Canute	son of Sweyn I of Denmark, who conquered England in 1013
1035–40	Harold I	son of Canute
1040–42	Hardicanute	son of Canute

West Saxon kings (restored)
1042–66	Edward the Confessor	son of Ethelred II
1066	Harold II	son of Godwin

Norman kings
1066–87	William I	illegitimate son of Duke Robert the Devil
1087–1100	William II	son of William I
1100–35	Henry I	son of William I
1135–54	Stephen	grandson of William II

House of Plantagenet
1154–89	Henry II	son of Matilda (daughter of Henry I)
1189–99	Richard I	son of Henry II
1199–1216	John	son of Henry II
1216–72	Henry III	son of John
1272–1307	Edward I	son of Henry III
1307–27	Edward II	son of Edward I
1327–77	Edward III	son of Edward II
1377–99	Richard II	son of the Black Prince

House of Lancaster
1399–1413	Henry IV	son of John of Gaunt
1413–22	Henry V	son of Henry IV
1422–61, 1470–71	Henry VI	son of Henry V

House of York
1461–70, 1471–83	Edward IV	son of Richard, Duke of York
1483	Edward V	son of Edward IV
1483–85	Richard III	brother of Edward IV

House of Tudor
1485–1509	Henry VII	son of Edmund Tudor, Earl of Richmond
1509–47	Henry VIII	son of Henry VII
1547–53	Edward VI	son of Henry VIII
1553–58	Mary I	daughter of Henry VIII
1558–1603	Elizabeth I	daughter of Henry VIII

House of Stuart
1603–25	James I	great-grandson of Margaret (daughter of Henry VIII)
1625–49	Charles I	son of James I
1649–60	*the Commonwealth*	

House of Stuart (restored)
1660–85	Charles II	son of Charles I
1685–88	James II	son of Charles I
1689–1702	William III and Mary	son of Mary (daughter of Charles I); daughter of James II
1702–14	Anne	daughter of James II

House of Hanover
1714–27	George I	son of Sophia (grand-daughter of James I)
1727–60	George II	son of George I
1760–1820	George III	son of Frederick (son of George II)
1820–30	George IV (regent 1811–20)	son of George III

| 1830–37 | William IV | son of George III |
| 1837–1901 | Victoria | daughter of Edward (son of George III) |

House of Saxe-Coburg

| 1901–10 | Edward VII | son of Victoria |

House of Windsor

1910–36	George V	son of Edward VII
1936	Edward VIII	son of George V
1936–52	George VI	son of George V
1952–	Elizabeth II	daughter of George VI

European Commission Presidents from 1958

term	name	nationality
1958–66	Walter Hallstein	German
1966–70	Jean Rey	Belgian
1970–72	Franco Malfatti	Italian
1972–73	Sicco Mansholt	Dutch
1973–77	François-Xavier Ortoli	French
1977–81	Roy Jenkins	British
1981–85	Gaston Thorn	Luxembourg
1985–95	Jacques Delors	French
1995–	Jacques Santer	Luxembourg

Kings of France 751–1848

reign	name

Carolingian House (* Robertian House)

751–68	Pepin the Short
768–814	Charlemagne
814–40	Louis I, the Pious
840–77	Charles I, the Bald
877–79	Louis II, the Stammerer
879–82	Louis III
879–84	Carloman
884–88	Charles II, the Fat
888–93	Eudes
893–922	Charles III, the Simple
922–23	Robert I
923–36	Rudolf
936–54	Louis IV of Outremer
954–86	Lothair
986–87	Louis V, the Sluggard

Capetian House

987–96	Hugh Capet
996–1031	Robert II, the Pious
1031–60	Henry I
1060–1108	Philip I
1108–37	Louis VI, the Fat
1137–80	Louis VII, the Younger
1180–1223	Philip II (Philip Augustus)
1223–26	Louis VIII, the Lion
1226–70	St Louis IX
1270–85	Philip III, the Bold
1285–1314	Philip IV, the Fair
1314–16	Louis X, the Stubborn
1316	John I
1316–22	Philip V, the Tall
1322–28	Charles IV, the Fair

House of Valois

1328–50	Philip VI
1350–64	John II, the Good
1364–80	Charles V, the Wise
1380–1422	Charles VI, the Mad

1422–61	Charles VII, the Victorious
1461–83	Louis XI
1483–98	Charles VIII
1498–1515	Louis XII
1515–47	Francis I
1547–59	Henry II
1559–60	Francis II
1560–74	Charles IX
1574–89	Henry III

House of Bourbon

1589–1610	Henry IV
1610–43	Louis XIII
1643–1715	Louis XIV
1715–74	Louis XV
1774–92	Louis XVI (deposed)
1792–1803	First Republic
1804–14	House of Bonaparte (First Empire)
1814–24	Louis XVIII
1824–30	Charles X (deposed)
1830–48	Louis Philippe I (deposed)

French Fifth Republic Presidents and Prime Ministers from 1959

term	name	party
presidents		
1959–69	General Charles de Gaulle	Gaullist
1969–74	Georges Pompidou	Gaullist
1974–81	Valéry Giscard d'Estaing	Republican/ Union of French Democracy
1981–95	François Mitterand	Socialist
1995–	Jacques Chirac	Neo-Gaullist RPR
prime ministers		
1959–62	Michel Debré	Gaullist
1962–68	Georges Pompidou	Gaullist
1968–69	Maurice Couve de Murville	Gaullist
1969–72	Jacques Chaban-Delmas	Gaullist
1972–74	Pierre Messmer	Gaullist
1974–76	Jacques Chirac	Gaullist
1976–81	Raymond Barre	Union of French Democracy
1981–84	Pierre Mauroy	Socialist
1984–86	Laurent Fabius	Socialist
1986–88	Jacques Chirac	Neo-Gaullist RPR
1988–91	Michel Rocard	Socialist
1991–92	Edith Cresson	Socialist
1992–93	Pierre Bérégovoy	Socialist
1993–95	Edouard Balladur	Neo-Gaullist RPR
1995–97	Alain Juppé	Neo-Gaullist RPR
1997–	Lionel Jospin	Socialist

Political Leaders of Germany from 1949

Federal Republic

term	chancellor	party
1949–63	Konrad Adenauer	Christian Democrat
1963–66	Ludwig Erhard	Christian Democrat
1966–69	Kurt Kiesinger	Christian Democrat
1969–74	Willy Brandt	Social Democrat
1974–82	Helmut Schmidt	Social Democrat
1982–	Helmut Kohl	Christian Democrat

Democratic Republic

term	Communist Party leader
1949–50	Wilhelm Pieck
1950–71	Walter Ulbricht
1971–89	Erich Honecker
1989	Egon Krenz

prime ministers
1989–90	Hans Modrow
1990–91	Lothar de Maizière

House of Habsburg

reign	name

emperors of Austria
1804–35	Francis (Franz) I (of Austria) and II (as Holy Roman emperor until 1806)
1835–48	Ferdinand

emperors of Austria-Hungary
1848–1916	Franz Josef
1916–18	Charles (Karl; abdicated)

Holy Roman Emperors

reign	name

Carolingian kings and emperors
800–14	Charlemagne (Charles the Great)
814–40	Louis the Pious
840–55	Lothair I
855–75	Louis II
875–77	Charles II, the Bald
881–87	Charles III, the Fat
891–94	Guido of Spoleto
892–98	Lambert of Spoleto (co-emperor)
896–901	Arnulf (rival)
901–05	Louis III of Provence
905–24	Berengar
911–18	Conrad I of Franconia (rival)

Saxon kings and emperors
918–36	Henry I, the Fowler
936–73	Otto I, the Great
973–83	Otto II
983–1002	Otto III
1002–24	Henry II, the Saint

Franconian (Salian) emperors
1024–39	Conrad II
1039–56	Henry III, the Black
1056–1106	Henry IV
1077–80	Rudolf of Swabia (rival)
1081–93	Hermann of Luxembourg (rival)
1093–1101	Conrad of Franconia (rival)
1106–25	Henry V
1126–37	Lothair II

Hohenstaufen kings and emperors
1138–52	Conrad III
1152–90	Frederick Barbarossa
1190–97	Henry VI
1198–1215	Otto IV
1198–1208	Philip of Swabia (rival)
1215–50	Frederick II
1246–47	Henry Raspe of Thuringia (rival)
1247–56	William of Holland
1250–54	Conrad IV
1254–73	no ruler (the Great Interregnum)

rulers from various noble families
1257–72	Richard of Cornwall (rival)
1257–73	Alfonso X of Castile (rival)
1273–91	Rudolf I, Habsburg
1292–98	Adolf I of Nassau
1298–1308	Albert I, Habsburg
1308–13	Henry VII, Luxembourg
1314–47	Louis IV of Bavaria
1314–25	Frederick of Habsburg (co-regent)
1347–78	Charles IV, Luxembourg
1378–1400	Wenceslas of Bohemia
1400	Frederick III of Brunswick
1400–10	Rupert of the Palatinate
1411–37	Sigismund, Luxembourg

Habsburg emperors
1438–39	Albert II
1440–93	Frederick III
1493–1519	Maximilian I
1519–56	Charles V
1556–64	Ferdinand I
1564–76	Maximilian II
1576–1612	Rudolf II
1612–19	Matthias
1619–37	Ferdinand II
1637–57	Ferdinand III
1658–1705	Leopold I
1705–11	Joseph I
1711–40	Charles VI
1742–45	Charles VII of Bavaria

Habsburg-Lorraine emperors
1745–65	Francis I of Lorraine
1765–90	Joseph II
1790–92	Leopold II
1792–1806	Francis II

Inca Emperors

reign	name	relationship
the kingdom of Cuzco		
c. 1200?	Manco Capac	traditional founder of Cuzco and the Inca royal house
	Sinchi Roca	son
	Lloque Yupanqui	son
	Mayta Capac	son
	Capac Yupanqui	son
	Inca Roca	son
	Yahuar Huaca	son
	Viracocha Inca	son
the empire		
1438–71	Pachacuti	son; abdicated, died 1471
1471–93	Topa Inca	son
1493–1524	Huayna Capac	son
1524–32	Huascar	son; deposed, died 1532
1532	Atahualpa	brother; deposed, died 1533 in the Spanish conquest of the Inca Empire
the Vilcabamba state		
1533	Topa Hualpa	brother
1533–45	Manco Inca	brother
1545–60	Sayri Tupac	son
1560–71	Titu Cusi Yupanqui	brother

1571–72	Tupac Amaru	brother; deposed, died 1572 in the Spanish conquest of the Vilcabamba state

Emperors of India

reign	name

Mauryan emperors

325–297 BC	Chandragupta Maurya
297–72 BC	Bindusara
272–68 BC	interregnum
268–32 BC	Asoka
232–24 BC	Dasaratha
224–15 BC	Samprati
215–02 BC	Salisuka
202–195 BC	Devavarman
195–87 BC	Satadhanvan
187–85 BC	Brihadratha

Gupta emperors

AD 320–50	Chandragupta I
350–76	Samudragupta
376–415	Chandragupta II
415–55	Kumaragupta I
455–70	Skandagupta
470–75	Kumaragupta II
475–500	Budhagupta
500–15	Vainyagupta
515–30	Narasimhagupta
530–40	Kumaragupta III
540–50	Vishnugupta

Mogul emperors

Great Moguls

1526–30	Babur (Zahiruddin Muhammad)
1530–56	Humayun (Nasiruddin Muhammad)*
1556–1605	Akbar (Jalaluddin Muhammad)
1605–27	Jahangir (Nuruddin)
1627–28	Dewar Baksh
1628–58	Shah Jahan (Shihabuddin; dethroned)
1658–1707	Aurangzeb (Muhiyuddin)

lesser Moguls

1707	Azam Shah
1707–12	Shah Alam I (Muhammad Mu'azzam)
1712	Azim-ush Shan
1712–13	Jahandar Shah (Muhammad Muizzuddin)
1713–19	Farrukh Siyar (Jalaluddin Muhammad)
1719	Rafi ud-Darajat (Shamsuddin)
1719	Rafi ud-Daula Shah Jahan II
1719	Nikusiyar
1719–48	Muhammad Shah (Nasiruddin)
1748–54	Ahmad Shah Bahadur (Abu al-Nasir Muhammad)
1754–60	Alamgir II (Muhammad Azizuddin)
1760	Shah Jahan III
1760–1806	Shah Alam II (Jalaluddin Ali Jauhar; deposed briefly in 1788)
1806–37	Akbar Shah II (Muhiyuddin)
1837–58	Bahadur Shah II (Abul al-Zafar Muhammad Sirajuddin; banished)

* Humayun was defeated 1540 and expelled from India until 1555, leaving N India under the control of Sher Shah Suri (died 1545), Islam Shah, and Sikandar Shah.

Governors-General/Viceroys of India

term	name
1858–62	C J Canning, 1st Earl Canning
1862–63	J Bruce, 8th Earl of Elgin and Kincardine
1864–69	John L M Lawrence, 1st Earl Lawrence
1869–72	R S Bourke, 6th Earl of Mayo
1872–76	T G Baring, 1st Earl of Northbrook
1876–80	E R Bulwer-Lytton, 1st Earl of Lytton
1880–84	G F S Robinson, Earl and Marquess of Ripon
1884–88	F Hamilton-Temple-Blackwood, Earl and Marquess of Dufferin and Ava
1888–94	H C K Petty-Fitzmaurice, 5th Marquess of Lansdowne
1894–99	V A Bruce, 9th Earl of Elgin and Kincardine
1899–1905	G N Curzon, 1st Earl and Marquess Curzon of Kedleston
1905–10	G J Elliot-Murray-Kynynmond, Earl of Minto
1910–16	C Hardinge, 1st Baron Hardinge of Penhurst
1916–21	F J N Thesiger, 1st Viscount Chelmsford
1921–26	R D Isaacs, Marquess of Reading
1926–31	E F L Wood, Earl of Halifax
1931–36	F Freeman-Thomas, Earl and Marquess of Willingdon
1936–43	V A J Hope, 2nd Marquess of Linlithgow
1943–47	A P Wavell, Viscount and Earl Wavell
1947–48	Louis, 1st Earl Mountbatten of Burma

Prime Ministers of India

term	name	party
1949–64	Jawaharlal Nehru	Congress
1964–66	Lal Bahadur Shastri	Congress
1966–77	Indira Gandhi	Congress (I)
1977–79	Morarji Desai	Janata
1979–80	Charan Singh	Janata/Lok Dal
1980–84	Indira Gandhi	Congress (I)
1984–89	Rajiv Gandhi	Congress (I)
1989–90	Viswanath Pratap Singh	Janata Dal
1990–91	Chandra Shekhar	Janata Dal (Socialist)
1991–96	P. V. Narasimha Rao	Congress
1996	Atal Behari Vaj Payee	Bharatiya Janata
1996–97	H. D. Deve Gowda	Janata Dal
1997	Inder Kumar Gujral	United Front coalition

Prime Ministers of Ireland from 1922

term	name	party
1922	Michael Collins	Sinn Fein
1922–32	William T Cosgrave	Fine Gael
1932–48	Eamonn de Valera	Fianna Fáil
1948–51	John A Costello	Fine Gael
1951–54	Eamonn de Valera	Fianna Fáil
1954–57	John A Costello	Fine Gael
1957–59	Eamonn de Valera	Fianna Fáil
1959–66	Sean Lemass	Fianna Fáil
1966–73	Jack Lynch	Fianna Fáil
1973–77	Liam Cosgrave	Fine Gael
1977–79	Jack Lynch	Fianna Fáil
1979–81	Charles Haughey	Fianna Fáil
1981–82	Garrett Fitzgerald	Fine Gael
1982	Charles Haughey	Fianna Fáil
1982–87	Garrett Fitzgerald	Fine Gael
1987–92	Charles Haughey	Fianna Fáil
1992–94	Albert Reynolds	Fiánna Fáil
1994–97	John Bruton	Fine Gael
1997–	Bertie Ahern	Fiánna Fáil

Prime Ministers of Israel

term	name	party
1948–55	David Ben Gurion	Mapai
1955	M Sharett	Mapai
1955–63	David Ben Gurion	Mapai
1963–69	Levi Eshkol	Mapai/Labour
1969–74	Golda Meir	Labour
1974–77	Yitzhak Rabin	Labour
1977–83	Menachem Begin	Likud
1983–84	Yitzhak Shamir	Likud
1984–86	Shimon Peres	Labour
1986–92	Yitzhak Shamir	Likud
1992–95	Yitzhak Rabin	Labor
1995–96	Shimon Peres	Labor
1996–	Binjamin Netanyahu	Likud

Kings of Italy 1861–1946

reign	name
1861–78	Victor Emmanuel II
1878–1900	Umberto I
1900–46	Victor Emmanuel III
1946	Umberto II (abdicated)

Emperors of Japan

reign	era name*	personal name	relationship
legendary and Yamato periods (to AD 710)			
40–10 BC	Jimmu		semimythical founder of the dynasty
10 BC–AD 20	Suizei		son
20–50	Annei		son
50–80	Itoku		son
80–110	Kōshō		son
110–40	Kōan		son
140–70	Kōrei		son
170–200	Kōgen		son
200–30	Kaika		son
230–58	Sujin		son
258–90	Suinin		son
290–322	Keikō		son
322–55	Seimu		son
355–62	Chūai		nephew
362–94	Ōjin		son
394–427	Nintoku		son
427–32	Richū		son
432–37	Hanzei		brother
437–54	Ingyō		brother
454–57	Ankō		son
457–89	Yūraku		brother
489–94	Seinei		son
494–97	Kenzō		grandson of Richū
497–504	Ninken		brother
504–10	Buretsu		son
510–27	Keitai		fifth in descent from Ōjin
527–35	Ankan		son
535–39	Senka		brother
539–71	Kimmei		brother
572–85	Bidatsu		son
585–87	Yōmei		brother
587–92	Sushun		brother
593–628	Suiko		sister
629–41	Jomei		grandson of Bidatsu
642–45	Kōgyoku		niece; abdicated
645–54	Kōtoku		brother
655–61	Saimei		ex-empress Kōgyoku
661–72	Tenji		son of Jomei
672	Kōbun		son
672–86	Temmu		son of Jomei
686–97	Jitō		daughter of Tenji; abdicated, died 703
697–707	Mommu		grandson of Temmu
Nara period (710–84)			
707–15	Gemmei		daughter of Tenji; abdicated, died 721
715–24	Genshō		sister of Mommu; abdicated, died 748
724–49	Shōmu		son of Mommu; abdicated, died 756
749–58	Kōken		daughter; abdicated
758–64	Junnin		grandson of Temmu; deposed, died 765
764–70	Shōtoku		ex-empress Kōken
770–81	Kōnin		grandson of Tenji; abdicated, died 782
Heian period (794–1185)			
781–806	Kammu		son
806–09	Heizei		son; abdicated, died 824
809–23	Saga		brother; abdicated, died 842
823–33	Junna		brother; abdicated, died 840
833–50	Nimmyō		son of Saga
850–58	Montoku		son
858–76	Seiwa		son; abdicated, died 881
876–84	Yōzei		son; deposed, died 949
884–87	Kōkō		son of Nimmyō
887–97	Uda		son; abdicated, died 931
897–930	Daigo		son; abdicated, died 930
930–46	Suzaku		son; abdicated, died 952
946–67	Murakami		brother
967–69	Reizei		son; abdicated, died 1011
969–84	En'yū		brother; abdicated, died 991
984–86	Kazan		son of Reizei; abdicated, died 1008
986–1011	Ichijō		son of En'yū; abdicated, died 1011
1011–16	Sanjō		son of Reizei; abdicated, died 1017
1016–36	Go-Ichijō		son of Ichijō
1036–45	Go-Suzaku		brother; abdicated, died 1045
1045–68	Go-Reizei		son
1068–73	Go-Sanjō		brother; abdicated, died 1073
1073–87	Shirakawa		son; abdicated, died 1129
1087–1107	Horikawa		son
1107–23	Toba		son; abdicated, died 1156

1123–42	Sutoku	son; abdicated, died 1164
1142–55	Konoe	brother
1155–58	Go-Shirakawa	brother; abdicated, died 1192
1158–65	Nijō	son; abdicated, died 1165
1165–68	Rokujō	son; abdicated, died 1176
1168–80	Takakura	son of Go-Shirakawa; abdicated, died 1181
1180–85	Antoku	son

Kamakura period (1192–1333)

1183-98	Go-Toba	brother; abdicated, died 1239
1198–1210	Tsuchimikado	son; abdicated, died 1231
1210–21	Juntoku	brother; abdicated, died 1242
1221	Chūkyō	son; deposed, died 1234
1221–32	Go-Horikawa	grandson of Takakura; abdicated, died 1234
1232–42	Shijō	son
1242–46	Go-Saga	son of Tsuchimikado; abdicated, died 1272
1246–60	Go-Fukakusa	son; abdicated, died 1304
1260–74	Kameyama	brother; abdicated, died 1305
1274–87	Go-Uda	son; abdicated, died 1324
1287–98	Fushimi	son of Go-Fukakusa; abdicated, died 1317
1298–1301	Go-Fushimi	son; abdicated, died 1336
1301–08	Go-Nijō	son of Go-Uda
1308–1318	Hanazono	son of Fushimi, abdicated, died 1348

Nambokuchō period (1336–92)
The Southern Court

1318–39	Go-Daigo	son of Go-Uda
1339–68	Go-Murakami	son
1368–83	Chōkei	son; abdicated, died 1394
1383–92	Go-Kameyama	brother; abdicated, died 1424

The Northern Court

1331–33	Kōgon	son of Go-Fushimi; deposed, died 1364
1336–48	Kōmyō	brother; abdicated, died 1380
1348–51	Sukō	son of Kōgon; abdicated, died 1398
1352–71	Go-Kōgon	brother; abdicated, died 1374
1371–82	Go-En'yū	son; abdicated, died 1393

Muromachi period (1392–1568)

1382–1412	Go-Komatsu	son; abdicated, died 1433
1412–28	Shōkō	son
1428–64	Go-Hanazono	great-grandson of Sukō; abdicated, died 1471

1464–1500	Go-Tsuchimikado	son
1500–26	Go-Kashiwabara	son
1526–57	Go-Nara	son
1557–86	Ōgimachi	son; abdicated, died 1593

Edo period (1603–1868)

1586–1611	Go-Yōzei	grandson; abdicated, died 1617
1611–29	Go-Mizunoo	son; abdicated, died 1680
1629–43	Meishō	daughter; abdicated, died 1696
1643–54	Go-Kōmyō	brother
1655–63	Go-Sai	brother; abdicated, died 1685
1663–87	Reigen	brother; abdicated, died 1732
1687–1709	Higashiyama	son; abdicated, died 1710
1709–35	Nakamikado	son; abdicated, died 1737
1735–47	Sakuramachi	son; abdicated, died 1750
1747–62	Momozono	son
1762–71	Go-Sakuramachi	sister; abdicated, died 1813
1771–79	Go-Momozono	son of Momozono
1780–1817	Kōkaku	great-grandson of Higashiyama; abdicated, died 1840
1817–46	Ninkō	son
1846–67	Kōmei	son

modern period (from 1867)

1867–1912	Meiji	Mutsuhito	son
1912–26	Taishō	Yoshihito	son
1926–89	Shōwa	Hirohito	son; regent 1921–26
1989–	Heisei	Akihito	son

* Many emperors changed their era names for parts of their reign; for example, Higashiyama was known as Genroku 1688–1704 and as Hōei 1704–09.

Prime Ministers of Japan from 1945

term	name	party
1945–46	Kijurō Shidehara	coalition
1946–47	Shigeru Yoshida	Liberal
1947–48	Tetsu Katayama	coalition
1948	Hitoshi Ashida	Democratic
1948–54	Shigeru Yoshida	Liberal
1954–56	Ichirō Hatoyama	Liberal*
1956–57	Tanzan Ishibashi	LDP
1957–60	Nobusuke Kishi	LDP
1960–64	Hayato Ikeda	LDP
1964–72	Eisaku Satō	LDP
1972–74	Kakuei Tanaka	LDP
1974–76	Takeo Miki	LDP
1976–78	Takeo Fukuda	LDP
1978–80	Masayoshi Ohira	LDP
1980–82	Zenkō Suzuki	LDP
1982–87	Yasuhiro Nakasone	LDP
1987–89	Noboru Takeshita	LDP
1989	Sōsuke Uno	LDP
1989–91	Toshiki Kaifu	LDP

1991–93	Kiichi Miyazawa	LDP
1993–94	Morohiro Hosokawa	JNP-led coalition
1994–96	Tomiichi Murayama	SDPJ-led coalition
1996–	Ryutaro Hashimoto	LDP

* The conservative parties merged 1955 to form the Liberal Democratic Party (LDP, Jiyū-Minshūtō).

Presidents of Mexico from 1913

term	name
1913–17	V Huerta
1917–20	V Carranza
1920–24	General A Obregon
1924–34	P Calles
1934–40	General L Cardenas
1940–46	General M Avila Camacho
1946–52	M Aleman Valdes
1952–58	A Ruiz Cortines
1958–64	A Lopez Mateos
1964–70	G Diaz Ordaz
1970–76	L Echeverria Alvarez
1976–82	J Portillo y Pacheco
1982–88	M de la Madrid Hurtado
1988–94	Carlos Salinas de Gortari
1994–	Ernesto Zedillo Ponce de Léon

Prime Ministers of New Zealand from 1891

term	name	party
1891–93	J Ballance	Liberal
1893–1906	R J Seddon	Liberal
1906	W Hall-Jones	Liberal
1906–12	Joseph Ward	Liberal
1912	T Mackenzie	Liberal
1912–25	W F Massey	Reform
1925–28	J G Coates	Reform
1928–30	Joseph Ward	United
1930–35	G W Forbes	United
1935–40	M J Savage	Labour
1940–49	P Fraser	Labour
1949–57	S G Holland	National
1957	K J Holyoake	National
1957–60	Walter Nash	Labour
1960–72	K J Holyoake	National
1972	J Marshall	National
1972–74	N Kirk	Labour
1974–75	W Rowling	Labour
1975–84	R Muldoon	National
1984–89	D Lange	Labour
1989–90	G Palmer	Labour
1990	M Moore	Labour
1990–	J Bolger	National

Presidents/Heads of State of Nigeria from 1963

term	name
1963–66	Nnamdi Azikiwe
1966	Maj-Gen J Aguiyi-Ironsi
1966–75	Lt-Col Yakubu Gowon
1975–76	General M Ramat Mohammed
1976–79	Lt-Gen Olusegun Obasanjo
1979–83	A Shehu Shagari
1983–85	Maj-Gen Muhammadu Buhari
1985–93	Maj-Gen Ibrahim Babagida
1993	Ernest Shonekan
1993–	Gen Sani Abacha

Ottoman Emperors 1280–1924

reign	Osmanli dynasty
1280–1324	Osman I
1324–62	Orhan
1362–89	Murad I
1389–1402	Bayezid I, the Thunderbolt (deposed)
1402–03	Isa (claimed Anatolia)
1402–11	Suleiman (claimed Rumelia)
1409–13	Mesa (claimed Rumelia)
1413–21	Mehmed I (claimed Anatolia, 1402-13)
1421–51	Murad II (abdicated in favour of Mehmed II 1444–46)
1451–81	Mehmed II, the Conqueror
1481–1512	Bayezid II (deposed)
1512–20	Selim I, the Grim
1520–66	Suleiman I, the Magnificent
1566–74	Selim II, the Sot
1574–95	Murad III
1595–1603	Mehmed III
1603–17	Ahmed I
1617–18	Mustafa I (deposed)
1618–22	Osman II
1622–23	Mustafa I (restored; deposed)
1623–40	Murad IV
1640–48	Ibrahim (deposed)
1648–87	Mehmed IV (deposed)
1687–91	Suleiman II
1691–95	Ahmed II
1695–1703	Mustafa II (deposed)
1703–30	Ahmed III (deposed)
1730–54	Mahmud I
1754–57	Osman III
1757–74	Mustafa III
1774–89	Abdulhamid I
1789–1807	Selim III (deposed)
1807–08	Mustafa IV (deposed)
1808–39	Mahmud II
1839–61	Abdulmecid I
1861–76	Abdulaziz (deposed)
1876	Murad V (deposed)
1876–1909	Abdulhamid II (deposed)
1909–18	Mehmed V Resad
1918–22	Mehmed VI Vahiduddin (deposed)
1922–24	Abdulmecid II (deposed)

Popes from 1492

pontificate	papal name
1492–1503	Alexander VI
1503	Pius III
1503–13	Julius II
1513–21	Leo X
1522–23	Hadrian VI
1523–34	Clement VII
1534–49	Paul III
1550–55	Julius III
1555	Marcellus II
1555–59	Paul IV
1559–65	Pius IV
1566–72	Pius V
1572–85	Gregory XIII
1585–90	Sixtus V
1590	Urban VII
1590–91	Gregory XIV
1591	Innocent IX

1592–1605	Clement VIII
1605	Leo XI
1605–21	Paul V
1621–23	Gregory XV
1623–44	Urban VIII
1644–55	Innocent X
1655–67	Alexander VII
1667–69	Clement IX
1670–76	Clement X
1676–89	Innocent XI
1689–91	Alexander VIII
1691–1700	Innocent XII
1700–21	Clement XI
1721–24	Innocent XIII
1724–30	Benedict XIII
1730–40	Clement XII
1740–58	Benedict XIV
1758–69	Clement XIII
1769–74	Clement XIV
1775–99	Pius VI
1800–23	Pius VII
1823–29	Leo XII
1829–30	Pius VIII
1831–46	Gregory XVI
1846–78	Pius IX
1878–1903	Leo XIII
1903–14	Pius X
1914–22	Benedict XV
1922–39	Pius XI
1939–58	Pius XII
1958–63	John XXIII
1963–78	Paul VI
1978	John Paul I
1978–	John Paul II

Roman Emperors 27 BC–AD 285

reign   *name*

Julio-Claudian emperors

27 BC–14 AD	Augustus
14–37	Tiberius I
37–41	Caligula (Gaius Caesar)
41–54	Claudius I
54–68	Nero
68–69	Galba

Flavian emperors

69–79	Vespasian
79–81	Titus
81–96	Domitian

the Five Good Emperors

96–98	Nerva
98–117	Trajan
117–38	Hadrian
138–61	Antoninus Pius
161–69*	Lucius Verus
161–80*	Marcus Aurellus

* divided voluntarily between two brothers

despotic emperors

180–92	Commodus
193	Pertinax
193	Didius Julianus

the Severi

193–211	Septimus Severus
211–17	Caracalla
217–18	Macrinus
218–22	Elagabalus
222–35	Severus Alexander

the soldier emperors

235–38	Maximus the Thracian
238–44	Gordian III
244–49	Philip I, the Arabian
249–51	Decius
251–53	Trebonianus Gallus
253–68	Gallienus
268–70	Claudius II
270–75	Aurelian
275–76	Tacitus
276	Florian
276–82	Probus
282–83	Carus
283–85	Carinus

Tsars of Russia 1547–1917

reign   *name*

House of Rurik

1547–84	Ivan the Terrible
1584–98	Theodore I
1598	Irina

House of Gudonov

1598–1605	Boris Gudonov
1605	Theodore II

usurpers

1605–06	Dimitri III
1606–10	Basil IV
1610–13	interregnum

House of Romanov

1613–45	Michael Romanov
1645–76	Alexis
1676–82	Theodore III
1682–96	Peter I and Ivan V (brothers)
1689–1725	Peter I, the Great*
1725–27	Catherine I
1727–30	Peter II
1730–40	Anna Ivanovna
1740–41	Ivan VI
1741–62	Elizabeth
1762	Peter III
1762–96	Catherine II, the Great
1796–1801	Paul I
1801–25	Alexander I
1825–55	Nicholas I
1855–81	Alexander II
1881–94	Alexander III
1894–1917	Nicholas II

* The title of 'tsar' was replaced by 'emperor' from 1721.

Kings and Queens of Scotland 1005–1603

(from the unification of Scotland to the union of the crowns of Scotland and England)

reign   *name*

Celtic kings

1005	Malcolm II
1034	Duncan I
1040	Macbeth

1057	Malcolm III Canmore
1095	Donald Ban (restored)
1097	Edgar
1107	Alexander I
1124	David
1153	Malcolm IV
1165	William the Lion
1214	Alexander II
1249	Alexander III
1286–90	Margaret of Norway

English domination

| 1292–96 | John Baliol |
| 1296–1306 | annexed to England |

House of Bruce

| 1306 | Robert I, the Bruce |
| 1329 | David II |

House of Stuart

1371	Robert II
1390	Robert III
1406	James I
1437	James II
1460	James III
1488	James IV
1513	James V
1542	Mary
1567	James VI
1603	union of crowns

The Ten Gurus (Religious Teachers) of Sikhism

period	name	born
c. 1500–39	Guru Nanak	1469
1539–52	Guru Angad	1504
1552–74	Guru Amar Das	1495
1574–81	Guru Ram Das	1534
1581–1606	Guru Arjan*	1563
1606–44	Guru Hargobind	1595
1644–61	Guru Har Rai	1630
1661–64	Guru Har Krishan	1656
1664–75	Guru Tej Bahadur*	1621
1675–1708	Guru Gobind Singh	1666

* Executed by Muslim rulers for refusing to renounce the Sikh faith.

Prime Ministers and Presidents of South Africa

term	name
prime ministers	
1910–19	General L Botha
1919–24	General Jan Smuts
1924–39	General James Hertzog
1939–48	General Jan Smuts
1948–54	Daniel Malan
1954–58	J Strijdon
1958–66	Hendrik Verwoerd
1966–78	Balthazar Johannes Vorster
1978–84	Pieter Botha
presidents*	
1984–89	Pieter Botha
1989–94	F. W. de Klerk
1994–	Nelson Mandela

* The post of prime minister was abolished 1984 and combined with that of president.

Monarchs of Spain from 1516

reign	name
House of Habsburg	
1516–56	Charles I
1556–98	Philip II
1598–1621	Philip III
1621–65	Philip IV
1665–1700	Charles II
House of Bourbon	
1700–46	Philip V
1746–59	Ferdinand VI
1759–88	Charles III
1788–1808	Charles IV
1808	Ferdinand VII (deposed)
1808–13	Joseph Napoleon*
1813–33	Ferdinand VII (restored)
1833–68	Isabel II
1868–70	provisional government
1870–73	Amadeus I † (abdicated)
1873–74	first republic
1874–86	Alfonso XII
1886–1931	Alfonso XIII (deposed)
1931–39	second republic
1939–75	fascist state, General Francisco Franco head of state
1975–	Juan Carlos I

* House of Bonaparte　† House of Savoy

Prime Ministers of the United Kingdom from 1721

term	name	party
1721–42	Sir Robert Walpole	Whig
1742–43	Earl of Wilmington	Whig
1743–54	Henry Pelham	Whig
1754–56	Duke of Newcastle	Whig
1756–57	Duke of Devonshire	Whig
1757–62	Duke of Newcastle	Whig
1762–63	Earl of Bute	Tory
1763–65	George Grenville	Whig
1765–66	Marquess of Rockingham	Whig
1767–70	Duke of Grafton	Whig
1770–82	Lord North	Tory
1782	Marquess of Rockingham	Whig
1782–83	Earl of Shelburne	Whig
1783	Duke of Portland	coalition
1783–1801	William Pitt the Younger	Tory
1801–04	Henry Addington	Tory
1804–06	William Pitt the Younger	Tory
1806–07	Lord Grenville	coalition
1807–09	Duke of Portland	Tory
1809–12	Spencer Perceval	Tory
1812–27	Earl of Liverpool	Tory
1827	George Canning	coalition
1827–28	Viscount Goderich	Tory
1828–30	Duke of Wellington	Tory
1830–34	Earl Grey	Tory
1834	Viscount Melbourne	Whig
1834–35	Sir Robert Peel	Whig
1835–41	Viscount Melbourne	Whig
1841–46	Sir Robert Peel	Conservative
1846–52	Lord Russell	Liberal
1852	Earl of Derby	Conservative
1852–55	Lord Aberdeen	Peelite
1855–58	Viscount Palmerston	Liberal

1858–59	Earl of Derby	Conservative
1859–65	Viscount Palmerston	Liberal
1865–66	Lord Russell	Liberal
1866–68	Earl of Derby	Conservative
1868	Benjamin Disraeli	Conservative
1868–74	W E Gladstone	Liberal
1874–80	Benjamin Disraeli	Conservative
1880–85	W E Gladstone	Liberal
1885–86	Marquess of Salisbury	Conservative
1886	W E Gladstone	Liberal
1886–92	Marquess of Salisbury	Conservative
1892–94	W E Gladstone	Liberal
1894–95	Earl of Rosebery	Liberal
1895–1902	Marquess of Salisbury	Conservative
1902–05	Arthur James Balfour	Conservative
1905–08	Sir H Campbell-Bannerman	Liberal
1908–15	H H Asquith	Liberal
1915–16	H H Asquith	coalition
1916–22	David Lloyd George	coalition
1922–23	Andrew Bonar Law	Conservative
1923–24	Stanley Baldwin	Conservative
1924	Ramsay MacDonald	Labour
1924–29	Stanley Baldwin	Conservative
1929–31	Ramsay MacDonald	Labour
1931–35	Ramsay MacDonald	national coalition
1935–37	Stanley Baldwin	national coalition
1937–40	Neville Chamberlain	national coalition
1940–45	Sir Winston Churchill	coalition
1945–51	Clement Attlee	Labour
1951–55	Sir Winston Churchill	Conservative
1955–57	Sir Anthony Eden	Conservative
1957–63	Harold Macmillan	Conservative
1963–64	Sir Alec Douglas-Home	Conservative
1964–70	Harold Wilson	Labour
1970–74	Edward Heath	Conservative
1974–76	Harold Wilson	Labour
1976–79	James Callaghan	Labour
1979–90	Margaret Thatcher	Conservative
1990–97	John Major	Conservative
1997–	Tony Blair	Labour

United Nations Secretaries-General

term	name	nationality
1946–53	Trygve Lie	Norwegian
1953–61	Dag Hammarskjöld	Swedish
1961–71	U Thant	Burmese
1972–81	Kurt Waldheim	Austrian
1982–92	Javier Pérez de Cuéllar	Peruvian
1992–96	Boutros Boutros Ghali	Egyptian
1997–	Kofi Annan	Ghanaian

Presidents of the USA

term	name	party
1789–97	George Washington	Federalist
1797–1801	John Adams	Federalist
1801–09	Thomas Jefferson	Democratic Republican
1809–17	James Madison	Democratic Republican
1817–25	James Monroe	Democratic Republican
1825–29	John Quincy Adams	Democratic Republican
1829–37	Andrew Jackson	Democrat
1837–41	Martin Van Buren	Democrat
1841	William Henry Harrison	Whig
1841–45	John Tyler	Whig
1845–49	James Knox Polk	Democrat
1849–50	Zachary Taylor	Whig
1850–53	Millard Fillmore	Whig
1853–57	Franklin Pierce	Democrat
1857–61	James Buchanan	Democrat
1861–65	Abraham Lincoln	Republican
1865–69	Andrew Johnson	Democrat
1869–77	Ulysses S Grant	Republican
1877–81	Rutherford B Hayes	Republican
1881	James A Garfield	Republican
1881–85	Chester Alun Arthur	Republican
1885–89	Grover Cleveland	Democrat
1889–93	Benjamin Harrison	Republican
1893–97	Grover Cleveland	Democrat
1897–1901	William McKinley	Republican
1901–09	Theodore Roosevelt	Republican
1909–13	William Howard Taft	Republican
1913–21	Woodrow Wilson	Democrat
1921–23	Warren Gamaliel Harding	Republican
1923–29	Calvin Coolidge	Republican
1929–33	Herbert C Hoover	Republican
1933–45	Franklin Delano Roosevelt	Democrat
1945–53	Harry S Truman	Democrat
1953–61	Dwight D Eisenhower	Republican
1961–63	John F Kennedy	Democrat
1963–69	Lyndon B Johnson	Democrat
1969–74	Richard M Nixon	Republican
1974–77	Gerald R Ford	Republican
1977–81	James Earl Carter	Democrat
1981–89	Ronald Reagan	Republican
1989–93	George Bush	Republican
1993–	Bill Clinton	Democrat

Presidents and Communist Party Leaders of the USSR

term	name

Communist Party leaders

1917–22	V I Lenin
1922–53	Joseph Stalin
1953–64	Nikita Khrushchev
1964–82	Leonid Brezhnev
1982–84	Yuri Andropov
1984–85	Konstantin Chernenko
1985–91	Mikhail Gorbachev

presidents

1917–22	V I Lenin
1922–46	Mikhail Kalinin
1946–53	N Shvernik
1953–60	Marshal K Voroshilov
1960–64	Leonid Brezhnev
1964–65	A Mikoyan
1965–77	N Podgorny
1977–82	Leonid Brezhnev
1982–83	V Kuznetsov (acting)
1983–84	Yuri Andropov
1984	V Kuznetsov (acting)
1984–85	Konstantin Chernenko
1985	V Kuznetsov (acting)
1985–89	Andrei Gromyko
1989–91	Mikhail Gorbachev

Appendix 2
Global and Regional Organizations

The Commonwealth

joined	country
in Africa	
1966	Botswana
1965	British Indian Ocean Territory
1995	Cameroon
1965	Gambia
1957	Ghana
1963	Kenya
1966	Lesotho
1964	Malawi
1968	Mauritius
1995	Mozambique
1990	Namibia
1960	Nigeria*
1931	St Helena
1976	Seychelles
1961	Sierra Leone
1910	South Africa**
1968	Swaziland
1961	Tanzania
1962	Uganda
1964	Zambia
1980	Zimbabwe

* suspended from membership 1995
** withdrawn from membership 1961 and readmitted 1994

joined	country
in the Americas	
1931	Anguilla
1981	Antigua and Barbuda
1973	Bahamas
1966	Barbados
1982	Belize
1931	Bermuda
1931	British Virgin Islands
1931	Canada
1931	Cayman Islands
1978	Dominica
1931	Falkland Islands
1974	Grenada
1966	Guyana
1962	Jamaica
1931	Montserrat
1983	St Christopher-Nevis
1979	St Lucia
1979	St Vincent and the Grenadines
1962	Trinidad and Tobago
1931	Turks and Caicos Islands

joined	country
in the Antarctic	
1936	Australian Antarctic Territory
1931	British Antarctic Territory
1931	Falkland Island Dependencies
1931	Ross Dependency

joined	country
in Asia	
1972	Bangladesh
1984	Brunei
1947	India
1957	Malaysia
1982	Maldives
1947*	Pakistan
1965	Singapore
1948	Sri Lanka

* Left 1972 and rejoined 1989

joined	country
in Australasia and the Pacific	
1931	Australia
1931	Cook Islands
1931	Norfolk Island
1979	Kiribati
1968	Nauru
1931	New Zealand
1931	Niue
1975	Papua New Guinea
1931	Pitcairn Islands
1978	Solomon Islands
1931	Tokelau
1970	Tonga
1978	Tuvalu
1980	Vanuatu
1970	Western Samoa

joined	country
in Europe	
1931	Channel Islands
1961	Cyprus
1931	Gibraltar
1964	Malta
1931	Isle of Man
1931	United Kingdom

Members of the United Nations

joined	country
1946	Afghanistan
1955	Albania
1962	Algeria
1993	Andorra
1976	Angola
1981	Antigua and Barbuda
1945	Argentina †
1992	Armenia
1945	Australia †
1955	Austria
1992	Azerbaijan
1973	Bahamas
1971	Bahrain
1974	Bangladesh
1966	Barbados
1945	Belarus †
1945	Belgium †
1981	Belize
1960	Benin
1971	Bhutan
1945	Bolivia †

1992	Bosnia-Herzegovina	1992	Kyrgyzstan
1966	Botswana	1955	Laos
1945	Brazil †	1991	Latvia
1984	Brunei	1945	Lebanon †
1955	Bulgaria	1966	Lesotho
1960	Burkina Faso	1945	Liberia †
1962	Burundi	1955	Libya
1955	Cambodia	1990	Liechtenstein
1960	Cameroon	1991	Lithuania
1945	Canada †	1945	Luxembourg †
1975	Cape Verde	1993	Macedonia, former Yugoslav Republic of
1960	Central African Republic	1960	Madagascar
1960	Chad	1964	Malawi
1945	Chile †	1957	Malaysia
1945	China †	1965	Maldives
1945	Colombia †	1960	Mali
1975	Comoros	1964	Malta
1960	Congo	1991	Marshall Islands
1945	Costa Rica †	1961	Mauritania
1992	Croatia	1968	Mauritius
1945	Cuba †	1945	Mexico †
1960	Cyprus	1991	Micronesia
1993	Czech Republic••••	1992	Moldova
1945	Denmark †	1993	Monaco
1977	Djibouti	1961	Mongolia
1978	Dominica	1956	Morocco
1945	Dominican Republic †	1975	Mozambique
1945	Ecuador †	1948	Myanmar (Burma)
1945	Egypt †	1990	Namibia
1945	El Salvador †	1955	Nepal
1968	Equatorial Guinea	1945	Netherlands †
1993	Eritrea	1945	New Zealand †
1991	Estonia	1945	Nicaragua †
1945	Ethiopia †	1960	Niger
1945	Fiji	1960	Nigeria
1955	Finland	1991	North Korea
1945	France †	1945	Norway †
1960	Gabon	1971	Oman
1965	Gambia	1947	Pakistan
1992	Georgia	1994	Palau
1973/1990	Germany *	1945	Panama †
1957	Ghana	1975	Papua New Guinea
1945	Greece †	1945	Paraguay †
1974	Grenada	1945	Peru †
1945	Guatemala †	1945	Philippines †
1958	Guinea	1945	Poland †
1974	Guinea-Bissau	1955	Portugal
1966	Guyana	1971	Qatar
1945	Haiti †	1955	Romania
1945	Honduras †	1991	Russian Federation **
1955	Hungary	1962	Rwanda
1946	Iceland	1983	St Christopher and Nevis
1945	India †	1979	St Lucia
1950	Indonesia	1980	St Vincent and the Grenadines
1945	Iran †	1975	São Tomé e Principe
1945	Iraq †	1945	Saudi Arabia †
1955	Ireland	1992	San Marino
1949	Israel	1960	Senegal
1955	Italy	1976	Seychelles
1960	Ivory Coast	1961	Sierra Leone
1962	Jamaica	1965	Singapore
1956	Japan	1993	Slovak Republic****
1955	Jordan	1992	Slovenia
1963	Kenya	1978	Solomon Islands
1963	Kuwait	1960	Somalia
1992	Kazakhstan	1945	South Africa †

1991	South Korea	1964	Zambia
1955	Spain	1980	Zimbabwe
1955	Sri Lanka		
1956	Sudan		† founder member
1975	Surinam		* represented by two countries until unification in 1990
1968	Swaziland		** became a separate member upon the demise of the
1946	Sweden		USSR, which was a founder member 1945
1945	Syria †		*** suspended 1992
1961	Tanzania		**** joined as founder member Czechoslovakia 1945
1946	Thailand		
1960	Togo		
1962	Trinidad and Tobago		
1956	Tunisia		
1992	Turkmenistan		
1945	Turkey †		
1962	Uganda		
1945	Ukraine †		
1971	United Arab Emirates		
1945	United Kingdom †		
1945	United States of America †		
1945	Uruguay †		
1992	Uzbekistan		
1981	Vanuatu		
1945	Venezuela †		
1977	Vietnam		
1976	Western Samoa		
1947	Yemen *		
1945	Yugoslavia †***		
1960	Zaire		

Members of the European Union

joined	country
1995	Austria
1957	Belgium
1973	Denmark
1995	Finalnd
1957	France
1957	Germany
1981	Greece
1973	Ireland
1957	Italy
1957	Luxembourg
1957	Netherlands
1986	Portugal
1986	Spain
1995	Sweden
1973	United Kingdom

Appendix 3
Political Thinkers and Economists

Significant Political Thinkers

lived	name	chief work published
551–479 BC	Confucius	The Analects
c. 428–347	Plato	The Republic, The Laws
384–22	Aristotle	Constitution of the Athenians, Politics
1225–1274	St Thomas Aquinas	Summa contra Gentiles/Against the Errors of the Infidels 1259–64
1469–1527	Niccolò Machiavelli	Il principe/The Prince 1532
		Discorsi/Discourses 1531
1588–1679	Thomas Hobbes	The Leviathan 1651
1632–1704	John Locke	Treatise on Civil Government 1690
1712–1778	Jean-Jacques Rousseau	Du Contrat social/Social Contract 1762
1729–1797	Edmund Burke	Thoughts on the Present Discontents 1770
		Reflections on the Revolution in France 1790
1737–1809	Thomas Paine	The Rights of Man 1791
1748–1832	Jeremy Bentham	Fragments on Government 1776
1770–1831	Georg Wilhelm Friedrich Hegel	Philosophie des Rechts/Philosophy of Right 1821
1772–1837	Charles Fourier	Le nouveau Monde industriel/ The New Industrial World 1829
1806–1873	John Stuart Mill	On Liberty 1859
1809–1865	Pierre Joseph Proudhon	Qu'est-ce que la propriété?/What is Property? 1840
1818–1883	Karl Marx	The Communist Manifesto (with F Engels) 1848
		Das Kapital/Capital 1867–95
1820–1895	Friedrich Engels	The Communist Manifesto (with K Marx) 1848
		Origins of the Family, Private Property, and the State 1884
1869–1948	Mohandas K Gandhi	Collected Works 1958

1876–1924	Vladimir Ilyich Lenin	*What Is to be Done?* 1902
		Imperialism 1917
1889–1945	Adolf Hitler	*Mein Kampf/My Struggle* 1925–27
1891–1937	Antonio Gramsci	*Quaderni di carcere/Prison Notebooks* 1947
1893–1976	Mao Zedong	*Little Red Book* 1960
1899–1992	Friedrich August von Hayek	*The Road to Serfdom* 1944

1772–1823	David Ricardo	*Principles of Political Economy* 1817
1818–1883	Karl Marx	*Das Kapital/Capital* 1867–95
1834–1910	Léon Walras	*Elements d'économie politique pure/ Elements of Pure Political Economy* 1874–77
1842–1924	Alfred Marshall	*Principles of Economics* 1890
1883–1946	John Maynard Keynes	*The General Theory of Employment, Interest and Money* 1936
1883–1950	Joseph Schumpeter	*Capitalism, Socialism and Democracy* 1942
1908–	John Kenneth Galbraith	*The Affluent Society* 1958
1912–	Milton Friedman	*Inflation: Causes and Consequences* 1953

Ten Great Economists

lived	name	chief work published
1723–1790	Adam Smith	*The Wealth of Nations* 1776
1766–1834	Thomas Malthus	*Essay on the Principle of Population* 1798

Appendix 4
The World at War

Significant Wars and Battles

period	war/battle	contestants/ military result
499–48 BC	Greek/Persian Wars	Greek cities' revolt against Persian Empire.
490 BC	Marathon	Persian army defeated by Athenians.
431–04 BC	Peloponnesian War	Athens against Sparta.
343–41, 326–04 BC	Samnite Wars	Latins against Samnites, southern neighbours of Rome.
333 BC	Issus	Alexander the Great of Macedonia defeated Persian king Darius.
326 BC	Hydaspes	Alexander the Great defeated Indian ruler Porus.
264–146 BC	Punic Wars	Rome against Carthage.
216 BC	Cannae	Roman legionaries defeated by Carthaginian general Hannibal.
215–11 BC	First Macedonian War	Rome against Macedonia.
202 BC	Zama	Carthaginian troops defeated by Romans.
58–51 BC	Gallic Wars	Campaigns by Julius Caesar to establish Roman rule west of the river Rhine.
53 BC	Carrhae	Roman forces under general Crassus defeated by Parthians.
48 BC	Pharsalus	Pompey defeated by Julius Caesar.
AD 101, 105–06	Dacian Wars	Rome conquered Dacia.
378	Adrianople	Roman forces defeated by Visigoths.
410	Rome	City captured and sacked by Goths.
451	Chalons	Forces of Attila the Hun defeated by Romans and Visigoths.
628	Nineveh	Victory for the Byzantine ruler Heraclius over Persians.
732	Tours	French victory over Arabs.
955	Lechfeld	Magyars defeated by forces of Holy Roman emperor Otto I.
1066	Hastings	Defeat of army of Harold, king of England, by that of William the Conqueror, from Normandy.
1071	Manzikert	Byzantine forces defeated by Seljuk Turks.
1096–1291	Crusades	European rulers and Muslims.

1191–92	Tarain	Muhammad Ghuri defeated Indian leader Prithviraja near Delhi.
1214	Bouvines	Army led by Philip II of France defeated the forces of Holy Roman emperor Otto IV.
1215	Beijing	Victory of Genghis Khan over Chinese forces.
1240	Kiev	Russian defeat by Batu Khan's Golden Horde.
1243	Kosedagh	Seljuk Turks defeated by Mongols.
1260	Ain Jalut	Mongols' westward advance halted by defeat near Damascus.
1302	Courtrai	French defeat by Flemish forces.
1337–1453	Hundred Years' War	England against France.
1346	Crécy	English victory over French forces.
1380	Kulikov	Mongols defeated by forces of Dmitri IV of Moscow.
1389	Kosovo	Ottoman victory over Serb forces.
1396	Nicopolis	Ottoman victory over Crusaders on river Danube.
1398	Panipat	Indian forces defeated by Mongols led by Tamerlane.
1402	Ankara	Ottoman forces under Bayezid I defeated by Tamerlane's Mongols.
1415	Agincourt	French forces defeated by English army under Henry V.
1429	Orléans	French victory over English forces.
1448	Kosovo	Ottoman victory over Hungarians.
1450	Formigny	French victory over English troops.
1519–21	Aztec-Spanish War	Conquest of Mexico led by Cortés.
1525	Pavia	Victory of Habsburg imperial forces over French army in Lombardy.
1526	Panipat	Ibrahim Lodi, Afghan ruler of Delhi, defeated by Babur, founder of the Mogul empire.
1526	Mohács	Ottoman victory over Hungarians.
1532–34	Inca-Spanish War	Conquest of Peru by Pizarro's forces.
1540	Kanauj	Defeat of Indian ruler Humayn by Sher Shah.
1563–70	Seven Years' War of the North	Denmark and Sweden.
1591	Tondibi	Moroccan victory over forces of Songhai empire.
1592	Seoul	Japanese victory over Korean forces.
1618–48	Thirty Years' War	Protestants against Catholics in central Europe.
1665	War of Devolution	French attempt to seize Spanish Netherlands.
1687	Mohács	Austro-Hungary victory over Ottoman Turkish forces.
1700–21	Great Northern War	Sweden against Denmark, Poland, and Russia.
1701–14	War of the Spanish Succession	Britain, Austria, the Netherlands, Portugal, and Denmark against France, Spain, and Bavaria.
1702–13	Queen Anne's War	War of the Spanish Succession fought in America.
1704	Blenheim	British victory over French and Bavarian forces.
1706	Ramillies	British victory over French forces.
1708	Oudenarde	French forces defeated by British, Austrian, and Dutch.
1709	Malplaquet	French forces defeated by British and Holy Roman Empire troops.
1709	Poltava	Russian victory over Swedish forces.
1733–38	War of the Polish Succession	Russia and Poland against France.
1739	War of Jenkins's Ear	Britain against Spain.
1740–48	War of the Austrian Succession	Austria, Britain, the Netherlands, and Savoy against Bavaria, France, Prussia, and Spain.
1745	Fontenoy	British, Dutch, and Hanoverian forces defeated by the French.
1755–63	French and Indian War	France and Britain in North America; both sides enlisted American Indian support.
1756–63	Seven Years' War	Britain and Prussia against Austria, France, and Russia.
1757	Plassey	British victory over northern Indian forces.
1759	Plains of Abraham	British victory over French forces near Québec, Canada.
1759	Minden	French forces defeated by British, Hanoverian, and Hessian troops in Westphalia.
1761	Panipat	Afghan victory over Marathas near Delhi.
1764	Buxar	North Indian imperial coalition defeated decisively by British East India Company.

1775–83	American Revolution	Revolt of Britain's North American colonies.
1775	Bunker Hill	Defeat of the colonists by British troops.
1777	Saratoga Springs	Colonists' victory.
1781	Yorktown	Defeat of British forces by North American colonists.
1792–1802	French Revolutionary Wars	France against Austria, Britain, and Prussia.
1792	Valmy	French victory over Prussian army.
1798	Pyramids	French victory over Mameluke army in Egypt.
1803–15	Napoleonic Wars	Continuation of the French Revolutionary Wars.
1805	Austerlitz	French victory over Austrian and Russian forces.
1806	Jena	Defeat of Prussian troops by French army.
1808–14	Peninsular War	War caused by Napoleon's invasion of Portugal and Spain.
1812	Salamanca	British victory over French forces.
1812	Borodino	French victory over Russian forces.
1812–15	War of 1812	Britain against USA.
1813	Leipzig	Defeat of French forces by Austrian, Prussian, Russian, and Swedish troops.
1815	Waterloo	Defeat of Napoleon by British, German, Dutch, and Belgian troops.
1821–70	Italian Wars of Independence	Italian states against the occupying Austrians.
1824	First Anglo-Burman War	British annexation of Burmese territory.
1839–42	First Opium War	Britain against China.
1846–48	Mexican War	USA against Mexico.
1854–56	Crimean War	Britain and France against Russia.
1854	Balaclava	Russian defeat of British forces.
1854	Inkerman	Russian advance repulsed by British.
1856–60	Arrow War	China against the West.
1865–70	Paraguay War	Paraguay against Argentina, Brazil, and Uruguay.
1866	Seven Weeks' War	Austria against Prussia.
1866	Sadowa	Prussian defeat of Austria.
1870–71	Franco-Prussian War	France against Prussia.
1879–83	Pacific War	Bolivia and Peru against Chile.
1881	South African War	Britain against Boers.
1881	Majuba Hill	Boer victory over British forces.
1882–89	British Egyptian and Sudan campaigns	Egyptian and Sudanese nationalists against British colonizers.
1882	Tel-el-Kebir	British victory over Egyptian forces.
1885	Khartoum	Sudanese victory over British forces.
1894–95	Sino-Japanese War	Japan and China.
1898	Omdurman	British victory over Sudanese dervishes.
1898	Spanish-American War	US-backed Cuban revolutionaries and Spanish colonial rulers.
1899–1902	Boer War	British and the South African Boers.
1899–1900	Mafeking	British garrison besieged by Boers.
1904–05	Russo-Japanese War	Russia and Japan.
1912–13	Balkan War	Bulgaria, Greece, Montenegro, and Serbia against Turkey.
1914–18	World War I	Central European Powers (Austria-Hungary, Germany, and allies) against the Triple Entente (Britain, France, and Russia) and their allies, including the USA.
1914	Tannenberg	German victory over Russian forces.
1914	Marne	German offensive halted by French army.
1916	Somme	Indecisive result.
1916	Verdun	German onslaught withstood by French army.
1917	Passchendaele	Indecisive British assault.
1918	Marne	German forces defeated by those of Triple Entente.
1918	Amiens	Victorious Triple Entente offensive.
1918	Vittorio Veneto	British and Italian victory over Austrian forces.
1939–45	World War II	Axis powers (Italy, Japan, and Nazi Germany) against the Allied powers (Britain, the Commonwealth, France, the USA, the USSR, and China).
1940	Battle of Britain	Conflict between German and British air forces.
1942	Singapore	Japanese victory over British forces.
1942	Tobruk	German victory over British forces.
1942	El Alamein	British defeat of German and Italian forces.
1942–43	Stalingrad	German forces defeated by Soviet Red Army.
1944	Anzio	Allied invasion of Italy.
1944	Arnhem	Partial success for Allies against German forces.
1944	Battle of the Bulge	Failed German counteroffensive.

1945	Iwo Jima	American victory over Japanese forces.
1946–54	Indochina War	French colonial forces against the Vietminh (Vietnamese nationalists).
1948–49	Arab-Israeli War	Arab attack on new Israeli state.
1950–53	Korean War	North Korea against US-led United Nations coalition.
1954	Dien Bien Phu	Vietminh defeat of French forces.
1954–62	Algerian War of Independence	Algerian independence war against French colonizers.
1954–75	Vietnam War	US-backed South Vietnamese armed forces against Chinese-backed North Vietnam and South Vietnamese guerrillas.
1967	Six-Day War	Israel against its Arab neighbours.
1973	Yom Kippur War	Egypt and Syria against Israel.
1980–88	Iran-Iraq War	Iran against Iraq.
1982	Falklands War	Argentina against Britain.
1991	Gulf War	US-led UN coalition against Iraq.

Notable Naval Battles

year	site	conflict
480 BC	Salamis	Greek victory over Persian fleet.
405 BC	Aegospotami	Athenian fleet defeated by Spartans.
31 BC	Actium	Fleets of Antony and Cleopatra of Egypt defeated by Roman fleet of Octavian.
AD 1340	Sluis	British victory over French navy.
1457	Matelino	Victory of papal fleet over Ottoman navy.
1571	Lepanto	Defeat of Ottoman Empire by the Holy League (Italian states and Spain).
1588	Gravelines	British defeat of Spanish Armada.
1591	Azores	British victory over Spanish fleet.
1592	Yellow Sea	Japanese victory over Korean navy.
1666	Four Days' War	Dutch victory over British navy.
1759	Quiberon Bay	British victory during Seven Years' War.
1782	Les Saintes	British victory over French navy off Dominica in the Caribbean.

1797	Cape St Vincent	British victory over French and Spanish fleets off SW Portugal.
1798	Nile (Aboukir Bay)	French defeat by British navy.
1801	Copenhagen/Baltic	British victory over Danish fleet.
1805	Trafalgar	British victory over French navy.
1813	Lake Erie	American victory over British fleet.
1905	Tsushima	Japanese victory over Russian fleet.
1914	Falkland Islands	British victory over German navy.
1916	Jutland	British against German navy (indecisive result).
1942	Midway	Defeat of Japanese navy in Pacific by USA.

Civil Wars and Related Battles

period	civil war/battle	conflict
c. 800 BC	Mahābhārata	Kaurava and Pandava families' rivalry on Upper Ganges plain.
88–c. 28 BC	Roman Civil Wars	Military factions in power struggle.
AD 220–65	Three Kingdoms War	In China, civil war between the Wei, Shu, and Wu kingdoms.
1180–85	Gempei War	In Japan, Minamoto clan rose against rival Taira.
1185	Dannoura	Naval defeat of Taira by Minamoto forces.
1265	Evesham	English royal forces led by Prince Edward defeated the army of Simon de Montfort in second Barons' War.
1298	Falkirk	English forces of Edward I put down Scottish revolt of William Wallace.
1314	Bannockburn	English defeated by Scots forces under Robert the Bruce.
1331–36	Genkō War	Japanese imperial forces put an end to the Kamakura shogunate.
1333	Halidon Hill	Nationalist Scots defeated by Edward Baliol.
1336–92	Nambokuchō	Japanese succession dispute between Northern Court in Kyoto and Southern Court in Yoshino.
1355–67	Chu Yuan-chang	Rebellion In China, uprising against Mongol Yuan dynasty.
1455–85	Wars of the Roses	English wars between the houses of Lancaster and York.
1460	Wakefield	Victory of Lancaster over York.

1464	Hexham	Yorkist victory over forces of Henry Beaufort.
1467–77	Ōnin War	Kyoto area of Japan devastated by feudal factions.
1471	Barnet	Defeat of Lancaster by York.
1485	Bosworth Field	Defeat of Yorkist king Richard III by Henry (VII).
1513	Flodden Field	Defeat of the Scots by the English army.
1556	Panipat	Mogul forces of Akbar defeated a Hindu army near Delhi.
1562–98	French Wars of Religion	Catholics versus Protestants (Huguenots) and fight for control of the expiring Valois dynasty.
1600	Sekigahara	Victory of Tokugawa Ieyasu over rivals ensured him control of Japan.
1642–49	English Civil War	Parliamentarians under Oliver Cromwell against Royalists.
1642	Edgehill	Indecisive result.
1644	Marston Moor	Royalist defeat by Parliamentarians and Scots.
1645	Naseby	Defeat of Royalists by Cromwell's troops.
1648–52	The Fronde	Revolts against French absolutism during the minority of Louis XIV.
1685	Sedgemoor	Duke of Monmouth's rebellion crushed by forces of James II.
1698	Killiecrankie	Victory for supporters of James II.
1690	Boyne	Deposed James II defeated by William III of Great Britain and Ireland.
1715	The Fifteen	Unsuccessful Jacobite rebellion by Scots against Hanoverian king George I.
1745–46	The Forty-Five	Unsuccessful Jacobite rebellion by Scots against English crown.
1745	Prestonpans	English forces defeated by Jacobites in Scotland.
1746	Culloden	Defeat of the Jacobite rebels.
1850–64	Taiping Rebellion	Opposition to Manchu dynasty in China.
1857–58	Indian Mutiny	Revolt of Indian soldiers against British colonizers.
1861–65	American Civil War	Secession of Southern states (Confederacy) from North (Union).
1861–62	Bull Run	Confederate army victories.
1863	Gettysburg	Union victory over the Confederacy.
1865	Appomattox	Confederate army surrender.
1927–37 and 1946–49	Chinese Civil War	Communist overthrow of Guomindang nationalist government.
1948–49	Huai-Hai	Communist victory over nationalist forces.
1936–39	Spanish Civil War	Right-wing Nationalist revolt against left-wing Republican government.
1937	Guernica	Defeat of Basques by Nationalists supported by Nazi Germany.
1944–49	Greek Civil War	US-sponsored royalist suppression of socialist movement.
1948–55	Burmese (Myanmar) Civil War	Ethnic separatists and communists against socialist government.
1948–	Karen insurgence in Burma	Separatist movement of ethnic group.
1950–62	Indonesian Civil War	Revolts in Sumatra and the South Moluccas against the dominance of Java.
1955–72	Sudanese Civil War	Muslim north against non-Muslim south.
1959–75	Laotian and Vietnamese Civil Wars	Communists against right-wing governments.
1960–67	Congolese Civil War	Secession attempt by Katanga from the Republic of the Congo (now Zaire).
1961–75	Angolan War of Independence	Three nationalist movements against Portuguese colonial rulers.
1961–	Kurdish revolts	Separatist uprisings by Kurds especially in Iraq and Iran.
1962–70	North Yemen Civil War	Royalists against republicans.
1962–	Irian Jaya conflict	Popular resistance in W New Guinea to Indonesian rule.
1963–68	Cypriot Civil War	Turkish community in Cyprus withdrew recognition of Greek Cypriot government.
1963–	Eritrean revolt	Secessionist movement in N Ethiopia.
1965–79	Zimbabwe Civil War	Popular resistance to white-only rule in what was then Rhodesia.
1964–74	Mozambique War of Independence	Nationalist opposition to Portuguese colonial rule.
1965–	Chad Civil War	Resistance by Muslim north to government
1966–89	Namibian War of Independence	Popular resistance to South African rule.
1967–70	Nigerian (Biafran) Civil War	Attempted secession of state of Biafra.
1969–	Northern Ireland Troubles	Civil insurgence against British rule in Northern Ireland.

1970–93	Cambodian Civil Wars	Communist Khmer Rouge against US-backed right wing and other groups
1975–89	Angolan Civil Wars	Cuban-backed left and South African-backed right-wing forces.
1975–	Lebanese Civil War	Christian Phalangists, Muslim militias, Druse socialists, Syrian and Israeli interventions.
1975–	Western Sahara dispute	Partition of territory between Morocco and Mauritania rejected by Polisario separatist guerrillas.
1975–	East Timor guerrilla war	Popular resistance to Indonesian rule.
1976–92	Mozambique Civil War	Right-wing insurgence backed by South Africa.
1977–91	Ogaden secession	Somalian-backed breakaway from Ethiopia.
1977–	Sri Lanka guerrilla war	Ethnic Tamil separatist rebellion.
1978–90	Nicaraguan Civil War	US-sponsored right wing guerrilla war to overthrow socialist government.
1979–	Afghan War	Muslim guerrillas (muja-heddin) against communist government and one another.
1984–	Indian separatist unrest	Sikhs in Punjab; Muslims in Kashmir, disputed with Pakistan.
1987–	Palestinian Intifada	Arab resistance movement in Israel-occupied West Bank and Gaza.
1990–	Liberian Civil War	Government overthrown by rival armed groups.
1991–	Somalian Civil War	Government overthrown by rival armed groups.
1992–	Yugoslavian Civil War	Disintegration of republic amid interethnic violence.

Appendix 5
Significant Political Upheavals

date	convulsion/revolution
1381	Peasants' Revolt against poll tax in England
1524	Peasants' War in Germany
1637–38	Shimabara uprising in S Japan
1649–60	English Revolution
1688–89	'Glorious Revolution' (English)
1775–83	American Revolution
1789–99	French Revolution
1848	European revolutions
1868–89	Meiji Restoration (Japan)
1871	Paris Commune
1910–17	Mexican Revolution
1911	Chinese Revolution
1917	Russian Revolution
1945–49	Indonesian Revolution
1949	Chinese Revolution
1952–60	Mau Mau revolt (Kenya)
1953–59	Cuban Revolution
1970–73	Chilean Revolution
1974–75	Ethiopian Revolution
1978–79	Nicaraguan Revolution
1979	Iranian Revolution
1989–91	Anticommunist counter-revolutions (Eastern Europe and Asia)

Appendix 6
Natural and Human-Made Disasters

The Ten Worst Recorded Cyclones and Floods in History

date	flood/cyclone	region affected	est death toll
Aug 1931	flood	China (Huang He/Yellow River)	3,700,000
Sept 1887	flood	China (Huang He/Yellow River)	900,000
13 Nov 1970	cyclone	East Pakistan (Bangladesh)	500,000
1939	flood	China (north)	400,000
1642	flood	China (Kaifeng)	300,000
7 Oct 1737	cyclone	India (Bengal)	300,000
1881	cyclone	Vietnam (Haiphong)	300,000
23 April 1969	flood	China (Shandong peninsula)	200,000
30 April 1991	cyclone	Bangladesh	126,000
1228	flood	Netherlands	100,000

Earthquakes: The Ten Most Deadly Earthquakes of the 20th Century

date	location	magnitude (Richter scale)	death toll
28 July 1976	Tangshan (China)	8.2	242,000
22 May 1927	Nan-Shan (China)	8.3	200,000
28 Dec 1908	Messina (Italy)	7.5	140,000
1 Sept 1923	Tokyo (Japan)	8.3	140,000
5 Oct 1948	USSR	7.3	110,000
16 Dec 1920	Gansu (China)	8.6	100,000
26 Dec 1932	Gansu (China)	7.6	70,000
31 May 1970	Huaras (Peru)	7.7	67,000
20 June 1990	Iran	7.7	50,000
26 Dec 1939	Erzincan (Turkey)	7.9	45,000

*now in Pakistan

Serious Earlier Recorded Earthquakes

date	location	est death toll
373 BC	Helice (Greece)	not known
AD 526	Antioch (Syria)	not known
553 or 555	Constantinople	not known
26 Oct 740	Thrace and Asia Minor	not known
856	Corinth (Greece)	45,000
1038	Shanxi (China)	not known
1170	Sicily (Italy)	15,000
27 Sept 1290	Gulf of Chihli (China)	100,000
26 Jan 1531	Lisbon (Portugal)	30,000
24 Jan 1556	Shanxi (China)	830,000
8 Sept 1596	Japan	not known
1693	Naples & Sicily (Italy)	150,000
30 Dec 1703	Japan	200,000
1731	Beijing	100,000
11 Oct 1737	Calcutta (India)	300,000
1 Nov 1755	Lisbon (Portugal)	50,000
5 Feb 1783	Calabria (Italy)	50,000
4 Feb 1797	Quito (Ecuador)	41,000
1822	Aleppo (Syria)	20,000
14 Aug 1868	Peru	25,000

The Ten Worst Epidemics in History

date	epidemic	region affected	est death toll
AD 542–650	plague	('plague of Justinian') Europe and Asia	80 million
1347–51	plague	(Black Death) W Europe*	65 million
1918–19	influenza	the world (especially India)	25–40 million
17th century	plague	India	not known
1897–1930	plague	India	12 million
1518 and after	smallpox & measles	Meso-America	not known
1485–1550	'English sweats'	Britain and W Europe	4 million
1556–60	influenza	Europe	not known
1500 and after	syphilis	W Europe	not known
1914–15	typhus	E Europe	3 million

*also affected Asia in 14th century

Famines: The Worst Famines of the 19th and 20th Centuries

date	country/region affected	est death toll
1959–61	China	20.0 million
1876–79	China (north)	10.0 million
1932–34	USSR (Ukraine and Kazakhstan)	6.0 million
1876–78	India (especially south)	5.0 million
1896–97	India	5.0 million
1928–29	China (Gansu, Henan, and Shanxi)	3.0 million
1921–22	USSR (Ukraine and Volga)	3.0 million
1975–78	Cambodia	2.0 million
1943	China (Henan)	2.0 million
1892–94	China	2.0 million
1860–61	India (north)	2.0 million
1866–70	India	2.0 million
1899–1900	India	2.0 million
1946–47	USSR (Ukraine)	2.0 million
1943–44	India (Bengal)	1.5 million
1888–92	Ethiopia	not known
1984–85	Ethiopia	1.0 million
1967–69	Nigeria (Biafra)	1.0 million
1837–38	India (north)	0.8 million
1845–50	Ireland ('Great Potato Famine')	0.8 million
1891–92	Russia	0.7 million
1941–43	USSR (siege of Leningrad/St Petersburg)	0.6 million
1877–78	Brazil (Ceara state)	0.5 million
1920–21	China (north)	0.5 million
1973	The Sahel and Ethiopia	0.4 million
1991–92	Somalia	0.3 million
1987–88	Sudan	0.2 million

Serious Earlier Recorded Famines

date	country/region affected	est death toll
1064–72	Egypt	not known
1315–17	central and W Europe	not known
1333–37	China	4.0 million
1330s–40s	India	not known
1557	Russia	not known
1594–98	India and other parts of Asia	not known
1629–30	India (western)	not known
1650–52	Russia	not known
1693	France	not known
1739–41	Ireland	0.5 million
1769	France	not known
1769–70	India (Bengal)	3–10 million
1770	E Europe	not known
1790–92	India	not known

Worst Known Nuclear-Power Accidents

year	power station	type of accident
1957	Windscale (UK)	radioactive leak after fire destroyed the reactor's core
1976	Greifswald (East Germany)	near meltdown of the reactor
1979	Three Mile Island (USA)	release of thousands of gallons of radioactive water and a plume of radioactive gas after the near meltdown of a pressurized-water reactor
1979	Church Rock (USA)	leak of 100 million gallons of radioactive water
1986	Chernobyl (Ukraine)	explosion spread radioactive pollution and contamination across central, northern, and western Europe
1992	St Petersburg (Russia)	leak of radioactive iodine from a Chernobyl-type reactor

The Ten Most Serious Recorded Volcanic Eruptions in History

date	volcano/country	est death toll
26 Aug 1883	Krakatoa (Indonesia)	36,000
8 May 1902	Mont Pelée (Martinique)	30,000
13 Nov 1985	Nevada del Ruiz (Colombia)	23,000
25 March 1669	Etna (Sicily)	20,000
24 Aug 1979	Vesuvius (Italy)	16,000
1169	Etna (Sicily)	15,000
5 April 1815	Tambora (Java)	12,000
1792	Unzen-Dake (Japan)	10,000
June–Aug 1783	Skaptar (Iceland)	10,000
May 1919	Kelud (Indonesia)	5,000

Appendix 7
Political Assassinations

year	victim
514 BC	Hipparchus of Athens
338 BC	Artaxerxes III of Persia
336 BC	Philip II of Macedon
44 BC	Julius Caesar, Roman dictator
AD 41	Caius Caligula, Roman emperor
54	Claudius I, Roman emperor
946	Edmund I of England
1170	St Thomas à Becket, archbishop of Canterbury
1327	Edward II of England
1437	James I of Scotland
1483	Edward V of England
1488	James III of Scotland
1584	William the Silent of Orange (Netherlands)
1589	Henry III of France
1610	Henry IV of France
1792	Gustavus III of Sweden
1793	Jean Paul Marat, French revolutionary leader
1801	Paul I, tsar of Russia
1812	Spencer Perceval, British prime minister
1865	Abraham Lincoln, US president
1881	Alexander II, tsar of Russia
1881	James Garfield, US president
1882	Lord Frederick Cavendish, chief secretary for Ireland
1894	Sadi Carnot, French president
1901	William McKinley, US president
1903	Alexander I of Serbia
1911	Peter Stolypin, Russian prime minister
1914	Archduke Francis Ferdinand of Austria-Hungary
1914	Jean Jaurès, French socialist leader
1918	Nicholas II, tsar of Russia
1920	Venustiano Carranza, Mexican president
1922	Walther Rathenau, German foreign minister
1922	Michael Collins, Irish republican leader
1924	Giacomo Matteotti, Italian socialist leader
1934	Engelbert Dollfuss, Austrian chancellor
1934	Alexander I of Yugoslavia
1940	Leon Trotsky, exiled Russian communist leader
1945	Benito Mussolini, Italian dictator
1948	Mohandas Karamchand Gandhi, Indian nationalist leader
1948	Count Folke Bernadotte, Swedish United Nations mediator in Palestine

1951	Liaquat Ali Khan, Pakistani prime minister	1975	Sheik Mujibur Rahman, Bangladeshi president
1956	Anastasio García Somoza, Nicaraguan president	1978	Mohammad Daud Khan, president of Afghanistan
1958	Faisal II, king of Iraq	1979	Lord Mountbatten of Burma, admiral of the fleet
1959	Solomon Bandaranaike, Sri Lankan prime minister	1979	Park Chung-hee, president of South Korea
1961	Dag Hammarskjöld, Swedish UN secretary general	1981	Maj-Gen Zia ur-Rahman, president of Bangladesh
1961	General Rafael Trujillo, Dominican Republic dictator	1981	Anwar Sadat, president of Egypt
1963	Ngo Dinh Diem, president of South Vietnam	1982	Bachir Gemayel, president-elect of Lebanon
1963	John F Kennedy, US president	1983	Benigno Aquino, Filipino opposition leader
1965	Malcolm X, US black nationalist leader	1983	Maurice Bishop, prime minister of Grenada
1966	Abubakar Tafawa Balewa, Nigerian prime minister	1984	Indira Gandhi, Indian prime minister
1966	Hendrik Verwoerd, South African prime minister	1986	Olof Palme, Swedish prime minister
1968	Martin Luther King, US civil-rights campaigner	1988	General Mohammea Zia ul-Haq, president of Pakistan
1968	Robert Kennedy, US senator	1991	Rajiv Gandhi, former Indian prime minister
1969	Tom Mboya, Kenyan political leader	1993	Ranasinghe Premadasa, Sri Lankan prime minister
1973	Salvador Allende, president of Chile	1993	Melchior Ndadaye, president of Burundi
1975	Ibn Abdul Aziz Faisal, king of Saudi Arabia	1994	Cyprien Ntaryamira, president of Burundi
		1994	Juvenal Habyarimana, president of Rwanda
		1995	Yitzhak Rabin, Israeli prime minister

Appendix 8
World Population and Urbanization

Estimated World Population by Region, 200 BC–AD 1994 (millions)

date	Africa	the Americas	Asia	Europe	Oceania	total
200 BC	14	3	105	26	0.8	149
AD 1	16	4	115	31	1.0	167
200	17	5	130	36	1.1	190
400	19	6	130	31	1.2	188
600	21	7	140	26	1.3	196
800	25	8	155	29	1.4	219
1000	33	9	185	36	1.5	265
1200	38	11	250	58	1.7	359
1400	43	13	235	60	1.9	353
1600	55	12	375	100	2.1	545
1700	61	13	415	120	2.3	612
1800	70	24	625	180	2.5	902
1900	110	145	970	390	6.7	1,622
1950	205	325	1,450	515	14	2,509
1994	708	764	3403	726	31	5630

The World's Largest Cities, 200 BC–1995 (population in millions)

top five 200 BC		top five AD 100		top five AD 622	
Pataliputra (India)	0.35	Rome (Italy)	0.65	Constantinople (Turkey)	0.50
Alexandria (Egypt)	0.30	Loyang (China)	0.50	Changan (China)	0.45
Seleucia (Syria)	0.30	Alexandria (Egypt)	0.40	Loyang (China)	0.40
Changan (China)	0.25	Seleucia (Persia)	0.30	Ctesiphon (Persia)	0.25
Loyang (China)	0.20	Changan (China)	0.25	Alexandria (Egypt)	0.20

top five 1000		top five 1400		top five 1600	
Córdoba (Spain)	0.45	Nanjing (China)	0.47	Beijing (China)	0.71
Constantinople (Turkey)	0.45	Cairo (Egypt)	0.45	Constantinople (Turkey)	0.70
Kalfeng (China)	0.40	Vijayanagar (India)	0.35	Agra (India)	0.50
Xian (China)	0.30	Hangzhou (China)	0.33	Cairo (Egypt)	0.40
Kyoto (Japan)	0.20	Beijing (China)	0.32	Osaka (Japan)	0.40

top five 1800		top five 1900		top five 1950	
Beijing (China)	1.10	London (UK)	6.48	New York (USA)	12.30
London (UK)	0.95	New York (USA)	4.24	London (UK)	8.86
Guangzhou (China)	0.80	Paris (France)	3.33	Tokyo (Japan)	7.55
Constantinople (Turkey)	0.57	Berlin (Germany)	2.42	Paris (France)	5.90
Paris (France)	0.55	Chicago (USA)	1.72	Shanghai (China)	5.41

top ten 1985	
Tokyo-Yokohama (Japan)	25.43
Mexico City (Mexico)	16.90
São Paulo (Brazil)	14.91
New York (USA)	14.60
Seoul (South Korea)	13.67
Osaka-Kobe-Kyoto (Japan)	13.56
Buenos Aires (Argentina)	10.75
Calcutta (India)	10.46
Bombay (India)	10.14
Rio de Janeiro (Brazil)	10.12

top ten 1995	
Tokyo-Yokohama (Japan)	26.84
São Paulo (Brazil)	16.42
New York (USA)	16.33
Mexico City (Mexico)	15.64
Bombay (India)	15.09
Shanghai (China)	15.08
Los Angeles (USA)	12.41
Beijing (China)	12.36
Calcutta (India)	11.67
Seoul (South Korea)	11.64

top ten 2000 (projected)	
Tokyo-Yokohama (Japan)	28.70
Bombay (India)	18.10
São Paulo (Brazil)	17.80
Shanghai (China)	17.20
New York (USA)	16.60
Mexico City (Mexico)	16.40
Beijing (China)	14.20
Jakarta (Indonesia)	14.10
Lagos (Nigeria)	13.50
Los Angeles (USA)	13.10

top ten 2015 (projected)	
Tokyo-Yokohama (Japan)	28.70
Bombay (India)	27.40
Lagos (Nigeria)	24.40
Shanghai (China)	23.40
Jakarta (Indonesia	21.20
São Paulo (Brazil)	20.80
Karachi (Pakistan)	20.60
Beijing (China)	19.40
Dhaka (Bangladesh)	19.00
Mexico City (Mexico)	18.80

World Chronology

ASIA and AUSTRALASIA

2.5 million BC

800,000 *Homo erectus* began colonizing Asia.
c. 50,000 Modern humans in Asia.

30,000 Tools in use in Japan.
30,000–10,000 Aboriginal migration to Australia from S India, Sri Lanka and SE Asia.
c. 10,000 Harvesting of wild seeds in SW Asia.

c. 7500 First agriculture in SW Asia.

c. 4000 Rice grown in China. Indus valley became a population centre.

2850 Start of legendary 'golden age' in China.
2800–2200 Sage Kings period in China.

c. 2500 Indus civilization began in India.
2500–250 Jomon culture in Japan.
2200–1700 Xia dynasty in China.

c. 1760–c. 1122 Shang dynasty in China.

c. 1500 Aryan invasion of India. Collapse of Indus civilization.
c. 1400 Iron Age under way in India and W Asia.
1285 Egyptians and Hittites fought over, then divided, Syria.
c. 1122–256 Zhou dynasty in China.

750 Foundation of Kushan kingdom.

660 Jimmu became first emperor of Japan.

570 Taoism founded.
560 Sakya Muni (later Buddha) born.
551 Confucius born.

500 Vedda conquered by Sinhalese in Sri Lanka.

403–221 'Warring states' period in China.

321–185 Mauryan dynasty in India.
313 Tibet founded.
300 Agriculture began in Japan.

221–206 Qin dynasty in China.

AFRICA and the MIDDLE EAST

2.5 million *Homo habilis* used stone tools in Africa.
1.7 million *Homo habilis* built first structured habitats.
1 million *Homo erectus* able to control fire.
c. 130,000 *Homo sapiens* in Africa.

c. 8500 Wheat and barley cultivated in Jordan.
c. 7500 Goats and sheep domesticated in Near East.
c. 7000 Walled settlement at Jericho.
c. 5000 Sumerians settled in Mesopotamia.

c. 3500 Height of Sumerian civilization.
c. 3000 Menes united Egypt. Semitic tribes occupied Assyria.
2600 Egyptians retaliated at Palestinian attacks on trade caravans. Semitic tribes in Syria and N Africa.
c. 2500 Great Pyramids at Giza built.
c. 2350 Sargon founded Akkadian Empire.
c. 2200 Tribesmen from Iran destroyed Akkadian Empire.
1925 Hittites conquered Babylon.

c. 1650 Hittite Old Kingdom established.
c. 1580 Hyksos driven out of Egypt. Egypt reunited under Ahmose.
1400–1200 Hittite New Empire.

c. 1250 Israelites under Moses left Egypt.
1200–332 Phoenicians built up empire.
1175 Egypt split into two kingdoms.
1100–612 Assyrian Empire in Mesopotamia.
1025 Hebrew monarchy founded.
970 Death of King David.
970–c. 937 Reign of King Solomon.
850 Phoenicians founded Carthage.

721 Assyrians conquered Israel.
689 Assyrians destroyed Babylon.
c. 625 End of Assyrian Empire.
550 Cyrus seized Median throne and began to build empire.
529 Persians conquered Egypt.
c. 522 Massacre of Magi priests in Persia.

332 Macedonians under Alexander the Great conquered Asia Minor, Phoenicia, Persia, and Egypt.

EUROPE

AMERICAS

2.5 million BC

2.5 million BC

800,000 Europe colonized by *Homo erectus*.
c. 130,000 *Homo erectus* in Europe, able to control fire.

60,000–35,000 Ice Age landbridge between Asia and Alaska allowed migration from Siberia towards America.

c. 35,000 Modern humans in Europe.

40,000 Probable arrival of modern humans in Australia.

c. 15,000 Date of cave wall paintings at Lascaux, France.

c. 23,000 Modern humans in Americas.
9000 South America settled by peoples from Central America.

10,000

8400 Domesticated dogs in America.
8000 Ciboney people of S America reached Hispaniola.

c. 6000 First farming communities appeared in SE Europe. S Sweden inhabited.

c. 5000 Domestication of llamas in South America. Agriculture developed in Mexico.

5000

5000–4000 Inuit people arrived in N America.

c. 3000 Minoan civilization in Crete. Athens first inhabited.

3000

2600 Maya civilization began in the Yucatán Peninsula.

2500 Agriculture developed in S America.

c. 2500 Stonehenge built in England.

c. 2200–1450 Middle Minoan age flourished because of control of sea.

2000

c. 1700 Bronze Age began in Europe.
1674 Hyksos invaded Europe.
c. 1580 Start of Mycenean civilization.

1500 Olmec civilization in Central America. Farming settlements developed in Peru.

c. 1300 First Celts appeared, in Upper Danube region.

1200 Sack of Troy.
1120 End of Mycenean civilization.

1200–800 Chavin culture blossomed in Peru (to 200).
1000–500 Zapotecs built ceremonial centre Monte Albán.

1000

c. 900 Etruscans settled in Italy.
c. 800 Building of Carthage.
776 First Olympic Games, in Greece.
753 Traditional date for founding of Rome.
736–716 First Messenian War.
650–630 Second Messenian War.

510 Roman republic founded.
499–404 Greek-Persian wars.
431–404 Peloponnesian wars.
4th century Gauls entered N Italy.
399 Death of Socrates.
359 Philip became king of Macedonia.

c. 500 Beginning of Maya civilization.

500

300 Olmec disappeared, replaced by regional cultures.

264–41 First Punic War (Rome and Carthage).
225 Romans defeated Gauls at Talamone.
218–201 Second Punic War.

ASIA and AUSTRALASIA

AFRICA and the MIDDLE EAST

	ASIA and AUSTRALASIA	AFRICA and the MIDDLE EAST
	206 Han dynasty began in China. **185–30** Shunga dynasty in India. **155–50** Indio-Greek kingdom in Indus valley, founded by Menander. **108** China annexed Korea.	**133** Asia Minor became a province of Rome. **64** Romans conquered Syria.
AD	**1st century** Kushans invaded India. **58** Buddhism introduced to China. **91** Han invaded Mongolia.	**4** Birth of Jesus Christ. **30** Jesus Christ crucified. **50** Rise of kingdom of Axum in NE Africa. **70** Revolt of Jews against Rome. Jerusalem sacked. **106** Jordan became part of Roman province of Arabia.
200	**200** Huns invaded Afghanistan, ruling to 540. **201–250** Andgra dynasty in S India. **220** End of Han dynasty in China. Three Kingdoms period to 581. **225** End of Andgra dynasty in S India. **270–550** Gupta Empire in India.	**220** Goths invaded Asia Minor and Balkan Peninsula. **224** Foundation of Sassanian Empire in Persia.
300	**4th century** Ainu people driven into N Japan.	**330** Constantine the Great shifted seat of power to Byzantium, renamed Constantinople, and briefly united Roman Empire.
400	**400–500** Mon kingdom in Burma.	
500	**c. 500** Huns secured control over NW India. **550** End of Gupta Empire.	**525** Abyssinians conquered Yemen. **534** Byzantines reconquered N Africa. **539–562** War between Byzantines and Persia. **570** Muhammad, founder of Islam, born in Mecca. **572–591** War between Byzantines and Persia. **575** Persians overthrew Abyssinians in Yemen.
600	**581–618** Sui dynasty united China. **600–650** Harsha dynasty in India. **607** First Japanese ambassadors to China. **618–907** Tang dynasty in China. **636** Rise of feudal nobility in Japan. **638** Burma founded. **644** China invaded Korea. **645** Reform in Japan at start of Nara period (645– 784).	**618** Persians conquered Egypt. **622** Flight of Muhammad to Medina. **633–41** Arabs conquered Persia. **632** Death of Muhammad. **637** Sassanian Empire destroyed by Muslims. **639–42** Arabs conquered Egypt. **650** Byzantine Empire partly overrun by Muslims. **661** Ommayad dynasty of the Islamic empire founded. **697** Arabs destroyed Carthage.
700	**c. 700–800** Hinduism drove Buddhism from India. **712** Moslems conquered Sindh. **740** Gurjara dynasty united N India and defeated the Arabs. **753–63** Rebellion by Anlu-shan increased China's vulnerability to invaders.	**750–1258** Abbasid caliphate founded in Baghdad. **760** Turkish Empire founded.
800	**800** Rajputs began to set up kingdom in India.	**809** Death of Haroun-al-Raschid began 200 years of chaos in Arab Empire.

EUROPE

AMERICAS

EUROPE	AMERICAS	
216 Hannibal crossed the Alps. **c. 200** Romans began to conquer Spain.		
149–46 Third Punic War. Carthage destroyed.		
	100 Teotihuacán established.	
60 First triumvirate formed. **50** Romans conquered Gaul. **43** Second triumvirate formed. **31** Battle of Actium. Roman Empire founded.		
		AD
43 Romans invaded Britain.		
98 Trajan became Roman emperor, with Empire at its largest. **122–26** Hadrian's Wall built.		
	200–1000 Arawak Indians migrated from NE South America to Caribbean.	**200**
268 Goths sacked Athens, Sparta, and Corinth.		
	300 Rise of Maya civilization in Central America.	**300**
360 Huns invaded Europe. **395** Roman Empire split into Western and Eastern (Byzantine) Empires. **c. 400–500** Picts, Saxons, Jutes, and Angles invaded Britain. **410** Goths sacked Rome. Romans withdrew from Britain. **470** Huns withdrew from Europe. **476** Fall of the (Western) Roman Empire. **481** Clovis founded Frankish kingdom. **496** Franks conquered Alemanni (Germany).		**400**
	500–1600 American Indians in Mississippi basin became farmers with small settlements. **550** Toltec kingdom continued Teotihuacán civilization.	**500**
	600–1000 Rise of Ayamará in Bolivia.	**600**
664 Synod of Whitby decided to adopt Roman, not Celtic, form of Christianity for Britain. **685** Picts stopped Northumbrians invading Scotland. **711** Moors invaded Spain. **720** Moors invaded France. **732** Moors driven out of France.		**700**
771 Charlemagne conquered Saxony and continued campaign for Carolingians. **793** Viking raids on Britain began. **800** Charlemagne crowned Holy Roman Emperor. **811** Bulars defeated Byzantines.		**800**

ASIA and AUSTRALASIA

AFRICA and the MIDDLE EAST

845 Buddhism proscribed in China.

867 Basil I began Macedonian dynasty of Byzantine empire (to 1056).

900

c. 907 Chola power established in S India.
907–960 Civil war in China.

960–1279 Song dynasty in China.

909 Fatimid dynasty founded in N Africa.

969 Fatimids conquered Egypt.

1000

1050–1200 Start of main Muslim invasions into India from Afghanistan. Collapse of Hindu kingdoms.

c. 1000 Rise of Kanem empire (N Nigeria).
1045 Byzantines conquered Armenia.
c. 1050 Almoravid empire in Morocco began. Egyptian anarchy ended by Badr al Jamali.
1054 Abdallah ben Yasim began Muslim conquest of W Africa. End of kingdom of Ghana.
1055 Seljuk Turks took over caliphate.
1061 Almoravids conquered N Africa.
1071 Turks conquered Anatolia.

1096–99 First Crusade.

1100

1100–1192 Civil war in Japan.

1127–1279 Southern Song dynasty in China.

1147–49 Second Crusade.
1160 Normans expelled from N Africa.
1171 Saladin conquered Egypt.
1174 Saladin launched Holy War against Christians.
1176 Turks defeated Byzantium over Asia Minor in Battle of Myriokephalon.
1189–92 Third Crusade.

1190 Mongol leader Genghis Khan began to build Mongol Empire in E Asia.
1192 Kamakura shogunate began in Japan.

1200

1205 Hōjō family set up feudal government in Japan.
1206 Delhi sultanate founded. Mogul state founded.
1221 Mongols attacked Delhi sultanate.
1234 Mongols destroyed Jin Empire.

c. 1200 Christian Sudan kingdoms invaded by Muslims.
1202 Fourth Crusade.
1204 Crusaders sacked Constantinople.
1212 Children's Crusade.
1240 Mali Empire founded in W Africa.
1244 Egyptian Khwarazmi took Jerusalem.
1250–1517 Mameluke dynasty in Egypt.

1258 Mongols took Baghdad.
1260–1368 Yuan dynasty in China.
1274 Kublai Khan failed in attempt to invade Japan.
1275–95 Marco Polo's travels.
1279 Moguls in control over whole of China.

1270 Ethiopia revitalized over next two centuries.

1281 Great Mongol attack on Japan, defeated.

1300

1291 End of the Crusades.
1300 Ottoman Empire founded.

1325–51 Sultanate of Delhi at its height under Muhammad ibn Tughluq.

EUROPE	AMERICAS
826 Arabs conquered Crete. **843** Treaty of Verdun broke up Frankish Empire. **844** Scotland unified under Kenneth MacAlpin. **855** Former Carolingian empire broken up. **874** Vikings settled in Iceland. **878** Treaty of Wedmore between Alfred and the Danes. **885–86** Viking siege of Paris. **900** Start of Christian reconquest of Spain. **907** Commercial treaties between Kiev and Constantinople. **959** Edgar crowned king of all England. **962** Otto I crowned Holy Roman Emperor. **985** Viking settlements in Greenland. **987** Capet became king of France. **991** Renewed Viking raids on England.	**850** Nahuas began invading from N Mexico. First Maya civilization in Yucatán and Guatemala collapsed. **985** Toltecs now controlled Mexico. **987–1185** League of Mayapán in South America.
1018 Byzantines conquered Bulgarians. **1023–91** Abbadid Muslim dynasty in Seville. **1054** Schism between Roman and Greek churches. **1061** Normans conquered Messina. **1066** Normans conquered England. **1077–1122** War between papacy and Holy Roman Empire. **1084** Normans sacked Rome. **1086** Domesday Book of England completed.	**1000** Chimú state formed in Peru. Peak of Mayan civilization in Yucatán. Caribs from South America destroyed Arawak culture in Caribbean. Viking Leif Ericsson said to have reached Nova Scotia.
1122 Concordat of Worms. **1127** Normans completed conquest of Sicily. **1143** Benjamin of Tudela travelled to India via Constantinople, returning via Egypt and Sicily. **1144** Republican rule established in Rome. **1147** Portugal became independent monarchy. **1169** English invaded Ireland. **1170** Thomas à Becket murdered. **1177** Peace of Venice between Pope and Holy Roman Emperor. **1183** Peace of Constance between Pope, Holy Roman Emperor and the Lombards.	**1100** Nahuas in control of central Mexican plateau. **1168** Toltec capital Tula fell to the Aztecs. **1180** Toltec state fell to nomadic tribes. **1194** Chichen Itzá fell.
1204 King John of England lost Normandy to France. **1215** Magna Carta. **1223** Mongols overan S steppes of Russia. **1236** Arabs lost Córdoba to Castile. **1240** Mongols took Moscow and Kiev. **1241** Mongols defeated Germans and invaded Poland and Hungary, but later withdrew from Europe. **1259** Treaty of Paris (France and England). **1265** Birth of English Parliament **1282** Sicilians rose against Normans. **1294** Start of Franco-Scottish alliance.	**1200–50** Foundation of Aztec Empire in N Mexico. **1250** Inca settled at Cuzco, S Peru. Chimú established in N Peru.
1306 Robert Bruce became King Robert I of Scotland. **1314** Battle of Bannockburn, Robert defeated English.	**1327** Tenochtitlán founded by Aztecs.

900

1000

1100

1200

1300

	ASIA and AUSTRALASIA	AFRICA and the MIDDLE EAST
1350	1336 Kingdom of Vijayanagar founded in S India. 1339 Ashikaga shogunate in Japan. Political chaos. 1350 Siam founded. 1355 Illayas Shad established independent Bengal. 1363 Tamerlane began conquest of Asia. 1368 Mongol Yuan dynasty in China. 1368–1644 Ming dynasty in China.	1354 Turks took Gallipoli. 1375 Mamelukes captured Sis and overthrew Armenians. 1380 Tamerlane began series of conquests, including Persia, Georgia, Russia, and Egypt. 1390 Byzantines lost some territory to Turks.
1400	1396 Battle of Micopolis won by Bajazet. 1398–99 Tamerlane invaded India, annexing Punjab. 1401 Tamerlane conquered Damascus and Baghdad. 1403–24 Emperor Yongle extended territories in China. 1405–33 Zheng He's expeditions from China. 1428 First great peasant revolt in Japan.	1416 Venetians defeated Turks off Gallipoli.
1450	1447 Break up of Tamerlane's empire.	1442 First black slaves sent to Portugal. 1445 Diniz Diaz reached Cape Verde. 1448 Portuguese built first European fort on African coast, at Arguin (Mauritania). 1453 Turks with Mohammad II took Constantinople. 1455 Cadamosto explored Senegal. 1462 Castile captured Gibralta from Arabs. 1468 Songhai Empire began to grow in NW Africa. 1470 Portuguese reached Gold Coast of W Africa.
		1479 Peace of Constantinople: Venice ceded territory to Turks.
	1483 Russians began to explore Siberia. 1489 Yasuf Adilshah became last independent ruler of Bijapur. 1498 Vasco da Gama reached India.	1482 Portuguese set up trading base on Gold Coast (Ghana). 1484 Portuguese reached mouth of the Congo. 1488 Bartolomeu Diaz rounded Cape of Good Hope.
1500	1505 Trading contracts between India and Portugal. 1511 Portuguese reached Siam. Portuguese took Malacca. 1517 European traders gained access to China. 1526 Babur founded Mogul dynasty (to 1761), and conquered most of India. 1529 Treaty of Saragossa: Spain and Portugal divided up Far East.	1501–1736 Safavid dynasty in Persia. 1505 Portuguese reached Mozambique. 1507 Cadamosto explored Gambia. 1516–17 Turks conquered Egypt. 1521 Tartars from Crimea invaded S Russia as far as Moscow. 1531 Portuguese trading posts in Mozambique established.

EUROPE

AMERICAS

1337 Hundred Years' War began between England and France.
1348–49 Black Death in Europe.
1356 Ottoman Turks entered Europe.
1360 Treaty of Brétigny ended first stage of Hundred Years' War.
1378–1417 Great Schism of Rome and Avignon.

1358 Tlatelolco founded.

1350

1381 Peasants' Revolt in England.
1385 Portugal ensured independence from Spain.
1397 Union of Kalmar united Sweden, Norway, and Denmark (to 1520).

1401 Union of Poland and Lithuania.

1400–1500 Aztec empire grew to cover most of Mexico.

1400

1410 Battle of Tannenberg.
1415 Battle of Agincourt.

1428 Aztecs in control of central basin of Mexico.
1438 Inca rebuilt Cuzco and began expansion.
1440 Aztecs crowned Montezuma I. Battle of Cuzco: Inca defeated Chanca.
1441 Mayapán fell to Xius. Maya broken up into smaller states.

1450

1453 End of Hundred Years' War.
1454 Peace of Lodi between Venice and Milan.
1455–85 Wars of the Roses.
1456 Turks conquered Athens.
1459 Turks overran Serbia.
1463 Turks conquered Bosnia. Turks at war with Venice (to 1479).

1475 Turkey took over Crimea.

1476 Inca conquered Chimú (Ecuador).
1479 Treaty of Alvaovas between Spain and Portugal about Atlantic islands.
1480 Inca took over Bolivia.

1480 Ivan III of Moscow overthrew Mongols.
1481 Spanish Inquisition established.
1482 Peace of Arras.

1483 Burgundy and Brittany annexed by France.

1484 Inca conquered N and central Chile, and NW Argentina.

1492 Spain conquered Granada from Muslims.

1492 Columbus reached West Indies.
1494 Treaty of Tordesillas.
1496 Aztecs captured Tehuantepec.
1497 Cabot landed at Newfoundland. Spanish settled Hispaniola.
1500 Aztecs took Soconuscuo, threatening Mayan territory.
1505 Spanish conquered Puerto Rico.
1511–26 Inca pacified N territories.

1504 Treaty of Lyons: France ceded Naples to Spain.
1511 Holy League formed.
1512–22 War between Russia and Poland.
1517 Protestant Reformation began.
1520 Field of the Cloth of Gold
1521 Diet of Worms.
1526 League of Cognac: France, Florence, Venice, Milan, and papacy against Charles V.
1529 Peace of Cambrai.

1500

1519–21 Aztec empire fell to Cortés.

1532 Portuguese began to settle in Brazil.
1532–33 Inca fell to Pizarro.

ASIA and AUSTRALASIA	AFRICA and the MIDDLE EAST
	1551 Turks took Tripoli.
1555 Accession of Akbar in India.	
	1569 Turks captured the Yemen.
	1574 Portuguese began colonizing Angola.
1575 Akbar conquered Bengal.	
1582 Japan united under Hideyoshi.	
1592–93 Hideyoshi's invasion of Korea repelled.	**1591** Morocco conquered Songhay.
1600 English East India Company formed. **1602** Dutch East India Company formed. **1603** Tokugawa shogunate began in Japan, based in Tokyo. **1606** First European sighting of Australia, from a Dutch ship. **1609** Portugal took Ceylon from Dutch. **1615** Tribes in N China started forming military groupings, later called Manchus. **1619** Dutch empire founded in East Indies.	**1602–18** Turkey and Persia at war.
	1621 Iraq reoccupied by Persia.
1624 Japan expelled Spanish.	
1627 Korea became a tributary state of China.	
1632 Portuguese withdrew from Bengal.	**1633** Portuguese expelled from Abyssinian territory. **1637** French settlements set up in Senegal. **1638** Dutch took Mauritius.
1637 Russian explorers reached Pacific coast. **1639** Dutch took Trincomalee (in Ceylon) from Portuguese. Japan expelled Portuguese traders. **1641** Japan isolated itself from the rest of the world (to 1853). Dutch ousted Portuguese from Malacca. **1642** Tasman landed at Tasmania. **1644–1912** Qing (Manchu) dynasty in China.	
	1650 Rise of Ashanti in W Africa. **1652** Dutch founded Cape colony.
1658 Dutch took over rule of Ceylon from Portuguese. **1658–1707** Aurangzeb Empire in India.	
1664 French East India Company formed.	

Left margin markers: **1575**, **1600**, **1625**, **1650**

EUROPE

AMERICAS

EUROPE	AMERICAS	
1534 Henry VIII broke with Rome. Jesuits founded. **1536** Union of England and Wales.	**1534** French reached Canada. **1536–1609** French and British began to penetrate Spanish Caribbean. **1538** Spain conquered Bolivia. **1539** Spain annexed Cuba.	
1541 Turks conquered Hungary. **1547** Ivan the Terrible became tsar of Russia. **1552** Russia conquered Tatar state.	**c. 1545** Silver found in Peru and Mexico.	
1562–98 French Wars of Religion. **1563–70** Sweden and Denmark at war. **1568** Dutch Revolt began. **1571** Battle of Lepanto.	**1565** Spanish settled Florida. **1567** Portuguese founded Rio de Janeiro.	
1579 United Provinces (Dutch) proclaimed independence from Spain in Union of Utrecht. **1580** Spain conquered Portugal.	**1575** Frobisher reached Frobisher Bay, Canada.	**1575**
1588 English defeated Spanish Armada. **1589** Bourbon dynasty began in France. **1595–98** Franco-Spanish War. **1598** Edict of Nantes.	**1584** Raleigh annexed Virginia.	
1603 James I king of England and Scotland.		**1600**
	1605 French settled in Nova Scotia. England claimed Barbados. **1607** English founded Jamestown, Virginia. **1608** Quebec founded.	
1613–1917 Romanov dynasty in Russia. **1618** Outbreak of Thirty Years' War.		
	1619 First American legislature at Virginia. **1620** *Mayflower* arrived in New England. **1621** Dutch West India Company founded. Dutch took over Guyana. **1624–54** Dutch-Portuguese wars over Brazil. **1625** Dutch founded New Amsterdam. **1627** England secured Barbados. **1630** Great migration to the New World began. **1630–40** English and French made claims on West Indies possessions.	**1625**
1635 French entered Thirty Years' War against Spain.	**1634** English Catholics founded Maryland.	
1640 Portugal and Catalonia rebelled against Spain.		
1642–48 English Civil War. **1645–69** Turkey won war with Venice over Crete. **1648** Treaty of Westphalia ended Thirty Years' War. **1649** Charles I executed. Britain a republic to 1660.	**1642** Montreal founded.	
1652–54 First Anglo-Dutch war. **1654–67** Russo-Polish war **1656–59** Anglo-Spanish war. **1657–59** Dutch Republic and Portuguese at war. **1659** Treaty of Pyrenees ended Franco-Spanish war. **1660** Charles II restored in England. **1661–64** Turkey and Holy Roman Empire at war.	**1650** French began colonizing Canada. **1654** Portuguese drove Dutch from Brazil. **1655** English took Jamaica from Spanish. **1664** English seized New Amsterdam from Dutch.	**1650**

ASIA and AUSTRALASIA

AFRICA and the MIDDLE EAST

1665 Battle of Ambuila: Portuguese killed king of the Kongo kingdom.

1668 England acquired Bombay.

1669 Hindus persecuted in India by Aurangzeb.

1670

1674 Sivaji defeated Mongols. Maratha kingdom invaded.
1676–78 Sikh uprisings in India.
1683 Taiwan (Formosa) incorporated into China.
1685 All Chinese ports opened to foreign trade.

1689 Treaty of Nerchinsk between China and Russia over boundaries.

1690 Mogul conquests of S India almost complete.
1693 China invaded Mongolia.

1699 Sultanate of Oman established on E coast of Africa.

1700

c. 1700 British East India Company took control of key Indian ports.

1707 Death of Mogul emperor Aurangzeb: power struggle in India to 1761.

1711 Russo-Turkish war.

1714 Tripoli gained independence from Turkey.

1720 Chinese invaded Tibet.

1725

1729 Arabs took Mombasa from Portugal.
1734–35 Turko-Persian war.
1735–95 Chinese expanded into Turkestan, Annam (Vietnam), Burma, and Nepal.
1736–39 Russo-Turkish war.

1739 Persians pillaged Delhi.

1747 Afghanistan united.

1750

1750 Ngwane III conquered Swaziland.

1751 Britain captured Arcot, India, from French. China invaded Tibet.
1752 Fall of Toungoo dynasty in Burma.
1756 Black hole of Calcutta.
1757 Battle of Plassey: Britain defeated nawab of Bengal.
1759 China occupied E Turkestan.
1760 French defeated in India leaving British supreme.
1761 Battle of Panipat ended Maratha attempt to dominate India.

EUROPE	AMERICAS	
1665–67 Second Anglo-Dutch war. **1667–68** War of Devolution by France against Spain. **1668** Triple Alliance of England, Netherlands, and Sweden against France. Spain recognized Portugal's independence. **1670** Secret Treaty of Dover between England and France. **1672–74** Third Anglo-Dutch war. **1678** Treaty of Nijmegen marked peak of Louis XIV's ambitions. **1683** Turkey's defeat at Vienna ended advance of Islam into Europe. **1685** Edict of Nantes revoked. Huguenot exodus. **1688** Revolution in England. **1688–97** War of the League of Augsburg (France against Grand Alliance). **1690** Battle of the Boyne in Ireland. **1695–96** Russo-Turkish war. **1697** Peace of Ryswick marked defeat of France by Grand Alliance. **1699** Turks lost Hungary to Austria. **1700–21** Great Northern War. **1701** Act of Settlement. **1701–13** War of the Spanish Succession. **1704** Britain captured Gibraltar. **1707** Union of England and Scotland. **1709** Battle of Poltava. **1713** Treaty of Utrecht. **1715** Jacobite rising. Death of Louis XIV. **1718** England declared war on Spain. **1721** Proclamation of the Russian Empire. **1725** Treaty of Vienna (Pragmatic Sanction). **1727–28** Spanish siege on Gibraltar. **1727–29** War between Britain and Spain. **1731** Treaty of Vienna (England, Holland, Spain, and Holy Roman emperor). **1740** Accessions of Frederick the Great and Maria Theresa. **1740–48** War of the Austrian Succession. **1745** Peace of Dresden. **1745–46** Last Jacobite uprising in Britain. **1762** Accession of Catherine the Great. **1763** Peace of Paris ended Seven Years' War.	**1670** Hudson's Bay Company founded. **1681** Pennsylvania colony founded by Quakers. **1683** Peace treaty between William Penn and North American Indians. **1697** French gained Haiti. **1699** French began to colonize Louisiana. **1710** British captured Nova Scotia from French. **1711** French captured Rio de Janeiro. **1713** British gained Newfoundland, Hudson Bay. **1733** Dawes gained control of Santa Cruz. Georgia became the 13th British crown colony. **1739** New Granada parted from Peru. **1750** Spanish-Portuguese treaty over South America. **1754** Seven Years' (French and Indian) War between Europeans in North America. **1758–60** British conquered French Canada. **1761** Britain gained control of West Indies. **1763** Peace of Paris: France lost American possessions to Britain. Ottawa Indians fought British.	**1670** **1700** **1725** **1750**

ASIA and AUSTRALASIA	AFRICA and the MIDDLE EAST

1770

1767–69 First Mysore War.
1768 Cook landed in New Zealand and E coast of Australia.
1769 Burmese recognized Chinese sovereignty.
1770 Cook claimed New South Wales as a colony.

1775–82 First Maratha War.

1776 Dutch Afrikaners met Bantu.

1780–84 Second Mysore War.

1784 India Act. Burma conquered Arakan.
1786 British took Malacca.
1787 First European settlement of Freetown.
1788 Colonization of Australia began at Botany Bay.
1790–92 Third Mysore War.

1792 British took Cape of Good Hope.

1794 Slave trade in French colonies ended.

1796 British took Ceylon.

1798 French invaded Egypt.

1799 Kingdom of Mysore divided between Britain and Hyderabad.
1800–50 Laos broken up into several states.

1800

1801 French defeated Turks at Heliopolis, but later left Egypt.
1801–24 Osei Bonsu reduced powers of Ashanti chiefs.
1803–05 First Maratha War in India.
1804 Castle Hill rising in New South Wales.
1804–08 Uthman dan Fodio led jihad against the Hausa.
1804–08 Japan rejected Russian and British trading attempts.
1805 Mehemet Ali proclaimed pasha of Egypt.
1806 Sepoy mutiny at Vellore, India.
1806 Britain seized Cape Colony from Dutch.

1810 Fulani Empire of Sokoto (Nigeria) established.
1811 Massacre of Mamelukes.

1812 Chinese edict against Christianity.
1817 Ceylon revolt suppressed by British.

1814 Cape Province sold to British.

1817–18 Second Maratha War.

1818 Zulu kingdom formed by Shaka. Sheik Ahmuda's jihad.
1819 Singapore founded as British colony. Kashmir conquered by Ranjit Singh.
1820 Ali Pasha's revolt crushed by Turks.
1820–22 Egypt conquered Sudan.
1822 Liberia founded for freed slaves. Mzilika rebelled against Shaka.
1824 Assam ceded to Britain.
1824–26 First Anglo-Burmese War.
1824 Mzilika led Ndebele to western Transvaal. First Ashanti War.
1824–51 General Chakri of Siam founded new dynasty.

1825

1825–50 Java War.

EUROPE	AMERICAS	
	1765 Britain imposed Stamp Act on American colonies.	
	1768–71 Cook explored Pacific.	
		1770
1772 First partition of Poland.		
1774 Turkey left Crimea.	**1773** Boston Tea Party. **1774** Declaration of Rights and Grievances. **1775–83** American War of Independence. **1776** Declaration of Independence issued. Viceroyalty of River Plate founded. **1780–81** Peruvian Indians revolted against Spanish. **1781** Battle of Yorktown. **1784** US began trade with China. **1787–89** US constitution formed.	
1789 French Revolution began.	**1789** Washington first US president. **1791** Canada divided in Upper and Lower Canada, and allowed representative government.	
1792 Russian Empire extended to Black Sea. **1793** Execution of Louis XVI. Start of Revolutionary War. Second partition of Poland. **1793–94** Reign of Terror in France. **1795** Poland ceased to exist.	**1795** Treaty of San Lorenzo between US and Spain over border rights. **1796** Britain captured Guyana.	
1799 Napoleon seized power as first consul.		
	1800 Jefferson became US president. **1800–15** Tripolitan War.	**1800**
1801 Act of Union (Britain and Ireland). **1802** Peace of Amiens (Britain and France). **1803** Britain and France at war again.	**1803** Louisiana Purchase of large tract of land from France. **1804** Haiti independent. **1804–06** Lewis and Clark expedition in US to find land route to Pacific.	
1804 Napoleon became emperor of the French.		
1805 Battles of Trafalgar and Austerlitz. **1806** Battle of Jena. End of Holy Roman Empire. **1807** Treaty of Tilsit. Treaty of Fontainebleau. Slave trade abolished by Britain. **1808** Peninsular War started. Treaty of Bucharest ended Russo-Turkish war. Russia seized Finland. **1811** Luddite riots began in England. **1812** Napoleon's retreat from Russia. **1813** Quadruple Alliance. Battle of Leipzig.	**1807** Colombian Independent Movement started in Venezuela. **1809** Ecuador became part of Colombia. **1811** Paraguay and Venezuela gained independence. Battle of Tippecanoe. **1812–14** Anglo-American war.	
1814 Congress of Vienna. Restoration of Bourbons in France. **1815** Napoleon's Hundred Days. Battle of Waterloo. German Confederation formed.	**1814** Treaty of Ghent. **1815** Battle of New Orleans. **1816** United Provinces of South America. Argentine independent. **1818** Chile independent. **1819** Colombia independent. **1820** Missouri compromise.	
1818 Congress of Aix-la-Chapelle. **1819** Peterloo massacre in England.		
1821–32 Greek War of Independence.	**1821** Mexico, Central America, and Peru proclaimed independence. **1822** Brazil independent. **1823** Monroe Doctrine.	
1825 Decembrist uprising.	**1825** Bolivia independent.	**1825**

ASIA and AUSTRALASIA	AFRICA and the MIDDLE EAST
1826 Straits Settlements formed by East India Company. **1828** Western Australia founded.	**1826–7** Sheikh Ahmadu conquered Timbuktu. **1827** Battle of Navarino: Turkish and Egyptian fleets destroyed.

1830

1830 Britain gained Mysore. **1830–54** Russia conquered Kazakhstan.	**1830** Algeria became a French colony.
1834 South Australia founded. **1836** Uprising in Japan.	**1836** Great Trek by Boers.
1837 Colonization of New Zealand began. **1838** Myall Creek massacre. **1838–42** First Afghan War.	**1838** Massacre of Zulus at Battle of Blood River.
1839–42 First Opium War.	**1839** Mehemet Ali defeated Ottomans. Tanzimat Reforms began.

1840

1840 Treaty of Waitangi. Britain annexed New Zealand. **1841** Britain occupied Hong Kong. **1841–43** Reforms in Japan. **1842** Treaty of Nanking opened up Chinese trade with West, creating treaty ports. Massacre at Khyber Pass during British retreat from Afghanistan. **1843** French occupied Tahiti. Britain conquered Sind. **1845–49** Britain annexed Punjab. Sikh Wars.	**1840** Said ibn Sayyid took over Zanzibar. Matabeleland founded. Natal proclaimed. **1841** Mehemet Ali recognized as hereditary ruler of Egypt, virtually independent of Ottomans. **1842** French occupied Tahiti. **1843** Orange Free State founded. Natal became a British colony. **1846–53** Xhosa War. **1847** Liberia independent.

1850

1850 Victoria separated from New South Wales. **1850–64** Taiping Rebellion in China. **1852–54** Second Burmese War (with Britain). **1853** Britain annexed Nagpur. **1855** Treaty of Peshawar (Afghanistan and Britain). **1855–60** Second Opium War (China and Britain). **1856** Britain annexed Oudh. Tasmania became self-governing. US Admiral Perry entered Japanese ports. **1857–58** Indian Mutiny suppressed. **1858** Treaty of Aigun: Russia gained Amur from China.	**1850** Britain bought Danish settlements in W Africa. **1850–53** Anglo-Kaffir War. **1851** British occupied Lagos. **1853** Russo-Turkish war over Palestine. **1854** Orange Free State founded. **1856** Natal became a crown colony. **1856–57** Persia at war with Britain after taking Herat (Afghanistan). **1859** Morocco and Spain at war.

1860

1860 End of Opium War: Britain and France occupied Beijing. Peking Pact signed. **1860–70** Second Maori War. **1863** Cambodia became a French protectorate. **1867** Convict transportation to Australia ended.	**1861** Lagos ceded to Britain. **1862** Messina conquered by Tukolor al-Hajj Umar.

EUROPE

AMERICAS

EUROPE	AMERICAS	
	1826 First Pan-American Congress in Panama.	
1827–29 Russo-Turkish war.		
	1828 Uruguay independent. Treaty of Rio de Janeiro. Andrew Jackson elected US president.	
1830 Revolutions in France, Poland, Belgium, Italy.	**1830** Partition of Gran Columbia. Removal of	**1830**
1831 Young Italy movement formed.	American Indians to reservations began.	
1832 First Reform Act (Britain).	**1832** Black Hawk War. Britain occupied Falkland	
1833 Prussian Zollverein formed.	Islands.	
1834 Slavery ended in British colonies.		
	1836 Battles of the Alamo and San Jacinto. Texas gained independence from Spain.	
1837 Accession of Queen Victoria.	**1837** Papineau and Mackenzie rebellions. Montreal rebellion.	
	1838 Durham Report. First crossing of Atlantic by steamship.	
1839 First Chartist petition.	**1839** Central America split into numerous states.	
	1840 Act of Union for Canada.	**1840**
	1842 Oregon Trail opened up. Webster-Ashburton Treaty	
1845–51 Irish potato famine.	**1845** Texas annexed by US.	
1846 Corn Laws repealed.	**1846** Oregon Treaty.	
	1846–48 Mexican-American War.	
1847 Il Risorgimento founded.	**1848** Californian Gold Rush. Hawaii granted	
1848 Revolutions throughout Europe. Communist Manifesto published.	independence. Maya Indian revolt in Mexico suppressed.	
	1850 New US states compromised over slavery. California joined US.	**1850**
	1851 Cuba unsuccessfully declared independence.	
1852 Fall of 2nd Republic in France. Napoleon III took power.		
1854–56 Crimean War	**1853–54** Gadsdon Purchase.	
	1854 Elgin Treaty re Canadian trade by US and Britain.	
1856 Congress of Paris.		
	1858–61 Mexican War of Reform.	
1859 France and Sardinia at war with Austria.		
1860 Carlist uprising in Spain.	**1860** Confederacy formed by Southern states.	**1860**
1861 Emancipation of Russian serfs. Unification of Italy.	**1861–65** American Civil War.	
1862 Bismarck prime minister of Prussia.		
1863 Greek revolution.	**1863** Dutch abolished slavery in colonies. Slavery abolished in US. France occupied Mexico.	
1864 Denmark and France at war with Prussian alliance.	**1864–70** Triple Alliance (Paraguayan) War.	
	1865 Rebellion in Jamaica.	
1866 Austro-Prussian War. Crete revolted against Turks.		
1867 Second Great Reform Act in Britain. Garibaldi's march on Rome.	**1867** Alaska purchased by US from Russia. Dominion of Canada established. French left Mexico.	
	1867–70 Reconstruction Acts in US.	

	ASIA and AUSTRALASIA	AFRICA and the MIDDLE EAST
1870	1868 Meiji dynasty restored in Japan.	1868 Basutoland became a British protectorate. 1869 Suez Canal opened. 1871 Britain annexed Kimberley diamond fields.
	1874 Britain annexed Fiji. 1876 Korea independent. 1877 Queen Victoria became empress of India. Satsuma rebellion in Japan. 1878–80 Second Anglo-Afghan War.	1873–74 Second Ashanti War. 1874 Gold Coast (Ghana) colony founded by Britain. 1877 Britain annexed Transvaal. 1877–79 Last Xhosa War. 1879 Zulu Wars. Britain and France took control of Egypt.
1880	1880 French annexed Tahiti. 1882 French captured Hanoi. 1883–85 Sino-French War. 1885 Anglo-Russian crisis over Afghan boundary. Indian National Congress met. 1885–86 Anglo-Burmese War: Britain annexed Upper Burma, and rest joined India. 1887 French Indochina established.	1881 First South African War. Revolt in Egypt. French invaded Tunis. 1882 French left Egypt to British, who occupied Cairo. 1883 Britain left Sudan. 1884 Berlin Conference accelerated European 'scramble for Africa'. Germany acquired SW Africa, Togoland, Cameroons. 1885 Germany annexed Tanganyika and Zanzibar. 1886 Royal Niger Company formed. 1887 Ethiopia and Italy at war.
1890	1893 Durrand Agreement (India and Afghanistan frontier defined). 1894–95 Sino-Japanese War over Korea. 1896 Manchuria Convention (Russia and China). 1898 Hundred Days' reform in China.	1889 Italy gained protectorate over Ethiopia. 1890 Rhodesia formed. Britain annexed Uganda. Zanzibar Settlement (Britain and Germany). 1891 Anglo-Portuguese Convention on E Africa. Anglo-Italian agreement on NE Africa. 1892 Anglo-German agreement over Cameroons. 1893 Matabele War: French gained Ivory Coast. 1895–96 Ethiopia won war with Italy. 1896 French annexed Madagascar. Britain won last Ashanti War. 1898 Fashoda Incident. Britain agreed 99-year lease on New Territories (Hong Kong). 1899–1902 Second South African War.
1900	1900 Boxer Rebellion in China. 1901 Australian Commonwealth established. US took over Philippines. Russia occupied Manchuria. 1902 Anglo-Japanese treaty. 1904–05 Russo-Japanese War. 1905 Partition of Bengal. Battle of Mukden. 1907 New Zealand an independent dominion. Dutch conquered Sumatra. 1908 Dutch took over Bali. Muslim League formed. 1909 Indian Councils Act.	1900 North and South Nigeria became British protectorates. Britain annexed Orange Free State and Transvaal. First Pan-African Conference. 1902 End of South African War. 1903 Britain occupied North Nigeria (Sokoto). 1904 Germans massacred Herero rebels, SW Africa. 1905 Moroccan crisis (France and Germany). 1906 Revolution in Iran. Algeciras Conference.
1910	1910 Japan annexed Korea. China ended slavery. 1911–12 Revolution in China: republic established.	1908 Young Turk Revolution. Belgium took over Congo Free State. 1910 South Africa became independent dominion. 1911 Agadir Crisis (Germany and France over Morocco). Italy conquered Libya. Italy and Turkey at war to 1912. 1914 Egypt and Cyprus declared British protectorates.

EUROPE

1868 Military rising in Spain.

1870 Third Republic in France. Italy annexed Rome.
1870–71 Franco-Prussian War.
1872–76 2nd Carlist uprising in Spain.

1876 Turks massacred Bulgarians.
1877–78 Russo-Turkish War.
1878 Congress of Berlin.

1879 Treaty of San Stefano (Russia and Turkey).
Dual Alliance (Austria and Germany).

1882 Triple Alliance (Italy, Germany, and Austria)
formed.

1886 Treaty of Bucharest ended Serbo-Bulgarian
War.
1887 Reinsurance Treaty of neutrality between
Germany and Russia.
1889 Great London Dock Strike.

1893 Franco-Russian alliance.
1894–1906 Dreyfus Affair in France.

1897 Greece and Turkey at war over Crete.

1904 Entente Cordiale (Britain and France).

1905 Revolution in Russia. Sweden and Norway
split.
1907 Triple Entente (France, Britain, and Russia).

1910 Revolution in Portugal.

1912 Treaty of Lausanne.
1914 Start of World War I between Central Powers
and Allies (France and Germany). Battle of
Tannenburg.

AMERICAS

1868 Ku Klux Klan formed.
1868–78 Cuba and Spain at war.
1869–70 Red River Rebellion.
1871 British Columbia and Vancouver joined
Dominion of Canada.
1871–86 Military conflict with Apaches.
1873 Spain ended slavery in Puerto Rico.

1876 Battle of Little Big Horn.

1879 War of the Pacific: Chile beat Peru and Bolivia,
which lost its coastline.
c. 1880 End of Indian wars in Argentina and Chile.

1886 Spain ended slavery in Cuba.

1888 Slavery ended in Brazil.
1889 Brazil a republic.

1893 US overthrew Hawaiian government.

1895 Cuba rebelled against Spain.

1898 Spanish-American War over Cuba. US
annexed Hawaii.

1902 Cuba fully independent. Anglo-German force
seized Venezuelan fleet.
1904 Treaty between Bolivia and Chile.

1906–09 US occupied Cuba.

1909–11 Civil war in Honduras.
1910 Revolution in Mexico.

1912 Arizona and New Mexico joined US.
1914 Panama Canal opened.

1870

1880

1890

1900

1910

ASIA and AUSTRALASIA

AFRICA and the MIDDLE EAST

1915

1915 Twenty-one demands by Japan on China.

1916–18 Mesopotamia campaign.
1918 Britain captured Syria.

1919 Punjab riots. Amritsar Massacre.

1920

1921 Breakaway Chinese government set up under Sun Yat-sen.

1926 Chiang Kai-shek firmly in control in China.
1927 Chiang Kai-shek began purge of communists.

1930

1931 Mukden Incident. Japan occupied Manchuria to 1932.
1932 Indian Congress declared illegal.

1933 Japan left League of Nations.
1934–35 Long March by Chinese communists.
1935 Burma separated from India. Philippines became self-governing.
1936 Japan signed Anti-Comintern Pact with Germany.

1937–45 Japan invaded China.

1940

1941 Japan attacked Pearl Harbor and began to overrun SE Asia. China joined Allies in World War II.
1942 Japan conquered Singapore.

1944 Battle of Leyte Gulf.
1945 Atomic bombs dropped on Japan, which surrendered. US and USSR troops entered Korea.
1946–49 Civil war in China.
1947 Indonesia established. India, Pakistan, and Laos independent.
1948 Korea divided. Burma independent.

1949

1919 Ottoman Empire dismantled. Arab Revolt in Egypt.
1920 Kenya a British colony. Turkish Revolution.

1921–58 Hashemite kingdom in Iraq.
1922 End of British protectorate in Egypt.

1923 Turkish republic founded. Palestine, Transjordan, and Iraq mandated to Britain: Syria to France.
1924 N Rhodesia became a British protectorate.

1926 Independent Lebanon established.

1929 Major Arab-Jewish conflict in Palestine.

1932 Saudi Arabia established.

1935–36 Ethiopia occupied by Italy.

1936 Arab-Jewish conflict in Palestine.

1940 Italy expelled from Somalia, Eritrea, and Ethiopia.
1941 World War II reached N Africa.

1942 Battle of El Alamein.
1943 End of Axis resistance in N Africa.

1946 Jordan independent.

1948 Israel established.
1948 Apartheid began in South Africa.
1948–49 First Arab-Israeli War.

EUROPE

AMERICAS

EUROPE	AMERICAS	
1915 Italy joined Allies. Bulgaria joined Central Powers.		**1915**
1915–16 Gallipoli campaign.		
1916 Battles of Verdun, Jutland, and the Somme. Portugal and Romania joined war against Germany. Easter Rising in Ireland.	**1916** US bought Danish West Indies (Virgin Islands).	
1917 Revolutions in Russia.	**1917** US declared war on Germany. US bought Dutch West Indies.	
1918 Central Powers surrendered. Civil wars began in Ireland (to 1921), and Russia (to 1922).		
1919 Treaty of Versailles.	**1919** Woodrow Wilson advocated League of Nations.	
1920 League of Nations formed.	**1920** US Senate rejected Versailles settlement. Civil war in Mexico.	**1920**
1921 Irish Free State created in S Ireland.	**1920–33** Prohibition in US.	
1922 USSR formed. Mussolini prime minister in Italy.		
1923 French occupied Ruhr.		
	1924 US limited immigration and barred Japanese.	
1925 Locarno Conference.		
	1927 Kellogg-Briand pact.	
	1927–30 Cristeros Revolt in Mexico.	
1927 Kellogg-Briand pact.	**1928** Chaco War (Paraguay and Bolivia).	
1929 Yugoslavia created.	**1929** Wall Street Crash.	
1929–33 Great Depression.		
1930 Statute of Westminster in Britain.	**1930** Revolutions in Argentina and Brazil.	**1930**
	1932 Ottawa Conference.	
	1932–35 Bolivia and Paraguay at war.	
1933 Hitler became chancellor of Germany.	**1933** Roosevelt's New Deal.	
1934 Balkan Pact.		
1936 Rome-Berlin Axis formed. Germany and Japan signed Anti-Comintern Pact.		
1936–39 Spanish Civil War.		
1937 Italy joined Anti-Comintern Pact.		
1938 Munich Crisis.		
1939 Italy conquered Albania. Germany signed non-aggression pact with USSR. USSR invaded Finland. Germany invaded Czechoslovakia and Poland. Start of World War II.		
1940 Germany invaded France. Italy joined war against Allies. Germany began exterminating Jews.		**1940**
1941 Germany invaded USSR.	**1941** Japan bombed Pearl Harbor. US entered World War II.	
	1942 Brazil entered World War II.	
1943 Italy surrendered. USSR drove Germans back.		
1944 Normandy landings.		
1945 End of World War II.	**1945** United Nations formed.	
1945–48 Communist takeover in E Europe.		
1946–49 Greek Civil War.		
1948–49 Berlin blockade.	**1948** Organization of American States formed. Marshall Plan of aid for Europe.	
1949 North Atlantic Treaty Alliance formed. Germany divided into E and W. Comecon formed.		**1949**

ASIA and AUSTRALASIA	AFRICA and the MIDDLE EAST
1950 **1950–53** Korean War.	**1950** Anglo-Egyptian dispute over Suez Canal and Sudan.
1951 China occupied Tibet. French defeated by Vietminh. Colombo plan for economic development in S and SE Asia. Japan signed treaties of peace with 49 nations. **1954** Vietnam independent and divided into North and South, which began a war. Laos and Cambodia independent. SEATO (SE Asian Treaty Organization) formed (to 1977). **1956** French recognized Moroccan and Tunisian independence. **1957** Malaya independent. **1958** Singapore independent.	**1951** British troops entered canal zone. **1952** Moroccan uprising against French. **1952–55** Mau Mau campaign in Kenya. **1953** Egypt became a republic. **1954–62** Algerian War of Independence. **1955** Baghdad Pact (Iran, Iraq, and Turkey). **1956** Suez Crisis, and Canal nationalized. Morocco, Sudan, and Tunisia independent. **1957** Suez Canal reopened. Ghana independent. **1958** Revolution in Iraq. Egypt and Sudan formed United Arab Republic, which Yemen joined.
1960 **1959** China crushed uprising in Tibet, and had border clashes with India.	**1959** China crushed uprising in Tibet, and had **1960** South Africa became a republic. Sharpeville massacre. Nigeria and Belgian Congo independent.
1962 Sino-Indian border clashes.	
1963 Military coup in S Vietnam.	**1963** Organization of African Unity formed. Kenya independent.
1964–66 War between Indonesia and Malaysia.	**1964** Tanzania founded. Malawi and Zambia independent. Palestine Liberation Organization formed.
1965 US marines entered Vietnam. India and Pakistan at war over Kashmir. **1966–76** Cultural Revolution in China.	**1965** White Rhodesian government formed.
1968 Tet Offensive in Vietnam.	**1967** Six-day Arab-Israeli War. Suez Canal shut. **1967–70** Biafra War in Nigeria. **1969** Libyan revolution.
1970	**1970** Civil war in Jordan.
1971 Fighting in Indochina spread into Laos and Cambodia. Tension between India and Pakistan. Bangladesh proclaimed. China joined United Nations. **1972** Sri Lanka independent.	**1972** Lebanese Civil War. Uganda expelled Asians.
1973 US troops left Vietnam.	**1973** Arab-Israeli (Yom Kippur) War. Oil prices raised. **1974** Oil crisis.
1975 End of Vietnam War.	**1975** Suez Canal re-opened. Portuguese colonies gained independence.
1976 North and South Vietnam reunited.	**1976** Civil war in Angola. Soweto riots in South Africa.
1977 Military coup in Pakistan.	**1977** Israeli and Egyptian leaders visited each other's countries. Israel settled on West Bank.
1978 Military junta seized power in Afghanistan.	**1978** Camp David agreement. Border troubles between Israel and Lebanon.
1979 Civil war in Afghanistan. Russia entered Afghanistan. Chinese invaded Vietnam. **1979–88** Vietnam invaded Cambodia.	**1979** Islamic Revolution in Iran. Egypt and Israel signed peace treaty.
1980	**1980** Rhodesia independent (Zimbabwe). **1980–88** Iran-Iraq War. **1981** President Sadat of Egypt assassinated. **1982** Israel invaded Lebanon. Numerous atrocities in Beirut.
1984 UK affirmed agreement to return Hong Kong to China in 1997.	**1984** Ethiopian famine. Foreign nationals left Beirut.

EUROPE

AMERICAS

EUROPE	AMERICAS	
1950 East Germany and Poland agreed frontier.	**1950–54** McCarthy anti-communist campaign.	**1950**
1951 Schuman Plan (France and Germany). **1952** End of Allied occupation of West Germany. Greece and Turkey joined NATO. **1953** Death of Stalin in USSR. **1954** Warsaw Pact formed. West Germany joined NATO.	**1953** Coup in Colombia. **1954** Revolution in Guatemala.	
1956 Soviet troops crushed uprising in Hungary. Polish revolt. **1957** European Economic Community established by six countries through Treaty of Rome.	**1956–57** Cuban Civil War. **1957** US Civil Rights Act. **1958** Alaska joined US. West Indies Federation formed. **1959** Cuban Revolution. Hawaii joined US. **1960** US invasion of Cuba failed.	**1960**
1961 Berlin Wall built.	**1961** Cuban Missile Crisis. Latin American Free Trade Association formed. **1962** Jamaica and Trinidad independent.	
1963 French vetoed British application to join EEC. Nuclear Test Ban Treaty signed in Moscow. **1964** Greek-Turkish tension over Cyprus.	**1963** Nuclear Test Ban Treaty. US President Kennedy assassinated. Race riots in Birmingham, Alabama. **1964** US Civil Rights Act.	
1966 France left NATO. **1967** Military coup in Greece. **1969** Violence in Northern Ireland.	**1968** Martin Luther King assassinated. **1969** US put men on the Moon.	**1970**
1972 British direct rule introduced in Northern Ireland. USSR signed SALT I accord. **1973** Britain, Ireland, and Denmark entered EEC. **1973–75** Helsinki Conference. **1974** Portuguese dictactorship overthrown. Partition of Cyprus. Northern Irish terrorism spread to British mainland. **1975** Democracy restored in Spain. Helsinki Agreement.	**1972** US signed SALT I accord. **1973** Military coup in Chile. **1974** Watergate scandal in US.	
1979 USSR signed SALT II accord. **1980** Solidarity formed in Poland.	**1979** US signed SALT II accord. Sandinistas overthrew Somoza in Nicaragua.	**1980**
1981 Greece joined EC. **1982** Spain joined NATO. Falklands War (Britain and Argentina).	**1982** Falklands War (Argentina and Britain). **1983** US invaded Grenada.	

ASIA and AUSTRALASIA   AFRICA and the MIDDLE EAST

1985

1986 Overthrow of President Marcos in Philippines.   **1986** US bombed Libya.

1989 Soviet troops left Afghanistan. Democracy demonstrations in China crushed.

1990

1990 Dismantling of apartheid in South Africa began. Iraq invaded Kuwait.
1991 Gulf War. Middle East peace talks began.

1992 Muslims replaced communists to rule Afghanistan.

1992 South Africa voted for majority rule: continued unrest. Civil war and famine in Somalia: US intervened.

1993 North Korea withdraws from nuclear non-proliferation treaty.

1993 Peace agreement between Israel and PLO.

1994 Civil war in Rwanda. Non-racial elections in South Africa.

1995

1995 Ethnic clashes in Burundi. Israeli prime minister Rabin assassinated.

1997

1997 Hong Kong reverts to Chinese control.

EUROPE	AMERICAS	
1985 Gorbachev came to power in USSR.		**1985**
1986 Spain and Portugal joined EC.	**1986** Irangate scandal broke.	
1987 USSR signed Intermediate Nuclear Forces treaty.	**1987** US signed Intermediate Nuclear Forces treaty.	
1989 Berlin Wall opened. Revolutions in E Europe against communist rule.		
1990 Germany reunified. Free elections in Hungary, Romania, Bulgaria, and Czechoslovakia.		**1990**
1991 Civil war in Yugoslavia. USSR broke up into republics. Warsaw Pact disbanded. Gorbachev resigned.	**1991** US signed START treaty. New constitution in Colombia. Military coup in Haiti.	
1992 Yugoslavia broke up amid civil war. EC crisis over Maastricht Treaty. Czechoslovakia split into two.	**1992** Rio de Janeiro hosted Earth Summit.	
1993 ECs single market comes into force.		
1994 IRA cessation of violence.	**1994** US invades Haiti.	
	1995 Inauguration of Mercosur (Southern Common Market). Bombing in Oklahoma City, USA.	**1995**
		1997